The authoritative
source book of
urban data and
developments

**The
Municipal
Year
Book**

1994

ICMA

The Municipal Year Book

1994

Washington, D.C.

International
City/County
ICMA
Management
Association

For eighty years ICMA has been the professional association of appointed administrators serving local governments. Its primary goals include strengthening the quality of local government through professional management and developing and disseminating new concepts and approaches to management through a wide range of information services, training programs, and publications.

As an educational and professional association, ICMA is interested in the dissemination and application of knowledge for better local government management. To further these ends, the association supports a comprehensive research, data collection, and information dissemination program to facilitate reference and research by local government officials, university professors and students, researchers, and others concerned with local affairs.

Comprehensive Research, Data Collection, and Information Dissemination Program

The Municipal Year Book

Urban Data Service
   Baseline Data Reports
   Special Data Issues
   Survey data resources
Management Information Service
   Monthly management reports
   Inquiry service
   Special reports

Research Projects and Publications

Volume 61, 1994

ISBN: 0-87326-969-1
ISSN: 0077-2186

Library of Congress Catalog Card Number: 34-27121

Printed in the United States of America

The views expressed in this *Year Book* are those of individual authors and are not necessarily those of the International City/County Management Association.

Suggested citation for use of material in this *Year Book*: Jane S. Author [and John N. Other], "Title of Article," in *The Municipal Year Book 1994* (Washington, DC: International City/County Management Association, 1994), 00–000.

Table of Contents

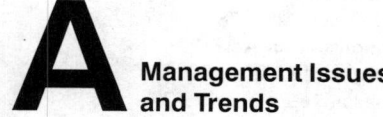

D Directories

E References

Acknowledgments

The Municipal Year Book, which provides local government officials with information on local government management, represents an important part of ICMA's extensive research program. Each year, ICMA surveys local officials on a variety of topics, and the data derived from their responses constitute the primary information source for the *Year Book*. Authors from local, state, and federal government agencies; universities; public interest groups; and ICMA staff prepare articles that describe the data collected and examine trends and developments affecting local governments.

We would like to express our appreciation to the thousands of city and county managers, clerks, finance officers, personnel directors, police chiefs, fire chiefs, and other officials who patiently and conscientiously responded to ICMA questionnaires. It is only because of their time-consuming efforts that we are able to provide the information in this volume.

Barbara H. Moore is the director of publications, Evelina R. Moulder is the editor of *The Municipal Year Book*. Other ICMA staff members who contributed to this publication are Haywood J. Talcove, director of survey design and evaluation; Lisa Huffman, research associate; Aubrey Charles, director of data processing; Dawn Leland, director of publications production; Brian Derr, assistant director of publications production; and Yvonne Rodgers, research secretary.

William H. Hansell, Jr.
Executive Director
ICMA

Inside the Year Book

For local governments, 1993 ended on an optimistic note. Economic indicators look promising, home sales are on the rise, and local government revenues will soon reflect the stronger economy. Congress passed legislation that will benefit local governments, and state aid to localities was not cut back as much in 1993 as it had been in previous years. This edition of *The Municipal Year Book* looks at technologies and practices that can increase local governments' productivity and help them benefit from the recovery.

Management Issues and Trends

Information is the key to success in this age of technology. One of the most important surveys conducted by ICMA in 1993 is on local government computer technology. In "Computers in Local Government" (A/1), Kenneth Kraemer and Donald Norris explore the technologies local governments are using and planning. The article covers computer applications, budgets, productivity, and acquisition in local government.

TQM has been shown not only to contain costs but to increase service effectiveness. In "Total Quality Management in Local Government" (A/2), Jonathan West, Evan Berman, and Anita Cava examine which services most often use TQM, the factors prompting implementation, the strategies used to ensure employee involvement, and many more facets of this highly acclaimed management approach.

Contracting with the private sector continues to be the most commonly used alternative service delivery method. It also continues to have vocal supporters and opponents. Based on a comprehensive ICMA survey covering 62 city and county services, in their article, "Alternative Service Delivery in Local Governments, 1982–1992" (A/3) Rowan Miranda and Karlyn Andersen examine service delivery methods, factors prompting privatization, activities used to ensure success, obstacles to privatization, and evaluating contractors.

The debate over term limitations for state and federal elected officials has captured the headlines in recent years. Although there has been substantial research on turnover at the state and federal levels, little exists on local officials. In "Term Limits and Turnover Among Local Officials" (A/4) Tari Renner and Victor DeSantis present research that explores the patterns of turnover and term limitations among elected local officials and turnover among appointed local government managers/CAOs.

Problems confronting local governments are seldom limited to the legal boundaries of the jurisdiction. Strict liquor laws in one state do not prevent youth from purchasing liquor in a city across the state line. Many local governments band together to address problems of their region or metropolitan area. In "Profiles of Regional Councils and Their Executive Directors" (A/5), Sherman Wyman describes the legal basis, sources of revenue, issues, and programs of these regional councils. A profile of the regional council executive director is developed using survey data on authority, responsibility, and time spent on specific functions.

The Intergovernmental Dimension

David Berman, in "State-Local Relations: Patterns, Politics, and Problems" (B/1), looks at state and local relations—focusing on local authority, mandates, state aid to local governments, local revenues, and state activity in the areas of education, environmental protection, and land use and transportation planning.

In "Supreme Court Cases Affecting Local Governments" (B/2), Charles Wise and Rosemary O'Leary cover decisions that have implications for local governments. Among the subjects covered are religion and free speech, corrections, minority set-aside programs, forfeiture of property, local taxation, civil rights, attorneys fees, cable television regulation, housing, overtime pay, health insurance, and voting rights.

The Brady Bill, NAFTA, the Family and Medical Leave Act, the "Motor-Voter" bill, empowerment zones and enterprise communities, the National Service Act, and the HUD Demonstration Act are among the numerous pieces of legislation covered by Eugene Boyd in "Congressional Actions Affecting Local Governments" (B/3).

Staffing and Compensation

One of the most basic managerial concerns is compensation. This section provides salary data for a variety of positions held by local officials.

In "Salaries of Municipal Officials for 1993," Evelina Moulder looks at the salaries of 21 municipal officials (C/1). The article is based on the results of the salary survey conducted by ICMA in July 1993.

Moulder also uses the salary survey results to evaluate the salaries of 12 county managerial positions in "Salaries of County Officials for 1993" (C/2).

"Police and Fire Personnel and Expenditures, 1993" presents the following in tabular form: total personnel, the number of uniformed personnel, hours worked per week, entrance and maximum salaries, information on longevity pay, and a breakdown of departmental expenditures (C/3). Gerard Hoetmer compares the 1993 data with the results of the 1992 survey.

Directories

The directories section (D/1/1 through D/1/10) encourages *Year Book* users to turn to sources beyond the *Year Book*—state municipal leagues, state agencies for community affairs, state management associations, and colleagues in other municipalities, counties, and regional councils—to exchange information and set up informal networks. *The Year Book* directories provide the names of nearly 70,000 contacts in United States local governments and a means of getting in touch with them—a phone number and in some cases an address.

A special directory in the *Year Book* is "Professional, Special Assistance, and Educational Organizations Serving Local and State Governments" (D/2). The organizations included in this directory provide educational and research services to members or others on a cost-of-service basis and in this way strengthen professionalism in government administration.

References

The "Sources of Information" (E/1), prepared by Eleanor Ferrall, provides bibliographic listings of the latest books and periodicals in 2 basic reference categories and 15 functional area categories: basic references; basic statistical resources; emergency management; environment and energy; fire protection; housing; human resources and services; information technologies; intergovernmental relations; law enforcement and criminal justice; local government organization and management; personnel and labor relations; planning and development; public finance; public works and utilities; recreation and leisure; and transportation and roads. Online data sources are included.

PROFESSIONAL MUNICIPAL MANAGEMENT

Professional municipal management in the United States and Canada has its roots in the council-manager plan, as does ICMA. The first appointment to a position similar to a city manager was 86 years ago, in 1908, in Staunton, Virginia, where a "general manager" was employed to oversee the administrative functions of the municipality. The first adoption of the council-manager plan in the United States is usually considered to have been in Sumter, South Carolina, in 1912, and in Canada during the next year at Westmount, Québec. Dayton, Ohio, in 1914, was the first community of substantial size to adopt the council-manager plan, and in 1930 Durham County, North Carolina, became the first county to institute professional management.

The council-manager plan grew steadily from 1914, slowed only as a result of the difficulties of war and depression. By 1918 there were 98 council-manager municipalities. In 1930 the total had increased to 418, and by 1945, it had reached 622. By the end of 1969, 2,252 municipalities in the United States and Canada were using the council-manager plan. Since that time the number of places using the plan has increased by 807 so that by December 1993 ICMA had verified the existence of the plan in 2,926 cities and counties in the United States and 133 in Canada.

During the 1960s, the profile of local government had begun to show significant changes. Not only were there new problems, but variations in organization and structure became evident. Many cities, towns, and counties began providing for an appointed official responsible for overall administrative affairs without adopting the council-manager plan as it was originally conceived. Similarly, the development of councils of governments and regional councils brought new and innovative structures to local government. It became obvious to ICMA that, in many cities, professional management positions were being developed that did not vary significantly from the role of the traditional city and county manager positions provided for in the council-manager plan.

Therefore, in July 1969, the International City Managers' Association changed its name to the International City Management Association and provided for full professional recognition of these positions. To distinguish these municipalities from those recognized as council-manager municipalities, they were designated "general management municipalities." Criteria were established for recognition, and the incumbents in these positions were made eligible for Corporate (voting) Membership in ICMA. Similarly, ICMA began recognizing state municipal leagues in the spring of 1986. In 1991, ICMA changed its name to the International City/County Management Association.

Between June 1969 and December 1993 ICMA recognized 1,411 governments in the United States and Canada under the general management criteria. Included in this total are 1,046 municipalities, 203 counties, 142 councils of governments, and 18 leagues.

Figure 1 shows the numbers of council-manager and general management recognitions since 1983. The numbers include recognitions in the United States and Canada.

Recognized Municipalities

All management executives are selected by municipalities on the basis of relevant education and experience. Although professional management is defined by a common set of functions, the association has not sought to control entrance into the profession by requiring completion of a specified education program. The primary emphasis has been on demonstrated competence in a position with significant management responsibility and authority.

These professional positions are defined by a set of criteria describing the characteristics of overall professional management. The present criteria provide for recognition of a position in the council-manager form of government and a position of general management that applies to a wide variety of governmental forms, councils of government, and state municipal leagues.

Table 1 indicates, by ICMA regions, the number of municipalities in which there is a recognized professional manager. ICMA regions are determined by the Executive Board in accordance with the relative number of corporate members in the various geographic areas. The ICMA regions are *Northeast*: Connecticut, Delaware, the District of Columbia, Maine, Maryland, Massachusetts, New Hampshire, New Jersey, New York, Pennsylvania, Rhode Island, and Vermont; *Southeast*: Alabama, Florida, Georgia, Kentucky, Mississippi, North Carolina, South Carolina, Tennessee, Virginia, and West Virginia; *Midwest*: Illinois, Indiana, Iowa, Michigan, Minnesota, Missouri, Ohio, and Wisconsin; *Mountain-Plains*: Arizona, Arkansas, Colorado, Idaho, Kansas, Louisiana, Montana, Nebraska, New Mexico, North Dakota, Oklahoma, South Dakota, Texas, Utah, and Wyoming; *West Coast*: Alaska, California, Hawaii, Nevada, Oregon, and Washington. The Canadian information is reported as for an independent region. (Although all members in countries outside of North America are currently represented in the association through a region which includes Canada, data for these countries are excluded from the table.) Further information on these recognized places, including legal basis, title of position, form of government, and year of recognition, is presented in the annual ICMA publication, *Who's Who in Local Government Management*.

Organizational Goals

Beginning in the fall of 1983, the association underwent an extensive self-analysis and strategic planning process that resulted in a revision

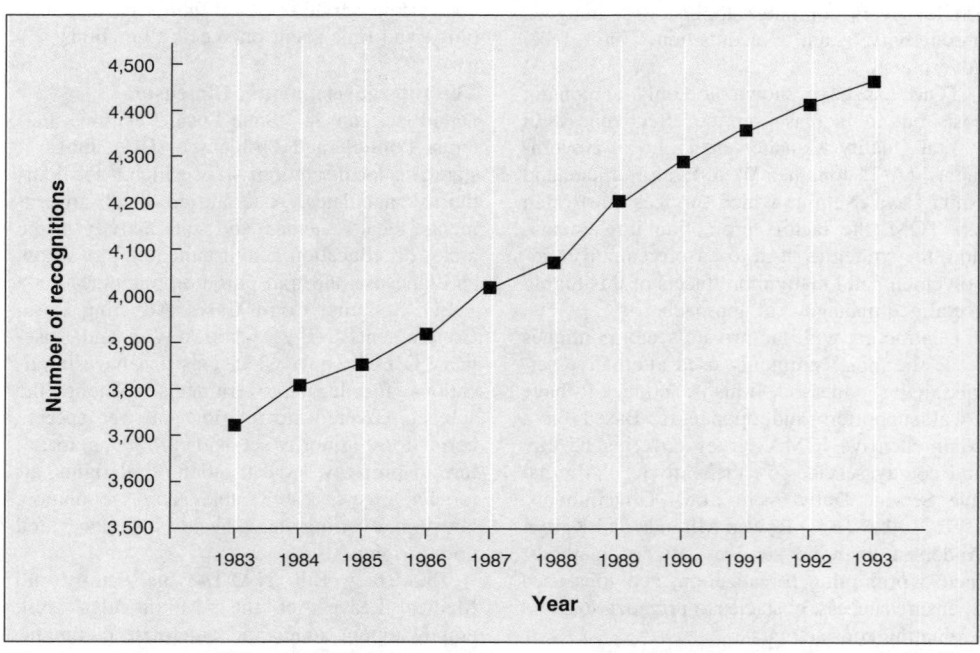

Figure 1 *Council-manager and general management recognitions in the United States and Canada, 1983–1993*

Table 1   RECOGNIZED LOCAL GOVERNMENTS, COUNCILS OF GOVERNMENTS, AND LEAGUES BY ICMA REGION[1]

ICMA region	Council-manager (CM)			General management (GM)					Total CM and GM
	Cities, towns, etc.	Counties	Total CM	Cities, towns, etc.	Counties	COGs	State municipal leagues	Total GM	
Northeast	589	5	594	338	27	10	4	379	973
Southeast	599	82	681	113	93	39	6	251	932
Midwest	541	14	555	323	32	27	3	385	940
Mountain-Plains	565	12	577	160	15	40	3	218	795
West Coast	502	17	519	82	36	23	2	143	662
U.S. total	2,796	130	2,926	1,016	203	139	18	1,376	4,302
Canada total	127	6	133	30	2	3	0	35	168
Grand total	2,923	136	3,059	1,046	205	142	18	1,411	4,470

[1]Data in this table are as of 30 November 1993.

of ICMA's organizational goals. Adopted by the executive board in January 1985, these goals, the framework for ICMA services, are as follows:

1. To provide professional development programs and publications for local government professionals that improve their skills, increase their knowledge of local government, and strengthen their commitment to the values and ideals of professional management.

2. To support professional management in all forms of local government and specifically to encourage local governments in the United States and in other countries to adopt and retain the council-manager or the general management plan.

3. To improve the recruiting process for professional local government administrators, in order to ensure the future of the profession and increase professional management opportunities for women and minorities.

4. To serve as a national and international clearinghouse for the collection, analysis, and dissemination of local government-related information and to conduct research and offer contractual technical consulting services in areas that address local government needs.

5. To promote professional local government management by working in cooperation with and serving as a resource for public interest groups directly involved in the formulation of public policy.

6. To offer services and programs and to provide a communications network to respond to personal, professional, and family needs of members.

ORGANIZATION OF DATA

Most of the tabular data for *The Municipal Year Book 1994* were obtained from public officials through questionnaires developed and administered by the ICMA. ICMA's Municipal Data Service maintains a computer-based information file of all data collected through ICMA surveys.

Every city[1] of 2,500 and over in population, all recognized places under 2,500 population, and all counties 2,500 and over were surveyed by questionnaire for sections C1, C2, and D1/9 and D1/10 of this *Year Book*. However, not every city and county were surveyed for each local government function and activity included in the other sections. Questionnaires are reviewed by local authorities and pretested before they are prepared in final form. All governments surveyed for each study receive a mail questionnaire; if they do not respond to the first mailing, a second request is sent.

All survey questionnaires are edited to eliminate respondent errors and to assure that questionnaire responses are keypunched as accurately as possible for computer tabulation. *Year Book* authors determine the analysis and the tables required from the computer as the basis for their articles.

Government Definitions

At the beginning of 1987, there were 83,237 governments in the United States. Fifty-one of these are nonlocal governments; the remainder are all local governments—counties, municipalities, townships, school districts, and special districts.

A municipality, by census definition, is a "political subdivision within which a municipal corporation has been established to provide general local government for a specific population concentration in a defined area." This definition includes all active governmental units officially designated as cities, boroughs (except in Alaska), villages, or towns (except in Minnesota, New York, New England, and Wisconsin). The definition generally includes all places incorporated under the procedures established by the several states.

Counties are the primary political administrative divisions of the state. In Louisiana these units are called parishes. Alaska has county-type governments called boroughs. There are certain unorganized areas of some states that are not included in the *Year Book* data base, which have a county designation from the Census Bureau for strictly administrative purposes. These comprise 12 areas in Alaska; 2 areas in South

Dakota; 5 areas in Rhode Island; 8 areas in Connecticut; and 1 area in Montana.[3]

Year Book Data Base

Unless otherwise noted, this edition of the *Year Book* uses the 1990 Census Bureau figures for placing local governments in the United States into population groups for tabular presentation.

Using the 1990 census data, it is possible to show information for 6,608 cities and other urban places 2,500 and over in population and 592 council-manager and general management places under 2,500 population. Although the selection of cities 2,500 and over in population largely corresponds to the criteria established by the Bureau of the Census, there are some variations. Selection of council-manager and general management places under 2,500 population is based on recognition by ICMA. *The Year Book* data base shows 3,043 counties.

City Classification

Table 2 details the distribution of all municipalities of 2,500 and over in population (and all municipalities udner 2,500 recognized by ICMA as providing for the council-manager plan or providing for a position of overall general management) by population, geographic region and division, metro status, and form of government.

Population

The population categories are self-explanatory.

Geographic Classification

Nine geographic divisions and four regions are used by the Bureau of the Census (Figure 2). The nine divisions are *New England*: Connecticut, Maine, Massachusetts, New Hampshire, Rhode Island, and Vermont; *Mid-Atlantic*: New Jersey, New York, and Pennsylvania; *East North Central*: Illinois, Indiana, Michigan, Ohio, and Wisconsin; *West North Central*: Iowa, Kansas, Minnesota, Missouri, Nebraska, North Dakota, and South Dakota; *South Atlantic*: Delaware, the District of Columbia, Florida, Georgia, Maryland, North Carolina, South Carolina, Virginia, and West Virginia; *East South Central*: Alabama, Kentucky, Mississippi, and Tennessee; *West South Central*: Arkansas, Louisiana, Oklahoma, and Texas; *Mountain*: Arizona, Colorado, Idaho, Montana, New Mexico, Nevada, Utah, and Wyoming; and *Pacific Coast*: Alaska, California, Hawaii, Oregon, and Washington.

For *The Year Book* the regions are further consolidated as follows: *Northeast*: Connecticut, Maine, Massachusetts, New Hampshire, New Jersey, New York, Pennsylvania, Rhode Island, and Vermont; *North Central*: Illinois, Indiana, Iowa, Kansas, Michigan, Minnesota, Missouri, Nebraska, North Dakota, Ohio, South Dakota, and Wisconsin; *South*: Alabama, Arkansas, Delaware, the District of Columbia, Florida, Georgia, Kentucky, Louisiana, Maryland, Mississippi, North Carolina, Oklahoma, South Carolina, Tennessee, Texas, Virginia, and West Virginia; and *West*: Alaska, Arizona, California, Colorado, Hawaii, Idaho, Montana, Ne-

Table 2   CUMULATIVE DISTRIBUTION OF U.S. MUNICIPALITIES

Classification	All cities	Cities 2,500 & over	Cities 5,000 & over	Cities 10,000 & over	Cities 25,000 & over	Cities 50,000 & over	Cities 100,000 & over	Cities 250,000 & over	Cities 500,000 & over	Cities over 1,000,000
Total, all cities	7,200	6,608	4,613	2,810	1,212	533	195	64	25	8
Population group										
Over 1,000,000	8	8	8	8	8	8	8	8	8	8
500,000–1,000,000	17	17	17	17	17	17	17	17	17	
250,000–499,999	39	39	39	39	39	39	39	39		
100,000–249,999	131	131	131	131	131	131	131			
50,000–99,999	338	338	338	338	338	338				
25,000–49,999	679	679	679	679	679					
10,000–24,999	1,598	1,598	1,598	1,598						
5,000–9,999	1,803	1,803	1,803							
2,500–4,999	1,995	1,995								
Under 2,500[1]	592									
Geographic region										
Northeast	1,984	1,840	1,344	779	281	97	24	6	3	2
North Central	2,091	1,916	1,280	782	310	125	40	14	6	2
South	2,099	1,905	1,249	729	293	139	65	24	9	2
West	1,026	947	740	520	328	172	66	20	7	2
Geographic division										
New England	797	707	529	327	128	46	10	1	1	0
Mid-Atlantic	1,187	1,133	815	452	153	51	14	5	2	2
East North Central	1,360	1,272	890	558	224	89	25	8	6	2
West North Central	731	644	390	224	86	36	15	6	0	0
South Atlantic	883	783	521	315	142	66	29	9	3	0
East South Central	470	430	284	149	47	15	11	4	2	0
West South Central	746	692	444	265	104	58	25	11	4	2
Mountain	371	326	224	129	71	38	15	7	1	0
Pacific Coast	655	621	516	391	257	134	51	13	6	2
Metro status										
Central	516	515	515	514	484	327	160	64	25	8
Suburban	3,860	3,673	2,766	1,702	607	201	35			
Independent	2,824	2,420	1,329	594	121	5				
Form of government										
Mayor-council	3,562	3,306	2,044	1,120	441	201	83	36	20	6
Council-manager	2,992	2,711	2,158	1,460	718	319	106	26	5	2
Commission	162	155	117	80	26	9	6	2		
Town meeting	412	365	234	105	7	0				
Rep. town meeting	72	71	60	45	20	4				

[1] Municipalities recognized by ICMA as providing for the council-manager plan or providing for a position of overall general management. Also includes municipalities with populations that dropped below 2,500 between the 1980 and 1990 U.S. censuses.

vada, New Mexico, Oregon, Utah, Washington, and Wyoming.

Metro Status

Metro status refers to the status of a municipality within the context of the U.S. Office of Management and Budget definition of a metropolitan statistical area. The criteria allow for three levels of classification: metropolitan statistical areas, primary metropolitan statistical areas, and consolidated statistical areas.

Metropolitan Statistical Areas (MSAs) These areas have either a city of at least 50,000 population or a Bureau of the Census urbanized area of at least 50,000 *and* a total metropolitan statistical area population of at least 100,000. Each MSA has at least one central city and one central county and may include outlying counties with economic and social ties to the central components of the area. Outlying counties must also meet requirements relating to community level and "urban character" to be included in an MSA.

MSAs are not closely associated with other metropolitan statistical areas and are surrounded by nonmetropolitan counties.

Primary Metropolitan Statistical Areas (PMSAs) Metropolitan statistical areas of over 1,000,000 population can be designated as primary metropolitan statistical areas. There must be local support for separate recognition and at least 60% of the area's population must be urban; less than 50% of its residents are permitted to commute to jobs outside the country for it to be considered a PMSA.

If any area within a metropolitan statistical area is recognized as a primary metropolitan statistical area, the remaining area of that statistical area is designated as a separate primary metropolitan statistical area.

Consolidated Metropolitan Statistical Areas (CMSAs) A metropolitan statistical area in which primary statistical areas have been identified is designated as a consolidated metropolitan statistical area. If no primary metropolitan statistical areas are identified within an MSA, the term metropolitan statistical area applies.

In New England, the city and town are administratively more important than the county, and a wide range of data is compiled locally for such entities. Here, towns and cities are the units used in defining metropolitan statistical areas. Because cities and towns are generally

smaller in area than counties, the total MSA population requirement is lower in the six New England states (75,000) than in the other states (100,000).

The Office of Management and Budget currently identifies 353 metropolitan areas. Of this number 262 are MSAs, and 71 are PMSAs. There are 20 CMSAs.

Central cities are the core cities of an MSA and must have a population of at least 25,000 and meet two commuting requirements: At least 50% of the employed residents of the city must work within the city, and there must be at least 75 jobs for each 100 residents who are employed. Cities between 15,000 and 25,000 population may also be considered central cities if they are at least one-third the size of the MSA's largest city and meet the commuting requirements. Suburban cities are the other cities, towns, and incorporated places in an MSA. Independent cities are incorporated places not located in an MSA.

Form of Government

Form of government relates primarily to the organization of the legislative and executive

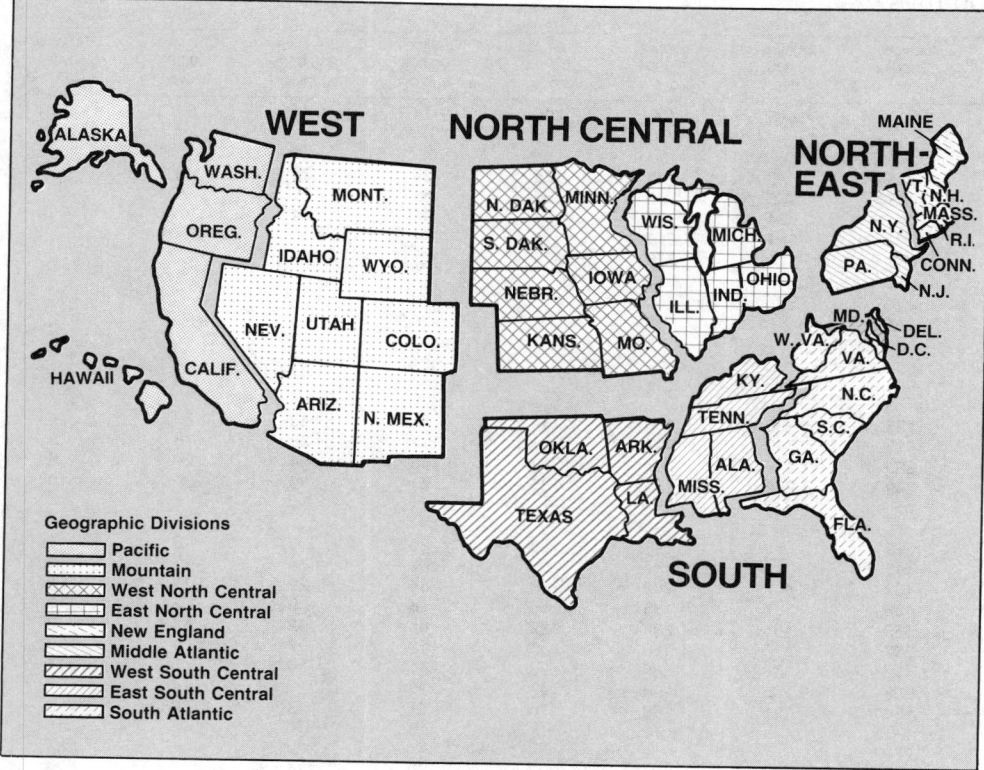

Figure 2   *U.S. Bureau of the Census grographic regions and divisions*

Form of Government

For counties, form of government relates to structural organizations of the legislative and executive branches of counties; counties are classified as being with or without an administrator. There are three basic forms of county government: commission, council-administrator, and council-elected executive.

The *commission form* of county government is characterized by a governing board that shares the administrative and, to an extent, legislative responsibilities with several independently elected functional officials. Counties with this form of government are designated as being without an administrator.

Counties with the *council-administrator form*, in which an administrator is appointed by, and responsible to, the elected council to carry out directives, are designated under form of government as ''with administrator.'' The *council-elected executive form* features two branches of government: the executive and the legislative. The independently elected executive is considered the formal head of the county. This form of government is also included in the designation ''with administrator.''

The use of varying types of local government is an institutional response to the needs, requirements, and articulated demands of citizens at the local level. Within each type of local government, structures are developed to provide adequate services. These structural adaptations are a partial result of the geographic location, population, metropolitan status, and form of government of the jurisdiction involved.

branches of municipalities and townships. In the *mayor-council form*, an elected mayor generally acts as the chief executive officer with the amount of administrative authority dependent on state law and variations in local organization. These variations include the scope of the powers of the elected council and the delegation of some authority to appointed professional administrators, to special boards, and to commissions.

Many cities with a mayor-council form of government have an appointed city administrator. These officials are appointed by the elected representatives (council) and are responsible to them for the execution of their duties. However, their administrative authority is limited—they often do not directly appoint department heads or other key city personnel, and their responsibility for budget preparation and administration, although significant, is subordinate to that of the elected officials.

Under the *council-manager form*, a manager is appointed by and responsible to an elected council to serve as chief administrative officer to oversee personnel, development of the budget, proposing policy alternatives, and general implementation of policies and programs adopted by the council.

The *commission form* of government operates with an elected commission performing both legislative and executive functions, generally with departmental administration divided among the commissioners.

The *town meeting form* of government is a system in which all qualified voters of a mu-

nicipality meet annually (or more often if necessary) to set policy and choose selectmen to carry out the basic policies they have established.

Under the *representative town meeting form* of government, the voters select a large number of citizens to represent them at the meeting(s). All citizens can participate in the meeting(s), but only the representatives actually have a direct vote.

County Classification

Counties are the primary political administrative divisions of the states. The county-type governments in Alaska are called boroughs. Table 3 details the distribution of counties thoughout the nation, using the same categories as Table 3. The population categories are self-explanatory, and the geographic regions are described in the discussion of Table 3.

Metropolitan Status

For counties, metro status refers to the status of a county within the context of the U.S. Office of Management and Budget definition of a metropolitan statistical area (MSA). ''Metro'' means a county is located within an MSA; ''nonmetro'' indicates that it is located outside of the boundaries of an MSA.

Counties that are located in an MSA are classified in a way similar to that for cities. Central counties are those in which central cities are located. Suburban counties are the other counties located within an MSA. Counties not located in an MSA are considered independent.

USES OF STATISTICAL DATA

The Municipal Year Book uses primary and secondary data sources. ICMA collects and publishes the primary source data. Secondary source data refers to data collected by another organization. Most of the primary source data are collected through survey research. ICMA develops questionnaires on a variety of subjects during a given year and then pretests and refines them to increase the validity of each survey instrument. Once completed, the surveys are sent to officials in all cities above a given population level (i.e., 2,500 and above, 10,000 and above, etc.). Surveys are sent to the appropriate officials. For example, city managers or chief administrative officers receive the *Organizational Structure and Decision Making* survey, and finance officers receive the *Police and Fire Personnel and Expenditures* survey.

ICMA conducts the city, county, and councils of governments salary surveys and the *Police and Fire Personnel and Expenditures* survey every year. The other research projects are conducted every several years, and some are one-time efforts to provide information on subjects of current interest.

LIMITATIONS OF THE DATA

Regardless of the subject or type of data presented, they should be read cautiously. All pol-

Table 3   CUMULATIVE DISTRIBUTION OF U.S. COUNTIES

Classification	All counties	Counties 2,500 & over	Counties 5,000 & over	Counties 10,000 & over	Counties 25,000 & over	Counties 50,000 & over	Counties 100,000 & over	Counties 250,000 & over	Counties 500,000 & over	Counties over 1,000,000
Total, all counties	3,043	2,928	2,752	2,315	1,408	796	418	174	80	25
Population group										
Over 1,000,000	25	25	25	25	25	25	25	25	25	25
500,000–1,000,000	55	55	55	55	55	55	55	55	55	
250,000–499,999	94	94	94	94	94	94	94	94		
100,000–249,999	244	244	244	244	244	244	244			
50,000–99,999	378	378	378	378	378	378				
25,000–49,999	612	612	612	612	612					
10,000–24,999	907	907	907	907						
5,000–9,999	437	437	437							
2,500–4,999	176	176								
Under 2,500[1]	115									
Geographic region										
Northeast	196	196	195	190	180	134	87	43	20	4
North Central	1,053	1,009	918	740	417	208	112	38	16	5
South	1,374	1,344	1,299	1,111	637	329	145	54	24	6
West	420	379	340	274	174	125	74	39	20	10
Geographic division										
New England	52	52	52	50	46	28	20	8	5	1
Mid-Atlantic	144	144	143	140	134	106	67	35	15	3
East North Central	436	435	432	403	282	153	84	29	13	4
West North Central	617	574	486	337	135	55	28	9	3	1
South Atlantic	545	540	532	461	296	172	85	32	13	2
East South Central	362	360	357	312	156	65	19	7	3	0
West South Central	467	444	410	338	185	92	41	15	8	4
Mountain	276	242	206	153	76	49	23	11	4	1
Pacific Coast	144	137	134	121	98	76	51	28	16	9
Metro status										
Central	336	336	336	336	336	327	277	134	63	24
Suburban	347	347	347	344	303	212	107	40	17	1
Independent	2,360	2,245	2,069	1,635	769	257	34			
Form of government										
Without administrator	2,338	2,227	2,053	1,646	884	404	164	49	22	6
With administrator	705	701	699	669	524	392	254	125	58	19

[1]Includes recognized counties and those with populations that dropped below 2,500 between the 1980 and 1990 censuses.

icy, political, and social data have strengths and limitations. These factors should be considered in any analysis and application. Statistics are no magic guide to perfect understanding and decision-making, but they can shed light on particular subjects and questions in lieu of haphazard and subjective information. They can clarify trends in policy expenditures, processes, and impacts, and consequently, assist in evaluating the equity and efficiency of alternative courses of action. Statistical data are most valuable when one remembers their imperfections, both actual and potential, while drawing conclusions.

For example, readers should examine the response bias for each survey. Surveys may be sent to all municipalities above a certain population threshold, but not all of them are necessarily returned. Jurisdictions that fail to respond are rarely mirror images of those that do. ICMA reduces the severity of this problem by maximizing the opportunities to respond through second and (sometimes) third requests. But although this practice mitigates the problem, response bias invariably appears. Consequently, ICMA always includes a "Survey Response" table in each article that analyzes a particular survey. This allows the reader to examine the patterns and degrees of response bias through a variety of demographic and structural variables.

Other possible problems can occur with survey data. Local governments have a variety of record-keeping systems. Therefore, some of the data (particularly those on expenditures) may lack uniformity. In addition, no matter how carefully a questionnaire is refined, problems such as divergent interpretations of directions, definitions, and specific questions invariably arise. However, when inconsistencies or apparently extreme data are reported, every attempt is made to verify these responses through follow-up telephone calls.

TYPES OF STATISTICS

There are basically two types of statistics: descriptive and inferential.

Descriptive
Most of the data presented in this volume are purely descriptive. Descriptive statistics summarize some characteristics of a group of numbers. A few numbers represent many. If you want to find out something about the age of a city's work force, for example, it would be quite cumbersome to read a list of several hundred numbers (each representing the age of individual employees). It would be much easier to have

a few summary descriptive statistics such as the mean (average) or the range (the highest value minus the lowest value). These two "pieces" of information would not convey all of the details of the entire data set, but they can help and are much more useful and understandable than complete numerical lists.

There are essentially two types of descriptive statistics: measures of central tendency and measures of dispersion.

Measures of Central Tendency These types of statistics indicate the most common or typical value of a data set. The most popular examples are the mean and median. The mean is simply the arithmetic average. It is calculated by summing the items in a data set and dividing by the total number of items. For example, given the salaries of $15,000, $20,000, $25,000, $30,000 and $35,000, the mean is $25,000 ($125,000 divided by 5).

The mean is the most widely used and intuitively obvious measure of central tendency. However, it is sensitive to extreme values. A few large or small numbers in a data set can produce a mean that is not representative of the "typical" value. Consider the example of the five salaries above. Suppose the highest value was not $35,000 but $135,000. The mean of the data set would now be $45,000 ($225,000 di-

vided by 5). This figure, however, is not representative of this group of numbers because it is substantially greater than four of the five values and is $90,000 below the high score. A data set such as this is "positively skewed" (it has one or more extremely high scores). Under these circumstances (or when the data set is "negatively skewed," with extremely low scores), it is more appropriate to use the median as a measure of central tendency.

The median is the middle score of a data set that is arranged in order of increasing magnitude. Theoretically, it represents the point that is equivalent to the 50th percentile. For a data set with an odd number of items, the median has the same number of observations above and below it (i.e., the third value in a data set of five or the eighth value in a data set of fifteen). With an even number of cases, the median is the average of the middle two scores (i.e., the second and third values in a data set of four or the seventh and eighth values in a data set of fourteen). In the example of the five salaries used above, the median is $25,000 regardless of whether the largest score is $35,000 or $135,000. When the mean exceeds the median, the data set is positively skewed. If the median exceeds the mean, then it is negatively skewed.

Measures of Dispersion This form of descriptive statistics indicates how widely scattered or spread out the numbers are in a data set. Some common measures of dispersion are the range and the interquartile range. The range is simply the highest value minus the lowest value. For the numbers 3, 7, 50, 80, and 100, the range is 97 (100 − 3 = 97). For the numbers 3, 7, 50, 80, and 1,000, it is 997 (1,000 − 3 = 997). The interquartile range is the value of the third quartile minus the value of the first quartile. Quartiles divide a data set into four equal parts similar to the way percentiles divide a data set into 100 equal parts. Consequently, the third quartile is equivalent to the 75th percentile, and the first quartile is equivalent to the 25th percentile. The interquartile range is essentially the range of the middle 50% of the data.

Inferential

Inferential statistics permit the social and policy researcher to make inferences about whether or not a correlation exists between two (or more) variables in a population based on data from a sample. Specifically, inferential statistics provide the probability that the sample results could have occurred by chance if there were really no relationship between the variables in the population as a whole. If the probability of random occurrence is sufficiently low (below the researcher's preestablished significance level), then the null hypothesis, that there is no association between the variables, is rejected. This lends indirect support to the research hypothesis that a correlation does exist. If they can rule out chance factors (the null hypothesis), then researchers conclude that they have found a "statistically significant" relationship between the two variables under examination.

Significance tests are those statistics that permit inferences about whether or not variables are correlated but provide nothing directly about the strength of such correlations. Measures of association, on the other hand, indicate how strong relationships are between variables. These statistics range from a high of +1.0 (for a perfect positive correlation), to zero (indicating no correlation), to a low of −1.0 (for a perfect negative correlation).

Some common significance tests are the Chi Square and difference-of-means tests. Some common measures of association are Yule's Q, Sommer's Gamma, Lambda, Cramer's V, Pearson's C, and the correlation coefficient. Consult any major statistics textbook for further information on these tests and measures.[2]

Inferential statistics are used less frequently in this volume than descriptive statistics. However, whenever possible, the data have been presented so that the user can calculate inferential statistics whenever appropriate.

SUMMARY

All social, political, and economic data are collected with imperfect techniques in an imperfect world. Therefore, users of such data should be continuously cognizant of the strengths and weaknesses of the information from which they are attempting to draw conclusions. Readers should note the limitations of the data published in this volume. Particular attention should be paid to the process of data collection and potential problems such as response bias.

---

[1]The terms *city* and *cities*, as used in this volume, refer to cities, villages, towns, townships, and boroughs.

[2]For additional information on statistics see Tari Renner's *Statistics Unraveled: A Practical Guide to Using Data in Decision Making* (Washington, D.C.: International City/County Management Association, 1988).

A Management Issues and Trends

Computers in Local Government

Kenneth L. Kraemer
University of California, Irvine

Donald F. Norris
*University of Maryland Graduate School,
Baltimore County*

Findings

Population size continues to be a factor in differentiating the use of computing among cities.

There is a shift toward greater use of microcomputers and local area networks among all cities, regardless of size.

Blanket procurement agreements are used more often by large cities than by small jurisdictions.

As municipalities become more advanced in their use of computer technology, the role that computers play in the management and operations of local governments is likely to increase. Although historically computing has been focused primarily on internal administration, new applications are expected to extend the technology outward to citizens in their homes, offices, and schools. Examples of such applications include IBM's 24-Hour City Hall program, public access to government databanks, public conferencing and communication networks, information kiosks, electronic bill paying, and smart cards for social services payments. During the next decade, municipalities will become interconnected with other governments and with business, education, and health institutions through the national information highways being planned by the federal government and major telecommunications companies. But what is the current state of computing in municipalities? Does it constitute a revolution or an evolution?

This article, based on data from ICMA's 1993 *Survey of Computer Technology in Local Government*, attempts to answer that question by comparing current and planned computer use and practices. The last major surveys of computing in cities were conducted in 1985—one by ICMA[1] and another by the Center for Research on Information Technology and Organizations at the University of California, Irvine.[2]

METHODOLOGY

The ICMA survey was mailed to 7,135 cities; 2,527 responded, for an overall response rate of 35% (Table 1/1). The response rate does not vary significantly among different population groups. Moreover, the proportion of municipalities in the sample is approximately equal to their proportion in the population. Thus, although the sample is broadly representative of the population of all municipalities, it is heavily weighted toward small cities (under 25,000 in population), which represent 80% of the sample and of the population (Table 1/1 A). This means

that it is important to pay attention to city size when interpreting the data.

The respondents from small jurisdictions are primarily city managers, chief administrative officers (CAOs), and finance officers (63%). The primary respondent in medium-size (population from 25,000 to 249,999) and large cities (population 250,000 and above) is the MIS/data processing manager (66% or more). The respondents have been in their positions an average of seven years; three-fifths are men and two-fifths are women, with higher proportions of women respondents in small jurisdictions (not shown).

Responses were examined by population size, geographic division, and metropolitan status. Only population size was determined to be a consistent factor affecting differences in response, and therefore, nearly all responses are shown by size only. In addition, although the survey gathered data at nine levels of population size, only three levels (and sometimes five levels) are used. This enables comparison with data from past surveys and, more importantly, defines the natural breaks in the responses.

County governments were not surveyed this year. Previous surveys have shown that the character of computing is nearly identical in cities and counties.[3] The major differences are in computer application. Counties perform certain functions, such as health and social services, that most cities do not perform. However, since cities are representative in most other areas covered by this survey, it was decided to focus on municipalities and to place emphasis on a good response rate.[4]

About 97% of responding municipalities now use computers (Table 1/2), with smaller jurisdictions showing a pronounced rate of increase. For example, approximately 42% of the cities from 10,000 to 49,999 in population used computers in 1975,[5] compared to about 93% in 1985, and 97% in 1993. Although no similar comparison is possible for jurisdictions under 10,000 in population, 93% of the responding jurisdictions surveyed in that population group report computer use in 1993. By the year 2000,

Table 1/1   SURVEY RESPONSE

Classification	No. cities surveyed (A)	No. responding	% of (A)
Total, all cities[1]	7,135	2,527	35.4
Population group			
Over 1,000,000	8	3	37.5
500,000–1,000,000 ..	16	8	50.0
250,000–499,999	40	18	45.0
100,000–249,999	131	55	42.0
50,000–99,999	334	128	38.3
25,000–49,999	674	284	42.1
10,000–24,999	1,590	580	36.5
5,000–9,999	1,794	586	32.7
2,500–4,999	1,989	649	32.6
Under 2,500	559	216	38.6
Geographic division[2]			
New England	793	258	32.5
Mid-Atlantic	1,180	322	27.3
East North Central ...	1,349	481	35.7
West North Central ..	719	340	47.3
South Atlantic	868	330	38.0
East South Central ..	470	120	25.5
West South Central ..	746	201	26.9
Mountain	367	165	45.0
Pacific Coast	643	310	48.2
Metro status[3]			
Central	509	200	39.3
Suburban	3,825	1,348	35.2
Independent	2,801	979	35.0

[1]The term *cities* refers also to towns, townships, villages, and boroughs.

[2]*Divisions: New England*—the states of Connecticut, Maine, Massachusetts, New Hampshire, Rhode Island, and Vermont; *Mid-Atlantic*—the states of New Jersey, New York, and Pennsylvania; *East North Central*—the states of Illinois, Indiana, Michigan, Ohio, and Wisconsin; *West North Central*—the states of Iowa, Kansas, Minnesota, Missouri, Nebraska, North Dakota, and South Dakota; *South Atlantic*—the states of Delaware, Florida, Georgia, Maryland, North Carolina, South Carolina, Virginia, and West Virginia, plus the District of Columbia; *East South Central*—the states of Alabama, Kentucky, Mississippi, and Tennessee; *West South Central*—the states of Arkansas, Louisiana, Oklahoma, and Texas; *Mountain*—the states of Arizona, Colorado, Idaho, Montana, Nevada, New Mexico, Utah, and Wyoming; *Pacific Coast*—the states of Alaska, California, Hawaii, Oregon, and Washington.

[3]*Metro status: Central*—core city of an MSA; *Suburban*—incorporated city located within an MSA; *Independent*—city located outside of an MSA.

there may not be a single jurisdiction that does not use computers. There is no significant difference in the percentage of jurisdictions using computers by region of the country or by metropolitan status (data not shown).

ORGANIZATIONAL ARRANGEMENTS

Government computing systems are organized in three ways: in-house, shared, or outsourced (Table 1/3). Under *in-house arrangements*, the computer systems are owned by the government and operated by government personnel. Nearly all municipalities (95%) continue to use this arrangement, which has been the most commonly used since computers were first introduced in local government.

Two-thirds of respondents with in-house arrangements report a single computing department; one-third report more than one. As might be expected, large cities tend to have multiple departments, and small jurisdictions tend to have a single department or no formal computing department. The proportion of municipalities with multiple computing departments (33%) is somewhat higher than it was in 1985 (23%), continuing the trend toward decentralization that characterized computing during the 1980s (not shown). Among municipalities with one computing department, 39% are located in finance, 30% in administration, and one-fourth are independent departments. Approximately 6% are located in public works or in another department (Table 1/4).

In *shared arrangements*, one government provides services to others (e.g., Douglas County and Omaha, Nebraska) or several governments band together to create a cooperative or nonprofit corporation (e.g., San Diego Data Processing Corporation) to provide computing services to the members. Few municipalities (approximately 6%) use this arrangement currently, and few have used it historically.

The practice of contracting out all or part of computing services is *outsourcing*. A municipality might contract management of all facilities, contract with a service bureau for an application, contract with staff to develop programs, or contract for computer time by entering a time-sharing agreement. Outsourcing has not proved popular and is used currently by few jurisdictions responding (approximately 3%). Usage is highest among the large governments where the complexity and cost of computing sometimes prompt local officials to turn to outsourcing. There is an impression that outsourcing is on the rise because of a few prominent cases in industry (Kodak, General Dynamics). However, current and historical data suggest it is unlikely to become a major trend in the future (see section on management). Orange County, California, is one of the few successful examples of long-term outsourcing in local government.

COMPUTING RESOURCES

The survey data clearly demonstrate that municipalities use a combination of mainframe computers, minicomputers, and microcomputers. For analysis and presentation purposes, mainframes and minicomputers have been combined into one category and the various types of microcomputers into another category.

Mainframes and Minicomputers

All of the large cities and 92% of the medium-size cities use mainframes and/or minicomputers, as compared to 54% of the small jurisdictions (Table 1/5). At the same time, there is a discernible shift occurring from mainframes/minicomputers to microcomputers. Overall, 14% of the municipalities have abandoned larger computers for smaller ones, and 18% indicate they are considering the shift, which suggests that the shift is not dramatic. While the proportion of small municipalities considering the shift is

---

Table 1/1A   REPRESENTATIVENESS OF RESPONDENTS

Classification	No. surveyed (A)	No. responding	% of (A)	% of total no. surveyed	% of total no. responding
Total, all cities	7,135	2,527	35	100	100
Population group					
Large cities: 250,000 and over	64	29	45	1	1
Medium-size cities: 25,000–249,999	1,139	467	41	19	19
Small cities: under 25,000	5,932	2,031	34	80	80

Table 1/2   COMPUTER USE IN CITIES

Classification	Computer users (% of respondents)[1]		
	1975	1985	1993
Total, all cities	51	97	97
Population group[2]			
100,000 and over	98	100	100
50,000–99,999	92	100	100
10,000–49,999	42	93	97
Under 10,000	...	...	93

Source for 1975 and 1985 data: Kenneth L. Kraemer et al., *The Future of Information Systems in Local Governments* (Irvine, CA: Public Policy Research Organization, University of California, 1986).
[1] In 1975, there were 2,294 responses; in 1985, 754; in 1993, 2,465.
[2] The 1975 and 1985 surveys were not sent to cities under 10,000 in population.

Table 1/3   ORGANIZATIONAL ARRANGEMENTS FOR COMPUTING

Classification	No. reporting (A)	In-house (%)	Share with other government (%)	Outsource (%)
Total, all cities	2,465	95	6	3
Population group				
250,000 and over	27	100	19	7
25,000–249,999	459	99	9	3
Under 25,000	1,979	94	6	3

Table 1/4   LOCATION OF SINGLE COMPUTING DEPARTMENTS

Classification	No. reporting (A)	Independent % of (A)	Finance % of (A)	Administration % of (A)	Public works % of (A)	Other department % of (A)
Total, all cities	1,585	26	39	30	1	5
Population group						
250,000 and over	25	64	16	4	0	16
25,000–249,999	408	31	41	21	1	6
Under 25,000	1,152	23	38	34	1	4

Table 1/5   TYPES OF COMPUTERS

Classification	No. reporting (A)	Mainframe/ minicomputer		Microcomputers	
		Cities reporting % of (A)	Average no. computers	Cities reporting % of (A)	Average no. computers
Total, all cities	2,367	61	1	92	34
Population group					
250,000 and over	28	96	3	100	655
25,000–249,999	461	92	2	94	96
Under 25,000	1,878	54	1	91	11

Table 1/6   SHIFT FROM MAINFRAMES/MINICOMPUTERS TO MICROCOMPUTERS

Classification	No. reporting (A)	Have abandoned mainframe/ minicomputer for microcomputers % of (A)	No. reporting (B)	Considering abandoning mainframe/ minicomputer for microcomputers % of (B)
Total, all cities	2,283	14	1,667	18
Population group				
250,000 and over	28	14	23	57
25,000–249,999	462	11	386	24
Under 25,000	1,793	15	1,258	16

Table 1/7   TYPES OF MICROCOMPUTERS

Classification	No. reporting	Average micros (No.)	Total micros (No.)	% of total micros
Total, all cities	2,527	34	84,802	100
Type of microcomputer				
IBM-PC and compatibles	1,922	40	77,072	91
Apples/MacIntoshes	314	12	3,605	4
Workstations	535	8	4,125	5

Table 1/8   CITY SIZE AND TYPES OF MICROCOMPUTERS

Classification	Ratio of micros to employees	IBM-PCs compatibles No. reporting	Average micros (No.)	Apples/ Macintoshes No. reporting	Average micros (No.)	Workstations No. reporting	Average micros (No.)
Total, all cities	1:8	1,922	40	314	12	535	8
Population group							
250,000 and over	1:93	25	727	15	47	16	8
25,000–249,999	1:19	404	102	118	18	123	11
Under 25,000	1:3	1,493	12	181	4	396	7

Table 1/9   LOCAL AREA NETWORKS (LANs)

Classification	No. reporting (A)	Have LANs No. reporting	% of (A)	Number of LANs No. reporting	Average no. LANs
Total, all cities	2,409	1,159	48	1,058	2.6
Population group					
250,000 and over	28	28	100	27	22
25,000–249,999	461	334	72	316	3
Under 25,000	1,920	797	42	715	2

Table 1/10   INTERCONNECTION OF COMPUTERS IN CITIES

Classification	Micro to LANs No. reporting	Average % of computers connected	Mainframe/mini to LANs No. reporting	Average % of computers connected	LAN to LAN No. reporting (A)	% of (A) connected
Total, all cities	1,035	60	375	75	530	64
Population group						
250,000 and over	25	53	17	64	24	33
25,000–249,999	317	44	189	79	224	55
Under 25,000	693	67	169	72	282	73

almost the same as those that have already made the shift, the proportions of medium and large cities are two and four times greater, respectively.

In each population group, the percentages of jurisdictions that have already abandoned mainframes/minicomputers are similar, which indicates that for some applications, micros are a good substitute.

The reality is that there are some functions that the larger systems perform better or that microcomputers cannot currently perform. Also, some local governments have made large investments in the applications that run on mainframes and minicomputers and would gain no advantage by moving these applications to microcomputers. For example, it is estimated that Douglas County, Nebraska, would require 150 person years (30 analysts/programmers working 50 years) to replace its mainframe systems; the estimate for San Diego is 220 person years.[6] Local officials are well-advised to consider carefully the costs and benefits of radical shifts in computer technologies.

Microcomputers
There is a shift toward greater use of microcomputers among *all* jurisdictions regardless of size. In ICMA's 1983 survey, only 13.2% of the responding jurisdictions used micros, and they used only one on average.[7] In 1993, 92% report use of microcomputers. The overall average is 34 microcomputers per jurisdiction, but the average varies greatly by size (Table 1/6).

Most of the microcomputers used in municipalities are IBM-PCs or compatibles (91%) rather than Apples/Macintoshes (4%) or workstations (5%) (Table 1/7). However, among municipalities having each of these types of microcomputers, the average number is 40 for IBM-PCs and compatibles (1,922 cities), 12 for Apples/Macintoshes (314 cities), and 8 for workstations (535 cities) (Table 1/8).

The average number of workstations in municipalities is more or less the same regardless of size, whereas the average number of PCs and Apples/Macs fluctuates with population. This variation suggests that the demand and justification for the more powerful and expensive workstations are related to the task needs of larger cities, which use them for engineering work (mapping, computer-aided design) and specialized applications such as geographic information systems (GIS).

The ratio of microcomputers to employees provides a measure of the extent of computing within municipalities. The overall ratio is 1:8, with the large cities having fewer microcomputers per employee than the small jurisdictions (not shown). However, the large cities also have many computer terminals attached to their mainframes and minicomputers, so the ratio of end-user devices to employees is probably around 1:40 or even 1:20.

Local Area Networks (LANs)
About one-half (48%) of the responding municipalities have local area networks (LANs) connecting at least some of their microcomputers

necting at least some of their microcomputers (Table 1/9). All of the cities 250,000 and above in population have LANs, and about two-fifths of those below 25,000 in population have LANs. Overall, the average number of LANs per city is three, but the large cities have about ten times more LANs than smaller jurisdictions. The LAN, minicomputer, and microcomputer data indicate that the larger cities are using more innovative and varied computing technology than much of the popular computing literature suggests.

Interconnection of Computers and Networks

Among the cities that have LANs, an average of 60% of the microcomputers are connected, with the proportion being greatest (67%) in the small municipalities. This pattern is similar for mainframes and minicomputers (Table 1/10). Three-fourths of the mainframes/minicomputers are interconnected with LANs. In addition, nearly two-thirds (64%) of the LANs are connected to one another so that electronic messages and data can be exchanged. The highest percentage of municipalities reporting LAN to LAN connections (73%) have populations under 25,000. This is probably because few of these municipalities have mainframes or minicomputers connecting their end-user devices, so they must rely on LANs.

Approximately 70% of the jurisdictions report using Novell's Netware to support their LANs; 12% report using IBM's OS/2 LAN Server; and 5% report using Apple's Appletalk or Appleshare (data not shown). Approximately one-fourth use "other" LAN software. (The total of these percentages exceeds 100% because jurisdictions that have more than one network can use more than one type of network software.)

COMPUTING EXPENSES

Municipalities spend about 4% of their total operating budgets on computing, with the larger cities spending approximately 7% and the smaller ones spending approximately 2%. The comparable overall figure for counties is 4% of total operating budget,[8] and for service firms in industry it is approximately 2% of total revenues and 8% of total operating expenses.

Budget Shares for Computer Resources

The budget shares allocated to different computing resources such as hardware and personnel show change from earlier surveys. The major comparable change is in hardware spending, which since 1985 has declined from 27% of total computing expenses to 22%. Personnel expenses consume approximately 50% of the budget, and purchased software, outside services, and all other each consume from 8% to 11% (Table 1/11). (Although only 690 responding municipalities provided complete budget information, the results are similar to those of previous analyses and are, therefore, probably reliable.)

Computing Efficiency and Labor-Capital Ratios

A central issue in computing services is determining the relative efficiency of computing departments. The ratio of labor (personnel) expenditures to capital (hardware) expenditures measures the *internal* productivity of computing departments. Although this ratio shows nothing about the re-

Table 1/11   ALLOCATION OF COMPUTING EXPENDITURES

	Percent of total computing budget		
Classification	Cities (%)	Counties[1] (%)	Services firms[2] (%)
Budget element			
Hardware	22	10	29
Personnel	51	56	43
Purchased software	8	23	8
Outside services	11	...	9
All other	8	11	11
Labor/capital ratio	2.3	5.6	1.42

Note: 690 cities; 40 counties; and 50 service firms reported.
[1]Source: Patricia T. Fletcher, Stuart I. Bretschneider, and Donald A. Marchand, *Managing Information Technology: Transforming County Governments in the 1990s* (New York: Syracuse University, 1992).
[2]Source: Kenneth L. Kraemer, Vijay Gurbaxani, and Nicholas Vitalari, *Performance Benchmarks for Information Systems in Corporations* (Irvine, CA: Center for Research on Information Technology and Organizations, University of California, 1993).

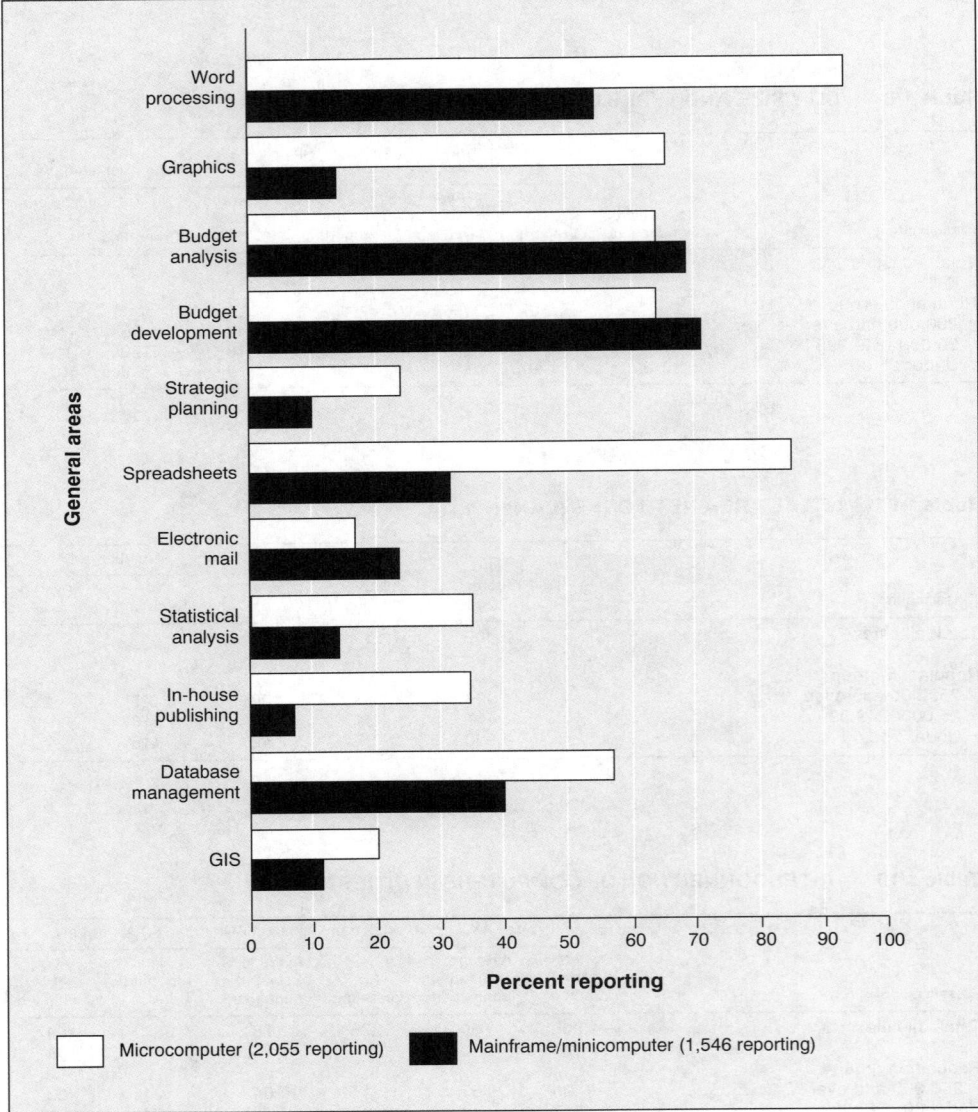

Figure 1/1   *Current computer applications in general areas*

turn on investment or the business value of computing in the local government as a whole, it does measure production efficiency. It does so by reflecting the capital intensity of the production process underlying the delivery of information services.

Economists have used this measure with considerable success to explain differences in productivity in other sectors of the economy. In particular, it is argued that different ratios of labor and capital can be used to produce any given amount of output. For a given set of labor and capital costs, there is an optimal ratio of labor to capital. As the amount of capital to labor is increased toward the optimal point, output increases. However, when the optimal point is exceeded, the increases in productivity are too small to compensate for the costs of the incremental capital investment.

Labor-Capital Substitution and Computing Productivity

Since the unit costs of hardware (capital costs) are dropping rapidly relative to personnel costs, one way to improve the productivity of computer-based information systems is by continually substituting capital equipment for labor. However, it is difficult to determine the optimal ratio of labor to capital in light of rapidly changing costs and technologies.

In such circumstances, estimates of the labor-capital expenditure ratios for cities that are leading-edge users of computing can have considerable value. These ratios provide a productivity benchmark for computing managers. In the absence of special circumstances, a ratio that is significantly higher than the norm suggests the possibility of computing service inefficiencies, which should be further investigated. Moreover, the ratio of these expenditures over time can also serve as a valuable planning tool for managers who need to project future investments in hardware and personnel.

Labor-Capital Ratios for Computing

Municipalities spend about 2.3 times as much on computing personnel as on hardware (Table 1/11). In the county survey, software and maintenance costs for operating systems are included in the purchased software budget rather than in the hardware budget. Consequently, hardware spending is extremely low and throws off the labor-capital calculation. A more realistic comparison is with service firms in industry, which spend approximately 1.4 times as much on labor as on capital. The magnitude of their corporate labor-capital ratio is consistent with other studies of computing budgets. These studies show that while the unit costs of hardware have decreased at the rate of 20% per year, personnel unit costs have increased slowly in inflation-adjusted terms. The average labor expenditure is about 1.5 times the hardware expenditure. This labor-capital ratio has not changed in the last five years.

Expectations about Future Budgets

Approximately 60% of the reporting municipalities expect their budgets for computing to be the same next year; 18% expect an increase; and 22% expect a decrease (data not shown).

Among those expecting a decrease, 75% indicate they will cut expenditures for hardware; 60% will purchase less software; and 27% will cut expenditures for outside services. Only 13% indicate they will cut expenditures for personnel (not shown), suggesting that local governments are reluctant to cut staff, even in the face of declining budgets.

Computing Personnel

The average number of computer personnel for reporting jurisdictions is eight. The large cities have an average of 72; the small municipalities average 5 computer personnel (not shown). It is possible that these figures underreport the number of city staff serving in computing roles because some staff perform computing functions for themselves and others but are not counted as computing personnel.

COMPUTER APPLICATIONS

There are general and specific uses for computers in local government. The general uses are for common applications such as word processing; the specific applications are found in specialized functional areas, such as engineering.

General Areas

Computers are *currently* used by 50% or more of the responding municipalities in the following general areas: word processing, graphics, budget analysis, budget development, spreadsheets, and database management (Figure 1/1). Regardless of the percentage reporting use, the percentage reporting use of microcomputers is higher than the percentage using mainframes/ minicomputers in eight of the eleven common

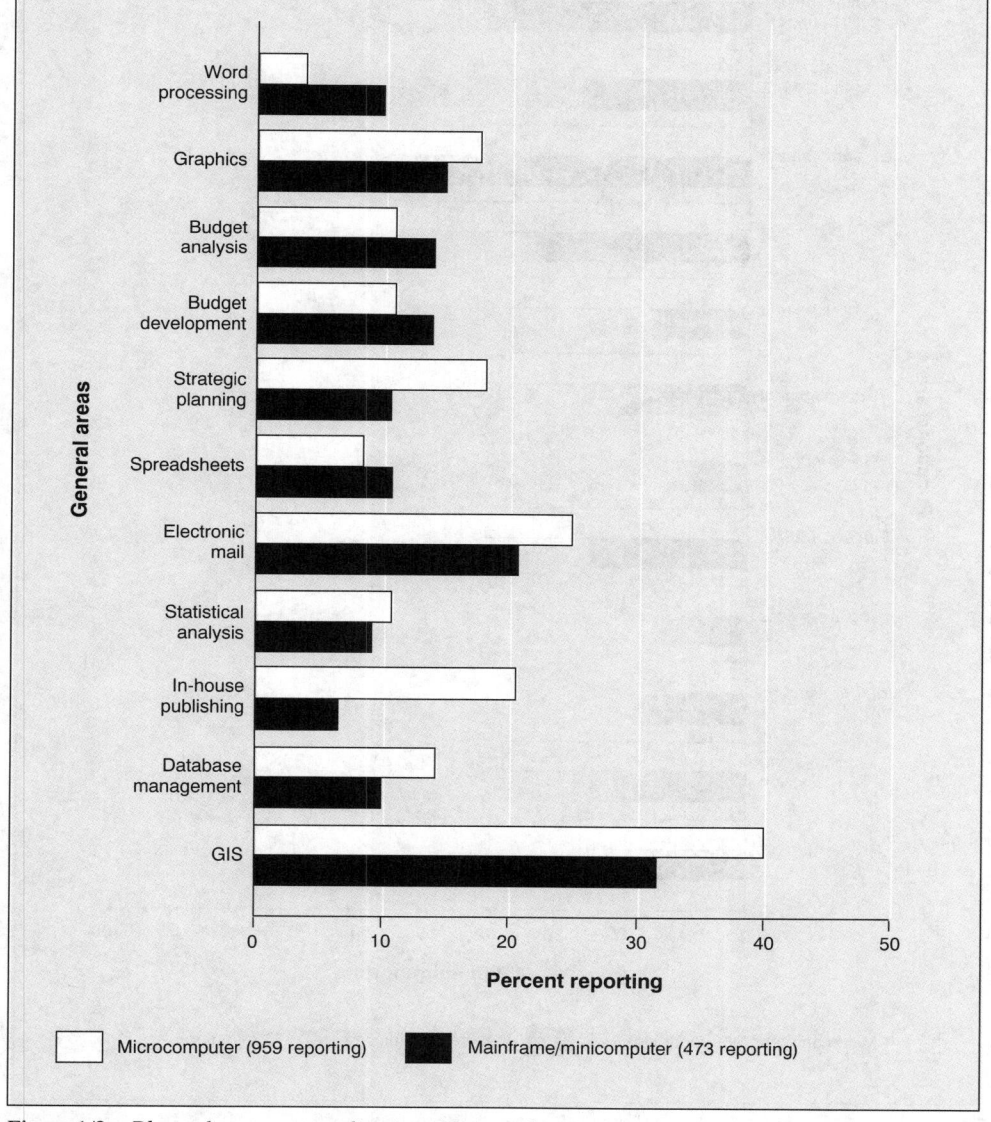

Figure 1/2 *Planned computer applications in general areas*

applications. At least one-fifth of the cities are *planning* to use computers within the next two years in three areas: electronic mail, geographic information systems (GIS), and in-house publishing (Figure 1/2).

Functional Areas

At least 50% of the cities report *current* use of computers in finance, utility services, personnel, administration/office support, and law enforcement (Figure 1/3). Higher percentages of jurisdictions use microcomputers than use mainframes in ten of the fifteen functional areas. Microcomputers tend to be used more in areas historically left out by the larger systems— planning and community development, engineering, fire, parks and recreation, and libraries.

Land records management, public works, and planning and community development have been identified for *future* computer applications in the next two years by significant percentages of respondents (Figure 1/4).

MANAGEMENT OF INFORMATION TECHNOLOGY

The rapid growth and broad reach of information technology present a management challenge. Initially users often made independent purchasing decisions, which resulted in expensive systems that did not "talk to each other." The need for systematic acquisition and planning became apparent.

Acquisition

City officials who might become involved in decisions about the acquisition of information technology range from the MIS/DP director to the department heads and from the city manager to the mayor and council. An indirect indication of the relative influence of these different positions is the proportion of respondents that identify them as decisionmakers. Fifty percent or more of the respondents identify the city manager or chief administrative officer, the MIS/DP director, and department heads as being involved in acquisition decisions (Table 1/12).

The relative influence of these three positions varies by size of jurisdiction. In municipalities with populations under 25,000, the chief administrative officer is the only decisionmaker identified by at least 50% of respondents (Table 1/12). In municipalities with populations from 25,000 to 249,999, 70% report the MIS/DP director as decisionmaker; no other role is identified by 50% of the respondents. And in cities 250,000 and over, 89% report the MIS/DP director and 64% report the department heads as decisionmakers. The dynamics of decision making are undoubtedly more complex than suggested by this comparison, but it is likely that this snapshot captures much about the relative influence of different actors.

Municipalities obtain computer applications by producing them with an in-house systems development staff, by purchasing packaged applications, and by contracting out for development. Approximately 75% use off-the-shelf

packages, 59% contract out for development, and 34% develop in-house. The method of obtaining applications is probably determined by a combination of need, availability, and cost.

The proportion of large cities using in-house development (89%) is much greater than that of small jurisdictions (25%), mainly because they use different types of computer systems. Most small municipalities use microcomputers for which there is a large inventory of software that does not require customization. In contrast, large

cities use mainframes and minicomputers in addition to microcomputers and have an inventory of their own applications built over many years.

Procurement Practices

Although outsourcing is frequently offered as a way of economizing on computing expenditures, it was shown earlier that at most 9% of the cities now contract out for services. (That is only if shared arrangements with other governments and the use of service bureaus and time-

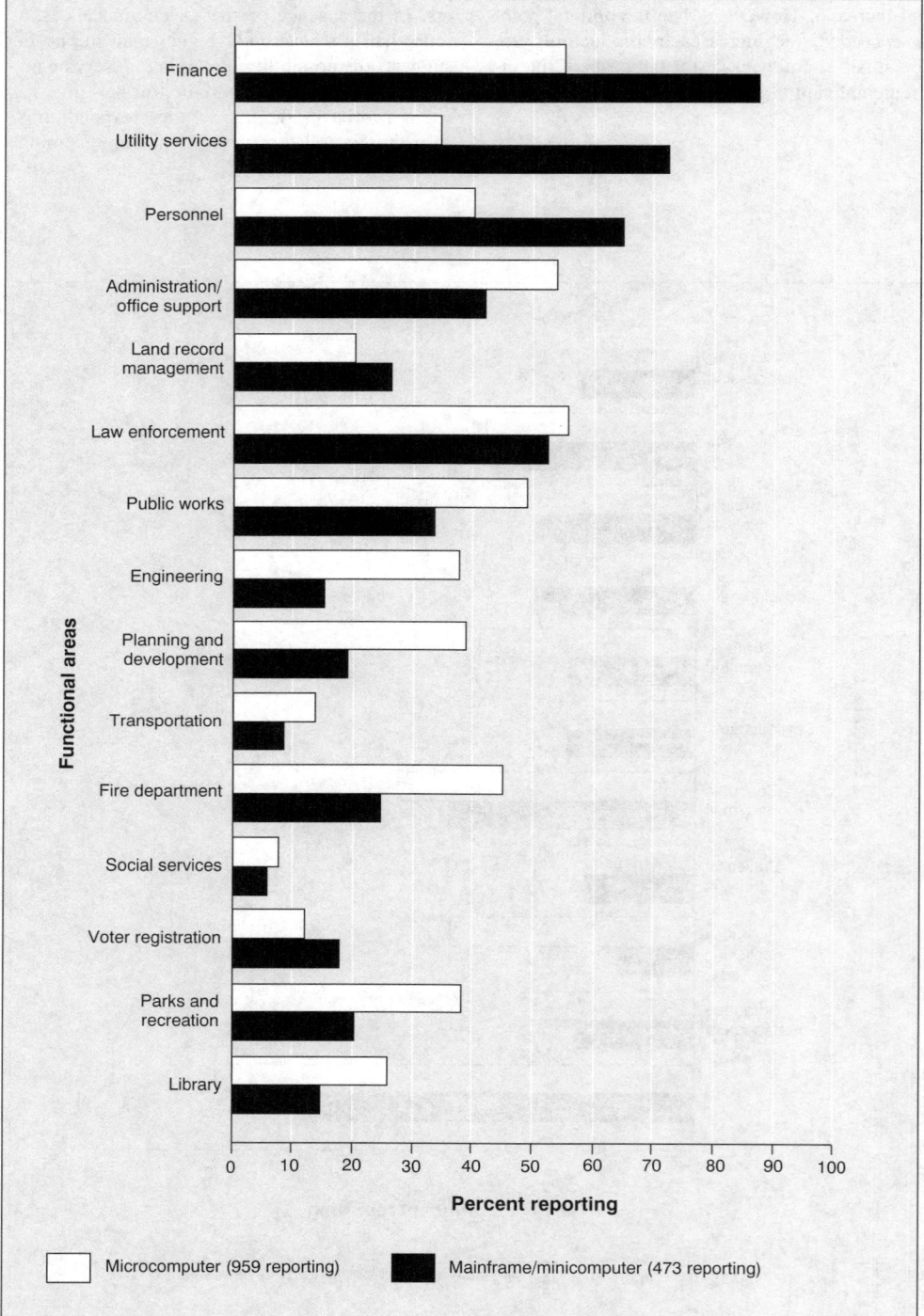

Figure 1/3 *Current computer applications in functional areas*

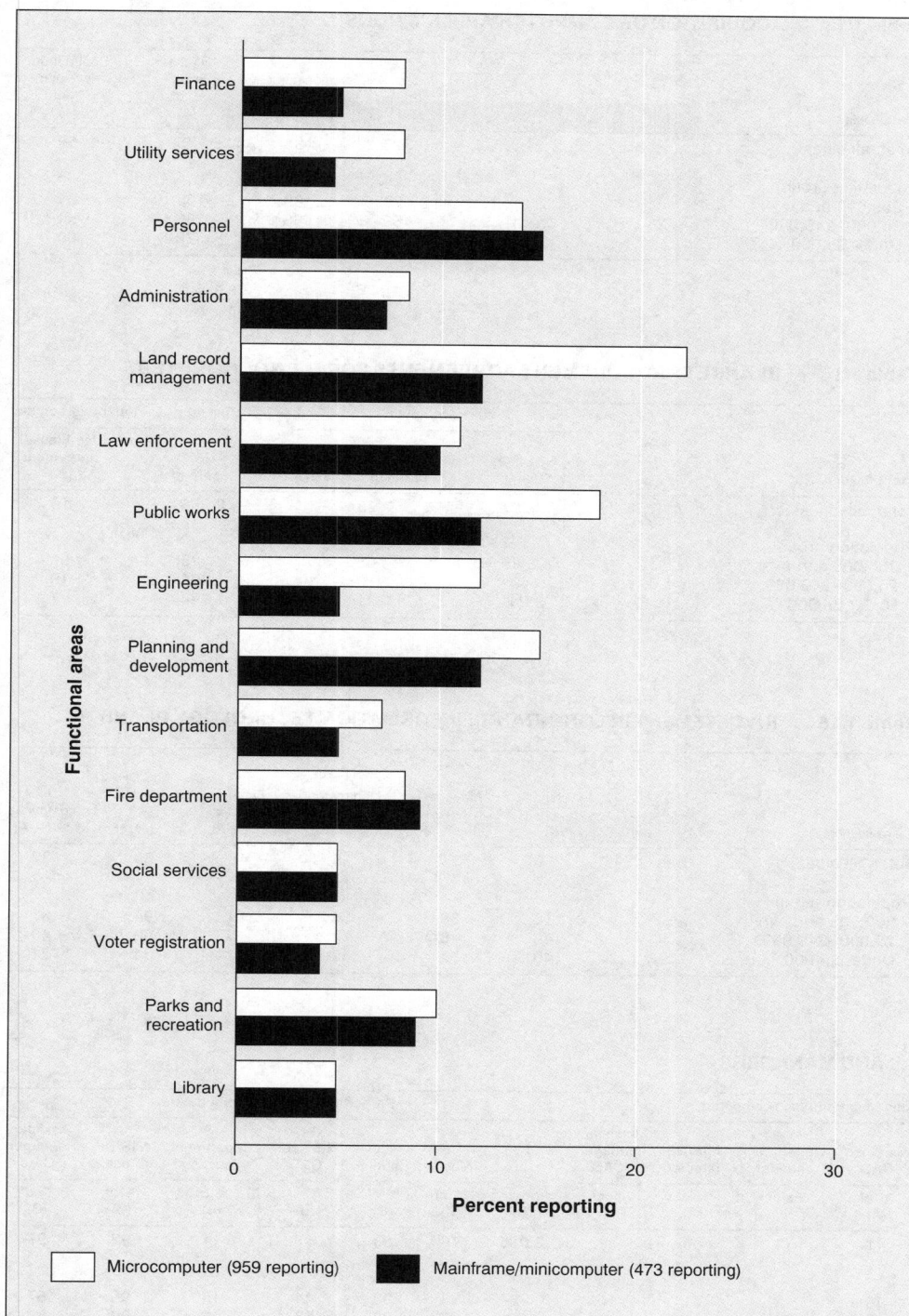

Primary reasons for dissatisfaction with blanket procurement agreements
1. *Failure of vendors to deliver equipment according to specifications*
2. *Failure of vendors to deliver on time*
3. *Lack of flexibility*
4. *Poor quality of equipment*
5. *Poor quality of support*
6. *Slow responsiveness in dealing with problems*
7. *Lack of a single point of contact for problems and issues that arise*

Figure 1/4   *Planned computer applications in functional areas*

sharing arrangements are included in the calculations.) It was also shown earlier that about 11% of computing budgets are spent for "outside services," which include contracts for training, software development, time-sharing, etc. Only 2% of municipalities indicate they are "likely" or "very likely" to consider contracting out whereas 93% indicate they are "unlikely" or "very unlikely" to consider it (data not shown).

Many municipalities (59%) contract out for application development in addition to making their own applications and buying others off-the-shelf (Table 1/13). Both now and in the future, regardless of the type of computer system used, municipalities will contract out for GIS and engineering applications (calculations, computer-aided design, and computer-aided drafting).

Approximately 75% of the municipalities can purchase computers under state government contracts (not shown). But according to the majority (76%), the contracts only "sometimes" enable local governments to purchase at a price lower than they could negotiate independently. There are no significant differences in these results by size of municipality.

Close to 10% of the municipalities have blanket procurement agreements for microcomputers (Table 1/14). The use of blanket agreements is related to city size, with 57% of the large cities and only 7% of the small cities having such agreements. However, given that the small municipalities have only ten microcomputers on average and that price competition for microcomputers is keen in major urban areas, this practice probably makes sense. The larger cities probably use blanket agreements because the size of their procurements gives them additional bargaining power and because blanket agreements can be an indirect way of achieving standardization of technology platforms, which provides uniform computer configurations rather than multiple configurations.

Among the 221 jurisdictions that use blanket procurement agreements, 70% are satisfied or very satisfied, 23% are neutral, and only 7% are dissatisfied or very dissatisfied. In general, more of the larger cities than the smaller ones are dissatisfied with procurements.

The emphasis by city officials on accepting the "lowest bid" in blanket procurements rather than the "best overall bid" is identified as a major concern, one that could be at the root of all other concerns.

Long-Range Plan for Information Technology
Overall, only 13% of the municipalities have a long-range information technology plan (Table 1/15). This figure is misleading, however, because many small municipalities in the sample have only ten microcomputers on average and probably don't need a long-range plan. For the large cities especially, the scope, scale, complexity, and level of information technology investment clearly warrant long-range plans. Moreover, long-range plans are probably advan-

tageous for all but the small jurisdictions because the information technology plan can include:

1. An inventory of existing technology,
2. An assessment of present technology standards and an identification of future needs,
3. An explicit statement of strategy for the use of the technology,
4. The identification of department and user needs related to the strategy,
5. An estimate of the costs of additional technology,
6. A justification for the investment, and
7. A procurement and implementation schedule.

In decisions about long-range plans, the city manager/CAO, finance director, MIS/DP director, and department heads are important players (Table 1/16). Their importance varies with city size as does the importance of those involved in acquisition. Small jurisdictions report the city manager/CAO (57%), department heads (59%), and finance director (54%) involved in developing the long-range information technology plan. In medium-size jurisdictions, 80% report MIS/DP director involvement and 73% report department head involvement; no other role is identified by at least 50% of the respondents. In large cities, 94% report the MIS/DP director and 56% report department heads as decisionmakers. Thus, it appears that a clearly definable and limited number of actors are involved in developing information technology plans and in acquisition decisions, even though others might participate to some degree.

COMPUTER USERS

When computers were first introduced in cities, they were used primarily by staff rather than by

Table 1/12 DECISION MAKERS FOR PURCHASES OF INFORMATION TECHNOLOGY

Classification	No. reporting (A)	Manager/ CAO % of (A)	Asst. mgr./ CAO % of (A)	Mayor % of (A)	Council members % of (A)	MIS/ DP director % of (A)	Dept. heads % of (A)	User committees % of (A)	Other % of (A)
Total, all cities	2,387	53	8	21	41	24	43	10	8
Population group									
250,000 and over	28	36	14	11	43	89	64	21	7
25,000–249,999	463	38	15	20	36	70	46	19	7
Under 25,000	1,896	56	6	22	43	12	42	8	8

Table 1/13 ACQUISITION OF COMPUTER APPLICATIONS

Classification	No. reporting (A)	In-house development % of (A)	Off-the-shelf % of (A)	Contract out for development % of (A)
Total, all cities	2,323	34	75	59
Population group				
250,000 and over	28	89	93	61
25,000–249,999	458	68	86	54
Under 25,000	1,837	25	72	60

Table 1/14 BLANKET PROCUREMENT AGREEMENTS FOR MICROCOMPUTERS

Classification	Microcomputers		Blanket procurement agreement	
	No. cities using	Avg. number of microcomputers	No. reporting	Use blanket agreement (%)
Total, all cities	2,527	34	2,386	10
Population group				
250,000 and over	29	655	28	57
25,000–249,999	467	96	464	19
Under 25,000	2,031	10	1,894	7

Table 1/15 LONG-RANGE PLAN FOR INFORMATION TECHNOLOGY

Classification	No. reporting (A)	Long-range plan in place % of (A)
Total, all cities	2,305	13
Population group		
250,000 and over	28	61
25,000–249,999	449	32
Under 25,000	1,828	8

Table 1/16 INVOLVEMENT IN LONG-RANGE INFORMATION TECHNOLOGY PLANS

Classification	No. reporting (A)	Manager/ CAO % of (A)	Department heads % of (A)	Finance director % of (A)	MIS/DP director % of (A)	User committee % of (A)
Total, all cities	299	51	65	48	59	32
Population group						
250,000 and over	16	38	56	19	94	31
25,000–249,999	143	46	73	45	80	43
Under 25,000	140	57	59	54	34	21

Table 1/17 COMPUTER USE AMONG OFFICIALS AND MANAGERS

Classification	Proportion using mainframe/minicomputers							Proportion using microcomputers						
	No. reporting (A)	Mayor % of (A)	Council % of (A)	Manager/ CAO % of (A)	Department heads % of (A)	MIS/DP director % of (A)	Assistant manager/ CAO % of (A)	No. reporting (B)	Mayor % of (B)	Council % of (B)	Manager/ CAO % of (B)	Department heads % of (B)	MIS/DP director % of (B)	Assistant manager/ CAO % of (B)
Total, all cities	1,506	63	67	41	11	83	31	2,035	78	68	57	11	92	37
Population group														
250,000 and over	26	58	100	46	8	81	50	27	93	93	44	15	96	67
25,000–249,999	422	80	90	45	14	85	47	451	87	93	53	12	96	57
Under 25,000	1,058	56	57	39	10	82	24	1,557	75	60	58	11	90	31

management and elected officials. In the 1993 survey, however, three-fifths or more of the respondents report that the mayor and council use computers, and two-fifths or more report that the manager/CAO uses computers (Table 1/17). The most surprising finding is the low proportion of jurisdictions reporting that department heads use computers (11%). There is not much difference in users by type of computer system or by city size.

Eighty-two percent of respondents using mainframes/minicomputers indicate their overall experience has met or exceeded expectations (data not shown). Ninety percent of those rating microcomputers indicate their experience has met or exceeded expectations. Given this favorable overall view, it is interesting to examine the respondents' perceptions about the benefits of computer use.

Perceived Benefits

In general, most respondents report that computers have a positive impact on worklife, decision making, operations, and finances (Figure 1/5). At least 51%, and often considerably more, of the respondents agree or strongly agree that computer use has improved employee job performance, creativity, and morale, even though some report that computing has increased frustration. Approximately 80% think that computer use improves decision making, and 70% or more report that it enables in-depth analysis. Three-fifths or more believe that computer use has improved communication, timeliness, and quality. Close to 70% feel that computer use reduces costs, even though only approximately 15% report that computers eliminate jobs.

The greatest difference in perceived impacts of mainframes/minicomputers and microcomputers is in employee worklife. One-half or more of the respondents think that mainframes enhance employee creativity and morale, whereas 71% think that microcomputers improve morale and about 90% believe they enhance creativity.

Perceived Problems

Fewer than two-fifths of the respondents perceive technical problems with computing. Fewer than one-half perceive behavioral problems, except in two areas (Figure 1/6). Personnel training is identified as a problem with microcomputers by 57% of the respondents and as a problem with mainframes/minicomputers by 50% of the respondents. Underutilization of equipment capacity is reported as a problem with microcomputers by 55% of the respondents.

Our field research provides insights into the relation between these issues. Assuming that resistance to use is not an issue, underutilization of microcomputer capacity can result from the nature of the work and from lack of adequate training. Because employees do many different things in their jobs—from attending meetings and visiting field sites to answering telephones—most work on microcomputers a maximum of four to six hours per day. Moreover, a detailed study of computer use shows that most people use about 10% of the capabilities of the software with which they are *most familiar*. Modern software packages, such as word processing, are designed for broad markets, so the software comes with far greater capabilities than most people need most of the time. Nonetheless, most people could use more than they do of the hardware and software capabilities at their disposal.

Inadequate training, both initial and ongoing, is the primary reason for this underutilization. A study of computer use among 3,000 municipal employees finds that computer literacy is significantly correlated with computer use for a wide range of tasks (e.g., updating files, record searching, text processing, graphics, statistical analysis, financial calculations, and programming). The study also shows that 30% of municipal employees are self-taught, 37% are taught by coworkers, and 33% are taught by computer professionals. All three methods are equally effective for initial training, but for ongoing training, formal courses are significantly correlated with greater computer use. Thus, city officials could increase computer utilization by providing more formal training for employees.[9]

FUTURE DIRECTIONS FOR TECHNOLOGY

Forty percent of the respondents consider their communities technologically progressive, 20% consider themselves static, and 40% consider themselves in the middle. These self-characterizations appear to be consistent with the reality of technologies actually in use or being considered. Although across all jurisdictions, an average of one in eighteen possible information

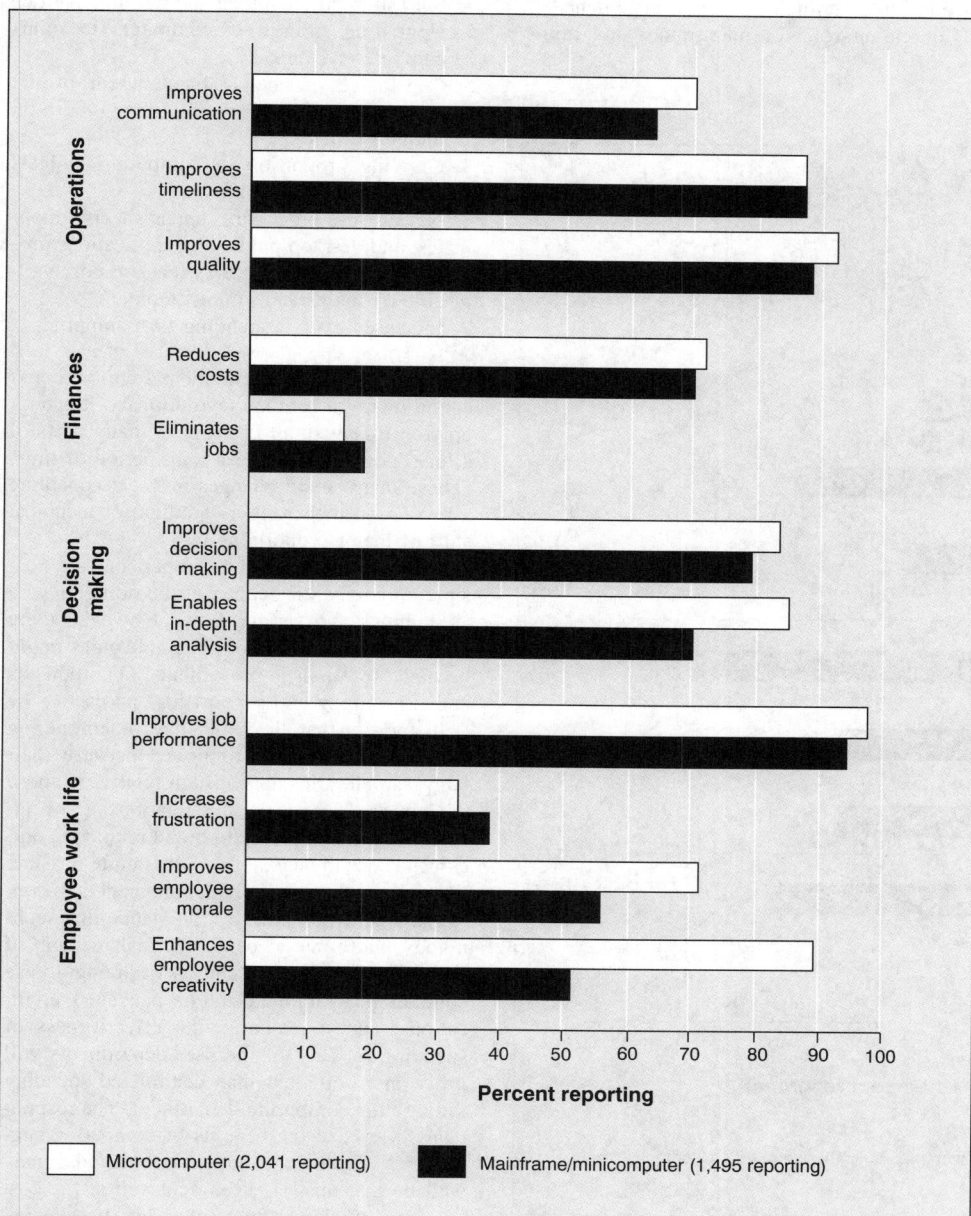

Figure 1/5 *Impact of computers*

technologies is being used and one being considered, the jurisdictions that characterize themselves as technologically progressive are using more of the technologies than those that characterize themselves as technologically static.

Municipalities are also making choices about the kinds of technologies they are using. To illustrate these choices, the technologies are grouped into three categories.

1. Citizen/public technologies that support direct service delivery to citizens, including 24-Hour City Hall, video arraignment, smart-traffic monitoring systems, smart-coded toll booths and parking, and smart highways.
2. Staff-support technologies that affect the internal administration and operation of the government. These include scanners, imaging, interactive video training, finger print ID, bar code technology, and electronic mail.
3. Infrastructure technologies that support greater technical sophistication and innovation. Among these are portable computers,

fax boards in computers, CD ROM, multimedia, optical disk, virtual reality, smart public buildings, wireless LANs, wide area networks, fiber optics, and GIS.

On average, municipalities are directing their future use of information technology toward building information infrastructure. They are less interested in developing citizen/public technologies (direct service delivery) or staff support technologies.

CONCLUSION

The character of computing in cities reflects both stability and change. The following stable features are highlighted in the survey results:

1. Continued use of computing primarily through in-house computing departments rather than through outside arrangements
2. Continuing role for mainframes and mini-

computers, at least in those jurisdictions currently using these systems
3. Stable distribution of spending for computing, particularly between hardware and personnel expenses
4. Continuation of benefits accompanying computer use primarily in the areas of decision making, operational performance, and employee worklife
5. Continuation of problems accompanying computer use, primarily in the areas of user training and user frustration with rapid technological changes

Change is evident in the following features:

1. Continuous growth in the number of municipalities using computers
2. Spread of computing to smaller and smaller municipalities
3. Spread of computing to more functions and to more end users
4. Shift to microcomputers in all municipalities
5. Upgrading from microcomputers to minicomputer systems
6. Considered or actual abandonment of the mainframe/minicomputer among some municipalities
7. Growing proportion of computing budgets placed in user departments
8. Newer word processing, spreadsheets, graphics, and desktop publishing applications provided by microcomputers that are not available on mainframes/minicomputers
9. Increased overall spending for computing

In short, the change in municipal computing is evolutionary rather than revolutionary. It is built up from many small changes in many parts of a local government over a long period of time. (These many small changes may yet constitute a revolution if there is a paradigm or technical shift of major proportions.)

In most areas in which comparisons are possible, municipalities appear to be doing as well as counties and service firms. However, there are two areas in which considerable gains might be made by small improvements: (1) efficiency and (2) training and support for end users.

It appears that the efficiency of computing departments could be improved because their labor-capital ratios appear high relative to those of industry. However, the relationship of investments in computing to broad municipal outcomes needs to be examined. It is quite possible that action taken by individual managers to consolidate hardware and staff, to standardize technology platforms, to centralize management of LANs and provision of end-user training, to use contract programmers and/or packaged applications, and to examine the effectiveness of spending by each of the user departments will prove more efficient than centralized spending through the computing department. The respondents' views of the benefits of computing suggest that effectiveness has been achieved. It may well be that this has been achieved at the cost of some efficiency but that it has been a net positive tradeoff.

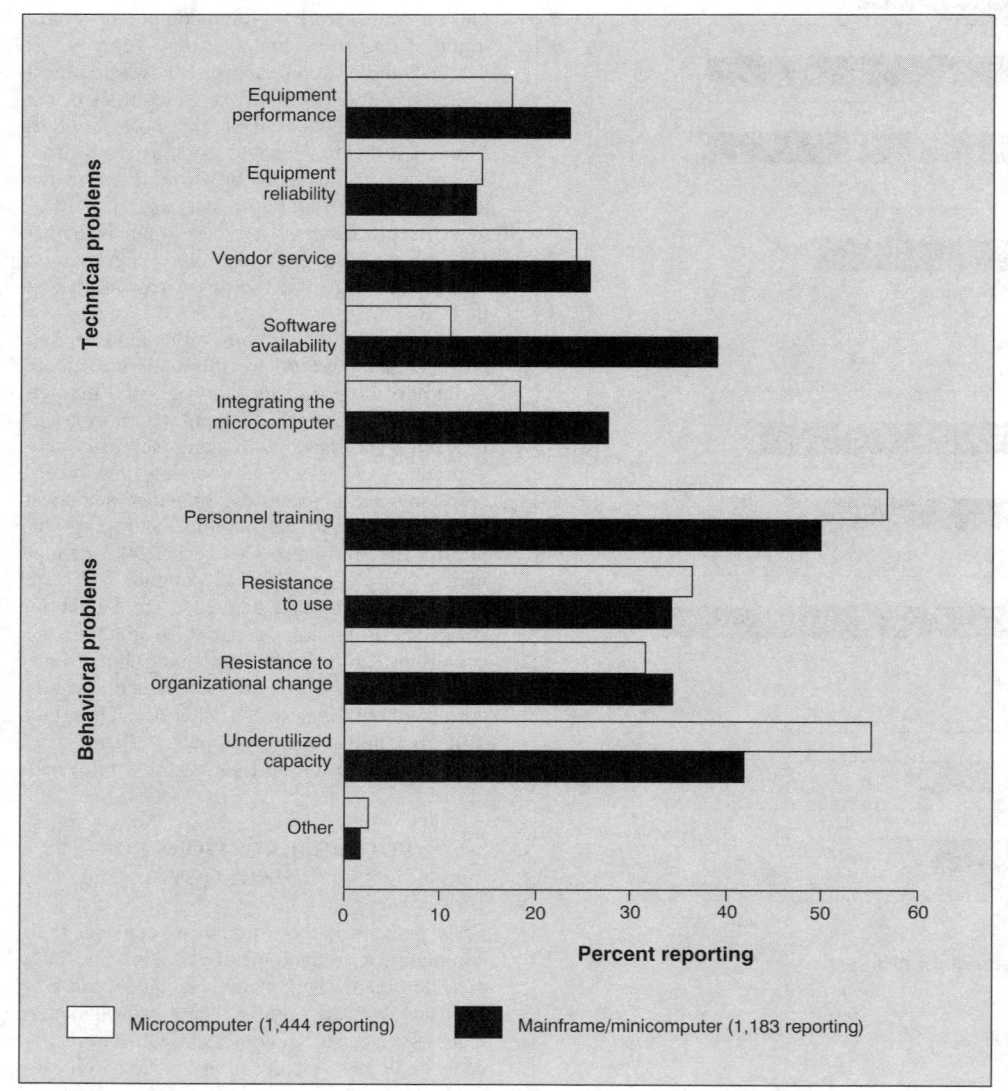

Figure 1/6   *Perceived problems with computing*

Providing more computer training and support for end users could result in substantial gains in personal productivity and reduction of employee frustration. The comments of respondents specifically identified the following aspects of computing as frustrating: initial use of the computer or of new applications; loss of files; loss of work through user errors; problems due to errors or "bugs" in the software; overuse of the computer for things better done manually; poorly written manuals; lack of time to learn on one's own; lack of formal training; and lack of top management support for training time or resources. Training and support to relieve user frustration would increase the productivity and effectiveness of municipal managers and staff.

The 1993 ICMA *Survey of Computer Technology in Local Government* is a rich storehouse of information, not all of which could be explored within the space of this chapter. For example, the patterns of small municipalities are sufficiently varied to warrant examination in a separate report. Similarly, the relationship between management practices and computing benefits warrants fuller examination.

[1]John Scoggins, Thomas H. Tidrick, and Jill Auerback, "Computer Use in Local Government," *The Municipal Year Book 1985* (Washington, DC: International City Management Association, 1985): 33–45.

[2]Kenneth L. Kraemer et al., *The Future of Information Systems in Local Governments* (Irvine, CA: Public Policy Research Organization, University of California, 1986).

[3]For recent information on computing in counties, see Patricia T. Fletcher, Stuart I. Bretschneider, and Donald A. Marchand, *Managing Information Technology: Transforming County Governments in the 1990s* (New York: Syracuse University, 1992).

[4]Kraemer et al., 1986.

[5]Kenneth L. Kraemer, William H. Dutton, and Joseph R. Matthews, *Municipal Computers*, Urban Data Service Report, vol. 7, no. 11 (Washington, DC: International City Management Association, 1975).

[6]Irvine Research Corporation, *Right-Sizing Study of the Douglas County Computer Center* (Omaha, NE: Automated Information Systems, 1993) and San Diego Data Processing Corporation, *Technical Strategy* (San Diego, CA: SDDPC, 1992).

[7]Donald F. Norris and Vincent J. Webb, *Microcomputers*, Baseline Data Report vol. 15, no. 7 (Washington, DC: International City Management Association, July 1983).

[8]Fletcher, Bretschneider, and Marchand.

[9]Alana Northrop et al., *Management Policy for Greater Computing Benefits: The Versatility of Training* (Irvine, CA: Center for Research on Information Technology and Organizations, University of California, 1993).

Total Quality Management in Local Government

Jonathan P. West
Evan M. Berman
Mike E. Milakovich
Department of Political Science
Graduate Program in Public Administration
University of Miami, Florida

Findings

Quality improvement activities are most often implemented in police departments.

Seventy-four percent of survey respondents identified citizen complaints as the most important reason for their concern about quality and productivity improvement.

Employee resistance to change is the most often reported barrier to implementing quality improvement.

In recent years, Total Quality Management (TQM) has gained popularity as an important, new approach to management in both the public and private sectors. This set of management strategies, techniques and tools is being adopted by public agencies in many municipal service areas. Local government administrators coping with increased responsibilities, decreased funding, and widespread public cynicism recognize that TQM will help them to contain costs and increase service effectiveness.

This study reports the results from a national survey about the implementation of TQM in local government and the factors that prompt cities to adopt its strategies. Entrenched bureaucracies often resist the organizational change required by TQM, an approach that differs sharply from traditional styles of management and requires important alterations in organizational culture and leadership actions.

What is TQM? Most definitions of quality management are applied to the private manufacturing sector.[1] In practice, the meaning of TQM depends on one's perspective. For a city manager, TQM can "... create an environment that inspires excellence in management and fosters the professional and personal development of all employees" (ICMA Declaration of Ideals) in which it is possible to "strive for personal professional excellence and encourage professional development of associates" (ASPA Code of Ethics). For a city council member, TQM is a vehicle to hold government accountable. For an academic, TQM is a body of knowledge about improving management systems. Perhaps the most that can be agreed upon is *how* TQM is applied in practice. In its purest form, TQM has an explicit focus on (1) the needs of internal and external customers, (2) continual improvement in meeting these needs, (3) a system-wide perspective on objectives and processes, (4) a bias toward objective measurement, and (5) increased employee empowerment and teamwork.[2] Although significant improvements in organizational effectiveness can also be accomplished when some, but not all five elements are

implemented, such partial applications are not considered true TQM.

The literature on TQM includes selected case studies illustrating municipal government attempts to improve organizational effectiveness, but most of them describe partial applications, such as the one found in the best-seller, *Reinventing Government*. The authors, David Osborne and Ted Gaebler, describe how a parks and recreation employee from Visalia, California, took advantage of an opportunity to purchase a much-needed swimming pool for the city by drawing on agency funds that were held over from the previous year. While this example does not show the use of objective measurement, it does show customer-oriented thinking on the part of an empowered employee. A different example comes from the surveys conducted by some police forces such as those in Brighton, Colorado, and Madison, Wisconsin, on community feelings of safety and satisfaction with police services, which enable police to deploy their resources to meet constituent priorities more efficiently.[3] These cases show how customer-oriented thinking and a systematic and objective view of agency services result in improved performance.

Although TQM has assumed cult-like status among its most ardent followers, it is not without critics.[4] One concern is that TQM may be undemocratic in its focus on customers rather than constituents. Public agencies cannot ignore the reality that services must be responsive to the needs of all constituents, particularly in such areas as parole programs, road taxes, and transportation, where the interests of paying customers and constituents sharply diverge.[5] A second potential problem arises because many early TQM applications involved manufacturing, in which product variability is considered something to be minimized. However, local government services should not impose service uniformity in instances where individualized treatment is required. This idea is nicely captured by the statement, "If you treat everyone the same, what varies is satisfaction. To achieve

equal satisfaction, you must vary treatment."[6] A third worry is that TQM may be a fad that has been oversold by proponents[7] and that it may fail to meet expectations when put to the test.[8] Despite these concerns, TQM is being applied in the public sector with increasing frequency.[9]

Finally, it is useful to note the direct links between TQM and previous productivity improvement approaches.[10] Both TQM and its predecessor, organizational excellence, focus on similar objectives of action-orientation, closeness to citizens, employee orientation, flatter organizational structure (agility), clearly stated values, and entrepreneurship.[11] However, TQM also attempts to overcome employee resistance to change by improving the quality of work life, specifically by reducing uncertainty and fear among employees. Of the two approaches, TQM has a stronger focus on clients, and is more apt to advocate specific techniques and to stress continual quality improvement (QI).

METHODOLOGY

In the spring of 1993, a mail survey was sent to city managers/chief administrators in all U.S. municipalities with populations of 25,000 and over.[12] Mailing labels were provided by the International City/County Management Association (ICMA). The survey procedure included three follow-up mailings, as well as telephone reminders. In addition, another 100 telephone interviews were completed with municipal executives concerning TQM activities in their cities. Of the 1,211 jurisdictions surveyed by mail, 433 useable responses (36%) were received (Table 2/1).

The greatest percentage of respondents is from the largest cities and from those with a population ranging from 250,000 to 499,999. Within the regional classification, the highest response rate is for western municipalities (43%) and the lowest for municipalities in the Northeast (23%). The response rate for council-manager jurisdictions is higher (42%) than that

of mayor-council jurisdictions (26%). Because the number of respondents reporting QI in at least one area and having commission, town meeting, and representative town meeting forms of government is so small, the results are difficult to interpret. Throughout this article comparisons are made only between jurisdictions with the mayor-council and council-manager forms of government.

As we designed the survey and analyzed the pilot results we sought to minimize the problems of both false negatives and false positives. The first problem would occur if respondents who were implementing comprehensive quality improvement programs, but not calling them TQM, responded negatively when asked if they were using TQM. False positive responses would occur if respondents who were implementing limited productivity improvement initiatives, but not TQM, responded positively when asked about TQM. To minimize the first concern we substituted the label "quality improvement" (QI) for TQM. A precise definition of QI was provided in the survey instrument (see below) to avoid the second pitfall. This definition encompassed the essential elements of TQM without using that label.

The survey instrument covered three central concepts: quality improvement, employee empowerment, and customer orientation/service. The bulk of this chapter focuses on quality improvement (QI), which is defined in the survey as "a comprehensive management approach to quality and productivity improvement, such as Total Quality Management and other strategies, which include all of the following:

1. Commitment to customer-driven quality,
2. Employee participation in quality improvement,
3. Actions based on facts, data and analysis,
4. Commitment to continuous improvement, and
5. Systemic perspective as a starting point."

Before answering the substantive questions in the survey, respondents were asked to indicate their familiarity with quality improvement efforts in their municipality using a three-item scale: not familiar (0), familiar (1) and very familiar (2). Respondents in municipalities using QI were very familiar (mean = 1.59) with their local QI efforts. An examination of Table 2/1 reveals that a majority (55%) of jurisdictions responding to our survey are implementing QI in at least one municipal service. Larger cities are more likely than smaller ones to be using QI. Those located in the South are more likely than those in the other three regions to be involved in QI efforts. Moreover, council-manager cities are more likely than mayor-council jurisdictions to be undertaking quality improvement initiatives.

In addition, respondents were asked about the way QI is administered. Twenty-four percent indicate that their municipality has a central coordinating staff for quality and productivity improvement efforts, and the larger cities are more likely than others to have staff to coordinate the program. Within the organization, this unit is most commonly located in the personnel department.

GOVERNMENT SERVICES

One way jurisdictions demonstrate their concern with total quality improvement is to implement service-specific QI efforts. Are some government services "leaders" and others "laggards" in undertaking quality improvement initiatives? We provided respondents with a list of 25 municipal services and asked whether quality improvement efforts meeting the five requirements in our definition are underway in these functional areas.[13] Table 2/2 shows that the most frequent use of QI occurs in eleven services, including traditional functions that define the scope of local government: police, recreation, parks, water/sewer, solid/hazardous waste, streets, fire, and fleet vehicles, as well as staff services such as personnel, budget, and data processing. Between 26 and 36% of all respondents report QI initiatives in these 11 services. Table 2/2 reports the use of QI in the remaining 14 service areas as well.

The two columns to the right of the QI column in Table 2/2 report similar results for customer service and employee empowerment activities. Customer service is defined in the questionnaire as "performance objectives that emphasize responsiveness to customers and customer satisfaction. In this survey, the strategy also requires minimally a systematic method of addressing customer satisfaction." Employee empowerment is defined on the survey as a "formal or structured approach which enables individuals and teams to make important decisions about their own work and work environment. Empowerment is generally used to increase responsiveness and innovation." Respondents were advised that empowerment and customer orientation are part of TQM (QI) implementation, and that TQM (QI) includes these elements and more. Customer service is used more frequently in various services (ranging from a low of 8% for gas to a high of 60% for police) than employee empowerment (range = 4% to 41%), and both of these are implemented more frequently than the broader, more comprehensive "total" QI approach (range = 4% to 36%). However, in the case of each of these productivity improvement efforts, results reported in the three columns of Table 2/2 show marked similarities in the rankings across the 25 municipal services. In other words, the rank ordering of government services from most frequent use (police) to least frequent (gas) is based on data from column one for QI; however, the rankings of services would have been very similar had they been derived from data in column two (customer service) or column three (employee empowerment). The services most

Table 2/1   SURVEY RESPONSE AND SAMPLE CHARACTERISTICS

Characteristics	Cities surveyed		Cities responding			Cities Using TQM[1]	
	No. (A)	(%)	No. (B)	(%)	% of (A)	No. (C)	% of (B)
Total[2]	1,211	100	431	100	36	237	55
Population group							
Over 1,000,000	8	1	4	1	50	4	100
500,000–1,000,000	16	1	5	1	31	4	80
250,000–499,999	40	3	23	5	58	16	70
100,000–249,999	131	11	61	14	47	39	64
50,000–99,999	337	28	126	29	37	62	49
25,000–49,999	679	56	212	49	31	112	53
Geographic region[3]							
Northeast	281	23	64	15	23	33	52
North Central	310	26	110	26	35	53	48
South	292	24	116	27	40	78	67
West	328	27	141	33	43	73	52
Form of government[4]							
Mayor-council	442	36	114	26	26	56	49
Council-manager	719	59	305	71	42	172	56
Commission	23	2	7	2	30	4	57
Town meeting and rep. town meeting	27	2	5	1	19	5	100

[1]TQM is adopted in at least one municipal function.

[2]The term cities refers also to towns, townships, villages, and boroughs.

[3]Geographic regions: Northeast—the New England and Mid-Atlantic divisions, which include the states of Connecticut, Maine, Massachusetts, New Hampshire, New Jersey, New York, Pennsylvania, Rhode Island, and Vermont; North Central—the East and West North Central divisions, which include the states of Illinois, Indiana, Iowa, Kansas, Michigan, Minnesota, Missouri, Nebraska, North Dakota, Ohio, South Dakota, and Wisconsin; South—the South Atlantic and the East and West South Central divisions, which include the states of Alabama, Arkansas, Delaware, Kentucky, Florida, Georgia, Louisiana, Maryland, Mississippi, North Carolina, Oklahoma, South Carolina, Tennessee, Texas, Virginia, and West Virginia, and the District of Columbia; West—the Moun-

tain and Pacific Coast divisions, which include the states of Alaska, Arizona, California, Colorado, Hawaii, Idaho, Montana, Nevada, New Mexico, Oregon, Utah, Washington, and Wyoming.

[4]Forms of government: Mayor-council—an elected council serves as the legislative body with a separately elected head of government; Council-manager—the mayor and council make policy and an appointed administrator is responsible for the administration of the city; Commission—a board of elected commissioners serves as the legislative body and each commissioner is responsible for administration of one or more departments; Town meeting—qualified voters meet to make basic policy and choose a board of selectmen to carry out the policy; Representative town meeting—representatives selected by citizens vote at meetings, which may be attended by all town citizens.

likely to adopt any one of these three innovations (QI, CS, EE) are those most likely to adopt the other and, similarly, those least likely to adopt one are least likely to adopt the others. By focusing the remainder of the chapter exclusively on QI, we are using the most conservative and the most comprehensive of the three measures of municipal productivity efforts.

A clearer picture of the kinds of jurisdictions that are implementing QI in the ten leading municipal service areas can be seen in Table 2/3. Not surprisingly, respondents from larger cities generally use QI more frequently than their small city counterparts in providing these services. This pattern holds for all nine of the line services, but not for the two staff services—notably personnel and budget. Also, respondents from the South report more frequent use of QI for all 11 services. This finding of TQM activity in the South is consistent with results from a November 1992 survey of TQM implementation in each state.[14] In the areas of police, personnel, and finance/budgeting, officials from municipalities with a mayor-council form of government are less likely than those from council-manager municipalities to report quality improvement initiatives.

REASONS FOR CONCERN

A combination of external and internal pressures usually spurs an organization to focus on quality improvement. Table 2/4 shows respondents' perceptions of the relative importance of 20 either external or internal factors that relate to quality in their jurisdictions. The factors reported as very important (top of scale) from both categories are response to citizen complaints, interest of the city manager, desire to improve employee productivity, budget pressures, and strategic planning. Other items of importance include community planning activities, voter demands, a desire to promote good public relations, and interest or initiative from senior managers and employees. Interest expressed by mayors, city council persons, and agency directors in the internal environment are additional factors promoting quality-related initiatives. The nature, distribution and relative importance of these factors are discussed in the following sections.

External Forces

Forces in the external environment affect the perceptions, strategies, and action steps of any organization.[15] Table 2/5 shows the percentages of respondents who ranked external factors as a two or a three on the four-point importance scale with zero indicating not important and three indicating very important. These percentages appear in the ''yes'' column in Table 2/5. A majority of respondents rate three out of nine external forces as important to their concern about quality: citizen complaints, community planning activities, and voter demands. Respondents from municipalities of 100,000 and over in population are less likely than smaller juris-

dictions to cite the importance of media discussion as a factor affecting their concern about quality. Officials from cities in the 100,000 to 499,999 population range are less likely than those in either the largest or the smaller jurisdictions to identify demands from other governments, professional associations, or local capabilities as a reason for concern about quality improvements.

Respondents from the Northeast are more likely than those from other regions to attribute their interest in quality to success stories in business, to voter demands, or to citizen complaints. Respondents in the South are more receptive to the cues and demands from other

governments as a stimulus to quality efforts. Media discussion of quality issues is least influential in the North Central region.

Respondents from jurisdictions with mayor-council governments are more likely than those from council-manager jurisdictions to attribute greater importance to voter demands, citizen complaints, success stories in business, and local capabilities as factors affecting quality improvement initiatives. Officials from council-manager jurisdictions give greater importance to media discussion of productivity. The highest percentages of both council-manager and mayor-council jurisdictions responding indicate that community planning activities and citizen

Table 2/2   QUALITY IMPROVEMENT ACTIVITIES IN MUNICIPAL GOVERNMENT SERVICE AREAS

Government services[1]	Quality improvement (% reporting)	Customer service (% reporting)	Employee empowerment (% reporting)
Most frequent use			
Police	35	59	41
Recreation	30	56	36
Parks	29	52	35
Personnel services	30	44	35
Financial/budgetary reporting	29	39	31
Water/sewer	28	47	28
Streets	28	50	33
Solid/hazardous waste	27	44	26
Fire	27	45	29
Fleet/vehicles	25	36	27
Data processing	25	37	28
Moderate use			
Traffic	23	43	27
Buildings	19	30	22
Emergency services	19	33	21
Libraries	16	32	19
Animal control	13	32	18
Taxes	13	29	16
Transit	13	24	14
Least frequent use			
Convention centers	9	16	10
Public health	9	15	10
Social welfare	7	14	9
Electricity	7	12	7
Prison/jails	6	9	7
Museums	6	12	8
Gas	4	8	4

[1]431 respondents provided data

Selected positive comments about QI

''We were able to turn a General Fund deficit into a surplus using QI methods.''

''We have initiated a monthly interview/survey in our customers' homes/ businesses to identify their needs vis-a-vis city services.''

''We have had positive results both with employee buy-in and raising customer satisfaction and positive perceptions.''

''We are reorganizing the balance of the workforce and then will create quality improvement teams for continuous process improvement.''

''Good customer service follow-up tracking procedure implemented.''

''QI activities have now become departmentalized as a result of the new reorganization.''

''[Our city's] experience has been very successful. Customer service has reached an all time high.''

complaints are the most influential external factors prompting concern about quality.

Internal Forces

Forces within the municipal government also influence the attention given to quality-related concerns.[16] Of the 11 internal factors affecting quality improvement in local government presented in Table 2/6, a majority of respondents identify ten on the importance scale: interest by the city manager, mayor, city council members, or employees; initiatives by senior managers or agency directors; and desire to improve employee productivity, to respond to budget pressures, to plan strategically, or to promote public relations. The only item not reported by a majority was the success of pilot programs. Almost nine out of ten respondents think their jurisdic-

tion's interest in quality is linked to the interests of the city manager (89%) or to the goal of improved employee productivity (87%). Seven of these internal forces are important to higher percentages of officials from cities 500,000 and over than to those from medium and small municipalities.

Municipal strategic planning is identified as an important spur to QI by respondents in the South, West, and North Central regions, while pilot program success is more important to respondents in the Northeast. Budget pressures encourage interest in quality improvement, especially among respondents from the South. In addition, respondents from jurisdictions in the South, West, and Northeast are more likely than those from the North Central region to link their concern about quality with the promotion of pub-

lic relations. Respondents from mayor-council cities give greater importance to interest by the mayor and initiatives from both senior managers and agency directors than do respondents from council-manager cities, who attribute greater importance to city manager interest and to employee interest.

IMPLEMENTING QUALITY GOALS AND PROCESSES

What strategies are used to implement new quality goals and processes in local government? The literature suggests that municipalities may rely on organizational reforms, training, use of outside resources, and a host of other approaches to introduce QI.[17] Initially, respondents from jurisdictions where QI is being implemented were provided with a list of 21 strategies and asked to indicate which of these they have used during the last four years. A majority of respondents from jurisdictions implementing QI indicate use of 16 of the 21 strategies (Table 2/7). Identification of customer needs, increased coordination among units (or cross-functional management),[18] monitoring of internal performance and customer satisfaction, reformulation of mission statements, and training of employees in techniques are among the most frequently used strategies for implementing QI goals and processes. Other widely used approaches are training in techniques for senior managers, performance measures, implementation teams, and budgets for quality and productivity improvement. Benchmarking, which we define as "measuring performance against best-in-class units, including other departments or municipalities, and determining how the best in class achieve those performance levels," is one of the more advanced quality tools used in the private sector. In local government, however, benchmarking is one of the least used approaches to introduce QI.

Selected negative comments about QI

"There is a lot of 'faddishness' related to TQM and QI at present! We are trying to adopt the pieces that work well ... without undue stress on the process, itself."

"We need a lot of training but have ... little motivation to fight one more budget battle for the 'latest' panacea for organizational productivity-quality concerns."

"The organization leadership is not consumed by QI and especially empowerment. There is not a critical mass of department heads to implement these initiatives on a large scale."

"... the organization ... is under siege from elected officials who think employees are the problem, not the solution."

"Employee resistance [is] strong due to implementation during budget cutbacks—recessionary economy. Lack of funds to reward employee teams; lack of supervisory commitment to allow employee participation."

"Our biggest problem was benchmarking against other municipalities."

"I do not believe QI as it was formulated in the private sector is totally transferable to the public sector."

Table 2/3 QUALITY IMPROVEMENT ACTIVITIES BY CITY CLASSIFICATION

Classification	No. reporting (A)	Police % of (A)	Recreation % of (A)	Parks % of (A)	Personnel services % of (A)	Financial/ budget % of (A)	Solid/hazardous waste % of (A)	Water/sewer % of (A)	Streets % of (A)	Fire % of (A)	Fleet/vehicles % of (A)	Data processing % of (A)
Total	431	35	30	29	30	29	27	28	28	27	25	25
Population group												
Over 1,000,000	4	75	50	75	25	50	100	75	50	75	50	50
500,000–1,000,000	5	60	40	60	60	20	40	40	60	40	80	20
250,000–499,999	23	30	48	48	39	26	39	52	30	30	35	35
100,000–249,999	61	33	34	33	38	36	30	25	25	33	31	31
50,000–99,999	126	33	25	24	20	28	21	26	25	25	21	22
25,000–49,999	212	36	30	28	32	29	26	25	29	25	24	23
Geographic region												
Northeast	64	33	33	31	27	31	33	28	28	22	25	27
North Central	110	29	20	20	27	23	19	20	25	21	20	19
South	116	41	41	39	40	37	36	38	32	38	36	32
West	141	35	29	28	26	28	22	25	27	25	21	22
Form of government												
Mayor-council	114	29	28	29	26	25	30	29	27	25	27	25
Council-manager	305	36	31	29	30	31	25	27	28	26	24	24
Commission	7	43	14	14	43	29	29	29	14	57	14	14
Town meeting and rep. town meeting	5	100	80	60	80	60	60	60	60	60	60	60

Implementation of new performance measures and formation of quality councils are organizational reforms found more often in jurisdictions with populations 250,000 and over. Officials from jurisdictions of this size are also more likely to use productivity models adopted elsewhere and to monitor customer satisfaction. Those from jurisdictions with populations of 50,000 or less are least likely to offer training in team skills and awareness training for em-

ployees; those from the largest cities (500,000 or more) are least likely to visit other sites to learn about quality initiatives. In addition, use of consultants is reported most often by those in jurisdictions with populations ranging from 250,000 to 499,999.

Reformulating agency missions, monitoring customer satisfaction, training in team skills, and awareness training for senior managers and for employees are strategies used less frequently

in the Northeast than in the other three geographic regions. However, respondents from the Northeast are more likely than those from other regions to use increased coordination, quality budgets, and benchmarking. Respondents from southern cities report greater use of most of the strategies, especially the following five: forming quality councils, identifying customer needs, implementing pilot projects, and training employees and senior managers in techniques. Reliance on outside resources such as consultants and visits to other locales are reported least frequently by administrators from North Central municipalities.

Adoption of new performance measures and increased coordination are reported more frequently by mayor-council than by council-manager jurisdictions; however, administrators from council-manager locales report more frequent attempts to reformulate mission statements, support grass roots initiatives, provide awareness training, train employees and senior managers in QI techniques, and implement productivity models already adopted elsewhere.

ENSURING EMPLOYEE INVOLVEMENT

A different set of strategies needs to be considered for involving employees in municipal quality improvement initiatives. Empowerment, monetary and nonmonetary incentives, organizational development, and performance enhancement initiatives can be critical to QI success. Three of these strategies are used in seven of ten cities: recognizing achievement (75%), basing decisions on objective data

Table 2/4 IMPORTANCE OF REASONS FOR CONCERN ABOUT QUALITY AND PRODUCTIVITY IMPROVEMENT IN YOUR ORGANIZATION

Reasons	No. reporting (A)	Importance Not imp. 0 (% of A)	1 (% of A)	2 (% of A)	Very imp. 3 (% of A)
External					
Citizen complaints	231	9	18	24	50
Community planning activities	221	11	19	43	27
Voter demands	224	22	20	28	30
Success stories in business	216	21	42	25	12
Local capabilities (e.g., of colleges	208	42	31	20	7
Media discussion	218	41	32	20	7
Professional associations	216	38	37	23	2
Used by other nearby governments	201	43	33	22	2
Demands from other governments	211	52	30	14	4
Internal					
City manager's interest	212	5	7	30	59
Increasing employee productivity	233	3	10	40	47
Budget pressures	229	5	16	34	45
City strategic planning	226	11	17	32	40
Public relations	220	13	24	36	28
Initiatives from senior managers	223	16	22	44	18
Employee interest	228	8	33	35	24
Mayor's interest	219	22	19	27	32
Council's interest	223	17	24	34	25
Initiatives from agency directors	220	19	23	38	20
Pilot program success	196	26	32	32	10

Table 2/5 IMPORTANCE OF EXTERNAL FORCES INFLUENCING CONCERN ABOUT QUALITY AND PRODUCTIVITY IN YOUR ORGANIZATION

Classification	Community planning activities No. reporting (A)	Yes % of (A)	Voter demands No. reporting (B)	Yes % of (B)	Citizen complaints No. reporting (C)	Yes % of (C)	Demands from other governments No. reporting (D)	Yes % of (D)	Used by other governments No. reporting (E)	Yes % of (E)	Media discussion No. reporting (F)	Yes % of (F)	Professional associations No. reporting (G)	Yes % of (G)	Success stories in business No. reporting (H)	Yes % of (H)	Local capabilities No. reporting (I)	Yes % of (I)
Total	221	70	224	58	231	74	211	18	201	24	218	27	216	25	216	37	208	27
Population group																		
Over 1,000,000	4	100	4	100	4	100	4	25	4	25	3	0	4	25	4	75	4	25
500,000–1,000,000	4	75	4	100	4	75	4	25	4	25	4	0	4	50	4	75	4	25
250,000–499,999	12	75	16	50	16	56	14	14	14	21	15	7	13	15	15	27	13	15
100,000–249,999	36	69	35	43	37	70	32	6	31	16	35	20	33	12	35	23	34	18
50,000–99,999	60	68	59	58	61	78	53	25	49	33	56	27	56	27	59	32	53	28
25,000–49,999	105	70	106	61	109	78	104	19	99	22	105	32	106	28	99	39	100	31
Geographic region																		
Northeast	33	64	32	72	33	85	31	19	30	17	33	30	32	28	30	50	29	31
North Central	49	63	49	45	53	66	47	9	41	12	47	17	49	22	50	28	48	25
South	71	70	73	64	74	80	68	31	67	37	73	33	70	29	73	44	68	32
West	68	78	70	54	71	68	65	12	63	21	65	25	65	22	63	29	63	21
Form of government																		
Mayor-council	53	70	53	64	56	79	51	16	48	21	52	21	52	25	52	42	50	34
Council-manager	159	70	162	54	166	71	151	19	144	25	157	27	155	24	157	33	150	23
Commission	4	50	4	75	4	75	4	0	4	0	4	50	4	25	4	75	3	67
Town meeting and rep. town meeting	5	80	5	100	5	100	5	0	5	0	5	60	5	60	3	67	5	40

Note: The "yes" column reports the percentages of respondents who ranked the factor as a two or a three on a four point scale, with zero indicating *not important* and three indicating *very important*.

(78%), and involving employees in implementation (81%) (Table 2/8). Monitoring of employee satisfaction, consistency in the use of new performance measures, use of labor-management committees, and employee career development programs are in moderate use. Sharing savings from improvements with employees (i.e., gainsharing) is the least frequently used (15%) of the 12 employee involvement efforts covered.

There is no discernible pattern of variation among jurisdictions of different population sizes in the use of strategies for ensuring employee involvement in municipal quality initiatives. Respondents from the Northeast report fewer efforts than colleagues from other regions to recognize employee achievements, reward group

performance, share savings from improvements with employees, and monitor employee satisfaction. Employee career development programs and use of labor-management committees are reported most often by CAOs from North Central municipalities. The highest percentage of respondents involving employees in the implementation of QI and in developing a plan for cultural change is in the West.

Quality circles and consistent use of performance measures are reported with greater frequency by respondents from mayor-council jurisdictions, while development of plans for cultural change and employee involvement are cited more often by those from council-manager jurisdictions.

GARNERING SUPPORT

Decisions to pursue new goals, modify existing processes, and involve employees may fail to have the desired effect if insufficient attention is paid to garnering support from critical players on the municipal scene. Respondents were asked about their efforts to gain support for QI from managers (city manager/CAO, senior managers, agency directors), politicians (mayor, council members, other political leaders) and other influential actors (community activists, private citizens). All of these strategies are used extensively with the exception of obtaining support from other political leaders and influential private citizens (Table 2/9). Obtaining support

Table 2/6 IMPORTANCE OF INTERNAL FORCES INFLUENCING CONCERN ABOUT QUALITY AND PRODUCTIVITY IN YOUR ORGANIZATION

Classification	City strategic planning No. reporting (A)	Yes % of (A)	Budget pressures No. reporting (B)	Yes % of (B)	Mayor interest No. reporting (C)	Yes % of (C)	Council member interest No. reporting (D)	Yes % of (D)	City manager interest No. reporting (E)	Yes % of (E)	Employee interest No. reporting (F)	Yes % of (F)
Total	226	72	229	79	219	59	223	59	212	89	228	59
Population group												
Over 1,000,000	4	75	4	100	4	75	4	50	3	100	4	50
500,000–1,000,000	4	75	4	100	4	100	4	75	2	100	4	75
250,000–499,999	14	64	16	75	15	67	15	53	15	80	14	57
100,000–249,999	38	63	37	70	35	49	37	46	37	84	36	56
50,000–99,999	59	71	60	88	58	62	59	64	54	93	61	54
25,000–49,999	107	76	108	76	103	57	104	61	101	89	109	63
Geographic region												
Northeast	32	59	33	85	28	61	28	61	22	82	33	52
North Central	50	68	51	65	50	50	50	52	48	85	52	54
South	74	76	74	92	73	66	75	64	71	90	72	64
West	70	76	71	73	60	57	70	57	71	92	71	62
Form of government												
Mayor-council	54	74	55	80	55	75	55	60	37	68	55	49
Council-manager	163	72	165	78	158	53	163	58	168	93	164	63
Commission	4	25	4	75	4	75	4	75	3	67	4	25
Town meeting and rep. town meeting	5	60	5	100	2	100	1	100	4	100	5	80

Classification	Initiatives from agency directors No. reporting (G)	Yes % of (G)	Initiatives from senior managers No. reporting (H)	Yes % of (H)	Pilot program success No. reporting (I)	Yes % of (I)	Public relations No. reporting (J)	Yes % of (J)	Improve employee productivity No. reporting (K)	Yes % of (K)
Total	220	58	223	62	196	42	220	64	234	87
Population group										
Over 1,000,000	3	67	4	75	4	25	3	100	4	100
500,000–1,000,000	4	100	4	75	4	50	4	75	4	100
250,000–499,999	15	60	15	47	14	57	15	40	16	69
100,000–249,999	36	61	37	59	27	33	35	63	39	95
50,000–99,999	57	51	59	58	51	37	57	62	60	85
25,000–49,999	105	59	104	66	96	45	106	64	110	87
Geographic region										
Northeast	32	63	32	69	28	64	32	66	33	88
North Central	50	58	50	64	41	17	50	54	53	81
South	72	60	72	71	64	45	72	71	76	92
West	66	55	69	48	63	44	66	62	71	86
Form of government										
Mayor-council	53	68	53	70	50	46	54	69	56	84
Council-manager	158	55	161	58	137	39	157	61	118	88
Commission	4	25	4	50	4	25	4	50	4	75
Town meeting and rep. town meeting	5	80	5	100	5	80	5	100	5	100

Note: The "yes" column reports the percentages of respondents who ranked the factor as a two or a three on a four point scale, with zero indicating *not important* and three indicating *very important*.

Table 2/7   STRATEGIES USED TO IMPLEMENT QUALITY IMPROVEMENT

Classification	Increasing coordination		Reformulating mission		Implementing new performance measures		Forming a quality council		Identifying customer needs		Monitoring internal performance		Monitoring customer satisfaction	
	No. reporting (A)	Yes % of (A)	No. reporting (B)	Yes % of (B)	No. reporting (C)	Yes % of (C)	No. reporting (D)	Yes % of (D)	No. reporting (E)	Yes % of (E)	No. reporting (F)	Yes % of (F)	No. reporting (G)	Yes % of (G)
Total	216	79	217	71	217	65	215	45	217	85	216	75	218	74
Population group														
Over 1,000,000	3	100	4	75	4	75	4	75	4	75	4	75	4	100
500,000–1,000,000	4	75	4	50	4	100	4	75	4	100	4	100	4	100
250,000–499,999	15	73	15	87	15	73	15	60	14	79	15	67	15	87
100,000–249,999	34	85	33	76	33	64	33	55	35	86	34	85	34	82
50,000–99,999	57	84	57	79	56	61	55	45	56	89	56	71	58	81
25,000–49,999	103	74	104	64	105	64	104	38	104	84	103	73	103	64
Geographic region														
Northeast	30	83	31	58	31	61	31	35	32	84	31	74	32	69
North Central	46	76	46	67	47	64	45	38	47	81	45	71	46	83
South	69	81	68	76	69	67	68	57	69	91	69	77	68	72
West	71	76	72	75	70	64	71	42	69	83	71	75	72	74
Form of government														
Mayor-council	51	84	52	63	51	73	52	38	53	87	52	79	53	75
Council-manager	157	76	156	74	157	62	154	47	155	85	155	74	156	73
Commission	4	75	4	50	4	75	4	75	4	75	4	50	4	100
Town meeting and rep. town meeting	4	100	5	80	5	40	5	40	5	80	5	60	5	80

Classification	Mid-level implementation teams		Budgets for quality improvements		Conducting a pilot implementation		Supporting grass roots initiatives		Comprehensive top-down planning		Benchmarking		Training in techniques for employees	
	No. reporting (H)	Yes % of (H)	No. reporting (I)	Yes % of (I)	No. reporting (J)	Yes % of (J)	No. reporting (K)	Yes % of (K)	No. reporting (L)	Yes % of (L)	No. reporting (M)	Yes % of (M)	No. reporting (N)	Yes % of (N)
Total	216	65	215	62	214	55	213	51	216	46	214	40	219	69
Population group														
Over 1,000,000	3	100	4	75	3	100	3	67	4	75	4	25	4	75
500,000–1,000,000	4	75	4	25	4	75	4	50	4	25	4	50	4	75
250,000–499,999	15	53	15	60	15	67	15	47	15	40	15	53	15	80
100,000–249,999	34	68	35	63	34	74	33	48	34	62	33	45	35	80
50,000–99,999	56	71	54	57	55	47	55	51	55	44	56	27	57	68
25,000–49,999	104	61	103	65	103	49	103	51	104	42	102	43	104	64
Geographic region														
Northeast	31	68	29	69	31	52	31	39	31	48	31	55	31	68
North Central	45	64	47	64	47	49	45	42	46	39	45	42	46	63
South	69	70	69	62	66	62	67	58	68	53	67	40	70	81
West	71	59	70	57	70	53	70	54	71	42	71	31	72	63
Form of government														
Mayor-council	51	65	49	59	52	54	51	41	52	46	52	40	52	63
Council-manager	156	65	157	63	153	55	153	54	155	46	153	39	158	70
Commission	4	75	4	50	4	25	4	75	4	50	4	25	4	100
Town meeting and rep. town meeting	5	60	5	60	5	80	5	40	5	20	5	80	5	100

Classification	Training in techniques for managers		Training in team skills		Awareness training for managers		Awareness training for employees		Use of consultants		Visits to other sites		Productivity models elsewhere	
	No. reporting (O)	Yes % of (O)	No. reporting (P)	Yes % of (P)	No. reporting (Q)	Yes % of (Q)	No. reporting (R)	Yes % of (R)	No. reporting (S)	Yes % of (S)	No. reporting (T)	Yes % of (T)	No. reporting (U)	Yes % of (U)
Total	220	66	219	64	218	56	217	51	218	59	212	43	216	40
Population group														
Over 1,000,000	3	67	4	75	4	75	4	75	4	50	4	25	4	75
500,000–1,000,000	4	50	4	75	4	50	4	50	4	0	4	25	4	75
250,000–499,999	15	67	15	73	15	80	15	80	15	93	14	50	15	47
100,000–249,999	36	83	35	77	34	65	34	59	35	51	33	48	34	38
50,000–99,999	57	70	56	75	56	57	56	46	56	61	55	44	56	39
25,000–49,999	105	59	105	52	105	50	104	45	104	59	102	41	103	38
Geographic region														
Northeast	31	58	31	45	31	42	31	32	31	65	31	45	31	29
North Central	47	60	47	74	46	54	46	48	46	43	43	33	46	28
South	71	77	70	73	69	59	69	55	70	67	68	49	69	51
West	71	63	71	58	72	61	71	56	71	59	70	43	70	43
Form of government														
Mayor-council	51	61	52	58	52	48	52	38	52	56	51	35	52	27
Council-manager	160	67	158	67	157	59	156	55	157	58	152	44	155	45
Commission	4	100	4	75	4	75	4	75	4	100	4	75	4	75
Town meeting and rep. town meeting	5	80	5	40	5	40	5	20	5	100	5	60	5	20

from the city manager/CAO and other senior administrators as well as endorsements from mayors and council members are most often cited. An effort is made by slightly over 50% to secure backing from agency directors and community participants in a majority of municipalities undertaking QI.

Which jurisdictions lead in gaining support for QI activities? Strategies for ensuring agency directors' backing are most common in cities with populations of 250,000 and over, although overall they are used by 56% of respondents. Support of senior managers is sought by all cities with populations of 500,000 and over. Efforts to obtain support via community participation and involvement of influential private citizens are reported least often by respondents

in the North Central region. Strategies designed to gain support from agency directors are used most often by respondents in the Northeast. Predictably, administrators from council-manager jurisdictions are much more likely to pursue efforts to gain city manager support, while those from mayor-council jurisdictions more frequently strive to secure mayoral backing and support from other political leaders (excluding council members).

BARRIERS TO QUALITY IMPROVEMENT INITIATIVES

The literature on public sector productivity and quality improvement devotes considerable at-

tention to obstacles and barriers encountered in implementation.[19] Political, budgetary, and technological obstacles need to be anticipated as do organizational/managerial barriers and those associated with the municipal workforce. Twenty-two barriers were listed on the survey instrument, and respondents were asked to rate the importance of each on a three-point scale, with zero indicating not important and two indicating very important. Ten items are identified as important barriers, determined by combining the percentages of items receiving a one or two on the importance scale (Table 2/10). Competing demands on employee time, employee resistance to change, inadequate rewards for employees, inadequate team building skills, and inadequate employee empowerment are among the biggest

Table 2/8   STRATEGIES FOR ENSURING EMPLOYEE INVOLVEMENT IN QUALITY IMPROVEMENT

Classification	Recognizing achievement		Rewarding group performance		Sharing savings		Decisions based on objective data		Consistency in use of performance measures		Monitoring employee satisfaction	
	No. reporting (A)	Yes % of (A)	No. reporting (B)	Yes % of (B)	No. reporting (C)	Yes % of (C)	No. reporting (D)	Yes % of (D)	No. reporting (E)	Yes % of (E)	No. reporting (F)	Yes % of (F)
Total	219	75	219	29	218	15	220	78	217	46	216	47
Population group												
Over 1,000,000	3	100	4	50	3	100	4	75	3	67	1	100
500,000–1,000,000	4	75	4	25	4	50	4	50	4	25	4	50
250,000–499,999	15	87	15	27	15	20	15	80	14	57	15	47
100,000–249,999	34	91	34	38	35	11	34	91	34	44	34	41
50,000–99,999	59	69	58	22	58	10	59	73	57	44	58	48
25,000–49,999	104	71	104	29	103	17	104	78	105	46	104	48
Geographic region												
Northeast	32	56	31	16	31	10	32	75	31	45	31	39
North Central	48	77	48	29	48	17	48	75	48	52	49	43
South	69	84	70	37	70	17	69	80	68	44	67	52
West	70	74	70	26	69	14	71	80	70	43	69	49
Form of government												
Mayor-council	53	75	52	25	52	13	53	77	51	53	51	45
Council-manager	157	75	158	30	157	17	158	78	157	44	156	48
Commission	4	75	4	50	4	00	4	75	4	25	4	75
Town meeting and rep. town meeting	5	80	5	00	5	00	5	100	5	40	5	20

Classification	Assessing unit readiness		Involving employees		Labor-management committee		Quality circles		Career development		Planning for cultural change	
	No. reporting (G)	Yes % of (G)	No. reporting (H)	Yes % of (H)	No. reporting (I)	Yes % of (I)	No. reporting (J)	Yes % of (J)	No. reporting (K)	Yes % of (K)	No. reporting (L)	Yes % of (L)
Total	216	37	221	81	216	48	217	33	217	46	217	32
Population group												
Over 1,000,000	3	67	3	100	3	33	4	50	2	100	2	50
500,000–1,000,000	4	25	4	75	4	50	4	25	4	00	4	00
250,000–499,999	15	47	15	87	13	23	15	40	15	67	15	47
100,000–249,999	34	47	35	86	35	43	36	36	34	44	34	35
50,000–99,999	56	32	59	81	59	54	56	36	58	45	58	34
25,000–49,999	104	34	105	79	102	50	102	28	104	44	104	28
Geographic region												
Northeast	31	32	31	74	32	53	31	29	31	35	31	19
North Central	48	31	50	68	49	63	46	33	48	54	48	23
South	68	49	70	86	66	29	70	39	69	49	69	35
West	69	30	70	90	69	54	70	29	69	41	69	41
Form of government												
Mayor-council	52	40	52	75	53	51	52	40	51	49	51	22
Council-manager	155	35	160	83	154	45	156	31	157	45	157	34
Commission	4	25	4	100	4	100	4	25	4	25	4	50
Town meeting and rep. town meeting	5	40	5	80	5	60	5	20	5	40	5	40

obstacles. This is an intriguing finding. Each of these barriers relates to employees and each is mutually reinforcing. The picture portrayed by these results is one of employees who are already so absorbed by work-related responsibilities that additional QI efforts seem burdensome. Inadequate employee skills and lack of empowerment suggest that even if these employees could cope with demands on their time, they may be unable to make the important decisions about their own work environment that QI often requires. The absence of adequate rewards for those who undertake quality-related initiatives also makes it easy to understand why employees may be resistant to change. While this picture may be overdrawn and off the mark for particular jurisdictions, local governments will need to think strategically about ways to overcome these barriers to QI implementation.

Political challenges; turnover of political leaders; inadequate understanding of quality concepts; union resistance; inadequate top management support for QI; and the inability to evaluate programs, to shift people, or to document savings are the barriers identified as important more often by managers from cities with populations 500,000 and over than from smaller municipalities. It may be that larger cities identify more barriers because they are implementing more QI.

Higher percentages of managers from the Northeast and the South attribute importance to QI barriers than do managers from the two other regions. The percentages of respondents in the Northeast region identifying a barrier as significant are higher for 10 of the 22 options and higher among respondents from the South for 12 of the 22. In addition, the percentages identifying 14 of the 22 barriers as problematic are higher in mayor-council than council-manager jurisdictions. This is consistent with the previ-

ously reported findings regarding municipal adoption of QI strategies, which show that mayor-council jurisdictions are engaged in fewer quality-related activities than are council-manager jurisdictions.

IMPACT OF QUALITY IMPROVEMENT

Despite the barriers to QI, some cities have achieved success in quality improvements. Many recently established QI programs are just beginning to bear fruit. Sixty-five percent of cities have adopted QI programs since 1991, so it is understandable that 37% of cities indicate that it is too early to speak with confidence about specific impacts resulting from their QI initiatives. Nevertheless, Table 2/11 shows results to date, focusing on both performance objectives and organizational processes. Large majorities indicate positive results on indicators in both of these categories; very few indicate negative results. The most notable impacts are improvements in the following performance objectives: quality of product/service, productivity/efficiency, customer satisfaction, amount of service to customer, timeliness of service, and communication throughout the unit. Organizational process enhancements, such as more unit-wide communication, better group decision-making capabilities, improvements during a period of resource constraints, better informed decision making, greater commitment to stakeholders, higher employee morale, and use of new performance measures are identified in seven out of ten jurisdictions.

Four results of QI efforts are assessed more positively by respondents from cities with 250,000 or more population than by those from smaller municipalities: improvement in group decision-making capability, stimulating high-

quality performance, and assessment of productivity and quality goals.

Respondents from the North Central region show the highest percentage favorably assessing QI's impact on customer satisfaction. Although the highest percentages of respondents reporting positive results in quality of service and productivity are from the Northeast, in general respondents from northeastern jurisdictions give fewer high marks than those from other geographic regions to other QI results, which fits with findings reported earlier showing fewer QI strategies used and more barriers present in this region.

The most clear-cut pattern reported in Table 2/12 is between form of government and quality improvement results. More positive assessments of the impact of QI on such performance indicators as productivity and efficiency, quality of product and service, and, to a lesser extent, customer satisfaction are provided by managers from mayor-council governments than are given by those from council-manager governments. Responses on the organizational process items follow a similar pattern. Respondents from mayor-council governments more frequently say that QI is a stimulus to high quality performance, improved timeliness of internal processes, and improvements despite resource constraints. This finding that fewer positive results are found in council-manager jurisdictions is perplexing given the greater number of quality-related activities in such locales as well as the wider range of QI strategies used and the small number of barriers encountered. It could be inferred from the findings that even though fewer mayor-council jurisdictions have been able to implement QI, officials have made correspondingly greater efforts to ensure substantial political and managerial support, and have used targeted (e.g., employee involvement) strategies to help achieve effective results.

Table 2/9   STRATEGIES FOR ENSURING POLITICAL SUPPORT FOR LOCAL GOVERNMENT QUALITY INITIATIVES

| | Obtain support from/through | | | | | | | | | | | | | | | |
| | City manager/ CAO | | Senior managers | | Agency directors | | Mayor | | City council members | | Other political leaders | | Community participation | | Private citizens | |
Classification	No. reporting (A)	Yes % of (A)	No. reporting (B)	Yes % of (B)	No. reporting (C)	Yes % of (C)	No. reporting (D)	Yes % of (D)	No. reporting (E)	Yes % of (E)	No. reporting (F)	Yes % of (F)	No. reporting (G)	Yes % of (G)	No. reporting (H)	Yes % of (H)
Total	207	86	222	85	218	56	218	76	222	75	217	40	218	53	219	44
Population group																
Over 1,000,000	2	100	4	100	3	67	3	100	3	100	2	100	3	100	3	67
500,000–1,000,000	4	50	4	100	4	75	4	75	4	75	4	25	4	75	4	25
250,000–499,999	15	80	15	87	15	73	15	87	15	73	15	27	15	40	15	53
100,000–249,999	33	85	34	85	34	53	34	74	35	69	35	43	34	62	34	44
50,000–99,999	55	93	60	87	57	54	59	75	59	73	58	38	57	49	59	46
25,000–49,999	98	84	105	82	105	53	103	76	106	77	103	41	105	52	104	41
Geographic region																
Northeast	24	71	32	88	32	72	30	67	32	72	30	40	32	56	32	47
North Central	46	78	50	84	48	54	48	83	49	76	48	40	47	32	48	29
South	67	88	69	84	69	52	69	80	70	79	69	41	68	59	68	49
West	70	93	71	85	69	52	71	72	71	72	70	39	71	61	71	48
Form of government																
Mayor-council	40	58	53	83	53	66	52	88	53	70	50	52	53	58	53	49
Council-manager	160	93	160	84	156	51	158	72	160	76	158	35	156	51	157	41
Commission	3	67	4	100	4	50	4	100	4	100	4	75	4	75	4	50
Town meeting and rep. town meeting	4	100	5	100	5	80	4	50	5	80	5	40	5	60	5	80

Table 2/10   IMPORTANCE OF BARRIERS IN IMPLEMENTING QUALITY IMPROVEMENTS IN YOUR ORGANIZATION

Classification	Political challenges No. reporting (A)	Yes % of (A)	Turnover of political officials No. reporting (B)	Yes % of (B)	Lack of voter support No. reporting (C)	Yes % of (C)	Inadequate rewards for employees No. reporting (D)	Yes % of (D)	Inadequate funds No. reporting (E)	Yes % of (E)	Inadequate training funds No. reporting (F)	Yes % of (F)	Inadequate team building No. reporting (G)	Yes % of (G)	Inadequate understanding No. reporting (H)	Yes % of (H)
Total	221	69	225	59	212	48	219	81	211	76	218	76	222	78	218	72
Population group																
Over 1,000,000	4	100	4	75	3	67	4	75	4	100	4	75	3	67	4	75
500,000–1,000,000	4	75	4	75	4	25	4	100	4	100	4	100	4	100	4	75
250,000–499,999	14	71	14	36	14	50	13	100	14	79	14	79	13	92	14	71
100,000–249,999	37	60	39	54	36	23	38	79	36	75	38	74	38	79	37	73
50,000–99,999	58	74	59	61	57	54	58	90	59	76	58	83	60	78	58	67
25,000–49,999	104	65	105	62	98	53	102	74	94	73	100	72	104	76	101	73
Geographic region																
Northeast	33	70	32	81	31	58	33	88	30	80	31	90	33	76	33	64
North Central	48	67	49	55	47	40	47	66	47	53	49	59	49	78	49	61
South	72	74	75	60	71	46	74	92	69	87	73	81	73	85	72	82
West	68	66	69	51	63	49	65	75	65	78	65	77	67	73	64	72
Form of government																
Mayor-council	55	69	54	69	51	47	53	87	53	85	53	89	54	80	53	77
Council-manager	157	69	162	54	152	46	157	78	150	73	156	72	159	79	156	70
Commission	4	75	4	75	4	75	4	75	4	50	4	50	4	50	4	50
Town meeting and rep. town meeting	5	80	5	100	5	80	5	100	4	100	5	100	5	80	5	80

Classification	Inadequate statistical capabilities No. reporting (I)	Yes % of (I)	Unable to document savings No. reporting (J)	Yes % of (J)	Unable to evaluate progress No. reporting (K)	Yes % of (K)	Lack of positive examples and models No. reporting (L)	Yes % of (L)	Demands on employee time No. reporting (M)	Yes % of (M)	Employee resistance to change No. reporting (N)	Yes % of (N)	Resistance to measures No. reporting (O)	Yes % of (O)
Total	212	56	216	63	221	64	216	56	220	86	224	83	211	67
Population group														
Over 1,000,000	3	67	4	100	4	100	4	25	4	75	4	75	4	75
500,000–1,000,000	4	75	4	100	4	75	4	75	4	75	4	100	4	50
250,000–499,999	13	62	14	64	14	64	13	38	14	86	14	79	14	79
100,000–249,999	37	57	35	57	36	56	37	62	36	92	38	95	34	68
50,000–99,999	56	54	58	59	59	61	59	53	59	92	60	83	60	67
25,000–49,999	99	55	101	65	104	66	99	58	103	82	104	81	95	66
Geographic region														
Northeast	33	67	33	70	33	73	32	53	33	79	33	82	31	84
North Central	46	41	46	48	50	44	48	56	49	80	50	80	48	58
South	69	65	70	70	71	68	72	58	72	96	74	86	66	67
West	64	50	67	64	67	72	64	53	66	83	67	85	66	67
Form of government														
Mayor-council	52	62	53	60	54	63	52	54	55	85	55	82	54	65
Council-manager	151	52	154	64	158	63	155	55	156	87	160	84	149	67
Commission	4	50	4	75	4	75	4	75	4	50	4	100	4	75
Town meeting and rep. town meeting	5	100	5	80	5	100	5	80	5	80	5	100	4	100

Classification	Union resistance No. reporting (P)	Yes % of (P)	Inadequate employee empowerment No. reporting (Q)	Yes % of (Q)	Demands on leaders' time No. reporting (R)	Yes % of (R)	Goal conflict No. reporting (S)	Yes % of (S)	Unable to shift personnel No. reporting (T)	Yes % of (T)	Inadequate top management support No. reporting (U)	Yes % of (U)	Traditional hierarchical structure No. reporting (V)	Yes % of (V)
Total	212	50	217	78	219	80	201	65	218	62	222	57	220	73
Population group														
Over 1,000,000	3	67	4	100	4	100	3	100	3	67	4	100	4	100
500,000–1,000,000	4	75	4	75	4	75	4	50	4	75	4	75	4	75
250,000–499,999	13	38	13	69	14	86	12	75	14	57	14	50	14	79
100,000–249,999	36	42	37	78	37	84	36	72	37	59	37	51	36	92
50,000–99,999	57	54	59	85	59	83	49	73	58	64	60	63	60	78
25,000–49,999	99	51	100	75	101	75	97	58	102	63	103	53	102	61
Geographic region														
Northeast	31	84	29	90	33	85	29	62	33	82	33	48	33	67
North Central	49	55	48	75	50	68	45	51	49	45	50	48	48	71
South	67	33	73	79	71	87	65	78	71	62	72	69	72	79
West	65	48	67	75	65	78	62	65	65	59	67	55	67	70
Form of government														
Mayor-council	53	77	51	82	55	85	48	65	55	75	55	58	53	81
Council-manager	150	39	157	76	155	79	144	67	154	58	158	56	158	71
Commission	4	25	4	75	4	50	4	75	4	75	4	50	4	50
Town meeting and rep. town meeting	5	100	5	100	5	60	5	40	5	40	5	60	5	60

Note: The "yes" column shows the percentages of respondents who ranked the barrier a one or a two on the importance scale.

CONCLUSIONS

Five lessons that can help minimize risk and reduce uncertainty for managers in cities wishing to proceed with QI can be extracted from the examples of best practices in municipalities with experience in quality improvement.[20] First, municipalities can start the QI process by emphasizing customer or citizen service or employee empowerment in those government service areas deemed ready and appropriate for cultural change. Such actions result in service-specific models that will help to develop experienced champions who can serve as internal consultants and change agents in other parts of the organization. These models and individuals will be useful as the focus of reform broadens to more comprehensive quality improvement and as management innovations are diffused throughout the government. Our findings suggest that customer service initiatives are currently found more often than either empowered employees or full-blown QI. Government service areas most receptive to a customer service emphasis are the same ones that are most amenable to employee empowerment and QI.

The second lesson to emerge from our findings is that some service areas are more logical starting places for QI than others. Police, recreation, parks, personnel, and budgeting are five line and staff units that are most appropriate for a full QI thrust as well as for starting more limited customer service and employee empowerment efforts. The first three are front-line services that require rapport with constituents, while the other two are administrative services that can better serve their internal customers by streamlining procedures.

Third, managers need to identify driving forces that help push and sustain the QI thrust and the restraining forces that must be overcome if such efforts are to succeed. City man-

Table 2/11 REPORTING POSITIVE RESULTS OF QUALITY IMPROVEMENT EFFORTS ON MUNICIPAL PERFORMANCE INDICATORS AND PROCESSES

Classification	Quality of service No. reporting (A)	Positive % of (A)	Productivity No. reporting (B)	Positive % of (B)	Customer satisfaction No. reporting (C)	Positive % of (C)	Amount of service to customer No. reporting (D)	Positive % of (D)	Timeliness No. reporting (E)	Positive % of (E)	Cost reduction No. reporting (F)	Positive % of (F)	Increased communication No. reporting (G)	Positive % of (G)	Improved group decision making No. reporting (H)	Positive % of (H)	Stimulated high quality performance No. reporting (I)	Positive % of (I)
Total	181	89	175	85	172	83	182	82	172	79	168	75	197	84	187	78	180	61
Population group																		
Over 1,000,000	4	100	4	100	4	100	3	100	3	100	4	100	4	75	4	100	4	75
500,000–1,000,000	3	100	3	67	3	100	3	100	2	100	3	67	4	100	4	100	4	75
250,000–499,999	12	75	11	91	11	82	11	82	11	82	12	83	12	92	11	82	10	80
100,000–249,999	29	90	29	86	28	86	29	83	28	79	26	92	30	83	28	75	30	63
50,000–99,999	45	93	46	85	44	84	46	85	44	80	42	71	55	84	51	73	49	49
25,000–49,999	88	86	82	84	82	82	90	78	84	77	81	68	92	83	89	80	83	64
Geographic region																		
Northeast	25	92	24	92	24	75	27	78	24	75	25	64	30	80	26	81	27	59
North Central	40	90	38	89	36	92	40	78	38	79	35	71	46	89	42	74	42	52
South	61	87	56	82	58	79	60	87	57	77	57	75	61	84	63	78	55	69
West	55	87	57	82	54	87	55	80	53	83	51	80	60	82	56	80	56	61
Form of government																		
Mayor-council	44	98	41	95	40	88	42	86	39	79	40	78	50	86	44	82	42	71
Council-manager	130	85	128	82	126	83	133	80	126	79	123	74	138	83	135	76	131	58
Commission	4	75	4	75	3	67	3	67	4	75	2	50	4	75	3	100	3	67
Town meeting and rep. town meeting	3	100	2	100	3	100	4	75	3	100	3	67	5	100	5	100	4	50

	Ability to improve in spite of constraints on resources No. reporting (J)	Positive % of (J)	Improved decision making due to availability of information No. reporting (K)	Positive % of (K)	Improved timeliness of internal processes No. reporting (L)	Positive % of (L)	Movement of decision making to lower level No. reporting (M)	Positive % of (M)	Commitment to stakeholders No. reporting (N)	Positive % of (N)	Morale No. reporting (O)	Positive % of (O)	Goal assessment No. reporting (P)	Positive % of (P)	New performance measures No. reporting (Q)	Positive % of (Q)
	171	70	191	70	185	63	182	68	174	72	191	70	175	57	178	72
	4	75	4	75	3	67	4	75	3	100	4	75	4	75	3	100
	3	67	4	50	4	100	4	75	3	67	4	50	4	75	4	75
	11	82	11	55	10	70	11	64	11	82	11	55	9	67	11	82
	26	69	30	70	30	67	29	59	30	70	30	70	28	57	27	78
	43	60	51	69	49	53	50	64	47	70	51	69	47	55	49	59
	84	74	91	73	89	64	84	73	80	73	91	73	83	55	84	75
	22	64	30	63	27	56	24	63	27	63	30	63	25	44	25	64
	40	58	43	67	42	62	42	71	38	68	43	67	41	51	38	68
	57	79	61	74	61	64	58	67	55	80	61	74	54	61	60	77
	52	73	57	70	55	65	58	67	54	72	57	70	55	64	55	73
	39	79	48	71	47	70	41	73	43	72	48	71	41	59	43	77
	126	67	134	69	132	60	134	66	125	71	134	69	127	57	129	71
	4	50	4	25	3	67	4	75	4	100	4	25	3	67	4	50
	2	100	5	100	3	67	3	67	2	100	5	100	4	50	2	100

Note: The "yes" column shows the percentages of respondents who ranked the results as +1 and +2 on a five point scale, which ranged from −2 (very negative) to +2 (very positive).

ager or CAO support, a pervasive concern about increasing productivity, budget pressures, and a decision to make QI part of city strategic planning activities are critical driving forces originating from inside the organization. Citizen complaints, voter demands, and community planning activities are motivating forces pressuring the organization from the outside. Restraining forces can be categorized as political, budgetary, technological, managerial, or worker-related. Knowledge of the field of forces unique to a particular municipal jurisdiction or critical decision process enables "transformational" leaders and managers to mold their strategies to the particular situation.

The fourth lesson is that QI strategies can be selected from a set of strategic packages, each appropriate to a particular purpose. If inadequate knowledge of QI is a key barrier to improved productivity, then awareness training, training in techniques, or training in skills targeted at either managers, employees, or both may be combined with various empowerment strategies (e.g., use of monetary or nonmonetary incentives, performance data, or organizational/ employee development programs) to bring about desired changes. Results from our survey provide a menu of such strategies with information on how frequently various selections have been tried. Of the more than 40 strategies we consider, the findings highlight the critical importance of three—obtaining managerial support, identifying customer needs, and involving employees with implementation.

The fifth lesson deals with the results on municipal performance objectives and organizational processes expected from QI. While it is too early to gauge long-range impacts of QI in many municipalities, results to date suggest gains in service quality, customer satisfaction, and employee productivity. In addition, organizational changes such as increased communication, improved group decision-making capabilities, and high performance despite resource constraints are among the positive results that managers have identified.

It is impossible to say definitively whether TQM, or QI as we refer to it, will have lasting effects on municipal government. Preliminary indications from the baseline data provided by this study are that QI can be adapted to a variety of local government settings in response to a mix of internal and external driving forces. In many cities, a broad array of implementation strategies have been used with promising results despite a formidable combination of restraints and barriers.

[1] W. Edwards Deming, *Out of Crisis* (Cambridge, MA: MIT Center for Advanced Engineering Study, 1986); Joseph Juran, *Juran on Leadership for Quality* (New York: McGraw-Hill, 1988); Kaoru Ishikawa, *What is Total Quality Control? The Japanese Way* (Englewood Cliffs, NJ: Prentice Hall, 1985).

[2] Mike Milakovich, *Beyond Total Quality: Service Organizations Survival Guide* (Westport, CT: Quorum Books, forthcoming); Mike Milakovich, "Total Quality Management for Public Service Productivity Improvement," in Marc Holzer, ed., *Public Productivity Handbook* (New York: Marcel Dekker, 1992): 577–602.

[3] David Osborne and Ted Gaebler, *Reinventing Government* (Reading, MA: Addison-Wesley, 1992); Joe Sensenbrenner, "Quality Comes to City Hall," *Harvard Business Review* (March-April 1991): 64–75; Robert A. Galloway, "Quality Improvement and Heightened Self Improvement: The Brighton Police Story," *National Productivity Review* (Autumn 1992): 453–61.

[4] J. Walters, "The Cult of Total Quality," *Governing* (May 1992): 38–42.

[5] James E. Swiss, "Adapting Total Quality Management (TQM) to Government," *Public Administration Review* (July/August 1992): 356–62; see also George Frederickson, "Painting Bull's-Eyes around Bullet Holes," *Governing* vol. 6, no. 1 (October 1992): 13.

[6] Kenneth B. Johnston, *Beyond Bureaucracy: A Blueprint and Vision for Government That Works* (Homewood, IL: Business One Irvin, 1993): 29.

[7] Robert B. Denhardt, *The Pursuit of Excellence: Strategies for Managerial Success* (Belmont, CA: Wadsworth, 1993).

[8] Fred R. Bleakley, "Many Companies Try Management Fads, Only to See Them Flop," *Wall Street Journal* (July 6, 1993): 1.

[9] Milakovich, *Beyond Total Quality*.

[10] Holzer, ed., *Public Productivity*.

[11] P. Epstein and D. Cutchin, "The Achieving Organization," *National Civic Review* vol. 79, no. 3 (May 1988): 207–21; David Carr and Ian Littman, *Excellence in Government* (Washington, DC: Coopers and Lybrand, 1990); W. Duncan, P. Ginter and S. Caper, "Excellence in Public Administration: Four Transferable Lessons from the Private Sector," *Public Productivity and Management Review* vol. 14, no. 3 (1991): 227–36.

[12] The address labels used in this survey typically included the name of the city manager or municipal executive; where the name was not known the address label included the position title of the chief administrative officer.

[13] Municipalities were classified as implementing QI if respondents indicated that one or more government services in their jurisdiction was engaged in a comprehensive management approach to quality and productivity improvement, such as TQM or other activities, including the five elements of our definition (see Methodology section).

[14] See Robert S. Kravchuk, "Total Quality Management in the States: A 50-State Survey," paper presented at the Northeast Regional Conference of the American Society for Public Administration, 11–13 November 1992, Boston, MA. Kravchuk's survey results identified seven southern states among the 15 top-ranked states using a composite index of TQM implementation status. Those seven states were Arkansas, Texas, West Virginia, Maryland, Oklahoma, Delaware, and Florida.

[15] Mary E. Guy, "Productive Work Environments," in Holzer, ed., *Public Productivity*, 321–33.

[16] Ibid.

[17] Steven Cohen and Ronald Brand, *Total Quality Management in Government* (San Francisco: Jossey-Bass, 1993).

[18] A. Keith Smith, "Total Quality Management in the Public Sector," *Quality Progress* vol. 26, no. 7 (July 1993): 57–65.

[19] David Ammons, "Productivity Barriers in the Public Sector," in Holzer, ed., *Public Productivity*, 117–38.

[20] Richard Rose, *Lesson Drawing in Public Policy* (Chatham, NJ: Chatham House, 1993).

Alternative Service Delivery In Local Government, 1982–1992

Rowan Miranda
Karlyn Andersen
University of Pittsburgh

Findings

In some areas, most notably crime prevention/patrol and the operation and maintenance of recreational facilities, the exclusive use of local government employees has increased substantially since 1982.

Local governments adopting various forms of private service delivery encounter obstacles almost 50% of the time.

Periodic taxpayer revolts and more than a decade of fiscal strain have led local officials to reexamine the provision and delivery of services. Mandates from state and federal governments, of course, often require localities to provide a service, but should the local government always deliver the service or is there a more efficient, cost-effective approach? If contracting out is desirable, should the government contract with for-profits or nonprofits? How many services could be delivered through intergovernmental agreements? Which services are citizens willing to purchase directly from the marketplace or produce themselves?

More than three decades ago, in their influential study of the organization of metropolitan government, Ostrom, Tiebout, and Warren argued that the "separation of the provision of public goods and services from their production opens the greatest possibility for redefining economic functions in a public service economy."[1] The separation of *provision* (i.e., responsibility) from *production* (i.e., delivery) has more recently been recast by the authors of *Reinventing Government* as *steering* versus *rowing*.[2] The separation of these processes results in a range of alternative service delivery approaches (ASDAs), which are more commonly referred to as forms of privatization even though the private sector is not always involved.[3] Although ASDAs are not new, interest in new ways of delivering services is likely to persist as long as fiscal pressures continue. Lately, an increase in federal mandates has prompted local governments to consider contracting out, particularly for clean up of toxic waste and other activities that require technical expertise and sophisticated equipment. However, even when the potential cost savings from alternative service delivery approaches seem compelling, governments may fear a loss of control over the quality of the service.

The International City/County Management Association (ICMA) conducted surveys on alternative service delivery in 1982 and 1988. This article examines the use of ASDAs by cities and counties in 1992 and the service delivery trends for selected services. Because an analysis of the 1988 survey results does not show major changes in the use of ASDAs between 1982 and 1988,[4] only the 1982 data are used for comparisons in this article.

METHODOLOGY

In order to gather information on which services local governments are providing and on the service delivery arrangements, ICMA designed and conducted a nationwide survey of municipalities and counties in the fall of 1992. The survey was mailed to the chief administrative officers of all municipalities 10,000 and over in population and all counties 25,000 and over in population. Additionally, as was done with the 1982 and 1988 surveys, a sample was drawn of one in eight jurisdictions and counties with pop-

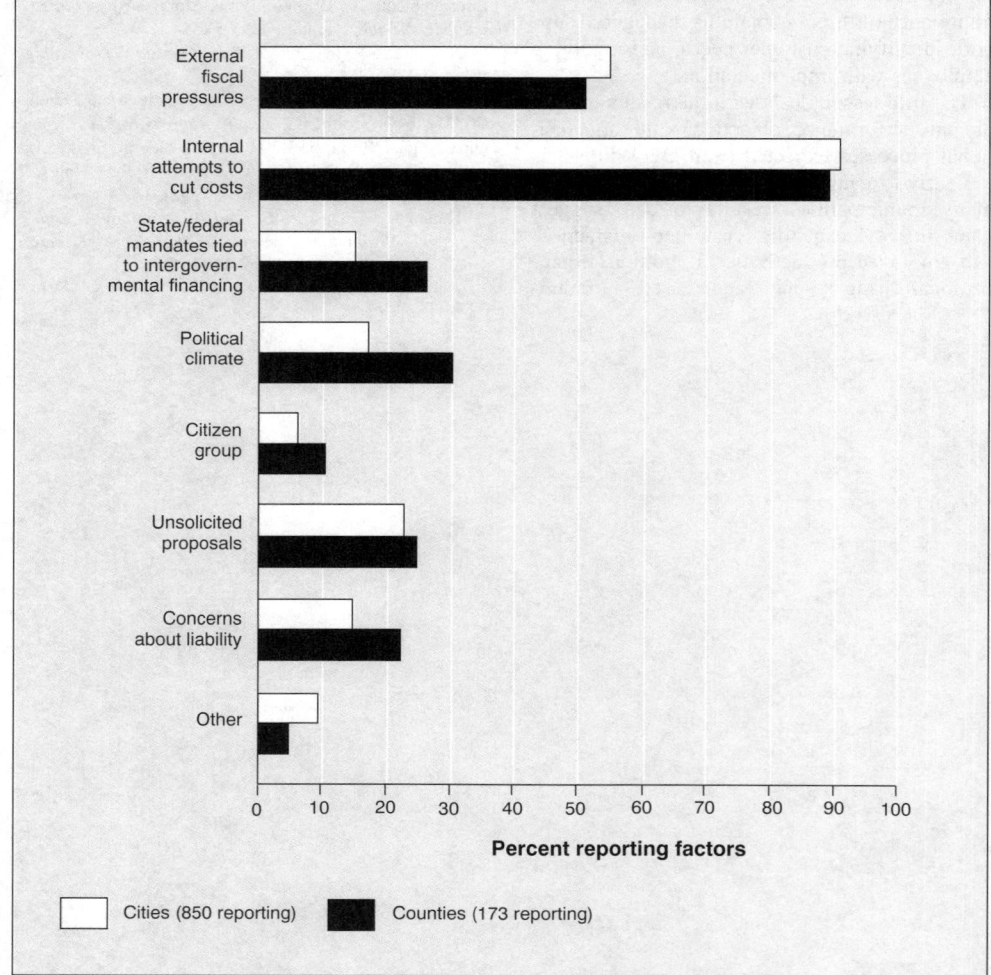

Figure 3/1   *Factors prompting consideration of private service delivery*

ulations from 2,500 to 10,000 and from those under 2,500 that are recognized by ICMA.[5]

Responses were received from 1,504 municipalities and counties for an overall response rate of 31% (Table 3/1). The response rate for municipalities (36.8%) is more than twice the response rate of counties (17.6%); 81% of all survey responses are from municipalities. Response rates also vary by population, geographic region, and metropolitan status of the responding local governments. Although the overall response rates are reasonable for mail surveys, the differences in response rates by specific characteristics of the jurisdiction suggest that the data are subject to self-selection bias that may affect the results.

The 1992 survey content is similar to that of the 1982 survey although the response rate in 1982 was higher for both municipalities (46%)

Table 3/1   SURVEY RESPONSE

Classification	No. cities and counties surveyed (A)	No. responding	% of (A)
Total, all cities and counties[1]	4,935	1,504	30.5
Population group			
Over 1,000,000	33	6	18.2
500,000–1,000,000 ..	72	21	29.2
250,000–499,999	133	41	30.8
100,000–249,999	374	110	29.4
50,000–99,999	711	210	29.5
25,000–49,999	1,282	361	28.2
10,000–24,999	1,700	568	33.4
5,000–9,999	307	97	31.6
2,500–4,999	255	65	25.5
Under 2,500	68	25	36.8
Geographic division[2]			
New England	416	97	23.3
Mid-Atlantic	669	159	23.8
East North Central ...	948	283	29.9
West North Central ..	489	182	37.2
South Atlantic	715	264	36.9
East South Central ..	381	59	15.5
West South Central ..	540	135	25.0
Mountain	267	111	41.6
Pacific Coast	510	214	42.0
Metro status[3]			
Central	844	280	33.2
Suburban	2,243	771	34.4
Independent	1,848	453	24.5

[1]The term *cities* refers also to towns, townships, villages, and boroughs.
[2]*Divisions: New England*—the states of Connecticut, Maine, Massachusetts, New Hampshire, Rhode Island, and Vermont; *Mid-Atlantic*—the states of New Jersey, New York, and Pennsylvania; *East North Central*—the states of Illinois, Indiana, Michigan, Ohio, and Wisconsin; *West North Central*—the states of Iowa, Kansas, Minnesota, Missouri, Nebraska, North Dakota, and South Dakota; *South Atlantic*—the states of Delaware, Florida, Georgia, Maryland, North Carolina, South Carolina, Virginia, and West Virginia, plus the District of Columbia; *East South Central*—the states of Alabama, Kentucky, Mississippi, and Tennessee; *West South Central*—the states of Arkansas, Louisiana, Oklahoma, and Texas; *Mountain*—the states of Arizona, Colorado, Idaho, Montana, Nevada, New Mexico, Utah, and Wyoming; *Pacific Coast*—the states of Alaska, California, Hawaii, Oregon, and Washington.
[3]*Metro status: Central*—core city of an MSA; *Suburban*—incorporated city located within an MSA; *Independent*—city located outside of an MSA.

and counties (22%). The 1982 survey collected information on a broader range of service delivery approaches: The categories "self-help," "vouchers," and "incentives" were excluded from the 1992 survey because the number of respondents reporting use of these methods in both 1982 and 1988 was minimal.

SERVICE DISCONTINUATION

Despite tighter fiscal constraints faced by local governments, there is little evidence to indicate that load-shedding has increased. Many municipal and county services are mandated by law, which makes shedding more difficult and encourages local governments to look to ASDAs to reduce costs. For most services, approximately 1% to 6% of responding jurisdictions indicate that services had been discontinued. The proportion of counties reporting load-shedding is even less—approximately 1% to 2% in most service areas. There are, however, some exceptions to this trend, especially for solid waste related functions.

Discontinuation of residential and commercial solid waste collection and solid waste disposal increased for both responding groups. Shedding of parking meter maintenance/collection functions and prison operations by municipalities also increased substantially from 1982. At the county level, hospital services are the most popular candidate for service shedding. The 1992 results show that nearly 1 in 10 counties discontinued hospital operations.

A reverse trend can be seen in the support function area. A higher percentage in 1992 than in 1982 report that building/grounds maintenance, building security, tax bill processing and assessing, and delinquent tax collection are handled by local government employees. This increase may be attributed to a different group of respondents or local government employees may have resumed these activities.

SERVICE PROVISION

A list of services covered by the survey is shown in Table 3/2. Municipalities are generally responsible for more functions than counties. Municipalities and counties show the highest percentages providing public safety operations, especially crime prevention/patrol and police/fire communications, and support functions, including building and grounds maintenance, payroll, and personnel services.

Municipal provision of public works/transportation and public safety has remained relatively stable since 1982, although some decreases have occurred in residential and commercial solid waste disposal (Table 3/3). Parking meter maintenance/collection is another service discontinued by a noticeably higher percentage of jurisdictions reporting in 1992 than in 1982. Municipal provision of health and human services, especially sanitary inspections and operations of mental health/retardation programs, has increased substantially. Counties have increased their role in providing inspection/code enforcement.

USE OF PUBLIC EMPLOYEES

In general, a modest majority of local governments report service delivery by their employees exclusively (Figure 3/1). In many service areas, there has been a decrease in the exclusive use of local government employees over the past decade, and there appears to be a significant decrease in the partial use of government employees as well. Table 3/4 illustrates the specific services that public managers believe are best delivered exclusively or in-part by local government employees. The combined municipal and county data in Table 3/4 show that exclusive use of public employees is highest in the public safety area. In crime prevention/patrol, the percentage of jurisdictions reporting exclusive use of employees has increased 14 percentage points and the percent reporting partial use of employees has decreased 14 percentage points since 1982. In 1992, approximately 75% of local governments report exclusive use of government employees for operation and maintenance of recreational facilities compared with 58% in 1982. Nearly 80% of local governments report exclusive use of local employees for data processing services, an increase of 15 percentage points since 1982. Some of the increase in governmental production of this service could be related to the declining costs of data processing in instances where mainframes are replaced by personal computers.

Despite the increase for data processing functions, most support functions reveal substantial decreases in exclusive use of government employees. Tax bill processing/assessing and delinquent tax collection are two areas in which the exclusive use of government employees has decreased. Other noticeable decreases have occurred in public works/transportation services, including street repair services, street and parking lot cleaning, traffic signal installation and maintenance, and tree trimming and planting. With the exception of traffic signal installation/maintenance, many of these services show increases in the partial use of government employees, which implies a greater use of ASDAs.

Both exclusive and partial use of public employees have declined in health and human services, especially in child welfare programs; partial use of public employees in this area dropped from 37% in 1982 to 19% in 1992, and exclusive use dropped 10 percentage points during that same time period. Municipalities and counties also report substantial decreases in partial use of employees for elderly, public health, drug/alcohol treatment, and mental health/retardation programs. Some of the movement away from government involvement in these services is probably related to declining federal aid. The Community Development Block Grant (CDBG) was the lifeblood of many nonprofit and for-profit agencies that contracted with municipalities to provide human services. As funding for the CDBG was scaled back, contracts with external producers were cut back.

CONTRACTING

Contracting is the oldest and most popular method of alternative service delivery. Under this approach, government maintains responsibility for a service but contracts with a for-profit or nonprofit organization to actually deliver the service. Contracting is especially desirable when competition exists among firms and when there is a mechanism to measure service quality. Contracting allows more flexibility than typically allowed by direct government service delivery. For example, as intergovernmental aid increases, services can also; as it decreases, services can be reduced. By contrast, rules imposed by collective bargaining often prevent government agencies from expanding or cutting back on labor as easily.

Complete service delivery can be contracted out, or local government employees can perform some of the functions and the private firm can deliver the rest. For example, a private firm may contract to provide residential solid waste collection trucks and drivers, while local government employees perform the actual hauling of garbage onto the trucks. The private firm may be able to maintain the trucks at lower cost than the local government can and may want to protect its investment with its own drivers, but the local government employees may perform the actual pick-up more economically and efficiently. One of the byproducts of contracting is that it can provide an external benchmark for evaluating the performance of public agencies.

Some jurisdictions allow employees to respond to RFPs when they are sent out. Phoenix, Arizona, is perhaps the most publicized example of this practice. The city employees' proposal for service delivery has been the one selected in several instances.

Contracting, which was once limited to specialized areas such as legal and insurance services, is now the most frequently used alternative service delivery approach. Although the reported use of contracting varies across service areas, contracts have been used for every service local governments provide (Table 3/5). Are some services better suited for production by nonprofits? Local governments report the greatest use of nonprofits in the delivery of health and human services and cultural and arts programs, which suggests that perhaps these services are strong candidates for contracting out. Some 41% of municipalities and counties report using contracts for cultural and arts program operations, and 37% report contracts for museum operations. In recent years, Pittsburgh has increased contracts with nonprofits for some cultural and arts programs as an attempt to export some of the tax-burden for these services to suburbanites. This is accomplished because the nonprofits rely on user fees rather than exclusively on property taxes, so a greater share of the financial burden is shifted to people from the suburbs who take advantage of the cultural opportunities.

Local governments are more likely to use for-profit organizations to deliver most public works/transportation services, public utilities,

Table 3/2 SERVICES PROVIDED BY CITIES AND COUNTIES, 1982 AND 1992

Service	Cities (%)		Counties (%)	
	1982	1992	1982	1992
Public works/transportation				
Residential solid waste collection	76	68	37	33
Commercial solid waste collection	67	53	32	29
Solid waste disposal	67	63	65	67
Street repair	97	99	69	78
Street/parking lot cleaning	94	94	34	40
Snow plowing/sanding	76	80	54	59
Traffic sign/signal installation/maintenance	92	94	64	71
Parking meter maintenance/collection	42	31	5	7
Tree trimming/planting	87	93	52	59
Cemetery administration/maintenance	43	46	21	24
Inspection/code enforcement	96	99	58	80
Parking lot/garage operation	49	44	17	19
Bus transit system operation/maintenance	28	35	23	24
Paratransit system operation/maintenance	31	31	27	25
Airport operation	29	35	31	45
Water distribution	...	83	...	39
Water treatment	...	77	...	34
Sewage collection and treatment	...	86	...	40
Disposal of sludge	...	75	...	40
Disposal of hazardous materials	...	54	...	41
Public utilities				
Electric utility operation and management	...	34	...	12
Gas utility operation and management	...	29	...	12
Utility meter reading	77	64	22	23
Public safety				
Crime prevention/patrol	96	99	77	92
Police/fire communication	95	98	85	89
Fire prevention/suppression	92	96	53	67
Emergency medical service	76	86	60	71
Ambulance service	69	79	57	66
Traffic control/parking enforcement	95	96	39	47
Vehicle towing and storage	79	77	40	34
Health and human services				
Sanitary inspection	50	68	58	77
Insect/rodent control	58	61	50	56
Animal control	85	87	70	79
Animal shelter operation	69	70	60	68
Daycare facility operation	21	30	31	28
Child welfare programs	19	32	72	69
Programs for elderly	62	67	75	82
Operation/management of hospitals	16	26	34	37
Public health programs	32	46	70	83
Drug/alcohol treatment programs	26	44	62	78
Operation of mental health/retardation programs/facilities	17	39	66	77
Prisons/jails	...	59	...	97
Operation of homeless shelters	...	36	...	39
Parks and recreation				
Operation and maintenance of recreation facilities	91	95	61	72
Parks landscaping and maintenance	93	95	65	73
Operation of convention centers and auditoriums	26	33	15	22
Cultural and arts programs				
Operation of cultural and arts programs	41	53	29	30
Operation of libraries	63	73	66	66
Operation of museums	25	40	32	36
Support functions				
Buildings/grounds maintenance	94	99	92	93
Building security	84	82	83	80
Fleet management and vehicle maintenance				
heavy equipment	94	98	84	88
emergency vehicles	90	95	74	82
all other vehicles	92	97	85	88
Payroll	96	99	96	98
Tax bill processing	99	81	90	97
Tax assessing	79	75	83	93
Data processing	82	97	80	95
Delinquent tax collection	61	81	89	97
Title records/plat map maintenance	...	79	...	95
Legal services	91	93	83	92
Secretarial services	94	98	86	94
Personnel services	94	98	88	94
Public relations/information	89	96	76	81

Table 3/3   SERVICE DISCONTINUATION, 1982 AND 1992

Service	Cities (%) 1982	Cities (%) 1992	Counties (%) 1982	Counties (%) 1992
Public works/transportation				
Residential solid waste collection	2	10	1	5
Commercial solid waste collection	5	12	1	6
Solid waste disposal	8	12	3	7
Street repair	0	1	1	2
Street/parking lot cleaning	1	2	1	4
Snow plowing/sanding	0	1	1	3
Traffic sign/signal installation/maintenance	2	2	1	2
Parking meter maintenance/collection	10	22	1	3
Tree trimming/planting	2	2	1	1
Cemetery administration/maintenance	1	3	2	3
Inspection/code enforcement	1	1	1	0
Parking lot/garage operation	1	3	1	3
Bus transit system operation/maintenance	4	5	1	3
Paratransit system operation/maintenance	3	4	1	2
Airport operation	3	3	2	2
Water distribution	...	1	...	2
Water treatment	...	2	...	2
Sewage collection and treatment	...	2	...	2
Disposal of sludge	...	4	...	3
Disposal of hazardous materials	...	4	...	3
Public utilities				
Electric utility operation and management	...	2	1	2
Gas utility operation and management	...	2	1	1
Utility meter reading	1	2	0	2
Public safety				
Crime prevention/patrol	0	0	2	1
Police/fire communication	2	1	1	4
Fire prevention/suppression	1	1	1	1
Emergency medical service	3	2	2	2
Ambulance service	4	3	2	3
Traffic control/parking enforcement	0	1	1	1
Vehicle towing and storage	2	2	1	1
Health and human services				
Sanitary inspection	5	3	2	1
Insect/rodent control	3	3	2	2
Animal control	3	3	1	2
Animal shelter operation	3	4	3	3
Daycare facility operation	1	2	3	2
Child welfare programs	2	2	2	1
Programs for elderly	3	1	2	2
Operation/management of hospitals	2	3	5	9
Public health programs	2	2	3	0
Drug/alcohol treatment programs	2	1	4	2
Operation of mental health/retardation programs/facilities	1	1	1	2
Prisons/jails	...	6	...	0
Operation of homeless shelters	...	1	...	1
Parks and recreation				
Operation and maintenance of recreation facilities	2	1	1	3
Parks landscaping and maintenance	1	1	1	3
Operation of convention centers/auditoriums	1	2	1	2
Cultural and arts programs				
Operation of cultural and arts programs	1	2	1	3
Operation of libraries	4	2	1	3
Operation of museums	2	2	2	5
Support functions				
Buildings/grounds maintenance	7	1	1	2
Building security	5	1	0	1
Fleet management and vehicle maintenance				
heavy equipment	1	1	0	2
emergency vehicles	0	1	1	2
all other vehicles	0	1	0	1
Payroll	1	1	0	1
Tax bill processing	7	2	1	1
Tax assessing	6	3	1	1
Data processing	1	0	1	2
Delinquent tax collection	5	2	1	1
Title records/plat map maintenance	...	1	...	1
Legal services	1	1	1	1
Secretarial services	0	0	0	1
Personnel services	0	0	0	1
Public relations/information	0	0	1	2

public safety, parks and recreation, and support functions. In 1992, for example, 54% of municipalities and counties report contracts with for-profit firms for commercial solid waste disposal—an increase of 13 percentage points since 1982. The greatest increase in contracting with for-profit firms occurred in day care provision. More than half (54%) of governments surveyed currently contract with a for-profit firm for day care, an increase of 21 percentage points from 1982.

Contracts with for-profit firms have decreased since 1982 for tax bill and data processing (from 22% to 5% and from 22% to 8%, respectively). The reduction in contracts for data processing may be explained by the lower cost of information processing in the personal computer age.

OTHER GOVERNMENTS AND AUTHORITIES

Intergovernmental agreements refers to formal arrangements in which one government pays another to deliver designated services. *Authorities* are legally distinct entities usually created to operate enterprise-type functions. Unfortunately, because the survey asks only whether a service is provided by "another government or authority," the responses do not necessarily demonstrate that a formal intergovernmental agreement exists. For these reasons, the 1992 data can be used to demonstrate only whether the service is delivered by another government or authority. Consequently, the data should be interpreted cautiously.

Service delivered by another government or authority is most frequently reported in the areas of public works and transportation and health and human services (Table 3/6). Nearly half (49%) the bus transit systems are provided through another government or authority, and approximately one-third of respondents use this approach for sewage collection and treatment and for disposal of sludge and hazardous materials. In the health and human services area, the use of other governments or authorities is widespread for child welfare programs (63%) and mental health/retardation programs (67%). Support functions use this service delivery alternative for tax bill processing (38%), tax assessing (51%), and title records/plat map maintenance (44%).

Reported use of another government or authority has grown substantially for many services. The largest gains from 1982 to 1992 occurred in child welfare programs (from 26% to 63%), mental health programs (from 32% to 67%), and public health programs (from 28% to 57%). Cultural and arts programs also experienced noticeable increases in the use of this approach since 1982. Although this approach generally increased across service areas, marginal decreases are discernible for support functions, building/grounds maintenance, building security, and legal services.

FRANCHISES AND CONCESSIONS

Under this approach, a jurisdiction or county awards to one or more producers the right to service a particular area. Citizens pay for the service directly to the firm. The role of governments is limited to ensuring that firms meet specific price and quality criteria. Examples of franchises include cable TV, electric power, residential solid waste collection, and taxi service. Under *exclusive* franchises, services are produced by private, regulated monopolies; *nonexclusive* franchises allow competition for customers. Concessions are closely related to franchises.

Survey results show minimal use of franchises and concessions as an alternative approach to service delivery (Table 3/7). The highest use of this approach is for residential (13%) and commercial (14%) solid waste collection and electric (15%) and gas (20%) utility operations. Use of franchises and concessions for all other service categories is under 8%. While this service delivery approach remains a viable alternative for a limited number of services, slightly smaller percentages of jurisdictions in 1992 report use of franchises/concessions for all services except solid waste disposal.

SUBSIDIES

This approach allows governments to make financial or in-kind contributions to private and nonprofit organizations enabling them to charge citizens lower prices. Local governments frequently use subsidies for health and human service programs as well as cultural and arts programs. Subsidies allow local governments to have a considerable amount of flexibility in particular service areas. When times are good, municipalities and counties can increase support for a service; when times are bad, resources can be cut back.

Municipal and county use of subsidies has not been widespread. The 1992 results show that use of subsidies is under 9% for most services (Table 3/8). The most common use of subsidies is in cultural and arts programs; however, in 1992 only 9% of municipalities and counties used subsidies in this area compared with 17% in 1982. Similar decreases have occurred with museum and library operations. This trend is also apparent in several health and human services, particularly day care operations and mental health programs where use of subsidies has decreased from 15% to 5%. The decline in the use of subsides is probably related to cutbacks in federal aid to municipalities and counties.

VOLUNTEERS

Although the use of volunteers in local government is not new, only recently have broad appeals been made for volunteers. Volunteers serve government agencies by dealing with clients directly or by assisting with administrative and managerial work. The volunteer fire department is the classic example. Volunteers are also used to fill library, school crossing guard,

Table 3/4   USE OF PUBLIC EMPLOYEES, 1982 AND 1992

| | Combined city and county responses | | | |
| | 1982 | | 1992 | |
Service	Exclusive (%)	In-part (%)	Exclusive (%)	In-part (%)
Public works/transportation				
Residential solid waste collection	48	12	47	10
Commercial solid waste collection	28	24	23	22
Solid waste disposal	35	14	32	12
Street repair	65	33	43	52
Street/parking lot cleaning	84	11	70	19
Snow plowing/sanding	79	19	76	22
Traffic sign/signal installation/maintenance	53	37	43	34
Parking meter maintenance/collection	72	7	80	10
Tree trimming/planting	53	39	44	46
Cemetery administration/maintenance	68	16	67	15
Inspection/code enforcement	82	14	83	15
Parking lot/garage operation	73	16	68	16
Bus transit system operation/maintenance	24	20	25	10
Paratransit system operation/maintenance	19	28	23	12
Airport operation	37	25	36	17
Water distribution	...	...	75	9
Water treatment	...	...	67	6
Sewage collection and treatment	...	...	57	18
Disposal of sludge	...	...	43	10
Disposal of hazardous materials	...	...	16	24
Public utilities				
Electric utility operation and management	...	...	32	2
Gas utility operation and management	...	...	12	3
Utility meter reading	64	23	65	10
Public safety				
Crime prevention/patrol	74	22	88	8
Police/fire communication	75	16	72	14
Fire prevention/suppression	69	18	70	10
Emergency medical service	39	27	43	19
Ambulance service	30	19	33	9
Traffic control/parking enforcement	90	7	88	8
Vehicle towing and storage	7	14	5	9
Health and human services				
Sanitary inspection	49	13	42	14
Insect/rodent control	44	22	34	17
Animal control	61	16	59	13
Animal shelter operation	36	13	34	7
Daycare facility operation	7	19	6	14
Child welfare programs	26	37	16	19
Programs for elderly	18	57	21	45
Operation/management of hospitals	16	8	9	4
Public health programs	25	35	25	20
Drug/alcohol treatment programs	10	30	7	17
Operation of mental health/retardation programs/ facilities	13	25	7	11
Prisons/jails	...	...	39	17
Operation of homeless shelters	...	...	0	5
Parks and Recreation				
Operation and maintenance of recreation facilities	58	35	75	19
Parks landscaping and maintenance	76	20	74	20
Operation of convention centers/auditoriums	68	15	57	15
Cultural and arts programs				
Operation of cultural/arts programs	11	46	17	39
Operation of libraries	48	20	49	10
Operation of museums	21	25	19	12
Support functions				
Buildings/grounds maintenance	73	25	66	32
Building security	85	11	78	15
Fleet management and vehicle maintenance				
heavy equipment	59	37	55	37
emergency vehicles	59	34	52	36
all other vehicles	63	32	56	36
Payroll	86	11	92	5
Tax bill processing	64	23	53	11
Tax assessing	54	14	41	8
Data processing	64	23	80	15
Delinquent tax collection	59	16	48	13
Title records/plat map maintenance	...	...	42	20
Legal services	41	29	38	25
Secretarial services	94	5	90	9
Personnel services	90	8	91	8
Public relations/public information	87	12	85	13

Table 3/5   USE OF PRIVATE AND NONPROFIT CONTRACTING, 1982 AND 1992

Service	For-profit 1982 (%)	For-profit 1992 (%)	Nonprofit 1982 (%)	Nonprofit 1992 (%)
Public works/transportation				
Residential solid waste collection	34	37	0	1
Commercial solid waste collection	41	54	0	1
Solid waste disposal	26	32	2	1
Street repair	26	29	1	1
Street/parking lot cleaning	9	17	0	1
Snow plowing/sanding	...	10	...	0
Traffic sign/signal installation/maintenance	25	24	2	1
Meter maintenance/collection	...	6	...	0
Tree trimming/planting	30	31	1	2
Cemetery administration/maintenance	10	11	8	6
Inspection/code enforcement	6	5	1	0
Parking lot/garage operation	...	13	...	2
Bus transit system operation/maintenance	...	14	...	8
Paratransit system operation/maintenance	22	20	20	15
Airport operation	...	16	...	3
Water distribution	...	5	...	1
Water treatment	...	4	...	1
Sewage collection and treatment	...	5	...	1
Disposal of sludge	...	17	...	2
Disposal of hazardous materials	...	35	...	3
Public utilities				
Electric utility operation and management	...	37	...	4
Gas utility operation and management	...	53	...	5
Utility meter reading	...	18	...	2
Public safety				
Crime prevention/patrol	...	1	...	1
Police/fire comunication	...	1	...	1
Fire prevention/suppression	...	1	...	3
Emergency medical service	13	14	10	8
Ambulance service	23	27	9	10
Traffic control/parking enforcement	1	1	1	1
Vehicle towing and storage	78	83	0	3
Health and human services				
Sanitary inspection	...	2	...	0
Insect/rodent control	...	14	...	1
Animal control	6	5	8	9
Animal shelter operation	13	11	17	23
Daycare facility operation	33	54	34	35
Child welfare programs	5	4	22	13
Programs for elderly	4	6	28	24
Operation/management of hospitals	...	31	...	30
Public health programs	7	5	25	8
Drug/alcohol treatment programs	6	20	38	34
Operation of mental health/retardation programs/facilities	6	15	38	29
Prisons/jails	...	1	...	0
Operation of homeless shelters	...	5	...	54
Parks and recreation				
Operation and maintenance of recreation facilities	8	5	9	3
Parks landscaping and maintenance	9	10	2	2
Operation of convention centers/auditoriums	...	8	...	6
Cultural and arts programs				
Operation of cultural and arts programs	...	7	...	41
Operation of libraries	1	1	10	4
Operation of museums	...	2	...	37
Support functions				
Buildings/grounds maintenance	19	20	1	2
Building security	7	12	1	1
Fleet management and vehicle maintenance				
heavy equipment	...	27	...	2
emergency vehicles	...	27	...	3
all other vehicles	...	25	...	2
Payroll	...	4	...	1
Tax bill processing	22	5	2	1
Tax assessing	6	6	4	1
Data processing	22	8	2	1
Delinquent tax collection	10	8	3	1
Title records/plat map maintenance	...	8	...	1
Legal services	48	47	2	3
Secretarial services	...	5	...	0
Personnel services	5	4	1	0
Public relations/public information	...	6	...	1

Table 3/6   USE OF OTHER GOVERNMENTS AND AUTHORITIES, 1982 AND 1992

Service	Combined city and county responses 1982 (%)	1992 (%)
Public works/transportation		
Residential solid waste collection	8	2
Commercial solid waste collection	7	2
Solid waste disposal	29	27
Street repair	5	5
Street/parking lot cleaning	3	3
Snow plowing/sanding	4	5
Traffic sign/signal install/maint	14	19
Parking meter maint/collect	3	8
Tree trimming/planting	4	4
Cemetery admin/maint	4	7
Inspection/code enforcement	6	7
Parking lot/garage oper	7	8
Bus transit system oper/maint	38	49
Paratransit system oper/maint	26	38
Airport operation	24	35
Water distribution	...	16
Water treatment	...	26
Sewage collection and treatment	...	33
Disposal of sludge	...	33
Disposal of hazardous materials	...	37
Public utilities		
Electric utility oper/mgt	...	13
Gas utility oper/mgt	...	11
Utility meter reading	8	8
Public safety		
Crime prevention patrol	5	7
Police/fire communication	14	21
Fire prevention/suppression	8	13
Emergency medical service	16	20
Ambulance service	16	18
Traffic control/parking enforcement	4	7
Vehicle towing and storage	2	2
Health and human services		
Sanitary inspection	33	48
Insect/rodent control	27	42
Animal control	18	21
Animal shelter operation	28	29
Daycare facility operation	15	18
Child welfare programs	26	63
Programs for elderly	21	34
Operation/mgt of hospitals	21	39
Public health programs	28	57
Drug/alcohol treatment programs	28	52
Operation of mental health/ retardation programs/facilities	32	67
Prisons/jails	...	53
Operation of homeless shelters	...	40
Parks and recreation		
Oper/maint of rec facilities	8	11
Parks landscaping maintenance	5	8
Oper of conv centers/auditoriums	9	23
Cultural and arts program		
Oper of cultural and arts prog	11	16
Operation of libraries	26	39
Operation of museums	15	26
Support functions		
Buildings/grounds maintenance	4	2
Building security	3	2
Fleet mgt/vehicle maint		
heavy equipment	2	2
emergency vehicles	3	4
all other vehicles	2	2
Payroll	2	1
Tax bill processing	10	38
Tax assessing	27	51
Data processing	...	6
Delinquent tax collection	18	38
Title records/plat map maintenance	...	44
Legal services	6	3
Secretarial services	1	1
Personnel services	2	1
Public relations/information	1	1

Table 3/7   **SELECTED USE OF FRANCHISES IN CITIES AND COUNTIES, 1982 AND 1992**

Service	Combined city and county responses	
	1982 (%)	1992 (%)
Public works/transportation		
Residential solid waste collection	15	13
Commercial solid waste collection	17	14
Solid waste disposal	5	7
Parking lot/garage operation	2	2
Bus transit system operation/ maintenance	4	2
Paratransit system operation/ maintenance	4	3
Airport operation	9	6
Water distribution	...	1
Water treatment	...	1
Disposal of hazardous materials	...	1
Public utilities		
Electric utility operation and management	...	15
Gas utility operation and management	...	20
Utility meter reading	10	4
Public safety		
Emergency medical service	3	1
Ambulance service	4	2
Vehicle towing and storage	7	5
Parks and recreation		
Operation and maintenance of recreation facilities	...	2
Operation of convention centers and auditoriums .	3	1
Cultural and arts programs		
Operation of cultural and arts programs	...	2
Operation of museums	...	1

Note: Only those services for which at least 1% of local governments reported franchises in 1992 are listed.

Table 3/8   **SELECTED USE OF SUBSIDIES, 1982 AND 1992**

Service	Combined city and county responses	
	1982 (%)	1992 (%)
Public works/transportation		
Bus transit system operation/ maintenance	8	3
Paratransit system operation/ maintenance	13	5
Airport operation	2	1
Public safety		
Emergency medical service	5	1
Ambulance service	7	2
Health and human services		
Animal control	1	1
Animal shelter operation ...	3	2
Day care facility operation .	15	5
Child welfare programs	8	4
Programs for elderly	13	6
Operation/management of hospitals	4	2
Public health programs	8	1
Drug/alcohol treatment programs	12	5
Operation of mental health programs	15	5
Operation of homeless shelters	...	8
Cultural and arts programs		
Operation of cultural and arts programs	17	9
Operation of libraries	6	3
Operation of museums	16	8

Note: Only those services for which at least 1% of local governments reported use of subsidies in 1992 are listed.

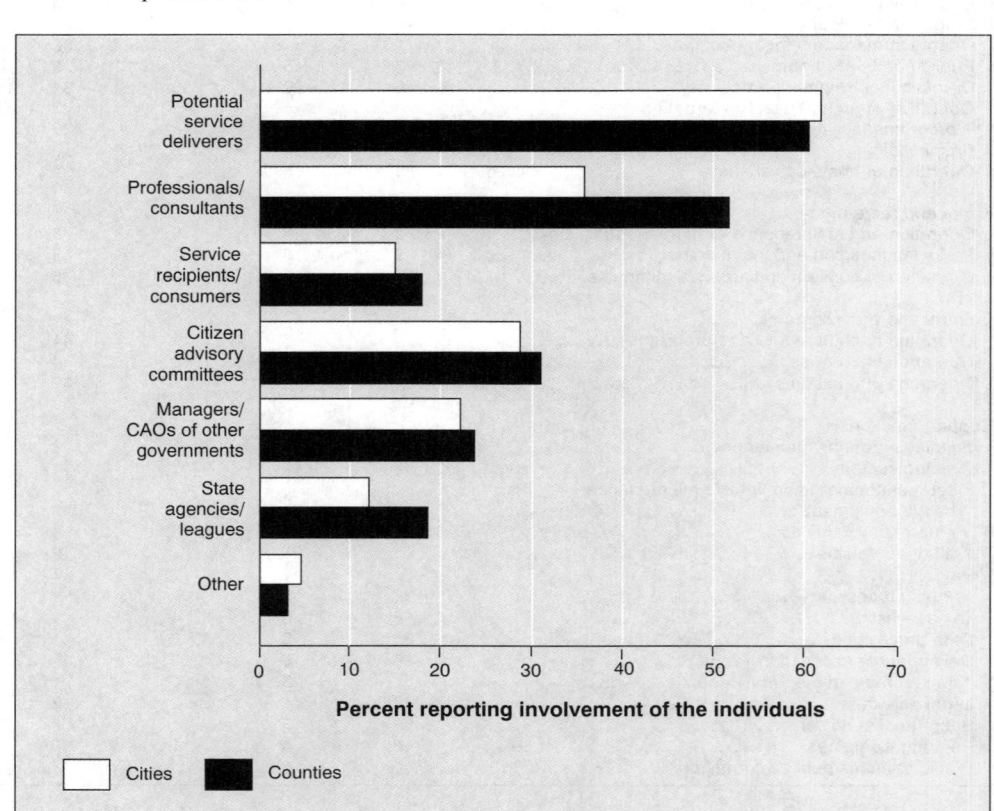

Figure 3/2   *Local government involvement in evaluating the feasibility of service delivery by the private sector*

Figure 3/3   *Outside involvement in evaluating the feasibility of service delivery by the private sector*

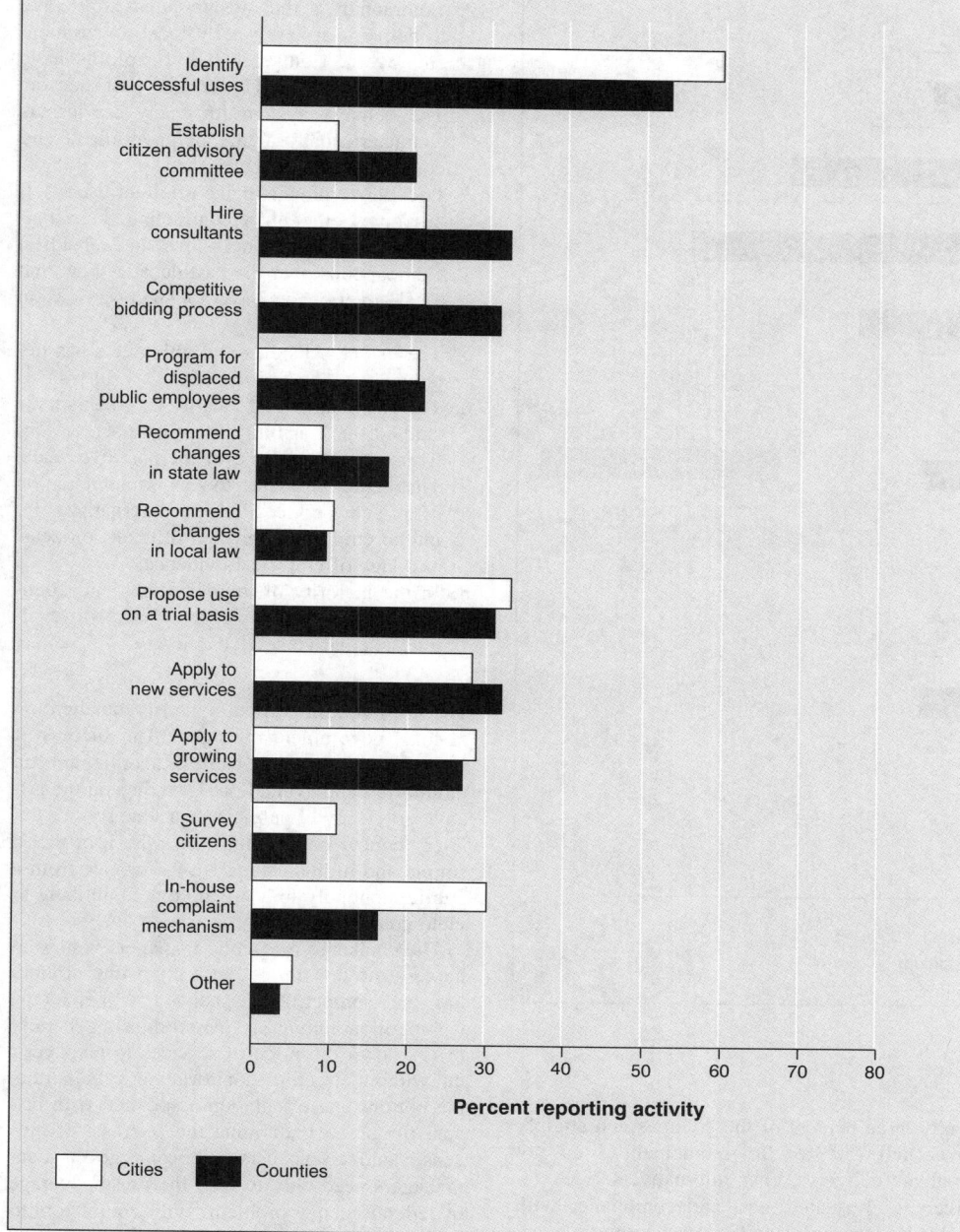

Figure 3/4   *Activities used to ensure success in implementing service delivery by the private sector*

feasibility of private service delivery (Figure 3/3). Elected officials and finance/accounting officers are identified as primary players by approximately 50% of the respondents. Management and budget analysts are more involved in the process at the county level (41%) than at the municipal level (22%). A greater proportion of the counties cite management/budget analysts as being more involved in evaluating feasibility than assistant managers. This trend is different for municipalities, where 39% respond that the assistant managers are more involved.

The survey also collected information on which individuals and groups outside the local government are involved in evaluating the feasibility of private service delivery (Figure 3/4). The vendors, or potential service deliverers, are the most frequently identified outside actors involved in evaluating service delivery. Professionals/consultants and citizen advisory committees are also cited by a large proportion of the respondents.

Half the municipalities and a slightly smaller proportion of counties indicate that some action is taken to ensure success in implementing private service delivery approaches. The identification of successful private alternatives in other jurisdictions is reported by the highest percentage of municipalities and counties, followed by private service delivery on a trial basis (Figure 3/5). Both groups of respondents report that they are likely to apply private alternatives to new or growing services as opposed to firmly established services. Municipalities are more

Table 3/9   SELECTED USE OF VOLUNTEERS, 1982 AND 1992

Service	Combined city and county responses	
	1982 (%)	1992 (%)
Public works/transportation		
Tree trimming/planting	3	3
Cemetery administration/ maintenance	3	3
Paratransit system operation/maintenance ..	7	2
Public safety		
Crime prevention patrol ...	9	4
Police/fire communication .	2	2
Fire prevention/suppression	17	14
Emergency medical service	15	12
Ambulance service	14	10
Health and human services		
Animal shelter operation ..	2	2
Daycare facility operation .	4	1
Child welfare programs ...	6	3
Programs for elderly	18	11
Public health programs	7	2
Drug/alcohol treatment programs	6	4
Operation of mental health/ retardation programs	...	2
Operation of homeless shelters	...	8
Operation/management of hospitals	2	1
Parks and recreation		
Operation/maintenance of Recreation Facilities	4	5
Parks landscaping and maintenance	4	3
Operation of convention centers/auditoriums	2	2
Cultural and arts programs		
Operation of cultural and arts programs	31	17
Operation of libraries	11	5
Operation of museums	20	14

Note: Only those services for which at least 1% of local governments reported use of volunteers in 1992 are listed.

anu counsellor positions in health and human service programs.

Municipalities and counties continue to use volunteers to staff a broad range of services. Use of volunteers is highest in operation of cultural and arts programs and in museum operations (Table 3/9). Public safety is another area where volunteers are used, especially in fire prevention and suppression.

While use of volunteers is likely to continue, a downward trend is apparent. Significant decreases in the use of volunteers have occurred in almost all service areas reported on by survey respondents. The most noticeable decline is in cultural and arts programs, where the proportion of governments using volunteers was 31% in 1982 compared with 17% in 1992. Programs for the elderly also have declined in volunteer use, from 18% in 1982 to 11% in 1992.

The number of jurisdictions reporting each type of service delivery approach is found in the appendix.

FEASIBILITY OF SERVICE DELIVERY BY THE PRIVATE SECTOR

Regardless of whether municipalities and counties have actually used private service delivery, 71% of responding jurisdictions and 63% of counties have studied the feasibility of this option. The survey defines *private* as the use of for-profit firms, nonprofit organizations, and private industries.

Various factors prompt decisions to study private service delivery options. Figure 3/2 shows that both municipalities (91%) and counties (89%) report "internal attempts to decrease costs" as the primary reason and external fiscal pressures as the second strongest reason for considering private service delivery alternatives. The percentage of counties identifying the rest of the factors covered in the survey as influential is consistently higher than the percentage of municipalities attributing a significant role to these factors.

Managers/CAOs and department heads are named as the primary actors in evaluating the

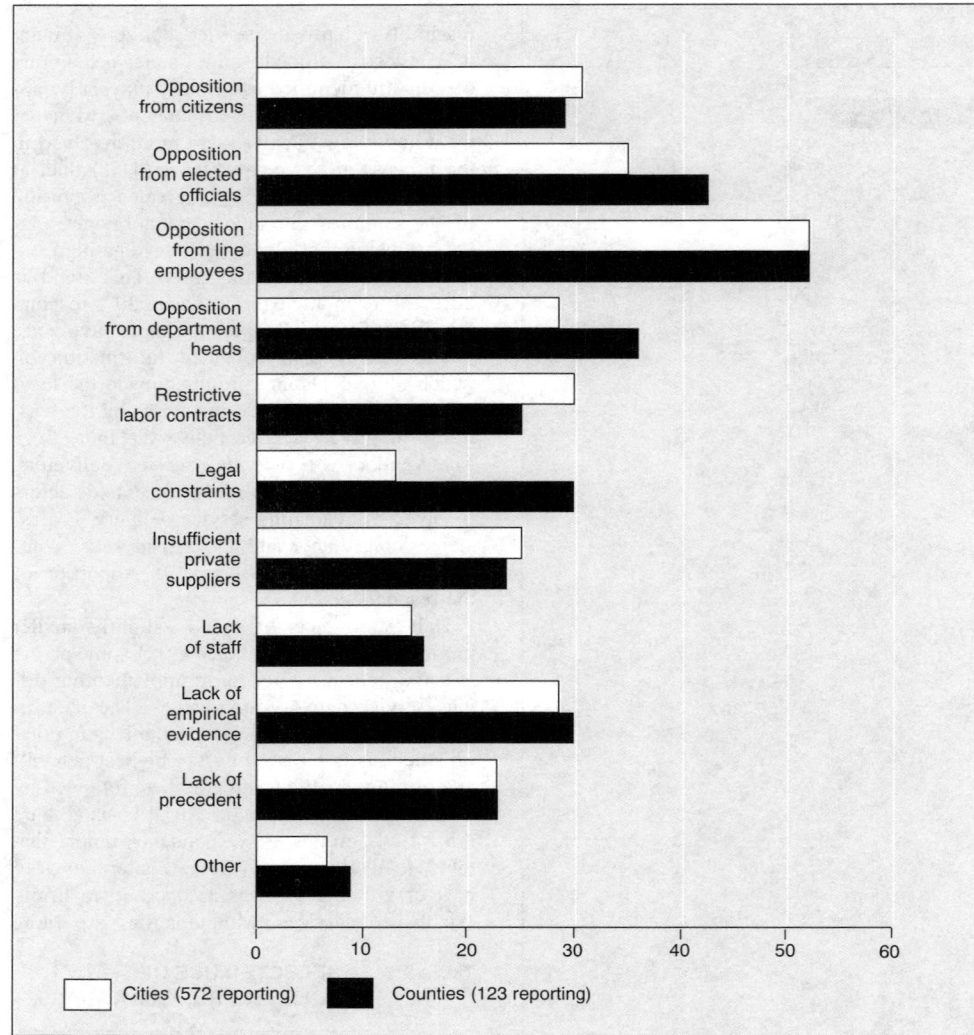

Figure 3/5 *Obstacles to private service delivery*

likely than counties to survey their citizens and to have a complaint mechanism in-house. Alternatively, counties are more likely to establish citizen advisory committees and to hire consultants. Recommending changes in state and local laws are less popular activities for both groups.

Local governments adopting various forms of private service delivery encounter obstacles to their implementation slightly less than 50% of the time. Most of the opposition comes from line employees (54%) and elected officials (45% of counties and 37% of municipalities). Municipalities are more apt to receive opposition from citizens than counties are; the latter receive more opposition from department heads (not shown). The data indicate that restrictive labor contracts are more of an obstacle for municipalities than counties, while legal constraints appear to pose a greater obstacle for counties. Almost one-third of each group cite the lack of empirical evidence as an obstacle to private service delivery.

Once private service delivery is adopted, the majority of local governments do not systematically evaluate service delivery alternatives.

Sixty-three percent of the counties and slightly over half (50.3%) the municipalities do not evaluate delivery. When alternative service delivery is evaluated, cost and compliance with delivery standards are the most important factors that are addressed. Nearly two-thirds of municipalities (64%) and about half the counties (51%) evaluate citizen satisfaction with service delivery. Given recent efforts toward customer-driven government, these figures will probably increase.

Analysis of data/records and field observations are widely cited as approaches to evaluate service delivery (not shown). Monitoring of citizen complaints is used more at the municipal than at the county level.

SUMMARY

Comparisons of the 1982 and 1992 surveys show both continuity and change in service delivery.

1. The majority of the services provided by both municipalities and counties are delivered by local government employees.

2. Contracting is the most popular alternative to delivery of services by local government employees. Contracts with for-profits have generally increased over the past decade. The delivery system for many services is characterized by a mix of government and contract production.
3. Local governments make minimal use of alternatives other than contracting, i.e., franchises, vouchers, concessions, and subsidies.
4. Comparisons over the past decade show that local governments have not shed services on a widespread basis.
5. The use of subsidies and volunteers has declined over the past decade.
6. The vast majority of local governments have studied the feasibility of private service delivery arrangements over the past five years.
7. The major obstacles to the implementation of private service delivery alternatives are public employees, elected officials, citizens, and lack of empirical evidence.
8. In the majority of municipalities and counties, there is little systematic effort to evaluate alternative service delivery.

The last point, in particular, merits the attention of local government managers. The success of alternative service delivery is contingent on monitoring and evaluation. If studies on the relative efficiency of public and private service delivery concur on anything, it is the idea that a simple and militant transfer of a service from a public monopoly to a private one is unlikely to yield cost savings.

The challenge for public managers is how to harness the powers of the bottom-line orientation and competition associated with markets. Competition among service producers generally drives down the price of services to taxpayers, but without effective monitoring and evaluation, the bottom-line orientation associated with private firms can undermine the interests of citizens and taxpayers. Local government managers need only to read the press coverage of federal agency problems with contractors to appreciate the need for monitoring and evaluation if contracting is to be cost effective.

1. See Vincent Ostrom, Charles Tiebout, and Robert Warren "The Organization of Metropolitan Areas: A Theoretical Inquiry," *American Political Science Review* vol. 55, no. 4 (1961): 831–42.

2. David Osborne and Ted Gaebler, *Reinventing Government* (Reading, MA: Addison-Wesley, 1992).

3. See E.S. Savas, *Privatization: The Key to Better Government* (Chatham, NJ: Chatham House, 1987).

4. See Elaine Morley, "Patterns in the Use of Alternative Service Delivery Approaches," *The Municipal Year Book 1989* (Washington, DC: International City Management Association, 1989): 33–44. Findings from the 1982 Survey are reported in Harry Hatry and Carl Valente, "Alternative Service Delivery Approaches Involving Increased Use of the Private Sector," *The Municipal Year Book 1983* (Washington, DC: International City Management Association, 1983): 199–217.

5. The term *recognition* refers to a formal process whereby ICMA ascertains that a local government provides for an appointed professional manager.

Appendix   SERVICE DELIVERY APPROACHES OF CITIES AND COUNTIES

Local government services	No. reporting	Your employees entirely (No.)	Your employees in part (No.)	Another government or authority (No.)	Private for profit (No.)	Private non-profit (No.)	Franchises/ concessions (No.)	Subsidies (No.)	Volunteers (No.)
Public works/transportation									
Residential solid waste collection	912	426	89	20	338	11	121	0	3
Commercial solid waste collection	712	166	157	15	381	6	98	1	0
Solid waste disposal	922	290	109	251	296	7	61	4	4
Street repair	1,370	583	712	67	397	7	8	1	0
Street/parking lot cleaning	1,203	842	231	37	198	8	10	0	1
Snow plowing/sanding	1,035	783	229	48	107	3	2	2	0
Traffic sign/signal installation/ maintenance	1,297	559	440	242	313	9	9	2	0
Parking meter maintenance and collection	344	276	34	28	19	1	1	0	0
Tree trimming and planting on public rights of way	1,251	546	569	47	384	20	6	6	38
Maintenance and administration of cemeteries	574	384	86	41	65	37	2	6	15
Inspection/code enforcement	1,379	1,139	200	90	75	4	2	0	2
Operation of parking lots and garages	525	358	84	42	70	12	8	3	0
Operation/maintenance of bus transit system	437	107	44	213	62	35	8	15	3
Operation/maintenance of paratransit system	395	89	48	151	77	60	10	19	7
Operation of airports	513	185	85	179	83	13	30	4	4
Water distribution	1,079	805	94	168	53	9	11	0	0
Water treatment	988	658	63	258	41	10	10	0	0
Sewage collection and treatment	1,113	631	199	363	51	13	6	1	1
Disposal of sludge	971	420	97	319	167	15	6	2	0
Disposal of hazardous materials	710	114	173	264	251	23	7	4	7
Public utilities									
Utility operation and management									
Electricity	414	134	9	53	154	18	60	1	0
Gas	351	43	11	40	187	17	71	1	0
Utility meter reading	784	513	77	61	141	14	31	2	1
Public safety									
Crime prevention/patrol	1,406	1,243	109	92	12	8	0	1	53
Police/fire communications	1,388	997	192	291	9	14	2	4	30
Fire prevention/suppression	1,299	913	123	168	11	34	2	6	182
Emergency medical service	1,200	512	229	240	164	99	11	16	144
Ambulance service	1,102	359	103	203	297	113	25	18	112
Traffic control/parking enforcement	1,243	1,094	96	85	10	6	0	1	10
Vehicle towing and storage	993	50	86	24	820	25	52	1	1
Health and human services									
Sanitary inspection	981	416	133	474	15	4	0	5	0
Insect/rodent control	848	289	146	359	119	8	1	5	0
Animal control	1,226	726	156	251	66	109	8	12	3
Operation of animal shelters	988	339	70	283	104	230	7	16	23
Operation of daycare facilities	417	26	57	75	223	144	3	19	2
Child welfare programs	545	86	105	344	22	69	1	20	16
Programs for the elderly	977	201	441	334	61	238	7	56	107
Operation/management of hospitals	390	33	15	152	120	118	0	8	4
Public health programs	741	182	148	422	40	62	0	10	15
Drug and alcohol treatment programs	704	50	122	369	141	236	2	33	27
Operation of mental health/mental retardation programs and facilities	635	41	67	422	96	187	1	29	10
Prisons/jails	939	363	160	494	10	2	2	10	2
Operation of homeless shelters	510	3	24	205	24	274	3	41	43
Parks and recreation									
Operation and maintenance of recreation facilities	1,308	978	244	142	68	44	20	13	61
Park landscaping and maintenance	1,309	965	259	109	124	22	1	5	42
Operation of convention centers and auditoriums	421	240	61	97	33	24	6	5	9
Cultural and arts programs									
Operation of cultural and arts programs	679	113	263	111	44	277	16	60	115
Operation of libraries	1,019	501	104	401	10	43	1	27	55
Operation of museums	542	102	63	142	11	198	5	44	78
Support functions									
Buildings and grounds maintenance	1,401	917	449	22	277	23	4	1	20
Building security	1,129	881	165	23	131	15	2	1	2
Fleet management/vehicle maintenance									
Heavy equipment	1,357	751	500	24	365	31	1	1	0
Emergency vehicles	1,290	674	459	49	350	41	1	0	7
All other vehicles	1,350	758	485	25	343	32	1	1	0
Payroll	1,422	1,312	73	13	59	7	1	0	0
Tax bill processing	1,197	631	134	454	58	7	2	3	0
Tax assessing	1,110	455	84	560	62	6	1	2	0
Data processing	1,376	1,103	205	79	114	12	1	0	2
Collection of delinquent taxes	1,198	574	151	456	100	14	2	2	0
Title records/plat map maintenance	1,153	483	227	504	88	6	0	2	0
Legal services	1,322	505	328	43	618	33	7	4	2
Secretarial services	1,386	1,252	130	8	75	2	0	0	7
Personnel services	1,392	1,272	112	16	54	6	0	0	4
Public relations/public information	1,326	1,120	175	19	84	9	1	2	12

A4

Term Limits and Turnover Among Local Officials

Victor S. DeSantis
University of North Texas

Tari Renner
Illinois Wesleyan University

Findings

Only 8.4% of responding local governments report term limits for council members.

The reelection rate of incumbents is higher in at-large elections than in district or mixed elections.

The existence of a separately elected mayor appears to conditionally affect the relationship between city council and manager turnover.

The American public's concern about the accountability of government officials appears to have grown in recent years. Large numbers of voters continue to indicate in public opinion surveys that they are frustrated with government actions and suspicious of elected officeholders.

In 1992, voters defeated an incumbent president and registered a near-record protest vote for an antiestablishment third party candidate. Ross Perot's 19% of the vote was the highest received by any non-major-party candidate since Theodore Roosevelt ran as the Progressive Bull Moose nominee in 1912. The number of incumbent members of the U.S. House of Representatives who were defeated for reelection increased substantially in 1992. This reversed a generation-long trend toward decreasing competitiveness in House elections where incumbents sought another term. As a result, there were more new members in the House after the 1992 elections than in any election year since 1948.

The state and local elections of 1993 showed few signs that voter anger with incumbents and the status quo had subsided. The two states holding off-year gubernatorial elections (New Jersey and Virginia) shifted political party control of the chief executive office from Democratic to Republican hands. The nation's two largest cities (New York and Los Angeles) also shifted party control of their mayoral positions by defeating either the incumbent or the incumbent party.

Perhaps the most important long-run consequence of the 1993 elections, however, was the adoption of term limitations on public officials through referendums in several states. This marks the fourth year in a row that additional states have instituted term limits. Only one referendum attempt has failed during this period (Washington State in 1991), and that decision was reversed by the voters in a subsequent election.

These reforms appear to be the most effective strategy to ensure that the tenure of public officials is limited and, therefore, that turnover is maximized. Voters seeking mandatory turnover

among their elected officials have supported these restrictions apparently to save themselves from their own decisions at the ballot box. The assumption seems to be that policy-making institutions need constant membership change to remain responsive because incumbents over time become increasingly insulated from their constituents' interests.

This research project explores the patterns of turnover and term limitations among local government elected officials and turnover among appointed managers/chief administrative officers (CAOs). Although there is a substantial body of research in the field examining turnover and incumbency reelection prospects among executive and legislative officials at other levels of government, there is very little systematic evidence regarding local public officeholders.

The situation at the local level is unique and particularly warrants separate attention because many municipalities have nonelected, appointed chief executives with generally unspecified terms of service. In addition, the patterns and trends apparent for elected incumbents at other levels may not exist among local government officials. The advantages of incumbency, for example, may not be as strong given that incumbents' name recognition is likely to be lower, their constituencies smaller, and campaign costs lower than at other levels. It may be comparatively easy (from both an organizational and financial perspective) to successfully challenge an incumbent under these circumstances. It is also possible that the tendency for local public service positions to be part-time and volunteer, rather than full-time and career, results in more voluntary turnover of incumbents and less longevity than at other levels of government.

METHODOLOGY

The data for this exploratory research were collected through ICMA's 1991 *Municipal Form of Government* survey. The survey instrument was sent to city clerks in all 6,579 jurisdictions with populations of 2,500 and over and to 562

jurisdictions with fewer than 2,500 people that ICMA recognizes as providing for a position of professional management. Officials who did not respond to the first survey instrument received a second survey instrument. This article is based on the responses from jurisdictions with a population of 25,000 and above; 914 responded out of 1,205 for a 75% response rate (Table 4/1).

LENGTH OF MAYORAL TERMS

Overall, a plurality (48.4%) of mayors have terms of four or more years (Table 4/2). Approximately one-third of the responding municipalities indicate that their mayors have two-year terms (33.1%). One- and three-year terms are the least likely to be reported with 14.8% and 3.7%, respectively.

Although we cannot be certain from the data presented, the single-year mayoral term is probably found in jurisdictions in which the position rotates annually among members of the elected legislative body or in which the legislature elects the mayor from among its members. When the data are arrayed by form of government, the results are consistent with this possibility. While almost no mayor-council municipalities (1.7%) have one-year terms, more than one-fifth of the municipalities with other forms of government report one-year terms. Previous research using ICMA data has

Table 4/1   SURVEY RESPONSE

Classification	No. of cities surveyed (A)	No. reporting	% of (A)
Total, all cities	1,205	914	75.9
Population group			
Over 1,000,000	8	2	25.0
500,000–1,000,000 ..	16	8	50.0
250,000–499,999	40	32	80.0
100,000–249,999	133	100	75.2
50,000–99,999	334	255	76.4
25,000–49,999	674	517	76.7

Table 4/2   LENGTH OF TERM FOR MAYOR

Classification	No. reporting (A)	One year No.	One year % of (A)	Two years No.	Two years % of (A)	Three years No.	Three years % of (A)	Four years or more No.	Four years or more % of (A)
Total, all cities[1]	891	132	14.8	295	33.1	33	3.7	431	48.4
Population group									
Over 1,000,000	2	0	0.0	0	0.0	0	0.0	2	100.0
500,000–1,000,000	8	0	0.0	2	25.0	0	0.0	6	75.0
250,000–499,999	32	0	0.0	9	28.1	1	3.1	22	68.8
100,000–249,999	99	7	7.1	36	36.4	4	4.0	52	52.5
50,000–99,999	248	35	14.1	85	34.3	10	4.0	118	47.6
25,000–49,999	502	90	17.9	163	32.5	18	3.6	231	46.0
Geographic division[2]									
New England	80	9	11.3	59	73.8	6	7.5	6	7.5
Mid-Atlantic	104	19	18.3	17	16.3	0	0.0	68	65.4
East North Central	158	9	5.7	34	21.5	1	0.6	114	72.2
West North Central	71	5	7.0	18	25.4	2	2.8	46	64.8
South Atlantic	110	11	10.0	39	35.5	8	7.3	52	47.3
East South Central	31	0	0.0	3	9.7	0	0.0	28	90.3
West South Central	83	2	2.4	47	56.6	15	18.1	19	22.9
Mountain	57	3	5.3	20	35.1	0	0.0	34	59.6
Pacific Coast	197	74	37.6	58	29.4	1	0.5	64	32.5
Form of government[3]									
Mayor-council	303	5	1.7	65	21.5	2	0.7	231	76.2
Council-manager	566	119	21.0	226	39.9	28	4.9	193	34.1
Commission	13	4	30.8	2	15.4	0	0.0	7	53.8
Town meeting	1	1	100.0	0	0.0	0	0.0	0	0.0
Rep. town meeting	8	3	37.5	2	25.0	3	37.5	0	0.0

[1]The term *cities* refers also to towns, villages, boroughs, and townships.

[2]*Divisions: New England*—the states of Connecticut, Maine, Massachusetts, New Hampshire, Rhode Island, and Vermont; *Mid-Atlantic*—the states of New Jersey, New York, and Pennsylvania; *East North Central*—the states of Illinois, Indiana, Michigan, Ohio, and Wisconsin; *West North Central*—the states of Iowa, Kansas, Minnesota, Missouri, Nebraska, North Dakota, and South Dakota; *South Atlantic*—the states of Delaware, Florida, Georgia, Maryland, North Carolina, South Carolina, Virginia, and West Virginia, plus the District of Columbia; *East South Central*—the states of Alabama, Kentucky, Mississippi, and Tennessee; *West South Central*—the states of Arkansas, Louisiana, Oklahoma, and Texas; *Mountain*—the states of Arizona, Colorado, Idaho, Montana, Nevada, New Mexico, Utah, and Wyoming; *Pacific Coast*—the states of Alaska, California, Hawaii, Oregon, and Washington.

[3]*Form of government: Mayor-council*—an elected council serves as the legislative body with a separately elected head of government; *Council-manager*—the mayor and council make policy and an appointed administrator is responsible for the administration of the city; *Commission*—a board of elected commissioners serves as the legislative body and each commissioner is responsible for administration of one or more departments; *Town meeting*—qualified voters meet to make basic policy and choose a board of selectmen to carry out the policy; *Representative town meeting*—representatives selected by citizens vote at meetings, which may be attended by all town citizens.

Table 4/3   LENGTH OF TERM FOR COUNCIL MEMBERS ELECTED AT LARGE

Classification	No. reporting (A)	Two years No.	Two years % of (A)	Three years No.	Three years % of (A)	Four years or more No.	Four years or more % of (A)
Total, all cities	706	158	22.4	50	7.1	498	70.5
Population group							
Over 1,000,000	2	0	0.0	0	0.0	2	100.0
500,000–1,000,000	3	0	0.0	0	0.0	3	100.0
250,000–499,999	23	5	21.7	1	4.3	17	73.9
100,000–249,999	71	16	22.5	3	4.2	52	73.2
50,000–99,999	211	51	24.2	12	5.7	148	70.1
25,000–49,999	396	86	21.7	34	8.6	276	69.7
Geographic division							
New England	77	56	72.7	18	23.4	3	3.9
Mid-Atlantic	81	3	3.7	5	6.2	73	90.1
East North Central	116	27	23.3	1	0.9	88	75.9
West North Central	46	6	13.0	1	2.2	39	84.8
South Atlantic	87	23	26.4	10	11.5	54	62.1
East South Central	15	5	33.3	0	0.0	10	66.7
West South Central	64	36	56.3	15	23.4	13	20.3
Mountain	37	1	2.7	0	0.0	36	97.3
Pacific Coast	183	1	0.5	0	0.0	182	99.5
Form of government							
Mayor-council	204	64	31.4	4	2.0	136	66.7
Council-manager	479	92	19.2	33	6.9	354	73.9
Commission	11	1	9.1	2	18.2	8	72.7
Town meeting	3	0	0.0	3	100.0	0	0.0
Rep. town meeting	9	1	11.1	8	88.9	0	0.0

[1]Not one respondent reported a one-year term.

shown that choosing a mayor from among the council members and/or rotating the mayoral position among council members are common selection methods in all forms of government except mayor-council. In fact, the percentages of jurisdictions using these techniques of mayoral selection within each form of government are very similar to the percentages with single-year terms.[1] The patterns of mayoral terms vary by population group. Odd-year terms (one and three years) are least likely to be found in the largest cities. The percentages of respondents reporting four-year terms, on the other hand, consistently decline with population size, from 100% in jurisdictions with populations greater than 1,000,000 to 46% in jurisdictions with populations from 25,000 to 49,999. There appears to be no consistent pattern among population groups for jurisdictions using two-year terms.

The geographic patterns are not as clear-cut. Single-year terms are most likely to be found among Pacific Coast municipalities where a plurality (37.6%) of the 197 responding jurisdictions report one-year mayoral terms. They are least likely among cities in the East South Central division where none of the respondents indicates using one-year terms. Three-year terms are unlikely in all areas of the country. It is only in West South Central jurisdictions that the proportion exceeds 10%. Two-year terms are reported in the overwhelming majority of New England jurisdictions (73.8%) and by a smaller majority (56.6%) of West South Central jurisdictions. They are least likely in the East South Central division. Four-year terms are comparatively common in all geographic divisions except New England (7.5%). They are most likely, however, to be found in jurisdictions in the East South Central division (90.3%).

The distribution of responses by form of government shows that more than three-fourths (76.2%) of the mayor-council cities have four-year terms. Virtually all jurisdictions that do not report four-year terms have two-year terms (21.6%). A small plurality of council-manager cities (39.9%) report having two-year terms rather than four-year terms (34.1%). As noted earlier, a disproportionate number of jurisdictions with other forms of government report single-year mayoral terms.

LENGTH OF CITY COUNCIL TERMS

Tables 4/3 and 4/4 show the term length data for city councils elected at-large and by district, respectively. The data are separated by election system type because the patterns differ for each. None of the responding jurisdictions indicates that any at-large council members have single-year terms; only one jurisdiction with election by district reports a one-year term. A solid majority (70.5%) of jurisdictions with at-large council members elect members to four-year terms and 22.4% elect them to two-year terms. Only 7.4% use three-year intervals. This contrasts with the aggregate pattern for council members elected by ward or district. Although

the majority of respondents (59.3%) with district elections report four-year terms, the percent is lower than the percent reporting four-year terms and at-large elections for council members (70.5%). Alternatively, the proportion of respondents reporting council members serving two-year terms is higher for those elected by district (36.6%) than at-large (22.4%). Only 3.9% of responding jurisdictions holding district elections report three-year terms for council members. It is also apparent that, regardless of election system, council members are much less likely than mayors to serve in odd-year intervals.

Use of four-year terms appears to decline slightly with population size for council members elected at large; the decline is less consistent for council members elected by district. The geographic division patterns are similar for both election systems. New England communities are the most likely to use two-year terms, although the proportion of district legislators serving two-year terms, (89.6%) is noticeably higher than the proportion of at-large legislators (72.7%) serving two-year terms. Pacific Coast and Mountain jurisdictions report the highest use of four-year terms for at-large council members (99.5% and 97.3%, respectively). Mountain and East South Central cities report the highest proportions of council members elected by district for four-year terms (94.4% and 89.5%, respectively). The form-of-government differences show that council-manager jurisdictions are slightly more likely than mayor-council jurisdictions to use four-year terms for their council members, regardless of election method.

TERM LIMITATIONS FOR MAYORS

It is clear that the overwhelming majority of cities with populations 25,000 and over (89%) do not have term limits on the mayor (Table 4/5). The 11% that report term limits are not uniformly distributed among different types of cities. The reporting of these restrictions appears to be positively associated with population size (with the exception of the two respondents with populations more than one million). One-half of the cities reporting with populations from 500,000 to 1,000,000 indicate mayoral term limits. This figure declines consistently with population size down to 7.9% for the jurisdictions with populations from 25,000 to 49,999.

The variation from the 11% average is even less dramatic among geographic divisions for jurisdictions with term limits. The proportion with mayoral term limits ranges from a high of 22.0% in the West South Central area to 3.6% in New England. Overall, the northern tier respondents are less likely to report having term limitations than the Sun Belt and western respondents.

Council-manager jurisdictions are the most likely to have mayoral term limits (12.7%) followed by mayor-council jurisdictions (8.9%). No jurisdiction with the commission, town

meeting, or representative town meeting form of government reports mayoral term limits.

CITY COUNCIL

Table 4/6 displays the data for legal limitations on consecutive council terms. Overall, a slightly

smaller proportion of municipalities have term limits on council members than on mayors. Only 8.4% of respondents report having term limits for the council.

City council term limits, like mayoral term limits, are positively related to the population size of the responding jurisdictions (with the exception of the two cities responding with pop-

Table 4/4   TERM LENGTH FOR COUNCIL ELECTED BY WARD OR DISTRICT

| | | Length of term for council elected by ward or district | | | | | | | |
| | | One year | | Two years | | Three years | | Four years or more | |
Classification	No. reporting (A)	No.	% of (A)	No.	% of (A)	No.	% of (A)	No.	% of (A)
Total, all cities	413	1	0.2	151	36.6	16	3.9	245	59.3
Population group									
500,000–1,000,000	6	0	0.0	2	33.3	0	0.0	4	66.7
250,000–499,999	22	0	0.0	7	31.8	0	0.0	15	68.2
100,000–249,999	51	0	0.0	12	23.5	2	3.9	37	72.5
50,000–99,999	120	0	0.0	48	40.0	7	5.8	65	54.2
25,000–49,999	214	1	0.5	82	38.3	7	3.3	124	57.9
Geographic division									
New England	48	0	0.0	43	89.6	2	4.2	3	6.3
Mid-Atlantic	45	0	0.0	11	24.4	0	0.0	34	75.6
East North Central	88	0	0.0	32	36.4	2	2.3	54	61.4
West North Central	49	0	0.0	17	34.7	3	6.1	29	59.2
South Atlantic	55	0	0.0	16	29.1	3	5.5	36	65.5
East South Central	19	0	0.0	2	10.5	0	0.0	17	89.5
West South Central ...	48	0	0.0	26	54.2	5	10.4	17	35.4
Mountain	36	1	2.8	1	2.8	0	0.0	34	94.4
Pacific Coast	25	0	0.0	3	12.0	1	4.0	21	84.0
Form of government[1]									
Mayor-council	206	0	0.0	83	40.3	5	2.4	118	57.3
Council-manager	206	1	0.5	67	32.5	11	5.3	127	61.7
Commission	1	0	0.0	1	100.0	0	0.0	0	0.0

[1]Town meeting and rep. town meeting jurisdictions report only at-large elections.

Table 4/5   LEGAL LIMIT ON CONSECUTIVE TERMS FOR MAYOR

| | | Legal limit on consecutive terms for mayor | | | |
| | | Yes | | No | |
Classification	No. reporting (A)	No.	% of (A)	No.	% of (A)
Total, all cities	896	99	11.0	797	89.0
Population group					
Over 1,000,000	2	0	0.0	2	100.0
500,000–1,000,000	8	4	50.0	4	50.0
250,000–499,999	32	10	31.3	22	68.8
100,000–249,999	98	17	17.3	81	82.7
50,000–99,999	251	28	11.2	223	88.8
25,000–49,999	505	40	7.9	465	92.1
Geographic division					
New England	84	3	3.6	81	96.4
Mid-Atlantic	104	7	6.7	97	93.3
East North Central	156	10	6.4	146	93.6
West North Central	72	5	6.9	67	93.1
South Atlantic	109	18	16.5	91	83.5
East South Central	31	5	16.1	26	83.9
West South Central ...	82	18	22.0	64	78.0
Mountain	57	9	15.8	48	84.2
Pacific Coast	201	24	11.9	177	88.1
Form of government					
Mayor-council	303	27	8.9	276	91.1
Council-manager	569	72	12.7	497	87.3
Commission	13	0	0.0	13	100.0
Town meeting	2	0	0.0	2	100.0
Rep. town meeting	9	0	0.0	9	100.0

ulations greater than one million). One-half of the cities with populations from 500,000 to 1,000,000 report term limits for council members. This proportion consistently declines until it reaches 6.5% in the population group from 25,000 to 49,999.

The differences in council limits by geographic division are similar, but not identical, to those of mayoral limits. The range is from 16.9% in the West South Central division to 0.0% in the East South Central division. The overall geographic pattern appears to reflect an East/West distinction for council limits with the latter the most likely to report having term restrictions. The mayoral differences reflect a Frost Belt/Sun Belt distinction.

The form-of-government differences that relate to city council term limitations are virtually identical to those of mayors. Council-manager cities are the most likely to report having these restrictions (11.4%). Only 3.3% of mayor-council communities have terms limits for city council members. Not one respondent with commission, town meeting, or representative town meeting form of government reports a limit on consecutive terms for council members.

TURNOVER AND TENURE

Turnover can, of course, be either voluntary or involuntary regardless of whether the official is a mayor, city council member, or city manager. Even without term limits, involuntary turnover may occur when voters defeat an incumbent elected official or when the city council votes to fire a city manager or place pressure upon the manager to resign. On the other hand, elected officials may decide not to seek reelection in order to retire or to pursue other ventures, including higher office. The same can be said of city managers, who may leave voluntarily because of retirement, other personal reasons, or to advance their careers by serving another, usually larger, community.

Mayors
The longevity of mayors is examined in Table 4/7, which shows the number of years that the incumbent has served. The overall average is 5.43 years. The maximum is 36 years and the minimum is zero (apparently for newly elected mayors).

The two cities with populations greater than 1,000,000 report incumbents with 18 and 19 years of service, for an average of 18.5 years. However, the consistency of average years of mayoral service by each of the other population, geographic, and form-of-government categories is surprising. There is remarkably little variation regardless of these characteristics.

City Managers
Survey respondents were asked in which year their current city manager/CAO was appointed. Table 4/8 shows the data on appointments in 1991. Jurisdictions with newly created city manager or CAO positions were excluded from this analysis. Only those reporting new appointments that related to turnover are included.

Overall, turnover was reported in 29.1% of the jurisdictions. This closely corresponds to the findings of a recent study of Florida cities conducted by Ruth DeHoog and Gordon Whitaker in which they found that approximately one-fourth of the jurisdictions had manager turnover in a one-year period.[2]

The limited number of cases in the top two population categories does not permit us to draw meaningful conclusions from the ICMA survey data. Below that level, however, it appears that incidence of manager turnover tends to decline with population size. Respondents from cities with populations from 25,000 to 49,999, for example, show the lowest rate of turnover among the four lower population cat-

Table 4/6   LIMIT ON CONSECUTIVE TERMS OF COUNCIL MEMBERS

| Classification | No. reporting (A) | Limit on consecutive terms of council members | | | |
| | | Yes | | No | |
		No.	% of (A)	No.	% of (A)
Total, all cities	898	75	8.4	823	91.6
Population group					
Over 1,000,000	2	0	0.0	2	100.0
500,000–1,000,000	8	4	50.0	4	50.0
250,000–499,999	32	6	18.8	26	81.3
100,000–249,999	99	13	13.1	86	86.9
50,000–99,999	250	19	7.6	231	92.4
25,000–49,999	507	33	6.5	474	93.5
Geographic division					
New England	87	3	3.4	84	96.6
Mid-Atlantic	104	1	1.0	103	99.0
East North Central	156	8	5.1	148	94.9
West North Central	71	4	5.6	67	94.4
South Atlantic	108	8	7.4	100	92.6
East South Central	31	0	0.0	31	100.0
West South Central ...	83	14	16.9	69	83.1
Mountain	57	7	12.3	50	87.7
Pacific Coast	201	30	14.9	171	85.1
Form of government					
Mayor-council	300	10	3.3	290	96.7
Council-manager	572	65	11.4	507	88.6
Commission	13	0	0.0	13	100.0
Town meeting	3	0	0.0	3	100.0
Rep. town meeting	10	0	0.0	10	100.0

Table 4/7   YEARS IN OFFICE OF CURRENT MAYOR

| Classification | No. reporting | Years in office of current mayor | | |
		Average no.	Maximum no.	Minimum no.
Total, all cities	839	5.43	36.00	0.00
Population group				
Over 1,000,000	2	18.50	19.00	18.00
500,000–1,000,000	8	2.25	8.00	1.00
250,000–499,999	29	3.72	11.00	1.00
100,000–249,999	94	5.45	28.00	1.00
50,000–99,999	234	5.52	32.00	0.00
25,000–49,999	472	5.49	36.00	0.00
Geographic division				
New England	78	4.94	21.00	1.00
Mid-Atlantic	98	5.77	34.00	0.00
East North Central	148	5.54	31.00	0.00
West North Central	71	5.68	30.00	1.00
South Atlantic	102	5.42	22.00	1.00
East South Central	31	6.10	23.00	1.00
West South Central ...	77	4.42	18.00	1.00
Mountain	52	4.19	24.00	0.00
Pacific Coast	182	5.96	36.00	1.00
Form of government				
Mayor-council	283	5.95	29.00	0.00
Council-manager	533	5.15	36.00	0.00
Commission	13	4.92	23.00	1.00
Town meeting	2	6.50	7.00	6.00
Rep. town meeting	8	6.75	19.00	2.00

egories, with jurisdictions with populations from 250,000 to 499,999 showing the highest.

Among the geographic divisions, the East South Central cities report no manager turnovers in 1991. The respondents from New England have the highest among the categories (37.9%).

The form-of-government figures indicate that greater turnover occurred among appointed executives in mayor-council communities (36.5%) than in council-manager jurisdictions (28.0%). This is consistent with anecdotal evidence and case studies that suggest turnover among mayors influences the likelihood of city manager turnover. The remaining categories have too few cases to draw substantive conclusions.

City Councils

An examination of city councils must include the individual council members. The analysis, therefore, requires slightly different data to examine longevity and turnover. Table 4/9 presents the average percent of council members that are serving all or part of one, two, three, four, or more than four terms. Overall, an average of 47.0% are in their first term, 24.2% in their second term, 13.8% in their third term, and 6.0% in their fourth term. An average of only 9% are serving more than four terms. The jurisdictions with populations greater than 1,000,000 report the highest percentage (53.3%) of council members serving more than four terms, but the most consistent population differences are apparent for the one- and two-term categories. Perhaps consistent with political norms of volunteerism (as opposed to careerism) in smaller jurisdictions, cities with populations less than 500,000 appear to have more members in their first or second terms than do the larger jurisdictions. However, these differences may exist because incumbents are more likely to be reelected in larger cities than in smaller ones, not because of more voluntary decisions not to seek reelection. Although they are less consistent, the same could be said of the slight regional and form-of-government differences. Since few communities have term limitations on their city councils, are the seniority differences between jurisdictions a function of voluntary retirements or of varying reelection patterns of incumbents?

This and other questions regarding city council incumbency and turnover are important and cannot be definitively addressed in this project. However, the data in Table 4/10 provide some clues. Overall, nearly 84% of city council incumbents were successful in their reelection bids, and only 16% were defeated. This is actually lower than the reelection rates for the U.S. House of Representatives and appears more comparable to the lower rate among U.S. Senators. Perhaps more important is the minimal variation in council incumbency reelection patterns by either population group, geographic division, or form of government.

CAUSES OF TURNOVER

There is little systematic research examining the causes, characteristics, and consequences of turnover among local government officials. What factors appear to produce high or low turnover? Does turnover depend upon whether the officials are elected or appointed?

City Councils

Although there is little controversy about what constitutes voluntary or involuntary retirement of city council members (those who do not seek reelection voluntarily retire, those defeated involuntarily retire), virtually all the systematic evidence that exists on the subject focuses exclusively on a single jurisdiction or region. James Vanderleeuw, for example, has recently examined city council incumbency reelection patterns in New Orleans from 1965 to 1985.[3]

Table 4/8   CITY MANAGER/CAO TURNOVER IN 1991

| Classification | No. reporting (A) | City manager/CAO turnover in 1991 | | | |
| | | No turnover occurred | | Turnover occurred | |
		No.	% of (A)	No.	% of (A)
Total, all cities	375	266	70.9	109	29.1
Population group					
Over 1,000,000	1	1	100.0	0	0.0
500,000–1,000,000	2	0	0.0	2	100.0
250,000–499,999	11	6	54.5	5	45.5
100,000–249,999	50	35	70.0	15	30.0
50,000–99,999	112	74	66.1	38	33.9
25,000–49,999	199	150	75.4	49	24.6
Geographic division					
New England	29	18	62.1	11	37.9
Mid-Atlantic	34	24	70.6	10	29.4
East North Central	49	36	73.5	13	26.5
West North Central	35	29	82.9	6	17.1
South Atlantic	51	34	66.7	17	33.3
East South Central	7	7	100.0	0	0.0
West South Central ...	42	29	69.0	13	31.0
Mountain	27	18	66.7	9	33.3
Pacific Coast	101	71	70.3	30	29.7
Form of government					
Mayor-council	52	33	63.5	19	36.5
Council-manager	318	229	72.0	89	28.0
Commission	1	1	100.0	0	0.0
Town meeting	3	3	100.0	0	0.0
Rep. town meeting	1	0	0.0	1	100.0

Table 4/9   NUMBER OF TERMS SERVED BY COUNCIL MEMBERS

| Classification | Council members serving all or part of | | | | |
| | One term | Two terms | Three terms | Four terms | More than four terms |
	Mean %	Mean %	Mean %	Mean %	Mean %
Total, all cities	47.0	24.2	13.8	6.0	9.0
Population group					
Over 1,000,000	26.7	13.3	3.3	3.3	53.3
500,000–1,000,000	42.0	20.4	17.0	8.8	11.9
250,000–499,999	45.1	26.6	14.5	7.3	6.6
100,000–249,999	46.9	24.0	15.2	5.7	8.3
50,000–99,999	43.3	24.8	14.8	7.1	10.1
25,000–49,999	49.3	23.9	13.0	5.4	8.4
Geographic division					
New England	40.0	20.5	18.4	7.6	13.5
Mid-Atlantic	52.6	21.3	12.0	4.6	9.5
East North Central	43.4	25.1	14.6	6.1	10.8
West North Central	46.7	24.6	12.2	5.4	11.1
South Atlantic	39.9	26.4	13.6	8.1	12.0
East South Central	43.7	28.7	8.6	5.5	13.5
West South Central ...	48.4	25.2	13.7	5.8	6.9
Mountain	54.9	24.7	11.4	5.0	4.0
Pacific Coast	51.6	23.7	14.4	5.4	4.8
Form of government					
Mayor-council	44.7	23.5	14.2	6.7	11.1
Council-manager	48.3	24.7	13.5	5.7	7.8
Commission	45.5	21.8	9.1	5.5	18.2
Town meeting	46.7	26.7	6.7	6.7	13.3
Rep. town meeting	51.7	16.7	27.5	4.2	0.0

In this project, we seek to explore whether the likelihood of council incumbency defeat in a jurisdiction's most recent election is associated with any of the following:

1. Form of government
2. Mayoral veto power
3. Existence of standing committees on the council
4. Whether the elections for council seats are staggered or simultaneous
5. Partisan elections
6. Election system type (at-large, mixed, district)
7. Geographic region, metropolitan status, and population size of the jurisdiction

The form-of-government and mayoral veto power variables are included in order to examine the impact of basic structural differences on the reelection success of council incumbents. We expect lower reelection rates in council-manager and commission jurisdictions than in mayor-council governments because without a separation of powers we assume that responsibility is more clearly concentrated in the council as a unit and that incumbents are less likely to be able to fashion a style that is individual and independent of city government.

The structural characteristics of the councils are included to distinguish them on the basis of activity and institutionalization. We suggest that incumbency will be more valuable as institutionalization increases. It is possible that as city councils come to resemble state legislatures or Congress in activity, the council member positions become more secure. A member's name recognition, ability to raise campaign contributions, and obtain interest group endorsements will presumably increase as a result.

The election system characteristics of the jurisdiction are presumed to have several effects. Simultaneous election of all council members should result in lower incumbency reelection than staggered elections. Because the council is perceived as a unit when all members are elected at the same time, it is difficult to present individual style. Partisan elections and at-large elections are also expected to be associated with lower incumbency reelection success. Political party organizations and labels on the ballot are presumed to increase competition and reduce the probability that an incumbent will get a free ride. At the very least, something other than simple name recognition exists as a possible voting cue in partisan systems. At-large elections are hypothesized to have a harmful effect upon an incumbent's reelection prospects because the constituencies are likely to be broader and more diverse. Alternatively, at-large could be more costly than district elections and incumbents could have an easier time because of their greater ability to raise money.

Each of the three demographic variables included in the model is also hypothesized to have an impact. Southern cities are presumed to be more likely to reelect incumbents than non-Southern communities. The traditionalist political background of the region is expected to produce greater deference to the status quo. Population size is hypothesized to have a negative effect upon incumbency reelection due to the larger, more diverse constituency. Larger and more diverse constituencies may, however, increase campaign costs and thereby increase the incumbent advantage. Metropolitan central jurisdictions are assumed to have more competition and more vulnerable incumbents than suburban jurisdictions. And the latter are expected to have lower incumbency reelection rates than nonmetropolitan independent jurisdictions.

Table 4/11 shows the data on reelection of city council incumbents. The patterns are generally in the directions hypothesized, but most of the differences are not substantial. The gap between categories exceeds 10% for population size, form of government, election systems, election timetable (staggered-simultaneous) and whether or not the city has partisan or nonpartisan elections. On the other hand, region and the presence of permanent standing committees on a council appear to have a negligible effect upon whether any incumbents are defeated in a jurisdiction.

One pattern that stands out is the consistent decrease in incumbency reelection rates from at-large to mixed and district election systems. This suggests that incumbents may benefit from at-large elections because challengers may be less able to raise funds. It is also possible, of course, that these differences are attributable to something else, such as partisanship. Since we know that at-large systems are disproportionately nonpartisan, it may be the latter and not the former variable that is having the real effect.

Table 4/11   CITY COUNCIL INCUMBENCY RE-ELECTION PATTERNS

Variables	At least one council incumbent defeated in last election (%)
Total, all variables	53.1
Demographic variables	
Population	
500,000 and over	90.0
250,000–499,999	62.5
100,000–249,999	54.5
50,000–99,999	54.7
25,000–49,999	50.8
Region	
South	50.4
Non-south	54.0
Metropolitan status	
Central	57.7
Suburban	50.6
Independent	47.9
Structural variables	
Form of government	
Mayor-council	62.0
Council-manager	48.6
Election systems	
At-large	49.3
Mixed	54.1
District	61.6
Election timetable	
Staggered	47.6
Simultaneous	67.5
Party labels	
Partisan	63.4
Non-partisan	49.9
Mayoral veto	
No	50.3
Yes	58.9
Council standing committees	
No	52.6
Yes	53.6

Table 4/10   INCUMBENTS SUCCESSFUL IN REELECTION BIDS

Classification	No. reporting	Successful incumbents Average (%)	Maximum (%)	Minimum (%)
Total, all cities	782	83.89	100.00	14.29
Population group				
Over 1,000,000	1	87.50	87.50	87.50
500,000–1,000,000	8	82.97	100.00	50.00
250,000–499,999	28	81.76	100.00	33.33
100,000–249,999	93	82.36	100.00	20.00
50,000–99,999	218	83.49	100.00	20.00
25,000–49,999	434	84.56	100.00	14.29
Geographic division				
New England	80	86.20	100.00	28.57
Mid-Atlantic	75	80.72	100.00	20.00
East North Central	144	84.98	100.00	16.67
West North Central	67	83.40	100.00	20.00
South Atlantic	95	84.89	100.00	25.00
East South Central	28	79.86	100.00	20.00
West South Central	74	87.41	100.00	33.33
Mountain	49	81.31	100.00	14.29
Pacific Coast	170	82.76	100.00	33.33
Form of government				
Mayor-council	268	82.00	100.00	14.29
Council-manager	495	84.57	100.00	16.67
Commission	10	86.00	100.00	50.00
Town meeting	2	100.00	100.00	100.00
Rep. town meeting	7	100.00	100.00	100.00

This underscores the need for a preliminary multivariate analysis including all of the possible factors.

Table 4/12 presents the data in a logistic regression (logit) model. It examines the reelection of city council incumbents as a function of all of the other variables combined and of each individually. A logistic regression enables an analysis of the effect of combined variables or of individual variables by controlling for each of the other variables. The impact of the combined variables in the model is statistically significant at the .0001 level, which means that the probability is one in ten thousand that patterns in the data could have occurred by chance. However, the goodness of the fit measure is weak (.3664). Goodness of fit indicates strength of the correlation between the *combined* variables and ranges from a low of .0000 to a high of 1.000. Because the goodness of the fit is weak, we can conclude that although the patterns in the data probably did not occur by chance, the effect of the combined variables upon the reelection of council incumbents is weak.

The only independent variable that is significant at the .05 level is whether the elections are staggered or simultaneous. There is a significant

Table 4/12   LOGIT ANALYSIS OF CITY COUNCIL INCUMBENCY

Model significance = .0000
Goodness of fit = .3664

Structural variables	Significance
Form of government	0.0741
Partisan elections	0.0995
Staggered/simultaneous elections	0.0007
At-large elections (%)	0.9306
Council meetings	0.7440
Mayoral veto	0.2836
Council size	0.3331
Standing committees	0.1795
Demographic variables	
Population size	0.0934
Region	0.1300
Central/noncentral city	0.6749
Independent/nonindependent city	0.6626

decrease in reelection of incumbents in jurisdictions with simultaneous elections. Three other independent variables—form of government, party on ballot, and population size—result in relationships that are likely to occur by chance only between 5% and 10% of the time. The remaining variables are not significant using any of the conventional significance levels. Significance tests indicate the probability of obtaining a particular sample result or pattern by chance if there is really no relationship in the population from which the sample was drawn.

It is clear that there are other factors than those included in this model that account for the diversity of reelection patterns for council incumbents. We are unable to make good predictions about city council incumbent reelection using the factors in our model. Subsequent research might seek to examine additional socioeconomic characteristics such as education, income and unemployment levels or population diversity, personal and occupational characteristics of the incumbents themselves, or policy outputs of the city such as per capita taxation and municipal debt.

City Managers

It is clear from the existing research on city manager turnover that it is difficult to distinguish between voluntary and involuntary turnover. Few managers are overtly fired by their councils. But this does not mean that they are not pushed into resignation to avoid formal dismissal from their position. Others may chose to resign before potential disagreements escalate. Of course, a manager's resignation may also be voluntary. Recent research by DeHoog and Whitaker suggests, however, that a clear majority of manager turnovers are involuntary.[4]

Although determinations about reasons for turnover are difficult to make, the existing research suggests possible causes. DeHoog and Whitaker have found clear linkages between manager turnover and elections that change the composition of the city council.[5] In addition, the existence of a separately elected mayor appears to conditionally affect the relationship between city council and manager turnover. Apparently, "elections were likely to change the balance on

the council only in cities with elected mayors who opposed the manager."[6] While the results of DeHoog and Whitaker's projects are limited by their small number of cases and the fact that they all come from Florida, a more recent national study supports most of their conclusions and finds that (1) the greater the length of time an elected mayor has served, the less likely the jurisdiction has experienced city manager turnover; (2) managers with greater budgetary authority are less likely to experience turnover than those with weaker authority; but (3) the appointment power of managers is not significantly associated with manager turnover.[7]

CONCLUSION

This exploratory research project seeks to shed some light on term limitations and turnover among local government officials.

It is our hope that future scholars will give this subject the attention it deserves. Local governments are clearly at the front line of virtually every major policy area in America. They are responsible for implementing many, if not most, federal and state programs. It is, therefore, vital for scholars, practitioners and activists to obtain an understanding of the selection and accountability processes within these often ignored governments.

[1] See Tari Renner, *Elected Executives: Authority and Responsibility*, Baseline Data Report vol. 20, no. 3 (Washington, DC: International City/County Management Association, May/June 1988): 7.

[2] Ruth Hoogland DeHoog and Gordon Whitaker, "Political Conflict or Advancement: Alternative Explanations of City Manager Turnover," *Journal of Urban Affairs* vol. 12, no. 4 (1990): 361–77.

[3] James Vanderleeuw, "The Influence of Racial Transition on Incumbency Advantage in Local Elections," *Urban Affairs Quarterly* vol. 27 (1991): 36–50.

[4] See DeHoog and Whitaker, 1990.

[5] See DeHoog and Whitaker, 1990, and DeHoog and Whitaker, "City Managers Under Fire: How Conflict Leads to Turnover," *Public Administration Review* vol. 51, no. 2 (1991): 156–65.

[6] DeHoog and Whitaker, 1991: 162.

[7] Tari Renner and Victor DeSantis, "City Manager Authority and Turnover: Is There a Linkage?" Paper presented at the 1993 annual meeting of the American Political Science Association, Washington, DC.

^A5

Profiles and Prospects: Regional Councils and Their Executive Directors

Sherman M. Wyman
University of Texas at Arlington

Findings

Regional councils are interested in an opportunity to operate public services and to have the power to veto local projects.

Taxing and enforcement powers are not sought by the majority of councils of governments.

The regional economy, transportation, environment, and infrastructure are identified by regional councils as the most important issues.

Many of today's regional councils had their genesis in the domestic policies and programs of the Johnson administration in the 1960s.[1] When Lyndon Johnson assumed office in 1963 there were 160 federal domestic grant assistance programs. By the end of 1966 the tally was 379. During this period, over 200 new regional councils were formed to serve as stewards of federal largess.[2] Johnson's domestic programs mandated regional planning and regional grant review. The years since Johnson, however, most notably those of President Reagan's New Federalism, brought a severe shrinkage in federal domestic funding and a concomitant reduction in the creation of new councils.

The withdrawal of federal money and influence prompted shifts in the program and policy orientation of many regional councils and changed the political and administrative demands on appointed professional council directors. Regional councils have shifted from an emphasis on planning and regulation to a focus on member service, which includes a strong commitment to the achievement of regional goals.

This new direction in regionalism is the principal catalyst for the research that provides the basis for this article. It is hoped that the survey results discussed below will illuminate the current status of regional councils and their directors and also provide data for further analysis.

METHODOLOGY

In the fall of 1990, the National Association of Regional Councils; Robert Weaver, Executive Director of the Texas Concho Valley Council of Governments; and the School of Urban and Public Affairs at the University of Texas at Arlington collaborated on the design and distribution of the survey instrument used in this study.

Questionnaires were mailed to 502 executive directors of regional councils.[3] A total of 283 useable questionnaires were received, representing a return rate of 56%. Responses were received from every state in the U.S. except the

four that in 1990 had no councils: Alaska, Hawaii, Rhode Island, and New Jersey. (New Jersey has subsequently adopted state-enabling legislation and established several councils.)

All of the row and column table data are drawn from the completed questionnaires. There are, therefore, variations due to skipped responses, both within and between tables. As each of the four major analytic categories—population, region, age of council, and budget—provide a context for analysis, they are referred to as the *contextual categories*. The total responses for each of the contextual variables are: population 280, region 282, age of council 283, and budget 275.

THE EXECUTIVE DIRECTOR'S ROLE

This section focuses on several dimensions of the executive director's role. Topics include appointment of the executive director, the extent of the director's authority over management functions, and time devoted to several key professional areas, including attitudes about relating to governing boards and general membership.

Executive Director Appointment

Five directors report that their source of appointment is a president or chairperson of the regional council. No obvious pattern emerges to suggest that any of the contextual categories contribute significantly to the unusual practice of direct appointment by a chief officer.

Overall, the number of executive directors appointed by executive boards is slightly less than the number appointed by the full membership (Table 5/1). Both types of appointment are fairly balanced in the population and age of council ranges. However, from a geographic perspective, almost two-thirds of the southeastern and 57% of the western councils require full membership approval of their executive directors. Some bias toward full membership approval also is exhibited among councils with budgets of $500,000 to $2.5 million.

While termination agreements and employment contracts have become increasingly com-

mon in council-manager governments of all sizes, they are not widespread among regional council executive directors. Moreover, the directors who report either a termination agreement or a contract are distributed fairly widely throughout the ranges in all four contextual categories. Even among the nine respondents from councils with budgets of more than $10 million, only two report employment agreements. It appears that even among executive directors with large budgets, neither termination agreements nor employment contracts are as yet common practice.

Executive Director's Authority

Respondents were asked to indicate the extent of their authority over seven management functions, ranging from budget preparation and hiring and firing of staff to appointing committees and executing contracts.

The vast majority of respondents have total authority for budget preparation and execution (Table 5/2). While a few respondents indicate only ''limited'' budget preparation and execution authority, those indicating they had only ''some'' authority in both of these areas range from a few directors of councils of government (COGs) serving the largest population groups to surprisingly higher numbers among councils serving smaller populations. It may be that the leadership of some smaller councils is intimately involved in the budget preparation and execution functions of their directors.

In terms of geography, larger numbers of the directors in the Northeast, Southeast, and Midwest regions report only modest control over budget preparation. However, in the area of budget execution, only northeastern and midwestern directors report significantly less authority than their counterparts in other areas.

In concert with the results by population size, directors with smaller budgets report less control over preparation and execution. Again, this result probably reflects the closer membership scrutiny possible in smaller systems.

Full authority over staff hiring and firing is found less often among council directors serving smaller populations. Midwestern and north-

The author greatly appreciates the conscientious research assistance of Su Chuang and Kazuyo Sekio.

Table 5/1   SOURCE AND NATURE OF APPOINTMENT

| | Who Appoints Regional Council Directors | | | | | | | | Employment Agreement | | | | | |
| | President or Chairperson | | Executive board | | Full membership | | Other | | Written termination agreement | | Employment contract | | Neither | |
Classification	No. reporting	% of total	No. reporting	% of total	No. reporting	% of total	No. reporting	% of total	No. reporting	% of total	No. reporting	% of total	No. reporting	% of total
Population														
Total respondents	5	1.8	124	44.8	139	50.2	9	3.2	9	3.2	21	7.5	249	89.2
Over 1,000,000	2	6.5	15	48.4	13	41.9	1	3.2	1	3.1	5	15.6	26	81.3
500,000–1,000,000	0	0.0	19	46.3	21	51.2	1	2.4	0	0.0	4	9.8	37	90.2
250,000–499,999	0	0.0	19	37.3	28	54.9	4	7.8	2	3.8	5	9.6	45	86.5
100,000–249,999	2	1.8	50	45.9	55	50.5	2	1.8	3	2.8	4	3.7	102	93.6
50,000–99,999	0	0.0	14	42.4	18	54.5	1	3.0	2	6.1	2	6.1	29	87.9
Under 50,000	1	8.3	7	58.3	4	33.3	0	0.0	1	8.3	1	8.3	10	83.3
Region[1]														
Total respondents	5	1.8	126	45.2	139	49.8	9	3.2	9	3.2	22	7.8	250	89.0
Northeast	2	4.9	21	51.2	16	39.0	2	4.9	2	4.8	4	9.5	36	85.7
Southeast	0	0.0	26	36.1	44	61.1	2	2.8	1	1.4	6	8.3	65	90.3
Midwest	2	2.5	38	47.5	37	46.3	3	3.8	2	2.5	7	8.8	71	88.8
Southwest	0	0.0	27	55.1	22	44.9	0	0.0	1	2.0	2	4.1	46	93.9
Northwest	1	50.0	1	50.0	0	0.0	0	0.0	0	0.0	0	0.0	2	100.0
West	0	0.0	13	37.1	20	57.1	2	5.7	3	8.3	3	8.3	30	83.3
Age of regional council														
Total respondents	5	1.8	126	45.0	140	50.0	9	3.2	9	3.2	22	7.8	251	89.0
1–14 years	2	18.2	6	54.5	3	27.3	0	0.0	0	0.0	2	18.2	9	81.8
15–25 years	3	1.3	101	44.9	115	51.1	6	2.7	8	3.5	17	7.5	201	88.9
More than 25 years	0	0.0	19	43.2	22	50.0	3	6.8	1	2.2	3	6.7	41	91.1
Budget														
Total respondents	5	1.8	122	44.9	136	50.0	9	3.3	9	3.3	22	8.0	244	88.7
$99,999 or less	2	66.7	0	0.0	1	33.3	0	0.0	0	0.0	0	0.0	3	100.0
$100,000–$249,999	0	0.0	20	57.1	15	42.9	0	0.0	2	5.7	2	5.7	31	88.6
$250,000–$499,999	2	3.1	28	43.8	30	46.9	4	6.3	3	4.6	4	6.2	58	89.2
$500,000–$999,999	0	0.0	16	38.1	25	59.5	1	2.4	0	0.0	3	7.0	40	93.0
$1,000,000–$2,499,999	0	0.0	21	38.9	32	59.3	1	1.9	1	1.9	5	9.3	48	88.9
$2,500,000–$4,999,999	0	0.0	20	52.6	17	44.7	1	2.6	0	0.0	4	10.3	35	89.7
$5,000,000–$9,999,999	0	0.0	13	48.1	12	44.4	2	7.4	3	11.1	2	7.4	22	81.5
$10,000,000 and above	1	11.1	4	44.4	4	44.4	0	0.0	0	0.0	2	22.2	7	77.8

[1]Regions: *Northeast:* Maine, New Hampshire, Vermont, Massachusetts, Connecticut, New York, Pennsylvania; *Southeast:* West Virginia, Maryland, Delaware, Virginia, North Carolina, South Carolina, Georgia, Florida, Alabama, Mississippi, Tennessee, Kentucky; *Midwest:* Ohio, Michigan, Indiana, Illinois, Wisconsin, Minnesota, North Dakota, South Dakota, Nebraska, Iowa, Kansas, Missouri; *Southwest:* Louisana, Arkansas, Oklahoma, Texas, Colorado, Utah, New Mexico, Arizona; *Northwest:* Wyoming, Montana, Idaho; *West:* Washington, Oregon, Nevada, California.

Table 5/2   DIMENSIONS OF EXECUTIVE DIRECTOR'S AUTHORITY

| | Budget preparation responsibility | | | | Budget execution responsibilities | | | | Hiring and firing staff | | | |
| | No. reporting (A) | Total % of (A) | Some % of (A) | Limited % of (A) | No. reporting (B) | Total % of (B) | Some % of (B) | Limited % of (B) | No. reporting (C) | Total % of (C) | Some % of (C) | Limited % of (C) |
Classification												
Population												
Total respondents	279	85.3	14.0	0.7	277	83.0	15.2	1.8	277	77.3	19.5	3.2
Over 1,000,000	32	81.3	18.8	0.0	32	87.5	9.4	3.1	31	90.3	9.7	0.0
500,000–1,000,000	41	85.4	14.6	0.0	41	92.7	7.3	0.0	41	87.8	9.8	2.4
250,000–499,999	52	88.5	11.5	0.0	52	76.9	21.2	1.9	52	92.3	7.7	0.0
100,000–249,999	109	90.8	7.3	1.8	107	86.9	11.2	1.9	108	72.2	21.3	6.5
50,000–99,999	33	75.8	24.2	0.0	33	78.8	18.2	3.0	33	54.5	45.5	0.0
Under 50,000	12	58.3	41.7	0.0	12	41.7	58.3	0.0	12	50.0	41.7	8.3
Region												
Total respondents	281	85.1	14.2	0.7	279	82.8	15.1	2.2	279	77.1	19.7	3.2
Northeast	42	73.8	26.2	0.0	42	66.7	26.2	7.1	41	65.9	29.3	4.9
Southeast	72	83.3	15.3	1.4	71	91.5	7.0	1.4	72	81.9	16.7	1.4
Midwest	80	82.5	16.3	1.3	79	78.5	20.3	1.3	79	65.8	26.6	7.6
Southwest	49	93.9	6.1	0.0	49	83.7	14.3	2.0	49	89.8	10.2	0.0
Northwest	2	100.0	0.0	0.0	2	100.0	0.0	0.0	2	100.0	0.0	0.0
West	36	94.4	5.6	0.0	36	91.7	8.3	0.0	36	86.1	13.9	0.0
Age of regional council												
Total respondents	282	85.1	14.2	0.7	280	82.5	15.4	2.1	280	76.8	20.0	3.2
1–14 years	11	81.8	18.2	0.0	11	90.9	9.1	0.0	10	90.0	10.0	0.0
15–25 years	226	85.0	14.2	0.9	224	81.3	16.5	2.2	225	75.1	21.3	3.6
More than 25 years	45	86.7	13.3	0.0	45	86.7	11.1	2.2	45	82.2	15.6	2.2
Budget												
Total respondents	275	85.5	13.8	0.7	273	82.8	15.0	2.2	273	76.9	19.8	3.3
$99,999 or less	3	66.7	33.3	0.0	3	66.7	33.3	0.0	2	50.0	50.0	0.0
$100,000–$249,999	35	68.6	28.6	2.9	35	71.4	22.9	5.7	35	54.3	37.1	8.6
$250,000–$499,999	65	83.1	16.9	0.0	64	76.6	20.3	3.1	64	70.3	26.6	3.1
$500,000–$999,999	43	86.0	14.0	0.0	43	76.7	20.9	2.3	43	79.1	16.3	4.7
$1,000,000–$2,499,999	54	88.9	9.3	1.9	54	85.2	13.0	1.9	54	81.5	16.7	1.9
$2,500,000–$4,999,999	39	92.3	7.7	0.0	38	97.4	2.6	0.0	39	87.2	10.3	2.6
$5,000,000–$9,999,999	27	96.3	3.7	0.0	27	96.3	3.7	0.0	27	92.6	7.4	0.0
$10,000,000 and above	9	88.9	11.1	0.0	9	88.9	11.1	0.0	9	88.9	11.1	0.0

eastern directors apparently enjoy somewhat less staff authority than their counterparts in other regions. A slightly higher proportion of respondents from the youngest and oldest councils indicate total control over hiring and firing. Moreover, a larger portion of executive directors with the largest budgets, and presumably staffs, exercise more authority over personnel decisions.

Authority over agenda preparation varies less among the contextual categories than the responses to budget preparation and budget execution (Table 5/2). Detail of the population and budget responses indicates that there is somewhat less authority over agendas as population decreases. No clear differences emerge among regions.

One major countertrend in the agenda preparation data is the less-than-total authority reported by 53 directors whose councils were founded 15 to 25 years ago. All directors from councils less than 14 years in age report complete authority over agendas, and 89% of respondents from councils more than 25 years in age report total responsibility for agenda preparation. The percentages of respondents indicating authority to *recommend* committee appointments in most of the contextual categories are consistently higher than those indicating authority to *appoint* committees. However, the difference between the number of directors in all four contextual categories who report "some" authority and the few who report "total" authority to appoint committees is impressive.

In contrast to their authority in budget preparation and execution, directors of the most recently established councils and those with the smallest budgets report more committee appointment authority than most of their colleagues directing older, larger regional councils.

In the area of contract execution, most directors in all four categories exhibit evenly distributed authority between the "total" and "some" options. However, proportionately less authority is reported by directors in two subcategories: those from the Northeast and those with budgets from $250,000 to $499,999 (Table 5/2).

Time Spent on Key Activities

Time use by city managers has been the subject of a number of studies. But because little, if any, reliable information exists on regional council executive directors, the survey gathered information on the amount of time directors devote to several key professional activities.

The total response results for each of the four contextual factors indicates that approximately one-third of the respondents consistently devote considerable time to *personnel* activities, and about one-half indicate they spend considerable time on *finance* (Table 5/3).

Somewhat contrary to conventional wisdom, directors in councils with the largest populations and budgets choose to spend more time on staff rather than to delegate this function to a deputy or personnel officer. A somewhat similar pattern emerges regarding the amount of time spent on finance, although directors from councils serving larger populations with larger budgets do not as consistently indicate a heavy time commitment.

The total responses for each of the four contextual factors under *grantsmanship* suggests that this activity, in general, receives less time than finance and about the same as personnel. Directors of councils serving smaller populations and those with smaller budgets spend a much larger proportion of their time on grants than do those serving councils with larger budgets and larger populations. But, over one-fourth of the southeastern directors and 40% of the western directors (perhaps reflecting generous state and membership support) report they spend no time in this area; larger proportions of the directors of younger and older councils also report spending less time on grantsmanship.

Time spent on *board-officer relations* is equal to time spent on finance and second only to *member government relations*, which demand the highest time commitment. This pattern may well reflect the increased level of member service activities that characterizes today's councils in contrast to the focus on planning, control, and grant administration dominating the 1960s and 1970s.

It is difficult to explain the results of the few directors who report "no time" spent on these two critical membership areas. Possibly these directors delegate board-officer and member government responsibilities to another staff member, or perhaps these functions are performed by the council president.

Finally, as budget size increases directors devote more time to member government relations. However, this pattern is not reflected consistently by population size.

In contrast to the extensive time spent on board-officer and member government relations, a moderate amount of time is spent on *community leader* interaction in all contextual cat-

Table 5/2 (continued)

	Preparing agendas				Recommending committees				Appointing committees				Executing contracts			
		Total	Some	Limited		Total	Some	Limited		Total	Some	Limited		Total	Some	Limited
No. reporting (D)	% of (D)	% of (D)	% of (D)	No. reporting (E)	% of (E)	% of (E)	% of (E)	No. reporting (F)	% of (F)	% of (F)	% of (F)	No. reporting (G)	% of (G)	% of (G)	% of (G)	
276	79.3	19.9	0.7	260	36.9	52.7	10.4	199	7.0	45.2	47.7	267	45.3	46.4	8.2
31	83.9	16.1	0.0	31	32.3	61.3	6.5	22	13.6	54.5	31.8	30	36.7	60.0	3.3
41	87.8	12.2	0.0	39	46.2	43.6	10.3	30	6.7	53.3	40.0	40	37.5	50.0	12.5
52	71.2	28.8	0.0	49	30.6	61.2	8.2	35	5.7	40.0	54.3	48	43.8	50.0	6.3
108	81.5	16.7	1.9	99	38.4	52.5	9.1	80	6.3	42.5	51.3	106	56.6	36.8	6.6
32	78.1	21.9	0.0	30	33.3	43.3	23.3	23	8.7	26.1	65.2	32	31.3	53.1	15.6
12	58.3	41.7	0.0	12	41.7	50.0	8.3	9	0.0	88.9	11.1	11	36.4	54.5	9.1
278	78.4	20.9	0.7	262	36.6	53.1	10.3	199	7.0	45.2	47.7	269	45.0	46.8	8.2
41	68.3	31.7	0.0	40	30.0	55.0	15.0	35	8.6	42.9	48.6	41	31.7	48.8	19.5
71	83.1	16.9	0.0	67	40.3	50.7	9.0	48	10.4	43.8	45.8	68	47.1	48.5	4.4
79	72.2	25.3	2.5	72	29.2	58.3	12.5	54	0.0	44.4	55.6	76	39.5	52.6	7.9
49	81.6	18.4	0.0	47	46.8	46.8	6.4	36	11.1	44.4	44.4	46	54.3	39.1	6.5
2	100.0	0.0	0.0	1	0.0	100.0	0.0	1	0.0	100.0	0.0	2	50.0	50.0	0.0
36	88.9	11.1	0.0	35	40.0	51.4	8.6	25	8.0	52.0	40.0	36	55.6	38.9	5.6
279	78.5	20.8	0.7	264	36.4	53.4	10.2	200	7.0	45.0	48.0	270	44.8	47.0	8.1
11	100.0	0.0	0.0	9	44.4	44.4	11.1	6	33.3	66.7	0.0	10	40.0	50.0	10.0
223	75.3	23.8	0.9	211	37.4	50.7	11.8	157	4.5	47.8	47.8	217	45.2	46.5	8.3
45	88.9	11.1	0.0	44	29.5	68.2	2.3	37	13.5	29.7	56.8	43	44.2	48.8	7.0
272	78.7	20.6	0.7	256	36.3	53.1	10.5	194	7.2	45.4	47.4	263	44.9	46.8	8.4
3	100.0	0.0	0.0	3	66.7	33.3	0.0	3	33.3	33.3	33.3	3	33.3	66.7	0.0
35	77.1	20.0	2.9	29	34.5	55.2	10.3	19	0.0	68.4	31.6	30	33.3	56.7	10.0
64	70.3	29.7	0.0	62	30.6	54.8	14.5	51	3.9	41.2	54.9	63	30.2	52.4	17.5
43	79.1	20.9	0.0	40	27.5	55.0	17.5	33	3.0	45.5	51.5	43	44.2	48.8	7.0
53	81.1	17.0	1.9	52	38.5	51.9	9.6	37	10.8	32.4	56.8	54	50.0	44.4	5.6
38	84.2	15.8	0.0	37	43.2	54.1	2.7	29	10.3	55.2	34.5	37	56.8	37.8	5.4
27	92.6	7.4	0.0	25	48.0	48.0	4.0	18	11.1	38.9	50.0	25	64.0	36.0	0.0
9	55.6	44.4	0.0	8	37.5	50.0	12.5	4	25.0	75.0	0.0	8	62.5	37.5	0.0

Table 5/3   TIME SPENT ON COUNCIL ACTIVITIES

Classification	Personnel				Finance				Grantsmanship			
	No. reporting (A)	Considerable % of (A)	Moderate % of (A)	None % of (A)	No. reporting (B)	Considerable % of (B)	Moderate % of (B)	None % of (B)	No. reporting (C)	Considerable % of (C)	Moderate % of (C)	None % of (C)
Population												
Total respondents	277	29.5	58.4	11.9	277	48.7	45.1	6.1	271	29.2	50.2	20.7
Over 1,000,000	30	23.3	73.3	3.4	30	36.7	63.3	0.0	30	16.7	56.7	26.7
500,000–1,000,000	41	26.8	53.7	19.5	41	51.2	39.0	9.8	40	23.0	47.8	30.0
250,000–499,999	52	21.2	75.0	3.8	52	51.9	42.3	5.8	50	20.0	62.0	18.0
100,000–249,999	110	37.3	50.9	11.8	110	54.5	39.1	6.4	108	35.2	44.4	20.4
50,000–99,999	32	31.3	49.9	18.8	32	37.5	62.5	0.0	32	34.4	56.3	9.3
Under 50,000	12	15.4	68.3	25.0	12	33.3	41.7	25.9	11	63.6	27.2	18.2
Region												
Total respondents	279	29.7	58.4	11.8	280	48.2	45.7	6.1	273	28.9	50.5	20.5
Northeast	41	24.4	61.0	14.6	42	47.6	38.1	14.3	40	25.0	65.0	10.0
Southeast	71	36.7	56.3	7.0	71	49.3	47.8	2.8	69	30.4	43.5	26.1
Midwest	80	25.0	63.8	4.2	80	46.3	50.0	3.7	78	42.5	44.9	12.8
Southwest	49	30.6	55.1	14.3	49	51.0	42.9	6.1	49	24.5	55.1	20.4
Northwest	2	50.0	0.0	50.0	2	50.0	50.0	0.0	2	50.0	50.0	0.0
West	36	29.6	55.6	13.9	36	47.2	44.4	8.4	35	5.7	54.3	40.0
Age of regional council												
Total respondents	280	29.6	58.6	11.8	280	48.5	45.4	6.1	274	28.8	50.7	20.4
1–14 years	10	20.0	30.0	50.0	10	30.0	30.0	40.0	11	27.3	45.4	27.3
15–25 years	225	30.6	57.8	11.6	225	56.7	44.9	4.4	222	31.1	49.1	19.4
More than 25 years	45	26.7	68.9	4.4	45	42.2	51.1	6.7	41	15.9	58.5	24.4
Budget												
Total respondents	272	29.4	59.2	11.4	272	48.5	45.6	5.9	272	28.7	49.6	21.7
$99,999 or less	2	0.0	50.0	50.0	2	50.0	50.0	0.0	3	100.0	0.0	0.0
$100,000–$249,999	35	11.1	62.9	25.7	35	28.6	60.0	11.4	36	47.2	25.0	27.8
$250,000–$499,999	64	21.9	60.9	17.2	64	51.5	43.8	4.7	64	37.5	56.2	6.3
$500,000–$999,999	43	32.6	51.1	16.3	43	55.8	34.9	9.3	42	31.0	45.2	23.8
$1,000,000–$2,499,999	54	33.3	64.8	1.9	54	55.6	44.4	0.0	54	22.3	48.1	29.6
$2,500,000–$4,999,999	39	41.0	56.4	2.6	39	38.5	53.8	7.7	38	21.1	55.2	23.7
$5,000,000–$9,999,999	26	34.6	65.4	0.0	26	50.0	42.3	7.7	26	3.9	76.9	19.2
$10,000,000 and above	9	55.6	33.3	11.1	9	66.7	33.3	0.0	9	0.0	44.4	55.6

Table 5/4   ATTITUDES TOWARD KEY DIRECTOR ROLE DIMENSIONS

Classification	Council formulates and director implements						Maintain neutrality on divisive issues					
	No. reporting (A)	Strongly agree % of (A)	Agree % of (A)	Disagree % of (A)	Strongly disagree % of (A)	Unsure % of (A)	No reporting (B)	Strongly agree % of (B)	Agree % of (B)	Disagree % of (B)	Strongly disagree % of (B)	Unsure % of (B)
Population												
Total respondents	277	5.8	36.5	44.4	11.6	1.8	275	7.6	36.0	44.7	5.1	6.9
Over 1,000,000	32	0.0	25.0	50.0	25.0	0.0	31	0.0	29.0	54.9	12.9	3.2
500,000–1,000,000	40	10.0	37.5	42.5	7.5	2.5	40	5.0	30.0	55.0	5.0	5.0
250,000–499,999	52	5.8	42.3	38.5	11.5	1.9	52	5.8	46.1	36.5	5.8	5.8
100,000–249,999	109	6.4	37.6	43.1	11.9	0.9	107	9.3	34.6	43.9	4.7	7.5
50,000–99,999	33	3.0	30.3	54.5	6.1	6.1	33	15.2	39.3	36.4	0.0	9.1
Under 50,000	11	9.0	45.5	45.5	0.0	0.0	12	8.3	33.3	50.0	0.0	8.3
Region												
Total respondents	280	6.1	36.4	44.3	11.4	1.8	278	7.6	36.0	45.0	5.0	6.5
Northeast	42	9.5	31.0	47.6	9.5	2.4	40	0.0	25.0	60.0	5.0	10.0
Southeast	73	8.2	39.7	44.1	9.6	1.4	72	8.3	44.4	38.4	5.6	2.8
Midwest	79	5.1	34.2	46.8	11.4	2.5	79	8.9	31.6	46.8	5.1	7.6
Southwest	49	6.1	40.8	40.8	10.2	2.0	49	14.3	42.9	34.7	2.0	6.1
Northwest	2	0.0	50.0	50.0	0.0	0.0	2	0.0	50.0	50.0	0.0	0.0
West	45	0.0	34.3	45.7	20.0	0.0	36	2.8	30.6	50.0	8.3	8.3
Age of regional council												
Total respondents	280	5.7	36.4	44.3	11.4	1.8	278	7.9	35.5	45.0	5.0	6.5
1–14 years	11	0.0	45.5	45.5	9.1	0.0	11	18.2	36.3	45.5	0.0	0.0
15–25 years	224	5.7	37.9	43.4	10.7	2.2	222	7.2	36.9	45.0	4.1	6.8
More than 25 years	45	6.7	28.9	48.9	15.6	0.0	45	8.9	28.9	44.4	11.1	6.7
Budget												
Total respondents	273	5.9	35.9	44.7	11.7	1.8	270	7.4	35.2	45.6	5.2	6.7
$99,999 or less	3	0.0	100.0	0.0	0.0	0.0	3	33.3	66.7	0.0	0.0	0.0
$100,000–$249,999	34	5.9	35.3	48.6	8.8	0.0	34	5.9	26.9	58.9	0.0	8.8
$250,000–$499,999	65	12.3	36.9	44.7	4.6	1.5	65	7.7	36.9	43.1	3.1	9.2
$500,000–$999,999	43	0.0	39.5	44.2	11.6	4.7	40	10.0	32.5	47.5	2.5	7.5
$1,000,000–$2,499,999	54	5.6	38.9	40.7	12.9	1.9	53	7.5	34.0	45.3	5.7	7.5
$2,500,000–$4,999,999	39	7.7	25.6	46.2	17.9	2.6	39	5.1	38.5	41.0	15.4	0.0
$5,000,000–$9,999,999	27	0.0	25.9	48.1	25.9	0.0	27	7.4	40.7	40.7	7.4	3.8
$10,000,000 and above	8	0.0	50.0	50.0	0.0	0.0	9	0.0	33.3	55.6	0.0	11.1

Table 5/3   (continued)

	Board-officer relations				Member government relations				Community leaders				Public		
	Considerable	Moderate	None		Considerable	Moderate	None		Considerable	Moderate	None		Considerable	Moderate	None
No. reporting (D)	% of (D)	% of (D)	% of (D)	No. reporting (E)	% of (E)	% of (E)	% of (E)	No. reporting (F)	% of (F)	% of (F)	% of (F)	No. reporting (G)	% of (G)	% of (G)	% of (G)
279	48.0	47.7	4.3	278	65.5	30.6	4.0	277	43.0	46.6	10.5	278	36.1	50.9	13.0
31	54.8	45.2	0.0	31	48.4	48.4	3.2	30	50.0	36.7	13.3	31	19.4	54.8	25.8
41	65.9	45.1	0.0	41	78.0	17.1	4.9	41	46.3	43.9	9.8	41	41.5	51.2	7.3
52	36.5	61.5	2.0	52	63.4	30.8	5.8	52	40.4	46.1	13.5	52	34.6	53.8	11.6
111	51.4	41.4	7.2	110	69.1	30.9	0.0	110	45.5	46.3	8.2	110	39.1	47.3	13.6
32	34.4	56.2	9.4	32	62.4	31.3	6.3	32	25.0	59.4	15.6	32	25.0	62.5	12.5
12	25.0	75.0	0.0	12	50.0	25.0	25.0	12	50.0	50.0	0.0	12	66.7	25.0	8.3
280	48.2	47.5	4.3	280	65.0	31.1	3.9	279	42.7	47.0	10.4	279	35.5	51.3	13.3
42	38.1	67.1	4.8	42	61.9	31.0	7.1	42	38.1	47.6	14.3	41	22.0	65.9	12.2
71	54.9	43.7	1.4	71	71.8	28.2	0.0	71	43.7	42.3	14.1	71	39.4	49.3	11.3
80	41.3	52.5	6.2	80	61.3	33.8	5.0	79	55.7	40.5	3.8	80	40.0	51.3	8.8
49	51.0	42.9	6.1	49	67.3	24.5	8.2	49	32.7	55.1	12.2	49	38.8	44.9	16.3
2	50.0	50.0	0.0	2	50.0	50.0	0.0	2	50.0	50.0	0.0	2	100.0	0.0	0.0
36	58.3	38.9	2.8	36	61.1	38.9	0.0	36	30.0	58.3	11.1	36	25.0	50.0	25.0
281	48.0	47.7	4.3	281	64.8	31.3	3.9	280	42.3	47.1	10.4	280	35.7	51.1	13.2
11	36.4	54.5	9.1	11	63.6	27.3	9.1	11	42.5	45.5	9.0	10	20.0	40.0	40.0
225	47.6	48.0	4.4	225	65.3	30.7	4.0	225	40.4	48.4	11.1	225	36.4	1.1	12.4
45	53.3	44.4	2.2	45	62.2	35.6	2.3	44	52.3	40.9	6.8	45	35.6	53.3	11.1
273	47.6	48.0	4.4	273	65.3	30.8	4.0	272	43.0	46.7	10.3	272	36.3	51.1	12.9
3	0.0	66.7	33.3	3	33.3	66.7	0.0	3	33.3	66.7	0.0	2	100.0	0.0	0.0
35	28.6	60.0	11.4	35	60.0	25.7	14.3	35	45.7	45.7	8.6	35	42.9	40.0	17.1
64	39.1	56.2	4.7	64	59.3	39.1	1.6	64	31.3	57.8	10.9	64	25.0	67.2	7.8
43	44.2	51.1	4.7	43	65.1	32.6	2.3	43	39.5	44.2	16.3	43	37.2	48.8	14.0
54	51.9	48.1	0.0	54	66.7	29.6	3.7	54	64.8	27.8	7.4	54	44.4	50.0	5.6
39	59.0	35.9	5.1	39	66.6	30.8	2.6	39	38.5	51.2	10.3	39	30.8	51.3	17.9
25	69.2	30.8	0.0	26	80.8	19.2	0.0	25	28.0	60.0	12.0	26	34.6	34.6	30.8
9	77.8	22.2	0.0	9	77.8	11.1	11.1	9	66.7	33.3	0.0	9	44.4	55.6	0.0

Table 5/4   (continued)

	Work informally to achieve agreement on council plans				
		Strongly agree	Agree	Disagree	Strongly disagree	Unsure
Classification	No. reporting (C)	% of (C)	% of (C)	% of (C)	% of (C)	% of (C)
Population						
Total respondents	279	36.6	57.3	4.3	1.0	0.7
Over 1,000,000	32	62.5	37.5	0.0	0.0	0.0
50,000–1,000,000	41	31.7	58.5	7.3	2.4	0.0
250,000–499,999	52	34.6	63.5	0.0	0.0	1.9
100,000–249,999	109	37.6	54.1	5.5	1.8	0.9
50,000–99,000	33	15.2	78.8	6.1	0.0	0.0
Under 50,000	12	41.7	50.0	8.3	0.0	0.0
Region						
Total respondents	281	36.7	57.3	4.3	1.1	0.7
Northeast	42	38.1	52.4	7.1	2.4	0.0
Southeast	72	34.7	58.3	2.8	1.4	2.8
Midwest	80	40.0	52.5	7.5	0.0	0.0
Southwest	49	32.7	63.3	2.0	2.0	0.0
Northwest	2	0.0	10.0	0.0	0.0	0.0
West	36	38.9	61.1	0.0	0.0	0.0
Age of regional council						
Total respondents	282	69.1	30.5	0.0	0.0	0.4
1–14 years	11	54.5	45.5	0.0	0.0	0.0
15–25 years	226	32.7	60.0	4.4	1.3	0.9
More than 25 years	45	51.1	42.2	6.7	0.0	0.0
Budget						
Total respondents	275	69.8	30.2	0.0	0.0	0.4
$99,999 or less	3	33.3	66.7	0.0	0.0	0.0
$100,000–$249,999	35	37.1	6.0	2.9	0.0	0.0
$250,000–$499,999	65	30.8	60.0	6.2	1.5	1.5
$500,000–$999,999	43	37.2	55.8	4.7	2.7	0.0
$1,000,000–$2,499,999	54	27.8	63.0	7.4	0.0	1.9
$2,500,000–$4,999,999	39	41.0	56.4	0.0	2.6	0.0
$5,000,000–$9,999,999	27	66.9	33.3	0.0	0.0	0.0
$10,000,000 and above	9	22.2	77.8	0.0	0.0	0.0

egories. Community leaders appear, however, to receive somewhat more time from directors than the *public* does.

With the exception of finance, the highest rated categories are those requiring interpersonal and political skills rather than technical and analytic competencies. Interestingly, this emphasis is substantially inverse to the theoretical and quantitative-analytical competencies emphasized in the university public administration, planning, and business curricula from which council directors are expected to hold degrees.

DIRECTOR'S ROLE IN POLICY MAKING

The responses to three of the survey questions on the director's role in policy making are particularly revealing. Results are reported in Table 5/4.

These questions were:

1. Should directors concern themselves only with the implementation of council objectives and leave formulation of objectives to the council?
2. Should directors maintain a neutral stand on issues dividing the membership?
3. Should directors work informally with council members to achieve agreement on council activities?

On the first question concerning the director's role as strictly an *implementor* of policy, the total responses for each of the four contextual categories indicate that a narrow majority of directors (approximately 56%) disagree with the perception that their role is solely implementation of policy.

The detailed results under the population category suggest that directors of regional councils serving a population of more than one million do not see their role as strictly implementation. However, this pattern is not reflected in the budget responses. Directors with the largest budgets are evenly split over this issue, although those administering budgets in the middle ranges tend somewhat more toward disagreement.

The next question, should directors maintain a *neutral stand* on potentially divisive issues, garnered a response pattern generally similar to that of the first question. An even narrower majority (50.1%) disagree with the notion that directors should maintain a neutral stand on divisive issues. Directors with smaller populations are somewhat more inclined toward a neutral position, but the highest percentage of respondents (100%) who agree with maintaining neutrality have budgets under $1 million (Table 5/4).

Finally, the directors were asked about their attitudes toward *working informally* to realize agreement on council plans and issues. Here, in contrast to the results on style and neutrality, the general and detailed responses indicate agreement in every contextual category.

FUNCTIONAL DIMENSIONS OF REGIONAL COUNCILS

Tables 5/5 through 5/12 feature information, both factual and perceptual, about the anatomy of regional councils. Subjects treated range from information on membership, revenues, voting patterns, legal bases, and policy preferences to the directors' perceptions of the council's importance and primary function.

Membership Proportions

In order to develop a clearer picture of the makeup of council memberships, the directors were asked to indicate (1) what percentage of eligible municipalities and counties in their regions were council members, (2) the percentage of the total regional population that resides in member municipalities, and (3) the percentage of their member municipalities with populations of 10,000 or less.

With respect to municipality and county membership, as the total responses indicate, close to 95% of the councils enjoy 75% to 100% membership from these jurisdictions (not shown).

The substantial majority of small jurisdiction membership is dramatically demonstrated in the data on member jurisdictions of 10,000 or less. Here, regardless of the contextual category, the preponderance of small jurisdictions is striking. Indeed, the diversity of policy expectations imposed by a membership mix of many small communities with a few larger ones is probably the single overarching challenge to effective,

stable council leadership throughout the United States.

Membership Composition

Two major patterns are evident in the membership composition results. First, in contrast to municipalities and counties, a paucity of school and special district membership is evident in all contextual categories (not shown). Second, contrary to the impression held by many students of regionalism, the total membership of the councils represented in this survey contains approximately an equal number of municipalities and counties.

Council's Primary Functions

In an effort to track the change in the nature of regional council activities, respondents were asked to characterize the functional emphasis of their council. The overall results indicate that the dual planning and service role is the most common, although a significant portion of directors see their council's primary function as service (Table 5/5).

Directors of councils with populations of 500,000 and above report planning as the primary function. This trend is also noted by directors with the largest budgets.

Possibly reflecting the limited functions historically assigned to councils of governments by the northeastern states, the largest number of these directors see planning as their council's primary function; however, a significant number note both roles. A number of western directors also favor planning, possibly in response to the

Table 5/5 COUNCILS' PRIMARY FUNCTION AND IMPORTANCE OF GOVERNING BOARD MEMBERS

Classification	No. reporting (A)	Planning % of (A)	Service % of (A)	Both % of (A)	No. reporting (B)	Often important % of (B)	Sometimes important % of (B)	Seldom important % of (B)
Population								
Total respondents	278	30.2	27.0	42.8	278	60.8	35.3	4.0
Over 1,000,000	32	62.5	6.3	31.3	32	62.5	37.5	0.0
500,000–1,000,000	41	51.2	12.2	36.6	41	51.2	43.9	4.9
250,000–4999,999	51	23.5	27.5	49.0	52	59.6	38.5	1.9
100,000–249,999	109	18.3	33.9	47.7	109	64.2	32.1	3.7
50,000–99,999	33	24.2	36.4	39.4	32	62.5	28.1	9.4
Under 50,000	12	25.0	41.7	33.3	12	58.3	33.3	8.3
Region								
Total respondents	280	30.4	26.4	43.2	280	60.0	36.1	3.9
Northeast	42	47.6	19.0	33.3	42	40.5	45.2	14.3
Southeast	71	28.2	29.6	42.3	72	66.7	33.3	0.0
Midwest	80	22.5	31.3	46.3	80	61.3	35.0	3.8
Southwest	49	18.4	30.6	51.1	48	70.8	27.1	2.1
Northwest	2	50.0	0.0	50.0	2	100.0	0.0	0.0
West	36	47.2	13.9	38.9	36	50.0	47.2	2.8
Age of regional council								
Total respondents	280	30.4	26.4	43.2	281	60.5	35.6	3.9
1–14 years	11	27.3	36.4	36.4	11	63.6	36.4	0.0
15–25 years	225	26.7	29.8	43.6	225	60.4	36.0	3.6
More than 25 years	44	50.0	6.8	43.2	45	60.0	33.3	6.7
Budget								
Total respondents	275	30.2	27.3	42.5	274	59.9	36.1	4.0
$99,999 or less	3	0.0	33.3	66.7	3	66.7	33.3	0.0
$100,000–$249,999	35	28.6	31.4	40.0	34	58.8	35.3	5.9
$250,000–$499,999	65	29.2	29.2	41.5	65	52.3	40.0	7.7
$500,000–$999,999	43	39.5	23.3	37.2	43	58.1	34.9	7.0
$1,000,000–$2,499,999	54	35.2	27.8	37.0	54	61.1	37.0	1.9
$2,500,000–$4,999,999	39	20.5	33.3	46.2	39	71.8	28.2	0.0
$5,000,000–$9,999,999	27	18.5	22.2	59.3	27	63.0	37.0	0.0
$10,000,000 and above	9	55.6	0.0	44.4	9	55.6	44.4	0.0

constant growth which, until very recently, has characterized their region.

Directors of councils that have been in existence for 15 years or more indicate both planning and service more often than their counterparts directing regional councils that were established more recently.

The nature and size of new council service activities is an issue that is now being confronted in the offices of councils across the country. At the heart of the issue is the willingness of council members and taxpayers to financially and politically support a wide variety of new service offerings ranging from data collection and analysis to high school dropout programs, regional transit operations, and regional training centers.

Importance of Governing Board

Because councils are expanding into new areas and becoming increasingly dependent on local support, respondents were asked about their perception of the importance of their governing board members in the conduct of regional policy making and affairs.

The total response results in each contextual category show well over one-half of the respondents feel their leaders are often important regional players. More than one-third of directors see their key board members as "sometimes" influential.

The detailed data for each of the four contextual categories show similar patterns throughout the population, age, and budget categories (Table 5/5). But from a regional perspective, higher percentages of northwestern and southwestern directors see their leaders as more often influential. Western and northeastern directors see their board members as relatively less important in regional affairs, perhaps reflecting the typically urbanized, more fragmented nature of many of these councils.

Legal Bases

The survey instrument included a question about the various statutes and local agreements that provide the legal basis for regional councils.

As the overall distribution of responses indicates, general planning agency legislation is by far the most widely used (Table 5/6). Interlocal, voluntary, and nonprofit agreements are reported by the next highest percentage of respondents, suggesting that locally driven rather than state initiated alliances have contributed to the formation of many councils. Often general or specific legislation was subsequently passed by the state legislature. Other regional councils were initially formed under voluntary agreements among municipalities, counties, and districts without the benefit of state legislation.

Although interstate regional councils have received considerable attention in the literature on regionalism, only four respondents indicate their councils are supported by interstate compacts. And finally, the overall results indicate that in some states economic development was the motivation for the development of some regional councils.

When the responses are examined by region, the relatively high percentage of respondents from the West reporting joint exercise of powers reflects the joint powers legislation in California. Councils in existence more than 15 years are widely supported by planning agency legislation, and several councils also report they use various local agreements or are covered by a metropolitan planning act.

Finally, almost half of the youngest councils indicate that an interlocal agreement act is their principal legal justification. With the exception of those councils with the largest and smallest budgets, budget size does not have any obvious connection to the type of legal basis.

Sources of Revenue

Revenue structure is a critical and changing feature of the anatomy of contemporary regional councils. Severe reductions in federal funding have forced many councils to seek larger portions of funds from state and local sources. To provide a picture of the relative levels of revenue source dependency, each respondent was asked to indicate the percentage of regional council revenues derived from four key sources: federal, state, and member governments, and fees for services.

In general, the largest revenue provider in each contextual category is the federal government, followed, with some important exceptions, by state and then member governments (Table 5/7). Revenue from fees for services generally ranks as the smallest source, although directors in the Northwest region report that service charges constitute a major portion of their total revenues.

Table 5/6 LEGAL BASIS OF COUNCIL

Classification	No. reporting (A)	Planning agency act % of (A)	Council of government act % of (A)	Nonprofit corporation % of (A)	Interlocal agreement act % of (A)	Joint exercise of powers act % of (A)	Economic development act % of (A)	Interstate compact % of (A)	Metropolitan planning act % of (A)	Other enabling legislation % of (A)	Voluntary agreement % of (A)
Population											
Total respondents	280	37.9	12.1	17.1	18.9	10.4	13.2	1.4	5.4	8.2	17.5
Over 1,000,000	32	28.1	9.4	15.6	18.8	18.8	8.3	3.1	6.3	0.0	31.3
500,000–1,000,000	41	29.3	19.5	9.8	14.6	9.8	4.9	2.4	0.0	12.2	19.5
250,000–499,999	52	42.3	9.6	13.5	15.4	7.7	17.3	0.0	3.8	3.8	9.6
100,000–249,999	110	40.9	13.6	23.6	21.8	10.9	18.2	0.9	8.2	12.7	17.3
50,000–99,999	33	42.4	6.1	9.1	24.2	6.1	9.1	3.0	6.1	6.1	18.2
Under 50,000	12	33.3	8.3	25.0	8.3	8.3	8.3	0.0	0.0	0.0	8.3
Region											
Total respondents	282	37.6	12.4	17.0	18.8	10.6	13.1	1.4	5.3	8.2	17.4
Northeast	42	38.1	11.9	14.3	7.1	7.1	7.1	2.4	7.1	11.9	14.3
Southeast	72	43.1	15.3	18.1	11.1	5.6	13.9	1.4	1.4	4.2	19.4
Midwest	81	45.7	14.8	16.0	21.0	9.9	11.1	1.2	8.6	8.6	9.9
Southwest	49	32.7	8.2	28.6	34.7	2.0	22.4	0.0	4.1	4.1	20.4
Northwest	2	0.0	50.0	50.0	50.0	50.0	0.0	0.0	0.0	0.0	50.0
West	36	16.7	5.6	2.8	19.4	36.1	11.1	2.8	5.6	16.7	27.8
Age of regional council											
Total respondents	283	37.8	12.7	16.6	18.7	10.6	13.1	1.4	5.3	8.1	17.3
1–14 years	11	18.2	9.1	27.3	45.5	9.1	9.1	0.0	0.0	0.0	36.4
15–25 years	227	39.2	14.1	17.2	18.5	11.9	15.0	1.3	4.4	8.4	16.3
More than 25 years	45	35.6	6.7	11.1	13.3	4.4	4.4	2.2	11.1	8.9	17.8
Budget											
Total respondents	275	37.5	12.7	16.4	19.3	10.9	12.4	1.5	5.5	8.4	17.5
$99,999 or less	3	0.0	0.0	33.3	0.0	33.3	33.3	0.0	0.0	33.3	0.0
$100,000–$249,999	35	48.6	8.6	17.1	14.3	5.7	8.6	0.0	11.4	2.9	14.3
$250,000–$499,999	65	44.6	7.7	13.8	16.9	10.8	10.8	3.1	4.6	12.3	12.3
$500,000–$999,999	43	39.5	11.6	16.3	20.9	14.0	14.0	0.0	7.0	11.6	14.0
$1,000,000–$2,499,999	54	27.8	20.4	18.5	25.9	9.3	16.7	0.0	9.3	5.6	20.4
$2,500,000–4,999,999	39	35.9	15.4	17.9	28.2	10.3	10.3	2.6	0.0	7.7	23.1
$5,000,000–$9,999,999	27	25.9	14.8	11.1	11.1	11.1	11.1	3.7	0.0	3.7	25.9
$10,000,000 and above	9	44.4	11.1	22.2	0.0	22.2	11.1	0.0	0.0	11.1	22.2

Table 5/7   SOURCES OF REVENUE

Classification	Federal government		State government		Member government		Service charges	
	No. reporting	Average (%)	No. reporting	Average (%)	No. reporting	Average (%)	No. reporting	Average (%)
Population								
Over 1,000,000	31	43.3	29	21.2	31	22.5	26	17.8
500,000–1,000,000	38	37.7	36	23.6	38	27.5	32	14.2
250,000–499,999	45	52.8	43	22.6	47	22.0	31	13.4
100,000–249,999	90	40.0	85	30.5	102	23.2	73	22.8
50,000–99,999	29	37.3	27	33.1	31	27.1	24	19.1
Under 50,000	8	32.0	8	53.3	10	31.9	6	16.3
Region								
Northeast	36	38.1	40	28.1	42	29.2	25	15.2
Southeast	62	45.2	68	25.8	68	18.8	45	20.0
Midwest	72	38.5	53	21.6	75	27.7	66	22.6
Southwest	41	50.5	39	33.2	40	17.1	33	10.5
Northwest	2	43.6	0	0.0	2	57.5	0	0.0
West	29	33.8	29	29.6	33	36.7	23	13.7
Age of regional council								
1–14 years	8	39.6	6	46.2	11	32.5	6	24.8
15–25 years	194	42.0	186	28.1	206	23.7	153	17.8
More Than 25 Years	41	40.2	38	23.9	44	26.4	33	20.2
Budget								
$99,999 or less	3	68.3	0	0.0	3	23.3	1	25.0
$100,000–$249,999	25	35.5	22	38.9	33	34.4	19	25.9
$250,000–$499,999	54	29.9	55	30.1	63	31.2	46	24.9
$500,000–$999,999	39	37.0	37	26.6	42	28.9	34	15.7
$1,000,000–$2,499,999	51	45.8	46	26.0	52	18.9	39	17.5
$2,500,000–$4,999,999	35	55.1	35	23.4	34	14.2	27	11.6
$5,000,000–$9,999,999	25	53.9	24	22.1	24	14.4	19	13.6
$10,000,000 and above	8	35.1	8	36.1	7	14.1	6	11.3

Note: Respondents were asked to record the percent of revenue from each source; cell data are means of scores.

Member government contributions exceed state government revenues in several of the regional, population, and budget subcategories. As the competition for state government funds continues to increase, councils will undoubtably more frequently and creatively seek revenue from local jurisdictions.

Councils serving larger populations generally realize a larger share of their revenue from direct federal grants, pass-through programs, and contracts. However, the budget data do not consistently support this pattern. Councils with budgets of $10 million or more rank federal support slightly lower than state support, and the three councils with the smallest budgets show an average of 68.3% of revenue coming from the federal government. Moreover, although the length of time the council has been in existence does not seem to matter, the regional results suggest that southwestern, northwestern, and southeastern councils are somewhat more dependent on federal largess than are the other regions.

As the competition for federal and state dollars continues to mount, higher membership levies and charges for service could become the only real revenue options for council stability, let alone growth.

Voting Apportionment

Voting apportionment has been a source of tension between large and small member jurisdictions. Respondents were asked to indicate which of the following common approaches best describes their member voting apportionment formula:

1. Each member has an equal vote
2. Voting is in proportion to population
3. Voting is a combination
4. Another formula is employed

Overall results show *equal apportionment* as the method used by the majority. Second in popularity is a combination of equal and proportionate voting, with proportionate and other formula about tied for third place.

Detail of the four contextual categories, however, reveals some important distinctions (Table 5/8). Equal voting power is typically more popular among councils with smaller populations

Table 5/8   VOTING APPORTIONMENT

Classification	No. reporting (A)	Equal % of (A)	Proportionate population % of (A)	Combination % of (A)	Other % of (A)
Population					
Total respondents	272	60.3	10.7	19.5	9.6
Over 1,000,000	32	43.8	15.6	34.4	6.3
500,000–1,000,000	41	61.0	19.5	17.1	2.4
250,000–499,999	50	60.0	10.0	14.0	16.0
100,000–249,999	105	57.1	10.5	20.0	12.4
50,000–99,999	32	75.0	0.0	18.8	6.3
Under 50,000	12	91.7	0.0	8.3	0.0
Region					
Total respondents	274	59.9	10.6	19.7	9.9
Northeast	41	75.6	2.4	19.5	2.4
Southeast	69	62.3	15.9	15.9	5.8
Midwest	79	60.8	10.1	21.5	7.6
Southwest	48	47.9	12.5	27.1	12.5
Northwest	2	100.0	0.0	0.0	0.0
West	35	48.6	8.6	14.3	28.6
Age of regional council					
Total respondents	275	60.0	10.5	19.6	9.8
1–14 years	11	100.0	0.0	0.0	0.0
15–25 years	220	58.2	10.9	21.8	9.1
More than 25 years	44	59.1	11.4	13.6	15.9
Budget					
Total respondents	268	59.7	10.8	19.8	9.7
$99,999 or less	3	100.0	0.0	0.0	0.0
$100,000–$249,999	35	68.6	5.7	22.9	2.9
$250,000–$499,999	63	61.9	14.3	14.3	9.5
$500,000–$999,999	41	65.9	14.6	9.8	9.8
$1,000,000–$2,499,999	54	55.6	9.3	20.4	14.8
$2,500,000–$4,999,999	37	51.4	8.1	27.0	13.5
$5,000,000–$9,999,999	26	57.7	7.7	26.9	7.7
$10,000,000 and above	9	33.3	22.2	44.4	0.0

Table 5/9 IMPORTANCE OF ISSUES

| | Organizational | | | | | | Membership | | | | Revenue | |
| | Representation | | Voting apportionment | | Committee structure | | Eligibility | | Withdrawal of members | | Dues assessment | |
Classification	No. reporting	Mean	No. reporting	Mean	No. reporting	Mean	No. reporting	Mean	No. reporting	Mean	No. reporting	Mean
Population												
Over 1,000,000	18	3.5	18	3.4	19	3.0	14	3.8	16	4.2	18	2.7
500,000–1,000,000	20	3.3	19	3.3	17	3.5	15	4.5	20	3.7	21	3.0
250,000–499,999	19	3.3	16	4.2	20	4.2	18	4.2	18	3.9	28	2.6
100,000–249,999	41	3.6	36	4.3	37	4.0	40	4.5	43	3.8	69	2.4
50,000–99,999	18	2.8	15	3.3	15	3.8	14	3.9	17	3.5	22	2.8
Under 50,000	4	2.0	2	2.5	3	3.7	4	3.3	1	5.0	2	1.5
Average of means	...	3.1	...	3.5	...	3.7	...	4.0	...	4.0	...	2.5
Region												
Northeast	15	3.5	13	4.6	15	3.8	12	4.3	11	4.0	23	2.6
Southeast	33	3.5	29	4.2	31	3.9	28	4.5	32	4.2	44	3.0
Midwest	30	3.2	28	3.3	33	3.5	32	3.9	35	3.1	44	2.3
Southwest	21	3.1	20	3.6	18	4.1	19	4.4	35	3.1	44	2.3
Northwest	1	1.0	1	1.0	0	0.0	0	0.0	1	2.0	26	2.8
West	21	3.3	16	3.3	15	3.7	15	4.0	17	4.3	1	4.0
Average of means	...	2.9	...	3.3	...	3.2	...	3.5	...	3.7	22	2.4
											...	2.9
Age of regional council												
1–14 years	5	2.4	4	3.3	4	2.8	3	4.3	6	3.3	7	1.9
15–25 years	94	3.3	83	3.7	85	3.9	83	4.3	90	3.8	127	2.6
More than 25 years	23	3.6	21	3.7	24	3.8	21	3.5	21	3.7	28	2.7
Average of means	...	3.1	...	3.6	...	3.5	...	4.0	...	3.6	...	2.4
Budget												
$99,999 or less	1	5.0	1	5.0	1	2.0	1	5.0	1	5.0	1	1.0
$100,000–$249,999	16	3.3	17	3.5	16	3.7	16	4.4	16	3.8	19	2.4
$250,000–$499,999	15	3.5	18	4.2	23	3.9	20	4.2	24	3.0	41	2.2
$500,000–$999,999	18	3.4	17	3.6	14	3.9	14	4.6	20	4.1	26	2.8
$1,000,000–$2,499,999	25	2.9	21	3.8	23	4.1	26	4.2	22	3.9	36	2.7
$2,500,000–$4,999,999	20	3.2	17	3.5	18	3.3	18	3.8	20	4.1	21	3.0
$5,000,000–$9,999,999	10	4.0	11	4.1	12	3.8	8	4.5	9	4.9	12	3.0
$10,000,000 and above	5	3.6	4	3.0	4	3.3	3	3.0	3	3.3	4	3.8
Average of means	...	3.5	...	3.8	...	3.5	...	4.2	...	4.0	...	2.7

| | Power | | | | | | | | Intergovernmental relations | |
| | Dominance by one jurisdictions | | Dominance by a coalition of jurisdiction | | Executive director | | Board and officers | | Conflicts with other governments/agencies | |
	No. reporting	Mean	No. reporting	Mean	No. reporting	Mean	No. reporting	Mean	No. reporting	Mean
Population / Total respondents										
Over 1,000,000	16	2.9	17	3.2	15	4.4	16	3.9	21	2.1
500,000–1,000,000	17	3.7	19	3.4	14	4.0	14	3.8	26	2.6
250,000–499,999	18	3.9	16	4.4	17	4.2	18	3.6	29	2.4
100,000–249,999	51	3.4	37	3.9	41	4.2	41	4.0	66	2.7
50,000–99,999	15	3.3	12	4.0	14	3.4	17	3.7	22	2.7
Under 50,000	2	2.5	1	5.0	4	2.8	6	2.0	6	2.7
Average of means	...	3.3	...	4.0	...	3.9	...	3.5	...	2.5
Region / Total respondents										
Northeast	16	3.2	13	3.6	14	3.9	17	3.2	24	2.4
Southeast	31	3.8	30	4.1	31	4.2	29	3.7	45	2.6
Midwest	34	3.1	28	3.6	32	4.1	31	3.8	46	2.3
Southwest	21	3.5	15	4.3	15	3.8	20	3.9	46	2.3
Northwest	1	1.0	0	0.0	1	3.0	0	0.0	29	2.7
West	17	3.4	18	3.6	13	4.5	15	4.3	0	0.0
Average of means	...	3.0	...	3.2	...	3.9	...	3.2	25	3.1
									...	2.2
Age of regional council / Total respondents										
1–14 years	5	2.0	5	3.2	5	4.6	4	4.5	7	1.9
15–25 years	97	3.5	79	3.8	84	4.0	88	3.7	137	2.6
More than 25 years	19	3.4	21	3.8	18	4.1	21	3.9	28	2.8
Average of means	...	3.0	...	3.6	...	4.2	...	4.0	...	2.4
Budget / Total respondents										
$99,999 or less	1	1.0	1	5.0	1	5.0	1	5.0	1	1.0
$100,000–$249,999	18	3.4	12	4.3	18	3.7	18	3.4	24	3.3
$250,000–$499,999	29	3.1	24	3.6	23	3.8	25	3.6	38	2.4
$500,000–$999,999	17	3.6	13	4.0	15	4.2	16	3.9	29	2.3
$1,000,000–$2,499,999	22	3.5	23	3.7	24	4.1	21	3.7	33	2.5
$2,500,000–$4,999,999	17	3.5	17	3.5	14	4.6	17	4.0	26	2.4
$5,000,000–$9,999,999	11	3.9	10	4.3	7	5.0	9	4.9	14	3.0
$10,000,000 and above	5	2.8	4	3.8	4	3.8	5	2.4	5	3.0
Average of means	...	3.1	...	4.0	...	4.3	...	3.9	...	2.5

Note: Respondents were asked to score "1" to "5" with "5" the most important.

and smaller budgets. Moreover, it is quite popular among the youngest councils (100%) and those in the Northeast and Northwest. These regional preferences may be due to state-mandated formulas.

Where it is used, the combination approach appears to be equally popular among councils in all population ranges except the smallest. All regions except the Northwest show use of the combination approach. Councils with budgets of $10 million or more also favor a combination approach, probably to balance the representational demands of their central cities and urban counties with those of members from smaller jurisdictions.

Table 5/10 POLICY AND PROGRAM STATUS

Classification	No. reporting (A)	Economic development Policy % of (A)	Economic development Program % of (A)	Transportation Policy % of (A)	Transportation Program % of (A)	Solid waste Policy % of (A)	Solid waste Program % of (A)	Land use/ development Policy % of (A)	Land use/ development Program % of (A)	Housing Policy % of (A)	Housing Program % of (A)
Population											
Total respondents	280	68.2	72.1	66.1	68.6	60.4	60.7	58.2	58.9	51.8	41.4
Over 1,000,000	32	43.8	50.0	87.5	84.4	62.5	56.3	68.8	78.1	59.4	37.5
500,000–1,000,000	41	73.2	82.9	82.9	87.8	53.7	61.0	78.0	63.4	68.3	43.9
250,000–499,999	52	76.9	78.8	67.3	69.2	75.0	73.1	51.9	55.8	46.2	32.7
100,000–249,999	110	64.5	72.7	54.5	61.8	56.4	63.6	48.2	52.7	42.7	37.3
50,000–99,999	33	75.8	66.7	60.6	57.6	63.6	39.4	63.6	63.6	57.6	60.6
Under 50,000	12	91.7	75.0	66.7	50.0	41.7	50.0	66.7	50.0	66.7	66.7
Region											
Total respondents	282	67.7	71.6	65.6	68.4	59.6	60.6	57.4	58.5	51.4	41.8
Northeast	42	61.9	52.4	88.1	83.3	66.7	69.0	73.8	81.0	76.2	54.8
Southeast	72	72.2	81.9	52.8	62.5	70.8	72.2	58.3	58.3	43.1	47.2
Midwest	81	74.1	79.0	70.4	70.4	53.1	58.0	56.8	58.0	58.0	39.5
Southwest	49	65.3	79.6	51.0	49.0	57.1	61.2	46.9	36.7	36.7	26.5
Northwest	2	100.0	100.0	0.0	0.0	50.0	0.0	50.0	50.0	0.0	0.0
West	36	52.8	44.4	77.8	88.9	47.2	36.1	52.8	63.9	47.2	44.4
Age of council											
Total respondents	283	67.8	71.4	66.1	68.9	59.4	60.8	58.0	59.0	51.9	42.0
1–14 years	11	72.7	63.6	36.4	36.4	45.5	27.3	18.2	36.4	18.2	27.3
15–25 years	227	68.7	73.1	62.1	64.8	59.0	61.7	56.4	54.6	52.4	42.7
More than 25 years	45	62.2	64.4	93.3	97.8	64.4	64.4	75.6	86.7	57.8	42.2
Budget											
Total respondents	275	67.6	72.0	66.2	68.7	59.6	60.4	57.8	59.3	52.4	42.2
$99,999 or less	3	100.0	66.7	33.3	0.0	33.3	0.0	0.0	0.0	66.7	0.0
$100,000–$249,999	35	65.7	65.7	62.9	60.0	57.1	57.1	57.1	60.0	51.4	45.7
$250,000–$499,999	65	70.8	69.2	69.2	69.2	61.5	56.9	63.1	60.0	52.3	40.0
$500,000–$999,999	43	65.1	67.4	69.8	76.7	51.2	58.1	53.5	48.8	58.1	37.2
$1,000,000–$2,499,999	54	68.5	75.9	68.5	72.2	59.3	63.0	55.6	59.3	55.6	48.1
$2,500,000–$4,999,999	39	64.1	79.5	61.5	64.1	64.1	61.5	59.0	69.2	43.6	41.0
$5,000,000–$9,999,999	27	70.4	77.8	63.0	66.7	63.0	77.8	59.3	59.3	40.7	33.3
$10,000,000 and above	9	55.6	66.7	66.7	88.9	77.8	55.6	66.7	77.8	77.8	77.8

Classification	Water quality Policy % of (A)	Water quality Program % of (A)	Infrastructure improvements Policy % of (A)	Infrastructure improvements Program % of (A)	Natural resources Policy % of (A)	Natural resources Program % of (A)	Open space Policy % of (A)	Open space Program % of (A)	Wastewater Policy % of (A)	Wastewater Program % of (A)
Population										
Total respondents	49.6	46.1	47.5	59.3	33.9	34.3	32.5	19.6	32.5	31.1
Over 1,000,000	71.9	65.6	40.6	43.8	31.3	34.4	53.1	31.3	53.1	53.1
500,000–1,000,000	63.4	63.4	48.8	58.5	51.2	48.8	51.2	24.4	43.9	36.6
250,000–499,999	36.5	30.8	38.5	57.7	30.8	36.5	26.9	15.4	19.2	21.2
100,000–249,999	42.7	40.9	50.0	63.6	29.1	29.1	21.8	18.2	30.9	32.7
50,000–99,999	54.5	51.5	51.5	63.6	33.3	30.3	30.3	12.1	24.2	21.2
Under 50,000	50.0	33.3	66.7	58.3	41.7	33.3	41.7	25.0	33.3	8.3
Region										
Total respondents	49.3	46.1	47.5	58.9	33.3	31.9	31.9	19.5	31.9	30.9
Northeast	73.8	64.3	59.5	45.2	52.4	33.3	52.4	33.3	31.0	19.0
Southeast	45.8	47.2	41.7	55.6	25.0	34.7	26.4	13.9	36.1	45.8
Midwest	43.2	42.0	53.1	67.9	35.8	38.3	33.3	24.7	34.6	30.9
Southwest	49.0	44.9	44.9	59.2	30.6	26.5	24.5	6.1	26.5	28.6
Northwest	100.0	50.0	50.0	100.0	50.0	50.0	0.0	0.0	100.0	50.0
West	38.9	33.3	36.1	58.3	25.0	30.6	27.8	22.2	22.2	16.7
Age of regional council										
Total respondents	49.8	46.3	47.7	58.7	33.9	33.9	32.5	19.8	32.2	30.7
1–14 years	45.5	45.5	27.3	36.4	18.2	27.3	9.1	0.0	36.4	36.4
15–25 years	46.3	44.9	47.6	57.7	32.2	30.4	30.0	20.7	30.0	28.6
More than 25 years	68.9	53.3	53.3	68.9	46.7	53.3	51.1	20.0	42.2	40.0
Budget										
Total respondents	49.5	46.2	47.3	59.3	33.8	34.2	32.4	19.3	32.0	30.5
$99,999 or less	100.0	66.7	100.0	66.7	0.0	0.0	0.0	0.0	66.7	66.7
$100,000–$249,999	40.0	40.0	51.4	57.1	25.7	25.7	31.4	17.1	22.9	28.6
$250,000–$499,999	50.8	40.0	47.7	52.3	32.3	32.3	27.7	20.0	32.3	21.5
$500,000–$999,999	44.2	41.9	48.8	55.8	23.3	23.3	34.9	25.6	30.2	16.3
$1,000,000–$2,499,999	51.9	57.4	51.9	64.8	42.6	38.9	33.3	16.7	35.2	40.7
$2,500,000–$4,999,999	48.7	43.6	43.6	66.7	38.5	41.0	28.2	10.3	35.9	35.9
$5,000,000–$9,999,999	51.9	51.9	33.3	66.7	40.7	48.1	40.7	22.2	25.9	37.0
$10,000,000 and above	66.7	55.6	33.3	44.4	44.4	44.4	55.6	44.4	44.4	55.6

The proportionate approach results also indicate that this formula is used more often by councils with populations of 100,000 and above. Finally, approximately 10% of councils report an "other" method such as extra representation for their largest cities and at-large seats for region-wide representation.

Importance of Issues

Although policy issues of importance to a particular council can span a wide spectrum, eleven core issues were identified as common to the deliberations of regional councils. These subjects can be organized under five general categories:

1. Organizational concerns
2. Membership
3. Revenues
4. Power
5. Intergovernmental relations

The average results for each of these five categories suggest that revenue and intergovernmental issues do not generate as much significant discussion as power, membership, and organizational issues (Table 5/9). This finding may in part be explained by the fact that even with an older council, voting apportionment and committee structure, for example, are subjects ripe for demonstrations of organizational influence. Surprisingly, conflicts with other governments and member dues assessments are rated as less important.

Both the eligibility and withdrawal of members are often key to the maintenance of a delicate, political, regional equilibrium; not surprisingly both receive high ratings.

There seems to be no effective solution to the perceived or real concerns about dominance by a single jurisdiction or by a coalition. Constant sensitivity and genuinely inclusive behavior are perhaps the best preventive measure. But as the results suggest, this concern is probably endemic to regional council governance.

Finally, it is notable that the directors report that board and officer as well as their own powers generate considerable discussion. Those in a position of leadership on a regional council are always likely to be targets of criticism from a large and diverse membership.

In the detailed population results, as population size decreases, all the issues became less important. However, the budget range data do not consistently reflect this pattern.

Policy and Program Status

The ever broadening role of councils is impressively displayed by a listing of the many policy and program areas with which councils are involved on a daily basis. Respondents were asked to identify areas in which they had *articulated a policy* and areas in which they had an *active program*. The pattern of responses mirrors federal funding, although, as indicated earlier in this study, in such areas as transportation, training, education, economic development, and housing, a significant number of councils have developed programs that move beyond the activity levels supported by federal funds.

The results for several program-policy areas, such as in economic development, transportation, and housing, indicate that active programs actually exceed adopted policy (Table 5/10). In most cases, this is probably the result of the hasty development of a program in response to the sudden availability of funds without earlier adoption of a formal policy.

A number of patterns in the data are important. Councils in the Southwest and Southeast have articulated policy and implemented programs across many of the areas. Moreover, they report stronger policy and program commitment to such human service areas as substance abuse, employment, and health.

The population range results show that regional councils serving more populous areas have adopted more policies and programs in transportation, water, wastewater, solid waste, open space, and air. But their smaller counterparts show relatively equal or even more policy and/or program activity in economic development, land use, and most of the human service areas. Some of these trends may be explained by the need for and availability of targeted federal funds to depressed, less populated regions. Nevertheless, the magnitude of the difference is striking.

Councils that have been functioning for 15 years or more generally report fairly active policy and program effort in all areas.

Directors with larger budgets report proportionately more policies and programs for all areas. The void of policy and program activity in many areas among the three councils with the smallest budgets reflects their relatively focused mission.

Table 5/10 continued

Classification	Employment training Policy % of (A)	Employment training Program % of (A)	Air quality Policy % of (A)	Air quality Program % of (A)	Substance abuse Policy % of (A)	Substance abuse Program % of (A)	Health services/facilities Policy % of (A)	Health services/facilities Program % of (A)	Education Policy % of (A)	Education Program % of (A)
Population										
Total respondents	30.4	30.7	22.5	15.7	17.9	10.7	14.6	11.8	7.1	9.3
Over 1,000,000	18.8	21.9	62.5	56.3	15.6	18.8	15.6	18.8	9.4	6.3
500,000–1,000,000	22.0	14.6	41.5	24.4	22.0	7.3	14.6	4.9	9.8	9.8
250,000–499,999	36.5	36.5	13.5	9.6	19.2	3.8	13.5	9.6	3.8	11.5
100,000–249,999	36.4	39.1	9.1	7.3	16.4	11.8	15.5	11.8	6.4	10.9
50,000–99,999	24.2	24.2	18.2	6.1	18.2	12.1	12.1	15.2	6.1	0.0
Under 50,000	25.0	25.0	25.0	8.3	16.7	16.7	16.7	16.7	16.7	16.7
Region										
Total respondents	29.8	30.1	22.0	15.2	17.4	10.3	14.2	11.3	6.7	8.9
Northeast	16.7	9.5	38.1	16.7	9.5	2.4	7.1	9.5	9.5	14.3
Southeast	40.3	44.4	13.9	6.9	30.6	11.1	19.4	12.5	11.1	6.9
Midwest	19.8	21.0	18.5	13.6	8.6	12.3	12.3	7.4	6.2	11.1
Southwest	46.9	49.0	18.4	14.3	26.5	10.2	24.5	16.3	4.1	8.2
Northwest	0.0	0.0	0.0	0.0	0.0	50.0	0.0	50.0	0.0	0.0
West	25.0	22.2	33.3	36.1	8.3	11.1	2.8	11.1	0.0	2.8
Age of regional council										
Total respondents	30.0	30.0	22.3	16.3	17.7	10.6	14.5	11.7	7.1	9.2
1–14 years	36.4	18.2	18.2	9.1	18.2	9.1	18.2	18.2	9.1	18.2
15–25 years	30.8	32.6	18.9	13.7	19.4	9.7	16.7	11.9	7.0	9.3
More than 25 years	24.4	20.0	40.0	31.1	8.9	15.6	2.2	8.9	6.7	6.7
Budget										
Total respondents	29.8	30.2	22.9	16.7	17.8	10.5	14.5	11.6	6.5	9.5
$99,999 or less	0.0	0.0	0.0	0.0	0.0	0.0	0.0	0.0	0.0	0.0
$100,000–$249,999	20.0	17.1	14.3	8.6	11.4	17.1	8.6	8.6	14.3	11.4
$250,000–$499,999	10.8	16.9	16.9	7.7	9.2	3.1	4.6	6.2	1.5	7.7
$500,000–$999,999	25.6	25.6	20.9	11.6	18.6	7.0	18.6	11.6	7.0	4.7
$1,000,000–$2,499,999	29.6	24.1	33.3	22.2	20.4	9.3	22.2	13.0	9.3	9.3
$2,500,000–$4,999,999	46.2	48.7	20.5	23.1	30.8	20.5	17.9	15.4	2.6	15.4
$5,000,000–$9,999,999	63.0	66.7	25.9	33.3	18.5	11.1	14.8	18.5	3.7	11.1
$10,000,000 and above	66.7	55.6	55.6	33.3	33.3	22.2	33.3	22.2	22.2	11.1

THE FUTURE

Predictions from journalists and scholars about the future of regional council government run the gamut. Some argue that the size and influence of councils will shrink, others that council influence will diminish in some activity areas and grow in others, and a few speculate that continued growth, particularly of the urban councils, is inevitable.

In order to introduce expert perspectives into the discussion, council directors were asked about future prospects for regional councils.

Expectations for the Future of Councils

Responses reflect a general sense that significant change will occur in the activities and roles of regional councils in the next ten years. Moreover, the overall pattern of responses to the question on optimism about the future is generally positive.

Directors of councils serving large populations are somewhat more expectant of change and optimistic about the future than those from smaller councils (Table 5/11). Directors in councils serving large, urbanized areas are used to overseeing a wide range of programs, are typically more senior, and have experienced a process of almost continuous change and growth along with the region they serve.

Western directors, although beset by problems of shrinking revenues and, until recently, growth, are the most hopeful about change. Along with their counterparts in the Southeast, the western group is also slightly more optimistic about the future.

The three respondents with budgets of under $99,999 are considerably less optimistic than directors with greater resources.

Importance of Policy-Program Areas Over the Next Decade

Respondents were asked to rate the importance of seven major policy-program areas to their region over the next decade.

The regional economy ranks as the most important, followed by transportation, environment, and infrastructure (Table 5/12). In the next tier are housing and education, with substance abuse and health issues ranked least important.

This profile for the future does not differ measurably from the general pattern of current policy-program status results in Table 5/10. Economic development policy and programs will dominate agendas of regional councils, followed by transportation, utilities, and housing. Human service needs will continue to attract the least attention.

Reflecting their more focused mission, the directors of small councils rate such social service areas as substance abuse and education as relatively less important than do directors of councils serving large populations.

Directors of councils in the West do not indicate that regional economies are important areas for future policy or programs, although, along with their northeastern counterparts, they indicate significant concern about the future of their transportation systems.

In general, directors of the relatively new councils rate many areas, except the environment and housing, as less important in the future than do their colleagues from older councils. Directors from councils with the largest budgets note future concern with regional economy, transportation, environment, and infrastructure, while the two respondents with the smallest budgets are most concerned about economy and infrastructure.

Changes in Organization Structure, Operating Authority, and Powers

Sharing the power of local self determination has always been a difficult issue for regional governments, and discussions among local professionals and elected officials frequently center around the structure and authority of councils. However, particularly in regions beset by continued interjurisdictional disputes, redundant service offerings, and fragmented planning and policy making, the rationale for stronger regional direction is compelling.

In order to measure director support for new areas of council authority, respondents were asked to indicate which additional powers should be given to regional councils. These ranged from the authority to tax, enforce codes and regulations, and enact laws to direct election of members, veto power over local projects of regional significance, and general authority to operate services.

The overall pattern of the results indicates considerable support for the opportunity to operate public services and the power to veto local projects (Table 5/13). Authority to tax and to enforce garners about half as much support as the two most popular areas, while law making and direct member elections are rated as least needed.

Councils serving populations of all sizes are generally enthusiastic about operating more services and holding veto power over local projects. However, enforcement support declines somewhat among the councils in smaller regions. Western directors are considerably less enthusiastic about service operation than their counterparts in all other regions, but they, along with directors in the Northeast and Northwest, are the strongest advocates for a veto.

Authority to tax is more popular in the Northeast, Midwest, and Northwest. Enforcement powers rate very high among western and northwestern directors.

Directors of the 11 younger councils consistently report relatively high levels of support for taxing, enforcement, and veto authority, while directors with councils that have been in existence for more than 25 years are most enthusiastic about taxing authority and the veto.

The budget size results for the highest bracket are particularly revealing. In the $10 million or over category, local veto and taxing authority are, respectively, the most popular. Interestingly,

---

Table 5/11   THE FUTURE OF REGIONAL COUNCILS

Classification	Change expected in next ten years[1]		Optimism about the future[2]	
	No. reporting	Mean	No. reporting	Mean
Population				
Over 1,000,000	29	1.5	32	1.3
500,000–1,000,000	40	1.8	41	1.3
250,000–499,999	51	1.9	52	1.3
100,000–249,999	104	1.7	109	1.4
50,000–99,999	33	1.7	33	1.4
Under 50,000	12	1.8	12	1.8
Average of means	. . .	1.7	. . .	1.4
Region				
Northeast	41	1.8	41	1.4
Southeast	69	1.7	72	1.2
Midwest	75	1.7	80	1.4
Southwest	48	1.8	49	1.4
Northwest	2	2.5	2	2
West	35	1.3	36	1.3
Average of means	. . .	1.8	. . .	1.5
Age of regional council				
1–14 years	11	1.7	11	1.5
15–25 years	219	1.7	225	1.4
More than 25 years	41	1.7	45	1.3
Average of means	. . .	1.7	. . .	1.4
Budget				
$99,999 or less	3	2.0	3	2.0
$100,000–$249,999	34	1.8	34	1.6
$250,000–$499,999	64	1.8	65	1.4
$500,000–$999,999	43	1.7	43	1.4
$1,000,000–$2,499,999	49	1.6	53	1.3
$2,500,000–$4,999,999	38	1.7	39	1.2
$5,000,000–$9,999,999	24	1.8	27	1.1
$10,000,000 and above	9	1.6	9	1.2
Average of means	. . .	1.8	. . .	1.4

[1]Respondents were asked to select "Much" (1), "Some" (2), "Little" (3), or "None" (4).

[2]Respondents were asked to select "Definitely" (1), "Somewhat" (2), or "Not Very" (3).

Table 5/12   IMPORTANCE OF POLICY AND PROGRAM AREAS

Classification	Regional economy No. reporting	Mean	Transportation No. reporting	Mean	Substance abuse and health No. reporting	Mean	Environment No. reporting	Mean	Education No. reporting	Mean	Infrastructure No. reporting	Mean	Housing No. reporting	Mean
Population														
Over 1,000,000	32	1.9	31	1.5	28	3.4	30	2.1	28	2.5	32	2.6	32	3.6
500,000–1,000,000	39	1.9	41	1.9	36	4.1	40	1.7	36	4.0	40	2.2	39	3.5
250,000–499,999	51	2.1	52	3.0	51	3.9	52	3.1	51	3.2	51	2.6	51	3.8
100,000–249,999	109	1.8	108	2.8	103	4.0	108	2.6	105	3.4	109	2.2	108	3.3
50,000–99,999	32	1.7	32	2.9	29	5.1	31	2.1	29	4.2	30	2.4	31	2.9
Under 50,000	11	2.7	11	2.5	10	4.4	11	2.9	11	4.6	11	3.0	11	3.4
Average of means	...	2.0	...	2.4	...	4.2	...	2.4	...	3.7	...	2.5	...	3.3
Region														
Northeast	41	1.9	41	1.8	37	4.6	41	2.1	38	4.2	41	2.6	42	3.0
Southeast	70	1.8	70	2.5	67	3.9	69	2.2	67	3.0	70	2.1	70	3.2
Midwest	79	1.9	80	2.7	73	3.8	78	2.5	75	3.3	79	2.3	78	3.2
Southwest	49	1.5	49	3.2	49	4.3	49	3.1	49	3.7	49	2.5	49	4.1
Northwest	1	1.0	1	5.0	1	9.0	1	1.0	1	9.0	1	1.0	1	5.0
West	35	2.7	36	2.2	32	4.0	36	2.5	32	3.5	35	3.1	34	3.5
Average of means	...	1.8	...	2.9	...	4.9	...	2.2	...	4.5	...	2.3	...	3.7
Age of regional council														
1–14 years	10	2.7	9	3.0	9	5.0	9	2.2	8	4.5	10	2.2	10	3.5
15–25 years	222	1.9	224	2.7	211	4.1	222	2.5	214	3.5	222	2.4	223	3.4
More than 24 years	44	1.9	45	1.9	40	3.7	44	2.3	41	3.0	44	2.3	42	3.3
Average of means	...	2.2	...	2.5	...	4.3	...	2.3	...	3.7	...	3.3	...	3.4
Budget														
$99,999 or less	2	1.0	1	7.0	2	6.0	1	5.0	1	3.0	2	1.0	2	5.0
$100,000–$249,999	35	2.1	35	2.7	31	4.1	33	2.7	33	3.8	34	2.4	34	3.3
$250,000–$499,999	62	1.9	64	2.5	58	4.6	62	2.5	59	3.8	61	2.4	62	3.4
$500,000–$999,999	42	2.2	42	2.2	40	3.8	43	2.2	42	3.6	43	2.2	42	3.0
$1,000,000–$2,499,999 ..	52	1.8	53	2.4	51	3.8	53	2.4	51	3.2	53	2.8	52	3.4
$2,500,000–$4,999,999 ..	39	1.6	39	2.7	37	3.8	39	2.6	37	3.3	39	2.5	39	3.8
$5,000,000–$9,999,999 ..	27	1.8	27	2.8	26	4.1	27	2.7	26	3.2	27	2.5	27	3.9
$10,000 and above	9	1.4	9	1.7	8	4.0	9	1.8	7	3.7	9	1.9	9	2.9
Average of means	...	1.8	...	3.0	...	4.4	...	2.7	...	3.5	...	2.2	...	3.6

Note: Respondents were asked to score "1" (Very important) to "10" (Not very important).

Table 5/13   AUTHORITY NEEDED

Classification	No. reporting (A)	Taxing No. reporting	Taxing % of (A)	Enforcement No. reporting	Enforcement % of (A)	Law making No. reporting	Law making % of (A)	Direct election of members No. reporting	Direct election of members % of	Veto over local projects No. reporting	Veto over local projects % of (A)	Operate services No. reporting	Operate services % of (A)
Population													
Total respondents	280	71	25.4	57	20.4	22	7.9	24	8.6	104	37.1	115	41.1
Over 1,000,000	32	11	34.4	8	25.0	5	15.6	4	12.5	18	56.3	10	31.3
500,000–1,000,000	41	12	29.3	14	34.1	3	7.3	3	7.3	21	51.2	13	31.7
250,000–499,999	52	6	11.5	8	15.4	2	3.8	3	5.8	16	30.8	22	42.3
100,000–249,999	110	33	30.0	20	18.2	8	7.3	11	10.0	28	25.5	53	48.2
50,000–99,999	33	7	21.2	6	18.2	2	6.1	2	6.1	17	51.5	11	33.3
Under 50,000	12	2	16.6	1	8.3	2	16.6	1	8.3	4	33.3	6	50.0
Region													
Total respondents	282	72	25.5	59	20.9	21	7.4	24	8.5	106	37.6	115	40.8
Northeast	42	14	33.3	12	28.6	4	2.4	4	9.5	23	54.8	18	42.9
Southwest	72	9	12.5	10	13.9	2	2.8	5	6.9	21	29.2	34	47.2
Midwest	81	30	37.4	13	16.0	7	8.6	7	8.6	26	32.1	28	34.6
Southwest	49	10	20.4	7	14.3	2	4.1	4	8.2	14	28.6	26	53.1
Northwest	2	1	50.0	1	50.0	0	0.0	0	0.0	1	50.0	1	50.0
West	36	8	22.2	16	44.4	6	16.7	4	11.1	21	58.3	8	22.2
Age of regional council													
Total respondents	283	72	25.4	59	20.8	22	7.8	24	8.5	101	35.7	107	37.8
1–14 years	11	5	45.5	6	54.5	2	18.2	2	18.2	6	54.5	4	36.4
15–25 years	227	54	23.7	43	18.9	16	7.0	19	8.3	81	35.6	9	42.3
More than 25 years	45	13	28.8	10	22.2	4	8.8	3	6.6	14	31.1	6	13.3
Budget													
Total respondents	275	72	26.2	58	21.1	21	7.6	24	8.7	104	37.8	114	41.5
$99,999 or less	3	0	0.0	0	0.0	0	0.0	0	0.0	0	0.0	0	0.0
$100,000–$249,000	35	11	31.4	5	14.3	3	8.6	3	8.6	10	28.6	12	34.3
$250,000–$499,999	65	16	24.6	17	26.2	2	3.1	5	7.7	26	40.0	27	41.5
$500,000–$999,999	43	12	27.9	13	30.2	4	9.3	4	9.3	15	34.9	17	39.5
$1,000,000–$2,499,999	54	15	27.8	9	16.7	5	9.3	4	7.4	22	40.7	25	46.3
$2,500,000–$4,999,999	39	8	20.5	8	20.5	3	8.0	4	10.3	14	35.9	16	41.0
$5,000,000–$9,999,999	27	5	18.5	6	22.2	3	11.1	2	7.4	10	37.0	13	48.1
$10,000,000 and above	9	5	55.6	0	0.0	1	11.1	2	22.2	7	77.8	4	44.4

among this big budget group the support for both of these is greater than that for service authority.

To conclude, directors generally embrace the future possibility of authority to veto local projects of regional significance and to operate services. They are somewhat less enthusiastic about taxing and enforcement powers, preferring to leave these typically politically volatile areas to their local government and district members. And finally, although the direct election of members and even law making have been subjects for speculation, the results emphatically suggest that indirect representation and control by collaboration and negotiation rather than by edict will continue to be the way of doing regional business in the future.

Council Dominance

Particularly in metropolitan areas, councils are no longer the only active agents in the region. Other entities seeking regional authority have emerged, ranging from private sector associations and foundations to environmental coalitions and citizen groups. Organizations for economic development include subregional associations of municipalities and their chambers of commerce and business-supported associations with regionwide mandates to enhance trade and attract new firms.

Given this new competition and the lingering uncertainties about the acceptable role and scope of councils, the final section of the survey asked directors whether councils will be the dominant regional structure in the future and whether another organization could assume the council's role.

Overall, the directors are somewhat tentative about the future of their councils as dominant regional structures (Table 5/14). As a group, they are not certain that another dominant organization would assume the role.

Possibly in response to the emergence of new regional and subregional groups in their heavily populated regions, directors of councils in the two highest population brackets are slightly less positive about the future dominance of councils than their colleagues in smaller population ranges. Regional differences on the dominance question show more pessimism in the Northeast and Northwest, with southeastern directors providing the highest level of optimism. The age of the respondent's council category does not produce any striking differences, but the size of budget does. The three directors with the smallest budgets are least positive, although those with increasingly larger budgets are not markedly more enthusiastic with one exception. Directors with budgets of $5 million to $9.9 million are the most positively inclined group.

The prospect of an alternative regional organization is generally devalued by respondents in all population brackets, although the 12 respondents with the smallest populations are a little less certain. Northwestern directors are substantially less concerned than those in other regions about the probability of another regional structure, as are those with budgets of $99,999 or less.

CONCLUSION

Several patterns of behavior are revealed in this study about the roles of executive directors. Probably reflecting an expanded service emphasis, directors spend large amounts of time tending to the needs of their member governments. Board-officer and community leader relations also are heavy consumers of director energy.

When queried about the appropriate style for board relationships, about half of the directors prefer a conservative "implementor" posture, and an equal number prefer to remain neutral on issues that are potentially divisive for their memberships. However, most suggest they are comfortable with informal contacts outside of scheduled meetings to achieve agreement on plans and issues.

The shift in the mission of many regional councils to an emphasis on membership service may not be well served by an implementation brand of executive director leadership that leaves program and policy direction largely to the executive board. Indeed, in many cases the future success of councils as dominant regional entities could be dependent on executive directors who are responsive and even provocative in relations with their members and assertive in advocating member needs.

Major trends from the returns on functional activities suggest that in many councils continuing tension among members is often expressed as perceived dominance by a few larger entities over the majority, smaller members. This en-

demic problem, however, has not precluded many councils from addressing a broad policy and program agenda with physical and environmental initiatives at the top of the list.

Many directors advocate the provision of more services to their members and veto power over local projects of regional significance. But they are less insistent on taxing and enforcement authority, preferring to rely on their membership for revenue as well as law and code enforcement. Future additional service programming will be premised on membership needs rather than federal and state initiatives.

In sum, tomorrow's regional councils will be member-driven. They will share the responsibility for regional policy advocacy and service with other regional coalitions and special interest organizations. Their directors will offer leadership for an expanded range of regional issues, while equitably administering programs to the increasingly diverse social, economic, and political needs of both their large and small constituencies.

[1]"Regional council" is used in this report to describe multipurpose regional governments also known as councils of governments, regional planning commissions, development councils, planning and development districts, etc.

[2]"Federalism and the Local Planning Agenda," in E. Blaine Liner, ed., *Local Agenda Setting Processes: Part I*, Monograph #85-10 (Cambridge, MA: Lincoln Institute of Land Policy, 1985), 6–7.

[3]*1989 Directory of Regional Councils in the United States*, National Association of Regional Councils, 1700 K Street, N.W., Suite 1300, Washington, DC 20006, 1989.

Table 5/14   COUNCIL DOMINANCE

Classification	Dominant regional structure		Another organization	
	No. reporting	Mean	No. reporting	Mean
Population				
Over 1,000,000	32	1.9	26	2.5
500,000–1,000,000	41	1.9	30	2.6
250,000–499,999	52	1.6	29	2.7
100,000–249,999	108	1.6	63	2.5
50,000–99,999	33	1.8	21	2.9
Under 50,000	12	1.8	6	2.3
Average of means	. . .	1.8	. . .	2.6
Region				
Northeast	37	2.0	28	1.6
Southeast	81	1.6	44	2.6
Midwest	76	1.7	47	2.6
Southwest	49	1.7	31	2.6
Northwest	5	2.0	2	3.5
West	27	1.9	22	2.5
Average of means	. . .	1.8	. . .	2.6
Age of regional council				
1–14 years	11	2.0	7	2.7
15–25 years	225	1.7	140	2.6
More than 25 years	44	1.8	30	2.6
Average of means	. . .	1.8	. . .	2.6
Budget				
$99,999 or less	3	2.3	2	3.5
$100,000–$249,999	34	1.8	24	2.5
$250,000–$499,999	65	1.8	44	2.4
$500,000–$999,999	43	1.7	26	2.8
$1,000,000–$2,499,999	54	1.7	35	2.6
$2,500,000–$4,999,999	39	1.6	21	2.5
$5,000,000–$9,999,999	27	1.4	17	3.0
$10,000,000 and above	9	1.8	7	2.4
Average of means	. . .	1.8	. . .	2.7

Note: Response options were "Definitely" (1), "Perhaps" (2), "Probably" (3), and "No" (4).

B The Intergovernmental Dimension

State-Local Relations: Patterns, Politics, and Problems

David R. Berman
Arizona State University

Findings

About one-third of the states require full or partial reimbursement of the costs of mandates imposed on local governments.

Local officials are being presented with new growth management responsibilities that require them to resolve conflicts among groups with divergent interests.

"We, the locally elected officials who are accountable to the public, have little or no control over how most of our budget dollars are spent. This is simply unfair. It is a problem that must be addressed."[1] Thus spoke Milwaukee County (Wisconsin) Executive F. Thomas Ament as he joined other local officials in kicking off a campaign to raise public awareness of the mandate problem. Local officials throughout the nation have complained that federal and state officials in recent years have responded to their own financial problems by passing the costs for programs on to local governments. To add insult to injury, local officials have generally had to get along with less federal and state financial assistance.

Last year brought some relief in regard to mandates, though progress was uneven, and some increases in state aid. Perhaps the most striking aspect of intergovernmental politics in 1993, however, was increased evidence that local officials are willing and able to fight challenges to their authority and financial well being. On the mandate front, local governments waged extensive lobbying campaigns, put together comprehensive assessments of the financial impacts of the mandates, alerted the public through media campaigns, and, by attaching notices to tax and utility bills blaming mandates for increased taxes, initiated and campaigned for antimandate ballot measures and brought court suits challenging the validity of mandates. Local governments also fought back on other issues. In California, for example, several counties refused to comply with a law transferring property tax revenues from them to the state. Some have sued the state over the tax shift.

This article looks first at some broad developments affecting the shape of intergovernmental relations and then at state actions affecting local authority and finances in both general and specific policy areas.

BROAD PATTERNS AND DEVELOPMENTS

Local governments function in an intergovernmental system in which the actions taken by one level of government have direct and indirect implications for the others. In this complex system, financial and regulatory decisions made at the national level vitally affect the relations between state and local governments.

Changes in Federal Policy

Changes in federal grant and regulatory policies that began in the late 1970s and escalated over the 1980s dramatically rearranged the broad pattern of intergovernmental relations in this country. One basic change was the decline in federal aid to state and local governments. Federal aid equaled around 27% of state-local spending in 1978. By 1989 this had fallen to around 17%.[2]

Direct federal aid to local governments went from a high of $22 billion in 1981 to a low of $17 billion in 1988 before rebounding to about $18 billion in the early 1990s. The percent of the average municipal government budget provided by federal funds fell from around 16% to 8% over the 1980s. From 1980 to 1993, federal aid to municipalities declined from $63.60 per capita to $29.40 per capita, a drop of around 54%.[3] Cuts were particularly steep for priority municipal programs—including low-income housing, wastewater treatment, public transit, and job training. County governments have been hit as hard, if not harder, by cuts in federal aid in recent years.[4]

This decline in federal aid has been accompanied by increased costs to state and local governments. The costs have come in part as a result of citizen pressure to replace the lost federal revenues for various programs and in part from federal mandates requiring states and localities to provide services the federal government once supported.

The shift in federal policy from granting subsidies to introducing regulatory mandates began in the mid-1970s. Since then, states and localities have encountered costly federal mandates in policy areas such as air and water quality, solid waste, hazardous waste, transportation standards, labor management, health-care, and courts and corrections. Among recent examples of congressional legislation creating unfunded mandates are the Americans with Disabilities Act, the Safe Drinking Water Act, and the National Voter Registration Act. The last of these, popularly known as the Motor Voter Bill, requires states to encourage greater voter registration and will cost state and local governments an estimated average of $20 million a year for its first five years.[5]

Local governments, the targets of what some call "shift and shaft federalism," wind up paying many of these costs.[6] Thus, when Congress decides to increase Medicaid coverage or expand environmental protection, it forces the states to pay more for their share of the increased costs or risk losing the program. State governments comply by passing the increased costs on to their local governments.

Some observers contend state and local governments have been abandoned by Congress which, they feel, has an obligation to protect these levels from the intrusion of national authority.[7] Others, including state and local officials and their organizations, have condemned the federal courts for allowing an erosion of state and local authority.[8] Indeed, U.S. Supreme Court decisions have facilitated the growth in mandates. The landmark ruling in this respect is the 1985 case *Garcia* v. *San Antonio Metropolitan Transit District*. Here the Supreme Court reversed an earlier decision by holding that the question of whether the federal Fair Labor Standards Act applies to state and local employees is to be answered by Congress rather than the courts. The result of such rulings is that Congress has had a free hand to impose costly mandates on state and local governments. In *Missouri* v. *Jenkins* (1991) a divided Court (5 to 4) went even further by upholding the right of federal courts to order local governments to increase taxes if necessary to remedy constitutional violations even when raising taxes conflicts with state laws limiting local taxing authority. The Court has also told state and local governments that their only protection against restrictions on their use of tax exempt financing is through the congressional political process (*South Carolina* v. *Baker*, 1987).

In various periods of history the federal government has been willing to help local officials by involving them in the formation of national policies directed at their problems. Local officials and the organizations that represent them were, however, out of the loop in Washington during the Reagan-Bush years, when the federal government largely abandoned its role as an intergovernmental partner. No longer accepted as

cogovernors or partners, state and local officials were viewed as members of a large constituency pleading for special causes, albeit ones with particularly large appetites.[9]

Local officials have not altogether abandoned the idea of a restored federal-local partnership. Indeed, there have been some bright spots in this regard. One example is the Intermodal Surface Transportation Efficiency Act, signed late in 1991, which calls for a federal-state-local partnership in a coordinated approach to transportation, air quality, and growth management problems.[10]

Changes in the national administration brought about by the 1992 presidential election may produce a stronger partnership emphasis. Speaking to national associations of local officials, President Clinton has called for more flexibility and less micromanagement and regulation from the federal level and has initiated a policy of avoiding further unfunded mandates on local governments.[11] Some action is also likely in Congress. By late 1993, 24 proposals had been introduced in Congress to provide state and local governments relief from unfunded mandates.

However, local officials probably cannot expect drastic changes in federal aid policies in the immediate future. Confronted with public resistance to increased taxes and a massive debt problem, it is unlikely that the federal government will find it either economically or politically feasible to resume an active role in financing state and local programs. One result of this is to encourage local officials to forge more effective relations with their state governments. In this era of "fend-for-yourself federalism," lobbying efforts at the state level have become even more important.

Politics and Policy in the States

Since federal policy began to change in the late 1970s, localities have turned to their states for help in making up for lost federal revenues. The initial state response was generally positive but, as economic conditions worsened and as demands for greater expenditures for education, health care, and corrections increased, state financial aid to local governments in many parts of the country began to vanish. Faced with their own budgetary problems, states shifted more and more of the costs to local governments. Indeed, individual states impose many more mandates on their local governments than does the federal government, though, as noted above, some of the more expensive mandates are federal requirements passed on by the states to localities.

Over the last few decades, economic, political, and legal pressures have also brought about a greater interest by state officials in matters such as education and land use planning traditionally handled on the local level. Through improvements in staffing, state legislatures have increased their institutional capacities to become involved in these matters. Critics of these centralizing trends see the states doing, at best, a spotty job in helping their localities and warn against the danger of inaction and overload at the state level.

While many of the most important decisions affecting local government are made by state legislators and administrators, one should not overlook the importance of state courts in this respect. Over the years, state courts have built up an enormous body of case law affecting local governments and have had an increasingly important impact on local taxing, spending, and regulatory powers in general and in such policy areas as education, environmental protection, land use planning, and housing.

Voters in the various states and localities have also become more involved in directly conferring and limiting state and local power. Many important financial decisions are fought out before the voters in initiative and referendum campaigns. Voters have generally come down on the side of local officials on the mandate question. On the other hand, the downside of "ballot budgeting" from the local point of view is that voters have commonly resisted proposals to reduce property tax pressures and bring more equity to school financing. They have also raised havoc by approving tax and spending limitation measures. In Colorado, municipal officials are still trying to determine the ultimate meaning of the Taxpayers Bill of Rights or "TABOR" amendment to the state constitution. Approved by the voters in the November 1992 election, the amendment requires voter approval for certain state and local government tax revenue increases and debt; restricts property, income, and other taxes; and limits the rate of increase in state and local government spending. Following passage of the amendment, one observer noted: "In Colorado the use of the initiative process has turned out to be a wild card for the entire state and for the local budget process. . . . When the results were in, the verdict was mayhem."[12]

THE STATES AND LOCAL AUTHORITY

State courts commonly view local governments as the "legal creatures" of their states. Applying Dillion's Rule (after John F. Dillion, a judge in Iowa in the nineteenth century) the courts commonly concluded that local governments possess only the powers expressly granted them by the state and that these powers must be narrowly construed. From time to time, however, state courts have taken a more liberal view. Last year, for example, the Supreme Court of South Carolina gave a liberal construction of the home rule authority conferred upon municipalities by the state constitution in a decision upholding the right of the town of Hilton Head Island to adopt a real estate transfer fee. Also last year a court in Maine confirmed that municipalities have extremely broad home rule powers to adopt local ordinances and charter provisions by virtue of a statute implementing the home rule provision in the state constitution.

Many of the questions concerning local authority wind up in court. Many more, however, are settled in the state legislature. Generally, state legislators, regardless of the nature of their constituencies, ideologies, or party identification, have been reluctant to relinquish control over local governments. Attitudes concerning the fundamentals of state-local relations seem to be very much a product of Miles' Law: "Where you stand depends on where you sit."[13] From where they sit, local officials usually see more local autonomy to be a good thing. From where they sit, state legislators often see more local autonomy as something that might bring undesirable results.[14] Businesses and various other groups also worry about the effects of giving local governments more discretion. They find it easier and more comfortable to deal with a single state legislative body than with a multitude of local governmental authorities.

Late in 1992, a gubernatorial commission in Virginia recommended a limited expansion of local governmental authority. Thanks in part to the opposition of the business community, however, the legislature did not even consider the commission's recommendations.[15] Also in 1992, the Wyoming legislature turned down a home rule bill sponsored by the Wyoming Association of Municipalities. Nevertheless, pressures of urbanization and suburbanization are encouraging states to extend home rule powers to county governments.[16] In November 1992, Arizona voters approved a constitutional amendment giving home rule to its two largest counties (Maricopa and Pima). Thirty-eight of the 48 states with county governments now grant counties some form of home rule. Only 18 did so in 1965.

In practice, the amount of local discretion varies by region, type of local governmental unit, and by the type of function performed.[17] The tradition of local self government is, for example, stronger in New England than in the South. Municipalities, on the whole, enjoy greater self government than do counties and other units of local government. Generally, local units are freer to create their own structure and organization than they are to determine what functions they may perform or how they may raise and spend revenues. As Christopher Hamilton and Donald Wells have noted, "One of the factors in understanding the actions of local governments is to see how the 'legal cards' are stacked against them inside the states."[18]

Scope of State Involvement

Because of the inferior legal status of local governments, states have virtually unlimited ability to intervene in local affairs by stipulating rules and requirements, mandating the performance of certain functions, and prohibiting local governments from taking certain types of actions.

The importance of state governments to localities is shown, in part, in the routine passage of legislation affecting local authority, procedures, and finances. The number of legislative proposals a local government organization feels compelled to monitor varies from state to state and from year to year within a given state. In 1992, for example, the League of Cities monitored more than 600 of the 2,560 bills introduced in the Florida legislative session. Meanwhile, the Oregon County Association tracked 1,494 bills out of 3,137 considered by the legislature. After screening 2,798 bills and resolutions introduced in the North Carolina legislature in 1993, the North Carolina League of Municipalities identified 615 or 22% as legislation that affected

municipalities and merited watching. On the average, probably around 20% of the hundreds of measures introduced in state legislatures significantly affect local governments.[19]

State laws extend into several areas. They condition the general level of local authority and the types of structures local governments can adopt. State laws also commonly prescribe voter registration procedures and qualifications and set regulations on local elections. On matters of finance, state laws often set debt limits, mandate public hearings for adopting budgets, institute referendums for bond issues, and outline the method for assessing property. On personnel matters, most local governments have to abide by state laws regulating training and workers' compensation for their employees. Open meeting and open record requirements are among the most frequent types of regulations affecting the governing process, followed by incorporation, annexation, consolidation, and intergovernmental service agreements. Most new state laws have been enacted in the areas of financial and personnel management.[20]

State legislators in nearly every session tinker around with laws they think will make local government more accountable, effective, and efficient. When it comes to mandates, however, a stronger motivation may simply be to shift the costs of programs to local governments. In the case of prohibitions, legislative action may be a matter of acceding to a demand of some private group anxious to avoid local taxes or regulations.

The Mandate Problem

In recent years, states have relied on their legislative and regulatory authority to compel local units to assume responsibilities for various programs and services. Local officials support the goals of many mandates and even find that such intervention has valuable results, for example, in setting minimum standards for jails.[21] In some cases, local officials also welcome the political cover that mandates give them as they try to carry out programs that are unpopular with segments of their communities (for example, low income housing).

Other mandates, however, are considered objectionable because they distort local priorities, impair managerial flexibility, and impose costs that have to be picked up out of local revenues. A range of studies indicates that localities dedicate anywhere from 20% to 80% of their expenditures to implementing federal and state mandates.[22]

Local officials have to be constantly on guard against legislation that dumps expensive or inefficient state programs on them.[23] Some of the routine shifts cost relatively little money, though their aggregate effects can be staggering. The big ticket items in areas such as health care, education, and environmental protection can overwhelm the budgets of local governments.

Local officials and organizations that represent them constantly seek state payments to cover the costs of new mandates. Sometimes they are successful. At other times, legislatures give local governments more authority to raise the revenues needed to meet the costs of new

mandates. In the latter case, coping with a new mandate means that local officials run the risk of incurring the wrath of the taxpayers.

Other strategies for coping with mandates center on the mandate process. More than 40 states require agencies or commissions on intergovernmental relations to estimate the costs imposed on localities by state laws or regulations. These are fiscal note requirements. In several states fiscal notes are used in conjunction with a requirement that the state reimburse localities for the expense of undertaking the required activity. In others they are used simply to call attention to the costs to be incurred by local governments.

Research suggests that the usefulness of the fiscal note process in either situation is impaired by problems of securing timely and reliable cost estimates and by the disinclination of legislators to pay much attention to the estimates even if they are available and reasonably accurate. Preparation of reliable cost estimates in time to influence legislative decision making (at least before the full committee has to vote on a proposed mandate) has been frustrated by the lack of staff, time, and expertise.[24] Because of these limitations, many measures with a potential financial impact on local government may not even be identified.

When used alone (that is, without a reimbursement requirement), fiscal notes appear to have a limited effect on legislative behavior. Even assuming that the process makes legislators more aware of the real financial burden they are passing along to local governments, this knowledge does not mean that they will refuse to impose the costs. The costs, after all, are not assumed by the state but by local governments. Fiscal notes when used as the sole antimandate strategy appear of little value in providing local governments with lobbying ammunition.[25]

About one-third of the states require reimbursement or partial reimbursement of the costs of mandates imposed on local governments. In some places, such as California, the state must either pick up the costs for mandated programs or give localities the added authority to raise taxes to finance them. Most states allow unreimbursed costs following a two-thirds or three-fourths vote of the legislature. Reimbursement can be required either by statute or by voter-approved state constitutional amendments. Voters appear more likely to approve such measures when proponents link them to the goals of reducing local property taxes and preserving local control over spending priorities.[26]

Reimbursement requirements placed in the constitution with the backing of the voters may be more effective in influencing legislative behavior than simple statutes requiring the same thing. In practice, the usefulness of reimbursement programs established through the process of constitutional amendment depends greatly on implementing statutes passed by the legislature that detail the process of reimbursement.[27] Legislatures normally have considerable discretion in interpreting the constitutional provisions; the problem is in the details found in the implementing statutes.

Mandate reimbursement, whether required by statute or by constitution, appears more effective than simple cost estimation in deterring unfunded mandates. The Florida legislature, for example, has generally shied away from even considering unfunded mandates since 1990 when the voters approved a constitutional amendment prohibiting such measures without a two-thirds vote in both houses.[28] This suggests that the real force of reform through constitutional amendment may be that it reflects public antimandate sentiment. As time goes by, the deterrent effect brought about by the expression of public opinion may well diminish.

The major effect of reimbursement provisions appears to be in deterring or modifying mandates to make them less expensive rather than in providing extensive funding for mandates.[29] In some states, legislatures have simply ignored the requirements—there is no penalty for doing so—or have evaded them by earmarking part of the funding already allocated for state aid to localities as mandate reimbursement. Mandate reimbursement costs are, in effect, deducted from what would have gone into local aid programs.[30]

Mandate reform in some states is driven by evidence of popular support. In Nevada, the county association led the effort to place an advisory referendum against unfunded mandates on the ballot. It passed with better than 80% of the vote. The legislature responded by passing a bill against unfunded mandates that requires the legislature to identify a specific funding source for any new or expanded program. In 1992, 80% of those who voted on the advisory question placed on the Illinois ballot by the Illinois League of Cities also indicated that they did not want the state to impose unfunded mandates on local governments.[31] A constitutional amendment to restrict unfunded state mandates, the exact language of which is yet to be determined by the legislature, will be on the ballot in November 1994.

Success came in South Carolina in 1993 with passage of an unfunded mandates bill that provides that no country or municipality may be bound by any general law requiring it to spend funds unless the General Assembly has determined that the law fulfills a state interest and, with certain exceptions, the expenditure is approved by a two-thirds vote in each house. Legislation adopted in Connecticut provides a new procedure for establishing mandates and a ban on new mandates unless accompanied by full state funding. In Maine, the legislature implemented the antimandate amendment to the state constitution adopted by the voters in 1992 in a form agreeable to the Maine Municipal Association. Under the law, the state has to pay at least 90% of the costs it imposes on local governments unless that obligation is overridden by a two-thirds vote in both houses.

Other notable achievements applying to specific programs in 1993 came in Maryland, where the legislature adopted a statewide building code with the express provision that local governments would be reimbursed for any costs associated with the change. Maryland also guaranteed counties a minimum level of funding for local health services. In North Carolina, success

came more informally. Prior to the session, local officials met with legislative leaders and the governor and his staff to discuss the mandate problem. The chief executive and the legislative leaders said they would resist additional unfunded mandates. The result was that no unfunded mandates were passed in the 1993 session. In Utah, meanwhile, a review undertaken by the Utah Advisory Council on Intergovernmental Relations led to the elimination of eight state mandates found to be outdated or useless in that state.

On the negative side in 1993, a push by the Kansas Association of Counties and the League of Kansas Municipalities for a constitutional amendment that would force the state to reimburse local governments for mandated costs failed to get out of the legislature, though there was strong interest in the proposal. Likewise, measures proposed in North Carolina to limit unfunded mandates were defeated. The issue, however, is likely to be given further study.

States have considered or adopted a variety of antimandate measures in addition to fiscal note and reimbursement requirements. These include: requiring an agency such as the state advisory council on intergovernmental relations to compile and annually update a catalogue of all mandates, including the fiscal impact of new mandates, as a basic information base; requiring state agencies to regularly review current mandates to determine if any of these can be relaxed or eliminated; encouraging agencies to implement new mandates on an experimental basis to test out their effectiveness and impact before spreading them to all localities; and enabling the governor to suspend mandates upon the request of local governments should they be found to impose an unreasonable burden. Reforms along these lines were made last year in Virginia in response to recommendations made by the Joint Legislative Audit and Review Commission (JLARC), a legislative agency.[32]

Use of sunset legislation to review mandates every five or even ten years to see which ones have outlived their usefulness has been strongly recommended in a study conducted by Janet Kelly for the National League of Cities. The same study also suggests that local officials may have more success in fending off mandates by challenging the goal of mandated policy or the method of reaching that goal, rather than simply focusing on the costs being passed along to local governments. Kelly further suggests that the mandate problem is linked to the broader problem of increasing the ability of local governments to participate in and influence decisions made on the state level affecting them.[33]

State Preemption

Also of considerable concern to local officials are state mandates of a preemptory or "thou-shalt-not" nature. Such prohibitions frequently reflect the desire of a particular group to minimize if not avoid completely governmental taxation or regulation. Local officials, for example, regularly guard against state legislation that would exempt certain businesses from local sales taxes, or, at the request of businesses, completely preempt local sales tax authority.

Efforts to circumvent local authority have been especially intense on policies concerning controls over smoking, rents, guns, billboards, and pesticides. Tobacco companies have encouraged a move away from local legislation on smoking. States have often preempted local action through the passage of statewide clean air bills less stringent than the local ordinances they replace. Those opposed to rent controls have also lobbied at the state level seeking to prohibit local action. Thanks to the National Rifle Association, some 30 states prohibit local gun control ordinances. In some states, police chiefs have helped prevent preemption by pointing out that it simply makes it more difficult for them to fight crime.

Business groups that manufacture pesticides and businesses and agricultural groups that use pesticides have been active in state capitals in attempts to prevent local regulation of pesticide use. They argue that a multitude of restrictions on pesticide use would do injury to business and agriculture. Proponents of control argue that local regulations are needed to protect the environment and the health and welfare of citizens.[34] States are currently free to decide whether localities within their boundaries may regulate pesticide use. About half of the states have passed preemption laws. Legislation has been proposed in Congress to make such matters the exclusive concern of the national government and thus take the states as well as local governments out of the picture.

In 1993, as in the past several years, state legislatures engaged in preemptive actions. Alabama prohibited local governments from regulating pesticides and adopting rent control ordinances. The Arkansas legislature preempted local regulations on the ownership of handguns, local rent control ordinances, and local pesticide control ordinances. In North Carolina, the legislature preempted local authority to adopt and enforce local smoking ordinances. However, bills that would have prohibited municipalities and counties in North Carolina from phasing out nonconforming billboards and other land uses without paying monetary compensation were defeated. This was the third time in the last four sessions that the billboard issue had come up. In Georgia, an attempt to preempt all local ordinances regulating or restricting smoking failed. On financial matters, the Oregon legislature preempted local sales tax authority but let expire a preemption on local real estate transfer taxes, and the Missouri legislature preempted cigarette taxes for state use.

Related to the effort to secure preemptive legislation barring local activity has been a more focused drive to discourage local regulations by requiring localities to compensate property owners financially damaged by regulations. Several state courts are examining cases initiated by property rights advocates challenging the regulatory authority of state and local governments. In California, the question has been whether a local rent control ordinance on a mobile-home-park owner amounts to a regulatory taking that requires the city to compensate the owner. In South Carolina, property owners have challenged beachfront regulations on sim-

ilar grounds. Environmentalists fear expansion of such protections could come at the expense of a broader public interest in shoreline protection.

Property rights advocates, realtors, and developers who are unhappy with various land use regulations have also pushed for legislation requiring compensation for limitations these regulations place on the use of private property. Environmentalists and state and local officials have expressed considerable alarm over such measures as the Property Rights Protection Act passed in 1992 in Arizona, which limits governmental regulatory authority. This measure will be on the ballot in 1994. Wyoming legislators defeated similar legislation last year.

THE STATES AND LOCAL REVENUES

State aid to local governments consists of grants and shared taxes. Grants are usually designated for education, transportation, or other programs; most states also provide unrestricted grants for general purposes. In regard to shared taxes, the states act essentially as tax collectors. They return all or a portion of the yield from a shared tax either according to an allocation formula or on the basis of origin of collection. States earmark much of the shared revenue for specific purposes. For example, a city's share of a state gas tax is usually spent on highway or street improvements.

Although state aid to local governments varies from state to state and fluctuates over time, it generally is a major source of local revenue. Local governments receive about four times as much from state governments as they do from the federal government, with state aid accounting for around 30% of all city and county revenue.[35] Analysts credit differences among the states to a wide range of factors, ranging from per capita income to the percentage of Democrats in the state legislature. The importance of particular factors varies with different types of assistance programs.[36]

Most state aid (over 60%) goes to support education, a function most often performed by independent school districts. City or county governments administer school systems in only a few places, for example, Maryland, North Carolina, and Virginia. Following education in funding are public welfare (12% of the total), general local government support (around 10%), and highways (4%).[37] State aid has also begun to appear in relatively new areas, such as corrections, housing, and transit. Yet, relatively little state aid (only about one out of every eight dollars) goes to cities to support traditional municipal programs.[38] State aid has had a modest equalization effect in reducing the revenue gap between poorer and wealthier localities.[39] Only a handful of states, however, have made a conscious effort to target funds on the basis of local needs.

During the 1980s, localities turned to their states for financial help because of declines in federal aid, increased mandates, strains on local revenues, and growth in citizen demands for services. The states generally responded with

increases in state aid, though, upon inspection, this response has been less impressive than it first appears.

Total state aid to local governments jumped from around $83 billion in 1980 to close to $130 billion in 1986, and $172 billion in 1990. Studies indicate that the growth of state aid over the 1980s, while substantial, generally lagged behind the growth in state economies during the period.[40] Moreover, as states experienced trouble balancing their budgets in the late 1980s and early 1990s, the percentage behind increase in state aid began to dwindle. From 1985 to 1991, state aid increase lagged behind increases in state and local spending.[41] Over the past decade, with good reason, local officials have had little confidence in the states' willingness to provide adequate funding for the programs local governments have to administer.[42] As the economy worsened, examples of state concern with the fiscal problems of local governments became rarer and rarer.

Several state legislatures have cut direct aid to localities. Last year, however, with a general economic upturn in many parts of the country (California and some New England states being the principal exceptions) there was evidence that the trend may be now slightly reversing.[43] In many states, cities and counties held their own on aid and in others the outcome, while not spectacular, was an improvement over recent legislative sessions. In New York, legislators approved the governor's recommendation to keep revenue sharing equal to 1992–93 levels. From 1988–89 to 1992–93, revenue sharing had been reduced by 52%, or some $535 million.[44] After an intensive lobbying effort, Maine municipal officials preserved programs that share state revenues with municipalities and help provide property tax relief. In the previous session, legislators had cut deeply into the revenue sharing funds. In Maryland, the negative trend also was somewhat arrested in that no additional cuts in state aid were evidenced. In a more positive action, the New Hampshire legislature ended a decade-long drought in any increases in general property tax relief aid by enacting a new program to share 75% of an increased rooms and meals sales tax with communities. The general assembly in North Carolina restored automatic statutory allocation status to various local revenue sources that the legislature had brought into the annual appropriations process in 1990 to improve the state's balance sheet. The funds are scheduled to be automatically allocated to local governments, outside the appropriation process, in fiscal year 1995–96.

There was more positive news last year: Vermont towns ended up with two new state-funded highway programs that will provide property tax relief and improve the highway system; the Virginia assembly approved the distribution in 1994 of $20 million in recordation taxes (taxes levied when recording a deed) to local governments for education and transportation purposes; the Illinois legislature made a temporary income tax increase permanent (counties and municipalities will receive a portion of those revenues); and the Washington legislature reenacted and permanently funded the City/County Criminal Justice Assistance Act for cities and counties.

A look at the total range of actions by state legislatures shows that some of the gains in aid mentioned above were countered by losses created by new mandates or revenue restrictions. Moreover, municipalities and counties in Arkansas, Arizona, and a few other states experienced cuts in at least some state aid or tax sharing programs in 1993.

Locally Derived Revenues

Since the mid 1980s, tax revenues at the local level have generally been increasing at a faster rate than they have at the state level.[45] Locally raised revenues have increased, in part, to make up for the loss of intergovernmental aid and increased costs due to unfunded mandates and local service demands.

Among local governments, counties have experienced the largest increases in tax revenues, jumping about 58% between 1985 and 1990. This is due to increased county expenses arising from the growth in demand for health and social service programs administered by counties and to a general tendency to shift responsibilities from cities and towns to counties.[46] Counties have also had a greater incentive to raise taxes because they have been hit especially hard by the cutback in federal aid.[47]

Property tax increases accounted for much of the growth in revenues at the local level. Revenues from local property taxes increased nationally by an astounding 128% from 1980 to 1990 and have continued to increase in the 1990s above the inflation rate. Increased revenues from this source have resulted mostly from increases in assessed values rather than from tax rate increases.[48] The burden has been particularly difficult for homeowners. Indeed, because of the collapse of commercial property values around the nation, much of the burden for paying the tax has shifted from the owners of commercial property to owners of residential property.[49]

As a consequence of this growth, the property tax has, once again, become one of the most unpopular taxes in the country.[50] Not surprisingly, demands are made on the state level for property tax relief in the form of limits or caps on increases in assessments or rates. At the same time, the utility of the property tax as a revenue producer in many jurisdictions continues to suffer from exemptions made at the state level that reduce its base. Counties often find that 60% or more of the property tax base has been exempted.[51] Figures are nearly as bad for many jurisdictions in states like New York. Governments, educational institutions, religious bodies, charitable organizations, and hospitals are all owners of tax exempt property. The major exemptions in regard to residential property are for veterans and the elderly.[52]

Many local governments have sought to move away from reliance on the property tax and toward a more diversified local revenue structure in which they use the sales tax, user fees, and local income taxes. States in recent years have allowed local governments more dis-

cretion in raising revenues, though this is often subject to voter approval. Counties have had more difficulty securing additional revenue authority. Proposals expanding the taxing powers of counties so they approach those enjoyed by municipalities have failed in Alabama, Florida, Maryland, and Virginia. In the last of these, a study commission has concluded: ''Differences between city and county taxing authority exist due to historical distinctions in the levels of services provided. However, increased urbanization and suburbanization of Virginia's localities have blurred these distinctions. Many counties are now required to provide levels of services similar to cities. Consequently, taxing authority between cities and counties should be equalized.''[53]

Over the last two decades, user fees have become a popular means of financing a variety of services, particularly in fast growing Sun Belt states.[54] Fees are commonly levied for hospital charges, sewage and sanitation, and air transportation. Because the notion that the direct user of a service should pay for has become a relatively acceptable way of raising revenues, local governments can usually levy fees without a grant of permission from state legislatures. Last year in Missouri, the state supreme court upheld the constitutionality of a new statewide local use tax of 1.5%. The tax will produce about $30 million annually in new revenue.

Localities also have considerable discretion in imposing impact fees on developers to offset the costs of building or expanding facilities such as roads, sewers, and parks and to serve the growth engendered by projects. Several states, however, have acted in recent years to ensure that fees are reasonable and related to reliable estimates of the impact of particular developments.

State Assumption and Cost Reimbursement

State legislatures could help financially strapped localities not only by increasing aid and extending revenue sources but also by assuming responsibility for programs now financed out of local revenues. This has been done in recent years in the areas of courts and corrections, indigent health care, and cash welfare assistance. Shifting total responsibility for a program to the state provides financial relief to local governments but results in a loss of local control. Some observers have suggested, for example, that a state financed and administered court system might not be as effective as a decentralized one that can respond to the diverse values among communities within the state. Rather than assume full financial and administrative responsibility for courts, states could provide relief through grants in aid and cost reimbursement plans and continue to give local governments some control over the administration of the system.[55]

It may, of course, be difficult to persuade the states either to assume responsibilities or share costs. Last year, for example, bills that would have required the state of Maryland to assume the funding and administration of orphans' courts and election boards did not secure legislative approval. On the other hand, the state

of Pennsylvania temporarily assumed the costs of mental health forensic services, the Utah legislature established a phase-in period of four years for full funding of a program to repay counties for the cost of housing state prisoners in county jails, and Virginia came up with a program reimbursing municipalities and counties for part of the cost of constructing jails.

THREE AREAS OF STATE ACTIVITY

Among the policy areas in which state actions have become of increasing importance to local governments are education, environmental protection, and land use and transportation planning.

Education: Problems of Equity and Finance

Traditionally, local governments have provided the bulk of support for elementary and secondary education out of local property taxes. The share borne by state governments, however, has increased over the last several years and now slightly surpasses the amount supplied by local taxes. As states move toward picking up a larger share of education expenditures, city and county officials who do not have responsibilities in the area of education have had reason to worry about the safety of their revenues coming from the states.

Growth of state financial responsibility has been accompanied by an increase in state regulations designed to improve the quality of education and to cap local educational expenditures. Research suggests that shifting to the state level has been most pronounced in states where property tax pressures have been the greatest and where resistance to state control has historically been the weakest.[56]

State aid to education has increased for two primary reasons: to reduce reliance on the local property taxes, and to equalize expenditures among school districts. Courts in about half of the states have added to the pressure by bringing into question the validity of spending disparities between rich and poor school districts. Equalization plans in Texas, Kansas, and other states have encountered the wrath of wealthier counties and have become the subject of court suits. Texas voters in May 1993 overwhelmingly rejected an equalization plan, called a "Robin Hood" plan by its opponents, which would have taken money from the richer districts and given it to the poorer ones. The legislature put together a new plan to meet a court imposed deadline, but this plan also faces a court challenge. The new plan reduces the disparity in property value in school districts between the richest and the poorest from 590 to 1 to 29 to 1.

While reliance on the states to assume more of the cost of education is likely to continue, particularly because of the pressure for equalization, there is also growing discontent with increases in the level of state taxes and increasing demands for expenditures in the areas of health care and corrections.[57] In 1993, California, Maryland, Montana, and Vermont cut aid to education. On the other hand, Colorado, Kansas, Minnesota, Mississippi, Tennessee, and Wyoming made double digit increases to education.

In Kansas, where the state began to fund education through a statewide property tax, aid jumped by 32.2%.[58] In Tennessee, the legislature relieved pressure on local property taxes by permanently extending a half-cent increase in the state's sale tax to provide some $230 million for local education systems (grades K-12).

Among the most dramatic developments in state-local financial relations last year was the decision of the Michigan legislature to eliminate the use of property taxes to fund elementary and secondary education. This action was taken even though lawmakers did not have a plan to replace the revenues. The state gave itself about nine months to come up with plans to reform the school system and to determine how to replace the some $6.3 billion lost in property tax revenues. In the fall of 1993 it appeared that the state was likely to replace the loss with a mixture of sin, sales and, once again, property taxes. Along with a different funding mix for education, the state may be heading for a more decentralized system of education based on the voucher system.

The legislative action followed several years of experimenting with reform of the property tax system. Michigan has had a relatively high property tax burden, and voters in recent years have regularly rejected proposed increases to pay for increased school costs. Several schools have, as a result, been on the brink of closing and one actually did close for a short period. In June 1993 voters rejected a proposal that would have increased the state sales tax by 50% in exchange for a cap on local property taxes and a guaranteed minimum of $4,800 spending in school aid for every pupil.

Property taxes and education also grabbed the headlines in California last year. Here, however, it was a matter of the legislature transferring $2.6 billion in property tax revenues from local governments to the state. The transferred funds were earmarked for education. The move was necessary, state officials argued, to make up for declining revenues and to keep education funding at its current level. Without the transfer, the state would have had to raise taxes or take money out of the general fund to pay for education and, because of this, cut the level of other state services. In making the tax shift, the legislature also, in effect, brought an end to the bailout it had given counties and cities as the result of the adoption of the property-tax limitation measure, Proposition 13, in 1978. The state, with financial needs of its own, could no longer afford the subsidy.

To help offset this loss of revenues, the legislature repealed some expensive local mandates and extended a temporary half-cent sales tax increase to January 1994 (an action expected to generate some $700 million for local governments) and agreed to let voters decide in November on a county-by-county basis if they want to make the sales tax increase permanent.

California county governments were particularly hard hit by the loss of property tax revenue. Collectively they lost $2.2 billion of the $2.6 billion—the rest came from cities, special districts, and redevelopment agencies. Some counties reacted in dramatic fashion to this tax grab by directing[58] their auditors not to turn the

money over to the state and by taking the state to court on the grounds that the action had violated county rights under the state constitution.[59]

Changes in the pattern of state-local financial relations in Oregon have also been under way since the adoption of a severe property-tax-limitation measure—Initiative Measure Number 5—by the voters in November 1990. The measure shifted funding for education from local property taxes to the state over a five-year phase-in period. The leading question is, where will the state find the revenue to met its new responsibilities in education? The initial response of the legislature was to cut programs across the board to eliminate waste. Some have called for more fundamental tax reform, including the often rejected sales tax.[60] Since the 1930s, Oregon voters have regularly rejected proposals for a state sales tax, most recently in an advisory vote in 1990, in which 63% of those who voted turned down the idea. In November 1993 voters rejected a proposal that would have dedicated the revenues from a 5% sales tax exclusively to education. Voters would have been given a chance to terminate the tax after four years.[61]

Environmental Protection: The Solid Waste Problem

Much of the discontent found on the local level in recent years has been directed at the effects, though not necessarily the broader goals, of environmental mandates. Some local officials, for instance, have contended that many of the testing requirements under the Safe Drinking Water Act as amended in 1986 are unnecessary and, thus, impose unnecessary costs. Under federal and state mandates, local officials have to come up with revenues to comply with federal regulations regarding not only the safety of drinking water but also such matters as underground storage tanks and the disposal of solid wastes.

State governments are often in the business of passing legislation making it possible for local governments to comply with regulations issued by the Environmental Protection Agency. Last year, for example, the Tennessee legislature gave cities with populations of 100,000 and above the authority to regulate storm water discharges and to establish fees to be used to fund municipal compliance with the federal Water Quality Act and the Clean Water Act. The legislation also requires that any charge rendered as a result of the act must contain the following statement, printed in bold-face type: "THIS TAX HAS BEEN MANDATED BY CONGRESS."

Municipalities around the nation are placing similar inserts in utility bills, often suggesting that state as well as federal officials are to be held accountable. Local officials have also challenged EPA and state regulations in court. In Missouri, for example, the state Municipal League has filed a lawsuit claiming mandated state environmental fees and permits violate a state constitution provision that prohibits state-mandated costs on local governments.

Since the mid 1980s, several industrial states—California, Florida, New York, and Pennsylvania—have adopted stringent and costly environmental standards for landfills. These regulations affect about 20% of the land-

fills currently in operation.[62] Under the federal Resource and Recovery Act, landfills throughout the nation are to be upgraded by standards worked out by the Environmental Protection Agency. These standards affect the location, design, operation, and closing of landfills and are to take effect in 1994. State governments may apply their own regulations as long as they meet federal standards and are approved by the EPA. State agencies are to develop landfill permit programs to determine if landfills comply with environmental standards before they issue permits for waste disposal. Ultimately, implementation of the regulations will require some localities to close down existing dumps. Others will have to come up with the funds to upgrade landfills. Because of the expense involved, many localities will pool their resources and create new regional landfills that can meet the standards.

Faced with difficulties regarding landfills, a growing number of states have given attention to the recovery of solid wastes for reuse or conversion into fuel. Several states have also adopted mandatory recycling laws that require the formulation of waste-management plans, local source separation and recycling programs, and specific statewide reductions in solid waste by a certain year. In 1992, North Dakota joined several other states by passing legislation to establish a state solid waste management plan and state solid waste management districts. Under the landmark California Integrated Waste Management Act of 1989, local officials must plan and coordinate their efforts toward the goals of diverting 25% of the waste stream from landfills by 1995 and 50% by the year 2000.

The economic feasibility of recovery programs is a major problem for some local governments, especially smaller ones in rural areas that have relied almost entirely on landfills (which now are to become far more expensive). Other communities face the problem of finding a market for the recovered material or energy. Achievement of waste reduction goals in California and elsewhere requires supportive action on the state level, including technical assistance, assistance in developing markets for materials, and action to change packaging standards.[63] Ultimately, however, it may be that some states have established unrealistic goals.

Land Use and Transportation Planning
State legislatures have also been encouraging municipalities and counties to develop land-use growth management plans that are consistent with state comprehensive plans. Such plans focus on the interrelated goals of controlling growth, combating environmental problems such as air and water pollution, and providing an adequate infrastructure. Florida's law has controversial concurrency requirements that limit new development to places where an adequate infrastructure is already in place or will be in place concurrent with the development. Changes in the state's growth management act last year require increased cooperation among cities and counties that change their individual comprehensive plans.[64]

Some observers object to the "top down" approach taken by the states to land use planning and worry about the adverse impact on lo-cal authority.[65] Local officials are being presented with new growth management responsibilities that require them to resolve conflicts among groups and individuals with divergent interests.[66] Another problem with state-imposed comprehensive planning is that it sometimes ignores the limitations on the ability of local governments to do the job. The ability to plan land use and to implement plans requires a level of professionalism, organization, and management expertise that is very often lacking in local governmental units, especially smaller ones in nonmetropolitan areas.[67]

As noted earlier, the federal Intermodal Surface Transportation Efficiency Act (ISTEA) encourages the participation of local governments in the development and implementation of state transportation plans. In many states it is too early to judge how this is working out. Thus far, information gathered from Year Book correspondents suggests a mixed picture. Local officials in some states have discovered that state agencies want to exclude them from meaningful participation and are unhappy about the distribution of funds. Local officials in other states are upbeat about the actual or potential effect of the act in increasing their involvement in transportation planning and execution. In some states, such as Ohio, ISTEA appears to have added to the ability of local governments and the state to continue a history of cooperation. In Maine, the state's Sensible Transportation Policy Act preceded ISTEA and went one step further by establishing Regional Transportation Advisory Committees to advise the department of transportation on a wide range of transportation issues and to work with the department throughout the transportation planning process. State and local officials and private citizens who represent diverse transportation concerns will serve on the committees.

PARTNERSHIPS AND RESPONSIBILITIES

Historically, local officials, working individually or through associations, have had considerable influence on the development of state and federal policies affecting them, the distribution of state and federal funds, and the extent to which state and federal policies are implemented.[68] The bottom line may be, as Hamilton and Wells note, that when it comes to state-local and federal-local relations, local units "are not passive objects allowing themselves to be willy-nilly shoved anywhere. The shoved can and do sometimes become the shovers."[69]

Yet, from the local point of view, the last several years may be best described as "combat federalism." Local governments have had to struggle to exert influence over the framing of policies and the implementation of programs affecting them. Largely in response to the growing mandate problem, they have become more assertive and aggressive.

Certainly one law of intergovernmental relations is that in periods of economic stress, local officials can expect less intergovernmental aid and more of the costs of government to be shifted their way. Recent years also lead one to predict that in times of economic stress, relief coming to localities from the states is particularly likely to take the form of authorizing increased local taxing authority so that local government officials will be forced to take the heat for raising taxes.

Local officials throughout the country have voiced their concerns about the quality of state-local relations. In a National League of Cities survey of local officials, 43% of the respondents rated the response of their state to the needs of municipalities as poor or failing. On the other end of the scale, about 16% rated the response good, and only 3% rated it excellent.[70] Local officials—county as well as city, appointed as well as elected—have been critical of the loss of local government authority, the lack of sufficient discretion to generate revenues, the lack of state financial aid and technical assistance, the lack of support of state agencies and, perhaps most of all, the growth of unfunded mandates.[71]

The growing responsibilities and problems of both state and local governments have prompted several states to create blue ribbon commissions in the last few years. These examine such topics as the efficiency of state and local tax systems, state aid to local government, and the structure of local finances.[72] Last year, a local government reform effort growing out of a study conducted by a private nonprofit corporation in North Dakota produced far reaching "tool chest" legislation.[73] The act provided several new or improved means through which citizens, governing officials, or both together can renovate local governments. Among the tools covered by the legislation and available to all units of local government are those on the joint use of powers and the transfer of powers. Also in the legislation is a new advisory study process through which citizens and leaders can examine local governance options and special tools for counties and cities in such areas as home rule.

Short of facilitating a renovation of local governments, state legislatures could help financially strapped localities by increasing aid (and targeting it to the places most in need), assuming the costs of programs now financed out of local revenues, easing the burden of costly mandates, and allowing greater discretion in raising revenues. In the last respect, they could come to the financial aid of local governments not only by authorizing new revenue sources but also by eliminating state laws that remove certain types of property from the local property tax or certain items from the local sales or income tax base. States could additionally help by passing legislation allowing localities to save expenses by consolidating services with other jurisdictions or by engaging in other types of creative cost sharing partnerships. Particularly useful are comprehensive privatization statutes now found in several states that make it easier for local governments to form public-private agreements. Another positive step is to make it easier for local governments to participate in federal programs. Last year, for example, the Georgia legislature gave municipalities and counties increased powers to take advantage of federal grant and loan programs for housing, transportation, and other purposes.

The recurrent disputes between state and local governments over finances and authority and over the relative merits of centralization and decentralization are not likely to abate in the immediate future. Fortunately, several states have established state-local panels or commissions to examine such problems, an example other states might well consider following. In any given state, one can find problems of considerable importance to the state as a whole that are being addressed by local officials who lack the perspectives and the resources to cope with them. At the same time, in any given state, one can no doubt find decisions being made at the state level that should be made at the local level in light of the needs and priorities of particular communities. While the sorting out of responsibilities is a difficult task, positive steps toward this end and toward the overall improvement of state-local cooperation are imperative.

[1]F. Thomas Ament, quoted in "Local Governments Declare War on Unfunded Federal Mandates," *County News* (August 16, 1992): 1, 5, at 5.

[2]Though grants have increased since the mid-1980s up to around 22% of state and local spending, the recent increases represent a shift away from grants giving state and local officials an opportunity to pursue programs based on their own assessment of needs. Rather, the increased aid is mostly entitlements for individuals that require state and local officials to provide benefits under federal rules to all those who qualify. Much of the increase in federal aid, moreover, has gone to states rather than to local governments. See Brenda Avoletta and Phillip M. Dearborn, "Federal Grants-in-Aid Soar in the 1990s, But Not for Locals or General Purposes," *Intergovernmental Perspective* (Summer 1993): 32–33.

[3]National League of Cities, *Fiscal Conditions in 1993* (Washington, DC, July 1993).

4. See "Special Districts Buck Trend of Declining Federal Aid," *Intergovernmental Perspective* (Fall 1990): 3–4.

[5]Tommy Neal, "Just Another Mandate," *State Legislatures* (July 1993): 59–60.

[6]On "shift and shaft federalism" see Steven D. Gold and Sarah Ritchie, "State Policies Affecting Cities and Counties in 1991: Shifting Federalism," *Public Budgeting & Finance* (Spring 1992): 23–46.

[7]See Rodney E. Hero, "The U.S. Congress and American Federalism: Are 'Subnational' Governments Protected?" *Western Political Quarterly* 42 (March 1989): 93–106 and sources cited therein.

[8]David R. Berman and Barbara Greene, "Counties and the National Agenda," in David R. Berman, ed., *County Governments in an Era of Change* (Westport CT: Greenwood Press, 1993): 123–34; and Richard C. Kearney and Reginald S. Sheehan, "Supreme Court Decision Making: The Impact of Court Composition on State and Local Government Litigation," *Journal of Politics* 54 (1992): 1008–25.

[9]See, for example, Alan Ehrenhalt, "As Interest in Its Agenda Wanes, a Shrinking Urban Bloc in Congress Plays Defense," *Governing* (July 1989): 21–25; Jonathan Walters, "Lobbying for the Good Old Days," *Governing* (June 1991): 33–37; Charles H. Levine and James A. Thurber, "Reagan and the Intergovernmental Lobby: Iron Triangles, Cozy Subsystems and Political Conflict," in Allan J. Cigler and Burdett A. Loomis, eds., *Interest Group Politics* (Washington, DC: Congressional Quarterly Press, 1986): 202–20; and B. J. Reed, "The Changing Role of Local Advocacy in National Politics," *Journal of Urban Affairs* 5 (Fall 1983): 287–98.

[10]Bruce D. McDowell, "Reinventing Surface Transportation: New Intergovernmental Challenges," *Intergovernmental Perspective* (Winter 1992): 6–8, 18.

[11]Laura Turner, "Clinton's Pledge to the Mayors: 'New Partnership' with Cities," *Nation's Cities Weekly* (June 28, 1993): 1; and Beverly Scholtterbeck, "Administra-

tion's Plan for Reinventing Government Appears to Serve Counties Well," *County News* (September 13, 1993): 1.

[12]John A. Straayer, "Direct Democracy and Fiscal Mayhem in Colorado," *Comparative State Politics* (February 1993): 6–12.

[13]Rufus E. Miles, "The Origin and Meaning of Miles' Law," *Public Administration Review* 38 (September/October 1978): 399–403.

[14]David R. Berman, Lawrence L. Martin, and Laura Kajfez, "County Home Rule: Does Where You Stand Depend on Where You Sit?" *State and Local Review* (Spring 1985): 232–34.

[15]See *Report of The Governor's Advisory Commission on the Dillion Rule and Local Government*, J. Granger MacFarlane, Chairman, submitted to Lawrence Douglas Wilder, Governor, Commonwealth of Virginia, November 1, 1992.

[16]See Berman, ed., *County Governments*.

[17]See Joseph F. Zimmerman, *State-Local Relations: A Partnership Approach* (New York: Praeger, 1983) and David R. Berman and Lawrence L. Martin, "State-Local Relations: An Examination of Local Discretion," *Public Administration Review* (March/April 1988): 637–41.

[18]Christopher Hamilton and Donald T. Wells, *Federalism, Power, and Political Economy: A New Theory of Federalism's Impact on American Life* (Englewood Cliffs, NJ: Prentice Hall, 1990): 131.

[19]David R. Berman, "State Actions Affecting Local Governments," *The Municipal Year Book 1990* (Washington, DC: International City/County Management Association, 1990): 56.

[20]See U.S. Advisory Commission on Intergovernmental Relations, *State Laws Governing Local Government Structure and Administration* (Washington, DC: GPO, March 1993). This report shows the extent of involvement and recent trends.

[21]See, for example, Joel A. Thompson and G. Larry Mays, "The Impact of State Standards and Enforcement Procedures on Local Jail Performance," *Policy Studies Review* 8 (Autumn 1988): 55–71.

[22]Estimates of the amount spent by state and local governments on federal mandates vary widely. Part of this variation is due to differences in how researchers define mandate. Generally, researchers focus on the costs of requirements that state and local officials undertake certain functions or follow certain procedures. Sometimes listed in the category of mandates, however, are regularly occurring state directives that prohibit local officials from becoming involved in certain policy areas or taking actions such as raising revenues. Prohibitions on revenue raising can have as devastating an impact on local finances as requirements that local governments spend funds. See, for example, Paul Flowers and John T. Torbert, *Mandate Costs: A Kansas Case Study* (Topeka, KS: Kansas Association of Counties, 1993). On the definition of mandates and the different forms they may take, see Janet M. Kelly, *State Mandates: Fiscal Notes, Reimbursement, and Anti-Mandate Strategies* (Washington, DC: National League of Cities, 1992); Max Neiman and Catherine Lovell, "Federal and State Mandating: A First Look at the Mandate Terrain," *Administration and Society* (November 1982): 343–72; and Max Neiman and Catherine Lovell, "Mandating as a Policy Issue—The Definitional Problem," *Policy Studies Journal* (Spring 1981): 667–80; and Advisory Commission on Intergovernmental Relations, *State Mandating of Local Expenditures* (Washington, DC: GPO, 1978).

[23]In 1992, for example, county officials in Delaware battled successfully against legislation handling them responsibility for expensive animal control services. In Montana, on the other hand, the legislature shifted costs for court-ordered psychiatric evaluations to counties at an estimated cost of $513,454 statewide. Last year, the Arkansas legislature forced counties to begin picking up a portion of the costs incurred by the state in the transporting of bodies to the state crime lab for autopsies. This legislation will probably cost the counties at least $100,000. In Arizona, the legislative action was more costly. It increased county responsibility for funding the local share of federal health programs, an action costing some $13 million for fiscal 1993–94. Maine municipalities were able to avoid assuming responsibility for 20%

of the cost of teachers' retirement when it was pulled from the budget, but the issue is likely to surface again next year.

[24]Kelly, op. cit.

[25]See generally Ann Calvares Barr, "Cost Estimations as an Anti-Mandate Strategy," in Michael Fix and Daphne Kenyon, eds., *Coping with Mandates: What Are the Alternatives?* (Washington, DC: The Urban Institute Press, 1990): 57–61. See also *Legislative Mandates: State Experiences Offer Insights for Federal Action* (Washington, DC: General Accounting Office, 1988) and Kelly, op. cit.

[26]Susan A. McManus, "Mad About Mandates: The Issue of Who Should Pay for What Resurfaces in the 1990's," *Publius* (Summer 1991): 59–75.

[27]Kelly, op. cit.: 42.

[28]The legislature has yet to implement the 1990 constitutional amendment. In its 1993 session the legislature, responding to Hurricane Andrew, passed an emergency planning act that will cost county governments millions of dollars.

[29]Joint Legislative Audit and Review Commission, *Intergovernmental Mandates and Financial Aid to Local Governments* (Richmond, Commonwealth of Virginia, 1992, House Document No. 56).

[30]See Richard H. Horte, "State Experiences with Mandate Reimbursement," in Fix and Kenyon, eds., op. cit.: 57–61; and Kelly, op. cit.

[31]Linda Wagar, "A Declaration of War," *State Government News* (April 1993): 18–22.

[32]Joint Legislative Audit and Review Commission, op. cit.

[33]Kelly, op. cit.

[34]Carla Smallwood, "A Struggle for Control," *American City & County* (January 1993): 60–71.

[35]*City Government Finances in 1988–89*, GF89–4, and *County Government Finances in 1988–89*, GF89–8, issued by the United States Bureau of the Census.

[36]Keith J. Mueller, "Explaining Variation in State Assistance Programs to Local Communities: What to Expect and Why," *State and Local Review* (Fall 1987): 101–7. Compare this with David R. Morgan and Robert E. England, "State Aid to Cities: A Causal Inquiry," *Publius* 14 (Spring 1984): 67–82.

[37]See David Kellerman, "State Aid to Local Governments, Fiscal 1990," in *The Book of the States, 1992–93* (Lexington, KY: 1992): 632–34.

[38]Randy Arndt, "NLC Study Shows Lag on City Aid," *Nation's Cities Weekly* 12 (September 1988): 1, 9.

[39]See Thomas R. Dye and Thomas L. Hurley, "The Responsiveness of Federal and State Governments to Urban Problems," *Journal of Politics* 40 (February 1978): 196–207; and John P. Pelissero, "State Aid and City Needs: An Examination of Residual State Aid to Large Cities," *Journal of Politics* 46 (August 1984): 916–35. For a more pessimistic view, see Robert M. Stein and Keith E. Hamm, "A Comparative Analysis of the Targeting Capacity of State and Federal Intergovernmental Aid Allocations: 1977, 1982," *Social Science Quarterly* 68 (September 1987): 447–77; and David R. Morgan and Mei-Chiang Shih, "Targeting State and Federal Aid to City Needs," *State and Local Government Review* (Spring 1991): 60–67.

[40]Helen F. Ladd, "The State Aid Decision: Changes in State Aid to Local Governments, 1982–1987," *National Tax Journal*, (December 1991): 477–96. For earlier assessments of the performance of the states, see Helen F. Ladd and John Yinger, *America's Ailing Cities* (Baltimore: Johns Hopkins University Press, 1989) and Steven D. Gold, "A Better Scoreboard: States Are Helping Local Governments," *State Legislatures* (April 1990): 27–28.

[41]Steven D. Gold, "Local Taxes Outpace State Taxes," *PA Times* (July 1993): 15, 17.

[42]See, for example, William L. Waugh, Jr., "States, Counties, and the Questions of Trust and Capacity," *Publius* 18 (1988): 189–98.

[43]On earlier trends, see Jonathan Walters, "Cities Have a Simple Message for States This Year: Set Us Free," *Governing* (January 1992): 40–43.

[44]"Rebuilding Revenue Sharing: The Key to Property Tax Relief," *Public Policy Report*, New York State Conference of Mayors and Municipal Officials (February 1993): 1.

[45]For analysis of this growth, see Gold, "Local Taxes Outpace State Taxes," and Gold, "Passing the Buck," *State Legislatures* (January 1993): 36–38.

[46]Gold, "Local Taxes Outpace State Taxes."

[47]Steven D. Gold, "The State of State-Local Relations," *State Legislatures* (August 1988): 17–20.

[48]Phillip M. Dearborn, "Local Property Taxes: Emerging Trends," *Intergovernmental Perspective* (Summer 1993): 10–12.

[49]News item in *Governing* (August 1993): 13. Based on "The Effect of the Collapse of Commercial Property Values on Local Government Revenues and Tax Burdens," Urban Land Institute, Washington, DC.

[50]U. S. Advisory Commission on Intergovernmental Relations, *Changing Public Attitudes on Government and Taxes* (Washington, DC: GPO, 1990, 1991, 1992. In the 1992 study the property tax and the federal income tax tied as the worst tax.

[51]John P. Thomas, "Financing County Government: An Overview," *Intergovernmental Perspective* (Winter 1991): 10–13.

[52]See *Government Finance Review* (June 1991): 4.

[53]See Joint Legislative Audit and Review Commission, *op. cit.* On the need for counties in unincorporated areas to have municipal-type revenue sources, see John P. Thomas, op. cit.

[54]See generally Donald Levitan and Adam D. Silverman, "User Fees: Current Practice," *Management Information Report*, vol. 24 (December 1992), published by the International City/County Management Association.

[55]Barbara Todd, "Counties in the Federal System: The State Connection," *Intergovernmental Perspective* (Winter 1991): 21–25.

[56]Kenneth K. Wong, "Fiscal Support for Education in the American States: The Parity-to-Dominance View Examined," *American Journal of Education*, (August 1989): 329–57.

[57]Hal Hovey, "State and Local Tax Policy: Looking Ahead," *Intergovernmental Perspective* (Fall 1990): 5–8.

[58]National Conference of State Legislatures, *State Budget and Tax Actions*, 1993. See also Karen Diegmueller, "Budget Shifts Hurting Public Colleges, Survey Finds," *Education Week* (August 4, 1993): 30.

[59]Among the general sources on the California situation are Mary Beth Barber, "Local Government Hits the Wall: Proposition 13 Finally Comes Home to Roost," *California Journal* (August 1993): 13–15; A.G. Block, Danielle Starkey, and Steve Scott, "The 1993–94 Budget: Pete Wilson and Willie Brown Delivered, but Was It a Knockout Punch for California?" *California Journal* (August 1993): 7–11; Danielle Starkey, "Stung By a Grab of Property Taxes by the State, County Governments are Fighting Back," *California Journal* (August 1993): 21–23; and Hugh Mields, Jr., "The Property Tax: Local Revenue Mainstay," *Intergovernmental Perspective* (Summer 1993): 16–18.

[60]Donald J. Stabrowski, "Oregon and Measure Five: One Year Later," *Comparative State Politics* (October 1992): 33–38.

[61]Meg Sommerfeld, "Oregon Parents Push Sales Tax to Raise Funds for Schools," *Education Week* (September 8, 1993): 32.

[62]Tom Arrandale, "The Changing World of Landfills," *Governing* (August 1993): 59–71.

[63]Linda Morse, "California—How Can We Get to 50 Percent?" *Public Management* (*PM*) (October 1991): 4–10.

[64]Recent studies on state programs include Scott A. Bollens, "State Growth Management: Intergovernmental Frameworks and Policy Objectives," *Journal of the American Planning Association* 58 (Autumn 1992): 454–66; Forster Ndubisi and Mary Dyer, "The Role of Regional Entities in Formulating and Implementing Statewide Growth Policies," *State and Local Government Review* 24 (Fall 1992): 117–27; and Dennis E. Gale, "Eight State-Sponsored Growth Management Programs: A Comparative Analysis," *Journal of the American Planning Association* 58 (Autumn 1992): 425–39.

[65]See, for example, Eileen Shanahan, "Going it Jointly: Regional Solutions for Local Problems," *Governing* (August 1991): 70–75.

[66]See, for example, Barbara Sheen Todd and Robert M. Jones, "Building Consensus on Development Issues," *Intergovernmental Perspective* (Winter 1992): 19–22, 38.

[67]See generally Jane Elizabeth Decker, "Management and Organizational Capacities for Responding to Growth in Florida's Nonmetropolitan Counties," *Journal of Urban Affairs*, vol. 9 (1987): 47–61; and Robyne S. Turner, "Intergovernmental Growth Management: A Partnership Framework for State-Local Relations," *Publius* (Summer 1990): 79–85.

[68]Michael J. Rich, "Distributive Politics and the Allocation of Federal Grants," *American Political Science Review* 83 (March 1989): 198–213; Richard P. Nathan, "State and Local Governments under Federal Grants: Toward a Predictive Theory," *Political Science Quarterly* 98 (Spring 1983): 47–57; and Hamilton and Wells, op. cit.

[69]Hamilton and Wells, op. cit.: 153.

[70]William Barnes and David Dickinson, "Federal, State Levels Get Poor Rating from Local Officials," *Nation's Cities Weekly* (January 20, 1992): 7. See also *The Status of America's Cities: The Eighth Annual Opinion Survey of Municipal Elected Officials*, Research Report on America's Cities Series (Washington, DC: National League of Cities, 1992).

[71]Victor S. DeSantis, "State, Local, and Council Relations: Managers' Perceptions," *Baseline Data Report*, vol. 23, no. 2 (March-April 1991, International City/ County Management Association, Washington, DC). Relevant survey data is also found in William L. Waugh and Gregory Strieb, "County Capacity and Intergovernmental Relations" and Tanis J. Salant, "Shifting Roles in County-State Relations," which appear as chapters in David R. Berman, ed., *County Government*.

[72]See "Formulating State Tax Policy: The Tax Study Process," The Urban Institute, *Policy and Research Report* (Summer 1989): 18–19.

[73]For background, see Bruce Levi and Larry Spears, "North Dakota: Building a Consensus on the Future," *Intergovernmental Perspective* (Winter 1993): 35–37.

THE YEAR BOOK
STATE CORRESPONDENTS

Alabama *Perry C. Roquemore, Jr.*
Alabama League of Municipalities
Arizona *Catherine F. Connolly*
League of Arizona Cities and Towns
Jerry Orrick
County Supervisors Association of Arizona
Arkansas *Jeff Sikes* Association of Arkansas Counties
Don A. Zimmerman Arkansas Municipal League
California *John Masterson*
League of California Cities
Colorado *Samuel D. Mamet*
Colorado Municipal League
Geoff Withers
Colorado Division of Local Government
Connecticut *Gian-Carl Casa*
Connecticut Conference of Municipalities
Florida *James C. Shipman*
Florida Association of Counties
Lynn Tipton Florida League of Cities
Georgia *Walter E. Summer*
Georgia Municipal Association
Illinois *Thomas G. Fitzsimmons*
Illinois Municipal League
Indiana *Nicolas J. Pasyanos*
Association of Indiana Counties
Michael F. Roeder
Indiana Association of Cities and Towns
Iowa *Susan E. Crowley*
General Assembly of Iowa
Staff League of Iowa Municipalities
Kansas *Beverly Bradley and Anne Smith*
Kansas Association of Counties
Kentucky *Karen Garrison*

Kentucky Association of Counties
Louisiana *Susan Gordon*
Louisiana Municipal Association
Maine *Dana F. Connors*
Maine Department of Transportation
Bob Devlin Maine Municipal Association
Maryland *David Bliden*
Maryland Association of Counties
Stephen McHenry Maryland Municipal League
Michigan *John D. Niemela*
Michigan Municipal League
Minnesota *Terry Lindeke* Minnesota ACIR
Missouri *Gary S. Markenson*
Missouri Municipal League
Nevada *Thomas J. Grady*
Nevada Association of Cities
Robert Hadfield Nevada Association of Counties
New Hampshire *John B. Andrews*
New Hampshire Municipal Association
New Mexico *Pat Romero*
New Mexico Association of Counties
Regina Romero New Mexico Municipal League
New York *Staff*
New York State Association of Counties
Peter Baynes
New York State Conference of Mayors
North Carolina *Ellis Hankins*
North Carolina League of Municipalities
North Dakota *Robert E. Johnson*
North Dakota League of Cities
John Walstad North Dakota ACIR
Ohio *John Coleman* Ohio Municipal League
Oklahoma *John Henry Ward*

Association of County Commissioners of Oklahoma
Oregon *Robert Cantine*
Association of Oregon Counties
Staff League of Oregon Cities
Pennsylvania *Douglas Hill*
Pennsylvania State Association of County Commissioners
South Carolina *Andrew G. Smith*
South Carolina ACIR
Kathleen K. Williams
South Carolina Association of Counties
J. Milton Pope
Municipal Association of South Carolina
Tennessee *Bob Wormsley*
Tennessee County Services Association
Dennis W. Huffer
Tenn. Municipal League Risk Mgt. Pool
John F. Norman Tennessee ACIR
Utah *Wayne C. Parker* Utah ACIR
Vermont *Steven E. Jeffrey*
Vermont League of Cities and Towns
Virginia *James D. Campbell*
Virginia Association of Counties
Robert H. Kirby Virginia ACIR
Clay Wirt Virginia Municipal League
Washington *Cathie J. Halpin*
Department of Community Development
State of Washington.
West Virginia *Lisa Dooley*
West Virginia Municipal League
Wisconsin *Kathy L. Bull*
League of Wisconsin Municipalities
Wyoming *Staff*
Wyoming Association of Municipalities

B2

Supreme Court Cases Affecting Local Governments

Charles R. Wise
School of Public and Environmental Affairs
Indiana University, Bloomington

Rosemary O'Leary
Maxwell School of Citizenship
and Public Affairs
Syracuse University

During the 1992–1993 term, the U.S. Supreme Court decided 126 cases. Twenty-four of these cases have significant implications for local governments. This article reviews the major holdings of those cases in areas that will or could have an impact on local government. Cases reviewed cover such subjects as religion and free speech, search and seizure, corrections, minority set-aside programs, forfeiture of property, local taxation, civil rights, attorney's fees, cable television regulation, housing, overtime pay, environment, health insurance, and voting rights.

FIRST AMENDMENT CASES

Several cases involved the constitutional issues of religious freedom and free speech, which are established under the First Amendment.

Religious Freedom

In *Church of Lukumi Babalu Ave.* v. *City of Hialeah* [113 S. Ct. 2217 (1993)], the Court reviewed ordinances of the City of Hialeah, Florida, dealing with the ritual slaughter of animals. The church alleged that the three ordinances violated the First Amendment's religion clause. In analyzing such ordinances, the Court uses a two-stage approach. At the first stage it seeks to determine if the law is sufficiently neutral and generally applicable to various kinds of conduct so that it need not be justified by a compelling governmental interest, even if the law has the incidental effect of burdening a particular religious practice. If the law passes the first stage, it is upheld without the Court subjecting it to the second stage. A law failing to satisfy the first stage must be justified by a compelling governmental interest and must be narrowly tailored to advance that interest.

The second stage of analysis determines if the law "advanced interests of the highest order" and was "narrowly tailored in pursuit of those interests."

In assessing the Hialeah ordinances at the first stage, the Court indicated that it (and by inference lower courts in future cases) may determine from both direct and circumstantial evidence the city council's objective in passing the ordinances. "Relevant evidence includes, among other things, the historical background of the decision under challenge, the specific series of events leading to the enactment or official policy in question, as well as the legislative or administrative history, including contemporaneous statements made by members of the decisionmaking body." The Court's first stage analysis led the majority to conclude that the ordinances had as their object the suppression of religion. The majority stated that the ordinances' text constituted "religious gerrymandering" in that they proscribed religious killing of animals. They were also overbroad, and disclosed animosity to Santeria Church adherents and their religious practices.

The general applicability of the ordinances was then assessed by the Court, which found that each of the ordinances were underinclusive in advancing the city's avowed interests in pro-

> **Amendment I**
> *Congress shall make no law respecting an establishment of religion, or prohibiting the free exercise thereof; or abridging the freedom of speech, or of the press; or the right of the people peaceably to assemble, and to petition the Government for a redress of grievances.*

tecting public health and preventing cruelty to animals. The ordinances were applicable only to religious killings and did not prohibit secular killing of animals. If the intent of the ordinances was really to protect the public health and to prevent cruelty to animals, then killing of animals for reasons other than religious would have been addressed. The ordinances thus pursued the city's governmental interests only against conduct motivated by religious belief.

Having failed the first stage analysis, the ordinances were subjected to second stage analysis. The Court's analysis concluded that the city's interests could be achieved by more narrowly drafted ordinances that burdened religion to a far lesser degree. The absence of narrow tailoring sufficed to establish the invalidity of the ordinances.

This case highlights the Supreme Court's approach to local government regulation of activities with religious components.

The second case involves the sometimes difficult tradeoffs associated with the First Amendment's religion and free speech clauses. In *Lambs Chapel* v. *Center Moriches School District* [113 S.Ct. 2141 (1993)], a church brought suit alleging that a school district violated its constitutional rights by refusing the church's request to use school facilities for a film series on family values and child rearing with a religious orientation. Pursuant to state law, the school district had issued regulations for the use of school property when the property is not in use for school purposes. Among the permitted uses was the holding of "social, civic, and recreational meetings and entertainments, and other uses pertaining to the welfare of the community; but such meetings, entertainment, and uses shall be non-exclusive and open to the general public." Another rule provided that "the school premises shall not be used by any group for religious purposes." The issue in this case was whether denying the church use of the school

to show the film for public viewing and for assertedly religious purposes violated the Free Speech Clause of the First Amendment.

The Court stated that the film dealt with a subject otherwise permissible under the school district's regulation, and use of the school for the film viewing was denied solely because the film dealt with the subject from a religious standpoint. The Court held that denial on that basis was plainly invalid under the principle that the First Amendment forbids the government to regulate speech in ways that favor some viewpoints or ideas at the expense of others. As to the argument that the district's decision was designed to avoid a charge of establishment of religion, the Court concluded that such fears were unfounded and observed that the showing of the film would not have been during school hours, would not have been sponsored by the school, and would have been open to the public, not limited to church members.

In *Zobrest* v. *Catalina Foothills School District* [113 S.Ct. 2462 (1993)], a boy deaf since birth had asked the public school district in which he lived to provide a sign-language interpreter to accompany him to classes at a Roman Catholic high school pursuant to the Individuals with Disabilities Education Act (IDEA), 20 U.S.C. sec. 1400 et seq. The Ninth Circuit decided that provision of an interpreter who was a public employee would violate the freedom of religion Establishment Clause of the First Amendment.

The Supreme Court held that the Establishment Clause does not bar the school district from providing the requested interpreter. The Court said that government programs that neutrally provide benefits to a broad class of citizens defined without reference to religion are not readily subject to Establishment Clause challenge just because sectarian institutions may also receive the financial benefit.

The Court concluded that the service at issue in this case is part of a general government program that distributes benefits neutrally to any child qualifying as "handicapped" under IDEA, without regard to the "sectarian-nonsectarian, or public-nonpublic nature" of the school the child attends. The Court concluded that the IDEA creates a neutral government program dispensing aid to individual handicapped children, not to schools. The Court stated that when a government offers a neutral service on the premises of a sectarian school as part of a general program that is in no way skewed towards religion, it follows under previous decisions that provision of that service does not offend the Establishment Clause. The Court's reasoning is not confined to the school context; it could be applied to any local government service.

Freedom of Speech

The First Amendment Rights of publishers of free magazines, distributed in part through news racks on city property, were the subject of *City of Cincinnati* v. *Discovery Network, Inc., et al.* [113 S.Ct. 1505 (1993)]. In that case, the City of Cincinnati, in the interest of safety and aesthetics, revoked permission previously granted to publishers of free commercial magazines to distribute their publications through freestanding newsracks located on public property. Calling the publications "commercial handbills" whose distribution on public property was prohibited by a pre-existing city ordinance, the city continued to allow daily newspapers to be sold on public property.

The Supreme Court, in a 6 to 3 decision, upheld the lower courts by finding that the city's "selective and categorical ban" on the distribution of "commercial handbills" in newsracks on public property violated First Amendment protections of free speech. In announcing its decision, the Court emphasized several points. First, the city had drawn an unreasonable distinction between commercial speech, such as that printed in the free magazines (which the city obviously viewed as having a low value), and noncommercial speech, such as that printed in daily newspapers (which the city obviously viewed as having high value). This different treatment of the two types of works is not content neutral and so violates the First Amendment. Further, such disparate treatment negates the city's claimed safety concerns. Hence, the city did not meet its burden of establishing a reasonable fit between its legitimate interests in safety and aesthetics and the means it chose to serve those interests.

FOURTEENTH AMENDMENT: EQUAL PROTECTION

In *Northeastern Florida Contractors* v. *Jacksonville* [113 S.Ct.2297 (1993)], an association of contractors challenged a city ordinance entitled "Minority Business Enterprise Participation," which required that 10% of the amount spent on city contracts be set aside each fiscal year for minority business enterprises (MBEs). The action against the city and its Mayor pursuant to 42 U.S.C. sec. 1983 claimed that the ordinance violated the Equal Protection Clause of the Fourteenth Amendment. Although the District Court ruled in favor of the contractors'

> **Amendment XIV**
>
> *All persons born or naturalized in the United States, and subject to the jurisdiction thereof, are citizens of the United States and of the State wherein they reside. No State shall make or enforce any law which shall abridge the privileges or immunities of citizens of the United States; nor shall any State deprive any person of life, liberty, or property, without due process of law; nor deny to any person within its jurisdiction the equal protection of the laws.*

association, the Court of Appeals held that the association could not establish standing to sue because it failed to allege that one or more of its members would have been awarded a contract but for the challenged ordinance and therefore there was no "injury."

The Supreme Court's review of applicable case law resulted in the following proposition: When the government erects a barrier that makes it more difficult for members of one group to obtain a benefit than it is for members of another group, in order to establish standing to sue, a member of the group seeking to challenge the barrier does not have to allege that without the barrier he or she would have obtained the benefit. The Court concluded that the "injury in fact" in an equal protection case of this variety is the denial of equal treatment resulting from the imposition of the barrier, not the ultimate inability to obtain the benefit. The Supreme Court thus reversed the Court of Appeals and granted standing to the contractors' association to challenge the minority set-aside ordinance.

FOURTH AMENDMENT: SEARCH AND SEIZURE

Two cases were decided that focused on the U.S. Constitution's bar of unreasonable searches and seizures.

Minnesota v. *Dickerson* [113 S.Ct. 2130 (1993)] resolved a conflict between the state and federal courts over whether contraband detected by sense of touch during a patdown search may be admitted into evidence. A police officer, having stopped a man in the course of a lawful investigation, conducted a patdown frisk for weapons. As the officer pat-searched the front of the suspect's body, he felt a small lump in the front pocket. The officer examined the lump with his fingers, and as it slid, it felt like a lump of crack cocaine in cellophane. The officer then reached into the suspect's pocket and retrieved a small plastic bag containing crack cocaine. The Court of Appeals disallowed the search.

The Supreme Court reversed the Court of Appeals. The Court referred to the "plain-view" doctrine. Under that doctrine, if police are lawfully in a position from which they view an object, if its incriminating character is immediately apparent, and if the officers have a lawful right of access to the object, they may seize it without a warrant. The Court stated that this doctrine had an obvious application by analogy to cases in which an officer discovers contraband through the sense of touch during an otherwise lawful search.

The Court held if a police officer lawfully pats down a suspect's outer clothing and feels an object whose contour or mass makes its identity immediately apparent, there has been no invasion of the suspect's privacy beyond that already authorized by the officer's search for weapons; if the object is contraband, its warrantless seizure would be justified by the same practical considerations that inhere in the plain-view context.

The second search and seizure case involved the removal of a mobile home from a trailer court. In the case of *Soldal et ux.* v. *Cook County, Illinois, et al.* [113 S.Ct. 548 (1992)], the owner of a mobile home that was illegally torn from its foundation and towed to another lot while law enforcement officers looked on, filed suit under 42 U.S.C. section 1983 of the federal Civil Rights Act. The owner claimed that the manager and the owners of the mobile home lot conspired with deputy sheriffs to unreasonably seize and remove the home in violation of the Fourth and Fourteenth Amendments. Although an eviction proceeding had been scheduled, the action was taken two weeks prior to the actual eviction hearing. Cook County, Illinois, Sheriff's Department deputies, who were asked to oversee the eviction by the mobile home manager, later testified that they knew there was no eviction order and that the actions were illegal. Despite these facts, however, they refused to accept a complaint for criminal trespass made by the mobile home owner Soldal or to otherwise interfere with the eviction. At a later date, a judge found that the eviction was unauthorized and the badly damaged trailer was returned to the lot.

The lower courts found for the defendants, reasoning, among other things, that while the action was a seizure in the literal sense of the word, it was not a seizure as contemplated by the Fourth Amendment because it did not invade petitioner's property. Thus, the sole issue before the Supreme Court in this case was whether the seizure and removal of the trailer home involved Soldal's Fourth Amendment rights.

In a unanimous decision, the Court held that the actions in this case constituted a seizure invoking the protection of the Fourth Amendment because there was a meaningful interference with Soldal's possessory interest in his property. Whether the Amendment was in fact violated, however, is now a decision for the lower courts, as the case was reversed and remanded for a determination of whether the seizure was reasonable under the circumstances.

EIGHTH AMENDMENT: FORFEITURE

Forfeiture of property pursuant to federal and state laws is compelling the courts to define

conditions and limits. Local governments have a stake in the federal civil forfeiture statute, because local law enforcement agencies share in the proceeds of successful forfeiture actions arising from joint federal-local law enforcement operations, which are civil actions that arise out of criminal trials. Two forfeiture cases decided by the Supreme Court signal the Court's entry into the issue of setting limits in the area.

Austin v. *United States* [113 S.Ct. 2801 (1993)] focuses on the issue of limits in such forfeiture actions. This case arose out of a criminal action in South Dakota court against a defendant who was found guilty of possession of cocaine with intent to distribute and was sentenced to seven years' imprisonment. A month later the United States filed an *in rem* action in the United States District Court seeking forfeiture of the defendant's mobile home and auto body shop under 21 U.S.C. sec. 881(a)(4) and (a)(7), which provide for forfeiture of conveyances and of real property used to facilitate the sale of controlled substances and related materials. The defendant challenged the forfeiture, arguing that the Eighth Amendment should be applied to civil forfeitures and that the Court should employ a multifactor test in determining whether a forfeiture is "excessive" within the meaning of the Eighth Amendment. Both the District Court and the Court of Appeals had rejected his argument that forfeiture of his property invoked the Eighth Amendment's Excessive Fines Clause and could be applied to *in rem* civil forfeitures.

After reviewing U.S. and British law at the time of the Eighth Amendment's adoption and its own previous decisions in interpreting the Amendment, the Supreme Court concluded that forfeiture generally and statutory *in rem* forfeiture in particular, historically and currently are understood as punishment within the meaning of the Eighth Amendment. The Court declined, however, to establish a multifactor test for determining whether a forfeiture is constitutionally excessive in this case, preferring to allow the lower courts to first consider the question. It is, thus, fully predictable that forfeiture actions will be challenged significantly as the trial courts and the courts of appeals attempt to develop criteria for determining excessive forfeitures.

The second forfeiture case involved the "innocent owner" defense. The pivotal issue in the case of *United States* v. *A Parcel of Land, Buildings, Appurtenances and Improvements Known as 92 Buena Vista Avenue, Rumson, New Jersey, et al.* [113 S.Ct. 1126 (1993)] was whether an owner's lack of knowledge that her home had been purchased with the proceeds of illegal drug transactions constitutes a defense to a forfeiture proceeding under the Comprehensive Drug Abuse Prevention and Control Act of 1970. In a 6 to 3 decision, the Supreme Court held that such lack of knowledge is a valid defense. It is now up to the defendant to convince a trial court that she is indeed innocent.

In 1982, Joseph Brenna gave the defendant $240,000 to purchase a home that she and her three children have occupied since that time.

The defendant is the sole owner of the property. Drug enforcement officials found probable cause that the funds used to buy the house were the proceeds of illegal drug sales. Although the defendant maintained a personal relationship with Brenna from 1981 until 1987, she swore that she had no knowledge of the illegal origins of the $240,000.

The U.S. government maintained, among other things, that because the money in question was a gift, the defendant was not really an owner and, therefore, could not claim to be an "innocent land owner" under the statute. The Supreme Court, however, held that the fact that the funds used to purchase the home were a gift does not disqualify the defendant from claiming that she is an innocent land owner.

The United States also argued that the statute transferred ownership of the house to the United States at the moment when the proceeds of the illegal drug transaction were used to pay for the property. Again the Court disagreed, maintaining, among other things, that the government must first win a forfeiture judgment. To hold otherwise would effectively eliminate the innocent owner defense in "almost every imaginable case in which proceeds could be forfeited," the Court wrote.

EIGHTH AMENDMENT: CRUEL AND UNUSUAL PUNISHMENT

Another Eighth Amendment case, although arising in the context of state prisons, nonetheless has direct applicability to local jails. *Helling et al.* v. *McKinney* [113 S.Ct. 2475 (1993)] dealt with a civil rights suit brought by a state prisoner under 42 U.S.C. sec. 1983 alleging violation of the Eighth Amendment's bar against "cruel and unusual punishment" due to his exposure to environmental tobacco smoke. The trial magistrate had ruled that the prisoner had no constitutional right to a smoke-free environment but could state a claim for deliberate indifference to serious medical needs if he could prove the underlying facts. The magistrate held that the respondent had, however, failed to present evidence showing either medical problems that were traceable to cigarette smoke or deliberate indifference to medical needs. The Court of Appeals disagreed and held that the prisoner had stated a viable cause for action under the Eighth Amendment.

The question for the Supreme Court was whether the Appeals court had erred in holding that McKinney had stated an Eighth Amendment claim by alleging that his compelled exposure to environmental tobacco smoke (ETS)

Amendment IV

The right of the people to be secure in their persons, houses, papers, and effects, against unreasonable searches and seizures, shall not be violated, and no Warrants shall issue, but upon probable cause, supported by Oath or affirmation, and particularly describing the place to be searched, and the persons or things to be seized.

Amendment VIII

Excessive bail shall not be required, nor excessive fines imposed, nor cruel and unusual punishments inflicted.

poses an unreasonable risk to his health. The State argued that unless the prisoner could prove that he is currently suffering serious medical problems caused by exposure to ETS, there can be no violation of the Eighth Amendment. That Amendment, it was argued, does not protect against prison conditions that merely "threaten to cause health problems in the future, no matter how grave and imminent the threat."

The Supreme Court held that there could be a cause of action under the Eighth Amendment and disagreed with the State that threat to future health could not be considered. The majority observed, "It would be odd to deny an injunction to inmates who plainly proved an unsafe, life-threatening condition in their prison on the grounds that nothing yet had happened to them." The Court remanded the case in order to allow the prisoner to attempt to prove his assertion that the level of ETS to which he had been involuntarily exposed is such that his future health is unreasonably endangered. However, the Court enunciated standards that must be used to assess the proof of the allegation. The objective element the prisoner must prove is that he himself is exposed to unreasonably high levels of ETS. That requires more than a scientific or statistical inquiry into the seriousness of the potential harm and the likelihood that such injury to health will actually be caused by exposure to ETS. It also requires a court to assess whether society considers the risk that the prisoner complains of to be so grave that it violates contemporary standards of decency to expose *anyone* unwillingly to such a risk. The subjective factor that must be proved is deliberate indifference on the part of prison authorities. This should be determined in light of the authorities' current attitudes and conduct.

MILITARY SERVICE AND LOCAL TAXATION

Conroy v. *Aniskoff* [113 S.Ct.1562 (1993)] dealt with interpretation of provisions of the Soldiers' and Sailors' Civil Relief Act that affect whether local government tax authorities can sell property owned by a uniformed member of the armed forces who has not paid taxes. At issue in the case was whether the provision in sec. 525 of the Act that the "period of military service shall not be included in computing any period . . . provided by any law for the redemption of real property sold or forfeited to enforce any obligation, tax, or assessment."

An Army officer who was on active duty continuously from 1966 until the time of trial had purchased a parcel of vacant land in a town in Maine. He had paid taxes on the property for ten years but had failed to pay local real estate taxes for three consecutive years. Thereafter, the town followed the state statutory procedures and sold the property. The officer brought suit against the town and the two purchasers claiming that he was in military service, and federal law prevented the town from acquiring good title to the property, even though the state's pro-

cedures had been followed. The trial court rejected the claim and followed a line of decisions that refused to exclude the period of military service in computing the redemption period unless the taxpayer could show that "military service resulted in hardship excusing timely legal action." The trial court said that it would be absurd and illogical to exclude from computation periods of time for career service personnel who had not been handicapped by their military status. The Maine Supreme Judicial Court agreed.

The Supreme Court in interpreting the statute reversed the lower courts. It stated that when reading sec. 525 in the context of the entire statute, it could find no support for the town's argument that it implicitly conditions its protection of military personnel on a demonstration of hardship or prejudice resulting from military service. It concluded that the Act's legislative history confirmed a congressional intent to protect all military personnel on active duty, not just those whose lives have been temporarily disrupted by the service.

CIVIL RIGHTS SUITS

The Supreme Court reviewed four cases brought against government entities and their employees for alleged violations of constitutional rights. Two of these cases further elucidated standards to be used by lower courts in processing such cases. The two additional cases focused on the conditions under which personnel employed in the judicial process should be accorded absolute immunity in civil rights suits as opposed to qualified immunity.

Absolute immunity (meaning the official can not be sued for money damages) has been carefully limited by the Supreme Court to a few officials, who in the Court's judgement require full exemption from liability. The Court employs a "functional approach" to the issue of whether a particular type of official should be accorded absolute immunity or qualified immunity instead. The functional approach has led the Court to accord absolute immunity to those engaged in acts of a judicial, prosecutorial, or legislative nature. Others are accorded qualified or "good faith" immunity. Whether an official will be excused from liability on the basis of qualified immunity depends on the "objective legal reasonableness" of the action, assessed in light of the legal rules that were clearly established at the time the action was taken. Qualified immunity is really a defense that must be pleaded by the official in response to a suit; the defendant must demonstrate his or her good faith by objectively proving that there has been no violation of clearly established law.

The Supreme Court undertook consideration of these issues in *Antoine* v. *Byers and Anderson, Inc., et al.* [113 S. Ct. 2167 (1993)] in order to resolve conflicting interpretations among the Circuit Courts of Appeals over whether court reporters should be accorded absolute immunity from civil rights suits or only qualified immunity. Although the court reporter sued in this

case was employed in the federal system, the principles apply to state and local court reporters as well as other court employees.

In *Antoine*, a convicted bank robber had appealed his conviction and ordered a copy of the trial transcript from the court reporter. Over two years later, the court reporter had yet to provide the transcript. The reporter then explained that she had lost many of her trial notes, although additional notes and tapes later were discovered. Eventually another reporter produced a partial transcript. As a result of the delay the prisoner's appeal was not heard until four years after his conviction. The prisoner filed suit seeking damages from the court reporter, but the District Court granted summary judgement to dismiss on the ground that the reporter was entitled to absolute immunity. The Court of Appeals affirmed and declared that "the tasks performed by a court reporter in furtherance of her statutory duties are functionally part and parcel of the judicial process."

The Supreme Court refused to accord absolute immunity to the court reporter. The justices stated that they were not persuaded that the functional approach to immunity required them to extend absolute immunity to court reporters because they are a part of the judicial function. Instead, they reasoned that when absolute immunity is extended to judicial employees other than judges, it is because the judgements of such employees in the course of their work is "functionally comparable" to those of judges because they too "exercise a discretionary judgement" as part of their function. The justices concluded that the function performed by court reporters is not in this category.

The second case concerned the immunity available to prosecutors. In *Buckley* v. *Fitzsimmons* [113 S.Ct.2606 (1993)], a prosecutor was sued pursuant to 42 U.S.C. sec. 1983 for allegedly fabricating evidence during a preliminary investigation of a highly publicized rape and murder case and for allegedly making false statements at a press conference announcing the return of an indictment against a defendant. The issue before the Court was whether the prosecutor enjoyed absolute immunity for either or both claims. The Court assumed the allegations were true only for purposes of addressing the prosecutor's claim to absolute immunity.

Employing its functional analysis the Court reiterated, based on previous cases involving prosecutors, that a prosecutor's administrative duties and those investigatory functions that do not relate to an advocate's preparation for the initiation of a prosecution or for judicial proceedings are not entitled to absolute immunity. The Court found that the false evidence charge arose out of actions by the prosecutor in investigating the case and declared that a prosecutor may not shield his investigative work with the aegis of absolute immunity merely because, after a suspect is eventually arrested, indicted, and tried, that work may be retrospectively described as "preparation" for a possible trial. The Court observed that when the functions of prosecutors and detectives are the same, the im-

munity that protects them is also the same, i.e., qualified immunity.

As to the second charge, the Court found that the prosecutor's statements to the media also were not entitled to absolute immunity. The Court reasoned that comments to the media have no functional tie to the judicial process just because they are made by a prosecutor.

In both of the cases in which absolute immunity was an issue, the Supreme Court has demonstrated its continuing proclivity to be very sparing in according absolute immunity to any officials and is carefully defining the circumstances in which the lower courts can accord it.

A third civil rights case focused on a procedural issue in the courts' handling of civil rights cases against local governments and their officials. The circumstances that provoked the case involved the search of a home. In the case of *Leatherman et al.* v. *Tarrant County et al.* [113 S.Ct. 1160 (1993)], homeowners who were the subject of a narcotics search filed suit under 42 U.S.C. section 1983 of the federal Civil Rights Act. The suit named local officials, a county, and two municipalities, alleging that the search of the plaintiffs' home violated the Fourth Amendment of the U.S. Constitution. The homeowners also alleged that the basis for such municipal liability was failure to train adequately the police officers involved.

A federal district court dismissed the homeowners' suit because of technical flaws. The homeowners' pleading, while comporting with the Federal Rules of Civil Procedure (FRCP), did not meet the more detailed pleading requirements mandated by the Court of Appeals. The Court of Appeals upheld the dismissal of the suit on this basis. At issue were the rules mandated by the Court of Appeals, which had requirements more stringent than the Federal Rules of Civil Procedure. The pivotal issue examined by the Supreme Court, then, was whether a federal court may demand more detailed and more stringent pleadings than are required in the FRCP when a municipality is sued under section 1983. In a unanimous decision, the Supreme Court overturned the lower courts and held that a federal court may not demand a more rigorous pleading standard in suits against municipalities under section 1983 than are required under the FRCP. In the absence of formal amendments to the FRCP, the Court reasoned, the lower courts could gather additional information in such suits, if needed, through such mechanisms as pre-trial discovery.

ATTORNEY'S FEES

Local governments and officials involved in civil rights suits pursuant to 42 U.S.C. sec. 1983 (commonly referred to as sec. 1983 suits) can be held liable to pay the fees for the attorney of the plaintiff, pursuant to 42 U.S.C. sec. 1988, the Civil Rights Attorney's Fees Award Act. In *Ferrar* v. *Hobby* [113 S.Ct. 566 (1992)], the Supreme Court made a significant pronouncement in defining the circumstances under which local officials and local governments as defendants in

civil rights cases will be required to pay the fees for attorneys for the plaintiff. In this case against multiple state and local defendants, the owner of a private school sought $17 million in compensatory damages. The trial court had awarded nothing, but the Court of Appeals found that one of the six defendants had deprived the plaintiff of a civil right and remanded for entry of judgement for nominal damages. The plaintiffs then sought attorney's fees under sec. 1988. The District Court then awarded fees of $280,000, expenses of $27,932, and $9,730 in prejudgment interest. The Court of Appeals reversed the fee award and held that the plaintiffs were not "prevailing parties" and therefore were ineligible for fees under sec. 1988.

The Supreme Court disagreed with the Appeals court in part and held that a plaintiff who wins nominal damages is a prevailing party. However, more significantly, the Court stated that while the "technical" nature of a nominal damages award does not affect the court's determination of whether the plaintiff was a prevailing party, it does bear on the propriety of the fees awarded. The Court pronounced that in some circumstances even a plaintiff who formally prevails under sec. 1988 should receive no attorney's fees and that a plaintiff who seeks compensatory damages but receives no more than nominal damages is often such a prevailing party.

The Court pronounced the basis for determining fees by saying that "the most critical factor" in determining the reasonableness of a fee award "is the degree of success obtained." In previous cases the Court had issued instructions for lower courts in calculating the fee amounts including 12 factors to be considered. Here, however, the Court declared that having considered the amount and nature of damages awarded, a trial court may lawfully award low fees or no fees at all without reciting the 12 factors bearing on reasonableness or multiplying the number of hours reasonably expended by a reasonable hourly rate. The Court concluded that in the case of a plaintiff recovering only nominal damages because of his failure to prove an essential element of his claim for monetary relief, the only reasonable fee is usually no fee at all. The Court thus agreed with the Court of Appeals' reversal of the District Court's fee award.

CABLE TELEVISION

Federal Communications Commission v. *Beach Communications, Inc.* [113 S.Ct. 2096 (1993)] affects local governments' role in regulating cable television. The Cable Communications Policy Act provides for cable television systems to be franchised by local government authorities but exempts facilities serving "only subscribers in one or more multiple unit dwellings under common ownership, control, or management, unless such facilities use any public right of way." The FCC ruled that a satellite master antenna television system in an apartment complex is subject to local franchise requirements, if its transmission lines interconnect separately

owned and managed buildings or if its lines use or cross any public right-of-way. The Court of Appeals invalidated the FCC's ruling on the basis that it violated the Due Process Clause of the Fifth Amendment. The Supreme Court reversed and declared that the FCC's common ownership distinction is constitutional. The disputed systems will therefore be subjected to local franchise requirements.

SECTION 8 HOUSING

Most local governments are familiar with the Section 8 housing program created in 1974 by a congressional amendment to the federal Housing Act. Through the Section 8 program, Congress hoped to aid low-income families in obtaining decent places to live by subsidizing private landlords who would rent to low-income tenants. The statute requires that the rent charged is to be based on "the fair market rental" value of the dwelling, plus a modest addendum to compensate landlords for the expense of participating in the program.

When the U.S. Department of Housing and Urban Development (HUD) suspected in the 1980s that the rental payments made to some landlords under this program were well above prevailing market rates for comparable housing, it initiated several "comparability studies" to ascertain private market rents for similar housing. Based on these studies, HUD limited the rent payments it would make under the Section 8 contracts with landlords. The Department of Housing and Urban Development Reform Act of 1989 (Reform Act), confirmed HUD's right to limit rent adjustments through the use of these comparability studies.

Several landlords sued HUD, arguing that this section of the Reform Act violated the Due Process Clause of the Fifth Amendment of the U.S. Constitution because it stripped them of rights to automatic rent increases written into their long-term contracts. The lower courts agreed with the landlords. In a unanimous decision, however, the Supreme Court reversed the lower courts and held for HUD [*Cisneros, Secretary of Housing and Urban Development et al.* v. *Alpine Ridge Group et al.* [113 S.Ct. 1989 (1993)]. Examining the plain language of the landlords' contracts with HUD, the Court found that there was no wording prohibiting the use of comparability studies to impose an independent cap on rental adjustments. Indeed, the Court found language in the contracts that clearly allowed comparison with similar private market units.

FAIR LABOR STANDARDS ACT AND OVERTIME PAY

The issue of whether 400 deputy sheriffs in Harris County, Texas, were entitled to wages or extra time off under the Fair Labor Standards Act (FLSA) for overtime work was decided in the case of *Lynwood Moreau et al.* v. *Johnny Kevenhagen, Sheriff, Harris County, Texas, et al.* [113 S.Ct. 1905 1993)].

The FLSA generally requires employers to pay their employees for overtime work at a rate of one and a half times the employees' regular wages. However, in 1985, Congress amended the FLSA to provide a limited exception to this rule for state and local government agencies. Under the 1985 amendments, public employers may compensate employees who work overtime with extra time off instead of overtime pay in certain circumstances. There are only two instances under the FLSA when a public agency may provide compensatory time, or "comp time," in lieu of overtime pay: if there is a collective bargaining agreement with a union agreeing to such provisions (subclause I) or absent such a collective bargaining agreement, if there is an agreement or understanding arrived at between the employer and the employee before the performance of the work (subclause II).

Several pivotal facts complicate the situation in Harris County, Texas. First, each deputy sheriff's employment terms and conditions are set forth in individual agreements. Each individual agreement incorporates by reference the Harris County regulations that provide that deputies shall receive comp time for overtime work. Such an arrangement would seem to put the deputy sheriffs squarely under the second condition above. At the same time, however, each deputy sheriff is a member of the Harris County Deputy Sheriff's Union, which has represented the deputies for years with the county in such areas as processing grievances and handling workers' compensation claims. The existence of a union would seem to put the deputy sheriffs squarely under the first condition above. However, the union is prohibited by Texas law from entering into a collective bargaining agreement with the county.

The deputy sheriffs filed suit maintaining that the county violated the FLSA by providing comp time rather than overtime pay, absent an agreement with their union representative authorizing the substitution pursuant to subclause I, above. Hence, the main issue addressed by the Court was whether the deputies are a union pursuant to subclause I (even though collective bargaining is prohibited under Texas Law) or whether they fall under the subclause II exception. The lower courts found for the county and upheld the comp-time provision in individual contracts pursuant to subclause II.

In a unanimous decision, the Supreme Court affirmed the decision of the lower courts. Reasoning that the deputy sheriffs did not have a union representative authorized by law, the Court found that the deputies could not have negotiated a union agreement under subclause I. Accordingly, they were covered by subclause II, so the comp-time provisions negotiated by the county in the individual deputy sheriff's contracts were fully supported by the FLSA.

OPERATION RESCUE AND ABORTION CLINICS

The original plaintiffs in the case of *Jayne Bray et al.* v. *Alexandria Women's Health Clinic et al.* [113 S.Ct. 753 (1993)] were clinics that perform abortions and organizations that support legalized abortions. The original defendants were primarily members of Operation Rescue, a group that organizes anti-abortion demonstrations in which participants trespass on and obstruct general access to the premises of abortion clinics. The plaintiffs filed suit pursuant to 42 U.S.C. section 1985 of the Civil Rights Act of 1871 to stop Operation Rescue from conducting demonstrations at abortion clinics in the Washington, D.C., metropolitan area. Both lower courts held, among other things, that Operation Rescue violated section 1985 by conspiring to deprive women seeking abortions of the right to interstate travel.

The Supreme Court, however, in a split decision, reversed the decisions of the lower courts. Legal precedent, the Court wrote, establishes that to successfully file suit under section 1985, the plaintiffs must demonstrate at least two things, neither of which was demonstrated here. First, the plaintiffs must show that some racial or class-based discriminatory resentment or hostility lay behind the defendants' actions. Although the Court acknowledged that sex-based discrimination would fit the intent of the statute, the Court concluded that the defendant's demonstrations are not directed specifically at women but are intended to protect the victims of abortion, stop the practice of abortion, and reverse the legalization of abortion. Second, the plaintiffs must demonstrate that the conspiracy in question was "aimed at" interfering with rights that are protected against private and official encroachment. While the right to interstate travel is constitutionally protected, the Court reasoned, the plaintiffs failed to establish that Operation Rescue's actions were "aimed at" that right. When looked at in its entirety, the case firmly establishes that section 1985 does not provide a federal cause of action against persons obstructing access to abortion clinics under this factual situation.

DISTRICT OF COLUMBIA HEALTH INSURANCE

In 1991, the District of Columbia began requiring employers who provide health insurance for their employees to provide equivalent health insurance coverage for injured employees eligible for workers' compensation benefits. The Greater Washington Board of Trade, a nonprofit corporation that sponsors health insurance coverage for its employees, filed suit against the District of Columbia and Mayor Sharon Pratt Kelly maintaining that this new requirement was preempted by the federal Employee Retirement Income Security Act of 1974 (ERISA). While the lower courts were split on this topic, the Supreme Court decided in an 8 to 1 decision that ERISA does supersede such regulation. Basing its decision on a fairly straightforward reading of the federal statute, the Court held that there was a connection to the federal law, even if the new regulation was not purposely designed to affect it [*District of Columbia et al.* v. *Greater Washington Board of Trade,* 113 S.Ct. 580 (1992)].

BOSTON HARBOR CLEANUP

The saga of the cleanup of Boston Harbor continues, with the latest chapter written by the Supreme Court in the case of *Building and Construction Trades Council of the Metropolitan District* v. *Associated Builders and Contractors of Massachusetts/Rhode Island, Inc., et al.* [113 S.Ct. 1190 (1993)]. The Massachusetts Water Resources Authority (MWRA) is an independent government agency charged by the Massachusetts Legislature with providing water-supply services, sewage collection, and treatment and disposal services for the eastern half of Massachusetts. Following a lawsuit arising out of its failure to prevent the pollution of Boston Harbor as mandated by the Clean Water Act, the MWRA was ordered to clean up the Harbor. The cleanup project is expected to cost $6.1 billion over 10 years. The court that decided the original case ordered cleanup to proceed without interruption, making no allowance for delays from causes such as labor disputes.

MWRA has the primary responsibility for the cleanup. In the spring of 1988, MWRA selected Kaiser Engineers, Inc., as its project manager. Part of Kaiser's responsibilities included advising the MWRA on the development of a labor-relations policy that would maintain worker harmony and stability throughout the duration of the project. To that end, Kaiser suggested to MWRA that Kaiser be permitted to negotiate an agreement with the Building and Construction Trades Council (BCTC) and affiliated organizations that would assure such labor stability. With MWRA's permission, Kaiser negotiated such an agreement.

In March 1990, a contractors' association filed a charge with the National Labor Relations Board (NLRB) maintaining that the agreement violated the National Labor Relations Act (NLRA). The NLRB's General Counsel found no wrongdoing. In the same month, however, the Associated Builders and Contractors of Massachusetts/Rhode Island, Inc. (ABC), an organization representing nonunion construction industry employers, filed suit against MWRA, Kaiser, and BCTC alleging, among other things, that parts of the negotiated agreement were preempted by the NLRA. Although the District Court found for the MWRA, the Court of Appeals came to the opposite conclusion.

The Supreme Court, in an unanimous decision, reversed the Court of Appeals and held that the parts of the negotiated agreement in question were not pre-empted by the NLRA. After concluding that the NLRA contains no express pre-emption provision, the Court examined the possibility that pre-emption might be inferred by looking at the totality of the laws and circumstances. The Court found no implied pre-emption and concluded that the negotiated agreement was a valid project labor agreement.

REDISTRICTING CASES

Three cases concerning voting districts were decided by the Court. In the case of *Shaw et al.* v. *Reno, Attorney General et al.*, [113 S.Ct. 2816 (1993)], when North Carolina gained a congressional seat as a result of the 1990 census, the General Assembly enacted a reapportionment plan that included one majority-black congressional district. After the Attorney General of the United States objected to the plan pursuant to the Voting Rights Act of 1965, the General Assembly passed new legislation creating a second majority-black district. A lawsuit by some North Carolina residents followed, alleging that the revised plan, which contains district boundary lines of dramatically irregular shape, constitutes an unconstitutional racial gerrymander. Although the lower courts upheld the plan for diverse reasons, in a 6 to 3 decision, the Supreme Court reversed and remanded. Reasoning, among other things, that a plan that expressly distinguishes among citizens on account of race must be narrowly tailored to further a compelling governmental interest, the Court returned the case to the lower court to determine whether the plan used racial classifications as a way of promoting equal opportunity without violating the Fourteenth Amendment's Equal Protection Clause.

An opposite claim initially was made in the case of *Growe, Secretary of State of Minnesota, et al.* v. *Emison et al.*, [113 S.Ct. 1075 (1993)]. In that case, new congressional districts drawn in response to the 1990 census were challenged in both state and federal courts as diluting the minority group vote and as being malapportioned in violation of the Voting Rights Act. The Minnesota state legislature reacted to the suits by adopting a new legislative districting plan, which contained numerous drafting errors. A second round of lawsuits was filed in federal court. In a long and convoluted process, the state and federal courts became entwined in a tug-of-war, with both courts taking action concerning the redistricting plan. Before the state court could issue a congressional plan, the federal court adopted its own plan and issued an order halting any further action by the state court. The federal court found, in effect, that the state court's legislative plan violated the Voting Rights Act because it did not contain a "super-majority minority" Senate district. The federal court's plan contained such a district, designed to create a majority composed of at least three separately identifiable minority groups.

The pivotal question addressed by the Supreme Court, then, was whether the federal court erred both in interfering with state court reapportionment efforts and in concluding that the state court's plan violated the Voting Rights Act. In a unanimous decision, the Court reversed the federal court, holding that it indeed acted improperly. Reasoning that states have the primary duty to perform such a task, the Court said that federal courts must defer to a state when there is evidence that adequate action was being taken. Further, the Court found no evidence of vote-fragmentation in the state court's plan.

In the third redistricting case of *Voinovich, Governor of Ohio, et al.* v. *Quilter, Speaker Pro Tempore of Ohio House of Representatives, et al.*, [113 S.Ct. 1149 (1993)], the main issue addressed by the Supreme Court was whether Ohio's creation of several legislative districts dominated by minority voters violated the Voting Rights Act and the Fourteenth and Fifteenth Amendments of the Constitution. Black voters maintained that by packing black voters in a few districts with a disproportionately large black voter population, the plan deprived them of a larger number of districts in which they would have been influential members. The state of Ohio justified much of its action by pointing to its constitutional policy in favor of preserving county boundaries.

In a unanimous decision, the Court reversed lower courts when it found no evidence of intentional discrimination. The Court held that the plaintiffs could prevail on a dilution claim only if they show that, under the totality of the circumstances, the state's apportionment scheme has the effect of diminishing or abridging the voting strength of the protected class. The case was remanded to the District Court for further fact finding and analysis.

SUMMARY

This chapter has presented highlights of 24 Supreme Court cases decided in 1992–1993. The rulings discussed here permeate many aspects of local government management: public health regulation, handicapped services, contracting, criminal justice services, corrections, the taxation of property, the administration of ballot requirements, housing, employee pay and benefit administration, and environmental cleanup. While case summaries are presented to inform local government managers and other interested readers about the most significant aspects of these very important cases, they do not constitute legal advice. Local government managers and officials who find themselves in similar situations are urged to seek the advice of a qualified attorney.

B 3

Congressional Actions Affecting Local Governments

Eugene P. Boyd
Congressional Research Service
The United States Library of Congress

Significant Legislation

Family and Medical Leave Act
National Voter Registration Act
Economic Stimulus Package
Empowerment Zones/Enterprise Communities
Disaster Relief
National Service Act
HUD Demonstration Act
Gun Control and Crime Bills
NAFTA

The first session of the 103d Congress adjourned on 18 November 1993 after passage of the Brady bill, a gun control measure that had been the target of a Senate Republican filibuster. The session was filled with legislative victories, compromises, and disappointments for local government officials. The Congress and the newly elected Clinton administration debated and acted on a number of issues affecting local governments, including disaster relief for communities devastated by flooding of the Mississippi River and its tributaries, a short-range economic stimulus proposal designed to jump start stagnant local economies, "ready-to-go" public works projects, family and medical leave, and empowerment zone legislation.

The first session of the 103d Congress convened on 5 January 1993 with the expectation that the legislative gridlock that had delayed action on a number of issues during the 102d Congress would dissipate with the Democratic party in control of both houses of Congress and the White House. However, the honeymoon was short-lived, as the administration sought a consensus on a number of issues, including America's roles in Somalia and Bosnia and gays in the military, and scrambled to limit the damage caused by the failure of several cabinet nominees to pay social security taxes for child care services.

On 17 February 1993, in his first address to the recently convened 103d Congress, President Bill Clinton outlined his administration's short- and long-term budget and economic agendas. The president's proposals were detailed in a document titled *A Vision of Change for America*, which was released the night of the address and included themes that were raised during the 1992 presidential campaign.

At the end of the first session of the 103d Congress, municipal governments could point to both large and small victories such as passage of the Brady hand gun control legislation, empowerment zones, national service, disaster relief, a homeless demonstration initiative, and the defeat of the BTU tax. However, Congress also continued a troubling and costly practice of enacting unfunded federally mandated legislation, such as motor voter and family and medical leave legislation. Municipal governments

were also disappointed by the demise of the administration's short-term economic stimulus plan, which would have given $9 billion to grant programs controlled by local governments to be used for employment-generating public works projects. The initiative was substantially scaled back, and, in the process, the image of one significant program, Community Development Block Grants, was tarnished. The program was labeled "pork barrel" spending during the Senate Republicans' successful filibuster of the initial stimulus proposal (H.R. 1335).

The second session of the 103d Congress may focus on a number of issues of particular interest to local governments, including community development banks, unfunded federal mandates, and government reorganization.

CHILDREN AND FAMILIES

The 103d Congress passed several significant measures that will help local governments address the needs and problems of children and families. Though the administration was unsuccessful in its attempt to increase fiscal year (FY) 1993 funding for child immunization programs and Head Start, Congress authorized such funding in the Omnibus Budget Reconciliation Act (OBRA) that was passed later in the year. Congress also authorized the following: (1) family and medical leave legislation; (2) family preservation legislation; (3) an increase in the earned income tax credit for poor working families as a part of OBRA; and (4) legislation requiring states to undertake criminal background checks for child care providers, including those employed in facilities supported or sponsored by local governments.

On 5 February 1993 President Clinton signed the Family and Medical Leave Act (P.L. 103-3), ending an eight-year legislative campaign by organized labor and women's groups. With the exception of hand gun control and enterprise zone legislation, which have been debated in Congress since 1986 and 1982, respectively, perhaps no other recent legislative proposal has endured as long a fight for passage. Much like federal enterprise zone legislation, while Congress and the administration debated, each year

states continued to pass and implement their versions of such legislation. At least eight states and three communities have passed parental and medical leave legislation.

Though federal family and medical leave legislation was passed during the 101st and 102d Congresses, the measures were vetoed by President Bush, who argued that they were intrusive and costly to business. Opponents of family leave cited a study funded by the Ford Foundation of the state experience with parental leave. The study found that one-quarter to one-third of the employers surveyed in Wisconsin, Minnesota, and Rhode Island experienced increased medical costs in implementing state-mandated parental leave.[1] Supporters of federal legislation have argued that the legislation at worst is a zero-sum gain for employers and at best may produce a net saving to business owners.[2]

Family and medical leave legislation (H.R. 2 and S. 5) and motor voter legislation were supported by the Clinton/Gore ticket during the presidential campaign of 1992.[3] These issues were placed on the fast track by the House and Senate Democratic leadership to give the president easy and early legislative victories in hopes of building legislative momentum. Within 31 days of convening, the 103d Congress passed and President Clinton signed the Family and Medical Leave Act.

P.L. 103-3 is the product of years of debate and compromise. It is substantially less liberal than the original bill, which was introduced in 1985. Under that bill employers with as few as five employees would have been required to allow up to 26 weeks of unpaid leave.

P.L. 103-3 requires employers, including local governments, with 50 or more employees to allow qualified employees to take up to 12 weeks of unpaid leave within any 12-month period for the birth or adoption of a child or for the serious illness of a child, spouse, parent, or the employee. To qualify for family or medical leave employees must have been employed by the local government for at least 12 months and must have worked at least 1,250 hours during that period. The law requires a local government to grant recurrent leave to employees for planned medical treatment for themselves or a

family member with a serious illness. The law (1) allows employees to substitute any accumulated annual or sick leave for which they would be paid for any of the 12 weeks of the unpaid family or medical leave mandated by this act; (2) limits spouses employed by the same local government or private employer to no more than 12 weeks of leave within any 12-month period to care for a newborn or adopted child or a family member; and (3) requires employees, whenever possible, to notify employers at least 30 days in advance of the date leave will be taken.

When leave is requested because of the employee's or a family member's ill health, the request must be supported by certification from the health care provider. The certification must include information about the nature of the illness, the date the illness commenced, and the projected duration of the illness. In addition, when an employee is requesting medical leave because of a health condition, he or she must also submit a doctor's statement that the employee is unable to perform his or her job because of that condition. When the leave is to be used to care for an ill family member, the act requires that the certification be accompanied by a statement that the employee is needed to care for the family member and include an estimate of the amount of time such care may be needed. In instances in which intermittent leave or leave on a reduced work schedule will be used for planned medical treatment, the certification document must include a treatment schedule, including the dates and duration of such treatments.

The local government or private employer may require a second opinion from another health care provider of its choosing if there is some question about the validity of the initial certification. The expense of the second opinion must be borne by the local government. If the first and second opinions conflict, a third and binding opinion may be sought from a doctor chosen by the employee and local government, but paid for by the local government. Neither the second nor third opinions may be rendered by a doctor who is regularly employed by the local government or private employer. In addition, employers may require an employee to submit to a reasonable recertification process during the leave period.

The law also provides employment protection to employees. An employee who exercises his or her right to family or medical leave is entitled to return to the position held prior to taking leave or an equivalent position with equivalent benefits, pay, status, and other terms and conditions. The law prohibits the use of coercion or intimidation by others to prevent an employee from exercising the right to family or medical leave. If the employer violates the rights of the employee to medical or family leave, the employer may be liable for money damages equal to wages, salaries, or other compensation denied by the employer's action and any actual monetary losses resulting directly from the violation. In addition, an employee may not lose any benefits accrued before taking

leave, and the employee may continue to be covered under the employer's medical insurance during the leave period. However, if an employee fails to return to work after leave has expired, the employer may be entitled to the repayment of health coverage premiums paid during the leave period. The act allows employers to exempt the highest paid 10 percent of its employees if the employer believes that granting such leave will cause him or her economic injury.

The act establishes a Commission on Leave, which is to be composed of 12 voting members, selected House and Senate leaders of the majority and minority parties, and 4 ex officio members (the secretaries of Health and Human Services, Commerce, and Labor, and the administrator of the Small Business Administration). The commission is charged with studying existing and proposed family and medical leave policies and their potential costs, benefits, and impact on productivity, job creation, and business growth. The commission is to submit a report to Congress within two years of its first meeting.

Later during the legislative year Congress passed the Omnibus Budget Reconciliation Act of 1993 (P.L. 103-66), authorizing the appropriation of $1 billion over five years for activities that will support the preservation of families and expand the Earned Income Tax Credit for the working poor. Family preservation funds are to be awarded to states, U.S. territories, and Indian tribes that submit detailed plans describing community-based activities that will be undertaken to support the welfare of children and families, strengthen the stability of families, enhance child development, and increase parents' confidence and competence in parenting skills. The act limits state administrative expenses to 10 percent of a grant allocation and prohibits grant funds from being used in place of other federal or nonfederal funds that support existing programs and activities. Funds are to be allocated to states based on the average monthly number of children receiving food stamp benefits.

The Earned Income Tax Credit (EITC) was championed by the Clinton administration as a means of helping the working poor out of poverty and as an important part of the administration's welfare reform efforts. The EITC, a refundable income tax credit available to working poor families with children, is the second largest source of cash aid to this group. Amendments to the EITC were included in OBRA, which was passed by the 103d Congress in early August 1993. OBRA extends EITC benefits to childless taxpayers between the ages of 24 and 65 who are not claimed as dependents by another taxpayer, increases the EITC for families with two or more children, and extends the income range in which the credit applies. The EITC is important to local governments because it may indirectly affect the need for housing, social welfare, and other services supplied by local governments by reducing poverty among the working poor.

NATIONAL VOTER REGISTRATION ACT

The National Voter Registration Act (P.L. 103-31) was signed by President Clinton on 20 May 1993. Similar legislation was passed by the 102d but vetoed by President Bush. The legislation, which was opposed by state and local governments, makes it easier to register to vote in elections for federal offices. The National Voter Registration Act, also known as the "motor voter" bill, mandates that states and local governments establish procedures to permit voter registration at the time an individual is applying for or renewing a driver's license, or by mail, or at designated federal, state, local, or nongovernmental office locations.[4] The new law permits, but does not mandate, a state or local government to use offices that provide public assistance, unemployment compensation, and services to persons with disabilities as voter registration locations. The act allows the removal of voters' names from the register only in the case of death, criminal conviction, mental incapacity, or change of residence outside the jurisdiction of the voter registrar. Voters who have changed addresses within the same jurisdiction may vote at either the old or new polling place and individuals may file suit against state or local officials for failure to comply with the act's provisions.

State and local officials opposed the bill as too costly and cited it as another example of an unfunded federal mandate. According to the Congressional Budget Office the act will cost states and local governments $20 to $25 million a year for the first five years plus an additional $60 million to $70 million in start-up costs to computerize local registration files. Opponents of the act argued that it places mandatory requirements on state and local governments without providing funds to meet the mandates, that the law will contribute to voter fraud, and that studies of state legislation indicate that the law will not increase voter participation appreciably. The National League of Cities and the National Association of Counties, in lobbying against the bill (H.R. 2), supported Senate amendments that would have changed voter registration from mandatory to voluntary and provided financial grants or reimbursement to cover implementation costs. The amendment, supported by Senate Republicans, was defeated. The act's requirements become effective on 1 January 1995.

ECONOMIC STIMULUS

Perhaps the most difficult legislative defeat for local governments during the first session of the 103d Congress was the downsizing of the administration's short-term economic stimulus package. As signed by the President on 2 July 1993, P.L. 103-50 appropriates about $3.5 billion in emergency supplemental funding for FY 1993. Approximately $2.5 billion will come from transfers and rescissions in existing programs, so net new funding is about $1 billion.

A substantial part of the new spending is slated to support government operations in Somalia and Kuwait.

P.L. 103-50 provides slightly more than $1.5 billion in domestic spending. Of the $1.126 billion available for community development assistance, $581.8 came from transfers and rescissions, and approximately $221.5 million is targeted for disaster assistance activities. P.L. 103-50 appropriates $220 million for a summer jobs program, which includes $50 million for a new Youth Fair Chance Program, $250 million for rural water and waste disposal loans, $35 million for rural water and waste disposal grants, and $150 million for Byrne Discretionary Grants to be used by states and local governments to hire additional police.

P.L. 103-50, dubbed the "grandson of stimulus," provides far less funding than envisioned in H.R. 1335, the original stimulus legislation. The proposals in H.R. 1335 allocated $16.3 billion in supplemental FY 1993 appropriations. According to the administration, these funds would have been used to create 500,000 jobs and provide a downpayment on the president's long-term economic investment strategy. Over $9 billion would have been allocated to states and local governments to be used primarily in public works, summer youth employment, and community development activities.

The president's proposal, which was supported by local officials, was passed by the House on 19 March 1993, about two weeks after it was introduced. The administration and the House and Senate Democratic leadership hoped to complete work on the stimulus package before the Easter recess scheduled for April 2, so that funds would be available in time to provide summer employment for youth and before the onset of cold weather and the end of the construction season in northern communities. However, consideration of the bill did not go as smoothly in the Senate. The bill was the target of amendments by conservative Democrats and a successful filibuster by Republicans who argued that the bill would not create the projected number of jobs, that the package represented spending above the targets set by the Budget Enforcement Act of 1990 and would add to the deficit, and that many of the spending proposals in the package would not create jobs. It would take another three months beyond the initial 2 April 1993 target date before Congress completed action on supplemental emergency funding for FY 1993. The measure that emerged—P.L. 103-50—bears scant resemblance to the ambitious plan put forth earlier in the legislative session.

TAX ISSUES

In passing OBRA 1993, P.L. 103-66, the 103d Congress enacted several tax-related provisions that will affect municipal governments. The law, which was signed by the president on 10 August 1993, was a major victory for the Clinton administration, culminating a national debate that began in February 1993 when the president announced his budget and economic agenda before a joint session of Congress. The act passed by narrow margins in both houses of Congress, with Vice President Gore casting the deciding vote in the Senate. One of the central issues in the debate over tax and spending priorities was the use of a broad-based energy tax to fund the president's long-term investment program and deficit reduction. The administration favored a so-called "BTU tax" that would have been tied to energy consumption. The BTU tax, which was included in the House-passed version of OBRA (H.R. 2264), would have generated $71 billion in revenues; $10 billion of that amount would have come from levies on state and local services. During conference consideration of H.R. 2264, the BTU tax was rejected in favor of a 4.3 cent increase in the fuel consumption tax, with an exemption for state and local governments.

OBRA includes provisions authorizing the creation of empowerment zones and enterprise communities and related tax provisions intended to revitalize economically distressed areas through the use of tax incentives to spur business investment. The act includes other tax-related provisions affecting municipal governments, including

1. permanent extension of local government authority to issue mortgage revenue bonds and small issue industrial development bonds;
2. permanent extension of the low-income housing tax credits;
3. extension of the limitation on the federal deductibility of state and local taxes; and
4. extension of the current 2.5 cent tax on gas through 1999, with the revenues raised to go to mass transit and highway trust fund accounts.

Several of these provisions were included in H.R. 11, which was passed in the final days of the 102d Congress but was vetoed by President Bush.

Other provisions of OBRA extend employer-sponsored education assistance and the targeted jobs tax credits through 1994 and also the Earned Income Tax Credit. Excluded from the final version of the act were provisions that would have preempted state and municipal authority to impose property taxes on FCC license holders or to annex or provide utility services in territories served by rural electric cooperatives.

The inclusion of provisions authorizing empowerment zones (EZs) and enterprise communities (ECs), which was embraced by conservatives and liberals, Democrats and Republicans, ends a decade-long effort to enact federal legislation in this area. Congress passed similar legislation last year in response to the Los Angeles riots, which was vetoed by President Bush.

At issue when EZs and ECs were taken up in the conference committee on OBRA were the number of each type of zone to be created and the trade-offs between enacting the administration's plan and reducing the budget deficit. The administration's proposal was introduced as a stand-alone legislative initiative on 5 May 1993, but was then rolled into the House's version of OBRA (H.R. 2264), which passed on 27 May 1993. EZs and ECs were not included in the Senate version of OBRA in the interest of deficit reduction. However, the measure survived attempts by Senate conservatives to eliminate it during conference consideration of OBRA and was included in the House and Senate conference report.

The act establishes a two-tiered level of assistance. Neighborhoods selected as EZs will receive the major portion of tax incentives and grants, while those designated as ECs will receive a less generous package. The act calls for the designation of 9 (6 urban and 3 rural) empowerment zones. At least 1 of the 6 urban zones must be located in an area with a population of 500,000 or less, one additional zone must be located in a two-state area; the population of this two-state zone must not exceed 50,000. In addition, 95 (65 urban and 30 rural) ECs will be selected. The Department of Housing and Urban Development (HUD) is charged with selecting urban EZs and ECs, while rural designations will be handled by the Department of Agriculture. Nominations are to be made jointly by state and local governments, and all EZs and ECs will be designated before 1996. Selected communities will retain their status as EZs or ECs for a period not to exceed ten years.

EZs and ECs may be multijurisdictional. In the case of urban areas, the designated area may not exceed 20 square miles and the population of the area may not exceed 200,000 persons or 10 percent of the population of the most populous city located in the nominated area. In rural areas, the designated area may not exceed 1,000 miles, and the population of the designated area may not exceed 30,000 persons. Areas seeking designation must meet certain poverty, unemployment, and general distress thresholds.

Communities and states seeking EZ or EC designations also must submit a strategic plan that (1) delineates a coordinated and integrated economic, physical, and social plan for the targeted area; (2) identifies state, municipal, and private resources, including financial resources, that will be used to implement the plan; (3) describes the roles of community and municipal institutions in developing and implementing the strategic plan; and (4) establishes the criteria to be used to measure the success of the strategic plan.

The law provides several tax credits to spur business development and expansion in EZs and ECs. Several of the tax credits, including an employer wage tax credit and Section 179 expensing, will be available for use in EZs only. In addition, the law sets aside $720 million of the $1 billion in new funding for social service block grants to states for use in EZs. Qualified zone businesses may receive a 20 percent wage credit against the first $15,000 in wages and training expenses for each qualified person employed in the zone. Qualified zone businesses will be allowed to increase expensing to the lesser of $20,000 or the value of the property subject to the expensing. Current Section 179 provisions allow non-zone businesses to deduct

the full cost of certain assets up to $10,000 in the year they are put into service, rather than depreciating them over several years.

ECs receive a more modest bundle of incentives and assistance. The 95 communities selected will be eligible to receive $280 million of the $1 billion in social service block grants. The grants are to be made to states and must be used to support activities aimed at (1) promoting self-sufficiency among zone residents; (2) assisting families and children in the targeted area through the provision of job training related to housing construction; (3) supporting after-school, community development, or economic development activities; and (4) funding drug and alcohol prevention and treatment programs. In addition, the act provides incentives that may be used by both ECs and EZs, including the issuance of up to $3 million in a new tax-exempt private activity bond to each qualified business and a 5 percent tax credit for cash contributions of up to $2 million annually to any of 20 HUD-designated community development corporations.

The EZ and EC provisions of P.L. 103-66 are expected to cost the federal government between $2.5 billion and $3.5 billion in foregone taxes plus an additional $1 billion in social service block grant assistance.

In addition to the creation of EZs and ECs, P.L. 103-66 includes two provisions that also represent a fundamental change in the use of the tax code as a social policy vehicle, namely the increase in the EITC and the creation of the Family Preservation Act. These three provisions mark significant efforts by the federal government to improve the lives of the poor.

DISASTER RELIEF

On 6 August 1993, one month after completing action on an FY 1993 emergency supplemental appropriations measure (P.L. 103-50), the 103d Congress completed action on a second emergency supplemental appropriations bill (H.R. 2667). The bill, which was signed by the president on 12 August 1993 as P.L. 103-75, appropriates $6.2 billion in disaster relief assistance to victims of the Midwest floods of 1993. Approximately 11 percent ($665.4 million) of the funds appropriated are targeted to community development programs, with 62 percent ($400 million) of this amount allocated to community development block grants and economic development administration activities.

In addition, one day before action was completed on H.R. 2667, the Senate passed legislation designed to give lending institutions and bank regulatory agencies greater flexibility in helping meet the credit needs in areas damaged by the flooding of the Mississippi and its tributaries. The legislation, the Depository Institutions Disaster Relief Act of 1993 (P.L. 103-76), was signed by the president on 12 August 1993. The act allows the Federal Reserve Board to grant exceptions to provisions of the Truth in Lending Act in areas damaged by flooding if such areas have been declared disaster areas by

the president and if the board determines that the exception can reasonably be expected to alleviate hardships caused by the flooding and that such alleviation outweighs possible adverse effects. The act gives the board six months from the date of enactment of P.L. 103-76 to grant such exceptions and allows the exceptions to remain in place until 1 October 1994.

NATIONAL SERVICE ACT

On 1 March 1993 President Clinton, in a speech at Rutgers University, outlined his national service proposal in broad terms. The idea of providing educational funds in return for community service was one of the cornerstones of his campaign. National service would allow participants to receive financial support for college or job training by working in projects sponsored by states, local governments, or nonprofit organizations, including universities. Approved projects would be designed to address unmet educational, environmental, human, and public safety needs. All those who wished to participate could do so, and participants could earn up to $10,000 annually in education benefits. As proposed by the administration, national service would provide program participants with financial assistance for education and job training while helping to rebuild neighborhoods, improve lives, and enhance the nation's long-term economic prospects. In his address at Rutgers, President Clinton equated the concept of national service with the GI bill passed shortly after World War II and generally credited with facilitating a postwar education boom that helped sustain the country's economic dominance in the postwar era.

Opponents of national service argued against universal coverage and in favor of means-tested eligibility. In addition, opponents contended that national service would reduce the amount of funds available for other grant programs, such as Pell Grants, that help students pay for college or trade schools.

Nearly 60 days after the Rutgers speech, the Clinton administration's national service proposal was introduced in the House (H.R. 2010) and the Senate (S. 919). Despite an attempted filibuster by Senate Republicans, the conference report authorizing national service legislation passed the Senate on 6 September 1993 and was signed by President Clinton on 21 September as the National and Community Service Act of 1993 (P.L. 103-82). The act creates a National Service Trust Program and establishes the Corporation for National and Community Service (CNCS). The CNCS is charged with distributing funds to states, local governments, and nonprofit sponsors of approved national service programs; approving state, local government, and nonprofit national service programs; and overseeing, monitoring, and evaluating approved programs. Approved programs must address critical educational, human, public safety, or environmental needs of an area; must not involve the dislocation of existing workers; and should provide individuals participating in such

programs with the training necessary to carry out their responsibilities. Recipients may use funds for the following types of activities:

1. community corps, and year-round or summer youth corps;
2. campus-based programs that involve college and university students;
3. preprofessional training programs in which students agree to participate in a national service program upon graduation;
4. a professional corps program that recruits and places participants with certain skills or professional backgrounds in communities with an inadequate number of such professionals;
5. skill development for disadvantaged youth and programs to meet low-income housing and neighborhood development needs of low-income areas; and
6. community service programs designed to meet needs of rural communities.

CNCS funds may be used to cover the costs of planning or operating national service programs carried out by qualified applicants or to expand or replicate existing programs. Planning grants will be limited to one year, while operational assistance may be made available for up to three years.

The VA-HUD Independent Agencies Appropriations Act (P.L. 103-137) appropriated $370 million to carry out national service activities in FY 1994. P.L. 103-82 provides for the following distribution of funds: (1) 33.5 percent to states with approved national service plans based on the population of the state relative to all states with approved plans (the District of Columbia and Puerto Rico are included in the definition of state); (2) 33.5 percent on a competitive basis to states; (3) 1 percent to U.S. territories and possessions; (4) 1 percent to Indian tribes; and (5) such sums as the CNCS deems necessary to provide technical assistance, disaster services (not to exceed $10 million), challenge grants, or to assist in the establishment of state commissions on national and community service. CNCS and other federal funds used to establish state commissions may not exceed 85 percent of the initial year's operation cost of such a commission and may not exceed 50 percent of the cost by a state's fifth year of operation. The remaining funds shall be allocated by the CNCS to federal agencies, local governments, Indian tribes, and nonprofit organizations on a competitive basis. Federal agencies may receive no more than one-third of the funds made available under a competitive grant category.

Applicants eligible to receive assistance from the CNCS, including local governments, must submit an application that describes (1) the type of activities that will be undertaken; (2) other sources of funds that will be used in conjunction with CNCS funds; (3) how the projects to be conducted will address unmet needs of the targeted community; (4) the plan to be used to recruit participants, including disabled and economically disadvantaged persons; (5) how proposed projects build on existing programs; (6)

how proposed projects build an ethic of civil responsibility and leadership in project participants; (7) how projects conform to national service priorities established by the CNCS; (8) the applicant's past experience in operating comparable programs; and (9) the number and type of proposed positions in which participants will receive national service education awards, the jobs in which participants will be placed, and the tasks they will perform.

Individuals selected to participate in national service projects intended to address unmet needs of selected areas must be at less 17 years of age. Participants will be selected on a non-discriminatory and nonpolitical basis. Participants in national service projects, including those administered by local governments, are eligible to receive health care, child care allowances, stipends, and education awards. CNCS grants may cover 85 percent of the health care costs, 100 percent of the child care allowance, 85 percent of the stipend, up to the VISTA subsistence allowance, which is based on the minimum wage, and an education award of up to $4,725 for one year of full-time participation in a national service project. Participants have up to seven years to use their education award.

HUD DEMONSTRATION ACT

On 6 October 1993 the 103d Congress completed action on H.R. 2517, the HUD Demonstration Act of 1993, a little-noticed act that authorizes $200 million to address the problems associated with homelessness. Signed by the president on 12 October 1993, P.L. 103-120 authorizes the Department of Housing and Urban Development (HUD) to develop, in cooperation with states, local governments, and nonprofit organizations, innovative and comprehensive strategies for assisting homeless individuals and families. Funds may be awarded directly to states, municipal governments, or nonprofit organizations. In awarding funds to states and local governments HUD is to consider the extent of homelessness in the jurisdiction, the extent to which existing public and private services for the homeless would benefit from additional resources; the demonstrated ability of the state or local government grantee to work with HUD, nonprofits, and community residents in designing and implementing a homeless initiative; and the level of financial and other resource commitments from nongovernmental sources. In addition, HUD is to seek geographic diversity in awarding the grants.

Recipients of the funds must develop a comprehensive strategy to be designed in cooperation with HUD, other governmental entities, nonprofit organizations, foundations, and the community. The elements of the proposed plan should (1) identify the specific projects and activities to be carried out and specify activities to be funded by the grants provided under this act; (2) identify other sources of funds that will be used to implement a comprehensive homeless assistance strategy; and (3) include a statement of cooperation from entities that will be participating in developing and implementing a strategy. The act also provides grants to states, local governments, and nonprofit organizations to fund innovative projects. These projects should serve as model programs that can be replicated in other jurisdictions.

The act also authorizes funding for other programs, including $165 million to help poor families move to areas of greater economic opportunity and away from high crime and poverty areas, and $25 million in matching grants to help community development corporations (CDCs) and community housing development organizations (CHDOs) with community development and housing projects. Funds may be used for training and education to enhance the technical and administrative capabilities of CDCs and CHDOs, and for loans, grants, and predevelopment assistance to implement community development and affordable housing activities benefiting low-income persons. CDCs and CHDOs that receive assistance under this part must provide a match from private sources equal to three times the amount received. The act establishes a demonstration program using project-based Section 8 assistance to attract pension funds and extends the statute authorizing the National Commission on Manufactured Housing through FY 1994.

GUN CONTROL AND CRIME

During the final days of the first session of the 103d Congress, the House and Senate passed the Brady handgun control bill, which was supported by organizations, such as the National League of Cities, representing municipal governments. After eight years of debate Congress passed P.L. 103-159, instituting a five-day waiting period and criminal background checks for persons seeking to purchase a handgun. In an emotional signing ceremony at the White House in November 1993, President Clinton signed the measure in the presence of the bill's namesake, Jim Brady, who was injured in the assassination attempt on President Reagan in March 1981.

In September 1993, two months before the passing of handgun control legislation, the Democratic chairmen of the House and Senate Judiciary committees introduced comprehensive anti-crime legislation. Absent from the Senate bill (S. 1488), but included in the House bill (H.R. 3131), was the handgun control measure.

The Senate anti-crime bill, which was redrafted as S. 1607 and amended during floor debate, includes provisions that would authorize community policing programs and the hiring of 100,000 state and local police officers; promote alternative sentencing such as boot camps for nonviolent criminals and youths; support innovative juvenile delinquency prevention programs and drug and gang prevention programs; fund jail construction; support state and local government efforts to combat domestic violence and violence against women; and ban the production, transfer, and sale of assault weapons and large-capacity ammunition feeding devices. The total funding authorization level is $22.3 billion, which doubles the amount requested by the administration and would be made available through the Violent Crime Reduction Trust Fund established by the bill. The increase in spending for anti-crime efforts would have to be offset by reductions in other discretionary programs, such as transportation, housing, or community development, to comply with deficit reduction targets. The Senate completed action and passed its version of a comprehensive anti-crime bill on 19 November 1993.

In an effort to expedite consideration of non-controversial anti-crime legislation, the House divided its original anti-crime bill, H.R. 3131, into six separate measures (H.R. 3350—H.R. 3355). During the last week of October 1993, the House approve four of the five measures. One measure (H.R. 3355) would provide $3.5 billion to hire 50,000 policemen for community policing activities. Funds could also be used for proactive crime prevention and intervention efforts. Funds would be awarded to state and local governments or local government consortiums representing populations in excess of 100,000 persons. Another bill, H.R. 3354, would provide $100 million for substance abuse treatment for inmates in state and local correctional facilities. The House also passed H.R. 3353, which would provide $100 million to reduce drug and other criminal activity by juvenile gangs.

The House and Senate approaches in passing anti-crime legislation have resulted in a legislative mix-and-match that will have to be resolved during the second session of the 103d Congress if anti-crime legislation is to be passed. The House's piecemeal approach to crime legislation coupled with the Senate's comprehensive effort makes the convening of a conference unlikely until the House completes action on a number of germane legislative proposals.

OTHER LEGISLATIVE PROPOSALS

The House and Senate are poised to complete action on a number of legislative issues that affect municipal governments during the second session of the 103d Congress. Among these are the administration's health care reform proposal, resolution of Senate and House anti-crime measures, reauthorization of housing and community development programs, unfunded federal mandates, community development banking legislation, welfare reform, and the administration's proposal to reinvent government. These and other measures will be considered within a budget and deficit reduction context that will essentially freeze discretionary spending, pitting programs and national priorities against each other for limited resources.

NAFTA

On 17 December 1992 the North American Free Trade Agreement (NAFTA) was signed by President Bush and the leaders of Canada and Mexico. Nearly a year later Congress passed and

President Clinton signed P.L. 103–182, which implements NAFTA. Unlike a treaty, which requires two-thirds of the Senate to vote for passage before it may be implemented, legislation implementing a trade agreement must pass both houses of Congress by simple majorities before it may be implemented. NAFTA and its supplemental agreements on labor, the environment, and import surges are intended to remove trade barriers between Canada, Mexico, and the United States and lead to economic expansion. NAFTA, which became effective 1 January 1994, includes provisions that eliminate all tariffs between Canada, Mexico and the United States within 15 years, eliminate barriers and discrimination in the trade of services, eliminate many restrictions on investment between the three countries, that institute special procedures to investigate unfair trade practices including antidumping matters, and that address issues related to intellectual property rights. Though the agreement involved U.S. trade with Canada and Mexico, the principle focus of congressional debate was on the impact of the agreement on trade with Mexico.

The congressional debate over ratification of NAFTA cast traditional political allies as adversaries. NAFTA, which was supported by president Clinton, a Democrat, was opposed by traditional Democratic allies such as labor, and a significant number of congressional Democrats, including those in leadership positions. The Administration achieved its NAFTA victory with significant support from congressional Republicans who voted to ratify the agreement based on the party's long standing support of free trade. Opponents of NAFTA argued that the agreement will result in lower U.S. wages and a loss of U.S. jobs to Mexico and will weaken some local economies as jobs and factories are relocated to Mexico, with its lower wages and its poor enforcement of environmental laws.

Supporters of NAFTA acknowledge that the agreement may result in the loss of jobs in some sectors of the economy such as apparel, but they counter that the agreement will result in jobs gains in agriculture, machinery, and metal products sectors. The majority of studies project that the agreement will result in a positive but negligible net increase in U.S. employment in the short term. For instance, a 1993 study by the Institute for International Economics projects that NAFTA could result in a net gain of 170,000 jobs by 1995. It should be noted that the extent of employment gains or losses resulting from U.S. companies moving to or expanding their operations in Mexico is dependent on several factors including U.S./Mexican wage differentials (wages in Mexico average one/seventh the wages paid U.S. workers). Supporters of NAFTA also argue that by creating jobs in Mexico the agreement will slow the rate of illegal immigration into the U.S.

---

[1]Charles Dervarics, ''Family Leave: Is It Good Business?'' *State Legislatures*, August 1991:31.

[2]Ibid; 33.

[3]Governor Bill Clinton and Senator Al Gore, ''Children,'' *Putting People First: How We Can All Change America.* (Time Books, 1992): 51.

[4]Twenty-seven states have some form motor voter registration; twenty-eight states allow people to register by mail.

C Staffing and Compensation

Salaries of Municipal Officials, 1993

Evelina R. Moulder
International City/County Management Association

Findings

For each position covered in the survey, the average salary is highest in the West region.

The average salary of city managers in central cities is 26% higher than the average salary for managers in suburban jurisdictions.

For virtually every position covered in this article, the average salary decreases as population size decreases.

It is often said that local governments experience the fluctuations in the economy a year or two after the private sector does. Home sales, new home construction, and corporate profits are on the rise, which have a positive effect on local revenues, but the salaries of local government managers and department heads have not yet benefited from the improved economy.

METHODOLOGY

The data in this article are based on the results of ICMA's annual salary survey, which was mailed in the summer of 1993 to all cities with populations of 2,500 and over and to all ICMA-recognized cities with populations under 2,500.[1] Of the 7,200 cities that received surveys, 4,570 responded, for a survey response rate of 63.5% (Table 1/1).

SALARY TRENDS

Numerous factors contribute to variations in salary among local government management personnel in similar positions. A city with a high number of employees, an airport, a sea port, a university, and several chemical manufacturing plants will need top level staff with particular expertise: The city will be willing to offer a higher salary to attract the talents required. As with positions in the private sector and in federal and state government, experience and education are also considered in determining salaries.

Table 1/2 shows the average annual salary for each of 19 municipal positions, as well as percentage changes over the course of six years. (Only jurisdictions that responded to each survey conducted in the six years from 1988 to 1993 are included in the table.) A general downward trend emerges when the percentage increases for each positions are examined from year to year. Over the six-year period, the average salary increase for the position of assistant city manager/assistant CAO shows a drop of four percentage points from the high (8%) increase in average salary from 1988 to 1989 and

the low (4%) increase from 1992 to 1993. From 1988 to 1993, however, the average salaries for assistant city managers show the highest percentage of increase (32%) among all positions. Of the nineteen positions, only two—superintendent of parks and chief appointed administrator—show a higher percentage of increase in average salary in 1993 than they did in 1992. For all other positions, the percentage of increase remained the same or decreased.

Table 1/1 SURVEY RESPONSE

	No. cities[1] surveyed (A)	No. cities responding No.	No. cities responding % of (A)
Total, all cities	7,200	4,570	63.5
Population group			
Over 1,000,000	8	5	62.5
500,000–1,000,000	17	13	76.5
250,000–499,999	39	26	66.7
100,000–249,999	131	94	71.8
50,000–99,999	338	240	71.0
25,000–49,999	679	507	74.7
10,000–24,999	1,598	1,082	67.7
5,000–9,999	1,803	1,146	63.6
2,500–4,999	1,995	1,129	56.6
Under 2,500	592	328	55.4
Geographic region[2]			
Northeast	1,984	1,082	54.5
North Central	2,091	1,443	69.0
South	2,099	1,278	60.9
West	1,026	767	74.8
Geographic division[3]			
New England	797	455	57.1
Mid-Atlantic	1,187	627	52.8
East North Central	1,360	919	67.6
West North Central	731	524	71.7
South Atlantic	883	601	68.1
East South Central	470	259	55.1
West South Central	746	418	56.0
Mountain	371	252	67.9
Pacific Coast	655	515	78.6
Metro status[4]			
Central	516	371	71.9
Suburban	3,860	2,459	63.7
Independent	2,824	1,740	61.6
Form of government[5]			
Mayor-council	3,562	1,984	55.7
Council-manager	2,992	2,211	73.9
Commission	162	99	61.1
Town meeting	412	233	56.6
Rep. town meeting	72	43	59.7

POPULATION GROUP

Population is clearly a factor in average salaries across the Untied States. For virtually every position shown in this article, the average salary decreases as population size decreases. With few exceptions, the decrease in average salary is a steady progression. The exceptions occur among responding cities with populations from 500,000 to 1 million, which show slightly lower

[1]The term *cities* is used in this and the following tables to refer to cities, villages, towns, townships, and boroughs.

[2]*Geographic regions: Northeast*—the New England and Mid-Atlantic Divisions, which include the states of Connecticut, Maine, Massachusetts, New Hampshire, New Jersey, New York, Pennsylvania, Rhode Island, and Vermont; *North Central*—the East and West North Central Divisions, which include the states of Illinois, Indiana, Iowa, Kansas, Michigan, Minnesota, Missouri, Nebraska, North Dakota, Ohio, South Dakota, and Wisconsin; *South*—the South Atlantic and the East and West South Central Divisions, which include the states of Alabama, Arkansas, Delaware, Florida, Georgia, Kentucky, Louisiana, Maryland, Mississippi, North Carolina, Oklahoma, South Carolina, Tennessee, Texas, Virginia, and West Virginia, plus the District of Columbia; *West*—the Mountain and Pacific Coast Divisions, which include the states of Alaska, Arizona, California, Colorado, Hawaii, Idaho, Montana, Nevada, New Mexico, Oregon, Utah, Washington, and Wyoming.

[3]*Geographic divisions: New England*—the states of Connecticut, Maine, Massachusetts, New Hampshire, Rhode Island, and Vermont; *Mid-Atlantic*—the states of New Jersey, New York, and Pennsylvania; *East North Central*—the states of Illinois, Indiana, Michigan, Ohio, and Wisconsin; *West North Central*—the states of Iowa, Kansas, Minnesota, Missouri, Nebraska, North Dakota, and South Dakota; *South Atlantic*—the states of Delaware, Florida, Georgia, Maryland, North Carolina, South Carolina, Virginia, and West Virginia, plus the District of Columbia; *East South Central*—the states of Alabama, Kentucky, Mississippi, and Tennessee; *West South Central*—the states of Arkansas, Louisiana, Oklahoma, and Texas; *Mountain*—the states of Arizona, Colorado, Idaho, Montana, Nevada, New Mexico, Utah, and Wyoming; *Pacific Coast*—the states of Alaska, California, Hawaii, Oregon, and Washington.

[4]*Metro status: Central*—the city(ies) appearing in the metropolitan statistical area (MSA) title; *Suburban*—the city(ies) located with an MSA; *Independent*—the city(ies) not located within an MSA.

[5]*Form of government: Mayor-council*—an elected council serves as the legislative body with a separately elected head of government; *Council-manager*—the mayor and council make policy and an appointed administrator is responsible for the administration of the city; *Commission*—a board of elected commissioners serves as the legislative body and each commissioner is responsible for administration of one or more departments; *Town meeting*—qualified voters meet to make basic policy and choose a board of selectmen to carry out the policy; *Representative town meeting*—representatives selected by citizens vote at meetings, which may be attended by all town citizens.

Table 1/2   AVERAGE SALARIES OF MUNICIPAL OFFICIALS

Title	No. of cities included[1]	1988 ($)	1989 ($)	Increase from 1988 (%)	1990 ($)	Increase from 1989 (%)	1991 ($)	Increase from 1990 (%)	1992 ($)	Increase from 1991 (%)	1993 ($)	Increase from 1992 (%)
Mayor	1,232	8,011	8,432	5	9,001	7	9,340	4	9,790	5	10,120	3
City manager	911	51,628	54,778	6	58,183	6	60,937	5	63,245	4	65,073	3
Chief apptd. administrator/CAO	409	41,751	44,141	6	46,866	6	49,719	6	51,683	4	54,022	5
Asst. city mgr./asst. CAO	264	42,753	46,275	8	49,550	7	51,999	5	54,287	4	56,315	4
City clerk	1,079	28,005	29,597	6	31,307	6	32,667	4	33,984	4	35,261	4
Chief financial officer	585	42,758	45,445	6	48,395	6	50,656	5	52,683	4	54,470	3
Treasurer	75	30,729	32,749	7	33,659	3	35,374	5	37,084	5	39,089	5
Director of public works	930	39,030	41,180	6	43,580	6	45,826	5	47,811	4	49,488	4
Engineer	265	43,820	46,408	6	49,242	6	51,948	5	53,985	4	55,546	3
Police chief	1,223	38,345	40,402	5	42,885	6	44,880	5	46,998	5	48,602	3
Fire chief	626	38,618	40,900	6	43,450	6	45,542	5	47,755	5	49,378	3
Planning director	367	41,546	43,879	6	46,590	6	49,221	6	51,054	4	52,772	3
Personnel director	317	39,334	41,767	6	44,517	7	47,069	6	49,152	4	51,003	4
Director of parks/recreation	344	39,421	41,714	6	44,229	6	46,498	5	48,743	5	50,164	3
Superintendent of parks	186	32,275	33,967	5	35,698	5	37,789	6	38,906	3	40,412	4
Director of recreation	119	31,600	33,079	5	35,495	7	37,406	5	39,144	5	40,389	3
Librarian	374	31,607	33,501	6	35,619	6	37,326	5	38,840	4	40,497	4
Director of info. services/data proc.	131	41,196	43,545	6	46,374	6	48,666	5	51,041	5	52,611	3
Purchasing director	204	31,987	33,771	6	36,028	7	37,640	4	39,693	5	40,802	3

[1]This table is based on salary data for each of the six years 1988 to 1993. Number of cities included are those that have consistently reported data for the position indicated for each of the six years.

Table 1/3   VARIATION IN SALARIES BY POPULATION SIZE

Population group	Public works director		Police chief		Chief financal officer	
	No. reporting	Average salary ($)	No. reporting	Average salary ($)	No. reporting	Average salary ($)
Over 1,000,000	4	91,426	5	102,154	4	92,614
100,000–249,999	79	76,196	81	78,802	88	75,264
5,000–9,999	714	39,490	820	41,599	442	37,832

average salaries than do the jurisdictions in the population group from 250,000 to 499,999. Table 1/3 shows the variation in salaries among population groups for three positions chosen randomly. The average salary for each position in the population group of over 1 million is more than double the average salary for the same position in jurisdictions with populations from 5,000 to 9,999. Population size alone is not the determinant of salary, but population and the complexity of service delivery, the types of services delivered, and the many competing needs of a large population contribute to higher salaries for upper management positions in large cities.

GEOGRAPHIC REGION

Region is also a factor in salary, although the patterns are not so clear cut. The cost of living is reported to be highest on the West Coast; housing costs are definitely highest. For each of the 20 positions covered, the average salary is highest in the West region. For 16 of the 20 positions, the lowest average salary is in the South region (not shown).

The most pronounced difference is in the average salary for the position of assistant city manager/CAO. The Northeast region shows the lowest average salary ($37,785); the highest salary is in the West ($69,212). The $31,427 difference is 83% of the average salary for the assistant manager in the Northeast. This is an

extreme example. For the other positions, the difference between the lowest and highest average salary among the regions is anywhere from 20% to 50% of the lowest salary.

One might speculate that salaries are higher in the West region because it has more cities with high populations than the other regions have. This is not the case: The West region has 29 cities with populations of 250,000 and above; the South has 35 cities of that size; the North Central region, 22; and the Northeast region, 11. (See Table 2 in "Inside the Year Book.") The South has more of the larger cities and the lowest average salaries in general for these positions.

METRO STATUS

When compared with the average salaries of suburban and independent jurisdictions, central city salaries have long been the highest. Central cities are the core cities of a Metropolitan Statistical Area (MSA) and must have a population of at least 25,000 and meet certain employment requirements in order to be so classified.[2] Because central cities by definition employ at least 50% of their residents and because there must be at least 75 jobs per 100 residents of central cities, they have to provide services to residential and business customers. The vast array of services that these cities provide combined with the management issues that accompany a diverse constituency require management staff of

the highest caliber. Salary affects the ability of a local government to attract such expertise.

When the position of mayor is excluded from the comparisons (because the numbers are skewed), the greatest disparity in dollars between the average salary for position in a central city and in a suburban jurisdiction is found in the city manager position ($18,049). The average salary of the manager of the central city is 26% higher than the suburban manager's average salary. The least difference is in the average salary for an engineer, which is greater by $3,508 in central cities than in suburban jurisdictions.

FORM OF GOVERNMENT

In general, salaries are higher for positions in council-manager and representative town meeting forms of government. In both of these forms, a high level of responsibility and authority is placed on the manager and department heads. The exception is for the position of mayor, which commands a much higher salary in mayor-council and commission governments.

SUMMARY

In general, the percentage gains in local appointed officials' salaries have decreased in the last several years. As the economy continues to improve, salaries of local officials should reflect the overall economic picture.

The following listing (Table 1/4) presents the average salaries of municipal officials by population group, geographic region, form of government, and metro status.

---

[1]Governments recognized by ICMA have the council-manager form of government or provide for a general management position.

[2]Suburban cities are incorporated jurisdictions within an MSA that do not meet the criteria for central city classification. Independent cities are incorporated places not located in an MSA.

Table 1/4 SALARIES OF MUNICIPAL OFFICIALS: 1 JULY 1993

Salary data for the 21 municipal positions in this table are based on information reported by municipal officials as of 1 July 1993. Data are reported by position title only. Although job responsibilities are generally similar, the titles do not necessarily indicate identical duties and responsibilities.

For the position of city manager, data are shown for only those municipalities recognized by ICMA as having the council-manager form of government. For the position of chief administrative officer (CAO), data are shown for all other reporting municipalities.

Except for the position of mayor, which does include part-time salaries, this table excludes

(1) salaries of part-time officials, (2) salaries for vacant positions, (3) salaries of acting officials, (4) those paid in whole or in part by fees, and (5) all salaries below $8,000. All salaries below $100 for the position of mayor are also excluded. Salaries are presented by ten population groups and are further classified by geographic region, city type, and form of government. Cities under 2,500 population include only cities recognized by ICMA as providing for a position of overall professional management or as having the council-manager form of government.

Classifications having fewer than three cities reporting are excluded because meaningful statistics cannot be computed. Consequently the

number reporting in some subcategories does not always equal the total reporting. Quartiles are not shown when only three cities reported. The median represents either the value of the middle observation or, when there is an even number of observations, the mean of the two middle observations. The first and third quartile observations represent the value of the observation below which 25% and 75% of the number of observations fall, respectively, and are calculated around the median, such that an equal number of observations fall between the median and first quartile and the median and the third quartile.

| Title of official | No. cities reporting | Distribution of 1993 salaries | | | | Title of official | No. cities reporting | Distribution of 1993 salaries | | | |
		Mean ($)	First quartile ($)	Median ($)	Third quartile ($)			Mean ($)	First quartile ($)	Median ($)	Third quartile ($)
All cities						**All cities continued**					
Mayor						City type					
Total	3,865	10,467	2,000	4,200	9,241	Central	166	67,728	54,172	66,333	81,422
Geographic region						Suburban	647	51,510	36,000	47,412	62,734
Northeast	915	10,684	1,450	2,750	7,000	Independent	252	36,215	25,200	36,115	43,675
North Central	1,332	10,286	2,100	4,539	9,000	Form of government					
South	1,024	11,390	2,400	5,000	12,000	Mayor-council	210	38,019	24,277	35,184	47,446
West	594	8,947	3,000	4,800	8,000	Council-manager	809	54,589	38,837	50,012	68,004
City type						Commission	9	41,926	23,393	33,750	51,582
Central	332	33,633	7,200	24,018	53,760	Town meeting	31	29,304	19,658	29,782	35,000
Suburban	2,025	8,969	2,200	4,200	7,937	Rep. town meeting	6	43,944	32,692	48,650	53,646
Independent	1,508	7,379	1,500	3,600	7,200	**City clerk**					
Form of government						Total	3,351	32,932	24,000	30,878	39,936
Mayor-council	1,832	15,301	3,000	6,000	18,000	Geographic region					
Council-manager	1,698	5,150	3,600	6,000	6,000	Northeast	772	32,220	23,232	31,739	40,177
Commission	92	12,370	3,000	4,800	11,193	North Central	1,002	31,198	23,982	29,880	37,000
Town meeting	203	11,147	1,000	2,000	6,550	South	1,006	30,431	22,742	28,417	35,829
Rep. town meeting	40	6,936	1,500	2,200	3,100	West	571	41,342	29,820	38,904	51,840
City manager						City type					
Total	1,964	63,865	47,154	60,634	78,000	Central	314	44,527	33,900	41,749	53,976
Geographic region						Suburban	1,709	34,791	25,750	33,259	42,122
Northeast	342	54,098	40,537	51,409	68,000	Independent	1,328	27,798	21,424	26,705	32,865
North Central	471	59,844	46,500	57,050	72,000	Form of government					
South	650	59,859	45,900	57,243	72,339	Mayor-council	1,444	30,510	22,156	28,718	36,902
West	501	79,508	60,600	78,500	96,043	Council-manager	1,607	35,784	26,205	33,150	43,149
City type						Commission	73	33,799	25,098	31,500	41,600
Central	198	86,970	73,793	84,409	98,324	Town meeting	188	26,342	19,448	26,956	32,432
Suburban	1,032	68,921	52,530	67,000	83,686	Rep. town meeting	39	35,227	29,000	35,000	43,514
Independent	734	50,523	40,697	49,476	60,500	**Chief financial officer**					
Form of government						Total	2,068	48,616	35,496	46,357	60,024
Mayor-council	98	58,951	45,900	54,119	70,207	Geographic region					
Council-manager	1,795	64,920	48,000	61,651	79,000	Northeast	485	45,280	33,408	44,382	57,255
Commission	8	41,526	36,950	38,425	46,500	North Central	524	46,205	35,230	44,831	57,200
Town meeting	56	41,205	27,000	38,450	53,508	South	589	45,242	33,322	42,820	55,661
Rep. town meeting	7	68,788	65,526	70,000	73,359	West	470	58,973	42,882	58,000	74,572
Chief appointed administrator						City type					
Total	1,485	48,168	35,457	46,300	58,886	Central	320	62,616	51,209	61,307	74,110
Geographic region						Suburban	1,164	49,847	36,805	48,445	61,446
Northeast	454	49,263	35,143	48,358	61,000	Independent	584	38,490	29,907	37,880	45,828
North Central	543	48,002	36,615	46,350	57,757	Form of government					
South	323	43,779	31,711	40,000	52,205	Mayor-council	660	44,437	32,330	42,857	54,391
West	165	54,292	42,270	52,500	65,544	Council-manager	1,256	51,805	38,237	50,503	63,458
City type						Commission	38	39,701	24,172	34,018	52,722
Central	92	65,307	49,843	62,743	78,488	Town meeting	91	38,269	27,852	37,960	47,199
Suburban	879	50,397	37,640	49,600	62,000	Rep. town meeting	23	50,004	38,000	46,460	57,864
Independent	514	41,288	31,837	40,041	49,200	**Director of economic development**					
Form of government						Total	746	48,381	35,244	45,726	59,647
Mayor-council	1,007	48,003	35,000	46,000	59,512	Geographic region					
Council-manager	310	50,347	37,565	48,629	60,000	Northeast	128	44,662	35,030	43,875	52,100
Commission	39	45,598	35,265	42,093	53,000	North Central	263	42,888	31,799	40,872	52,908
Town meeting	101	43,415	32,916	42,000	51,975	South	182	47,005	34,156	45,892	57,312
Rep. town meeting	28	50,679	35,000	51,892	63,278	West	173	60,932	45,450	60,000	75,000
Asst. city mgr./asst. CAO						City type					
Total	1,065	50,419	35,000	46,500	63,134	Central	189	56,996	44,183	56,468	67,267
Geographic region						Suburban	337	51,257	38,522	48,500	61,404
Northeast	192	37,785	27,780	35,430	44,779	Independent	220	36,576	27,853	36,396	42,471
North Central	295	45,358	35,339	45,245	54,210	Form of government					
South	308	46,667	32,881	43,255	57,469	Mayor-council	273	43,593	32,160	41,267	52,590
West	270	69,212	52,008	69,277	87,925						

Table 1/4   SALARIES OF MUNICIPAL OFFICIALS: 1 JULY 1993
continued

Title of official	No. cities reporting	Distribution of 1993 salaries			
		Mean ($)	First quartile ($)	Median ($)	Third quartile ($)
All cities continued					
Council-manager	440	52,084	38,513	50,009	62,986
Commission	12	42,853	35,000	39,098	47,000
Town meeting	15	33,418	29,000	32,000	36,212
Rep. town meeting	6	43,119	35,000	43,606	46,539
Treasurer					
Total	973	34,020	21,424	30,889	44,000
Geographic region					
Northeast	345	31,657	19,260	30,182	41,272
North Central	295	31,695	22,000	29,700	40,526
South	181	34,457	22,307	29,949	44,960
West	152	43,376	24,530	40,146	58,380
City type					
Central	159	50,751	39,700	49,781	62,686
Suburban	490	33,539	21,644	31,543	43,830
Independent	324	26,537	20,000	25,578	31,830
Form of government					
Mayor-council	385	32,269	20,000	28,554	41,254
Council-manager	446	37,273	24,772	33,591	47,900
Commission	25	26,833	18,928	20,758	28,188
Town meeting	93	26,953	16,464	26,848	35,442
Rep. town meeting	24	36,515	30,024	37,803	45,990
Director of public works					
Total	2,946	45,912	32,884	42,801	56,000
Geographic region					
Northeast	659	45,810	35,028	44,100	55,500
North Central	768	45,454	35,000	43,044	54,708
South	974	40,337	28,735	37,260	48,960
West	545	56,642	39,314	53,768	71,952
City type					
Central	316	63,170	51,492	61,345	74,184
Suburban	1,558	48,224	35,472	45,484	57,924
Independent	1,072	37,465	28,678	35,853	44,372
Form of government					
Mayor-council	1,198	41,819	30,766	39,167	50,004
Council-manager	1,563	49,297	35,135	46,199	59,892
Commission	45	44,324	32,000	41,600	50,336
Town meeting	109	41,040	31,066	40,300	49,250
Rep. town meeting	31	52,848	38,588	56,010	62,990
Engineer					
Total	1,075	50,670	42,224	49,939	59,748
Geographic region					
Northeast	204	49,023	40,144	50,000	60,850
North Central	314	48,845	42,956	49,370	56,430
South	324	48,270	40,707	48,996	55,933
West	233	57,909	45,038	55,393	69,742
City type					
Central	260	55,800	46,300	54,933	63,237
Suburban	513	52,292	44,376	51,718	62,480
Independent	302	43,498	37,608	44,224	49,660
Form of government					
Mayor-council	356	46,062	38,480	45,818	55,196
Council-manager	657	53,214	44,491	51,715	61,285
Commission	23	48,202	41,000	44,964	63,237
Town meeting	22	51,058	48,158	50,960	55,675
Rep. town meeting	17	51,690	47,147	53,123	55,590
Police chief					
Total	3,319	46,688	33,782	43,179	56,506
Geographic region					
Northeast	699	51,868	39,166	51,000	63,744
North Central	976	44,036	33,686	42,000	52,416
South	1,106	40,748	29,500	37,717	48,600
West	538	56,983	40,368	52,881	70,056
City type					
Central	336	63,995	50,501	62,087	75,150
Suburban	1,648	51,308	38,825	49,368	61,190
Independent	1,335	36,630	28,600	35,048	42,500
Form of government					
Mayor-council	1,389	42,402	30,000	38,714	51,459
Council-manager	1,724	49,991	36,979	46,500	60,012
Commission	66	42,840	30,424	38,449	49,083
Town meeting	106	49,158	40,419	49,594	55,822
Rep. town meeting	34	54,092	48,842	55,393	65,100
Fire chief					
Total	1,835	46,320	33,841	43,860	56,716
Geographic region					
Northeast	293	48,172	36,397	47,341	59,020
North Central	515	45,266	35,783	44,520	55,400
South	714	40,422	29,515	37,677	48,334
West	313	59,776	42,156	56,716	74,424

Title of official	No. cities reporting	Distribution of 1993 salaries			
		Mean ($)	First quartile ($)	Median ($)	Third quartile ($)
All cities continued					
City type					
Central	329	60,870	48,563	59,570	71,115
Suburban	827	49,122	36,702	47,413	58,396
Independent	679	35,857	28,579	35,072	42,342
Form of government					
Mayor-council	692	42,424	31,140	39,814	51,553
Council-manager	1,006	49,176	35,854	46,584	60,179
Commission	39	42,096	30,576	40,539	50,000
Town meeting	71	42,793	34,172	45,150	54,386
Rep. town meeting	27	55,154	46,575	55,416	65,404
Planning director					
Total	1,276	48,620	35,507	45,294	59,280
Geographic region					
Northeast	232	44,267	34,392	43,504	52,050
North Central	20	46,290	35,535	44,097	56,460
South	405	43,769	32,698	41,338	51,915
West	359	58,721	43,212	58,488	72,264
City type					
Central	263	58,365	44,558	57,396	70,572
Suburban	667	50,184	37,590	46,888	61,916
Independent	346	38,197	30,499	37,611	44,904
Form of government					
Mayor-council	376	43,875	33,100	41,814	52,050
Council-manager	827	51,335	37,700	48,697	62,987
Commission	16	51,212	32,060	55,536	67,551
Town meeting	39	37,280	29,640	39,203	45,031
Rep. town meeting	18	45,242	31,287	45,729	52,762
Personnel director					
Total	1,039	45,733	32,712	44,040	56,179
Geographic region					
Northeast	117	44,906	33,508	42,885	52,300
North Central	239	45,708	36,170	45,411	54,142
South	439	40,032	27,000	38,200	49,857
West	244	56,413	42,200	56,058	70,183
City type					
Central	294	54,734	42,650	52,274	66,676
Suburban	466	46,713	33,743	44,967	57,510
Independent	279	34,613	25,500	34,000	42,885
Form of government					
Mayor-council	320	42,162	28,665	40,009	51,126
Council-manager	685	47,553	34,740	46,178	59,091
Commission	19	41,525	25,480	38,272	55,664
Town meeting	6	42,646	31,309	37,133	53,302
Rep. town meeting	9	45,168	39,632	45,100	50,034
Risk manager					
Total	367	44,254	34,164	43,764	53,015
Geographic region					
Northeast	28	40,612	32,000	41,570	48,834
North Central	67	43,449	38,272	43,928	50,590
South	154	39,895	31,661	39,850	48,480
West	118	51,265	43,082	51,528	60,012
City type					
Central	172	47,842	38,541	46,140	56,400
Suburban	134	44,377	35,375	43,913	52,338
Independent	61	33,868	26,054	33,290	41,100
Form of government					
Mayor-council	91	40,243	29,692	39,817	49,419
Council-manager	266	45,671	37,763	44,919	53,747
Commission	10	43,069	37,196	44,466	46,500
Director of parks and recreation					
Total	1,424	42,974	30,302	39,708	52,823
Geographic region					
Northeast	234	38,956	30,154	36,938	47,930
North Central	357	41,476	31,200	39,748	51,190
South	537	38,909	27,789	36,082	47,672
West	296	55,333	40,710	53,622	69,619
City type					
Central	249	56,356	45,811	54,108	67,970
Suburban	701	44,467	32,431	41,685	53,650
Independent	474	33,738	25,334	32,471	40,008
Form of government					
Mayor-council	507	38,250	27,851	35,500	47,352
Council-manager	854	46,252	32,953	43,790	56,881
Commission	23	42,367	23,093	38,314	54,519
Town meeting	26	29,857	20,000	29,925	36,000
Rep. town meeting	14	39,516	31,287	34,909	46,976
Superintendent of parks					
Total	838	38,116	27,581	35,766	45,468

Table 1/4   SALARIES OF MUNICIPAL OFFICIALS: 1 JULY 1993
continued

Title of official	No. cities reporting	Distribution of 1993 salaries Mean ($)	First quartile ($)	Median ($)	Third quartile ($)
All cities continued					
Geographic region					
Northeast	126	39,998	31,090	39,473	46,122
North Central	247	36,625	27,879	35,198	43,915
South	260	31,461	23,619	29,688	37,820
West	205	47,198	35,220	43,586	56,932
City type					
Central	187	44,405	34,204	43,836	53,636
Suburban	385	39,712	30,094	38,731	47,681
Independent	266	31,386	23,360	29,487	35,915
Form of government					
Mayor-council	285	34,449	25,832	31,970	41,549
Council-manager	513	40,001	29,494	37,627	47,669
Commission	13	42,474	27,123	40,893	56,036
Town meeting	17	39,613	29,400	38,362	47,780
Rep. town meeting	10	37,766	27,853	40,999	43,626
Director of recreation					
Total	660	36,443	25,438	34,403	46,200
Geographic region					
Northeast	163	33,402	22,594	33,524	42,438
North Central	187	35,486	25,427	33,958	45,200
South	173	32,686	24,079	30,846	40,308
West	137	46,112	32,472	43,680	58,392
City type					
Central	148	43,845	33,900	41,648	53,172
Suburban	321	37,980	26,000	37,727	48,257
Independent	191	28,124	20,737	27,396	34,112
Form of government					
Mayor-council	235	33,316	23,254	31,286	42,182
Council-manager	370	39,405	28,000	37,950	49,171
Commission	16	33,394	23,000	27,960	40,808
Town meeting	28	25,627	17,507	26,176	31,761
Rep. town meeting	11	35,600	25,272	36,576	47,580
Librarian					
Total	1,108	37,758	25,377	34,940	47,220
Geographic region					
Northeast	297	40,346	30,580	38,745	48,311
North Central	292	35,613	25,064	34,000	44,647
South	295	31,487	19,812	28,600	39,865
West	224	45,381	27,504	41,035	57,948
City type					
Central	154	54,722	44,558	52,425	67,000
Suburban	524	40,598	28,573	38,206	49,476
Independent	430	28,222	20,600	27,292	35,000
Form of government					
Mayor-council	384	35,225	22,714	31,550	44,410
Council-manager	603	39,872	26,780	36,836	50,000
Commission	27	34,210	19,656	28,787	52,457
Town meeting	73	33,502	28,000	32,687	41,601
Rep. town meeting	21	42,716	33,000	38,685	48,765
Director of information services					
Total	635	47,626	35,859	46,612	57,396
Geographic region					
Northeast	103	46,311	36,367	44,911	55,000
North Central	150	46,059	36,150	46,147	53,826
South	240	45,036	32,535	43,387	53,551
West	142	54,611	42,974	54,782	66,156
City type					
Central	234	55,475	44,000	53,583	67,250
Suburban	244	47,560	38,200	47,227	55,900
Independent	157	36,030	27,872	34,396	42,974
Form of government					
Mayor-council	201	46,655	34,528	43,607	57,631
Council-manager	405	48,438	37,440	47,882	57,675
Commission	11	45,167	28,350	50,618	60,008
Town meeting	9	33,816	31,341	34,308	40,189
Rep. town meeting	9	49,587	43,691	49,895	55,000
Purchasing director					
Total	697	38,266	26,749	37,024	47,237
Geographic region					
Northeast	110	38,546	29,725	38,500	46,897
North Central	131	40,744	32,760	40,768	48,417
South	323	34,464	25,156	31,512	41,467
West	133	44,826	32,064	46,224	57,340
City type					
Central	237	45,666	36,084	44,280	55,120
Suburban	268	38,287	28,077	38,174	47,180
Independent	192	29,101	22,524	26,546	34,332
Form of government					
Mayor-council	237	36,498	25,214	34,000	46,092

Title of official	No. cities reporting	Distribution of 1993 salaries Mean ($)	First quartile ($)	Median ($)	Third quartile ($)
All cities continued					
Council-manager	443	39,248	28,848	38,700	48,000
Commission	11	39,663	25,355	38,272	55,577
Town meeting	4	23,889	15,546	16,977	18,408
Over 1,000,000					
Mayor					
Total	5	110,661	110,000	115,000	130,000
City type					
Central	5	110,661	110,000	115,000	130,000
Form of government					
Mayor-council	4	122,001	115,000	122,500	130,000
Chief appointed administrator					
Total	3	98,216	. . .	100,900	. . .
City type					
Central	3	98,216	. . .	100,900	. . .
Form of government					
Mayor-council	3	98,216	. . .	100,900	. . .
Asst. city mgr./asst. CAO					
Total	3	94,434	. . .	94,896	. . .
City type					
Central	3	94,434	. . .	94,896	. . .
City clerk					
Total	3	70,140	. . .	74,521	. . .
City type					
Central	3	70,140	. . .	74,521	. . .
Chief financial officer					
Total	4	92,614	85,738	92,027	98,316
City type					
Central	4	92,614	85,738	92,027	98,316
Form of government					
Mayor-council	3	94,905	. . .	98,316	. . .
Director of economic development					
Total	3	93,549	. . .	94,248	. . .
City type					
Central	3	93,549	. . .	94,248	. . .
Form of government					
Mayor-council	3	93,549	. . .	94,248	. . .
Treasurer					
Total	4	73,530	66,500	71,959	77,418
City type					
Central	4	73,530	66,500	71,959	77,418
Form of government					
Mayor-council	3	72,233	. . .	66,500	. . .
Director of public works					
Total	4	91,426	85,738	92,027	98,316
City type					
Central	4	91,426	85,738	92,027	98,316
Form of government					
Mayor-council	3	93,322	. . .	98,316	. . .
Engineer					
Total	3	85,828	. . .	85,738	. . .
City type					
Central	3	85,828	. . .	85,738	. . .
Police chief					
Total	5	102,154	100,900	108,347	110,000
City type					
Central	5	102,154	100,900	108,347	110,000
Form of government					
Mayor-council	4	100,606	100,900	105,450	110,000
Fire chief					
Total	5	96,781	82,600	103,704	106,850
City type					
Central	5	96,781	82,600	103,704	106,850
Form of government					
Mayor-council	4	94,264	82,600	93,152	103,704
Planning director					
Total	4	94,315	97,802	97,804	97,806
City type					
Central	4	94,315	97,802	97,804	97,806
Form of government					
Mayor-council	3	93,152	. . .	97,806	. . .
Personnel director					
Total	5	88,581	84,000	92,532	95,472
City type					
Central	5	88,581	84,000	92,532	95,472
Form of government					
Mayor-council	4	86,858	84,000	88,266	92,532

Table 1/4 SALARIES OF MUNICIPAL OFFICIALS: 1 JULY 1993
continued

Title of official	No. cities reporting	Distribution of 1993 salaries			
		Mean ($)	First quartile ($)	Median ($)	Third quartile ($)
Over 1,000,000 continued					
Risk manager					
Total	4	70,615	74,040	75,729	77,418
City type					
Central	4	70,615	74,040	75,729	77,418
Form of government					
Mayor-council	3	68,347	. . .	74,040	. . .
Director of parks and recreation					
Total	3	83,678	. . .	83,450	. . .
City type					
Central	3	83,678	. . .	83,450	. . .
Librarian					
Total	4	86,368	84,100	85,410	86,720
City type					
Central	4	86,368	84,100	85,410	86,720
Form of government					
Mayor-council	3	88,090	. . .	86,720	. . .
Director of information services					
Total	4	92,065	76,208	80,080	83,952
City type					
Central	4	92,065	76,208	80,080	83,952
Form of government					
Mayor-council	4	92,065	76,208	80,080	83,952
Purchasing director					
Total	5	72,814	68,300	68,370	70,924
City type					
Central	5	72,814	68,300	68,370	70,924
Form of government					
Mayor-council	4	73,925	68,300	69,612	70,924
500,000 - 1,000,000					
Mayor					
Total	12	89,624	85,000	91,356	100,000
Geographic region					
North Central	4	91,343	90,711	91,356	92,000
South	5	78,290	75,000	90,705	100,000
West	3	106,223	. . .	100,000	. . .
City type					
Central	12	89,624	85,000	91,356	100,000
Form of government					
Mayor-council	11	90,499	85,000	92,000	100,000
Chief appointed administrator					
Total	9	83,536	72,114	82,268	90,605
Geographic region					
North Central	4	69,932	70,126	71,120	72,114
South	4	96,886	90,605	92,551	94,496
City type					
Central	9	83,536	72,114	82,268	90,605
Form of government					
Mayor-council	9	83,536	72,114	82,268	90,605
Asst. city mgr./asst. CAO					
Total	3	96,428	. . .	90,305	. . .
City type					
Central	3	96,428	. . .	90,305	. . .
City clerk					
Total	9	61,965	41,540	70,756	72,800
Geographic region					
North Central	4	52,021	41,540	51,315	61,090
South	3	67,176	. . .	72,800	. . .
City type					
Central	9	61,965	41,540	70,756	72,800
Form of government					
Mayor-council	7	58,464	41,518	61,090	72,439
Chief financial officer					
Total	12	82,927	72,114	79,193	87,727
Geographic region					
North Central	4	75,250	70,658	71,386	72,114
South	5	77,136	77,662	80,724	81,756
West	3	102,814	. . .	102,264	. . .
City type					
Central	12	82,927	72,114	79,193	87,727
Form of government					
Mayor-council	10	81,213	70,658	76,879	87,727
Director of economic development					
Total	10	71,565	60,000	65,510	81,885
Geographic region					
North Central	3	60,677	. . .	60,000	. . .
South	6	70,146	65,099	68,845	81,885

Title of official	No. cities reporting	Distribution of 1993 salaries			
		Mean ($)	First quartile ($)	Median ($)	Third quartile ($)
500,000 - 1,000,000 continued					
City type					
Central	10	71,565	60,000	65,510	81,885
Form of government					
Mayor-council	8	64,915	60,000	63,915	65,920
Treasurer					
Total	9	75,794	65,110	71,770	87,727
Geographic region					
North Central	3	63,043	. . .	57,158	. . .
South	4	72,191	70,000	70,885	71,770
City type					
Central	9	75,794	65,110	71,770	87,727
Form of government					
Mayor-council	8	74,226	65,110	70,885	81,885
Director of public works					
Total	11	78,372	69,615	76,095	88,152
Geographic region					
North Central	4	74,211	69,615	70,865	72,114
South	5	74,155	73,913	81,197	82,056
City type					
Central	11	78,372	69,615	76,095	88,152
Form of government					
Mayor-council	9	72,840	69,615	73,913	81,197
Engineer					
Total	8	63,823	61,841	62,827	68,087
Geographic region					
North Central	4	61,309	59,301	60,651	62,000
South	4	66,338	63,653	65,870	68,087
City type					
Central	8	63,823	61,841	62,827	68,087
Form of government					
Mayor-council	7	64,106	59,301	63,653	71,770
Police chief					
Total	12	89,616	76,591	90,629	95,111
Geographic region					
North Central	4	81,700	74,630	82,982	91,333
South	5	85,982	76,952	90,605	90,653
West	3	106,228	. . .	118,380	. . .
City type					
Central	12	89,616	76,591	90,629	95,111
Form of government					
Mayor-council	10	86,636	76,095	83,779	95,111
Fire chief					
Total	10	81,991	74,811	76,776	80,246
Geographic region					
North Central	4	77,859	70,356	75,301	80,246
South	4	77,042	76,591	76,776	76,960
City type					
Central	10	81,991	74,811	76,776	80,246
Form of government					
Mayor-council	10	81,991	74,811	76,776	80,246
Planning director					
Total	10	71,182	59,301	66,198	76,095
Geographic region					
North Central	4	62,424	59,301	61,781	64,260
South	4	68,322	62,976	67,196	71,415
City type					
Central	10	71,182	59,301	66,198	76,095
Form of government					
Mayor-council	8	67,013	59,301	66,198	71,415
Personnel director					
Total	11	70,513	57,130	76,095	81,885
Geographic region					
North Central	4	59,936	51,000	54,995	58,989
South	5	72,480	65,000	77,662	80,724
City type					
Central	11	70,513	57,130	76,095	81,885
Form of government					
Mayor-council	9	66,391	57,130	65,000	77,662
Risk manager					
Total	5	52,066	39,817	54,330	54,996
Geographic region					
North Central	3	41,737	. . .	39,817	. . .
City type					
Central	5	52,066	39,817	54,330	54,996
Form of government					
Mayor-council	4	45,052	39,817	47,074	54,330
Director of parks and recreation					
Total	9	71,610	65,000	71,770	76,095

Table 1/4   **SALARIES OF MUNICIPAL OFFICIALS: 1 JULY 1993**
continued

Title of official	No. cities reporting	Distribution of 1993 salaries			
		Mean ($)	First quartile ($)	Median ($)	Third quartile ($)
500,000 - 1,000,000 continued					
Geographic region					
North Central	3	66,955	. . .	65,000	. . .
South	5	73,506	67,600	71,770	81,300
City type					
Central	9	71,610	65,000	71,770	76,095
Form of government					
Mayor-council	8	70,398	65,000	69,685	72,114
Superintendent of parks					
Total	3	64,562	. . .	63,250	. . .
City type					
Central	3	64,562	. . .	63,250	. . .
Director of recreation					
Total	4	58,596	47,250	55,125	63,000
City type					
Central	4	58,596	47,250	55,125	63,000
Form of government					
Mayor-council	3	50,083	. . .	47,250	. . .
Librarian					
Total	4	74,348	67,000	71,459	75,917
City type					
Central	4	74,348	67,000	71,459	75,917
Form of government					
Mayor-council	3	66,663	. . .	67,000	. . .
Director of information services					
Total	9	75,096	68,796	75,068	81,286
Geographic region					
North Central	3	68,282	. . .	64,260	. . .
South	4	74,380	71,770	73,419	75,068
City type					
Central	9	75,096	68,796	75,068	81,286
Form of government					
Mayor-council	7	71,913	64,260	71,770	81,286
Purchasing director					
Total	7	64,205	54,144	64,728	73,597
Geographic region					
North Central	4	58,348	54,144	56,723	59,301
South	3	72,015	. . .	69,431	. . .
City type					
Central	7	64,205	54,144	64,728	73,597
Form of government					
Mayor-council	6	63,334	54,144	62,015	73,597
250,000 - 499,999					
Mayor					
Total	25	48,225	17,000	41,621	74,471
Geographic region					
North Central	6	55,456	36,900	58,804	74,471
South	10	42,917	5,000	26,003	71,464
West	9	49,303	24,000	41,621	77,938
City type					
Central	25	48,225	17,000	41,621	74,471
Form of government					
Mayor-council	10	76,670	69,996	72,968	95,580
Council-manager	13	24,930	12,000	17,000	35,006
City manager					
Total	13	114,431	103,706	118,560	120,000
Geographic region					
South	6	115,221	104,520	113,083	124,250
West	6	116,047	103,706	119,158	120,000
City type					
Central	13	114,431	103,706	118,560	120,000
Form of government					
Council-manager	12	113,988	103,706	112,411	120,000
Chief appointed administrator					
Total	10	85,294	77,188	86,727	94,785
Geographic region					
North Central	4	82,944	83,000	86,727	90,454
South	4	91,746	94,785	95,147	95,508
City type					
Central	10	85,294	77,188	86,727	94,785
Form of government					
Mayor-council	9	85,549	77,188	90,454	94,785
Asst. city mgr./asst. CAO					
Total	15	84,760	77,188	86,994	97,049
Geographic region					
North Central	3	68,822	. . .	77,597	. . .
South	5	84,739	77,188	78,229	97,049
West	7	91,606	86,994	92,023	104,962

Title of official	No. cities reporting	Distribution of 1993 salaries			
		Mean ($)	First quartile ($)	Median ($)	Third quartile ($)
250,000 - 499,999 continued					
City type					
Central	15	84,760	77,188	86,994	97,049
Form of government					
Mayor-council	6	72,790	59,010	71,948	79,092
Council-manager	9	92,740	86,994	92,023	97,049
City clerk					
Total	23	61,254	51,072	60,686	68,160
Geographic region					
North Central	4	58,529	59,999	61,159	62,319
South	9	59,396	56,472	60,686	63,461
West	10	64,017	51,072	60,488	78,083
City type					
Central	23	61,254	51,072	60,686	68,160
Form of government					
Mayor-council	8	53,076	48,062	54,573	59,467
Council-manager	13	66,173	58,300	61,432	78,083
Chief financial officer					
Total	24	81,462	76,586	79,507	88,320
Geographic region					
North Central	6	77,431	68,951	75,934	85,712
South	9	81,187	76,586	79,622	89,621
West	9	84,423	78,600	82,668	84,214
City type					
Central	24	81,462	76,586	79,507	88,320
Form of government					
Mayor-council	8	78,873	79,353	79,507	83,174
Council-manager	14	84,114	76,586	83,441	92,019
Director of economic development					
Total	19	75,530	66,534	75,530	83,126
Geographic region					
North Central	3	81,534	. . .	83,126	. . .
South	8	70,331	65,241	67,111	76,608
West	8	78,477	71,114	74,628	81,082
City type					
Central	19	75,530	66,534	75,000	83,126
Form of government					
Mayor-council	8	72,982	66,534	74,628	76,608
Council-manager	10	77,621	66,959	74,760	91,436
Treasurer					
Total	20	64,371	59,188	63,253	72,217
Geographic region					
North Central	3	57,007	. . .	58,342	. . .
South	8	61,798	59,395	61,754	64,522
West	9	69,112	66,602	67,680	75,936
City type					
Central	20	64,371	59,188	63,253	72,217
Form of government					
Mayor-council	9	64,147	58,342	61,524	72,217
Council-manager	10	64,349	59,188	63,253	73,848
Director of public works					
Total	22	85,422	75,844	84,116	90,802
Geographic region					
North Central	5	81,506	75,844	83,126	86,130
South	9	85,212	79,504	83,595	85,284
West	8	88,105	78,499	90,068	95,238
City type					
Central	22	85,422	75,844	84,116	90,802
Form of government					
Mayor-council	10	85,218	71,630	83,361	91,836
Council-manager	11	86,236	75,844	85,284	90,334
Engineer					
Total	16	71,584	63,896	72,518	77,352
Geographic region					
South	6	71,907	62,650	72,560	77,352
West	8	70,301	63,896	72,518	74,768
City type					
Central	16	71,584	63,896	72,518	77,352
Form of government					
Mayor-council	6	73,723	60,928	78,828	83,174
Council-manager	9	69,914	63,896	71,115	74,004
Police chief					
Total	22	82,037	74,486	80,922	88,320
Geographic region					
North Central	6	76,114	71,084	75,973	83,029
South	9	83,150	79,716	81,168	90,132
West	7	85,682	77,089	81,570	95,238
City type					
Central	22	82,037	74,486	80,922	88,320

Table 1/4   SALARIES OF MUNICIPAL OFFICIALS: 1 JULY 1993
continued

Title of official	No. cities reporting	Distribution of 1993 salaries			
		Mean ($)	First quartile ($)	Median ($)	Third quartile ($)
250,000 - 499,999 continued					
Form of government					
Mayor-council	9	79,204	71,084	80,675	83,126
Council-manager	11	85,719	77,089	81,168	94,765
Fire chief					
Total	25	80,456	69,757	78,280	88,320
Geographic region					
North Central	6	73,763	67,525	73,155	78,117
South	10	80,974	72,245	80,960	90,132
West	9	84,343	69,757	82,992	99,451
City type					
Central	25	80,456	69,757	78,280	88,320
Form of government					
Mayor-council	10	76,877	68,682	78,221	83,126
Council-manager	14	83,939	72,245	83,070	97,408
Planning director					
Total	23	77,111	67,568	76,226	88,192
Geographic region					
North Central	5	70,354	67,568	71,396	76,226
South	8	73,926	61,524	72,193	88,192
West	10	83,038	75,120	79,998	88,300
City type					
Central	23	77,111	67,568	76,226	88,192
Form of government					
Mayor-council	7	71,419	63,814	71,396	79,579
Council-manager	14	81,631	75,600	81,474	89,379
Personnel director					
Total	23	77,269	68,000	78,754	84,876
Geographic region					
North Central	6	76,070	68,000	79,403	83,912
South	9	78,322	70,171	78,374	85,010
West	8	76,984	68,690	77,136	83,174
City type					
Central	23	77,269	68,000	78,754	84,876
Form of government					
Mayor-council	9	76,664	70,171	80,051	83,174
Council-manager	12	79,268	71,267	80,312	85,010
Risk manager					
Total	22	59,374	49,816	59,335	63,958
Geographic region					
North Central	5	58,549	49,816	60,865	63,958
South	10	57,680	48,134	54,933	60,798
West	7	62,384	53,700	61,090	65,438
City type					
Central	22	59,374	49,816	59,335	63,958
Form of government					
Mayor-council	7	58,353	49,932	60,865	65,852
Council-manager	13	60,564	49,816	56,487	63,958
Director of parks and recreation					
Total	20	79,043	71,677	82,638	84,490
Geographic region					
North Central	3	69,534	. . .	70,682	. . .
South	9	77,763	71,500	79,812	84,490
West	8	84,050	82,101	83,227	87,028
City type					
Central	20	79,043	71,677	82,638	84,490
Form of government					
Mayor-council	6	81,720	79,812	83,385	83,919
Council-manager	12	79,837	71,677	82,691	84,637
Superintendent of parks					
Total	18	61,089	53,577	57,076	67,574
Geographic region					
North Central	5	69,625	56,036	67,574	86,052
South	5	54,732	49,358	54,468	55,207
West	8	59,728	54,574	58,657	59,529
City type					
Central	18	61,089	53,577	57,076	67,574
Form of government					
Mayor-council	7	63,191	54,468	58,116	68,785
Council-manager	10	60,123	50,731	57,202	63,240
Director of recreation					
Total	14	58,848	51,229	59,437	64,402
Geographic region					
North Central	5	66,992	63,277	64,402	70,548
South	4	52,856	44,892	54,480	64,068
West	5	55,497	52,811	54,574	58,116
City type					
Central	14	58,848	51,229	59,437	64,402
Form of government					
Mayor-council	6	63,187	58,116	64,235	67,412

Title of official	No. cities reporting	Distribution of 1993 salaries			
		Mean ($)	First quartile ($)	Median ($)	Third quartile ($)
250,000 - 499,999 continued					
Council-manager	6	53,453	44,892	50,010	52,811
Librarian					
Total	12	74,283	72,145	76,741	83,174
Geographic region					
North Central	3	78,784	. . .	78,000	. . .
South	4	72,817	70,075	72,904	75,732
West	5	72,755	72,145	83,174	84,876
City type					
Central	12	74,283	72,145	76,741	83,174
Form of government					
Mayor-council	5	81,544	78,000	83,174	83,919
Council-manager	7	69,097	67,711	72,145	75,732
Director of information services					
Total	23	74,307	62,280	73,884	81,684
Geographic region					
North Central	5	67,842	57,632	69,758	77,484
South	10	77,026	69,468	76,953	81,684
West	8	74,948	68,958	72,000	83,174
City type					
Central	23	74,307	62,280	73,884	81,684
Form of government					
Mayor-council	9	74,219	69,758	73,008	79,622
Council-manager	13	75,853	62,280	74,283	84,239
Purchasing director					
Total	25	61,796	56,042	60,540	67,100
Geographic region					
North Central	6	61,383	53,000	61,656	73,963
South	9	61,007	56,042	59,076	66,602
West	10	62,754	57,395	60,815	72,095
City type					
Central	25	61,796	56,042	60,540	67,100
Form of government					
Mayor-council	9	59,642	56,568	59,076	63,214
Council-manager	14	63,704	56,042	63,345	72,371
100,000 - 249,999					
Mayor					
Total	88	36,431	11,847	24,518	62,000
Geographic region					
Northeast	9	70,636	54,636	67,650	90,372
North Central	20	49,753	32,760	55,000	65,828
South	27	38,112	12,500	20,104	65,494
West	32	17,065	7,800	10,724	21,000
City type					
Central	62	43,362	16,500	43,500	65,828
Suburban	26	19,903	7,560	10,724	18,000
Form of government					
Mayor-council	31	64,622	54,636	65,828	78,499
Council-manager	53	17,167	7,800	13,801	21,486
Commission	4	73,196	55,000	73,021	91,042
City manager					
Total	59	107,861	99,500	104,432	117,708
Geographic region					
North Central	9	96,358	91,811	97,050	101,150
South	19	104,329	98,748	102,201	113,527
West	31	113,365	102,300	114,504	121,032
City type					
Central	33	103,823	93,840	101,150	113,069
Suburban	26	112,986	102,201	113,288	121,124
Form of government					
Council-manager	57	107,854	99,782	104,432	117,708
Chief appointed administrator					
Total	18	72,891	56,713	68,007	82,555
Geographic region					
Northeast	7	71,552	56,713	75,000	82,555
North Central	5	59,111	54,075	61,311	62,608
South	4	80,997	69,014	75,701	82,388
City type					
Central	17	71,297	56,713	67,000	82,388
Form of government					
Mayor-council	18	72,891	56,713	68,007	82,555
Asst. city mgr./asst. CAO					
Total	60	81,622	68,035	85,253	93,976
Geographic region					
Northeast	3	64,661	. . .	63,064	. . .
North Central	11	64,048	50,563	64,765	78,482
South	18	81,194	75,720	80,834	89,600
West	28	90,618	85,391	91,640	102,168

Table 1/4   SALARIES OF MUNICIPAL OFFICIALS: 1 JULY 1993
continued

Title of official	No. cities reporting	Distribution of 1993 salaries			
		Mean ($)	First quartile ($)	Median ($)	Third quartile ($)
100,000 - 249,999 continued					
City type					
Central	36	77,372	65,686	80,550	89,600
Suburban	24	87,996	76,032	91,958	103,280
Form of government					
Mayor-council	7	62,186	47,446	62,064	83,472
Council-manager	52	83,943	73,867	87,120	96,174
City clerk					
Total	86	53,642	44,796	53,277	61,500
Geographic region					
Northeast	9	50,281	41,746	50,000	61,091
North Central	19	52,875	43,216	53,134	58,632
South	28	51,264	44,796	50,115	60,377
West	30	57,355	51,840	57,359	65,529
City type					
Central	59	52,587	43,216	51,126	62,379
Suburban	27	55,947	52,104	57,312	61,500
Form of government					
Mayor-council	27	50,725	37,787	50,000	61,500
Council-manager	55	55,593	47,500	57,288	62,842
Commission	4	46,499	43,216	45,003	46,790
Chief financial officer					
Total	88	75,264	65,140	76,119	83,683
Geographic region					
Northeast	8	70,895	64,514	67,539	72,318
North Central	20	67,042	59,595	67,233	74,235
South	29	72,314	64,200	74,172	79,801
West	31	84,456	76,512	83,169	91,094
City type					
Central	60	72,635	64,514	74,197	81,296
Suburban	28	80,898	75,406	79,501	90,946
Form of government					
Mayor-council	28	68,090	58,510	66,609	77,500
Council-manager	56	79,190	74,172	78,660	88,804
Commission	4	70,525	69,893	70,094	70,294
Director of economic development					
Total	61	68,337	58,423	66,477	76,525
Geographic region					
Northeast	8	60,907	60,759	62,847	65,000
North Central	15	59,703	50,564	63,190	67,760
South	15	64,886	53,804	65,000	74,604
West	23	78,802	69,024	81,228	89,556
City type					
Central	43	63,936	55,405	63,190	71,365
Suburban	18	78,850	69,024	75,969	87,516
Form of government					
Mayor-council	24	60,026	50,564	58,212	70,000
Council-manager	35	74,284	65,745	71,674	82,715
Treasurer					
Total	50	57,417	51,292	59,238	66,299
Geographic region					
Northeast	7	55,653	41,750	59,795	65,795
North Central	13	54,557	46,924	53,307	60,713
South	14	57,407	47,882	56,849	66,402
West	16	60,522	58,169	64,116	70,860
City type					
Central	37	57,088	47,026	59,795	65,874
Suburban	13	58,354	53,592	58,169	69,408
Form of government					
Mayor-council	17	53,571	46,155	58,510	65,795
Council-manager	30	59,365	53,307	60,324	69,408
Commission	3	59,738	. . .	60,713	. . .
Director of public works					
Total	79	76,196	66,685	78,000	89,128
Geographic region					
Northeast	8	64,968	55,196	64,132	70,000
North Central	20	66,971	59,636	68,971	74,984
South	27	73,385	61,381	75,016	82,030
West	24	90,789	86,914	91,090	95,653
City type					
Central	56	72,303	61,381	72,792	83,472
Suburban	23	85,675	78,000	88,204	95,000
Form of government					
Mayor-council	29	66,233	55,196	69,274	75,941
Council-manager	47	82,925	74,380	83,331	91,581
Commission	3	67,080	. . .	66,685	. . .
Engineer					
Total	74	67,951	60,840	68,416	77,340

Title of official	No. cities reporting	Distribution of 1993 salaries			
		Mean ($)	First quartile ($)	Median ($)	Third quartile ($)
100,000 - 249,999 continued					
Geographic region					
Northeast	7	64,782	55,196	67,554	77,512
North Central	20	63,395	60,840	63,102	71,531
South	26	63,295	57,456	62,895	72,821
West	21	79,110	75,592	78,228	83,664
City type					
Central	52	66,587	59,413	65,450	75,115
Suburban	22	71,173	63,066	73,045	80,712
Form of government					
Mayor-council	24	62,006	54,694	61,343	72,868
Council-manager	46	70,939	62,893	72,763	78,617
Commission	4	69,253	64,418	69,330	74,241
Police chief					
Total	81	78,802	70,470	78,686	90,881
Geographic region					
Northeast	7	70,335	64,955	68,097	86,959
North Central	18	67,257	61,797	69,615	76,287
South	29	75,035	72,642	76,368	80,668
West	27	92,739	87,168	92,854	98,040
City type					
Central	59	75,792	68,097	76,807	87,168
Suburban	22	86,873	76,287	89,609	98,040
Form of government					
Mayor-council	27	68,908	58,718	69,274	76,368
Council-manager	50	84,949	78,062	82,957	92,854
Commission	4	68,738	62,098	62,668	63,237
Fire chief					
Total	79	73,231	62,871	71,424	82,620
Geographic region					
Northeast	8	69,669	64,955	68,686	75,000
North Central	19	64,650	61,651	63,500	70,470
South	29	67,519	61,360	68,316	77,073
West	23	88,761	82,573	91,800	96,880
City type					
Central	59	70,564	62,000	68,759	78,806
Suburban	20	81,099	74,592	82,597	95,628
Form of government					
Mayor-council	29	65,326	56,788	66,516	70,470
Council-manager	46	78,834	69,014	78,289	87,867
Commission	4	66,107	60,618	61,928	63,237
Planning director					
Total	71	71,967	62,315	72,868	82,620
Geographic region					
Northeast	7	67,749	51,190	69,274	84,362
North Central	18	64,312	57,524	63,915	71,365
South	24	70,874	63,336	71,909	77,256
West	22	80,764	74,901	81,360	86,832
City type					
Central	50	70,270	60,648	72,585	80,100
Suburban	21	76,007	64,890	74,604	88,690
Form of government					
Mayor-council	22	67,210	55,358	67,019	82,875
Council-manager	45	74,652	66,269	76,720	82,620
Commission	4	67,921	67,551	69,062	70,572
Personnel director					
Total	82	66,388	54,184	68,294	77,508
Geographic region					
Northeast	8	58,224	45,423	47,683	72,868
North Central	19	57,255	47,955	55,664	68,159
South	27	65,177	58,094	67,932	72,747
West	28	76,085	69,394	77,536	81,402
City type					
Central	57	63,337	51,126	65,580	72,681
Suburban	25	73,344	68,159	75,750	82,101
Form of government					
Mayor-council	28	59,388	47,955	56,362	71,115
Council-manager	50	70,803	65,580	70,658	77,976
Commission	4	60,206	55,664	59,717	63,770
Risk manager					
Total	57	50,142	41,770	50,590	58,781
Geographic region					
Northeast	4	45,311	41,770	44,774	47,778
North Central	15	42,512	31,868	43,526	50,590
South	17	45,771	40,456	43,000	51,756
West	21	60,051	56,543	59,218	65,688
City type					
Central	45	48,566	41,196	50,436	57,838
Suburban	12	56,054	49,635	57,033	61,416

Table 1/4 continued   SALARIES OF MUNICIPAL OFFICIALS: 1 JULY 1993

Title of official	No. cities reporting	Mean ($)	First quartile ($)	Median ($)	Third quartile ($)
100,000 - 249,999 continued					
Form of government					
Mayor-council	17	42,380	31,868	41,196	48,379
Council-manager	37	54,205	49,635	56,256	60,753
Commission	3	44,022	...	43,526	...
Director of parks and recreation					
Total	62	67,873	56,118	68,190	77,425
Geographic region					
Northeast	6	66,453	53,000	63,598	81,804
North Central	14	58,483	51,831	56,059	67,038
South	26	65,437	59,000	68,714	73,332
West	16	80,583	74,901	82,366	85,692
City type					
Central	47	65,390	55,000	66,223	72,704
Suburban	15	75,655	69,526	76,564	85,351
Form of government					
Mayor-council	20	61,641	53,000	57,559	69,992
Council-manager	38	71,527	63,912	71,212	81,507
Commission	4	64,329	63,475	63,623	63,770
Superintendent of parks					
Total	48	53,626	48,720	54,490	61,344
Geographic region					
Northeast	3	44,152	...	49,756	...
North Central	10	51,323	43,874	53,279	58,457
South	18	48,772	41,595	50,337	54,163
West	17	61,791	59,590	61,526	65,484
City type					
Central	32	52,008	46,634	51,756	59,349
Suburban	16	56,861	53,711	57,642	63,528
Form of government					
Mayor-council	14	47,493	38,340	48,807	57,033
Council-manager	31	56,460	50,532	58,457	63,528
Commission	3	52,950	...	58,097	...
Director of recreation					
Total	39	54,713	44,991	55,024	61,344
Geographic region					
Northeast	3	58,620	...	55,218	...
North Central	9	47,605	44,991	50,128	52,723
South	14	47,329	40,808	45,935	55,034
West	13	66,684	57,459	68,170	70,104
City type					
Central	26	51,894	44,695	52,046	58,457
Suburban	13	60,351	50,762	57,396	69,805
Form of government					
Mayor-council	11	50,073	43,325	51,369	56,700
Council-manager	25	57,260	47,174	55,056	68,170
Commission	3	50,502	...	55,034	...
Librarian					
Total	49	66,406	57,847	67,053	78,634
Geographic region					
Northeast	4	69,265	58,000	70,736	83,472
North Central	11	59,820	54,999	58,804	68,548
South	16	58,123	51,912	59,572	67,053
West	18	77,157	71,200	79,115	81,768
City type					
Central	31	63,142	57,233	60,859	71,370
Suburban	18	72,027	65,787	77,180	79,760
Form of government					
Mayor-council	14	60,902	54,999	59,507	68,548
Council-manager	31	69,873	57,948	71,244	79,601
Commission	4	58,797	58,161	58,548	58,934
Director of information services					
Total	63	64,125	56,597	66,211	73,068
Geographic region					
Northeast	6	60,137	45,984	64,946	71,538
North Central	15	57,688	53,539	57,911	62,315
South	27	65,078	57,049	68,890	75,219
West	15	70,443	67,172	69,780	75,904
City type					
Central	47	63,131	55,338	62,259	73,068
Suburban	16	67,046	62,315	70,327	72,467
Form of government					
Mayor-council	23	59,572	49,292	59,911	71,927
Council-manager	37	67,072	61,193	67,956	73,300
Commission	3	62,699	...	62,259	...
Purchasing director					
Total	64	53,655	44,650	54,948	60,907
Geographic region					
Northeast	8	52,200	42,318	55,662	62,408
North Central	14	48,062	43,029	51,129	53,952
100,000 - 249,999 continued					
South	25	50,571	41,704	53,696	56,904
West	17	63,480	60,120	62,376	64,991
City type					
Central	47	52,032	42,318	53,832	59,714
Suburban	17	58,142	53,874	59,478	64,356
Form of government					
Mayor-council	25	49,770	38,364	51,459	59,714
Council-manager	37	56,444	51,840	55,686	62,376
50,000 - 99,999					
Mayor					
Total	203	24,034	6,000	12,000	45,600
Geographic region					
Northeast	39	42,094	15,000	47,000	59,000
North Central	54	25,535	7,004	13,999	49,427
South	45	23,667	7,200	12,000	47,500
West	65	12,205	5,940	7,420	14,030
City type					
Central	97	28,198	7,200	16,800	49,427
Suburban	103	20,100	6,000	9,600	28,020
Independent	3	24,427	...	14,030	...
Form of government					
Mayor-council	68	47,828	44,000	52,000	60,000
Council-manager	132	11,149	5,940	8,107	13,284
City manager					
Total	161	91,363	79,512	90,420	102,120
Geographic region					
Northeast	9	79,930	62,666	83,000	89,500
North Central	35	84,227	76,000	86,794	90,100
South	45	86,222	77,256	87,504	94,680
West	72	99,474	88,000	102,036	111,000
City type					
Central	74	85,964	76,003	86,231	93,280
Suburban	84	96,465	86,676	96,052	109,334
Independent	3	81,689	...	83,000	...
Form of government					
Mayor-council	6	84,556	70,000	79,255	111,000
Council-manager	155	91,626	80,000	90,812	102,120
Chief appointed administrator					
Total	45	61,882	49,400	61,818	73,577
Geographic region					
Northeast	20	60,214	46,000	57,772	73,500
North Central	13	65,587	55,037	64,979	75,000
South	9	56,634	45,576	50,000	61,818
West	3	72,689	...	73,902	...
City type					
Central	26	58,330	44,400	55,715	72,252
Suburban	19	66,742	55,037	66,523	74,493
Form of government					
Mayor-council	38	58,510	46,000	56,881	72,252
Council-manager	6	83,006	72,500	82,315	99,000
Asst. city mgr./asst. CAO					
Total	134	71,385	59,155	70,542	84,432
Geographic region					
Northeast	9	57,789	48,034	54,800	60,000
North Central	35	62,033	54,861	63,876	70,408
South	31	68,687	60,424	67,414	78,270
West	59	80,424	70,600	82,896	92,364
City type					
Central	61	65,920	57,200	65,625	76,953
Suburban	72	75,912	61,227	76,818	90,252
Form of government					
Mayor-council	12	52,541	48,034	52,696	58,229
Council-manager	121	73,398	61,227	72,000	85,806
City clerk					
Total	208	46,884	37,315	45,983	56,400
Geographic region					
Northeast	35	45,889	38,808	45,847	55,521
North Central	55	43,411	36,920	43,368	49,193
South	55	42,179	31,798	40,345	51,438
West	63	54,578	44,503	56,640	63,972
City type					
Central	106	42,263	33,000	41,133	48,127
Suburban	100	51,628	41,668	52,774	61,904
Form of government					
Mayor-council	59	40,828	31,798	41,126	47,797
Council-manager	146	49,322	39,546	48,057	59,463
Chief financial officer					
Total	214	66,203	57,089	66,089	75,767

Table 1/4   SALARIES OF MUNICIPAL OFFICIALS: 1 JULY 1993
continued

Title of official	No. cities reporting	Distribution of 1993 salaries			
		Mean ($)	First quartile ($)	Median ($)	Third quartile ($)
50,000 - 99,999 continued					
Geographic region					
Northeast	33	60,655	52,596	58,242	68,000
North Central	53	62,621	57,136	64,418	69,179
South	57	60,365	53,227	58,692	67,708
West	71	76,143	66,634	77,952	84,456
City type					
Central	111	61,435	53,674	60,642	69,004
Suburban	99	71,497	59,952	69,552	81,094
Independent	4	67,499	68,591	69,279	69,966
Form of government					
Mayor-council	57	57,132	49,868	55,572	65,125
Council-manager	154	69,468	60,000	68,510	78,713
Director of economic development					
Total	100	59,197	48,027	57,804	69,444
Geographic region					
Northeast	18	50,134	41,475	47,862	53,180
North Central	25	56,438	52,080	59,654	64,633
South	24	53,304	43,680	51,781	59,912
West	33	70,518	60,068	69,444	83,712
City type					
Central	49	53,279	42,177	52,080	61,724
Suburban	49	65,236	53,180	63,204	76,274
Form of government					
Mayor-council	29	47,515	39,600	44,340	53,180
Council-manager	70	64,027	52,042	62,633	74,684
Treasurer					
Total	83	46,024	37,576	47,797	53,628
Geographic region					
Northeast	22	44,659	27,000	44,438	59,223
North Central	24	47,701	45,957	47,890	52,051
South	17	41,824	36,123	40,560	49,940
West	20	49,085	34,960	51,564	55,000
City type					
Central	44	44,641	38,232	46,371	52,305
Suburban	38	47,496	37,409	48,288	57,102
Form of government					
Mayor-council	28	39,700	27,000	41,652	48,676
Council-manager	54	49,384	43,300	49,861	55,000
Director of public works					
Total	192	66,797	56,652	65,606	76,428
Geographic region					
Northeast	31	58,634	48,500	58,000	72,367
North Central	53	65,254	58,088	66,510	70,969
South	52	59,604	52,499	58,864	67,400
West	56	79,456	65,776	82,994	90,156
City type					
Central	100	62,723	55,712	61,788	70,876
Suburban	89	71,356	58,770	70,764	85,969
Independent	3	67,376	. . .	61,422	. . .
Form of government					
Mayor-council	54	57,751	48,000	56,441	64,916
Council-manager	135	70,255	59,472	69,580	80,270
Engineer					
Total	156	58,610	49,837	57,493	64,752
Geographic region					
Northeast	21	55,716	46,374	51,363	65,057
North Central	46	56,876	51,415	57,216	62,903
South	49	53,606	48,961	53,712	60,302
West	40	68,252	53,254	66,548	80,193
City type					
Central	90	53,585	47,973	54,571	58,552
Suburban	63	65,588	53,148	63,996	74,100
Independent	3	62,803	. . .	65,027	. . .
Form of government					
Mayor-council	41	52,662	43,984	49,032	59,339
Council-manager	113	60,716	52,956	58,396	65,242
Police chief					
Total	197	68,251	58,244	66,102	74,954
Geographic region					
Northeast	32	66,320	57,000	65,202	75,710
North Central	58	63,015	57,803	63,161	70,304
South	55	62,333	55,000	60,540	71,136
West	52	81,541	68,172	80,412	94,356
City type					
Central	108	62,496	55,000	61,998	69,222
Suburban	85	75,653	63,502	71,640	88,097
Independent	4	66,359	59,285	66,438	73,590
Form of government					
Mayor-council	57	59,729	51,064	58,477	66,366

Title of official	No. cities reporting	Distribution of 1993 salaries			
		Mean ($)	First quartile ($)	Median ($)	Third quartile ($)
50,000 - 99,999 continued					
Council-manager	137	71,699	60,948	69,245	79,500
Fire chief					
Total	179	63,644	54,002	61,380	71,500
Geographic region					
Northeast	26	61,764	52,257	60,854	72,302
North Central	56	60,379	57,096	61,079	66,929
South	54	57,332	49,859	56,500	63,211
West	43	76,961	65,750	74,496	86,963
City type					
Central	105	59,254	51,129	58,844	66,367
Suburban	71	70,332	57,902	68,000	80,875
Independent	3	58,997	. . .	57,601	. . .
Form of government					
Mayor-council	53	56,379	48,499	55,619	63,226
Council-manager	53	66,694	57,000	64,646	73,283
Planning director					
Total	165	59,637	50,500	58,728	67,736
Geographic region					
Northeast	22	53,387	42,210	54,394	64,949
North Central	44	56,665	51,041	58,037	61,900
South	47	52,978	43,472	52,893	62,987
West	52	70,816	62,300	71,106	80,352
City type					
Central	89	54,546	44,201	54,724	63,001
Suburban	72	65,992	53,813	64,217	75,093
Independent	4	58,532	57,845	60,393	62,941
Form of government					
Mayor-council	42	49,580	39,624	45,601	56,364
Council-manager	120	63,165	53,118	62,200	70,470
Personnel director					
Total	179	56,382	46,920	55,177	63,984
Geographic region					
Northeast	25	50,104	43,389	48,142	61,007
North Central	49	54,794	51,070	56,077	60,528
South	55	51,725	46,304	51,828	58,475
West	50	66,199	53,328	68,124	75,540
City type					
Central	99	52,931	45,845	51,938	60,415
Suburban	77	60,824	51,200	59,279	70,188
Independent	3	56,236	. . .	52,720	. . .
Form of government					
Mayor-council	50	47,841	38,741	46,925	56,092
Council-manager	128	59,650	51,254	57,894	66,096
Risk manager					
Total	95	46,680	38,471	45,136	53,063
Geographic region					
Northeast	5	48,324	43,012	45,240	55,369
North Central	21	44,378	41,288	44,367	45,780
South	40	43,057	36,208	42,340	49,190
West	29	53,062	45,700	52,338	60,012
City type					
Central	61	44,409	37,336	44,367	50,782
Suburban	32	51,070	42,999	48,006	56,136
Form of government					
Mayor-council	14	43,590	36,603	41,362	45,485
Council-manager	80	47,237	39,850	45,584	53,172
Director of parks and recreation					
Total	153	58,206	48,113	55,931	69,120
Geographic region					
Northeast	20	50,135	46,000	48,607	55,369
North Central	38	55,092	48,591	54,321	62,542
South	48	52,316	46,051	51,126	60,340
West	47	70,174	58,200	71,478	79,622
City type					
Central	85	53,582	46,244	52,685	60,451
Suburban	65	64,224	50,960	65,184	74,672
Independent	3	58,807	. . .	52,294	. . .
Form of government					
Mayor-council	40	48,872	43,076	49,051	54,108
Council-manager	112	61,419	50,835	60,173	71,219
Superintendent of parks					
Total	110	45,673	36,693	44,580	52,530
Geographic region					
Northeast	15	41,771	34,204	41,061	51,457
North Central	27	45,691	40,214	45,445	50,091
South	34	38,583	31,344	37,878	44,761
West	34	54,471	43,896	54,230	62,191
City type					
Central	67	42,447	36,061	41,600	49,246
Suburban	40	51,242	44,761	50,083	58,188

Table 1/4 continued **SALARIES OF MUNICIPAL OFFICIALS: 1 JULY 1993**

Title of official	No. cities reporting	Mean ($)	First quartile ($)	Median ($)	Third quartile ($)
50,000 - 99,999 continued					
Independent	3	43,465	...	41,681	...
Form of government					
Mayor-council	26	40,810	35,675	40,319	44,522
Council-manager	83	47,099	37,560	46,529	53,617
Director of recreation					
Total	87	46,353	36,240	45,445	54,600
Geographic region					
Northeast	14	43,319	37,691	41,970	46,755
North Central	21	43,658	36,918	45,445	49,619
South	25	38,091	33,529	36,358	44,638
West	27	57,673	50,112	56,602	61,110
City type					
Central	53	42,087	34,105	41,600	48,385
Suburban	31	53,958	43,937	51,438	59,376
Independent	3	43,145	...	43,680	...
Form of government					
Mayor-council	23	40,074	31,276	37,691	43,937
Council-manager	63	48,476	38,683	46,916	56,248
Librarian					
Total	104	56,593	48,311	54,669	63,190
Geographic region					
Northeast	26	53,350	46,000	52,929	61,606
North Central	29	57,007	52,000	55,618	59,708
South	24	47,281	44,558	48,952	53,136
West	25	68,426	54,858	71,411	79,622
City type					
Central	56	52,559	46,080	52,341	58,300
Suburban	46	62,189	51,314	58,847	74,672
Form of government					
Mayor-council	32	53,131	45,971	52,393	58,519
Council-manager	70	58,055	48,959	55,125	64,620
Director of information services					
Total	136	52,547	45,775	52,313	59,545
Geographic region					
Northeast	20	54,638	45,580	51,460	60,918
North Central	37	49,776	45,009	50,570	54,742
South	47	49,380	44,875	49,878	55,484
West	32	59,096	53,144	60,337	65,112
City type					
Central	86	51,055	45,580	51,168	57,263
Suburban	46	54,956	46,376	52,510	62,632
Independent	4	56,919	59,545	60,337	61,128
Form of government					
Mayor-council	36	48,967	43,607	47,328	52,494
Council-manager	98	53,610	47,272	52,902	60,093
Purchasing director					
Total	143	44,415	39,000	44,956	49,862
Geographic region					
Northeast	24	45,754	39,494	46,653	52,308
North Central	36	44,212	40,768	45,119	47,545
South	48	41,547	35,616	42,254	46,669
West	35	47,641	42,066	47,382	53,147
City type					
Central	86	42,499	36,140	43,359	47,545
Suburban	54	47,439	43,412	46,945	50,748
Independent	3	44,938	...	44,090	...
Form of government					
Mayor-council	37	41,512	32,108	44,340	47,314
Council-manager	104	45,225	39,728	45,200	50,175
25,000 - 49,999					
Mayor					
Total	445	16,897	4,200	7,368	18,591
Geographic region					
Northeast	109	21,008	3,600	7,211	40,000
North Central	129	18,085	6,000	8,799	35,000
South	95	17,489	5,197	9,600	20,000
West	112	11,027	3,600	4,812	9,528
City type					
Central	109	23,768	6,000	12,000	43,523
Suburban	260	13,665	4,000	6,000	12,000
Independent	76	18,101	4,800	9,069	32,055
Form of government					
Mayor-council	155	34,863	12,000	39,192	51,367
Council-manager	267	6,906	3,600	5,400	8,400
Commission	9	15,158	4,000	6,000	8,400
Town meeting	6	19,968	2,000	4,000	48,000
Rep. town meeting	8	1,927	1,200	1,668	2,000

Title of official	No. cities reporting	Mean ($)	First quartile ($)	Median ($)	Third quartile ($)
25,000 - 49,999 continued					
City manager					
Total	294	81,220	71,505	79,247	89,054
Geographic region					
Northeast	48	74,893	68,575	73,430	80,000
North Central	65	75,929	67,000	77,000	84,506
South	75	76,737	67,600	77,380	83,988
West	106	90,501	79,620	88,311	100,000
City type					
Central	61	76,630	67,469	77,380	82,992
Suburban	175	85,797	74,900	84,866	93,600
Independent	58	72,239	64,118	73,180	80,000
Form of government					
Mayor-council	8	83,162	77,000	78,124	97,832
Council-manager	280	81,381	71,858	80,000	89,054
Town meeting	4	70,806	66,465	69,553	72,640
Chief appointed administrator					
Total	119	63,561	52,200	65,520	75,155
Geographic region					
Northeast	50	61,913	49,600	64,125	75,000
North Central	39	62,460	51,000	63,800	73,780
South	13	62,045	53,757	63,051	73,275
West	17	72,094	62,830	73,088	80,004
City type					
Central	20	53,817	42,000	50,422	63,514
Suburban	83	67,923	58,289	70,000	78,563
Independent	16	53,112	36,329	58,678	68,040
Form of government					
Mayor-council	81	61,014	45,000	62,830	75,000
Council-manager	26	70,247	60,547	68,060	77,991
Commission	5	67,950	62,568	68,054	75,755
Rep. town meeting	7	65,062	60,308	72,000	74,388
Asst. city mgr./asst. CAO					
Total	209	58,042	45,400	54,400	68,292
Geographic region					
Northeast	37	45,699	36,957	44,000	51,582
North Central	58	51,400	45,097	51,894	55,494
South	46	54,659	47,157	54,590	61,436
West	68	72,712	62,076	70,393	81,072
City type					
Central	40	56,226	46,125	55,041	65,772
Suburban	139	59,954	45,933	54,984	71,642
Independent	30	51,604	42,475	50,763	59,575
Form of government					
Mayor-council	24	52,780	42,253	51,895	61,436
Council-manager	180	58,981	45,620	54,992	69,300
Rep. town meeting	3	54,072	...	53,646	...
City clerk					
Total	396	40,765	32,333	40,688	47,900
Geographic region					
Northeast	97	42,608	35,952	42,628	48,498
North Central	111	35,090	27,862	34,374	43,410
South	88	38,224	29,774	38,099	44,227
West	100	47,515	38,004	46,481	55,316
City type					
Central	97	37,795	29,556	37,000	44,215
Suburban	225	43,535	35,472	43,372	50,529
Independent	74	36,239	30,500	34,261	42,885
Form of government					
Mayor-council	130	37,579	30,000	37,000	44,448
Council-manager	245	42,171	33,048	41,772	48,724
Commission	7	45,795	33,446	43,808	55,855
Town meeting	5	45,508	43,644	46,148	47,112
Rep. town meeting	9	41,977	41,500	42,620	45,000
Chief financial officer					
Total	382	57,119	46,774	56,845	65,448
Geographic region					
Northeast	101	55,383	46,738	55,614	63,500
North Central	97	52,557	44,088	53,340	60,858
South	89	53,086	46,115	52,392	59,467
West	95	67,403	58,092	67,284	74,572
City type					
Central	91	52,028	42,180	51,573	58,830
Suburban	224	61,195	51,821	60,095	69,377
Independent	67	50,408	42,700	50,503	58,767
Form of government					
Mayor-council	108	51,437	41,250	49,882	61,338
Council-manager	261	59,734	51,000	58,192	67,706
Commission	4	45,840	33,500	47,989	62,478
Town meeting	4	55,092	51,808	54,654	57,499
Rep. town meeting	5	54,025	51,500	55,533	57,864

Table 1/4   SALARIES OF MUNICIPAL OFFICIALS: 1 JULY 1993
continued

Title of official	No. cities reporting	Distribution of 1993 salaries			
		Mean ($)	First quartile ($)	Median ($)	Third quartile ($)
25,000 - 49,999 continued					
Director of economic development					
Total	164	52,806	41,895	52,797	61,175
Geographic region					
Northeast	38	51,068	43,886	49,010	57,500
North Central	56	49,598	41,394	50,914	59,280
South	30	46,672	39,344	43,500	53,604
West	40	63,548	56,712	64,343	69,720
City type					
Central	56	48,130	37,765	45,499	56,595
Suburban	84	56,871	48,500	57,358	62,986
Independent	24	49,487	40,830	50,641	56,712
Form of government					
Mayor-council	54	47,285	38,525	44,392	56,433
Council-manager	108	55,733	48,115	56,797	62,688
Treasurer					
Total	131	40,753	32,448	40,894	47,586
Geographic region					
Northeast	55	40,689	34,990	41,468	47,000
North Central	38	36,641	31,200	38,418	44,000
South	12	38,273	31,152	36,325	44,960
West	26	48,044	32,939	47,241	59,952
City type					
Central	39	40,622	34,127	39,700	48,069
Suburban	65	42,640	33,013	44,000	51,676
Independent	27	36,400	29,317	38,500	44,242
Form of government					
Mayor-council	56	38,310	28,805	38,418	46,546
Council-manager	65	42,258	33,204	41,988	47,936
Rep. town meeting	8	44,447	42,620	44,438	46,539
Director of public works					
Total	389	59,026	48,759	58,434	67,581
Geographic region					
Northeast	101	55,841	47,700	56,666	62,990
North Central	101	56,825	48,672	57,300	63,201
South	98	52,526	46,500	51,684	60,362
West	89	72,297	64,501	70,983	79,920
City type					
Central	102	54,458	45,827	53,715	61,800
Suburban	214	63,076	52,627	62,382	70,848
Independent	73	53,539	46,000	52,208	62,000
Form of government					
Mayor-council	126	53,534	45,000	52,345	61,800
Council-manager	244	62,032	51,506	60,757	70,562
Commission	7	51,821	41,600	45,000	56,424
Town meeting	4	57,089	54,920	56,890	58,859
Rep. town meeting	8	61,120	56,666	62,268	62,990
Engineer					
Total	261	52,387	45,000	52,125	59,924
Geographic region					
Northeast	61	49,846	43,158	51,715	57,238
North Central	75	51,240	45,000	50,544	57,803
South	73	48,846	43,000	50,323	54,835
West	52	61,991	54,036	61,892	68,928
City type					
Central	80	48,497	41,000	48,696	54,684
Suburban	121	56,643	49,962	56,592	64,600
Independent	60	48,989	42,936	49,064	54,742
Form of government					
Mayor-council	72	47,918	41,755	46,525	54,835
Council-manager	175	54,570	48,141	53,976	62,500
Commission	5	44,795	41,000	49,404	53,248
Rep. town meeting	7	49,761	47,000	52,523	55,487
Police chief					
Total	405	59,788	50,049	58,600	68,399
Geographic region					
Northeast	106	62,716	53,583	61,425	69,842
North Central	116	54,703	46,154	55,006	62,537
South	103	53,330	44,990	52,333	61,661
West	80	71,597	61,510	70,878	80,004
City type					
Central	109	54,213	45,695	51,557	61,510
Suburban	212	65,921	57,073	63,959	71,400
Independent	84	51,546	42,936	50,799	59,628
Form of government					
Mayor-council	138	54,902	43,292	53,800	63,615
Council-manager	248	62,244	52,780	61,680	69,300
Commission	7	60,313	50,000	57,700	73,926
Town meeting	3	77,033	. . .	82,316	. . .
Rep. town meeting	9	60,892	58,767	60,308	61,600

Title of official	No. cities reporting	Distribution of 1993 salaries			
		Mean ($)	First quartile ($)	Median ($)	Third quartile ($)
25,000 - 49,999 continued					
Fire chief					
Total	326	54,569	45,000	53,382	62,000
Geographic region					
Northeast	65	55,245	47,555	55,472	62,000
North Central	99	51,395	44,484	51,300	58,580
South	99	49,187	42,154	47,964	55,000
West	63	67,315	56,892	66,900	76,200
City type					
Central	111	51,696	43,937	50,751	58,376
Suburban	144	59,844	51,885	59,048	67,596
Independent	71	48,360	41,600	46,818	55,896
Form of government					
Mayor-council	111	48,838	40,983	47,045	56,232
Council-manager	200	57,355	48,318	55,682	65,964
Commission	4	51,398	50,000	52,500	55,000
Rep. town meeting	9	61,594	58,767	62,000	66,929
Planning director					
Total	286	53,109	42,766	51,516	62,667
Geographic region					
Northeast	64	49,435	40,554	46,839	57,028
North Central	69	48,464	41,859	47,424	56,460
South	73	47,394	41,054	46,000	52,778
West	80	65,270	56,613	65,128	72,924
City type					
Central	75	48,339	39,282	46,230	55,076
Suburban	157	57,217	46,175	56,460	66,948
Independent	54	47,793	40,830	45,340	54,218
Form of government					
Mayor-council	81	47,827	38,502	44,304	57,648
Council-manager	193	55,637	45,777	53,720	64,705
Rep. town meeting	8	44,552	43,418	45,729	47,000
Personnel director					
Total	282	46,441	38,045	45,958	53,033
Geographic region					
Northeast	50	43,439	34,595	41,906	50,034
North Central	68	43,926	38,045	45,649	49,895
South	94	42,587	35,354	43,004	49,249
West	70	56,204	47,237	57,620	64,368
City type					
Central	91	43,873	35,734	43,392	51,803
Suburban	129	50,282	41,544	48,828	57,700
Independent	62	42,219	34,341	43,091	49,000
Form of government					
Mayor-council	87	42,636	34,595	41,708	50,960
Council-manager	185	48,327	40,679	47,676	54,719
Commission	4	43,554	40,328	43,816	47,304
Rep. town meeting	4	47,005	45,100	47,550	50,000
Risk manager					
Total	92	42,566	32,983	43,141	50,000
Geographic region					
Northeast	10	39,548	32,609	40,602	48,834
North Central	12	43,365	42,831	43,864	45,881
South	42	37,033	29,692	35,586	43,535
West	28	51,602	43,403	49,872	57,540
City type					
Central	33	42,144	31,388	43,236	51,120
Suburban	42	43,644	37,800	43,576	50,460
Independent	17	40,721	33,134	41,100	43,403
Form of government					
Mayor-council	22	39,285	29,692	39,334	47,539
Council-manager	68	43,607	37,637	43,294	50,460
Director of parks and recreation					
Total	284	50,495	40,435	48,851	58,596
Geographic region					
Northeast	57	46,487	35,905	45,501	52,958
North Central	74	46,419	36,576	46,379	55,635
South	78	46,575	39,677	46,237	52,225
West	75	61,640	50,551	62,640	69,168
City type					
Central	74	47,423	36,576	47,175	53,925
Suburban	148	54,289	43,455	52,916	62,899
Independent	62	45,106	36,750	44,712	51,626
Form of government					
Mayor-council	89	45,587	36,060	44,735	52,907
Council-manager	184	53,369	43,801	52,165	62,143
Commission	5	43,101	33,883	40,560	52,826
Rep. town meeting	5	40,884	35,913	40,000	44,568
Superintendent of parks					
Total	187	43,054	32,305	40,446	47,669

Table 1/4 **SALARIES OF MUNICIPAL OFFICIALS: 1 JULY 1993**
continued

Title of official	No. cities reporting	Distribution of 1993 salaries			
		Mean ($)	First quartile ($)	Median ($)	Third quartile ($)
25,000 - 49,999 continued					
Geographic region					
Northeast	40	43,452	35,600	42,829	50,000
North Central	49	39,561	33,404	39,744	45,097
South	58	33,792	26,557	31,933	40,020
West	40	60,362	41,390	49,302	57,084
City type					
Central	56	37,742	27,879	37,146	45,000
Suburban	92	44,666	37,009	42,177	51,300
Independent	39	46,876	29,702	36,940	42,557
Form of government					
Mayor-council	52	37,981	29,786	35,410	42,276
Council-manager	127	44,918	33,788	41,076	49,181
Rep. town meeting	4	45,919	43,626	45,313	47,000
Director of recreation					
Total	151	39,695	29,896	39,393	47,712
Geographic region					
Northeast	36	40,480	36,057	39,882	47,000
North Central	47	39,283	29,158	38,960	47,800
South	41	32,366	26,000	32,507	40,500
West	27	50,498	40,381	50,532	60,510
City type					
Central	45	36,379	29,184	36,790	40,788
Suburban	74	43,960	36,057	42,702	52,305
Independent	32	34,498	26,834	33,328	40,381
Form of government					
Mayor-council	54	35,357	26,891	33,808	44,620
Council-manager	93	42,241	33,293	40,621	50,278
Rep. town meeting	3	38,017	. . .	37,413	. . .
Librarian					
Total	180	46,193	37,616	44,142	52,728
Geographic region					
Northeast	63	48,371	40,482	47,000	55,000
North Central	33	44,086	39,971	44,016	47,216
South	46	37,947	31,000	37,358	44,268
West	38	54,394	40,348	51,528	66,276
City type					
Central	41	43,601	35,934	42,779	48,516
Suburban	96	49,222	40,500	45,758	55,000
Independent	43	41,901	33,696	40,000	51,000
Form of government					
Mayor-council	49	44,077	36,961	40,837	47,183
Council-manager	116	46,864	37,616	44,712	52,848
Commission	4	50,567	46,720	49,748	52,776
Town meeting	4	49,027	46,819	48,060	49,301
Rep. town meeting	7	45,769	40,482	48,308	51,829
Director of information services					
Total	194	45,856	38,252	45,737	52,584
Geographic region					
Northeast	40	44,317	38,200	43,508	54,000
North Central	49	43,758	36,624	43,929	49,774
South	54	43,318	35,632	43,258	50,000
West	51	51,767	45,276	51,948	61,560
City type					
Central	58	45,748	38,686	43,549	52,584
Suburban	89	49,228	42,923	49,975	55,780
Independent	47	39,606	32,365	40,352	46,888
Form of government					
Mayor-council	59	43,084	35,712	42,000	48,804
Council-manager	126	47,328	40,060	47,099	53,300
Town meeting	3	33,583	. . .	31,677	. . .
Rep. town meeting	4	48,540	49,895	51,948	54,000
Purchasing director					
Total	161	38,202	31,900	38,040	43,596
Geographic region					
Northeast	44	38,325	32,157	39,032	43,197
North Central	27	36,545	28,968	36,247	40,928
South	64	35,950	29,116	36,272	40,102
West	26	45,261	39,036	44,737	51,900
City type					
Central	61	36,174	31,962	36,084	40,196
Suburban	66	40,522	36,058	40,201	46,224
Independent	34	37,338	27,223	36,025	44,365
Form of government					
Mayor-council	52	35,950	29,116	36,240	40,966
Council-manager	106	39,400	32,537	39,000	44,766
10,000 - 24,999					
Mayor					
Total	917	11,211	3,000	5,400	11,800

Title of official	No. cities reporting	Distribution of 1993 salaries			
		Mean ($)	First quartile ($)	Median ($)	Third quartile ($)
10,000 - 24,999 continued					
Geographic region					
Northeast	243	10,462	2,299	3,500	8,000
North Central	312	12,976	3,600	6,620	15,000
South	243	12,297	3,600	6,475	13,200
West	119	5,892	3,600	4,320	6,612
City type					
Central	20	15,737	4,800	7,200	30,000
Suburban	605	10,618	2,999	5,000	9,600
Independent	292	12,130	2,652	6,000	16,500
Form of government					
Mayor-council	392	18,425	5,400	10,287	33,000
Council-manager	437	4,382	2,100	3,600	6,000
Commission	31	8,600	3,200	5,000	13,000
Town meeting	43	16,994	1,200	2,341	40,712
Rep. town meeting	14	10,398	1,500	2,100	5,000
City manager					
Total	516	66,550	56,656	65,072	74,401
Geographic region					
Northeast	93	65,966	55,250	62,000	76,840
North Central	129	63,688	55,125	63,340	70,005
South	187	63,221	55,000	62,525	71,236
West	107	76,326	65,004	72,769	85,785
City type					
Central	13	66,163	59,161	63,525	70,000
Suburban	334	69,509	58,850	68,250	77,750
Independent	169	60,732	52,624	60,600	66,950
Form of government					
Mayor-council	20	67,211	58,850	66,767	77,175
Council-manager	481	66,616	56,656	65,004	74,401
Town meeting	8	65,926	58,300	65,540	72,500
Rep. town meeting	5	67,631	65,526	66,163	70,331
Chief appointed administrator					
Total	342	56,004	45,251	56,892	66,194
Geographic region					
Northeast	135	57,653	45,320	57,885	70,580
North Central	119	56,832	48,670	57,200	66,350
South	60	48,555	38,600	51,511	60,000
West	28	60,498	52,003	59,407	67,500
City type					
Central	6	46,659	35,265	47,443	60,000
Suburban	253	57,906	48,641	58,896	68,904
Independent	83	50,881	43,739	54,384	59,982
Form of government					
Mayor-council	230	56,098	45,094	57,242	66,350
Council-manager	58	59,058	52,003	58,925	68,000
Commission	18	43,749	36,733	41,249	52,765
Town meeting	28	56,829	49,912	55,560	64,785
Rep. town meeting	8	55,840	52,132	56,500	60,000
Asst. city mgr./asst. CAO					
Total	307	45,591	36,142	43,962	53,640
Geographic region					
Northeast	64	40,733	32,453	39,337	46,000
North Central	100	43,891	37,359	43,941	48,000
South	93	43,538	36,000	43,000	52,000
West	50	59,026	46,296	57,612	71,724
City type					
Central	7	46,905	38,345	43,118	47,000
Suburban	231	46,946	36,558	45,635	54,787
Independent	69	40,921	34,216	40,032	46,000
Form of government					
Mayor-council	58	39,948	32,000	37,701	46,296
Council-manager	232	47,559	38,319	45,802	54,432
Commission	4	31,518	23,393	26,181	28,968
Town meeting	11	39,550	32,453	37,639	49,306
City clerk					
Total	807	34,990	28,336	34,064	40,800
Geographic region					
Northeast	224	35,554	28,527	35,000	41,226
North Central	231	33,373	27,811	32,568	38,917
South	247	32,830	26,656	32,136	37,841
West	105	42,423	34,385	40,843	50,556
City type					
Central	17	32,688	29,148	30,905	35,000
Suburban	540	35,974	29,725	34,979	41,521
Independent	250	33,020	26,330	32,178	38,670
Form of government					
Mayor-council	305	33,705	27,433	33,000	39,130
Council-manager	417	36,212	29,000	34,882	41,567
Commission	19	33,635	26,718	34,234	41,504
Town meeting	51	32,315	27,243	33,202	38,288

Table 1/4   **SALARIES OF MUNICIPAL OFFICIALS: 1 JULY 1993**
continued

Title of official	No. cities reporting	Mean ($)	First quartile ($)	Median ($)	Third quartile ($)
10,000 - 24,999 continued					
Rep. town meeting	15	37,917	29,000	37,295	46,911
Chief financial officer					
Total	643	46,664	38,432	45,740	54,272
Geographic region					
Northeast	184	47,131	37,500	46,164	57,000
North Central	175	44,613	37,957	45,000	51,493
South	191	44,008	36,500	43,148	51,432
West	93	55,058	45,000	52,704	62,232
City type					
Central	18	44,705	41,685	45,000	47,873
Suburban	442	48,236	39,000	47,956	57,060
Independent	183	43,061	37,109	42,779	49,496
Form of government					
Mayor-council	209	42,770	34,512	42,888	51,396
Council-manager	374	49,044	40,748	47,726	56,604
Commission	14	34,878	24,172	36,768	46,656
Town meeting	34	48,046	41,343	45,740	55,823
Rep. town meeting	12	50,169	40,209	45,630	48,866
Director of economic development					
Total	207	42,609	35,124	41,500	49,088
Geographic region					
Northeast	36	39,370	34,866	40,500	44,859
North Central	71	40,044	35,044	40,872	45,909
South	67	42,507	34,044	41,017	50,000
West	33	51,868	44,000	48,817	57,382
City type					
Central	8	32,831	30,612	32,625	33,625
Suburban	127	44,399	36,207	43,500	50,000
Independent	72	40,539	35,044	40,034	47,316
Form of government					
Mayor-council	65	40,589	35,044	41,000	45,909
Council-manager	129	44,461	37,004	44,075	50,449
Commission	4	33,899	36,632	36,914	37,196
Town meeting	6	33,746	31,580	33,433	35,030
Rep. town meeting	3	36,123	...	35,000	...
Treasurer					
Total	232	31,847	23,338	31,569	41,216
Geographic region					
Northeast	101	31,793	19,250	32,220	42,135
North Central	69	29,740	24,507	30,500	37,061
South	38	33,379	24,690	30,444	42,312
West	24	35,706	23,868	32,706	46,380
City type					
Central	5	24,616	19,000	24,587	26,000
Suburban	152	32,539	20,904	32,561	42,920
Independent	75	30,925	25,655	29,978	39,084
Form of government					
Mayor-council	86	29,380	20,000	29,839	37,380
Council-manager	94	34,676	26,146	32,320	43,830
Commission	12	20,612	17,250	20,475	25,480
Town meeting	32	32,975	23,163	35,431	42,180
Rep. town meeting	8	37,453	29,036	35,821	49,507
Director of public works					
Total	755	48,386	40,000	47,880	55,700
Geographic region					
Northeast	199	50,463	41,728	49,380	58,220
North Central	202	48,018	41,637	48,381	54,972
South	249	43,317	35,000	42,515	50,678
West	105	57,178	47,273	56,724	65,708
City type					
Central	20	48,138	40,081	47,538	55,928
Suburban	496	50,361	42,000	49,551	57,720
Independent	239	44,308	36,929	44,134	51,840
Form of government					
Mayor-council	273	46,160	37,939	45,200	54,096
Council-manager	424	49,535	41,443	48,630	57,055
Commission	15	42,159	31,817	40,539	49,317
Town meeting	30	52,230	45,839	51,364	60,294
Rep. town meeting	13	55,969	45,518	58,220	60,806
Engineer					
Total	364	46,998	40,516	47,729	52,795
Geographic region					
Northeast	86	50,675	41,092	50,785	61,285
North Central	112	44,917	41,500	47,212	51,246
South	117	44,506	39,500	45,385	50,552
West	49	51,257	43,077	49,080	57,411
City type					
Central	11	39,053	27,640	43,786	47,465

Title of official	No. cities reporting	Mean ($)	First quartile ($)	Median ($)	Third quartile ($)
10,000 - 24,999 continued					
Suburban	216	49,319	43,000	49,917	55,780
Independent	137	43,978	39,000	44,628	49,660
Form of government					
Mayor-council	125	43,359	36,666	44,940	51,285
Council-manager	205	48,827	42,377	48,686	53,087
Commission	8	42,876	41,483	43,738	46,384
Town meeting	18	51,538	48,776	50,960	54,369
Rep. town meeting	8	50,909	48,654	53,147	55,590
Police chief					
Total	843	50,418	41,818	49,305	57,630
Geographic region					
Northeast	214	57,453	48,183	55,553	66,868
North Central	244	48,476	43,407	48,543	54,421
South	284	44,495	37,000	42,541	50,814
West	101	56,858	47,353	55,104	64,548
City type					
Central	20	47,798	42,500	47,058	52,613
Suburban	540	53,977	45,600	52,579	60,450
Independent	283	43,813	37,656	43,000	48,984
Form of government					
Mayor-council	310	48,282	38,304	47,684	55,516
Council-manager	461	51,373	42,806	49,560	58,300
Commission	21	41,582	38,213	40,000	47,000
Town meeting	37	57,981	50,429	56,180	66,072
Rep. town meeting	14	59,523	50,000	55,393	68,608
Fire chief					
Total	605	44,121	35,984	43,056	50,331
Geographic region					
Northeast	118	48,487	41,243	47,162	57,073
North Central	182	43,163	37,428	43,926	50,000
South	235	39,842	33,841	38,479	45,084
West	70	53,616	42,156	51,750	64,272
City type					
Central	14	41,989	38,833	41,199	43,632
Suburban	348	47,410	39,222	46,893	54,269
Independent	243	39,534	33,900	38,755	44,107
Form of government					
Mayor-council	224	41,609	34,222	41,158	48,037
Council-manager	323	44,980	37,040	43,584	50,150
Commission	14	39,721	33,500	37,395	43,638
Town meeting	32	50,421	49,423	52,315	59,699
Rep. town meeting	12	56,238	48,941	51,269	64,319
Planning director					
Total	403	43,911	34,320	42,000	50,009
Geographic region					
Northeast	88	43,725	36,445	43,611	48,774
North Central	92	41,059	34,320	41,229	47,163
South	147	39,404	32,477	37,981	45,360
West	76	56,297	44,544	54,686	66,504
City type					
Central	12	41,138	35,277	39,933	44,096
Suburban	256	46,315	36,102	43,564	52,293
Independent	135	39,599	32,243	39,564	45,032
Form of government					
Mayor-council	113	39,362	31,000	40,000	45,242
Council-manager	261	46,039	35,842	43,222	53,200
Commission	4	30,336	22,734	27,279	31,824
Town meeting	19	42,804	36,445	41,939	46,911
Rep. town meeting	6	49,576	34,333	48,375	66,600
Personnel director					
Total	299	37,195	29,363	35,745	43,070
Geographic region					
Northeast	30	39,341	26,561	36,500	44,342
North Central	71	36,797	30,237	37,600	44,640
South	151	34,492	27,000	33,134	39,102
West	47	45,113	36,420	41,567	52,533
City type					
Central	8	31,671	27,230	31,280	34,070
Suburban	166	39,485	30,975	37,786	45,949
Independent	125	34,509	26,830	34,229	40,116
Form of government					
Mayor-council	88	33,416	25,000	33,295	40,260
Council-manager	198	39,042	32,032	37,659	44,658
Commission	5	25,084	23,355	24,482	26,000
Town meeting	4	42,894	31,309	36,787	42,265
Rep. town meeting	4	38,373	35,000	37,316	39,632
Risk manager					
Total	62	35,524	27,011	33,449	44,000

Table 1/4 SALARIES OF MUNICIPAL OFFICIALS: 1 JULY 1993
continued

Title of official	No. cities reporting	Distribution of 1993 salaries Mean ($)	First quartile ($)	Median ($)	Third quartile ($)
10,000 - 24,999 continued					
Geographic region					
Northeast	7	32,828	19,050	31,001	41,369
North Central	7	33,295	26,077	30,000	44,000
South	31	34,053	25,376	32,867	42,057
West	17	40,234	30,617	37,296	51,612
City type					
Suburban	35	38,134	30,000	37,196	47,421
Independent	25	30,926	24,669	30,604	36,924
Form of government					
Mayor-council	14	30,226	24,100	28,993	33,608
Council-manager	46	37,458	27,934	36,479	45,572
Director of parks and recreation					
Total	484	39,955	32,431	38,576	47,267
Geographic region					
Northeast	103	36,589	29,338	35,587	44,360
North Central	129	40,592	34,970	40,508	47,164
South	183	36,964	30,368	36,055	43,142
West	69	51,718	43,221	50,100	60,962
City type					
Central	11	38,098	30,050	36,480	42,328
Suburban	304	41,336	33,000	39,831	49,067
Independent	169	37,590	30,717	36,534	44,000
Form of government					
Mayor-council	175	36,858	30,002	36,534	43,092
Council-manager	286	42,230	33,801	40,609	49,490
Commission	4	30,949	28,787	30,694	32,600
Town meeting	14	32,939	24,804	33,719	41,395
Rep. town meeting	5	44,990	33,000	46,976	50,447
Superintendent of parks					
Total	262	34,972	27,500	33,994	41,575
Geographic region					
Northeast	47	39,116	31,336	38,440	45,825
North Central	88	34,791	28,668	33,775	41,765
South	78	28,780	23,200	29,117	33,000
West	49	41,179	35,592	39,396	46,666
City type					
Central	9	29,597	27,350	29,856	34,386
Suburban	158	36,988	29,700	36,034	43,586
Independent	95	32,128	25,575	31,361	37,305
Form of government					
Mayor-council	88	34,034	26,800	31,970	40,817
Council-manager	155	35,135	28,944	34,538	42,218
Commission	5	30,659	26,506	31,347	32,650
Town meeting	9	43,747	33,541	45,825	50,098
Rep. town meeting	5	34,950	27,853	40,146	40,340
Director of recreation					
Total	202	33,877	25,619	32,620	40,078
Geographic region					
Northeast	60	33,957	27,265	32,643	40,241
North Central	65	32,347	24,263	32,430	40,003
South	44	31,504	24,789	28,904	36,483
West	33	39,909	32,508	37,404	41,652
City type					
Central	5	29,498	25,743	27,265	30,630
Suburban	123	36,234	27,322	34,900	45,000
Independent	74	30,256	25,020	30,317	35,256
Form of government					
Mayor-council	76	33,457	25,020	32,209	40,020
Council-manager	101	35,505	27,851	34,178	40,700
Commission	7	25,704	22,728	27,800	31,946
Town meeting	13	28,604	18,097	28,133	37,727
Rep. town meeting	5	32,538	25,272	31,169	47,580
Librarian					
Total	324	36,771	29,496	35,301	42,899
Geographic region					
Northeast	106	40,993	33,380	39,624	47,965
North Central	92	35,417	29,330	35,040	40,000
South	83	30,984	24,675	30,222	37,195
West	43	40,427	30,873	39,468	46,248
City type					
Central	6	34,106	29,268	35,747	38,820
Suburban	192	39,122	31,545	38,094	45,246
Independent	126	33,314	28,121	32,000	39,096
Form of government					
Mayor-council	105	36,656	28,800	35,326	43,654
Council-manager	170	36,691	29,496	35,608	42,236
Commission	9	29,745	27,801	28,787	31,357
Town meeting	31	38,081	32,869	37,222	44,340
Rep. town meeting	9	42,128	33,075	37,967	48,110

Title of official	No. cities reporting	Distribution of 1993 salaries Mean ($)	First quartile ($)	Median ($)	Third quartile ($)
10,000 - 24,999 continued					
Director of information services					
Total	147	37,272	29,224	36,553	43,533
Geographic region					
Northeast	29	41,353	35,217	41,626	48,911
North Central	31	37,052	33,300	37,900	41,241
South	68	34,845	27,650	34,080	42,121
West	19	40,085	29,616	38,064	47,695
City type					
Central	7	30,953	26,650	28,551	34,528
Suburban	71	40,387	32,316	39,900	47,695
Independent	69	34,708	28,368	34,776	40,955
Form of government					
Mayor-council	40	36,163	29,224	36,339	40,623
Council-manager	97	37,843	29,983	37,011	43,928
Commission	3	27,204	. . .	28,350	. . .
Town meeting	3	32,585	. . .	35,217	. . .
Rep. town meeting	4	45,573	43,691	44,646	45,600
Purchasing director					
Total	168	31,162	24,023	29,682	36,810
Geographic region					
Northeast	24	31,123	19,000	30,217	41,369
North Central	25	37,244	30,160	34,000	42,280
South	102	29,164	22,699	27,635	34,332
West	17	34,260	27,539	32,064	42,744
City type					
Central	6	26,235	17,868	27,717	33,259
Suburban	81	34,318	25,480	32,635	40,456
Independent	81	28,370	22,893	26,965	33,228
Form of government					
Mayor-council	56	29,438	21,000	27,563	34,735
Council-manager	109	32,161	25,356	31,000	37,132
5,000 - 9,999					
Mayor					
Total	965	7,010	2,000	3,600	6,700
Geographic region					
Northeast	268	6,120	1,500	2,350	4,000
North Central	319	7,089	2,400	4,500	7,200
South	252	8,930	2,400	4,800	9,600
West	126	4,861	2,400	3,600	6,000
City type					
Suburban	547	6,516	2,000	3,600	6,000
Independent	417	7,672	1,800	3,840	7,812
Form of government					
Mayor-council	465	9,356	3,000	5,500	10,200
Council-manager	399	3,138	1,200	2,400	3,999
Commission	23	7,296	3,000	5,000	6,500
Town meeting	70	13,889	1,500	2,900	31,372
Rep. town meeting	8	2,727	2,400	2,550	2,975
City manager					
Total	454	53,947	45,449	51,944	60,060
Geographic region					
Northeast	100	48,585	41,870	46,980	52,134
North Central	111	53,069	46,500	52,530	57,881
South	151	52,016	45,000	50,102	58,765
West	92	64,004	52,100	61,700	74,976
City type					
Suburban	242	56,945	46,750	54,059	65,000
Independent	212	50,525	44,132	49,658	56,000
Form of government					
Mayor-council	32	52,939	46,500	50,283	56,719
Council-manager	411	54,197	45,312	52,000	60,278
Town meeting	9	49,669	41,689	47,507	60,680
Chief appointed administrator					
Total	420	46,537	38,000	46,142	54,075
Geographic region					
Northeast	138	45,401	35,178	44,575	53,747
North Central	141	47,505	40,560	47,000	53,640
South	90	43,030	35,637	41,918	52,000
West	51	53,125	46,800	52,012	61,693
City type					
Suburban	287	47,489	38,000	46,800	56,238
Independent	132	44,640	38,000	45,207	50,971
Form of government					
Mayor-council	272	45,895	37,960	45,822	54,029
Council-manager	93	50,895	43,013	49,555	57,769
Commission	9	38,926	32,915	37,960	46,000
Town meeting	40	42,613	35,178	42,000	49,587

Table 1/4 SALARIES OF MUNICIPAL OFFICIALS: 1 JULY 1993
continued

Title of official	No. cities reporting	Distribution of 1993 salaries				Title of official	No. cities reporting	Distribution of 1993 salaries			
		Mean ($)	First quartile ($)	Median ($)	Third quartile ($)			Mean ($)	First quartile ($)	Median ($)	Third quartile ($)
5,000 - 9,999 continued						**5,000 - 9,999 continued**					
Rep. town meeting	6	45,672	41,110	48,262	51,460	**Director of public works**					
Asst. city mgr./asst. CAO						Total	714	39,490	31,803	38,812	45,500
Total	201	36,099	26,850	35,066	42,793	Geographic region					
Geographic region						Northeast	186	40,999	33,990	40,000	46,833
Northeast	50	29,888	25,000	30,589	35,987	North Central	159	40,287	35,208	40,000	44,983
North Central	50	35,261	26,083	36,148	43,474	South	251	35,053	28,000	33,614	41,000
South	71	35,533	28,371	35,110	41,950	West	118	45,476	37,141	44,544	50,596
West	30	49,186	36,000	48,908	58,176	City type					
City type						Suburban	415	41,029	33,180	40,425	47,820
Suburban	126	37,516	27,362	35,493	44,900	Independent	299	37,354	30,864	37,010	43,000
Independent	75	33,718	26,083	33,830	39,600	Form of government					
Form of government						Mayor-council	296	37,907	30,000	37,326	44,013
Mayor-council	49	28,665	22,623	26,285	35,448	Council-manager	363	40,681	32,960	39,549	46,860
Council-manager	141	39,448	31,512	37,274	46,578	Commission	11	38,615	26,600	38,314	48,456
Town meeting	10	27,228	21,000	29,664	32,633	Town meeting	38	41,110	35,505	40,218	46,047
City clerk						Rep. town meeting	6	36,895	33,088	36,969	38,295
Total	798	29,809	23,955	29,026	34,750	**Engineer**					
Geographic region						Total	145	39,698	33,624	41,253	47,736
Northeast	211	29,138	23,000	29,000	33,740	Geographic region					
North Central	234	29,915	24,624	29,622	34,739	Northeast	23	36,878	14,000	36,000	55,675
South	236	28,055	23,012	27,014	32,629	North Central	45	39,440	34,299	41,600	46,000
West	117	34,343	27,922	33,780	39,996	South	41	37,368	31,000	38,943	46,446
City type						West	36	44,477	39,509	44,091	48,600
Suburban	431	30,574	24,000	30,000	36,000	City type					
Independent	367	28,910	23,857	27,672	33,478	Suburban	72	41,403	32,947	43,110	49,774
Form of government						Independent	73	38,017	34,000	39,509	44,433
Mayor-council	360	29,881	23,400	28,446	35,300	Form of government					
Council-manager	346	30,289	24,401	29,597	35,098	Mayor-council	55	34,932	25,000	37,856	44,433
Commission	18	31,589	26,000	30,843	33,850	Council-manager	85	42,681	36,000	43,000	49,500
Town meeting	66	26,528	23,336	27,531	31,185	Commission	4	37,860	41,340	41,694	42,047
Rep. town meeting	8	28,853	25,474	31,699	32,280	**Police chief**					
Chief financial officer						Total	820	41,599	33,800	39,621	47,170
Total	442	37,032	29,798	36,025	43,236	Geographic region					
Geographic region						Northeast	204	47,190	37,600	43,004	54,590
Northeast	115	33,084	26,523	32,408	39,957	North Central	220	39,962	34,479	39,261	44,941
North Central	102	36,759	30,160	36,582	42,563	South	272	36,334	30,305	35,751	40,400
South	129	35,323	29,172	34,020	39,737	West	124	46,852	39,756	44,649	53,350
West	96	44,346	36,168	43,311	49,560	City type					
City type						Suburban	439	45,667	37,400	43,192	52,250
Suburban	254	38,371	30,160	37,095	46,000	Independent	381	36,911	30,977	36,300	41,095
Independent	188	35,223	29,172	35,216	40,285	Form of government					
Form of government						Mayor-council	341	40,149	31,100	38,575	44,976
Mayor-council	150	35,898	28,900	35,760	43,500	Council-manager	423	42,295	35,172	40,174	47,604
Council-manager	244	38,750	30,300	36,942	45,011	Commission	14	38,166	28,200	36,123	38,314
Commission	7	29,673	30,160	30,840	36,107	Town meeting	37	48,116	42,611	48,019	53,455
Town meeting	37	32,043	26,848	31,341	39,480	Rep. town meeting	5	42,963	38,868	43,000	48,842
Rep. town meeting	4	33,762	33,975	34,451	34,926	**Fire chief**					
Director of economic development						Total	406	34,537	28,367	33,904	39,953
Total	98	37,173	30,000	36,224	40,790	Geographic region					
Geographic region						Northeast	60	35,232	30,558	35,196	40,734
Northeast	20	34,611	26,600	35,422	39,675	North Central	109	33,471	27,616	34,154	40,000
North Central	41	35,123	30,000	35,856	40,643	South	175	32,089	26,628	31,500	36,504
South	17	37,730	28,800	35,000	45,093	West	62	42,647	34,770	40,050	51,397
West	20	43,465	35,004	38,100	45,600	City type					
City type						Suburban	173	37,187	30,700	37,000	44,576
Suburban	36	40,678	32,323	37,381	43,843	Independent	233	32,569	27,616	32,477	36,600
Independent	62	35,138	30,000	35,000	40,223	Form of government					
Form of government						Mayor-council	157	32,822	26,770	32,406	37,555
Mayor-council	38	35,184	30,000	35,850	40,238	Council-manager	211	35,515	29,744	34,952	40,169
Council-manager	49	39,110	32,323	37,200	44,532	Commission	10	33,059	25,000	33,194	45,277
Commission	4	33,663	31,720	33,360	35,000	Town meeting	26	37,272	34,172	39,369	45,150
Town meeting	6	35,188	31,045	33,781	40,000	**Planning director**					
Treasurer						Total	205	37,432	29,609	35,000	43,700
Total	230	27,756	20,400	26,753	34,630	Geographic region					
Geographic region						Northeast	38	33,102	27,999	33,750	40,110
Northeast	102	27,539	19,073	25,845	33,353	North Central	33	32,073	26,250	32,111	38,821
North Central	61	27,787	22,371	27,500	34,750	South	65	34,637	30,246	33,196	39,567
South	43	28,796	21,296	28,000	35,440	West	69	45,013	33,684	43,700	56,424
West	24	26,738	20,696	22,686	32,640	City type					
City type						Suburban	115	40,697	30,828	38,600	46,272
Suburban	139	29,365	21,306	28,000	36,106	Independent	90	33,260	26,457	33,622	38,610
Independent	91	25,298	20,011	24,003	30,293	Form of government					
Form of government						Mayor-council	59	33,130	27,372	32,698	40,238
Mayor-council	86	27,029	20,176	24,620	32,760	Council-manager	130	39,794	30,000	35,321	46,272
Council-manager	99	29,718	21,232	28,208	35,440	Commission	3	34,065	. . .	32,060	. . .
Commission	4	22,065	20,758	22,381	24,003	Town meeting	12	34,355	34,216	37,730	40,159
Town meeting	36	24,934	19,329	23,222	31,988	**Personnel director**					
Rep. town meeting	5	26,292	16,000	31,795	33,353	Total	125	29,720	20,953	26,280	36,560

Table 1/4
continued   SALARIES OF MUNICIPAL OFFICIALS: 1 JULY 1993

Title of official	No. cities reporting	Distribution of 1993 salaries			
		Mean ($)	First quartile ($)	Median ($)	Third quartile ($)
5,000 - 9,999 continued					
Geographic region					
North Central	15	36,247	26,242	34,070	48,149
South	84	27,048	20,085	24,814	29,910
West	24	35,116	24,458	35,053	45,994
City type					
Suburban	57	31,201	22,506	26,338	38,000
Independent	68	28,478	20,085	26,081	33,545
Form of government					
Mayor-council	37	24,596	18,678	23,067	28,000
Council-manager	85	32,058	23,296	28,459	38,000
Commission	3	26,673	. . .	25,480	. . .
Risk manager					
Total	19	33,972	26,000	39,419	41,357
Geographic region					
South	9	33,723	21,140	33,902	45,130
West	8	38,246	39,419	39,600	39,879
City type					
Suburban	10	36,515	26,686	39,444	50,648
Independent	9	31,146	26,000	33,902	39,879
Form of government					
Mayor-council	5	20,329	16,640	21,140	27,000
Council-manager	14	38,845	33,902	39,805	45,130
Director of parks and recreation					
Total	278	30,710	24,455	30,090	35,880
Geographic region					
Northeast	40	27,832	19,981	29,500	33,666
North Central	61	31,994	26,730	32,438	36,025
South	126	28,985	22,797	27,080	33,610
West	51	35,693	29,256	32,757	42,696
City type					
Suburban	121	32,588	25,400	31,073	38,930
Independent	157	29,262	23,330	28,510	33,280
Form of government					
Mayor-council	107	28,263	22,491	28,000	34,000
Council-manager	150	33,099	25,750	31,137	38,700
Commission	7	24,801	20,800	23,000	25,400
Town meeting	10	25,093	18,540	28,183	32,536
Rep. town meeting	4	30,965	30,692	30,990	31,287
Superintendent of parks					
Total	134	28,563	23,236	28,304	33,482
Geographic region					
Northeast	16	31,234	28,000	29,423	37,500
North Central	45	28,638	23,979	29,947	31,221
South	38	23,366	18,021	23,318	27,372
West	35	32,890	27,581	33,492	37,848
City type					
Suburban	52	30,102	24,204	29,231	35,740
Independent	82	27,587	22,000	27,581	31,221
Form of government					
Mayor-council	53	27,207	22,885	28,517	30,971
Council-manager	75	29,259	22,880	27,830	34,534
Town meeting	5	33,417	29,400	32,323	38,362
Director of recreation					
Total	118	25,273	17,534	24,361	31,123
Geographic region					
Northeast	38	24,004	11,000	24,545	31,761
North Central	28	25,070	17,900	24,132	30,288
South	30	25,730	19,996	24,187	29,432
West	22	27,099	20,530	27,914	32,472
City type					
Suburban	58	27,030	14,110	27,650	33,780
Independent	60	23,574	18,800	24,061	29,744
Form of government					
Mayor-council	42	22,463	13,152	21,714	30,462
Council-manager	61	28,116	19,996	25,464	32,822
Commission	3	18,491	. . .	16,500	. . .
Town meeting	10	21,039	13,060	22,046	26,421
Librarian					
Total	260	28,466	22,131	27,654	33,816
Geographic region					
Northeast	74	30,758	25,991	30,485	37,023
North Central	64	28,775	24,024	28,448	33,476
South	68	23,766	19,000	22,056	26,873
West	54	30,875	23,753	29,004	36,099
City type					
Suburban	125	30,513	23,298	29,971	37,023
Independent	135	26,570	21,386	26,000	30,900
Form of government					
Mayor-council	91	27,481	21,024	27,019	34,016

Title of official	No. cities reporting	Distribution of 1993 salaries			
		Mean ($)	First quartile ($)	Median ($)	Third quartile ($)
5,000 - 9,999 continued					
Council-manager	133	29,077	22,680	27,571	33,904
Commission	5	21,117	18,000	19,656	25,271
Town meeting	27	29,599	25,875	30,580	35,768
Rep. town meeting	4	32,080	31,287	32,144	33,000
Director of information services					
Total	45	33,738	21,216	30,169	40,189
Geographic region					
Northeast	6	28,942	24,752	28,955	34,308
North Central	4	22,550	18,079	21,406	24,732
South	22	32,398	20,168	24,565	35,859
West	13	41,660	31,886	42,974	48,828
City type					
Suburban	17	34,759	25,501	31,390	43,000
Independent	28	33,118	21,112	29,005	35,859
Form of government					
Mayor-council	17	33,556	22,000	25,501	31,390
Council-manager	24	34,401	21,216	33,252	43,000
Town meeting	3	35,279	. . .	34,308	. . .
Purchasing director					
Total	86	25,567	20,640	25,079	28,884
Geographic region					
Northeast	8	25,133	19,939	25,501	27,992
North Central	12	21,506	19,136	23,619	25,355
South	49	25,904	21,068	25,156	28,920
West	17	27,666	20,640	26,459	31,616
City type					
Suburban	36	25,184	20,508	25,147	28,920
Independent	50	25,843	20,675	25,079	28,872
Form of government					
Mayor-council	29	23,497	19,136	23,462	26,025
Council-manager	52	26,894	21,257	25,679	30,014
Commission	3	28,711	. . .	25,355	. . .
2,500 - 4,999					
Mayor					
Total	962	4,556	1,277	2,681	4,800
Geographic region					
Northeast	197	4,335	1,000	1,500	3,720
North Central	387	3,968	1,500	3,000	4,800
South	275	5,314	1,500	3,000	6,000
West	103	5,161	1,800	3,600	6,300
City type					
Suburban	408	4,473	1,495	3,000	4,800
Independent	554	4,616	1,200	2,500	5,000
Form of government					
Mayor-council	583	5,428	1,800	3,600	6,000
Council-manager	290	2,418	1,000	1,800	3,000
Commission	19	3,988	2,080	3,500	4,500
Town meeting	63	6,716	1,000	1,450	3,504
Rep. town meeting	7	2,553	1,700	2,500	3,000
City manager					
Total	303	45,235	36,923	44,000	50,376
Geographic region					
Northeast	54	39,073	30,500	36,605	45,000
North Central	87	44,392	39,500	43,148	47,278
South	108	43,196	36,732	42,318	49,004
West	54	56,835	47,000	52,250	65,825
City type					
Suburban	125	48,443	38,430	46,737	56,000
Independent	178	42,983	36,420	42,558	47,650
Form of government					
Mayor-council	18	47,000	42,432	45,896	50,789
Council-manager	265	45,779	37,500	44,290	50,615
Town meeting	18	35,655	29,702	34,500	43,260
Chief appointed administrator					
Total	418	37,797	30,000	37,453	46,000
Geographic region					
Northeast	90	33,808	25,000	32,250	41,600
North Central	158	39,481	33,644	39,202	46,000
South	118	35,672	27,431	35,000	43,451
West	52	44,402	34,500	41,677	52,416
City type					
Suburban	196	38,797	30,285	38,429	47,329
Independent	222	36,913	30,000	35,912	42,500
Form of government					
Mayor-council	278	37,227	29,000	37,054	45,003
Council-manager	101	41,346	34,000	40,000	47,652
Commission	5	36,512	27,867	39,000	46,275

Table 1/4 **SALARIES OF MUNICIPAL OFFICIALS: 1 JULY 1993**
continued

Title of official	No. cities reporting	Distribution of 1993 salaries				Title of official	No. cities reporting	Distribution of 1993 salaries			
		Mean ($)	First quartile ($)	Median ($)	Third quartile ($)			Mean ($)	First quartile ($)	Median ($)	Third quartile ($)
2,500 - 4,999 continued						**2,500 - 4,999 continued**					
Town meeting	29	32,924	27,000	31,350	37,420	Geographic region					
Rep. town meeting	5	27,319	22,700	29,130	34,750	Northeast	114	34,542	28,000	32,000	40,100
Asst. city mgr./asst. CAO						North Central	163	34,329	30,000	33,700	38,688
Total	106	31,178	21,500	28,549	38,000	South	214	29,925	24,960	28,744	34,389
Geographic region						West	108	38,995	30,390	35,034	44,000
Northeast	18	25,138	19,589	24,146	29,782	City type					
North Central	30	29,134	22,940	27,990	36,590	Suburban	258	35,891	29,500	34,013	41,183
South	36	27,743	20,274	28,155	33,138	Independent	341	31,933	26,000	30,713	36,200
West	22	44,526	33,678	43,050	57,000	Form of government					
City type						Mayor-council	326	32,634	26,400	31,214	37,156
Suburban	50	34,164	25,001	31,051	41,196	Council-manager	234	35,449	29,500	33,667	39,312
Independent	56	28,511	20,000	25,032	35,463	Commission	5	31,763	27,100	33,000	36,217
Form of government						Town meeting	32	31,204	25,148	29,747	36,700
Mayor-council	44	25,543	19,552	24,117	28,497	**Engineer**					
Council-manager	55	36,976	28,386	35,360	43,035	Total	42	38,392	32,409	39,311	45,483
Town meeting	6	22,041	18,657	21,795	24,292	Geographic region					
City clerk						Northeast	4	27,543	18,000	28,590	39,179
Total	804	25,549	19,750	24,900	29,839	North Central	9	36,695	30,014	38,500	45,256
Geographic region						South	7	38,756	33,000	35,722	39,624
Northeast	166	24,316	17,801	22,253	30,000	West	22	40,943	36,345	44,286	47,520
North Central	271	25,885	21,000	25,543	29,617	City type					
South	259	23,786	18,870	23,108	28,000	Suburban	16	35,329	18,000	39,312	46,600
West	108	30,831	23,328	28,752	36,384	Independent	26	40,277	33,000	39,311	44,562
City type						Form of government					
Suburban	315	27,228	20,633	25,750	32,500	Mayor-council	21	39,106	35,443	44,100	46,286
Independent	489	24,467	19,171	24,000	28,523	Council-manager	19	37,506	25,284	36,600	44,491
Form of government						**Police chief**					
Mayor-council	458	24,952	19,171	24,000	29,120	Total	733	33,666	27,093	32,123	38,000
Council-manager	267	27,557	22,410	26,250	30,796	Geographic region					
Commission	19	26,656	16,920	23,441	33,915	Northeast	116	37,686	30,160	34,446	42,000
Town meeting	55	20,734	14,400	19,822	26,729	North Central	241	33,637	28,475	33,120	37,648
Rep. town meeting	5	21,769	18,500	22,992	25,854	South	265	29,426	24,483	28,422	32,500
Chief financial officer						West	111	39,652	32,376	37,799	44,268
Total	212	32,304	23,962	31,019	38,500	City type					
Geographic region						Suburban	285	37,607	30,853	36,192	42,900
Northeast	40	28,666	23,000	26,789	33,408	Independent	448	31,159	25,938	30,035	35,000
North Central	55	30,363	21,994	29,660	38,500	Form of government					
South	58	29,405	22,089	29,184	34,599	Mayor-council	407	31,927	25,350	30,461	35,848
West	59	39,430	30,000	36,000	46,656	Council-manager	282	36,243	30,000	35,000	40,116
City type						Commission	14	28,887	23,500	27,050	32,000
Suburban	103	33,387	24,048	32,479	39,096	Town meeting	26	36,445	30,160	35,525	42,137
Independent	109	31,280	23,000	30,060	36,870	Rep. town meeting	4	27,562	26,465	28,233	30,000
Form of government						**Fire chief**					
Mayor-council	77	29,900	23,000	29,472	34,446	Total	168	29,961	22,670	28,216	34,674
Council-manager	116	34,898	25,729	33,170	40,920	Geographic region					
Commission	5	22,192	19,800	23,700	27,560	Northeast	14	28,665	25,914	29,627	34,600
Town meeting	14	27,646	19,750	25,391	31,000	North Central	31	31,119	25,150	30,529	35,783
Director of economic development						South	88	25,278	20,551	24,959	30,430
Total	68	30,065	25,000	28,146	34,617	West	35	41,230	31,322	40,620	52,208
Geographic region						City type					
Northeast	7	27,348	25,000	25,000	30,000	Suburban	59	34,586	25,300	32,775	42,500
North Central	38	28,018	25,000	27,572	32,000	Independent	109	27,458	21,546	26,642	31,322
South	13	29,466	17,950	25,181	39,292	Form of government					
West	10	40,526	28,291	39,834	50,000	Mayor-council	82	27,932	20,551	26,651	33,758
City type						Council-manager	69	32,850	24,648	30,430	36,678
Suburban	20	33,972	26,000	30,966	37,580	Commission	5	28,915	24,700	27,600	32,000
Independent	48	28,438	24,197	26,754	31,071	Town meeting	10	27,537	12,400	27,000	42,000
Form of government						**Planning director**					
Mayor-council	34	28,035	23,769	26,962	32,000	Total	93	33,115	26,000	31,440	39,519
Council-manager	31	32,374	25,000	30,000	39,292	Geographic region					
Town meeting	3	29,223	. . .	26,728	. . .	Northeast	12	22,568	16,000	23,780	28,500
Treasurer						North Central	11	29,888	21,840	28,000	38,688
Total	171	24,103	17,929	22,800	29,000	South	30	29,394	24,987	29,030	33,748
Geographic region						West	40	39,957	32,500	38,090	44,268
Northeast	50	20,971	16,000	20,000	28,272	City type					
North Central	62	23,490	18,750	25,500	27,827	Suburban	38	34,500	26,859	32,000	39,374
South	32	22,358	17,929	22,255	24,960	Independent	55	32,158	25,700	30,349	40,000
West	27	33,379	21,236	26,470	47,756	Form of government					
City type						Mayor-council	39	32,853	27,500	34,000	39,374
Suburban	70	25,605	18,500	25,610	30,024	Council-manager	47	35,028	23,400	30,000	42,063
Independent	101	23,062	17,500	21,096	26,438	Town meeting	6	22,850	16,000	23,729	29,000
Form of government						**Personnel director**					
Mayor-council	76	22,145	17,000	20,820	26,046	Total	32	32,317	20,230	26,454	42,684
Council-manager	70	27,937	20,950	26,000	30,264	Geographic region					
Commission	4	17,474	18,928	19,464	20,000	North Central	5	23,717	20,000	20,230	23,000
Town meeting	19	19,215	11,500	19,101	25,500	South	12	26,361	20,000	21,861	25,420
Director of public works						West	14	38,730	27,488	39,200	50,588
Total	599	33,638	27,224	32,065	37,908	City type					
						Suburban	11	37,594	23,000	37,400	47,756

Table 1/4 **SALARIES OF MUNICIPAL OFFICIALS: 1 JULY 1993**
continued

Title of official	No. cities reporting	Distribution of 1993 salaries			
		Mean ($)	First quartile ($)	Median ($)	Third quartile ($)
2,500 - 4,999 continued					
Independent	21	29,552	20,000	23,112	40,353
Form of government					
Mayor-council	8	30,262	20,000	23,744	40,353
Council-manager	23	33,024	20,800	25,420	44,410
Risk manager					
Total	11	30,505	18,400	30,538	39,000
Geographic region					
South	4	24,275	18,471	21,461	24,450
West	6	36,738	30,538	34,832	44,562
City type					
Suburban	3	35,578	. . .	31,000	. . .
Independent	8	28,602	18,400	27,494	38,664
Form of government					
Mayor-council	5	29,715	24,450	30,538	31,000
Council-manager	6	31,163	18,400	28,568	39,000
Director of parks and recreation					
Total	117	26,370	20,000	25,247	30,383
Geographic region					
Northeast	6	23,502	20,758	23,411	31,655
North Central	31	23,590	19,800	24,012	26,460
South	56	24,873	19,760	24,791	28,866
West	24	34,169	27,318	31,376	40,000
City type					
Suburban	46	27,524	23,856	26,431	31,655
Independent	71	25,622	19,800	24,850	29,232
Form of government					
Mayor-council	54	24,605	19,721	24,006	28,000
Council-manager	62	27,997	23,000	26,445	32,348
Superintendent of parks					
Total	65	25,198	19,760	23,923	28,000
Geographic region					
Northeast	4	33,301	31,090	32,979	34,867
North Central	17	24,646	20,640	24,186	27,700
South	27	21,190	18,000	21,500	25,662
West	17	30,210	20,072	28,000	36,500
City type					
Suburban	24	28,796	20,072	27,123	34,084
Independent	41	23,092	19,760	22,360	26,686
Form of government					
Mayor-council	40	24,551	19,774	23,319	28,000
Council-manager	23	26,327	19,327	25,500	27,280
Director of recreation					
Total	35	21,505	16,000	20,612	24,939
Geographic region					
Northeast	9	16,568	11,004	16,000	20,300
North Central	9	20,525	14,000	19,671	24,000
South	11	22,052	19,458	23,000	24,939
West	6	29,380	18,596	24,206	37,020
City type					
Suburban	21	21,112	12,000	20,300	24,000
Independent	14	22,095	17,172	21,631	27,800
Form of government					
Mayor-council	16	19,395	11,004	20,456	23,840
Council-manager	15	23,491	16,411	20,860	26,266
Town meeting	3	22,210	. . .	19,894	. . .
Librarian					
Total	144	21,146	15,036	18,788	25,194
Geographic region					
Northeast	20	24,438	20,000	23,650	30,640
North Central	50	20,266	15,775	18,736	24,675
South	43	16,384	12,480	15,808	18,824
West	31	27,049	16,598	25,000	36,108
City type					
Suburban	44	22,744	17,742	23,350	25,729
Independent	100	20,443	13,780	17,565	25,000
Form of government					
Mayor-council	70	19,906	15,397	18,360	24,024
Council-manager	61	22,376	14,100	19,866	25,786
Commission	3	16,054	. . .	16,361	. . .
Town meeting	10	23,856	16,547	23,779	32,085
Director of information services					
Total	12	28,922	19,320	22,855	35,688
Geographic region					
North Central	3	33,919	. . .	27,432	. . .
South	6	19,786	18,575	19,228	19,500
City type					
Suburban	4	29,400	27,432	31,560	35,688
Independent	8	28,683	19,320	20,000	25,210

Title of official	No. cities reporting	Distribution of 1993 salaries			
		Mean ($)	First quartile ($)	Median ($)	Third quartile ($)
2,500 - 4,999 continued					
Form of government					
Mayor-council	5	26,024	19,320	19,500	20,500
Council-manager	7	30,992	19,136	27,432	35,903
Purchasing director					
Total	36	24,626	18,304	21,381	28,848
Geographic region					
North Central	4	25,787	16,600	24,968	33,335
South	21	22,382	18,283	20,696	27,477
West	10	28,986	18,782	23,215	36,046
City type					
Suburban	13	25,192	18,480	25,601	28,848
Independent	23	24,305	17,638	20,696	31,200
Form of government					
Mayor-council	18	23,552	17,000	21,381	28,000
Council-manager	18	25,699	18,675	22,384	29,112
Under 2,500					
Mayor					
Total	243	2,426	800	1,500	2,800
Geographic region					
Northeast	49	1,278	550	800	1,250
North Central	99	2,076	900	1,500	2,600
South	71	3,578	1,200	1,800	4,200
West	24	2,802	1,200	2,100	4,800
City type					
Suburban	76	2,736	1,000	1,640	3,000
Independent	166	2,287	650	1,200	2,400
Form of government					
Mayor-council	113	3,403	1,200	2,000	3,999
Council-manager	105	1,736	600	1,200	1,975
Commission	3	987	. . .	600	. . .
Town meeting	21	808	600	700	1,000
City manager					
Total	161	37,703	28,000	35,020	45,154
Geographic region					
Northeast	38	28,526	21,630	27,800	35,000
North Central	34	40,219	32,600	38,641	45,722
South	58	36,946	26,518	33,234	45,864
West	31	47,612	35,600	43,000	58,920
City type					
Suburban	46	43,903	32,500	40,000	57,304
Independent	114	35,287	26,751	34,450	42,070
Form of government					
Mayor-council	11	34,947	28,000	29,196	34,900
Council-manager	131	39,666	29,870	37,200	46,694
Town meeting	17	24,004	17,500	23,000	30,000
Chief appointed administrator					
Total	101	34,371	28,200	33,000	40,000
Geographic region					
Northeast	14	33,819	23,000	30,878	35,175
North Central	58	33,922	28,500	32,980	38,000
South	20	32,929	26,989	32,500	41,113
West	9	41,327	37,030	41,838	49,700
City type					
Suburban	40	35,240	29,640	34,399	41,113
Independent	61	33,801	27,976	32,000	38,972
Form of government					
Mayor-council	69	33,484	27,810	31,837	38,500
Council-manager	26	36,482	32,960	35,000	41,113
Town meeting	4	33,598	30,000	30,378	30,755
Asst. city mgr./asst. CAO					
Total	27	25,973	18,000	22,000	28,704
Geographic region					
Northeast	10	22,048	19,658	20,896	23,922
North Central	6	20,690	18,000	20,750	27,040
South	7	26,240	16,000	21,000	36,930
West	4	43,247	41,904	43,512	45,120
City type					
Suburban	5	27,190	23,083	23,922	25,323
Independent	21	26,206	18,000	21,200	28,704
Form of government					
Mayor-council	7	18,090	16,000	18,000	23,000
Council-manager	16	31,612	22,000	27,470	37,500
Town meeting	4	17,215	14,600	17,129	19,658
City clerk					
Total	217	23,519	17,500	22,063	28,590
Geographic region					
Northeast	30	17,791	13,352	16,100	20,240

Table 1/4   SALARIES OF MUNICIPAL OFFICIALS: 1 JULY 1993
continued

Title of official	No. cities reporting	Mean ($)	First quartile ($)	Median ($)	Third quartile ($)
Under 2,500 continued					
North Central	72	24,258	19,000	22,784	27,500
South	80	22,422	17,266	20,857	26,766
West	35	29,414	21,660	28,590	35,532
City type					
Suburban	71	25,476	18,800	23,638	29,466
Independent	146	22,567	17,266	21,550	27,680
Form of government					
Mayor-council	88	22,257	17,835	20,000	25,750
Council-manager	115	25,141	18,837	23,188	29,466
Commission	3	22,760	. . .	26,479	. . .
Town meeting	11	16,858	12,000	16,500	18,000
Chief financial officer					
Total	47	29,452	20,550	27,108	36,617
Geographic region					
Northeast	3	29,799	. . .	33,500	. . .
North Central	10	26,234	21,393	24,793	26,416
South	22	27,306	19,000	26,620	34,195
West	12	35,982	28,000	38,849	42,240
City type					
Suburban	14	33,222	26,250	31,000	41,870
Independent	33	27,853	19,507	26,350	34,195
Form of government					
Mayor-council	10	25,648	18,000	20,411	27,108
Council-manager	34	30,946	22,538	30,000	37,296
Director of economic development					
Total	16	25,308	19,152	26,156	31,824
Geographic region					
North Central	9	25,086	19,152	26,312	31,824
West	5	26,585	15,000	30,098	37,429
City type					
Suburban	3	32,645	. . .	32,136	. . .
Independent	12	23,666	15,000	24,768	30,208
Form of government					
Mayor-council	10	21,667	11,845	22,576	30,208
Council-manager	6	31,376	23,224	31,117	39,800
Treasurer					
Total	43	21,259	15,600	21,000	28,000
Geographic region					
Northeast	7	25,219	17,500	30,000	32,000
North Central	20	19,490	15,000	20,000	22,932
South	13	19,803	15,600	19,500	22,000
West	3	30,119	. . .	31,830	. . .
City type					
Suburban	13	21,445	15,600	19,500	30,000
Independent	29	21,150	16,000	21,000	26,620
Form of government					
Mayor-council	16	20,869	15,600	19,873	23,192
Council-manager	22	21,044	15,000	21,334	26,620
Town meeting	4	24,441	17,888	24,080	30,272
Director of public works					
Total	181	30,206	24,621	28,543	34,000
Geographic region					
Northeast	19	27,635	22,000	26,000	30,900
North Central	59	29,953	25,938	28,690	33,500
South	69	28,035	23,172	27,000	31,487
West	34	36,488	27,900	33,800	42,053
City type					
Suburban	63	32,497	27,500	30,721	36,000
Independent	117	29,094	24,024	27,200	31,700
Form of government					
Mayor-council	72	28,692	22,933	27,412	31,574
Council-manager	102	31,639	25,532	29,140	35,474
Town meeting	5	23,493	18,200	25,000	26,000
Engineer					
Total	6	39,368	12,075	52,897	55,125
Geographic region					
West	4	54,033	54,876	55,001	55,125
City type					
Suburban	3	24,984	. . .	12,075	. . .
Independent	3	53,752	. . .	55,125	. . .
Form of government					
Mayor-council	3	25,096	. . .	12,075	. . .
Council-manager	3	53,639	. . .	54,876	. . .
Police chief					
Total	201	31,018	24,840	29,000	34,394
Geographic region					
Northeast	19	32,572	23,700	29,000	36,000

Title of official	No. cities reporting	Mean ($)	First quartile ($)	Median ($)	Third quartile ($)
Under 2,500 continued					
North Central	67	30,547	26,092	29,244	32,744
South	83	28,486	22,880	27,500	33,840
West	32	37,648	29,388	33,827	44,352
City type					
Suburban	65	35,768	28,870	33,840	40,000
Independent	135	28,776	23,161	27,640	32,250
Form of government					
Mayor-council	86	28,155	23,492	26,954	30,000
Council-manager	109	33,238	26,620	32,000	38,792
Commission	3	27,949	. . .	25,846	. . .
Town meeting	3	35,490	. . .	34,093	. . .
Fire chief					
Total	32	30,207	22,150	26,950	38,126
Geographic region					
North Central	7	29,348	23,232	29,000	36,000
South	19	26,673	21,767	23,597	30,000
West	5	42,313	38,126	41,904	52,369
City type					
Suburban	12	34,848	26,900	34,311	39,597
Independent	20	27,422	21,100	23,415	30,000
Form of government					
Mayor-council	12	27,016	22,020	26,752	29,000
Council-manager	19	31,557	22,150	28,054	40,278
Planning director					
Total	16	36,717	32,000	36,290	46,680
Geographic region					
North Central	3	33,160	. . .	32,000	. . .
South	6	31,281	23,654	30,772	38,834
West	7	42,901	35,950	45,000	49,123
City type					
Suburban	8	36,772	32,000	37,561	46,680
Independent	8	36,662	34,728	36,122	45,000
Form of government					
Council-manager	14	37,491	32,000	36,290	46,800
Director of parks and recreation					
Total	14	21,732	13,372	20,945	25,000
Geographic region					
North Central	3	16,120	. . .	12,000	. . .
South	5	17,382	13,372	13,600	19,610
West	4	31,857	25,000	30,149	35,298
City type					
Independent	12	21,060	13,372	19,230	24,844
Form of government					
Mayor-council	6	20,605	12,000	16,491	22,280
Council-manager	8	22,577	18,850	23,772	25,000
Superintendent of parks					
Total	9	27,656	17,326	23,712	38,582
Geographic region					
North Central	3	27,657	. . .	23,712	. . .
West	4	28,530	17,500	28,041	38,582
City type					
Suburban	3	39,985	. . .	42,210	. . .
Independent	6	21,492	16,000	17,413	23,712
Form of government					
Council-manager	8	28,149	17,326	25,993	38,582
Director of recreation					
Total	9	20,995	15,829	19,300	22,401
Geographic region					
South	3	20,215	. . .	19,343	. . .
West	3	26,233	. . .	19,300	. . .
City type					
Independent	8	21,957	18,900	19,322	22,401
Form of government					
Mayor-council	3	18,348	. . .	19,343	. . .
Council-manager	5	21,507	15,829	18,900	19,300
Librarian					
Total	27	18,052	12,480	15,163	23,664
Geographic region					
Northeast	3	22,576	. . .	26,780	. . .
North Central	8	15,424	13,000	14,500	15,163
South	9	15,670	12,480	14,560	19,062
West	7	22,179	14,100	23,664	28,428
City type					
Suburban	3	21,424	. . .	21,547	. . .
Independent	24	17,630	12,480	14,780	23,025
Form of government					
Mayor-council	12	16,569	13,000	15,082	19,062
Council-manager	13	18,844	12,480	20,600	23,664

Salaries of County Officials, 1993

Evelina R. Moulder
International City/County Management Association

Findings

Over the six-year period from 1988 to 1993, the position of county personnel director shows the highest percentage of increase (28%).

In general, counties with populations under 50,000 show average salaries that are below the national average.

For all positions except county administrator, the lowest average salary is in the North Central region.

In testimony before the House Human Resources and Intergovernmental Relations Subcommittee in May 1993, a county executive addressed the continuing fiscal hardships confronting counties. According to this testimony, counties are not yet experiencing the economic recovery that is making headlines in the news. It is, therefore, not surprising that the percentage of increase in average salaries for top-level county positions remains comparatively small.

METHODOLOGY

The data in this article are based on the results of ICMA's annual salary survey, which was mailed in the summer of 1993 to all counties with populations of 2,500 and over and to all ICMA-recognized counties with populations under 2,500.[1] Of the 3,107 counties that received surveys, 1,543 responded, for a survey response rate of 49.7% (Table 2/1).

TRENDS

Table 2/2 shows the percentage of increase in average salary for twelve county positions over a six-year period. In order to be included in this table, a jurisdiction must have responded to the salary survey for each of the six years covered in the survey (1988 through 1993). From 1992 to 1993 the percentage of increase for each position either remained what it had been the previous year or dropped. Among the four positions that show percentages of increase, only the position of purchasing director is noteworthy—an increase of four percentage points, from 1% in 1992 to 5% in 1993.

Over the six-year period the position of personnel director shows the highest percentage of increase (28%), followed by the position of chief financial officer (27%). Over that same period the lowest percentage of increase is for the position of director of welfare/human services (21%).

Table 2/1   SURVEY RESPONSE

Classification	No. counties surveyed (A)	No. counties responding No.	No. counties responding % of (A)
Total, all counties	3,107	1,543	49.7
Population group			
Over 1,000,000	27	13	48.1
500,000–1,000,000 ...	63	41	65.1
250,000–499,999	99	52	52.5
100,000–249,999	255	162	63.5
50,000–99,999	381	212	55.6
25,000–49,999	619	283	45.7
10,000–24,999	921	442	48.0
5,000–9,999	449	197	43.9
2,500–4,999	178	84	47.2
Under 2,500	115	57	49.6
Geographic region			
Northeast	200	95	47.5
North Central	1,055	584	55.4
South	1,423	597	42.0
West	429	267	62.2
Geographic division			
New England	54	18	33.3
Mid-Atlantic	146	77	52.7
East North Central	437	239	54.7
West North Central ...	618	345	55.8
South Atlantic	589	340	57.7
East South Central	364	90	24.7
West South Central ...	470	167	35.5
Mountain	280	166	59.3
Pacific Coast	149	101	67.8
Metro status			
Metro	725	408	56.3
Nonmetro	2,382	1,135	47.6

POPULATION

Population size of a county is an influential factor in salary. Size of a local government often affects the range of services provided and the complexity of management. Table 2/3 shows by population group the average salary for each county position covered in the survey. A downward trend in average salary is apparent as the population groups decrease in size. In general, jurisdictions with populations from 50,000 to 99,999 show average salaries that are slightly above the national average. Counties with populations under 50,000 show average salaries that are below the national average.

GEOGRAPHIC REGION

Geographic region seems to also play a part in the fluctuations among average salaries. For five of the twelve positions covered, the average salary is highest in the Northeast region (not shown). The average salaries for the remaining seven positions are highest in the West region. For all positions except county administrator, the lowest average salary is in the North Central region.

METRO STATUS

Metro counties, those located within a metropolitan statistical area, have higher average salaries than nonmetro counties. Metropolitan statistical areas (MSAs) have at least one central county and may include outlying counties with economic and social ties to the central cities and the central county in the MSA. Because population is a factor in defining an MSA, it is not surprising that the average salaries in metro counties would be higher.

SALARIES BY POSITION

Table 2/4 presents the average salaries for the twelve positions covered in the survey. The data are arrayed by population group, geographic region, and metro status.

---

[1] Governments recognized by ICMA have the council-manager form of government or provide for a general management position.

Table 2/2   AVERAGE SALARIES OF COUNTY OFFICIALS

Title	No. counties included	1988 ($)	1989 ($)	Increase from 1988 (%)	1990 ($)	Increase from 1989 (%)	1991 ($)	Increase from 1990 (%)	1992 ($)	Increase from 1991 (%)	1993 ($)	Increase from 1992 (%)
Governing board chair/president/county judge	491	15,774	16,505	5	17,277	5	17,934	4	19,025	6	19,498	2
County manager	102	59,721	62,993	5	66,719	6	69,292	4	70,876	2	74,031	4
County administrator	105	46,109	48,415	5	51,715	7	53,012	3	55,031	4	57,271	4
Clerk to the governing board	356	26,622	27,700	4	29,037	5	30,481	5	31,601	4	32,596	3
Chief financial officer	288	34,677	36,351	5	38,314	5	40,128	5	42,481	6	43,872	3
County health officer	141	45,048	46,804	4	48,873	4	51,249	5	53,867	5	56,106	4
Planning director	181	38,328	40,835	7	43,192	6	45,004	4	47,126	5	48,477	3
County engineer	55	48,766	51,626	6	54,807	6	57,477	5	58,865	2	60,534	3
Director of welfare/human services	171	42,657	44,990	5	47,486	6	49,228	4	50,180	2	51,533	3
Chief law enforcement official	423	35,912	37,955	6	39,605	4	41,424	5	43,038	4	44,492	3
Purchasing director	111	35,986	38,242	6	40,765	7	42,148	3	42,751	1	44,696	5
Personnel director	127	40,353	42,959	6	45,788	7	47,699	4	49,852	5	51,751	4

Note: Only those counties that have reported for each of the six years from 1988 through 1993 are included.

Table 2/3   SALARIES BY POPULATION GROUP

	Position											
	Governing board chair/president		County manager		County administrator		Clerk		Chief financial officer		Health officer	
Classification	No. reporting	Avg. salary ($)	No. reporting	Avg. salary ($)	No. reporting	Avg. salary ($)	No. reporting	Avg. salary ($)	No. reporting	Avg. salary ($)	No. reporting	Avg. salary ($)
Total, all counties	1,477	21,414	235	74,949	458	47,696	1,224	31,935	979	40,596	617	48,284
Population group												
Over 1,000,000	13	67,193	9	133,986	. . .	. . .	10	72,731	11	90,227	8	107,786
500,000–1,000,000	39	60,941	19	115,540	15	77,501	33	58,067	35	79,635	25	96,961
250,000–499,999	50	40,417	22	95,321	21	70,626	44	49,533	46	65,167	37	75,910
100,000–249,999	156	31,789	53	78,307	66	63,366	138	41,367	144	53,677	96	62,293
50,000–99,999	206	23,569	54	67,674	84	50,044	167	34,057	170	44,539	112	48,263
25,000–49,999	271	17,527	48	56,645	92	45,988	207	30,950	178	36,719	130	40,879
10,000–24,999	418	17,569	25	52,060	129	37,126	336	28,586	234	30,919	143	35,512
5,000–9,999	188	15,136	4	52,599	31	35,660	166	25,407	93	25,217	47	29,826
2,500–4,999	81	12,175	. . .	. . .	10	33,617	77	21,024	37	21,977	13	29,235
Under 2,500	55	11,226	. . .	. . .	8	27,361	46	22,201	31	23,471	6	22,726

	Position											
	Planning director		Engineer		Director welfare/ human services		Chief law enforcement official		Purchasing director		Personnel director	
Classification	No. reporting	Avg. salary ($)	No. reporting	Avg. salary ($)	No. reporting	Avg. salary ($)	No. reporting	Avg. salary ($)	No. reporting	Avg. salary ($)	No. reporting	Avg. salary ($)
Total, all counties	656	43,315	670	50,594	579	47,971	1,308	42,191	405	38,574	474	45,235
Population group												
Over 1,000,000	10	83,630	10	99,159	10	91,228	13	101,935	12	78,571	12	83,232
500,000–1,000,000	32	74,608	30	78,202	29	75,654	38	79,005	33	62,461	34	72,898
250,000–499,999	41	61,185	37	69,163	38	68,383	51	65,179	46	47,010	44	58,855
100,000–249,999	120	51,511	117	58,866	87	58,113	157	55,180	101	41,237	126	48,686
50,000–99,999	149	41,634	116	51,014	102	48,770	199	46,582	97	33,753	127	39,159
25,000–49,999	140	35,665	124	48,443	107	44,681	248	39,651	58	28,019	72	34,935
10,000–24,999	121	32,787	154	43,779	139	37,700	354	35,695	46	24,419	47	28,475
5,000–9,999	31	32,137	58	31,604	46	29,853	148	31,051	12	22,379	9	39,295
2,500–4,999	10	26,803	20	25,639	18	30,954	62	24,950	. . .	. . .	3	19,780
Under 2,500	. . .	. . .	4	25,391	3	29,477	38	26,049	. . .	. . .	. . .	. . .

Table 2/4 SALARIES OF COUNTY OFFICIALS: 1 JULY 1993

Salary data for the 12 selected county officials in this table are based on information reported by county officials as of 1 July 1993. Data are reported by position titles only, which while representing similar job responsibilities, do not purport to represent identical duties and responsibilities.

For the position of county manager, data are shown for only those counties recognized by ICMA as either having a council-manager form of government or providing for a position of overall general management. For the position of county administrator, data are shown for all other reporting counties.

Except for the position of governing board chairman/president/county judge which includes part-time salaries, this table excludes: (1) salaries of part-time officials, (2) salaries for vacant positions, (3) salaries of acting officials, (4) salaries of those paid in whole or in part by fees, and (5) all salaries below $8,000. Salaries are presented for ten population groups and are further classified by geographic region and county type.

Classifications having less than three counties reporting are excluded because meaningful statistics cannot be computed. Consequently the number reporting in some of the subcategories does not always equal the total reporting. Quartiles are not shown when only three counties reported.

Title of official	No. counties reporting	Distribution of 1993 salaries			
		Mean ($)	First quartile ($)	Median ($)	Third quartile ($)
All counties					
Governing board chair/ president/county judge					
Total	1,477	21,414	7,500	15,744	30,000
Geographic region					
Northeast	93	32,251	15,000	25,000	38,143
North Central	557	14,332	6,525	11,000	16,998
South	573	23,379	7,000	20,602	35,309
West	254	28,541	14,783	23,800	37,500
County type					
Metro	389	33,315	14,000	29,643	45,348
Nonmetro	1,088	17,159	6,750	13,690	24,102
County manager					
Total	235	74,949	55,000	71,377	90,950
Geographic region					
Northeast	13	76,448	62,500	72,800	90,950
North Central	40	69,386	48,984	66,445	84,942
South	134	72,337	52,400	67,197	87,299
West	48	86,471	67,156	79,962	105,000
County type					
Metro	130	87,332	65,160	85,206	104,776
Nonmetro	105	59,617	47,550	58,000	71,700
County administrator					
Total	458	47,696	31,852	46,019	59,130
Geographic region					
Northeast	50	50,577	36,168	47,127	65,000
North Central	97	47,094	33,936	47,000	56,743
South	224	46,488	31,500	45,364	58,140
West	87	49,820	30,000	44,437	65,000
County type					
Metro	161	59,373	44,500	57,000	74,027
Nonmetro	297	41,365	27,750	41,612	52,000
Clerk to the governing board					
Total	1,224	31,935	22,980	28,606	37,000
Geographic region					
Northeast	60	35,762	25,771	33,047	42,272
North Central	497	28,938	22,420	27,400	33,292
South	428	33,299	22,227	28,319	39,548
West	239	34,763	25,800	31,500	40,020
County type					
Metro	313	42,251	32,070	39,012	48,354
Nonmetro	911	28,390	22,001	26,544	32,254
Chief financial officer					
Total	979	40,596	26,304	36,925	50,799
Geographic region					
Northeast	80	44,021	32,392	38,977	55,733
North Central	340	35,020	24,210	30,870	42,081
South	379	42,233	27,250	40,200	52,293
West	180	46,162	28,800	41,149	58,232
County type					
Metro	324	55,977	42,210	52,301	68,905
Nonmetro	655	32,988	23,362	30,477	40,073
County health officer					
Total	617	48,284	30,000	42,108	62,599
Geographic region					
Northeast	37	59,940	46,084	53,745	67,761
North Central	298	38,414	27,000	34,660	46,410
South	173	58,514	39,000	54,825	79,499
West	109	55,075	29,028	46,805	78,996
County type					
Metro	229	64,441	45,000	60,949	82,914
Nonmetro	388	38,748	26,624	34,864	45,555
Planning director					
Total	656	43,315	30,985	40,935	52,752
Geographic region					
Northeast	71	45,498	32,550	43,844	55,157

Title of official	No. counties reporting	Distribution of 1993 salaries			
		Mean ($)	First quartile ($)	Median ($)	Third quartile ($)
All counties continued					
North Central	184	36,416	26,812	34,000	43,083
South	233	45,096	33,191	43,000	53,102
West	168	47,477	32,532	45,396	58,008
County type					
Metro	289	52,054	38,812	48,586	63,995
Nonmetro	367	36,432	28,092	34,802	44,720
County engineer					
Total	670	50,594	40,000	50,000	60,594
Geographic region					
Northeast	41	58,973	43,260	62,905	71,021
North Central	314	46,424	38,600	47,358	55,125
South	192	51,186	40,000	50,227	61,628
West	123	57,521	44,553	55,920	67,836
County type					
Metro	262	60,876	47,741	59,256	71,032
Nonmetro	408	43,991	35,000	45,000	53,684
Director of welfare/human services					
Total	579	47,971	36,170	46,202	57,389
Geographic region					
Northeast	58	51,593	37,477	51,169	62,152
North Central	194	44,918	33,524	46,830	55,068
South	211	46,980	35,931	43,832	54,970
West	116	53,068	37,690	48,636	63,523
County type					
Metro	225	60,269	47,382	58,000	71,000
Nonmetro	354	40,154	32,328	41,000	48,801
Chief law enforcement official					
Total	1,308	42,191	30,524	38,403	49,289
Geographic region					
Northeast	88	45,469	32,124	38,092	55,650
North Central	487	36,804	28,500	34,784	42,955
South	509	44,506	33,425	42,479	51,551
West	224	47,357	32,972	41,916	54,765
County type					
Metro	384	56,394	42,300	52,048	67,774
Nonmetro	924	36,289	28,600	35,000	42,480
Purchasing director					
Total	405	38,574	26,295	35,127	48,256
Geographic region					
Northeast	49	39,344	29,000	39,000	46,500
North Central	67	38,209	27,981	35,019	49,080
South	221	35,746	23,839	32,622	43,992
West	68	47,568	34,032	44,767	56,508
County type					
Metro	241	44,635	32,302	42,943	54,285
Nonmetro	164	29,666	20,800	28,040	36,000
Personnel director					
Total	474	45,235	31,305	42,410	56,460
Geographic region					
Northeast	58	46,660	34,840	46,082	55,039
North Central	108	44,225	32,122	41,660	53,450
South	200	43,356	30,000	40,734	55,009
West	108	48,957	33,926	48,371	58,697
County type					
Metro	265	52,172	38,220	51,137	64,083
Nonmetro	209	36,438	25,854	35,736	45,428
Over 1,000,000					
Governing board chair/ president/county judge					
Total	13	67,193	49,874	66,840	90,740

Table 2/4   SALARIES OF COUNTY OFFICIALS: 1 JULY 1993
continued

Title of official	No. counties reporting	Distribution of 1993 salaries Mean ($)	First quartile ($)	Median ($)	Third quartile ($)
Over 1,000,000 continued					
Geographic region					
South	5	65,142	56,000	73,212	90,740
West	6	63,300	47,196	54,624	82,056
County type					
Metro	13	67,193	49,874	66,840	90,740
County manager					
Total	9	133,986	113,000	135,512	140,628
Geographic region					
West	6	137,843	127,556	137,436	140,628
County type					
Metro	9	133,986	113,000	135,512	140,628
Clerk to the governing board					
Total	10	72,731	58,531	67,664	80,518
Geographic region					
West	6	70,268	58,531	63,380	69,180
County type					
Metro	10	72,731	58,531	67,664	80,518
Chief financial officer					
Total	11	90,227	82,512	89,376	100,568
Geographic region					
South	4	90,609	89,376	93,688	98,000
West	5	92,828	85,634	91,291	100,568
County type					
Metro	11	90,227	82,512	89,376	100,568
County health officer					
Total	8	107,786	96,512	101,408	121,888
Geographic region					
West	5	119,534	104,340	121,888	122,820
County type					
Metro	8	107,786	96,512	101,408	121,888
Planning director					
Total	10	83,630	78,166	85,181	93,060
Geographic region					
South	3	77,331	. . .	80,340	. . .
West	6	87,435	78,166	91,104	93,060
County type					
Metro	10	83,630	78,166	85,181	93,060
County engineer					
Total	10	99,159	87,618	97,704	107,052
Geographic region					
West	6	109,858	88,317	106,556	114,768
County type					
Metro	10	99,159	87,618	97,704	107,052
Director of welfare/human services					
Total	10	91,228	63,523	99,850	103,280
Geographic region					
South	4	74,214	56,388	70,694	85,000
West	6	102,571	97,322	102,814	112,452
County type					
Metro	10	91,228	63,523	99,850	103,280
Chief law enforcement official					
Total	13	101,935	91,392	99,000	111,238
Geographic region					
South	5	89,278	74,136	91,392	99,000
West	6	115,364	99,985	108,629	127,452
County type					
Metro	13	101,935	91,392	99,000	111,238
Purchasing director					
Total	12	78,571	62,400	73,850	82,518
Geographic region					
South	5	71,089	61,488	73,699	74,000
West	6	87,024	62,400	80,155	103,776
County type					
Metro	12	78,571	62,400	73,850	82,518
Personnel director					
Total	12	83,232	78,554	89,679	91,728
Geographic region					
South	5	68,936	60,000	67,884	78,554
West	5	92,076	90,002	90,204	91,728
County type					
Metro	12	83,232	78,554	89,679	91,728
500,000 - 1,000,000					
Governing board chair/ president/county judge					
Total	39	60,941	45,000	58,542	73,112

Title of official	No. counties reporting	Distribution of 1993 salaries Mean ($)	First quartile ($)	Median ($)	Third quartile ($)
500,000 - 1,000,000 continued					
Geographic region					
Northeast	7	61,071	29,682	52,500	90,000
North Central	9	60,484	54,440	58,542	67,704
South	14	55,885	45,000	55,831	73,112
West	9	69,162	45,000	62,340	68,850
County type					
Metro	39	60,941	45,000	58,542	73,112
County manager					
Total	19	115,540	105,000	115,000	123,630
Geographic region					
North Central	3	109,597	. . .	105,580	. . .
South	9	117,708	107,101	117,594	137,509
West	5	118,526	115,000	115,000	123,630
County type					
Metro	19	115,540	105,000	115,000	123,630
County administrator					
Total	15	77,501	67,210	76,770	90,000
Geographic region					
Northeast	4	74,404	65,166	77,583	90,000
North Central	4	74,761	67,600	71,799	75,997
South	4	73,386	70,717	75,309	79,900
West	3	90,773	. . .	84,550	. . .
County type					
Metro	15	77,501	67,210	76,770	90,000
Clerk to the governing board					
Total	33	58,067	45,000	60,000	66,963
Geographic region					
Northeast	5	50,888	36,900	45,000	66,150
North Central	9	54,320	41,995	60,100	61,038
South	11	59,977	45,461	50,171	87,210
West	8	64,143	60,000	63,634	70,000
County type					
Metro	33	58,067	45,000	60,000	66,963
Chief financial officer					
Total	35	79,635	69,205	80,000	86,288
Geographic region					
Northeast	6	71,649	51,817	72,071	77,843
North Central	9	72,509	61,038	76,564	81,452
South	12	81,014	73,468	81,259	91,800
West	8	91,574	80,000	85,867	95,000
County type					
Metro	35	79,635	69,205	80,000	86,288
County health officer					
Total	25	96,961	85,000	98,550	115,154
Geographic region					
Northeast	4	83,341	76,663	89,746	102,829
North Central	5	82,484	81,788	83,892	89,128
South	10	101,544	93,768	100,183	115,154
West	6	110,466	100,464	110,799	115,732
County type					
Metro	25	96,961	85,000	98,550	115,154
Planning director					
Total	32	74,608	64,355	71,762	83,025
Geographic region					
Northeast	6	62,428	52,500	54,298	65,166
North Central	6	72,834	64,355	73,847	81,121
South	12	78,849	71,400	72,689	92,196
West	8	78,713	70,000	77,786	89,724
County type					
Metro	32	74,608	64,355	71,762	83,025
County engineer					
Total	30	78,202	71,032	74,348	90,117
Geographic region					
Northeast	6	70,998	46,920	71,748	86,790
North Central	6	76,579	72,993	74,123	81,432
South	12	79,900	71,032	75,317	91,467
West	6	83,631	74,484	78,048	95,000
County type					
Metro	30	78,202	71,032	74,348	90,117
Director of welfare/human services					
Total	29	75,654	64,260	73,772	83,660
Geographic region					
Northeast	5	72,681	58,714	71,460	73,772
North Central	7	69,644	53,937	67,288	79,518
South	11	72,778	64,260	69,205	83,624
West	6	90,415	82,992	87,520	94,260

Table 2/4 **SALARIES OF COUNTY OFFICIALS: 1 JULY 1993**
continued

Title of official	No. counties reporting	Distribution of 1993 salaries			
		Mean ($)	First quartile ($)	Median ($)	Third quartile ($)
500,000 - 1,000,000 continued					
County type					
Metro	29	75,654	64,260	73,772	83,660
Chief law enforcement official					
Total	38	79,005	69,205	76,448	94,429
Geographic region					
Northeast	7	69,165	57,000	58,526	87,138
North Central	8	67,088	55,469	73,845	74,210
South	13	85,750	73,112	93,010	95,111
West	10	86,658	70,000	86,426	96,368
County type					
Metro	38	79,005	69,205	76,448	94,429
Purchasing director					
Total	33	62,461	53,859	59,099	67,288
Geographic region					
Northeast	6	53,380	41,558	53,885	66,150
North Central	8	55,304	51,538	54,646	57,147
South	13	65,796	58,931	60,986	68,946
West	6	73,859	54,285	74,254	95,000
County type					
Metro	33	62,461	53,859	59,099	67,288
Personnel director					
Total	34	72,898	64,083	71,381	83,025
Geographic region					
Northeast	5	74,945	65,000	70,953	72,512
North Central	8	66,564	57,798	62,711	70,625
South	14	72,872	65,795	71,898	83,025
West	7	78,725	66,256	77,124	90,688
County type					
Metro	34	72,898	64,083	71,381	83,025
250,000 - 499,999					
Governing board chair/ president/county judge					
Total	50	40,417	22,783	35,150	47,923
Geographic region					
Northeast	12	48,185	24,535	36,064	73,000
North Central	14	37,890	22,783	32,639	46,179
South	18	36,637	16,476	38,250	43,999
West	6	42,118	32,437	39,042	50,000
County type					
Metro	50	40,417	22,783	35,150	47,923
County manager					
Total	22	95,321	88,848	95,976	102,762
Geographic region					
North Central	6	93,233	88,100	100,801	102,762
South	12	95,711	91,072	95,298	97,904
West	4	97,282	92,705	96,221	99,736
County type					
Metro	22	95,321	88,848	95,976	102,762
County administrator					
Total	21	70,626	52,452	74,027	85,367
Geographic region					
Northeast	10	69,541	48,000	73,260	85,367
North Central	5	70,604	52,452	76,942	82,173
South	4	63,675	57,900	58,100	58,299
County type					
Metro	21	70,626	52,452	74,027	85,367
Clerk to the governing board					
Total	44	49,533	39,012	44,623	60,670
Geographic region					
Northeast	9	47,821	42,482	44,845	49,300
North Central	13	45,630	40,904	44,282	48,354
South	16	57,274	35,172	59,191	77,660
West	6	39,913	33,883	37,998	42,074
County type					
Metro	44	49,533	39,012	44,623	60,670
Chief financial officer					
Total	46	65,167	54,871	67,423	75,876
Geographic region					
Northeast	12	63,709	52,610	59,782	75,751
North Central	13	62,979	57,293	66,950	70,000
South	15	65,205	54,871	63,020	77,272
West	6	72,725	70,345	72,108	77,563
County type					
Metro	46	65,167	54,871	67,423	75,876
County health officer					
Total	37	75,910	63,169	78,837	89,096

Title of official	No. counties reporting	Distribution of 1993 salaries			
		Mean ($)	First quartile ($)	Median ($)	Third quartile ($)
250,000 - 499,999 continued					
Geographic region					
Northeast	6	72,986	56,607	76,747	87,752
North Central	12	67,528	61,900	68,026	74,188
South	15	79,671	73,536	84,674	90,738
West	4	91,338	94,115	95,855	97,594
County type					
Metro	37	75,910	63,169	78,837	89,096
Planning director					
Total	41	61,185	53,102	61,380	71,396
Geographic region					
Northeast	10	62,936	57,990	67,176	74,500
North Central	11	61,819	55,260	64,168	71,396
South	15	57,546	51,605	55,121	63,050
West	5	67,203	63,918	64,313	71,739
County type					
Metro	41	61,185	53,102	61,380	71,396
County engineer					
Total	37	69,163	59,133	70,969	79,581
Geographic region					
Northeast	8	68,617	58,176	72,511	75,000
North Central	11	73,034	69,709	72,993	81,120
South	12	65,620	59,133	66,706	70,969
West	6	69,879	51,105	74,801	83,961
County type					
Metro	37	69,163	59,133	70,969	79,581
Director of welfare/human services					
Total	38	68,383	56,355	67,194	79,955
Geographic region					
Northeast	9	65,254	58,032	60,650	70,000
North Central	9	71,571	58,000	74,214	82,400
South	13	61,749	48,000	56,355	69,500
West	7	80,627	67,038	79,955	90,709
County type					
Metro	38	68,383	56,355	67,194	79,955
Chief law enforcement official					
Total	51	65,179	54,763	66,228	77,268
Geographic region					
Northeast	13	58,892	40,000	61,125	72,104
North Central	14	63,023	53,927	62,185	71,084
South	17	67,211	63,898	70,506	80,880
West	7	76,231	56,400	74,804	92,934
County type					
Metro	51	65,179	54,763	66,228	77,268
Purchasing director					
Total	46	47,010	37,740	46,234	52,000
Geographic region					
Northeast	11	45,238	32,636	39,250	57,959
North Central	13	47,539	43,030	49,080	56,547
South	16	46,321	40,671	44,397	48,473
West	6	50,953	45,011	47,819	51,376
County type					
Metro	46	47,010	37,740	46,234	52,000
Personnel director					
Total	44	58,855	49,504	57,871	71,000
Geographic region					
Northeast	10	57,011	49,400	55,481	57,990
North Central	13	61,556	57,776	63,000	71,868
South	16	55,421	47,753	55,290	61,526
West	5	66,506	57,990	71,063	72,093
County type					
Metro	44	58,855	49,504	57,871	71,000
100,000 - 249,999					
Governing board chair/ president/county judge					
Total	156	31,789	15,000	30,267	43,328
Geographic region					
Northeast	25	37,765	16,026	36,905	48,522
North Central	46	24,565	10,000	21,911	40,675
South	62	30,698	13,510	27,320	42,887
West	23	42,680	33,756	42,580	53,220
County type					
Metro	137	31,529	14,560	29,864	43,329
Nonmetro	19	33,659	15,000	36,167	42,580
County manager					
Total	53	78,307	65,160	75,876	88,358

Table 2/4 continued   SALARIES OF COUNTY OFFICIALS: 1 JULY 1993

Title of official	No. counties reporting	Mean ($)	First quartile ($)	Median ($)	Third quartile ($)
100,000 - 249,999 continued					
Geographic region					
Northeast	3	85,100	. . .	90,950	. . .
North Central	13	70,098	60,000	69,590	77,430
South	29	79,393	65,160	75,237	94,761
West	8	85,161	80,623	81,321	91,312
County type					
Metro	44	77,521	65,154	75,269	87,299
Nonmetro	9	82,147	75,000	80,000	91,956
County administrator					
Total	66	63,366	49,878	60,319	73,500
Geographic region					
Northeast	13	54,359	44,000	52,742	59,000
North Central	20	55,477	48,000	54,236	60,000
South	23	71,093	49,878	72,263	77,000
West	10	73,081	62,124	71,469	74,530
County type					
Metro	58	63,047	48,730	58,186	73,500
Nonmetro	8	65,678	62,733	69,354	73,229
Clerk to the governing board					
Total	138	41,367	32,916	39,800	47,070
Geographic region					
Northeast	18	33,834	29,848	34,974	40,926
North Central	43	38,716	34,898	39,511	43,500
South	59	43,657	32,786	39,600	53,118
West	18	47,725	40,020	48,816	56,460
County type					
Metro	123	40,444	32,916	39,552	46,462
Nonmetro	15	48,930	32,786	42,582	66,384
Chief financial officer					
Total	144	53,677	44,000	52,500	62,530
Geographic region					
Northeast	22	44,334	34,718	42,171	55,733
North Central	41	49,870	42,240	50,000	54,183
South	61	57,736	45,735	55,402	68,311
West	20	59,381	53,175	59,623	65,083
County type					
Metro	125	53,141	43,485	52,022	62,192
Nonmetro	19	57,207	46,592	55,733	66,384
County health officer					
Total	96	62,293	51,167	58,378	78,255
Geographic region					
Northeast	10	54,291	46,544	53,138	59,200
North Central	41	55,225	49,622	55,000	60,637
South	29	67,014	53,543	70,803	82,246
West	16	76,849	70,008	79,344	86,132
County type					
Metro	85	61,470	51,167	58,128	77,000
Nonmetro	11	68,654	51,160	62,599	86,918
Planning director					
Total	120	51,511	43,000	48,592	60,153
Geographic region					
Northeast	19	49,750	43,399	47,997	58,531
North Central	31	44,771	38,812	44,144	51,547
South	47	52,376	43,000	50,066	63,143
West	23	60,282	47,946	60,300	68,676
County type					
Metro	102	50,661	41,605	47,822	59,780
Nonmetro	18	56,325	46,030	50,928	66,384
County engineer					
Total	117	58,866	49,000	60,049	68,460
Geographic region					
Northeast	14	53,202	37,929	55,500	63,982
North Central	31	59,689	52,000	62,274	68,560
South	50	57,165	48,240	55,741	63,765
West	22	65,173	54,247	67,974	72,197
County type					
Metro	101	58,490	49,677	59,592	68,460
Nonmetro	16	61,238	48,672	62,670	68,112
Director of welfare/human services					
Total	87	58,113	46,308	57,712	67,232
Geographic region					
Northeast	16	53,759	44,943	52,460	62,809
North Central	24	56,826	52,270	56,823	62,299
South	32	56,800	44,323	54,822	69,963
West	15	67,620	59,758	69,950	79,227
County type					
Metro	75	57,738	46,308	57,712	67,232

Title of official	No. counties reporting	Mean ($)	First quartile ($)	Median ($)	Third quartile ($)
100,000 - 249,999 continued					
Nonmetro	12	60,458	49,390	56,932	64,872
Chief law enforcement official					
Total	157	55,180	45,432	52,324	61,658
Geographic region					
Northeast	24	44,453	34,122	40,317	51,283
North Central	46	51,610	45,432	51,250	55,000
South	64	59,159	48,712	54,974	72,876
West	23	62,441	52,000	62,016	69,972
County type					
Metro	138	54,366	45,431	52,000	60,570
Nonmetro	19	61,094	52,000	56,900	75,213
Purchasing director					
Total	101	41,237	33,113	39,895	46,824
Geographic region					
Northeast	18	36,135	28,718	33,567	43,982
North Central	18	38,217	31,428	39,212	43,992
South	52	42,543	34,917	39,948	49,024
West	13	47,258	38,328	44,523	51,096
County type					
Metro	88	40,965	32,572	39,647	45,613
Nonmetro	13	43,075	35,002	42,016	46,904
Personnel director					
Total	126	48,686	39,288	47,320	57,531
Geographic region					
Northeast	19	44,661	36,362	46,079	50,601
North Central	31	45,957	39,765	45,150	53,450
South	56	48,565	36,156	46,476	58,801
West	20	57,079	50,374	56,466	66,384
County type					
Metro	107	48,005	38,220	46,511	57,398
Nonmetro	19	52,524	45,594	51,580	62,025
50,000 - 99,999					
Governing board chair/president/county judge					
Total	206	23,569	9,000	21,500	36,000
Geographic region					
Northeast	22	19,564	11,000	19,225	29,622
North Central	59	17,544	6,056	14,935	31,040
South	89	24,539	8,436	24,000	40,000
West	36	33,493	22,546	36,516	42,108
County type					
Metro	82	26,053	12,000	24,725	37,540
Nonmetro	124	21,926	7,500	19,228	34,400
County manager					
Total	54	67,674	57,512	68,015	75,254
Geographic region					
Northeast	7	67,438	60,125	65,411	78,604
North Central	8	53,204	47,150	48,917	56,930
South	33	70,977	60,996	71,970	76,295
West	6	69,079	64,220	69,413	75,000
County type					
Metro	21	73,715	60,996	74,651	79,795
Nonmetro	33	63,830	54,178	65,411	72,130
County administrator					
Total	84	50,044	38,800	49,242	58,500
Geographic region					
Northeast	12	37,663	25,253	38,994	46,000
North Central	22	46,440	35,858	46,500	56,743
South	33	53,499	42,500	52,000	61,417
West	17	56,739	49,884	57,036	62,784
County type					
Metro	37	48,337	35,192	47,000	57,960
Nonmetro	47	51,388	43,267	50,102	61,417
Clerk to the governing board					
Total	167	34,057	27,508	33,800	37,679
Geographic region					
Northeast	10	31,415	28,048	31,377	34,170
North Central	52	32,750	29,921	32,883	36,500
South	73	34,782	23,843	33,540	38,664
West	32	35,349	31,527	35,190	37,788
County type					
Metro	57	32,983	28,048	33,800	36,608
Nonmetro	110	34,613	27,120	33,744	37,788
Chief financial officer					
Total	170	44,539	36,694	42,081	51,210

Table 2/4 continued SALARIES OF COUNTY OFFICIALS: 1 JULY 1993

Title of official	No. counties reporting	Distribution of 1993 salaries: Mean ($)	First quartile ($)	Median ($)	Third quartile ($)
50,000 - 99,999 continued					
Geographic region					
Northeast	17	39,473	33,094	38,584	48,371
North Central	47	40,045	35,195	38,240	44,352
South	78	47,066	37,440	45,846	53,289
West	28	48,122	39,420	46,173	54,745
County type					
Metro	62	46,577	36,752	44,604	53,289
Nonmetro	108	43,370	36,694	41,666	50,736
County health officer					
Total	112	48,263	38,292	45,000	55,094
Geographic region					
Northeast	10	53,468	45,000	50,117	63,441
North Central	46	41,045	33,480	42,021	46,758
South	39	50,459	34,999	45,200	67,357
West	17	59,698	49,362	54,816	68,256
County type					
Metro	45	45,575	33,480	44,376	54,791
Nonmetro	67	50,069	39,600	45,225	57,239
Planning director					
Total	149	41,634	33,483	40,222	47,757
Geographic region					
Northeast	18	40,823	32,621	39,910	43,000
North Central	39	37,248	30,000	35,547	42,224
South	59	42,547	34,112	42,156	47,882
West	33	45,625	36,727	45,384	54,508
County type					
Metro	58	41,774	32,621	39,413	47,882
Nonmetro	91	41,544	33,483	40,956	47,757
County engineer					
Total	116	51,014	43,000	52,980	59,892
Geographic region					
Northeast	11	53,231	35,995	62,885	65,000
North Central	37	52,080	43,800	53,130	61,422
South	44	48,362	41,596	48,400	54,180
West	24	53,218	44,553	55,874	58,200
County type					
Metro	46	51,039	41,826	52,915	60,594
Nonmetro	70	50,998	43,752	53,571	59,892
Director of welfare/human services					
Total	102	48,770	41,626	50,858	56,700
Geographic region					
Northeast	16	47,365	38,000	49,919	58,228
North Central	27	52,101	47,632	52,352	57,512
South	41	46,962	40,000	48,414	54,970
West	18	49,138	38,400	55,476	58,947
County type					
Metro	41	50,790	40,000	54,475	61,241
Nonmetro	61	47,411	42,979	50,767	55,248
Chief law enforcement official					
Total	199	46,582	38,453	44,887	51,996
Geographic region					
Northeast	20	43,315	31,399	38,722	50,000
North Central	56	43,787	38,413	43,327	47,520
South	86	48,805	41,600	47,391	52,842
West	37	47,409	36,721	46,800	52,000
County type					
Metro	79	46,979	38,392	44,723	52,328
Nonmetro	120	46,320	38,880	44,944	51,720
Purchasing director					
Total	97	33,753	25,000	32,302	39,915
Geographic region					
Northeast	12	33,696	23,332	31,804	39,447
North Central	16	28,967	22,666	28,341	32,222
South	55	33,598	24,778	32,302	40,165
West	14	39,879	34,032	36,915	45,696
County type					
Metro	42	33,811	23,625	32,868	41,704
Nonmetro	55	33,709	26,219	31,830	39,286
Personnel director					
Total	127	39,159	31,305	37,906	47,327
Geographic region					
Northeast	16	38,074	30,005	36,675	45,881
North Central	25	37,699	31,704	36,525	45,552
South	56	37,859	31,018	36,258	43,618
West	30	43,380	36,414	42,067	52,166
County type					
Metro	52	38,687	29,388	35,059	49,000
Nonmetro	75	39,486	33,585	39,600	46,404

Title of official	No. counties reporting	Distribution of 1993 salaries: Mean ($)	First quartile ($)	Median ($)	Third quartile ($)
25,000 - 49,999					
Governing board chair/president/county judge					
Total	271	17,527	6,500	14,030	25,853
Geographic region					
Northeast	19	21,795	6,000	25,405	31,839
North Central	104	13,419	5,912	12,974	18,904
South	113	18,119	6,000	9,996	27,315
West	35	25,508	15,600	25,000	33,800
County type					
Metro	41	19,674	6,000	15,000	25,405
Nonmetro	230	17,145	6,869	13,828	26,174
County manager					
Total	48	56,645	46,056	53,150	66,394
Geographic region					
North Central	8	50,735	42,685	45,528	51,500
South	32	55,909	49,000	53,150	60,000
West	7	67,429	60,000	68,684	78,995
County type					
Metro	12	61,036	52,400	56,375	68,289
Nonmetro	36	55,182	45,000	52,266	61,980
County administrator					
Total	92	45,988	35,000	46,892	54,906
Geographic region					
Northeast	7	28,150	21,000	27,341	31,494
North Central	26	45,357	40,000	47,425	54,906
South	48	46,962	40,000	46,991	53,978
West	11	54,584	40,000	58,700	72,530
County type					
Metro	13	44,515	30,187	42,889	59,130
Nonmetro	79	46,231	39,975	47,000	54,906
Clerk to the governing board					
Total	207	30,950	25,000	29,536	35,618
Geographic region					
Northeast	10	26,585	23,625	26,021	27,000
North Central	90	29,325	26,660	29,786	32,127
South	74	31,165	23,700	27,383	37,560
West	33	36,221	28,475	37,000	43,200
County type					
Metro	24	33,798	27,034	31,390	38,617
Nonmetro	183	30,577	24,504	29,300	34,800
Chief financial officer					
Total	178	36,719	29,174	35,660	43,179
Geographic region					
Northeast	16	25,600	22,091	25,446	32,392
North Central	68	34,239	28,750	33,080	38,536
South	70	38,256	31,421	36,850	45,436
West	24	46,673	38,640	44,274	49,812
County type					
Metro	27	40,998	31,421	41,000	49,004
Nonmetro	151	35,954	28,968	35,190	40,073
County health officer					
Total	130	40,879	26,562	38,959	48,477
Geographic region					
Northeast	3	50,543	...	49,875	...
North Central	69	33,278	22,638	35,514	41,953
South	37	56,127	40,715	48,707	78,200
West	21	37,608	15,944	36,910	46,536
County type					
Metro	18	45,973	35,772	43,452	67,000
Nonmetro	112	40,060	26,562	38,318	46,536
Planning director					
Total	140	35,665	28,776	33,579	43,875
Geographic region					
Northeast	11	31,288	23,252	31,000	34,351
North Central	51	29,718	22,390	30,306	36,797
South	49	37,110	30,984	33,504	45,219
West	29	45,344	36,000	44,880	50,440
County type					
Metro	28	37,290	30,466	34,422	46,124
Nonmetro	112	35,259	28,613	33,456	42,307
County engineer					
Total	124	48,443	42,336	50,000	57,132
Geographic region					
North Central	65	48,730	42,857	51,491	55,952
South	34	44,747	38,000	43,271	54,761
West	24	53,883	46,920	53,892	62,700
County type					
Metro	21	49,729	42,696	50,756	57,441
Nonmetro	103	48,181	41,663	49,987	57,132

Table 2/4 SALARIES OF COUNTY OFFICIALS: 1 JULY 1993
continued

Title of official	No. counties reporting	Distribution of 1993 salaries			
		Mean ($)	First quartile ($)	Median ($)	Third quartile ($)
25,000 - 49,999 continued					
Director of welfare/human services					
Total	107	44,681	39,000	45,718	52,000
Geographic region					
Northeast	7	37,033	32,466	34,400	42,344
North Central	49	45,311	43,143	47,986	52,000
South	38	44,753	41,844	44,805	50,616
West	13	46,219	38,899	52,216	54,864
County type					
Metro	22	47,109	44,260	48,200	52,442
Nonmetro	85	44,053	38,899	45,372	51,300
Chief law enforcement official					
Total	248	39,651	33,243	38,480	44,865
Geographic region					
Northeast	16	30,632	27,045	30,568	33,100
North Central	102	37,301	32,880	35,993	41,046
South	97	42,172	35,000	42,284	48,840
West	33	43,876	36,820	42,000	52,000
County type					
Metro	37	43,920	35,290	42,144	52,454
Nonmetro	211	38,902	32,880	37,589	43,497
Purchasing director					
Total	58	28,019	20,500	26,583	32,906
Geographic region					
North Central	6	26,458	24,000	25,581	30,288
South	41	24,919	19,070	23,359	28,911
West	10	40,710	29,120	43,437	48,838
County type					
Metro	15	29,482	19,070	30,160	36,200
Nonmetro	43	27,509	20,500	25,417	30,288
Personnel director					
Total	72	34,935	27,000	33,325	42,422
Geographic region					
Northeast	4	32,140	28,850	31,000	33,150
North Central	23	35,412	29,702	36,689	41,352
South	28	30,924	23,832	27,221	40,353
West	17	41,554	30,950	42,282	53,009
County type					
Metro	11	38,139	34,115	40,353	45,000
Nonmetro	61	34,357	26,752	32,000	42,360
10,000 - 24,999					
Governing board chair/ president/county judge					
Total	418	17,569	7,000	14,573	23,800
Geographic region					
Northeast	4	10,860	6,090	9,045	12,000
North Central	164	11,852	7,875	11,700	15,750
South	184	20,416	5,040	20,023	31,500
West	66	24,241	15,000	22,677	33,000
County type					
Metro	26	16,148	4,528	9,385	23,085
Nonmetro	392	17,663	7,231	14,756	23,800
County manager					
Total	25	52,060	42,408	49,000	60,180
Geographic region					
South	15	45,160	40,525	45,150	49,627
West	9	64,803	56,527	67,156	72,108
County type					
Nonmetro	23	51,892	41,800	49,000	62,500
County administrator					
Total	129	37,126	25,002	35,000	46,500
Geographic region					
North Central	18	31,683	26,780	31,500	35,000
South	89	37,590	24,000	35,025	48,668
West	20	40,448	29,393	38,000	44,460
County type					
Metro	15	50,474	37,750	52,000	65,218
Nonmetro	114	35,369	24,500	33,397	45,000
Clerk to the governing board					
Total	336	28,586	23,435	27,329	32,230
Geographic region					
Northeast	3	23,485	. . .	23,017	. . .
North Central	150	27,976	24,668	27,305	30,240
South	121	27,730	20,160	24,926	32,563
West	62	31,978	28,000	30,917	35,120

Title of official	No. counties reporting	Distribution of 1993 salaries			
		Mean ($)	First quartile ($)	Median ($)	Third quartile ($)
10,000 - 24,999 continued					
County type					
Metro	22	33,442	25,355	32,115	40,000
Nonmetro	314	28,246	23,340	27,066	31,500
Chief financial officer					
Total	234	30,919	24,340	28,233	35,397
Geographic region					
Northeast	3	27,824	. . .	32,000	. . .
North Central	93	27,952	24,668	27,306	30,250
South	92	30,396	21,000	26,971	40,054
West	46	38,163	28,752	34,920	44,520
County type					
Metro	17	39,670	28,387	40,054	45,436
Nonmetro	217	30,233	24,150	27,851	34,848
County health officer					
Total	143	35,512	27,331	32,725	39,000
Geographic region					
North Central	84	31,320	26,624	31,150	34,591
South	36	45,537	31,476	38,882	59,250
West	22	35,124	26,707	33,502	45,400
County type					
Metro	11	50,799	32,725	39,000	80,000
Nonmetro	132	34,238	27,298	32,037	37,836
Planning director					
Total	121	32,787	24,586	31,260	38,196
Geographic region					
Northeast	3	28,265	. . .	25,059	. . .
North Central	34	26,322	22,000	26,481	30,000
South	42	35,550	29,476	34,391	42,382
West	42	35,579	24,540	34,116	46,134
County type					
Metro	17	37,178	30,000	34,122	43,222
Nonmetro	104	32,069	24,500	30,172	38,000
County engineer					
Total	154	43,779	36,636	45,992	51,378
Geographic region					
North Central	98	44,541	42,000	46,000	51,498
South	30	40,517	30,000	41,186	50,000
West	26	44,671	36,600	46,023	55,068
County type					
Metro	16	44,067	40,480	46,114	50,000
Nonmetro	138	43,746	36,600	45,992	51,378
Director of welfare/human services					
Total	139	37,700	32,631	38,264	43,825
Geographic region					
North Central	55	36,074	23,352	38,635	44,538
South	53	37,860	34,529	37,390	39,936
West	29	40,659	36,000	41,000	47,599
County type					
Metro	10	40,662	34,864	38,280	39,037
Nonmetro	129	37,470	32,328	38,160	44,281
Chief law enforcement official					
Total	354	35,695	30,042	35,000	41,031
Geographic region					
Northeast	3	33,144	. . .	36,085	. . .
North Central	140	33,579	30,000	33,875	36,701
South	156	36,701	29,000	36,720	43,412
West	55	38,368	32,604	37,800	42,120
County type					
Metro	27	41,705	35,000	40,000	47,352
Nonmetro	327	35,199	29,705	34,483	40,446
Purchasing director					
Total	46	24,419	17,080	22,950	28,931
Geographic region					
North Central	4	22,293	20,887	24,434	27,981
South	30	22,287	15,000	19,032	28,931
West	11	31,624	22,000	26,052	35,815
County type					
Metro	5	24,678	17,105	17,451	28,551
Nonmetro	41	24,388	17,080	23,900	28,931
Personnel director					
Total	47	28,475	20,220	25,000	39,072
Geographic region					
North Central	7	23,503	12,000	24,000	31,000
South	23	27,935	16,720	25,000	39,102
West	16	31,594	22,092	28,375	41,500
County type					
Metro	5	38,206	29,000	30,424	52,499

Table 2/4 continued   **SALARIES OF COUNTY OFFICIALS: 1 JULY 1993**

Title of official	No. counties reporting	Distribution of 1993 salaries			
		Mean ($)	First quartile ($)	Median ($)	Third quartile ($)
10,000 - 24,999 continued					
Nonmetro	42	27,316	20,220	24,814	35,736
5,000 - 9,999					
Governing board chair/ president/county judge					
Total	188	15,136	6,295	11,238	20,190
Geographic region					
North Central	92	9,061	6,000	8,662	11,860
South	57	19,660	5,100	20,000	30,000
West	37	23,030	12,700	21,592	23,800
County type					
Nonmetro	187	15,185	6,295	11,275	21,592
County manager					
Total	4	52,599	47,550	51,600	55,650
County type					
Nonmetro	3	51,582	...	47,550	...
County administrator					
Total	31	35,660	23,000	31,852	42,504
Geographic region					
South	17	34,903	23,857	32,000	41,733
West	12	36,385	24,000	26,226	40,657
County type					
Nonmetro	31	35,660	23,000	31,852	42,504
Clerk to the governing board					
Total	166	25,407	20,689	23,451	28,000
Geographic region					
Northeast	3	35,309	...	24,926	...
North Central	81	23,061	21,108	22,893	24,578
South	47	26,030	18,492	22,573	30,124
West	35	29,150	23,646	28,000	32,000
County type					
Nonmetro	166	25,407	20,689	23,451	28,000
Chief financial officer					
Total	93	25,217	20,502	22,740	26,280
Geographic region					
North Central	40	22,438	21,013	22,484	23,500
South	27	22,372	18,000	20,500	25,608
West	24	31,892	22,429	26,640	33,000
County type					
Nonmetro	92	24,975	20,502	22,724	26,279
County health officer					
Total	47	29,826	24,814	27,710	31,673
Geographic region					
North Central	29	27,745	24,825	27,710	31,096
South	4	28,070	25,607	27,804	30,000
West	12	33,459	24,000	25,574	29,682
County type					
Nonmetro	47	29,826	24,814	27,710	31,673
Planning director					
Total	31	32,137	20,689	29,916	38,604
Geographic region					
Northeast	3	32,961	...	27,254	...
North Central	8	20,576	19,000	20,545	21,489
South	5	34,118	30,499	36,387	39,000
West	15	37,478	28,428	33,732	40,914
County type					
Nonmetro	30	31,713	20,689	29,458	36,387
County engineer					
Total	58	31,604	22,431	29,234	42,500
Geographic region					
North Central	47	30,849	22,431	29,131	41,475
South	5	28,777	21,000	24,907	28,916
West	6	39,871	36,076	41,368	48,564
County type					
Nonmetro	57	31,314	22,431	29,131	41,475
Director of welfare/ human services					
Total	46	29,853	19,542	32,014	38,196
Geographic region					
Northeast	3	31,326	...	35,000	...
North Central	14	25,195	15,888	26,346	33,524
South	17	29,220	19,983	30,643	36,350
West	12	35,817	32,000	37,312	42,000
County type					
Nonmetro	46	29,853	19,542	32,014	38,196
Chief law enforcement official					
Total	148	31,051	26,299	29,079	34,000

Title of official	No. counties reporting	Distribution of 1993 salaries			
		Mean ($)	First quartile ($)	Median ($)	Third quartile ($)
5,000 - 9,999 continued					
Geographic region					
Northeast	3	37,766	...	34,608	...
North Central	70	27,124	24,530	27,128	29,430
South	47	32,745	27,288	33,424	37,704
West	28	37,309	28,638	34,250	38,196
County type					
Nonmetro	147	30,999	26,232	29,000	34,000
Purchasing director					
Total	12	22,379	16,000	19,000	25,524
Geographic region					
South	9	21,948	16,000	18,000	25,524
County type					
Nonmetro	12	22,379	16,000	19,000	25,524
Personnel director					
Total	9	39,295	18,025	30,000	55,009
Geographic region					
West	5	45,824	20,384	30,000	59,535
County type					
Nonmetro	9	39,295	18,025	30,000	55,009
2,500 - 4,999					
Governing board chair/ president/county judge					
Total	81	12,175	6,060	8,858	18,000
Geographic region					
North Central	45	8,285	5,100	6,989	9,000
South	18	18,718	14,681	19,248	26,947
West	17	15,018	8,400	17,508	18,000
County type					
Nonmetro	81	12,175	6,060	8,858	18,000
County administrator					
Total	10	33,617	18,740	31,902	49,901
Geographic region					
South	4	43,041	49,901	50,833	51,764
West	6	27,333	18,740	28,650	33,204
County type					
Nonmetro	10	33,617	18,740	31,902	49,901
Clerk to the governing board					
Total	77	21,024	18,500	21,000	22,800
Geographic region					
North Central	42	20,426	18,576	20,724	21,477
South	14	19,137	15,590	18,298	23,344
West	20	23,904	21,182	24,763	25,800
County type					
Nonmetro	77	21,024	18,500	21,000	22,800
Chief financial officer					
Total	37	21,977	17,599	21,289	23,090
Geographic region					
North Central	18	21,752	18,156	20,911	22,050
South	12	19,657	14,798	17,422	23,693
West	6	27,435	23,090	25,800	27,758
County type					
Nonmetro	37	21,977	17,599	21,289	23,090
County health officer					
Total	13	29,235	21,996	25,584	31,503
Geographic region					
North Central	7	27,204	21,996	24,600	31,503
West	4	26,297	25,584	26,272	26,960
County type					
Nonmetro	13	29,235	21,996	25,584	31,503
Planning director					
Total	10	26,803	18,500	22,988	32,500
Geographic region					
North Central	3	29,358	...	21,210	...
West	6	26,910	21,975	27,500	32,500
County type					
Nonmetro	10	26,803	18,500	22,988	32,500
County engineer					
Total	20	25,639	19,669	23,562	26,650
Geographic region					
North Central	15	25,145	19,669	23,520	26,650
South	3	22,337	...	19,099	...
County type					
Nonmetro	20	25,639	19,669	23,562	26,650
Director of welfare/ human services					
Total	18	30,954	21,912	32,000	33,182

Table 2/4   **SALARIES OF COUNTY OFFICIALS: 1 JULY 1993**
continued

Title of official	No. counties reporting	Mean ($)	First quartile ($)	Median ($)	Third quartile ($)
2,500 - 4,999 continued					
Geographic region					
North Central	8	28,140	21,912	25,084	32,000
West	8	33,292	32,000	32,320	46,548
County type					
Nonmetro	18	30,954	21,912	32,000	33,182
Chief law enforcement official					
Total	62	24,950	20,507	24,102	27,758
Geographic region					
North Central	34	24,067	20,507	23,185	26,819
South	14	23,993	18,000	21,649	27,435
West	13	28,585	25,991	28,800	28,800
County type					
Nonmetro	62	24,950	20,507	24,102	27,758
Personnel director					
Total	3	19,780	. . .	19,200	. . .
Geographic region					
West	3	19,780	. . .	19,200	. . .
County type					
Nonmetro	3	19,780	. . .	19,200	. . .
Under 2,500					
Governing board chair/ president/county judge					
Total	55	11,226	4,800	7,200	18,000
Geographic region					
North Central	23	5,665	4,500	5,670	7,000
South	13	21,544	18,600	22,916	26,659
West	19	10,898	5,400	8,976	18,000
County type					
Nonmetro	55	11,226	4,800	7,200	18,000
County administrator					
Total	8	27,361	19,416	25,250	34,702
Geographic region					
West	6	29,435	19,416	30,101	39,573
County type					
Nonmetro	8	27,361	19,416	25,250	34,702
Clerk to the governing board					
Total	46	22,201	18,000	20,689	25,700

Title of official	No. counties reporting	Mean ($)	First quartile ($)	Median ($)	Third quartile ($)
Under 2,500 continued					
Geographic region					
North Central	16	20,244	18,600	20,195	21,105
South	11	20,890	16,640	18,000	23,296
West	19	24,607	18,993	22,905	25,800
County type					
Nonmetro	46	22,201	18,000	20,689	25,700
Chief financial officer					
Total	31	23,741	18,993	21,405	24,870
Geographic region					
North Central	10	21,448	19,000	21,022	23,400
South	8	23,271	20,400	22,599	23,296
West	13	25,793	18,993	21,405	25,800
County type					
Nonmetro	31	23,741	18,993	21,405	24,870
County health officer					
Total	6	22,726	15,000	21,690	26,376
Geographic region					
North Central	4	18,144	15,000	17,100	19,200
County type					
Nonmetro	6	22,726	15,000	21,690	26,376
County engineer					
Total	4	25,391	21,405	21,683	21,960
Geographic region					
North Central	3	26,720	. . .	21,960	. . .
County type					
Nonmetro	4	25,391	21,405	21,683	21,960
Director of welfare/human services					
Total	3	29,477	. . .	29,700	. . .
County type					
Nonmetro	3	29,477	. . .	29,700	. . .
Chief law enforcement official					
Total	38	26,049	22,575	25,971	28,000
Geographic region					
North Central	16	22,709	19,900	23,233	26,299
South	10	27,565	25,451	26,837	30,000
West	12	29,239	23,027	27,385	28,800
County type					
Nonmetro	38	26,049	22,575	25,971	28,000

^c**3**

Police and Fire Department Personnel and Expenditures, 1993

Gerard J. Hoetmer
International City/County Management Association

Findings

Since 1992, there has been a slight increase in the number of police personnel per thousand population; the number of fire personnel has remained virtually constant.

Total per capita expenditures for police departments increased 12.7% from 1992 to 1993; fire department expenditures increased 8.9%.

As the data in this report were being collected in January 1993, the Clinton administration was preparing for its inauguration. The resounding theme in the just-completed campaign had been the economy, which, although technically in a recovery since March 1991, was sputtering along at a snail's pace. The unemployment rate for all civilian employees was 7.1%, exactly the same as it had been in January 1992, a year earlier. Fortunately, inflation rates had remained steady in 1992: The Consumer Price Index for All Urban Consumers (CPI-U) hovered around 3.1%.

Local governments were especially hard-pressed, with cities on both coasts operating for all intents and purposes under recessionary conditions. Many local governments were forced to cut their expenditures during 1992 to meet much lower revenue projections; however, vital police and fire services were generally unaffected. As this report will show, individual salaries kept up with inflation, as did total salary and wage expenditures and all other expenditures for these services.

METHODOLOGY

The data in this report are based on responses to a mail survey conducted by ICMA in January 1993. Surveys were sent to the 2,795 municipalities in the United States with populations of 10,000 or more. The survey response rate is presented in Table 3/1 by population group, geographical division, and metro status. The overall response rate to the 1993 survey was 64.3%. Municipalities under one million in population

Table 3/1   SURVEY RESPONSE

	No. cities surveyed (A)	No. cities responding	% of (A)
Total, all cities[1]	2,795	1,798	64.3
Population group			
Over 1,000,000	8	4	50.0
500,000–1,000,000 ..	16	12	75.0
250,000–499,999	40	30	75.0
100,000–249,999	133	91	68.4
50,000–99,999	334	237	71.0
25,000–49,999	674	443	65.7
10,000–24,999	1,590	981	61.7
Geographic division[2]			
New England	327	158	48.3
Mid-Atlantic	448	234	52.2
East North Central ...	555	335	60.4
West North Central ..	225	171	76.0
South Atlantic	314	230	73.3
East South Central ...	149	85	57.1
West South Central ..	265	186	70.2
Mountain	129	98	76.0
Pacific Coast	383	301	78.6
Metro status[3]			
Central	510	353	69.2
Suburban	1,691	1,051	62.2
Independent	594	394	66.3

[1]The term *cities* refers also to towns, villages, boroughs, and townships.
[2]*Divisions: New England*—the states of Connecticut, Maine, Massachusetts, New Hampshire, Rhode Island, and Vermont; *Mid-Atlantic*—the states of New Jersey, New York, and Pennsylvania; *East North Central*—the states of Illinois, Indiana, Michigan, Ohio, and Wisconsin; *West North Central*—the states of Iowa, Kansas, Minnesota, Missouri, Nebraska, North Dakota, and South Dakota; *South Atlantic*—the states of Delaware, Florida, Georgia, Maryland, North Carolina, South Carolina, Virginia, and West Virginia, plus the District of Columbia; *East South Central*—the states of Alabama, Kentucky, Mississippi, and Tennessee; *West South Central*—the states of Arkansas, Louisiana, Oklahoma, and Texas; *Mountain*—the states of Arizona, Colorado, Idaho, Montana, Nevada, New Mexico, Utah, and Wyoming; *Pacific Coast*—the states of Alaska, California, Hawaii, Oregon, and Washington.
[3]*Metro status: Central*—core city of an MSA; *Suburban*—incorporated city located within an MSA; *Independent*—city located outside of an MSA.

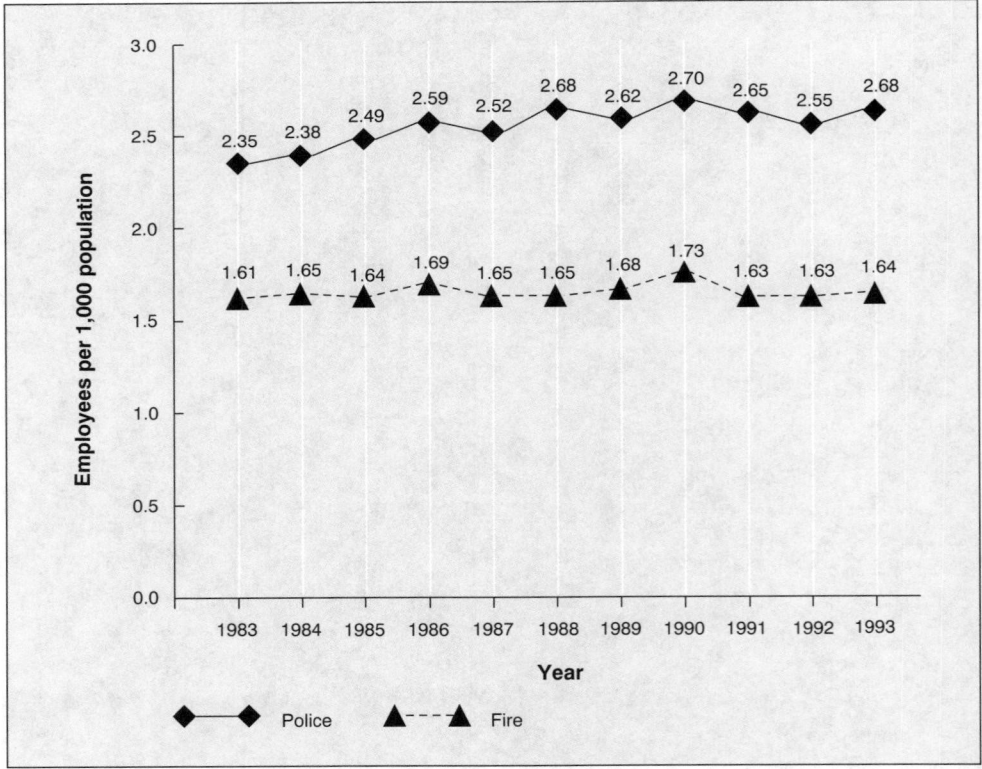

Figure 3/1   *Police and fire trends in employees per 1,000 population*

were more likely to respond to the survey than those over a million.

PERSONNEL

Data on the size of the workforce for each of the services, including both uniformed and civilian personnel, are presented in Table 3/2. For all jurisdictions reporting, the average number of police department employees is 127 and the average number of fire department employees is 90. Figure 3/1 shows a comparison of the average number of paid personnel from year to year in each department; however, these averages fluctuate each year, depending on the number of large cities that respond to the survey.

The number of employees per thousand population in police departments has remained fairly constant. During the early 1980s and the early 1990s, the number dropped because of the recession. Since the beginning of the current upturn in the economy the number has increased, from 2.55 per thousand in 1992 to 2.68 per thousand in 1993.

The number of fire personnel per thousand population has remained virtually constant over the past 12 years, at an average of 1.65 employees per thousand population. In 1993, there were 164 fire department personnel per thousand population. The range during the 11-year period was from a high of 1.73 per thousand in 1990 to a low of 1.61 per thousand in 1983.

Police departments in larger central cities tend to have more police officers per thousand population than do those in smaller and independent municipalities. The number of fire personnel differs very little between smaller and larger communities, except that cities with over one million in population tend to have a lower number per thousand simply because of their size.

Table 3/3 shows the average number of civilian personnel in police and fire departments in 1993. The civilian police personnel average was 33 per department, up from 30 in 1992; the civilian fire personnel average was 13. Fire department civilian personnel have been increasing steadily as a percentage of total personnel, although the percentage is still considerably lower than that of police departments. As of January 1993, police departments averaged 25.9% civilian personnel. Fire department averages have increased from 7.5% of total personnel in January 1988 to 9.7% in January 1991 to 14.4% in January 1993.

In 1993, for the first time, ICMA asked cities to indicate whether or not they had minimum crew size requirements on their fire apparatus or minimum staffing requirements on a fire department shift. Both areas have been major issues for fire labor organizations.

Table 3/4 shows that more than two-thirds (71.4%) of cities do not have minimum staffing requirements. Mid-Atlantic cities are the exception to the rule: Over 61% of the cities in this region have minimum staffing requirements per shift in their fire departments. The three cities

with over a million population also have minimums.

Table 3/5 shows that it is more likely for cities to have minimum crew size requirements than minimum staffing per shift; the majority of cities (51.6%) require crew size minimums. Of the cities that have minimum crew size requirements, Table 3/6 shows the average minimum crew requirements for pumpers, for ladders, and for other types of fire apparatus.

WORK WEEK

Police in all reporting cities average 40 regular work hours per week, while firefighters work an average of 51 hours (not shown). Work schedules vary greatly among cities. New England cities tend to run a 42-hour work week for firefighters while western cities generally remain on a 56-hour work week. Since Congress passed the Fair Labor Standards Act in 1986, many

Table 3/2   FULL-TIME PAID PERSONNEL, 1993[1]

	Police department			Fire department		
	No. cities reporting	Mean	Per 1,000 population	No. cities reporting	Mean	Per 1,000 population
Total, all cities	1,609	127	2.68	1,245	90	1.64
Population group						
Over 1,000,000	4	5,813	3.28	4	2,310	1.30
500,000–1,000,000	13	2,239	3.48	13	1,127	1.75
250,000–499,999	28	965	2.91	29	540	1.65
100,000–249,999	86	365	2.60	81	242	1.70
50,000–99,999	208	152	2.37	186	103	1.61
25,000–49,999	389	78	2.39	313	59	1.78
10,000–24,999	881	36	2.35	619	25	1.57
Geographic division						
New England	144	68	2.34	112	67	2.13
Mid-Atlantic	213	75	2.44	82	88	1.94
East North Central	308	100	2.51	258	71	1.61
West North Central	156	102	2.46	119	72	1.51
South Atlantic	203	176	3.70	175	106	2.04
East South Central	76	138	2.91	71	109	2.19
West South Central	180	156	2.52	163	107	1.63
Mountain	90	145	2.67	72	93	1.47
Pacific Coast	239	189	2.53	193	105	1.23
Metro status						
Central	338	393	2.91	326	233	1.67
Suburban	907	61	2.30	596	43	1.50
Independent	364	46	2.42	323	33	1.72

[1]Includes uniformed and civilian/nonuniformed personnel.

Table 3/3   CIVILIAN/NONUNIFORMED PERSONNEL, 1993

	Police department		Fire department	
	No. cities reporting	Mean personnel	No. cities reporting	Mean personnel
Total, all cities	1,455	33	880	13
Population group				
Over 1,000,000	4	1,381	4	250
500,000–1,000,000	13	478	13	250
250,000–499,999	27	250	28	46
100,000–249,999	86	91	81	15
50,000–99,999	200	40	174	9
25,000–49,999	368	19	275	6
10,000–24,999	757	9	305	4
Geographic division				
New England	128	14	86	8
Mid-Atlantic	171	14	49	4
East North Central	278	20	154	8
West North Central	146	29	63	14
South Atlantic	189	44	140	27
East South Central	69	35	46	12
West South Central	165	42	111	10
Mountain	82	47	58	15
Pacific Coast	227	55	173	12
Metro status				
Central	328	95	305	27
Suburban	799	17	407	6
Independent	328	11	168	5

communities have moved to an average 53-hour work week for fire personnel.

COMPENSATION

Tables 3/7 through 3/14 present salary data for full-time paid police officers and firefighters. Table 3/7 shows the mean entrance and maximum salaries for police officers and firefighters of all municipalities responding to ICMA surveys since 1983. The table also shows the percentage spread between entrance and maximum salaries and the number of years required to reach maximum salary.

Since 1983, entrance salaries have increased 52.0% for police officers and 49.8% for firefighters. Maximum salaries have risen more sharply—62.8% for police officers and 60.6% for firefighters. These higher percentage increases are reflected in the increased percentage spread as well as in the number of years it takes for police officers and firefighters to reach maximum salary. In the 1970s, police officers and firefighters usually reached maximum salary in four years; today it takes six years.

Tables 3/8 and 3/9 examine how responding cities of 500,000 and more in population compensate police officers and firefighters. These cities were selected for closer examination because large urban municipalities tend to set benchmark wage rates for the surrounding suburban communities.

Because of differences in the work week among the cities, hourly rates were compared. The overall mean entrance salary for police officers increased 2.2% in these large cities. (Note that this increase reflects the percentage change in hourly rates from cities reporting in both 1992 and 1993.) The average entrance salary increased 11.1% for firefighters. Two fire departments reporting in 1992 reduced their hourly work weeks. Firefighters' salary increases exceeded the 3.2% rate of inflation; police salary increases did not.

As of January 1993, entry-level police officers in reporting benchmark cities earned an average hourly rate of $13.35. All departments reported a 40-hour work week except Nashville/Davidson County, which reported a 42-hour work week. Entry-level firefighters in the benchmark cities received an average hourly rate of $10.37, with work weeks ranging from 40 to 56 hours.

Tables 3/10 and 3/11 show the following information for each service:

1. Annual entrance salary (base salary paid during the first 12 months with the department as a sworn police officer or firefighter, excluding uniform allowance, holiday pay, hazardous duty pay, or any other compensation).
2. Maximum annual base salary paid to sworn uniformed personnel who do not hold any promotional rank (excluding uniform allowance, holiday pay, hazardous duty pay, or any other compensation).

3. Mean number of years of service required to reach the maximum annual base salary.

When *all* reporting cities are included, since January 1992 mean entrance salaries have increased faster than the inflation rate in both services (not shown). Mean entrance salaries for police officers increased 5.0% and for firefighters, 5.3%. Maximum salaries increased faster than entrance salaries: for police officers, the increase was 6.2%; for firefighters, 6.8%.

Salary Trends
Increases in entrance and maximum salaries for police officers and firefighters are shown in Table 3/12, which includes salary data for municipalities that reported in each of the six years from 1988 through 1993. (Percentages in Table 3/12 have been rounded.)

Police entrance salaries increased 21.4% during the period; fire entrance salaries increased 20.8%. The inflation rate over the period was 23.2%. Thus, maximum salaries kept pace with inflation over the five years, increasing 25.4% for police officers and 25.4% for firefighters.

Longevity Pay
Tables 3/13 and 3/14 show the following information for each service:

1. Whether personnel can receive longevity pay (compensation beyond the regular maximum

---

Table 3/4   FIRE DEPARTMENTS' MINIMUM STAFFING REQUIREMENT

Classification	No. reporting (A)	Minimum staff				
		No.	% of (A)	No.	% of (A)	
		No		Yes		
Total, all cities	1,287	919	71.4	368	28.6	
Population group						
Over 1,000,000	3	3	100.0	0	0.0	
500,000–1,000,000	7	5	71.4	2	28.6	
250,000–499,999	22	17	77.3	5	22.7	
100,000–249,999	68	55	80.9	13	19.1	
50,000–99,999	172	150	87.2	22	12.8	
25,000–49,999	302	222	73.5	80	26.5	
10,000–24,999	713	467	65.5	246	34.5	
Geographic division						
New England	126	71	56.3	55	43.7	
Mid-Atlantic	149	58	38.9	91	61.1	
East North Central	251	184	73.3	67	26.7	
West North Central	129	88	68.2	41	31.8	
South Atlantic	174	148	85.1	26	14.9	
East South Central	61	54	88.5	7	11.5	
West South Central	155	123	79.4	32	20.6	
Mountain	70	51	72.9	19	27.1	
Pacific Coast	172	142	82.6	30	17.4	
Metro status						
Central	277	228	82.3	49	17.7	
Suburban	702	443	63.1	259	36.9	
Independent	308	248	80.5	60	19.5	

Table 3/5   MINIMUM NUMBER OF CREW PER FIRE APPARATUS

Classification	No. reporting (A)	Minimum number of crew members per apparatus				
		Yes		No		
		No.	% of (A)	No.	% of (A)	
Total, all cities	1,211	625	51.6	586	48.4	
Population group						
Over 1,000,000	3	3	100.0	0	0.0	
500,000–1,000,000	8	7	87.5	1	12.5	
250,000–499,999	21	17	81.0	4	19.0	
100,000–249,999	67	54	80.6	13	19.4	
50,000–99,999	161	123	76.4	38	23.6	
25,000–49,999	290	168	57.9	122	42.1	
10,000–24,999	661	253	38.3	408	61.7	
Geographic division						
New England	122	47	38.5	75	61.5	
Mid-Atlantic	142	49	34.5	93	65.5	
East North Central	234	102	43.6	132	56.4	
West North Central	111	52	46.8	59	53.2	
South Atlantic	163	105	64.4	58	35.6	
East South Central	61	36	59.0	25	41.0	
West South Central	144	74	51.4	70	48.6	
Mountain	69	40	58.0	29	42.0	
Pacific Coast	165	120	72.7	45	27.3	
Metro status						
Central	267	197	73.8	70	26.2	
Suburban	658	294	44.7	364	55.3	
Independent	286	134	46.9	152	53.1	

salary based on number of years of service).

2. Maximum annual salary, including longevity pay that personnel holding no promotional rank can receive.
3. Average number of years of service required to receive longevity pay.

Longevity pay is commonly used as an incentive to reduce employee turnover and to reward employees who have reached the maximum salary and have limited opportunities for promotion. Longevity pay may be a flat dollar amount, a percentage of base pay, a percentage of the maximum rate, or a normal step increase in the basic pay plan. The method of calculating longevity pay can have a significant effect on the burden that longevity pay will have on the personnel budget.

Over two-thirds of the municipalities responding to the survey have adopted longevity pay; however, there are significant differences among geographic areas. Although 70.1% of the cities reporting provide longevity pay for their police officers, only 35.1% of Pacific Coast jurisdictions do so. Similarly, 66.5% of all fire departments responding offer longevity pay, but only 31.8% of Pacific Coast city fire departments do.

On the average, longevity pay increases maximum salaries by 5.0% for police officers and 3.7% for firefighters. To be eligible for longevity pay, police officers and firefighters must serve an average of six years of service.

EXPENDITURES

Data on expenditures for police and fire departments appear in Tables 3/15 through 3/22.

Salaries and Wages

Table 3/15 shows salary and wage expenditures for all departmental personnel—permanent and temporary, full- and part-time. (The survey requested the gross amount of salaries and wages, including longevity pay, hazardous duty pay, holiday pay, etc., without deductions for income tax or employee contributions for social security or retirement programs.)

In 1993, average expenditures for salaries and wages for both civilian and uniformed personnel were $99.75 per capita for police departments and $63.28 per capita for fire departments. These expenditures had increased 8.7% for police departments and 7.1% for fire departments since the 1992 survey.

Smaller cities pay less on a per capita basis for police and fire salaries and wages than do larger cities. The range of salary and wage expenditures between the smallest and the largest population groups surveyed is greater in police departments than in fire departments. The salary range for police departments is from $74.94 per capita for the smallest population group to $151.21 for the largest, a 101.8% difference. The range for fire departments is from $49.66 per capita for the smallest jurisdictions to $82.37 for cities with 500,000 to a million in population, a 65.9% difference.

Employee Benefits

Data showing municipal contributions (as opposed to employee contributions) for employee benefits are presented in Tables 3/18 and 3/17. Table 3/16 shows contributions for federal, social security, and state- and city-administered employee retirement systems for uniformed and civilian personnel. Employee retirement benefits in police departments increased 6.4% per capita from the 1992 survey. Fire department expenditures for retirement increased 9.4% per capita.

Table 3/17 shows contributions to health, hospital, disability, and life insurance programs. Comparisons between years can be difficult because data from the very large cities can sometimes distort the relationships. (Table 3/22 gives a more accurate picture from year to year because it includes only the jurisdictions that responded every year that the survey was conducted.) Nevertheless, these expenditures have increased much more rapidly than other expenses. On a per capita basis, police department expenditures for health benefits have increased 25.4% over January 1992 figures and

Table 3/6   MINIMUM NUMBER OF CREW PER APPARATUS

Classification	Pumpers		Ladders		Other	
	No. reporting	Average minimum crew	No. reporting	Average minimum crew	No. reporting	Average minimum crew
Total, all cities	558	3.04	478	2.80	241	2.40
Population group						
Over 1,000,000	3	4.00	2	4.00	1	4.00
500,000–1,000,000	6	3.67	7	4.00	4	3.00
250,000–499,999	16	3.50	48	3.63	7	3.00
100,000–249,999	50	3.24	16	3.48	24	2.83
50,000–99,999	110	3.04	104	2.82	43	2.19
25,000–49,999	150	2.88	125	2.39	77	2.21
10,000–24,999	223	3.03	176	2.76	85	2.47
Geographic division						
New England	40	2.75	38	2.34	21	2.62
Mid-Atlantic	43	3.53	42	3.31	12	3.58
East North Central	89	2.89	83	2.64	44	2.39
West North Central	44	3.09	39	2.79	16	2.19
South Atlantic	93	3.01	79	2.62	39	2.64
East South Central	32	3.00	28	2.93	10	2.20
West South Central	70	3.00	58	2.78	28	2.50
Mountain	37	3.16	27	2.85	19	1.89
Pacific Coast	110	3.05	84	3.04	52	2.12
Metro status						
Central	179	3.10	168	2.96	80	2.53
Suburban	258	3.05	214	2.79	107	2.26
Independent	121	2.90	96	2.54	54	2.50

Table 3/7   COMPARISON OF MEAN ENTRANCE AND MAXIMUM SALARIES, 1983–1993

	Mean entrance salary ($)	Mean maximum salary ($)	Spread (%)	No. of years to maximum
Police				
1983	16,527	20,807	25.9	5
1984	17,115	21,681	26.7	5
1985	18,112	22,891	26.4	5
1986	18,897	24,204	28.1	5[1]
1987	19,825	25,484	28.5	5
1988	20,636	26,734	29.6	5
1989	21,356	27,850	30.4	5[1]
1990	22,350	29,139	30.4	6[1]
1991	23,474	30,881	31.6	6[1]
1992	23,921	31,891	33.3	6[1]
1993	25,126	33,880	34.8	6[1]
Fire				
1983	15,854	19,689	24.2	4
1984	16,436	20,500	24.7	5
1985	17,487	21,734	24.3	5
1986	18,054	22,776	26.2	5
1987	18,942	23,965	26.5	5
1988	19,713	25,010	26.9	5
1989	20,406	26,058	27.7	5
1990	21,062	27,076	28.6	6
1991	22,237	28,861	29.8	6
1992	22,559	29,601	31.2	6
1993	23,753	31,615	33.1	6

[1]Cities 100,000 and over in population averaged 6 or more years to reach maximum.

fire department expenditures for health benefits have increased 27.3%.

Police departments spent $18.91 per capita in 1993 for retirement and social security benefits, while fire departments spent $12.09 per capita. The figures were 14.5% of total police department personnel expenditures and 14.6% of total fire department personnel expenditures. Municipal expenditures for health, hospitalization, disability, and life insurance programs represent 8.9% of total police personnel expenditures and 9% of total fire department personnel expenditures.

Total Personnel Expenditures

Table 3/18 presents total personnel expenditures for civilian and uniformed personnel. These ex-penditures include salaries and wages; contributions to federal, social security, and state- and city-administered retirement systems; and contributions to health, hospital, disability, and life insurance programs. Average per capita expenditures for police personnel were $130.24 in 1993, an increase of 9.7% over 1992. Per capita fire personnel expenditures in 1993 were $82.80, an increase of 9% over 1992. Personnel expenditures represent 84% of total police department expenditures, a percentage that is consistent with the previous years' survey data. Fire personnel expenditures represent 89% of total fire department expenditures, which is also consistent with historical data.

Capital Outlay

Table 3/19 presents departmental expenditures for capital outlay, including purchase and replacement of equipment and purchase of land. Capital outlay expenditures are the most volatile departmental costs from year to year for both police and fire departments.

Per capita police department capital outlay expenditures decreased 5.8% from 1992 to 1993, while fire department capital outlay expenditures increased 5.2%. Table 3/22, shows average expenditures for police and fire departments for jurisdictions that reported from 1988 through 1992; the table shows the volatility of this expenditure category. Since 1988, police departments have decreased their capital outlay expenditures by 29%, while fire departments have increased theirs by 66%.

Other Expenditures

Expenditures for fuel, utilities, supplies, and other ongoing maintenance costs are shown in Table 3/20. These costs have risen very rapidly. Since 1992, police department maintenance expenses have risen 31.9% and fire department expenses have risen 8.3%. Since 1988 (Table 3/22), these costs have risen 24% and 126%, respectively.

TOTAL EXPENDITURES

Table 3/21 shows total personnel, capital outlay, and all other department expenditures. Total per capita expenditures for police departments increased 12.7% from 1992 to 1993, from $137.72 to $155.26; fire department expenditures increased 8.9%, from $85.25 to $92.85.

In Table 22, which shows the data from cities that responded to every survey since 1988, total expenditures for both departments have more than kept up with inflation. Since 1988, total police and fire department expenditures have increased 33% and 80%, respectively. This increase is much higher than the 23.2% increase in the inflation rate over the same period. Since 1992, responding cities have increased total expenditures for police departments by 2% and for fire departments by 17%.

Table 3/8   POLICE DEPARTMENT ENTRANCE SALARIES FOR BENCHMARK CITIES[1]

	Hourly rate[2] 1993 ($)	January 1992 entrance salary mean ($)[3]	January 1993 entrance salary mean ($)	1992–93 change (%)[4]
Total	13.35	26,778	27,814	2.2
Baltimore[5]	11.06	23,000	23,000	2.5
Cleveland	14.59	. . .	30,339	. . .
Columbus	10.71	21,975	22,277	1.4
Detroit	13.39	. . .	27,856	. . .
El Paso	10.65	. . .	22,145	. . .
Honolulu	13.10	. . .	27,240	. . .
Houston	13.11	24,754	27,259	10.2
Jacksonville	13.75	. . .	28,590	. . .
Los Angeles	15.94	35,315	33,157	−6.1
Milwaukee	12.96	. . .	26,954	. . .
Nashville/Davidson County	9.62[6]	. . .	21,012	. . .
Phoenix	13.36	27,789	27,789	0.0
San Antonio	12.72	26,448	26,448	0.0
San Diego	14.92	28,163	31,026	10.2
San Jose	17.50	. . .	36,400	. . .
Seattle	17.42	. . .	36,240	. . .
District of Columbia	12.07	. . .	25,108	. . .

[1]Cities 500,000 and over in population reporting in 1992 and 1993.
[2]Rates were calculated based on a 40-hour work week factored by 52 weeks.
[3]Only cities responding in both 1992 and 1993 are included.

[4]Percentage changes are based on hourly rates for cities responding in both 1992 and 1993 (total average for cities for both years was $12.84 and $13.12, respectively).
[5]Baltimore reduced its work week by one hour in 1993
[6]Nashville/Davidson County has a 42-hour work week.

Table 3/9   FIRE DEPARTMENT ENTRANCE SALARIES FOR BENCHMARK CITIES[1]

	Hourly rate[2] 1993 ($)	January 1992 entrance salary mean ($)[3]	January 1993 entrance salary mean ($)	1992–93 increase (%)[4]
Total	10.37[5]	25,332	26,767	11.1
Baltimore[6]	8.82	19,728	19,728	2.3
Cleveland	12.96	. . .	30,339	. . .
Columbus	7.72	18,751	19,261	2.8
Detroit	11.16	. . .	27,856	. . .
El Paso	7.47	. . .	21,739	. . .
Honolulu	8.31	. . .	24,192	. . .
Houston[7]	11.15	24,754	27,259	7.7
Jacksonville	8.49	. . .	24,732	. . .
Los Angeles	11.90	34,290	34,659	1.0
Milkwaukee	8.42	. . .	21,447	. . .
Nashville/Davidson County	7.48	. . .	20,622	. . .
Phoenix	9.50	27,664	27,664	0.0
San Antonio[8]	13.85	28,800	28,800	32.5
San Diego[9]	10.62	23,334	30,927	32.6
San Jose	11.95	. . .	34,800	. . .
Seattle	14.96	. . .	35,790	. . .
District of Columbia	11.55	. . .	25,227	. . .

[1]Cities 500,000 and over in population reporting in 1992 and 1993.
[2]Hourly work weeks vary among fire departments. Hourly rates are based on the actual work week in each city factored by 52 weeks.
[3]Only cities responding in both 1992 and 1993 are included.
[4]Percentage increases are based on hourly rates for cities responding in both 1992 and 1993. The overall average hourly rates for all benchmark cities responding in both 1992 and 1993 are $9.46 and $10.51, respectively.

[5]The average hourly rate for all benchmark cities in 1992 was $9.51.
[6]Baltimore reduced its work week by one hour in 1993.
[7]Houston increased its work week by one hour in 1993.
[8]San Antonio reduced its work week from 53 hours in 1992 to 40 in 1993.
[9]San Diego modified its classification system in 1993.

Table 3/10   POLICE OFFICERS' ANNUAL BASE SALARIES, 1 JANUARY 1993

	Entrance salary[1]				Maximum salary[2]				No. of years to reach maximum	
	No. of cities reporting	Mean ($)	First quartile ($)	Median ($)	Third quartile ($)	No. of cities reporting	Mean ($)	First quartile ($)	Median ($)	Third quartile ($)	No. of cities reporting	Mean ($)

	No. of cities reporting	Mean ($)	First quartile ($)	Median ($)	Third quartile ($)	No. of cities reporting	Mean ($)	First quartile ($)	Median ($)	Third quartile ($)	No. of cities reporting	Mean ($)
Total, all cities	1,592	25,128	20,800	24,904	28,461	1,501	33,882	28,417	33,342	39,000	1,305	6
Population group												
Over 1,000,000	4	29,825	27,259	27,856	31,026	4	38,590	34,896	35,669	36,795	3	8
500,000–1,000,000	13	27,196	22,277	26,954	28,590	13	38,029	33,660	36,816	40,608	13	9
250,000–499,999	28	28,574	23,904	26,580	30,776	27	39,064	34,563	39,021	41,460	25	9
100,000–249,999	86	28,232	23,355	26,706	33,036	86	37,605	32,170	36,893	42,288	82	7
50,000–99,999	207	27,329	22,675	27,024	31,300	194	36,572	31,174	36,798	41,800	179	6
25,000–49,999	384	26,089	21,424	25,892	29,361	373	35,022	29,597	34,521	40,040	332	6
10,000–24,999	870	23,711	19,906	23,364	27,095	804	32,041	26,611	31,297	36,846	671	6
Geographic division												
New England	146	26,033	23,152	26,053	28,704	137	32,025	28,838	31,260	35,277	129	4
Mid-Atlantic	209	26,857	24,047	26,555	29,500	195	39,775	34,270	38,829	44,237	189	5
East North Central	304	25,728	23,240	25,985	28,197	285	33,908	29,827	34,556	37,656	270	5
West North Central	156	23,193	20,000	23,080	25,740	151	31,130	25,932	30,648	36,085	126	6
South Atlantic	202	21,519	18,597	20,651	24,149	187	31,338	27,038	30,365	34,737	116	10
East South Central	76	18,714	17,289	18,665	20,167	71	26,178	21,308	25,541	28,224	53	10
West South Central	180	20,261	17,590	20,129	22,639	160	26,438	21,840	26,372	30,960	125	6
Mountain	89	23,537	20,640	23,293	26,879	82	33,168	28,580	33,629	36,893	71	9
Pacific Coast	230	33,219	29,000	34,044	37,224	233	41,545	36,852	42,156	46,208	226	4
Metro status												
Central	333	24,895	20,514	24,068	28,228	316	33,391	28,687	32,580	37,562	283	7
Suburban	898	26,838	23,000	26,522	29,736	849	36,531	31,344	36,475	41,090	747	5
Independent	361	21,090	18,262	20,316	23,962	336	27,650	24,133	27,344	30,200	275	7

[1] Entrance salary is defined as the base salary paid during the first 12 months with the department as a sworn police officer (excludes uniform allowance, holiday pay, or additional compensation).

[2] Maximum salary is the maximum amount paid to personnel who do not hold any promotional rank (excluding uniform allowance, holiday pay, hazard pay, or any additional compensation).

Table 3/11   FIREFIGHTERS' ANNUAL BASE SALARIES, 1 JANUARY 1993

	Entrance salary[1]				Maximum salary[2]				No. of years to reach maximum	
	No. of cities reporting	Mean ($)	First quartile ($)	Median ($)	Third quartile ($)	No. of cities reporting	Mean ($)	First quartile ($)	Median ($)	Third quartile ($)	No. of cities reporting	Mean ($)

	No. of cities reporting	Mean ($)	First quartile ($)	Median ($)	Third quartile ($)	No. of cities reporting	Mean ($)	First quartile ($)	Median ($)	Third quartile ($)	No. of cities reporting	Mean ($)
Total, all cities	1,212	23,755	19,809	23,854	28,560	1,137	31,616	26,272	30,710	36,759	976	6
Population group												
Over 1,000,000	4	30,175	27,259	27,856	30,927	4	40,119	35,669	36,795	40,488	3	7
500,000–1,000,000	13	25,719	20,622	24,732	28,800	13	35,288	31,836	33,696	37,337	13	7
250,000–499,999	29	27,151	23,292	25,392	29,111	28	37,834	33,503	36,552	41,208	26	9
100,000–249,999	81	26,486	21,692	26,120	30,723	80	35,477	30,408	34,440	40,713	76	6
50,000–99,999	185	25,722	20,926	25,515	29,535	172	34,306	29,122	34,588	38,952	157	6
25,000–49,999	308	24,546	20,232	24,076	27,852	293	32,486	27,310	31,580	37,320	259	6
10,000–24,999	592	22,101	18,393	21,228	25,364	547	29,271	24,396	28,510	33,627	442	6
Geographic division												
New England	109	24,979	22,495	24,657	27,641	104	30,445	27,144	29,947	32,682	99	4
Mid-Atlantic	77	25,530	22,905	24,947	28,135	72	36,206	30,620	35,535	41,637	69	5
East North Central	250	25,104	22,464	25,220	27,883	236	32,898	28,734	33,592	36,960	223	5
West North Central	114	21,646	18,708	21,168	24,076	110	29,020	24,447	28,315	32,630	89	7
South Atlantic	171	19,743	17,368	19,207	21,228	156	28,737	25,264	28,200	31,573	93	10
East South Central	70	18,162	16,475	18,200	19,703	66	25,542	21,319	24,838	27,824	50	9
West South Central	161	19,525	16,656	19,200	21,600	141	25,376	21,408	24,648	29,400	112	6
Mountain	70	22,968	20,070	22,783	25,992	65	31,749	27,219	32,435	35,808	57	8
Pacific Coast	190	31,366	27,852	31,668	34,626	187	39,611	35,892	39,828	42,984	184	4
Metro status												
Central	322	23,911	19,820	23,292	27,067	306	32,167	27,532	31,664	36,552	274	7
Suburban	576	25,712	21,307	25,501	29,194	547	34,214	29,077	34,450	38,712	470	5
Independent	314	20,004	17,201	19,677	23,000	284	26,017	23,096	25,946	28,841	232	6

[1] Entrance salary is defined as the base salary paid during the first 12 months with the department as a sworn police officer (excludes uniform allowance, holiday pay, or additional compensation).

[2] Maximum salary is the maximum amount paid to personnel who do not hold any promotional rank (excluding uniform allowance, holiday pay, hazard pay, or any additional compensation).

Table 3/12   TRENDS IN POLICE AND FIRE ENTRANCE AND MAXIMUM AVERAGE SALARIES

	No. of cities included[1]	1 Jan. 1988 ($)	1 Jan. 1989 ($)	Change from 1988 (%)	1 Jan. 1990 ($)	Change from 1989 (%)	1 Jan. 1991 ($)	Change from 1990 (%)	1 Jan. 1992 ($)	Change from 1991 (%)	1 Jan. 1993 ($)	Change from 1992 (%)	Change from 1988 (%)
Police													
Entrance salary	458	20,381	21,206	4	22,210	5	23,174	4	23,924	3	24,739	3	21
Maximum salary	419	26,599	27,862	5	29,357	5	30,787	5	32,106	4	33,361	4	25
Fire													
Entrance salary	359	19,218	19,950	4	20,818	4	21,711	4	22,475	4	23,209	3	21
Maximum salary	324	25,067	26,185	4	27,596	5	29,013	5	30,298	4	31,441	4	25

[1] Cities included in this table must have reported data on salaries and wages for each of the six years.

Table 3/13   LONGEVITY PAY FOR POLICE OFFICERS, 1 JANUARY 1993

	Personnel can receive longevity pay					Maximum salary including longevity					No. of years of service to receive longevity pay	
	No. of cities reporting	Yes		No		No. of cities reporting	Mean ($)	First quartile ($)	Median ($)	Third quartile ($)	No. of cities reporting	Mean
		No.	% of (A)	No.	% of (A)							
Total, all cities	1,548	1,086	70.1	462	29.8	863	35,576	29,990	34,760	40,955	957	5
Population group												
Over 1,000,000	4	3	75.0	1	25.0	3	41,922	36,973	37,913	37,913	3	5
500,000–1,000,000	13	11	84.6	2	15.3	11	38,734	35,757	37,691	39,708	11	7
250,000–499,999	25	21	84.0	4	16.0	19	39,620	35,088	39,886	43,615	19	7
100,000–249,999	86	54	62.7	32	37.2	48	37,341	32,377	36,057	42,907	50	5
50,000–99,999	200	136	68.0	64	32.0	112	36,473	31,175	34,920	41,675	124	5
25,000–49,999	374	262	70.0	112	29.9	212	36,953	31,060	35,755	42,295	235	6
10,000–24,999	846	599	70.8	247	29.1	458	34,250	28,450	33,382	39,478	515	5
Geographic division												
New England	144	124	86.1	20	13.8	98	33,178	29,366	33,057	37,198	115	6
Mid-Atlantic	209	201	96.1	8	3.8	168	42,745	36,000	42,221	47,028	181	5
East North Central	301	241	80.0	60	19.9	205	35,232	31,016	35,940	39,257	211	6
West North Central	148	92	62.1	56	37.8	72	33,502	28,877	31,864	40,065	84	6
South Atlantic	191	116	60.7	75	39.2	85	33,416	28,487	32,924	37,906	98	7
East South Central	72	41	56.9	31	43.0	22	26,819	23,400	27,500	28,978	34	5
West South Central	171	157	91.8	14	8.1	120	28,177	23,578	27,948	32,246	142	3
Mountain	87	35	40.2	52	59.7	27	35,189	29,052	35,544	39,320	30	5
Pacific Coast	225	79	35.1	146	64.8	66	43,536	39,010	43,488	48,175	62	8
Metro status												
Central	325	236	72.6	89	27.3	192	34,228	30,108	34,115	37,691	218	6
Suburban	875	628	71.7	247	28.2	503	38,258	33,048	37,734	42,800	552	6
Independent	348	222	63.7	126	36.2	168	29,088	25,240	28,718	31,610	187	5

Table 3/14   LONGEVITY PAY FOR FIREFIGHTERS, 1 JANUARY 1993

	Personnel can receive longevity pay					Maximum salary including logevity					No. of years of service to receive longevity pay	
	No. of cities reporting	Yes		No		No. of cities reporting	Mean ($)	First quartile ($)	Median ($)	Third quartile ($)	No. of cities reporting	Mean
		No.	% of (A)	No.	% of (A)							
Total, all cities	1,180	785	66.5	395	33.4	620	32,793	27,614	31,971	37,674	711	5
Population group												
Over 1,000,000	4	3	75.0	1	25.0	3	42,090	36,973	37,913	37,913	3	5
500,000–1,000,000	13	11	84.6	2	15.3	10	36,688	33,992	35,169	40,206	11	6
250,000–499,999	26	19	73.0	7	26.9	17	37,315	31,152	37,700	42,569	17	6
100,000–249,999	80	53	66.2	27	33.7	49	36,638	31,382	35,146	40,399	49	6
50,000–99,999	176	124	70.4	52	29.5	103	34,236	29,000	34,203	39,215	117	5
25,000–49,999	299	196	65.5	103	34.4	157	33,628	28,761	32,790	37,997	183	6
10,000–24,999	582	379	65.1	203	34.8	281	30,615	25,480	29,800	33,732	331	5
Geographic division												
New England	113	92	81.4	21	18.5	73	31,870	28,135	31,073	34,185	86	6
Mid-Atlantic	76	69	90.7	7	9.2	60	38,549	32,226	38,070	44,600	64	6
East North Central	254	201	79.1	53	20.8	169	34,295	29,834	34,537	38,125	178	5
West North Central	110	63	57.2	47	42.7	48	30,807	27,223	30,517	32,402	59	6
South Atlantic	160	94	58.7	66	41.2	70	30,868	26,744	30,237	34,860	84	6
East South Central	68	36	52.9	32	47.0	18	25,680	22,069	25,204	28,978	32	5
West South Central	152	140	92.1	12	7.8	107	27,078	22,976	26,181	30,744	130	3
Mountain	68	33	48.5	35	51.4	26	34,088	27,889	33,076	39,439	30	5
Pacific Coast	179	57	31.8	122	68.1	49	41,038	35,736	40,946	44,703	48	8
Metro status												
Central	311	227	72.9	84	27.0	184	32,950	28,481	32,158	36,812	213	6
Suburban	566	370	65.3	196	34.6	294	35,338	30,261	34,935	40,680	333	5
Independent	303	188	62.0	115	37.9	142	27,319	24,063	27,446	30,276	165	5

Table 3/15   EXPENDITURES FOR SALARIES AND WAGES (CIVILIAN AND UNIFORMED)

	Police			Fire		
	No. of cities reporting	Mean ($000)	Per capita ($)	No. of cities reporting	Mean ($000)	Per capita ($)
Total, all cities	1,208	5,117	99.75	946	3,663	63.28
Population group						
Over 1,000,000	4	268,009	151.21	3	149,055	73.61
500,000–1,000,000	9	100,681	144.58	8	56,570	82.37
250,000–499,999	26	36,173	108.69	27	21,958	67.03
100,000–249,999	71	13,375	95.52	67	9,535	66.45
50,000–99,999	163	5,053	79.42	152	3,470	54.48
25,000–49,999	297	2,519	76.70	232	1,916	57.26
10,000–24,999	638	1,162	74.94	457	791	49.66
Geographic division						
New England	76	2,678	85.44	54	2,707	75.82
Mid-Atlantic	130	3,834	114.22	48	4,985	87.31
East North Central	229	3,441	89.65	186	2,466	57.50
West North Central	131	3,592	83.10	96	2,807	55.36
South Atlantic	170	5,711	115.00	144	3,190	68.24
East South Central	60	3,296	71.52	58	3,401	62.05
West South Central	152	5,524	84.20	135	4,151	58.68
Mountain	76	5,615	94.10	64	3,488	53.03
Pacific Coast	184	9,705	118.62	161	5,660	67.13
Metro status						
Central	281	15,325	109.85	267	9,288	66.64
Suburban	641	2,378	88.41	431	1,740	59.39
Independent	286	1,225	63.50	248	948	47.87

Table 3/16   TOTAL MUNICIPAL CONTRIBUTIONS[1] TO SOCIAL SECURITY AND STATE/CITY ADMINISTERED EMPLOYEE RETIREMENT SYSTEMS[2]

	Police			Fire		
	No. of cities reporting	Mean ($000)	Per capita ($)	No. of cities reporting	Mean ($000)	Per capita ($)
Total, all cities	1,208	970	18.91	946	700	12.09
Population group						
Over 1,000,000	4	91,500	51.62	3	45,494	22.46
500,000–1,000,000	9	10,616	15.24	8	9,064	13.19
250,000–499,999	26	5,100	15.32	27	3,689	11.26
100,000–249,999	71	2,293	16.37	67	1,524	10.62
50,000–99,999	163	856	13.45	152	656	10.30
25,000–49,999	297	505	15.38	232	377	11.26
10,000–24,999	638	196	12.68	457	140	8.81
Geographic division						
New England	76	440	14.06	54	532	14.91
Mid-Atlantic	130	587	17.49	48	772	13.53
East North Central	229	747	19.46	186	589	13.74
West North Central	131	502	11.62	96	534	10.53
South Atlantic	170	734	14.78	144	512	10.96
East South Central	60	500	10.86	58	573	10.46
West South Central	152	748	11.40	135	590	8.34
Mountain	76	714	11.97	64	516	7.85
Pacific Coast	184	2,730	33.37	161	1,339	15.88
Metro status						
Central	281	2,956	21.19	267	1,779	12.76
Suburban	641	437	16.24	431	336	11.47
Independent	286	213	11.07	248	170	8.62

[1]The expenditures are the municipal contributions.
[2]The retirement systems are for civilian and uniformed employees.

Table 3/17   TOTAL MUNICIPAL CONTRIBUTIONS[1] FOR HEALTH, HOSPITALIZATION, DISABILITY, AND LIFE INSURANCE PROGRAMS[2]

	Police			Fire		
	No. of cities reporting	Mean ($000)	Per capita ($)	No. of cities reporting	Mean ($000)	Per capita ($)
Total, all cities	1,208	593	11.57	946	429	7.42
Population group						
Over 1,000,000	4	37,986	21.43	3	18,036	8.90
500,000–1,000,000	9	9,633	13.83	8	7,192	10.47
250,000–499,999	26	3,300	9.91	27	2,091	6.38
100,000–249,999	71	1,557	11.12	67	1,152	8.03
50,000–99,999	163	632	9.93	152	468	7.35
25,000–49,999	297	295	8.99	232	212	6.33
10,000–24,999	638	143	9.24	457	89	5.59
Geographic division						
New England	76	448	14.32	54	461	12.93
Mid-Atlantic	130	491	14.63	48	568	9.95
East North Central	229	616	16.05	186	396	9.23
West North Central	131	346	8.01	96	260	5.14
South Atlantic	170	496	9.99	144	330	7.05
East South Central	60	319	6.94	58	328	5.98
West South Central	152	517	7.88	135	480	6.79
Mountain	76	590	9.90	64	385	5.86
Pacific Coast	184	1,117	13.66	161	618	7.33
Metro status						
Central	281	1,725	12.36	267	1,083	7.77
Suburban	641	300	11.16	431	214	7.31
Independent	286	139	7.20	248	100	5.07

[1]The expenditures are the municipal contributions.
[2]The retirement systems are for civilian and uniformed employees.

Table 3/18   TOTAL PERSONNEL[1] EXPENDITURES[2]

	Police			Fire		
	No. of cities reporting	Mean ($000)	Per capita ($)	No. of cities reporting	Mean ($000)	Per capita ($)
Total, all cities	1,208	6,681	130.24	946	4,793	82.80
Population group						
Over 1,000,000	4	397,495	224.26	3	212,585	104.98
500,000–1,000,000	9	120,931	173.66	8	72,826	106.04
250,000–499,999	26	44,574	133.94	27	27,738	84.68
100,000–249,999	71	17,226	123.02	67	12,212	85.11
50,000–99,999	163	6,542	102.82	152	4,596	72.14
25,000–49,999	297	3,319	101.09	232	2,505	74.86
10,000–24,999	638	1,502	96.87	457	1,021	64.07
Geographic division						
New England	76	3,568	113.83	54	3,701	103.66
Mid-Atlantic	130	4,913	146.35	48	6,326	110.79
East North Central	229	4,804	125.16	186	3,452	80.48
West North Central	131	4,441	102.74	96	3,601	71.04
South Atlantic	170	6,942	139.78	144	4,033	86.26
East South Central	60	4,117	89.33	58	4,303	78.50
West South Central	152	6,790	103.49	135	5,222	73.83
Mountain	76	6,920	115.97	64	4,391	66.74
Pacific Coast	184	13,553	165.65	161	7,617	90.35
Metro status						
Central	281	20,008	143.41	267	12,151	87.17
Suburban	641	3,116	115.82	431	2,291	78.17
Independent	286	1,578	81.78	248	1,219	61.57

[1]Personnel refers to civilian and uniformed employees.
[2]Total personnel expenditures comprise salaries and wages (Table 3/15), contributions for Social Security and employee retirement programs (Table 3/16), and contributions for health and life insurance programs (Table 3/17).

Table 3/19   MUNICIPAL EXPENDITURES FOR CAPITAL OUTLAY[1]

	Police			Fire		
	No. of cities reporting	Mean ($000)	Per capita ($)	No. of cities reporting	Mean ($000)	Per capita ($)
Total, all cities	966	172	3.24	720	155	2.63
Population group						
Over 1,000,000	3	2,192	1.22	2	2,037	0.93
500,000–1,000,000	9	1,122	1.61	8	1,268	1.84
250,000–499,999	23	914	2.75	19	666	2.06
100,000–249,999	59	388	2.79	53	178	1.29
50,000–99,999	133	275	4.32	123	242	3.85
25,000–49,999	237	123	3.76	183	131	3.96
10,000–24,999	502	80	5.20	332	64	4.09
Geographic division						
New England	51	99	3.37	32	62	1.88
Mid-Atlantic	100	79	2.56	31	103	1.99
East North Central	178	232	5.56	144	184	3.94
West North Central	104	177	3.98	71	166	3.64
South Atlantic	143	130	2.55	117	110	2.41
East South Central	46	143	2.83	41	252	4.60
West South Central	119	186	3.12	103	161	2.39
Mountain	65	219	3.58	50	217	2.99
Pacific Coast	160	200	2.29	131	133	1.50
Metro status						
Central	228	426	2.94	215	324	2.38
Suburban	508	101	3.69	315	86	2.94
Independent	230	78	4.05	190	77	3.86

[1]The capital outlay expenditures include purchase and replacement of new and replacement equipment, land, existing structures, and/or new construction.

Table 3/20   ALL OTHER DEPARTMENT EXPENDITURES[1]

	Police			Fire		
	No. of cities reporting	Mean ($000)	Per capita ($)	No. of cities reporting	Mean ($000)	Per capita ($)
Total, all cities	1,208	1,283	25.02	946	581	10.05
Population group						
Over 1,000,000	4	94,505	53.32	3	5,601	2.76
500,000–1,000,000	9	26,442	37.97	8	7,189	10.46
250,000–499,999	26	6,419	19.28	27	2,462	7.51
100,000–249,999	71	3,034	21.67	67	1,602	11.16
50,000–99,999	163	1,025	16.12	152	516	8.09
25,000–49,999	297	658	20.06	232	613	18.33
10,000–24,999	638	296	19.14	457	178	11.17
Geographic division						
New England	76	307	9.81	54	283	7.93
Mid-Atlantic	130	562	16.74	48	417	7.30
East North Central	229	1,850	48.21	186	316	7.37
West North Central	131	693	16.05	96	368	7.27
South Atlantic	170	1,677	33.77	144	546	11.68
East South Central	60	800	17.36	58	569	10.38
West South Central	152	1,113	16.97	135	544	7.69
Mountain	76	1,154	19.35	64	569	8.66
Pacific Coast	184	1,898	23.20	161	1,236	14.66
Metro status						
Central	281	3,842	27.54	267	1,083	7.77
Suburban	641	573	21.32	431	492	16.80
Independent	286	360	18.68	248	196	9.90

[1]Includes fuel, utilities, supplies, and other expenditures not covered in Table 3/18 and 3/19.

Table 3/21   TOTAL EXPENDITURES[1]

	Police			Fire		
	No. of cities reporting	Mean ($000)	Per capita ($)	No. of cities reporting	Mean ($000)	Per capita ($)
Total, all cities	1,208	7,965	155.26	946	5,375	92.85
Population group						
Over 1,000,000	4	492,001	277.58	3	218,187	107.75
500,000–1,000,000	9	147,374	211.63	8	80,016	116.51
250,000–499,999	26	50,993	153.23	27	30,201	92.20
100,000–249,999	71	20,261	144.70	67	13,815	96.28
50,000–99,999	163	7,568	118.94	152	5,112	80.24
25,000–49,999	297	3,978	121.15	232	3,119	93.19
10,000–24,999	638	1,799	116.01	457	1,199	75.25
Geographic division						
New England	76	3,875	123.65	54	3,985	111.60
Mid-Atlantic	130	5,475	163.10	48	6,743	118.10
East North Central	229	6,655	173.38	186	3,768	87.85
West North Central	131	5,134	118.79	96	3,970	78.32
South Atlantic	170	8,620	173.56	144	4,579	97.95
East South Central	60	4,917	106.69	58	4,872	88.89
West South Central	152	7,903	120.47	135	5,766	81.52
Mountain	76	8,075	135.33	64	4,961	75.41
Pacific Coast	184	15,452	188.85	161	8,854	105.02
Metro status						
Central	281	23,850	170.95	267	13,235	94.95
Suburban	641	3,689	137.14	431	2,783	94.97
Independent	286	1,938	100.47	248	1,415	71.48

[1]Includes expenditures in Tables 3/18 through 3/20.

Table 3/22   TRENDS IN AVERAGE EXPENDITURES FOR POLICE AND FIRE DEPARTMENTS

	No. of cities[1] included	Annual expense 1988 ($000)	Annual expense 1989 ($000)	Change from 1988 (%)	Annual expense 1990 ($000)	Change from (%) 1988	Change from (%) 1989	Annual expense 1991 ($000)	Change from (%) 1988	Change from (%) 1990	Annual expense 1992 ($000)	Change from (%) 1988	Change from (%) 1991	Annual expense 1993 ($000)	Change from (%) 1992	Change from (%) 1988
Police																
Base salary, first year	458	20,381	21,206	4	22,210	9	5	23,174	14	4	23,924	17	3	24,739	3	21
Maximum base salary	419	26,599	27,862	5	29,357	10	5	30,787	16	5	32,106	21	4	33,361	4	25
Total salaries and wages	333	3,127	3,353	7	3,598	15	7	3,845	23	7	4,085	31	6	4,146	1	33
Capital outlay	272	251	200	−20	230	−8	15	185	−26	−20	163	−35	−12	178	9	−29
Total employee benefits	333	817	883	8	957	17	8	1,066	30	11	1,100	35	3	1,288	17	58
All other expenditures	333	662	690	4	724	9	5	794	20	10	974	47	23	821	−16	24
Total	333	4,814	5,080	6	5,450	13	7	5,848	21	7	6,280	30	7	6,383	2	33
Fire																
Base salary, first year	359	19,218	19,950	4	20,818	8	4	21,711	13	4	22,475	17	4	23,209	3	21
Maximum base salary	324	25,067	26,185	4	27,596	10	5	29,013	16	5	30,298	21	4	31,441	4	25
Total salaries and wages	269	2,637	2,857	8	2,985	13	4	3,114	18	4	3,310	26	6	3,643	10	38
Capital outlay	195	112	151	35	134	20	−11	158	41	18	136	21	−14	186	37	66
Total employee benefits	269	696	762	9	789	13	4	861	24	9	887	27	3	1,078	22	55
All other expenditures	269	368	406	10	434	18	7	476	29	10	546	48	15	832	52	126
Total	269	3,797	4,173	10	4,327	14	4	4,585	21	6	4,847	28	6	5,688	17	50

[1]Cities included in this table must have reported data on salaries and wages, capital outlays, contributions to retirement systems, insurance programs, and "all other expenditures" categories on the survey for each of the six years.

Table 3/23 POLICE AND FIRE DEPARTMENT PERSONNEL, SALARIES, AND EXPENDITURES FOR CITIES 10,000 AND OVER: 1993

This table comprises 1,798 cities 10,000 and over in population (based on U.S. Bureau of the Census 1990 population figures. Data were collected in the spring of 1993. All personnel and salary figures are as of 1 January 1993. Expenditure figures are for the fiscal year from 1 January 1992 to 1 January 1993. Leaders (. . . or . .) indicate data not reported or not applicable.

City: letter identifies municipal designation: "b," borough; "t," town; "tp," township; "v," village.

Service provision: The 1993 survey gathered data on service provision. The numbers that appear in parentheses following the jurisdiction name indicate the following: left, reflects information on the police department; right, reflects fire department. If there are no parentheses, the respondent did not answer this section. See key for detail.

Department: Letter identifies department to which the line of data pertains: "P," police department; "F," fire department.

Total personnel, no. uniformed, duty hours per week: Left, total actual (not authorized) number of full-time paid employees; middle, number of uniformed or sworn (not including civilian or non-uniformed) employees: regular workweek (in hours) for each department.

Entrance, maximum salary ($): Left, annual base salary of a full-time employee (patrol personnel, firefighter) during the first 12 months on the force; right, maximum annual base salary paid to a full-time employee not holding any promotional rank.

Longevity pay, maximum ($), no. years of service to receive longevity pay: Left, indicates whether municipality has longevity pay—extra compensation over the regular maximum salary based on the number of years of service–("Y" yes); center, maximum salary with longevity; right, the number of years of service required to receive longevity pay.

Total expenditures (A) ($): Sum of the other total figures (columns **B, E, F**). (This sum represents the total amount of department expenditures *reported* and may not, in all cases, be the complete expenditure figure for the department. Omissions can be found by examining the individual figures for each city.)

Total personnel expenditures (B) ($), % of (A): Left, sum of columns C and D; right, total personnel expenditures as a percentage of the total reported expenditures (**B ÷ A**).

Salaries and wages (C) ($): Amount of salaries and wages for all department personnel—regular, temporary, full-time, and part-time. (The gross amount is reported, including longevity pay, hazard pay, holiday pay, etc., without deduction of withholding for income tax or employee contributions for social security or retirement.)

City contributions to employee retirement, [to employee] insurance (D) ($): Left, amount the municipality contributes to federal social security, to a state-administered employee retirement system, and/or to a city-administered employee retirement system for civilian and uniformed personnel; right, amount the municipality contributes to health, hospital, or disability, and to life insurance programs for civilian and uniformed personnel.

Capital outlay (E) ($): Figure includes purchase and replacement of equipment, purchase of land and existing structures, and construction.

All other (F) ($): All other expenditures not reported in the above categories.

KEY

Numbers in parentheses after city names indicate how the service is provided.

Police and Fire (left and right numbers respectively)
1 full-time department
2 volunteer department
3 combined full-time paid and volunteer department
4 public safety department (consolidated police and fire)
5 special district provides service
6 regional service (multijurisdictional)
7 county provides service
8 contract with private company
9 other

(-) indicates data not reported or not available. In some instances the respondent indicated that a service was provided but did not indicate how. This is reflected as (-,-).

City (Service provision)	Depart-ment	Total personnel, no. uniformed, duty hours per week	Entrance, maximum salary ($)	Longevity pay, maximum ($), no. years to receive longevity pay	Total expendi-tures (A) ($)	Total personnel expendi-tures (B) ($), % of (A)	Salaries and wages (C) ($)	City contrib. to employee retirement, insurance (D) ($)	Capital outlay (E) ($)	All other (F) ($)
Over 1,000,000										
Detroit, Mich. (1,1)	P	4,364-3,848-40	27,856-36,795	Y-37,913-5	587,724	283,314-48	170,842	54,818-57,654	4,786	299,624
	F	1,724-1,372-48	27,856-36,795	Y-37,913-5	116,180	111,284-95	68,476	22,644-20,164	1,342	3,554
Houston, Tex. (1,1)	P	6,092-4,324-40	27,259-35,669	Y-36,973-1	345,936	318,422-92	270,328	27,402-20,692	...	27,514
	F	3,143-2,916-47	27,259-35,669	Y-36,973-1	182,636	178,488-97	144,556	21,022-12,910	...	4,148
Los Angeles, Calif. (1,1)	P	10,277-7,751-40	33,157-47,001	Y-50,879-10	888,813	847,125-95	522,727	265,959-58,439	1,535	40,153
	F	3,419-3,108-56	34,659-47,522	Y-51,385-10	359,820	347,985-96	234,133	92,817-21,035	2,732	9,103
San Diego, Calif. (1,1)	P	2,521-1,809-40	31,026-34,896	None	152,110	141,122-92	108,140	17,822-15,160	256	10,732
	F	955-844-56	30,927-40,488	None	...	...-..	...	...-...	762	...
500,000-1,000,000										
Baltimore, Md. (-,1)	P	3,411-2,859-40	23,000-32,414	Y-35,654-10	173,962	159,560-91	119,136	14,496-25,928	4	14,398
	F	1,797-52-43	19,728-31,973	Y-35,169-10	182,736	166,048-90	129,196	17,780-19,072	2,744	13,944
Cleveland, Ohio (1,1)	P	1,793-1,639-40	30,339-35,107	Y-35,757-5	...	...-..	...	...-...	...	...
	F	866-853-45	30,339-35,107	Y-35,757-5	...	...-..	...	...-...	...	...
Columbus, Ohio (1,1)	P	1,825-1,474-40	22,277-36,816	Y-37,691-8	106,942	95,413-89	66,257	16,812-12,344	1,184	10,345
	F	1,170-1,132-48	19,261-33,592	Y-33,992-6	68,015	63,950-94	42,641	14,422-6,887	375	3,690
El Paso, Tex. (1,1)	P	1,028-820-40	22,145-36,120	Y-36,745-1	...	...-..	...	...-...	3	...
	F	558-514-56	21,739-30,591	Y-31,971-1	...	...-..	...	...-...	1,649	...
Honolulu, Hawaii (1,1)	P	2,351-1,902-40	27,240-40,608	None	130,239	112,333-86	97,829	10,156-4,348	2,187	15,719
	F	1,043-1,009-56	24,192-31,836	Y-34,380-10	50,364	44,253-87	37,836	4,307-2,110	2,985	3,126
Jacksonville, Fla. (1,3)	P	2,150-1,262-40	28,590-41,172	Y-42,372-5	230,649	104,235-45	89,616	7,728-6,891	942	125,472
	F	957-901-53	24,732-33,696	Y-...-1	...	...-..	...	...-...	60	...
Milwaukee, Wis. (1,1)	P	2,528-2,061-40	26,954-36,500	Y-37,250-10	...	...-..	...	...-...	...	...
	F	1,650-1,591-49	21,447-36,500	None	...	...-..	...	...-...	...	...
Nashville-Davidson, Tenn. (1,1)	P	1,426-1,073-42	21,012-28,128	Y-28,978-5	...	...-..	...	...-...	1,706	...
	F	1,084-836-53	20,622-28,128	Y-28,978-5	58,526	54,800-93	41,000	9,000-4,800	126	3,600
Phoenix, Ariz. (1,1)	P	2,864-2,037-40	27,789-40,061	Y-41,661-8	159,650	133,133-83	111,989	9,864-11,280	2,704	23,813
	F	1,291-1,097-56	27,664-38,106	Y-40,206-7	87,322	71,020-81	58,986	5,876-6,158	2,599	13,703
San Antonio, Tex. (1,1)	P	2,011-1,587-40	26,448-33,660	Y-39,708-1	109,716	86,884-79	65,020	15,059-6,805	493	22,339
	F	1,306-1,208-53	28,800-32,580	Y-38,444-1	74,949	64,488-86	47,997	10,244-6,247	903	9,558

Table 3/23 continued POLICE AND FIRE DEPARTMENT PERSONNEL, SALARIES, AND EXPENDITURES FOR CITIES 10,000 AND OVER: 1993

City (Service provision)	Department	Total personnel, no. uniformed, duty hours per week	Entrance, maximum salary ($)	Longevity pay, maximum ($) no. years to receive longevity pay	Reported expenditures (in thousands)					
					Total expenditures (A) ($)	Total personnel expenditures (B) ($), % of (A)	Salaries and wages (C) ($)	City contrib. to employee retirement, insurance (D) ($)	Capital outlay (E) ($)	All other (F) ($)
500,000–1,000,000 continued										
San Jose, Calif. (1,1)	P	1,614-1,218-40	36,400-48,800	None	118,812	108,424-91	82,983	14,937-10,504	1,766	8,622
	F	725-608-56	34,800-46,700	None	60,266	58,312-96	43,660	8,247-6,405	54	1,900
Seattle, Wash. (1,3)	P	1,690-1,224-40	36,240-47,894	Y-51,314-5	104,289	89,234-85	77,052	5,108-7,074	521	14,534
	F	1,016-965-46	35,790-42,600	Y-46,860-5	68,099	59,744-87	51,244	2,636-5,864	363	7,992
Washington, D.C. (1,1)	P	4,417-3,744-40	25,108-37,094	Y-38,949-15	202,213	199,170-98	196,254	1,391-1,525	304	2,739
	F	1,200-642-42	25,227-37,337	Y-41,121-15	...	...-...	...	...-...	798	...
250,000–499,999										
Anaheim, Calif. (1,1)	P	519-351-40	33,654-45,094	..-...-..	...	...-...	...	...-...	258	...
	F	241-218-40	29,906-44,204	..-...-..	...	...-...	...	...-...	50	...
Arlington, Tex. (1,1)	P	508-391-40	28,350-33,600	Y-36,408-..	25,338	21,245-83	17,771	1,909-1,565	12	4,081
	F	299-268-56	27,054-32,100	Y-34,769-..	16,931	14,493-85	12,004	1,392-1,097	22	2,416
Austin, Tex. (1,1)	P	888-554-40	23,385-43,368	Y-...-1	68,873	60,959-88	51,221	7,008-2,730	1,051	6,863
	F	760-712-53	22,720-41,120	None	46,074	44,018-95	37,945	4,161-1,912	133	1,923
Birmingham, Ala. (1,1)	P	1,043-785-40	21,153-28,309	Y-29,509-6	42,760	38,740-90	31,874	2,931-3,935	19	4,001
	F	675-660-56	21,153-28,309	Y-29,509-6	29,555	27,538-93	23,291	2,013-2,234	...	2,017
Buffalo, N.Y. (1,1)	P	1,066-939-40	25,565-34,563	Y-35,763-5	66,269	63,574-95	50,255	9,851-3,468	653	2,042
	F	876-847-40	25,060-33,878	Y-35,078-5	51,779	50,006-96	39,108	7,666-3,232	214	1,559
Colorado Springs, Colo. (1,1)	P	646-459-40	26,580-38,664	Y-39,864-5	31,716	27,162-85	22,776	2,189-2,197	872	3,682
	F	381-336-52	24,936-36,552	Y-37,752-5	20,242	17,643-87	14,225	1,850-1,568	1,182	1,417
Corpus Christi, Tex. (1,1)	P	534-386-40	25,776-31,476	Y-32,916-1	26,409	23,033-87	18,046	3,316-1,671	249	3,127
	F	305-296-54	25,392-29,592	Y-31,152-1	14,066	13,159-93	10,190	2,002-967	27	880
Fort Worth, Tex. (1,1)	P	1,383-1,057-40	25,824-31,104	Y-32,304-1	60,234	50,109-83	42,846	3,580-3,683	755	9,370
	F	684-656-56	24,768-29,820	Y-31,020-1	34,314	28,610-83	24,653	2,078-1,879	146	5,558
Fresno, Calif. (1,1)	P	652-383-40	42,426-49,656	Y-49,956-..	70,664	61,811-87	47,050	12,219-2,542	503	8,350
	F	258-219-56	39,438-46,692	None	32,436	30,023-92	22,552	6,447-1,024	414	1,999
Kansas City, Mo. (1,1)	P	1,741-1,207-40	23,570-41,460	None	84,323	75,893-90	60,545	10,039-5,309	1,288	7,142
	F	807-754-49	23,292-39,912	None	44,550	40,238-90	31,619	6,192-2,427	673	3,639
Las Vegas, Nev. (6,1)	P	...-...-..	...-...	..-...-..	...	...-...	...	...-...	...	...
	F	376-348-56	24,932-40,175	Y-44,996-6	15,426	14,345-92	10,679	2,633-1,033	62	1,019
Long Beach, Calif. (1,1)	P	1,051-807-40	33,312-41,208	Y-44,368-10	...	...-...	...	...-...	17	...
	F	471-432-56	33,312-41,208	Y-44,368-10	...	...-...	...	...-...	57	...
Louisville, Ky. (1,1)	P	837-653-40	19,115-24,482	Y-27,911-5	23,263	19,253-82	15,051	2,831-1,371	172	3,838
	F	549-501-56	20,837-23,924	Y-26,573-5	14,264	13,345-93	10,329	1,984-1,032	48	871
Mesa, Ariz. (1,1)	P	646-427-40	29,380-39,650	Y-43,615-5	42,458	36,294-85	30,274	3,236-2,784	1,594	4,570
	F	283-255-56	26,611-35,854	Y-39,439-5	19,232	17,302-89	14,802	1,100-1,400	810	1,120
Miami, Fla. (1,1)	P	1,407-1,049-40	29,111-39,077	Y-45,197-..	29,430	26,254-89	20,905	2,923-2,426	22	3,154
	F	694-616-48	29,111-39,077	Y-45,197-..	16,581	15,707-94	12,849	1,534-1,324	12	862
Minneapolis, Minn. (1,1)	P	977-977-40	26,830-41,420	Y-42,569-9	36,292	34,989-96	28,603	3,817-2,569	3	1,300
	F	459-459-56	26,830-41,420	Y-42,569-9	18,806	18,693-99	15,398	2,033-1,262	...	113
Norfolk, Va. (3,1)	P	763-666-43	22,050-35,918	..-...-..	2,945	2,549-86	2,216	226-107	104	292
	F	473-465-52	21,000-34,208	..-...-..	1,710	1,610-94	1,392	150-68	...	100
Oakland, Calif. (1,1)	P	733-372-40	38,808-46,788	Y-50,273-7	103,678	91,232-87	58,094	23,431-9,707	406	12,040
	F	505-465-52	38,304-50,412	None	54,327	48,317-88	28,782	14,794-4,741	199	5,811
Oklahoma City, Okla. (1,1)	P	1,252-1,073-40	22,835-...	..-...-3	63,527	50,067-78	41,154	3,960-4,953	3,327	10,133
	F	883-848-40	19,450-...	..-...-3	49,834	38,834-77	31,309	3,482-4,043	5,000	6,000
Omaha, Nebr. (1,1)	P	764-614-37	30,776-39,525	Y-40,065-7	38,376	36,408-94	30,732	3,456-2,220	...	1,968
	F	544-534-56	27,037-37,190	Y-37,700-7	33,825	32,397-95	27,924	2,901-1,572	...	1,428
Pittsburgh, Pa. (1,1)	P	1,373-1,247-40	25,498-36,426	Y-39,886-4	76,289	64,919-85	53,187	5,906-5,826	...	11,370
	F	904-896-42	21,777-35,250	Y-38,070-4	53,971	46,473-86	37,613	4,705-4,155	...	7,498
Sacramento, Calif. (1,1)	P	879-568-40	32,463-47,875	Y-48,175-20	57,635	49,721-86	48,687	645-389	124	7,790
	F	478-442-56	31,615-46,627	Y-46,927-20	32,660	29,444-90	29,109	225-110	...	3,216
St. Louis, Mo. (1,1)	P	2,155-1,515-40	24,054-34,731	Y-...-1	88,800	78,000-87	67,100	3,600-7,300	3,000	7,800
	F	741-710-52	24,366-35,043	Y-...-1	34,800	34,300-98	23,300	8,900-2,100	...	500
St. Paul, Minn. (1,1)	P	688-176-40	34,263-44,243	None	41,383	36,197-87	29,026	6,917-254	1,247	3,939
	F	477-46-56	34,253-44,324	None	35,748	31,549-88	23,958	7,114-477	1,132	3,067
Santa Ana, Calif. (1,1)	P	882-635-40	48,237-58,655	None	61,578	43,070-69	36,395	2,138-4,537	1,652	16,856
	F	290-255-56	41,881-50,914	None	26,785	22,527-84	18,235	2,105-2,187	285	3,973
Tampa, Fla. (1,1)	P	1,045-797-40	27,290-39,021	Y-40,021-5	59,555	46,373-77	40,354	3,948-2,071	...	13,182
	F	540-495-52	24,985-33,503	Y-34,503-5	27,273	24,772-90	21,813	1,934-1,025	...	2,501
Toledo, Ohio (1,1)	P	737-685-40	30,278-38,606	Y-38,899-26	45,400	40,600-89	30,000	5,700-4,900	500	4,300
	F	517-508-48	26,821-38,611	Y-...-..	35,649	32,103-90	23,474	5,299-3,330	255	3,291
Tucson, Ariz. (1,1)	P	1,005-752-40	25,588-36,444	None	53,782	42,924-79	35,657	3,589-3,678	1,538	9,320
	F	461-433-56	25,588-36,444	None	24,510	22,480-91	18,899	1,809-1,772	339	1,691
Tulsa, Okla. (1,1)	P	864-750-40	23,904-33,360	Y-35,088-3	45,877	37,550-81	30,683	3,253-3,614	1,933	6,394
	F	745-710-52	24,940-33,000	Y-34,728-3	42,768	39,026-91	27,425	3,101-8,500	1,711	2,031
100,000–249,999										
Abilene, Tex. (1,1)	P	218-162-40	20,468-26,372	Y-27,572-1	8,319	7,153-85	5,956	779-418	183	983
	F	170-163-52	17,829-24,981	Y-26,181-1	6,320	5,749-90	4,837	568-344	76	495
Akron, Ohio (1,1)	P	502-434-40	28,683-33,446	Y-34,650-5	30,443	26,824-88	18,456	4,045-4,323	532	3,087
	F	434-392-40	28,683-33,446	Y-34,817-5	25,968	22,724-87	15,317	3,236-4,171	644	2,600
Alexandria, Va. (1,1)	P	369-261-40	27,995-45,676	None	22,796	19,816-86	14,854	3,567-1,395	124	2,856
	F	248-148-56	26,665-...	None	16,923	14,622-86	10,864	2,648-1,110	165	2,136
Allentown, Pa. (1,1)	P	256-204-40	24,056-32,170	Y-33,420-4	10,226	9,587-93	6,131	1,635-1,821	19	620
	F	148-146-40	22,927-31,469	Y-32,919-4	6,090	5,676-93	3,299	1,340-1,037	21	393

Table 3/23 continued

POLICE AND FIRE DEPARTMENT PERSONNEL, SALARIES, AND EXPENDITURES FOR CITIES 10,000 AND OVER: 1993

City (Service provision)	Depart-ment	Total personnel, no. uniformed, duty hours per week	Entrance, maximum salary ($)	Longevity pay, maximum ($), no. years to receive longevity pay	Reported expenditures (in thousands)					
					Total expenditures (A) ($)	Total personnel expenditures (B) ($), % of (A)	Salaries and wages (C) ($)	City contrib. to employee retirement, insurance (D) ($)	Capital outlay (E) ($)	All other (F) ($)
100,000-249,999 continued										
Amarillo, Tex. (1,1) ....P		253-179-40	20,940-29,412	Y-30,612-1	11,324	9,501-83	7,793	987-721	123	1,700
	F	210-206-56	19,512-27,648	Y-28,848-1	8,012	7,557-94	6,417	658-482	29	426
Anchorage, Alaska (3,1) ....P		423-272-40	44,273-57,470	None	...	...-..	...	...-...	146	...
	F	264-234-56	35,992-51,397	None	19,332	15,144-78	12,480	1,116-1,548	...	4,188
Ann Arbor, Mich. (1,1) ....P		221-187-40	25,896-36,962	Y-38,462-5	...	...-..	...	...-...	...	...
	F	113-107-54	28,213-35,960	Y-38,641-7	...	...-..	...	...-...	5	...
Aurora, Colo. (1,1) ....P		582-407-40	26,706-41,058	Y-42,558-5	28,956	25,656-88	20,928	2,628-2,100	...	3,300
	F	289-255-56	24,329-38,291	Y-39,791-5	6,486	4,686-72	2,190	1,416-1,080	...	1,800
Beaumont, Tex. (1,1) ....P		305-240-40	25,452-31,380	Y-31,860-1	13,505	10,194-75	1,828	3,958-4,408	870	2,441
	F	258-233-48	24,636-30,408	Y-30,744-1	21,278	19,998-93	15,184	1,594-3,220	500	780
Boise City, Idaho (1,1) ....P		214-169-40	21,240-33,420	None	11,913	9,382-78	7,645	961-776	541	1,990
	F	178-167-52	22,968-31,464	None	12,050	9,583-79	6,367	2,536-680	833	1,634
Bridgeport, Conn. (1,1) ....P		450-360-35	28,031-36,837	Y-37,212-5	17,889	17,247-96	11,680	2,063-3,504	...	642
	F	354-339-42	28,481-37,338	Y-37,713-5	16,085	14,857-92	9,997	1,861-2,999	...	1,228
Cedar Rapids, Iowa (1,1) ....P		213-170-40	24,249-30,648	Y-31,848-5	9,832	9,054-92	6,930	1,186-938	128	650
	F	160-150-53	24,860-29,743	Y-30,943-5	7,573	7,109-93	5,381	970-758	58	406
Chula Vista, Calif. (3,1) ....P		149-78-40	34,963-45,711	..-..-..	8,777	7,658-87	5,993	1,124-541	73	1,046
	F	80-76-56	31,677-41,346	..-..-..	3,623	3,233-89	2,509	520-204	5	385
Columbus-Muscogee, Ga. (1,1) ......P		472-369-40	15,642-29,078	None	17,876	15,838-88	11,962	2,518-1,358	646	1,392
	F	271-267-56	14,539-25,938	None	13,040	12,370-94	9,590	1,846-934	50	620
Concord, Calif. (1,5) ....P		183-136-40	36,510-44,380	None	...	...-..	...	...-...	22	...
	F	...-..-..	...-...	..-..-..	...	...-..	...	...-...	...	...
Dayton, Ohio (1,1) ....P		596-493-40	29,790-34,729	Y-35,451-5	...	...-..	...	...-...	789	...
	F	418-338-49	28,467-34,546	Y-35,146-5	...	...-..	...	...-...	497	...
Des Moines, Iowa (1,1) ....P		476-359-40	28,395-32,587	Y-34,337-5	25,714	21,661-84	16,962	2,570-2,129	102	3,951
	F	302-289-56	26,120-29,606	Y-31,382-5	13,939	13,112-94	10,071	1,722-1,319	140	687
Durham, N.C. (1,1) ....P		346-291-42	24,602-36,526	Y-37,026-5	19,554	17,236-88	13,334	2,168-1,734	252	2,066
	F	245-234-56	21,238-31,253	Y-32,753-5	11,582	10,934-94	8,760	1,316-858	28	620
El Monte, Calif. (1,1) ....P		148-115-40	35,658-42,288	Y-43,488-20	...	...-..	...	...-...	...	...
	F	73-65-56	32,556-38,604	Y-39,804-20	...	...-..	...	...-...	...	...
Elizabeth, N.J. (1,1) ....P		405-322-40	35,058-41,637	Y-45,801-5	23,600	22,903-97	18,182	2,696-2,025	...	697
	F	273-267-42	35,058-41,637	Y-45,801-5	16,154	15,800-97	12,542	1,893-1,365	...	354
Erie, Pa. (1,1) ....P		191-158-40	23,946-31,152	Y-33,644-4	...	...-..	...	...-...	...	...
	F	201-200-42	24,807-31,393	Y-33,858-4	...	...-..	...	...-...	...	...
Evansville, Ind. (1,1) ....P		270-249-..	25,985-31,564	Y-...-..	11,891	10,181-85	7,915	909-1,357	...	1,710
	F	276-273-..	25,409-30,177	Y-...-..	10,919	10,147-92	7,873	874-1,400	...	772
Fort Lauderdale, Fla. (1,1) ....P		698-445-..	29,474-41,808	Y-47,034-5	44,447	39,617-89	29,688	7,204-2,725	120	4,710
	F	279-264-..	27,805-35,219	Y-39,621-5	14,967	13,306-88	11,070	1,067-1,169	33	1,628
Fullerton, Calif. (1,1) ....P		220-142-40	37,767-48,200	None	17,263	15,467-89	11,415	2,372-1,680	208	1,588
	F	94-83-56	32,577-41,577	None	8,024	7,307-91	5,550	1,202-555	23	694
Garden Grove, Calif. (-,-) ....P		231-167-40	36,924-44,856	None	19,211	15,225-79	11,326	2,326-1,573	887	3,099
	F	94-89-56	30,480-37,080	None	9,247	7,789-84	5,547	1,182-1,060	21	1,437
Garland, Tex. (1,1) ....P		513-434-40	25,542-34,861	Y-36,057-1	...	...-..	...	...-...	34	...
	F	216-213-56	24,489-31,508	Y-32,704-1	...	...-..	...	...-...	146	...
Glendale, Calif. (1,1) ....P		303-209-..	40,404-52,788	None	31,080	25,472-81	19,226	3,514-2,732	60	5,548
	F	160-147-..	38,928-50,844	None	24,394	20,372-83	13,760	2,500-4,112	164	3,858
Greensboro, N.C. (1,1) ....P		552-425-40	22,008-35,016	Y-37,642-5	25,664	21,891-85	18,622	2,191-1,078	688	3,085
	F	361-352-56	19,980-31,728	Y-34,107-5	15,054	13,330-88	11,438	1,153-739	811	913
Hartford, Conn. (1,1) ....P		635-464-40	28,990-43,069	Y-43,254-6	33,534	31,558-94	26,653	2,219-2,686	500	1,476
	F	425-413-42	28,990-41,795	Y-41,980-6	24,654	23,587-95	18,888	2,154-2,545	35	1,032
Hollywood, Fla. (1,1) ....P		458-302-40	31,385-40,065	Y-48,077-10	...	...-..	...	...-...	...	...
	F	223-208-48	27,676-37,088	Y-52,187-10	...	...-..	...	...-...	...	...
Huntsville, Ala. (1,1) ....P		443-326-40	22,027-31,013	Y-31,583-5	18,495	16,358-88	13,150	1,898-1,310	17	2,120
	F	319-295-..	21,029-29,474	Y-30,044-5	12,936	12,302-95	9,918	1,429-955	...	634
Independence, Mo. (1,1) ....P		226-161-40	22,290-28,836	Y-32,436-5	10,028	9,386-93	7,555	1,042-789	89	553
	F	170-165-51	20,232-28,776	Y-32,402-5	9,850	9,692-98	7,267	1,760-665	3	155
Inglewood, Calif. (1,1) ....P		286-204-40	37,813-46,140	None	25,414	22,314-87	16,498	3,170-2,646	50	3,050
	F	90-86-56	28,905-43,035	None	10,088	8,912-88	6,488	1,362-1,062	54	1,122
Irvine, Calif. (1,7) ....P		189-126-40	38,614-52,129	None	10,162	8,315-81	6,459	1,194-662	2	1,845
	F	...-..-..	...-...	..-...-..	...	...-..	...	...-...	...	...
Irving, Tex. (1,1) ....P		362-256-40	25,704-34,440	Y-...-1	16,402	15,467-94	12,053	2,644-770	271	664
	F	252-243-53	25,704-34,440	Y-...-1	12,097	11,655-96	9,871	1,155-629	127	315
Jackson, Miss. (1,1) ....P		677-439-40	18,360-28,224	None	...	...-..	...	...-...	...	...
	F	367-340-56	21,000-27,540	None	...	...-..	...	...-...	616	2,517
Kansas City, Kan. (1,1) ....P		478-347-41	25,608-29,136	Y-30,336-5	22,918	19,785-86	15,440	2,294-2,051	439	1,028
	F	396-389-56	24,276-37,440	Y-38,640-5	20,616	19,149-92	14,989	2,296-1,864	...	3,916
Knoxville, Tenn. (1,1) ....P		...-..-40	...-...	Y-...-..	17,995	14,079-78	10,195	2,984-900	...	4,041
	F	...-..-56	...-...	Y-...-..	18,785	14,744-78	10,826	3,006-912	12	6,636
Lexington-Fayette, Ky. (1,1) ....P		525-401-40	19,404-27,333	Y-...-5	25,116	18,468-73	15,132	2,280-1,056	24	7,656
	F	441-408-56	19,404-27,333	Y-...-5	25,488	17,808-69	14,532	2,352-924	50	...
Lincoln, Nebr. (1,1) ....P		333-247-40	22,980-31,196	Y-32,377-5	...	...-..	...	...-...	234	...
	F	253-244-56	16,415-28,977	Y-30,177-..	...	...-..	...	...-...	733	3,725
Little Rock, Ark. (1,1) ....P		502-404-40	21,212-31,192	Y-31,942-1	21,389	16,931-79	14,506	1,218-1,207	608	2,512
	F	356-352-56	19,180-28,257	Y-28,977-1	15,192	12,072-79	10,706	739-627		

Table 3/23 continued

POLICE AND FIRE DEPARTMENT PERSONNEL, SALARIES, AND EXPENDITURES FOR CITIES 10,000 AND OVER: 1993

City (Service provision)	Department	Total personnel, no. uniformed, duty hours per week	Entrance, maximum salary ($)	Longevity pay, maximum ($), no. years to receive longevity pay	Reported expenditures (in thousands)					
					Total expenditures (A) ($)	Total personnel expenditures (B) ($), % of (A)	Salaries and wages (C) ($)	City contrib. to employee retirement, insurance (D) ($)	Capital outlay (E) ($)	All other (F) ($)
100,000-249,999 continued										
Livonia, Mich. (1,1) ....P	P	184-163-40	29,140-38,833	Y-40,783-5	7,622	6,727-88	5,078	1,279-370	...	895
	F	92-88-56	27,456-38,833	Y-40,783-5	3,574	3,315-92	2,820	287-208	...	259
Lubbock, Tex. (1,1) ....P	P	359-315-40	22,129-29,701	Y-30,901-1	17,620	14,258-80	11,384	2,062-812	702	2,660
	F	268-257-53	22,129-29,701	Y-30,901-1	12,202	10,893-89	8,920	1,370-603	59	1,250
Madison, Wis. (1,1) ....P	P	370-314-37	28,368-32,474	Y-43,186-4	24,390	20,540-84	15,720	3,133-1,687	31	3,819
	F	279-264-48	28,158-32,374	Y-43,056-4	18,989	17,254-90	11,869	4,102-1,283	56	1,679
Mobile, Ala. (1,1) ....P	P	544-439-40	19,860-30,804	None	21,126	15,506-73	12,870	2,537-99	50	5,570
	F	441-420-56	19,860-30,804	None	14,654	13,073-89	10,626	2,348-99	6	1,575
Modesto, Calif. (1,1) ....P	P	288-202-40	34,212-40,510	None	...	...-..	...	...-...	173	...
	F	164-151-56	34,992-42,528	None	...	...-..	...	...-...	63	...
Montgomery, Ala. (1,1) ....P	P	557-362-40	17,463-20,820	Y-...-..	20,792	18,714-90	16,172	1,040-1,502	128	1,950
	F	416-396-56	16,445-20,820	Y-...-..	13,005	10,711-82	8,938	717-1,056	894	1,400
Moreno Valley, Calif. (7,7) ....P	P	...-..-..	...-...	..-...-..	...	...-..	...	...-...	...	...
	F									
Ontario, Calif. (1,1) ....P	P	267-181-40	38,424-46,908	None	27,380	22,308-81	16,214	1,632-4,462	310	4,762
	F	137-114-53	38,232-46,680	None	19,750	16,296-82	12,396	528-3,372	598	2,856
Orange, Calif. (1,1) ....P	P	212-139-40	36,180-46,392	None	41,340	12,296-29	10,660	1,080-556	...	29,044
	F	147-115-55	36,156-43,956	None	27,832	10,628-38	8,852	1,180-596	168	17,036
Overland Park, Kan. (1,9) ....P	P	197-27-40	26,400-44,735	None	9,797	8,054-82	6,267	1,137-650	478	1,265
	F	...-..-..	...-...	..-...-..	...	...-..	...	...-...	...	...
Pasadena, Calif. (1,1) ....P	P	328-214-40	39,756-48,692	None	...	...-..	...	...-...	101	...
	F	178-167-56	27,854-48,504	None	...	...-..	...	...-...	137	...
Pasadena, Tex. (1,2) ....P	P	207-153-40	28,270-38,500	Y-...-1	14,577	11,148-76	8,247	1,720-1,181	238	3,191
	F	...-..-..	...-...	..-...-..	...	...-..	...	...-...	...	...
Paterson, N.J. (1,1) ....P	P	433-360-40	23,355-38,419	Y-43,029-5	21,616	20,311-93	18,129	104-2,078	...	1,305
	F	264-247-42	19,000-38,419	Y-43,029-5	14,480	13,295-91	12,004	24-1,267	400	785
Peoria, Ill. (1,1) ....P	P	281-205-40	25,473-39,729	Y-42,907-5	...	...-..	...	...-...	...	...
	F	210-202-57	24,949-35,324	Y-38,150-5	...	...-..	...	...-...	...	...
Plano, Tex. (1,1) ....P	P	246-184-40	29,082-35,398	Y-35,664-1	12,251	10,756-87	9,739	537-480	93	1,402
	F	183-168-50	28,935-33,072	Y-35,000-1	10,064	9,268-92	8,205	562-501	3	793
Pomona, Calif. (1,1) ....P	P	289-195-40	34,956-42,660	None	20,098	17,605-87	12,511	3,320-1,774	33	2,460
	F	145-119-56	34,956-42,660	None	12,961	11,894-91	8,570	2,142-1,182	20	1,047
Raleigh, N.C. (1,1) ....P	P	498-454-42	22,863-33,780	Y-35,300-5	...	...-..	...	...-...	...	...
	F	347-337-56	20,738-30,639	Y-32,018-5	...	...-..	...	...-...	...	...
Rancho Cucamonga, Calif. (-,1) .....P	P	...-..-..	...-...	..-...-..	...	...-..	...	...-...	...	...
	F	80-69-56	34,250-41,631	None	7,620	6,301-82	4,963	679-659	207	1,112
Reno, Nev. (1,1) ....P	P	432-287-40	26,922-36,893	Y-37,933-5	28,414	23,173-81	17,066	3,724-2,383	130	5,111
	F	210-203-56	28,376-38,514	Y-42,365-5	16,376	15,296-93	11,281	2,509-1,506	180	900
Richmond, Va. (1,1) ....P	P	712-621-40	26,702-37,726	None	16,708	13,951-83	11,356	1,806-789	...	2,757
	F	486-476-56	26,702-37,726	None	13,248	10,491-79	8,409	1,477-605	...	2,757
Riverside, Calif. (1,1) ....P	P	449-306-40	33,036-44,268	None	29,159	23,211-79	20,979	852-1,380	2,190	3,758
	F	201-185-56	31,668-42,432	None	12,977	11,508-88	10,477	433-598	402	1,067
Rochester, N.Y. (1,1) ....P	P	659-498-40	27,410-39,157	Y-40,307-3	46,793	42,910-91	33,751	6,933-2,226	50	3,833
	F	514-485-40	27,663-39,157	Y-40,307-3	32,136	30,935-96	24,565	4,634-1,736	5	1,196
St. Petersburg, Fla. (1,1) ....P	P	719-509-40	25,072-36,160	None	44,993	39,553-87	25,404	11,273-2,876	35	5,405
	F	327-305-52	22,179-31,779	None	21,356	19,308-90	11,840	5,960-1,508	140	1,908
Salem, Ore. (1,1) ....P	P	173-142-40	29,028-37,008	None	11,072	8,624-77	6,570	1,524-530	380	2,068
	F	140-130-56	23,916-33,864	None	8,372	7,392-88	5,614	1,296-482	142	838
Salinas, Calif. (1,1) ....P	P	184-137-40	33,072-40,224	None	15,048	11,914-79	9,444	1,546-924	516	2,618
	F	89-87-53	31,800-38,688	None	8,834	6,216-70	4,992	732-492	...	2,618
Salt Lake City, Utah (1,1) ....P	P	431-362-40	20,808-34,044	Y-35,544-6	21,944	19,482-88	14,450	3,632-1,400	334	2,128
	F	381-305-56	22,032-34,152	Y-35,352-7	...	...-..	...	...-...	158	...
San Bernardino, Calif. (1,1) ......P	P	415-267-40	37,356-44,808	None	25,964	23,162-89	16,210	3,731-3,221	133	2,669
	F	190-167-56	34,574-42,288	Y-43,188-10	13,823	13,308-96	9,666	2,394-1,248	108	407
Santa Rosa, Calif. (1,1) ....P	P	224-160-40	38,556-46,860	None	8,816	7,923-89	6,260	867-796	16	877
	F	114-108-56	35,328-42,384	None	4,681	4,320-92	3,280	615-425	22	339
Savannah, Ga. (1,1) ....P	P	463-374-40	20,372-30,698	Y-31,042-10	20,097	14,417-71	11,764	1,389-1,264	33	5,647
	F	206-199-56	17,689-29,526	Y-30,461-10	9,175	6,651-72	5,572	492-587	33	2,491
Scottsdale, Ariz. (1,8) ....P	P	311-225-40	29,328-41,621	None	18,190	14,871-81	12,010	1,841-1,020	279	3,040
	F	...-..-..	...-...	..-...-..	...	...-..	...	...-...	...	...
Simi Valley, Calif. (1,5) ....P	P	157-106-40	35,580-43,901	None	7,551	6,881-91	5,175	873-833	171	499
	F	...-..-..	...-...	..-...-..	...	...-..	...	...-...	...	...
Sioux Falls, S.D. (1,1) ....P	P	173-148-40	25,411-34,377	None	...	...-..	...	...-...	544	...
	F	159-147-53	22,880-31,118	None	...	...-..	...	...-...	380	...
South Bend, Ind. (1,1) ....P	P	298-233-48	21,300-25,220	None	11,132	10,208-91	8,920	654-634	312	612
	F	220-215-56	19,248-25,727	None	8,547	7,504-87	6,569	383-552	712	331
Springfield, Ill. (1,1) ....P	P	266-216-42	24,904-33,205	Y-36,526-5	13,440	12,180-90	10,135	1,375-670	250	1,010
	F	222-203-51	24,904-33,205	..-36,526-5	11,642	10,973-94	8,886	1,528-559	50	619
Springfield, Mo. (1,1) ....P	P	259-208-40	22,484-27,677	Y-28,877-5	9,552	8,964-93	7,368	1,068-528	120	468
	F	192-188-56	21,504-27,281	Y-28,481-5	7,416	7,128-96	5,844	804-480	36	252
Sterling Heights, Mich. (1,1) ....P	P	226-168-40	25,331-40,634	Y-43,234-..	14,678	13,681-93	9,998	2,224-1,459	410	587
	F	110-105-56	26,712-40,713	Y-43,313-..	7,743	7,121-91	5,162	1,203-756	110	512
Stockton, Calif. (1,1) ....P	P	477-325-40	32,772-40,020	Y-44,022-6	26,374	14,296-54	10,744	2,248-1,304	6,633	5,445
	F	236-211-56	31,200-38,112	Y-40,399-4	10,879	8,967-82	6,770	1,519-678	...	1,912

Table 3/23 POLICE AND FIRE DEPARTMENT PERSONNEL, SALARIES, AND EXPENDITURES FOR
continued CITIES 10,000 AND OVER: 1993

City (Service provision)	Department	Total personnel, no. uniformed, duty hours per week	Entrance, maximum salary ($)	Longevity pay, maximum ($), no. years to receive longevity pay	Total expenditures (A) ($)	Total personnel expenditures (B) ($), % of (A)	Salaries and wages (C) ($)	City contrib. to employee retirement, insurance (D) ($)	Capital outlay (E) ($)	All other (F) ($)
100,000-249,999 continued										
Sunnyvale, Calif. (4,4)	P	...-..-..	...-...	..-..-..	...	...-..	...	..-...	...	...
	F	...-..-..	...-...	..-..-..	...	...-..	...	..-...	...	...
Tacoma, Wash. (1,1)	P	388-346-40	32,531-42,031	Y-45,393-5	26,875	21,083-78	18,494	600-1,989	...	5,792
	F	367-346-40	32,187-43,347	Y-46,815-5	24,279	23,210-95	20,862	151-2,197	...	1,069
Tallahassee, Fla. (1,1)	P	439-308-40	24,695-34,894	None	21,368	16,594-77	14,215	1,593-786	139	4,635
	F	246-240-53	22,599-31,931	None	11,649	9,014-77	7,730	901-383	2	2,633
Tempe, Ariz. (1,1)	P	345-238-40	28,108-39,349	None	20,828	18,240-87	15,116	2,002-1,122	206	2,382
	F	131-117-56	27,037-37,451	None	8,296	7,724-93	6,732	516-476	2	570
Thousand Oaks, Calif. (7,7)	P	...-..-..	...-...	..-..-..	...	...-..	...	..-...	...	...
	F	...-..-..	...-...	..-..-..	...	...-..	...	..-...	...	...
Topeka, Kan. (1,1)	P	356-256-40	24,984-33,408	Y-34,115-4	17,326	14,656-84	12,124	1,808-724	511	2,159
	F	249-244-53	21,692-30,169	Y-31,627-5	10,983	10,497-95	8,675	1,398-424	79	407
Torrance, Calif. (1,1)	P	318-236-40	38,771-44,886	Y-48,096-7	29,909	22,759-76	19,842	1,301-1,616	47	7,103
	F	164-151-56	32,003-40,855	Y-50,567-7	18,771	15,177-80	13,790	776-611	42	3,552
Vallejo, Calif. (1,1)	P	196-131-40	44,307-53,856	None	17,860	13,108-73	9,893	2,268-947	19	4,733
	F	103-100-56	40,491-49,217	None	9,173	7,678-83	5,837	1,221-620	61	1,434
Waco, Tex. (1,1)	P	259-187-40	23,503-30,958	Y-32,158-25	11,052	9,478-85	7,748	1,471-259	...	1,574
	F	177-173-52	23,503-30,958	Y-32,158-25	8,021	7,384-92	6,159	1,048-177	2	635
Waterbury, Conn. (1,1)	P	343-292-40	30,212-38,116	Y-38,826-7	...	...-..	...	..-...	...	...
	F	280-274-42	30,723-38,188	Y-38,918-8	...	...-..	...	..-...	651	...
Winston-Salem, N.C. (1,1)	P	566-437-40	21,403-35,589	Y-38,258-5	27,082	22,423-82	16,084	4,264-2,075	29	4,630
	F	253-239-56	19,656-32,440	Y-34,873-5	10,093	8,993-89	7,031	1,050-912	50	1,050
Worcester, Mass. (1,1)	P	447-362-40	21,403-32,489	Y-33,114-10	22,917	21,689-94	15,889	2,740-3,060	...	1,228
	F	458-444-51	24,657-30,051	Y-30,806-5	22,927	22,109-96	15,957	2,904-3,248	...	818
Yonkers, N.Y. (1,1)	P	596-522-35	31,633-40,814	Y-44,487-9	45,992	45,202-98	35,200	5,302-4,700	75	715
	F	437-425-37	36,287-42,187	Y-45,984-9	31,810	31,106-97	24,500	2,806-3,800	...	704
50,000-99,999										
Albany, Ga. (1,1)	P	216-191-40	17,295-26,021	None	8,892	6,768-76	5,148	828-792	1,368	756
	F	171-159-56	15,885-23,908	None	5,502	5,472-99	4,128	684-660	12	18
Alhambra, Calif. (1,1)	P	150-94-40	34,044-41,376	None	13,548	10,272-75	7,402	1,654-1,216	48	3,228
	F	82-77-50	32,712-39,756	None	8,074	6,722-83	4,740	1,140-842	96	1,256
Antioch, Calif. (1,6)	P	115-82-40	37,908-44,952	None	...	...-..	...	..-...	...	...
	F	...-..-..	...-...	..-..-..	...	...-..	...	..-...	...	...
Arlington Heights v, Ill. (1,1)	P	140-106-40	31,692-42,471	Y-43,221-5	...	...-..	...	..-...	...	...
	F	95-92-50	30,183-40,448	Y-41,198-5	...	...-..	...	..-...	...	...
Arvada, Colo. (1,5)	P	168-116-40	25,200-39,940	None	9,797	7,764-79	6,504	649-611	840	1,193
	F	...-..-..	...-...	..-..-..	...	...-..	...	..-...	...	...
Asheville, N.C. (1,1)	P	186-169-40	18,860-32,219	Y-32,619-5	5,183	3,643-70	2,843	460-340	8	1,532
	F	179-175-56	18,860-30,659	Y-31,059-5	5,201	3,864-74	3,044	455-365	183	1,154
Baldwin Park, Calif. (1,7)	P	89-68-40	35,496-42,096	None	5,905	4,296-72	3,131	528-637	14	1,595
	F	...-..-..	...-...	..-..-..	...	...-..	...	..-...	...	...
Battle Creek, Mich. (1,1)	P	159-113-40	26,246-34,192	Y-35,192-7	22,160	7,882-35	5,978	1,176-728	13,000	1,278
	F	104-103-53	25,033-33,203	Y-34,203-7	15,966	5,184-32	3,774	858-552	10,320	462
Bayonne, N.J. (1,1)	P	174-174-40	27,099-...	Y-37,674-5	...	...-..	...	..-...	...	...
	F	168-168-42	24,947-...	Y-37,674-5	...	...-..	...	..-...	...	...
Baytown, Tex. (1,1)	P	133-104-40	22,992-...	Y-34,920-1	9,624	7,912-82	5,696	1,184-1,032	492	1,220
	F	75-71-52	23,688-34,236	Y-35,436-1	5,856	5,176-88	3,836	804-536	160	520
Beaverton, Ore. (1,1)	P	85-85-40	28,560-38,268	Y-40,181-15	6,250	5,728-91	4,583	760-385	25	497
	F	51-48-56	26,148-37,212	None	4,917	4,530-92	3,621	622-287	33	354
Bellevue, Wash. (1,1)	P	218-154-40	31,788-44,052	None	11,176	10,932-97	9,912	288-732	...	244
	F	173-149-50	33,564-42,696	None	10,296	8,940-86	8,148	216-576	...	1,356
Bellflower, Calif. (7,7)	P	...-..-..	...-...	..-..-..	...	...-..	...	..-...	...	...
	F	...-..-..	...-...	..-..-..	...	...-..	...	..-...	...	...
Bellingham, Wash. (1,1)	P	142-91-40	...-...	Y-...-5	...	...-..	...	..-...	...	...
	F	131-109-51	...-...	Y-...-10	...	...-..	...	..-...	...	...
Bethlehem, Pa. (1,1)	P	150-126-40	24,263-31,219	Y-32,468-4	6,883	6,435-93	5,375	522-538	156	292
	F	107-106-42	23,490-30,620	Y-31,870-4	5,311	5,202-97	3,815	947-440	16	93
Billings, Mont. (1,1)	P	116-98-40	20,678-30,480	None	5,089	4,367-85	3,430	443-494	161	561
	F	129-102-44	23,187-25,499	Y-25,769-1	5,389	4,500-83	3,597	475-428	441	448
Bloomington, Ill. (1,1)	P	94-87-40	28,470-41,184	..-..-..	5,368	4,666-86	3,704	754-208	270	432
	F	82-78-52	27,269-39,957	..-..-..	4,150	3,813-91	2,945	687-181	77	260
Bloomington, Ind. (1,1)	P	61-38-40	21,300-27,100	None	3,317	2,903-87	2,425	357-121	8	406
	F	82-81-40	22,738-26,038	Y-27,104-3	2,744	2,558-93	2,240	226-92	15	171
Boca Raton, Fla. (1,1)	P	206-127-40	29,785-44,137	Y-44,637-5	10,732	8,631-80	7,201	1,142-288	556	1,545
	F	154-145-42	23,478-40,076	Y-40,676-5	9,768	8,027-82	6,723	1,082-222	186	1,555
Bossier City, La. (1,1)	P	147-122-40	18,000-...	Y-...-3	...	...-..	...	..-...	542	...
	F	120-114-40	18,000-...	..-...-3	...	...-..	...	..-...	802	...
Bristol, Conn. (1,1)	P	107-100-38	31,090-38,241	None	9,812	8,980-91	5,682	2,081-1,217	126	706
	F	93-92-42	28,474-33,915	None	6,069	5,840-96	4,412	426-1,002	23	206
Brooklyn Park, Minn. (1,2)	P	69-61-40	26,292-40,428	Y-44,066-4	...	...-..	...	..-...	10	...
	F	...-..-..	...-...	..-..-..	...	...-..	...	..-...	...	...
Bryan, Tex. (1,1)	P	99-84-40	22,236-32,580	Y-32,680-1	4,845	3,660-75	3,083	437-140	130	1,055
	F	79-79-53	20,460-27,624	Y-27,724-1	3,466	3,003-86	2,532	360-111	75	388
Burbank, Calif. (1,1)	P	216-144-40	38,412-46,812	None	...	...-..	...	..-...	928	...

Table 3/23 continued   POLICE AND FIRE DEPARTMENT PERSONNEL, SALARIES, AND EXPENDITURES FOR CITIES 10,000 AND OVER: 1993

City (Service provision)	Department	Total personnel, no. uniformed, duty hours per week	Entrance, maximum salary ($)	Longevity pay, maximum ($) no. years to receive longevity pay	Total expenditures (A) ($)	Total personnel expenditures (B) ($), % of (A)	Salaries and wages (C) ($)	City contrib. to employee retirement, insurance (D) ($)	Capital outlay (E) ($)	All other (F) ($)
50,000-99,999 continued										
Burbank, Calif. (1,1) cont.	F	123-117-56	37,884-46,152	None	...	...-..	...	...-...	46	...
Camarillo, Calif. (-,7)	P	...-.-.	...-...	..-...-..	...	...-..	...	...-...	...	...
	F	...-.-.	...-...	..-...-..	...	...-..	...	...-...	...	...
Cambridge, Mass. (1,1)	P	230-199-40	22,405-32,238	Y-37,074-..	6,547	6,262-95	4,747	893-622	...	285
	F	252-248-42	23,968-34,495	Y-...-..	5,486	5,464-99	4,011	890-563	...	22
Cape Coral, Fla. (1,1)	P	...-.-.	...-...	..-...-..	7,131	6,322-88	4,900	908-514	187	622
	F	126-121-50	21,307-25,904	Y-27,717-10	6,744	6,013-89	4,477	1,113-423	104	627
Carlsbad, Calif. (1,1)	P	105-78-40	34,381-41,800	None	10,096	7,972-78	5,772	1,470-730	64	2,060
	F	78-69-56	31,928-38,792	None	7,504	6,786-90	4,954	1,222-610	...	718
Carrollton, Tex. (1,1)	P	178-52-40	28,787-33,342	Y-34,542-1	8,451	7,191-85	6,243	564-384	96	1,164
	F	114-112-50	27,900-32,305	Y-33,505-1	6,342	5,229-82	4,548	408-273	87	1,026
Carson, Calif. (7,5)	P	...-.-.	...-...	..-...-..	...	...-..	...	...-...	...	...
	F	...-.-.	...-...	..-...-..	...	...-..	...	...-...	...	...
Cerritos, Calif. (-,-)	P	...-.-.	...-...	..-...-..	...	...-..	...	...-...	...	...
	F	...-.-.	...-...	..-...-..	...	...-..	...	...-...	...	...
Champaign, Ill. (1,1)	P	126-114-40	32,559-35,813	Y-...-5	8,053	6,530-81	5,039	1,227-264	513	1,010
	F	90-80-53	32,377-35,615	Y-...-5	5,885	4,903-83	3,812	884-207	423	559
Chandler, Ariz. (1,1)	P	163-109-40	27,622-38,671	None	8,461	7,382-87	5,756	793-833	123	956
	F	79-75-56	25,544-35,762	None	4,851	3,754-77	3,243	105-406	96	1,001
Charleston, S.C. (1,1)	P	359-285-40	20,100-...	Y-34,300-1	15,302	12,566-82	10,077	1,417-1,072	113	2,623
	F	209-197-45	17,100-22,000	Y-...-1	7,078	6,575-92	5,154	731-690	60	443
Charleston, W.Va. (1,1)	P	171-148-40	18,120-22,436	Y-25,067-1	...	...-..	...	...-...	250	...
	F	...-.-.	...-...	..-...-..	...	...-..	...	...-...	...	...
Cheyenne, Wyo. (1,1)	P	101-77-40	17,942-30,760	Y-...-..	2,219	1,919-86	1,601	189-129	29	271
	F	84-83-48	20,926-25,438	Y-26,638-5	1,911	1,816-95	1,444	259-113	43	52
Chino, Calif. (1,5)	P	123-80-40	...-47,868	None	...	...-..	...	...-...	...	...
	F	...-.-.	...-...	..-...-..	...	...-..	...	...-...	...	...
Clarksville, Tenn. (1,1)	P	158-140-40	18,617-23,991	Y-24,641-5	4,639	4,433-95	3,502	646-285	190	16
	F	144-142-53	18,617-24,887	Y-25,137-5	4,351	4,183-96	3,308	636-239	18	150
Clearwater, Fla. (1,1)	P	337-260-40	24,698-35,671	None	5,004	4,247-84	3,443	537-267	36	721
	F	166-153-56	23,609-34,224	None	2,862	2,590-90	1,761	707-122	4	268
Cleveland Heights, Ohio (1,1)	P	112-96-40	29,501-33,561	Y-34,461-5	3,758	3,536-94	2,786	492-258	...	222
	F	80-79-52	29,263-33,343	Y-34,243-5	3,174	3,018-95	2,298	534-186	...	156
Clifton, N.J. (1,1)	P	150-131-40	30,438-52,019	Y-58,522-5	...	...-..	...	...-...	164	...
	F	125-121-42	27,451-43,503	Y-48,941-5	...	...-..	...	...-...	644	...
College Station, Tex. (1,1)	P	95-86-40	23,256-28,908	Y-30,108-1	...	...-..	...	...-...	...	...
	F	75-73-56	19,200-28,908	Y-30,108-1	...	...-..	...	...-...	...	...
Columbia, Mo. (1,1)	P	135-108-42	22,870-31,217	None	6,843	5,448-79	4,029	1,050-369	132	1,263
	F	108-106-56	20,746-28,315	Y-32,418-5	5,050	4,461-88	3,747	384-330	22	567
Compton, Calif. (1,1)	P	188-126-40	35,688-41,760	Y-...-..	7,885	7,007-88	4,610	1,316-1,081	55	823
	F	69-64-56	35,016-40,956	..-...-..	3,546	3,367-94	2,280	627-460	...	179
Coon Rapids, Minn. (1,1)	P	60-8-40	25,501-39,216	..-42,745-10	3,180	3,060-96	2,520	300-240	...	120
	F	28-28-56	25,501-39,238	..-42,769-10	1,908	1,884-98	1,548	168-168	...	24
Coral Springs, Fla. (1,2)	P	210-138-40	27,387-38,700	Y-41,675-10	4,315	3,828-88	3,043	468-317	4	483
	F	...-.-.	...-...	..-...-..	...	...-..	...	...-...	...	...
Corona, Calif. (1,1)	P	182-114-40	34,008-47,856	Y-48,606-5	8,067	7,116-88	4,961	902-1,253	115	836
	F	87-74-40	33,156-40,296	Y-40,946-5	4,227	4,043-95	2,881	595-567	5	179
Costa Mesa, Calif. (1,1)	P	201-140-40	38,364-46,632	..-...-..	19,094	15,854-83	11,743	2,336-1,775	...	3,240
	F	120-113-56	35,232-42,828	Y-42,873-5	10,426	9,451-90	7,164	1,129-1,158	7	968
Council Bluffs, Iowa (1,1)	P	105-88-39	22,657-28,873	Y-29,813-5	5,004	4,514-90	3,824	138-552	8	482
	F	88-87-56	21,228-26,580	Y-27,480-5	4,044	3,894-96	3,040	70-784	38	112
Cranston, R.I. (1,2)	P	210-142-37	28,880-32,471	Y-35,588-4	10,836	9,066-83	7,592	162-1,312	12	1,758
	F	...-.-.	...-...	..-...-..	...	...-..	...	...-...	...	...
Danville, Va. (1,1)	P	118-102-42	19,261-28,892	None	7,954	3,790-47	3,217	395-178	...	4,164
	F	119-118-52	19,261-28,892	None	2,634	2,033-77	1,632	197-204	347	254
Davenport, Iowa (1,1)	P	180-144-40	26,374-36,504	None	...	...-..	...	...-...	250	...
	F	154-152-56	25,623-35,294	None	...	...-..	...	...-...	125	...
Daytona Beach, Fla. (4,4)	P	...-.-.	...-...	..-...-..	...	...-..	...	...-...	...	...
	F	...-.-.	...-...	..-...-..	...	...-..	...	...-...	...	...
Decatur, Ill. (1,1)	P	142-138-40	26,168-33,053	Y-34,375-5	5,139	4,482-87	3,741	376-365	5	652
	F	108-107-56	26,422-32,424	Y-34,369-5	3,927	3,501-89	2,850	349-302	29	397
Denton, Tex. (3,1)	P	121-97-40	23,476-31,733	Y-...-1	7,347	6,405-87	5,303	600-502	...	942
	F	97-85-56	23,319-28,518	Y-...-1	6,262	5,376-85	4,658	458-260	...	886
Des Plaines, Ill. (1,1)	P	112-13-40	29,924-41,896	Y-44,354-10	7,002	5,571-79	4,334	547-690	...	1,431
	F	96-3-56	30,458-41,212	Y-43,760-10	4,731	3,975-84	3,498	416-61	...	756
Dothan, Ala. (1,1)	P	154-105-40	18,590-26,078	None	7,812	4,728-60	3,924	552-252	2,052	1,032
	F	117-115-40	18,590-26,078	None	10,332	3,684-35	3,036	420-228	6,288	360
Downey, Calif. (1,1)	P	154-121-40	33,498-41,499	Y-44,986-5	15,140	11,812-78	7,253	1,061-3,498	53	3,275
	F	84-71-56	30,150-37,351	Y-40,489-10	7,720	6,714-86	4,391	642-1,681	...	1,006
Dubuque, Iowa (1,1)	P	79-73-40	28,228-29,946	Y-31,388-6	4,328	4,021-92	2,807	664-550	29	278
	F	86-85-56	27,405-29,946	Y-31,965-5	4,527	4,299-94	3,135	614-550	35	193
East Lansing, Mich. (1,1)	P	...-.-.	...-...	..-...-..	...	...-..	...	...-...	...	...
	F	...-.-.	...-...	..-...-..	...	...-..	...	...-...	...	...
Edison tp, N.J. (4,4)	P	...-.-.	...-...	..-...-..	...	...-..	...	...-...	...	...

Table 3/23 continued POLICE AND FIRE DEPARTMENT PERSONNEL, SALARIES, AND EXPENDITURES FOR CITIES 10,000 AND OVER: 1993

City (Service provision)	Department	Total personnel, no. uniformed, duty hours per week	Entrance, maximum salary ($)	Longevity pay, maximum ($), no. years to receive longevity pay	Reported expenditures (in thousands)					
					Total expenditures (A) ($)	Total personnel expenditures (B) ($), % of (A)	Salaries and wages (C) ($)	City contrib. to employee retirement, insurance (D) ($)	Capital outlay (E) ($)	All other (F) ($)
50,000-99,999 continued										
Edison tp, N.J. (4,4) cont.	F	...-...-...	...-...	..-...-..	...	...-..	...	...-...	...	...
El Cajon, Calif. (3,1)	P	205-126-40	30,034-40,386	None	11,589	10,484-90	8,265	1,639-580	9	1,096
	F	85-79-56	28,093-35,961	None	5,749	5,068-88	3,877	959-232	14	667
Elgin, Ill. (1,1)	P	170-126-41	31,008-42,660	None	10,679	9,028-84	7,207	577-1,244	118	1,533
	F	104-102-52	30,744-40,980	None	6,287	5,843-92	4,494	547-802	43	401
Elyria, Ohio (1,1)	P	103-86-40	26,109-28,525	Y-34,230-..	6,612	5,880-88	4,488	828-564	276	456
	F	71-70-52	26,662-29,032	Y-34,838-..	5,148	4,848-94	3,480	876-492	84	216
Encinitas, Calif. (7,5)	P	...-...-..	...-...	..-...-..	...	...-..	...	...-...	...	...
	F	...-...-..	...-...	..-...-..	...	...-..	...	...-...	...	...
Euclid, Ohio (1,1)	P	166-98-40	27,786-33,800	Y-36,504-5	6,994	6,667-95	5,194	1,434-39	138	189
	F	101-97-48	27,140-35,153	Y-36,559-5	6,124	5,722-93	4,433	1,271-18	287	115
Evanston, Ill. (1,1)	P	...-...-..	...-...	..-...-..	...	...-..	...	...-...	...	...
	F	...-...-..	...-...	..-...-..	...	...-..	...	...-...	...	...
Fairfield, Calif. (3,3)	P	115-79-41	32,233-47,623	None	5,028	3,884-77	2,934	705-245	321	823
	F	48-46-40	23,686-40,500	None	1,641	1,276-77	953	250-73	42	323
Farmington Hills, Mich. (1,3)	P	141-97-40	27,610-39,750	Y-43,725-3	5,386	4,984-92	3,863	671-450	13	389
	F	20-16-40	24,952-37,420	Y-40,414-3	1,313	1,126-85	929	113-84	22	165
Fayetteville, N.C. (1,3)	P	291-196-40	20,048-29,471	Y-31,681-5	6,278	5,302-84	4,214	728-360	138	838
	F	156-152-56	18,184-26,730	Y-28,735-5	3,393	2,888-85	2,390	296-202	29	476
Fontana, Calif. (1,5)	P	109-58-40	36,987-50,163	Y-53,173-10	17,371	14,994-86	11,980	1,889-1,125	626	1,751
	F	...-...-..	...-...	..-...-..	...	...-..	...	...-...	...	...
Fort Collins, Colo. (1,6)	P	164-57-40	26,806-38,558	Y-38,588-..	10,357	8,071-77	6,492	932-647	136	2,150
	F	...-...-..	...-...	..-...-..	...	...-..	...	...-...	...	...
Fort Smith, Ark. (1,1)	P	152-115-40	18,054-22,818	Y-22,878-5	3,516	3,264-92	2,016	180-1,068	...	252
	F	111-109-56	17,123-22,015	Y-22,375-5	11,328	9,456-83	1,680	1,296-6,480	...	1,872
Gastonia, N.C. (1,1)	P	197-159-40	20,072-31,642	Y-32,292-5	...	...-..	...	...-...	278	...
	F	118-116-51	15,834-24,882	Y-25,532-5	...	...-..	...	...-...	512	...
Gloucester tp, N.J. (-,-)	P	64-64-40	23,350-43,933	Y-...-5	...	...-..	...	...-...	...	...
	F	...-...-..	...-...	..-...-..	...	...-..	...	...-...	...	...
Great Falls, Mont. (1,1)	P	95-63-40	20,400-27,214	Y-28,294-1	3,396	2,578-75	2,020	261-297	194	624
	F	65-64-48	19,296-28,848	Y-29,568-1	3,059	2,613-85	2,094	252-267	99	347
Greeley, Colo. (1,1)	P	134-85-40	24,600-37,562	None	...	...-..	...	...-...	...	...
	F	72-70-..	22,860-34,296	None	3,048	2,976-97	2,436	264-276	...	72
Greenville, S.C. (1,1)	P	183-147-43	18,491-25,875	Y-27,456-5	7,917	6,619-83	5,317	934-368	168	1,130
	F	150-142-40	18,491-25,875	Y-27,456-5	5,254	4,958-94	4,034	635-289	33	263
Greenwich t, Conn. (1,3)	P	177-158-35	32,578-41,090	Y-...-..	...	...-..	...	...-...	...	...
	F	77-75-42	30,398-38,341	Y-...-..	...	...-..	...	...-...	...	...
Gresham, Ore. (3,3)	P	118-89-40	28,560-38,280	None	5,083	3,403-66	2,662	472-269	61	1,619
	F	85-77-52	28,128-37,800	..-...-..	3,808	2,698-70	2,100	393-205	37	1,073
Hamden t, Conn. (1,1)	P	116-92-40	29,000-39,000	Y-...-5	...	...-..	...	...-...	12	...
	F	102-99-42	32,000-...	Y-33,000-5	...	...-..	...	...-...	...	...
Hamilton tp, N.J. (1,5)	P	191-164-40	28,687-45,033	Y-45,533-5	...	...-..	...	...-...	...	...
	F	...-...-..	...-...	..-...-..	...	...-..	...	...-...	...	...
Hamilton, Ohio (1,1)	P	119-102-37	25,920-33,472	Y-36,150-..	...	...-..	...	...-...	...	...
	F	106-105-51	26,314-33,980	Y-36,698-..	...	...-..	...	...-...	...	...
Hammond, Ind. (1,1)	P	225-185-40	22,675-27,982	Y-30,213-3	9,057	7,881-87	6,848	181-852	400	776
	F	178-174-52	20,549-27,987	Y-29,247-3	7,439	6,227-83	5,331	27-869	600	612
Harrisburg, Pa. (1,3)	P	227-174-40	28,222-30,826	Y-34,525-3	11,098	10,786-97	7,780	1,616-1,390	...	312
	F	107-103-42	26,589-...	Y-26,588-..	5,631	5,462-96	3,941	843-678	3	166
Hawthorne, Calif. (1,1)	P	150-92-40	38,256-45,568	None	7,467	6,224-83	4,871	856-497	18	1,225
	F	66-60-56	31,788-45,264	None	3,987	3,437-86	2,641	588-208	...	550
Henderson, Nev. (1,1)	P	148-109-40	31,031-41,585	None	4,433	4,212-95	3,056	728-428	1	220
	F	104-101-40	28,528-36,409	None	3,076	2,908-94	2,080	544-284	4	164
High Point, N.C. (1,1)	P	159-146-40	18,650-...	Y-29,000-1	...	...-..	...	...-...	...	...
	F	173-170-56	18,650-...	Y-29,000-1	...	...-..	...	...-...	...	...
Houma, La. (1,1)	P	66-51-40	12,500-18,375	Y-...-3	2,702	1,817-67	1,379	168-270	174	711
	F	50-49-53	13,750-20,590	Y-...-3	2,698	1,847-68	1,185	410-252	422	429
Huntington Park, Calif. (1,7)	P	86-54-..	37,800-48,852	None	3,131	2,937-93	2,190	610-137	90	104
	F	...-...-..	...-...	..-...-..	...	...-..	...	...-...	...	...
Irondequoit t, N.Y. (1,5)	P	66-52-..	30,722-...	Y-43,701-4	4,516	4,138-91	3,177	592-369	79	299
	F	...-...-..	...-...	..-...-..	...	...-..	...	...-...	...	...
Irvington tp, N.J. (1,1)	P	188-161-40	28,836-43,852	Y-43,862-5	...	...-..	...	...-...	...	...
	F	142-137-40	28,810-42,918	Y-...-5	...	...-..	...	...-...	...	...
Janesville, Wis. (1,1)	P	104-78-39	26,776-36,730	Y-...-2	7,757	7,548-97	5,268	1,500-780	108	101
	F	81-79-56	26,336-34,519	Y-...-2	7,051	6,216-88	4,248	1,272-696	...	835
Killeen, Tex. (1,3)	P	169-130-40	21,048-27,528	Y-27,816-1	8,112	7,036-86	5,872	840-324	20	1,056
	F	90-83-50	19,320-25,296	Y-25,584-1	4,832	4,260-88	3,520	556-184	152	420
La Crosse, Wis. (1,1)	P	55-55-37	29,230-...	Y-33,988-10	5,088	5,064-99	3,384	948-732	...	24
	F	100-100-56	25,072-...	Y-32,119-10	5,676	5,316-93	3,600	948-768	...	360
La Habra, Calif. (1,1)	P	90-62-40	36,922-44,879	Y-46,001-10	...	...-..	...	...-...	35	...
	F	38-37-56	33,263-40,433	Y-43,466-10	...	...-..	...	...-...	23	...
La Mesa, Calif. (1,1)	P	80-59-40	33,462-43,644	Y-...-..	5,459	4,727-86	3,393	755-579	168	564
	F	53-50-56	25,962-38,316	Y-...-..	3,791	3,237-85	2,326	548-363	9	545
Lafayette, La. (1,1)	P	234-178-40	18,028-...	None	8,963	6,147-68	5,198	520-429	895	1,921

Table 3/23 continued POLICE AND FIRE DEPARTMENT PERSONNEL, SALARIES, AND EXPENDITURES FOR CITIES 10,000 AND OVER: 1993

City (Service provision)	Department	Total personnel, no. uniformed, duty hours per week	Entrance, maximum salary ($)	Longevity pay, maximum ($) no. years to receive longevity pay	Reported expenditures (in thousands)					
					Total expenditures (A) ($)	Total personnel expenditures (B) ($), % of (A)	Salaries and wages (C) ($)	City contrib. to employee retirement, insurance (D) ($)	Capital outlay (E) ($)	All other (F) ($)
50,000-99,999 continued										
Lafayette, La. (1,1) cont.	F	195-169-40	15,574-...	None	6,355	4,950-77	4,161	416-373	844	561
Lake Charles, La. (1,1)	P	133-1-40	14,248-...	Y-...-1	5,664	3,924-69	2,850	841-233	231	1,509
	F	120-3-56	13,453-...	Y-...-1	4,828	4,191-86	2,814	1,146-231	27	610
Lakeland, Fla. (1,1)	P	289-253-42	24,068-33,852	Y-34,332-10	...	...-...	...	...-...	28	...
	F	119-115-50	20,779-29,245	Y-29,725-10	...	...-...	...	...-...	241	...
Lakewood, Calif. (9,5)	P	...-...-...	...-...	..-...-..	...	...-...	...	...-...	...	...
	F	...-...-...	...-...	..-...-..	...	...-...	...	...-...	...	...
Lakewood, Ohio (1,1)	P	109-88-40	29,662-35,902	Y-36,402-5	...	...-...	...	...-...	260	...
	F	85-83-51	28,906-35,902	Y-36,402-5	...	...-...	...	...-...	1,475	...
Lancaster, Calif. (-,5)	P	...-...-...	...-...	..-...-..	...	...-...	...	...-...	...	...
	F	...-...-...	...-...	..-...-..	...	...-...	...	...-...	...	...
Lancaster, Pa. (1,1)	P	125-100-48	23,898-31,067	None	6,254	6,024-96	4,905	961-158	6	224
	F	105-100-42	23,858-29,823	None	4,752	4,659-98	3,494	1,006-159	16	77
Largo, Fla. (1,1)	P	194-104-40	24,149-35,630	None	...	...-...	...	...-...	...	...
	F	125-102-50	20,910-31,628	None	...	...-...	...	...-...	...	...
Las Cruces, N.M. (1,1)	P	148-56-40	17,169-...	Y-30,713-6	5,972	4,839-81	3,731	648-460	92	1,041
	F	82-82-53	16,560-29,273	Y-...-6	3,757	3,223-85	2,455	458-310	51	483
Lawrence, Kan. (1,1)	P	127-103-40	24,235-31,024	Y-31,864-5	5,618	4,865-86	4,198	321-346	191	562
	F	88-85-56	22,617-29,677	Y-30,517-5	3,600	3,361-93	2,907	214-240	37	202
Lawton, Okla. (1,1)	P	191-152-40	19,177-25,147	Y-27,547-4	7,175	6,178-86	5,216	537-425	388	609
	F	121-119-50	19,236-27,937	Y-30,334-4	5,082	4,631-91	3,917	411-303	44	407
Livermore, Calif. (1,1)	P	83-60-40	38,796-47,160	None	4,433	3,924-88	2,883	580-461	...	509
	F	55-46-56	37,140-47,412	None	2,795	2,640-94	1,865	461-314	13	142
Lodi, Calif. (1,1)	P	105-70-40	29,000-35,000	None	6,862	5,893-85	4,307	944-642	105	864
	F	47-45-56	26,000-32,000	None	3,673	2,912-79	2,048	528-336	100	661
Longmont, Colo. (1,1)	P	109-81-...	28,344-37,296	None	5,591	4,839-86	3,980	387-472	41	711
	F	56-54-...	28,104-36,972	None	3,305	2,825-85	2,314	209-302	129	351
Longview, Tex. (1,1)	P	181-140-40	22,639-33,955	Y-...-1	2,519	2,195-87	1,760	279-156	...	324
	F	152-147-40	21,553-32,345	Y-...-1	2,078	1,949-93	1,640	162-147	20	109
Lorain, Ohio (1,1)	P	103-83-...	28,818-31,140	Y-33,440-...	...	...-...	...	...-...	1,100	...
	F	94-93-...	28,818-31,140	Y-33,440-...	...	...-...	...	...-...	600	...
Lynwood, Calif. (9,1)	P	...-...-...	...-...	..-...-..	...	...-...	...	...-...	...	...
	F	34-33-...	32,241-38,243	Y-40,043-5	1,358	1,330-97	972	300-58	3	25
Mc Allen, Tex. (1,1)	P	250-163-40	18,699-24,211	Y-...-1	2,917	2,515-86	2,099	283-133	12	390
	F	121-111-56	20,820-...	Y-...-1	1,407	1,259-89	1,027	168-64	10	138
Manchester t, Conn. (1,1)	P	122-95-40	33,439-41,750	Y-42,150-10	...	...-...	...	...-...	...	...
	F	73-70-42	33,948-41,017	Y-41,417-10	...	...-...	...	...-...	...	...
Manchester, N.H. (1,1)	P	233-180-40	27,590-31,844	Y-35,745-20	11,463	10,707-93	8,685	599-1,423	128	628
	F	249-229-42	25,515-29,914	Y-33,668-25	11,615	10,982-94	8,841	574-1,567	149	484
Mansfield, Ohio (1,1)	P	121-36-40	16,068-29,060	Y-29,160-3	2,658	2,292-86	1,938	90-264	...	366
	F	109-6-48	16,560-31,175	Y-31,275-1	...	...-...	...	...-...	87	...
Medford, Mass. (1,1)	P	110-104-41	28,397-32,057	Y-33,057-10	...	...-...	...	...-...	29	...
	F	134-131-42	29,272-32,682	Y-33,482-5	...	...-...	...	...-...	50	...
Melbourne, Fla. (1,1)	P	176-117-40	22,823-31,462	Y-33,091-15	5,409	5,100-94	4,350	504-246	42	267
	F	123-88-56	22,514-25,477	None	3,795	3,654-96	2,892	582-180	...	141
Merced, Calif. (3,1)	P	103-70-40	26,294-31,949	None	...	...-...	...	...-...	714	...
	F	54-50-56	25,520-31,028	None	...	...-...	...	...-...	271	...
Meriden, Conn. (1,1)	P	122-106-40	31,754-38,125	Y-38,475-5	8,668	8,273-95	5,469	2,098-706	155	240
	F	104-101-42	28,672-34,390	Y-34,790-5	7,447	7,245-97	4,399	2,105-741	...	202
Miami Beach, Fla. (1,1)	P	414-301-40	26,580-37,412	Y-41,527-7	...	...-...	...	...-...	...	...
	F	197-9-48	26,579-37,411	Y-41,526-7	...	...-...	...	...-...	...	...
Midland, Tex. (1,1)	P	186-154-40	22,056-26,700	Y-27,948-1	8,852	7,472-84	5,656	1,104-712	76	1,304
	F	155-151-56	21,600-24,576	Y-25,488-1	6,908	6,052-87	4,920	612-520	112	744
Midwest City, Okla. (1,1)	P	...-...-40	20,100-31,212	Y-32,412-...	4,796	4,194-87	3,336	587-271	3	599
	F	...-...-56	20,100-31,212	Y-34,245-...	3,783	3,443-91	2,904	312-227	1	339
Milpitas, Calif. (1,1)	P	103-78-40	41,151-50,020	None	9,134	7,710-84	5,788	1,211-711	184	1,240
	F	72-67-56	41,536-50,487	None	5,320	4,807-90	3,217	1,038-552	39	474
Mission Viejo, Calif. (-,7)	P	...-...-...	...-...	..-...-..	...	...-...	...	...-...	...	...
	F	...-...-...	...-...	..-...-..	...	...-...	...	...-...	...	...
Monroe, La. (1,-)	P	201-146-40	13,364-15,729	Y-16,629-1	...	...-...	...	...-...	219	...
	F	...-...-...	...-...	..-...-..	...	...-...	...	...-...	...	...
Montebello, Calif. (1,1)	P	132-91-...	35,376-45,144	None	6,432	5,340-83	4,008	596-736	62	1,030
	F	61-55-...	33,342-41,496	None	3,411	2,867-84	2,193	290-384	44	500
Monterey Park, Calif. (1,1)	P	118-77-40	36,420-44,196	None	4,995	4,371-87	3,208	618-545	12	612
	F	47-43-56	31,572-38,352	None	2,447	2,314-94	1,798	316-200	...	133
Mount Prospect v, Ill. (1,1)	P	90-70-40	26,167-29,874	Y-40,574-5	5,815	5,162-88	4,247	420-495	27	626
	F	76-68-50	28,747-41,696	Y-42,396-5	5,406	4,783-88	3,859	506-418	128	495
Muncie, Ind. (1,1)	P	120-115-40	23,624-...	Y-...-1	...	...-...	...	...-...	150	...
	F	120-119-47	23,624-...	Y-...-1	...	...-...	...	...-...	100	...
Napa, Calif. (1,1)	P	107-68-40	34,356-41,808	None	7,512	6,840-91	5,268	900-672	...	672
	F	52-46-56	31,812-40,380	None	4,560	4,200-92	3,156	672-372	120	240
Naperville, Ill. (1,1)	P	198-121-40	30,160-38,168	None	9,457	8,622-91	7,321	376-925	2	833
	F	132-124-56	28,373-40,720	None	7,394	6,350-85	5,535	99-716	71	973

Table 3/23 continued POLICE AND FIRE DEPARTMENT PERSONNEL, SALARIES, AND EXPENDITURES FOR CITIES 10,000 AND OVER: 1993

City (Service provision)	Department	Total personnel, no. uniformed, duty hours per week	Entrance, maximum salary ($)	Longevity pay, maximum ($), no. years to receive longevity pay	Reported expenditures (in thousands)					
					Total expenditures (A) ($)	Total personnel expenditures (B) ($), % of (A)	Salaries and wages (C) ($)	City contrib. to employee retirement, insurance (D) ($)	Capital outlay (E) ($)	All other (F) ($)
50,000-99,999 continued										
National City, Calif. (1,1) ....P		102-73-40	34,320-41,717	Y-41,837-5	8,369	7,969-95	6,851	1,108-10	...	400
	F	38-36-56	31,138-37,849	Y-37,969-5	3,333	3,192-95	2,749	428-15	...	141
New Bedford, Mass. (1,1) ....P		244-205-40	20,805-29,238	Y-29,888-10	...	...-..	...	...-...	...	...
	F	218-208-42	20,805-29,238	Y-29,888-10	...	...-..	...	...-...	10	...
New Britain, Conn. (1,1) ....P		162-151-40	34,153-37,200	Y-37,645-10	5,743	4,708-81	3,548	674-486	...	1,035
	F	148-148-42	31,976-35,183	Y-35,583-10	5,713	4,974-87	3,744	786-444	...	739
New Rochelle, N.Y. (1,1) ....P		211-172-36	30,377-43,907	Y-44,757-15	13,881	13,385-96	9,749	2,521-1,115	399	97
	F	...-..-39	...-...	..-...-..	...	...-..	...	...-...	...	...
Niagara Falls, N.Y. (1,1) ....P		...-..-..	...-...	..-...-..	...	...-..	...	...-...	...	...
	F	...-..-..	...-...	..-...-..	...	...-..	...	...-...	...	...
Norman, Okla. (1,1) ....P		158-130-40	18,717-25,083	Y-26,993-4	5,972	5,228-87	4,042	650-536	349	395
	F	110-108-56	18,943-25,385	Y-26,537-4	4,217	3,952-93	3,125	332-495	84	181
Norwalk, Calif. (7,5) ....P		...-..-..	...-...	..-...-..	...	...-..	...	...-...	...	...
	F	...-..-..	...-...	..-...-..	...	...-..	...	...-...	...	...
Norwalk, Conn. (1,1) ....P		198-176-40	31,300-37,680	Y-38,210-8	13,706	11,921-86	8,697	1,354-1,870	...	1,785
	F	139-131-42	31,301-37,181	Y-37,761-8	11,418	10,306-90	7,120	1,295-1,891	...	1,112
Oak Park v, Ill. (1,1) ....P		164-120-40	28,651-40,418	Y-40,898-5	8,968	8,218-91	6,881	777-560	27	723
	F	86-85-50	26,790-43,802	Y-44,702-10	5,673	5,407-95	4,153	964-290	21	245
Odessa, Tex. (1,1) ....P		241-173-40	18,600-23,844	Y-25,044-1	3,214	2,726-84	2,155	385-186	...	488
	F	170-155-56	18,090-22,704	Y-23,904-1	2,351	2,077-88	1,648	292-137	34	274
Ogden City, Utah (1,1) ....P		...-..-..	...-...	..-...-..	3,729	3,237-86	2,650	377-210	34	458
	F	...-..-..	...-...	..-...-..	3,509	2,979-84	2,523	278-178	35	495
Olathe, Kan. (1,1) ....P		107-83-40	24,368-36,798	..-...-..	5,915	4,941-83	3,911	498-532	76	898
	F	76-74-56	23,077-34,588	..-...-..	3,926	3,372-85	2,585	349-438	7	547
Oshkosh, Wis. (1,1) ....P		107-95-40	28,187-33,127	Y-...-..	5,117	4,760-93	3,336	893-531	132	225
	F	96-94-56	24,749-34,001	Y-34,337-20	5,177	4,956-95	3,508	886-562	34	187
Owensboro, Ky. (1,1) ....P		127-100-40	20,167-28,297	Y-30,297-5	5,583	4,719-84	3,528	678-513	229	635
	F	94-90-..	20,167-28,297	Y-30,297-5	4,244	3,759-88	2,810	528-421	117	368
Palm Bay, Fla. (1,1) ....P		151-97-40	20,988-28,687	Y-30,187-5	5,523	4,884-88	4,596	120-168	...	639
	F	117-106-56	18,061-...	Y-...-5	4,575	3,717-81	3,489	90-138	234	624
Palmdale, Calif. (7,7) ....P		...-..-..	...-...	..-...-..	...	...-..	...	...-...	...	...
	F	...-..-..	...-...	..-...-..	...	...-..	...	...-...	...	...
Palo Alto, Calif. (1,1) ....P		172-97-40	37,981-50,232	None	17,021	11,619-68	8,661	1,959-999	98	5,304
	F	114-112-56	36,483-47,944	None	13,041	9,589-73	6,978	1,825-786	186	3,266
Passaic, N.J. (3,3) ....P		152-149-40	32,554-44,900	Y-...-5	...	...-..	...	...-...	...	...
	F	112-112-42	32,992-45,509	Y-...-5	...	...-..	...	...-...	...	...
Pembroke Pines, Fla. (1,1) ....P		178-142-40	26,668-37,225	Y-38,369-10	9,708	8,595-88	7,011	909-675	15	1,098
	F	143-138-48	21,795-34,711	Y-35,855-10	7,761	7,014-90	5,643	765-606	135	612
Penn Hills, Pa. (1,2) ....P		77-56-..	25,582-36,483	Y-37,578-5	5,472	4,081-74	3,628	91-362	93	1,298
	F	...-..-..	...-...	..-...-..	...	...-..	...	...-...	...	...
Pensacola, Fla. (3,1) ....P		195-142-40	19,370-31,174	Y-34,294-5	7,868	6,836-86	5,524	872-440	114	918
	F	133-127-56	15,921-23,254	Y-25,579-5	4,851	4,131-85	3,224	697-210	43	677
Peoria, Ariz. (1,1) ....P		93-64-40	27,963-39,346	None	4,385	3,749-85	3,076	401-272	79	557
	F	59-55-56	26,815-36,141	None	3,531	2,693-76	2,376	129-188	495	343
Pico Rivera, Calif. (7,7) ....P		...-..-..	...-...	..-...-..	...	...-..	...	...-...	...	...
	F	...-..-..	...-...	..-...-..	...	...-..	...	...-...	...	...
Pine Bluff, Ark. (1,1) ....P		142-115-40	17,590-18,226	Y-23,986-1	4,308	3,840-89	3,192	348-300	...	468
	F	91-90-56	17,590-18,226	Y-23,986-1	2,979	2,832-95	2,448	192-192	3	144
Pleasanton, Calif. (1,1) ....P		92-64-40	41,640-50,724	None	8,200	7,529-91	5,668	1,093-768	19	652
	F	54-52-56	41,388-50,304	None	5,362	5,137-95	3,890	760-487	12	213
Plymouth, Minn. (4,4) ....P		...-..-..	...-...	..-...-..	...	...-..	...	...-...	...	...
	F	...-..-..	...-...	..-...-..	...	...-..	...	...-...	...	...
Pompano Beach, Fla. (1,1) ....P		318-63-40	28,747-40,449	Y-44,681-14	20,680	14,836-71	12,518	2,230-88	191	5,653
	F	139-136-48	25,989-36,569	Y-40,395-14	7,893	6,803-86	5,696	1,082-25	19	1,071
Pontiac, Mich. (4,4) ....P		...-..-..	...-...	..-...-..	...	...-..	...	...-...	...	...
	F	...-..-..	...-...	..-...-..	4,764	2,228-46	1,562	290-376	...	2,536
Port Arthur, Tex. (1,1) ....P		...-..-..	...-...	..-...-..	3,525	1,556-44	1,170	106-280	306	1,663
	F	...-..-..	...-...	..-...-..	1,933	1,687-87	1,185	176-326	...	246
Port St. Lucie, Fla. (1,5) ....P		118-93-40	23,462-31,347	None	...	...-..	...	...-...	...	...
	F	...-..-..	...-...	..-...-..	...	...-..	...	...-...	3	...
Portland, Me. (1,1) ....P		195-138-40	19,448-28,444	None	5,667	4,528-79	3,346	623-559	189	950
	F	242-186-42	18,564-27,560	None	3,766	3,266-86	2,409	429-428	22	478
Provo, Utah (1,1) ....P		102-70-40	23,236-30,704	Y-33,160-5	9,589	8,843-92	7,025	587-1,231	...	746
	F	63-2-56	23,236-...	Y-30,077-5	6,194	5,838-94	3,920	1,251-667	...	356
Pueblo, Colo. (1,1) ....P		219-174-40	22,884-30,636	Y-...-5	7,206	6,018-83	4,350	810-858	156	1,032
	F	139-137-56	22,308-28,200	Y-...-5	3,484	3,156-90	2,292	450-414	4	324
Redding, Calif. (1,1) ....P		151-151-40	29,307-39,145	None	3,988	3,456-86	2,216	593-647	7	525
	F	66-66-56	28,566-38,321	None	2,580	2,258-87	1,543	370-345	9	313
Redlands, Calif. (3,1) ....P		94-67-40	30,300-36,852	None	12,862	9,999-77	7,540	1,316-1,143	182	2,681
	F	56-53-56	28,500-34,632	None	6,696	5,054-75	3,766	704-584	42	1,600
Redondo Beach, Calif. (1,1) ....P		176-101-40	35,916-43,656	Y-...-..	9,824	7,258-73	5,428	1,243-587	78	2,488
	F	67-61-56	33,900-41,208	Y-45,324-5	6,840	5,437-79	4,199	813-425	71	1,332
Redwood City, Calif. (1,1) ....P		141-78-40	39,972-48,588	..-52,236-10						
	F	73-66-56	40,464-49,188	Y-52,872-15						

Table 3/23 continued   POLICE AND FIRE DEPARTMENT PERSONNEL, SALARIES, AND EXPENDITURES FOR CITIES 10,000 AND OVER: 1993

City (Service provision)	Department	Total personnel, no. uniformed, duty hours per week	Entrance, maximum salary ($)	Longevity pay, maximum ($) no. years to receive longevity pay	Reported expenditures (in thousands)					
					Total expenditures (A) ($)	Total personnel expenditures (B) ($), % of (A)	Salaries and wages (C) ($)	City contrib. to employee retirement, insurance (D) ($)	Capital outlay (E) ($)	All other (F) ($)
50,000-99,999 continued										
Rialto, Calif. (1,1)	P	148-104-40	37,824-45,996	None	10,755	9,166-85	7,074	1,493-599	267	1,322
	F	85-67-53	32,040-38,952	None	6,764	5,762-85	4,397	1,005-360	151	851
Richardson, Tex. (1,1)	P	229-229-40	27,978-34,200	Y-35,400-1	10,906	9,200-84	7,480	1,318-402	193	1,513
	F	132-132-52	28,092-32,496	Y-33,696-1	6,738	6,258-92	5,083	916-259	36	444
Richmond, Calif. (1,1)	P	247-172-40	40,608-46,848	Y-49,176-..	12,641	10,902-86	7,936	1,079-1,887	25	1,714
	F	108-105-40	37,632-45,600	Y-47,880-..	6,525	5,846-89	4,180	654-1,012	24	655
Rochester, Minn. (1,1)	P	119-94-42	29,726-39,617	None	7,497	6,948-92	5,164	1,242-542	137	412
	F	88-85-56	29,726-39,617	None	6,417	5,834-90	3,855	1,570-409	94	489
Rosemead, Calif. (9,5)	P	...-...-..	...-...	..-...-..	...	...-..	...	...-...	...	...
	F	...-...-..	...-...	..-...-..	...	...-..	...	...-...	...	...
Roseville, Mich. (1,1)	P	96-83-40	23,545-37,541	Y-41,295-5	6,785	6,237-91	4,658	802-777	116	432
	F	40-39-56	23,184-35,650	Y-39,215-5	3,039	2,704-88	2,009	325-370	162	173
Royal Oak, Mich. (1,1)	P	101-81-40	27,387-38,631	Y-42,494-5	4,186	3,863-92	2,952	568-343	10	313
	F	70-70-54	25,983-37,115	Y-40,827-5	2,696	2,606-96	1,982	396-228	14	76
Saginaw, Mich. (1,1)	P	147-130-40	26,124-33,862	Y-34,590-5	10,553	9,214-87	6,271	1,444-1,499	30	1,309
	F	100-94-54	22,885-35,380	Y-36,812-5	6,676	6,100-91	3,878	1,020-1,202	50	526
St. Charles, Mo. (1,1)	P	113-84-40	23,576-32,384	Y-32,904-10	5,459	4,645-85	3,578	572-495	...	814
	F	71-70-53	23,753-32,630	Y-...-..	3,855	3,651-94	2,739	588-324	...	204
St. Clair Shores, Mich. (1,1)	P	97-79-40	24,982-35,688	Y-39,257-5	...	...-..	...	...-...	...	...
	F	51-50-56	25,977-37,110	Y-40,821-5	...	...-..	...	...-...	...	...
St. Joseph, Mo. (1,1)	P	133-100-40	21,480-27,840	..-...-4	4,788	4,035-84	2,885	757-393	222	531
	F	124-122-52	21,042-26,604	Y-...-4	4,604	4,393-95	3,082	902-409	38	173
San Angelo, Tex. (1,1)	P	188-150-..	20,844-23,268	Y-23,316-1	7,941	6,285-79	5,013	891-381	735	921
	F	140-133-..	19,660-23,268	Y-23,316-1	4,719	4,524-95	3,537	705-282	27	168
San Buenaventura, Calif. (1,1)	P	185-108-40	34,218-40,584	None	...	...-..	...	...-...	47	...
	F	88-77-56	30,270-39,468	None	...	...-..	...	...-...	...	...
San Leandro, Calif. (1,1)	P	124-44-40	39,024-49,764	None	6,768	5,255-77	4,045	906-304	20	1,493
	F	94-5-56	34,212-45,888	None	5,030	4,357-86	3,317	783-257	34	639
San Mateo, Calif. (1,1)	P	138-99-40	39,041-46,550	None	13,379	11,847-88	9,780	1,346-721	208	1,324
	F	92-88-56	35,206-41,961	None	8,945	8,506-95	7,118	931-457	34	405
Sandy City, Utah (1,3)	P	91-27-40	19,240-...	None	...	...-..	...	...-...	50	...
	F	43-41-46	30,498-30,576	..-...-..	...	...-..	...	...-...	19	...
Santa Barbara, Calif. (1,1)	P	212-132-40	34,741-42,228	None	7,103	6,227-87	4,888	910-429	58	818
	F	119-112-50	33,556-40,787	None	4,451	4,012-90	3,091	697-224	15	424
Santa Clara, Calif. (1,2)	P	181-146-40	50,242-61,071	Y-64,126-10	...	...-..	...	...-...	30	...
	F	...-...-..	...-...	..-...-..	...	...-..	...	...-...	...	...
Santa Fe, N.M. (1,3)	P	121-80-40	20,150-36,116	Y-...-15	4,972	3,989-80	3,101	527-361	282	701
	F	91-86-60	20,150-37,922	..-...-15	2,812	2,402-85	1,897	329-176	135	275
Santa Maria, Calif. (3,3)	P	100-75-40	35,024-42,758	None	8,616	6,816-79	4,774	1,134-908	148	1,652
	F	34-31-56	33,320-40,677	None	2,903	2,443-84	1,765	368-310	48	412
Santee, Calif. (7,1)	P	...-...-..	...-...	..-...-..	...	...-..	...	...-...	...	...
	F	56-53-56	24,483-37,833	None	2,408	2,187-90	1,551	419-217	14	207
Sarasota, Fla. (4,4)	P	...-...-..	...-...	..-...-..	...	...-..	...	...-...	...	...
	F	...-...-..	...-...	..-...-..	...	...-..	...	...-...	...	...
Schenectady, N.Y. (1,1)	P	171-149-40	24,047-35,126	Y-36,651-5	8,302	7,949-95	6,168	985-796	32	321
	F	157-152-40	23,733-34,666	Y-36,341-5	8,365	8,150-97	5,965	1,379-806	9	206
Sioux City, Iowa (1,1)	P	137-115-40	24,549-30,869	Y-31,175-5	7,414	6,237-84	4,748	807-682	146	1,031
	F	120-116-56	23,679-30,795	Y-31,131-5	6,209	5,611-90	4,271	722-618	154	444
Somerville, Mass. (3,3)	P	131-124-40	26,061-31,283	Y-33,383-5	...	...-..	...	...-...	...	...
	F	154-152-42	27,103-32,534	Y-34,634-5	...	...-..	...	...-...	164	...
South Gate, Calif. (1,7)	P	121-88-36	37,380-55,392	Y-58,384-6	7,676	6,845-89	5,149	934-762	101	730
	F	...-...-..	...-...	..-...-..	...	...-..	...	...-...	...	...
Southfield, Mich. (1,1)	P	155-155-40	27,674-40,004	Y-43,204-3	12,397	11,197-90	8,081	1,955-1,161	14	1,186
	F	99-99-54	27,063-39,122	Y-42,252-3	7,882	7,460-94	5,228	1,266-966	37	385
Sparks, Nev. (1,1)	P	107-65-40	26,223-33,629	Y-36,129-5	7,972	6,700-84	4,620	1,084-996	6	1,266
	F	68-65-56	27,264-32,435	Y-34,935-5	5,908	5,336-90	3,640	962-734	14	558
Springfield, Ohio (1,1)	P	160-127-40	23,920-31,762	Y-...-5	6,973	3,460-49	2,428	417-615	1,803	1,710
	F	130-125-53	25,220-31,850	Y-...-5	3,387	3,107-91	2,098	497-512	...	280
Suffolk, Va. (1,3)	P	126-97-41	20,913-31,698	Y-...-6	5,850	3,744-64	3,089	557-98	...	2,106
	F	64-63-56	20,913-30,323	Y-...-6	4,096	2,097-51	1,732	312-53	4	1,995
Terre Haute, Ind. (1,1)	P	129-112-40	17,080-18,984	Y-...-2	...	...-..	...	...-...	...	...
	F	158-155-..	17,080-18,984	Y-...-2	...	...-..	...	...-...	...	...
Thornton, Colo. (1,1)	P	120-84-40	27,228-34,044	None	6,069	5,480-90	4,503	373-604	33	556
	F	53-50-56	25,668-...	Y-26,988-4	3,370	3,117-92	2,610	183-324	20	233
Trenton, N.J. (1,1)	P	431-374-40	29,932-38,832	Y-44,457-..	26,884	25,623-95	20,483	2,369-2,771	368	893
	F	282-271-40	29,535-38,305	Y-42,136-..	18,660	17,870-95	14,703	1,697-1,470	356	434
Troy, Mich. (1,3)	P	180-133-40	24,188-37,536	Y-40,176-4	14,281	11,671-81	8,505	2,245-921	373	2,237
	F	11-10-40	...-...	..-...-..	2,073	819-39	597	159-63	865	389
Tuscaloosa, Ala. (1,1)	P	213-187-40	19,180-27,299	Y-27,899-5	7,491	6,092-81	5,033	597-462	621	778
	F	148-146-60	19,180-27,299	Y-27,899-5	6,464	5,639-87	4,668	558-413	92	733
Tustin, Calif. (1,7)	P	244-209-..	39,044-47,458	Y-...-..	8,325	7,425-89	5,767	1,146-512	76	824
	F	...-...-..	...-...	..-...-..	...	...-..	...	...-...	...	...
Tyler, Tex. (3,1)	P	188-136-40	22,944-27,192	Y-28,392-1	7,563	7,440-98	5,772	888-780	4	119
	F	120-113-56	25,116-26,832	Y-28,032-1	5,189	4,609-88	3,831	432-346	75	505

Table 3/23 continued

POLICE AND FIRE DEPARTMENT PERSONNEL, SALARIES, AND EXPENDITURES FOR CITIES 10,000 AND OVER: 1993

City (Service provision)	Department	Total personnel, no. uniformed, duty hours per week	Entrance, maximum salary ($)	Longevity pay, maximum ($) no. years to receive longevity pay	Reported expenditures (in thousands)					
					Total expenditures (A) ($)	Total personnel expenditures (B) ($), % of (A)	Salaries and wages (C) ($)	City contrib. to employee retirement, insurance (D) ($)	Capital outlay (E) ($)	All other (F) ($)
50,000-99,999 continued										
Union City, Calif. (1,1)	P	87-59-40	37,392-45,456	None	6,550	5,968-91	4,729	871-368	...	582
	F	46-40-56	36,840-44,772	None	3,428	3,295-96	2,555	539-201	...	133
Union City, N.J. (4,4)	P	...-...-..	...-...	..-...-..	...	...-...	...	...-...	...	...
	F									
Upper Darby tp, Pa. (1,3)	P	123-107-40	28,756-35,756	Y-41,119-5	...	...-...	...	...-...	...	...
	F	29-26-40	28,756-35,756	Y-41,119-5	960	822-85	714	48-60	...	138
Vacaville, Calif. (1,1)	P	117-75-42	37,776-43,728	None	7,652	6,658-87	5,000	541-1,117	71	923
	F	56-51-57	32,676-37,824	None	4,302	3,404-79	2,528	273-603	336	562
Victoria, Tex. (1,1)	P	134-96-40	20,400-30,156	Y-31,356-1	4,800	3,948-82	3,072	564-312	...	852
	F	79-77-48	17,064-24,648	Y-25,848-1	2,748	2,292-83	1,824	324-144	...	456
Vineland, N.J. (1,3)	P	140-120-40	23,575-34,241	None	6,010	5,461-90	4,711	50-700	72	477
	F	27-27-56	21,100-35,191	None	1,316	1,053-80	910	3-140	26	237
Walnut Creek, Calif. (1,5)	P	107-78-40	41,040-49,848	None	...	...-...	...	...-...	132	...
	F	...-...-..	...-...	..-...-..	...	...-...	...	...-...	...	...
Warren, Ohio (1,1)	P	103-79-40	20,030-28,600	Y-28,825-5	3,804	3,540-93	2,808	552-180	84	180
	F	78-76-52	20,388-29,122	Y-29,332-5	2,162	2,114-97	1,296	638-180	24	24
Warwick, R.I. (1,1)	P	222-166-37	20,883-33,660	Y-38,205-4	15,576	14,740-94	8,500	4,940-1,300	20	816
	F	219-203-42	24,024-33,332	Y-37,165-6	20,495	19,496-95	9,100	8,996-1,400	20	979
Waterloo, Iowa (1,1)	P	139-118-40	23,317-31,075	Y-32,635-3	6,898	6,576-95	4,790	855-931	...	322
	F	122-112-53	22,296-29,048	Y-30,608-3	6,979	5,859-83	4,201	726-932	939	181
Waukegan, Ill. (1,1)	P	145-103-40	27,000-41,161	Y-...-..	6,002	5,464-91	4,740	72-652	28	510
	F	92-89-50	23,034-32,907	Y-35,427-1	3,406	3,152-92	2,681	13-458	44	210
Waukesha, Wis. (1,1)	P	133-96-40	29,982-36,996	Y-37,476-5	7,172	6,495-90	4,707	1,209-579	18	659
	F	93-91-52	22,989-36,960	Y-37,440-5	5,662	5,157-91	3,756	951-450	87	418
West Allis, Wis. (1,1)	P	153-129-38	24,667-37,601	None	9,435	8,968-95	6,365	1,868-735	95	372
	F	122-121-51	24,677-37,601	Y-37,901-5	7,755	7,421-95	5,218	1,579-624	90	244
West Covina, Calif. (1,1)	P	153-110-36	36,480-44,352	None	7,538	6,590-87	4,986	1,130-474	187	761
	F	75-70-56	33,300-40,488	None	4,104	3,662-89	2,775	653-234	61	381
West Hartford t, Conn. (1,1)	P	146-124-40	33,072-39,624	None	10,143	9,246-91	6,981	104-2,161	37	860
	F	106-105-42	33,072-39,624	None	8,050	7,616-94	5,937	27-1,652	20	414
West Haven, Conn. (1,5)	P	115-100-40	31,948-38,731	Y-...-5	...	...-..	...	...-...	...	...
	F	...-...-..	...-...	..-...-..	...	...-...	...	...-...	...	...
Westminster, Calif. (1,1)	P	150-108-40	40,000-48,000	Y-50,400-10	...	...-..	...	...-...	...	...
	F	74-70-56	38,000-46,500	Y-47,880-10	...	...-..	...	...-...	...	...
Westminster, Colo. (1,3)	P	159-111-45	27,024-38,184	Y-42,002-3	...	...-..	...	...-...	28	...
	F	79-77-56	25,094-34,593	Y-38,052-3	...	...-..	...	...-...	...	...
Weymouth t, Mass. (1,1)	P	104-93-40	24,879-29,115	Y-29,919-15	...	...-..	...	...-...	...	...
	F	92-89-42	24,873-30,053	Y-31,618-10	...	...-..	...	...-...	345	...
Wheaton, Ill. (1,1)	P	78-56-40	26,740-40,149	None	...	...-..	...	...-...	...	...
	F	24-23-56	27,883-36,943	None	...	...-..	...	...-...	2	...
Whittier, Calif. (3,7)	P	129-91-40	34,000-45,000	None	6,209	5,609-90	3,876	1,017-716	24	576
	F	...-...-..	...-...	..-...-..	...	...-..	...	...-...	...	...
Wichita Falls, Tex. (1,1)	P	248-175-40	26,039-...	Y-29,111-1	8,223	7,495-91	6,387	883-225	...	...
	F	157-152-54	19,993-22,802	Y-25,203-1	5,362	4,938-92	4,307	493-138	...	728
Wilmington, Del. (1,1)	P	324-273-40	27,652-37,314	None	12,292	10,209-83	7,692	1,579-938	10	424
	F	174-170-40	22,260-35,659	None	6,587	5,442-82	4,776	87-579	...	2,073
Wilmington, N.C. (1,1)	P	182-151-..	19,494-31,647	Y-32,440-5	13,668	6,093-44	5,059	747-287	...	1,145
	F	131-126-..	17,659-27,292	..-27,975-5	8,380	3,717-44	3,156	355-206	198	7,377
Woodbridge tp, N.J. (1,3)	P	185-185-40	28,000-...	...-...-..	...	...-..	...	...-...	38	4,625
	F	...-...-..	...-...	..-...-..	...	...-..	...	...-...	...	...
Yakima, Wash. (1,1)	P	146-107-40	32,104-41,890	Y-44,404-5	7,691	6,119-79	5,314	374-431	160	1,412
	F	79-69-40	31,555-40,532	Y-42,764-5	4,841	4,218-87	3,665	235-318	560	63
Yorba Linda, Calif. (9,7)	P	...-...-..	...-...	..-...-..	...	...-..	...	...-...	...	...
	F	...-...-..	...-...	..-...-..	...	...-..	...	...-...	...	...
Yuma, Ariz. (1,1)	P	127-99-40	27,275-36,681	..-...-..	7,468	6,096-81	5,103	587-406	194	1,178
	F	74-70-..	26,609-34,062	..-...-..	3,851	3,256-84	2,803	267-186	89	506
25,000-49,999										
Addison v, Ill. (1,5)	P	8-8-40	30,000-41,000	None	4,974	4,365-87	3,577	330-458	190	419
	F	...-...-..	...-...	..-...-..	...	...-..	...	...-...	...	...
Ames, Iowa (1,1)	P	67-50-40	25,680-31,045	Y-31,595-5	3,529	2,783-78	2,226	350-207	34	712
	F	53-46-48	24,484-29,106	Y-29,706-5	2,712	2,239-82	1,749	307-183	40	433
Andover t, Mass. (1,1)	P	60-46-38	26,450-31,683	Y-46,492-5	...	...-..	...	...-...	33	...
	F	61-60-42	26,408-31,185	Y-41,557-5	...	...-..	...	...-...	13	...
Annapolis, Md. (1,3)	P	148-109-40	24,981-30,365	Y-34,919-7	8,490	7,812-92	5,362	1,798-652	30	648
	F	96-94-50	23,792-28,919	Y-33,256-7	5,172	4,920-95	3,378	1,132-410	2	250
Anniston, Ala. (1,1)	P	111-83-40	18,450-21,216	Y-21,456-3	2,988	2,568-85	2,244	216-108	...	420
	F	73-73-56	18,200-20,946	Y-21,186-3	2,184	2,028-92	1,800	144-84	...	156
Apple Valley, Minn. (1,2)	P	50-34-..	27,336-39,060	Y-42,564-5	2,727	2,405-88	1,991	246-168	97	225
	F	...-...-..	...-...	..-...-..	...	...-..	...	...-...	...	...
Arcadia, Calif. (1,1)	P	94-75-40	38,220-46,464	None	8,316	7,226-86	5,316	1,290-620	...	1,090
	F	76-63-56	35,112-42,684	None	7,120	6,588-92	4,998	1,050-540	...	532
Arlington t, Mass. (1,1)	P	70-61-40	27,684-...	Y-18,000-5	...	...-..	...	...-...	70	...
	F	89-80-42	27,641-...	Y-18,000-5	...	...-..	...	...-...	202	...
Auburn, Ala. (4,4)	P	...-...-..	...-...	..-...-..	...	...-..	...	...-...	...	...

Table 3/23 continued POLICE AND FIRE DEPARTMENT PERSONNEL, SALARIES, AND EXPENDITURES FOR CITIES 10,000 AND OVER: 1993

City (Service provision)	Department	Total personnel, no. uniformed, duty hours per week	Entrance, maximum salary ($)	Longevity pay, maximum ($) no. years to receive longevity pay	Reported expenditures (in thousands)					
					Total expenditures (A) ($)	Total personnel expenditures (B) ($), % of (A)	Salaries and wages (C) ($)	City contrib. to employee retirement, insurance (D) ($)	Capital outlay (E) ($)	All other (F) ($)
25,000-49,999 continued										
Auburn, Ala. (4,4) cont.	F	...-.-..	...-...	..-.-..	...	...-..	...	...-...	...	...
Auburn, N.Y. (1,1)	P	67-60-40	31,539-35,941	Y-36,691-5	...	...-..	...	...-...	46	...
	F	70-69-40	26,385-36,810	Y-37,560-5	...	...-..	...	...-...	6	...
Auburn, Wash. (1,1)	P	90-67-40	31,837-40,259	Y-43,480-..	...	...-..	...	...-...	39	...
	F	67-63-47	31,139-40,627	Y-43,814-..	...	...-..	...	...-...	75	...
Augusta, Ga. (1,1)	P	202-171-40	17,288-26,727	Y-...-10	...	...-..	...	...-...	609	...
	F	136-136-40	17,288-23,072	None	...	...-..	...	...-...	57	...
Azusa, Calif. (3,9)	P	84-56-40	35,623-43,305	Y-44,356-7	6,999	6,051-86	4,114	1,299-638	148	800
	F	...-.-..	...-...	..-.-..	...	...-..	...	...-...	...	...
Bartlesville, Okla. (1,1)	P	77-50-40	20,238-27,123	Y-27,879-5	...	...-..	...	...-...	...	...
	F	60-59-56	18,346-24,344	Y-25,100-5	...	...-..	...	...-...	...	...
Bartlett t, Tenn. (3,3)	P	69-47-40	19,076-26,236	Y-27,810-..	...	...-..	...	...-...	...	...
	F	48-47-57	18,460-25,274	Y-...-10	...	...-..	...	...-...	...	...
Bay City, Mich. (1,1)	P	81-75-40	20,904-34,299	Y-35,506-5	...	...-..	...	...-...	...	...
	F	53-52-56	19,540-33,663	Y-34,863-5	...	...-..	...	...-...	...	...
Beavercreek, Ohio (1,9)	P	47-36-40	25,837-36,110	Y-36,410-7	...	...-..	...	...-...	...	...
	F	...-.-..	...-...	..-.-..	...	...-..	...	...-...	...	...
Bell, Calif. (3,7)	P	67-67-..	...-...	None	...	...-..	...	...-...	...	...
	F	...-.-..	...-...	..-.-..	...	...-..	...	...-...	...	...
Belleville, Ill. (1,1)	P	76-66-40	25,295-...	Y-31,741-20	2,929	2,612-89	2,014	378-220	78	239
	F	56-55-42	27,989-...	Y-33,948-20	2,212	2,023-91	1,408	452-163	102	87
Belleville tp, N.J. (1,1)	P	89-84-40	29,361-42,753	Y-47,028-5	6,369	5,661-88	4,419	359-883	350	358
	F	69-68-42	29,361-42,750	Y-47,025-5	4,579	4,471-97	3,491	282-698	...	108
Bellevue, Nebr. (1,2)	P	54-40-40	25,512-33,252	Y-35,352-7	...	...-..	...	...-...	...	...
	F	...-.-..	...-...	..-.-..	...	...-..	...	...-...	...	...
Beloit, Wis. (1,1)	P	95-74-40	...-...	None	5,820	5,090-87	3,422	1,037-631	28	702
	F	63-61-53	...-...	None	4,198	3,751-89	2,407	816-528	36	411
Beverly Hills, Calif. (1,1)	P	192-129-40	39,817-45,585	None	5,148	4,190-81	3,160	787-243	...	958
	F	81-76-56	37,469-46,551	None	9,036	7,132-78	5,340	1,187-605	62	1,842
Billerica t, Mass. (1,1)	P	56-52-40	28,656-31,974	Y-34,185-5	...	...-..	...	...-...	...	...
	F	69-68-48	29,512-31,974	Y-34,185-5	...	...-..	...	...-...	...	...
Biloxi, Miss. (4,4)	P	...-.-..	...-...	..-.-..	...	...-..	...	...-...	...	...
	F	...-.-..	...-...	..-.-..	...	...-..	...	...-...	...	...
Bismarck, N.D. (1,1)	P	93-66-40	23,592-30,336	Y-31,246-5	3,898	3,262-83	2,673	326-263	119	517
	F	64-10-53	23,592-30,336	Y-31,246-5	2,893	2,481-85	1,988	293-200	155	257
Blacksburg t, Va. (1,2)	P	61-48-..	19,000-29,000	None	2,623	2,219-84	1,702	291-226	57	347
	F	...-.-..	...-...	..-.-..	...	...-..	...	...-...	...	...
Blue Springs, Mo. (1,5)	P	75-51-40	21,792-32,016	..-.-..	3,201	2,886-90	2,236	279-371	...	315
	F	...-.-..	...-...	..-.-..	...	...-..	...	...-...	...	...
Bolingbrook v, Ill. (1,1)	P	92-64-40	Y-42,882-8	Y-42,882-8	5,220	4,542-87	3,639	496-407	152	526
	F	56-54-53	29,370-39,205	Y-40,605-8	3,939	3,129-79	2,488	247-394	505	305
Bountiful, Utah (1,1)	P	39-30-40	21,341-34,778	None	3,060	1,728-56	1,332	252-144	324	1,008
	F	14-13-58	20,070-32,670	None	2,694	708-26	552	108-48	1,536	450
Bowie, Md. (7,7)	P	...-.-..	...-...	..-.-..	...	...-..	...	...-...	...	...
	F	...-.-..	...-...	..-.-..	...	...-..	...	...-...	...	...
Bowling Green, Ohio (1,1)	P	42-31-40	21,424-29,619	Y-31,100-5	2,071	1,963-94	1,496	216-251	12	96
	F	25-24-52	23,201-29,646	None	1,477	1,420-96	1,011	248-161	3	54
Boynton Beach, Fla. (1,1)	P	137-114-40	28,184-34,278	Y-43,763-15	8,373	7,503-89	6,038	1,080-385	22	848
	F	94-87-48	22,505-27,310	Y-34,860-15	5,622	5,155-91	4,090	832-233	3	464
Bradenton, Fla. (1,1)	P	96-87-40	19,260-30,534	Y-...-5	3,172	3,039-95	2,361	345-333	16	117
	F	77-71-56	16,636-26,382	Y-...-5	2,526	2,322-91	1,800	306-216	3	201
Brea, Calif. (1,1)	P	132-105-40	36,094-46,316	None	...	...-..	...	...-...	218	...
	F	56-49-56	34,124-43,788	..-...-..	...	...-..	...	...-...	...	...
Brookfield, Wis. (1,1)	P	82-61-39	26,400-36,937	None	4,625	4,216-91	3,035	846-335	109	300
	F	54-53-56	26,160-36,684	None	3,242	2,959-91	2,121	591-247	101	182
Brunswick, Ohio (1,-)	P	37-29-40	26,600-33,100	Y-34,200-4	1,206	1,068-88	612	396-60	...	138
	F	...-.-..	...-...	None	...	...-..	...	...-...	19	...
Burlingame, Calif. (1,1)	P	52-46-40	34,996-42,536	None	...	...-..	...	...-...	133	...
	F	51-50-56	34,450-41,964	None	...	...-..	...	...-...	68	...
Burlington, Iowa (1,1)	P	51-37-..	20,736-25,356	Y-26,306-30	2,622	2,192-83	1,686	250-256	40	390
	F	49-49-41	23,052-26,496	Y-27,446-30	2,608	2,296-88	1,708	290-298	68	244
Burlington, N.C. (1,1)	P	120-89-40	18,204-26,520	Y-28,111-2	...	...-..	...	...-...	...	...
	F	77-76-56	17,424-25,380	Y-26,902-2	...	...-..	...	...-...	...	...
Burlington, Vt. (1,1)	P	121-93-40	20,412-30,353	..-...-..	...	...-..	...	...-...	...	...
	F	80-78-56	20,166-28,937	..-...-8	...	...-..	...	...-...	...	...
Campbell, Calif. (1,1)	P	55-40-40	37,813-51,062	None	3,339	1,886-56	1,561	199-126	51	1,402
	F	35-33-56	41,314-52,511	None	1,988	1,435-72	1,168	159-108	41	512
Cape Girardeau, Mo. (-,1)	P	80-58-40	19,000-25,441	None	6,888	3,258-47	2,844	234-180	456	3,174
	F	54-53-56	18,516-24,804	None	4,446	2,268-51	1,908	234-126	1,134	1,044
Carbondale, Ill. (1,1)	P	68-54-40	24,075-27,979	Y-31,610-5	2,259	1,983-87	1,564	329-90	7	269
	F	31-30-56	23,267-27,373	Y-30,809-5	1,542	959-62	657	262-40	20	563
Carol Stream v, Ill. (1,5)	P	63-63-40	28,341-40,294	None	2,718	2,664-98	2,172	324-168	...	54
	F	...-.-..	...-...	..-...-..	...	...-..	...	...-...	...	...
Carson City-Ormsby, Nev. (1,1)	P	101-75-40	24,431-34,521	None	3,133	2,811-89	2,136	457-218	3	319

Table 3/23 continued — POLICE AND FIRE DEPARTMENT PERSONNEL, SALARIES, AND EXPENDITURES FOR CITIES 10,000 AND OVER: 1993

City (Service provision)	Department	Total personnel, no. uniformed, duty hours per week	Entrance, maximum salary ($)	Longevity pay, maximum ($) no. years to receive longevity pay	Reported expenditures (in thousands)					
					Total expenditures (A) ($)	Total personnel expenditures (B) ($), % of (A)	Salaries and wages (C) ($)	City contrib. to employee retirement, insurance (D) ($)	Capital outlay (E) ($)	All other (F) ($)
25,000-49,999 continued										
Carson City-Ormsby, Nev. (1,1) cont.	F	57-54-56	24,668-34,856	None	1,883	1,716-91	1,293	303-120	5	162
Cary t, N.C. (1,1)	P	73-56-42	21,361-30,035	..-..-..	3,075	2,515-81	2,042	341-132	112	448
	F	73-71-53	19,364-27,227	..-..-..	2,760	2,366-85	1,891	337-138	43	351
Cathedral City, Calif. (1,1)	P	64-42-40	36,744-...	Y-54,024-6	...	...-..	...	...-...	...	...
	F	36-36-57	33,276-...	Y-43,524-6	...	...-..	...	...-...	...	...
Cedar Falls, Iowa (4,4)	P	...-..-..	...-...	..-..-..	...	...-..	...	...-...	...	...
	F	...-..-..	...-...	..-..-..	...	...-..	...	...-...	...	...
Ceres, Calif. (4,4)	P	...-..-..	...-...	..-..-..	...	...-..	...	...-...	...	...
	F	...-..-..	...-...	..-..-..	...	...-..	...	...-...	...	...
Cheltenham tp, Pa. (1,2)	P	84-78-40	27,416-34,270	Y-34,570-5	...	...-..	...	...-...	150	...
	F	...-..-..	...-...	..-..-..	...	...-..	...	...-...	...	...
Chesterfield, Mo. (3,5)	P	62-57-40	26,442-35,696	None	3,148	2,473-78	2,056	269-148	141	534
	F	...-..-..	...-...	..-..-..	...	...-..	...	...-...	...	...
Chicago Heights, Ill. (1,3)	P	105-77-..	29,206-34,623	Y-35,583-..	5,424	4,925-90	3,829	669-427	292	207
	F	69-66-56	28,115-33,941	Y-34,901-4	4,015	3,680-91	2,665	735-280	197	138
Chico, Calif. (1,3)	P	101-40-40	27,830-35,505	None	6,444	5,496-85	3,863	1,130-503	...	948
	F	47-2-56	24,752-30,110	None	3,624	3,135-86	2,183	712-240	...	489
Claremont, Calif. (3,7)	P	...-..-40	...-50,988	None	...	...-..	...	...-...	...	...
	F	...-..-..	...-...	..-..-..	...	...-..	...	...-...	...	...
Cleveland, Tenn. (1,1)	P	78-65-40	18,221-25,751	Y-...-1	2,606	2,004-76	1,677	190-137	144	458
	F	62-62-..	18,221-25,751	Y-...-1	2,194	1,826-83	1,522	176-128	101	267
Clinton, Iowa (3,1)	P	51-42-40	22,061-31,446	None	1,143	1,012-88	748	159-105	16	115
	F	45-45-52	20,209-29,539	None	1,119	993-88	727	160-106	37	89
Clovis, N.M. (1,1)	P	75-59-40	17,000-26,000	None	2,196	2,028-92	1,644	348-36	...	168
	F	65-63-56	17,000-26,000	None	1,949	1,908-97	1,512	360-36	12	29
Coconut Creek, Fla. (4,4)	P	...-..-..	...-...	..-..-..	...	...-..	...	...-...	...	...
	F	...-..-..	...-...	..-..-..	...	...-..	...	...-...	...	...
Colton, Calif. (3,1)	P	84-60-40	35,010-41,508	Y-42,338-2	6,265	5,180-82	3,875	868-437	139	946
	F	61-57-56	30,270-35,892	Y-36,610-2	4,457	3,919-87	2,898	680-341	34	504
Columbus, Ind. (1,1)	P	70-70-42	23,728-24,972	Y-29,022-2	2,888	2,588-89	2,019	363-206	36	264
	F	82-82-48	20,249-24,146	Y-28,196-2	3,188	2,964-92	2,422	280-262	38	186
Concord, N.H. (1,1)	P	...-..-40	24,773-33,925	None	...	...-..	...	...-...	...	...
	F	...-..-42	22,495-29,091	Y-30,091-10	...	...-..	...	...-...	...	...
Concord, N.C. (1,3)	P	88-66-..	21,258-32,365	Y-33,983-3	1,882	1,615-85	1,341	216-58	29	238
	F	97-96-..	19,261-29,307	Y-30,772-3	2,091	1,772-84	1,518	187-67	33	286
Conroe, Tex. (1,1)	P	78-61-40	21,840-29,161	Y-30,361-1	...	...-..	...	...-...	...	...
	F	50-48-53	21,840-29,151	Y-30,361-1	...	...-..	...	...-...	...	...
Coral Gables, Fla. (1,1)	P	181-50-40	28,925-38,763	Y-44,873-..	...	...-..	...	...-...	759	...
	F	192-70-48	28,265-37,879	Y-43,850-..	...	...-..	...	...-...	280	...
Coronado, Calif. (1,1)	P	59-42-40	30,864-41,364	Y-43,432-..	3,557	3,300-92	2,634	636-30	82	175
	F	34-32-56	29,208-37,272	..-39,135-..	2,270	1,997-87	1,609	383-5	80	193
Covina, Calif. (3,3)	P	69-69-40	37,464-45,540	None	...	...-..	...	...-...	...	...
	F	35-34-56	37,836-52,872	None	...	...-..	...	...-...	...	...
Culver City, Calif. (1,1)	P	153-117-40	37,554-48,552	None	13,079	10,183-77	7,558	1,862-763	...	2,896
	F	85-63-56	34,626-46,525	None	9,319	7,035-75	5,233	1,238-564	27	2,257
Cupertino, Calif. (-,5)	P	...-..-..	...-...	..-..-..	...	...-..	...	...-...	...	...
	F	...-..-..	...-...	..-..-..	...	...-..	...	...-...	...	...
Cypress, Calif. (1,7)	P	53-26-40	37,224-45,252	None	3,128	2,572-82	1,968	300-304	372	184
	F	...-..-..	...-...	..-..-..	...	...-..	...	...-...	...	...
Dana Point, Calif. (-,7)	P	36-35-40	42,000-50,877	None	...	...-..	...	...-...	...	...
	F	...-..-..	...-...	..-..-..	...	...-..	...	...-...	...	...
Danville, Calif. (7,5)	P	...-..-..	...-...	..-..-..	...	...-..	...	...-...	...	...
	F	...-..-..	...-...	..-..-..	...	...-..	...	...-...	...	...
Danville, Ill. (3,1)	P	74-59-41	25,838-29,870	Y-33,156-4	3,159	2,279-72	1,700	361-218	...	880
	F	64-61-..	22,978-28,723	Y-31,883-4	2,417	2,332-96	1,600	521-211	...	85
Dartmouth t, Mass. (1,-)	P	...-..-..	...-...	..-..-..	...	...-..	...	...-...	...	...
	F	...-..-..	...-...	..-..-..	...	...-..	...	...-...	...	...
Davis, Calif. (3,3)	P	72-53-40	30,443-36,999	..-..-..	2,393	1,843-77	1,262	364-217	1	549
	F	41-40-56	30,662-37,268	..-..-..	1,336	1,154-86	767	246-141	11	171
De Soto, Tex. (1,1)	P	63-45-40	23,520-30,840	Y-32,840-1	2,345	2,139-91	1,881	256-2	...	206
	F	48-47-53	22,920-28,920	Y-30,920-1	1,973	1,848-93	1,525	223-100	4	121
Deerfield Beach, Fla. (7,-)	P	...-..-..	...-...	..-..-..	...	...-..	...	...-...	...	...
	F	98-87-48	23,470-33,512	Y-36,193-5	5,623	5,008-89	3,881	856-271	270	345
Del Rio, Tex. (1,3)	P	70-54-40	16,604-21,799	Y-23,578-1	2,976	2,234-75	1,886	220-128	8	734
	F	41-40-53	16,604-21,799	Y-23,578-1	1,954	1,592-81	1,352	152-88	16	346
Delhi tp, Ohio (1,-)	P	27-24-40	29,514-37,398	Y-40,458-2	1,415	1,265-89	968	152-145	...	150
	F	14-13-50	28,422-34,239	Y-35,739-2	1,269	1,117-88	887	156-74	...	152
Delray Beach, Fla. (1,1)	P	208-137-40	27,487-38,756	None	10,177	8,388-82	6,710	1,203-475	...	1,789
	F	115-108-48	24,578-34,424	None	5,415	5,278-97	4,205	806-267	...	137
Delta Charter tp, Mich. (9,3)	P	...-..-..	...-...	..-..-..	...	...-..	...	...-...	...	...
	F	25-24-56	24,684-56,241	Y-58,209-15	2,095	1,590-75	1,268	201-121	20	485
Derry t, N.H. (1,1)	P	52-42-32	25,703-31,760	Y-...-5	1,446	1,343-92	1,142	45-156	29	74
	F	51-45-48	24,136-28,255	Y-...-5	1,587	1,322-83	1,069	70-183	105	160
Dover, N.H. (1,1)	P	64-46-41	27,447-...	Y-...-10	1,640	1,519-92	1,246	98-175	19	102

Table 3/23 continued   POLICE AND FIRE DEPARTMENT PERSONNEL, SALARIES, AND EXPENDITURES FOR CITIES 10,000 AND OVER: 1993

City (Service provision)	Department	Total personnel, no. uniformed, duty hours per week	Entrance, maximum salary ($)	Longevity pay, maximum ($) no. years to receive longevity pay	Reported expenditures (in thousands) Total expenditures (A) ($)	Total personnel expenditures (B) ($), % of (A)	Salaries and wages (C) ($)	City contrib. to employee retirement, insurance (D) ($)	Capital outlay (E) ($)	All other (F) ($)
25,000-49,999 continued										
Dover, N.H. (1,1) cont.	F	46-44-42	22,057-25,570	Y-26,600-5	1,264	1,087-85	916	38-133	13	164
Downers Grove v, Ill. (1,1)	P	94-70-40	31,096-41,672	None	5,130	4,254-82	3,737	136-381	47	829
	F	89-81-56	21,792-36,200	None	4,671	3,533-75	3,171	56-306	466	672
Dracut t, Mass. (1,1)	P	...-...-..	...-...	..-...-..	...	...-..	...	...-...-..	...	...
	F	...-...-..	...-...	..-...-..	...	...-..	...	...-...-..	...	...
Duncanville, Tex. (1,1)	P	73-48-40	25,974-32,640	Y-33,840-1	4,128	3,453-83	2,727	498-228	...	675
	F	54-53-56	24,774-31,068	Y-32,268-1	2,643	2,466-93	1,950	354-162	...	177
Dunedin, Fla. (3,1)	P	70-54-40	22,779-32,328	Y-32,388-8	4,136	3,211-77	2,476	535-200	...	925
	F	39-38-56	20,832-30,247	None	2,269	1,791-78	1,390	281-120	8	470
Eagan, Minn. (1,2)	P	72-52-40	28,800-39,900	Y-42,800-15	3,922	3,480-88	2,813	314-353	61	381
	F	...-...-..	...-...	..-...-..	...	...-..	...	...-...-..	...	...
East Brunswick tp, N.J. (1,2)	P	123-91-40	33,449-49,962	Y-56,956-5	...	...-..	...	...-...-..	...	...
	F	...-...-..	...-...	..-...-..	...	...-..	...	...-...-..	...	...
East Haven t, Conn. (3,3)	P	45-41-40	31,306-37,505	Y-38,065-5	2,023	1,791-88	1,363	197-231	48	184
	F	33-31-42	29,274-34,564	Y-35,064-5	1,846	1,626-88	1,228	177-221	10	210
Easton, Pa. (1,1)	P	56-48-40	25,688-29,151	Y-...-5	...	...-..	...	...-...-..	...	...
	F	45-44-..	25,688-29,151	Y-...-5	...	...-..	...	...-...-..	...	...
Eden Prairie, Minn. (1,2)	P	66-44-40	30,300-42,700	None	2,726	2,148-78	1,892	255-1	...	578
	F	...-...-..	...-...	..-...-..	...	...-..	...	...-...-..	...	...
Edina, Minn. (1,3)	P	56-48-40	30,886-38,808	Y-42,295-13	4,608	2,904-63	2,496	240-168	...	1,704
	F	29-28-55	24,076-37,618	Y-39,875-16	3,840	1,764-45	1,512	168-84	...	2,076
Edinburg, Tex. (1,2)	P	68-68-40	17,262-...	..-...-1	1,602	1,377-85	1,116	159-102	96	129
	F	...-...-..	...-...	..-...-..	...	...-..	...	...-...-..	...	...
El Centro, Calif. (1,1)	P	67-43-40	28,692-34,056	None	5,808	3,228-55	2,424	516-288	420	2,160
	F	41-38-56	27,492-35,184	None	4,020	2,292-57	1,680	408-204	288	1,440
Elk Grove Village v, Ill. (1,1)	P	111-98-40	29,000-41,000	None	...	...-..	...	...-...-..	385	...
	F	103-94-56	27,000-39,000	None	...	...-..	...	...-...-..	430	...
Elmira, N.Y. (1,1)	P	78-71-40	25,227-34,591	Y-34,791-15	...	...-..	...	...-...-..	...	...
	F	72-71-40	24,586-32,590	Y-32,790-15	...	...-..	...	...-...-..	...	...
Emporia, Kan. (1,3)	P	59-40-40	19,838-28,751	None	2,064	1,716-83	1,464	144-108	84	264
	F	47-46-53	18,613-29,453	None	2,052	1,740-84	1,428	144-168	24	288
Englewood, Colo. (4,4)	P	...-...-..	...-...	..-...-..	...	...-..	...	...-...-..	...	...
	F	...-...-..	...-...	..-...-..	...	...-..	...	...-...-..	...	...
Euless, Tex. (1,1)	P	87-56-40	25,080-32,100	Y-32,220-1	3,134	2,877-91	2,319	296-262	28	229
	F	46-44-..	22,968-29,400	Y-29,520-1	2,129	1,983-93	1,633	194-156	24	122
Eureka, Calif. (1,1)	P	57-40-40	25,968-31,560	Y-37,560-..	3,462	2,565-74	1,993	404-168	67	830
	F	50-...-56	23,464-28,531	None	2,981	2,156-72	1,770	218-168	91	734
Fairborn, Ohio (3,3)	P	53-41-40	27,019-35,235	Y-35,940-6	3,049	2,459-80	1,902	333-224	...	590
	F	45-44-54	25,721-33,705	Y-34,379-6	2,706	2,359-87	1,752	402-205	...	347
Fairfield, Ohio (1,-)	P	56-43-40	24,440-31,574	Y-34,091-5	2,497	2,472-98	1,608	680-184	1	24
	F	3-1-40	...-...	Y-...-1	...	...-..	...	...-...-..	4	...
Falls tp, Pa. (1,2)	P	60-50-40	24,115-40,192	Y-41,757-5	3,547	3,052-86	2,363	196-493	98	397
	F	...-...-..	...-...	..-...-..	...	...-..	...	...-...-..	...	...
Farmington, N.M. (1,1)	P	138-87-40	20,831-28,538	Y-...-5	4,868	4,105-84	3,359	563-183	185	578
	F	65-...-56	18,951-28,055	Y-...-5	3,064	2,431-79	1,968	352-111	180	453
Fayetteville, Ark. (1,1)	P	75-61-40	16,729-21,748	..-...-..	3,043	2,333-76	1,948	270-115	11	699
	F	60-59-56	14,742-20,174	..-...-..	2,106	1,834-87	1,531	215-88	5	267
Ferndale, Mich. (1,1)	P	58-52-40	30,409-38,283	Y-41,183-5	...	...-..	...	...-...-..	...	...
	F	34-34-53	28,148-37,667	Y-40,680-5	...	...-..	...	...-...-..	...	...
Flagstaff, Ariz. (1,3)	P	108-77-40	25,833-34,382	None	2,573	2,152-83	1,745	263-144	98	323
	F	78-2-56	24,273-32,323	None	5,153	4,646-90	3,877	484-285	157	350
Florence, Ala. (1,1)	P	112-83-40	17,423-20,497	None	...	...-..	...	...-...-..	189	...
	F	84-83-56	18,145-20,497	None	...	...-..	...	...-...-..	61	...
Folsom, Calif. (3,3)	P	42-33-..	27,516-33,444	Y-35,952-10	1,926	1,503-78	1,032	327-144	13	410
	F	45-44-..	26,856-32,652	Y-35,100-10	2,143	1,728-80	1,223	362-143	8	407
Fort Lee b, N.J. (1,2)	P	100-88-40	38,994-52,048	Y-59,848-4	22,709	7,100-31	6,200	400-500	100	15,509
	F	...-...-..	...-...	..-...-..	...	...-..	...	...-...-..	...	...
Fort Myers, Fla. (1,1)	P	177-129-40	23,899-36,358	Y-37,186-6	4,693	4,172-88	3,336	538-298	30	491
	F	125-97-52	23,860-35,964	Y-36,764-6	2,768	2,518-90	2,166	186-166	...	250
Fort Pierce, Fla. (1,5)	P	122-100-40	20,072-33,862	None	6,798	5,517-81	4,122	699-696	373	908
	F	...-...-..	...-...	..-...-..	...	...-..	...	...-...-..	...	...
Foster City, Calif. (3,3)	P	57-42-40	37,422-48,588	..-...-..	...	...-..	...	...-...-..	285	...
	F	39-37-..	40,158-47,628	..-...-..	...	...-..	...	...-...-..	306	...
Frankfort, Ky. (1,1)	P	57-52-40	18,762-25,216	Y-...-5	3,539	3,323-93	2,163	1,081-79	...	216
	F	64-62-56	18,762-24,481	Y-...-5	3,836	2,943-76	2,393	459-91	...	893
Franklin tp, N.J. (1,5)	P	83-83-40	26,387-42,128	Y-...-5	...	...-..	...	...-...-..	...	...
	F	...-...-..	...-...	..-...-..	...	...-..	...	...-...-..	...	...
Frederick, Md. (1,7)	P	105-89-40	24,270-34,232	None	3,540	3,022-85	2,093	534-395	154	364
	F	...-...-..	...-...	..-...-..	...	...-..	...	...-...-..	...	...
Freeport v, N.Y. (1,2)	P	...-...-..	...-...	..-...-..	...	...-..	...	...-...-..	...	...
	F	...-...-..	...-...	..-...-..	...	...-..	...	...-...-..	...	...
Gadsden, Ala. (1,1)	P	111-90-40	20,072-20,904	Y-22,576-10	5,126	4,161-81	3,073	669-419	235	730
	F	106-104-56	19,670-22,655	Y-24,468-10	5,965	4,196-70	3,111	662-423	1,240	529
Gahanna, Ohio (1,9)	P	43-38-40	21,211-35,713	Y-36,813-5	2,514	2,255-89	1,621	304-330	103	156

Table 3/23
continued

POLICE AND FIRE DEPARTMENT PERSONNEL, SALARIES, AND EXPENDITURES FOR CITIES 10,000 AND OVER: 1993

City (Service provision)	Department	Total personnel, no. uniformed, duty hours per week	Entrance, maximum salary ($)	Longevity pay, maximum ($), no. years to receive longevity pay	Total expenditures (A) ($)	Total personnel expenditures (B) ($), % of (A)	Salaries and wages (C) ($)	City contrib. to employee retirement, insurance (D) ($)	Capital outlay (E) ($)	All other (F) ($)
25,000-49,999 continued										
Gahanna, Ohio (1,9) cont.	F	...-..-..	...-...	..-...-..						
Gaithersburg, Md. (9,7)	P	22-20-40	26,003-43,242	None	1,290	1,042-80	809	146-87	111	137
	F	...-..-..	...-...	..-...-..		...-..		...-...		
Garden City, Mich. (1,1)	P	53-42-..	24,270-38,570	Y-...-1	1,715	1,516-88	1,241	111-164	13	186
	F	24-24-..	24,833-37,652	Y-...-1	844	749-88	611	56-82	10	85
Gardena, Calif. (1,1)	P	111-91-40	39,276-47,736	None	10,560	8,126-76	6,318	1,314-494	229	2,205
	F	52-48-56	39,564-48,084	None	5,229	4,640-88	3,615	777-248	33	556
Garfield Heights, Ohio (1,1)	P	56-56-40	28,057-35,327	Y-36,327-5	3,023	2,835-93	2,192	336-307		188
	F	48-48-51	26,617-34,804	Y-36,104-5	2,314	2,198-94	1,689	301-208	...	116
Gates t, N.Y. (1,5)	P	...-..-40	25,036-41,104	Y-42,104-4		...-..		...-...		
	F	...-..-..	...-...	..-...-..		...-..		...-...	...	...
Germantown, Tenn. (1,1)	P	61-49-43	21,303-30,094	None	2,994	2,322-77	1,862	258-202	16	656
	F	55-49-56	18,744-31,273	None	2,530	2,170-85	1,736	244-190	...	360
Gilbert t, Ariz. (1,-)	P	60-42-40	28,308-39,042	None	2,944	2,598-88	2,044	288-266	64	282
	F	20-19-..	26,957-37,170	None	...	...-..		...-...		
Gilroy, Calif. (1,1)	P	24-24-40	37,212-45,228	None		...-..		...-...		
	F	32-27-56	35,196-47,780	None		...-..		...-...		
Gladstone, Mo. (4,4)	P	...-..-..	...-...	..-...-..		...-..		...-...	...	...
	F	...-..-..	...-...	..-...-..		...-..		...-...		
Glastonbury t, Conn. (1,2)	P	72-52-40	32,376-39,727	Y-40,227-5	...	...-..		...-...		
	F	...-..-..	...-...	..-...-..	...	...-..		...-...	97	
Glendale Heights v, Ill. (1,5)	P	68-48-40	26,156-38,585	None	3,275	2,963-90	2,324	298-341	171	141
	F	...-..-..	...-...	..-...-..		...-..		...-...		
Glendora, Calif. (1,7)	P	75-52-40	41,000-50,000	..-50,050-..	5,301	4,086-77	3,029	741-316	106	1,109
	F	...-..-..	...-...	..-...-..	...	...-..		...-...		...
Glenview v, Ill. (1,1)	P	...-..-..	...-...	..-...-..	...	...-..		...-...	12	
	F	...-..-..	...-...	..-...-..	...	...-..		...-...	40	
Goldsboro, N.C. (1,1)	P	112-26-40	18,262-26,312	Y-27,364-5	...	...-..		...-...		
	F	80-80-50	17,368-25,064	Y-26,067-5	...	...-..		...-...		
Grand Forks, N.D. (1,1)	P	88-64-40	22,116-29,904	Y-30,924-6	3,587	3,441-95	2,761	292-388	108	38
	F	66-65-53	20,892-28,260	Y-29,280-6	2,957	2,717-91	2,221	241-255	57	183
Grand Island, Nebr. (1,1)	P	66-57-40	21,336-30,012	None	2,544	2,316-91	1,872	252-192	...	228
	F	55-54-54	20,292-28,560	None	2,268	2,088-92	1,728	192-168	48	132
Grand Junction, Colo. (1,1)	P	104-71-40	28,860-34,992	None	4,692	4,200-89	3,600	336-264	...	492
	F	65-62-56	25,992-32,496	None	3,720	3,024-81	2,448	264-312	...	696
Greenfield, Wis. (1,1)	P	77-77-..	...-...	..-...-..	...	...-..		...-...		
	F	52-52-..	...-...	..-...-..	...	...-..		...-...	850	
Greenville, N.C. (1,3)	P	147-31-40	18,772-29,723	Y-31,060-5	5,055	4,395-86	3,573	568-254	93	567
	F	110-107-56	18,520-29,723	Y-31,060-5	3,548	3,272-92	2,723	394-155	93	183
Groton t, Conn. (1,5)	P	70-61-40	29,800-36,200	Y-37,400-5	5,625	4,001-71	1,817	720-1,464	208	1,416
	F	...-..-..	...-...	..-...-..	...	...-..		...-...	...	...
Gulfport, Miss. (1,1)	P	112-70-40	17,289-19,084	Y-19,168-1	...	...-..		...-...	6	...
	F	101-100-57	17,289-19,084	Y-19,168-1	...	...-..		...-...	2	...
Hackensack, N.J. (1,1)	P	116-106-40	19,986-50,456	Y-56,763-4	3,236	3,136-96	2,620	280-236	...	100
	F	106-104-42	16,414-46,337	Y-50,347-4	2,172	2,112-97	1,640	260-212	...	60
Hagerstown, Md. (1,3)	P	112-100-40	20,236-28,685	Y-...-12	...	...-..		...-...	...	...
	F	56-53-48	18,956-27,251	Y-...-5	...	...-..		...-...		
Hallandale, Fla. (1,1)	P	113-87-40	30,307-41,057	Y-44,657-..	...	...-..		...-...		
	F	71-69-48	29,053-35,656	Y-39,256-..	...	...-..		...-...		
Hanford, Calif. (1,1)	P	50-36-40	30,476-35,849	None	2,852	2,514-88	1,782	364-368	36	302
	F	25-24-56	27,246-32,061	..-...-..	1,298	1,114-85	896	108-110	72	112
Harlingen, Tex. (1,1)	P	112-87-40	20,216-28,565	Y-29,765-1	5,372	4,536-84	3,412	636-488	...	836
	F	94-92-56	19,535-27,602	Y-28,802-1	3,776	3,376-89	2,628	360-388	28	372
Hattiesburg, Miss. (1,1)	P	135-91-40	13,880-25,541	None	3,958	3,113-78	2,673	256-184	381	464
	F	96-94-52	13,880-25,541	None	2,644	2,391-90	2,184	78-129	...	253
Hemet, Calif. (1,1)	P	64-27-40	32,286-38,280	None	2,196	1,784-81	1,225	296-263	2	410
	F	33-6-56	31,686-37,572	None	1,314	1,085-82	750	198-137	26	203
Hempfield tp, Pa. (9,2)	P	...-..-..	...-...	..-...-..	...	...-..		...-...	...	...
	F	...-..-..	...-...	..-...-..	...	...-..		...-...		
Hempstead v, N.Y. (1,2)	P	120-97-..	28,086-51,882	Y-53,832-6	6,719	6,291-93	4,923	768-600	128	300
	F	...-..-..	...-...	..-...-..	...	...-..		...-...	...	...
Henderson, Ky. (1,1)	P	56-50-40	18,241-23,920	Y-...-11	3,456	2,871-83	1,740	687-444	...	585
	F	60-58-56	18,241-23,920	Y-...-11	3,942	3,288-83	2,088	789-411	3	651
Hendersonville, Tenn. (1,1)	P	63-46-42	19,614-25,728	Y-27,628-2	2,730	2,400-87	2,048	178-174	6	324
	F	56-55-53	17,766-23,304	Y-25,204-2	2,262	2,048-90	1,750	150-148	32	182
Hickory, N.C. (1,1)	P	103-84-40	19,354-27,328	Y-...-5	3,436	2,820-82	2,345	365-110	214	402
	F	96-...-56	16,719-23,607	Y-...-5	3,645	2,715-74	2,316	292-107	279	651
Highland, Calif. (9,7)	P	...-..-..	...-...	..-...-..	...	...-..		...-...	...	...
	F	...-..-..	...-...	..-...-..	...	...-..		...-...		
Hillsboro, Ore. (1,1)	P	50-40-46	29,316-36,888	None	3,694	2,853-77	2,073	521-259	91	750
	F	48-...-56	37,432-...	None	3,248	2,583-79	1,880	470-233	127	538
Hilo, Hawaii (1,1)	P	453-335-40	27,240-35,892	None	...	...-..		...-...	685	
	F	...-..-..	...-...	..-...-..	...	...-..		...-...		
Hobbs, N.M. (1,1)	P	104-66-40	24,107-...	None	2,511	2,382-94	1,884	396-102	28	101

Table 3/23 continued   POLICE AND FIRE DEPARTMENT PERSONNEL, SALARIES, AND EXPENDITURES FOR CITIES 10,000 AND OVER: 1993

City (Service provision)	Department	Total personnel, no. uniformed, duty hours per week	Entrance, maximum salary ($)	Longevity pay, maximum ($) no. years to receive longevity pay	Reported expenditures (in thousands)					
					Total expenditures (A) ($)	Total personnel expenditures (B) ($), % of (A)	Salaries and wages (C) ($)	City contrib. to employee retirement, insurance (D) ($)	Capital outlay (E) ($)	All other (F) ($)
25,000-49,999 continued										
Hobbs, N.M. (1,1) (cont.)	F	71-69-56	22,043-...	None	1,855	1,764-95	1,341	351-72	11	80
Hoffman Estates v, Ill. (1,1)	P	117-88-40	27,000-38,847	None	5,577	5,145-92	4,242	498-405	199	233
	F	104-99-56	26,000-38,809	None	4,463	4,063-91	3,371	355-337	278	122
Hoover t, Ala. (1,1)	P	107-87-40	27,152-40,115	None	4,152	3,656-88	3,080	384-192	160	336
	F	115-114-53	27,152-40,115	None	4,496	4,272-95	3,584	440-248	...	224
Hopkinsville, Ky. (3,1)	P	52-46-40	19,832-24,232	..-...-..	1,620	1,292-79	1,020	185-87	94	234
	F	62-61-..	19,832-24,232	..-...-..	1,319	1,081-81	859	147-75	74	164
Hot Springs, Ark. (1,1)	P	90-74-40	15,747-19,839	Y-20,439-1	4,432	3,336-75	1,928	1,066-342	...	1,096
	F	77-75-53	14,590-18,382	Y-18,982-1	3,188	2,552-80	1,648	608-296	...	636
Huber Heights, Ohio (1,1)	P	41-38-40	24,283-34,477	Y-...-4	2,576	2,140-83	1,545	310-285	140	296
	F	45-44-56	22,212-32,281	Y-...-5	2,627	2,250-85	1,588	388-274	52	325
Huntsville, Tex. (1,-)	P	44-33-40	22,272-29,964	Y-30,276-1	1,678	1,434-85	1,224	122-88	85	159
	F	3-3-40	22,272-29,964	Y-30,276-1	270	172-63	144	23-5	21	77
Hurst, Tex. (1,1)	P	83-53-..	30,240-33,072	Y-34,272-1	4,164	3,768-90	2,700	696-372	192	204
	F	39-37-..	29,976-32,748	Y-33,948-1	2,088	1,920-91	1,368	360-192	84	84
Hutchinson, Kan. (1,1)	P	93-80-40	19,272-23,292	Y-23,417-2	3,765	2,824-75	2,137	533-154	163	778
	F	77-74-40	19,956-24,684	Y-24,834-2	3,202	2,723-85	2,066	516-141	326	153
Idaho Falls, Idaho (1,1)	P	104-75-40	22,776-33,342	Y-35,021-3	...	...-..	...	...-...	204	...
	F	87-85-56	22,783-32,798	Y-33,890-3	...	...-..	...	...-...	348	...
Imperial Beach, Calif. (7,1)	P	...-.-..	...-...	..-...-..	...	...-..	...	...-...	...	...
	F	12-12-56	28,032-35,784	None	936	798-85	499	211-88	...	138
Indio, Calif. (3,3)	P	69-47-40	31,059-37,733	Y-40,563-10	1,668	1,516-90	1,276	132-108	...	152
	F	32-30-56	26,928-32,699	Y-35,151-10	1,072	976-91	792	124-60	...	96
Inkster, Mich. (4,4)	P	...-.-..	...-...	..-...-..	...	...-..	...	...-...	...	...
	F	...-.-..	...-...	..-...-..	...	...-..	...	...-...	...	...
Jackson, Mich. (1,-)	P	83-64-..	26,180-33,721	Y-36,311-7	5,764	4,894-84	3,152	1,091-651	86	784
	F	56-53-..	24,613-31,862	Y-34,351-7	4,177	3,836-91	2,352	884-600	29	312
Jackson tp, N.J. (1,5)	P	54-39-40	27,174-49,408	Y-54,349-6	...	...-..	...	...-...	...	...
	F	...-.-..	...-...	..-...-..	...	...-..	...	...-...	...	...
Jackson, Tenn. (1,1)	P	150-96-40	19,926-28,828	Y-...-5	...	...-..	...	...-...	...	...
	F	170-161-50	...-...	Y-...-5	...	...-..	...	...-...	...	...
Jacksonville, Ark. (1,1)	P	66-52-40	17,000-22,300	None	1,981	1,610-81	1,380	218-12	61	310
	F	57-52-56	17,000-22,300	None	1,726	1,494-86	1,354	127-13	27	205
Jacksonville, N.C. (1,1)	P	107-87-40	16,848-...	..-...-..	4,267	3,234-75	2,627	423-184	339	694
	F	66-1-56	16,184-...	..-...-..	2,368	2,039-86	1,710	216-113	38	291
Jamestown, N.Y. (1,1)	P	68-64-40	26,503-31,132	Y-33,732-4	4,235	3,902-92	3,006	621-275	...	333
	F	76-75-40	23,272-28,841	Y-36,200-4	4,292	4,145-96	3,167	654-324	...	147
Johnson City, Tenn. (1,1)	P	147-129-40	17,773-27,689	Y-28,729-3	3,297	2,872-87	2,254	297-321	59	366
	F	77-75-56	16,265-25,340	Y-26,380-3	1,852	1,679-90	1,339	146-194	16	157
Johnston t, R.I. (1,1)	P	73-61-37	23,373-28,795	Y-29,658-5	...	...-..	...	...-...	...	...
	F	69-66-42	26,163-28,816	Y-31,368-5	...	...-..	...	...-...	...	...
Jonesboro, Ark. (1,1)	P	70-62-40	18,033-22,415	None	2,378	1,688-70	1,469	108-111	124	566
	F	66-65-53	18,033-22,415	None	2,004	1,708-85	1,470	113-125	67	229
Joplin, Mo. (1,1)	P	79-60-40	20,514-23,608	Y-23,908-5	13,212	2,316-17	1,980	276-60	2,664	8,232
	F	66-..-56	18,954-22,308	Y-22,608-5	11,184	1,920-17	1,620	252-48	2,760	6,504
Juneau, Alaska (1,3)	P	56-36-40	38,000-53,000	None	2,607	1,872-71	1,457	259-156	27	708
	F	36-35-56	34,000-45,000	None	1,810	1,049-57	781	168-100	459	302
Kannapolis, N.C. (1,3)	P	80-72-42	20,278-28,532	Y-35,231-2	3,781	2,739-72	2,476	125-138	249	793
	F	3-3-40	20,278-28,532	Y-35,231-2	314	163-51	144	15-4	34	117
Kennewick, Wash. (1,1)	P	69-55-40	28,728-38,964	Y-40,284-10	4,333	3,363-77	2,597	332-434	68	902
	F	54-52-50	27,852-36,684	Y-37,644-15	2,699	2,391-88	2,023	109-259	51	257
Kent, Ohio (1,1)	P	51-39-..	26,083-35,152	Y-35,632-10	3,265	2,609-79	1,947	360-302	213	443
	F	30-29-..	25,353-34,105	Y-34,585-10	2,160	1,599-74	1,132	271-196	327	234
Kent, Wash. (1,3)	P	125-81-40	32,100-40,188	Y-41,796-5	11,318	7,076-62	5,659	711-706	397	3,845
	F	142-125-51	34,836-43,812	Y-45,564-5	9,982	8,389-84	7,135	443-811	197	1,396
Kentwood, Mich. (1,1)	P	54-48-40	27,473-37,504	Y-39,004-5	3,253	2,498-76	1,891	442-165	164	591
	F	25-24-53	26,046-37,331	Y-38,531-5	1,448	1,118-77	922	122-74	17	313
Kingsport, Tenn. (1,1)	P	124-113-40	19,510-28,040	None	4,149	3,505-84	2,891	419-195	...	644
	F	97-95-..	19,510-28,040	None	3,284	2,975-90	2,449	338-188	...	309
Kingsville, Tex. (1,2)	P	43-43-40	18,122-20,796	Y-21,412-..	1,607	1,182-73	972	118-92	179	246
	F	...-.-..	...-...	..-...-..	...	...-..	...	...-...	...	...
Kinston, N.C. (1,1)	P	92-77-42	17,687-23,703	Y-24,651-5	1,805	1,591-88	1,301	205-85	20	194
	F	67-61-53	17,266-...	Y-21,302-5	1,147	1,006-87	838	104-64	2	139
Kirkland, Wash. (1,3)	P	75-55-..	34,296-44,700	Y-46,200-6	4,129	3,933-95	3,146	385-402	55	141
	F	63-59-..	36,456-43,656	None	4,353	3,429-78	2,776	318-335	98	826
Kirkwood, Mo. (1,1)	P	68-55-39	27,158-38,020	None	3,216	2,868-89	2,280	84-504	...	348
	F	42-41-56	24,814-34,738	None	...	...-..	...	...-...	...	...
Kissimmee, Fla. (1,1)	P	129-86-40	22,284-31,357	Y-32,924-9	5,856	5,208-88	3,621	1,386-201	75	573
	F	68-65-53	20,760-29,282	Y-30,746-9	3,540	3,246-91	2,112	1,029-105	36	258
Kokomo, Ind. (1,1)	P	137-97-40	26,091-27,291	Y-29,891-1	...	...-..	...	...-...	...	...
	F	116-115-56	25,856-27,156	Y-29,756-4	...	...-..	...	...-...	1	...
La Grange, Ga. (1,1)	P	84-78-..	18,879-29,288	None	3,139	2,547-81	2,069	173-305	129	463
	F	62-61-..	17,925-25,606	None	2,271	1,792-78	1,400	192-200	137	342
La Mirada, Calif. (7,5)	P	...-.-..	...-...	..-...-..	...	...-..	...	...-...	...	...

Table 3/23 continued — POLICE AND FIRE DEPARTMENT PERSONNEL, SALARIES, AND EXPENDITURES FOR CITIES 10,000 AND OVER: 1993

City (Service provision)	Department	Total personnel, no. uniformed, duty hours per week	Entrance, maximum salary ($)	Longevity pay, maximum ($), no. years to receive longevity pay	Total expenditures (A) ($)	Total personnel expenditures (B) ($), % of (A)	Salaries and wages (C) ($)	City contrib. to employee retirement, insurance (D) ($)	Capital outlay (E) ($)	All other (F) ($)
25,000-49,999 continued										
La Mirada, Calif. (7,5) cont.	F	...-...-...	...-...	..-...-..	...	...-...	...	...-...	...	...
La Porte, Tex. (3,3)	P	68-20-40	21,538-31,824	Y-...-1	2,148	1,819-84	1,437	228-154	20	309
	F	16-3-53	21,174-33,030	Y-...-1	756	534-70	416	84-34	38	184
La Puente, Calif. (-,5)	P	...-...-..	...-...	..-...-..	...	...-...	...	...-...	...	...
	F									
La Verne, Calif. (1,1)	P	56-39-40	35,124-42,684	None	4,439	3,793-85	2,730	258-805	78	568
	F	28-28-56	34,260-41,640	None	2,398	2,185-91	1,551	148-486	84	129
Lakewood tp, N.J. (1,3)	P	106-96-40	30,183-46,390	..-...-..						
	F									
Lancaster, Ohio (1,1)	P	87-63-40	...-...	Y-...-5						
	F	78-76-50	20,883-26,932	Y-...-5					96	
Lauderhill, Fla. (9,1)	P	...-...-..	...-...	..-...-..	...	...-...	...	...-...	71	...
	F	72-71-48	23,131-37,422	None	3,792	3,398-89	2,636	516-246	57	337
Lawndale, Calif. (7,5)	P	...-...-..	...-...	..-...-..	...	...-...	...	...-...	...	...
	F									
Lawrence tp, N.J. (1,3)	P	70-63-40	32,345-48,646	Y-50,976-..	...	...-...	...	...-...	...	...
	F	4-4-40	24,127-33,494	Y-35,494-..						
Layton, Utah (1,3)	P	51-10-40	21,072-28,512	Y-33,564-1	1,555	1,243-79	898	245-100	163	149
	F	15-14-53	22,000-24,000	None	571	427-74	321	75-31	66	78
League City, Tex. (3,2)	P	73-30-40	28,526-30,664	Y-...-1	2,433	2,045-84	1,659	226-160	87	301
	F	...-...-..	...-...	..-...-..						
Leavenworth, Kan. (1,1)	P	66-49-42	21,548-32,323	Y-32,923-5	2,760	2,016-73	1,716	144-156	...	...
	F	4-4-53	20,088-30,133	Y-30,733-5					...	744
Lee'S Summit, Mo. (1,1)	P	91-22-40	21,384-30,720	None	...	...-...	...	...-...	...	...
	F	79-8-56	19,728-27,996	None	...	...-...	...	...-...	...	...
Lenexa, Kan. (1,1)	P	93-55-40	25,068-36,816	None	...	...-...	...	...-...	...	...
	F	71-69-56	22,740-33,408	None	...	...-...	...	...-...	40	...
Lewiston, Idaho (1,1)	P	41-25-40	23,280-29,597	None	...	...-...	...	...-...	46	...
	F	44-41-56	22,085-27,529	Y-27,889-5						
Lewisville, Tex. (1,1)	P	111-80-40	25,728-30,938	Y-32,138-1	...	...-...	...	...-...	...	...
	F	81-79-56	23,789-29,545	Y-30,745-1						
Lima, Ohio (1,1)	P	103-78-40	22,022-26,419	Y-...-22	...	...-...	...	...-...	...	...
	F	74-72-53	22,447-26,260	Y-...-22						
Lincoln Park, Mich. (1,1)	P	66-61-40	27,000-35,000	Y-36,000-2	5,886	5,089-86	3,605	977-507	321	476
	F	37-36-50	30,000-38,000	Y-40,000-1	2,888	2,777-96	1,961	525-291	15	96
Linden, N.J. (1,1)	P	136-119-37	22,394-43,400	Y-44,600-..	7,915	7,591-95	6,468	404-719	50	274
	F	135-127-42	26,541-43,400	Y-44,600-..	8,343	7,715-92	6,907	24-784	7	621
Littleton, Colo. (1,1)	P	70-53-40	27,693-36,269	None	2,268	1,764-77	1,380	132-252	...	504
	F	106-95-56	25,395-36,245	None	3,498	2,988-85	2,286	216-486	6	504
Livingston tp, N.J. (1,2)	P	...-...-..	...-44,557	Y-49,013-5	...	...-...	...	...-...	90	...
	F	...-...-..	...-...	..-...-..						
Lombard v, Ill. (1,3)	P	80-61-40	28,132-39,065	None	...	...-...	...	...-...	...	...
	F	56-46-53	27,322-37,781	None	...	...-...	...	...-...	22	...
Lompoc, Calif. (1,1)	P	56-41-40	34,766-41,227	None	1,769	1,627-91	1,214	261-152	2	...
	F	26-25-56	33,087-39,236	None	955	844-88	623	142-79	20	122
Longview, Wash. (1,1)	P	55-49-..	32,172-39,540	Y-40,380-10	4,190	2,835-67	2,267	296-272	...	111
	F	39-38-..	32,160-37,848	Y-38,688-5	2,128	1,808-84	1,623	90-95	3	1,352
Los Gatos t, Calif. (3,5)	P	61-40-40	38,605-46,925	Y-49,296-..	4,201	3,669-87	3,024	65-580	16	304
	F	...-...-..	...-...	..-...-..					...	532
Loveland, Colo. (1,3)	P	79-52-40	28,608-36,240	None	3,772	3,156-83	2,679	291-186	...	616
	F	24-..-60	31,356-42,336	None	1,484	1,312-88	1,075	182-55	...	172
Lower Makefield tp, Pa. (1,2)	P	28-25-40	23,259-38,124	Y-39,224-5	1,755	1,548-88	1,261	96-191	6	201
	F	...-...-..	...-...	..-...-..						
Lower Paxton tp, Pa. (1,2)	P	50-45-40	24,940-36,761	Y-40,437-5	2,682	2,445-91	1,901	317-227	56	181
	F	...-...-..	...-...	..-...-..						
Lufkin, Tex. (1,1)	P	80-60-40	22,000-25,000	Y-27,400-1	...	...-...	...	...-...	...	...
	F	69-65-53	20,576-...	Y-22,976-1						
Lynnwood, Wash. (1,3)	P	65-46-40	33,247-39,127	Y-41,337-4	3,633	2,925-80	2,263	293-369	11	697
	F	35-34-48	33,868-40,026	Y-42,236-4	2,836	1,965-69	1,635	90-240	99	772
Mc Candless t, Pa. (1,2)	P	28-28-40	29,502-38,040	Y-...-1	1,891	1,492-78	1,031	306-155	66	333
	F	...-...-..	...-...	..-...-..						
Madison Heights, Mich. (1,1)	P	73-57-40	26,603-38,663	Y-41,757-5	5,520	4,543-82	3,299	639-605	251	726
	F	42-41-54	26,603-38,368	Y-41,438-5	2,948	2,575-87	1,770	373-432	70	303
Manalapan tp, N.J. (1,2)	P	63-46-40	28,959-40,165	Y-43,378-5	4,016	3,630-90	2,372	598-660	84	302
	F	...-...-..	...-...	..-...-..						
Manassas, Va. (1,3)	P	78-62-40	26,711-43,510	Y-...-..	4,837	3,959-81	3,213	515-231	22	856
	F	7-7-50	30,290-49,322	Y-...-..	439	322-73	262	45-15	15	102
Manhattan, Kan. (7,1)	P	...-...-..	...-...	..-...-..	...	...-...	...	...-...	...	...
	F	46-44-..	12,834-...	None	1,762	1,641-93	1,314	178-149	18	103
Manhattan Beach, Calif. (1,3)	P	73-59-40	36,480-45,672	None	6,943	5,085-73	3,873	937-275	29	1,829
	F	30-29-56	43,152-52,452	None	3,221	2,569-79	1,931	503-135	26	626
Manitowoc, Wis. (1,1)	P	73-63-37	26,436-29,964	Y-30,444-6	3,400	3,180-93	2,141	682-357	87	133
	F	46-45-51	25,716-29,844	Y-30,324-6	2,702	2,312-85	1,577	504-231	2	388
Mankato, Minn. (4,4)	P	...-...-..	...-...	..-...-..	...	...-...	...	...-...	...	...

Table 3/23 continued POLICE AND FIRE DEPARTMENT PERSONNEL, SALARIES, AND EXPENDITURES FOR CITIES 10,000 AND OVER: 1993

City (Service provision)	Department	Total personnel, no. uniformed, duty hours per week	Entrance, maximum salary ($)	Longevity pay, maximum ($) no. years to receive longevity pay	Reported expenditures (in thousands)					
					Total expenditures (A) ($)	Total personnel expenditures (B) ($), % of (A)	Salaries and wages (C) ($)	City contrib. to employee retirement, insurance (D) ($)	Capital outlay (E) ($)	All other (F) ($)
25,000–49,999 continued										
Mankato, Minn. (4,4) cont.	F	...-..-..	...-...	..-...-..	...	...-..	...	...-...	...	...
Manteca, Calif. (1,1) ....P	P	67-46-..	...-42,648	Y-47,448-10	4,293	3,917-91	3,049	426-442	4	372
	F	36-34-..	36,396-40,344	Y-42,553-10	2,652	2,333-87	1,739	379-215	10	309
Maple Heights, Ohio (1,1) ....P	P	59-43-40	25,355-33,810	Y-34,890-5	...	...-..	...	...-...	71	...
	F	39-39-51	25,564-33,842	Y-34,922-5	...	...-..	...	...-...	89	...
Maplewood, Minn. (1,9) ....P	P	57-47-40	25,358-...	..-...-..	3,577	2,820-78	2,234	340-246	224	533
	F	...-..-..	...-...	..-...-..	...	...-..	...	...-...	...	...
Marion, Ind. (1,1) ....P	P	70-60-40	19,165-23,957	None	7,140	3,162-44	2,442	102-618	90	3,888
	F	77-75-56	19,165-23,957	None	...	...-..	...	...-...	...	...
Marion, Ohio (1,1) ....P	P	64-47-40	24,960-30,846	Y-30,873-5	3,413	2,979-87	2,110	515-354	91	343
	F	65-65-48	22,389-29,652	Y-29,679-5	3,410	3,193-93	2,154	638-401	17	200
Marshalltown, Iowa (1,1) ....P	P	53-40-41	20,399-30,373	Y-...-10	5,458	1,848-33	1,428	228-192	1,008	2,602
	F	33-32-49	20,969-29,290	Y-30,715-10	5,086	1,260-24	948	156-156	1,224	2,602
Martinez, Calif. (1,7) ....P	P	55-43-..	36,816-43,644	Y-50,907-15	...	...-..	...	...-...	...	...
	F	...-..-..	...-...	..-...-..	...	...-..	...	...-...	...	...
Maryland Heights, Mo. (1,5) ......P	P	70-56-40	26,321-34,277	Y-...-4	3,178	2,737-86	2,292	323-122	75	366
	F	...-..-..	...-...	..-...-..	...	...-..	...	...-...	...	...
Massillon, Ohio (1,1) ....P	P	51-49-40	24,283-31,933	Y-...-..	...	...-..	...	...-...	...	...
	F	44-44-50	25,593-31,794	Y-...-..	...	...-..	...	...-...	...	...
Maywood, Calif. (1,7) ....P	P	27-27-40	36,216-44,040	Y-47,124-5	...	...-..	...	...-...	116	...
	F	...-..-..	...-...	..-...-..	...	...-..	...	...-...	...	...
Medford, Ore. (1,1) ....P	P	88-72-40	27,288-34,848	None	5,955	5,126-86	3,751	950-425	218	611
	F	66-65-56	28,044-35,076	None	4,011	3,629-90	2,622	668-339	43	339
Menlo Park, Calif. (1,5) ....P	P	60-42-..	...-...	..-...-..	2,812	2,491-88	2,072	276-143	37	284
	F	...-..-..	...-...	..-...-..	...	...-..	...	...-...	...	...
Menomonee Falls v, Wis. (1,3) ......P	P	72-55-40	29,931-35,991	Y-37,793-..	4,269	3,894-91	2,821	692-381	81	294
	F	6-5-50	25,945-30,529	Y-...-..	630	432-68	325	75-32	35	163
Mentor, Ohio (1,1) ....P	P	87-63-40	29,460-37,182	Y-38,682-5	5,042	4,420-87	3,357	618-445	65	557
	F	62-58-53	29,460-37,182	Y-38,682-5	5,402	4,010-74	3,144	626-240	626	766
Meridian, Miss. (1,1) ....P	P	123-93-..	16,598-24,648	..-...-..	3,688	2,862-77	2,346	314-202	144	682
	F	112-111-43	15,808-23,462	..-...-..	3,116	2,736-87	2,296	255-185	81	299
Merrillville, Ind. (1,2) ....P	P	54-48-40	21,934-27,895	Y-28,895-5	...	...-..	...	...-...	...	...
	F	...-..-..	...-...	..-...-..	...	...-..	...	...-...	...	...
Methuen t, Mass. (1,1) ....P	P	73-60-40	24,551-27,554	Y-28,079-5	3,482	3,230-92	2,866	13-351	124	128
	F	94-93-42	24,727-27,841	Y-...-1	4,277	4,111-96	3,636	7-468	38	128
Middletown, Ohio (1,1) ....P	P	118-34-40	27,297-34,344	Y-35,374-10	...	...-..	...	...-...	263	...
	F	75-75-53	25,983-34,679	Y-35,719-10	...	...-..	...	...-...	236	...
Middletown tp, Pa. (1,2) ....P	P	57-49-40	24,257-39,595	Y-42,565-5	3,930	3,680-93	2,681	367-632	51	199
	F	...-..-..	...-...	..-...-..	...	...-..	...	...-...	...	...
Midland, Mich. (1,1) ....P	P	53-50-42	24,283-36,781	Y-39,723-5	...	...-..	...	...-...	...	...
	F	41-40-56	21,620-34,883	Y-37,674-5	...	...-..	...	...-...	...	...
Milford t, Mass. (1,1) ....P	P	41-41-40	27,949-29,857	Y-32,647-10	...	...-..	...	...-...	78	...
	F	38-38-42	24,686-30,365	Y-30,428-5	...	...-..	...	...-...	9	...
Minot, N.D. (1,1) ....P	P	70-54-40	18,480-26,016	None	9,033	1,969-21	1,732	135-102	118	6,946
	F	46-45-56	18,480-26,016	None	...	...-..	...	...-...	36	...
Miramar, Fla. (1,1) ....P	P	104-87-40	27,258-46,612	Y-...-15	...	...-..	...	...-...	...	...
	F	65-59-50	23,919-38,962	Y-...-5	...	...-..	...	...-...	...	...
Mishawaka, Ind. (1,1) ....P	P	86-76-48	21,950-...	..-...-..	3,117	2,810-90	2,148	356-306	6	301
	F	90-89-56	21,950-...	..-...-..	3,333	3,239-97	2,531	348-360	18	76
Mission, Tex. (3,3) ....P	P	66-53-40	16,000-25,955	Y-27,155-25	1,762	1,258-71	1,054	136-68	99	405
	F	15-14-52	16,744-24,578	None	627	385-61	327	39-19	72	170
Moline, Ill. (1,1) ....P	P	92-70-40	27,067-35,282	Y-36,887-14	4,107	3,773-91	3,223	340-210	14	320
	F	68-67-56	27,067-33,933	Y-36,994-24	3,354	3,138-93	2,550	395-193	18	198
Montclair, Calif. (3,3) ....P	P	74-52-40	37,836-45,996	None	5,868	4,385-74	3,335	589-461	611	872
	F	46-38-56	32,448-39,444	None	3,982	3,020-75	2,304	443-273	499	463
Montclair tp, N.J. (1,1) ....P	P	116-99-40	26,085-40,105	..-45,238-5	7,374	6,875-93	5,256	914-705	...	499
	F	87-86-42	26,008-42,506	..-47,947-5	4,617	4,398-95	3,301	650-447	...	219
Monterey, Calif. (1,1) ....P	P	69-52-40	35,100-42,660	None	3,490	2,953-84	2,033	226-694	12	525
	F	49-46-56	32,340-39,312	None	2,382	2,095-87	1,433	184-478	15	272
Moorhead, Minn. (1,1) ....P	P	50-41-40	27,072-32,016	None	1,992	1,956-98	1,656	192-108	...	36
	F	38-32-56	24,792-28,536	None	1,488	1,404-94	1,176	132-96	...	84
Moorpark, Calif. (9,5) ....P	P	26-22-40	...-...	Y-...-10	...	...-..	...	...-...	3,500	...
	F	...-..-..	...-...	..-...-..	...	...-..	...	...-...	...	...
Mount Laurel tp, N.J. (1,5) ....P	P	45-29-40	29,215-38,540	Y-...-10	3,315	3,086-93	2,414	407-265	12	217
	F	...-..-..	...-...	..-...-..	...	...-..	...	...-...	...	...
Mt. Lebanon, Pa. (1,3) ....P	P	57-44-40	30,167-41,054	Y-41,604-4	2,230	2,141-96	1,586	121-434	...	89
	F	16-15-42	34,554-41,054	Y-41,604-4	698	646-92	473	36-137	...	52
Mount Pleasant t, S.C. (1,3) ....P	P	83-60-43	19,922-28,419	Y-...-3	1,446	1,240-85	1,056	170-14	11	195
	F	57-56-53	17,993-25,672	Y-...-3	1,008	864-85	744	100-20	20	124
Murfreesboro, Tenn. (1,1) ....P	P	122-98-37	18,504-21,308	Y-...-1	...	...-..	...	...-...	13	...
	F	139-136-52	17,738-21,253	Y-...-1	...	...-..	...	...-...	26	...
Murray, Utah (1,3) ....P	P	63-53-40	21,576-35,652	Y-...-..	3,556	2,763-77	2,133	415-215	138	655
	F	38-36-..	21,576-35,652	Y-...-..	2,134	1,642-76	1,292	221-129	244	248
Muskegon, Mich. (1,1) ....P	P	75-66-40	21,000-31,455	Y-31,955-5	4,332	3,664-84	2,584	599-481	1	667

Table 3/23 continued POLICE AND FIRE DEPARTMENT PERSONNEL, SALARIES, AND EXPENDITURES FOR CITIES 10,000 AND OVER: 1993

City (Service provision)	Depart-ment	Total personnel, no. uniformed, duty hours per week	Entrance, maximum salary ($)	Longevity pay, maximum ($) no. years to receive longevity pay	Reported expenditures (in thousands)					
					Total expendi-tures (A) ($)	Total personnel expendi-tures (B) ($), % of (A)	Salaries and wages (C) ($)	City contrib. to employee retirement, insurance (D) ($)	Capital outlay (E) ($)	All other (F) ($)
25,000-49,999 continued										
Muskegon, Mich. (1,1) cont.	F	37-36-54	21,000-31,580	Y-32,080-5	2,125	1,921-90	1,341	322-258	18	186
Nacogdoches, Tex. (1,3)	P	62-48-40	22,092-26,112	Y-27,312-1	2,207	1,817-82	1,465	251-101	74	316
	F	53-51-53	19,548-23,220	Y-24,420-1	2,088	1,826-87	1,480	259-87	49	213
Nampa, Idaho (1,1)	P	54-38-42	21,261-26,891	None	2,493	2,043-81	1,581	246-216	110	340
	F	31-1-56	21,252-28,008	None	1,662	1,414-85	918	366-130	22	226
Needham t, Mass. (1,1)	P	54-49-40	26,555-29,599	Y-...-5	...	...-..	...	...-...	...	...
	F	66-64-42	25,506-29,019	Y-...-5	...	...-..	...	...-...	...	...
Neptune tp, N.J. (1,5)	P	80-62-..	25,000-52,000	Y-54,400-..	5,445	4,985-91	3,800	617-568	100	360
	F	...-..-..	...-...	..-...-..	...	...-..	...	...-...	...	...
New Albany, Ind. (3,1)	P	61-58-38	22,912-24,260	Y-...-1	3,081	2,709-87	2,288	114-307	70	302
	F	74-73-56	23,669-25,320	Y-...-1	3,394	3,196-94	2,640	138-418	...	198
New Berlin, Wis	P	...-..-..	...-...	..-...-..	...	...-..	...	...-...	...	...
	F	...-..-..	...-...	..-...-..	...	...-..	...	...-...	...	...
New Braunfels, Tex. (1,1)	P	60-43-40	18,418-28,093	Y-30,045-1	2,496	1,884-75	1,572	216-96	312	300
	F	45-43-53	18,418-19,581	Y-21,531-1	834	768-92	642	90-36	...	66
New Brunswick, N.J. (1,1)	P	151-123-40	26,555-50,136	Y-51,640-20	...	...-..	...	...-...	...	...
	F	75-74-42	26,059-49,200	Y-...-20	...	...-..	...	...-...	...	...
New London, Conn. (1,1)	P	87-77-40	33,112-36,648	Y-37,198-5	5,057	4,676-92	3,841	336-499	64	317
	F	69-67-42	31,844-33,794	Y-34,294-5	3,645	3,387-92	2,731	161-495	10	248
Newark, Calif. (1,1)	P	70-50-40	46,884-56,976	None	...	...-..	...	...-...	...	...
	F	43-38-56	44,664-55,668	None	...	...-..	...	...-...	33	...
Newark, Del. (1,2)	P	66-51-40	25,378-33,048	Y-34,048-7	2,949	2,938-99	2,211	325-402	...	11
	F	...-..-..	...-...	..-...-..	...	...-..	...	...-...	...	...
Newark, Ohio (1,1)	P	66-59-..	18,324-27,060	Y-27,355-5	3,336	2,799-83	1,991	438-370	...	537
	F	79-71-..	17,742-27,664	Y-27,959-5	3,501	3,119-89	2,208	540-371	24	358
Newington t, Conn. (1,2)	P	52-49-40	32,942-42,094	Y-43,094-5	4,130	3,833-92	2,915	591-327	13	284
	F	...-..-..	...-...	..-...-..	...	...-..	...	...-...	...	...
Normal t, Ill. (1,1)	P	61-52-40	22,748-37,913	None	2,770	2,399-86	2,152	120-127	73	298
	F	40-40-..	25,389-39,589	None	2,265	1,870-82	1,506	272-92	150	245
North Attleborough t, Mass. (1,3)	P	39-33-40	24,709-28,134	Y-28,534-5	...	...-..	...	...-...	63	...
	F	50-46-42	25,099-29,947	Y-30,197-10	...	...-..	...	...-...	...	...
North Chicago, Ill. (1,1)	P	65-44-40	21,348-34,157	None	2,240	1,945-86	1,585	200-160	29	266
	F	27-26-50	20,948-33,516	None	1,012	866-85	712	90-64	42	104
North Las Vegas, Nev. (1,1)	P	274-177-40	31,094-40,818	Y-44,900-7	10,922	9,846-90	7,334	1,579-933	196	880
	F	63-61-56	29,330-40,175	Y-44,193-7	4,891	4,374-89	3,301	709-364	97	420
North Lauderdale, Fla. (4,4)	P	...-..-..	...-...	..-...-..	...	...-..	...	...-...	...	...
	F	...-..-..	...-...	..-...-..	...	...-..	...	...-...	...	...
North Miami, Fla. (1,7)	P	124-111-40	30,118-38,584	Y-38,658-5	7,604	6,759-88	5,207	1,216-336	...	845
	F	...-..-..	...-...	..-...-..	...	...-..	...	...-...	...	...
North Miami Beach, Fla. (1,-)	P	...-97-40	26,185-39,440	Y-40,440-7	...	...-..	...	...-...	321	...
	F	...-..-..	...-...	..-...-..	...	...-..	...	...-...	...	...
North Providence t, R.I. (1,1)	P	53-34-37	27,733-32,175	Y-34,427-5	3,668	3,301-89	2,500	515-286	28	339
	F	92-87-42	22,780-29,885	Y-32,276-5	4,918	4,650-94	3,565	640-445	...	268
North Richland Hills, Tex. (1,1)	P	100-72-40	26,616-...	Y-27,816-1	4,381	3,602-82	2,992	327-283	75	704
	F	65-63-56	26,616-34,956	Y-35,256-1	3,105	2,714-87	2,273	243-198	36	355
North Tonawanda, N.Y. (1,1)	P	53-50-40	28,534-33,937	Y-34,837-..	...	...-..	...	...-...	87	...
	F	61-59-40	29,378-34,943	Y-35,743-..	...	...-..	...	...-...	12	...
Northglenn, Colo. (1,5)	P	63-47-40	26,879-38,840	Y-39,320-7	...	...-..	...	...-...	...	...
	F	...-..-..	...-...	..-...-..	...	...-..	...	...-...	...	...
Norwich, Conn. (1,3)	P	70-61-40	24,435-29,658	None	4,765	3,802-79	3,040	357-405	9	954
	F	63-61-42	24,815-31,664	None	4,302	3,030-70	2,455	287-288	21	1,251
Novato, Calif. (1,5)	P	75-54-40	34,980-42,516	Y-...-..	...	...-..	...	...-...	...	...
	F	...-..-..	...-...	..-...-..	...	...-..	...	...-...	...	...
Oak Ridge, Tenn. (1,1)	P	59-47-40	21,986-31,699	Y-...-..	1,534	1,281-83	1,051	132-98	8	245
	F	43-42-52	21,986-31,699	Y-...-..	1,223	1,059-86	886	110-63	14	150
Oakland Park, Fla. (1,1)	P	109-81-40	26,736-37,621	Y-43,264-5	2,064	1,829-88	1,435	246-148	4	231
	F	46-43-48	26,058-35,045	Y-40,302-5	679	584-86	460	83-41	...	95
Ocala, Fla. (1,1)	P	188-123-40	19,807-31,579	Y-...-1	7,885	6,141-77	5,178	690-273	199	1,545
	F	113-105-56	17,991-28,833	Y-...-1	5,526	3,931-71	3,265	445-221	724	871
Orange Township, N.J. (1,1)	P	97-86-40	25,892-38,157	Y-...-5	...	...-..	...	...-...	...	...
	F	84-84-42	22,000-...	Y-47,363-5	...	...-..	...	...-...	...	...
Orland Park v, Ill. (1,-)	P	88-62-50	30,935-41,279	Y-42,579-..	4,834	3,934-81	3,336	149-449	62	838
	F	...-..-..	...-...	..-...-..	...	...-..	...	...-...	...	...
Ormond Beach, Fla. (1,1)	P	84-64-40	19,658-29,098	None	3,929	3,009-76	2,477	306-226	374	546
	F	40-39-56	17,831-26,394	None	1,899	1,648-86	1,282	263-103	30	221
Pacifica, Calif. (3,3)	P	48-36-40	26,952-43,104	None	2,160	1,784-82	1,364	252-168	11	365
	F	25-23-56	22,632-42,300	None	1,127	1,053-93	810	163-80	...	74
Paducah, Ky. (1,1)	P	70-63-40	20,352-26,940	Y-...-1	3,170	2,712-85	1,996	446-270	188	270
	F	87-82-40	21,565-25,059	Y-...-1	3,502	3,050-87	2,032	676-342	222	230
Palatine v, Ill. (1,1)	P	54-31-40	27,233-37,985	Y-38,935-8	5,597	4,739-84	3,994	702-43	1	857
	F	67-64-53	27,630-38,540	Y-39,490-8	6,424	5,837-90	3,812	1,576-449	56	531
Panama City, Fla. (1,1)	P	105-79-40	18,200-27,872	Y-...-4	4,416	3,353-75	2,719	393-241	299	764
	F	97-89-56	...-...	Y-...-4	3,621	3,147-86	2,534	390-223	71	403
Paramus b, N.J. (1,2)	P	91-67-40	28,400-58,055	Y-63,860-5	8,322	8,027-96	6,727	700-600	100	195

Table 3/23 continued POLICE AND FIRE DEPARTMENT PERSONNEL, SALARIES, AND EXPENDITURES FOR CITIES 10,000 AND OVER: 1993

City (Service provision)	Depart-ment	Total personnel, no. uniformed, duty hours per week	Entrance, maximum salary ($)	Longevity pay, maximum ($) no. years to receive longevity pay	Total expendi-tures (A) ($)	Total personnel expendi-tures (B) ($), % of (A)	Salaries and wages (C) ($)	City contrib. to employee retirement, insurance (D) ($)	Capital outlay (E) ($)	All other (F) ($)
25,000–49,999 continued										
Paramus b, N.J. (1,2) cont.	F	...-..-..	...-...	..-...-..	...	...-...	...	...-...	...	...
Park Ridge, Ill. (4,4)	P	...-..-..	...-...	..-...-..	...	...-...	...	...-...	...	...
	F	...-..-..	...-...	..-...-..	...	...-...	...	...-...	...	...
Parkersburg, W.Va. (1,1)	P	82-66-40	21,091-28,579	Y-...-1	2,973	2,359-79	1,854	261-244	187	427
	F	75-72-48	21,470-28,230	Y-...-1	2,707	2,414-89	1,875	292-247	11	282
Parsippany-Troy Hills tp, N.J. (1,2)	P	115-88-36	27,703-44,902	Y-49,392-15	7,961	7,407-93	6,585	22-800	30	524
	F	...-..-..	...-...	..-...-..	...	...-...	...	...-...	...	...
Pascagoula, Miss. (1,1)	P	82-82-40	17,448-25,779	None	2,810	2,384-84	1,881	243-260	145	281
	F	59-59-50	17,448-25,779	None	1,876	1,748-93	1,426	117-205	60	68
Peabody, Mass. (1,1)	P	86-86-40	23,736-26,972	Y-37,672-5	...	...-...	...	...-...	...	...
	F	100-100-40	23,964-27,232	Y-27,932-5	...	...-...	...	...-...	...	...
Pemberton tp, N.J. (1,2)	P	52-47-40	24,918-38,189	Y-42,765-5	...	...-...	...	...-...	...	...
	F	...-..-..	...-...	..-...-..	...	...-...	...	...-...	...	...
Pennsauken tp, N.J. (1,3)	P	127-94-40	32,251-38,085	Y-44,663-5	7,838	7,170-91	5,593	633-944	41	627
	F	10-9-48	32,251-38,085	Y-44,663-5	1,507	655-43	528	50-77	520	332
Petaluma, Calif. (1,1)	P	75-51-40	35,194-42,786	None	3,565	3,105-87	2,333	502-270	62	398
	F	51-49-56	35,507-43,158	None	2,346	2,195-93	1,592	406-197	4	147
Pinellas Park, Fla. (1,1)	P	107-70-40	23,234-34,445	None	5,600	4,500-80	3,704	580-216	...	1,100
	F	78-71-56	22,976-32,527	None	3,868	3,160-81	2,600	396-164	...	708
Piscataway tp, N.J. (1,5)	P	103-85-40	27,709-47,895	Y-52,684-..	6,631	6,343-95	4,715	789-839	50	238
	F	...-..-..	...-...	..-...-..	...	...-...	...	...-...	...	...
Pittsburg, Calif. (1,5)	P	73-66-40	36,036-43,812	None	...	...-...	...	...-...	9	...
	F	...-..-..	...-...	..-...-..	...	...-...	...	...-...	...	...
Placentia, Calif. (1,7)	P	67-51-40	37,601-46,405	Y-47,565-5	3,414	2,995-87	2,171	622-202	60	359
	F	...-..-..	...-...	...-...-..	...	...-...	...	...-...	...	...
Pleasant Hill, Calif. (1,5)	P	63-42-40	35,952-46,428	None	4,325	3,523-81	2,652	567-304	47	755
	F	...-..-..	...-...	..-...-..	...	...-...	...	...-...	...	...
Plum b, Pa. (1,2)	P	22-18-40	22,680-34,892	Y-36,142-5	3,156	2,619-82	878	1,735-6	13	524
	F	...-..-..	...-...	..-...-..	...	...-...	...	...-...	...	...
Plymouth t, Mass. (1,3)	P	96-83-40	26,613-30,290	Y-30,540-5	3,360	3,089-91	2,492	269-328	155	116
	F	114-109-42	23,828-28,511	Y-28,761-5	3,538	3,213-90	2,484	288-441	164	161
Ponca City, Okla. (1,1)	P	69-56-40	19,459-23,515	Y-...-..	...	...-...	...	...-...	...	...
	F	69-68-56	18,063-21,229	Y-21,239-..	...	...-...	...	...-...	67	...
Port Huron, Mich. (1,1)	P	70-51-40	31,058-35,604	Y-39,164-5	4,068	3,349-82	2,642	320-387	2	717
	F	56-54-56	29,821-34,543	Y-37,997-5	3,260	2,664-81	2,132	225-307	6	590
Port Orange, Fla. (9,9)	P	74-56-42	21,084-31,208	..-...-..	...	...-...	...	...-...	...	...
	F	51-49-53	18,673-27,636	..-...-..	...	...-...	...	...-...	22	...
Portage, Ind. (1,1)	P	51-37-40	20,852-26,624	Y-27,224-3	...	...-...	...	...-...	780	...
	F	43-42-..	20,852-27,014	Y-27,614-3	...	...-...	...	...-...	200	...
Portage, Mich. (3,3)	P	67-54-40	26,348-39,617	Y-42,588-5	...	...-...	...	...-...	...	...
	F	33-33-56	24,675-35,674	Y-35,724-5	...	...-...	...	...-...	...	...
Porterville, Calif. (3,3)	P	58-32-40	24,780-30,240	None	3,387	2,657-78	2,032	353-272	14	716
	F	29-28-56	21,996-26,832	None	3,329	3,122-93	2,820	132-170	6	201
Poughkeepsie, N.Y. (1,1)	P	91-80-40	...-...	..-...-..	5,419	4,947-91	3,826	827-294	90	382
	F	75-72-40	...-...	..-...-..	4,108	3,830-93	2,957	639-234	25	253
Poway, Calif. (-,3)	P	...-..-..	...-...	..-...-..	...	...-...	...	...-...	...	...
	F	35-33-56	30,204-40,764	None	3,468	1,395-40	1,066	193-136	8	2,065
Quincy, Ill. (1,1)	P	82-71-40	22,624-29,649	None	4,932	2,566-52	1,971	429-166	25	2,341
	F	65-61-40	22,624-30,149	None	4,471	2,431-54	1,756	495-180	...	2,040
Radnor tp, Pa. (1,2)	P	48-44-40	34,061-39,170	Y-41,741-3	3,903	3,670-94	2,649	361-660	31	202
	F	...-..-..	...-...	..-...-..	...	...-...	...	...-...	...	...
Rahway, N.J. (1,1)	P	78-74-40	29,772-43,476	Y-48,693-4	4,613	4,384-95	3,775	13-596	...	229
	F	60-59-42	26,547-42,026	Y-47,069-4	3,407	3,310-97	2,831	9-470	15	82
Rancho Palos Verdes, Calif	P	...-..-..	...-...	..-...-..	...	...-...	...	...-...	...	...
	F	...-..-..	...-...	..-...-..	...	...-...	...	...-...	...	...
Redmond, Wash. (1,1)	P	77-57-..	37,272-43,212	Y-44,292-6	5,445	3,690-67	3,015	372-303	...	1,755
	F	84-80-..	31,236-42,984	Y-44,703-6	4,932	3,992-80	3,282	385-325	2	938
Renton, Wash. (1,-)	P	108-81-..	...-...	Y-...-5	...	...-...	...	...-...	...	...
	F	119-108-..	36,600-45,084	Y-49,896-5	...	...-...	...	...-...	...	...
Reynoldsburg, Ohio (1,5)	P	50-38-40	20,280-32,157	Y-32,707-4	3,118	2,199-70	1,682	161-356	32	887
	F	...-..-..	...-...	..-...-..	...	...-...	...	...-...	...	...
Richfield, Minn. (1,1)	P	50-40-40	29,812-39,567	None	2,820	2,363-83	1,734	514-115	9	448
	F	50-50-55	32,880-40,651	Y-42,277-5	1,707	1,520-89	1,063	392-65	9	178
Richland, Wash. (1,1)	P	51-44-40	34,272-38,832	Y-39,072-10	3,372	2,400-71	2,040	132-228	...	972
	F	52-50-50	28,188-36,624	Y-40,286-20	3,204	2,844-88	2,400	132-312	...	360
Richmond, Ind. (1,1)	P	101-77-40	21,629-22,129	Y-25,414-1	3,936	3,756-95	2,544	972-240	...	180
	F	82-81-56	21,133-23,030	Y-25,030-2	3,972	3,300-83	2,328	780-192	36	636
Ridley tp, Pa. (1,2)	P	34-34-40	27,000-35,000	Y-...-..	2,269	2,093-92	1,510	208-375	87	89
	F	...-..-..	...-...	..-...-..	...	...-...	...	...-...	...	...
Rio Rancho, N.M. (4,4)	P	...-..-..	...-...	..-...-..	...	...-...	...	...-...	...	...
	F	...-..-..	...-...	..-...-..	...	...-...	...	...-...	...	...
Rochester, N.H. (1,-)	P	48-37-40	20,713-27,080	Y-27,380-3	1,250	1,018-81	840	45-133	23	209
	F	29-28-42	20,983-26,776	Y-27,376-3	1,075	617-57	498	39-80	347	111
Rock Hill, S.C. (1,1)	P	104-95-..	19,822-27,892	None	3,564	3,288-92	2,640	468-180	...	276

Table 3/23   POLICE AND FIRE DEPARTMENT PERSONNEL, SALARIES, AND EXPENDITURES FOR
continued   CITIES 10,000 AND OVER: 1993

City (Service provision)	Department	Total personnel, no. uniformed, duty hours per week	Entrance, maximum salary ($)	Longevity pay, maximum ($) no. years to receive longevity pay	Reported expenditures (in thousands)					
					Total expenditures (A) ($)	Total personnel expenditures (B) ($), % of (A)	Salaries and wages (C) ($)	City contrib. to employee retirement, insurance (D) ($)	Capital outlay (E) ($)	All other (F) ($)
25,000–49,999 continued										
Rock Hill, S.C. (1,1) cont.	F	69-68-..	17,784-25,022	None	2,148	2,076-96	1,656	300-120	...	72
Rock Island, Ill. (1,1)	P	110-81-40	22,258-29,827	Y-32,827-5	3,901	3,304-84	2,654	416-234	...	597
	F	62-61-48	21,403-33,204	Y-36,704-5	2,559	2,255-88	1,787	290-178	...	304
Rockville, Md. (1,7)	P	50-35-40	29,172-49,304	Y-57,769-12	2,589	2,419-93	2,022	281-116	25	145
	F	...-..-..	...-...	...-...-..	...	...-..	...	...-...	...	...
Rocky Mount, N.C. (1,1)	P	160-128-40	19,028-26,640	Y-27,306-5	3,385	3,004-88	2,326	527-151	76	305
	F	129-126-56	17,403-24,367	Y-24,976-5	3,143	2,576-81	2,024	412-140	451	116
Rohnert Park, Calif. (4,4)	P	...-..-..	...-...	..-...-..	...	...-..	...	...-...	...	...
	F	...-..-..	...-...	..-...-..	...	...-..	...	...-...	...	...
Rome, Ga. (1,1)	P	83-72-..	17,568-27,703	None	2,916	2,604-89	2,004	336-264	...	312
	F	150-145-..	17,568-27,703	None	4,644	3,732-80	2,880	348-504	...	912
Roseville, Calif. (3,1)	P	102-62-40	28,194-36,823	Y-38,644-10	3,444	2,734-79	1,984	395-355	63	647
	F	68-64-56	29,194-35,486	Y-35,736-15	2,373	1,949-82	1,355	321-273	38	386
Roseville, Minn. (1,2)	P	50-50-..	25,875-38,355	Y-41,288-4	2,949	2,454-83	2,080	245-129	226	269
	F	...-..-..	...-...	...-...-..	...	...-..	...	...-...	...	...
Ross tp, Pa. (1,2)	P	40-40-40	24,000-35,000	Y-45,000-5	...	...-..	...	...-...	...	...
	F	...-..-..	...-...	..-...-..	...	...-..	...	...-...	...	...
Roswell, Ga. (1,2)	P	141-99-40	20,426-26,125	Y-28,850-10	3,432	2,390-69	1,916	248-226	419	623
	F	...-..-..	...-...	...-...-..	...	...-..	...	...-...	...	...
Saginaw tp, Mich. (1,2)	P	42-39-40	23,795-36,156	..-...-..	2,808	2,226-79	1,656	305-265	59	523
	F	...-..-..	...-...	..-...-..	...	...-..	...	...-...	...	...
St. Louis Park, Minn. (1,1)	P	67-57-40	28,861-41,860	Y-...-..	3,216	2,688-83	2,052	324-312	...	528
	F	29-28-55	32,961-40,075	Y-41,911-5	1,320	1,116-84	816	132-168	...	204
St. Peters, Mo. (1,5)	P	63-52-40	22,963-35,131	None	3,085	2,586-83	2,089	246-251	79	420
	F	...-..-..	...-...	...-...-..	...	...-..	...	...-...	...	...
Salem, Mass. (1,-)	P	98-90-40	24,716-27,110	Y-28,010-10	4,928	4,893-99	4,227	410-256	...	35
	F	97-95-42	23,127-25,931	Y-26,600-5	4,758	4,063-85	3,377	434-252	321	374
Salem t, N.H. (1,1)	P	63-15-40	23,594-29,491	Y-...-5	3,556	3,244-91	2,523	166-555	...	312
	F	62-5-42	25,537-30,645	Y-...-5	3,691	3,438-93	2,599	189-650	...	253
Salina, Kan. (1,1)	P	77-65-40	20,342-26,562	Y-...-5	2,846	2,439-85	1,936	259-244	13	394
	F	85-81-56	19,394-25,276	Y-...-5	3,314	3,037-91	2,432	309-296	79	198
San Bruno, Calif. (1,1)	P	58-41-..	38,784-47,604	None	4,764	4,044-84	3,266	446-332	35	685
	F	34-33-..	35,268-43,272	None	2,614	2,122-81	1,654	283-185	196	296
San Carlos, Calif. (3,-)	P	50-35-40	38,015-46,208	None	3,963	3,352-84	2,700	416-236	80	531
	F	...-..-..	...-...	..-...-..	...	...-..	...	...-...	...	...
San Clemente, Calif. (1,1)	P	66-44-40	38,568-46,884	None	5,763	4,610-79	3,338	888-384	6	1,147
	F	43-31-56	28,368-39,828	None	3,800	3,117-82	2,313	558-246	16	667
San Gabriel, Calif. (1,1)	P	60-48-40	34,608-42,060	None	...	...-..	...	...-...	...	...
	F	34-33-56	31,848-38,712	None	...	...-..	...	...-...	...	...
San Marcos, Calif. (7,3)	P	...-..-..	...-...	..-...-..	...	...-..	...	...-...	...	...
	F	35-33-56	30,708-37,320	None	2,099	1,379-65	940	331-108	546	174
San Marcos, Tex. (1,3)	P	71-55-..	...-...	..-...-..	4,156	3,048-73	2,566	269-213	474	634
	F	33-32-..	18,019-22,000	Y-...-1	1,561	1,326-84	1,099	125-102	119	116
San Rafael, Calif. (1,1)	P	98-71-40	33,319-40,040	None	32,930	31,263-94	4,915	26,013-335	148	1,519
	F	92-86-56	31,973-38,418	None	16,926	16,257-96	4,753	11,053-451	18	651
Sandusky, Ohio (1,1)	P	46-39-40	20,856-29,652	Y-29,702-3	2,673	2,389-89	1,762	366-261	66	218
	F	55-55-52	25,056-28,644	Y-28,694-3	3,003	2,608-86	1,842	489-277	125	270
Sanford, Fla. (1,1)	P	101-83-43	20,232-30,421	None	4,374	3,624-82	2,934	517-173	71	679
	F	55-53-56	20,232-30,421	None	2,435	2,212-90	1,808	304-100	36	187
Santa Cruz, Calif. (1,1)	P	110-78-40	32,634-42,660	None	4,156	3,113-74	2,603	242-268	25	1,018
	F	45-44-56	27,924-38,448	None	1,841	1,416-76	1,213	102-101	12	413
Santa Paula, Calif. (1,3)	P	35-28-40	30,269-35,895	Y-...-..	3,108	2,496-80	1,896	416-184	178	434
	F	3-3-40	...-...	None	686	508-74	448	44-16	52	126
Saratoga, Calif. (7,5)	P	...-..-..	...-...	..-...-..	...	...-..	...	...-...	...	...
	F	...-..-..	...-...	..-...-..	...	...-..	...	...-...	...	...
Saratoga Springs, N.Y. (1,1)	P	70-62-40	24,755-...	Y-33,710-5	...	...-..	...	...-...	17	...
	F	55-51-40	25,994-31,521	Y-32,521-5	...	...-..	...	...-...	30	...
Saugus t, Mass. (1,1)	P	51-49-40	24,870-28,904	Y-29,771-5	1,939	1,787-92	1,229	429-129	64	88
	F	47-42-42	25,276-29,380	Y-30,261-5	1,647	1,538-93	1,048	382-108	69	40
Seal Beach, Calif. (1,7)	P	48-34-37	34,512-41,694	Y-48,396-10	1,918	1,737-90	1,398	197-142	...	181
	F	...-..-..	...-...	..-...-..	...	...-..	...	...-...	...	...
Seaside, Calif. (1,1)	P	53-45-..	32,000-39,800	Y-41,800-5	4,404	2,804-63	2,100	504-200	100	1,500
	F	27-26-..	28,600-36,400	Y-38,200-5	1,994	1,469-73	1,100	264-105	25	500
Shaler tp, Pa. (1,2)	P	30-21-40	28,080-37,946	Y-39,386-5	...	...-..	...	...-...	...	...
	F	...-..-..	...-...	..-...-..	...	...-..	...	...-...	...	...
Shawnee, Kan. (1,3)	P	67-55-41	23,878-37,045	None	3,497	2,770-79	2,199	359-212	155	572
	F	33-32-56	21,664-31,973	None	1,611	1,276-79	1,010	164-102	77	258
Shawnee, Okla. (1,1)	P	50-50-40	16,307-20,821	Y-21,819-4	1,738	1,564-89	1,316	126-122	79	95
	F	46-46-56	16,714-21,316	Y-22,480-4	1,768	1,586-89	1,308	147-131	14	168
Sheboygan, Wis. (1,1)	P	110-110-38	25,600-31,033	Y-32,431-15	6,136	5,608-91	3,801	1,125-682	113	415
	F	80-80-56	24,960-30,181	Y-31,533-15	4,356	4,046-92	2,643	899-504	167	143
Sherman, Tex. (1,1)	P	55-54-40	22,680-31,272	Y-32,772-..	...	...-..	...	...-...	...	...
	F	69-66-56	19,884-25,260	Y-26,760-..	...	...-..	...	...-...	...	...
Sierra Vista, Ariz. (4,4)	P	...-..-..	...-...	..-...-..	...	...-..	...	...-...	...	...

Table 3/23 continued

POLICE AND FIRE DEPARTMENT PERSONNEL, SALARIES, AND EXPENDITURES FOR CITIES 10,000 AND OVER: 1993

City (Service provision)	Depart-ment	Total personnel, no. uniformed, duty hours per week	Entrance, maximum salary ($)	Longevity pay, maximum ($) no. years to receive longevity pay	Reported expenditures (in thousands)					
					Total expendi-tures (A) ($)	Total personnel expendi-tures (B) ($), % of (A)	Salaries and wages (C) ($)	City contrib. to employee retirement, insurance (D) ($)	Capital outlay (E) ($)	All other (F) ($)
25,000–49,999 continued										
Sierra Vista, Ariz. (4,4) cont.	F	...-.-.	...-...	..-...-.	...	...-..	...	...-...	...	...
South Brunswick tp, N.J. (1,5)	P	85-62-40	32,171-46,991	Y-51,690-5	...	...-..	...	...-...	...	...
	F	...-.-.	...-...	..-...-.	...	...-..	...	...-...	...	...
Southington t, Conn. (3,3)	P	...-.-.	...-...	..-...-.	...	...-..	...	...-...	...	...
	F	...-.-.	...-...	..-...-.	...	...-..	...	...-...	...	...
Spartanburg, S.C. (1,1)	P	153-129-40	22,696-31,774	Y-...-5	5,741	4,506-78	3,354	770-382	18	1,217
	F	68-66-40	19,713-27,597	Y-...-5	2,990	2,604-87	2,078	374-152	18	368
Springdale, Ark. (9,9)	P	49-26-43	17,280-22,056	None	2,418	1,815-75	1,497	188-130	244	359
	F	58-57-56	17,280-22,056	..-...-..	1,870	1,512-80	1,357	45-110	136	222
Springfield, Ore. (1,1)	P	76-54-40	27,948-33,528	None	6,040	5,110-84	3,658	922-530	50	880
	F	74-60-56	26,292-33,516	None	6,732	5,154-76	3,710	1,006-438	318	1,260
Stanton, Calif. (7,7)	P	...-.-.	...-...	..-...-.	...	...-..	...	...-...	...	...
	F	...-.-.	...-...	..-...-.	...	...-..	...	...-...	...	...
State College b, Pa. (1,2)	P	72-55-40	28,146-33,575	Y-35,329-5	3,191	2,760-86	2,275	174-311	82	349
	F	...-.-.	...-...	..-...-.	...	...-..	...	...-...	...	...
Stillwater, Okla. (1,1)	P	82-60-40	18,990-28,080	None	6,448	2,634-40	2,158	236-240	38	3,776
	F	70-68-56	18,326-27,084	None						
Stow, Ohio (1,1)	P	36-30-40	26,000-33,850	Y-35,360-5	2,191	1,881-85	1,463	257-161	4	306
	F	40-35-56	25,900-33,650	Y-35,100-5	2,309	2,097-90	1,576	369-152	9	203
Stratford t, Conn. (1,1)	P	116-97-32	29,819-35,956	Y-36,808-5	...	...-..	...	...-...	696	...
	F	94-93-42	30,165-37,328	Y-38,138-5	...	...-..	...	...-...	706	...
Streamwood v, Ill. (1,-)	P	69-47-40	29,782-39,683	Y-40,477-7	3,669	3,180-86	2,588	317-275	164	325
	F	36-34-51	28,190-37,914	None	2,103	1,826-86	1,521	161-144	146	131
Strongsville, Ohio (1,1)	P	63-54-40	21,594-...	Y-...-5	2,975	2,654-89	2,120	324-210	...	321
	F	37-36-53	25,538-...	Y-37,771-5	2,441	2,077-85	1,565	365-147	...	364
Sumter, S.C. (3,1)	P	103-73-40	17,234-23,428	None	...	...-..	...	...-...	...	...
	F	65-65-60	15,825-22,155	None	...	...-..	...	...-...	...	...
Superior, Wis. (1,1)	P	57-54-40	23,628-33,675	Y-34,139-5	...	...-..	...	...-...	...	...
	F	46-44-56	21,379-29,815	Y-32,302-5	...	...-..	...	...-...	...	...
Tamarac, Fla. (7,1)	P	...-.-.	...-...	..-...-.	...	...-..	...	...-...	...	...
	F	42-40-48	23,780-...	None	2,445	2,374-97	1,882	366-126	...	71
Teaneck tp, N.J. (1,1)	P	101-93-39	26,348-44,237	Y-...-4	...	...-..	...	...-...	...	...
	F	109-107-42	24,000-46,500	Y-...-4	...	...-..	...	...-...	...	...
Temple, Tex. (1,1)	P	120-100-40	20,106-28,865	None	4,592	3,830-83	3,200	435-195	128	634
	F	98-95-56	19,003-24,860	None	3,250	3,003-92	2,500	332-171	...	247
Temple City, Calif. (7,5)	P	...-.-..	...-...	..-...-.	...	...-..	...	...-...	...	...
	F	...-.-.	...-...	..-...-.	...	...-..	...	...-...	...	...
Texarkana, Tex. (1,1)	P	89-81-40	20,275-24,669	Y-25,869-1	3,199	2,655-82	2,224	271-160	...	544
	F	74-73-56	19,311-23,487	Y-24,687-1	1,628	1,500-92	1,240	124-136	8	120
Tigard, Ore. (1,5)	P	51-44-40	27,996-33,492	Y-36,841-5	1,743	1,593-91	1,143	329-121	61	89
	F	...-.-..	...-...	..-...-.	...	...-..	...	...-...	...	...
Tinley Park v, Ill. (1,2)	P	63-51-40	25,390-40,584	..-41,544-5	4,208	3,643-86	2,927	389-327	189	376
	F	...-.-..	...-...	..-...-.	...	...-..	...	...-...	...	...
Titusville, Fla. (1,1)	P	102-74-40	20,779-29,141	None	4,564	3,715-81	2,839	525-351	196	653
	F	55-54-56	20,297-26,849	Y-27,577-10	2,658	2,261-85	1,714	333-214	13	384
Tracy, Calif. (1,1)	P	54-37-40	30,672-37,272	None	1,743	1,584-90	1,278	150-156	18	141
	F	26-25-56	28,248-34,320	None	2,456	1,752-71	1,428	168-156	8	696
Tulare, Calif. (1,1)	P	54-40-40	26,000-31,000	None	3,476	2,697-77	1,951	303-443	198	581
	F	29-27-56	22,000-26,000	None	1,492	1,275-85	942	159-174	9	208
Turlock, Calif. (1,3)	P	76-60-40	28,044-41,040	None	4,992	4,386-87	3,288	696-402	142	464
	F	28-26-56	25,488-39,540	None	2,878	2,126-73	1,596	378-152	532	220
Union tp, Ohio (1,1)	P	40-27-40	24,128-29,972	None	1,789	1,343-75	971	192-180	203	243
	F	14-14-40	23,500-29,000	None	1,491	1,055-70	789	170-96	157	279
Union tp, Ohio (-,-)	P	50-39-40	25,086-31,100	Y-...-5	2,268	2,112-93	1,548	360-204	...	156
	F	13-...-42	25,459-35,139	Y-...-5	1,476	1,308-88	972	252-84	72	96
University City, Mo. (1,1)	P	95-76-40	27,066-33,298	Y-34,270-10	2,645	2,022-76	1,885	18-119	118	505
	F	47-46-..	27,408-...	Y-...-10	...	...-..	...	...-...	...	...
Upper Arlington, Ohio (4,4)	P	...-.-..	...-...	..-...-.	...	...-..	...	...-...	...	...
	F	...-.-..	...-...	..-...-.	...	...-..	...	...-...	...	...
Upper Merion tp, Pa. (1,2)	P	70-53-40	27,737-39,624	Y-42,124-5	5,136	3,747-72	2,740	323-684	118	1,271
	F	...-.-..	...-...	..-...-.	...	...-..	...	...-...	...	...
Upper Moreland tp, Pa. (1,3)	P	45-36-40	30,285-38,153	Y-41,116-5	2,148	1,944-90	1,752	132-60	...	204
	F	3-...-40	26,832-31,600	None	...	...-..	...	...-...	...	...
Urbana, Ill. (1,1)	P	55-43-..	30,200-31,100	Y-35,500-..	3,098	2,411-77	1,986	379-46	...	687
	F	43-42-..	29,200-...	Y-32,100-..	2,193	1,934-88	1,558	340-36	...	259
Valdosta, Ga. (1,1)	P	94-73-40	17,991-26,267	Y-32,570-5	4,084	3,326-81	2,724	432-170	10	748
	F	87-85-56	17,991-26,267	Y-32,570-5	3,454	3,342-96	2,750	436-156	4	108
Vancouver, Wash. (1,1)	P	114-94-40	32,136-41,016	None	5,200	4,491-86	3,854	249-388	128	581
	F	77-75-40	30,780-40,524	None	4,036	3,728-92	3,244	177-307	39	269
Victorville, Calif. (7,1)	P	...-.-..	...-...	..-...-.	...	...-..	...	...-...	...	...
	F	45-24-53	27,660-33,696	Y-35,100-5	55,999	2,376-4	2,064	228-84	...	53,623
Walla Walla, Wash. (1,1)	P	58-38-40	27,588-35,220	Y-35,604-..	2,651	2,210-83	1,812	141-257	84	357
	F	48-46-53	25,596-33,888	Y-34,272-..	2,609	2,138-81	1,816	103-219	73	398
Walnut, Calif. (7,7)	P	...-.-..	...-...	..-...-.	...	...-..	...	...-...	...	...

Table 3/23 continued **POLICE AND FIRE DEPARTMENT PERSONNEL, SALARIES, AND EXPENDITURES FOR CITIES 10,000 AND OVER: 1993**

City (Service provision)	Department	Total personnel, no. uniformed, duty hours per week	Entrance, maximum salary ($)	Longevity pay, maximum ($) no. years to receive longevity pay	Total expenditures (A) ($)	Total personnel expenditures (B) ($), % of (A)	Salaries and wages (C) ($)	City contrib. to employee retirement, insurance (D) ($)	Capital outlay (E) ($)	All other (F) ($)
25,000-49,999 continued										
Walnut, Calif. (7,7) cont.	F	...-..-..	...-...	..-...-..	...	...-..	...	..-...	...	...
Washington (Glcstr) tp, N.J. (1,5)	P	70-65-36	29,031-...	Y-...-5	9,397	8,130-86	6,271	693-1,166	36	1,231
	F	...-..-..	...-...	..-...-..	...	...-..	...	..-...	...	...
Watertown, N.Y. (1,1)	P	67-64-40	24,928-31,375	Y-32,425-6	2,046	1,962-95	1,408	392-162	34	50
	F	83-82-40	23,854-30,024	Y-31,074-6	2,607	2,511-96	1,725	572-214	20	76
Watsonville, Calif. (1,1)	P	61-54-40	32,064-40,920	Y-...-..	3,553	3,169-89	2,339	537-293	...	384
	F	29-28-56	28,812-40,464	Y-...-..	2,175	1,775-81	1,300	336-139	...	400
Wausau, Wis. (1,1)	P	69-54-39	24,681-29,856	Y-30,336-5	2,582	2,484-96	1,800	432-252	2	96
	F	61-59-56	24,090-27,532	Y-28,012-5	2,724	2,484-91	1,812	408-264	72	168
Wellesley t, Mass. (1,1)	P	...-..-40	28,919-33,055	Y-33,755-15	...	...-..	...	..-...	243	...
	F	...-..-42	27,809-31,780	Y-32,480-10	...	...-..	...	..-...	37	...
West Des Moines, Iowa (1,3)	P	45-33-40	23,543-31,193	Y-32,793-20	3,013	2,335-77	1,779	294-262	163	515
	F	20-19-48	23,545-31,197	Y-31,997-20	1,147	708-61	507	103-98	192	247
West Hollywood, Calif. (7,7)	P	...-..-..	...-...	..-...-..	...	...-..	...	..-...	...	...
	F	...-..-..	...-...	..-...-..	...	...-..	...	..-...	...	...
West Lafayette, Ind. (1,1)	P	50-37-40	25,828-28,855	None	1,802	1,630-90	1,381	155-94	6	166
	F	33-33-51	25,828-28,855	None	1,229	1,166-94	984	120-62	11	52
West Milford tp, N.J. (1,2)	P	50-10-..	33,817-45,494	Y-50,043-4	3,485	2,444-70	2,205	41-198	813	228
	F	...-..-..	...-...	..-...-..	...	...-..	...	..-...	...	...
West Orange tp, N.J. (1,1)	P	101-90-40	24,706-41,009	Y-45,110-5	...	...-..	...	..-...	...	...
	F	77-75-42	24,598-41,156	Y-45,272-5	...	...-..	...	..-...	...	...
West Sacramento, Calif. (1,1)	P	86-63-40	29,256-35,712	None	3,656	2,880-78	2,032	448-400	136	640
	F	58-53-56	29,088-36,276	None	2,685	2,397-89	1,504	544-349	...	288
West Springfield t, Mass. (1,1)	P	...-..-..	23,306-27,016	Y-27,466-5	...	...-..	...	..-...	78	...
	F	67-67-..	22,823-26,542	Y-26,992-5	...	...-..	...	..-...	218	...
Westfield, Mass. (1,1)	P	68-65-37	22,811-...	Y-24,180-5	2,448	2,271-92	2,261	6-4	5	172
	F	78-77-42	22,811-28,773	Y-...-5	2,959	2,832-95	2,821	7-4	2	125
Wethersfield t, Conn. (1,2)	P	49-44-40	28,388-38,412	Y-38,912-5	2,080	2,018-97	1,572	135-311	...	62
	F	...-..-..	...-...	..-...-..	...	...-..	...	..-...	...	...
Wheat Ridge, Colo. (1,5)	P	82-58-40	25,956-36,096	None	...	...-..	...	..-...	...	...
	F	...-..-..	...-...	..-...-..	...	...-..	...	..-...	...	...
Wheeling v, Ill. (1,1)	P	77-52-40	31,392-42,314	Y-42,914-12	3,893	3,375-86	2,997	142-236	160	358
	F	43-41-53	27,995-39,555	Y-40,055-12	...	...-..	...	..-...	284	...
Wheeling, W.Va. (1,1)	P	81-80-40	20,244-20,972	Y-21,692-3	4,218	3,939-93	2,910	555-474	93	186
	F	97-93-56	20,244-20,972	Y-21,692-3	4,036	3,592-88	2,834	352-406	46	398
White Plains, N.Y. (4,4)	P	...-..-..	...-...	..-...-..	...	...-..	...	..-...	...	...
	F	...-..-..	...-...	..-...-..	...	...-..	...	..-...	...	...
Williamsport, Pa. (4,4)	P	...-..-..	...-...	..-...-..	...	...-..	...	..-...	...	...
	F	...-..-..	...-...	..-...-..	...	...-..	...	..-...	...	...
Wilmette v, Ill. (1,1)	P	60-43-40	33,680-42,374	Y-46,517-..	3,570	3,102-86	2,592	222-288	90	378
	F	45-44-50	32,168-42,374	Y-46,517-..	2,886	2,690-93	2,268	206-216	90	106
Wilson, N.C. (1,1)	P	102-86-40	19,328-28,813	Y-30,253-5	4,461	3,189-71	2,586	422-181	374	898
	F	88-86-56	18,407-27,442	Y-28,814-5	3,267	2,775-84	2,281	333-161	71	421
Windsor t, Conn. (1,2)	P	58-16-40	31,525-52,531	Y-...-5	4,364	3,907-89	2,942	579-386	300	157
	F	...-..-..	...-...	..-...-..	...	...-..	...	..-...	...	...
Winona, Minn. (1,3)	P	38-35-..	27,254-34,380	Y-35,755-5	1,290	999-77	918	9-72	81	210
	F	29-28-..	26,388-31,106	Y-32,350-5	...	...-..	...	..-...	3	...
Woodland, Calif. (1,1)	P	71-65-..	31,008-37,728	None	5,323	3,938-73	3,000	588-350	37	1,348
	F	42-40-..	28,284-34,416	None	2,979	2,413-81	1,806	397-210	56	510
Woonsocket, R.I. (1,1)	P	120-105-37	21,215-29,015	Y-31,047-5	4,321	3,997-92	2,202	1,146-649	62	262
	F	138-137-42	20,756-29,934	Y-32,029-5	5,203	4,623-88	2,907	1,092-624	84	496
York, Pa. (1,1)	P	93-93-40	22,305-31,772	Y-34,949-5	5,254	4,551-86	3,765	393-393	...	703
	F	74-72-42	22,252-30,473	Y-32,713-5	3,661	3,030-82	2,438	332-260	...	631
Yucaipa, Calif. (7,5)	P	...-..-..	...-...	..-...-..	...	...-..	...	..-...	...	...
	F	...-..-..	...-...	..-...-..	...	...-..	...	..-...	...	...
10,000-24,999										
Abbeville t, La. (1,1)	P	36-36-42	10,692-...	Y-16,032-3	1,112	768-69	639	56-73	64	280
	F	34-33-56	11,720-...	Y-20,808-3	949	804-84	645	88-71	16	129
Aberdeen, Wash. (9,9)	P	49-38-40	19,718-22,776	Y-...-..	1,829	1,604-87	1,304	198-102	56	169
	F	44-44-56	18,393-21,567	Y-...-..	1,204	951-78	801	83-67	196	57
Ada, Okla. (1,1)	P	41-32-40	18,300-21,156	Y-22,356-4	1,395	1,209-86	954	167-88	59	127
	F	32-32-56	19,176-21,432	Y-22,632-4	1,061	952-89	786	80-86	40	69
Adrian, Mich. (3,1)	P	38-32-40	23,633-30,629	Y-31,629-20	1,776	1,644-92	1,476	12-156	...	132
	F	22-22-54	24,314-30,310	Y-31,310-20	...	...-..	...	..-...	...	...
Agoura Hills, Calif. (8,5)	P	...-..-..	...-...	..-...-..	...	...-..	...	..-...	...	...
	F	...-..-..	...-...	..-...-..	...	...-..	...	..-...	...	...
Albany, Calif. (3,1)	P	37-33-40	36,888-43,260	None	...	...-..	...	..-...	26	...
	F	20-20-56	34,428-41,880	None	...	...-..	...	..-...	17	...
Albemarle, N.C. (1,1)	P	48-41-42	18,241-29,868	Y-31,361-..	1,488	1,200-80	960	192-48	12	276
	F	41-40-56	18,241-29,868	Y-31,361-..	1,185	1,056-89	864	168-24	9	120
Albert Lea, Minn. (1,3)	P	37-7-40	30,597-34,362	None	1,892	1,581-83	1,273	202-106	1	310
	F	21-..-56	23,442-31,450	Y-33,337-5	1,353	1,140-84	816	262-62	41	172
Albertville, Ala. (1,1)	P	36-27-42	13,315-20,674	None	...	...-..	...	..-...	23	...
	F	26-26-53	14,909-23,290	None	...	...-..	...	..-...	2	...

Table 3/23 continued   **POLICE AND FIRE DEPARTMENT PERSONNEL, SALARIES, AND EXPENDITURES FOR CITIES 10,000 AND OVER: 1993**

City (Service provision)	Department	Total personnel, no. uniformed, duty hours per week	Entrance, maximum salary ($)	Longevity pay, maximum ($) no. years to receive longevity pay	Reported expenditures (in thousands)					
					Total expenditures (A) ($)	Total personnel expenditures (B) ($), % of (A)	Salaries and wages (C) ($)	City contrib. to employee retirement, insurance (D) ($)	Capital outlay (E) ($)	All other (F) ($)
10,000-24,999 continued										
Albion, Mich. (4,4)	P	...-..-..	...-...	..-"-..	...	...-"..	...	...-"..	...	...
	F	...-..-..	...-...	..-"-..	...	...-"..	...	...-"..	...	...
Algonquin v, Ill. (1,5)	P	...-..-..	...-...	..-"-..	...	...-"..	...	...-"..	...	...
	F	...-..-..	...-...	..-"-..	...	...-"..	...	...-"..	...	...
Aliquippa b, Pa. (1,3)	P	19-19-40	12,000-25,368	Y-26,418-5	...	...-"..	...	...-"..	...	...
	F	9-9-42	12,000-25,246	Y-26,296-5	...	...-"..	...	...	...	...
Allen, Tex. (3,3)	P	36-25-..	23,808-30,960	Y-...-1	1,692	1,491-88	1,170	165-156	...	201
	F	30-29-..	22,344-29,040	Y-...-1	1,293	1,233-95	963	135-135	...	60
Allouez v, Wis. (7,3)	P	...-..-..	...-"..	..-"-..	...	...-"..	...	...-"..	...	...
	F	13-13-..	29,676-33,975	Y-34,286-5	...	...-"..	...	...-"..	8	...
Alpena, Mich. (1,1)	P	22-17-40	20,862-24,419	Y-25,884-8	1,021	798-78	655	49-94	70	153
	F	24-..-56	22,917-26,557	Y-28,150-8	1,327	1,050-79	868	52-130	49	228
Alpharetta, Ga. (1,3)	P	41-26-43	20,485-28,920	..-"-..	1,623	1,103-67	860	85-158	135	385
	F	13-12-53	20,485-28,920	..-"-..	789	540-68	432	41-67	22	227
Alvin, Tex. (1,2)	P	41-33-40	21,366-34,924	Y-...-1	1,725	1,413-81	1,218	182-13	84	228
	F	...-..-..	...-"..	..-"-..	...	...-"..	...	...-"..	...	...
American Fork, Utah (1,2)	P	19-17-40	20,640-...	None	864	746-86	537	131-78	14	104
	F	...-..-..	...-...	..-"-..	...	...-"..	...	...-"..	...	...
Amherst, Ohio (1,2)	P	15-15-40	23,057-28,729	Y-...-..	816	807-98	612	70-125	...	9
	F	...-..-..	...-...	..-"-..	...	...-"..	...	...-"..	...	...
Andover, Minn. (7,2)	P	...-..-..	...-...	..-"-..	...	...-"..	...	...-"..	...	...
	F	...-..-..	...-...	..-"-..	...	...-"..	...	...-"..	...	...
Andrews, Tex. (1,2)	P	14-13-40	19,452-28,428	Y-29,628-1	386	324-83	258	54-12	2	60
	F	...-..-..	...-...	..-"-..	...	...-"..	...	...-"..	...	...
Anoka, Minn. (1,3)	P	34-26-40	32,000-39,000	Y-42,000-4	1,981	1,700-85	1,444	170-86	14	267
	F	4-..-56	33,000-37,000	None	472	328-69	283	32-13	18	126
Apache Junction, Ariz. (1,5)	P	52-37-40	25,147-37,710	None	2,896	2,472-85	1,966	274-232	76	348
	F	...-..-..	...-...	..-"-..	...	...-"..	...	...-"..	...	...
Apopka, Fla. (1,3)	P	50-44-40	20,167-...	Y-...-..	...	...-"..	...	...-"..	...	...
	F	60-40-56	20,772-...	Y-...-..	...	...-"..	...	...-"..	...	...
Arcata, Calif. (3,5)	P	27-27-40	25,104-30,528	Y-32,054-5	2,265	1,980-87	1,692	180-108	1	284
	F	...-..-..	...-...	..-"-..	...	...-"..	...	...-"..	...	...
Ardmore, Okla. (1,1)	P	44-44-40	17,808-18,456	Y-...-..	...	...-"..	...	...-"..	59	...
	F	36-36-48	15,084-16,632	Y-...-..	...	...-"..	...	...-"..	82	...
Arkansas City, Kan. (1,1)	P	28-21-40	19,762-25,289	Y-...-3	1,231	1,038-84	788	127-123	67	126
	F	24-23-56	17,925-22,938	Y-...-3	1,076	929-86	685	116-128	69	78
Arnold, Mo. (1,5)	P	49-38-40	22,194-29,806	Y-30,998-10	2,129	1,809-84	1,410	219-180	135	185
	F	...-..-..	...-...	..-"-..	...	...-"..	...	...-"..	...	...
Artesia, Calif. (7,7)	P	...-..-..	...-...	..-"-..	...	...-"..	...	...-"..	...	...
	F	...-..-..	...-...	..-"-..	...	...-"..	...	...-"..	...	...
Artesia, N.M. (3,3)	P	35-26-40	20,664-25,344	Y-57,600-6	845	675-79	550	79-46	1	169
	F	18-17-53	20,664-25,344	Y-57,600-6	482	410-85	340	47-23	...	72
Asbury Park, N.J. (1,1)	P	64-56-40	23,000-39,759	Y-43,353-5	2,778	2,428-87	1,974	92-362	...	350
	F	47-42-42	28,135-43,057	Y-45,932-10	2,501	2,224-88	1,871	87-266	...	277
Asheboro, N.C. (1,1)	P	54-45-42	18,952-26,032	Y-28,635-3	1,668	1,458-87	1,163	185-110	48	162
	F	39-38-56	18,952-26,032	Y-28,635-3	1,224	1,125-91	932	115-78	...	99
Ashland t, Mass. (1,1)	P	20-19-37	24,973-31,576	Y-32,076-5	...	...-"..	...	...-"..	48	...
	F	15-14-42	29,829-31,746	Y-32,246-5	...	...-"..	...	...-"..	15	...
Ashland, Ohio (1,3)	P	39-29-40	22,672-27,602	None	1,794	1,542-85	1,224	218-100	48	204
	F	37-32-53	24,032-26,540	None	1,672	1,505-90	1,146	263-96	42	125
Ashland, Ore. (3,1)	P	32-24-40	26,826-31,812	None	2,087	1,587-76	1,170	229-188	9	491
	F	25-24-56	23,694-29,064	None	1,484	1,053-70	784	153-116	125	306
Ashtabula, Ohio (1,1)	P	40-34-40	22,869-...	Y-25,458-..	...	...-"..	...	...-"..	50	...
	F	26-26-56	27,297-28,613	Y-30,113-..	...	...-"..	...	...-"..	15	...
Aston tp, Pa. (1,2)	P	19-17-40	...-"..	Y-...-3	1,723	1,380-80	988	243-149	47	296
	F	...-..-..	...-"..	..-"-..	...	...-"..	...	...-"..	...	...
Astoria, Ore. (1,1)	P	24-16-..	22,740-27,348	Y-28,488-5	1,404	1,026-73	719	225-82	222	156
	F	19-18-..	22,644-27,216	Y-28,572-5	1,107	885-79	646	194-45	42	180
Atchison, Kan. (1,1)	P	31-22-40	17,000-22,000	Y-...-5	1,248	974-78	767	101-106	68	206
	F	29-29-56	17,000-22,000	Y-...-5	912	779-85	630	60-89	21	112
Athens, Tex. (1,1)	P	28-22-40	15,600-20,678	Y-...-1	935	708-75	596	66-46	40	187
	F	16-16-40	15,600-20,678	Y-...-1	632	512-81	433	48-31	6	114
Athol t, Mass. (4,4)	P	...-..-..	...-"..	..-"-..	...	...-"..	...	...-"..	...	...
	F	...-..-..	...-"..	..-"-..	...	...-"..	...	...-"..	...	...
Atlantic Beach, Fla. (1,3)	P	31-23-40	22,764-32,785	None	1,331	1,208-90	1,004	136-68	10	113
	F	14-14-53	20,224-27,422	None	450	401-89	335	36-30	8	41
Atwater, Calif. (1,3)	P	28-21-40	22,944-29,280	None	1,560	1,421-91	978	210-233	...	139
	F	8-8-56	19,740-25,188	None	452	404-89	276	68-60	...	48
Auburn, Calif. (1,3)	P	28-23-40	26,000-31,600	Y-34,760-7	...	...-"..	...	...-"..	386	...
	F	3-3-40	24,000-28,000	Y-31,000-7	...	...-"..	...	...-"..	49	...
Auburn, Me. (1,1)	P	52-52-40	18,565-23,712	Y-24,212-7	2,325	1,978-85	1,546	208-224	126	221
	F	69-69-42	17,785-21,385	Y-21,885-7	2,690	2,485-92	1,921	259-305	6	199
Auburn t, Mass. (1,3)	P	29-24-37	23,613-30,194	None	654	582-88	537	3-42	15	57
	F	5-4-50	28,370-34,450	None	...	...-"..	...	...-"..	...	...

Table 3/23 continued

POLICE AND FIRE DEPARTMENT PERSONNEL, SALARIES, AND EXPENDITURES FOR CITIES 10,000 AND OVER: 1993

10,000-24,999 continued

City (Service provision)	Department	Total personnel, no. uniformed, duty hours per week	Entrance, maximum salary ($)	Longevity pay, maximum ($), no. years to receive longevity pay	Reported expenditures (in thousands) Total expenditures (A) ($)	Total personnel expenditures (B) ($), % of (A)	Salaries and wages (C) ($)	City contrib. to employee retirement, insurance (D) ($)	Capital outlay (E) ($)	All other (F) ($)
Augusta, Me. (1,1)	P	47-39-42	20,540-24,804	Y-28,028-5	...	...-.	...	...-...	...	...
	F	41-40-48	20,644-24,388	None	...	...-.	...	...-...	...	...
Avondale, Ariz. (3,3)	P	40-27-40	19,802-26,562	None	791	701-88	555	73-73	...	90
	F	15-15-56	19,802-26,562	None	253	217-85	184	9-24	...	36
Babylon v, N.Y. (7,2)	P	...-.-..	...-...	..-.-..	...	...-.	...	...-...	...	...
	F	...-.-..	...-...	.-.-..	...	...-.	...	...-...	...	...
Bainbridge, Ga. (4,4)	P	...-.-..	...-...	.-.-..	...	...-.	...	...-...	...	...
	F	...-.-..	...-...	.-.-..	...	...-.	...	...-...	...	...
Baker, La. (1,1)	P	29-29-..	17,712-24,648	..-...-..	882	816-92	684	65-67	...	66
	F	15-15-..	17,712-24,648	..-...-..	486	457-94	381	32-44	...	29
Baldwin b, Pa. (1,2)	P	22-22-40	26,020-35,643	Y-37,425-5	...	...-.	...	...-...	309	...
	F	...-.-..	...-...	..	...	...-.	...	...-...	...	...
Ballwin, Mo. (1,5)	P	52-42-37	22,000-36,085	None	2,338	1,902-81	1,553	228-121	52	384
	F	...-.-..	...-...	.-...-..	...	...-.	...	...-...	...	...
Banning, Calif. (1,1)	P	43-29-40	29,229-35,528	..-...-..	1,596	1,381-86	930	370-81	30	185
	F	22-20-56	27,149-33,000	Y-33,600-5	953	838-87	606	188-44	1	114
Barstow, Calif. (1,5)	P	51-37-40	31,956-38,268	None	1,875	1,591-84	1,324	88-179	26	258
	F	...-.-..	...-...	.-...-..	...	...-.	...	...-...	...	...
Bartlett v, Ill. (1,5)	P	42-31-43	27,206-40,216	Y-42,203-..	6,607	1,562-23	1,274	97-191	4,166	879
	F	...-.-..	...-...	.-...-..	...	...-.	...	...-...	...	...
Bartow, Fla. (1,3)	P	56-41-40	27,928-...	Y-28,487-..	2,484	2,218-89	1,760	331-127	66	200
	F	13-13-48	25,715-...	Y-26,744-..	747	649-86	521	94-34	2	96
Batavia, Ill. (1,3)	P	39-33-..	26,483-40,186	None	...	...-.	...	...-...	...	...
	F	14-13-..	27,116-36,739	None	...	...-.	...	...-...	...	...
Batavia, N.Y. (1,1)	P	37-32-40	25,679-32,760	Y-33,760-5	1,838	1,744-94	1,262	325-157	17	77
	F	42-41-40	25,612-31,503	Y-32,503-5	2,125	2,020-95	1,461	369-190	21	84
Beachwood, Ohio (1,3)	P	39-31-40	30,756-36,348	Y-37,548-..	2,713	2,329-85	1,757	329-243	133	251
	F	32-32-53	31,986-37,802	Y-39,002-..	2,182	1,841-84	1,333	308-200	117	224
Beatrice, Nebr. (1,3)	P	27-20-40	20,316-25,932	None	929	821-88	662	84-75	3	105
	F	17-17-56	19,356-27,228	None	684	596-87	489	56-51	33	55
Beaver Falls, Pa. (1,3)	P	17-17-40	24,488-27,652	Y-27,789-5	1,096	1,022-93	641	255-126	22	52
	F	8-8-53	25,845-26,931	Y-27,068-5	473	431-91	251	120-60	...	42
Bedford t, Mass. (1,1)	P	27-26-37	27,527-30,726	Y-33,279-5	...	...-.	...	...-...	...	...
	F	23-22-42	29,985-33,185	Y-35,735-5	...	...-.	...	...-...	5	...
Bedford t, N.H. (1,3)	P	23-15-40	26,353-32,032	Y-33,532-5	804	756-94	630	60-66	...	48
	F	11-11-42	20,600-26,754	None	366	360-98	264	36-60	...	6
Bedford, Ohio (1,1)	P	27-27-40	...-...	Y-...-5	1,682	1,605-95	1,375	6-224	...	77
	F	20-20-48	...-...	Y-...-5	898	896-99	760	2-134	...	2
Bellaire, Tex. (1,1)	P	49-13-40	22,800-30,810	Y-32,010-25	2,285	1,837-80	1,444	143-250	72	376
	F	21-21-56	21,190-28,600	Y-29,800-25	993	790-79	670	68-52	67	136
Belle Glade, Fla. (1,3)	P	56-46-40	22,193-...	..-...-..	2,605	2,188-83	1,689	226-273	38	379
	F	16-15-52	19,160-...	..-...-..	781	652-83	520	57-75	39	90
Bellefontaine, Ohio (1,1)	P	29-22-40	22,350-29,000	Y-31,000-17	1,279	1,036-81	825	128-83	55	188
	F	16-16-56	22,350-29,000	Y-31,000-17	772	684-88	495	136-53	21	67
Bellefontaine Neighbors, Mo. (1,5)	P	24-24-..	20,268-25,596	None	...	...-.	...	...-...	...	...
	F	...-.-..	...-...	..-...-..	...	...-.	...	...-...	...	...
Belmont, Calif. (1,5)	P	41-29-40	37,428-50,052	None	...	...-.	...	...-...	...	...
	F	...-.-..	...-...	..-...-..	...	...-.	...	...-...	...	...
Belmont t, Mass. (1,1)	P	54-46-37	27,095-31,266	None	...	...-.	...	...-...	...	...
	F	64-57-48	29,877-30,077	None	...	...-.	...	...-...	...	...
Belton, Mo. (1,1)	P	37-28-40	21,829-29,254	Y-...-8	...	...-.	...	...-...	37	...
	F	21-20-53	20,790-27,861	Y-...-8	...	...-.	...	...-...	2	...
Belton, Tex. (1,3)	P	19-10-40	16,536-25,750	Y-...-1	867	656-75	527	82-47	23	188
	F	16-15-56	16,482-25,750	Y-...-1	541	417-77	340	51-26	13	111
Belvidere, Ill. (1,1)	P	27-25-42	23,480-29,498	Y-31,194-2	973	850-87	688	100-62	42	81
	F	20-20-56	23,480-29,498	Y-31,194-2	864	747-86	522	179-46	57	60
Bemidji, Minn. (1,3)	P	23-19-40	27,103-32,183	None	1,027	1,019-99	843	111-65	...	8
	F	6-6-48	24,852-28,260	None	219	204-93	168	20-16	...	15
Benbrook, Tex. (1,3)	P	40-31-40	26,229-31,881	Y-34,319-..	736	662-89	535	82-45	11	63
	F	4-..-40	30,148-36,645	Y-37,378-1	190	138-72	117	15-6	3	49
Bend, Ore. (1,1)	P	54-41-40	29,376-35,736	Y-42,024-..	3,616	2,994-82	2,196	531-267	92	530
	F	49-46-56	25,668-32,784	Y-38,700-..	3,662	3,037-82	2,254	533-250	111	514
Benicia, Calif. (1,1)	P	48-33-40	35,000-43,000	None	3,034	2,724-89	2,233	259-232	74	236
	F	36-35-56	31,500-38,000	None	2,502	2,220-88	1,800	222-198	47	235
Benton, Ark. (-,1)	P	32-28-42	15,840-19,781	None	1,216	1,024-84	830	103-91	63	129
	F	43-43-53	15,086-18,840	None	1,571	1,462-93	1,187	243-32	19	90
Bergenfield b, N.J. (3,3)	P	55-48-40	25,508-51,509	Y-55,630-5	1,848	1,812-98	1,482	132-198	...	36
	F	6-6-45	31,122-51,085	Y-55,172-5	324	192-59	156	12-24	...	132
Berkeley, Mo. (1,1)	P	39-39-40	24,831-36,686	None	2,099	1,948-92	1,600	236-112	...	151
	F	27-27-56	23,648-34,052	None	1,314	1,232-93	1,100	65-67	...	82
Berkeley Heights tp, N.J. (1,2)	P	31-25-40	28,924-41,129	Y-47,750-2	2,083	1,928-92	1,389	282-257	...	155
	F	...-.-..	...-...	..-...-..	...	...-.	...	...-...	...	...
Berkley, Mich. (4,4)	P	...-.-..	...-...	...-.-..	...	...-.	...	...-...	...	...
	F	...-.-..	...-...	..-...-..	...	...-.	...	...-...	...	...

Table 3/23 continued   POLICE AND FIRE DEPARTMENT PERSONNEL, SALARIES, AND EXPENDITURES FOR CITIES 10,000 AND OVER: 1993

					Reported expenditures (in thousands)					
City (Service provision)	Department	Total personnel, no. uniformed, duty hours per week	Entrance, maximum salary ($)	Longevity pay, maximum ($) no. years to receive longevity pay	Total expenditures (A) ($)	Total personnel expenditures (B) ($), % of (A)	Salaries and wages (C) ($)	City contrib. to employee retirement, insurance (D) ($)	Capital outlay (E) ($)	All other (F) ($)

10,000-24,999 continued

City (Service provision)	Dept	Personnel	Entrance, max salary	Longevity pay	(A)	(B)	(C)	(D)	(E)	(F)
Berlin t, Conn. (1,2)	P	51-42-40	31,237-38,110	Y-38,610-5	1,798	1,629-90	1,208	189-232	113	56
	F	...-...-..	...-...	..-...-..	...	...-..	...	...-..	...	...
Berlin, N.H. (1,3)	P	...-...-..	...-...	..-...-..	...	...-..	...	...-..	...	...
	F	...-...-..	...-...	..-...-..	...	...-..	...	...-..	...	...
Berwick b, Pa. (1,2)	P	15-11-40	15,000-26,582	Y-...-1	...	...-..	...	...-..	39	...
	F	...-...-..	...-...	..-...-..	...	...-..	...	...-..	...	...
Bethany, Okla. (1,1)	P	33-23-41	19,626-25,212	Y-26,112-5	1,526	1,376-90	1,018	166-192	14	136
	F	25-24-56	19,170-23,700	Y-24,600-5	1,096	1,046-95	804	90-152	4	46
Bethlehem tp, Pa. (1,2)	P	21-20-35	27,190-30,940	Y-31,940-5	1,205	1,068-88	788	157-123	30	107
	F	...-...-..	...-...	..-...-..	...	...-..	...	...-..	...	...
Beverly Hills v, Mich. (4,4)	P	...-...-..	...-...	..-...-..	...	...-..	...	...-..	...	...
	F	...-...-..	...-...	..-...-..	...	...-..	...	...-..	...	...
Big Rapids, Mich. (1,3)	P	15-14-48	24,000-28,000	Y-28,700-5	1,173	784-66	599	153-32	5	384
	F	9-9-56	23,000-26,000	Y-26,700-5	466	394-84	282	75-37	2	70
Birmingham, Mich. (1,1)	P	56-37-40	24,701-38,816	Y-42,698-5	1,961	1,692-86	1,303	152-237	29	240
	F	40-38-56	24,937-38,135	Y-41,949-5	1,435	1,241-86	950	104-187	10	184
Bloomingdale v, Ill. (1,5)	P	53-35-40	29,100-...	None	3,142	2,609-83	2,234	178-197	184	349
	F	...-...-..	...-...	..-...-..	...	...-..	...	...-..	...	...
Blue Ash, Ohio (4,1)	P	...-...-..	...-...	..-...-..	...	...-..	...	...-..	...	...
	F	...-...-..	...-...	..-...-..	...	...-..	...	...-..	...	...
Bogalusa, La. (1,1)	P	44-44-40	12,909-15,420	Y-...-20	1,385	1,315-94	1,110	100-105	...	70
	F	36-36-55	12,909-15,420	Y-...-20	2,603	2,577-99	893	1,595-89	...	26
Boone, Iowa (1,1)	P	15-14-42	22,074-27,285	Y-30,186-3	730	655-89	584	13-58	...	75
	F	13-13-53	21,507-26,597	Y-27,560-3	515	467-90	393	11-63	14	34
Boone t, N.C. (1,3)	P	31-31-42	20,221-27,195	Y-...-..	738	600-81	466	71-63	29	109
	F	5-5-40	...-...	None	220	97-44	79	12-6	61	62
Borger, Tex. (1,1)	P	28-20-40	19,524-24,996	Y-26,196-1	1,085	950-87	727	104-119	1	134
	F	22-22-54	18,600-23,808	Y-25,008-1	730	682-93	537	74-71	8	40
Bothell, Wash. (1,3)	P	44-30-40	30,516-39,936	None	2,678	1,882-70	1,604	257-21	152	644
	F	25-23-40	28,560-40,812	Y-42,036-15	2,124	1,797-84	1,471	130-196	40	287
Boulder City, Nev. (-,-)	P	27-22-40	27,313-35,646	Y-39,212-6	1,656	1,457-87	1,086	248-123	31	168
	F	15-14-56	26,705-34,472	Y-37,919-6	880	779-88	584	130-65	31	70
Bourbonnais v, Ill. (1,5)	P	22-16-40	22,651-34,528	Y-...-..	1,173	918-78	764	77-77	12	243
	F	...-...-..	...-...	..-...-..	...	...-..	...	...-..	...	...
Bourne t, Mass. (1,1)	P	32-28-37	21,276-28,891	Y-29,366-..	...	...-..	...	...-..	...	...
	F	26-25-42	20,650-28,510	Y-29,035-10	...	...-..	...	...-..	258	...
Bozeman, Mont. (1,1)	P	26-26-40	18,744-26,892	Y-29,052-1	1,307	1,140-87	940	95-105	61	106
	F	24-24-48	18,726-27,432	Y-30,132-1	1,111	984-88	820	84-80	6	121
Brainerd, Minn. (1,2)	P	22-18-40	27,196-30,522	Y-31,566-10	1,027	733-71	603	46-84	...	294
	F	...-...-..	...-...	..-...-..	...	...-..	...	...-..	...	...
Brenham, Tex. (1,3)	P	39-27-40	21,000-33,000	Y-35,000-1	1,322	1,120-84	914	109-97	19	183
	F	9-..-53	...-...	..-...-1	485	346-71	286	34-26	7	132
Brentwood b, Pa. (-,2)	P	11-11-40	14,070-32,918	Y-34,564-5	891	786-88	635	68-83	14	91
	F	...-...-..	...-...	..-...-..	...	...-..	...	...-..	...	...
Brentwood, Tenn. (1,1)	P	46-36-40	17,500-32,200	Y-...-5	2,306	1,856-80	1,558	174-124	178	272
	F	41-40-..	17,500-29,100	Y-...-5	2,076	1,496-72	1,240	138-118	32	548
Bridge View v, Ill. (3,3)	P	46-39-41	25,576-34,502	None	...	...-..	...	...-..	...	...
	F	33-32-40	25,116-35,346	Y-39,920-..	...	...-..	...	...-..	...	...
Bridgeton, Mo. (1,5)	P	67-56-40	27,726-33,842	None	3,514	3,017-85	2,422	326-269	196	301
	F	...-...-..	...-...	..-...-..	...	...-..	...	...-..	...	...
Brigantine, N.J. (1,1)	P	35-30-..	25,304-39,273	Y-43,200-5	4,337	4,207-97	1,691	2,264-252	30	100
	F	31-30-..	26,852-39,763	Y-43,740-5	1,913	1,741-91	1,313	205-223	75	97
Brigham City, Utah (1,2)	P	26-21-40	23,268-...	Y-25,097-1	1,390	1,206-86	920	160-126	72	112
	F	...-...-..	...-...	..-...-..	...	...-..	...	...-..	...	...
Bristol t, R.I. (1,2)	P	35-35-37	26,292-29,720	Y-33,366-5	1,993	1,404-70	1,066	185-153	45	544
	F	...-...-..	...-...	..-...-..	...	...-..	...	...-..	...	...
Bristol, Tenn. (1,1)	P	61-54-40	16,500-23,195	Y-23,890-10	1,865	1,521-81	1,237	162-122	99	245
	F	45-40-56	16,500-23,195	Y-23,890-10	1,607	1,443-89	1,175	156-112	44	120
Bristol, Va. (1,1)	P	58-43-40	18,063-24,638	Y-25,638-25	1,931	1,649-85	1,266	276-107	25	257
	F	48-47-53	18,063-24,638	Y-25,638-25	1,817	1,625-89	1,227	275-123	25	167
Broadview Heights, Ohio (1,2)	P	29-29-40	25,000-33,000	Y-...-5	...	...-..	...	...-..	65	...
	F	...-...-..	...-...	..-...-..	...	...-..	...	...-..	...	...
Brook Park, Ohio (1,1)	P	42-42-40	28,229-33,021	Y-33,221-3	...	...-..	...	...-..	...	...
	F	35-35-48	28,229-33,021	Y-33,221-5	...	...-..	...	...-..	...	...
Brookfield v, Ill. (1,1)	P	27-21-40	24,284-37,926	None	...	...-..	...	...-..	...	...
	F	16-15-52	24,572-37,926	None	...	...-..	...	...-..	...	...
Broomfield, Colo. (1,-)	P	56-41-..	26,220-38,616	None	2,861	2,432-85	2,010	221-201	178	251
	F	...-...-..	...-...	..-...-..	...	...-..	...	...-..	...	...
Brown Deer v, Wis. (1,1)	P	36-28-40	27,983-35,700	None	1,813	1,631-89	1,257	356-18	79	103
	F	17-17-56	28,215-35,913	None	965	725-75	600	117-8	21	219
Brownsville t, Tenn. (1,1)	P	23-23-40	13,700-...	None	...	...-..	...	...-..	...	...
	F	19-19-53	13,700-...	None	...	...-..	...	...-..	...	...
Brownwood, Tex. (1,1)	P	41-29-40	18,756-32,652	Y-33,252-1	1,079	939-87	765	124-50	35	105
	F	30-30-..	18,276-30,888	Y-31,704-1	860	793-92	641	110-42	4	63

Table 3/23 continued   POLICE AND FIRE DEPARTMENT PERSONNEL, SALARIES, AND EXPENDITURES FOR CITIES 10,000 AND OVER: 1993

City (Service provision)	Department	Total personnel, no. uniformed, duty hours per week	Entrance, maximum salary ($)	Longevity pay, maximum ($), no. years to receive longevity pay	Reported expenditures (in thousands)					
					Total expenditures (A) ($)	Total personnel expenditures (B) ($), % of (A)	Salaries and wages (C) ($)	City contrib. to employee retirement, insurance (D) ($)	Capital outlay (E) ($)	All other (F) ($)
10,000-24,999 continued										
Brunswick, Ga. (1,1)	P	82-65-43	17,804-25,667	None	2,555	2,303-90	2,051	164-88	22	230
	F	43-42-53	17,804-25,667	None	1,474	1,338-90	1,208	89-41	22	114
Bucyrus, Ohio (1,1)	P	24-18-40	23,962-26,374	Y-27,574-3	1,428	1,192-83	635	461-96	...	236
	F	14-14-..	20,275-25,240	Y-26,440-3	866	846-97	422	357-67	...	20
Burleson, Tex. (1,2)	P	40-32-40	22,693-31,762	Y-32,962-1	1,088	876-80	740	80-56	4	208
	F	...-..-..	...-...	..-...-..	...	...-..	...	...-...	...	...
Cadillac, Mich. (1,1)	P	21-17-40	25,099-28,027	Y-28,577-3	1,138	948-83	663	171-114	80	110
	F	10-10-53	23,510-26,092	Y-26,867-3	668	617-92	424	120-73	8	43
Caln tp, Pa. (1,2)	P	15-15-40	32,509-47,350	Y-...-5	2,665	743-27	598	70-75	4	1,918
	F	...-..-..	...-...	..-...-..	...	...-..	...	...-...	...	...
Cambridge, Md. (1,2)	P	50-39-37	19,642-25,700	None	1,144	1,038-90	817	160-61	20	86
	F	...-..-..	...-...	..-...-..	...	...-..	...	...-...	...	...
Camden, Ark. (1,1)	P	40-28-43	16,775-18,868	Y-...-..	1,706	1,526-89	1,252	118-156	...	180
	F	30-29-53	15,704-19,570	Y-...-..	1,392	1,248-89	1,056	72-120	...	144
Canandaigua, N.Y. (1,3)	P	31-25-37	25,670-30,691	Y-31,391-5	1,548	1,350-87	1,039	219-92	48	150
	F	16-16-40	23,114-29,474	Y-30,174-5	1,391	843-60	648	127-68	445	103
Canon City, Colo. (1,5)	P	32-22-40	21,986-26,796	Y-27,646-5	573	537-93	438	36-63	3	33
	F	...-..-..	...-...	..-...-..	...	...-..	...	...-...	...	...
Canton, Ill. (1,1)	P	28-20-40	20,860-29,800	Y-...-25	914	822-89	615	97-110	24	68
	F	16-15-56	21,080-27,830	Y-...-15	596	558-93	389	104-65	1	37
Canton t, Mass. (1,1)	P	41-39-40	24,400-28,800	Y-29,300-5	2,276	2,052-90	1,700	102-250	109	115
	F	43-42-40	24,400-28,800	..-29,300-5	2,317	2,052-88	1,700	102-250	142	123
Canyon, Tex. (1,3)	P	16-14-40	19,356-26,040	Y-27,240-1	441	393-89	327	45-21	6	42
	F	4-3-40	18,432-24,780	Y-25,980-1	...	...-..	...	...-...	...	...
Carlisle b, Pa. (1,2)	P	35-30-40	23,781-30,237	Y-...-4	1,667	1,424-85	1,278	54-92	48	195
	F	...-..-..	...-...	..-...-..	...	...-..	...	...-...	...	...
Carlsbad, N.M. (1,1)	P	70-48-..	18,000-27,726	None	2,849	2,503-87	1,902	430-171	...	346
	F	40-38-..	24,710-26,272	None	1,915	1,713-89	1,288	310-115	...	202
Carpentersville v, Ill. (1,5)	P	46-41-40	29,736-39,996	Y-40,596-1	2,712	2,204-81	1,857	192-155	100	408
	F	...-..-..	...-...	..-...-..	...	...-..	...	...-...	...	...
Carpinteria, Calif. (-,5)	P	16-14-..	...-...	..-...-..	...	...-..	...	...-...	...	...
	F	...-..-..	...-...	..-...-..	...	...-..	...	...-...	...	...
Carrboro t, N.C. (1,3)	P	29-2-42	21,891-33,152	None	...	...-..	...	...-...	...	...
	F	12-12-56	20,848-31,573	None	...	...-..	...	...-...	...	...
Carteret b, N.J. (1,3)	P	61-53-40	33,401-41,924	Y-58,623-4	...	...-..	...	...-...	...	...
	F	18-18-42	32,640-41,924	Y-58,623-4	...	...-..	...	...-...	...	...
Cartersville, Ga. (4,4)	P	...-..-..	...-...	..-...-..	...	...-..	...	...-...	...	...
	F	...-..-..	...-...	..-...-..	...	...-..	...	...-...	...	...
Carthage, Mo. (1,1)	P	26-20-42	18,360-21,252	None	1,037	849-81	693	81-75	36	152
	F	21-21-56	18,360-21,252	None	822	685-83	555	62-68	17	120
Casa Grande, Ariz. (3,1)	P	59-41-..	25,992-35,808	None	1,692	1,465-86	1,206	163-96	4	223
	F	13-12-..	25,992-35,808	None	738	620-84	569	24-27	5	113
Casselberry, Fla. (3,3)	P	50-44-40	21,973-31,358	Y-...-11	2,403	2,165-90	1,528	501-136	120	118
	F	21-20-56	21,172-30,188	Y-...-11	1,999	1,649-82	1,167	396-86	233	117
Cedar City, Utah (1,3)	P	18-17-..	20,424-32,651	None	841	689-81	488	115-86	41	111
	F	1-1-..	20,424-32,651	None	248	168-67	134	22-12	...	80
Cedar Hill, Tex. (3,3)	P	40-32-40	21,028-29,544	Y-...-1	2,092	1,524-72	1,118	161-245	72	496
	F	22-21-56	21,028-29,544	Y-...-1	1,074	835-77	620	89-126	49	190
Center tp, Pa. (-,2)	P	9-9-40	20,800-31,532	Y-31,832-5	...	...-..	...	...-...	...	...
	F	...-..-..	...-...	..-...-..	...	...-..	...	...-...	...	...
Centerville, Ohio (1,9)	P	39-31-40	27,528-35,984	Y-36,384-6	2,208	1,948-88	1,724	8-216	...	260
	F	...-..-..	...-...	..-...-..	...	...-..	...	...-...	...	...
Centerville, Utah (1,6)	P	10-10-43	21,672-25,884	None	...	...-..	...	...-...	39	...
	F	...-..-..	...-...	..-...-..	...	...-..	...	...-...	...	...
Central Falls, R.I. (1,1)	P	38-..-..	20,530-...	Y-26,364-4	...	...-..	...	...-...	50	...
	F	41-..-..	23,934-26,596	Y-27,969-5	...	...-..	...	...-...	50	...
Champlin, Minn. (3,-)	P	20-19-40	25,221-38,925	Y-42,428-4	955	852-89	678	97-77	8	95
	F	...-..-..	...-...	..-...-..	...	...-..	...	...-...	...	...
Chanhassen, Minn. (7,2)	P	...-..-..	...-...	..-...-..	...	...-..	...	...-...	...	...
	F	...-..-..	...-...	..-...-..	...	...-..	...	...-...	...	...
Charleston, Ill. (1,1)	P	36-28-..	19,908-33,252	Y-...-..	1,065	980-92	872	26-82	24	61
	F	32-32-..	19,548-32,280	Y-...-..	746	675-90	617	1-57	41	30
Chicago Ridge v, Ill. (1,3)	P	31-28-40	26,978-35,153	Y-40,764-4	1,967	1,633-83	1,358	103-172	28	306
	F	13-13-..	26,436-34,484	Y-39,988-4	823	703-85	587	44-72	2	118
Chickasha, Okla. (1,1)	P	43-33-40	16,247-21,190	Y-21,610-..	...	...-..	...	...-...	1	...
	F	40-39-56	16,656-23,965	Y-24,385-..	...	...-..	...	...-...	2	...
Chillicothe, Ohio (1,1)	P	54-48-40	20,800-24,731	Y-25,081-2	4,848	2,195-45	1,684	313-198	39	2,614
	F	50-49-56	20,297-24,694	Y-25,144-5	4,548	2,210-48	1,612	401-197	24	2,314
Chippewa Falls, Wis. (1,1)	P	35-25-40	26,077-28,448	Y-...-6	...	...-..	...	...-...	418	...
	F	26-25-56	25,364-28,234	Y-...-6	...	...-..	...	...-...	113	...
Christiansburg t, Va. (1,2)	P	35-27-40	18,000-24,000	Y-25,000-14	1,448	1,248-86	928	152-168	...	200
	F	...-..-..	...-...	..-...-..	...	...-..	...	...-...	...	...
Cinnaminson tp, N.J. (1,5)	P	31-23-40	29,024-34,825	Y-39,700-10	6,744	5,196-77	624	1,980-2,592	...	1,548
	F	...-..-..	...-...	..-...-..	...	...-..	...	...-...	...	...

Table 3/23 continued   POLICE AND FIRE DEPARTMENT PERSONNEL, SALARIES, AND EXPENDITURES FOR CITIES 10,000 AND OVER: 1993

| City (Service provision) | Depart-ment | Total personnel, no. uniformed, duty hours per week | Entrance, maximum salary ($) | Longevity pay, maximum ($) no. years to receive longevity pay | Reported expenditures (in thousands) | | | | | |
					Total expendi-tures (A) ($)	Total personnel expendi-tures (B) ($), % of (A)	Salaries and wages (C) ($)	City contrib. to employee retirement, insurance (D) ($)	Capital outlay (E) ($)	All other (F) ($)
10,000-24,999 continued										
Circleville, Ohio (1,3)	P	31-28-40	18,366-23,275	Y-...-5	708	651-91	570	54-27	27	30
	F	18-18-56	19,627-22,452	Y-...-5	417	384-92	336	33-15	...	33
Claremont, N.H. (1,1)	P	25-24-40	24,000-28,000	Y-28,450-..	1,333	907-68	769	33-105	260	166
	F	23-22-42	24,190-25,687	Y-26,137-..	...	...-..	...	...-...	...	...
Claremore, Okla. (1,1)	P	42-30-40	21,408-23,928	Y-25,186-3	1,497	1,221-81	1,037	153-31	90	186
	F	37-37-56	20,676-23,928	Y-25,176-3	1,363	1,136-83	1,006	109-21	79	148
Clark tp, N.J. (1,2)	P	50-45-40	32,226-42,968	Y-44,968-5	3,236	3,062-94	2,207	447-408	63	111
	F	...-..-..	...-...	..-...-..	...	...-..	...	...-...	...	...
Clarksburg, W.Va. (1,1)	P	35-35-40	16,683-22,692	Y-23,932-..	1,937	1,219-62	825	241-153	207	511
	F	41-41-..	16,683-22,692	Y-23,932-..	1,479	1,291-87	898	241-152	16	172
Clawson, Mich. (1,2)	P	24-22-40	25,000-37,921	Y-40,955-5	...	...-..	...	...-...	1	...
	F	...-..-..	...-...	..-...-..	...	...-..	...	...-...	...	...
Clayton, Mo. (1,1)	P	61-48-..	24,000-38,936	Y-...-..	...	...-..	...	...-...	...	...
	F	30-29-..	27,811-38,936	Y-...-..	...	...-..	...	...-...	...	...
Clearfield, Utah (1,3)	P	26-23-40	20,666-35,343	Y-...-..	1,330	1,064-80	799	179-86	75	191
	F	4-4-40	20,666-35,343	Y-...-..	411	270-65	215	36-19	32	109
Clearlake, Calif. (1,5)	P	22-15-40	25,620-31,260	Y-32,823-10	1,880	1,649-87	1,340	206-103	47	184
	F	...-..-..	...-...	..-...-..	...	...-..	...	...-...	...	...
Cleburne, Tex. (1,1)	P	50-36-40	22,694-26,261	Y-31,061-1	8,311	1,865-22	1,417	287-161	59	6,387
	F	43-41-48	21,599-24,391	Y-26,399-1	7,99	1,576-19	1,296	131-149	27	6,387
Clinton, Miss. (1,1)	P	44-32-40	17,944-24,838	None	1,286	997-77	844	107-46	79	210
	F	38-38-..	16,475-24,838	None	1,291	1,105-85	955	106-44	17	169
Coachella, Calif. (1,7)	P	27-19-41	30,420-36,984	None	...	...-..	...	...-...	90	...
	F	...-..-..	...-...	..-...-..	...	...-..	...	...-...	...	...
Cocoa, Fla. (1,1)	P	68-50-40	20,571-29,037	None	3,233	2,600-80	2,009	374-217	337	296
	F	40-...-50	20,228-28,210	None	1,938	1,655-85	1,302	218-135	103	180
Cocoa Beach, Fla. (1,1)	P	49-49-40	20,467-30,430	None	6,933	2,508-36	1,858	464-186	74	4,351
	F	30-30-56	18,841-28,654	None	6,098	1,636-26	1,277	271-88	111	4,351
Coeur D'Alene, Idaho (1,1)	P	53-47-40	24,162-30,084	None	2,263	2,112-93	1,704	292-116	...	151
	F	25-24-56	21,084-27,012	None	1,650	1,209-73	874	292-43	336	105
College Park, Ga. (1,1)	P	94-75-43	20,910-31,364	None	4,286	3,418-79	2,764	336-318	260	608
	F	61-60-53	20,910-31,364	None	2,773	2,255-81	1,826	221-208	374	144
College Park, Md. (7,2)	P	...-..-..	...-...	..-...-..	...	...-..	...	...-...	...	...
	F	...-..-..	...-...	..-...-..	...	...-..	...	...-...	...	...
Collierville t, Tenn. (3,3)	P	45-32-41	20,268-28,781	None	1,712	1,484-86	1,178	153-153	51	177
	F	29-..-56	19,273-26,075	None	1,236	1,058-85	860	120-78	46	132
Collingswood b, N.J. (1,3)	P	23-..-40	36,200-37,764	Y-39,652-..	...	...-..	...	...-...	...	...
	F	9-..-50	36,200-37,057	Y-38,910-..	...	...-..	...	...-...	...	...
Collinsville, Ill. (1,1)	P	41-33-40	33,348-33,654	Y-36,691-2	2,256	1,822-80	1,582	62-178	20	414
	F	25-25-42	28,578-32,127	Y-34,704-4	1,411	1,185-83	1,059	2-124	...	226
Colonial Heights, Va. (3,3)	P	49-36-42	20,694-29,119	Y-33,709-10	1,044	929-88	717	127-85	33	82
	F	13-1-40	20,694-29,119	Y-33,709-10	191	167-87	128	23-16	10	14
Columbia Heights, Minn. (1,3)	P	30-24-40	25,568-39,336	Y-42,156-4	...	...-..	...	...-...	...	...
	F	8-8-56	23,528-36,196	None	...	...-..	...	...-...	...	...
Columbus, Miss. (1,1)	P	...-..-40	19,703-21,319	Y-...-1	...	...-..	...	...-...	...	...
	F	...-..-56	19,703-21,319	Y-...-1	...	...-..	...	...-...	...	...
Columbus, Nebr. (1,3)	P	40-26-40	18,816-24,756	None	2,400	1,780-74	1,444	200-136	...	620
	F	12-12-53	17,760-24,396	None	952	660-69	548	64-48	12	280
Commerce, Calif. (7,7)	P	...-..-..	...-...	..-...-..	...	...-..	...	...-...	...	...
	F	...-..-..	...-...	..-...-..	...	...-..	...	...-...	...	...
Commerce City, Colo. (1,5)	P	56-44-40	29,940-...	Y-38,251-1	...	...-..	...	...-...	56	...
	F	...-..-..	...-...	..-...-..	...	...-..	...	...-...	...	...
Concord t, Mass. (1,1)	P	39-32-40	25,498-33,449	Y-34,049-5	...	...-..	...	...-...	81	...
	F	35-34-42	25,030-31,945	Y-32,545-5	...	...-..	...	...-...	163	...
Conneaut, Ohio (3,3)	P	23-23-40	21,611-24,086	Y-25,086-2	...	...-..	...	...-...	...	...
	F	12-12-48	18,520-22,439	Y-23,439-2	...	...-..	...	...-...	...	...
Connersville, Ind. (1,1)	P	36-32-40	20,107-25,133	Y-26,333-1	1,292	1,179-91	962	103-114	44	69
	F	42-42-..	23,980-24,481	Y-26,195-1	1,402	1,297-92	1,079	55-163	44	61
Cooper City, Fla. (1,1)	P	11-11-40	28,461-40,000	Y-41,000-..	759	570-75	489	78-3	144	45
	F	23-22-48	24,590-35,617	Y-36,367-10	1,488	1,056-70	828	144-84	372	60
Coos Bay, Ore. (1,1)	P	41-30-..	23,364-29,808	Y-31,895-15	...	...-..	...	...-...	75	...
	F	...-..-..	...-...	..-...-..	...	...-..	...	...-...	...	...
Coppell, Tex. (1,1)	P	34-27-40	27,159-32,461	Y-33,421-..	1,476	1,319-89	1,086	76-157	41	116
	F	33-32-48	24,917-29,781	Y-30,741-..	1,432	1,350-94	1,159	73-118	...	82
Copperas Cove, Tex. (1,3)	P	58-44-40	20,551-21,374	Y-21,886-1	...	...-..	...	...-...	...	...
	F	39-37-56	...-19,949	Y-20,893-1	2,573	2,100-81	1,440	492-168	65	408
Coralville, Iowa (1,2)	P	25-23-40	21,249-31,297	None	...	...-..	...	...-...	59	...
	F	...-..-..	...-...	..-...-..	...	...-..	...	...-...	...	...
Corcoran, Calif. (1,7)	P	19-15-40	23,736-29,708	Y-...-..	1,108	950-85	666	116-168	...	158
	F	...-..-..	...-...	..-...-..	...	...-..	...	...-...	...	...
Cordele, Ga. (1,1)	P	32-27-43	13,170-20,748	None	1,110	804-72	673	77-54	39	267
	F	23-..-57	12,968-20,446	None	561	453-80	365	47-41	27	81
Corsicana, Tex. (1,1)	P	44-34-40	21,300-22,500	Y-...-1	1,830	1,565-85	1,210	190-165	52	213
	F	35-33-56	21,048-22,356	Y-...-1	1,319	1,204-91	943	156-105	17	98

Table 3/23
continued

POLICE AND FIRE DEPARTMENT PERSONNEL, SALARIES, AND EXPENDITURES FOR CITIES 10,000 AND OVER: 1993

City (Service provision)	Depart-ment	Total personnel, no. uniformed, duty hours per week	Entrance, maximum salary ($)	Longevity pay, maximum ($) no. years to receive longevity pay	Total expendi-tures (A) ($)	Total personnel expendi-tures (B) ($), % of (A)	Salaries and wages (C) ($)	City contrib. to employee retirement, insurance (D) ($)	Capital outlay (E) ($)	All other (F) ($)
10,000-24,999 continued										
Cortland, N.Y. (1,3)	P	40-37-40	22,811-32,483	None	...	...-..	...	...-...	...	...
	F	39-38-40	22,811-32,483	None	...	...-..	...	...-...	...	...
Coshocton, Ohio (9,1)	P	...-..-..	...-...	..-...-..	...	...-..	...	...-...	...	...
	F	18-18-42	15,288-19,656	Y-...-..	...	...-..	...	...-...	...	...
Cottage Grove, Minn. (1,3)	P	20-12-..	29,184-38,376	Y-41,832-4	1,518	1,430-94	1,245	53-132	...	88
	F	6-5-40	26,076-35,928	Y-38,604-5	209	196-93	162	13-21	...	13
Country Club Hills, Ill. (1,5)	P	29-22-40	28,128-38,513	Y-41,305-..	3,670	2,323-63	1,784	337-202	77	1,270
	F	...-..-..	...-...	..-...-..	...	...-..	...	...-...	...	...
Covington, Ga. (1,1)	P	53-50-41	18,597-29,494	Y-...-20	2,383	1,653-69	1,363	208-82	211	519
	F	28-27-56	19,015-30,227	Y-...-20	1,360	1,091-80	978	66-47	40	229
Cranberry tp, Pa. (1,2)	P	17-15-40	...-...	..-...-..	...	...-..	...	...-...	...	...
	F	...-..-..	...-...	..-...-..	...	...-..	...	...-...	...	...
Crawfordsville, Ind. (1,1)	P	39-28-40	20,225-27,550	Y-...-25	1,365	1,203-88	942	118-143	42	120
	F	33-32-56	21,030-...	Y-27,655-1	1,269	1,171-92	900	130-141	12	86
Crest Hill, Ill. (1,-)	P	25-18-40	27,519-39,520	Y-40,300-6	1,064	914-85	751	75-88	...	150
	F	...-..-..	...-...	..-...-..	...	...-..	...	...-...	...	...
Crestwood, Mo. (1,1)	P	29-21-40	22,515-30,574	None	1,567	1,368-87	1,118	137-113	17	182
	F	30-29-56	22,515-30,574	None	1,332	1,241-93	1,024	121-96	4	87
Crystal, Minn. (1,2)	P	35-27-40	25,740-39,564	Y-43,125-4	2,356	2,049-86	1,517	316-216	115	192
	F	...-..-..	...-...	..-...-..	...	...-..	...	...-...	...	...
Cudahy, Calif. (9,7)	P	...-..-..	...-...	...-...	...	...-..	...	...-...	...	...
	F	...-..-..	...-...	..-...-..	...	...-..	...	...-...	...	...
Cudahy, Wis. (1,1)	P	42-8-..	27,552-37,345	Y-37,695-5	...	...-..	...	...-...	35	...
	F	...-..-..	...-...	..-...-..	...	...-..	...	...-...	...	...
Cullman, Ala. (3,1)	P	50-33-42	15,900-21,180	None	1,044	848-81	706	88-54	20	176
	F	29-28-53	16,200-21,500	None	724	643-88	534	70-39	3	78
Cumberland, Md. (1,1)	P	57-51-40	20,873-25,258	None	2,016	1,701-84	1,392	104-205	44	271
	F	59-58-40	18,793-25,264	None	2,007	1,906-94	1,431	221-254	9	92
Danville, Ky. (4,3)	P	...-..-..	...-...	..-...-..	...	...-..	...	...-...	...	...
	F	...-..-..	...-...	..-...-..	...	...-..	...	...-...	...	...
Daphne t, Ala. (1,3)	P	39-31-40	20,426-27,581	Y-...-..	1,213	962-79	795	91-76	4	247
	F	4-4-40	20,426-27,581	None	249	104-41	87	9-8	23	122
Darby b, Pa. (1,2)	P	13-13-40	14,000-...	Y-...-3	...	...-..	...	...-...	...	...
	F	...-..-..	...-...	..-...-..	...	...-..	...	...-...	...	...
Darby tp, Pa. (1,2)	P	12-11-40	32,000-33,000	Y-38,720-3	...	...-..	...	...-...	50	...
	F	...-..-..	...-...	..-...-..	...	...-..	...	...-...	...	...
Darien, Ill. (1,9)	P	33-28-40	25,551-39,909	Y-43,501-11	2,448	1,240-50	1,138	27-75	14	1,194
	F	...-..-..	...-...	..-...-..	...	...-..	...	...-...	...	...
De Land, Fla. (1,1)	P	76-56-42	18,886-27,643	Y-28,243-8	3,180	2,661-83	2,172	273-216	216	303
	F	24-23-56	17,139-25,076	Y-25,676-8	1,071	975-91	768	126-81	24	72
De Pere, Wis. (1,1)	P	33-25-38	26,952-36,444	Y-36,924-5	1,507	1,368-90	1,119	115-134	18	121
	F	28-28-50	26,913-35,280	Y-35,760-5	1,372	1,200-87	1,016	36-148	...	172
Decatur, Ga. (1,1)	P	56-12-40	21,195-29,827	None	1,238	1,115-90	897	98-120	6	117
	F	40-...-56	21,195-29,827	None	890	830-93	700	40-90	...	60
Dedham t, Mass. (1,1)	P	63-60-37	25,414-29,077	Y-30,936-5	...	...-..	...	...-...	...	...
	F	62-61-48	25,414-29,077	Y-30,936-5	...	...-..	...	...-...	...	...
Deerfield v, Ill. (1,5)	P	48-37-..	31,901-44,122	Y-...-..	...	...-..	...	...-...	...	...
	F	...-..-..	...-...	..-...-..	...	...-..	...	...-...	...	...
Defiance, Ohio (3,3)	P	28-23-40	21,690-29,716	Y-30,916-5	...	...-..	...	...-...	...	...
	F	18-18-56	22,242-28,090	Y-29,290-5	...	...-..	...	...-...	...	...
Del City, Okla. (1,1)	P	46-34-40	18,366-24,689	Y-25,289-9	...	...-..	...	...-...	...	...
	F	28-28-..	22,666-30,892	None	...	...-..	...	...-...	...	...
Delano, Calif. (1,7)	P	47-32-40	23,000-32,000	Y-32,840-..	...	...-..	...	...-...	...	...
	F	...-..-..	...-...	..-...-..	...	...-..	...	...-...	...	...
Delaware, Ohio (1,1)	P	43-32-40	23,858-29,869	Y-30,869-5	2,269	1,857-81	1,318	359-180	115	297
	F	33-32-50	23,716-29,697	Y-30,897-5	1,798	1,693-94	1,182	357-154	19	86
Delran tp, N.J. (1,2)	P	22-17-40	25,364-38,929	Y-...-4	1,764	1,425-80	1,200	91-134	100	239
	F	...-..-..	...-...	..-...-..	...	...-..	...	...-...	...	...
Deming, N.M. (1,3)	P	28-23-42	17,376-...	Y-17,876-1	1,062	533-50	372	73-88	319	210
	F	16-16-56	19,264-...	Y-19,764-1	351	328-93	232	43-53	...	23
Denison, Tex. (1,1)	P	50-42-..	16,140-27,072	Y-28,272-1	2,650	1,632-61	1,291	185-156	50	968
	F	58-53-..	14,112-21,228	Y-22,428-1	2,669	1,669-62	1,325	164-180	32	968
Dennis t, Mass. (1,-)	P	41-34-40	24,852-28,885	Y-...-5	1,032	936-90	815	72-49	62	34
	F	28-27-40	23,439-30,614	Y-31,532-5	752	717-95	643	35-39	6	29
Denville tp, N.J. (1,2)	P	34-5-40	33,388-...	Y-35,522-3	2,340	2,120-90	1,677	205-238	...	220
	F	...-..-..	...-...	..-...-..	...	...-..	...	...-...	...	...
Depew v, N.Y. (1,2)	P	39-31-40	22,000-35,000	Y-36,000-5	1,514	1,338-88	1,023	206-109	2	174
	F	...-..-..	...-...	..-...-..	...	...-..	...	...-...	...	...
Derby, Conn. (1,2)	P	29-29-40	36,180-38,572	Y-...-..	...	...-..	...	...-...	...	...
	F	...-..-..	...-...	..-...-..	...	...-..	...	...-...	...	...
Derby, Kan. (3,2)	P	32-24-40	20,400-29,160	Y-30,360-5	2,055	1,093-53	848	137-108	12	950
	F	...-..-..	...-...	..-...-..	...	...-..	...	...-...	...	...
Derry tp, Pa. (1,2)	P	34-27-40	24,112-32,149	Y-34,249-5	1,492	1,297-86	1,020	150-127	43	152
	F	...-..-..	...-...	..-...-..	...	...-..	...	...-...	...	...

Table 3/23 continued POLICE AND FIRE DEPARTMENT PERSONNEL, SALARIES, AND EXPENDITURES FOR CITIES 10,000 AND OVER: 1993

City (Service provision)	Depart-ment	Total personnel, no. uniformed, duty hours per week	Entrance, maximum salary ($)	Longevity pay, maximum ($) no. years to receive longevity pay	Reported expenditures (in thousands)					
					Total expendi-tures (A) ($)	Total personnel expendi-tures (B) ($), % of (A)	Salaries and wages (C) ($)	City contrib. to employee retirement, insurance (D) ($)	Capital outlay (E) ($)	All other (F) ($)
10,000-24,999 continued										
Des Moines, Wash. (3,7)	P	37-27-40	28,212-40,740	None	...	...-...	...	...-...	...	...
	F	...-...-..	...-...	..-...-..	...	...-...	...	...-...	...	...
Desert Hot Springs, Calif. (7,7)	P	...-...-..	...-...	..-...-..	...	...-...	...	...-...	...	...
	F	...-...-..	...-...	..-...-..	...	...-...	...	...-...	...	...
Dickinson, N.D. (1,3)	P	33-23-40	19,740-21,780	Y-...-5	1,112	952-85	762	157-33	32	128
	F	4-4-40	19,740-21,780	Y-...-5	254	192-75	148	36-8	9	53
Dixon, Calif. (1,3)	P	18-16-40	29,148-35,436	..-...-..	925	624-67	464	112-48	10	291
	F	4-4-40	25,992-31,584	..-...-..	196	72-36	58	9-5	2	122
Dixon, Ill. (1,3)	P	25-22-40	25,072-29,211	None	1,187	886-74	770	68-48	49	252
	F	16-16-56	26,114-29,211	None	922	711-77	588	91-32	178	33
Dodge City, Kan. (1,1)	P	50-36-42	19,339-26,571	Y-27,571-1	2,008	1,601-79	1,169	271-161	87	320
	F	22-22-..	17,239-22,847	Y-23,842-1	1,006	798-79	561	152-85	158	50
Douglas, Ariz. (1,1)	P	48-36-40	19,847-25,002	None	1,569	1,429-91	1,140	75-214	...	140
	F	23-22-56	19,847-25,002	None	884	820-92	635	77-108	...	64
Douglas, Ga. (3,3)	P	44-35-40	15,600-19,760	None	1,464	1,098-75	868	155-75	86	280
	F	29-29-56	15,600-19,760	None	905	803-88	645	109-49	17	85
Douglasville, Ga. (1,7)	P	45-37-42	17,778-...	..-...-..	1,119	872-77	658	130-84	...	247
	F	...-...-..	...-...	..-...-..	...	...-...	...	...-...	...	...
Dover t, N.J. (1,3)	P	30-27-40	26,973-46,700	Y-47,990-..	...	...-...	...	...-...	...	...
	F	4-4-40	23,534-40,686	..-46,686-..	...	...-...	...	...-...	...	...
Dover, Ohio (1,1)	P	22-19-40	25,792-28,662	Y-29,037-5	...	...-...	...	...-...	31	...
	F	13-13-56	22,174-24,984	Y-25,359-5	...	...-...	...	...-...	86	...
Doylestown tp, Pa. (1,2)	P	20-17-40	26,907-37,763	Y-37,913-1	1,357	1,094-80	796	150-148	67	196
	F	...-...-..	...-...	..-...-..	...	...-...	...	...-...	...	...
Dublin, Ohio (1,9)	P	50-8-40	24,118-35,935	Y-36,760-15	2,661	2,379-89	1,832	313-234	5	277
	F	...-...-..	...-...	..-...-..	...	...-...	...	...-...	...	...
Dumas, Tex. (1,3)	P	30-25-40	21,684-23,304	Y-23,352-1	944	893-94	714	128-51	23	28
	F	9-9-53	20,832-22,404	Y-22,452-1	289	261-90	209	37-15	26	2
Duncan, Okla. (1,1)	P	50-46-..	15,995-24,794	..-...-..	2,320	2,070-89	1,781	209-80	67	183
	F	41-40-..	15,226-23,629	..-...-..	1,477	1,390-94	1,213	107-70	18	69
Dunmore b, Pa. (1,3)	P	14-8-40	29,800-...	Y-29,901-5	810	750-92	600	30-120	50	10
	F	...-...-..	...-...	..-...-..	...	...-...	...	...-...	...	...
Durango, Colo. (1,1)	P	47-27-40	20,696-30,097	None	1,825	1,469-80	1,212	124-133	12	344
	F	16-15-56	19,656-28,828	None	741	605-81	509	48-48	12	124
Durham t, N.H. (1,1)	P	17-15-40	25,602-31,242	Y-...-5	...	...-...	...	...-...	...	...
	F	25-24-42	19,001-35,250	Y-...-5	...	...-...	...	...-...	...	...
Eagle Pass, Tex. (1,3)	P	58-45-40	15,401-18,644	Y-...-..	1,588	1,435-90	1,032	163-240	12	141
	F	31-30-56	15,788-19,254	Y-...-..	1,010	912-90	668	106-138	13	85
East Goshen tp, Pa. (6,6)	P	...-...-..	...-...	..-...-..	...	...-...	...	...-...	...	...
	F	...-...-..	...-...	..-...-..	...	...-...	...	...-...	...	...
Lake Station, Ind. (1,2)	P	24-19-40	22,165-27,539	Y-27,959-3	...	...-...	...	...-...	...	...
	F	...-...-..	...-...	..-...-..	...	...-...	...	...-...	...	...
East Grand Rapids, Mich. (4,4)	P	...-...-..	...-...	..-...-..	...	...-...	...	...-...	...	...
	F	...-...-..	...-...	..-...-..	...	...-...	...	...-...	...	...
East Hampton t, Conn. (1,2)	P	15-13-40	28,023-35,218	Y-...-5	898	832-92	649	113-70	...	66
	F	...-...-..	...-...	..-...-..	...	...-...	...	...-...	...	...
East Liverpool, Ohio (1,1)	P	27-22-40	14,587-23,288	Y-23,948-3	1,128	1,021-90	733	143-145	15	92
	F	32-32-48	14,587-23,288	Y-23,948-3	1,626	1,325-81	903	247-175	170	131
East Norriton tp, Pa. (1,2)	P	23-18-40	33,386-42,042	Y-43,513-5	...	...-...	...	...-...	...	...
	F	...-...-..	...-...	..-...-..	...	...-...	...	...-...	...	...
East Pennsboro tp, Pa. (1,2)	P	15-15-40	27,348-32,174	Y-33,774-1	822	722-87	560	89-73	24	76
	F	...-...-..	...-...	..-...-..	...	...-...	...	...-...	...	...
East Peoria, Ill. (1,3)	P	33-21-40	20,672-37,154	Y-41,205-3	...	...-...	...	...-...	...	...
	F	25-25-56	20,672-37,154	Y-41,205-3	...	...-...	...	...-...	...	...
East Ridge t, Tenn. (4,-)	P	...-...-..	...-...	..-...-..	...	...-...	...	...-...	...	...
	F	...-...-..	...-...	..-...-..	...	...-...	...	...-...	...	...
East Rockaway v, N.Y. (7,2)	P	...-...-..	...-...	..-...-..	...	...-...	...	...-...	...	...
	F	...-...-..	...-...	..-...-..	...	...-...	...	...-...	...	...
East Windsor t, Conn. (1,2)	P	22-5-40	28,273-...	Y-36,019-6	1,698	1,434-84	1,131	120-183	6	258
	F	...-...-..	...-...	..-...-..	...	...-...	...	...-...	...	...
Easthampton t, Mass. (1,1)	P	22-22-37	20,247-24,040	Y-24,540-10	...	...-...	...	...-...	...	...
	F	25-25-42	22,989-27,061	Y-27,561-10	...	...-...	...	...-...	...	...
Easton t, Mass. (1,1)	P	31-31-40	26,053-32,198	Y-32,598-5	1,862	1,632-87	1,456	21-155	...	230
	F	32-32-42	22,358-29,930	Y-30,330-5	1,603	1,488-92	1,310	18-160	...	115
Eden, N.C. (1,3)	P	49-42-..	18,008-24,133	Y-...-5	1,831	1,477-80	1,169	217-91	113	241
	F	17-17-..	18,008-24,133	Y-...-5	537	441-82	354	56-31	12	84
Edgewater, Fla. (1,3)	P	41-31-42	20,651-28,912	None	2,172	1,692-77	1,448	104-140	116	364
	F	10-9-42	19,630-27,482	None	884	512-57	440	32-40	4	368
Effingham, Ill. (1,3)	P	34-24-..	22,380-25,045	Y-25,087-..	...	...-...	...	...-...	...	...
	F	16-16-..	23,630-26,045	Y-26,087-..	...	...-...	...	...-...	...	...
Egg Harbor tp, N.J. (1,2)	P	79-60-40	24,821-38,472	Y-40,396-1	9,086	5,173-56	3,300	887-986	...	3,913
	F	...-...-..	...-...	..-...-..	...	...-...	...	...-...	...	...
El Cerrito, Calif. (1,1)	P	38-33-40	42,300-51,408	None	3,376	2,434-72	1,806	458-170	...	942
	F	27-26-56	41,568-50,532	None	1,998	1,712-85	1,294	310-108	...	286

Table 3/23 continued

POLICE AND FIRE DEPARTMENT PERSONNEL, SALARIES, AND EXPENDITURES FOR CITIES 10,000 AND OVER: 1993

City (Service provision)	Depart-ment	Total personnel, no. uniformed, duty hours per week	Entrance, maximum salary ($)	Longevity pay, maximum ($), no. years to receive longevity pay	Reported expenditures (in thousands)					
					Total expendi-tures (A) ($)	Total personnel expendi-tures (B) ($), % of (A)	Salaries and wages (C) ($)	City contrib. to employee retirement, insurance (D) ($)	Capital outlay (E) ($)	All other (F) ($)
10,000–24,999 continued										
El Dorado, Ark. (1,1)	P	55-46-40	20,175-23,420	Y-...-1	1,972	1,585-80	1,314	168-103	68	319
	F	55-48-53	21,109-24,338	Y-...-1	1,879	1,623-86	1,378	151-94	121	135
El Dorado, Kan. (4,4)	P	...-...-..	...-...	..-...-..	...	...-..	...	...-...	...	...
	F	...-...-..	...-...	..-...-..	...	...-..	...	...-...	...	...
El Paso De Robles, Calif. (3,3)	P	35-29-40	28,836-36,144	Y-38,292-5	2,579	2,037-78	1,446	440-151	66	476
	F	6-5-56	27,108-34,416	Y-...-3	554	300-54	212	63-25	8	246
El Reno, Okla. (1,1)	P	31-24-40	18,839-20,493	Y-22,893-3	1,220	1,048-85	836	134-78	96	76
	F	20-20-56	18,972-19,391	Y-20,591-3	782	704-90	592	60-52	12	66
El Segundo, Calif. (1,1)	P	91-66-40	39,377-50,829	None	6,493	5,395-83	4,488	586-321	10	1,088
	F	66-60-56	37,458-46,641	None	5,430	4,468-82	3,770	434-264	33	929
Elizabethton, Tenn. (1,1)	P	33-27-40	16,848-25,625	Y-26,111-..	1,514	1,180-77	970	132-78	55	279
	F	26-26-56	16,848-25,625	Y-26,111-..	1,087	934-85	773	105-56	1	152
Elk River, Minn. (1,3)	P	19-15-40	25,986-38,091	None	1,183	1,037-87	913	81-43	3	143
	F	1-1-40	37,041-48,037	None	201	126-62	121	4-1	4	71
Elko, Nev. (3,3)	P	38-34-37	26,892-33,432	Y-34,432-8	1,775	1,486-83	1,098	261-127	92	197
	F	16-16-56	30,156-32,076	Y-33,076-8	1,003	875-87	663	153-59	33	95
Ellington t, Conn. (6,2)	P	...-...-..	...-...	..-...-..	...	...-..	...	...-...	...	...
	F	...-...-..	...-...	..-...-..	...	...-..	...	...-...	...	...
Elmwood Park v, Ill. (3,3)	P	41-31-40	25,123-36,514	Y-39,435-3	1,681	1,656-98	1,488	72-96	1	24
	F	23-23-52	25,244-36,689	Y-39,624-3	1,045	1,032-98	948	24-60	1	12
Lake Elsinore, Calif. (7,7)	P	...-...-..	...-...	..-...-..	...	...-..	...	...-...	...	...
	F	...-...-..	...-...	..-...-..	...	...-..	...	...-...	...	...
Ennis, Tex. (3,3)	P	33-26-40	21,490-25,161	Y-25,229-1	1,236	1,114-90	896	123-95	63	59
	F	27-26-53	21,510-25,203	Y-25,271-1	1,013	959-94	772	106-81	15	39
Enterprise, Ala. (1,1)	P	49-37-43	14,664-19,985	None	1,579	1,247-78	988	128-131	35	297
	F	30-29-56	13,520-18,426	None	791	735-92	561	75-99	25	31
Erlanger, Ky. (1,2)	P	34-28-40	20,332-24,492	None	1,520	1,298-85	895	239-164	...	222
	F	...-...-..	...-...	..-...-..	...	...-..	...	...-...	...	...
Escanaba, Mich. (4,4)	P	...-...-..	...-...	..-...-..	...	...-..	...	...-...	...	...
	F	...-...-..	...-...	..-...-..	...	...-..	...	...-...	...	...
Essex t, Vt. (1,2)	P	31-25-40	22,236-30,884	Y-...-..	...	...-..	...	...-...	...	...
	F	...-...-..	...-...	..-...-..	...	...-..	...	...-...	...	...
Eufaula, Ala. (1,1)	P	41-41-40	15,370-...	..-...-..	1,125	881-78	688	88-105	36	208
	F	27-27-53	15,068-...	..-...-..	703	609-86	472	61-76	14	80
Eustis, Fla. (1,3)	P	41-11-42	19,822-29,203	Y-...-3	1,752	1,600-91	1,344	164-92	...	152
	F	18-1-50	17,992-26,520	Y-...-3	916	836-91	680	116-40	...	80
Evergreen Park v, Ill. (1,-)	P	67-54-40	27,436-40,636	Y-42,376-5	3,584	3,338-93	2,546	485-307	88	158
	F	3-3-40	...-...	..-...-..	1,102	898-81	785	88-25	41	163
Excelsior Springs, Mo. (1,1)	P	27-21-40	18,708-25,068	..-...-..	1,108	823-74	689	63-71	53	232
	F	11-11-40	18,708-25,068	..-...-..	673	488-72	410	50-28	57	128
Exeter t, N.H. (1,1)	P	29-22-40	25,900-29,000	Y-31,500-5	...	...-..	...	...-...	...	...
	F	19-18-42	24,500-30,900	Y-33,400-5	...	...-..	...	...-...	...	...
Exeter tp, Pa. (1,3)	P	19-19-42	26,557-34,791	Y-...-3	...	...-..	...	...-...	10	...
	F	1-1-40	...-...	Y-...-..	...	...-..	...	...-...	36	...
Fairfax, Va. (1,3)	P	73-59-40	28,019-43,466	None	5,316	4,704-88	3,300	1,068-336	96	516
	F	56-49-56	26,684-41,396	None	4,332	4,044-93	2,868	924-252	24	264
Fairhaven t, Mass. (1,3)	P	28-27-40	23,170-26,566	Y-27,416-10	1,356	1,212-89	1,066	50-96	37	107
	F	19-18-42	24,382-26,168	Y-27,346-..	740	678-91	608	31-39	16	46
Fairmont, Minn. (1,2)	P	16-16-40	26,000-28,000	Y-...-4	...	...-..	...	...-...	...	...
	F	...-...-..	...-...	..-...-..	...	...-..	...	...-...	...	...
Fairmont, W.Va. (1,1)	P	39-30-...	18,711-20,838	Y-21,538-4	2,156	1,490-69	996	324-170	28	638
	F	40-39-..	18,711-20,838	Y-21,538-4	2,524	1,834-72	1,330	300-204	...	690
Fairview tp, Pa. (1,2)	P	13-13-40	27,220-35,151	Y-37,551-4	726	583-80	484	37-62	15	128
	F	...-...-..	...-...	..-...-..	...	...-..	...	...-...	...	...
Fairview Heights, Ill. (1,-)	P	47-36-40	29,479-36,408	Y-38,028-1	8,557	1,297-15	1,032	97-168	...	7,260
	F	...-...-..	...-...	..-...-..	...	...-..	...	...-...	...	...
Fairview Park, Ohio (1,1)	P	29-28-40	29,088-36,381	Y-37,881-5	1,734	1,594-91	1,237	218-139	...	140
	F	26-26-49	28,930-36,185	Y-37,685-5	1,523	1,454-95	1,084	251-119	...	69
Fallsburg t, N.Y. (1,2)	P	23-19-40	21,008-29,016	Y-31,016-9	1,200	1,006-83	724	147-135	59	135
	F	...-...-..	...-...	..-...-..	...	...-..	...	...-...	...	...
Faribault, Minn. (3,3)	P	32-22-40	24,304-32,406	Y-35,006-5	1,789	1,479-82	1,113	257-109	33	277
	F	15-...-56	23,383-31,188	Y-33,683-5	1,036	933-90	651	221-61	8	95
Farmers Branch, Tex. (1,1)	P	73-59-40	29,016-34,524	Y-36,024-..	4,040	3,412-84	2,709	298-405	120	508
	F	62-62-56	29,016-34,524	Y-36,024-..	3,600	3,104-86	2,511	273-320	116	380
Farmington t, Conn. (1,3)	P	44-41-40	32,462-42,860	None	2,024	1,863-92	1,326	273-264	...	161
	F	6-6-40	30,346-37,532	None	636	195-30	135	24-36	...	441
Farmington, Mich. (4,4)	P	...-...-..	...-...	..-...-..	...	...-..	...	...-...	...	...
	F	...-...-..	...-...	..-...-..	...	...-..	...	...-...	...	...
Farmington, Mo. (1,3)	P	23-17-40	...-...	Y-...-..	...	...-..	...	...-...	51	...
	F	2-..-40	...-...	Y-...-..	...	...-..	...	...-...	110	...
Farragut t, Tenn. (7,9)	P	...-...-..	...-...	..-...-..	...	...-..	...	...-...	...	...
	F	...-...-..	...-...	..-...-..	...	...-..	...	...-...	...	...
Fergus Falls, Minn. (1,3)	P	22-18-40	23,580-28,980	Y-30,719-3	1,090	879-80	689	85-105	52	159
	F	2-2-40	...-...	None	178	130-73	102	8-20	1	47

Table 3/23 continued   POLICE AND FIRE DEPARTMENT PERSONNEL, SALARIES, AND EXPENDITURES FOR CITIES 10,000 AND OVER: 1993

City (Service provision)	Department	Total personnel, no. uniformed, duty hours per week	Entrance, maximum salary ($)	Longevity pay, maximum ($), no. years to receive longevity pay	Reported expenditures (in thousands)					
					Total expenditures (A) ($)	Total personnel expenditures (B) ($), % of (A)	Salaries and wages (C) ($)	City contrib. to employee retirement, insurance (D) ($)	Capital outlay (E) ($)	All other (F) ($)
10,000-24,999 continued										
Ferguson, Mo. (1,1)	P	58-51-40	23,379-28,417	Y-29,861-10	2,635	2,221-84	1,815	178-228	...	414
	F	25-25-56	22,754-27,658	..-29,063-10	1,122	978-87	807	75-96	...	144
Floral Park v, N.Y. (1,2)	P	45-36-..	27,000-52,249	Y-54,549-6	2,441	2,316-94	1,767	401-148	83	42
	F	...-..-..	...-...	..-...-..	...	...-..	...	...-...	...	...
Florence, Ky. (1,3)	P	47-44-40	20,310-32,245	None	2,478	2,274-91	1,631	412-231	...	204
	F	21-20-56	18,465-32,245	None	1,263	1,121-88	811	204-106	...	142
Forest Grove, Ore. (1,3)	P	20-20-40	27,264-34,080	None	1,156	986-85	784	128-74	10	160
	F	13-12-56	27,480-34,356	None	990	706-71	560	94-52	16	268
Forest Hill, Tex. (1,1)	P	26-16-..	21,516-35,184	Y-44,988-..	1,787	1,175-65	894	119-162	74	538
	F	15-13-..	21,516-35,184	Y-44,988-..	1,139	596-52	457	60-79	5	538
Forest Park, Ga. (4,4)	P	...-..-..	...-...	..-...-..	...	...-..	...	...-...	...	...
	F	...-..-..	...-...	..-...-..	...	...-..	...	...-...	...	...
Forest Park v, Ill. (3,3)	P	54-38-..	27,351-40,041	None	...	...-..	...	...-...	...	...
	F	26-24-..	23,362-38,747	None	...	...-..	...	...-...	...	...
Forrest City, Ark. (1,3)	P	36-27-43	17,796-18,408	..-19,008-1	1,335	769-57	625	59-85	78	488
	F	14-14-50	16,536-17,850	..-18,450-1	...	...-..	...	...-...	3	...
Fort Atkinson, Wis. (1,3)	P	23-15-39	28,044-33,744	Y-34,244-..	...	...-..	...	...-...	15	...
	F	4-4-54	27,096-29,880	Y-30,380-..	...	...-..	...	...-...	17	...
Fort Madison, Iowa (1,1)	P	26-21-40	17,555-23,795	Y-24,515-5	1,168	1,012-86	776	114-122	26	130
	F	20-20-56	16,554-23,096	Y-23,816-5	802	748-93	564	92-92	...	54
Fort Payne, Ala	P	30-27-40	13,633-20,621	None	...	...-..	...	...-...	...	...
	F	29-29-40	13,633-20,621	None	...	...-..	...	...-...	...	...
Fort Walton Beach, Fla. (3,4)	P	49-35-40	17,034-29,400	Y-...-3	809	729-90	577	87-65	37	43
	F	...-..-..	...-...	..-...-..	...	...-..	...	...-...	...	...
Fostoria, Ohio (1,1)	P	29-24-40	25,085-34,154	Y-36,886-..	1,653	1,533-92	1,227	168-138	...	120
	F	19-19-52	21,154-30,181	Y-32,595-..	907	840-92	664	101-75	...	67
Fountain Hills t, Ariz. (7,8)	P	...-..-..	...-...	..-...-..	...	...-..	...	...-...	...	...
	F	...-..-..	...-...	..-...-..	...	...-..	...	...-...	...	...
Frankfort, Ind. (1,1)	P	36-29-40	24,000-...	None	1,647	1,517-92	1,145	220-152	1	129
	F	39-33-56	24,000-...	None	1,697	1,620-95	1,208	247-165	...	77
Franklin, Ind. (1,1)	P	29-23-40	24,176-...	None	1,296	1,068-82	660	264-144	96	132
	F	33-33-..	23,176-24,176	None	1,812	1,308-72	804	312-192	228	276
Franklin t, Mass. (1,3)	P	37-31-40	26,236-28,844	Y-29,094-5	1,600	1,481-92	1,294	75-112	15	104
	F	27-23-42	24,050-27,144	Y-27,494-5	1,177	1,095-93	953	52-90	...	82
Murrysville, Pa. (1,2)	P	18-18-40	22,880-...	Y-...-..	...	...-..	...	...-...	42	...
	F	...-..-..	...-...	..-...-..	...	...-..	...	...-...	...	...
Franklin, Wis. (1,3)	P	41-31-38	28,585-36,521	Y-36,546-5	2,448	2,268-92	1,668	396-204	...	180
	F	21-21-56	25,293-36,187	Y-36,254-5	1,512	1,308-86	972	228-108	72	132
Fraser, Mich. (4,4)	P	...-..-..	...-...	..-...-..	...	...-..	...	...-...	...	...
	F	...-..-..	...-...	..-...-..	...	...-..	...	...-...	...	...
Fredericksburg, Va. (3,3)	P	80-57-..	22,220-32,833	None	1,700	1,389-81	1,111	186-92	55	256
	F	46-42-..	22,220-32,833	None	979	873-89	687	123-63	16	90
Fredonia v, N.Y. (1,1)	P	16-16-40	24,332-33,884	None	856	806-94	622	120-64	1	49
	F	6-6-44	23,500-29,000	None	338	253-74	196	29-28	9	76
Freehold b, N.J. (1,2)	P	32-32-40	27,977-42,302	Y-42,802-3	1,734	1,600-92	1,393	15-192	60	74
	F	...-..-..	...-...	..-...-..	...	...-..	...	...-...	...	...
Freehold tp, N.J. (1,2)	P	56-45-40	29,500-47,300	Y-...-5	...	...-..	...	...-...	...	...
	F	...-..-..	...-...	..-...-..	...	...-..	...	...-...	...	...
Freeport, Tex. (1,3)	P	39-32-40	18,000-31,000	Y-31,001-..	...	...-..	...	...-...	59	...
	F	5-5-50	19,292-24,528	Y-24,529-..	...	...-..	...	...-...	8	...
Fremont, Nebr. (1,3)	P	37-34-40	18,084-25,440	None	...	...-..	...	...-...	...	...
	F	28-28-..	17,220-24,228	None	...	...-..	...	...-...	...	...
Fremont, Ohio (1,1)	P	37-32-40	22,693-29,536	Y-...-..	2,559	2,207-86	1,056	967-184	...	352
	F	25-25-50	24,341-28,084	Y-...-..	947	858-90	672	66-120	1	88
Front Royal t, Va. (3,3)	P	36-26-40	21,861-30,576	None	1,512	1,328-87	993	215-120	32	152
	F	4-..-40	22,963-32,178	None	...	...-..	...	...-...	...	...
Fulton, Mo. (1,1)	P	25-23-40	16,500-22,000	None	732	568-77	452	46-70	...	164
	F	18-18-42	14,100-23,000	None	630	514-81	368	90-56	88	28
Fulton, N.Y. (1,1)	P	37-35-40	29,683-34,583	None	...	...-..	...	...-...	...	...
	F	40-40-40	21,065-33,733	None	...	...-..	...	...-...	...	...
Gaffney, S.C. (1,1)	P	24-24-42	18,000-25,215	None	...	...-..	...	...-...	36	...
	F	20-20-42	16,716-24,014	None	...	...-..	...	...-...	7	...
Gainesville, Ga. (1,1)	P	102-81-..	18,866-...	None	4,058	3,144-77	2,756	194-194	154	760
	F	66-65-..	18,879-...	None	1,848	1,596-86	1,368	116-112	10	242
Gainesville, Tex. (1,3)	P	39-30-40	17,352-24,900	Y-26,400-1	...	...-..	...	...-...	...	...
	F	27-27-..	16,512-23,124	Y-24,624-1	...	...-..	...	...-...	...	...
Gallup t, N.M. (1,1)	P	53-53-40	16,817-27,435	None	1,535	1,238-80	1,040	153-45	94	203
	F	42-41-42	15,421-26,688	None	960	897-93	742	108-47	8	55
Garden City, Kan. (1,3)	P	72-46-40	21,016-28,028	None	...	...-..	...	...-...	...	...
	F	7-7-52	16,536-22,259	None	...	...-..	...	...-...	...	...
Garden City v, N.Y. (1,3)	P	52-52-40	32,072-53,369	Y-54,894-6	4,192	3,798-90	3,003	571-224	103	291
	F	35-35-40	30,671-41,402	Y-42,602-8	3,049	2,247-73	1,797	296-154	325	477
Gardner, Mass. (1,1)	P	30-28-37	19,114-25,292	Y-26,192-5	...	...-..	...	...-...	...	...
	F	40-38-42	19,290-25,290	Y-...-5	...	...-..	...	...-...	...	...

Table 3/23 continued

POLICE AND FIRE DEPARTMENT PERSONNEL, SALARIES, AND EXPENDITURES FOR CITIES 10,000 AND OVER: 1993

City (Service provision)	Depart-ment	Total personnel, no. uniformed, duty hours per week	Entrance, maximum salary ($)	Longevity pay, maximum ($), no. years to receive longevity pay	Total expendi-tures (A) ($)	Total personnel expendi-tures (B) ($), % of (A)	Salaries and wages (C) ($)	City contrib. to employee retirement, insurance (D) ($)	Capital outlay (E) ($)	All other (F) ($)
10,000-24,999 continued										
Garner t, N.C. (1,2) ....P		36-33-43	20,800-32,261	Y-33,874-7	1,665	1,208-72	978	176-54	148	309
	F	...-...-...	...-...	..-...-..	...	...-..	...	...-...	...	...
Gautier, Miss. (4,4) ....P		...-...-...	...-...	..-...-..	...	...-..	...	...-...	...	...
	F	...-...-...	...-...	..-...-..	...	...-..	...	...-...	...	...
Geneva, N.Y. (1,3) ....P		34-34-40	26,323-30,454	Y-31,454-5	1,698	1,513-89	1,165	217-131	35	150
	F	22-22-43	25,896-30,454	Y-31,454-5	1,252	1,078-86	830	154-94	35	139
Georgetown, Ky. (1,3) ....P		35-28-40	17,500-...	Y-27,500-1	1,640	1,252-76	910	227-115	15	373
	F	20-20-56	17,500-...	None	402	329-81	248	57-24	43	30
Georgetown, Tex. (1,3) ....P		26-12-40	21,528-32,302	Y-35,662-1	1,511	1,181-78	950	125-106	44	286
	F	14-12-53	19,531-29,307	Y-32,667-1	702	407-57	330	43-34	58	237
Germantown v, Wis. (1,2) ......P		40-31-45	30,416-36,257	None	1,975	1,611-81	1,167	287-157	83	281
	F	...-...-...	...-...	..-...-..	...	...-..	...	...-...	...	...
Gillette, Wyo. (1,-) ....P		52-38-40	24,627-31,387	None	2,267	1,909-84	1,475	296-138	70	288
	F	...-...-...	...-...	..-...-..	...	...-..	...	...-...	...	...
Girard, Ohio (1,1) ....P		23-23-40	27,570-...	Y-...-1	1,208	1,096-90	844	100-152	...	112
	F	17-17-53	27,943-...	Y-...-1	992	932-93	676	112-144	...	60
Gladstone, Ore. (1,2) ....P		12-12-40	26,772-32,544	None	...	...-..	...	...-...	21	...
	F	...-...-...	...-...	..-...-..	...	...-..	...	...-...	...	...
Glassboro b, N.J. (1,3) ....P		42-42-40	36,756-...	Y-44,864-3	...	...-..	...	...-...	...	...
		4-4-40	29,000-...	..-30,160-3	...	...-..	...	...-...	...	...
Glen Cove, N.Y. (1,2) ....P		47-47-40	28,699-53,063	Y-55,063-6	...	...-..	...	...-...	67	...
	F	...-...-...	...-...	..-...-..	...	...-..	...	...-...	...	...
Glen Ellyn v, Ill. (-,2) ....P		42-33-40	27,934-39,083	None	...	...-..	...	...-...	...	...
	F	...-...-...	...-...	..-...-..	...	...-..	...	...-...	...	...
Glen Rock b, N.J. (1,2) ....P		24-20-40	25,000-55,132	Y-57,132-4	...	...-..	...	...-...	1	...
	F	...-...-...	...-...	..-...-..	...	...-..	...	...-...	...	...
Goffstown t, N.H. (1,3) ....P		26-22-40	25,418-38,355	Y-40,175-8	...	...-..	...	...-...	...	...
	F	12-12-45	23,189-35,872	Y-37,692-8	...	...-..	...	...-...	...	...
Golden, Colo. (1,3) ....P		33-9-40	27,295-36,849	None	1,831	1,457-79	1,226	131-100	28	346
	F	3-2-..	...-...	None	426	134-31	72	58-4	93	199
Golden Valley, Minn. (3,2) .....P		40-30-40	24,864-38,232	Y-41,676-4	2,208	1,956-88	1,620	180-156	...	252
	F	...-...-...	...-...	..-...-..	...	...-..	...	...-...	...	...
Goodlettsville, Tenn. (1,3) ......P		37-28-42	16,253-23,150	Y-23,400-1	1,585	1,149-72	918	94-137	...	436
	F	11-11-56	14,914-21,819	Y-22,069-1	432	309-71	245	24-40	...	123
Goose Creek, S.C. (1,1) ....P		41-41-43	17,823-27,812	..-...-..	1,285	1,026-79	872	106-48	31	228
	F	21-21-40	16,544-25,816	..-...-..	750	539-71	464	50-25	103	108
Gorham t, Me. (1,3) ....P		21-15-40	23,767-26,747	None	541	464-85	390	29-45	30	47
	F	6-6-40	...-...	None	265	172-64	158	7-7	27	66
Grandville, Mich. (1,2) ....P		21-18-40	25,618-34,556	Y-35,156-5	1,337	936-70	731	141-64	9	392
	F	...-...-...	...-...	..-...-..	...	...-..	...	...-...	...	...
Grants Pass, Ore. (4,4) ....P		...-...-...	...-...	..-...-..	...	...-..	...	...-...	...	...
	F	...-...-...	...-...	..-...-..	...	...-..	...	...-...	...	...
Green River, Wyo. (1,3) ....P		31-31-40	...-...	..-...-..	...	...-..	...	...-...	...	...
	F	2-2-40	...-...	..-...-..	...	...-..	...	...-...	...	...
Greenacres City, Fla. (4,4) ....P		...-...-...	...-...	..-...-..	...	...-..	...	...-...	...	...
	F	...-...-...	...-...	..-...-..	...	...-..	...	...-...	...	...
Greenbelt, Md. (1,7) ....P		57-43-..	25,584-27,684	None	3,302	2,604-78	1,953	476-175	105	593
	F	...-...-...	...-...	..-...-..	...	...-..	...	...-...	...	...
Greendale v, Wis. (1,1) ....P		32-25-39	26,160-37,016	Y-37,316-10	1,807	1,702-94	1,206	343-153	...	105
	F	19-19-56	25,140-36,649	Y-36,949-10	1,143	1,074-93	758	222-94	...	69
Greeneville t, Tenn. (1,1) ....P		38-38-40	18,863-24,619	Y-...-..	...	...-..	...	...-...	...	...
	F	36-36-40	18,863-24,619	None	...	...-..	...	...-...	...	...
Greenfield t, Mass. (1,3) ....P		38-35-40	19,802-25,522	None	...	...-..	...	...-...	...	...
	F	25-25-48	21,093-25,199	None	...	...-..	...	...-...	...	...
Greenville, Tex. (1,1) ....P		53-48-40	21,944-29,444	Y-30,644-1	2,387	2,034-85	1,637	255-142	95	258
	F	49-48-56	22,679-27,569	Y-28,769-1	2,320	1,874-80	1,547	172-155	363	83
Greenwood, S.C. (1,1) ....P		63-63-40	18,475-26,870	None	1,952	1,627-83	1,272	223-132	101	224
	F	46-46-35	16,325-23,859	None	1,312	1,225-93	969	135-121	6	81
Greer, S.C. (1,3) ....P		42-35-42	17,272-24,181	..-...-..	1,284	1,040-80	818	150-72	36	208
	F	23-23-53	15,920-22,288	..-...-..	744	570-76	452	82-36	110	64
Griffith t, Ind. (1,2) ....P		36-27-38	25,539-30,899	Y-...-3	1,704	1,548-90	1,476	36-36	...	156
	F	...-...-...	...-...	..-...-..	...	...-..	...	...-...	...	...
Griswold t, Conn. (-,2) ....P		...-...-...	...-...	..-...-..	...	...-..	...	...-...	...	...
	F	...-...-...	...-...	..-...-..	...	...-..	...	...-...	...	...
Grosse Pointe Woods, Mich. (4,4) ....P		...-...-...	...-...	..-...-..	...	...-..	...	...-...	...	...
	F	...-...-...	...-...	..-...-..	...	...-..	...	...-...	...	...
Grove City, Ohio (1,5) ....P		47-33-40	22,776-36,441	..-...-5	...	...-..	...	...-...	...	...
	F	...-...-...	...-...	..-...-..	...	...-..	...	...-...	...	...
Groves, Tex. (1,3) ....P		16-15-40	18,542-27,587	Y-28,787-1	928	677-72	524	89-64	30	221
	F	8-8-56	18,542-27,587	Y-28,787-1	534	439-82	342	58-39	13	82
Gulfport, Fla. (1,2) ....P		35-28-40	...-...	None	...	...-..	...	...-...	...	...
	F	...-...-...	...-...	..-...-..	...	...-..	...	...-...	...	...
Gurnee v, Ill. (1,3) ....P		36-33-42	28,950-42,775	Y-43,775-10	1,795	1,319-73	1,216	18-85	100	376
	F	17-16-48	28,950-42,775	Y-43,775-10	1,213	834-68	773	15-46	203	176

Table 3/23 continued

POLICE AND FIRE DEPARTMENT PERSONNEL, SALARIES, AND EXPENDITURES FOR CITIES 10,000 AND OVER: 1993

City (Service provision)	Department	Total personnel, no. uniformed, duty hours per week	Entrance, maximum salary ($)	Longevity pay, maximum ($), no. years to receive longevity pay	Total expenditures (A) ($)	Total personnel expenditures (B) ($), % of (A)	Salaries and wages (C) ($)	City contrib. to employee retirement, insurance (D) ($)	Capital outlay (E) ($)	All other (F) ($)
10,000-24,999 continued										
Haddon tp, N.J. (1,5)	P	...-..-..	...-...	..-...-..	...	...-..	...	...-...	...	...
	F	...-..-..	...-...	..-...-..	...	...-..	...	...-...	...	...
Haddonfield b, N.J. (1,3)	P	21-16-48	28,830-38,440	Y-42,284-5	...	...-..	...	...-...	55	...
	F	6-6-40	32,611-37,129	Y-40,841-5	...	...-..	...	...-...	8	...
Haines City, Fla. (1,1)	P	50-37-40	21,229-21,908	Y-...-5	1,560	1,344-86	1,152	96-96	...	216
	F	16-16-56	18,500-23,584	Y-...-5	516	408-79	360	24-24	...	108
Hamburg v, N.Y. (1,2)	P	22-16-40	19,000-39,003	Y-39,478-5	837	798-95	678	51-69	...	39
	F	...-..-..	...-...	..-...-..	...	...-..	...	...-...	...	...
Hammond, La. (1,1)	P	67-49-40	13,827-24,828	Y-...-9	2,405	1,574-65	1,339	133-102	134	697
	F	51-51-53	12,542-20,427	Y-...-9	1,748	1,350-77	1,089	184-77	134	264
Hampden tp, Pa. (1,2)	P	15-15-40	21,500-...	Y-...-5	...	...-..	...	...-...	...	...
	F	...-..-..	...-...	..-...-..	...	...-..	...	...-...	...	...
Hampton t, N.H. (1,1)	P	41-5-40	26,042-34,902	Y-...-..	2,382	2,336-98	2,055	112-169	...	46
	F	41-5-42	24,783-33,212	Y-...-..	2,147	2,097-97	1,773	125-199	...	50
Hampton tp, Pa. (1,2)	P	16-15-..	31,000-35,000	Y-35,500-5	...	...-..	...	...-...	50	...
	F	...-..-..	...-...	..-...-..	...	...-..	...	...-...	...	...
Hamtramck, Mich. (1,1)	P	52-52-40	21,908-30,416	Y-31,016-1	2,560	2,425-94	1,908	71-446	3	132
	F	39-39-50	21,908-30,416	Y-31,016-1	1,891	1,754-92	1,406	48-300	40	97
Hanahan, S.C. (3,3)	P	31-23-43	17,948-...	None	1,236	811-65	666	114-31	207	218
	F	27-26-36	14,886-...	None	1,101	675-61	531	94-50	260	166
Hannibal, Mo. (1,1)	P	45-34-40	16,358-18,828	Y-21,841-1	1,527	1,265-82	1,015	117-133	16	246
	F	39-39-52	16,358-18,828	Y-21,841-1	1,300	1,172-90	931	133-108	36	92
Hanover t, Mass. (1,3)	P	26-24-40	26,849-...	Y-27,199-15	...	...-..	...	...-...	16	...
	F	14-13-42	24,705-28,666	None	...	...-..	...	...-...	11	...
Hanover b, Pa. (1,3)	P	19-19-40	26,165-31,509	Y-35,509-6	1,320	1,100-83	800	50-250	30	190
	F	16-16-56	18,727-27,226	..-32,226-6	...	...-..	...	...-...	80	...
Harker Heights, Tex. (1,1)	P	30-24-40	16,444-18,844	Y-...-1	870	713-81	633	50-30	31	126
	F	18-18-53	16,444-18,844	Y-...-1	261	221-84	198	14-9	2	38
Harper Woods, Mich. (1,1)	P	42-35-40	28,139-41,081	Y-42,485-5	3,414	2,908-85	2,192	506-210	94	412
	F	21-20-56	27,190-38,576	Y-41,469-5	1,701	1,396-82	1,049	242-105	2	303
Harrison tp, Pa. (1,2)	P	11-11-40	29,853-35,122	Y-41,282-5	727	654-89	517	68-69	13	60
	F	...-..-..	...-...	..-...-..	...	...-..	...	...-...	...	...
Hastings, Nebr. (1,3)	P	45-37-40	18,927-24,902	None	1,326	1,244-93	971	114-159	...	82
	F	28-27-56	18,200-23,945	None	879	836-95	651	77-108	...	43
Havelock, N.C. (4,4)	P	...-..-..	...-...	..-...-..	...	...-..	...	...-...	...	...
	F	...-..-..	...-...	..-...-..	...	...-..	...	...-...	...	...
Havre, Mont. (1,1)	P	19-17-40	19,177-21,198	Y-21,518-1	678	570-84	442	64-64	8	100
	F	17-17-48	17,278-20,408	Y-20,715-1	674	626-92	490	62-74	2	46
Hawaiian Gardens, Calif. (9,9)	P	...-..-..	...-...	..-...-..	...	...-..	...	...	...	...
	F	...-..-..	...-...	..-...-..	...	...-..	...	...	...	...
Hays, Kan. (1,3)	P	36-12-40	21,324-27,576	Y-29,506-5	...	...-..	...	...-...	...	...
	F	17-17-56	21,324-27,576	Y-29,506-5	...	...-..	...	...-...	...	...
Hazel Crest v, Ill. (1,3)	P	31-24-40	27,976-39,510	Y-42,010-5	1,491	1,329-89	930	245-154	74	88
	F	10-9-..	26,593-39,510	Y-42,010-5	...	...-..	...	...-...	30	...
Hazel Park, Mich. (1,1)	P	42-36-40	24,983-36,994	Y-37,734-5	1,325	1,244-93	888	237-119	...	81
	F	20-20-53	21,420-36,759	Y-37,494-5	624	600-96	425	123-52	...	24
Hazelwood, Mo. (1,1)	P	51-40-40	25,286-37,432	None	1,768	1,239-70	1,058	80-101	11	518
	F	34-32-56	22,345-36,302	None	1,551	839-54	719	55-65	2	710
Hazleton, Pa. (1,3)	P	28-23-40	19,250-27,484	Y-...-..	1,823	1,642-90	722	641-279	...	181
	F	20-20-42	26,048-...	Y-...-..	1,421	1,283-90	534	569-180	25	113
Helena, Mont. (1,1)	P	42-38-..	17,712-23,700	Y-26,160-..	1,734	1,466-84	1,215	142-109	58	210
	F	34-33-..	18,600-23,868	Y-27,642-..	1,606	1,343-83	1,122	120-101	162	101
Henderson, N.C. (3,1)	P	54-49-42	17,369-24,048	..-...-..	2,195	1,513-68	1,289	148-76	186	496
	F	34-33-56	17,369-24,048	..-...-..	1,336	1,006-75	856	104-46	42	288
Henderson, Tex. (1,3)	P	29-23-40	18,416-21,510	Y-21,750-1	1,038	927-89	681	99-147	...	111
	F	16-16-48	15,824-16,673	Y-...-1	825	422-51	318	44-60	...	403
Hercules, Calif. (3,5)	P	22-18-40	35,136-44,832	None	912	702-76	546	99-57	66	144
	F	...-..-..	...-...	..-...-..	...	...-..	...	...-...	...	...
Hereford, Tex. (1,2)	P	29-24-..	21,768-29,712	Y-30,912-1	1,102	947-85	768	108-71	...	155
	F	...-..-..	...-...	..-...-..	...	...-..	...	...-...	...	...
Hermiston, Ore. (1,3)	P	22-22-40	23,235-26,796	None	1,053	851-80	619	133-99	46	156
	F	15-13-52	22,788-27,480	None	772	639-82	468	95-76	29	104
Hermosa Beach, Calif. (4,4)	P	...-..-..	...-...	..-...-..	...	...-..	...	...-...	...	...
	F	...-..-..	...-...	..-...-..	...	...-..	...	...-...	...	...
Herndon t, Va. (1,7)	P	43-34-40	27,886-46,607	None	1,558	1,347-86	1,087	183-77	55	156
	F	...-..-..	...-...	..-...-..	...	...-..	...	...-...	...	...
Hibbing, Minn. (1,3)	P	29-28-40	24,552-...	Y-...-5	1,652	1,513-91	1,020	330-163	51	88
	F	30-30-52	30,581-34,356	Y-37,104-5	1,472	1,414-96	1,078	136-200	2	56
Hilliard, Ohio (1,9)	P	45-31-40	20,510-32,913	Y-33,663-5	2,423	2,219-91	1,573	426-220	31	173
	F	...-..-..	...-...	..-...-..	...	...-..	...	...-...	...	...
Hillsborough t, Calif. (1,1)	P	...-..-..	37,080-45,072	None	1,688	1,292-76	910	214-168	18	378
	F	28-28-56	32,724-39,996	None	1,422	1,184-83	888	190-106	56	182
Hilton Head Island t, S.C	P	...-..-..	...-...	..-...-..	...	...-..	...	...-...	...	...
	F	...-..-..	...-...	..-...-..	...	...-..	...	...-...	...	...

Table 3/23   **POLICE AND FIRE DEPARTMENT PERSONNEL, SALARIES, AND EXPENDITURES FOR**
continued   **CITIES 10,000 AND OVER: 1993**

City (Service provision)	Depart-ment	Total personnel, no. uniformed, duty hours per week	Entrance, maximum salary ($)	Longevity pay, maximum ($) no. years to receive longevity pay	Reported expenditures (in thousands)					
					Total expendi-tures (A) ($)	Total personnel expendi-tures (B) ($), % of (A)	Salaries and wages (C) ($)	City contrib. to employee retirement, insurance (D) ($)	Capital outlay (E) ($)	All other (F) ($)
10,000-24,999 continued										
Hinesville, Ga. (1,1)	P	56-49-40	17,201-24,305	None	1,862	1,468-78	1,054	131-283	58	336
	F	17-17-40	17,201-24,305	None	609	456-74	299	40-117	86	67
Hingham t, Mass. (1,1)	P	45-41-40	28,400-31,260	None	...	...-..	...	...-...	98	...
	F	58-53-42	29,500-32,500	None	...	...-..	...	...-...	24	...
Hinsdale v, Ill. (1,1)	P	37-27-40	27,800-39,900	Y-40,400-10	1,806	1,573-87	1,385	28-160	114	119
	F	21-20-56	28,900-43,200	Y-43,700-10	1,134	1,078-95	983	7-88	28	28
Holly Hill, Fla. (1,3)	P	33-24-40	21,690-31,884	None	1,487	1,278-85	1,021	216-41	54	155
	F	9-9-56	19,968-30,821	None	427	347-81	312	22-13	21	59
Homewood, Ala. (1,1)	P	55-33-40	23,753-33,425	Y-...-6	1,131	1,028-90	858	130-40	...	103
	F	65-64-53	23,753-33,425	Y-...-6	1,156	1,101-95	917	138-46	...	55
Homewood v, Ill. (3,3)	P	49-38-40	28,446-39,944	Y-41,044-6	3,345	2,651-79	2,251	156-244	187	507
	F	15-13-56	28,728-40,332	Y-41,332-6	1,097	807-73	666	56-85	108	182
Hopatcong b, N.J. (1,2)	P	25-21-40	27,078-43,855	Y-46,925-5	1,570	1,480-94	1,120	214-146	27	63
	F	...-.-..								
Hopewell, Va. (1,1)	P	51-41-40	20,382-32,527	Y-34,135-11	2,364	1,968-83	1,548	264-156	192	204
	F	36-35-60	19,491-31,001	Y-32,527-11	1,932	1,500-77	1,200	192-108	252	180
Hudson t, N.H. (1,1)	P	39-30-40	22,464-31,595	Y-...-..	1,000	878-87	755	40-83	...	122
	F	27-24-42	21,373-27,295	Y-...-..	798	703-88	602	40-61	...	95
Hueytown, Ala. (1,1)	P	27-27-40	22,609-30,264	None	1,080	999-92	798	102-99	...	81
	F	25-25-52	22,609-30,264	None	1,029	963-93	759	102-102	...	66
Hutchinson, Minn. (1,2)	P	23-18-40	25,459-29,702	Y-32,510-5	1,740	1,596-91	1,356	132-108	48	96
	F	...-.-..		...-.-..						
Hyattsville, Md. (1,7)	P	34-27-40	25,000-31,000	Y-...-1	1,567	1,227-78	1,000	127-100	40	300
	F	...-.-..	...-..	...-.-..						
Independence, Ky. (1,5)	P	12-11-40	20,425-...	Y-...-..	698	442-63	314	58-70	4	252
	F	...-.-..	...-..	...-.-..	...	...-..	...	...-...	...	...
Indianola, Iowa (1,2)	P	15-13-40	21,145-26,957	Y-27,282-5	...	...-..	...	...-...	67	...
	F	...-.-..		...-.-..	...	...-..	...	...-...	...	...
Jacksonville, Ill. (1,1)	P	43-35-40	24,582-31,928	Y-33,205-6	...	...-..	...	...-...	...	...
	F	26-25-56	24,582-31,390	Y-32,290-7	...	...-..	...	...-...	...	...
Jacksonville, Tex. (1,3)	P	30-22-40	19,296-19,764	Y-20,964-25	682	616-90	458	76-82	...	66
	F	24-23-56	16,212-20,124	Y-21,324-25	702	510-72	390	64-56	50	142
Jacksonville Beach, Fla. (1,1)	P	68-48-40	24,429-35,974	Y-36,934-5	3,566	3,111-87	2,687	296-128	119	336
	F	33-31-56	21,228-24,227	Y-25,184-5	1,816	1,640-90	1,423	151-66	36	140
Jamestown, N.D. (1,3)	P	32-28-..	18,672-25,116	Y-26,120-5	1,201	968-80	827	84-57	5	228
	F	6-6-40	18,672-25,116	Y-26,120-5	317	229-72	198	19-12	13	75
Jasper, Ala. (1,3)	P	58-39-40	20,277-...	Y-...-5	1,619	1,319-81	1,024	140-155	65	235
	F	18-18-48	18,482-...	Y-...-5	719	505-70	385	53-67	76	138
Jeffersontown, Ky. (1,-)	P	45-38-40	22,795-34,053	Y-38,093-2	...	...-..	...	...-...	...	...
	F	...-.-..			...	...-..	...	...-...	...	...
Jennings, La. (3,3)	P	24-24-43	12,889-14,206	..-...-3	...	...-..	...	...-...	...	...
	F	12-12-53	13,504-15,378	..-...-3	...	...-..	...	...-...	...	...
Junction City, Kan. (1,1)	P	57-43-40	18,500-27,165	None	2,007	1,530-76	1,321	106-103	...	477
	F	32-31-56	17,015-24,725	None	883	847-95	730	59-58	...	36
Jupiter t, Fla. (1,7)	P	94-74-40	22,745-32,427	Y-33,177-9	3,050	2,746-90	2,160	324-262	46	258
	F	...-.-..	...-..	Y-...-..	...	...-..	...	...-...	...	...
Kalispell, Mont. (1,1)	P	36-12-40	25,065-29,477	None	2,382	1,265-53	1,031	99-135	50	1,067
	F	23-23-40	22,712-29,500	None	774	716-92	567	71-78	15	43
Kaysville, Utah (1,2)	P	12-10-40	21,780-32,556	None	647	523-80	387	94-42	45	79
	F	...-.-..	...-..	...-.-..	...	...-..	...	...-...	...	...
Kearney, Nebr. (1,3)	P	38-38-41	20,000-28,000	None	1,764	1,402-79	1,190	152-60	84	278
	F	3-3-40	19,000-27,000	None	262	140-53	120	14-6	28	94
Keizer, Ore. (3,5)	P	27-23-40	26,856-32,580	None	1,030	684-66	488	80-116	72	274
	F	...-.-..	...-..	...-.-..	...	...-..	...	...-...	...	...
Keller, Tex. (1,3)	P	33-22-40	23,263-...	Y-24,486-1	...	...-..	...	...-...	...	...
	F	18-17-56	23,263-...	Y-24,486-1	...	...-..	...	...-...	...	...
Kelso, Wash. (1,5)	P	27-23-40	29,448-38,640	Y-41,731-5	1,775	1,490-83	1,189	145-156	8	277
	F	...-.-..		...-.-..	...	...-..	...	...-...	...	...
Kenmore v, N.Y. (1,3)	P	25-25-40	36,607-51,640	Y-...-5	...	...-..	...	...-...	98	...
	F	3-3-40	23,601-37,113	Y-...-5	...	...-..	...	...-...	100	...
Keokuk, Iowa (1,1)	P	35-27-42	19,077-22,991	Y-24,431-5	1,142	922-80	717	127-78	35	185
	F	19-19-56	19,081-23,128	Y-24,568-5	784	628-80	483	100-45	76	80
Kernersville t, N.C. (9,1)	P	47-37-45	17,705-24,914	Y-...-..	1,024	746-72	588	108-50	3	275
	F	30-30-50	17,356-24,424	Y-...-..	840	511-60	415	61-35	13	316
Kerrville, Tex. (4,4)	P	...-.-..	...-..	...-.-..	...	...-..	...	...-...	...	...
	F	...-.-..	...-..	...-.-..	...	...-..	...	...-...	...	...
Kewanee, Ill. (1,1)	P	23-18-39	21,420-23,970	Y-24,880-..	...	...-..	...	...-...	85	...
	F	19-19-56	18,755-23,607	Y-26,017-5	...	...-..	...	...-...	10	...
Key West, Fla. (1,1)	P	102-74-40	30,598-58,439	None	5,567	5,100-91	4,000	743-357	217	250
	F	68-67-56	23,425-34,500	None	3,461	3,360-97	2,600	531-229	39	62
Kilgore, Tex. (1,1)	P	36-28-..	21,679-...	Y-...-1	...	...-..	...	...-...	...	...
	F	30-30-..	20,043-...	Y-...-1	...	...-..	...	...-...	...	...
Killingly t, Conn. (9,5)	P	...-.-..	...-..	...-.-..	...	...-..	...	...-...	...	...
	F	...-.-..	...-..	...-.-..	...	...-..	...	...-...	...	...

Table 3/23 continued   POLICE AND FIRE DEPARTMENT PERSONNEL, SALARIES, AND EXPENDITURES FOR CITIES 10,000 AND OVER: 1993

City (Service provision)	Depart- ment	Total personnel, no. uniformed, duty hours per week	Entrance, maximum salary ($)	Longevity pay, maximum ($) no. years to receive longevity pay	Reported expenditures (in thousands)					
					Total expendi- tures (A) ($)	Total personnel expendi- tures (B) ($), % of (A)	Salaries and wages (C) ($)	City contrib. to employee retirement, insurance (D) ($)	Capital outlay (E) ($)	All other (F) ($)
10,000-24,999 continued										
Kingman, Ariz. (1,3)	P	48-15-40	24,635-35,308	None	2,152	1,821-84	1,451	188-182	76	255
	F	28-26-53	23,462-33,627	None	1,407	1,076-76	885	69-122	65	266
Kingston, Pa. (1,3)	P	21-21-40	18,500-27,300	Y-...-3	1,507	693-45	602	21-70	50	764
	F	20-20-40	17,500-25,700	Y-...-3	1,208	569-47	493	17-59	75	564
Kirksville, Mo. (1,1)	P	28-22-40	16,268-21,801	Y-...-3	1,017	849-83	695	77-77	27	141
	F	22-21-57	14,121-18,923	Y-...-3	789	679-86	533	78-68	...	110
Klamath Falls, Ore. (1,5)	P	32-30-40	27,480-33,720	Y-...-..	2,018	1,657-82	1,255	273-129	69	292
	F	...-..-..	...-...	..-..-..	...	...-..	...	...-...	...	...
La Grande, Ore. (1,3)	P	24-13-40	24,000-30,000	None	1,479	1,338-90	1,060	218-60	26	115
	F	12-..-..	24,000-30,000	None	824	733-88	584	119-30	16	75
La Palma, Calif. (1,7)	P	30-25-32	35,328-47,340	None	2,893	2,401-82	1,788	426-187	164	328
	F	...-..-..	...-...	..-..-..	...	...-..	...	...-...	...	...
La Porte, Ind. (1,1)	P	43-38-..	21,076-22,076	Y-25,166-3	2,184	2,135-97	1,398	590-147	...	49
	F	43-43-..	21,076-22,076	Y-25,166-3	2,140	2,138-99	1,452	539-147	...	2
La Quinta, Calif. (7,7)	P	...-..-..	...-...	..-..-..	...	...-..	...	...-...	...	...
	F	...-..-..	...-...	..-..-..	...	...-..	...	...-...	...	...
Lacey, Wash. (1,7)	P	41-41-42	27,796-39,108	None	2,104	1,948-92	1,656	112-180	...	156
	F	...-..-..	...-...	..-..-..	...	...-..	...	...-...	...	...
Lackawanna, N.Y. (1,1)	P	43-43-40	25,441-30,241	Y-31,141-10	2,399	2,312-96	1,766	383-163	...	87
	F	51-51-40	22,905-28,996	Y-29,896-10	3,024	2,829-93	2,161	481-187	12	183
Laconia, N.H. (1,3)	P	39-31-40	23,525-30,035	Y-...-5	...	...-..	...	...-...	...	...
	F	32-30-42	24,177-26,710	Y-...-5	...	...-..	...	...-...	...	...
Laguna Beach, Calif. (1,1)	P	66-46-40	34,908-46,812	None	6,172	3,938-63	3,239	482-217	222	2,012
	F	40-39-56	29,772-37,764	None	3,723	2,790-74	2,292	346-152	133	800
Laguna Niguel, Calif. (7,7)	P	...-..-..	...-...	..-..-..	...	...-..	...	...-...	...	...
	F	...-..-..	...-...	..-..-..	...	...-..	...	...-...	...	...
Lake City, Fla. (1,1)	P	36-31-40	14,560-22,880	None	1,155	999-86	885	75-39	...	156
	F	35-32-52	13,520-21,632	None	786	675-85	579	69-27	12	99
Lake Forest, Ill. (1,1)	P	40-27-40	31,700-43,100	Y-43,700-5	2,154	2,058-95	1,686	258-114	18	78
	F	33-32-48	30,200-41,100	Y-41,700-5	3,018	2,958-98	1,044	1,842-72	...	60
Lake Havasu City, Ariz. (1,1)	P	70-51-40	23,171-33,093	None	2,387	1,911-80	1,565	137-209	98	378
	F	60-54-40	23,171-33,093	None	1,945	1,701-87	1,413	111-177	...	244
Lamesa, Tex. (1,3)	P	23-16-40	18,000-30,000	Y-31,200-3	...	...-..	...	...-...	...	...
	F	9-9-53	16,800-21,000	Y-22,200-3	...	...-..	...	...-...	...	...
Lansdale b, Pa. (1,2)	P	29-22-40	25,784-42,242	Y-48,156-5	1,859	1,629-87	1,239	172-218	12	218
	F	...-..-..	...-...	..-..-..	...	...-..	...	...-...	...	...
Lansdowne b, Pa. (1,2)	P	18-15-42	...-...	..-...-..	1,231	1,064-86	863	68-133	15	152
	F	...-..-..	...-...	..-..-..	...	...-..	...	...-...	...	...
Larkspur, Calif. (-,1)	P	...-..-..	...-...	..-..-..	...	...-..	...	...-...	...	...
	F	18-18-56	33,576-40,248	None	918	689-75	550	71-68	8	221
Las Vegas, N.M. (1,3)	P	...-..-..	...-...	..-..-..	...	...-..	...	...-...	...	...
	F	13-12-..	11,664-...	Y-...-..	388	339-87	282	41-16	...	49
Laurinburg, N.C. (1,3)	P	33-28-42	19,433-27,344	None	1,233	941-76	786	92-63	56	236
	F	4-4-..	18,508-26,042	None	248	169-68	144	15-10	6	73
Lawrenceville, Ga. (1,7)	P	47-38-40	24,606-...	None	...	...-..	...	...-...	...	...
	F	...-..-..	...-...	..-..-..	...	...-..	...	...-...	...	...
Leawood, Kan. (1,1)	P	57-41-40	21,536-35,766	Y-...-5	1,242	1,020-82	828	114-78	...	222
	F	40-39-53	19,810-32,758	Y-...-5	1,577	1,513-95	1,212	180-121	...	64
Lebanon, Ind. (1,1)	P	20-20-48	22,000-22,500	..-26,000-5	...	...-..	...	...-...	...	...
	F	19-19-48	22,000-22,500	..-26,000-5	847	832-98	488	311-33	...	15
Lebanon, Ohio (1,3)	P	28-28-40	23,566-...	Y-36,670-5	1,296	1,147-88	841	178-128	...	149
	F	1-1-40	39,170-40,541	Y-...-5	581	102-17	90	8-4	397	82
Lebanon, Ore. (1,5)	P	25-..-48	23,064-29,052	None	...	...-..	...	...-...	3	...
	F	...-..-..	...-...	..-..-..	...	...-..	...	...-...	...	...
Ledyard t, Conn. (1,3)	P	16-15-40	28,472-34,344	Y-...-..	916	780-85	650	82-48	50	86
	F	5-5-45	23,388-30,299	Y-30,849-5	415	200-48	164	16-20	77	138
Leesburg, Fla. (1,1)	P	59-47-40	20,301-25,917	None	2,608	1,764-67	1,397	242-125	111	733
	F	30-29-56	19,365-25,946	None	1,475	1,058-71	845	140-73	11	406
Leesburg t, Va. (1,9)	P	36-32-40	25,559-38,363	Y-...-..	1,828	1,728-94	1,346	194-188	10	90
	F	...-..-..	...-...	..-..-..	...	...-..	...	...-...	...	...
Lemon Grove, Calif. (7,1)	P	...-..-..	...-...	..-..-..	...	...-..	...	...-...	...	...
	F	22-21-56	31,649-37,533	None	859	747-86	586	109-52	...	112
Lemoore, Calif. (3,2)	P	26-21-40	25,296-32,460	None	1,516	1,216-80	915	247-54	7	293
	F	...-..-..	...-...	..-..-..	...	...-..	...	...-...	...	...
Lenoir, N.C. (1,1)	P	58-48-43	15,450-...	Y-15,604-..	...	...-..	...	...-...	...	...
	F	56-55-56	15,450-...	Y-15,604-..	...	...-..	...	...-...	...	...
Liberal, Kan. (3,3)	P	34-31-42	18,343-24,973	None	1,603	831-51	624	66-141	...	772
	F	11-11-53	18,052-19,374	None	460	275-59	203	18-54	...	185
Liberty, Mo. (1,1)	P	36-28-40	22,896-30,900	None	1,577	1,359-86	1,126	148-85	...	218
	F	27-27-56	22,896-30,900	None	1,265	1,113-87	903	146-64	...	152
Libertyville v, Ill. (1,3)	P	47-47-40	30,958-41,562	None	2,669	2,391-89	2,039	146-206	3	275
	F	30-30-56	28,044-37,584	None	2,075	1,839-88	1,591	100-148	42	194
Lighthouse Point, Fla. (4,1)	P	...-..-..	...-...	..-..-..	...	...-..	...	...-...	...	...

Table 3/23 — POLICE AND FIRE DEPARTMENT PERSONNEL, SALARIES, AND EXPENDITURES FOR
continued — CITIES 10,000 AND OVER: 1993

City (Service provision)	Department	Total personnel, no. uniformed, duty hours per week	Entrance, maximum salary ($)	Longevity pay, maximum ($), no. years to receive longevity pay	Total expenditures (A) ($)	Total personnel expenditures (B) ($), % of (A)	Salaries and wages (C) ($)	City contrib. to employee retirement, insurance (D) ($)	Capital outlay (E) ($)	All other (F) ($)
10,000-24,999 continued										
Lighthouse Point, Fla. (4,1) cont.	F	...-..-..	...-...	..-..-..	...	...-..	...	...-...	...	...
Lincoln, Ill. (1,1)	P	24-24-50	26,520-...	Y-31,824-2	...	...-..	...	...-...	22	...
	F	23-23-50	25,920-...	Y-30,480-2	774	589-76	530	6-53	10	175
Lincoln t, R.I. (1,5)	P	31-26-37	22,364-33,219	Y-36,042-3	1,099	984-89	761	173-50	...	115
	F	...-..-..	...-...	..-..-..						
Logansport, Ind. (1,1)	P	40-33-..	20,910-...	Y-21,910-1	1,418	1,385-97	1,153	23-209	...	33
	F	45-45-..	20,910-...	Y-21,910-1	1,720	1,659-96	1,276	143-240	8	53
Loma Linda, Calif. (9,3)	P	...-..-..	...-...	Y-...-..						
	F	18-16-..	25,776-36,264	Y-...-..	857	661-77	538	70-53	...	196
Londonderry t, N.H. (1,3)	P	43-11-40	25,801-31,225	Y-31,485-3	...	...-..	...	...-...	46	...
	F	30-..-48	20,848-31,292	Y-31,742-6	...	...-..	...	...-...	...	...
Longwood, Fla. (1,1)	P	34-30-43	19,437-27,256	..-28,006-..	1,666	1,466-87	1,066	342-58	4	196
	F	29-28-56	19,017-33,235	..-33,985-..	1,311	1,188-90	851	293-44	7	116
Los Alamitos, Calif. (1,7)	P	30-24-40	35,268-43,308	..-...-..						
	F	...-..-..	...-...	..-...-..	...	...-..	...	...-...	...	...
Louisville, Colo. (1,5)	P	24-21-40	25,042-33,806	None	1,230	1,089-88	873	95-121	5	136
	F	...-..-..	...-...		...	...-..	...	...-...	...	...
Loves Park, Ill. (1,2)	P	32-30-40	21,000-30,800	Y-33,264-5	1,059	1,012-95	798	118-96	5	42
	F	...-..-..	...-...	..-...-..						
Lower tp, N.J. (1,2)	P	50-40-40	22,495-40,491	Y-44,540-5	...	...-..	...	...-...	...	...
	F	...-..-..	...-...	..-...-..						
Lower Burrell, Pa. (1,2)	P	13-13-40	26,291-34,000	Y-...-..	...	...-..	...	...-...	64	...
	F	...-..-..	...-...	..-...-..	...	...-..	...	...-...	...	...
Lower Moreland tp, Pa. (1,2)	P	27-20-40	31,428-38,383	Y-42,221-20	1,478	1,395-94	1,084	118-193	27	56
	F	...-..-..	...-...	..-...-..						
Lower Providence tp, Pa. (1,2)	P	32-25-40	27,404-38,298	Y-40,548-5	1,524	1,411-92	1,082	157-172	34	79
	F	...-..-..	...-...	..-...-..						
Lower Southampton tp, Pa. (1,2)	P	27-24-40	18,000-24,710	Y-...-4	...	...-..	...	...-...	33	...
	F	...-..-..	...-...	..-...-..	...	...-..	...	...-...	...	...
Ludlow t, Mass. (1,1)	P	31-30-40	23,152-26,457	Y-26,557-5	1,428	1,367-95	1,125	178-64	...	61
	F	28-28-42	23,226-26,539	Y-26,639-5	1,346	1,302-96	1,064	166-72	...	44
Lumberton, N.C. (-,3)	P	70-60-42	15,871-16,674	Y-16,714-..	1,641	1,222-74	986	166-70	80	339
	F	58-57-51	15,871-16,674	Y-16,714-..	1,901	898-47	745	96-57	738	265
Lyndhurst tp, N.J. (1,2)	P	48-48-37	30,819-50,083	Y-53,089-4	3,863	3,568-92	2,800	368-400	40	255
	F	...-..-..	...-...	..-...-..	...	...-..	...	...-...	...	...
Lyndhurst, Ohio (1,1)	P	37-30-40	28,830-36,977	Y-...-6	2,283	1,971-86	1,522	274-175	86	226
	F	22-22-53	28,736-33,779	Y-...-6	1,404	1,289-91	959	222-108	28	87
Mc Alester, Okla. (1,1)	P	48-39-40	14,376-18,600	Y-20,844-3	1,687	1,571-93	1,280	191-100	2	114
	F	41-40-56	14,244-19,668	Y-20,160-3	2,075	2,016-97	1,214	718-84	6	53
Mc Henry, Ill. (1,5)	P	39-28-40	24,842-39,013	Y-40,574-6	1,809	1,639-90	1,231	296-112	68	102
	F	...-..-..	...-...	..-...-..	...	...-..	...	...-...	...	...
Mc Kinney, Tex. (1,1)	P	46-34-40	26,265-31,982	Y-33,182-1	1,902	1,674-88	1,386	189-99	3	225
	F	34-33-53	23,561-...	Y-29,874-1	1,596	1,413-88	1,179	159-75	3	180
Mc Minnville, Ore. (3,3)	P	29-25-40	25,632-32,724	Y-34,164-10	1,091	886-81	655	131-100	81	124
	F	12-..-40	25,632-32,724	Y-34,164-10	482	431-89	329	60-42	27	24
Mc Pherson, Kan. (1,1)	P	26-26-40	18,814-24,377	None	958	823-85	701	99-23	25	110
	F	16-16-56	15,463-24,111	None	675	570-84	484	68-18	40	65
Machesney Park v, Ill. (9,9)	P	...-..-..	...-...	..-...-..	...	...-..	...	...-...	...	...
	F	...-..-..	...-...	..-...-..	...	...-..	...	...-...	...	...
Macomb, Ill. (1,1)	P	29-24-40	23,176-26,923	Y-30,154-2	...	...-..	...	...-...	...	...
	F	21-21-56	23,907-25,857	Y-28,960-2	...	...-..	...	...-...	...	...
Madison, Ala. (1,1)	P	42-40-40	18,438-43,319	None	1,353	1,182-87	967	166-49	...	171
	F	27-26-53	18,438-43,319	None	820	761-92	624	106-31	...	59
Madison, Ind. (1,2)	P	28-23-40	18,700-21,666	Y-...-1	765	641-83	631	8-2	...	124
	F	...-..-..	...-...	..-...-..	...	...-..	...	...-...	...	...
Madisonville, Ky. (1,1)	P	...-..-..	...-...	..-...-..	...	...-..	...	...-...	...	...
	F	...-..-..	...-...	..-...-..	...	...-..	...	...-...	...	...
Magnolia, Ark. (1,1)	P	21-17-42	14,000-22,691	Y-23,051-2	638	538-84	447	45-46	...	100
	F	11-11-56	14,000-22,691	Y-23,051-2	316	301-95	254	10-37	...	15
Mamaroneck t, N.Y. (1,3)	P	41-40-38	25,000-49,000	Y-49,515-7	3,210	3,060-95	2,300	560-200	45	105
	F	14-14-39	22,000-45,790	Y-...-7	1,132	897-79	680	102-115	...	235
Mandan, N.D. (1,3)	P	30-24-42	18,500-...	..-...-..	...	...-..	...	...-...	...	...
	F	...-..-..	...-...	..-...-..	...	...-..	...	...-...	...	...
Mansfield t, Conn. (-,8)	P	4-3-40	30,000-34,000	Y-35,000-6	145	141-97	112	17-12	...	4
	F	...-..-..	...-...	..-...-..	...	...-..	...	...-...	...	...
Mansfield t, Mass. (1,1)	P	34-28-40	24,917-33,800	Y-34,200-5	...	...-..	...	...-...	2	...
	F	28-27-42	23,358-30,723	Y-31,073-5	...	...-..	...	...-...	3	...
Mansfield, Tex. (3,3)	P	44-16-40	22,000-30,327	Y-30,663-..	...	...-..	...	...-...	...	...
	F	23-1-50	21,000-28,948	Y-29,284-..	...	...-..	...	...-...	...	...
Manville b, N.J. (1,2)	P	25-23-40	36,615-...	Y-37,815-5	1,595	1,499-93	1,201	135-163	...	96
	F	...-..-..	...-...	..-...-..	...	...-..	...	...-...	...	...
Maple Shade tp, N.J. (1,2)	P	37-30-40	28,944-...	Y-37,300-7	...	...-..	...	...-...	...	...
	F	...-..-..	...-...	..-...-..	...	...-..	...	...-...	...	...
Maplewood tp, N.J. (1,1)	P	68-56-40	32,000-40,000	Y-44,000-5	2,348	1,770-75	1,398	126-246	500	78

Table 3/23 continued **POLICE AND FIRE DEPARTMENT PERSONNEL, SALARIES, AND EXPENDITURES FOR CITIES 10,000 AND OVER: 1993**

City (Service provision)	Depart-ment	Total personnel, no. uniformed, duty hours per week	Entrance, maximum salary ($)	Longevity pay, maximum ($) no. years to receive longevity pay	Total expendi-tures (A) ($)	Total personnel expendi-tures (B) ($), % of (A)	Salaries and wages (C) ($)	City contrib. to employee retirement, insurance (D) ($)	Capital outlay (E) ($)	All other (F) ($)
10,000-24,999 continued										
Maplewood tp, N.J. (1,1) cont.	F	37-36-42	32,000-40,000	Y-44,000-5	1,060	1,030-97	856	72-102	...	30
Marblehead t, Mass. (1,1)	P	39-37-38	22,150-27,135	Y-27,860-5	2,210	2,043-92	1,618	258-167	11	156
	F	42-42-42	22,150-27,135	Y-27,860-5	2,017	1,945-96	1,491	279-175	10	62
Marion, Iowa (1,1)	P	38-30-40	21,537-27,353	Y-28,053-5	1,588	1,356-85	1,082	100-174	36	196
	F	22-22-56	21,945-26,523	Y-27,223-5	906	839-92	668	59-112	...	67
Marquette, Mich. (1,1)	P	42-42-40	23,346-29,182	Y-29,512-5	1,647	1,430-86	1,289	3-138	59	158
	F	23-23-54	20,584-27,445	Y-27,660-5	1,118	780-69	701	5-74	41	297
Marshall, Mo. (1,3)	P	31-22-40	16,427-18,383	None	820	682-83	550	48-84	32	106
	F	17-17-56	14,999-18,157	None	696	451-64	355	42-54	180	65
Marshall, Tex. (1,1)	P	57-41-40	20,129-21,600	Y-22,800-1	857	364-42	314	34-16	...	493
	F	40-38-56	20,129-21,600	Y-22,800-1	...	...-...	...	...-...	...	...
Martinsburg, W.Va. (1,1)	P	51-41-40	...-...	..-..-..	...	...-...	...	...-...	...	...
	F	25-25-56	...-...	..-..-..	...	...-...	...	...-...	...	...
Marysville, Calif. (1,1)	P	...-..-..	...-...	..-..-..	...	...-...	...	...-...	...	...
	F	...-..-..	...-...	..-..-..	...	...-...	...	...-...	...	...
Marysville, Wash. (3,6)	P	44-23-48	29,166-37,020	Y-38,040-6	1,894	1,704-89	1,408	107-189	46	144
	F	...-..-..	...-...	..-..-..	...	...-...	...	...-...	...	...
Maryville, Mo. (4,4)	P	...-..-..	...-...	..-..-..	...	...-...	...	...-...	...	...
	F	...-..-..	...-...	..-..-..	...	...-...	...	...-...	...	...
Maryville, Tenn. (3,3)	P	37-31-40	18,907-52,686	None	1,870	1,344-71	1,098	104-142	28	498
	F	33-32-56	17,160-52,686	None	1,488	1,282-86	1,046	102-134	22	184
Massapequa Park v, N.Y. (7,9)	P	...-..-..	...-...	..-..-..	...	...-...	...	...-...	...	...
	F	...-..-..	...-...	..-..-..	...	...-...	...	...-...	...	...
Massena v, N.Y. (1,3)	P	23-23-40	18,500-30,039	Y-31,039-5	1,285	1,194-92	919	174-101	39	52
	F	8-8-42	28,217-30,794	Y-31,794-10	433	358-82	275	52-31	13	62
Matteson v, Ill. (1,3)	P	46-35-38	29,715-39,868	None	2,773	2,459-88	1,825	430-204	76	238
	F	23-22-56	29,772-39,945	None	1,617	1,477-91	1,121	233-123	61	79
Mauldin, S.C. (3,3)	P	33-27-40	16,447-26,949	None	1,382	994-71	808	120-66	142	246
	F	30-30-53	16,447-24,063	None	978	850-86	678	116-56	26	102
Maumee, Ohio (1,3)	P	51-40-40	25,452-32,383	Y-33,883-5	...	...-...	...	...-...	128	...
	F	4-4-..	...-...	..-..-..	...	...-...	...	...-...	35	...
Meadville, Pa. (1,3)	P	29-22-40	20,992-27,990	Y-30,089-6	1,021	925-90	772	39-114	24	72
	F	18-18-56	20,228-28,141	Y-28,985-5	1,067	739-69	511	163-65	214	114
Medford tp, N.J. (1,2)	P	42-33-40	24,484-41,981	Y-43,481-4	2,812	2,556-90	1,949	339-268	...	256
	F	...-..-..	...-...	..-..-..	...	...-...	...	...-...	...	...
Menasha, Wis. (1,1)	P	34-29-38	24,660-31,848	None	1,983	1,810-91	1,207	391-212	34	139
	F	29-29-56	27,516-32,808	None	1,651	1,572-95	1,055	328-189	11	68
Menomonie, Wis. (1,3)	P	31-26-42	26,424-28,944	Y-30,096-4	...	...-...	...	...-...	112	...
	F	21-20-56	23,184-28,788	Y-29,940-4	...	...-...	...	...-...	34	...
Mequon, Wis. (1,2)	P	37-36-40	30,942-35,766	Y-36,216-2	2,288	2,037-89	1,495	383-159	106	145
	F	...-..-..	...-...	..-..-..	...	...-...	...	...-...	...	...
Mercedes, Tex. (1,2)	P	26-19-43	14,352-16,057	Y-16,445-1	931	775-83	654	85-36	23	133
	F	...-..-..	...-...	..-..-..	...	...-...	...	...-...	...	...
Mercer Island, Wash. (4,4)	P	...-..-..	...-...	..-..-..	...	...-...	...	...-...	...	...
	F	...-..-..	...-...	..-..-..	...	...-...	...	...-...	...	...
Merriam, Kan. (1,3)	P	27-27-41	23,436-31,639	None	1,393	1,188-85	972	118-98	76	129
	F	15-15-56	22,134-29,881	None	777	683-87	538	67-78	40	54
Mexico, Mo. (4,4)	P	...-..-..	...-...	..-..-..	...	...-...	...	...-...	...	...
	F	...-..-..	...-...	..-..-..	...	...-...	...	...-...	...	...
Miami, Okla. (1,1)	P	35-28-40	15,828-19,542	None	1,301	895-68	760	68-67	364	42
	F	30-29-..	16,079-19,542	None	1,452	764-52	638	70-56	673	15
Miami Shores v, Fla. (3,7)	P	41-33-..	31,085-39,769	Y-...-5	1,153	827-71	637	174-16	...	326
	F	...-..-..	...-...	..-..-..	...	...-...	...	...-...	...	...
Middletown tp, Pa. (9,2)	P	...-..-..	...-...	..-..-..	...	...-...	...	...-...	...	...
	F	...-..-..	...-...	..-..-..	...	...-...	...	...-...	...	...
Middletown t, R.I. (1,1)	P	40-37-37	23,118-28,284	Y-...-5	1,238	1,067-86	808	247-12	...	171
	F	34-33-42	23,092-27,386	Y-...-5	1,070	912-85	695	205-12	...	158
Midvale, Utah (1,2)	P	24-22-40	19,476-32,868	None	...	...-...	...	...-...	154	...
	F	...-..-..	...-...	..-..-..	...	...-...	...	...-...	...	...
Milford t, N.H. (1,3)	P	23-21-40	23,332-29,540	Y-...-5	1,099	981-89	778	86-117	17	101
	F	1-1-40	...-...	Y-...-5	191	125-65	111	9-5	16	50
Mill Valley, Calif. (1,1)	P	22-16-40	34,452-41,880	None	...	...-...	...	...-...	14	...
	F	29-28-56	33,108-40,248	None	...	...-...	...	...-...	7	...
Millbrae, Calif. (1,1)	P	31-22-40	35,772-43,920	None	2,740	2,286-83	1,675	338-273	2	452
	F	24-23-56	36,984-45,408	None	1,945	1,758-90	1,228	337-193	2	185
Millburn tp, N.J. (1,3)	P	58-54-39	31,874-44,134	Y-...-5	...	...-...	...	...-...	...	...
	F	47-46-42	31,874-44,134	Y-...-5	...	...-...	...	...-...	...	...
Millington, Tenn. (1,1)	P	31-25-40	19,260-25,462	None	1,039	885-85	714	80-91	21	133
	F	18-18-56	17,565-23,190	None	548	493-89	394	43-56	4	51
Milwaukie, Ore. (1,1)	P	34-23-40	24,666-34,596	None	...	...-...	...	...-...	...	...
	F	25-25-56	24,996-35,688	None	...	...-...	...	...-...	12	...
Mineola v, N.Y. (7,2)	P	...-..-..	...-...	..-..-..	...	...-...	...	...-...	...	...
	F	...-..-..	...-...	..-..-..	...	...-...	...	...-...	...	...
Mineral Wells, Tex. (3,3)	P	31-25-40	20,928-23,568	Y-...-2	1,066	1,027-96	757	107-163	...	39

Table 3/23 continued **POLICE AND FIRE DEPARTMENT PERSONNEL, SALARIES, AND EXPENDITURES FOR CITIES 10,000 AND OVER: 1993**

City (Service provision)	Depart-ment	Total personnel, no. uniformed, duty hours per week	Entrance, maximum salary ($)	Longevity pay, maximum ($) no. years to receive longevity pay	Total expendi-tures (A) ($)	Total personnel expendi-tures (B) ($), % of (A)	Salaries and wages (C) ($)	City contrib. to employee retirement, insurance (D) ($)	Capital outlay (E) ($)	All other (F) ($)
10,000-24,999 continued										
Mineral Wells, Tex. (3,3) cont.	F	9-7-53	20,928-21,408	Y-...-2	262	235-89	179	27-29	...	27
Mitchell, S.D. (1,1)	P	30-22-40	18,396-23,749	..-...-..	1,011	866-85	710	104-52	53	92
	F	16-16-53	18,084-22,790	..-...-..	528	477-90	384	64-29	16	35
Moberly, Mo. (1,1)	P	38-32-..	14,789-20,550	None	1,176	1,009-85	820	104-85	50	117
	F	23-23-..	11,357-20,550	None	621	580-93	450	80-50	4	37
Monroe t, Conn. (1,2)	P	40-33-40	29,726-...	..-...-6	2,956	2,695-91	1,856	537-302	81	180
	F	...-..-..	...-...	..-...-..	...	...-..	...	...-...	...	...
Monroe, Mich. (1,1)	P	43-39-40	25,246-35,586	Y-...-5	1,217	1,105-90	1,013	70-22	2	110
	F	43-43-56	25,295-35,575	Y-...-5	1,021	971-95	897	54-20		50
Monroe, N.C. (4,4)	P	...-..-..	...-...	..-...-..	...	...-..	...	...-...	...	...
	F	...-..-..	...-...	..-...-..	...	...-..	...	...-...	...	...
Montgomery tp, Pa. (1,2)	P	28-...-40	30,500-...	None	648	213-32	126	74-13	113	322
	F	...-..-..	...-...	..-...-..	...	...-..	...	...-...	...	...
Montville tp, N.J. (1,5)	P	34-...-40	26,293-47,268	Y-49,631-5	2,461	2,180-88	1,725	207-248	25	256
	F	...-..-..	...-...	..-...-..	...	...-..	...	...-...	...	...
Moon tp, Pa. (1,2)	P	32-27-40	27,264-37,606	Y-39,106-21	1,797	1,575-87	1,347	25-203	54	168
	F	...-..-..	...-...	..-...-..	...	...-..	...	...-...	...	...
Moorestown tp, N.J. (1,5)	P	32-26-50	29,192-40,497	Y-43,737-5	2,486	2,342-94	1,958	194-190	69	75
	F	...-..-..	...-...	..-...-..	...	...-..	...	...-...	...	...
Morgan City, La. (1,1)	P	52-48-40	15,911-...	Y-...-1	1,515	1,197-79	1,030	100-67	300	18
	F	38-38-..	14,707-...	Y-...-1	1,037	1,024-98	885	80-59	...	13
Morgan Hill, Calif. (1,3)	P	32-20-40	35,550-42,156	None	3,554	3,059-86	2,297	490-272	7	488
	F	19-17-56	33,840-40,008	None	2,304	1,983-86	1,477	324-182	60	261
Morganton, N.C. (4,4)	P	...-..-..	...-...	..-...-..	...	...-..	...	...-...	...	...
	F	...-..-..	...-...	..-...-..	...	...-..	...	...-...	...	...
Morristown, Tenn. (1,1)	P	62-58-40	19,916-28,829	Y-...-5	2,519	2,041-81	1,646	143-252	61	417
	F	51-51-..	18,044-26,125	Y-...-5	2,174	1,768-81	1,413	122-233	...	406
Morton Grove v, Ill. (1,-)	P	63-46-37	32,150-42,421	Y-43,021-10	3,144	2,838-90	2,550	43-245	138	168
	F	44-42-49	31,519-42,421	Y-43,021-10	2,409	2,188-90	2,000	10-178	35	186
Moscow, Idaho (1,2)	P	33-24-..	23,022-29,700	Y-...-10	2,126	1,387-65	1,131	164-92	35	704
	F	...-..-..	...-...	..-...-..	...	...-..	...	...-...	...	...
Moses Lake, Wash. (3,3)	P	32-22-..	25,791-32,239	None	...	...-..	...	...-...	...	...
	F	15-14-..	24,501-30,626	None	...	...-..	...	...-...	...	...
Mount Pleasant, Mich. (4,4)	P	...-..-..	...-...	..-...-..	...	...-..	...	...-...	...	...
	F	...-..-..	...-...	..-...-..	...	...-..	...	...-...	...	...
Mount Pleasant, Tex. (1,3)	P	25-19-40	20,862-29,494	Y-...-1	780	720-92	600	72-48	...	60
	F	13-13-54	20,862-29,494	Y-...-1	528	372-70	312	36-24	...	156
Mount Vernon, Ill. (1,1)	P	37-31-40	23,240-27,917	None	1,691	1,270-75	1,174	40-56	114	307
	F	29-26-56	23,937-28,755	None	1,258	1,017-80	957	15-45	30	211
Mount Vernon, Ohio (1,1)	P	30-23-40	21,091-25,771	None	1,224	984-80	696	132-156	12	228
	F	30-29-48	21,103-25,833	None	1,392	1,260-90	900	204-156	12	120
Mount Vernon, Wash. (1,3)	P	37-31-40	27,345-34,061	None	6,336	5,676-89	1,584	2,028-2,064	60	600
	F	23-21-..	27,501-...	Y-33,390-5	...	...-..	...	...-...	...	...
Mountlake Terrace, Wash. (1,3)	P	36-29-..	31,907-38,854	None	...	...-..	...	...-...	2	...
	F	22-21-..	33,279-37,828	None	...	...-..	...	...-...	...	...
Mundelein v, Ill. (1,3)	P	32-23-..	31,600-41,500	None	...	...-..	...	...-...	...	...
	F	12-10-..	31,600-41,500	None	...	...-..	...	...-...	...	...
Muscatine, Iowa (1,1)	P	38-35-40	21,258-25,730	Y-26,210-5	...	...-..	...	...-...	33	...
	F	34-34-56	21,170-26,747	Y-27,227-5	...	...-..	...	...-...	4	...
Muskego, Wis. (1,2)	P	28-19-40	30,306-37,037	Y-37,217-5	1,698	1,470-86	1,086	279-105	53	175
	F	...-..-..	...-...	..-...-..	...	...-..	...	...-...	...	...
Mustang, Okla. (1,3)	P	19-19-42	20,000-21,300	Y-...-20	1,698	1,617-95	1,476	69-72	23	58
	F	5-5-41	18,500-21,500	Y-...-20	898	150-16	118	13-19	709	39
Myrtle Beach, S.C. (1,1)	P	130-96-40	18,274-26,466	None	4,408	3,682-83	3,001	503-178	46	680
	F	81-74-56	15,757-26,466	None	2,889	2,397-82	1,938	341-118	102	390
Narragansett t, R.I. (1,3)	P	46-36-38	22,889-26,557	Y-30,407-..	1,368	1,137-83	888	138-111	...	231
	F	36-35-42	20,313-25,148	Y-28,794-..	1,096	978-89	770	129-79	7	111
Natchez, Miss. (1,1)	P	69-54-40	16,050-19,262	None	1,817	1,490-82	1,276	117-97	...	327
	F	48-43-..	14,400-17,627	None	1,152	1,044-90	899	77-68	...	108
Natchitoches, La. (1,1)	P	50-47-40	13,512-...	..-...-..	1,321	1,071-81	842	171-58	113	137
	F	35-35-60	12,576-...	..-...-..	892	817-91	706	66-45	31	44
Neenah, Wis. (1,1)	P	50-41-39	28,884-33,564	Y-33,864-5	...	...-..	...	...-...	...	...
	F	42-42-56	28,848-32,244	Y-32,544-5	...	...-..	...	...-...	...	...
Nether Providence tp, Pa. (1,2)	P	13-13-..	25,031-35,758	Y-40,258-..	865	743-85	617	47-79	18	104
	F	...-..-..	...-...	..-...-..	...	...-..	...	...-...	...	...
New Bern, N.C. (1,3)	P	74-53-42	19,906-36,305	Y-...-5	2,618	2,073-79	1,694	275-104	191	354
	F	34-33-53	15,619-28,601	Y-...-5	1,992	1,659-83	860	745-54	94	239
New Canaan t, Conn. (1,3)	P	49-45-40	31,000-41,650	Y-...-5	...	...-..	...	...-...	...	...
	F	12-12-42	28,073-38,695	Y-...-5	...	...-..	...	...-...	...	...
New Carrollton, Md. (-,7)	P	2-2-40	29,442-50,261	Y-...-15	95	92-96	58	23-11	...	3
	F	...-..-..	...-...	..-...-..	...	...-..	...	...-...	...	...
New Castle, Ind. (1,1)	P	38-38-48	17,500-18,500	Y-21,000-3	...	...-..	...	...-...	...	...
	F	33-33-56	17,500-18,500	Y-21,000-3	...	...-..	...	...-...	...	...
New Fairfield t, Conn. (1,2)	P	13-13-40	26,100-36,846	Y-37,304-10	845	795-94	555	161-79	...	50

Table 3/23 continued

POLICE AND FIRE DEPARTMENT PERSONNEL, SALARIES, AND EXPENDITURES FOR CITIES 10,000 AND OVER: 1993

City (Service provision)	Department	Total personnel, no. uniformed, duty hours per week	Entrance, maximum salary ($)	Longevity pay, maximum ($) no. years to receive longevity pay	Total expenditures (A) ($)	Total personnel expenditures (B) ($), % of (A)	Salaries and wages (C) ($)	City contrib. to employee retirement, insurance (D) ($)	Capital outlay (E) ($)	All other (F) ($)
10,000-24,999 continued										
New Fairfield t, Conn. (1,2) cont.	F	...-.-..	...-...	..-...-..	...	...-...	...	...-...	...	...
New Hope, Minn. (1,-)	P	32-27-..	26,604-40,600	Y-42,960-16	2,318	1,656-71	1,345	162-149	2	660
	F	2-1-..	...-...	None	415	260-62	175	80-5	...	155
New Milford t, Conn. (1,2)	P	54-41-40	28,617-36,499	Y-36,899-10	...	...-...	...	...-...	55	...
	F	...-.-..	...-...	..-...-..	...	...-...	...	...-...	...	...
New Milford b, N.J. (1,2)	P	30-28-40	20,660-49,934	Y-53,929-4	...	...-...	...	...-...	50	...
	F	...-.-..	...-...	..-...-..	...	...-...	...	...-...	...	...
New Philadelphia, Ohio (1,1)	P	23-19-40	19,019-26,561	Y-26,861-5	...	...-...	...	...-...	2	...
	F	19-19-56	18,251-25,392	Y-25,692-5	...	...-...	...	...-...	...	...
Tinton Falls b, N.J. (1,2)	P	40-31-40	28,958-44,483	Y-49,376-4	2,328	2,202-94	1,867	135-200	47	79
	F	...-.-..	...-...	..-...-..	...	...-...	...	...-...	...	...
New Smyrna Beach, Fla. (1,1)	P	63-62-42	19,831-27,868	Y-28,787-5	2,508	2,016-80	1,620	180-216	132	360
	F	45-29-48	16,074-24,261	Y-24,961-5	1,872	1,536-82	1,272	96-168	60	276
New Ulm, Minn. (1,2)	P	...-3-40	27,851-29,661	Y-...-..	1,101	958-87	681	195-82	50	93
	F	...-.-..	...-...	..-...-..	...	...-...	...	...-...	...	...
Newberg, Ore. (1,3)	P	28-20-40	25,704-34,236	Y-34,536-10	1,573	1,230-78	899	234-97	61	282
	F	4-4-52	25,416-33,432	Y-33,732-10	589	269-45	199	55-15	200	120
Newberry, S.C. (1,3)	P	25-25-42	18,042-27,345	Y-28,439-..	598	552-92	445	81-26	...	46
	F	19-19-..	17,341-26,283	Y-27,334-..	375	332-88	264	48-20	...	43
Newnan, Ga. (1,1)	P	39-39-..	17,867-25,147	None	1,126	1,100-97	886	121-93	...	26
	F	25-25-..	18,035-25,410	None	646	641-99	515	76-50	...	5
Newport, Ky. (1,1)	P	54-43-40	19,011-23,650	None	2,302	1,963-85	1,450	304-209	75	264
	F	44-43-56	20,908-21,877	None	2,124	1,891-89	1,350	311-230	28	205
Newton, Iowa (3,3)	P	33-26-40	23,256-28,740	Y-29,640-8	1,684	1,478-87	1,096	176-206	54	152
	F	23-23-56	20,292-28,536	..-29,436-8	1,388	1,290-92	964	152-174	...	98
Newton, Kan. (1,1)	P	23-21-..	19,812-24,856	Y-25,480-2	...	...-...	...	...-...	47	...
	F	25-25-..	19,812-24,856	Y-25,480-2	...	...-...	...	...-...	78	...
Newtown tp, Pa. (1,2)	P	13-13-..	31,027-46,627	Y-...-..	917	748-81	554	94-100	...	169
	F	...-.-..	...-...	..-...-..	...	...-...	...	...-...	...	...
Niles, Mich. (3,3)	P	26-24-40	19,512-30,044	Y-33,048-5	1,361	1,080-79	874	85-121	175	106
	F	14-14-54	18,000-30,523	Y-33,575-5	740	660-89	518	77-65	25	55
Noblesville, Ind. (1,1)	P	...-.-..	...-...	Y-...-1	...	...-...	...	...-...	15	...
	F	...-.-..	...-...	Y-...-1	...	...-...	...	...-...	97	...
Norco, Calif. (7,1)	P	...-.-..	...-...	..-...-..	...	...-...	...	...-...	...	...
	F	20-..-56	27,876-35,352	Y-...-..	932	772-82	644	52-76	115	45
Norfolk, Nebr. (1,3)	P	50-36-..	20,448-...	None	1,976	1,484-75	1,218	166-100	249	243
	F	29-23-..	24,624-...	None	1,278	907-70	726	129-52	266	105
North Adams, Mass. (4,4)	P	...-.-..	...-...	..-...-..	...	...-...	...	...-...	...	...
	F	...-.-..	...-...	..-...-..	...	...-...	...	...-...	...	...
North Andover t, Mass. (1,1)	P	35-30-40	22,765-28,873	Y-...-..	...	...-...	...	...-...	273	...
	F	46-45-42	23,685-28,552	Y-29,352-..	...	...-...	...	...-...	90	...
North Branford t, Conn. (1,2)	P	21-20-40	28,080-36,358	Y-37,593-5	1,596	1,356-84	998	230-128	100	140
	F	...-.-..	...-...	..-...-..	...	...-...	...	...-...	...	...
North College Hill, Ohio (1,-)	P	13-12-40	25,126-30,659	None	966	910-94	688	167-55	...	56
	F	...-.-..	...-...	..-...-..	...	...-...	...	...-...	...	...
North Mankato, Minn. (1,2)	P	10-9-40	28,500-35,076	Y-36,830-4	614	464-75	377	47-40	35	115
	F	...-.-..	...-...	..-...-..	...	...-...	...	...-...	...	...
North Ogden, Utah (1,3)	P	10-10-40	17,178-25,983	Y-...-1	...	...-...	...	...-...	34	...
	F	7-7-56	17,178-25,983	Y-...-1	...	...-...	...	...-...	76	...
North Palm Beach v, Fla. (1,3)	P	45-36-40	21,500-35,344	Y-...-3	2,094	1,864-89	1,404	191-269	50	180
	F	3-..-40	21,500-35,344	Y-...-3	185	135-72	103	12-20	25	25
North Ridgeville, Ohio (1,1)	P	33-27-40	30,000-32,000	Y-34,000-3	1,748	1,594-91	1,251	133-210	...	154
	F	23-23-52	26,000-31,000	Y-33,000-3	1,190	1,113-93	853	105-155	4	73
North Royalton, Ohio (1,1)	P	40-31-40	28,267-34,819	Y-36,319-5	2,040	1,624-79	1,239	280-105	99	317
	F	24-23-51	28,866-34,785	Y-36,285-5	1,577	1,360-86	1,055	237-68	35	182
North St. Paul, Minn. (1,3)	P	16-14-40	24,695-38,400	Y-41,376-3	865	780-90	661	78-41	16	69
	F	1-1-40	...-...	..-...-..	144	48-33	40	5-3	16	80
Northport, Ala. (1,1)	P	47-40-40	18,231-21,070	Y-21,770-5	1,669	1,392-83	1,088	158-146	129	148
	F	37-37-53	17,680-20,560	Y-21,260-5	1,302	1,158-88	886	126-146	33	111
Norton t, Mass. (1,1)	P	17-15-..	22,432-27,390	Y-27,540-5	...	...-...	...	...-...	23	...
	F	21-20-..	20,924-27,985	Y-28,135-5	...	...-...	...	...-...	36	...
Norton Shores, Mich. (1,3)	P	25-25-40	27,684-33,457	Y-36,803-5	1,455	1,227-84	1,057	81-89	...	228
	F	10-1-48	24,689-29,425	Y-32,368-6	757	642-84	517	40-85	...	115
Norwalk, Ohio (1,1)	P	24-20-40	23,400-29,244	None	1,455	1,129-77	833	205-91	53	273
	F	14-14-56	26,189-30,710	None	847	712-84	495	155-62	53	82
Norwood, Ohio (1,1)	P	45-45-40	27,664-34,580	Y-...-5	...	...-...	...	...-...	...	...
	F	50-50-48	24,334-34,763	Y-...-5	...	...-...	...	...-...	...	...
O'Fallon, Ill. (1,2)	P	36-26-..	26,000-...	Y-35,000-..	...	...-...	...	...-...	82	...
	F	...-.-..	...-...	..-...-..	...	...-...	...	...-...	...	...
O'Fallon, Mo. (3,5)	P	33-33-40	23,920-29,770	None	2,662	1,575-59	1,252	143-180	618	469
	F	...-.-..	...-...	..-...-..	...	...-...	...	...-...	...	...
Oak Creek, Wis. (1,1)	P	46-40-..	30,533-37,656	Y-37,666-3	3,360	3,061-91	1,949	559-553	...	299
	F	34-33-..	30,983-36,634	Y-36,644-3	3,093	2,330-75	1,460	436-434	...	763
Oakdale, Calif. (1,1)	P	28-21-40	25,500-34,296	None	1,819	1,422-78	1,045	243-134	57	340

Table 3/23 continued POLICE AND FIRE DEPARTMENT PERSONNEL, SALARIES, AND EXPENDITURES FOR CITIES 10,000 AND OVER: 1993

City (Service provision)	Depart-ment	Total personnel, no. uniformed, duty hours per week	Entrance, maximum salary ($)	Longevity pay, maximum ($) no. years to receive longevity pay	Reported expenditures (in thousands)					
					Total expendi-tures (A) ($)	Total personnel expendi-tures (B) ($), % of (A)	Salaries and wages (C) ($)	City contrib. to employee retirement, insurance (D) ($)	Capital outlay (E) ($)	All other (F) ($)
10,000-24,999 continued										
Oakdale, Calif. (1,1) cont.	F	13-13-56	24,372-29,736	None	985	677-68	486	127-64	144	164
Ocean Springs, Miss. (1,1) ....P	P	37-28-40	16,661-20,676	Y-21,516-1	...	...-..	...	...-...	...	...
	F	26-26-48	16,641-20,651	Y-21,491-1	...	...-..	...	...-...	...	...
Ocoee, Fla. (1,3) ....P	P	40-32-40	20,892-27,997	Y-30,237-5	1,162	968-83	724	148-96	12	182
	F	28-27-52	20,892-27,997	Y-30,237-5	764	660-86	484	98-78	2	102
Oconomowoc, Wis. (1,3) ....P	P	26-20-40	28,020-33,852	Y-34,092-5	1,480	1,176-79	840	215-121	...	304
	F	4-3-40	28,968-32,607	Y-32,847-5	317	281-88	94	19-168	...	36
Ogdensburg, N.Y. (1,1) ....P	P	29-24-40	19,795-30,098	None	1,236	1,097-88	854	142-101	48	91
	F	35-35-40	24,689-27,960	Y-29,835-9	1,430	1,316-92	1,019	179-118	9	105
Okmulgee, Okla. (1,1) ....P	P	34-34-..	15,792-...	Y-...-2	...	...-..	...	...-...	...	...
	F	28-28-..	13,802-...	Y-...-2	784	718-91	556	60-102	...	66
Oneida, N.Y. (1,1) ....P	P	22-19-40	23,000-26,331	Y-27,731-10	1,202	1,110-92	733	163-214	48	44
	F	23-23-..	18,375-26,123	Y-28,123-5	1,175	1,127-95	734	181-212	...	48
Opelika, Ala. (1,4) ....P	P	87-70-43	19,691-26,343	..-26,993-5	4,548	2,616-57	2,016	276-324	...	1,932
	F	...-..-..	...-...	..-...-..	...	...-..	...	...-...	...	...
Opelousas, La. (1,1) ....P	P	47-39-32	13,998-...	None	1,013	597-58	454	118-25	13	403
	F	35-34-48	13,477-...	None	510	402-78	355	29-18	66	42
Orange, Tex. (1,1) ....P	P	57-44-40	23,388-28,716	Y-29,916-1	3,013	2,337-77	1,820	301-216	...	676
	F	47-46-53	23,568-26,808	Y-28,008-1	2,572	2,216-86	1,696	272-248	...	356
Orangeburg, S.C. (4,4) ....P	P	...-..-..	...-...	..-...-..	...	...-..	...	...-...	...	...
	F	...-..-..	...-...	..-...-..	...	...-..	...	...-...	...	...
Oregon, Ohio (1,3) ....P	P	43-40-40	29,244-35,900	Y-38,413-5	3,554	2,839-79	2,158	375-306	167	548
	F	12-9-40	30,576-38,251	None	1,493	1,035-69	798	166-71	253	205
Orinda, Calif. (-,5) ....P	P	13-12-40	37,200-43,788	Y-46,188-15	1,272	983-77	977	2-4	57	232
	F	...-..-..	...-...	..-...-..	...	...-..	...	...-...	...	...
Orono t, Me. (1,1) ....P	P	17-13-40	18,867-23,508	None	587	544-92	453	45-46	...	43
	F	15-14-53	17,160-21,840	None	736	608-82	511	48-49	...	128
Oroville, Calif. (1,3) ....P	P	30-21-40	26,000-31,000	None	...	...-..	...	...-...	...	...
	F	22-..-56	25,000-34,000	None	...	...-..	...	...-...	...	...
Oskaloosa, Iowa (1,1) ....P	P	19-17-40	18,647-24,812	Y-25,712-6	870	762-87	588	116-58	24	84
	F	18-18-56	18,824-24,447	Y-25,347-6	828	794-95	626	108-60	...	34
Ossining v, N.Y. (1,2) ....P	P	48-48-40	22,000-69,510	None	...	...-..	...	...-...	...	...
	F	...-..-..	...-...	..-...-..	...	...-..	...	...-...	...	...
Ottumwa, Iowa (1,1) ....P	P	37-31-40	19,594-25,376	Y-...-5	...	...-..	...	...-...	3	...
	F	33-33-56	21,168-25,248	Y-...-5	...	...-..	...	...-...	...	...
Overland, Mo. (1,5) ....P	P	61-12-40	24,852-31,716	Y-...-..	...	...-..	...	...-...	...	...
	F	...-..-..	...-...	..-...-..	...	...-..	...	...-...	...	...
Oviedo, Fla. (1,3) ....P	P	41-31-40	21,160-29,898	None	1,182	879-74	709	92-78	82	221
	F	22-21-56	21,160-29,898	None	754	580-76	479	56-45	...	174
Owatonna, Minn. (1,3) ....P	P	25-23-40	27,684-34,608	Y-35,819-10	1,386	1,233-88	1,021	125-87	70	83
	F	8-8-53	...-...	None	541	476-87	404	43-29	...	65
Oxford t, Mass. (1,-) ....P	P	21-16-..	23,017-30,738	None	2,301	2,190-95	741	321-1,128	15	96
	F	...-..-..	...-...	None	...	...-..	...	...-...	149	...
Oxford, Ohio (1,-) ....P	P	29-21-40	33,263-...	None	1,400	1,239-88	905	168-166	36	125
	F	...-..-..	...-...	..-...-..	65	41-63	29	9-3	7	17
Ozark, Ala. (1,3) ....P	P	42-39-40	15,000-19,000	None	1,265	956-75	780	102-74	...	309
	F	22-22-56	15,000-19,000	None	642	524-81	429	56-39	20	98
Painesville, Ohio (1,1) ....P	P	36-27-40	29,223-37,296	Y-41,026-..	2,115	1,797-84	1,451	222-124	65	253
	F	23-23-50	29,223-37,296	Y-41,026-..	1,551	1,297-83	1,007	195-95	37	217
Palatka, Fla. (1,3) ....P	P	44-31-40	17,372-25,667	Y-26,966-10	1,699	1,374-80	1,117	124-133	52	273
	F	17-17-56	16,170-23,268	Y-24,446-10	1,839	1,033-56	840	99-94	506	300
Palestine, Tex. (1,1) ....P	P	42-32-40	20,124-22,932	Y-24,732-1	1,474	1,327-90	1,035	146-146	5	142
	F	40-40-42	17,760-19,668	Y-21,468-1	1,370	1,296-94	998	139-159	...	74
Palm Beach Gardens, Fla. (1,1) ....P	P	95-75-40	25,921-34,737	Y-38,211-5	...	...-..	...	...-...	169	...
	F	38-36-48	20,966-28,200	Y-31,020-5	...	...-..	...	...-...	145	...
Palm Desert, Calif. (7,6) ....P	P	...-..-..	...-...	..-...-..	...	...-..	...	...-...	...	...
	F	...-..-..	...-...	..-...-..	...	...-..	...	...-...	...	...
Palos Verdes Estates, Calif. (1,-) .....P	P	35-22-39	33,804-42,372	Y-46,609-5	1,532	1,142-74	947	93-102	39	351
	F	...-..-..	...-...	..-...-..	...	...-..	...	...-...	...	...
Pampa, Tex. (1,1) ....P	P	35-27-40	19,635-27,518	Y-28,718-1	1,952	1,542-78	1,178	244-120	90	320
	F	34-33-50	18,677-25,157	Y-26,340-1	2,340	2,020-86	1,564	328-128	200	120
Papillion, Nebr. (1,2) ....P	P	16-15-40	22,189-27,878	Y-28,715-..	...	...-..	...	...-...	...	...
	F	...-..-..	...-...	..-...-..	...	...-..	...	...-...	...	...
Paradise Valley t, Ariz. (1,9) ....P	P	41-9-40	27,060-39,120	None	...	...-..	...	...-...	...	...
	F	...-..-..	...-...	..-...-..	...	...-..	...	...-...	...	...
Paragould, Ark. (1,3) ....P	P	33-28-40	16,970-18,447	Y-20,291-1	1,069	841-78	673	107-61	...	228
	F	19-19-..	17,500-19,021	Y-20,923-1	506	468-92	393	29-46	...	38
Park Forest v, Ill. (1,1) ....P	P	46-38-40	27,157-40,510	Y-41,026-..	1,877	1,666-88	1,088	496-82	40	171
	F	21-21-..	26,134-36,807	None	1,020	894-87	560	296-38	32	94
Parsons, Kan. (1,1) ....P	P	30-22-..	18,387-20,675	None	...	...-..	...	...-...	...	...
	F	20-20-..	11,752-14,248	None	...	...-..	...	...-..	...	...
Patchogue v, N.Y. (7,2) ....P	P	...-..-..	...-...	..-...-..	...	...-..	...	...-..	...	...
	F	...-..-..	...-...	..-...-..	...	...-..	...	...-..	...	...
Peachtree City, Ga. (1,3) ....P	P	39-29-40	20,877-29,498	Y-...-..	...	...-..	...	...-...	61	...

Table 3/23   **POLICE AND FIRE DEPARTMENT PERSONNEL, SALARIES, AND EXPENDITURES FOR**
continued   **CITIES 10,000 AND OVER: 1993**

City (Service provision)	Department	Total personnel, no. uniformed, duty hours per week	Entrance, maximum salary ($)	Longevity pay, maximum ($) no. years to receive longevity pay	Reported expenditures (in thousands)					
					Total expenditures (A) ($)	Total personnel expenditures (B) ($), % of (A)	Salaries and wages (C) ($)	City contrib. to employee retirement, insurance (D) ($)	Capital outlay (E) ($)	All other (F) ($)
10,000-24,999 continued										
Peachtree City, Ga. (1,3) cont.	F	20-19-..	...-...	..-...-..	...	...-..	...	...-...	...	...
Pearl, Miss. (1,3)	P	36-28-40	15,348-23,724	Y-...-14	...	...-..	...	...-...	40	...
	F	39-38-50	15,348-23,724	Y-...-14	...	...-..	...	...-...	500	...
Pearland, Tex. (1,2)	P	51-37-40	26,977-32,198	Y-32,246-1	2,074	1,720-82	1,488	221-11	122	232
	F	...-..-..	...-...	..-...-..	...	...-..	...	...-...	...	...
Pecos, Tex. (1,2)	P	24-17-40	18,684-22,836	Y-24,036-1	775	643-82	509	64-70	40	92
	F	...-..-..	...-...	..-...-..	...	...-..	...	...-...	...	...
Penn tp, Pa. (1,2)	P	17-16-40	22,941-31,021	Y-32,882-6	...	...-..	...	...-...	29	...
	F	...-..-..	...-...	..-...-..	...	...-..	...	...-...	...	...
Pepperell t, Mass. (1,3)	P	14-13-40	26,559-28,981	Y-32,863-5	...	...-..	...	...-...	...	...
	F	1-1-..	...-...	None	...	...-..	...	...-...	...	...
Pequannock tp, N.J. (1,2)	P	31-26-40	24,000-49,000	Y-50,000-5	...	...-..	...	...-...	30	...
	F	...-..-..	...-...	..-...-..	...	...-..	...	...-...	...	...
Perris, Calif. (1,7)	P	53-41-43	35,112-42,660	Y-...-10	3,880	3,039-78	2,411	465-163	80	761
	F	...-..-..	...-...	..-...-..	...	...-..	...	...-...	...	...
Peters tp, Pa. (1,3)	P	22-17-40	26,803-31,606	Y-32,874-5	...	...-..	...	...-...	...	...
	F	4-4-50	23,400-26,400	None	...	...-..	...	...-...	...	...
Phoenixville b, Pa. (1,2)	P	23-21-40	28,000-34,408	Y-...-5	...	...-..	...	...-...	30	...
	F	...-..-..	...-...	..-...-..	...	...-..	...	...-...	...	...
Picayune, Miss. (3,1)	P	35-22-40	14,676-21,276	None	1,082	819-75	634	97-88	48	215
	F	26-26-56	12,588-18,252	None	833	664-79	506	87-71	105	64
Piedmont, Calif. (3,3)	P	27-20-40	38,736-46,728	None	2,103	1,703-80	1,362	308-33	25	375
	F	22-22-56	36,828-42,336	None	1,943	1,645-84	1,311	303-31	70	228
Pierre, S.D. (1,2)	P	29-22-..	19,100-23,400	None	1,051	841-80	685	101-55	60	150
	F	...-..-..	...-...	..-...-..	...	...-..	...	...-...	...	...
Piqua, Ohio (1,1)	P	26-26-40	30,591-37,563	None	3,733	3,603-96	888	2,658-57	...	130
	F	26-26-56	30,035-36,421	None	3,056	2,696-88	1,370	1,216-110	250	110
Pittsburg, Kan. (1,1)	P	37-31-40	18,708-26,916	None	1,386	1,191-85	952	120-119	50	145
	F	31-31-56	18,708-26,916	None	1,049	1,001-95	798	103-100	7	41
Plainfield t, Conn. (1,2)	P	16-15-40	28,704-30,846	None	...	...-..	...	...-...	...	...
	F	...-..-..	...-...	..-...-..	...	...-..	...	...-...	...	...
Plainsboro tp, N.J. (1,5)	P	36-26-40	29,630-46,958	Y-49,258-7	...	...-..	...	...-...	...	...
	F	...-..-..	...-...	..-...-..	...	...-..	...	...-...	...	...
Plainview, Tex. (1,1)	P	37-30-..	17,472-...	Y-...-1	1,570	1,026-65	822	139-65	107	437
	F	35-34-..	16,308-...	Y-...-1	1,007	821-81	694	77-50	15	171
Plainville t, Conn. (1,2)	P	24-18-37	28,423-37,449	None	2,258	2,126-94	1,577	285-264	53	79
	F	...-..-..	...-...	..-...-..	...	...-..	...	...-...	...	...
Plant City, Fla. (1,1)	P	74-54-40	23,128-33,767	None	3,055	2,442-79	2,029	272-141	125	488
	F	30-29-..	20,953-28,873	None	1,653	994-60	832	106-56	16	643
Pleasantville, N.J. (1,1)	P	51-43-40	25,523-37,991	Y-41,030-4	...	...-..	...	...-...	...	...
	F	31-30-42	21,710-35,535	Y-38,378-5	...	...-..	...	...-...	...	...
Plymouth tp, Pa. (1,2)	P	39-32-40	29,132-40,615	Y-41,015-5	3,563	1,711-48	1,419	253-39	44	1,808
	F	...-..-..	...-...	..-...-..	...	...-..	...	...-...	...	...
Point Pleasant b, N.J. (1,2)	P	34-26-40	26,268-43,779	Y-...-24	2,381	2,230-93	1,706	294-230	56	95
	F	...-..-..	...-...	..-...-..	...	...-..	...	...-...	...	...
Poplar Bluff, Mo. (1,1)	P	44-39-..	21,624-25,164	None	1,998	1,773-88	1,518	62-193	134	91
	F	34-33-..	19,368-23,568	None	1,474	1,364-92	1,149	75-140	50	60
Port Angeles, Wash. (1,3)	P	52-29-40	30,336-36,120	Y-39,010-5	2,673	2,243-83	1,838	74-331	16	414
	F	24-23-52	30,444-39,060	..-...-..	1,447	1,183-81	1,018	26-139	5	259
Port Chester v, N.Y. (-,-)	P	57-57-40	23,100-45,318	Y-46,168-8	4,106	3,671-89	2,800	521-350	100	335
	F	13-13-40	22,000-38,468	Y-39,268-8	1,073	668-62	482	99-87	75	330
Port Neches, Tex. (1,1)	P	20-17-40	26,863-27,310	Y-...-1	1,521	859-56	660	112-87	502	160
	F	13-12-56	26,863-27,310	Y-...-1	1,164	539-46	413	70-56	472	153
Portsmouth, Ohio (1,1)	P	39-35-40	17,000-24,000	None	3,213	1,629-50	1,285	180-164	...	1,584
	F	39-34-53	19,000-24,000	None	3,930	2,400-61	1,928	274-198	...	1,530
Portsmouth t, R.I. (1,1)	P	27-27-37	20,849-27,167	Y-...-5	1,562	1,308-83	856	341-111	59	195
	F	26-26-42	23,776-26,486	Y-...-5	1,351	1,244-92	818	313-113	5	102
Potsdam v, N.Y. (1,3)	P	18-15-40	23,220-30,200	Y-30,300-..	...	...-..	...	...-...	...	...
	F	4-..-40	...-...	Y-25,100-1	...	...-..	...	...-...	...	...
Pottstown b, Pa. (1,3)	P	54-40-40	26,522-32,561	Y-32,968-5	2,327	1,997-85	1,707	90-200	...	330
	F	...-..-..	...-...	..-...-..	...	...-..	...	...-...	...	...
Prairie Village, Kan. (1,-)	P	47-38-40	23,080-35,562	None	2,518	1,953-77	1,574	225-154	92	473
	F	...-..-..	...-...	..-...-..	...	...-..	...	...-...	...	...
Presque Isle, Me. (1,3)	P	24-19-40	19,073-22,755	Y-25,875-7	...	...-..	...	...-...	...	...
	F	16-16-56	18,801-22,400	Y-25,600-7	...	...-..	...	...-...	...	...
Princeton b, N.J. (1,2)	P	39-34-39	33,068-44,567	Y-46,217-8	...	...-..	...	...-...	...	...
	F	...-..-..	...-...	..-...-..	...	...-..	...	...-...	...	...
Prior Lake, Minn. (1,2)	P	15-15-40	30,720-39,660	Y-43,229-..	963	820-85	692	81-47	34	109
	F	...-..-..	...-...	..-...-..	...	...-..	...	...-...	...	...
Pullman, Wash. (1,3)	P	32-24-40	28,944-34,368	None	...	...-..	...	...-...	...	...
	F	14-14-53	25,572-31,152	None	...	...-..	...	...-...	...	...
Punta Gorda, Fla. (3,3)	P	38-27-40	21,801-32,060	None	1,154	1,120-97	893	68-159	13	21
	F	24-21-40	19,775-29,224	None	966	948-98	765	55-128	...	18
Puyallup, Wash. (1,1)	P	54-41-..	...-44,268	None	3,800	3,311-87	2,650	345-316	23	466

Table 3/23 continued — POLICE AND FIRE DEPARTMENT PERSONNEL, SALARIES, AND EXPENDITURES FOR CITIES 10,000 AND OVER: 1993

City (Service provision)	Department	Total personnel, no. uniformed, duty hours per week	Entrance, maximum salary ($)	Longevity pay, maximum ($) no. years to receive longevity pay	Reported expenditures (in thousands)					
					Total expenditures (A) ($)	Total personnel expenditures (B) ($), % of (A)	Salaries and wages (C) ($)	City contrib. to employee retirement, insurance (D) ($)	Capital outlay (E) ($)	All other (F) ($)
10,000–24,999 continued										
Puyallup, Wash. (1,1) cont.	F	46-43-...	33,204-46,488	None	3,011	2,706-89	2,313	138-255	33	272
Ramsey b, N.J. (1,2)	P	32-29-40	14,000-51,539	Y-56,000-..	2,831	2,787-98	2,200	250-337	...	44
	F	...-...-..	...-...	..-...-..	...	...-..	...	...-...	...	...
Rantoul v, Ill. (1,2)	P	26-22-40	...-...	None	1,054	913-86	687	190-36	15	126
	F	...-...-..	...-...	..-...-..	...	...-..	...	...-...	...	...
Raritan tp, N.J. (1,2)	P	29-26-40	29,728-41,109	Y-44,398-5	1,748	1,564-89	1,334	100-130	23	161
	F	...-...-..	...-...	..-...-..	...	...-..	...	...-...	...	...
Ravenna, Ohio (1,1)	P	27-27-40	22,859-29,099	Y-30,299-5	1,449	1,227-84	946	168-113	62	160
	F	19-19-56	21,811-27,664	Y-28,864-5	1,073	894-83	647	161-86	75	104
Red Bluff, Calif. (1,3)	P	29-21-48	24,577-29,146	None	1,785	1,289-72	867	295-127	70	426
	F	11-10-49	24,577-29,146	None	906	503-55	331	118-54	43	360
Red Wing, Minn. (1,3)	P	26-24-40	29,736-35,328	Y-36,288-7	3,137	2,940-93	1,005	1,839-96	...	197
	F	27-27-56	27,768-34,272	..-...-..	1,461	1,349-92	971	280-98	...	112
Reidsville, N.C. (3,3)	P	51-51-..	19,973-28,104	Y-29,604-2	2,292	1,810-78	1,483	188-139	131	351
	F	22-22-..	19,022-26,765	Y-28,265-2	1,098	675-61	553	84-38	181	242
Rexburg, Idaho (3,3)	P	14-12-50	19,860-27,180	None	698	496-71	382	68-46	60	142
	F	6-6-50	18,360-27,180	None	364	317-87	217	81-19	16	31
Richmond Heights, Mo. (1,1)	P	35-32-40	25,404-39,211	Y-...-..	1,896	1,680-88	1,422	114-144	88	128
	F	22-22-53	26,674-45,392	Y-...-..	1,226	1,160-94	992	76-92	14	52
Ridgefield t, Conn. (1,3)	P	39-32-39	29,500-41,312	Y-42,512-5	2,878	2,450-85	1,856	360-234	204	224
	F	25-24-42	24,998-35,622	Y-36,822-5	1,606	1,458-90	1,092	222-144	...	148
Ridgeland, Miss. (1,1)	P	46-29-40	18,665-26,382	None	1,646	1,179-71	946	162-71	80	387
	F	35-30-53	18,665-26,382	None	1,103	847-76	677	116-54	82	174
River Edge b, N.J. (1,2)	P	27-24-40	23,820-48,540	Y-53,394-4	...	...-..	...	...-...	...	...
	F	...-...-..	...-...	..-...-..	...	...-..	...	...-...	...	...
River Falls, Wis. (1,2)	P	22-19-40	29,786-33,946	Y-34,546-..	1,236	1,062-85	763	192-107	55	119
	F	...-...-..	...-...	..-...-..	...	...-..	...	...-...	...	...
River Forest v, Ill. (1,1)	P	40-28-40	27,756-41,006	None	...	...-..	...	...-...	6	...
	F	21-21-56	25,044-40,058	None	...	...-..	...	...-...	8	...
Riverdale v, Ill. (-,2)	P	...-...-..	...-...	..-...-..	...	...-..	...	...-...	...	...
	F	...-...-..	...-...	..-...-..	...	...-..	...	...-...	...	...
Riverview, Mich. (1,-)	P	27-27-40	20,796-35,600	Y-36,100-5	...	...-..	...	...-...	35	...
	F	2-2-..	...-...	Y-...-5	...	...-..	...	...-...	29	...
Roanoke Rapids, N.C. (1,1)	P	42-42-42	17,403-...	Y-25,958-5	1,756	1,510-85	1,196	256-58	74	172
	F	29-29-54	16,574-...	Y-24,722-5	1,210	974-80	796	136-42	34	202
Robbinsdale, Minn. (1,2)	P	27-19-40	25,704-39,552	Y-43,112-4	1,126	886-78	660	56-170	2	238
	F	...-...-..	...-...	..-...-..	...	...-..	...	...-...	...	...
Robstown, Tex. (3,3)	P	20-20-40	18,768-23,520	Y-24,720-1	725	449-61	354	56-39	...	276
	F	10-10-52	18,036-22,272	Y-23,472-1	258	154-59	120	18-16	...	104
Rock Springs, Wyo. (1,1)	P	57-34-40	25,440-35,964	None	1,368	1,248-91	1,004	129-115	13	107
	F	37-36-53	29,958-32,356	Y-32,517-1	1,261	1,125-89	877	167-81	5	131
Rockland t, Mass. (1,1)	P	28-28-37	23,846-29,799	Y-30,199-10	...	...-..	...	...-...	33	...
	F	26-26-42	25,590-31,102	Y-31,502-10	...	...-..	...	...-...	29	...
Rocklin, Calif. (3,3)	P	40-27-40	27,756-33,912	Y-35,608-7	1,439	1,131-78	896	77-158	26	282
	F	17-17-56	37,901-46,065	Y-48,368-7	792	594-75	466	47-81	25	173
Rockville Centre v, N.Y. (1,2)	P	62-52-40	31,765-56,221	Y-57,771-6	...	...-..	...	...-...	87	...
	F	...-...-..	...-...	..-...-..	...	...-..	...	...-...	...	...
Rockwall, Tex. (1,2)	P	33-21-40	21,228-30,876	Y-...-1	...	...-..	...	...-...	2	...
	F	...-...-..	...-...	..-...-..	...	...-..	...	...-...	...	...
Rocky Hill t, Conn. (1,2)	P	32-29-40	29,000-36,000	Y-38,000-6	...	...-..	...	...-...	75	...
	F	...-...-..	...-...	..-...-..	...	...-..	...	...-...	...	...
Rocky River, Ohio (1,1)	P	3-3-40	27,908-36,483	Y-38,125-6	...	...-..	...	...-...	5	...
	F	29-29-56	27,908-36,483	Y-38,125-6	...	...-..	...	...-...	13	...
Rogers, Ark. (1,3)	P	56-42-40	15,558-19,822	None	2,102	1,685-80	1,321	211-153	113	304
	F	47-39-56	15,558-19,822	None	1,920	1,701-88	1,462	104-135	95	124
Rolla, Mo. (1,1)	P	36-24-40	16,625-22,492	None	1,190	911-76	745	101-65	67	212
	F	21-20-54	15,042-20,351	None	990	675-68	510	120-45	228	87
Rolling Meadows, Ill. (1,1)	P	76-58-39	28,780-41,464	None	...	...-..	...	...-...	155	...
	F	48-44-50	28,780-41,464	None	...	...-..	...	...-...	58	...
Romulus, Mich. (1,2)	P	62-57-40	27,983-37,716	None	9,503	3,741-39	2,835	428-478	192	5,570
	F	...-...-..	...-...	..-...-..	...	...-..	...	...-...	...	...
Roseburg, Ore. (1,1)	P	36-32-40	24,672-30,960	None	...	...-..	...	...-...	672	...
	F	32-31-56	26,232-31,884	None	...	...-..	...	...-...	240	...
Roselle v, Ill. (1,3)	P	44-31-40	28,425-40,254	None	2,831	2,310-81	1,813	285-212	23	498
	F	7-5-48	27,215-38,294	None	665	321-48	239	49-33	41	303
Roselle Park b, N.J. (1,2)	P	31-31-40	25,043-43,935	Y-47,005-5	...	...-..	...	...-...	...	...
	F	...-...-..	...-...	..-...-..	...	...-..	...	...-...	85	...
Rowlett, Tex. (1,1)	P	50-37-40	24,960-29,681	Y-30,881-25	...	...-..	...	...-...	85	...
	F	39-38-56	24,969-28,084	Y-29,284-25	...	...-..	...	...-...	29	...
Roy, Utah (1,3)	P	32-24-40	23,293-32,244	None	848	824-97	632	144-48	...	24
	F	21-20-53	22,184-30,708	None	696	600-86	472	96-32	...	96
Royal Palm Beach v, Fla. (1,1)	P	34-31-40	26,126-34,866	Y-...-5	1,747	1,390-79	1,134	171-85	60	297
	F	31-29-48	21,850-29,160	Y-...-5	1,574	1,278-81	1,028	170-80	38	258
Russellville, Ark. (1,3)	P	36-26-40	18,444-...	Y-27,500-..	976	968-99	768	104-96	...	8

Table 3/23 continued
POLICE AND FIRE DEPARTMENT PERSONNEL, SALARIES, AND EXPENDITURES FOR CITIES 10,000 AND OVER: 1993

City (Service provision)	Department	Total personnel, no. uniformed, duty hours per week	Entrance, maximum salary ($)	Longevity pay, maximum ($) no. years to receive longevity pay	Total expenditures (A) ($)	Total personnel expenditures (B) ($), % of (A)	Salaries and wages (C) ($)	City contrib. to employee retirement, insurance (D) ($)	Capital outlay (E) ($)	All other (F) ($)
10,000-24,999 continued										
Russellville, Ark. (1,3) cont.	F	37-37-53	18,444-...	Y-27,500-..	790	780-98	646	44-90	...	10
Ruston, La. (1,1)	P	46-40-43	14,760-...	None	1,557	1,231-79	912	202-117	89	237
	F	45-45-53	13,200-...	Y-14,400-2	1,507	1,192-79	965	84-143	24	291
Rye, N.Y. (1,3)	P	36-34-40	32,470-44,890	Y-46,780-9	...	...-..	...	...-...	...	...
	F	16-16-40	24,526-39,180	Y-41,438-9	...	...-..	...	...-...	...	...
Saddle Brook tp, N.J. (1,2)	P	35-33-37	31,500-60,400	Y-66,560-3	...	...-..	...	...-...	45	...
	F	...-..-..	...-...	..-..-..	...	...-..	...	...-...	...	...
Safety Harbor, Fla. (7,1)	P	...-..-..	...-...	..-..-..	...	...-..	...	...-...	...	...
	F	31-30-56	21,724-31,479	Y-32,479-5	1,964	1,484-75	1,020	352-112	30	450
St. Augustine, Fla. (3,1)	P	47-37-40	21,185-29,793	None	1,768	1,563-88	1,202	237-124	22	183
	F	27-26-56	20,269-28,074	None	1,089	1,022-93	744	201-77	1	66
St. Charles, Ill. (1,3)	P	58-48-41	26,970-41,148	None	4,037	3,260-80	2,609	458-193	129	648
	F	31-30-56	27,647-41,471	None	2,187	1,838-84	1,540	196-102	101	248
St. Cloud, Fla. (1,3)	P	42-22-42	21,590-29,277	None	1,797	1,451-80	1,129	218-104	83	263
	F	29-28-56	21,590-29,277	None	1,432	1,172-81	902	184-86	69	191
Salisbury, N.C. (1,1)	P	83-65-40	17,721-25,665	None	3,246	2,435-75	1,903	343-189	280	531
	F	64-..-56	16,867-24,428	None	1,949	1,665-85	1,425	75-165	10	274
San Benito, Tex. (3,3)	P	35-29-40	14,568-15,274	Y-17,094-1	1,127	949-84	689	63-197	...	178
	F	21-21-53	13,000-15,738	Y-17,226-1	528	468-88	342	39-87	...	60
San Fernando, Calif. (1,9)	P	48-34-40	33,828-41,904	Y-46,094-4	...	...-..	...	...-...	...	...
	F	...-..-..	...-...	..-..-..	...	...-..	...	...-...	...	...
San Juan, Tex. (1,2)	P	28-21-40	15,954-21,008	Y-21,058-1	1,376	535-38	420	32-83	185	656
	F	...-..-..	...-...	..-..-..	...	...-..	...	...-...	...	...
San Marino, Calif. (1,1)	P	32-26-40	33,396-40,752	None	1,878	1,705-90	1,373	231-101	18	155
	F	23-22-56	31,464-38,388	None	1,638	1,527-93	1,221	208-98	9	102
Sand Springs, Okla. (1,1)	P	30-27-40	18,360-19,440	Y-21,408-2	1,161	901-77	724	111-66	85	175
	F	28-28-56	15,636-20,160	Y-22,260-2	989	801-80	663	69-69	35	153
Sanford t, Me. (1,3)	P	46-33-40	20,114-23,993	Y-27,750-7	1,107	1,023-92	844	74-105	...	84
	F	42-1-48	21,187-...	Y-...-7	1,117	971-86	791	72-108	...	146
Sanford, N.C. (1,1)	P	75-62-40	18,735-26,472	Y-...-5	3,096	2,376-76	1,848	300-228	432	288
	F	47-46-40	18,735-26,472	Y-...-5	1,764	1,440-81	1,140	144-156	12	312
Santa Clarita, Calif. (7,7)	P	...-..-..	...-...	..-..-..	...	...-..	...	...-...	...	...
	F	...-..-..	...-...	..-..-..	...	...-..	...	...-...	...	...
Santa Fe Springs, Calif. (9,1)	P	...-..-..	...-...	..-..-..	...	...-..	...	...-...	...	...
	F	78-73-56	34,586-41,880	Y-41,902-3	3,870	3,608-93	2,242	826-540	8	254
Sapulpa, Okla. (3,1)	P	46-35-40	17,532-18,264	Y-25,224-1	...	...-..	...	...-...	...	...
	F	39-38-..	13,200-...	Y-25,234-1	...	...-..	...	...-...	...	...
Scarsdale v, N.Y. (1,3)	P	47-42-40	20,000-41,900	Y-42,650-17	3,152	3,010-95	2,338	392-280	26	116
	F	43-42-40	20,000-43,354	Y-44,104-17	2,904	2,611-89	2,008	357-246	181	112
Schererville t, Ind. (1,3)	P	30-22-40	23,760-...	None	1,568	1,323-84	1,036	214-73	68	177
	F	2-2-40	22,026-...	None	321	176-54	154	18-4	63	82
Schertz, Tex. (1,3)	P	24-18-..	16,128-19,669	Y-19,909-1	...	...-..	...	...-...	1	...
	F	6-6-..	15,095-18,283	Y-18,523-1	...	...-..	...	...-...	1	...
Schiller Park v, Ill. (1,3)	P	39-30-..	25,189-37,262	Y-39,497-4	...	...-..	...	...-...	...	...
	F	19-19-..	29,802-35,514	Y-37,644-4	...	...-..	...	...-...	...	...
Scituate t, Mass. (1,1)	P	29-22-40	26,185-29,447	Y-...-5	...	...-..	...	...-...	32	...
	F	48-42-42	27,418-30,224	Y-...-5	...	...-..	...	...-...	35	...
Scotch Plains tp, N.J. (1,2)	P	49-44-40	22,000-...	..-..-..	...	...-..	...	...-...	...	...
	F	...-..-..	...-...	..-..-..	...	...-..	...	...-...	...	...
Scott tp, Pa. (1,2)	P	24-19-40	28,989-36,235	Y-37,675-4	...	...-..	...	...-...	...	...
	F	...-..-..	...-...	..-..-..	...	...-..	...	...-...	...	...
Scottsbluff, Nebr. (1,2)	P	34-29-40	18,304-24,357	..-..-..	1,447	1,247-86	993	143-111	5	195
	F	...-..-..	...-...	..-..-..	...	...-..	...	...-...	...	...
Sebastian, Fla. (1,7)	P	31-23-40	24,398-30,576	None	1,370	1,085-79	901	108-76	109	176
	F	...-..-..	...-...	..-..-..	...	...-..	...	...-...	...	...
Sedalia, Mo. (1,1)	P	54-44-40	18,192-21,636	Y-...-3	1,632	1,228-75	1,026	83-119	57	347
	F	41-41-50	16,596-20,400	Y-...-3	1,162	1,046-90	890	55-101	6	110
Seguin, Tex. (3,3)	P	51-33-40	20,218-26,520	Y-27,720-1	2,327	2,121-91	1,821	192-108	2	204
	F	24-23-56	18,325-24,024	Y-25,224-1	744	672-90	537	93-42	...	72
Selma, Calif. (3,3)	P	39-28-40	25,064-36,103	None	2,667	2,121-79	1,551	327-243	21	525
	F	13-13-56	22,852-33,082	None	1,383	1,050-75	795	162-93	...	333
Seymour t, Conn. (1,2)	P	...-1-40	29,390-33,114	Y-34,107-5	1,939	1,658-85	1,242	185-231	41	240
	F	...-..-..	...-...	..-..-..	...	...-..	...	...-...	...	...
Shakopee, Minn. (1,2)	P	22-19-40	27,860-37,145	Y-39,485-14	1,288	991-76	886	100-5	54	243
	F	...-..-..	...-...	..-..-..	...	...-..	...	...-...	...	...
Sharonville, Ohio (1,3)	P	42-31-40	28,263-37,268	Y-...-..	2,887	2,261-78	1,730	317-214	...	626
	F	5-4-40	28,263-37,268	Y-...-..	857	591-68	483	83-25	...	266
Shelby, N.C. (3,3)	P	49-35-43	17,472-21,840	Y-22,240-5	...	...-..	...	...-...	...	...
	F	41-40-53	16,666-20,800	Y-21,200-5	...	...-..	...	...-...	...	...
Shelbyville, Ind. (1,1)	P	39-30-40	22,974-23,974	Y-28,769-1	1,751	1,449-82	1,073	135-241	71	231
	F	48-47-48	22,974-23,974	Y-28,769-1	2,355	1,866-79	1,344	229-293	52	437
Sheridan, Wyo. (1,1)	P	38-25-40	21,329-28,580	Y-30,380-5	1,848	1,368-74	1,080	108-180	300	180
	F	19-18-56	20,311-27,219	Y-29,019-5	984	912-92	636	168-108	24	48
Sherwood, Ark. (1,2)	P	59-41-40	20,315-26,164	None	2,365	1,685-71	1,372	202-111	241	439

Table 3/23 continued   POLICE AND FIRE DEPARTMENT PERSONNEL, SALARIES, AND EXPENDITURES FOR CITIES 10,000 AND OVER: 1993

City (Service provision)	Department	Total personnel, no. uniformed, duty hours per week	Entrance, maximum salary ($)	Longevity pay, maximum ($) no. years to receive longevity pay	Total expenditures (A) ($)	Total personnel expenditures (B) ($), % of (A)	Salaries and wages (C) ($)	City contrib. to employee retirement, insurance (D) ($)	Capital outlay (E) ($)	All other (F) ($)
10,000-24,999 continued										
Sherwood, Ark. (1,2) cont.	F	...-..-..	...-...	..-..-..	...	...-..	...	...-...	...	...
Shoreview, Minn. (-,-)	P	...-..-..	...-...	..-..-..	...	...-..	...	...	...	...
	F	...-..-..	...-...	..-..-..	...	...-..	...	...-..	...	...
Shorewood v, Wis. (1,1)	P	...-..-..	32,949-37,474	None	...	...-..	...	...-..	...	...
	F	...-..-56	32,949-37,474	None	...	...-..	...	...-..	...	...
Shrewsbury t, Mass. (1,-)	P	39-31-37	26,696-30,462	Y-30,812-5	...	...-..	...	...-...	60	...
	F	...-..-..	...-...	..-..-..	...	...-..	...	...-..	...	...
Sidney, Ohio (1,1)	P	41-30-40	25,168-32,490	Y-34,114-5	2,024	1,737-85	1,367	230-140	150	137
	F	30-30-54	24,902-32,155	Y-33,763-5	1,528	1,409-92	1,051	252-106	1	118
Sierra Madre, Calif. (1,2)	P	20-14-40	30,315-40,638	None	566	542-95	396	61-85	2	22
	F	...-..-..	...-...	..-..-..	...	...-..	...	...-..	...	...
Sikeston, Mo. (4,4)	P	...-..-..	...-...	..-..-..	...	...-..	...	...-..	...	...
	F	...-..-..	...-...	..-..-..	...	...-..	...	...-..	...	...
Silver City t, N.M. (4,4)	P	...-..-..	...-...	..-..-..	...	...-..	...	...-..	...	...
	F	...-..-..	...-...	..-..-..	...	...-..	...	...-..	...	...
Simpsonville t, S.C. (1,1)	P	...-..-..	...-...	..-..-..	891	760-85	621	109-30	...	131
	F	...-..-..	...-...	..-..-..	545	474-86	360	64-50	...	71
Smithfield t, R.I. (1,1)	P	44-38-40	22,789-26,811	Y-30,833-5	2,433	2,080-85	1,651	428-1	85	268
	F	40-34-42	21,257-26,656	Y-30,654-5	2,259	1,815-80	1,483	331-1	100	344
Smyrna t, Tenn. (1,4)	P	36-25-..	23,049-25,442	None	...	...-..	...	...-..	45	...
	F	...-..-..	...-...	..-..-..	...	...-..	...	...-..	...	...
Snellville, Ga. (4,7)	P	...-..-..	...-...	..-..-..	...	...-..	...	...-..	...	...
	F	...-..-..	...-...	..-..-..	...	...-..	...	...-..	...	...
Snyder, Tex. (1,3)	P	21-16-40	22,080-24,108	Y-25,632-1	894	687-76	542	108-37	50	157
	F	9-9-48	19,848-21,672	Y-21,720-1	628	313-49	246	50-17	69	246
Solana Beach, Calif. (9,1)	P	...-..-..	...-...	..-..-..	...	...-..	...	...-..	...	...
	F	23-21-56	30,558-37,674	..-..-..	1,921	1,826-95	1,258	362-206	3	92
Solon, Ohio (1,1)	P	53-40-40	30,726-36,728	Y-40,412-5	...	...-..	...	...-..	...	...
	F	43-42-40	25,213-36,914	Y-40,605-5	...	...-..	...	...-..	...	...
Somers Point, N.J. (1,2)	P	30-24-40	22,000-37,811	Y-40,311-3	...	...-..	...	...-..	14	...
	F	...-..-..	...-...	..-..-..	...	...-..	...	...-..	...	...
Somerset, Ky. (1,1)	P	29-29-40	...-...	..-..-..	...	...-..	...	...-..	...	...
	F	19-19-56	...-...	..-..-..	...	...-..	...	...-..	...	...
Somerset t, Mass. (1,2)	P	33-30-40	23,070-28,838	Y-30,138-5	1,243	1,114-89	1,097	4-13	68	61
	F	...-..-..	...-...	..-..-..	...	...-..	...	...-..	...	...
Somersworth, N.H. (1,3)	P	26-19-40	19,989-24,253	Y-24,877-5	1,409	1,190-84	717	40-433	29	190
	F	14-13-42	19,809-24,111	Y-25,151-5	628	528-84	439	24-65	5	95
South Burlington, Vt. (1,1)	P	33-33-40	...-...	..-..-..	...	...-..	...	...-..	...	...
	F	10-10-..	...-...	..-..-..	...	...-..	...	...-..	...	...
South Charleston, W.Va. (1,2)	P	30-30-40	16,712-23,129	None	...	...-..	...	...-..	33	...
	F	...-..-..	...-...	..-..-..	...	...-..	...	...-..	...	...
South Daytona, Fla. (1,1)	P	32-23-40	20,167-29,830	None	1,275	942-73	678	213-51	...	333
	F	12-12-53	19,207-28,409	None	558	444-79	321	102-21	...	114
South Euclid, Ohio (1,1)	P	...-..-..	...-...	..-..-..	...	...-..	...	...-..	...	...
	F	...-..-..	...-...	..-..-..	...	...-..	...	...-..	...	...
South Holland v, Ill. (1,3)	P	44-31-36	29,748-36,379	Y-39,499-5	...	...-..	...	...-..	42	...
	F	13-10-36	29,411-37,461	Y-40,581-5	...	...-..	...	...-..	274	...
South Kingstown t, R.I. (1,5)	P	66-43-37	21,400-32,443	Y-34,390-20	...	...-..	...	...-..	8	...
	F	...-..-..	...-...	..-..-..	...	...-..	...	...-..	...	...
South Lake Tahoe, Calif. (1,1)	P	73-53-40	...-...	None	...	...-..	...	...-..	...	...
	F	40-37-56	28,740-34,932	None	2,765	2,500-90	1,882	438-180	...	265
South Miami, Fla. (1,7)	P	59-49-40	27,180-34,689	Y-37,906-10	2,635	2,287-86	1,949	207-131	108	240
	F	...-..-..	...-...	..-..-..	...	...-..	...	...-..	...	...
South Milwaukee, Wis. (3,9)	P	32-31-38	33,575-37,016	Y-37,316-5	1,815	1,652-91	1,425	92-135	16	147
	F	...-..-..	32,436-36,060	Y-36,360-5	...	...-..	...	...-..	...	...
South Orange Village tp, N.J. (1,1)	P	61-53-37	26,948-38,390	Y-42,229-5	4,219	3,676-87	2,733	598-345	247	296
	F	32-32-42	22,732-41,748	Y-45,922-5	2,176	2,112-97	1,595	357-160	14	50
South Park tp, Pa. (1,2)	P	16-15-40	26,707-38,147	Y-40,054-5	1,019	768-75	628	26-114	38	213
	F	...-..-..	...-...	..-..-..	...	...-..	...	...-..	...	...
South Pasadena, Calif. (3,3)	P	47-30-40	32,256-39,204	Y-...-5	3,503	2,857-81	2,106	620-131	111	535
	F	27-27-56	31,452-38,232	Y-...-5	1,906	1,720-90	1,211	435-74	12	174
South Whitehall tp, Pa. (1,2)	P	38-34-40	22,789-31,995	Y-33,395-2	2,028	1,812-89	1,560	108-144	...	216
	F	...-..-..	...-...	..-..-..	...	...-..	...	...-..	...	...
South Windsor t, Conn. (1,2)	P	36-32-40	31,238-39,200	Y-39,420-5	2,446	2,220-90	1,802	226-192	96	130
	F	...-..-..	...-...	..-..-..	...	...-..	...	...-..	...	...
Southaven, Miss. (1,1)	P	43-43-43	17,971-19,594	None	2,633	1,566-59	842	361-363	166	901
	F	31-31-56	17,971-19,594	None	1,744	1,180-67	648	259-273	31	533
Spanish Fork, Utah (1,2)	P	16-16-40	23,800-27,900	..-..-..	1,171	584-49	462	117-5	359	228
	F	...-..-..	...-...	..-..-..	...	...-..	...	...-..	...	...
Sparta tp, N.J. (1,2)	P	34-27-42	26,085-45,952	Y-49,149-..	2,672	2,484-92	1,891	355-238	...	188
	F	...-..-..	...-...	..-..-..	...	...-..	...	...-..	...	...
Spencer, Iowa (1,3)	P	19-19-42	22,749-27,633	Y-28,533-..	...	...-..	...	...-..	45	...
	F	5-5-56	20,639-25,072	Y-...-..	...	...-..	...	...-..	18	...
Springettsbury tp, Pa. (1,3)	P	25-25-40	23,238-38,829	Y-...-3	...	...-..	...	...-..	60	...

| Table 3/23 | POLICE AND FIRE DEPARTMENT PERSONNEL, SALARIES, AND EXPENDITURES FOR |
| continued | CITIES 10,000 AND OVER: 1993 |

City (Service provision)	Depart-ment	Total personnel, no. uniformed, duty hours per week	Entrance, maximum salary ($)	Longevity pay, maximum ($) no. years to receive longevity pay	Total expendi-tures (A) ($)	Total personnel expendi-tures (B) ($), % of (A)	Salaries and wages (C) ($)	City contrib. to employee retirement, insurance (D) ($)	Capital outlay (E) ($)	All other (F) ($)
10,000-24,999 continued										
Springettsbury tp, Pa. (1,3) cont.	F	12-12-52	23,123-34,095	Y-...-3	...	...-...	...	...-...	...	...
Springfield, Tenn. (1,3)	P	34-28-40	17,202-23,442	None	1,232	964-78	748	105-111	64	204
	F	21-21-53	15,600-21,237	None	952	732-76	575	77-80	129	91
Springville, Utah (1,3)	P	19-19-40	18,500-27,287	None	...	...-...	...	...-...	37	...
	F	2-2-40	18,500-27,287	None	...	...-...	...	...-...	87	...
Starkville, Miss. (1,1)	P	37-36-40	17,443-21,215	..-...-..	1,312	1,003-76	812	142-49	102	207
	F	39-38-56	14,347-16,752	..-...-..	957	809-84	648	115-46	83	65
Statesboro, Ga. (1,3)	P	...-..-..	...-...	...-...-..	...	...-...	...	...-...	...	...
	F	...-..-..	...-...	...-...-..	...	...-...	...	...-...	...	...
Statesville, N.C. (3,1)	P	75-60-42	20,012-27,038	Y-27,788-5	2,764	2,307-83	1,830	349-128	97	360
	F	53-51-48	18,564-26,229	Y-26,979-5	2,045	1,710-83	1,426	179-105	24	311
Staunton, Va. (3,3)	P	60-56-40	17,973-25,644	None	1,191	945-79	712	159-74	71	175
	F	22-22-56	16,283-23,232	None	411	381-92	283	64-34	...	30
Sterling, Colo. (1,3)	P	23-16-42	18,411-25,209	None	1,144	972-84	798	67-107	45	127
	F	7-7-53	18,404-25,202	None	394	322-81	275	14-33	3	69
Sterling, Ill. (1,1)	P	25-14-40	19,250-28,269	None	...	...-..	...	...-...	20	...
	F	2-1-53	19,250-28,250	None	...	...	...	...	...	...
Steubenville, Ohio (1,1)	P	43-40-40	21,420-26,355	Y-...-5	...	...-..	...	...-...	59	...
	F	40-39-56	19,820-25,985	Y-...-5	...	...-..	...	...-...	63	...
Stevens Point, Wis. (1,1)	P	51-40-41	29,228-31,561	Y-32,101-5	4,248	3,420-80	2,292	576-552	300	528
	F	38-38-56	25,614-30,134	Y-30,794-5	3,324	2,832-85	1,932	492-408	...	492
Stoneham t, Mass. (1,1)	P	42-37-37	28,117-32,616	Y-33,766-5	...	...-..	...	...-...	...	...
	F	48-47-42	27,384-31,764	Y-33,035-5	...	...-..	...	...-...	...	...
Streator, Ill. (1,1)	P	30-23-37	21,628-35,873	..-...-..	1,248	1,040-83	872	37-131	38	170
	F	14-14-56	24,404-28,978	..-...-..	614	536-87	454	2-80	1	77
Stuart, Fla. (1,1)	P	58-44-40	21,439-31,382	Y-33,382-3	...	...-..	...	...-...	...	...
	F	27-21-53	19,226-27,556	Y-29,556-3	...	...-..	...	...-...	...	...
Sturgis, Mich. (1,1)	P	20-16-40	24,086-28,891	Y-29,391-5	1,142	998-87	838	71-89	...	144
	F	14-14-56	22,464-27,356	Y-27,856-5	817	721-88	594	62-65	...	96
Sudbury t, Mass. (1,1)	P	25-20-37	28,921-31,582	Y-32,845-6	822	780-94	701	2-77	...	42
	F	32-31-42	27,930-30,590	Y-31,814-6	904	860-95	765	1-94	...	44
Suffern v, N.Y. (1,2)	P	31-31-40	37,900-51,500	Y-...-3	2,306	2,109-91	1,631	304-174	100	97
	F	...-..-..	...-...	...-...-..	...	...-..	...	...-...	...	...
Suffield t, Conn. (1,3)	P	19-14-40	26,690-34,674	None	1,017	944-92	733	131-80	...	73
	F	4-4-40	27,109-...	None	277	226-81	177	27-22	...	51
Sugar Land, Tex. (1,1)	P	73-59-40	23,868-33,415	Y-34,615-..	2,553	2,133-83	1,776	132-225	27	393
	F	61-59-56	22,956-32,139	Y-33,339-..	2,328	1,965-84	1,647	120-198	6	357
Suisun City, Calif. (1,2)	P	33-23-40	29,710-39,814	..-...-..	1,932	1,572-81	1,212	204-156	...	360
	F	...-..-..	...-...	...-...-..	...	...-..	...	...-...	...	...
Sulphur, La. (1,1)	P	42-..-40	18,927-...	Y-15,454-3	1,735	1,055-60	892	80-83	352	328
	F	31-..-53	18,927-...	Y-15,454-3	1,204	1,023-84	874	71-78	29	152
Sulphur Springs, Tex. (1,2)	P	38-38-40	19,764-22,920	Y-23,064-1	...	...-..	...	...-...	...	...
	F	...-..-..	...-...	...-...-..	...	...-..	...	...-...	...	...
Summerville t, S.C. (1,3)	P	39-36-42	17,893-28,641	None	1,305	945-72	707	142-96	117	243
	F	33-33-42	16,000-34,000	None	1,041	833-80	608	122-103	9	199
Summit, N.J. (1,3)	P	54-40-40	...-...	Y-...-5	3,291	3,102-94	2,602	270-230	...	189
	F	36-30-42	...-...	Y-...-5	2,249	2,123-94	1,623	270-230	...	126
Sun Prairie, Wis. (1,2)	P	37-27-37	25,530-33,049	Y-...-5	1,151	1,090-94	874	213-3	...	61
	F	...-..-..	...-...	...-...-..	...	...-..	...	...-...	...	...
Sunnyside, Wash. (3,3)	P	27-19-48	25,428-29,436	Y-...-10	1,348	1,113-82	804	205-104	...	235
	F	11-10-52	26,280-30,444	Y-...-10	760	579-76	516	25-38	...	181
Susquehanna tp, Pa. (1,2)	P	32-30-40	26,000-32,256	Y-33,000-..	...	...-..	...	...-...	85	...
	F	...-..-..	...-...	...-...-..	...	...-..	...	...-...	...	...
Swampscott t, Mass. (1,1)	P	41-41-40	24,451-...	Y-...-5	...	...-..	...	...-...	34	...
	F	37-37-40	23,744-...	Y-23,747-5	...	...-..	...	...-...	...	...
Swatara tp, Pa. (1,2)	P	29-27-40	26,163-31,737	Y-34,386-4	...	...-..	...	...-...	26	...
	F	...-..-..	...-...	...-...-..	...	...-..	...	...-...	...	...
Sweetwater, Tex. (1,1)	P	25-21-..	19,788-21,840	Y-23,040-1	1,164	957-82	606	102-249	6	201
	F	25-24-..	19,788-21,840	Y-23,040-1	1,099	796-72	633	82-81	9	294
Tahlequah, Okla. (1,3)	P	31-23-40	15,859-17,059	..-...-..	752	661-87	525	85-51	31	60
	F	6-6-40	17,143-...	..-...-..	173	145-83	120	14-11	3	25
Takoma Park, Md. (1,7)	P	45-35-40	25,117-34,193	None	...	...-..	...	...-...	...	...
	F				...	...-..	...	...-...	...	...
Tarboro t, N.C. (1,3)	P	28-25-42	18,470-28,656	Y-29,802-..	1,030	830-80	686	111-33	9	191
	F	17-17-60	17,590-27,291	..-28,382-..	773	503-65	428	54-21	210	60
Tarpon Springs, Fla. (1,1)	P	57-43-40	22,510-31,514	None	2,589	2,187-84	1,839	231-117	12	390
	F	37-35-56	20,629-28,881	None	1,828	1,657-90	1,296	289-72	...	171
Taylor, Tex. (1,3)	P	16-16-40	20,612-...	Y-21,812-1	720	576-80	475	60-41	16	128
	F	16-16-54	20,114-...	Y-21,314-1	680	418-61	342	44-32	151	111
Taylorville, Ill. (3,3)	P	19-16-..	22,714-24,918	None	898	798-88	623	82-93	35	65
	F	11-11-..	21,494-24,735	None	454	401-88	307	48-46	12	41
Temple Terrace, Fla. (1,3)	P	54-37-42	23,358-32,697	Y-33,947-5	2,643	2,125-80	1,636	344-145	171	347
	F	30-29-56	19,219-...	Y-28,165-5	1,480	1,079-72	847	152-80	23	378
The Colony, Tex. (3,3)	P	30-22-42	23,880-31,344	None	542	437-80	360	52-25	12	93

Table 3/23 **POLICE AND FIRE DEPARTMENT PERSONNEL, SALARIES, AND EXPENDITURES FOR**
continued **CITIES 10,000 AND OVER: 1993**

City	Service provision	Department	Total personnel, no. uniformed, duty hours per week	Entrance, maximum salary ($)	Longevity pay, maximum ($) no. years to receive longevity pay	Reported expenditures (in thousands)					
						Total expenditures (A) ($)	Total personnel expenditures (B) ($), % of (A)	Salaries and wages (C) ($)	City contrib. to employee retirement, insurance (D) ($)	Capital outlay (E) ($)	All other (F) ($)
10,000-24,999 continued											
The Colony, Tex. (3,3) cont.		F	15-14-56	21,504-31,344	Y-...-1	264	209-79	174	25-10	3	52
The Dalles, Ore. (1,1)		P	16-14-40	23,592-27,996	None	1,004	798-79	570	160-68	8	198
		F	14-13-56	...-...	None	976	780-79	574	160-46	44	152
The Village, Okla. (1,1)		P	28-24-40	20,160-26,760	Y-27,365-3	1,224	1,146-93	908	140-98	...	78
		F	20-20-60	20,160-26,760	Y-27,365-3	928	824-88	678	74-72	...	104
Thibodaux, La. (1,2)		P	47-42-40	13,833-26,611	None	1,494	1,093-73	912	92-89	56	345
		F	...-...-...	...-...	...-...-..	...	...-..	...	...-...	...	...
Thomasville, Ga. (1,1)		P	47-40-42	16,314-26,907	None	1,697	1,325-78	1,147	112-66	...	372
		F	42-42-56	14,327-23,325	None	1,573	1,285-81	1,109	111-65	...	288
Thomasville, N.C. (1,1)		P	...-...-..	...-...	..-...-..	...	...-..	...	...-...	...	...
		F	...-...-..	...-...	...-...-..	...	...-..	...	...-...	...	...
Tiffin, Ohio (1,1)		P	40-28-40	21,796-27,594	Y-30,353-4	...	...-..	...	...-...	...	...
		F	27-26-52	21,410-27,121	Y-29,834-4	...	...-..	...	...-...	...	...
Tolland t, Conn. (-,3)		P	2-2-40	26,807-34,850	None	248	223-89	201	9-13	...	25
		F	4-4-40	26,807-34,850	None	259	168-64	121	15-32	...	91
Tonawanda, N.Y. (1,3)		P	35-31-40	27,000-33,000	Y-34,000-5	2,098	1,943-92	1,413	340-190	60	95
		F	30-29-40	27,000-33,000	Y-34,000-5	1,787	1,646-92	1,180	296-170	39	102
Tooele, Utah (1,2)		P	19-19-40	18,252-32,256	None	...	...-..	...	...-...	...	...
		F	...-...-..	...-...	..-...-..	...	...-..	...	...-...	...	...
Towamencin tp, Pa. (1,2)		P	20-19-40		...-...	...	...-..	...	...-...	...	...
		F	...-...-..	...-...	..-...-..	...	...-..	...	...-...	...	...
Traverse City, Mich. (1,1)		P	33-32-40	27,102-30,826	Y-32,989-10	2,095	1,647-78	1,262	257-128	15	433
		F	22-22-56	21,112-27,751	Y-29,702-10	1,280	1,015-79	780	150-85	19	246
Troy, Ohio (1,1)		P	38-36-..	24,467-33,873	Y-36,480-5	...	...-..	...	...-...	...	...
		F	31-30-..	24,467-33,873	Y-36,480-5	...	...-..	...	...-...	...	...
Tualatin, Ore. (1,5)		P	23-23-40	28,404-39,688	None	1,745	1,349-77	944	277-128	71	325
		F	...-...-..	...-...	..-...-..	...	...-..	...	...-...	...	...
Tukwila, Wash. (1,1)		P	71-59-40	36,042-42,524	None	5,395	3,969-73	3,216	415-338	115	1,311
		F	62-58-50	33,796-42,502	None	4,295	3,573-83	3,058	175-340	70	652
Tullahoma, Tenn. (1,3)		P	36-29-40	20,613-21,154	None	1,311	977-74	784	90-103	92	242
		F	29-29-40	20,218-20,613	None	1,101	787-71	661	75-51	51	263
Two Rivers, Wis. (-,-)		P	29-24-37	23,225-27,280	Y-28,644-6	1,523	1,352-88	959	272-121	45	126
		F	19-19-56	24,242-27,061	Y-28,414-6	962	898-93	631	183-84	19	45
University Heights, Ohio (1,1)		P	29-29-40	28,197-35,247	Y-37,714-3	2,459	1,807-73	1,353	265-189	40	612
		F	29-29-52	28,197-35,247	Y-37,714-3	2,290	1,610-70	1,189	274-147	530	150
University Park, Tex. (4,4)		P	...-...-..	...-...	..-...-..	...	...-..	...	...-...	...	...
		F	...-...-..	...-...	..-...-..	...	...-..	...	...-...	...	...
Upper Dublin tp, Pa. (1,2)		P	41-35-40	31,433-38,316	Y-42,316-5	2,338	2,153-92	1,613	184-356	14	171
		F	...-...-..	...-...	..-...-..	...	...-..	...	...-...	...	...
Upper St. Clair tp, Pa. (1,2)		P	33-27-40	26,686-38,210	Y-40,210-4	2,087	1,787-85	1,356	174-257	26	274
		F	...-...-..	...-...	..-...-..	...	...-..	...	...-...	...	...
Upper Southampton tp, Pa. (1,2)		P	...-...-40	29,125-37,380	Y-39,623-..	1,776	1,366-76	990	222-154	75	335
		F	...-...-..	...-...	..-...-..	...	...-..	...	...-...	...	...
Urbana, Ohio (1,1)		P	25-21-40	24,412-28,224	Y-29,710-2	1,094	983-89	684	131-168	...	111
		F	23-22-56	23,741-28,734	Y-30,259-2	1,098	1,059-96	700	169-190	...	39
Urbandale, Iowa (1,2)		P	40-33-40	24,762-29,718	Y-30,985-5	1,692	1,377-81	1,169	91-117	61	254
		F	...-...-..	...-...	..-...-..	...	...-..	...	...-...	...	...
Uvalde, Tex. (1,3)		P	26-22-40	19,270-24,040	Y-25,240-25	771	656-85	552	68-36	...	115
		F	3-3-56	16,620-20,745	Y-21,945-25	164	73-44	60	7-6	...	91
Uwchlan tp, Pa. (1,2)		P	...-19-..	37,144-41,883	Y-44,383-1	1,350	1,001-74	823	65-113	...	349
		F	...-...-..	...-...	..-...-..	...	...-..	...	...-...	...	...
Van Wert, Ohio (1,1)		P	27-21-40	19,600-26,094	Y-27,344-5	1,211	940-77	704	136-100	22	249
		F	20-20-..	21,340-25,010	Y-27,960-5	866	762-87	542	142-78	14	90
Vandalia, Ohio (1,3)		P	37-28-38	27,041-36,037	None	2,289	1,933-84	1,463	264-206	95	261
		F	5-5-40	27,248-32,552	None	683	430-62	350	57-23	113	140
Venice, Fla. (1,1)		P	61-40-40	22,000-33,000	None	3,287	2,406-73	1,891	400-115	...	881
		F	33-32-56	16,535-29,528	None	...	...-..	...	...-...	...	...
Vermillion, S.D. (1,3)		P	23-19-40	18,948-...	None	...	...-..	...	...-...	...	...
		F	1-1-40	20,000-...	...-...	...	...-..	...	...-...	...	...
Vero Beach, Fla. (1,7)		P	87-60-40	22,256-...	Y-29,994-1	...	...-..	...	...-...	...	...
		F	...-...-..	...-...	..-...-..	...	...-..	...	...-...	...	...
Vestavia Hills, Ala. (1,1)		P	35-34-40	23,733-31,803	Y-32,570-6	1,785	1,509-84	1,257	180-72	39	237
		F	49-48-52	23,733-31,803	Y-32,570-6	2,448	2,133-87	1,785	252-96	...	315
Vienna, W.Va. (1,2)		P	20-13-40	20,924-...	Y-31,158-1	817	569-69	467	13-89	37	211
		F	...-...-..	...-...	..-...-..	...	...-..	...	...-...	...	...
Wabash, Ind. (1,1)		P	25-19-..	24,418-...	Y-26,371-..	...	...-..	...	...-...	...	...
		F	31-31-..	24,418-...	Y-26,371-..	...	...-..	...	...-...	...	...
Wadsworth, Ohio (1,2)		P	29-24-40	26,894-33,592	Y-...-.	1,624	1,439-88	1,067	196-176	9	176
		F	...-...-..	...-...	..-...-..	...	...-..	...	...-...	...	...
Wakefield t, Mass. (1,1)		P	46-44-39	28,756-30,732	Y-54,132-5	...	...-..	...	...-...	...	...
		F	49-48-42	28,756-30,732	Y-54,132-5	...	...-..	...	...-...	...	...
Walker, Mich. (1,2)		P	37-29-40	26,727-37,251	Y-37,451-5	...	...-..	...	...-...	40	...
		F	...-...-..	...-...	..-...-..	...	...-..	...	...-...	...	...
Wall tp, N.J. (1,2)		P	64-49-40	25,155-49,678	Y-54,645-3	...	...-..	...	...-...	...	...

Table 3/23 continued **POLICE AND FIRE DEPARTMENT PERSONNEL, SALARIES, AND EXPENDITURES FOR CITIES 10,000 AND OVER: 1993**

City (Service provision)	Department	Total personnel, no. uniformed, duty hours per week	Entrance, maximum salary ($)	Longevity pay, maximum ($) no. years to receive longevity pay	Reported expenditures (in thousands)					
					Total expenditures (A) ($)	Total personnel expenditures (B) ($), % of (A)	Salaries and wages (C) ($)	City contrib. to employee retirement, insurance (D) ($)	Capital outlay (E) ($)	All other (F) ($)
10,000–24,999 continued										
Wall tp, N.J. (1,2) cont.	F	...-..-..	...-...	..-...-..	...	...-..	...	...-...	...	...
Warren tp, N.J. (1,2)	P	27-22-..	21,200-56,865	Y-79,200-..	1,704	1,556-91	1,188	223-145	30	118
	F	...-..-..	...-...	..-...-..	...	...-..	...	...-...	...	...
Warren t, R.I. (1,2)	P	21-21-..	24,512-27,693	Y-29,908-5	...	...-..	...	...-...	398	...
	F	...-..-..	...-...	..-...-..	...	...-..	...	...-...	...	...
Warrensburg, Mo. (1,3)	P	25-22-40	16,360-24,802	Y-25,052-5	1,062	880-82	723	71-86	61	121
	F	14-14-..	15,714-23,823	Y-24,063-5	665	539-81	436	52-51	26	100
Warrenville, Ill. (1,5)	P	17-17-40	27,000-...	..-...-..	1,093	875-80	676	138-61	41	177
	F	...-..-..	...-...	..-...-..	...	...-..	...	...-...	...	170
Warrington tp, Pa. (1,2)	P	18-16-40	20,500-36,935	Y-...-5	1,018	829-81	615	109-105	19	170
	F	...-..-..	...-...	..-...-..	...	...-..	...	...-...	...	...
Warsaw, Ind. (1,3)	P	40-32-40	21,890-26,000	Y-31,200-1	...	...-..	...	...-...	76	...
	F	26-26-56	21,890-26,000	Y-31,200-..	...	...-..	...	...-...	54	...
Wasco, Calif. (7,7)	P	...-..-..	...-...	..-...-..	...	...-..	...	...-...	...	...
	F	...-..-..	...-...	..-...-..	...	...-..	...	...-...	...	...
Washington, Ind. (1,1)	P	19-15-40	22,028-...	Y-23,028-1	1,232	1,058-85	854	118-86	88	86
	F	17-17-53	22,026-...	Y-23,026-1	1,021	943-92	762	105-76	22	56
Washington, Mo. (1,2)	P	...-..-..	...-...	..-...-..	968	726-75	592	68-66	95	147
	F	...-..-..	...-...	..-...-..	...	...-..	...	...-...	...	...
Washington (Morris) tp, N.J. (1,2)	P	28-26-40	28,024-44,452	Y-46,675-5	1,701	1,620-95	1,394	104-122	...	81
	F	...-..-..	...-...	..-...-..	...	...-..	...	...-...	...	...
Washington, Ohio (1,1)	P	23-16-40	20,051-24,731	Y-27,204-5	969	857-88	612	125-120	12	100
	F	13-13-56	20,091-23,977	Y-25,176-5	714	624-87	437	99-88	15	75
Watauga, Tex. (4,4)	P	...-..-..	...-...	..-...-..	...	...-..	...	...-...	...	...
	F	...-..-..	...-...	..-...-..	...	...-..	...	...-...	...	...
Waterford t, Conn. (1,3)	P	54-45-40	29,765-37,856	Y-38,456-5	3,946	3,273-82	2,406	540-327	61	612
	F	18-6-50	34,377-46,069	Y-46,669-5	2,277	1,299-57	1,022	163-114	83	895
Watertown t, Conn. (1,2)	P	33-33-40	34,200-...	Y-...-20	...	...-..	...	...-...	63	...
	F	...-..-..	...-...	..-...-..	...	...-..	...	...-...	...	...
Watertown, S.D. (1,1)	P	29-25-45	21,172-24,639	Y-26,499-1	1,078	968-89	757	115-96	31	79
	F	28-28-53	20,055-23,285	Y-25,145-1	970	808-83	712	1-95	9	153
Watertown, Wis. (1,1)	P	45-33-40	26,051-30,740	Y-30,915-8	1,933	1,721-89	1,243	309-169	65	147
	F	21-21-56	23,840-29,218	Y-29,393-8	1,133	1,069-94	805	193-71	7	57
Waterville, Me. (1,3)	P	37-30-42	17,829-24,366	Y-...-6	...	...-..	...	...-...	42	...
	F	25-21-51	19,677-23,137	Y-...-6	...	...-..	...	...-...	19	...
Waxahachie, Tex. (3,1)	P	43-34-..	22,027-23,129	Y-...-1	...	...-..	...	...-...	95	...
	F	33-33-..	22,279-23,360	Y-...-1	...	...-..	...	...-...	28	...
Waycross, Ga. (1,1)	P	64-49-43	15,221-20,143	None	...	...-..	...	...-...	1,518	...
	F	46-45-53	13,454-17,759	None	...	...-..	...	...-...	190	...
Wayne, Mich. (1,1)	P	51-38-40	28,386-36,078	Y-36,978-3	2,412	1,728-71	1,332	228-168	...	684
	F	21-20-..	29,020-35,169	Y-36,069-3	924	738-79	564	90-84	...	186
Waynesboro, Va. (3,3)	P	50-46-40	17,844-26,413	None	...	...-..	...	...-...	...	...
	F	23-22-56	15,253-23,481	None	...	...-..	...	...-...	...	...
Weatherford, Okla. (1,1)	P	29-29-40	19,760-21,840	Y-...-1	...	...-..	...	...-...	...	...
	F	13-13-53	19,136-21,528	Y-...-1	...	...-..	...	...-...	...	...
Weatherford, Tex. (1,3)	P	50-35-40	24,190-27,830	Y-29,030-..	2,026	1,607-79	1,293	222-92	45	374
	F	22-20-56	21,141-26,907	Y-28,107-..	919	758-82	609	106-43	6	155
Webster t, Mass. (1,2)	P	22-22-40	25,992-26,322	None	...	...-..	...	...-...	18	...
	F	...-..-..	...-...	..-...-..	...	...-..	...	...-...	...	...
Weirton, W.Va. (1,1)	P	39-39-40	20,020-21,043	Y-...-1	1,834	1,556-84	1,230	130-196	114	164
	F	16-16-40	15,662-16,453	Y-...-1	977	692-70	530	60-102	33	252
Wenatchee, Wash. (1,1)	P	48-35-40	30,000-38,000	Y-40,000-5	3,029	2,078-68	1,732	171-175	9	942
	F	40-32-48	31,000-39,000	..-...-..	2,279	1,884-82	1,709	52-123	8	387
Weslaco, Tex. (1,3)	P	51-41-40	15,642-20,426	Y-...-1	1,513	1,124-74	935	117-72	39	350
	F	30-29-42	11,690-15,267	Y-...-1	637	236-37	157	65-14	51	350
West Bend, Wis. (1,-)	P	60-46-40	28,036-34,095	Y-34,755-5	3,269	2,959-90	2,104	609-246	56	254
	F	27-27-56	26,014-31,259	Y-31,919-5	1,666	1,573-94	1,139	323-111	18	75
West Bradford tp, Pa. (9,2)	P	...-..-..	...-...	..-...-..	...	...-..	...	...-...	...	...
	F	...-..-..	...-...	..-...-..	...	...-..	...	...-...	...	...
West Chester b, Pa. (1,2)	P	53-35-40	29,083-43,595	Y-48,826-5	2,636	2,379-90	2,048	40-291	37	220
	F	...-..-..	...-...	..-...-..	...	...-..	...	...-...	...	...
West Chicago, Ill. (1,5)	P	31-26-40	24,500-38,421	None	2,074	1,664-80	1,256	217-191	...	410
	F	...-..-..	...-...	..-...-..	...	...-..	...	...-...	...	...
West Goshen tp, Pa. (1,2)	P	25-22-40	...-41,971	Y-45,442-5	...	...-..	...	...-...	...	...
	F	...-..-..	...-...	..-...-..	...	...-..	...	...-...	...	...
West Linn, Ore. (3,3)	P	22-19-40	26,640-34,632	..-...-..	856	689-80	502	108-79	9	158
	F	13-12-56	26,679-36,492	..-...-..	514	409-79	299	64-46	29	76
West Manchester tp, Pa. (1,2)	P	21-21-40	23,655-36,762	Y-38,624-..	...	...-..	...	...-...	300	...
	F	...-..-..	...-...	..-...-..	...	...-..	...	...-...	...	...
West Norriton tp, Pa. (1,3)	P	23-23-40	25,000-39,000	Y-...-3	...	...-..	...	...-...	47	...
	F	1-..-40	...-...	..-...-..	...	...-..	...	...-...	...	...
West St. Paul, Minn. (1,1)	P	26-22-40	25,750-39,603	Y-...-..	1,488	1,323-88	1,087	172-64	2	163
	F	20-20-53	26,623-38,031	Y-...-..	1,119	976-87	822	104-50	1	142
West University Place, Tex. (1,3)	P	27-20-40	22,308-31,812	Y-33,312-1	1,359	1,136-83	857	142-137	14	209

Table 3/23 continued **POLICE AND FIRE DEPARTMENT PERSONNEL, SALARIES, AND EXPENDITURES FOR CITIES 10,000 AND OVER: 1993**

City (Service provision)	Department	Total personnel, no. uniformed, duty hours per week	Entrance, maximum salary ($)	Longevity pay, maximum ($), no. years to receive longevity pay	Reported expenditures (in thousands)					
					Total expenditures (A) ($)	Total personnel expenditures (B) ($), % of (A)	Salaries and wages (C) ($)	City contrib. to employee retirement, insurance (D) ($)	Capital outlay (E) ($)	All other (F) ($)
10,000-24,999 continued										
West University Place, Tex. (1,3) cont.	F	19-19-53	20,784-29,268	Y-30,768-1	999	914-91	702	115-97	8	77
West Whiteland tp, Pa. (1,2)	P	18-16-42	23,000-43,899	Y-46,899-5	1,484	1,282-86	1,023	70-189	52	150
	F	...-...-...	...-...	..-...-..	...	...-..	...	...-...	...	...
West Windsor tp, N.J. (1,2)	P	46-36-40	32,474-48,338	Y-51,041-5	2,509	2,355-93	1,940	148-267	21	133
	F	...-...-...	...-...-..	..-...-..	...	...-..	...	...-...	...	...
Westbrook, Me. (1,3)	P	36-31-40	19,240-24,960	None	1,658	1,504-90	1,132	184-188	2	152
	F	25-20-42	18,775-25,237	None	1,153	1,050-91	787	133-130	6	97
Westbury v, N.Y. (7,5)	P	...-...-..	...-...	..-...-..	...	...-..	...	...-...	...	...
	F	...-...-..	...-...	..-...-..	...	...-..	...	...-...	...	...
Westchester v, Ill. (1,1)	P	45-26-40	26,408-39,287	Y-39,687-6	1,883	1,667-88	1,271	177-219	88	128
	F	24-24-57	27,237-39,562	Y-...-..	1,076	1,029-95	826	82-121	...	47
Westminster, Md. (1,9)	P	40-30-40	21,957-29,276	Y-29,776-..	1,825	1,482-81	1,146	214-122	109	234
	F	...-...-...	...-...	..-...-..	...	...-..	...	...-...	...	...
Westmont v, Ill. (1,3)	P	48-34-40	27,124-40,465	Y-43,000-5	2,470	2,176-88	1,711	165-300	100	194
	F	3-...-48	...-...	Y-...-5	720	582-80	477	74-31	4	134
Westport t, Conn. (4,4)	P	...-...-..	...-...	..-...-..	...	...-..	...	...-...	...	...
	F	...-...-..	...-...	..-...-..	...	...-..	...	...-...	...	...
Westport t, Mass. (1,1)	P	25-24-37	26,858-29,544	Y-...-10	...	...-..	...	...-...	34	...
	F	20-20-42	25,579-26,269	Y-...-10	...	...-..	...	...-...	64	...
Westwego, La. (3,3)	P	12-12-40	...-...	..-...-..	...	...-..	...	...-...	...	...
	F	9-9-40	...-...	..-...-..	...	...-..	...	...-...	...	...
White Bear Lake, Minn. (1,3)	P	...-...-..	...-...	..-...-..	...	...-..	...	...-...	...	...
	F	...-...-..	...-...	..-...-..	...	...-..	...	...-...	...	...
White Settlement, Tex. (1,2)	P	...-9-40	21,372-27,043	Y-35,407-..	1,471	1,094-74	842	134-118	36	341
	F	...-...-..	...-...	..-...-..	...	...-..	...	...-...	...	...
Whitefish Bay v, Wis. (1,1)	P	22-22-40	32,886-37,708	Y-38,008-5	3,596	1,102-30	847	250-5	755	1,739
	F	18-18-56	29,030-38,261	Y-38,561-5	2,251	977-43	713	258-6	616	658
Whitehall, Ohio (1,1)	P	42-32-40	22,859-33,592	Y-34,592-5	...	...-..	...	...-...	...	...
	F	34-29-56	22,859-33,592	Y-34,592-5	...	...-..	...	...-...	...	...
Whitehall tp, Pa. (1,2)	P	53-40-40	23,962-33,446	Y-34,766-5	...	...-..	...	...-...	67	...
	F	...-...-..	...-...	..-...-..	...	...-..	...	...-...	...	...
Whitemarsh tp, Pa. (1,2)	P	32-28-40	25,932-37,076	Y-38,201-5	...	...-..	...	...-...	...	...
	F	...-...-..	...-...	..-...-..	...	...-..	...	...-...	...	...
Whitewater, Wis. (1,-)	P	27-20-39	25,120-29,316	Y-30,316-3	1,686	1,345-79	993	230-122	101	240
	F	...-...-..	...-...	None	...	...-..	...	...-...	21	...
Whitman t, Mass. (3,3)	P	21-21-37	25,733-27,060	Y-27,260-10	...	...-..	...	...-...	14	...
	F	20-20-42	25,380-30,643	Y-30,843-10	...	...-..	...	...-...	34	...
Whitpain tp, Pa. (1,2)	P	29-25-40	26,132-41,941	Y-44,041-..	1,613	1,424-88	1,186	37-201	72	117
	F	...-...-..	...-...	..-...-..	...	...-..	...	...-...	...	...
Wilbraham t, Mass. (1,1)	P	24-23-37	28,361-29,788	Y-30,682-5	...	...-..	...	...-...	30	...
	F	22-...-42	26,457-29,024	Y-29,894-5	...	...-..	...	...-...	8	...
Williamsburg, Va. (1,3)	P	40-36-40	16,179-...	..-...-..	1,720	1,322-76	1,030	187-105	154	244
	F	26-25-56	16,179-...	..-...-..	1,214	1,035-85	811	148-76	27	152
Wilmington, Ohio (1,3)	P	24-17-40	17,326-27,872	None	1,408	1,005-71	726	133-146	169	234
	F	17-16-53	17,326-27,872	None	855	691-80	509	110-72	24	140
Wilton Manors, Fla. (1,2)	P	41-41-..	28,061-39,401	None	...	...-..	...	...-...	...	...
	F	...-...-..	...-...	..-...-..	...	...-..	...	...-...	...	...
Winchester t, Conn. (1,-)	P	21-11-40	...-...	None	1,663	1,306-78	821	309-176	57	300
	F	...-125-40	...-...	None	333	158-47	108	41-9	56	119
Winchester, Ky. (1,1)	P	39-28-40	17,123-27,824	Y-...-4	...	...-..	...	...-...	...	...
	F	52-51-56	17,120-27,824	Y-...-4	...	...-..	...	...-...	...	...
Windham t, Conn. (1,1)	P	35-31-40	26,500-35,046	Y-35,546-5	...	...-..	...	...-...	...	...
	F	27-26-42	24,461-33,007	Y-33,507-5	...	...-..	...	...-...	48	...
Windham t, Me. (1,-)	P	22-18-40	20,700-29,390	Y-29,990-10	...	...-..	...	...-...	...	...
	F	1-...-..	...-...	None	...	...-..	...	...-...	...	...
Windsor Locks t, Conn. (1,2)	P	25-23-37	30,716-36,475	..-37,075-5	...	...-..	...	...-...	...	...
	F	...-...-..	...-...	..-...-..	...	...-..	...	...-...	...	...
Winfield, Kan. (3,1)	P	19-15-..	19,656-24,460	None	1,016	882-86	672	130-80	39	95
	F	20-20-..	18,709-23,325	None	844	772-91	582	124-66	5	67
Winnetka v, Ill. (1,1)	P	35-25-40	31,632-42,468	Y-43,530-10	3,065	2,570-83	1,836	405-329	122	373
	F	23-22-52	34,380-42,468	Y-43,530-10	1,959	1,769-90	1,108	369-292	40	150
Winter Park, Fla. (1,1)	P	69-42-40	22,501-35,971	Y-...-5	...	...-..	...	...-...	...	...
	F	42-41-56	19,966-30,219	Y-...-5	...	...-..	...	...-...	...	...
Winter Springs, Fla. (1,1)	P	59-41-43	19,000-48,000	None	1,662	1,428-85	1,233	93-102	...	234
	F	35-34-56	18,000-47,000	None	1,347	1,110-82	975	75-60	...	237
Wisconsin Rapids, Wis. (1,1)	P	51-40-39	24,950-30,185	Y-30,582-15	2,335	2,151-92	1,545	444-162	...	184
	F	32-32-56	23,491-31,131	None	1,648	1,529-92	1,086	328-115	...	119
Wolcott t, Conn. (1,2)	P	22-15-40	30,410-35,277	Y-35,552-3	2,708	1,397-51	1,037	239-121	1,087	224
	F	...-...-..	...-...	..-...-..	...	...-..	...	...-...	...	...
Wood Dale, Ill. (1,-)	P	45-28-40	27,182-40,222	Y-41,022-15	2,028	1,812-89	1,416	132-264	84	132
	F	...-...-..	...-...	..-...-..	...	...-..	...	...-...	...	...
Woodburn, Ore. (1,5)	P	24-21-40	25,464-31,224	..-...-..	...	...-..	...	...-...	...	...
	F	...-...-..	...-...	..-...-..	...	...-..	...	...-...	...	...
Woodbury, Minn. (1,2)	P	23-22-40	27,708-38,064	Y-41,490-16	1,684	1,341-79	1,109	138-94	71	272

Table 3/23 continued

POLICE AND FIRE DEPARTMENT PERSONNEL, SALARIES, AND EXPENDITURES FOR CITIES 10,000 AND OVER: 1993

City	Service provision	Department	Total personnel, no. uniformed, duty hours per week	Entrance, maximum salary ($)	Longevity pay, maximum ($) no. years to receive longevity pay	Reported expenditures (in thousands)					
						Total expenditures (A) ($)	Total personnel expenditures (B) ($), % of (A)	Salaries and wages (C) ($)	City contrib. to employee retirement, insurance (D) ($)	Capital outlay (E) ($)	All other (F) ($)
10,000-24,999 continued											
Woodbury, Minn. (1,2) cont.		F	...-..-..	...-...	..-...-..	...	...-..	...	...-...	...	...
Woodstock, Ill. (1,3)	.P		39-29-40	26,917-40,373	None	2,018	1,770-87	1,414	242-114	89	159
		F	1-..-40	...-...	None	345	146-42	129	14-3	135	64
Woodward, Okla. (1,3)	.P		28-21-40	19,159-20,117	Y-22,517-1	1,680	1,592-94	1,318	170-104	4	84
		F	17-17-56	17,457-19,734	Y-22,134-1	1,200	1,152-96	976	96-80	...	48
Wooster, Ohio (1,1)	.P		40-36-40	29,078-31,512	None	2,469	1,918-77	1,461	278-179	20	531
		F	43-41-56	29,702-32,294	None	2,327	2,075-89	1,518	366-191	57	195
Worthington, Ohio (1,9)	.P		39-31-40	24,254-35,873	Y-36,673-5	...	...-..	...	...-...	...	...
		F	...-..-..	...-...	..-...-..	...	...-..	...	...-...	...	...
Wyckoff tp, N.J. (1,2)	.P		22-19-40	51,811-...	Y-56,992-5	...	...-..	...	...-...	...	...
		F	...-..-..	...-...	..-...-..	...	...-..	...	...-...	...	...
Xenia, Ohio (1,1)	.P		62-42-40	24,336-33,654	Y-34,054-5	3,321	2,627-79	2,059	354-214	276	418
		F	44-43-56	26,267-31,977	Y-32,377-5	2,336	1,921-82	1,442	327-152	181	234
Yarmouth t, Mass. (1,1)	.P		51-42-40	24,217-31,732	Y-31,992-5	...	...-..	...	...-...	101	...
		F	45-41-48	26,103-30,271	Y-30,496-5	...	...-..	...	...-...	105	...
York tp, Pa. (-,2)	.P		26-23-40	22,237-33,179	Y-36,497-4	1,525	1,353-88	1,025	78-250	49	123
		F	...-..-..	...-...	..-...-..	...	...-..	...	...-...	...	...
Yukon, Okla. (3,3)	.P		32-23-40	18,134-26,930	Y-...-5	1,352	1,206-89	880	138-188	6	140
		F	26-25-56	17,262-25,635	Y-...-5	1,178	1,116-94	830	88-198	...	62
Zion, Ill. (1,1)	.P		60-43-40	28,962-35,876	Y-36,626-..	3,200	2,586-80	2,072	303-211	111	503
		F	25-23-56	27,264-33,787	Y-34,537-..	1,070	729-68	545	142-42	217	124

D Directories

The Year Book Directories

The directories in this section of the *Year Book* contain the names of municipal and county officials in the United States as reported in the fall of 1993 along with the names of appointed chief administrative officers in other countries. In addition, this section includes directories for state municipal leagues; provincial associations and unions in Canada; state and territorial agencies for community affairs; provincial and territorial agencies for local affairs in Canada; state and provincial municipal management associations; state associations of counties; and directors of councils of governments recognized by ICMA.

The names of municipal and county managers and other chief appointed management executives for the United States and other countries are shown in directories 1/8, 1/9, and 1/10. Information on recognized places, including legal basis, title of position, form of government, and year of recognition, plus the number of administrators the community has had and information on the current administrator, is presented in the annual ICMA publication *Who's Who in Local Government Management.*

Information in directories 1/1 through 1/8 was obtained from the National League of Cities (1/1), the Federation of Canadian Municipalities (1/2), the Council of State Community Affairs Agencies (1/3), the Ontario Ministry of Municipal Affairs (1/4), ICMA files (1/5, 1/7, and 1/8), and the National Association of Counties (1/6), and is current as of November 1992 unless otherwise indicated. Information for Directory 1/9 was obtained by a *Year Book* mailing to all cities 2,500 and over in population, to recognized council-manager or general management places under 2,500 in July 1993, and to those communities whose populations dropped below 2,500 since the 1986 Census. Information for Directory 1/10 was obtained by a similar mailing to all county-type governments in July 1993.

The phone numbers in directories 1/7, 1/8, 1/9, and 1/10, preceded by the area code, are for the city hall, municipal building, or county building, or for some municipal or county official such as the manager, clerk, or mayor.

State Municipal Leagues
Directory 1/1 shows 49 state leagues of municipalities serving 49 states. (Hawaii does not have a league.) Information includes league address, name of the executive director, phone number, and year organized. State municipal leagues provide a wide range of research, consulting, training, publications, and legislative representation services for their cities.

Provincial and Territorial Associations and Unions in Canada
Directory 1/2 shows the organizations serving the provinces and territories of Canada. The name of the president and a permanent officer are shown along with the address and phone number.

State Agencies for Community Affairs
Directory 1/3 presents the name and address of 50 agencies for community affairs in the United States. It includes the name of the executive director or head of the agency. These agencies of state governments offer a variety of research, financial information, and coordination services for cities and other local governments.

Provincial and Territorial Agencies for Local Affairs in Canada
Directory 1/4 shows agencies for local affairs serving provinces and territories in Canada. The directory lists the name and address of the minister as well as the minister's phone number when available.

United States and International Municipal Management Associations
Directory 1/5 shows the name, president, address, and phone number of municipal management associations serving 48 of the United States, the District of Columbia, Canada, and 5 other countries.[1]

State Associations of Counties
Directory 1/6 shows the name, address, phone number, FAX number, name of executive director, and year organized for 50 county associations serving 47 states. (Two associations serve the state of Washington; three states do not have associations: Connecticut, Rhode Island, and Vermont.) Like their municipal league counterparts, these associations provide a wide range of research, training, consulting, publications, and legislative representation services.

Directors of Councils of Governments
Directory 1/7 gives the official name of the council of governments, the director, and the telephone number for COGs recognized by ICMA.

International Administrators
Directory 1/8 gives the name of the appointed administrator and phone number, if available, for the chief appointed administrator in communities overseas.

Municipal Officials in U.S. Cities
Directory 1/9 lists, alphabetically by state, all incorporated places in the United States 2,500 and over in population, those places under 2,500 recognized by ICMA, and those communities whose populations dropped below 2,500 since the 1986 Census. It shows the current form of government; the population (in thousands) according to the 1990 Census of Population estimates; municipal phone number; name of mayor; appointed administrator; city clerk; finance officer; fire chief; police chief; and public works director. Leaders (. .) in the population column mean that the population of the place is under 500.

County Officials in U.S. Counties
Directory 1/10 lists, alphabetically by state, all county-type governments. It shows the 1990 Census of Population estimates; the county telephone number; name of the board chairman, county judge, or president; appointed administrator; clerk to the governing board; chief financial officer; personnel director; and chief law enforcement official.

Other Local Government Directories
The names of municipal officials not reported in the *Year Book* are available in many states through directories published by state municipal leagues, state municipal management associations, and state associations of counties. Names and addresses of these leagues and associations are shown in directories 1/1, 1/5, and 1/6. In some states the secretary of state, the state agency for community affairs (Directory 1/3), or another state agency publishes a directory that includes municipal and county officials. In addition, several directories with national coverage are published for health officers, welfare workers, housing and urban renewal officials, and other professional groups.

---

[1]The states of Wyoming, North Dakota, South Dakota, Idaho, and Montana are served by the Great Open Spaces City Management Association. In addition, Idaho is also served by its own association.

Directory 1/1   STATE MUNICIPAL LEAGUES

State	Name of league and headquarters address	Name and title of executive director[1]	Phone number	Year first effort to cooperate[2]	Year first organized[3]
Alabama	Alabama League of Municipalities, P.O. Box 1270, Montgomery 36102	Perry Roquemore, ED	205 262-2566	1914	1930
Alaska	Alaska Municipal League, 217 Second Street, Suite 200, Juneau 99801	Kent E. Swisher, ED	907 586-1325	1950	1950
Arizona	League of Arizona Cities and Towns, 1820 West Washington Street, Phoenix 85007	John J. DeBolske, ED	602 258-5786	1925	1937
Arkansas	Arkansas Municipal League, P.O. Box 38, North Little Rock 72115	Don A. Zimmerman, ED	501 374-3484	1917	1934
California	League of California Cities, 1400 K Street, Suite 400, Sacramento 95814	Don Benninghoven, ED	916 444-5790	1898	1898
Colorado	Colorado Municipal League, 1660 Lincoln Street, Suite 2100, Denver 80264	Kenneth G. Bueche, ED	303 831-6411	1900	1923
Connecticut	Connecticut Conference of Municipalities, 900 Chapel Street, Suite 900, New Haven 06510-2807	Joel Cogen, ED	203 498-3000	...	1966
Delaware	Delaware League of Local Governments, P.O. Box 484, Dover 19903-0484	George C. Wright, ED	302 678-0991	1965	1965
Florida	Florida League of Cities, P.O. Box 1757, Tallahassee 32302-1757	Raymond C. Sittig, ED	904 222-9684	1922	1922
Georgia	Georgia Municipal Association, 201 Pryor Street, S.W., Atlanta 30303	James V. Burgess, Jr., ED	404 688-0472	1916	1934
Idaho	Association of Idaho Cities, 3314 Grace Street, Boise 83703	(Vacant)	208 344-8594	1918	1941
Illinois	Illinois Municipal League, P.O. Box 3387, Springfield 62708	Thomas G. Fitzsimmons, ED	217 525-1220	1899	1914
Indiana	Indiana Association of Cities and Towns, 150 West Market Street, Suite 728, Indianapolis 46204-2882	Michael J. Quinn, ED	317 237-6200	1891	1899
Iowa	League of Iowa Municipalities, 100 Court Avenue, Suite 209, Des Moines 50309	(Vacant)	515 244-7282	1898	1898
Kansas	League of Kansas Municipalities, 112 West Seventh Street, Topeka 66603	Christopher K. McKenzie, ED	913 354-9565	1910	1910
Kentucky	Kentucky League of Cities, 2201 Regency Road, Suite 100, Lexington 40503	Slyvia L. Lovely, ED	606 277-2886	1929	1929
Louisiana	Louisiana Municipal Association, P.O. Box 4327, Baton Rouge 70821	Charles J. Pasqua, ED	504 344-5001	1935	1937
Maine	Maine Municipal Association, 37 Community Drive, Augusta 04330	Christopher G. Lockwood, ED	207 623-8429	1936	1936
Maryland	Maryland Municipal League, 1212 West Street, Annapolis 21401	Jon C. Burrell, ED	301 268-5514	1937	1948
Massachusetts	Massachusetts Municipal Association, 60 Temple Place, Second Floor, Boston 02111	Geoffrey Beckwith, ED	617 426-7272	1961	1961
Michigan	Michigan Municipal League, P.O. Box 1487, Ann Arbor 48106	George D. Goodman, ED	313 662-3246	1899	1899
Minnesota	League of Minnesota Cities, 3490 Lexington Avenue North, St. Paul 55126-8044	Donald A. Slater, ED	612 490-5600	1903	1913
Mississippi	Mississippi Municipal Association, 600 East Amite Street, Jackson 39302	Al Sage, III, ED	601 353-5854	1918	1936
Missouri	Missouri Municipal League, 1913 William Street, Jefferson City 65109	Gary Markenson, ED	314 635-9135	1914	1927
Montana	Montana League of Cities and Towns, P.O. Box 1704, Helena 59624	Alec Hansen, ED	406 442-8768	1910	1932
Nebraska	League of Nebraska Municipalities, 1335 L Street, Lincoln 68508	Lynn Rox, ED	402 476-2829	1910	1910
Nevada	Nevada League of Cities, P.O. Box 2307, Carson City 89702	Gentty P. Etcheverry, ED	702 882-2121	...	1950
New Hampshire	New Hampshire Municipal Association, P.O. Box 617, Concord 03302-0617	John B. Andrews, ED	603 224-7447	1955	1961
New Jersey	New Jersey State League of Municipalities, 407 West State Street, Trenton 08618	John E. Trafford, ED	609 695-3481	1915	1915
New Mexico	New Mexico Municipal League, P.O. Box 846, Santa Fe 87504	William F. Fulginiti, ED	505 982-5573	...	1958
New York	New York State Conference of Mayors and Municipal Officials, 119 Washington Avenue, Albany 12210	Edward C. Farrell, ED	518 463-1185	1910	1910
North Carolina	North Carolina League of Municipalities, P.O. Box 3069, Raleigh 27602	David E. Reynolds	919 834-1311	1908	1922
North Dakota	North Dakota League of Cities, P.O. Box 2235, Bismarck 58502	Robert E. Johnson, ED	701 223-3518	1912	1927
Ohio	Ohio Municipal League, 175 South Third Street, Suite 510, Columbus 43215	John P. Coleman, ED	614 221-4349	1912	1952
Oklahoma	Oklahoma Municipal League, 201 N.E. 23rd Street, Oklahoma City 73105	William A. Moyer, ED	405 528-7515	1913	1913
Oregon	League of Oregon Cities, P.O. Box 928, Salem 97308	Richard C. Townsend, ED	503 588-6550	1913	1913
Pennsylvania	Pennsylvania League of Cities, 414 North Second Street, Harrisburg 17101	John A. Garner, Jr., ED	717 236-9469	1900	1900
Rhode Island	Rhode Island League of Cities and Towns, 1 State Street, Suite 502, Providence 02908	Daniel Beardsley, ED	401 272-3434	1959	1965
South Carolina	Municipal Association of South Carolina, P.O. Box 12109, Columbia 29211	J. McDonald Wray, ED	803 799-9574	1936	1939
South Dakota	South Dakota Municipal League, 214 East Capitol, Pierre 57501	Robert H. Miller, ED	605 224-8654	1925	1935
Tennessee	Tennessee Municipal League, 226 Capitol Boulevard, Room 710, Nashville 37219	Joseph A. Sweat, ED	615 255-6416	1913	1940
Texas	Texas Municipal League, 211 East Seventh Street, Suite 1020, Austin 78701-8283	Frank Sturzl, ED	512 478-6601	1913	1913

Directory 1/1   STATE MUNICIPAL LEAGUES
continued

State	Name of league and headquarters address	Name and title of executive director[1]	Phone number	Year first effort to cooperate[2]	Year first organized[3]
Utah	Utah League of Cities and Towns, 50 South 600 East, Suite 150, Salt Lake City 84102	Kenneth Bullock, ED	801 328-1601	1907	1907
Vermont	Vermont League of Cities and Towns, 12/ Main Street, Montpelier 05602	Steven E. Jeffrey, ED	802 229-9111	1967	1967
Virginia	Virginia Municipal League, P.O. Box 12164, Richmond 23241	R. Michael Amyx, ED	804 649-8471	1905	1905
Washington	Association of Washington Cities, 1076 South Franklin Street, Olympia 98501	Stan Finkelstein, ED	206 753-4137	1910	1910
West Virginia	West Virginia Municipal League, 1620 Kanawha Boulevard, Suite 1B, Charleston 25311	Betty Dean, ED	304 342-5564	1917	1935
Wisconsin	League of Wisconsin Municipalities, 122 West Washington Avenue, Suite 301, Madison 53703	Dan Thompson, ED	608 267-2380	1898	1898
Wyoming	Wyoming Association of Municipalities, P.O. Box 3110, Cheyenne 82003-3110	Carl Classen, ED	307 632-0398	. . .	1952

Note: Leaders (. . .) indicate information not available.
[1]Titles abbreviated as follows: AED, Acting Executive Director; ED, Executive Director; D, Director.

[2]The date in this column refers in most instances to the beginning of a loosely knit organization of cities on a cooperative basis for the purpose of presenting municipal problems before the legislature.

[3]This date is the year when an active organization, as now known, was established.

Directory 1/2   PROVINCIAL AND TERRITORIAL ASSOCIATIONS AND UNIONS IN CANADA

Province or territory	Association/union	President[1]	Permanent officer
Alberta	Alberta Association of Municipal Districts and Counties	Gordon Miller	Larry Goodhope, Executive Director 4504–101 Street Edmonton T6E 5G9 Phone: 403 436-9375
	Alberta Urban Municipalities Association	Mayor Bill Purdy P.O. Box 4607 Station SE Edmonton T6E 5G4	John E. Maddison, Executive Director P.O. Box 4607, Postal Station SE Edmonton T6E 5G4 Phone: 403 433-4431
British Columbia	Union of British Columbia Municipalities	Mayor Joyce Harder 10551 Shellbridge Way Suite 15 Richmond V6X 2W9 Phone: 604 270-8226 Fax: 604 660-2271	Richard Taylor, Executive Director 15-10551 Shellbridge Way, Suite 15 Richmond V6X 2W9 Phone: 604 270-8226
Manitoba	Manitoba Association of Urban Municipalities	Mayor Henry Wiebe 200, 611 Corydon Avenue Winnipeg R3L 0P3 Phone: 204 669-1256 Fax: 204 663-8875	Rochelle Zimberg, Executive Director-Room 201 611 Corydon Avenue Winnipeg R3L 0P3 Phone: 204 669-1256 Fax: 204 663-8875
	Union of Manitoba Municipalities	Jim Knight Box 536 Manitoba R1N 3B9 Phone: 204 686-2285	Jerome Mauws, Executive Director P.O. Box 397 Portage-la-Prairie R1N 3B7 Phone: 204 857-8666
New Brunswick	Provincial Municipal Council	Joseph G. Cormier 200 Prospect Street West, Suite 405 Fredericton E3B 2T8 Phone: 506 453-2152 Fax: 506 453-7954	David Ellis 200 Prospect Street West, Suite 405 Fredericton E3B 2T8 Phone: 506 453-2152 Fax: 506 453-7954
Newfoundland and Labrador	Newfoundland and Labrador Federation of Municipalities	Mayor Tibbo P.O. Box 5756 St. John's A1C 5X3 Phone: 709 753-6820 Fax: 709 738-0071	
Northwest Territories	Northwest Territories Association of Municipalities	Mayor Pat McMahon P.O. Box 580 Yellowknife X1A 2N4 Phone: 403 873-8359 Fax: 403 873-5801	Yvette Bungay, Executive Director 5201 50th Ave-Suite 904 Yellowknife X1A 3S9 Phone: 403 873-8359 Fax: 403 873-5801
Nova Scotia	Union of Nova Scotia Municipalities	Mayor John Coady	Kenneth R. B. Simpson, Executive Director 1809 Barrington Street, Suite 1106 Halifax B3J 3K8 Phone: 902 423-8331 Fax: 902 425-5592

Directory 1/2 **PROVINCIAL AND TERRITORIAL ASSOCIATIONS**
continued **AND UNIONS IN CANADA**

Province or territory	Association/union	President[1]	Permanent officer
Ontario	Association of Municipalities of Ontario	Ken Mathews 216 Ontario Street Kingston K7L 2Z3	Mable Dougherty, Executive Director 250 Bloor Street East, Suite 701 Toronto M4W 1E8 Phone: 416 929-7573 Fax: 416 929-7574
	Federation of Canadian Municipalities	Alderman Ron Harper	James W. Knight, Executive Director 24 Clarence Street, 2nd floor Ottawa K1N 5P3 Phone: 613 237-5221 Fax: 613 237-2965
Prince Edward Island	Federation of Prince Edward Island Municipalities	Councillor Cecil Murl	Lisa Doyle, Executive Director P.O. Box 98 Charlottetown C1A 7K2 Phone: 902 566-1493 Fax: 902 566-4701
Québec	Union des Conseils de Comités du Québec	Roger Nicolet 2954 boul. Laurier, Bureau 560 Ste-Foy G1V 4P2 Phone: 418 651-3343	Michelle Fernet, Directeur-général 2954 boul. Laurier, Bureau 560 Ste-Foy G1V 4P2 Phone: 418 651-3343
	Union des Municipalités du Québec	Ulrick Blacburn	Raymond L'Italien, Directeur-général 680, 680 Sherbrook West Montréal H3A 2M7 Phone: 514 282-7700 Fax: 514 282-7711
Saskatchewan	Saskatchewan Assocation of Rural Municipalities	Bernard Kirwan Box 77 Gull Lake Sachsketwen S0N 1A0 Phone: 306 672-3583	Darryl Chambers, Executive Director 2075 Hamilton Street Regina S4P 2E1 Phone: 306 757-3577
	Saskatchewan Urban Municipalities Association	Alderman Ted Cholod 200, 1819 Cornwall Street Regina S4P 2K4 Phone: 306 525-3727	Keith Schneider, Executive Director 200, 1819 Cornwall Street Regina S4P 2K4 Phone: 306 525-3727 Fax: 306 565-3552
Yukon	Association of Yukon Communities	Pat McMahon	Yvette Bungay, Executive Director 5201 50th Avenue Ste. 904 Yellowknife X1A 3S9 Phone: 403 873-8359 Fax: 403 873-5801

[1]Presidents without an address can be reached at the address of the permanent officer.

Directory 1/3 **STATE AGENCIES FOR COMMUNITY AFFAIRS**

State or territory	Agency and address	Name and title of executive director	State or territory	Agency and address	Name and title of executive director
Alabama	Department of Economic and Community Affairs 401 Adams Street, P.O. Box 5690 Montgomery 36103	Gene Anderson Director	Connecticut	Department of Housing 505 Hudson Street Hartford 06106	Henry S. Scherer, Jr. Commissioner
Alaska	Department of Community and Regional Affairs Post Office Box 112100 Juneau 99811	Edgar Blatchford Commissioner	Delaware	State Housing Authority 18 The Green P.O. Box 1401 Dover 19903	Susan Frank Director
Arizona	Department of Commerce 3800 North Central Street Suite 1400 Phoenix 85012	James E. Marsh Executive Director	Florida	Department of Community Affairs 2740 Centerview Drive Tallahassee 32399-2100	Linda L. Shelley Secretary
Arkansas	Industrial Development Commission 1 State Capitol Mall Little Rock 72201	Robert K. Middleton, III Director of Community Development	Georgia	Department of Community Affairs 1200 Equitable Building 100 Peachtree Street Atlanta 30303	Jim Higdon Commissioner
California	Department of Housing and Community Development P.O. Box 952051 Sacramento 94252-2051	Tim Coyle Director	Hawaii	Department of Planning and Economic Development P.O. Box 2359 Honolulu 96804	Roger A. Ulveling Director
Colorado	Department of Local Affairs 1313 Sherman Street 518 Centennial Building Denver 80203	Larry Kallenberger Executive Director	Idaho	Department of Commerce 700 West State Street State House Mall Room 108 Boise 83720	James Hawkins Director

Directory 1/3 continued   **STATE AGENCIES FOR COMMUNITY AFFAIRS**

State or territory	Agency and address	Name and title of executive director
Illinois	Department of Commerce and Community Affairs 620 East Adams Street Springfield 62701	Jan Grayson Director
Indiana	Department of Commerce One North Capitol, Suite 700 Indianapolis 46204-2243	Curt Wiley Director
Iowa	Department of Economic Development 200 East Grand Avenue Des Moines 50319	Allan Thoms Acting Director
Kansas	Department of Commerce and Housing 700 SW Harrison Street, #1300 Topeka 66603-3912	Dennis Schockley Director
Kentucky	Department of Local Government 1024 Capital Center Drive Frankfort 40601	Bruce Ferguson Commissioner
Louisiana	Division of Administration State Planning Office P.O. Box 94095 Baton Rouge 70804	Suzie Elkins Director
Maine	Department of Economic and Community Development 219 Capitol Street State House Station 130 Augusta 04333	Carolyn Manson Deputy Commissioner
Maryland	Department of Housing and Community Development 100 Community Place Crownsville 21032-2023	Patricia Payne Deputy Secretary
Massachusetts	Executive Office of Communities and Development 100 Cambridge Street 14th Floor Boston 02202	Mary Padula Deputy Director
Michigan	Office of Federal Grants Department of Commerce 525 West Ottawa, P.O. Box 30234 Lansing 48909	Richard Pastula Director
Minnesota	Department of Trade and Economic Development 121 7th Place E. 500 Metro Square St. Paul 55101-2146	Bob Benner Deputy Commissioner
Mississippi	Division of Community Development 1200 Walter Sillers Building P.O. Box 849 Jackson 39205	Alice Lusk Associate Director
Missouri	Department of Economic Development 301 West High Street Room 770, P.O. Box 1157 Jefferson City 65102	Carl Koupal Director
Montana	Department of Commerce 1424 Ninth Avenue, Capital Station Helena 59620	John Noal Director
Nebraska	Department of Economic Development Box 94666 301 Centennial Mall South Lincoln 68509	Jenne Rodriguez Director
Nevada	Commission on Economic Development Capitol Complex Carson City 89710	James L. Spoo Director
New Hampshire	Office of State Planning 2/ Beacon Street Concord 03301	David Scott Director
New Jersey	Department of Community Affairs South Broad and Front Street CN 806 Trenton 08625-0806	Stephanie Bush Commissioner

State or territory	Agency and address	Name and title of executive director
New Mexico	Local Government Division Department of Finance and Administration Bataan Memorial Building Room 201 Santa Fe 87501	Teodoro (Ted) Guambana Director
New York	Division of Housing and Community Renewal One Fordham Plaza, Fourth Floor Bronx 10458	Donald M. Halperin Commissioner
North Carolina	Division of Community Assistance Department of Commerce 1307 Glenwood Avenue Suite 250 Raleigh 27605	Robert Chandler Director
North Dakota	Office of Intergovernmental Assistance State Capitol, 14th Floor Bismarck 58505	Shirley R. Dykshoorn Director
Ohio	Department of Development 77 South High Street P.O. Box 1001 Columbus 43266-0101	Vincent Lombardi Director
Oklahoma	Department of Commerce P.O. Box 26980 Oklahoma City 73126-0980	Sherwood Washington Assistant Director
Oregon	Economic Development Department 775 Summer Street, N.E. Salem 97310	Yvonne Addington Director
Pennsylvania	Department of Community Affairs Commonwealth and Walnut 317 Forum Building Harrisburg 17120	Karen Miller Secretary
Puerto Rico	Municipal Services Administration G.P.O. Box 70167 San Juan 00936	Ms. Luc Delia Oquendo
Rhode Island	Governor's Office of Housing, Energy, and Intergovernmental Relations State House, Room 140 Providence 02903	Scott Wolfe Director
South Carolina	Division of Economic Development 1205 Pendleton Street Suite 308 Columbia 29201	Olney England Director
South Dakota	Governor's Office of Economic Development 711 Wells Avenue Pierre 57501-3335	Dave O'Hara Commissioner
Tennessee	Department of Economic and Community Development 320 Sixth Avenue North, Sixth Floor Nashville 37219-5308	Mike McGuire Assistant Commissioner
Texas	Department of Housing and Community Affairs P.O. Box 13941 Austin 78711-3941	Henry Flores Director
Utah	Department of Community and Economic Development 324 South State, Suite 500 Salt Lake City 84111	Carol Nixon Director
Vermont	Department of Housing and Community Affairs Pavilion Office Building Montpelier 05609	Elizabeth Mullikin Drake Commissioner
Virginia	Department of Housing and Community Development 501 North Second Street Richmond 23219	Neal Barber Director
Washington	Department of Community Development 906 Columbia Street, MS/GH-51 Olympia 98504-4151	Ms. Gene Liddell Director

Directory 1/3 continued

STATE AGENCIES FOR COMMUNITY AFFAIRS

State or territory	Agency and address	Name and title of executive director	State or territory	Agency and address	Name and title of executive director
West Virginia	Community Development Division West Virginia Development Office State Capitol Complex, Building 6, Room 553B Charleston 25305	Fred Cutlip Director	Wyoming	Division of Economic and Community Development Barrett Building Cheyenne 82002	George H. Gault Director
Wisconsin	Division of Community Development Department of Development 123 West Washington Avenue Madison 53703	Terry Grosenheider Administrator			

Directory 1/4

PROVINCIAL AND TERRITORIAL AGENCIES FOR LOCAL AFFAIRS IN CANADA

Province or territory	Minister address	Phone number	Province or territory	Minister address	Phone number
Alberta	Hon. R. Steve West Minister of Municipal Affairs 425 Legislative Building, Edmonton T5K 2B6	403 427-3744	Nova Scotia	Hon. Sandy Jolly Minister of Municipal Affairs P.O. Box 216 1505 Barrington St., 12th Fl. Maritime Centre Halifax B3J 2M4	902 424-5550
British Columbia	Hon. Darlene Marzari Municipal Affairs 306 Parliament Building Victoria, V8V 1X4	604 387-3602	Ontario	Hon. Ed Phillips Government Housing Leader Director of Management Board 777 Bay Street, 17th Floor Toronto M5G 2E5	416 585-7000
Manitoba	Hon. Linda McIntosh Minister of Urban Affairs and Housing Legislative Building, Room 317 450 Broadway Winnipeg R3C 0V8	204 945-0074	Prince Edward Island	Hon. Walter A. McEwen Minister of Community and Cultural Affairs P.O. Box 2000, Charlottetown C1A 7N8	902 368-5250
	Lenord Derkach Minister of Rural Development 301 Legislative Building, Winnipeg 450 Broadway R3C 0V8	204 945-3788	Québec	Hon. Claude Ryan Ministre des Affaires Municipales 20 Avenue Chaveau, Sector B, Third Floor, Québec G1R 4J3	418 691-2050
New Brunswick	Hon. Jan Barry Minister of Department of the Environment P.O. Box 6000, 364 Argyle Place Fredericton E3B 5H1	506 453-2558	Saskatchewan	Carol Carlson Minister of Community Services 303 Legislative Building Regina S4S 0B3	306 787-2635
	Hon. Marcelle Mersereau Minister of Municipal Affairs P.O. Box 6000, 364 Marysville Place Fredericton E3B 5H1	506 453-3001		Hon. Eldon Lautermilch Minister of Rural Development Legislative Building, Suite 306 Regina S4S 0B3	306 787-2260
Newfoundland	Authur Reid Minister of Municipal Affiars and Provincial Affairs P.O. Box 4750, St. John's A1C 5T7	709 729-3048	Yukon	Hon. Micky Fisher Yukon Government Administration Building P.O. Box 2703 Whitehorse Y1A 2C6	403 667-5811
Northwest Territories	Hon. Richard Nerysoo Min. of Education Culture Employment Program P.O. Box 1320, Yellowknife X1A 2L9	403 873-7658			

Directory 1/5

UNITED STATES AND INTERNATIONAL MUNICIPAL MANAGEMENT ASSOCIATIONS

State, province, or country	Association	President, address, phone number	State, province, or country	Association	President, address, phone number
Alabama	Alabama City Management Association	James Gould Administrative Assistant City of Alabaster P.O. Box 277 Alabaster 35007 205 664-6800	Arizona	Arizona City/County Management Association	Ken Buchanan Town Manager Town of Payson 303 North Beeline Highway Payson 85541 602 474-5242
Alaska	Alaska Municipal Management Association	Ginny Tierney City Manager City of Thorne Bay P.O. Box 19110 Thorne Bay 99919	Arkansas	Arkansas City Management Association	Bruno Rumbelow City Manager City of Texarkana P.O. Box 2711 Texarkana 75504 501 774-3161

Directory 1/5   **UNITED STATES AND INTERNATIONAL**
continued   **MUNICIPAL MANAGEMENT ASSOCIATIONS**

State, province, or country	Association	President, address, phone number	State, province, or country	Association	President, address, phone number
California	City Managers' Department, League of California Cities	Karen A. Smith City Manager City of Union City 34009 Alvarado Niles Road Union City 94587 510 471-3232	Maine	Maine Town and City Management Association	Richard Michaud Town Manager Town of Madison P.O. Box 190 Madison 04950 207 696-3971
Colorado	Colorado City/County Management Association	Steven Burkett City Manager City of Fort Collins P.O. Box 580 Fort Collins 80522 303 221-6505	Maryland	Maryland City and County Management Association	Norton Bonaparte Jr. Town Manager Town of Glenarden 8600 Glenarden Parkway Glenarden 20706 301 773-2100
Connecticut	Connecticut Town and City Management Association	Richard McGuire Administrative Officer Town of Woodbridge 11 Meetinghouse Lane Woodbridge 06525 203 389-3403	Massachusetts	Massachusetts Municipal Management Association	Mel Kleckner Executive Secretary Town of Belmont 455 Concord Avenue Belmont 02178 617 489-8213
Delaware	City Management Association of Delaware	Anne M. Alzapiedi City Administrator City of New Castle 220 Delaware Street New Castle 19720-4816 302 322-9812	Michigan	Michigan City Management Association	Kurt Kimball City Manager City of Grand Rapids 300 Monroe Avenue Grand Rapids 49503 616 456-3166
District of Columbia	District of Columbia Urban Management Association	Linda Cheatam Budget Director 1350 Pennsylvania Avenue, N.W. Washington, D.C. 20084 202 727-6343	Minnesota	Minnesota City/County Management Association	Edward Larson City Manager City of Morris P.O. Box 438 Morris 56267 612 589-3141
Florida	Florida City and County Management Association	Tom Bonfield City Manager City of Temple Terrace P.O. Box 16930 Temple Terrace 33687 813 989-7105	Mississippi	Mississippi City and County Management Association	Michael McPherson Director of Finance and Administration City of Ridgeland 304 Highway 51 P.O. Box 217 Ridgeland 39158 601 856-7113
Georgia	Georgia City/County Management Association	John Bennett City Manager City of Rome P.O. Box 1433 Rome 30163 706 236-4400	Missouri	Missouri City Management Association	David Johnston City Administrator City of Jefferson City 320 E. McCarthy Jefferson City 63501 314 634-6304
Idaho	Idaho City Management Association	Jan Vassar City Manager City of Lewiston P.O. Box 617 Lewiston 83501 208 746-3671	Nebraska	Nebraska City Management Association	Daniel Berlowitz City Administrator City of Seward P.O. Box 38 Seward 68434 402 643-2928
Illinois	Illinois City Management Association	Daniel Dubruiel Village Administrator Village of Matteson 3625 W. 215th Street Matteson 60443 708 748-1559	Nevada	Local Government Managers Association of Nevada	Donald L. Shalmy County Manager Clark County 225 Bridger Avenue Las Vegas 89155 702 455-3530
Indiana	Indiana Municipal Management Association	Ron Austin Town Manager Town of Lizton 206 N. Lebanon St. Lizton 46149 317 994-5500	New Hampshire	New Hampshire Municipal Management Association	Elizabeth Fox Administrative Assistant Town of East Swanzey P.O. Box 9 East Swanzey 03446 603 352-5143
Iowa	Iowa City/County Management Association	Tim Moerman City Administrator City of Jefferson 220 N. Chestnut Jefferson 50129 515 386-3111	New Jersey	New Jersey Municipal Management Association	Peter Miller Township Administrator Egg Harbor Township RD 2A Box 262 Egg Harbor 08221 609 926-4027
Kansas	Kansas Association of City Management	James G. Witt City Manager City of Dodge City 2601 Central, P.O. Box 880 Dodge City 67801-0880 316 225-8100	New Mexico	New Mexico City Management Association	John Strand City Manager City of Deming 1001 E. Dona Ana Road Deming 88030 505 546-8848
Kentucky	Kentucky City Management Association	William Fisher, Jr. City Manager City of Ashland P.O. Box 1839 Ashland, KY 41101-1839 606 327-2002	New York	Municipal Management Association of New York State	Joe Chiseri City Manager City of Poughkeepsie 21 Parkwood Boulevard Poughkeepsie 12603 914 451-4072

Directory 1/5   **UNITED STATES AND INTERNATIONAL**
continued   **MUNICIPAL MANAGEMENT ASSOCIATIONS**

State, province, or country	Association	President, address, phone number	State, province, or country	Association	President, address, phone number
North Carolina	North Carolina City and County Management Association	John Whitehurst County Manager County of Bertie P.O. Box 530 Windsor 27983 919 794-5300	West Virginia	West Virginia City Management Association	Mark Baldwin City Manager City of Wellsburg 70- 77th Street Wellsburg 26070 304 737-2104
Ohio	Ohio City Management Association	Cecil W. Osborn City Administrator 12105 Lawnview Avenue Springdale 45246 513 671-0885	Wisconsin	Wisconsin City Management Association	Charles Erickson Village Manager Village of Butler 12621 W. Hampton Avenue Butler 53007 414 783-2525
Oklahoma	City Management Association of Oklahoma	Alton Rivers City Administrator P.O. Box 309 Miami 74355 918 542-6685	Wyoming, North Dakota, South Dakota, Idaho, and Montana	Great Open Spaces City Management Association	Terri Ottens Administrative Officer City of Caldwell P.O. Box 1177 Caldwell, ID 83603 208 455-3000
Oregon	Oregon Section of ICMA	Harold Anderson City Manager City of Medford 411 West 8th Street Medford 97501 503 770-4432	Canada	Canadian Association of Municipal Administrators	Michael Boggs City Administrative Officer Regional Municipality of Niagara 2201 St. Davids Road P.O. Box 1042 Throld, ONL2V 4T7 Canada
Pennsylvania	Association for Pennsylvania Municipal Management	Ronald Wagenmann Township Manager Upper Merion Township 175 W. Valley Forge Road King of Prussia 19406 215 265-2600	Australia	The Institute of Municipal Management (Australia)	Stanley B. Fursman Town Clerk Mackay City Council POB 41 Mackay, Queensland Australia 4740 61-79-516466
Rhode Island	Rhode Island City and Town Managers Association	Thomas Bercher Town Manager Town of Burrillville 35 Howard Avenue Pascoag 02859-1136 401 568-4300	Europe	European City/ County Management Association	A. Jeffrey Greenwell Chief Executive Northamptonshire County Council County Hall Northampton MN1 1DN, England 44 604 236050 FAX 44 604 236223
South Carolina	South Carolina City and County Management Association	Dennis Harmon City Administrator City of Goose Creek P.O. Box 742 Goose Creek 29445 803 797-6220	Germany	Deutscher Städte- und Gemeindebund	Kaiserswerther Strasse 199/201 Düsseldorf 4000, Germany (49) 211/458-7223 Fax: (49) 211/458-7211
Tennessee	Tennessee City Management Association	Cindy Cameron City Manager City of Gatlinburg P.O. Box 5, Highway 321 Gatlinburg 37733 615 436-1400	Middle East	Middle East Section of ICMA	IULA-EMME Sultanahmet, Yerebatan Cad. 2 Istanbul, Turkey (90) 1/511-1010 Fax: (90) 1/522-4476
Texas	Texas City Management Association	Gordon Pierce City Manager City of Nacogdoches P.O. Drawer 630648 Nacogdoches 75963 409 564-4693	Israel	Union of Local Authorities in Israel	3 Heftman Street P.O. Box 20040 Tel-Aviv 61200 Israel (972) 3/219241 Fax: (972) 3/267447
Utah	Utah City Management Association	Roger Handy City Administrator Brigham City Corporation P.O. Box A, 20 N. Main Brigham City 84302 801 734-2001	New Zealand	New Zealand Society of Local Government Managers	P. Michael Willis General Manager Palmerston North City Council Private Bag Palmerston North, 5301 New Zealand
Vermont	Vermont Town and City Management Association	William Finger Town Manager Town of West Rutland P.O. Box 392 West Rutland 05777 802 438-2263	United Kingdom	The Society of Local Authority Chief Executives (SOLACE)	John S. Horsnell Chief Executive Isle of Wight Council City Hall, High Street Newport Isle of Wight, P03O, 1UD United Kingdom 44 983-823102
Virginia	Virginia Local Government Management Association	Robert O'Neill City Manager City of Hampton 22 Lincoln Street Hampton 23669 804 727-6392			
Washington	Washington City/County Management Association	Joni Earl Deputy County Executive Snohomish County Courthouse 3000 Rockefeller Everett 98201 206 388-3460			

Directory 1/6   **STATE ASSOCIATIONS OF COUNTIES**

State	State association and address	Name and title of executive director	Phone number FAX	Year first organized
Alabama	Association of County Commissions of Alabama 100 North Jackson Street, Montgomery 36104	O. H. "Buddy" Sharpless, Executive Director	205 263-7594 205 263-7678	1929
Alaska	Alaska Municipal League 217 2nd Street, Suite 200, Juneau 99801-1267	Kent E. Swisher, Executive Director	907 586-1325 907 463-5480	1950
Arizona	Arizona Association of Counties 1910 West Jefferson, Suite 1, Phoenix 85007	Archie Stephens, Executive Director	602 252-6563 602 254-0969	1968
	County Supervisors Association of Arizona 1570 West Van Buren, Phoenix 85007	P. Jerry Orrick, Executive Director	602 252-5521 602 253-3227	. . .
Arkansas	Association of Arkansas Counties 314 South Victory Street, Little Rock 72201	James Baker, Executive Director	501 372-7550 501 372-0611	1968
California	State Association of Counties 1100 K Street, Suite 101, Sacramento 95814	Steve Swendiman, Executive Director	916 327-7500 916 441-5507	1895
Colorado	Colorado Counties, Inc. 1177 Grant Street, Denver 80203	Peter King, Executive Director	303 861-4076 303 861-2818	1915
Delaware	Delaware Association of Counties 414 Federal Street, Dover 19901	. . .	302 736-2040 302 736-2262	. . .
Florida	Florida Association of Counties P.O. Box 549, Tallahassee 32302	James C. Shipman, Executive Director	904 224-3148 904 222-5839	1929
Georgia	Association of County Commissioners of Georgia 2 Peachtree Street, N.W., Suite 2600, Atlanta 30303	Jerry R. Griffin, Executive Director	404 522-5022 404 525-2477	1914
Hawaii	Hawaii State Association of Counties 200 South High Street, Wailuku 96793	Gwen Yoshimi-Ohashi, Executive Director	808 243-7744 808 243-7686	1959
Idaho	Idaho Association of Counties P.O. Box 1623, Boise 83701	Daniel G. Chadwick, Executive Director	208 345-9126 208 345-0379	1960
Illinois	Illinois Association of County Board Members 413 West Monroe Street, Springfield 62704	Paul Bitschenauer, Executive Director	217 528-5331	1973
	Urban Counties Council of Illinois 215 East Adams, Suite 300, Springfield 62705	W. Michael McCreery, Executive Director	217 544-5585 217 544-5571	. . .
Indiana	Association of Indiana Counties, Inc. 101 West Ohio, Suite 710, Indianapolis 46204	Richard J. Cockrum, Executive Director	317 684-3710 317 684-3713	1958
Iowa	Iowa State Association of Counties 701 East Court Avenue, Des Moines 50309	Paul Coates, Executive Director	515 244-7181 515 244-6397	1971
Kansas	Kansas Association of Counties 1275 S.W. Topeka Boulevard, Topeka 66612	John T. Torbert, Executive Director	913 233-2271 913 233-4830	. . .
Kentucky	Kentucky Association of Counties 400 King's Daughters Drive, Frankfort 40601-4106	John Griggs, Executive Director	502 223-7667 502 223-1502	1973
Louisiana	Police Jury Association of Louisiana 707 North Seventh Street, Baton Rouge 70802	James T. Hays, Executive Director	504 343-2835 504 343-0050	1923
Maine	Maine County Commissioners Association Three Wade Street, Augusta 04330	Robert Howe, Executive Director	207 623-4697 207 622-4437	1939
Maryland	Maryland Association of Counties 169 Conduit Street, Annapolis 21401	David Bliden, Executive Director	301 269-0043 301 268-1775	1951
Massachusetts	County Commissioners and Sheriffs of Massachusetts 2 Main Street, Room 3, Worcester 01608	Michael J. Donoghue, Executive Director	508 798-7725 508 798-7737	. . .
Michigan	Michigan Association of Counties 935 North Washington Avenue, Lansing 48906	James N. Callahan, Executive Director	517 372-5374 517 482-4599	1898
Minnesota	Association of Minnesota Counties 125 Charles Avenue, St. Paul 55103-2108	James A. Mulder, Executive Director	612 224-3344 612 224-6540	1909
Mississippi	Mississippi Association of Supervisors P.O. Box 1314, Jackson 39215	Eddie Washington, Executive Director	601 353-2741 601 353-2749	1929
Missouri	Missouri Association of Counties P.O. Box 234, Jefferson City 65102	Juanita Donehue, Executive Director	314 634-2120 314 634-3549	1972
Montana	Montana Association of Counties 2711 Airport Road, Helena 59601	Gordon Morris, Executive Director	406 442-5209 406 442-5238	1909

Directory 1/6 STATE ASSOCIATIONS OF COUNTIES
continued

State	State association and address	Name and title of executive director	Phone number FAX	Year first organized
Nebraska	Nebraska Association of County Officials 625 South 14th Street, Suite A, Lincoln 68508	Jack D. Mills, Executive Director	402 434-5660 402 434-5673	1937
Nevada	Nevada Association of Counties 308 North Curry Street, Suite 205, Carson City 89703	Robert S. Hadfield, Executive Director	702 883-7863 702 883-7398	1945
New Hampshire	New Hampshire Association of Counties 16 Centre Street, Concord 03301	John Disko, Executive Director	603 224-9222 603 224-8312	1947
New Jersey	New Jersey Association of Counties 214 West State Street, Trenton 08608	Linda Spalinski, Executive Director	609 394-3467 609 989-8567	1921
New Mexico	New Mexico Association of Counties 1215 Paseo De Peralta, Santa Fe 87501	Donna K. Smith, Executive Director	505 983-2101 505 983-4396	1926
New York	New York State Association of Counties 150 State Street, Albany 12207	Edwin L. Crawford, Executive Director	518 465-1473 518 465-0506	1925
North Carolina	North Carolina Association of County Commissioners 215 North Dawson Street, Raleigh 27602-1488	C. Ronald Aycock, Executive Director	919 832-2893 919 733-1065	1908
North Dakota	North Dakota Association of Counties P.O. Box 417, Bismarck 58502	Mark A. Johnson, Executive Director	701 258-4481 701 258-2469	1906
Ohio	County Commissioners Association of Ohio 175 South Third Street, Suite 500, Columbus 43215-5134	Larry L. Long, Executive Director	614 221-5627 614 221-6986	1880
Oklahoma	Association of County Commissioners of Oklahoma 818 N.W. 63rd Street, Oklahoma City 73116-7604	John Ward, Executive Director	405 840-9582 405 840-5122	. . .
Oregon	Association of Oregon Counties P.O. Box 12729, Salem 97309	Robert Cantine, Executive Director	503 585-8351 503 373-7876	1906
Pennsylvania	Pennsylvania State Association of County Commissioners 17 North Front Street, Suite 120, Harrisburg 17101	Douglas E. Hill, Executive Director	717 232-7554 717 232-2162	1886
South Carolina	South Carolina Association of Counties P.O. Box 8207, Columbia 29202-8207	Michael B. Cone, Executive Director	803 252-7255 803 252-0379	1967
South Dakota	South Dakota Association of County Commissioners 207 East Capitol, Suite 203, Pierre 57501	Dennis Hanson, Executive Director	605 224-4554 605 224-5364	1914
Tennessee	Tennessee County Services Association 226 Capitol Boulevard Building, Suite 700, Nashville 37219	Robert M. Wormsley, Executive Director	615 242-5591 615 244-3340	1954
Texas	Texas Association of Counties P.O. Box 2131, Austin 78768	Sam Seale, Executive Director	512 478-8753 512 478-0519	1969
Utah	Utah Association of Counties 4021 South-700 East, Suite 180, Salt Lake City 84107	L. Brent Gardner, Executive Director	801 265-1331 801 265-9485	1923
Virginia	Virginia Association of Counties 1001 East Broad Street, Suite 1120, Richmond 23219	James D. Campbell, Executive Director	804 788-6652 804 788-0083	1935
Washington	Washington Association of County Officials 206 Tenth Avenue S.E., Olympia 98501	Fred Saeger, Executive Director	206 753-7319 206 753-2842	1959
	Washington State Association of Counties 206 Tenth Avenue S.E., Olympia 98501	Gary Lowe, Executive Director	206 753-1886 206 753-2842	1908
West Virginia	West Virginia Association of Counties 211 Washington Street East, Charleston 25301	John Hoff, Executive Director	304 346-0591 304 346-0592	1960
Wisconsin	Wisconsin Counties Association 802 West Broadway, Suite 308, Madison 53713-1897	Mark Rogacki, Executive Director	608 266-6480 608 221-3832	1935
Wyoming	Wyoming County Commissioners Association P.O. Box 86, Cheyenne 82003	B. G. "Jerry" Michie, Executive Director	307 632-5409 307 632-6533	1968

Directory 1/7 DIRECTORS OF COUNCILS OF GOVERNMENTS
RECOGNIZED BY ICMA[1]

Regional council	Appointed administrator	Phone number
ALABAMA-4		
Birmingham Regional Planning Commission	Paul G. Dentiste	205 251-8139
Central Alabama Regional Planning and Development Commission	Janet M. Tate	205 262-4300
East Alabama Regional Planning and Development Commission	James W. Curtis	205 237-6741
South Central Alabama Development Commission	. . .	205 281-2196
ARIZONA-5		
District 4 COG	. . .	602 782-1886
Maricopa Association of Governments	. . .	602 254-6308
Northern Arizona COG	. . .	602 774-1895
PIMA Association of Governments	Thomas L. Swanson	602 792-1093
Southeastern Arizona Governments Organization	. . .	602 432-5301

Regional council	Appointed administrator	Phone number
ARKANSAS-3		
Metroplan	Jim McKenzie	501 372-3300
Northwest Arkansas Regional Planning Commission	Larry R. Wood	501 751-7125
White River Planning and Development District	. . .	501 793-5233
CALIFORNIA-14		
Alameda County Waste Management Authority	. . .	510 639-2481
Association of Bay Area Governments	Revan A. F. Tranter	415 464-7900
Association of Monterey Bay Area Governments	Nicolas Papadakis	408 624-2117
Central Sierra Planning Council	. . .	209 532-8768
Council of Fresno County Governments	William E. Briam	209 233-4148
Sacramento Area COG	. . .	916 441-5930
San Diego Association of Governments	. . .	619 595-5300

Directory 1/7 DIRECTORS OF COUNCILS OF GOVERNMENTS
continued RECOGNIZED BY ICMA[1]

Regional council	Appointed administrator	Phone number
San Joaquin County COG	...	805 861-2191
Santa Barbara County Association of Governments	Gerald R. Lorden	805 568-2546
South Bay Regional Public Communications Authority	Dennis R. Warren	213 973-1802
Southern California Association of Governments	Mark A. Pisano	213 236-1800
Stanislaus Area Association of Governments	Greg Steel	209 525-7830
Transportation Corridor Agency COG	William Woollett, Jr.	714 557-3298
Tulare County Association of Governments	George E. Finney	209 733-6303
COLORADO-2		
Denver Regional COG	Robert D. Farley	303 455-1000
Northwest Colorado COG	...	303 668-5445
CONNECTICUT-1		
Connecticut River Estuary Regional Planning Agency	Stanley V. Greimann	203 388-3497
DISTRICT OF COLUMBIA-1		
Metropolitan Washington COG	Ruth R. Crone	202 962-3200
GEORGIA-4		
Atlanta Regional Commission	B. Harry West	404 656-7700
Coastal Georgia Regional Development Center	Vernon D. Martin	912 264-7363
Middle Georgia Regional Development Center	...	912 744-6160
Southeast Georgia Regional Development Center	Lace Futch	912 285-6097
IDAHO-2		
Panhandle Area Council	...	208 772-0584
Southeast Idaho COG	Scott B. McDonald	208 233-4032
ILLINOIS-10		
Bi-State Regional Commission	Gary B. Vallem	309 793-6300
Champaign County Regional Planning Commission	Robert Soltau	217 328-3313
Greater Egypt Regional Planning and Development Commission	A. S. Kirkikis	618 549-3306
North Central Illinois COG	John Henning	815 875-3396
Northeastern Illinois Planning Commission	Phillip D. Peters	312 454-0400
Northwest Municipal Conference	...	708 253-6323
South Central Illinois Regional Planning and Development Commission	...	618 548-4234
South Suburban Mayors' and Managers' Association	...	708 957-6970
Southwestern Illinois Metropolitan Regional Planning Commission	Thomas A. Wobbe	618 344-4250
Tri-County Regional Planning Commission	John F. Boyle	309 694-9330
INDIANA-2		
Michiana Area COG	...	219 287-1829
Northwestern Indiana Regional Planning Commission	James E. Ranframz	219 923-1060
IOWA-4		
East Central Intergovernmental Association	Bill Baum	319 556-4166
Midas COG	Stephen F. Hoesel	515 576-7183
Siouxland Interstate Metropolitan Planning Council	Donald M. Meisner	712 279-6286
Southern Iowa Economic Development Association	...	515 682-8741
KANSAS-1		
North Central Regional Planning Commission	...	913 738-2218
KENTUCKY-6		
Barren River Area Development District	...	502 781-2381
Big Sandy Area Development District	...	606 886-2374
Bluegrass Area Development District	...	606 272-6656
Lincoln Trail Area Development District	James E. Greer	502 769-2393
Northern Kentucky Area Development District	Deanna Skees	606 283-1885
Purchase Area Development District	...	502 247-7171
LOUISIANA-2		
Lafayette Areawide Planning Commission	Roger K. Hedrick	318 237-0216
Shreve Area COG	...	318 226-6488
MAINE-1		
Greater Portland COG	John Dana Bubier	207 774-9891

Regional council	Appointed administrator	Phone number
MARYLAND-2		
Baltimore Regional COG	...	301 383-5830
Tri-County Council for Southern Maryland	Gary V. Hodge	301 884-2144
MASSACHUSETTS-1		
Merrimack Valley Planning Commission	...	617 374-0519
MICHIGAN-1		
Southeast Michigan COG	...	313 961-4266
MISSISSIPPI-1		
Central Mississippi Planning and Development District	...	601 981-1511
MISSOURI-4		
East-West Gateway Coordinating Council	...	314 421-4220
Mid-America Regional Council	David A. Warm	816 474-4240
Ozark Foothills Regional Planning Commission	...	314 785-6402
South Central Ozark COG	...	417 256-8123
NEW MEXICO-1		
Southwest New Mexico COG	...	505 388-1974
NEW YORK-1		
Capital District Regional Planning Commission	Chungchin Chen	518 272-1414
NORTH CAROLINA-7		
Centralina COG	E. Lee Armour	704 372-2416
Land-of-Sky Regional Council	Robert E. Shepherd	704 254-8131
Lumber River COG	...	919 738-8104
Neuse River COG	...	919 638-3185
Piedmont Triad COG	Randall Billings	919 294-4950
Region L COG	...	919 446-0411
Western Piedmont COG	R. Douglas Taylor	704 322-9191
OHIO-4		
Miami Valley Regional Planning Commission	...	513 223-6323
Ohio Mid-Eastern Governments Association	John A. Quinlan	614 439-4471
Ohio-Kentucky-Indiana Regional COG	James Q. Duane	513 621-7060
Toledo Metropolitan Area COG	William L. Knight	419 241-9155
OKLAHOMA-3		
Association of Central Oklahoma Governments	Zach D. Taylor	405 848-8961
Central Oklahoma Economic Development District	...	405 273-6410
Northern Oklahoma Development Association	...	405 237-4810
OREGON-6		
Lane COG	George Kloeppel	503 687-4283
Metropolitan Service District	...	503 221-1646
Mid-Columbia Economic Development District	Betty J. Mills	503 296-2266
Mid-Willamette Valley COG	Alan H. Hershey	503 588-6177
Oregon Cascade West COG	William R. Wagner	503 757-6851
Umpqua Regional COG	Richard J. Dolgonas	503 440-4231
PENNSYLVANIA-3		
Allegheny League of Municipalities	...	412 355-5986
North Central Pennsylvania Regional Planning and Development Commission	...	814 773-3162
Northwest Pennsylvania Regional Planning and Development Commission	...	814 437-3024
SOUTH CAROLINA-4		
Central Midlands Regional Planning Council	Donald R. Hinson	803 798-1243
Lower Savannah COG	...	803 649-7981
South Carolina Appalachian COG	Robert M. Strother	803 242-9733
Upper Savannah COG	...	803 229-6627
SOUTH DAKOTA-2		
Northeast COG	Faye Kann	605 622-2595
Planning and Development District Three	...	605 665-4408
TENNESSEE-2		
Chattanooga Area Regional COG/ Southeast Tennessee Development District	...	615 266-5781
East Tennessee Development District	Robert E. Freeman	615 584-8553

Directory 1/7 continued **DIRECTORS OF COUNCILS OF GOVERNMENTS RECOGNIZED BY ICMA[1]**

Regional council	Appointed administrator	Phone number
TEXAS-17		
Alamo Area COG	Al J. Notzon	512 225-5201
Ark-Tex COG	James C. Fisher Jr.	501 774-3481
Capital Area Planning Council	. . .	512 443-7653
Central Texas COG	. . .	817 939-1801
Coastal Bend COG	John P. Buckner	512 883-5743
Concho Valley COG	Robert R. Weaver	915 944-9666
Deep East Texas COG	Walter G. Diggles	409 384-5704
East Texas COG	Glynn J. Knight	214 984-8641
Heart of Texas COG	Leon A. Willhite	817 756-6631
Houston-Galveston Area Council	. . .	713 627-3200
Lower Rio Grande Valley Development Council	. . .	512 682-3481
Nortex Regional Planning Commission	. . .	817 322-5281
North Central Texas COG	Mike Eastland	817 461-3300
Panhandle Regional Planning Commission	. . .	806 372-3381
South Plains Association of Governments	. . .	806 762-8721
Texoma Regional Planning Commission	. . .	214 786-2955
West Central Texas COG	Brad Helbert	915 672-8544
UTAH-1		
Five County Association of Governments	John S. Williams	801 673-3548
VIRGINIA-8		
Central Shenandoah Planning District Commission	. . .	703 885-5174
Central Virginia Planning District Commission	Dennis G. Gragg	804 845-3491
Crater Planning District Commission	Dennis K. Morris	804 861-1666
Hampton Roads Planning District Commission	Arthur L. Collins	804 461-3200
Northern Neck Planning District Commission	. . .	804 529-7400
Northern Virginia Planning District Commission	G. Mark Gibb	703 642-0700
Southside Planning District Commission	William Park	804 447-7101
West Piedmont Planning District Commission	. . .	703 638-3987
WASHINGTON-4		
Benton-Franklin Regional Council	. . .	509 943-9185
Intergovernmental Resource Center	Dean Lookingbill	206 699-2361
Puget Sound COG	Mary McCumber	206 464-7090
Skagit COG	W. Kelley Moldstad	206 757-4514
WEST VIRGINIA-3		
Bel-O-Mar Regional Council and Interstate Planning Commission	. . .	304 242-1800
Mid-Ohio Valley Regional Council	. . .	304 485-3801
Region One Planning and Development Council	. . .	304 425-9508
WISCONSIN-2		
East Central Wisconsin Regional Planning Commission	Kenneth J. Theine	414 729-1100
West Central Wisconsin Regional Planning Commission	. . .	715 836-2918
WYOMING-1		
Fremont County Association of Governments	Mike Morgan	317 856-8589
CANADA-1		
Québec Urban Community (Québec)	. . .	418 681-9611

[1]This directory is limited to those councils of governments that have been recognized by ICMA as of November 1992 as providing for a position of overall professional management.

Directory 1/8 **INTERNATIONAL CHIEF APPOINTED ADMINISTRATORS**

Local government	Appointed administrator	Phone number
AUSTRALIA		
New South Wales		
Baulkam Hills Shire	David W. Mead	612-821-9222
Bankstown	Arthur B. Heiler	612-707-9524
Blue Mountains	Graham C. Collins	614-782-0777
Botany	John F. Patterson	612-317-0555
Byron Shire	Barry F. Pullinger	. . .
Caringbah	Douglas J. Chapman	
Hawkesbury	Garry M. McCully	614-587-7000
Hunters Hill	William E. G. Phipson	612-816-1555
Lake Macquarie	John R. Rankin	614-921-0220
Lane Cove	Alan W. Byleveld	612-911-3555
Lismore	Paul T. Muldoon	616-625-0420
Lithgow	Stuart W. McPherson	616-352-1077
Liverpool	John H. Walker	612-821-9222
Manly	Wayne A. Collins	612-976-1500
Mosman	Vivian H. R. May	612-960-0900
Penrith	Barry B. Long	614-732-7620
Queanbeyan	Hugh H. Percy	616-298-0223
Rockdale	Stephen J. Blackadder	612-567-5573
Singleton Shire	John A. Flannery	616-572-1866
Sutherland Shire	John W. Rayner	612-710-0359
Tweed Shire	John F. Griffin	616-672-0415
Wollongong	Roderick J. Oxley	614-227-7111
Woollahra	Denis W. McGuinn	612-391-7000
Wyong Shire	John S. Dawson	614-353-1333
Northern Territory		
Alice Springs	Allan R. McGill	618-952-2733
Darwin	David K. Wormald	618-982-2505
Queensland		
Cairns	Noel P. Briggs	617-050-2481
Gold Coast	Robert H. Brown	617-581-6379
Mackay	Stanley B. Fursman	617-951-6466
Miriam Vale Shire	James S. Nixon	617-931-1278
Rockhampton	Robin D. Noble	617-931-1278
Stanthorpe Shire	Rowland W. Edwards	617-681-1799
Warwick	John P. Cuddihy	617-661-2333
South Australia		
Adelaide	Michael J. Llewellyn-Smith	618-203-7234
Brighton	John L. Chenoweth	618-296-6966
Burnside	Rodney W. S. Donne	618-366-4200
Happy Valley	John D. Christie	618-270-2655
Noarlunga	Christopher Catt	618-384-0626
Port Adelaide	Keith Beamish	618-479-841
Salisbury	Stephen C. Hains	618-259-1212
Unley	Keith R. Adams	613-372-5103
Woodville	Geoffrey T. Whitbread	618-348-6111
Tasmania		
Clarence	Stewart A. Wardlaw	612-440-640
Devonport	David E. Sales	614-240-511
Dorset	Thomas B. Ransom	613-522-444
Hobart	Garry R. Storch	612-382-711
Huon	Thomas P. O'Connor	610-264-1211
Launceston	Robert G. Campbell	613-371-102
Ulverstone	Alfred R. Mott	614-425-1099
Victoria		
Alberton Shire	Garry J. Stephens	615-182-5100
Altona	John Francis Shaw	613-316-1221
Ballan Shire	David G. Carey	615-368-1001
Ballarat	David R. Peile	615-338-602
Ballarat Shire	Jeremy W. M. Johnson	615-338-1477
Barrabool Shire	Mervyn W. Hair	615-261-4202
Benalla	William S. Jaboor	615-762-1533
Bendigo	Ray J. Burton	615-443-1677
Berwick	Neil B. Lucas	613-705-5200

Directory 1/8 INTERNATIONAL CHIEF APPOINTED ADMINISTRATORS
continued

Local government	Appointed administrator	Phone number
Box Hill	Ian G. Port	613-895-9611
Brighton	Raymond J. Cobain	613-591-8688
Bulla Shire	John W. Watson	613-744-9253
Buninyong Shire	Peter Mangan	. . .
Castlemaine	Barry P. Rochford	615-407-2161
Coburg	Joseph R. Diffen	613-350-0210
Cranbourne Shire	Terence Vickerman	615-996-1000
Creswick Shire	Bruce T. Crago	615-345-2000
Croyden	Terence L. Maher	613-724-3201
Dandenong	Colin G. Dickie	613-212-1010
Doncaster and Templestowe	Donald O. McLean	613-840-9202
Eaglehawk	Barry Secombe	615-446-8966
Essendon	Peter R. Seamer	614-332-4388
Flinders Shire	Larry M. Jones	615-986-0111
Frankston	Adrian H. Butler	613-784-1800
Gisborne Shire	Terence H. Larkins	. . .
Hamilton	Russell J. Worland	615-573-0444
Hawthorn	Kenneth J. McNamara	613-810-2401
Keilor	Peter J. Black	. . .
Kew	Malcolm D. Hutchinson	613-862-2466
Kilmore Shire	Peter O. Anderson	615-782-1322
Knox	Robert G. Seiffert	618-818-222
Lilydale Shire	Warwick I. Heine	613-735-8333
Lowan Shire	Robert J. Foster	615-391-1811
Maldon Shire	Richard T. Walsh	615-475-2633
Malvern	Peter A. Akers	613-823-1222
Marong	Graeme L. Elvey	615-435-2202
Melton Shire	Lindsay A. Merritt	613-747-7200
Metcalfe Shire	Maxwell B. Watson	615-423-2302
Mildura	Damian B. Goss	615-022-2777
Moe	Peter G. Lerstang	615-127-3666
Moorabbin	Douglas I. Owens	. . .
Mordialloc	Jonathan F. Edwards	613-584-4366
Mornington Shire	Jan B. Cover	615-975-4155
Morwell	Ronald H. Waters	615-134-4744
Northcote	David Niven	. . .
Numurkah Shire	Lindsay G. Mitchell	615-862-1222
Prahran	Greg N. Maddock	615-727-0888
Preston	Kelvin L. Spiller	613-479-4602
Richmond	David G. Williams	613-420-9655
Ringwood	John D. Paech	. . .
St. Kilda	Jude R. Munro	613-536-1333
Sandringham	John L. Purdey	613-598-8111
Sherbrooke Shire	Dennis E. Stevens	613-212-8222
South Melbourne	Noel F. Kropp	613-695-8201
Springvale	Bryan A. Payne	613-549-1117
Strathfieldsaye Shire	Barry W. Edwards	054-343-9555
Sunshine	John P. James	613-313-3300
Swan Hill Shire	Neil L. Noelker	615-032-0333
Warragul	Geoffrey C. Davey	615-623-0211
Warrnambool	Vernon G. Robson	615-554-7800
Waverley	John N. Webster	613-566-0282
Werribee	John T. Kerr	613-742-0703
Whittlesea	Lindsay G. Esmonde	613-401-0333
Woorayl Shire	John F. Dyer	615-662-9200

Western Australia

Albany Shire	Wayne F. Scheggia	619-841-2311
Gnowangerup Shire	Philip A. Anning	619-827-1007
Kalamunda Shire	Edward H. Kelly	619-293-2111
Kalgoorlie-Boulder	Leslie P. Strugnell	619-021-2544
Kwinana	Robert K. Smillie	619-419-2222
Melville	Garry G. Hunt	619-364-0666
Narrogin	Patrick John Walker	619-881-1944
Peppermint Grove Shire	Graham D. Partridge	619-384-0099
Perth	Reginald F. Dawson	619-265-3260
Swan Shire	Eric W. Lumsden	619-274-9801

CANADA
Alberta

Airdrie	Deryl Kloster	403-948-8821
Banff	James Bennett	403-762-1200
Bonnyville	J. D. Crisp	. . .
Brooks	Kevin Bridges	403-362-3333
Calgary	Robert A. Welin	403-268-5634
Cochrane	Martin J. Schmitke	403-932-2075
Drumheller	R. M. Romanetz	403-823-6300
Edmonton	J. Richard Picherack	403-496-8222
Fort McMurray	Glen Laubenstein	403-743-7022
Fort Saskatchewan	Paul Benedetto	403-992-6212
Gibbons	Maisie Metrunec	403-923-3331

Local government	Appointed administrator	Phone number
Grande Prairie	Robert W. Robertson	. . .
Lacombe	Robert D. Jenkins	403-782-6666
Leduc	Glenn Pitman	403-980-7101
Lethbridge	Bryan Horrocks	403-320-3901
Medicine Hat	Allan T. Hagan	403-529-8228
Ponoka	Gordon C. Harris	403-783-3341
Rainbow Lake	Julie M. Burge	. . .
Red Deer	H. Michael Day	403-342-8156
Rocky View Municipal District	F. Dale Clark	403-230-1401
St. Albert	Norbert Van Wyk	403-459-1607
Spruce Grove	John A. Cosgrove	403-962-2611
Strathmore	Dwight J. Stanford	403-934-3133
Sylvan Lake	P. J. Grimson	. . .

British Columbia

Abbotsford District	Rick Beauchamp	. . .
Burnaby	A. L. Parr	604-294-7103
Castlegar	Gary Williams	. . .
Coquitlam	Norman A. Cook	604-526-3611
Esquimalt Township	Sandy T. Gray	604-385-2461
Fort St. John	Colin J. Griffith	. . .
Kamloops	Joseph E. Martignago	604-828-3498
Kelowna	Ronald Born	604-763-6011
Langley Township	Jim F. Godfrey	604-534-3211
Maple Ridge District	Jerry A. Sulina	604-463-5221
Matsqui District	Hedda Cochran	604-853-2281
Mission District	Glen C. Robertson	604-826-6271
Nanimo	Gerald D. Berry	604-755-4401
Nanimo Regional District	Kelly D. Daniels	. . .
North Vancouver	A. Kenneth Tollstam	. . .
Parksville	Grant G. McRadu	604-248-6144
Penticton	Tim Wood	604-492-3043
Pitts Meadows	Ken J. Wiesner	604-465-2413
Port Alberni	D. R. Walker	604-723-2146
Port Hardy District	Phyllis Belaire	. . .
Port Moody	Leslie T. Harrington	. . .
Prince George	George Paul	604-561-7607
Prince Rupert	William J. Smith	604-627-6937
Richmond	John Y. Carline	604-276-4153
Squamish	R. A. (Bob) Miles	604-892-5217
Surrey	Douglas A. Lychak	604-591-4122
Vancouver	Ken F. Dobell	604-873-7627
Vancouver Regional District	Ben Marr	604-828-3498
Vernon	Blake M. Kimura	. . .
Victoria	Colin F. Crisp	604-385-5711
West Vancouver District	J. Douglas Allan	604-922-1211
White Rock	Wayne W. Baldwin	604-531-9111

Manitoba

Brandon	Earl E. Backman	204-729-2204
Portage la Prairie	William G. Newell	204-239-8336
Steinbach	Jack Kehler	204-326-9877
Winnipeg	Richard L. Frost	204-986-2375

New Brunswick

Bathurst	Edward Childs	506-548-0414
Campbellton	Ronald F. Mahoney	506-753-7767
Dalhousie	Michael Allain	. . .
Fredericton	John C. Robison	506-452-9500
Moncton	Lawrence E. Strang	506-853-3333
Newcastle	Doug Chase	506-627-2512
Oromocto	Wayne Carnell	506-357-8487
St. Andrews	Jacques Dube	506-529-4501
St. John	John Brown	506-658-2877

Newfoundland

Gander	Jake Turner	709-651-2949
Labrador City	Cecil E. Vincent	709-944-2621
St. John's	William K. Mann	. . .

Northwest Territories

Iqaluit	Kathryn E. Garven	819-979-5381
Yellowknife	Douglas B. Lagore	403-920-5600

Nova Scotia

Bedford	Dan R. English	902-832-8312
Halifax	Donald Murphy	902-421-6500
Halifax County Municipality	Ken R. Meech	. . .
Halifax Metropolitan Authority	R. Mort Jackson	. . .
Port Hawkersbury	Colin J. MacDonald	902-625-0116

Directory 1/8   INTERNATIONAL CHIEF APPOINTED ADMINISTRATORS
continued

Local government	Appointed administrator	Phone number
Ontario		
Ajax	D. J. Low	416-683-4550
Ancaster	A. Bruce Davidson	416-648-4401
Aurora	James B. Currier	416-727-1375
Brampton	Al Solski	416-874-2625
Burlington	W. Michael Fenn	416-335-7608
Cambridge	Donald N. Smith	519-740-4518
Chatham	Hugh J. Thomas	519-436-3241
Clarence Township	Richard R. Lalonde	613-488-2570
Cornwall	Hugh John Cook	613-932-6252
Cobourg	Bryan W. Baxter	416-372-4301
Flamborough	Blayne C. Rennick	416-689-7351
Fort Erie	Kenneth Paul Zurby	. . .
Halton Regional Municipality	J. S. Burke	416-827-2151
Hamilton-Wentworth Region	W. McMillin Carson	416-546-4263
Hawkesbury	Theodore J. Proulx	613-632-0105
Kirkland Lake	Lionel J. Sherratt	705-567-9361
Kitchener	Tom McKay	519-741-2290
London	John E. Fleming	519-661-5493
Markham	John Morand	416-477-7000
Mississauga	G. Stanley Spencer	416-896-5550
Muskoka District Municipality	Bill Calvert	705-645-2231
Nepean	Robert Letourneau	. . .
Niagara-on-the-Lake	Lew Holloway	416-468-3266
Niagara Regional Municipality	Michael H. Boggs	416-984-3602
Oakville	Harry E. Henderson	416-845-6601
Oro Township	Robert W. Small	. . .
Oshawa	Curtis W. Keil	. . .
Ottawa	David S. O'Brien	613-564-1429
Ottawa-Carleton Regional Municipality	C. M. Beckstead	. . .
Peel Regional Municipality	Michael R. Garrett	416-791-9400
Peterborough	David L. Hall	705-748-8811
Richmond Hill	Charles D. Weldon	416-771-2505
Rockcliffe Park	Murray E. MacLean	613-749-9791
Rockland	Jean D. Vachon	613-446-6022
Sault Ste. Marie	Allan A. Jackson	705-759-5348
Scarborough	Donald W. Roughley	416-396-7278
Sudbury	William Rice	705-674-3131
Thunder Bay	Bruce Thom	807-625-2223
Toronto	Michael L. Nixon	416-392-0495
Toronto, Metropolitan	Dale E. Richmond	416-392-8681
Vanier	Daniel Ouimet	613-747-2501
Waterloo	Robert L. Byron	519-747-8702
Waterloo Regional Municipality	Gerald A. Thompson	519-885-9425
Welland	Volker Kerschl	. . .
Whitby	William H. Wallace	. . .
Windsor	Hilary G. Payne	519-994-2728
York Regional Municipality	Bob Forhan	416-895-1231
Prince Edward Island		
Charlottetown	Harry Gaudet	. . .
Summerside	Terry Murphy	902-436-4222
West Royalty	Donna Waddell	902-368-1025
Québec		
Anjou	Serge Gosselin	514-352-4440
Aylmer	Denis Hubert	819-684-5372
Baie-d'Urfe	Richard White	514-457-5324
Beaconsfield	Georges Krcmery	514-697-4660
Brossard	Richard Labrècque	514-676-0201
Chandler	David C. Johnstone	418-689-2221
Charlesbourg	Michel Lavoie	418-624-7804
Dollard-des-Ormeaux	Wesley Lancaster	514-684-1010
Drummondville	Marc Y. Beaulieu	819-478-6557
Gatineau	Claude Doucet	819-243-2310
Granby	Robert Duval	514-372-6671
Hull	Paul Preseault	819-595-7131
Jonquière	Jean-Marc Gagnon	418-548-0615
Kirkland Lake	Jacques Chan	. . .
La Salle	Robert Barbeau	514-367-6200
Longueuil	Jean Verdy	514-646-8210
Mirabel	Yves Lacroix	514-476-0360
Montreal	Pierre Le François	514-872-2996
Montreal-Est	Rejean Guillette	. . .
Mount Royal	Duncan E. Campbell	514-340-2900
Outremont	J. R. Victor Mainville	514-495-6223
Pierrefonds	Louis Morin	514-620-5111
Pointe-Claire	Tom Buffitt	514-630-1200

Local government	Appointed administrator	Phone number
Québec	Denis DeBelleval	416-691-6560
Repentigny	Michel Dagenais	
St.-Lambert	Richard J. Shuttleworth	514-672-4444
St.-Laurent	Pierre Lebeau	. . .
Shawinigan-Sud	Charles J. Mills	819-536-5671
Westmount	Bruce St. Louis	514-935-8531
Saskatchewan		
La Ronge	John H. Wade	. . .
Lloydminster	Roger H. Brekko	306-825-6184
Moose Jaw	Jim Penrod	306-694-4427
Prince Albert	Len Cantin	306-922-7300
Regina	A. R. Linner	306-777-7314
Yukon		
Dawson	Carol Metz-Murray	403-993-5434
Faro	S. Bruce Peever	604-994-2728
Whitehorse	Bryce Walt	403-667-6401
ENGLAND		
Berkshire		
Reading Borough	Sylvie Pierce	44-734-390113
Windsor and Maidenhead Borough	Geoffrey B. Blacker	44-628-798888
East Sussex		
East Sussex County	Robin M. Beechey	. . .
Eastbourne Borough	Michael D. Blanch	44-323-415009
Greater Manchester		
Salford	Roger C. Rees	. . .
Hertfordshire		
Stevenage Borough	Howard L. Miller	44-438-766225
Welwyn/Hatfield	David W. Riddle	44-707-331212
Isle of Wight		
Isle of Wight County	John S. Horsnell	44-983-823102
Kent		
Dover District	John P. Moir	44-304-821199
Kent County	Paul R. Sabin	44-622-694000
Turnbridge Wells	Rodney J. Stone	44-892-526121
Lancashire		
Ribble Valley Borough	Ossie Hopkins	44-810-200251
Lincolnshire		
South Kesteven District	Kenneth R. Cann	44-411-476591
London		
City of London	Samuel Jones	44-713-321400
Croydon Borough	Roger D. Jefferies	44-816-864433
Kingston Borough	Robert J. McCloy	44-815-475001
Leduc	Glenn Pitman	403-980-7101
Lethbridge	Bryan Horrocks	403-320-3901
Merseyside		
Knowsley Metropolitan Borough	David G. Henshaw	44-514-433772
Sefton Metropolitan Borough	Graham J. Haywood	44-519-342057
Middlesex		
Spelthorne Borough	Michael B. Taylor	44-784-446250
Norfolk		
South Norfolk District	Adrian Kellett	44-5-083-1122
Northamptonshire		
Daventry District	Robert J. Symons	44-327-71100
East Northamptonshire District	Roger K. Heath	44-933-41200
Northampton Borough	Roger J. B. Morris	44-604-233500
Northamptonshire County	A. Jeffrey Greenwell	44-604-236050
Nottinghamshire		
Mansfield District	Richard P. Goad	44-623-656656
Oxfordshire		
Cherwell District	Grahame J. Handley	44-295-252535

Directory 1/8   INTERNATIONAL CHIEF APPOINTED ADMINISTRATORS
continued

Local government	Appointed administrator	Phone number	Local government	Appointed administrator	Phone number
Shropshire			Ruapehu District	Clifford J. Houston	64-7-895-8188
Oswestry Castle View			South Taranaki District	Desmond R. Beaven	64-628-8010
Borough	David A. Towers	44-691-654411	Taranaki Region	Basil G. Chamberlain	64-676-57127
			Tararua District	Max C. Griffiths	64-6-374-8068
Warwickshire			Tauranga District	Alan N. Bickers	64-757-77010
Stratford-on-Avon District	Ian B. Prosser	44-789-260101	Timaru District	Leslie Baker	64-3-684-8199
Warwick District	Michael J. Ward	44-926-450000	Waikato District	John C. Fitzpatrick	64-7-856-3199
			Wairoa	Peter J. Freeman	64-0724-7309
West Sussex			Waitakere	Mark O. Dacombe	64-9-837-3700
Worthing Borough	Michael J. Ball	44-903-239999	Wanganui District	Colin J. Whitlock	64-345-8529
			Wellington	Angela C. Griffin	64-801-3462
Worcester			Western Bay of Plenty		
Redditch Borough	Stella E. Manzie	44-052-764252	District	John B. Skinner	64-75-718-008
ISRAEL			**SCOTLAND**		
Beer-Sheva	Haim Gurfinkel	972-5-772179	Skye and Lochalsh District	David H. Noble	44-478-2341
Dimona	Yehoshwa Klein	972-5-7563104			
Lod	Albert Sivan	972-8-222396	**SOUTH AFRICA**		
			National Transvaal Regional		
MARSHALL ISLANDS			Services Council	Jack A. Botes	27-01521-71015
Kwajalein Atoll	Abon A. Jeadrik	692-873-3008	Pietermaritzburg	Granville G. Shenker	27-331-95109
Majuro	James A. Alloway	. . .			
			SWEDEN		
NETHERLANDS			Malung	Olof E. Almkleven	46-280-18100
Amsterdam	Klaas Kooiker	31-20-552-3300	Partille	Ulf C. G. Dermark	46-3136-1138
			Sigtuna	Laris-Goran Sorqvist	46-8-5912600
NEW ZEALAND			Umea	Bert Aasa	46-90-161240
Auckland	Bruce T. W. Anderson	64-9-379-2020	Vasteras	Hans B. V. Granquist	46-21-160000
Banks Peninsula District	John W. Stott	64-3-288-065			
Buller District	Darryl C. Griffin	64-289-7239	**SWITZERLAND**		
Central Otago District	Patrick T. Cooney	64-3-448-6979	Chur	Dieter Heller	41-8121-4111
Dunedin	Murray F. Douglas	64-3-477-4000			
Far North District	Warwick L. Bennett	. . .	**TURKEY**		
Hauraki District	I. Keith Laurenson	64-7-862-8609	Iula Eastern Mediterranean/		
Manukau	Colin J. B. Dale	64-9-263-7100	Middle East Region	Selahattin Yildirim	90-1-511-10-10
Nelson	Joseph M. Rudhall	64-3-546-0200			
New Plymouth District	Kinsley N. Sampson	64-6-758-8099	**WALES**		
North Shore	Keven L. Tate	64-9-486-8400	Cardiff	Roger E. Paine	44-222-822051
Palmerston North	P. Michael Willis	64-6-351-4435	Radnorshire District	Geoffrey C. Read	44-597-824773
Papakura	Thomas McLean	64-929-98870			
Rangitikei District	Pamela H. Taylor	64-652-8174			
Rotorua District	Allen E. Hansen	64-73-484199			

Directory 1/9   OFFICIALS IN ALL U.S. MUNICIPALITIES 2,500 AND OVER

The data for the directory of municipal officials were collected by ICMA during the summer of 1993 through a mail survey. The 7,200 municipalities surveyed include all incorporated places 2,500 and over, those places under 2,500 that are recognized by ICMA as having either the council-management form of government or a position of overall general management, and those communities whose populations had dropped below 2,500 since the 1986 Census.

In addition to the names of officials (and the municipal phone number), data on race and sex are collected for 20 positions shown in Tables 1/9/a and 1/9/b. Only the names of the mayor, appointed administrator, city clerk, finance officer, fire chief, police chief, and public works director are shown in the municipal directory that follows. All data collected other than the name and phone number are treated with confidentiality, and only aggregate data are presented below.

Sex and Race of Municipal Officials. Tables 1/9/a and 1/9/b present a breakdown of each sex by race and ethnicity for the municipal officials. Given the level of detail shown, it is possible to reaggregate these data for other displays that would show race and sex characteristics for the total number of officials reporting.

The positions shown are most often held by males with the exception of municipal clerk and librarian. Whites are predominant in each position shown. Other than whites, blacks (male and female combined) are more dominant in each of the positions than other minority group members.

The Directory. For convenience, the directory shows the names of municipalities in alphabetical order within each state. Other items indicated in the directory for each municipality are the type of municipality (city, village, town, township, borough, or plantation), form of government, population, and municipal phone number.

Table 1/9/a   MALE MUNICIPAL OFFICIALS BY RACE AND ETHNICITY

Position	Total reporting (A)	Total males No. (B)	Total males % of (A)	White No.	White % of (B)	Black No.	Black % of (B)	American Indian No.	American Indian % of (B)	Asian No.	Asian % of (B)	Other No.	Other % of (B)	Race not reported No.	Race not reported % of (B)	Hispanic No.	Hispanic % of (B)
Elected mayor/president	4,537	3,930	86.6	3,469	88.3	93	2.4	19	0.5	8	0.2	23	0.6	318	8.1	66	1.7
Chief appointed administrative officer/ manager	3,587	3,167	88.3	2,775	87.6	36	1.1	13	0.4	10	0.3	18	0.6	315	9.9	63	2.0
Assistant manager/assistant CAO	1,111	740	66.6	596	80.5	38	5.1	1	0.1	2	0.3	5	0.7	98	13.2	24	3.2
Clerk	4,116	1,060	25.8	620	58.5	17	1.6	4	0.4	2	0.2	8	0.8	409	38.6	14	1.3
Chief financial officer	3,036	1,977	65.1	1,599	80.9	19	1.0	11	0.6	20	1.0	19	1.0	309	15.6	41	2.1
Director of economic development	1,044	863	82.7	682	79.0	28	3.2	7	0.8	4	0.5	15	1.7	127	14.7	25	2.9
Treasurer	3,011	1,570	52.1	1,165	74.2	14	0.9	7	0.4	6	0.4	12	0.8	366	23.3	20	1.3
Director of public works	3,815	3,770	98.8	3,103	82.3	55	1.5	22	0.6	16	0.4	26	0.7	548	14.5	72	1.9
Engineer	1,933	1,907	98.7	1,606	84.2	10	0.5	5	0.3	21	1.1	19	1.0	246	12.9	26	1.4
Police chief	4,284	4,260	99.4	3,431	80.5	106	2.5	29	0.7	5	0.1	21	0.5	668	15.7	63	1.5
Fire chief	3,657	3,656	100.0	2,954	80.8	37	1.0	17	0.5	2	0.1	16	0.4	630	17.2	49	1.3
Planning director	2,056	1,725	83.9	1,376	79.8	32	1.9	7	0.4	12	0.7	13	0.8	285	16.5	37	2.1
Personnel director	2,096	1,174	56.0	910	77.5	51	4.3	6	0.5	3	0.3	8	0.7	196	16.7	25	2.1
Risk manager	995	667	67.0	543	81.4	13	1.9	2	0.3	3	0.4	6	0.9	100	15.0	16	2.4
Director of parks and recreation	2,188	1,874	85.6	1,455	77.6	46	2.5	8	0.4	4	0.2	8	0.4	353	18.8	24	2.6
Superintendent of parks	1,407	1,350	95.9	1,071	79.3	33	2.4	3	0.2	5	0.4	19	1.4	219	16.2	50	3.7
Director of recreation	1,405	1,010	71.9	775	76.7	34	3.4	4	0.4	0	0.0	9	0.9	188	18.6	22	2.2
Librarian	1,833	594	32.4	290	48.8	1	0.2	2	0.3	1	0.2	4	0.7	296	49.8	7	1.2
Director of data processing/info. serv.	928	647	69.7	515	79.6	8	1.2	3	0.5	7	1.1	8	1.2	106	16.4	16	2.5
Purchasing director	1,467	1,004	68.4	797	79.4	30	3.0	2	0.2	8	0.8	4	0.4	163	16.2	22	2.2

Table 1/9/b   FEMALE MUNICIPAL OFFICIALS BY RACE AND ETHNICITY

Position	Total reporting (A)	Total females No. (B)	Total females % of (A)	White No.	White % of (B)	Black No.	Black % of (B)	American Indian No.	American Indian % of (B)	Asian No.	Asian % of (B)	Other No.	Other % of (B)	Race not reported No.	Race not reported % of (B)	Hispanic No.	Hispanic % of (B)
Elected mayor/president	4,537	607	13.4	573	94.4	13	2.1	3	0.5	1	0.2	6	1.0	11	1.8	13	2.1
Chief appointed administrative officer/ manager	3,587	420	11.7	387	92.1	15	3.6	2	0.5	1	0.2	3	0.7	12	2.9	8	1.9
Assistant manager/assistant CAO	1,111	371	33.4	330	88.9	21	5.7	3	0.8	0	0.0	4	1.1	13	3.5	11	3.0
Clerk	4,116	3,056	74.2	2,861	93.6	70	2.3	22	0.7	7	0.2	22	0.7	74	2.4	78	2.6
Chief financial officer	3,036	1,059	34.9	990	93.5	22	2.1	7	0.7	8	0.8	7	0.7	25	2.4	19	1.8
Director of economic development	1,044	181	17.3	165	91.2	8	4.4	1	0.6	1	0.6	2	1.1	4	2.2	3	1.7
Treasurer	3,011	1,441	47.9	1,359	94.3	30	2.1	8	0.6	5	0.3	3	0.2	36	2.5	18	1.2
Director of public works	3,815	45	1.2	35	77.8	7	15.6	1	2.2	1	2.2	0	0.0	1	2.2	1	2.2
Engineer	1,933	26	1.3	24	92.3	1	3.8	0	0.0	1	3.8	0	0.0	0	0.0	0	0.0
Police chief	4,284	24	0.6	24	100.0	0	0.0	0	0.0	0	0.0	0	0.0	0	0.0	1	4.2
Fire chief	3,657	1	0.0	1	100.0	0	0.0	0	0.0	0	0.0	0	0.0	0	0.0	0	0.0
Planning director	2,056	331	16.1	306	92.4	7	2.1	1	0.3	4	1.2	5	1.5	8	2.4	7	2.1
Personnel director	2,096	922	44.0	816	88.5	57	6.2	7	0.8	3	0.3	9	1.0	30	3.3	37	4.0
Risk manager	995	328	33.0	301	91.8	11	3.4	2	0.6	0	0.0	3	0.9	11	3.4	12	3.7
Director of parks and recreation	2,188	314	14.4	290	92.4	12	3.8	1	0.3	1	0.3	3	1.0	7	2.2	6	1.9
Superintendent of parks	1,407	57	4.1	53	93.0	1	1.8	0	0.0	0	0.0	3	5.3	0	0.0	3	5.3
Director of recreation	1,405	395	28.1	360	91.1	15	3.8	2	0.5	1	0.3	3	0.8	14	3.5	8	2.0
Librarian	1,833	1,239	67.6	1,177	95.0	9	0.7	8	0.6	10	0.8	4	0.3	31	2.5	14	1.1
Director of data processing/info. serv.	928	281	30.3	255	90.7	11	3.9	4	1.4	3	1.1	0	0.0	8	2.8	2	0.7
Purchasing director	1,467	463	31.6	413	89.2	21	4.5	4	0.9	3	0.6	3	0.6	19	4.1	18	3.9

Directory 1/9
continued

OFFICIALS IN U.S. MUNICIPALITIES 2,500 AND OVER

Form of government
CM Council-manager
CO Commission
MC Mayor-council
RT Representative town meeting
TM Town meeting

Municipal designation
b borough
pl plantation
t town
tp township
v village

Population
Note: The only jurisdictions under 2,500 in population that are listed are those recognized by ICMA.
Population figures are not rounded up; 14,500 will appear as 14.
(..) Less than
500 population
Other codes
. . . . Data not reported or not applicable

City, 1990 population figures (000 omitted), form of government	Municipal phone number	Mayor	Appointed administrator	City clerk	Finance officer	Fire chief	Police chief	Public works director
ALABAMA (135)								
Abbeville (3)	MC 205 585-6444	(not reporting)						
Alabaster (15)	MC 205 664-6800	Roger N Wheeler	James S Gould	Catherine Sarris	. . . .	John C Cochran	Larry R Rollan	Jack Zuiderhoek
Albertville (15)	MC 205 891-8206	(not reporting)						
Alexander City (15)	MC 205 329-8426	Ben R Cleveland	. . . .	George H Gordon	George H Gordon	Marvin L Still	Lynn E Royall	. . . .
Aliceville (3)	MC 205 373-6611	(not reporting)						
Andalusia (9)	MC 205 222-3311	Paul T Armstrong	. . . .	Roland Carter	Roland Carter	Joseph B Lee	Jerry Williamson	James B Hogg
Anniston (27)	CM 205 236-3422	David Dethrage	Tom Wright	Alan B Atkinson	Tom Wright	Louis Lefoy	Wayne Chandler	Charles D Johnson
Arab t (6)	MC 205 586-3544	(not reporting)						
Athens (17)	MC 205 233-8720	Dan Williams	. . . .	Mignon Bowers	. . . .	Craig Wilson	Wayne Harper	Larry Elkins
Atmore (8)	MC 205 368-2253	Howard Shell	. . . .	Sharon Robbins		Charles Rutherford	Glenn Carlee	. . . .
Attalla (7)	MC 205 538-9986	(not reporting)						
Auburn (34)	CM 205 887-4900	Jan Dempsey	Douglas J Watson	. . . .	Levi Knapp	R Blankenship	Edwin Downing	John Holmes
Bay Minette (7)	MC 205 937-5502	(not reporting)						
Bessemer (33)	CO 205 424-4060	Quitman Mitchell	. . . .	Hugh Mitchell Jr	. . . .	Pete Kendricks	Ray Adams	. . . .
Birmingham (266)	MC 205 254-2000	(not reporting)						
Boaz (7)	MC 205 593-8105	Bruce Sanford	. . . .	Mike Montgomery	Mike Montgomery	Jackie Nicholson	Bill Robinson	Kenneth Richey
Brent (3)	MC 205 926-4643	(not reporting)						
Brewton (6)	MC 205 867-3281	(not reporting)						
Bridgeport t (3)	MC 205 495-3892	(not reporting)						
Brighton (5)	MC 205 425-8934	(not reporting)						
Brundidge t (2)	MC 205 735-2385	Jimmy Ramage	. . . .	Linda M Holeman		David Barbaree	Joe Connell	. . . .
Centreville (3)	MC 205 926-4995	(not reporting)						
Chickasaw (7)	MC 205 452-6450	J C Davis Jr	. . . .	Cathy Neal	. . . .	. . . .	C E Hollinghead	Sam Rawls
Childersburg (5)	MC 205 378-5521	B J Meeks	. . . .	Frank E Humber	. . . .	Douglas Blair	Kenneth Flowers	. . . .
Citronelle (4)	MC 205 866-7973	Rannel Presnell	. . . .	Diane D Barnett	. . . .	Larry W Griffin	Clarence Parker	Kenneth Patrick
Clanton (8)	MC 205 755-1105	(not reporting)						
Columbiana (3)	MC 205 669-5800	Lewis B Walker	. . . .	Linda T Humber	. . . .	Johnny Howard Jr	Richard Todd	James Palmer
Cordova t (3)	MC 205 483-9266	(not reporting)						
Cullman (13)	MC 205 739-1212	(not reporting)						
Dadeville t (3)	MC 205 825-9242	(not reporting)						
Daleville (5)	MC 205 598-2345	Gene Hughes	Jeffrey Moon	Angelia Filmore	Dawn Dallas	. . . .	Wess Etheredge	Ray Sartin
Daphne t (11)	CO 205 621-9000	E Harry Brown	. . . .	Ruth P Martin	Kimberly S Morrow	Andrew M Hanson	Joseph H Hall	William H Eady Sr
Decatur (49)	MC 205 355-7410	(not reporting)						
Demopolis (8)	MC 205 289-0577	Austin Caldwell	. . . .	Dolly S Ward	. . . .	Mike Fuqua	Charles Avery	Clarence Brooker
Dothan (54)	CM 205 793-0100	Alfred J Saliba	Donald J Marnon	Delma R Lee	Willie C Houston	Gerald McDaniel	Harold G Locke	James C Kilgore
East Brewton t (3)	MC 205 867-6092	Terry D Clark	. . . .	Karen H Singleton	. . . .	Guyland Langham	Wilson Mallard	Steve Dunaway
Elba (4)	MC 205 897-2333	(not reporting)						
Enterprise (20)	MC 205 347-1211	John W Henderoon	Carl W Griffin	Carl W Griffin	. . . .	Billy Joe Watson	Michael Lolley	Joseph Ward
Eufaula (13)	MC 205 687-1206	(not reporting)						
Evergreen (4)	MC 205 578-1574	(not reporting)						
Fairfield (12)	MC 205 788-2492	Larry P Langford	. . . .	Melvin Turner	. . . .	Charley Carnes	Laird Sharpe	Danny Fields
Fairhope (8)	MC 205 928-2136	(not reporting)						
Fayette (5)	MC 205 932-5367	(not reporting)						
Florence (36)	MC 205 760-6400	Eddie Frost	. . . .	Steven W Eason	. . . .	Charles Cochran	Richard Thompson	. . . .
Foley (5)	MC 205 943-1545	Arthur A Holk	A Perry Wilbourne	A Perry Wilbourne	. . . .	Joseph A Bouzan	James W Anderson	. . . .
Fort Payne (12)	MC 205 845-1524	David Stout	. . . .	Jim McGee	Elaine Teague	Chester Harrison	Frank Parker	. . . .
Fultondale (6)	MC 205 841-6456	(not reporting)						
Gadsden (43)	CO 205 549-4500	(not reporting)						
Gardendale (9)	MC 205 631-8789	G William Noble	. . . .	Euel Fountain	. . . .	C G Doss	W O Campbell	W L Phillips
Geneva (5)	MC 205 684-2485	Hugh Herring Jr	Sheron Enfinger	Jennifer Aycock	. . . .	Ben Latimer	Frankie Lindsey	James Dixon
Glencoe t (5)	MC 205 492-1425	John A Sewell	. . . .	Carol Surtees	. . . .	Jerry Lay	B J Alexander	Charles Hodge
Graysville (2)	MC 205 674-5643	Wayne Tuggle	. . . .	Judy Flippo	. . . .	Randy Reid	Charles Melton	Paul Busby
Greensboro (3)	MC 205 624-8119	John C Jay Jr	Rebecca Townsend	Marjorie Davis	. . . .	. . . .	Gary A Bice	. . . .
Greenville (7)	MC 205 382-2647	C E Smith	. . . .	Linda Vandenbosch	Linda Vandenbosch	Michael Phillips	Lonzo Ingram	Herbert Gregory
Gulf Shores (3)	MC 205 968-2425	(not reporting)						
Guntersville (7)	MC 205 582-2120	(not reporting)						
Haleyville (4)	MC 205 486-3121	Larry Gilliland	A M Yarbrough	A M Yarbrough	. . . .	Leon Bridges	Kyle Reogas	. . . .
Hamilton t (6)	MC 205 921-2121	E T Sims Jr	. . . .	Barbara Partain	. . . .	Billy Loden	Tommy Wooten	. . . .
Hartford (2)	MC 205 588-2245	(not reporting)						
Hartselle (11)	MC 205 773-2535	(not reporting)						
Headland (3)	MC 205 693-3365	Sara W Holman	. . . .	Elizabeth White	. . . .	. . . .	Charles Helms	. . . .
Heflin t (3)	MC 205 463-2291	(not reporting)						
Hokes Bluff t (4)	MC 205 492-2414	(not reporting)						
Homewood (23)	MC 205 877-8620	(not reporting)						
Hoover t (40)	MC 205 978-5500	Frank S Skinner	Samuel A Harper	Linda H Crump	Richard K Smith	Thomas E Bradley	David A Cummings	Steve Brown
Hueytown (15)	MC 205 491-7010	(not reporting)						
Huntsville (160)	MC 205 532-7332	Steve R Hettinger	. . . .	Charles E Hagood	William D Newton	Darryel F Cothren	Richard V Ottman	Richard C Liles
Irondale (9)	MC 205 956-9200	David Krider	Glenda Cox	Glenda Cox	Glenda Cox	John McDanal	Wallace Gibson	Tommy Anderson
Jackson (6)	MC 205 246-2461	Norma Beard	Jesse H J Miller	Cathy Larrimore	Jesse H J Miller	Neal Bradley	William Taylor	Clifford Dolbear
Jacksonville (10)	MC 205 435-7611	George Douthit	. . . .	Jeanne Jordan	. . . .	Fermond King	Thomas Thompson	. . . .
Jasper (14)	MC 205 221-2100	(not reporting)						
Lafayette (3)	MC 205 864-7181	David Ennis	. . . .	Charles Jennings	Charles Jennings	. . . .	Robert F Lumpkin	Jack Bailey
Lanett (9)	CM 205 644-2141	(not reporting)						
Leeds (10)	MC 205 699-2585	Lynn A Maxey	. . . .	Kenneth R Ray	. . . .	Vester M Arnold	Charles A Hudson	Robert Parker Jr

MUNICIPAL OFFICIALS IN U.S. CITIES OVER 2,500

City, 1990 population figures (000 omitted), form of government	Municipal phone number	Mayor	Appointed administrator	City clerk	Finance officer	Fire chief	Police chief	Public works director
ALABAMA (135) continued								
Linden (3)	MC 205 295-4121	(not reporting)						
Lipscomb (3)	MC 205 428-6374	(not reporting)						
Livingston (4)	CM 205 652-2505	(not reporting)						
Luverne (3)	MC 205 335-3741	John D Harrison	. . . .	Bonnie N King	. . . .	Frank Turner Jr	Ronald K Cochran	Fred L Moman
Madison (15)	MC 205 772-5600	Charles E Yancura	. . . .	Betty T Benson	Lillie M Causey	Charles P Wallace	Cecil E Moses	Merlyn R Adkins
Marion (4)	MC 205 683-6545	(not reporting)						
Midfield (6)	MC 205 923-7578	(not reporting)						
Millbrook (6)	MC 205 285-6428	Arvil T Minor	. . . .	Arthur E Elsner		. . . .	Danny C Pollard	Morris Sherrill
Mobile (196)	MC 205 470-7727	Michael C Dow	Bobby Bostwick	Richard L Smith	Barbara S Malkove	Edward A Berger	Harold Johnson	. . . .
Monroeville (7)	MC 205 575-2081	Anne H Farish	. . . .	Toni L McKelvey	. . . .	Eddie Everette	William C Dailey	Lyle Salter
Montevallo (4)	MC 205 665-2555	Ralph W Sears	Steven D Gibbs	. . . .	. . . .	Alan Blackmon	Allen Needham	Howard Harkins
Montgomery (187)	MC 205 241-4417	(not reporting)						
Moulton t (3)	MC 205 974-5191	Barbara Coffey	. . . .	Bobbie Grant	. . . .	Johnny Moses	J C Holliday	. . . .
Mountain Brook (20)	CM 205 870-3532	(not reporting)						
Muscle Shoals t (10)	CO 205 383-5675	Charles Mitchell	. . . .	Clair Stratford	. . . .	Dean Lesley	David Underwood	Johnny Wisdom
Northport (17)	CM 205 339-7000	Wayne Rose	Charles T Swann	. . . .	Marcus Powell	Paul Evans	Dempsey Marcum	Larry Boshell
Oneonta (5)	MC 205 274-2150	Danny B Hicks	Martha J Walker	. . . .	. . . .	C Montgomery	David Odom	Marvin Sloan
Opelika (22)	MC 205 705-5100	Bobby J Freeman	Bob Shuman	Zane E Burleson	Mitch Price	Charlie Moore	Tommy Mangham	Boalman Johnson
Opp (7)	MC 205 493-4572	James A Moore	Charles McGowan	Betty Kelley	. . . .	Hank Gwaltney	Johnny Metcalf	. . . .
Oxford t (9)	MC 205 831-7510	Leon Smith	. . . .	Shirley Henson	. . . .	Eugene Smallwood	Stanley Merrill	. . . .
Ozark (13)	MC 205 774-5393	Billy J Blackmon	. . . .	William Blackwell	. . . .	. . . .	Alan Benefield	. . . .
Pelham t (10)	MC 205 663-3901	(not reporting)						
Pell City (8)	MC 205 338-2244	Lawrence Fields	. . . .	Peggy Lee	. . . .	Greg Barnes	Joe Davis	Wayne Duck
Phenix City (25)	CM 205 298-5649	(not reporting)						
Piedmont (5)	MC 205 447-9007	Vera Stewart	Brent Morrison	Brent Morrison		Robert Holbrook	. . . .	
Pleasant Grove (8)	MC 205 744-7221	(not reporting)						
Prattville (20)	MC 205 361-3600	David D Whetstone	. . . .	Eugene Champion	. . . .	Donald McGough	Alfred Wadsworth	Kenneth DeRamus
Prichard (34)	MC 205 457-3381	(not reporting)						
Rainbow City t (8)	MC 205 442-2511	Sue L Glidewell	. . . .	Barbara Wester	Sue L Glidewell	Russell E Wimpee	Morris Alexander	Charles Foster
Rainsville t (4)	MC 205 638-6331	Roy Sanderson	. . . .	Judy Lewis	. . . .	Ronnie Helton	Billy R Williams	. . . .
Red Bay (3)	MC 205 356-4473	Billy M Bolton	Charlene Fancher	Cindy Green	. . . .	Ogene Harrison	Charles Garrison	Alan Bostick
Roanoke (6)	MC 205 863-4129	(not reporting)						
Roosevelt (..)	MC 205 426-1261	(not reporting)						
Russellville (8)	MC 502 726-5000	(not reporting)						
Saraland (12)	MC 205 675-5103	Frank Pridgen Jr	. . . .	Barbara Timothy	. . . .	Ravon E Allen	Gerald V Young	Cecil B Smith
Satsuma (5)	MC 205 675-1440	(not reporting)						
Scottsboro (14)	MC 205 574-3100	(not reporting)						
Selma (24)	MC 205 874-2105	(not reporting)						
Sheffield (10)	CO 205 383-0250	(not reporting)						
Southside t (6)	MC 205 442-2255	(not reporting)						
Stevenson (2)	MC 205 437-3000	James W Matthews	Bettye Jackson	Bettye Jackson	. . . .	Mack Morris	James Kerby	. . . .
Sumiton t (3)	MC 205 648-3261	(not reporting)						
Sylacauga (13)	MC 205 245-3421	(not reporting)						
Talladega (18)	MC 205 362-8186	(not reporting)						
Tallassee (5)	MC 205 283-6571	(not reporting)						
Tarrant City (8)	MC 205 841-2758	(not reporting)						
Thomasville (4)	MC 205 636-5827	(not reporting)						
Troy (13)	CO 205 566-0177	(not reporting)						
Trussville t (8)	MC 205 655-7478	Charles Grover	. . . .	Lynn B Honeycutt	. . . .	David Griffith	Irving A Nash	Lewis V Simpson
Tuscaloosa (78)	MC 205 349-0125	Alvin P DuPont	. . . .	Byron Findley Jr	James M Wright	Thomas M Davis	Ken W Swindle	Richard Curry
Tuscumbia (8)	CO 205 383-5463	(not reporting)						
Tuskegee (12)	MC 205 727-2180	Johnny Ford	. . . .	Hattie King	James C B Samuel	Luther Curry	David Warren	William Foster
Union Springs (4)	MC 205 738-2720	Durden Dean	. . . .	Doris Roten	. . . .	Thomas May	E L Love	Willie Parker
Valley (8)	MC 205 756-3131	Bobby L Crowder	Charles W Story	Martha N Cato	. . . .	. . . .	Jack A Manley	Jack A Manley
Vernon (2)	MC 205 695-7718	(not reporting)						
Vestavia Hills (20)	MC 205 978-1000	C Pat Reynolds	. . . .	Thelma Moon	T M Jones	Bill Towers	Douglas Jefferson	Perry Glass
Warrior (3)	MC 205 647-0521	Rena Hudson	. . . .	Joyce B Brooks	. . . .	Claude Watson	Michael H Thrash	. . . .
Weaver t (3)	MC 205 820-1125	W E Kimbrough	. . . .	Nanette M Estes	. . . .	Bill Smith	Gary Carroll	Rickey L Steele
Wetumpka (5)	MC 205 567-5147	(not reporting)						
Winfield (4)	MC 205 487-4337	William D Sager	. . . .	June East	. . . .	Ray Westbrook	Thomas E Fields	Denver L Miles
York (3)	MC 205 392-5231	Joseph F Stegall	. . . .	Janice R Pringle	Janice R Pringle	Stephen Lang	Cleveland Brown	John E Stallings
ALASKA (29)								
Anchorage (226)	MC 907 343-4425	Tom Fink	Larry Crawford	Lejane Ferguson	Jerry Anderson	Larry Langston	Kevin O'Leary	Ken Canfield
Barrow (3)	MC 907 852-5211	(not reporting)						
Bethel (5)	CM 907 543-2297	James H Feaster	William J Hunter	Jane Elam	Lawrence Elam	George Young	Chris Liu	Ron Kwiatkowski
Cordova (2)	CM 907 424-6200	Kelly Weaverling	Gary Lewis	Lynda Plant	Don Walter	Dewey Whetsell	Kevin Clayton	Jeff Currier
Dillingham (2)	CM 907 842-5211	Tom Tilden	Henry E Graper Jr	Vivian Braswell	. . . .	Lance Nunn	Ralph Taylor	Steve D Hardin
Fairbanks (31)	CM 907 459-6781	James C Hayes	Robert R Wolting	Toni W Nigro	Barbara Koneczny	. . . .	Michael E Pulice	David D Jacoby
Fort Yukon (1)	CM 907 662-2379	Vera B James	David C Smith	Vickie Thomas	Walter J Peter	Grafton Bergman	Zelma Fairchild	Grafton Bergman
Galena (1)	CM 907 656-1301	(not reporting)						
Homer (4)	CM 907 235-8121	Harry Gregoire	Richard J Leland	Mary L Shannon	Val Koeberlein	Robert Purcell	Michael Daugherty	Hugh Bevan
Juneau (27)	CM 907 586-5240	Jamie Parsons	Mark Palesh	Patty Ann Polley	Craig Duncan	Larry Fanning	Mike Gelston	Ernie Mueller
Kenai (6)	CM 907 283-7530	John Williams	Thomas Manninen	Carol Freas	Charles Brown	David Burnett	Daniel Morris	Keith Kornelis
Ketchikan (8)	CM 907 225-3111	Alaire E Stanton	John L Pearson	Karen C Miles	Robert E Newel	David O'Sullivan	Daniel Anslinger	Fred D Monrean
Kodiak (6)	CM 907 486-8640	Walter E Johnson	Gary Bloomquist	Marcella H Dalke	Roy A Deebel	Mike Dolph	Jack McDonald	John E Sullivan
Kotzebue (3)	CM 907 442-2877	Willie Goodwin Jr	Jeff S Smith	Sally J Melton	Judith F Bennett	Ronald Monson	Lawrence Wallace	Clinton Rabern
Mountain Village (1)	MC 907 591-2929	(not reporting)						
Nome (4)	CM 907 443-5242	John K Handeland	Paul R Day	Linda E Conley	Caroline Reardon	Robert K Lewis	Robert L Kauer	Paul R Day
Palmer (3)	CM 907 745-3271	George Carte	David L Soulak	David L Soulak	George Castaneda	Daniel Contini	Ronald Otte	Vic Gretzinger
Petersburg (3)	CM 907 772-4519	D A Coon	William Robinson	Patricia Curtiss	. . . .	N Fredricksen	Marvin Ronimous	Eli Lucas
Seldovia (..)	CM 907 234-7643	Gerald W Willard	Ivan L Widom	Frances L Eckoldt	. . . .	. . . .	A W Anderson	John Mickelson
Seward (3)	CM 907 224-3331	David Crane	Bradley T Jones	Linda Murphy	Rick Gifford	John Gage	Tom Walker	David Calvert
Sitka (9)	MC 907 747-3294	Dan Keck	Gary Paxton	Melinda Jenkins	John Sweeney	Doug Karpstein	John Newell	Richard Smith
Skagway (1)	MC 907 983-2297	Stan Selmer	James Filip	Lorene Gordon	. . . .	Carl Mulvihill	David Sexton	. . . .
Soldotna (3)	CM 907 262-9107	William S Reeder	R L Underkofler	Patricia Burdick	Joel L Wilkins	. . . .	Walter Bonner	David Bunnell
St. Mary's (..)	CM 907 438-2515	(not reporting)						
Unalaska (3)	CM 907 581-1251	Frank Kelty	Mark Earnest	Debra Dushkin	Tom Graham	. . . .	Glenn Herbst	Roe Sturgulewski
Valdez (4)	CM 907 835-4313	John Harris	Douglas Griffin	Jeanne Donald	. . . .	Charles Lundfelt	Bert Cottle	Lee Schlitz
Whittier (1)	CM 907 472-2337	Kelly Carlisle	Gary Williams	Carolyn Fisher	Roger Casad	Roy Swanson	Max Hurlbut	Richard Amerman
Wrangell (2)	MC 907 874-2381	Edward Rilatos Jr	Duane Gasaway	Franette Vincent	Jeff Jabusch	Timothy Buness	Brent Moody	Robert Caldwell
Yakutat (1)	CM 907 784-3323	Daryl James	Carl L Hille	Mona Swanson	Martha R Ross	Larry Powell	Richard Brown	Raymond Mapes

Directory 1/9 continued **MUNICIPAL OFFICIALS IN U.S. CITIES OVER 2,500**

City, 1990 population figures (000 omitted), form of government	Municipal phone number	Mayor	Appointed administrator	City clerk	Finance officer	Fire chief	Police chief	Public works director
ARIZONA (65)								
Apache Junction (18)	CM 602 982-8002	(not reporting)						
Avondale (16)	CM 602 932-2400	(not reporting)						
Benson (4)	CM 602 586-2245	(not reporting)						
Bisbee (6)	CM 602 432-5446	(not reporting)						
Buckeye t (5)	CM 602 256-2488	Joseph Schettino	Fred C Carpenter	Fred C Carpenter	Fred C Carpenter	Alan Calvert	Harry Bishop	Ron Long
Camp Verde t (6)	CM 602 567-6631	Carter Rogers	Jack Niner	. . . .	Dane Bullard	. . . .	Chuck Devine	. . . .
Casa Grande (19)	CM 602 421-8600	Bob Mitchell	Kent A Myers	Gloria Haro	Frank N Brown	Randy Baldridge	Don Maxon	Robert Jackson
Cave Creek t (3)	CM 602 488-1400	R E Bartholomew	Carl J Stephani	Carl J Stephani				
Chandler (91)	CM 602 786-2740	Coy Payne	John M Pinch	Carolyn H Dunn	Barry H Webber	James P Roxburgh	Ronald Danielson	George E Selvia
Chino Valley t (5)	CM 602 636-2646	(not reporting)						
Clifton t (3)	CM 602 865-4146	David McCullar	Mark Fooks	Espie Castaneda	. . . .	Nazario Hernandez	Kenneth Stephens	Nazario Hernandez
Coolidge (7)	CM 602 723-5361	Michael L Minter	Martin A Colburn	Lucy Fitzpatrick	. . . .	Mickey S McHugh	Meredith D Jenson	Donald Peters
Cottonwood (6)	CM 602 634-5526	Joseph Jones	Brian Mickelsen	Marianne Kistner	Robert Lynch	Don Eberle	Roy Finch	Timothy Costello
Douglas (13)	CM 602 364-7501	Elizabeth Ames	Adriana M Garza	Victor Stevens	Victor Stevens	John Harris	Charles Austin	Ben Laforge
Eagar t (4)	CM 602 333-4128	George Pena	Bill Greenwood	Karen Merrill	Cynthia Snyder	Howard Carlson	Lester James	Douglas Pike
El Mirage (5)	CM 602 972-8116	Maggie Reese	Jose G Solarez	Rosalinda Herrera	Jose G Solarez	Eddie Rios	Ed Calles	. . . .
Eloy (7)	CM 602 466-9201	Armida Flores	John F Vidaurri	Mary Ridgell	Jean Carlisle	Lonnie Madewell	James Griffith	Charles Coyle
Flagstaff (46)	CM 602 774-5281	Chris Bavasi	Dave Wilcox	Linda Butler	Mary Jo Jenkins	Dean Treadway	Gary Latham	Bill Menard
Florence t (8)	MC 602 868-5889	Oscar Padilla	Brett Nelson	Victoria Celaya	Sara Lawrence	Rick Evans	Tom Rankin	Pat Granillo
Fountain Hills t (10)	CM 602 837-2003	John Cutillo	. . . .	Cassie Hansen	. . . .	. . . .	. . . .	. . . .
Gila Bend t (2)	MC 602 683-2255	(not reporting)						
Gilbert t (29)	CM 602 892-0802	Wilburn Brown	Kent Cooper	Phyllis Alberty	Marc Anderson	John Garcilaso	Fred Dees	Chuck Strand
Glendale (148)	CM 602 435-4121	Elaine Scruggs	Martin Vanacour	Lavergne Behm	Arthur Lynch	John Nunes	Robert Forry	Ken Reedy
Globe (6)	CM 602 425-2442	(not reporting)						
Goodyear (6)	CM 602 932-3910	Carl K Gow	Stephen Cleveland	Barbara Dunaway	Jean Pace	Mark Gaillard	Peter Nick	Lynn Kartchner
Guadalupe t (5)	CM 602 730-3080	(not reporting)						
Hayden t (1)	CM 602 356-7801	(not reporting)						
Holbrook (5)	CM 602 524-2927	Richard Mester	William A Kelly	William A Kelly	Blaine Hatch	Jack Hillebert	Kenneth Moore	. . . .
Kearny t (2)	CM 602 363-5547	Ken Huish	Terry Hinton	Lorraine Birkett	Lorraine Birkett	Dale Huddleston	Terry Hinton	Ray Burgess
Kingman (13)	CM 602 753-5561	Carol Anderson	Lou Sorensen	Charlene Ware	James Jordan	Chuck Osterman	Carrol Brown	Ed Covington
Lake Havasu City (24)	CM 602 855-2116	Richard L Hileman	Larry D Price	Ann R Sayne	Carol Mitchell	Robert Ward	Victor M Wilkins	William R Madigan
Litchfield Park (..)	CM 602 935-5033	(not reporting)						
Mesa (288)	MC 602 644-2365	Wong	Luster	Hogue	Ayers	Oliver	Meeks	Crandall
Miami t (2)	MC 602 473-4403	(not reporting)						
Nogales (19)	MC 602 287-6571	Jose L Canchola	Fernando Castro	Fernando Castro	Chris Byroad	Hector Robles	Jose Luis Alday	Manuel Ruiz
Oro Valley t (7)	CM 602 297-2591	(not reporting)						
Page (7)	CM 602 645-8861	Gary Scaramazzo	Curtis A Shook	Kaye Findlay	Wilkie L Miller	Terry B Allen	Richard C Obergh	Carl E Elleard
Paradise Valley t (12)	CM 602 948-7411	J David Hann	John L Baudek	. . . .	Lenore Lancaster	. . . .	Donald Lozier	. . . .
Parker t (3)	MC 602 669-9265	(not reporting)						
Payson (8)	CM 602 474-5242	B Craig Swartwood	Ken Buchanan	Linda Foster	Wiliam R Ingram	Charles Jacobs	Gordon Gartner	Colin Walker
Peoria (51)	CM 602 412-7000	Kenenth Forgia	Peter C Harvey	Janice Graziano	Jorge G Cruz Aedo	Michael Fusco	Michael Strope	Kevin Kadlec
Phoenix (983)	CM 602 262-6941	(not reporting)						
Pinetop-Lakeside t (2)	CM 602 368-8696	Larry Vicario	Paul M Watson	Leslee M Wessel	Wm A Beecroft	. . . .	Terry Ringey	. . . .
Prescott (26)	CM 602 445-3500	Daiton Rutkowski	Mark C Stevens	Marie Watson	N Carl Tenney	Ronald Prince	Robert Reed	Thomas Long
Prescott Valley t (9)	CM 602 772-9207	Harvey Skoog	Kenneth Rittmer	Linda J Thorson	Linda J Thorson	. . . .	Charles E Seder	Larry Tarkowski
Quartzsite t (2)	CM 602 927-4333	(not reporting)						
Safford (7)	CM 602 428-2762	Van Talley	Kip Bingham	Sherrie Farar	Ron Jacobson	Dick Bingham	Dennis Thompson	Robert Porter
Scottsdale (130)	CM 602 994-2690	H Drinkwater	Richard Bowers	Sonia Robertson	James Jenkins	. . . .	M Heidingsfield	. . . .
Show Low (5)	CM 602 537-5724	(not reporting)						
Sierra Vista (33)	CM 602 458-3315	Richard Archer	James Whitlock	Sandra Kenny	Mary Abrahams	. . . .	Arthur Montgomery	George Michael
Snowflake t (4)	CM 602 536-7103	Ray Caldwell	Roy W Hunt	Barbara Bigler	Roy W Hunt	John Hagelstien	Carl W Schaefer	Jim Langston
Somerton (5)	MC 602 627-8866	Vivan Robinson	Enrique Castillo	Enrique Castillo	Mark Ryan	Paul Deanda	Terry Hollis	Edmundo Mendez
South Tucson (5)	CM 602 792-2424	Shirley Villegas	William L Ponder	Dolores Robles	William L Ponder	Henry Vega	. . . .	Rene Gastelum
St. Johns (3)	CM 602 337-4517	(not reporting)						
Superior t (3)	MC 602 689-5752	(not reporting)						
Surprise t (7)	CM 602 583-1000	Roy Villanueva	Richard McComb	. . . .	Vito Tedeschi	Robert Weekley	Garvin Arrell	Herschell Morrow
Tempe (142)	CM 602 350-8276	Harry Mitchell	Terry Zerkle	Helen Fowler	Patrick Flynn	Cliff Jones	David Brown	Jim Jones
Thatcher t (4)	MC 602 428-2290	(not reporting)						
Tolleson (4)	CM 602 936-7111	Charles P Hayes	Ralph Velez	Rosemarie M Booth	Bruce Johnson	Arthur Wendell	Rick Patschieder	Manuel Dominguez
Tucson (405)	CM 602 791-4241	George Miller	Michael Brown	Kathleen Detrick	Kay Gray	Fred Shipman	Elaine Hedtke	. . . .
Wickenburg t (5)	CM 602 684-5451	Dallas C Gant	Ben J Nardelli	Edna C Grieves	Tom Candelaria	Joe T Walters	William Willmann	Coney Orosco
Willcox (3)	CM 602 384-4271	Sandra L Ousley	Mac D Manning Jr	Cristina G Whelan	Larry D Rains	Daniel Ritenour	V E Jones	Rene L Diaz
Williams (3)	CM 602 635-4451	Calder W Chapman	Matt Winkel	Marian C Rock	Jill Brown	Jerry Fuller	John Cardani	. . . .
Winslow (8)	MC 602 289-2422	Georgia Metzger	Baldev Josan	Linda Samson	Ken Mitchell	Boney Candelaria	Wayne Wagner	Ray Moss
Yuma (55)	CM 602 783-1278	Robert Tippett	Douglas Lowe	. . . .	Robert Stull	Philip Mele	William Robinson	Larry Hunt
ARKANSAS (92)								
Alma (3)	MC 501 632-4119	(not reporting)						
Arkadelphia (10)	CM 501 246-9864	(not reporting)						
Ashdown (5)	MC 501 898-2622	(not reporting)						
Atkins (3)	MC 501 641-2900	(not reporting)						
Augusta (3)	MC 501 347-5656	(not reporting)						
Bald Knob (3)	MC 501 724-6371	(not reporting)						
Barling (4)	MC 501 452-1556	(not reporting)						
Batesville (9)	MC 501 698-2400	James F Barnett	. . . .	Denise Johnston	. . . .	Bobby Davis	. . . .	Sanford St John
Beebe (4)	MC 501 882-3365	Philip Petray	. . . .	Rebecca Short	. . . .	Bill Nick	Lester Parchman	. . . .
Benton (18)	MC 501 776-5900	Jimmy F Presnall	. . . .	Margaret Ramsey	John P Walden	Sam McCallie	Richard Elmendorf	. . . .
Bentonville (11)	MC 501 271-3112	Don M O'Neal	. . . .	Terry Coberly	William Spurlock	Leon Reece	James Allen	. . . .
Berryville (3)	MC 501 423-4414	(not reporting)						
Blytheville (23)	MC 501 763-3602	(not reporting)						
Booneville (4)	MC 501 675-3811	Brian Mueller	. . . .	Melinda Smith	. . . .	David Hardin	Ricky West	. . . .
Brinkley (4)	MC 501 734-1382	(not reporting)						
Bryant (5)	MC 501 847-0292	Roy Bishop	. . . .	Wanda Smith	Mary Jane Alpe	Van B Alexander	James A Hipps	. . . .
Cabot (8)	MC 501 843-3566	Jay D Smith	. . . .	Marva Verkler	. . . .	Calr Pickard	Paul Eddy	. . . .
Camden (14)	CM 501 836-6436	Steve Crumpler	Charles W Bell	Preston L Woods	Preston L Woods	W Phillip Seaton	Micheal Paladino	Harlan B Benson
Carlisle (2)	MC 501 552-3120	Pat Clyburn	. . . .	Brenda Wright	. . . .	Joe Cunningham	Steve Lee	Rick Sumner
Clarksville (6)	MC 501 754-6486	(not reporting)						
Conway (26)	MC 501 327-3392	(not reporting)						
Corning (3)	MC 501 857-6716	(not reporting)						
Crossett (6)	MC 501 364-4131	(not reporting)						
Dardanelle (4)	MC 501 229-4500	(not reporting)						
De Queen (5)	CM 501 584-3445	(not reporting)						
De Witt (4)	MC 501 946-2191	(not reporting)						
Dermott (5)	MC 501 538-5251	Frank Henry Jr	. . . .	Kathryn McDaniel	. . . .	Morris Parker	Jerry Melton	Carrol Jackson

Directory 1/9
continued

**MUNICIPAL OFFICIALS
IN U.S. CITIES OVER 2,500**

City, 1990 population figures (000 omitted), form of government	Municipal phone number	Mayor	Appointed administrator	City clerk	Finance officer	Fire chief	Police chief	Public works director
ARKANSAS (92) continued								
Dumas (6)	MC 501 382-2121	Lewis R Baker	. . . .	Mary S Howard	. . . .	David Byrd	Everett Cox	. . . .
Earle (3)	MC 501 792-8909	(not reporting)						
El Dorado (23)	MC 501 862-7911	(not reporting)						
England (3)	MC 501 842-3911	Roy Cox	Ruth Baker	Ruth Baker	. . . .	Gene Harp	Randy Krablin	. . . .
Eudora (3)	MC 501 355-4436	(not reporting)						
Fayetteville (42)	CM 501 521-7700	(not reporting)						
Fordyce (5)	MC 501 352-2198	(not reporting)						
Forrest City (13)	MC 501 633-1692	Danny W Ferguson	. . . .	Christine Gates	. . . .	Bobby G Johnson	James Goff	Clovis Macon
Fort Smith (73)	CM 501 784-2201	(not reporting)						
Gosnell (4)	MC 501 532-8544	(not reporting)						
Greenwood (4)	MC 501 996-2742	Joe W Siegmund	. . . .	Linda Bryant	. . . .	Kenneth Bryan	Robert Hicks	. . . .
Gurdon (2)	MC 501 353-2514	(not reporting)						
Hamburg (3)	MC 501 853-5300	Boyce E Harrod	. . . .	Brenda S Graham	. . . .	Tab Harrod	David L Sims	Earle Benson
Harrison (10)	MC 501 741-2525	William Gregg	. . . .	Ray Noell	Richard McComas	Tom Walker	Wayne Cone	Frank Gelinas
Heber Springs (6)	MC 501 362-6647	Edward Roper	. . . .	Norma J Martin	. . . .	F D Valentine	Fred L Byford	Royce V Riggs
Helena (7)	MC 501 338-9831	Joann D Smith	. . . .	Louise Galloway	. . . .	Jeff Wages	Boyd Williams	Dennis Sullivan
Hope (10)	CM 501 777-6701	. . . .	David Meriwether	Leneta Hare	Debra Cummings	Joe Don Webb	Richard Thomas	. . . .
Hot Springs (32)	CM 501 321-6800	Melinda Baran	Gus Pappas	Lance Hudnell	Jim Scott	Arval Sanders	Martin White	Jim Atchley
Hoxie (3)	MC 501 886-2742	(not reporting)						
Jacksonville (29)	MC 501 982-3181	Tommy Swaim	. . . .	Lula Mae Leonard	Paul Mushrush	Rick Ezell	Don Tate	James Spears
Jonesboro (47)	MC 501 932-1052	(not reporting)						
Lake Village (3)	MC 501 265-2228	Joanne H Vencill	. . . .	Harolyn Keith	. . . .	Larry Donaldson	. . . .	. . . .
Little Rock (176)	CM 501 371-4510	(not reporting)						
Lonoke (4)	MC 501 676-6123	Jack W Wheat	Delilah Chivers	John Latimer	Delilah Chivers	David Evans Jr	Floyd R Van Horn	Tony Scroggins
Magnolia (11)	MC 501 234-1375	George Wheatley	. . . .	Judy Whitelaw	. . . .	Herschel Hampton	Larry Taylor	Roy Waters
Malvern (9)	MC 501 332-3638	(not reporting)						
Manila (3)	MC 501 561-4437	(not reporting)						
Marianna (6)	MC 501 295-2700	Martin Chaffin	Dorothy Willis	Dorothy Willis	. . . .	Jack R Gentry	Barry V Downs	Jack Dilks Jr
Marion (4)	MC 501 739-3071	(not reporting)						
Marked Tree (3)	MC 501 358-3216	Lawrence Ashlock	. . . .	Paul Hutchins	. . . .	Danny Johnson	Orbie James Crum	Clifton Parham
Maumelle (..)	CM 501 851-2500	. . . .	Gerald Boon	Beverly Masters	. . . .	. . . .	Norman Moseley	Robert Cogdell
Mc Gehee (5)	MC 501 222-3160	Rosalie Gould	. . . .	Frances Sims	. . . .	. . . .	Clifford Madsen	. . . .
Mena (5)	MC 501 394-4585	(not reporting)						
Monticello (8)	MC 501 367-3415	Harold West	. . . .	Glenda F Nichols	Reva L Abbolt	Raymond Chisom	Robert Maxwell	Charles Quimby
Morrilton (7)	MC 501 354-3484	(not reporting)						
Mountain Home (9)	MC 501 425-5116	John Ayers	Sherry Harris	. . . .	. . . .	Dale Harris	Paul Doak	. . . .
Nashville (5)	MC 501 845-7400	(not reporting)						
Newport (7)	MC 501 523-2167	Wayne Beard	. . . .	Elwanda Templeton	. . . .	Harry Benish Jr	David Stewart	Burt Willard
North Little Rock (62)	MC 501 758-6126	Patrick H Hays	Joe Smith	Mary L Munns	Bob Sisson	Charles Redding	William P Nolan	John Blodgett
Osceola (9)	MC 501 563-5102	(not reporting)						
Ozark (3)	MC 501 667-2238	Vernon McDaniel	. . . .	Larhonda Melton	. . . .	. . . .	Lonnie C Ellison	. . . .
Paragould (19)	MC 501 239-7510	Charles Partlow	. . . .	Goldie Wide	. . . .	Eddie Brown	Dennis Hyde	Jacksie Jamison
Paris (4)	MC 501 963-2450	(not reporting)						
Piggott (4)	MC 501 598-2388	(not reporting)						
Pine Bluff (57)	MC 501 543-1840	(not reporting)						
Pocahontas (6)	MC 501 892-3924	John Patrick	. . . .	Elizabeth Penn	. . . .	Jerry Matheny	Charles Meridith	. . . .
Prescott (4)	MC 501 887-2210	(not reporting)						
Rogers (25)	MC 501 621-1117	John W Sampier	. . . .	Sandra Fearman	. . . .	Kenneth Riley	Charles Jones	. . . .
Russellville (21)	MC 501 968-2098	Woody Harris	. . . .	Helen Price	. . . .	Ray Hobby	John Waterson	Les Church
Searcy (15)	MC 501 268-2483	(not reporting)						
Sheridan (3)	MC 501 942-3921	(not reporting)						
Sherwood (19)	MC 501 835-5319	Bill Harmon	. . . .	Bobbie Chapman	. . . .	. . . .	Jim Crockett	Denver Gentry
Siloam Springs (8)	CM 501 524-5136	M L Van Poucke Jr	. . . .	Peggy Woody	. . . .	Wayne Brashear	Albert Gregory	Richard Stone
Springdale (30)	MC 501 750-8114	Charles McKinney	. . . .	Mida Neff	. . . .	Dan White	Gary Payne	. . . .
Stamps (2)	MC 501 533-4771	Linda B Conlin	. . . .	Gayla Teague	. . . .	James Good	Al Dyer	. . . .
Stuttgart (10)	MC 501 673-3535	H E Raines	. . . .	Mitri Greenhill	Jane Jackson	Edward Lynch	Aubrey Roswell	Frank Dent
Texarkana (23)	CM 501 774-3161	Danny Gray	Bruno Rumbelow	Sandra Powell	Frank Pryor	Mark McCarty	Robert Harrison	Ronald Homeyer
Trumann t (6)	MC 501 483-5355	(not reporting)						
Van Buren (15)	MC 501 474-1541	(not reporting)						
Waldron (3)	MC 501 637-3181	(not reporting)						
Walnut Ridge (4)	MC 501 886-6638	(not reporting)						
Warren (6)	MC 501 226-6743	R Gregg Reep	. . . .	Bertia M Lassiter	R Gregg Reep	Bob Stedman	Bob Outlaw	. . . .
West Helena (10)	MC 501 572-2528	Bob Teeter	. . . .	Renee Knowlton	. . . .	Earl Meiers	Johnny Goings	H T Wilborn
West Memphis (28)	MC 501 732-7500	Keith Ingram	. . . .	Dan Craft	Wyman Morgan	Mac Holmes	Bobby Sanders	Ward Wimbish
Wynne (8)	MC 501 238-9171	James C Luker	. . . .	. . . .	. . . .	Dan Curtner	Lynn Rodgers	Henry Williams
CALIFORNIA (429)								
Adelanto (9)	MC 619 246-2300	Mary Scarpa	Pat Chamberlaine	Sharon Gasaway	Michael Sakamoto	Gary Long	Robert Gardner	. . . .
Agoura Hills (20)	CM 818 597-7300	Ed Kurtz	Terry Matz	Patricia Manning	Elaine Graves	. . . .	. . . .	V Mastrosimone
Alameda (76)	CM 510 748-4521	E William Withrow	William Norton	Diane Felsch	Zenda James	Robert LaGrone	William Schmitz	Robert Warnick
Albany (16)	CM 510 528-5710	(not reporting)						
Alhambra (82)	CM 818 570-5007	. . . .	Julio Fuentes	Frances Moore	Derek Hanway	Raymond Brooks	Russell Siverling	Terry James
Alturas (3)	CM 916 233-2512	(not reporting)						
American Canyon (8)	CM 707 647-4360	(not reporting)						
Anaheim (266)	CM 714 254-5100	Thomas Daly	. . . .	Lee Sohl	George Ferrone	Jeffrey Bowman	. . . .	Gary Johnson
Anderson (8)	CM 916 378-6626	Peter A Smolenski	William A Murphy	Jacqueline Sharp	Carol Martin	. . . .	Phil Raner	Gary Lighthall
Angels (2)	CM 209 736-2181	(not reporting)						
Antioch (62)	CM 510 778-3501	Joel Keller	David Rowlands	Florence Rundall	John Tasker	. . . .	David Lewis	Stanford Davis
Apple Valley t (..)	CM 619 240-7051	Kathy Davis	Wayne Lamoreaux	Eunice Puckett	Kevin Smith	. . . .	Mike Cardwell	Bruce Williams
Arcadia (48)	CM 818 574-5400	Joseph Ciraulo	Donald R Duckwort	June Alford	James Dale	Gerald Gardner	Neal Johnson	Joseph Lopez
Arcata (15)	CM 707 822-5953	Victor Schaub	Alice Harris	Alice Harris	Daphne Hodgson	. . . .	Mel Brown	Stephen J Leiker
Arroyo Grande (14)	CM 805 489-1303	M P Gallagher	C Christiansen	Nancy A Davis	David Bacon	Kurt Latipow	Rick Terborch	Van W Laurn
Artesia (15)	CM 310 865-6262	James A Van Horn	Paul J Philips	Patricia Mitchell	. . . .	. . . .	. . . .	Chuck Bernal
Arvin (9)	CM 805 854-3134	Jess Ortiz	Thomas A Payne	Gola Manasco	Joseph Hanna	. . . .	. . . .	Terry Freeman
Atascadero (23)	MC 805 461-5010	Marty Kudlac	Andrew J Takata	Lee Price	Mark Joseph	Michael P McCain	Richard H McHale	. . . .
Atherton t (7)	CM 415 325-4457	. . . .	Judy Kelsey	Julie Mitchum	Melissa Eddy	. . . .	Patrick Rolle	Troy Henderson
Atwater (22)	CM 209 357-6314	(not reporting)						
Auburn (11)	CM 916 823-4211	D C Taylor	Nicholas Willick	Rebecca Bearry	Richard Crimbly	Howard Leal	Michael Morello	Richard Plecker
Avalon (3)	CM 310 510-0220	Hugh T Smith	Chuck Prince	Shirley Davy	David Batt	Jack Goslin	. . . .	Dick Gosselin
Avenal (10)	CM 209 386-5766	Kelly Granger	Russ Carlsen	Esther O Strong	. . . .	. . . .	. . . .	Jerry Watson
Azusa (41)	CM 818 334-5125	Eugene Moses	Henry Garcia	Adolph Solis	Geoffrey Craig	. . . .	Byron Nelson	. . . .
Bakersfield (175)	CM 805 326-3773	. . . .	. . . .	. . . .	. . . .	. . . .	. . . .	. . . .
Baldwin Park (69)	CM 818 960-4011	Fidel A Vargas	Donald E Penman	Linda L Gair	Carl L Yeats	. . . .	Carmine R Lanza	Sid J Mousavi

Directory 1/9 continued **MUNICIPAL OFFICIALS IN U.S. CITIES OVER 2,500**

City, 1990 population figures (000 omitted), form of government		Municipal phone number	Mayor	Appointed administrator	City clerk	Finance officer	Fire chief	Police chief	Public works director
CALIFORNIA (429) continued									
Banning (21)	CM	714 922-1295	Gary E Reynolds	Raymond Schweitzer	Lucille Elizondo	Willis S Olson	Carl Sparks	Russ Cross	Paul Toor
Barstow (21)	CM	619 256-3531	Malvin Wessel	....	Donna Sluder	Evelyn Radel	....	Robert Sessions	....
Beaumont (10)	CM	714 845-4321	Jan Lega	Dayle Keller	Dayle Keller	Ronney Wong	....	Patrick Smith	....
Bell (34)	CM	213 588-6211	Ray Johnson	Robert Rizzo	Patricia Casjens	E Van Note	....	Michael Trevis	Annette Peretz
Bell Gardens (42)	CM	310 806-4500	Frank Duran	Charles Gomez	Lucie Recio	....	....	Andy Romero	S Steinbrecher
Bellflower (62)	CM	310 804-1424	(not reporting)						
Belmont (24)	MC	415 595-7408	David Bomberger	Richard Haffey	Dorothy Hall	Sandra Salerno	Richard Latreille	Michael Oliver	John Hopkins
Belvedere (2)	CM	415 435-3838	Kenenth G Johnson	Edmund San Diego	Edmund San Diego	Edmund San Diego	....	Gary Lester	....
Benicia (24)	CM	707 746-4210	Ernest Cirrochi	Michael Warren	Frances Greco	Alan Nadritch	Ken Hanley	Otto Giuliani	Virgil Mustain
Berkeley (103)	CM	510 644-6960	Ilona Hancock	Weldon Rucker	Renata Tubman	Philip Kamlarz	Gary Cates	Daschel Butler	Vicki Elmer
Beverly Hills (32)	CM	310 285-1000	....	Mark Scott	Jean Ushijima	Don Oblander	Bill Daley	Marv Iannone	Dan Webster
Big Bear Lake (5)	CM	714 866-5831	Walt Dwyer	Stephen L Wright	Kathy Jefferies	....	Ed Kimbrough	....	Thomas Covey
Bishop (3)	CM	619 873-5863	Roger Rogers	Richard F Pucci	Richard F Pucci	Richard F Pucci	Phillip Moxley	Frederick Coburn	Andrew Boyd
Blythe (8)	CM	619 922-6161	Thomas Farrage	Lester B Nelson	J Newell Sorensen	Patricia Stewart	Ray Pease	Larry Vandiver	Charles Hull Jr
Bradbury (1)	MC	818 358-3218	Audrey Hon	Keene Wilson	Claudia Vestal	....	....	....	....
Brawley (19)	CM	619 344-9111	(not reporting)						
Brea (33)	CM	714 990-7600	Burnie Dunlap	Frank Benest	Elaine Capps	Lawrence Hurst	William Simpkins	Donald Forkus	Patrick McCarron
Brentwood (8)	CM	510 634-6900	Arthur Gonzales	Donald Russell	Vilma Ring	....	....	Larry Shaw	David Bryan
Brisbane (3)	CM	415 467-1515	Lee J Panza	Robin Leiter	Angelina Reyes	Gul Ramchandani	Scott Kenley	Tom Hitchcock	Jim Thompson
Brooktrails (Csd) tp (3)	MC	707 459-2494	Bill Edmonson	Paul Williams	....	....	Dave Thomen	....	....
Buena Park (69)	CM	714 562-3500	(not reporting)						
Burbank (94)	CM	818 953-9700	George E Battey	Robert R Ovrom	Margaret Lauerman	John K Nicoll	Michael W Davis	David P Newsham	Ora Lampman
Burlingame (27)	CM	415 696-7206	A C Harrison	Dennis Argyres	Judith Malfatti	Rahn Becker	Malcolm Towns	Alfred Palmer	Ralph Kirkup
Calabasas (..)	CM	818 878-4225	Marvin Lopata	Charles R Cate	Robin Parker	Sheila Cumberland	....	....	....
Calexico (19)	CM	619 756-2110	Antonio P Tirado	Alejandro Armenta	Lourdes Cordova	Judith Hashem	Carlos Escalante	Torivio Flores	Mariano Martinez
California City (6)	MC	619 373-8661	Richard L Moser	Stephan A West	Helen Dennis	Terry L Hicks	Richard Hall	Wayne Dickerson	Kenneth Redfern
Calimesa (12)	CM	714 795-9801	Shirley Morton	Dennis R Halloway	....	....	....	....	Duane Fessenden
Calipatria (3)	MC	714 348-2293	(not reporting)						
Calistoga (4)	CM	707 942-2800	(not reporting)						
Camarillo (52)	CM	805 388-5307	Charlotte Craven	J William Little	Marilyn Thiel	Anita Bingham	....	Ray Abbott	John Elwell
Campbell (36)	CM	408 866-2100	Barbara Conant	Mark Ochenduszko	Anne Bybee	Gretchen Conner	....	James Cost	Robert Kass
Capitola (10)	CM	408 475-7300	Ronald Graves	Stephen Burrell	Pamela Greeninger	Ardath Fugate	....	Donald Braunton	Fred Braun
Carlsbad (63)	CM	619 434-2852	Claude Lewis	Raymond Patchett	Lee Rautenkranz	James Elliott	D Van Der Maaten	Robert Vales	....
Carmel-By-The-Sea (4)	CM	408 624-2781	Kennedy White	Jere Kersnar	W Jeanne Brehmer	....	Bill Hill	John J McGilvray	James Cullem
Carpinteria (14)	CM	805 684-5405	Michael Ledbettor	Paul Marangella	Jayne Diaz	John Thornberry	....	....	Bob Hisbet
Carson (84)	CM	213 830-7600	(not reporting)						
Cathedral City (30)	MC	619 770-0340	Carol Engelhard	Bruce Liedstrand	Kammy Hill	Dudley Haines	George Truppelli	Ron Johnson	....
Ceres (26)	CM	209 538-5700	Richard McBride	Gary A Napper	....	Carlos Sanchez	....	Gail W Peterson	Joachim Hollstein
Cerritos (53)	CM	213 860-0311	John Crawley	Art Gallucci	Caroline Dellamas	Becky Lingad	....	....	Vince Brar
Chico (40)	CM	916 895-4800	Jim Owens	Tom Lando	Barbara Evans	....	Charles Lowden	Michael Dunbaugh	Robert Nunes
Chino (60)	CM	714 591-9800	....	Richard Rowe	....	....	....	Patrick Connolly	Robert Beardsley
Chowchilla (6)	CM	209 665-8615	Eric Haupt	Scott Lambers	Nancy Red Bump	Connie Wright	Harry Turner	Al Lucchesi	Doug Lackey
Chula Vista (135)	CM	619 691-5031	(not reporting)						
Claremont (33)	CM	714 399-5440	Diann Ring	Glenn Southard	Barbara Royalty	John Stark	....	Robert Moody	Marcia Goldstein
Clayton (7)	CM	510 672-3622	William Walcutt	Thomas Steele	Frances Douglas	Thomas Steele	....	Norm Venturino	....
Clearlake (12)	CM	707 994-8201	C Constable	Daniel Obermeyer	Sharon Goode	....	....	Robert Chalk	....
Cloverdale (5)	CM	707 894-2521	John Doble	Bob Perrault	Michele Winterbot	....	James Miner	Robert Dailey	Fred Browne
Clovis (50)	CM	209 297-2300	Dave Lawson	Kathy Millison	Michael Prandini	Michael Prandini	Dennis Byrns	Joseph Maskovich	Ronald Peterson
Coachella (17)	CM	619 398-3502	(not reporting)						
Coalinga (8)	CM	209 935-1533	Alfonso Bonilla	....	Trish O'Halloran	Thomas Fus	Fred Frederickson	John DeAngelis	Alan Jacobsen
Colton (40)	CM	714 370-5000	(not reporting)						
Colusa (5)	CM	916 458-4740	Frank Jaconetti	Gay Rainsbarger	Gay Rainsbarger	Marianne Neal	Randall Dunn	Thomas A Gwinnup	Millard Totman
Commerce (12)	CM	213 722-4805	Ruth Aldaco	Lou Shepard	Linda Oliveri	Tom Bachman	Jimmy Ryland	....	Sam Johnson
Compton (90)	CM	310 605-5500	Omar Bradly	Howard Caldwell	Charles Davis	Helen Tyler	Milford Fonza	Hourie Taylor	Angel Espiritu
Concord (111)	CM	415 671-3000	....	Farrel Stewart	Lynnet L Keihl	P Ron Howard	....	Michael Maehler	Michael Vogan
Corcoran (13)	CM	209 992-2151	Terry Kwast	Donald Pauley	Connie Harris	Joyce Venegas	....	....	John Cook
Corning (6)	CM	916 824-7020	Ross Turner	Stephen Kimbrough	Darlene Dickison	Stephen Kimbrough	Robert Pryatel	Anthony Cardenas	Terry Snow
Corona (76)	CM	714 736-2205	Richard Deininger	William Garrett	D Lingenfelter	Helen Bell	Robert McNabb	John Cleghorn	Joseph Palencia
Coronado (27)	CM	619 522-7300	....	....	....	Jack Van Sambeek	....	....	....
Corte Madera t (8)	CM	415 927-5050	(not reporting)						
Costa Mesa (96)	CM	714 754-5223	Sandra Genis	Allan Roeder	....	Susan Temple	James Reed	David Snowden	William Morris
Cotati (6)	CM	707 792-4600	Richard Cullinen	Bonnie Long	Sara Anna	Vance Ashe	....	Lester Wasko	Steve Nommsen
Covina (43)	CM	818 331-0111	Henry M Morgan	John R Thomson	Mary Jo Southall	Stan McCartney	....	John Lentz	....
Crescent City (4)	CM	707 464-7483	....	Stephen Casey	Kathleen Smith	Carol Leuthold	Don Olson	Richard Metcalf	David Gustafson
Cudahy (23)	CM	213 773-5143	Alex F Rodriguez	Jack M Joseph	Jack M Joseph	Aurora C Martinez	....	....	Daniel A Pulone
Culver City (39)	CM	310 202-5745	Mike Balkman	Jody Hall Esser	Pauline Dolce	Robert Norquist	Michael Olson	Ted Cooke	Gary Audet
Cupertino (40)	CM	408 252-4505	....	Donald D Brown	....	Blaine Snyder	....	....	Bert S Viskovich
Cypress (43)	CM	714 229-6681	Gail H Kerry	Darrell L Essex	Darrell L Essex	Richard M Storey	....	Daryl M Wicker	Donald E Donovan
Daly City (92)	CM	415 991-8000	Albert M Teglia	David R Rowe	Lorraine D'Elia	Donald W McVey	Michael V Orloff	Thomas G Reese	V Lee Yarborough
Dana Point (..)	CM	714 248-9890	(not reporting)						
Danville (31)	CM	510 820-4699	Mike Shimansky	....	Patti Muck	....	....	....	....
Davis (46)	CM	916 757-5644	Lois Wolk	John Meyer	Bette Racki	Susan Miller	William Berger	Pillip Coleman	David Pelz
Del Mar (5)	CM	619 755-9313	D Elliot Parks	L Breake Esparza	Patti Barnes	....	James Baker	....	Richard Andrews
Delano (23)	CM	805 721-3300	Art B Armendariz	Joseph L Corbett	Jeanne C Bumatay	Wiley Jung	....	Gerald Gruver	Eddie Ahumada
Desert Hot Springs (12)	CM	619 329-6411	(not reporting)						
Dinuba (13)	CM	209 591-1203	Ray Fudge	Ed Todd	Antonia Mashall	Ken Grover	Myles Chute	Ed Hernandez	Dan Meinert
Dixon (10)	CM	916 678-7000	(not reporting)						
Dos Palos (4)	CM	209 392-2174	Ron Skinner	Darrell Fonseca	Patricia Mann	Vickie Lewis	Dewayne Jones	Tom Saavedra	Hub Ballinger
Downey (91)	CM	310 904-7293	Robert Brazelton	Gerald Caton	Judith McDonnell	Lowell Williams	Ronald Irwin	Gregory Caldwell	Richard Redmayne
Duarte (21)	CM	818 357-7931	(not reporting)						
Dublin (23)	CM	510 833-6650	Peter W Snyder	Richard C Ambrose	Kay Keck	Paul S Rankin	Karl Diedman	Jim Rose	Lee S Thompson
Dunsmuir (2)	CM	916 235-4822	Len Albright	Alan Harvey	Ann Smith	Ted Marconi	Sid Nystrom	....	....
East Palo Alto (23)	CM	415 853-3100	(not reporting)						
El Cajon (89)	CM	619 441-1736	Joan Shoemacker	Robert T Acker	Marilynn Linn	James Kell	Richard Hardy	Jack Smith	Marvin Munzenmair
El Centro (31)	CM	619 337-4548	Jack Terrazas	Abdel Salem	Rita Noden	Philip Carr	R Feuerstein	Ralph Cordova	Danny Brammer
El Cerrito (23)	CM	510 215-4300	W Mae Ritz	Gary F Pokorny	Linda M Giddings	Julie K Brown	Stephen Cutright	Daniel Givens	....
El Monte (106)	MC	818 580-2001	Patricia Wallach	Gregory Korduner	Rose Griffith	Marvin Louie	Leslie George	Wayne Clayton	Juan Mireles
El Paso De Robles (19)	CM	805 238-0400	Christian Iversen	Richard Ramirez	Richard Ramirez	Michael Compton	Doug Hamp	John Nelson	John McCarthy
El Segundo (15)	CM	213 322-4670	Carl Jacobson	James Morrison	Cindy Mortesen	Steve Klotzsche	David Sloan	Tim Grimmond	....
Emeryville (6)	CM	415 596-4300	Nora Davis	John Flores	....	Cesario Jinayon	Ray Vittori	Joe Colleti	Harry Hecht
Encinitas (..)	CM	619 944-5050	John T Davis	Warren H Shafer	Jane Pool	James F Benson	....	....	Robert A Nelson
Escalon (4)	CM	209 838-3556	(not reporting)						
Escondido (109)	CM	619 741-4641	Jerry Harmon	Doug Clark	Jeanne Bunch	Clay Phillips	Miles Julihn	Vince Jimno	Mike Adams

Directory 1/9 continued	MUNICIPAL OFFICIALS IN U.S. CITIES OVER 2,500

City, 1990 population figures (000 omitted), form of government	Municipal phone number	Mayor	Appointed administrator	City clerk	Finance officer	Fire chief	Police chief	Public works director
CALIFORNIA (429) continued								
Eureka (27)	CM 707 443-7331	Nancy Flemming	John E Arnold	Sally Goetz	David W Tyson	Vern Cooney	Arnold Millsap	....
Exeter (7)	CM 209 592-9244	William N Brooks	Roy G Chace	Roy G Chace	....	....	John Kunkel	Howard Ricks
Fairfax t (7)	CM 415 453-1584	(not reporting)						
Fairfield (77)	CM 707 428-7400	(not reporting)						
Farmersville (6)	CM 209 747-0458	Al Vanderslice	Steve Thompson	Lucille Scott	....	....	Garry Meek	Ron Mathis
Fillmore (12)	CM 805 524-3701	Michael McMahan	Roy Payne	Noreen Withers	Allan Coates	Pat Askren	Richard Purnell	John Kozar
Firebaugh (4)	CM 209 659-2043	Marcia Sablan	Keyth Durham	Shiaeko Hall	Nancy Walker	Johm Borboa	Rod Lake	Dave Wilson
Folsom (30)	CM 916 355-7200	(not reporting)						
Fontana (88)	CM 714 350-7650	Gary E Boyles	Gregory Devereaux	Kathleen Montoya	Loron C Cox	....	Edward Stout	Kenneth Jeske
Fort Bragg (6)	CM 707 961-2825	(not reporting)						
Fortuna (9)	CM 707 725-6125	(not reporting)						
Foster City (28)	CM 415 349-1200	(not reporting)						
Fountain Valley (54)	CM 714 965-4400	Laurann Cook	Raymond Kromer	Jay Palazzo	Elizabeth Fox	Richard Jorgensen	Elvin Miali	Wayne Osborne
Fremont (173)	CM 510 790-6883	Bill Ball	Roger Anderman	Sharon Whitten	David Millican	Dan Lydon	Craig Steckler	Tom Blalock
Fresno (354)	CM 209 498-1575	Jim Patterson	Michael A Bierman	Jacqueline L Ryle	James K Katen	Bud Armstrong	....	....
Fullerton (114)	CM 714 738-6300	Molly McClanahan	James Armstrong	Anne York	Barbara Henderson	Marc Martin	Patrick McKinley	Robert Hodson
Galt (9)	MC 209 745-2961	Steven J Sekelsky	Peter Cosentini	Carol Cowley	Inez Kuriu	....	Doug Matthews	Robert Kawasaki
Garden Grove (143)	CM 714 741-5000	Frank Kessler	George Tindall	Carolyn Morris	Anthony Andrade	George Cahill	Stan Knee	....
Gardena (50)	CM 213 217-9500	Donald L Dear	Kenneth W Landau	May Y Doi	Richard Roxburgh	Craig S Pedego	Richard Propster	Kenneth C Ayers
Gilroy (31)	MC 408 848-0400	Donald Gage	Jay Baksa	Susanne Steinmetz	Noble Shaw	Art Gillespie	Roy Sumisaki	Norman Allen
Glendale (180)	CM 818 548-2110	Larry Zarian	David Ramsay	Aileen Boyle	Brian Butler	Richard Hinz	James Anthony	George Miller
Glendora (48)	CM 818 914-8200	Robert Kuhn	Arthur E Cook	Jo Ann Sharp	L Schroeder	....	Paul Butler	Richard Cantwell
Gonzales (5)	CM 408 675-5000	Harold Wolgamott	Carla Pew	Susan Warner	Rene M Vise	Rick Rubbo	Ray Green	Carlos Lopez
Grand Terrace (11)	CM 714 824-6621	(not reporting)						
Grass Valley (9)	MC 916 273-2203	Bill Hullender	Gene Haroldsen	Bobbi Poznik	Wes Peters	Jeff Brady	Mel Mousen	Rudi Golnik
Greenfield (7)	CM 408 674-5591	Roy Morris	Arturo Delacerda	Ann Rathbun	Arturo Delacerda	....	J M Romo	John Alves
Gridley (5)	MC 916 846-5695	Frank Hall	John W Slota	John W Slota	John W Slota	Woody Allshouse	Jack Storne	Ed Melton
Grover City (12)	CM 805 473-4567	Lowell Forister	Penelope Culbreth	Patricia Risoldi	Brian Johnson	Robert Cassel	David Brown	Thomas Sullivan
Guadalupe (5)	CM 805 343-1340	Rennie Pili	Bennie Gonzales	Nancy Etteddgue	Brad Whitty	Henry Lawrence	Chris Nartatez	Bennie Gonzales
Gustine (4)	CM 209 854-6471	(not reporting)						
Half Moon Bay (9)	CM 415 726-5566	Larry Patterson	Mark Weiss	....	Fred Wright	....	Dennis Wick	Mike Smith
Hanford (31)	CM 209 585-2500	John Lehn	Jan E Reynolds	Karen McAlister	Tom Dibble	Wesley P Yeary	Brian L DeCuir	Gary Misenhimer
Hawaiian Gardens (14) ...	CM 310 420-2641	(not reporting)						
Hawthorne (71)	CM 213 970-7902	(not reporting)						
Hayward (111)	CM 510 293-5000	Michael Sweeney	Jesus Armas	....	Perry Carter	Michael Bradley	Joseph Brann	Robert Bauman
Healdsburg (9)	CM 707 431-3316	Carla Howell	Michael A Wilson	Maria A Curiel	Kurt Hahn	Robert Taylor	Joseph J Palla	Richard J Pusich
Hemet (36)	CM 714 765-2300	Kenneth Wolford	Joseph P Guzzetta	Brenda Weckerle	Steve Temple	William Dahlquist	Milton L Evanson	Rocky Carns
Hercules (17)	CM 415 799-8200	(not reporting)						
Hermosa Beach (18)	CM 310 318-0239	(not reporting)						
Hesperia (50)	CM 619 947-1000	Mike Lampignano	....	Meg Vall	Don Fraser	....	Bill Abernathy	....
Highland (34)	CM 714 864-6861	John Timmer	Sam J Racadio	Debbie Anderson	Karin Grance	....	....	Ernie Wong
Hillsborough t (11)	CM 415 579-3800	Jean E Auer	Robert M Davidson	Eleanor M Giorgi	James F Coyne	Kenneth Newman	Robert McNichol	Jack B Rush
Hollister (19)	CM 408 637-8221	Seth Irish	Hugh R Riley	Arnold A Carrillo	Philip S Molina	Dan Holsapple	Camerino Sanchez	....
Holtville (5)	CM 619 356-4574	....	Karen G Stauffer	....	....	....	....	....
Hughson (3)	CM 209 883-4054	Jim Sexton	Troy C Presley	Mary Jane Cantrel	....	....	Len Etherington	Ronald Bremer
Huntington Beach (182) ..	CM 714 536-5265	(not reporting)						
Huntington Park (56)	CM 213 582-6161	Ric Loya	Donald L Jeffers	Marilyn A Boyette	Edward S Chow	....	Frank Sullivan	Neil B Poole
Huron (5)	CM 209 945-2241	James Dempsey	John D Luthy	John D Luthy	Stephen Jorgensen	....	Gerald Tucker	Matt Bumguardner
Imperial (4)	CM 619 355-4371	Randy Hines	....	Patricia Cano	Janell Hodgkin	....	Avis Moore	Bayani Mauricio
Imperial Beach (27)	CM 619 423-8300	Michael B Bixler	Murray L Warden	Cynthia M Tjarks	Robert F Hain	John Holsenback	....	C David Ewing
Indian Wells (3)	CM 619 346-2489	William Arenstein	George J Watts	....	Charlie Francis	....	....	Jeanette Peck
Indio (37)	CM 619 342-6580	Jeff Holt	Frederick M Diaz	Karen Dodd	David P Culver	Ken Hammond	Tom Ramirez	Allyn Waggle
Inglewood (110)	CM 213 412-5301	Edward Vincent	Paul Eckles	Hermanita Harris	Nick Rives	Julian Ysais	Oliver Thompson	William Mahar
Irvine (110)	CM 714 724-6000	(not reporting)						
Irwindale (1)	CM 818 962-3381	(not reporting)						
Kerman (5)	CM 209 846-9384	Scott Barber	....	Edith M Forsstrom	Edward Watanabe	....	Raymond Sands	Kenneth Moore
King City (8)	CM 408 385-3281	John L Myers	Blaine Michaelis	Marjorie Sarina	Roberto Moreno	Floyd Owens	David Torres	Harlan Butler
Kingsburg (7)	CM 209 897-5821	Gordon Satterberg	Barbara Carpenter	Barbara Carpenter	Don Jensen	Ed Morgan	James Taylor	John White
La Canada Flintridge (19)	CM 818 790-8880	Jim Edwards	Gabrielle Pryor	Patricia Anderson	Gabrielle Pryor	....	....	Fullmer Chapman
La Habra (51)	CM 213 905-9700	William Mahoney	Lee Risner	Sharie Apodaca	Sheri Peasley	Ben Wilkins	Steve Staveley	Elray Hanna
La Habra Heights (6)	CM 310 694-6302	(not reporting)						
La Mesa (53)	CM 619 463-6611	Art Madrid	David Wear	Anita Underwood	Dennis Hackett	Chris Carlson	Walter Mitchell	Cecil Leonardo
La Mirada (40)	CM 213 943-0131	Wayne Rew	Gary Sloan	Gail Vasquez	Rick Patton	....	....	....
La Palma (15)	CM 714 523-7700	Eva G Miner	Pamela M Gibson	Brigitte Charles	Pamela M Gibson	....	David S Barr	Ismile Noorbaksh
La Puente (37)	CM 818 339-2106	....	Robert Gutierrez	....	Ted Abo	....	....	....
La Quinta (11)	CM 619 564-2246	(not reporting)						
La Verne (31)	CM 714 596-8726	Jon Blickenstaff	Martin Lomeli	Kathy Hamm	Ron Clark	Robert Miller	Ron Ingels	Brian Bowcock
Lafayette (24)	CM 415 284-1968	....	Robert Adams	Sue Jusaitis	Steven Falk	....	Greg Moore	....
Laguna Beach (23)	CM 714 497-3311	Lida Lenney	Kenneth C Frank	Verna Rollinger	Rob Clark	....	Neil J Purcell	Terry Brandt
Laguna Niguel (..)	CM 714 362-4300	Thomas Wilson	Tim Casey	Juanita Zarilla	Dennis Miura	....	....	Ken Montgomery
Lake Elsinore (18)	CM 714 674-3124	Gary Washburn	Ron Molendyk	Vicki Kasad	Bob Boone	Terry Schmutz	Wayne Daniel	Frank Tecca
Lake Forest (..)	CM 714 707-5583	(not reporting)						
Lakeport (4)	MC 707 263-5615	Howard Van Lente	....	Janel Chapman	Larry Jack	Chuck Hinchcliff	James Campbell	Michael Stevenson
Lakewood (74)	CM 213 866-9771	(not reporting)						
Lancaster (97)	CM 805 723-6000	(not reporting)						
Larkspur (11)	CM 415 927-5000	....	Harlan Barry	Nancy Anthony	Gail Green	Robert B Sinnott	Phillip Green	Mark Miller
Lathrop (7)	CM 209 858-2860	A Sangalang	John Bingham	Sue Wilcox	Rodney Davenport	....	....	Wilce Martin
Lawndale (27)	CM 310 970-2120	Harold Hoffman	Patrick Importuna	Neil Roth	Jan Rush	....	....	Mehrdad Kapanpour
Lemon Grove (24)	CM 619 464-6934	Brian Cochran	Jack D Shelver	Christine Taub	Christine Taub	William Wright	....	Les R Ruh
Lemoore (14)	CM 209 924-5398	John Luis	Allen Goodman	Helen Murray	Harry Empey	Manuel Luis	Ken Marvin	David Wlaschin
Lincoln (7)	CM 916 645-3314	Roberta Babcock	William J Malinen	Linda Stackpoole	Robert Sesnon	Vernon Losh	Ernest Klevesahl	....
Lindsay (8)	MC 209 562-5927	Valeriano Soucedo	William R Drennen	Bobbi Paul	Kenny Walker	Bert Garzelli	Bert Garzelli	Tom McCurdy
Live Oak (4)	MC 916 695-2112	Keith Combs	....	Lorie Adams	....	....	....	Donald Dosser
Livermore (57)	CM 510 373-5100	Cathie Brown	Lee Horner	Carol Greany	Monica Potter	....	Ron Scott	John Hines
Livingston (7)	CM 209 394-8041	Russ Winton	Tim Kerr	Woody Campini	Tim Kerr	....	....	Gary Petty
Lodi (52)	CM 209 334-5634	(not reporting)						
Loma Linda (17)	CM 714 799-2800	Robert Christman	Peter R Hills	P Brynes O'Camb	John Morris	Peter R Hills	....	A R Cablay
Lomita (19)	CM 310 325-7110	....	Walker J Ritter	Dawn Tomita	Walker J Ritter	....	....	Walker J Ritter
Lompoc (38)	CM 805 736-1261	Joyce Howerton	Gene L Wahlers	Maureen Bosking	John Walk	Ron Reid	Robert Hebert	Larry McPherson
Long Beach (429)	CM 310 590-6475	(not reporting)						
Los Alamitos (12)	CM 310 431-3538	Ron Bates	Robert Dunek	....	Richard Patino	....	....	Jerry Andersen
Los Altos (26)	CM 415 948-1491	Penelope Lave	Dianne Gershuny	Carol Scharz	Sherry Lambach	Dick Landrum	Lucy Carlton	Bruce Bane
Los Altos Hills t (8)	CM 415 941-7222	Robert Johnson	Les M Jones	Patricia Dowd	Les M Jones	....	....	Jeff Peterson

Directory 1/9 continued **MUNICIPAL OFFICIALS IN U.S. CITIES OVER 2,500**

City, 1990 population figures (000 omitted), form of government		Municipal phone number	Mayor	Appointed administrator	City clerk	Finance officer	Fire chief	Police chief	Public works director
CALIFORNIA (429) continued									
Los Angeles (3485)	MC	213 485-2121	(not reporting)						
Los Banos (15)	CM	209 826-5119	(not reporting)						
Los Gatos t (27)	CM	408 354-6829	Joanne Benjamin	David Knapp	Marian Cosgrove	Mark Linder	. . . .	Larry Todd	Michael LaRocca
Lynwood (62)	CM	310 603-0220	Paul H Richards	Faustin Gonzales	Andrea Hooper	Alfretta Earnest	Gerald Wallace	. . . .	Emilio Murga
Madera (29)	CM	209 661-5400	(not reporting)						
Mammoth Lakes t (..)	CM	619 934-8983	David Watson	Glenn Thompson	Anita Hatter	Tracy Fuller	. . . .	Bruce Mac Afee	Bob Warren
Manhattan Beach (32)	CM	310 545-5621	Connie Sieber	Bill Smith	Win Underhill	Eunice Kramer	Keith Hackamack	Ted Mertens	. . . .
Manteca (41)	CM	209 239-8400	Franklin Warren	David M Jinkens	Joann Tilton	Leticia Espinoza	Charles Rule	W Weatherford	Michael Brinton
Marina (26)	CM	408 384-3715	Edith Johnsen	John Longley	Joy Junsay	Marty Silguero	Travis Jackson	Roger Williams	Vince Dimaggio
Martinez (32)	CM	510 372-3500	Michael Mensini	James Jakel	Gus Kramer	Ronald Peterson	. . . .	Gerald Boyd	Marcia Raines
Marysville (12)	MC	916 741-6633	Frank Crawford	Alan J Bengyel	Alan J Bengyel	Sherri Emitte	Rick Tye	Jack Simpson	Ben Bramer
Maywood (28)	MC	213 562-5000	Thomas H Engle	Ronald L Lindsey	Samuel Pena	Michael Williams	. . . .	Theodore Heidke	Edward W Ahrens
Mc Farland (7)	CM	805 792-3091	(not reporting)						
Mendota (7)	MC	209 655-3291	Fidel DeLa Cruz	Daniel F Ayala	Rosemary Ramirez	Elena R Martin	. . . .	. . . .	Louie Garcia
Menlo Park (28)	CM	415 858-3360	Gail L Slocum	Janet M Dolan	Jaye M Carr	Uma Chokkalingam	. . . .	Bruce C Cumming	Daniel V Freitas
Merced (56)	CM	209 385-6834	Jim Lindsey	James Marshall	Dorothy Penner	Brad Grant	Ken Mitten	Patrick Lunney	Nick Pinhey
Mill Valley (13)	CM	415 388-4033	. . . .	Doug Dawson	Mary Herr	. . . .	. . . .	Peter Brindley	Ed Marshall
Millbrae (20)	CM	415 259-2334	P Van Iderstine	James Erickson	Alicia Espinoza	Hector Luin	Brian Kelly	Michael Parker	Lou Sandrini
Milpitas (51)	CM	408 942-2310	Peter McHugh	Lawrence Moore	Gail Blalock	Lawrence Sabo	Michael Harwood	J Frank Acosta	. . . .
Mission Viejo (73)	CM	714 582-2489	. . . .	Fred Sorsabal	Ivy Joseph	Irwin Bornstein	. . . .	. . . .	Dennis Wilberg
Modesto (165)	CM	209 577-5200	Richard Lang	J Edward Tewes	Norrine Coyle	Kevin Riper	Doug Hannink	Paul Jefferson	Marshall Elizer
Monrovia (36)	CM	818 359-3231	Robert Bartlett	Rodney Gould	Linda Proctor	Kenneth Nordhoff	Ernest Mitchell	Joseph Santoro	Robert Bammes
Montclair (28)	CM	714 626-8571	Larry Rhinehart	Lee McDougal	Margaret Crawford	Ned Crutcher	Loren Pettis	Guy Eisenbrey	Carl Sawtell
Monte Sereno (3)	CM	408 354-7635	Dorothea Bamford	Rosemary Pierce	Fay Furtado	Rosemary Pierce	. . . .	Robert Stith	Rosemary Pierce
Montebello (60)	CM	213 887-1200	William Molinari	Richar Torres	Maryanne Saucede	Ted Nix	Robert Fager	G Steve Simonian	Ayyad Ghobrial
Monterey (32)	CM	408 646-3761	(not reporting)						
Monterey Park (61)	CM	818 307-1255	Marie Purvis	Chris Jeffers	David Barron	David Dong	Ernest Pruett	Daniel Cross	Nels Palm
Moorpark (25)	CM	805 529-6864	. . . .	Steven Kueny	Lillian Hare	Richard Hare	. . . .	. . . .	Ken Gilbert
Moraga t (16)	CM	510 376-2590	Susan L Noe	Ross G Hubbard	Ross G Hubbard	Michael Medvedoff	. . . .	Barry Kalar	Daniel I Bernie
Moreno Valley (119)	CM	909 243-3000	Cynthia Crothers	Norm King	Alicia Chavez	Rick Teichert	Bob Green	Sue Hansen	Barry McClellan
Morgan Hill (24)	CM	408 779-7271	Joe Martucci	David C Biggs	Betty Busk	Michael Shelton	Bradley Spencer	Steven Schwab	Gordon Siebert
Morro Bay (10)	CM	805 772-1214	William Yates	Forrest Henderson	Bridgett Davis	Rudy Hernandez	Jeffrey Jones	David Howell	Jon G Crawford
Mount Shasta (3)	CM	916 926-3464	Russ Porterfield	Al Meneni	Prudence Simon	Keith Samse	Joseph Spini	Robert K Montz	Daniel R Avila
Mountain View (67)	CM	415 966-6000	. . . .	Kevin C Duggan	Kathy Koliopoulos	Robert Locke	Hugh Holden	Brown Taylor	Larry Janda
Napa (62)	MC	707 257-9500	(not reporting)						
National City (54)	CM	619 336-4200	George H Waters	Thom G McCabe	Lori A Peoples	Alejandro Caloza	Randy L Kimble	Kent R Reesor	Curtis R Williams
Needles (5)	CM	619 326-2113	Roy A Mills	Leon H Berger	. . . .	Virginia Tasker	John Clark	Leroy Morgan	. . . .
Nevada City (3)	CM	916 265-2496	(not reporting)						
Newark (38)	CM	510 793-1400	David W Smith	Paul H B Tong	Thelma Metcalf	Neil Grasso	. . . .	Dennis Gleeson	Kenneth Buck
Newman (4)	CM	209 862-3725	Janet Carlsen	Steve Hollister	Steve Hollister	Fidel Fabela	Mel Souza	Larry Bussard	Ernie Garza
Newport Beach (67)	CM	714 644-3309	(not reporting)						
Norco (23)	CM	714 735-6840	Larry Cusimano	George Lambert	Dianna Higdon	Carolyn Bartleman	Dave Carlson	. . . .	Joseph Schenk
Norwalk (94)	CM	310 929-2677	(not reporting)						
Novato (48)	CM	415 897-4300	Harry Morre	Roderick Wood	Shirley Gremmels	Richard Hill	. . . .	Brian Brady	Vi Grinsteiner
Oakdale (12)	CM	209 847-3031	Elma Garcia	Bruce Bannerman	Rebecca A Peluso	Marge Cruz	Jack Criswell	David Sundy	Michael Pettinger
Oakland (372)	CM	415 273-3301	Elihu Harris	Craig Kocian	Ceda Floyd	Gary Breaux	Philip Ewell	Joseph Samuels	Terry Roberts
Oceanside (128)	CM	619 966-4485	(not reporting)						
Ojai (8)	CM	805 646-5581	Steve Olsen	Andrew S Belknap	Cyndi Reynolds	Cyndi Reynolds	. . . .	. . . .	W S Moore
Ontario (133)	CM	714 986-1151	James Fatland	Michael Milhiser	D Arterburn	David Bentz	David Lee	Lowell Stark	Mike Teal
Orange (111)	CM	714 744-2203	Norman E Beyer	. . . .	Marilyn Jensen	Jeanne Arehart	Ed Rowlett	John Robertson	Frank V Page
Orange Cove (6)	CM	209 626-4488	Victor Lopez	Alan J Bengyel	June Lopez	Jose Garay	. . . .	. . . .	Gabe Jimenez
Orinda (17)	CM	415 254-3900	Bobbie Landers	Thomas Sinclair	Thomas Sinclair	Elizabeth Stewart	. . . .	. . . .	John Lisenko
Orland (5)	CM	916 865-4741	. . . .	Al Calonico	Laura Blevins	. . . .	Rick Nunes	William Olney	Jerry Troxel
Oroville (12)	CM	916 538-2401	Dennis D Diver	Shelton T Enochs	Shelton T Enochs	Paul A Kayson	Dean J Hill Sr	Gary H Grant	John M Crump
Oxnard (142)	CM	805 385-7430	Manuel Lopez	Vernon Hazen	Jose Martinez	Rudolph Muravez	Richard Smith	Harold Hurtt	. . . .
Pacific Grove (16)	CM	408 373-1576	(not reporting)						
Pacifica (38)	CM	415 738-7300	Bonnie K Wells	Daniel Pincetich	Daniel Pincetich	Pollyann Wallace	Gary Stofan	Charlie English	Scott Holmes
Palm Desert (23)	CM	619 346-0611	Jean Benson	Bruce Altman	Sheila Gilligan	Paul Gibson	Eric Vogt	Steve Bloomquist	Richard Folkers
Palm Springs (40)	CM	619 323-8215	Lloyd Maryanov	Rob Pakins	Judith Sumich	Thomas Kanarr	Thomas Robertson	Donald Burnett	David Strecker
Palmdale (69)	CM	805 273-3162	James Ledford Jr	Robert W Toone Jr	Victoria Denham	Bill Ramsey	. . . .	. . . .	Steve Williams
Palo Alto (56)	CM	415 329-2392	(not reporting)						
Palos Verdes Estates (14)	CM	310 378-0383	Michael Moody	James Hendrickson	Barbara Culver	Bill Yeomans	. . . .	Gary Johansen	Tim D'Zmura
Paradise t (25)	CM	916 872-6282	Chester L Hubb	Kenenth Whorton	Frances Rutledge	Paul A Eckert	. . . .	Leonard Trombley	Jon A Lander
Paramount (48)	CM	213 220-2000	Manuel Guillen	William Holt	. . . .	. . . .	. . . .	. . . .	Harry Babbitt
Parlier (8)	MC	209 646-3545	(not reporting)						
Pasadena (132)	CM	818 405-4000	(not reporting)						
Patterson (9)	CM	209 892-2041	Pat Maisetti	Jeffrey C Parker	Tammy A Ulibarri	Edard Oborn	Richard Gaiser	William Middleton	Ignacio Lopez
Perris (21)	CM	714 943-6100	Robert Fletcher	Mike Napolitano	Betian Hynes	Larry L Weaver	. . . .	Gil Olivarria	. . . .
Petaluma (43)	CM	707 778-4345	Patti M Hilligos	John Scharer	Patrica Bernard	David Spilman	Terry Krout	Dennis Dewitt	William P Miller
Pico Rivera (59)	MC	310 942-2000	Alberto Natividad	D Courtemarche	Chris Schaefer	Randy L Rassi	. . . .	. . . .	Enrique Acevedo
Piedmont (11)	MC	510 420-3040	Katy Foulkes	Geoff Grote	Ann Swift	Mark Bichsel	Ron Christensen	John Mollan	Larry Rosenberg
Pinole (17)	CM	415 724-9000	(not reporting)						
Pismo Beach (8)	CM	805 773-4657	(not reporting)						
Pittsburg (48)	CM	510 439-4850	(not reporting)						
Placentia (41)	CM	714 993-8141	Maria Moreno	Robert D'Amato	Edmund Ponce	Howard Longballa	. . . .	Manuel Ortega	C Becker
Placerville (8)	CM	916 642-5200	Kathi Lisman	Robert Semple	Bob Gilmore	. . . .	. . . .	Robert Harmon	Michael W Foster
Pleasant Hill (32)	CM	510 671-5270	Kimberly N Brandt	Joseph M Tanner	Doris P Nilsen	Richard Ricci	. . . .	James R Nunes	Leary Wong
Pleasanton (51)	CM	510 484-8000	Ben Tarver	Deborah Acosta	Peggy Ezidro	Susan Rossi	George Withers	William Eastman	Joseph Elliott
Pomona (132)	CM	714 620-2052	Eddie Cortez	. . . .	E Villeral	Jose Sanchez	John Parker	Lloyd Wood	Robert Deloach
Port Hueneme (20)	CM	805 488-3625	Orvene Carpenter	John R Velthoen	Karen Jackson	James F Hanks	. . . .	John Hopkins	John J Duffy
Porterville (30)	CM	209 782-7466	(not reporting)						
Portola (2)	CM	916 832-4216	Joseph Moctezuma	Stacey Mac Donald	Judith Martini	. . . .	. . . .	. . . .	Verlin Woods
Portola Valley (4)	CM	415 851-1700	(not reporting)						
Poway (44)	CM	619 748-6600	. . . .	J L Bowersox	M K Wahlsten	P A Stewart	M A Sanchez	. . . .	J R Williams
Rancho Cucamonga (101)	CM	714 989-1851	Dennis Stout	Jack Lam	Debra Adams	Susan Neely	Dennis Michael	. . . .	Wm Joe O'Neil
Rancho Mirage (10)	CM	619 324-4511	Alan Seman	Patrick M Pratt	Barbara E Dohn	Scott Morgan	. . . .	. . . .	Eldon K Lee
Rancho Palos Verdes (42)	CM	310 377-0360	Susan Brooks	Paul Bussey	Jo Purcell	Brent Mattingly	. . . .	. . . .	Trent Pulliam
Red Bluff (12)	CM	916 527-2605	Velma Trujillo	Dennis W Fischer	Susan M Elston	Ray D Harrington	. . . .	Richard A Bull	Gary B Antone
Redding (66)	CM	916 225-4000	Carl Arness	R Christofferson	Connie Strohmayer	Linda Downing	Paul Bailey	Robt Blankenship	Robert Galusha
Redlands (60)	CM	714 798-7510	Charles Demirjyn	Gary Luebbers	Lorrie Poyzer	Steve Chapman	Mel Enslow	Lou Nelson	Ronald Mutter
Redondo Beach (60)	CM	310 372-1171	(not reporting)						
Redwood City (66)	CM	415 780-7300	(not reporting)						
Reedley (16)	CM	209 637-4200	(not reporting)						

Directory 1/9 continued | **MUNICIPAL OFFICIALS IN U.S. CITIES OVER 2,500**

City, 1990 population figures (000 omitted), form of government		Municipal phone number	Mayor	Appointed administrator	City clerk	Finance officer	Fire chief	Police chief	Public works director
CALIFORNIA (429) continued									
Rialto (72)	CM	714 820-2525	(not reporting)						
Richmond (87)	CM	510 620-6602	George Livingston	Jay Goldstone	Eula Barnes	Ken Jett	Floyd Cormier	Earnest Clements	Larry Loder
Ridgecrest (28)	MC	619 371-3700	Kevin Corlett	Damon B Edwards	Pamela Snyder	Roger Ward	. . . .	Randy Narramore	Jerry Lo
Rio Dell (3)	CM	209 764-3532	(not reporting)						
Rio Vista (3)	CM	707 374-6451	(not reporting)						
Ripon (7)	MC	209 599-2108	Jim Dale	Leon Compton	Lynette Van Laar	. . . .	. . . .	Tom Scheidecker	Dale Ramey
Riverbank (9)	CM	209 869-3671	Noel Price	Brian Cox	Elise Cunningham	Vernon Whorton	. . . .	Jerry McBride	Randal Dodd
Riverside (227)	CM	714 782-5312	(not reporting)						
Rocklin (19)	CM	916 632-4000	Kathy Lund	Carlos A Urrutia	Sandra Tocci	Rex E Miller	James Pennington	Gary A Prince	Arch Moosakhanian
Rohnert Park (36)	CM	707 795-2411	. . . .	Joseph D Netter	. . . .	Michael Harrow	. . . .	Robert E Dennett	Roland L Brust
Rolling Hills (2)	CM	310 377-1521	Jody Murdock	Craig Nealis	Craig Nealis	Nan Huang	. . . .	. . . .	. . . .
Rolling Hills Estates (8)	CM	310 377-1577	Kenneth Servis	Douglas Prichard	Douglas Prichard	Judy Smith	. . . .	. . . .	Samuel Wise
Rosemead (52)	CM	818 288-6671	Robert W Bruesch	Frank G Tripepi	Janice Warner	Karen Ogawa	Marc McConnell	Robert Mirabella	Jeff Stewart
Roseville (45)	CM	916 774-5204	(not reporting)						
Ross t (2)	MC	415 453-1453	(not reporting)						
Sacramento (369)	CM	916 264-5726	(not reporting)						
Salinas (109)	CM	408 758-7201	Alan D Styles	David R Mora	Ann Camel	John Copeland	. . . .	Tecumseh D Nelson	John Fair
San Anselmo (12)	CM	415 258-4600	Paul Chignell	Jean Bonander	Caroline Foster	Jean Bonander	. . . .	Bernard Del Santo	Wayne Bush
San Bernardino (164)	MC	714 384-5493	Tom Minor	Shauna Clark	Rachel Clark	Barbara Pachon	William Wright	Daniel Robbins	Roger Hardgrave
San Bruno (39)	CM	415 877-8897	Ed Simon	. . . .	Terri Rasmussen	Molly Smith	Tom Ott	Frank Hedley	Lee Ritzman
San Buenaventura (93)	CM	805 654-7800	Greg Carson	John Baker	Barbara Kam	Terry Adelman	Vern Hamilton	Richard Thomas	Ronald Calkins
San Carlos (26)	CM	415 593-8011	Paul Sivley	Mike Garvey	Margaret Hanley	Brian Moura	Richard Latreille	Clifford Gerst	Parviz Mokhtari
San Clemente (41)	MC	714 361-8200	Truman Benedict	Mike Parness	Myrna Erway	. . . .	Gene Begnell	. . . .	Mike Sorg
San Diego (1111)	CM	619 236-5555	Susan Golding	John R McGrory	Charles Abdelnour	Patricia Frazier	Robert E Osby	Gerald R Sanders	George Loveland
San Dimas (32)	CM	714 599-6713	Terry Dipple	Donald Pruyn	Pamela Jackson	Hertha Nissell	. . . .	. . . .	Frank Basile
San Fernando (23)	CM	818 898-1200	. . . .	Mary Strenn	. . . .	Michael Moon	. . . .	Dominick Rivetti	Michael Drake
San Francisco (724)	MC	415 557-4990	Frank Jordan	R Nothenberg	John Taylor	Edward Harrington	Joseph Medina	Anthony Ribera	John Cribbs
San Gabriel (37)	CM	818 308-2802	James Castaneda	P Michael Paules	Cynthia A Bookter	Tracey L Butler	Gene E Murry	David A Lawton	John E Nowak
San Jacinto (16)	CM	714 654-7337	Henry Hafliger	Pamela S Easter	Richard Brewer	Anna Vega	Ross Chadwick	. . . .	Les Evans
San Jose (782)	CM	408 277-4000	Susan Hammer	Leslie R White	Patricia L Ohearn	John V Guthrie	. . . .	Louis Cobarruviaz	Ralph A Qualls Jr
San Juan Bautista (..)	CM	408 623-4661	Priscilla Hill	Dennis McDuffie	Jade Dunnick	. . . .	. . . .	. . . .	. . . .
San Juan Capistrano (26)	CM	714 493-1171	Gil Jones	G Scarborough	Cheryl Johnson	Cynthia Pendleton	. . . .	. . . .	William Huber
San Leandro (68)	MC	510 577-3200	J Faria	M A Oliver	A Calvert	J J Jermanis	W McCammon	E J P Maginnis	R Taylor
San Luis Obispo (42)	CM	805 781-7250	Peg Pinard	John Dunn	Diane Gladwell	Bill Statler	Robert Neumann	Jim Gardiner	Michel McClusley
San Marcos (39)	CM	619 744-4020	Lee B Thibadeau	Rick Gittings	Sheila A Kennedy	G L Cano	Harry Townsend	. . . .	Richard Wygant
San Marino (13)	CM	818 300-0700	Eugene H Dryden	Keith R Till	Carol Robb	. . . .	John Demonaco	Frank J Wills	Virgil Nichols
San Mateo (85)	CM	415 377-3350	Jane Baker	Arne Croce	Norma Gomez	John DeRussy	Gary Schmitz	Don Phipps	Arch Perry
San Pablo (25)	CM	510 215-3000	(not reporting)						
San Rafael (48)	CM	415 485-3070	(not reporting)						
San Ramon (35)	CM	415 275-2211	(not reporting)						
Sanger (17)	CM	209 875-2587	Elliott Martinez	Oliver L Drummond	Harriett Stephens	Raymond Steine	Ronald Karle	Gregory Cooper	Edward Larrabee
Santa Ana (294)	CM	714 647-5200	Daniel Young	David Ream	Janice Guy	Rod Coloma	Allen Carter	Paul Walters	Jim Ross
Santa Barbara (86)	CM	805 963-0611	Sheila Lodge	Sandra Lizarraga	Sandra Lizarraga	Mark Paul	Monroe Rutherford	Richard Breza	David H Johnson
Santa Clara (94)	CM	408 984-3000	Everett Souza	J Sparacino	Judy Boccignone	Kristin Machnick	Gerald Simon	Frank Vasquez	Robert Mortenson
Santa Clarita (11)	CM	805 259-2489	. . . .	George Caravalho	Donna Grindey	Steve Stark	. . . .	. . . .	Jeff Kolin
Santa Cruz (49)	CM	408 429-3616	Neal Connerty	Richard Wilson	Emma Solden	Jack Ness	Ed Ekers	Jack Bassett	Larry Erwin
Santa Fe Springs (16)	CM	213 868-0511	(not reporting)						
Santa Maria (61)	CM	805 925-0951	(not reporting)						
Santa Monica (87)	CM	213 458-8301	(not reporting)						
Santa Paula (25)	CM	805 933-4201	Margaret Ely	Arnold Dowdy	Arnold Dowdy	Cindy Kretzer	Paul Skeels	Walt Adair	Norm Wilkinson
Santa Rosa (113)	CM	707 524-5274	Maureen Casey	Kenneth Blackman	. . . .	Stan Lindsay	Tony Pini	Salvatore Rosano	Rosalind Daniels
Santee (53)	CM	619 258-4100	(not reporting)						
Saratoga (28)	CM	408 867-3438	Karen Tucker	Harry Peacock	Betsy Cory	Patricia Shriver	. . . .	. . . .	Larry Perlin
Sausalito (7)	CM	415 289-4100	. . . .	. . . .	Janet F Tracy	Carl Tregner	Stephen Bogel	William Fraass	. . . .
Scotts Valley (9)	CM	408 438-2324	Gina Koshland	Chuck Comstock	Judi Coffman	Jack Dilles	. . . .	Stephen Walpole	Ken Anderson
Seal Beach (25)	CM	310 431-2527	Gwen Forsythe	Jerry Bankston	Joanne Yeo	E Stoddard	. . . .	William Stearns	. . . .
Seaside (39)	CM	408 899-6200	Lancelot McClair	Charles McNeely	Arlene Soto	Mike Brooks	Chuck Streeter	Chuck Richardson	Richard Guillen
Sebastapol (7)	CM	707 823-7863	Lynn Hamilton	Paul Berlant	. . . .	Ron Puccinelli	John Zanzi	Dwigt Crandall	Larry Koverman
Selma (15)	CM	209 896-1064	Robert L Allen	Manuel A Esquibel	Judy L Bier	Judy L Bier	Roy E Peak	Thomas Whiteside	Steven R Harper
Shafter (8)	CM	805 746-6361	Linda Gragg	Wade G McKinney	Dolores Robinson	Jo Barrick	. . . .	Greg Greeson	John D Guinn
Sierra Madre (..)	CM	818 355-7135	Clem Bartolai	James McRea	N Shollenberger	David Cain	Edward Tracy	I E Betts	Kev Tcharkoutian
Signal Hill (8)	CM	310 426-7333	Carol Churchill	Douglas LaBelle	Rebecca Burleson	Vicki Baker	. . . .	Michael McCrary	Richard Lundahl
Simi Valley (100)	CM	805 583-6700	Gregory Stratton	Marlin Koester	Alice Redondo	John McMillan	. . . .	Lindsey Miller	Ronald Coons
Solana Beach (13)	CM	619 755-2998	M Schlesinger	Michael W Huse	Deb Harrington	Barb Castleberry	William Roebuck	. . . .	. . . .
Soledad (7)	CM	408 678-3963	Fred Ledesma	Blair King	. . . .	Betty Burns	Graig Stephens	Thomas Engstrom	Clarence Nielsen
Solvang (5)	CM	805 688-5575	Kenneth Palmer	Michael Montoya	Debbie Glover	Bobbie Goodwin	Howard Peterson	. . . .	David Serge
Sonoma (8)	CM	707 938-3681	Phyllis Carter	Brock Arner	Eleanor Berto	. . . .	Mike Cahill	John Gurney	Dick Rowland
Sonora (4)	MC	209 532-4541	. . . .	Greg Applegate	. . . .	Pat Perry	Guy Mills	Ralph Hamilton	Rick Green
South El Monte (21)	MC	818 579-6540	. . . .	Raul T Romero	Kathy L Gonzales	Lou A Delgado	. . . .	. . . .	Steve A Henley
South Gate (86)	CM	213 563-9500	Mary Ann Buckles	Todd W Argow	Nina A Banuelos	Karen M Plover	. . . .	Ronald P George	James A Biery
South Lake Tahoe (22)	CM	916 573-2000	Kevin Cole	Kerry Miller	Angela Peterson	James Deaton	Jim Plake	Dave Solaro	Carol Drawbaugh
South Pasadena (24)	CM	818 799-9101	James C Hodge	Ken Farfsing	Jeannine Gregory	Barbara James	William Eisele	Tom Mahoney	Jim Van Winkle
South San Francisco (54)	CM	415 877-8500	Roberta Teglia	. . . .	Barbara Battaya	Amy Margolis	Andrew Stark	James Datzman	Ronald Parini
St. Helena (5)	CM	707 963-2741	(not reporting)						
Stanton (30)	CM	714 220-2220	(not reporting)						
Stockton (211)	CM	209 944-8233	(not reporting)						
Suisun City (23)	CM	707 421-7300	James P Spering	Chet J Wystepek	Sharon Ventura	Sergio Fabian	John Malmquist	Thomas D Alder	David M Cosper
Sunnyvale (117)	CM	408 730-7500	Patricia Castillo	Thomas F Lewcock	Thomas F Lewcock	Amy Chan	Regan Williams	Regan Williams	Marvin Rose
Susanville (7)	MC	916 257-2174	Lino Callegari	Harry Jensen	Mary Fahlen	Jay W Rice	Steve Rose	Lee Sanford	Harry Harvey
Taft (6)	CM	805 763-1222	Kenneth Knost	Eric Ziegler	Norma Robinson	Nellie Bazzell	Vance Brannon	Charles Scott	Bill Kytola
Tehachapi (6)	CM	805 822-2200	LaVonne D Booth	Steven R Minton	Kathryn L Koski	Steven R Minton	Antonio A Anthony	. . . .	Tex R Shehan
Temple City (31)	CM	818 285-2171	Mary Manning	Denise Ovrom	Lynne Pahner	F Maldonado	. . . .	. . . .	Bill Hart
Thousand Oaks (104)	CM	805 496-8605	Judith A Lazar	Grant R Brimhall	Nancy Dillon	Robert S Biery	. . . .	. . . .	John P Clement
Tiburon t (8)	CM	415 435-0956	Michael Friedman	Robert L Kleinert	Therese Hennessy	Richard Stranzl	. . . .	Peter Herley	Tony Iacopi
Torrance (133)	CM	213 618-5880	Cathryn Geissert	LeRoy Jackson	John Bramhall	Mary Giordano	Scott Adams	Joe DeLadurantey	Richard Garcia
Tracy (34)	CM	209 836-2572	Clyde Bland	Michael E Locke	Sharon Smith	. . . .	Terrell Estes	Jared Zwickey	. . . .
Truckee t (10)	CM	915 582-7700	(not reporting)						
Tulare (33)	CM	209 685-2300	Claude Retherford	W Lynn Dredge	W Lynn Dredge	Edwin Warren	Al Miller	Roger Hill	John Tindel
Turlock (42)	CM	209 668-5615	Curt Andre	Steven Kyte	Linda Leitaker	Larrie Sweet	Robert Carlson	. . . .	Thomas Tinsley
Tustin (51)	CM	714 544-8890	(not reporting)						
Ukiah (15)	CM	707 463-6200	Fred Schneiter	Charles L Rough	Cathy McKay	Louise Burt	. . . .	Fred Keplinger	Rick Kennedy
Union City (54)	CM	510 471-3232	. . . .	Karen Smith	. . . .	Michael Lynch	. . . .	Albert Guzman	Larry Cheeves
Upland (63)	CM	714 982-1352	Robert Nolan	Kevin Northcraft	Sheryll Schroeder	Phyllis Proctor	Gary Edwards	Gary Hart	Raul Rojas

Directory 1/9 continued — MUNICIPAL OFFICIALS IN U.S. CITIES OVER 2,500

City, 1990 population figures (000 omitted), form of government		Municipal phone number	Mayor	Appointed administrator	City clerk	Finance officer	Fire chief	Police chief	Public works director
CALIFORNIA (429) continued									
Vacaville (71)	CM	707 449-5100	(not reporting)						
Vallejo (109)	CM	707 648-4575	Anthony Intintoli	Walt Graham	A Villarante	Kenneth Campo	Michael Turnick	Gerald Galvin	John Duane
Victorville (41)	CM	619 955-5000	James Busby	James L Cox	Carolee Stotko	Adair M Most	Rodolfo Cabriales	. . . .	Guy W Patterson
Villa Park (6)	CM	714 998-1500	Bob Bell	Fred Maley	J Kaysene Miller	Fred Maley	. . . .	. . . .	Ronald Hagley
Visalia (76)	CM	209 738-3318	. . . .	Ray Forsyth	Leslie Caviglia	Tim Hansen	Doug Dawson	Bruce McDermott	Britt Fussel
Vista (72)	CM	619 726-1340	Gloria McClellan	Morris Vance	Jo Seibert	Frank Rowlen	Roger Purdie	. . . .	William Basham
Walnut (29)	CM	714 595-7543	William Choctaw	Linda Holmes	Beverly Sherwood	Chris Londo	. . . .	. . . .	John Davidson
Walnut Creek (61)	CM	510 943-5800	Gene Wolfe	Donald Blubaugh	Barbara Rivara	Arlene Hildebrand	. . . .	Karel Swanson	Kevin Roberts
Wasco (12)	CM	805 758-3003	(not reporting)						
Waterford (5)	MC	209 874-2328	(not reporting)						
Watsonville (31)	CM	408 728-6011	Oscar Rios	Steven Salomon	L Washington	Eric Frost	Gary Smith	Terrence Medina	John Cooper
Weed (3)	CM	916 938-5020	James Gubetta	. . . .	Deborah Salvestri	M Kelly McKinnis	Darin Quigley	Martin Nicholas	Ronald Servia
West Covina (96)	CM	818 814-8400	Richard Jennings	James Starbird	. . . .	Abraham Koniarsky	Richard Greene	Ronald Holmes	Harry Thomas
West Hollywood (36)	CM	310 854-7400	Sal Guarriello	Paul Brotzman	Vivian Love	Paul Arevalo	. . . .	. . . .	. . . .
West Sacramento (..)	CM	916 373-5800	Wesley A Beers	Joseph M Goeden	Helen Kanowsky	Leigh Keicher	Al Iannone	Melvin Nelson	Larry Gossett
Westlake Village (7)	CM	818 706-1613	James E Emmons	Raymond B Taylor	Raymond B Taylor	. . . .	. . . .	. . . .	. . . .
Westminster (78)	CM	714 898-3311	Charles Smith	Jerry Kenny	Mary Lou Morey	Brian Mayhew	. . . .	James Cook	Donald Vestal
Whittier (78)	CM	310 945-8200	Bob Henderson	Thomas G Mauk	Gertrude Hill	Clara Wong	. . . .	Brad Hoover	David Mochizuki
Willits (5)	CM	707 459-4601	Virginia Stranske	Gordon Logan	. . . .	Robert Brown	. . . .	Robert Foster	Richard Seanor
Willows (6)	CM	916 934-7041	Michael Murray	Russell Melquist	Russell Melquist	Sharon Barker	Bradley Mallory	Robert Shadley	Jon Barker
Windsor t (13)	CM	707 838-1000	Julie Adamson	Berton Wills	. . . .	Sandra Sato	. . . .	Jmaes Piccinini	John Johnson
Winters (5)	CM	916 795-4910	J Robert Chapman	Merrell Watts	Nanci G Mills	Nanci G Mills	. . . .	Steve Godden	George Hicks
Woodlake (6)	CM	209 564-8055	(not reporting)						
Woodland (40)	CM	916 661-5800	Elaine Rominger	Kris Kristensen	Jean Winnop	Peter Woodruff	John Buchanan	. . . .	Gary Wegener
Woodside t (5)	CM	415 851-6790	Barbara Seitle	Susan George	Ruth Swanson	Susan George	Mike Fuge	Don Horsley	. . . .
Yorba Linda (52)	CM	714 961-7100	John Gullixson	Arthur Simonian	Carolyn Wallace	Gordon Vessey	Larry Holmes	Donald Forkus	Roy Stephenson
Yountville t (3)	CM	707 944-8851	(not reporting)						
Yreka (7)	CM	916 842-4386	(not reporting)						
Yuba City (27)	CM	916 741-4601	Karen Cartoscelli	Jeffrey Foltz	Robyn Kain	Colby Smith	Randy Lavelock	Roy Harmon	John Wright
Yucaipa (..)	CM	714 797-2489	William Semans	John Tooker	Juanita Brown	Gregory Franklin	Ray Snodgrass	Monte Lindquist	John McCarty
Yucca Valley t (..)	CM	619 369-7207	Joan Burnside	Sue Tsuda	. . . .	Dean Beyer	. . . .	. . . .	. . . .
COLORADO (88)									
Alamosa (8)	CM	719 589-2593	(not reporting)						
Arvada (89)	CM	303 421-2550	Robert Frie	Neal Berlin	Diana Tangsrud	Robert Gibson	. . . .	Patrick Ahlstrom	Ronald Culbertson
Aspen (5)	CM	303 920-5199	John S Bennett	Amy L Margerum	Kathryn S Koch	. . . .	Wayne Vandemark	Thomas Stephenson	Robert Gish
Aurora (222)	CM	303 695-7000	Paul E Tauer	John Pazour	Donna Young	John Gross	Raymond Barnes	James Everett	Darrell Hogan
Avon t (2)	CM	303 949-4280	Albert Reynolds	William James	Patty Meyhart	Valerie McCoy	Charlie Moore	Art Dalton	Larry Brooks
Boulder (83)	CM	303 441-3388	Leslie Durgin	Tim Honey	Alisa Lewis	Kate Simson	Larry Donner	Tom Koby	David Rhodes
Breckenridge t (1)	CM	303 453-2251	Stephen C West	Gary R Martinez	Mary Jean Loufek	Donald O Taylor	. . . .	A Kiburas	Terry L Perkins
Brighton (14)	CM	303 654-1643	Don Hamstra	Ted Anderson	Marianne Thomas	J Denise Hahl	. . . .	Robert Galloway	Nick Adeh
Broomfield (25)	MC	303 469-3301	Robert J Schulze	George D DiCiero	Vicki D Marcy	J Michael Urie	. . . .	Thomas C Deland	Marvin D Thurber
Brush (4)	MC	303 842-5001	Lawrence Coughlin	Rod Wensing	Cathryn Smith	. . . .	Stan Krueger	Kenneth Baker	Rowena Pennell
Buena Vista t (2)	MC	303 395-8643	(not reporting)						
Burlington t (3)	MC	303 346-8652	Rol Hudler	Tracy Tillman	Phyllis Collins	Phyllis Collins	. . . .	Carrol Johnston	Rich Winslow
Canon City (13)	CM	719 269-9011	Roger Jensen	Steve Thacker	Terry Kimbrel	Jim Allan	Dan Brixey	Martin Stefanic	Jim Patton
Carbondale (3)	MC	303 963-2733	James H Luttrell	Davis S Farrar	Suzanne Cerise	Nancy J Barnett	. . . .	Alfred L Williams	Peter Ware
Castle Rock t (9)	CM	303 660-1015	Mark C Williams	Ronald Mitchell	Sally A Misare	Gary R Higbee	Joe Schum	Tony Lane	David N Hoagland
Cherry Hills Village (5)	CM	303 789-2541	Joan R Duncan	Charles S Coward	. . . .	Cheryl Bohn	. . . .	Les Langford	Bob Jaramillo
Colorado Springs (281)	CM	719 578-6686	Robert Isaac	R Zickefoose	Carmen Hartin	David Nickerson	Louis Roman	Lorne Kramer	David Zelenok
Commerce City (16)	CM	303 289-3627	David Busby	Steven S Crowell	Betty Martin	. . . .	. . . .	James Sanderson	Gregg Clements
Cortez (7)	CM	303 565-3402	Roger W Smith	William A Ray Jr	E Reynolds	Kathi Moss	. . . .	Roy Lane	Bruce Smart
Craig (8)	CM	303 824-8151	. . . .	Donald R Birkner	. . . .	. . . .	. . . .	. . . .	. . . .
Crested Butte t (1)	CM	303 349-5338	(not reporting)						
Del Norte t (2)	MC	719 657-2708	Terry S Blackmon	Patsy E Moreland	Patsy E Moreland	. . . .	. . . .	Jeff Sailee	Don Waller
Delta (4)	CM	303 874-7566	Robert Harding	Stephen Shutt	Mary L Williams	Chris Sasse	. . . .	Paul Suppes	Ron Alexander
Denver (468)	MC	303 640-2613	Wellington Webb	Bruce Alexander	Arie Taylor	Elizabeth Orr	Richard Gonzales	David Michaud	Mike Musgrave
Durango (12)	CM	303 247-5622	Lynn Shine	Robert F Ledger	Linda Yeager	Sherry Eilbes	Michael Dunaway	R Chris Wiggins	Otha Rogers
Eagle t (2)	CM	303 328-6354	Bill Cunningham	William Powell	Marilene Miller	William Powell	John Boyd	Phil Biersdorfer	Duston Walls
Edgewater (5)	MC	303 238-7803	(not reporting)						
Englewood (29)	CM	303 762-2370	Clyde Wiggins	Lorraine Hayes	Pat Crow	Frank Gryglewicz	Allan Stanley	Allan Stanley	Charles Esterly
Estes Park t (3)	CM	303 586-5331	H B Dannels	Gary Klaphake	V O'Connor	Monte Vavra	Jack Rumley	David Racine	William Linnane
Evans (6)	CM	303 339-5344	(not reporting)						
Federal Heights t (9)	MC	303 428-3526	Mark J Stickel	Eugene C Wieneke	Phyllis Gray	Eugene C Wieneke	James Kroupa	Lester Acker	Leland McDermott
Florence (3)	CM	303 784-4848	Frank W Tedesko	Kenneth F Bruch	Doris E Williams	Patricia A Mock	. . . .	Guy E Orazem	Martin Duran
Fort Collins (88)	CM	303 221-6500	Ann Azari	Steven C Burkett	Wanda Krajicek	Alan Krcmarik	John Mulligan	Fred Rainguet	. . . .
Fort Lupton (5)	MC	303 857-6694	Eugene S Reynolds	David Yamada	Barbara Rodgers	Rose M Bowles	. . . .	George Ward	. . . .
Fort Morgan (9)	MC	303 867-3001	James Zwetzig	. . . .	Elizabeth Gilbert	Wayne Kellogg	Steve Enfante	Harold Davisson	Michael Gay
Fountain (10)	CM	719 382-8521	(not reporting)						
Frisco t (2)	CM	303 668-5276	James Spenst	Elizabeth Black	Vivian Touve	. . . .	. . . .	E G Falconetti	Tim Mack
Fruita (4)	MC	303 858-3663	B Waldschmidt	. . . .	Margaret Steelman	. . . .	. . . .	Kris Monson	Jay Ingelhart
Glendale (2)	CM	303 759-1513	Stephen P Ward	Gary L Sears	Jo Ann Skaggs	. . . .	Richard McGowan	Kenneth E Burge	Robert D Taylor
Glenwood Springs (7)	CM	303 945-2575	(not reporting)						
Golden (13)	CM	303 279-3331	Marvin L Kay	Michael C Bestor	Susan Brooks	Ann Zelnio	Bob Burrell	Russell Cook	Dan Hartman
Grand Junction (29)	CM	303 244-1551	Reford Theobold	Mark Achen	Stephanie Nye	Ronald Lappi	Michael Thompson	Darold Sloan	James Shanks
Greeley (61)	CM	303 350-9710	William Morton	Paul Grattet	Betsy Holder	Timothy Nash	Gary Novinger	Ronald Wood	William Sterling
Greenwood Village (8)	CM	303 773-0252	Rollin D Barnard	Dinah L Lewis	Dave G Manzanares	Cathy A Fromm	. . . .	Rick Waugh	Larry A Prehm
Gunnison (5)	CM	303 641-2444	James Gelwicks	Robert Filson	Margaret Anderson	Terry Lowell	. . . .	Stu Ferguson	Kenneth Coleman
Hayden t (1)	CM	303 276-3741	Richard D Roberts	Daniel R Ellison	Janet Lea Hays	Judy Muldoon	Bryan Rickman	Cyril J Lenahan	Jack A Rickman
Julesburg t (1)	CM	303 474-3344	(not reporting)						
La Junta (8)	CM	719 384-5991	Ardeth Sneath	Daniel F Noller	Jan Schooley	Doris Houghton	Rodney Davidson	Charles Widup	Joe Kelley
Lafayette (15)	CM	303 665-5588	Larry T Gupton	Brian E Rick	Beverly A Smith	M E Hornbacher	John Hunter	Leo R Carrillo	Tim Paranto
Lakewood (126)	CM	303 987-7000	Linda Morton	Michael J Rock	Karen Goldman	Linda O'Banion	. . . .	Charles Johnston	Richard Plastino
Lamar (8)	MC	719 336-4376	Jack Bowman	David Lock	Eric Pearson	Aaleta Newman	Jeff Anderson	John Hall	Bill Thrailkill
Las Animas (2)	MC	719 456-0422	Keith E Varner	. . . .	Leslie J Uncel	. . . .	. . . .	Jerry L Butler	John F Trent
Leadville (3)	MC	303 486-0349	(not reporting)						
Limon t (2)	CM	719 775-2346	Michael Liggett	Delmar Beattie	Cary Lohmeier	. . . .	Galen Harrela	James Trahern	William Layton
Littleton (34)	CM	303 795-3700	Susan Thornton	Andrew McMinimee	Janice Owen	Marvin Thrasher	Mike Doyle	Craig Camp	Charles Blosten
Longmont (52)	CM	303 776-6050	Fred Wilson	. . . .	Valeria Skitt	Jim Golden	Steve Trunck	. . . .	Barbara Huner
Louisville (12)	CM	303 666-6565	Tom Davidson	Annette A Brand	Maj Lis Kemper	S Asti Caranci	. . . .	Rod Leesman	Tom Phare
Loveland (37)	CM	303 962-2000	. . . .	Roger W Fraser	Victoria Sheneman	. . . .	Richard L Minor	Thomas F Wagoner	. . . .
Manitou Springs (5)	MC	719 685-5596	Dan Wecks	James G Pratt	Lois J Greenman	. . . .	Steve Hart	John Humphrey	Gary Smith
Meeker t (2)	CM	303 878-5344	Jon L Hertzke	Sharon Day	Carmen Orris	Sharon Day	. . . .	Si Woodruff	Dwight Frantz

MUNICIPAL OFFICIALS IN U.S. CITIES OVER 2,500

City, 1990 population figures (000 omitted), form of government	Municipal phone number	Mayor	Appointed administrator	City clerk	Finance officer	Fire chief	Police chief	Public works director
COLORADO (88) continued								
Monte Vista (4)	CM 719 852-2692	Michael J Lister	Arthur Scibelli	Janeen Martinez	Elaine M Johnsen	. . . .	Frank R Martinez	Joseph P Kurys
Montrose (9)	CM 303 249-4534	Bob Kreamelmeyer	Ted Barkley	Mary Watt	Leona James	. . . .	Gerald Hoey	Larry Ryser
Morrison t (..)	MC 303 697-8749	Mary C Poe	. . . .	Sharon Blackstock	. . . .	. . . .	Robert Wasko	Dewayne Rhodig
Northglenn (27)	CM 303 451-8326	Donnie Parsons	James Landeck	Joan Baker	Scott Wright	. . . .	C A Gunderson	Bruce Shipley
Pagosa Springs t (..)	MC 303 264-4151	Ross Aragon	Jay Harrington	Jacquelyn Schick	. . . .	. . . .	Don Volger	Chris Gallegos
Palisade tp (2)	CM 303 464-5602	(not reporting)						
Pueblo (99)	CM 719 584-0800	Fay Kastelic	Lewis Quigley	Marian Mead	Billy Martin	Greg Miller	Bill Young	Tom Cvar
Rangely t (2)	MC 303 675-8476	Frances Green	Donald Peach	Daniel Cooley	Daniel Cooley	. . . .	Jerry Reese	John Kenney
Rifle (5)	CM 303 625-2121	David Ling	. . . .	Ellen Berggren	Nancy Black	. . . .	Daryl Meisner	Bob Whittington
Rocky Ford (4)	MC 719 254-7414	(not reporting)						
Salida (5)	MC 719 539-2311	Nancy E Sanger	Patsy R Brooks	Anthony E Gentile	. . . .	James M Gray	Darwin L Hibbs	William C Lambert
Sheridan (5)	MC 303 762-2200	Dale W Patton	Thomas H Palmer	Delores J Heath	. . . .	Mark Wallace	Jack Van Arsdol	John Christensen
Silverthorne t (2)	CM 303 468-2637	. . . .	Dallas D Everhart	. . . .	. . . .	. . . .	. . . .	. . . .
Snowmass Village t (1)	CM 303 923-3777	. . . .						
Steamboat Springs (7)	CM 303 879-2060	Mary T Brown	Harvey M Rose	Deborah Carey	Brian Funderburk	James Haugsness	Roger Jensen	Kirk A Madsen
Sterling (10)	CM 303 522-9700	Edith Evans	Randy Gustafson	James Thompson	James Thompson	Charles Miner	Larry Graham	Joe Kiolbasa
Telluride t (1)	CM 303 728-3071	(not reporting)						
Thornton (55)	CM 303 538-7245	M Carpenter	Jack Ethredge	Nancy Vincent	Keith Tillman	Charles Long	James Nursey	Bud Elliot
Trinidad (9)	CM 719 846-9843	. . . .	William Cordova	Lydia Shea	Rose Butler	Richard George	Jim Montoya	Terry Haugen
Vail (4)	CM 303 479-2100	(not reporting)						
Walsenburg (3)	MC 719 738-1048	Jay D Crook	. . . .	P Sterk Conder	H C Summers	Curtis Montoya	Octaviano Vigil	. . . .
Westminster (75)	CM 303 430-2400	Nancy Heil	Bill Christopher	Michele Gallegos	Susann Stubbs	Jim Cloud	Dan Montgomery	Ron Hellbusch
Wheat Ridge (29)	MC 303 234-5900	Ray J Winger Jr	Robert C Middaugh	Wanda Sang	. . . .	. . . .	Jack Hurst	Robert Goebel
Windsor t (5)	CM 303 686-7476	Thomas R Jones	Glen E Welden	P J Nazarenus	. . . .	. . . .	John E Michaels	Terry J Walker
Winter Park t (1)	CM 303 726-8081	Nick Teverbaugh	Daryl K Shrum	Nancy Anderson	Daryl K Shrum	. . . .	. . . .	Tom Russell
Woodland Park (5)	CM 719 687-9246	Clarke D Becker	Don E Howell	Cindy Morse	Kelly McCullar	. . . .	John W Hogue	Jim Schultz
Wray (2)	CM 303 332-4431	Jack Sloniker	Robert Snedeker	Chuck Murphy	Robert Snedeker	Eldon Dryden	Rick Schorzman	Randy Wells
Yuma (3)	CM 303 848-3878	Donald R Starnes	Douglas Lasater	Ronda Wright	. . . .	Daniel Baucke	Fred Gonzalez	. . . .
CONNECTICUT (151)								
Ansonia (18)	MC 203 736-5900	(not reporting)						
Ashford t (4)	TM 203 429-2750	William Falletti	. . . .	. . . .	. . . .	R E Whitehouse	. . . .	John A Balazs
Avon t (14)	CM 203 677-2634	Richard W Hines	Philip K Schenck	C LaMonica	Glenn S Klocko	Harvey Reeser	James Martino Jr	Rudolph W Fromm
Barkhamsted t (3)	TM 203 379-8285	(not reporting)						
Beacon Falls t (5)	TM 203 729-4340	Leonard D'Amico	. . . .	Francis X Doiron	. . . .	William Lee	Leonard D'Amico	Frank Del Vecchio
Berlin t (17)	TM 203 828-7000	(not reporting)						
Bethany t (5)	TM 203 393-2100	(not reporting)						
Bethel t (18)	MC 203 794-8501	Clifford J Hurgin	. . . .	Jane D Shannon	Barry R Curina	. . . .	John Basile	Hemraj Khona
Bethlehem t (3)	TM 203 266-7677	(not reporting)						
Bloomfield t (19)	CM 203 243-8971	(not reporting)						
Bolton t (5)	MC 203 649-8066	Michael W Emerita	John C Guinan	Susan Depold	. . . .	. . . .	. . . .	Danotto Rattazzi
Branford t (28)	RT 203 488-8394	(not reporting)						
Bridgeport (142)	MC 203 576-7600	(not reporting)						
Bristol (61)	MC 203 584-7665	William T Stortz	. . . .	. . . .	Theodore Hamilton	Anthony D Basile	William R Kohnke	Ronald H Smith
Brookfield t (14)	TM 203 775-7300	Bonnie P Smith	. . . .	Ruth B Burr	Raymond Bolek	. . . .	John W Anderson	Ronald Klimas
Brooklyn t (7)	TM 203 774-9452	Donald S Francis	. . . .	Leona Mainville	. . . .	. . . .	Donald S Francis	Leonard Albee
Burlington t (7)	TM 203 673-6789	Theodore Scheidel	. . . .	. . . .	Arthur W Johanson	Richard Higley	Theodore Scheidel	Albert Wilusz
Canterbury t (4)	TM 203 546-9377	(not reporting)						
Canton t (8)	TM 203 693-4093	Kathleen Corkum	. . . .	Shirley Krompegal	Richard Mahoney	. . . .	John LaDucer	Richard Negro
Cheshire t (26)	CM 203 271-6660	Sandra Mouris	Edward O'Neill	Mae Tabor	Michael Milone	Chris Bowman	George Merraim	Thomas Crowe
Chester t (3)	TM 203 526-9553	(not reporting)						
Clinton t (13)	TM 203 669-9333	(not reporting)						
Colchester t (11)	TM 203 537-3461	Jenny Contols	. . . .	. . . .	Margaret Wasicki	Jess McMinn	. . . .	Mark Decker
Columbia t (5)	TM 203 228-0110	Adella G Urban	. . . .	Eleanor V Vickers	Paula Stahl	Jerry James	Adella G Urban	Peter Naumec
Coventry t (10)	CM 203 742-6324	Richard Ashley	John A Elsesser	Ruth Benoit	John A Elsesser	. . . .	Frank Trzaskos	. . . .
Cromwell t (12)	TM 203 632-3410	(not reporting)						
Danbury (66)	MC 203 797-4598	Gene F Eriquez	Basil Friscia	Michael Seri	Dominic Setaro	Antonio Legardo	Nelson A Macedo	. . . .
Danielson b (4)	RT 203 774-6058	(not reporting)						
Darien t (18)	RT 203 656-7300	Henry Sanders	Norman A Lucas	M Van Sciver	John Fletcher	. . . .	Hugh McManus	Robert Steeger
Deep River t (4)	TM 203 526-2028	Richard H Smith	. . . .	Jean M Ressler	. . . .	Steve David	. . . .	Richard H Smith
Derby (12)	MC 203 734-9203	Dino DiMauro Jr	. . . .	. . . .	. . . .	Anthony Gian	Donald Germain	Gary Parker
Durham t (6)	TM 203 349-3452	(not reporting)						
East Granby t (4)	TM 203 653-2576	Charles W Chatey	. . . .	E W Birmingham	. . . .	Albert Brown	Charles W Chatey	Stewart Dewey
East Haddam t (7)	TM 203 873-8615	(not reporting)						
East Hampton t (10)	CM 203 267-4468	. . . .	Alan Bergren	Pauline Markham	Carol Souppa	Phil Visintainer	Eugene Rame	Robert Drewry
East Hartford t (50)	MC 203 289-2781	Susan G Kniep	. . . .	Brian Fitzgerald	Paul Narbowski	Dave Dagon	Jim Shay	Jack Petkus
East Haven t (26)	MC 203 468-3204	Henry J Luzzi	Louis A Zullo	Elizabeth C Leary	Barbara J Avard	Wayne Sandford	James Criscuolo	Raymond J Farina
East Lyme t (15)	TM 203 739-6931	(not reporting)						
East Windsor t (10)	TM 203 623-8122	Walter Gudzunas	. . . .	Claire Badstubner	. . . .	. . . .	Thomas Laufer	David Fisck
Easton t (6)	TM 203 268-6291	Anthony Colonnese	. . . .	Elizabeth Pander	Joy Haller	David Buchanan	Gerard Hance	Edward Nagy
Ellington t (11)	TM 203 875-0787	Donald V Landmann	. . . .	D Mac Intosh	N J DiColeto Jr	. . . .	. . . .	Peter Michaud
Enfield t (46)	CM 203 745-0371	Francis A Burke	A Louis Hayward	S Olechnicki	V Santacroce	. . . .	Hebert Foy	Walter Markett
Essex t (6)	TM 203 767-8201	Bruce Glowac	. . . .	Betty Gaudenzi	. . . .	. . . .	. . . .	. . . .
Fairfield t (53)	RT 203 256-3000	J Durrell	. . . .	M Toth	J Leahy	D Gardiner	R Sullivan	R White
Farmington t (21)	CM 203 673-8200	B Stockwell	Thomas J Wontorek	Edgar King	Daniel P Costello	Vincent Dipietro	Leroy Bangham	James Bonini
Glastonbury t (28)	CM 203 659-2711	Charles L Monaco	Richard J Johnson	Edward Friedeberg	G Ted Ellis	Bernard Dennler	James M Thomas	. . . .
Granby t (9)	CM 203 653-2538	. . . .	W F Smith Jr	. . . .	H C Laraway	. . . .	J P Marron Sr	W P Lyons
Greenwich t (58)	RT 203 622-7710	(not reporting)						
Griswold t (10)	TM 203 376-0233	Donald E Burdick	. . . .	Ellen Dupont	. . . .	. . . .	. . . .	. . . .
Groton t (45)	CM 203 441-6600	Linda Krause	Ronald LeBlanc	Barbara Tarbox	Sal Pandolfo	. . . .	Thomas Falvey	Gary Schneider
Groton (10)	MC 203 441-2103	(not reporting)						
Guilford t (20)	TM 203 453-8015	Edward J Lynch	. . . .	Shirley Bohan	Philip Russell	C Herrschaft	Kenneth Cruz	Raymond Tardie
Haddam t (7)	TM 203 345-8531	Jane W Blau	. . . .	. . . .	. . . .	. . . .	Jane W Blau	Philip Goff
Hamden t (52)	MC 203 287-2500	(not reporting)						
Hartford (140)	CM 203 722-6340	(not reporting)						
Harwinton t (5)	TM 203 485-9051	Marie Knudsen	. . . .	Cherie D Shanley	. . . .	Fred Gottschall	. . . .	Thomas Pollack
Hebron t (7)	TM 203 228-9406	John Hibbard	Robert E Lee	Marian Celio	Joanne Gyure	Bruce Degray	. . . .	Earl Woodworth
Jewett City b (3)	MC 203 376-2443	(not reporting)						
Killingly t (16)	CM 203 774-8601	(not reporting)						
Killingworth t (5)	TM 203 663-1765	(not reporting)						
Lebanon t (6)	TM 203 642-6100	Joyce Okonuk	. . . .	J McGillicuddy	Thomas Wentworth	Robert Cady	. . . .	Thomas Conley
Ledyard t (15)	MC 203 464-8740	Joseph A Lozier	Gloria Hosmer	Patricia Karns	Anna M Johnson	George Chapman	Joseph A Lozier	Joseph A Lozier
Lisbon t (4)	TM 203 376-3400	Daniel W Teper	. . . .	Barbara Burzycki	Nancy Gosselin	Ricky Hamel	Daniel W Teper	Wayne K Natzel

Directory 1/9
continued

MUNICIPAL OFFICIALS
IN U.S. CITIES OVER 2,500

City, 1990 population figures (000 omitted), form of government	Municipal phone number	Mayor	Appointed administrator	City clerk	Finance officer	Fire chief	Police chief	Public works director
CONNECTICUT (151) continued								
Litchfield t (8)	TM 203 567-5133	Craig A Miner	. . . .	Evelyn N Goodwin	Norma Waldvogel	. . . .	Craig A Miner	David P Thompson
Madison t (15)	TM 203 245-5602	Thomas R Rylander	. . . .	Betty Anne Lynch	. . . .	. . . .	James Cameron	S Mac Millan
Manchester t (52)	CM 203 647-3123	(not reporting)						
Mansfield t (21)	CM 203 429-3336	Fred A Cazel Jr	Martin H Berliner	Joan Gerdsen	Jeffrey H Smith	. . . .	Martin H Berliner	Lon R Hultgren
Marlborough t (6)	TM 203 295-9547	(not reporting)						
Meriden (59)	CM 203 630-4037	Angelo D'Agostino	Roger Kemp	Irene Masse	Edward Murphy	Robert Raby	Robert Kosienski	Joseph Franco
Middlebury t (6)	TM 203 758-1770	Edward B St John	. . . .	. . . .	Karl A Mandl	Edmond E Bailly	Patrick J Bona	Edward B St John
Middlefield t (4)	MC 203 349-3449	David G Webster	. . . .	Frances Pac	. . . .	Terry Parmelee	David G Webster	David G Webster
Middletown (43)	MC 203 344-3401	(not reporting)						
Milford (48)	MC 203 783-3200	(not reporting)						
Monroe t (17)	MC 203 452-5400	Kenneth S Heitzke	. . . .	Kay Inderdohnen	Jeffrey Whone	. . . .	Robert Wesche	Sherwood Lovejoy
Montville t (17)	MC 203 848-3030	Wayne D Scott	. . . .	Margaret Skinner	Michael Hillsberg	. . . .	Wayne D Scott	David King
Naugatuck t (31)	MC 203 729-4571	Robert C Paolino	Brian J Powell	Kara M Keating	Jack Tedesco	William Mallone	William Long	Hank Witkoski
New Britain (75)	MC 203 826-3303	(not reporting)						
New Canaan t (18)	TM 203 972-2311	Louis J Moreno	Peter G Murphy	Mary Ritter	C Rothschild	. . . .	Eric Dam	Frank Denicola
New Fairfield t (13)	TM 203 746-8101	Cheryl D Reedy	. . . .	Diana Peck	Gail R Redenz	Peter Benzinger	. . . .	Thomas Dube
New Hartford t (6)	TM 203 379-3389	Bryce Gresczyk	Roxanne Carroll	Pat Halloran	Barbara Schaffer	. . . .	. . . .	Victor Vincent
New Haven (130)	MC 203 787-8200	John C Daniels	L S Turner	Sally Brown	Ralph W Halsey	John Smith	Nicholas Pastore	Vanessa Burns
New London (29)	CM 203 447-5200	William Satti	Richard Brown	Clark Vander Lyke	Donald E Gray Jr	Ronald Samul	. . . .	. . . .
New Milford t (24)	MC 203 355-6000	(not reporting)						
Newington t (29)	MC 203 666-4661	Rodney Mortensen	Keith Chapman	Roberta Jenkins	Joan McGovern	Joseph Kalasky	Thomas G Ganley	Keith Chapman
Newtown t (21)	MC 203 270-4201	Zita McMahon	. . . .	Cynthia Curtis	Benjamin B Spragg	. . . .	Michael DeJoseph	Frederick Hurley
North Branford t (13)	CM 203 488-7203	Joanne Wentworth	Frank Connolly	Lisa Valenti	Gregory Brown	Ralph Thomas	Matthew Canelli	John Volpe
North Canaan t (3)	TM 203 824-7313	(not reporting)						
North Haven t (22)	TM 203 239-5321	Anthony Rescigno	. . . .	Elinor Pedalino	Vincent Palmeri	John Obier	Kevin Connolly	Richard Gillen
North Stonington t (5)	TM 203 535-0793	(not reporting)						
Norwalk (78)	MC 203 854-7724	Frank Esposito	. . . .	Kathryn Senie	Jack E Miller	John Yost	Carl Labianca	Dominck Digangi
Norwich (37)	CM 203 886-2381	Charles Witt	William Tallman	Beverly Muldoon	A Sanquedolce	Thomas Kirby	Richard Abele	Walter Wadja
Old Lyme t (7)	TM 203 434-1605	James R Rice	. . . .	Irene A Carnell	. . . .	. . . .	. . . .	Olcott Harris
Old Saybrook t (10)	TM 203 388-3401	(not reporting)						
Orange t (13)	TM 203 795-0751	Dorothy L Berger	. . . .	Jean V Mitchell	. . . .	Kenneth Mitchell	Joseph Rowley	John Kazmarski
Oxford t (9)	TM 203 888-2543	Edward Oczkowski	Carl Serus	C Koskelowski	. . . .	Victor Noll	Edward Oczkowski	. . . .
Plainfield t (14)	TM 203 564-4071	(not reporting)						
Plainville t (17)	CM 203 793-0221	Donald St Pierre	John P Bohenko	Peter Lennon	Judy Doneiko	Joseph Watkins	Francis Roche	Caryl P Bradt
Plymouth t (12)	MC 203 585-4002	David M Denis	. . . .	Janet P Scoville	Manuel Gomes	Richard Kruezer	David A Damon	Anthony Lorezetti
Pomfret t (3)	TM 203 974-0191	Stanley S Sheldon	. . . .	Nora V Johnson	. . . .	Gordon Spink Jr	. . . .	Fred R Sirrine
Portland t (8)	TM 203 342-2880	(not reporting)						
Preston t (5)	TM 203 887-5581	Parke C Spicer	. . . .	Hattie Wucik	Morris Fishbone	. . . .	. . . .	Parke C Spicer
Prospect t (8)	MC 203 758-4461	Robert Chatfield	. . . .	Pat Vaillancourt	. . . .	. . . .	. . . .	. . . .
Putnam (9)	MC 203 928-5529	Maxine Mann	. . . .	Lucille Herrick	. . . .	Norman Bernier	Edward Perron	. . . .
Putnam t (..)	TM 203 928-6608	Daniel S Rovero	. . . .	Lillian M Newth	. . . .	. . . .	. . . .	Gerard Beausoleil
Redding t (8)	TM 203 938-2002	H Bielawa	. . . .	P Creigh	M Wiesner	. . . .	. . . .	R Harker
Ridgefield t (21)	TM 203 438-7301	Sue Manning	. . . .	Dora Cassavechia	Jay Wahlberg	Richard Nagle	Thomas Rotunda	Frank Serfilippi
Rocky Hill t (17)	CM 203 563-1451	(not reporting)						
Salisbury t (4)	TM 203 435-9512	Louis Trotta	Linda Stevens	Laura Johnson	Carl Williams	Donald Reid	. . . .	William Pickert
Seymour t (14)	TM 203 888-2511	R Koskelowski	R Koskelowski	Norma Drummer	Janice Hallaman	Frank Critchett	Michael Metzler	Sal Vicari
Sharon t (3)	MC 203 364-5789	Robert Moeller	Tina M Pitcher	Linda A Wasley	. . . .	. . . .	. . . .	. . . .
Shelton (35)	MC 203 736-2681	Mark A Lauretti	Sandra Nesteriak	. . . .	Louis Marusic	Richard Tallberg	Robert White	Paul DiMauro
Simsbury t (22)	TM 203 651-3751	(not reporting)						
Somers t (9)	TM 203 763-0837	Robert B Percoski	. . . .	Claire Walker	. . . .	Edward Pagani	Robert B Percoski	Kenneth Anderson
South Windsor t (22)	MC 203 644-2511	Lincoln Streeter	Jean E Zurbrigen	Marilyn W Burger	George Spring Jr	William R Lanning	Gary K Tyler	Michael J Gantick
Southbury t (16)	MC 203 264-0606	(not reporting)						
Southington t (39)	CM 203 276-2665	James Verderame	John Weichsel	Y Depaolo	Edward Brickett	Thomas J Murphy	William Perry	. . . .
Sprague t (3)	TM 203 822-3000	Thomas McAvoy Jr	. . . .	Mary M Stefon	Edmand F Conde	Robert A Tardif	. . . .	Mark M Benson
Stafford t (11)	TM 203 684-2130	(not reporting)						
Stafford Springs b (4)	MC 203 684-3827	(not reporting)						
Stamford (108)	MC 203 977-4070	Stanley Esposito	. . . .	Lois Pont Briant	Patrick O'Connor	Ronald Graner	. . . .	Michael Pavia
Stonington t (17)	TM 203 535-4721	(not reporting)						
Stratford t (49)	CM 203 385-4007	. . . .	Mark Barnhart	Patrici Ulatowski	Edward Gomeau	Roger Macey	Robert Mossman	Michael Hudzik
Suffield t (11)	TM 203 668-7397	Lorette Russell	. . . .	Dorothy McCarty	. . . .	Thomas Bellmore	Murray Phelps Jr	. . . .
Thomaston t (7)	TM 203 283-4421	Eugene McMahon	. . . .	Arlene Foley	. . . .	Clifford Brammer	Edward Grabherr	Gerald Grohoski
Thompson t (9)	TM 203 923-9561	(not reporting)						
Tolland t (11)	CM 203 871-3600	. . . .	John B Harkins	Elaine Bugbee	John B Harkins	Ronald Littell	Ronald Littell Sr	William Sevcik
Torrington (34)	MC 203 489-2228	Delia Donne	Rosalie Bellemare	Frank Vitalo	Richard Friday	Marquam Johnson	Mahlon Sabo	Matthew Dominy
Trumbull t (32)	MC 203 452-5000	(not reporting)						
Vernon t (30)	MC 203 872-8591	(not reporting)						
Wallingford t (41)	MC 203 294-2080	William Dickinson	. . . .	Kathryn Wall	Thomas Myers	Wayne Lefebvre	Douglas Dortenzio	Henry McCully
Washington t (4)	TM 203 868-2786	Alan Chapin	. . . .	Doris Welles	. . . .	Mark Lyon	. . . .	. . . .
Waterbury (109)	MC 203 574-6890	(not reporting)						
Waterford t (18)	RT 203 442-0553	(not reporting)						
Watertown t (20)	CM 203 274-5411	. . . .	John Salomone	Mary Canty	Frank Nardelli	O'Neill Burrows	John Carroll	Phillip Deleppo
West Hartford t (60)	CM 203 523-2000	(not reporting)						
West Haven (54)	MC 203 937-3500	H Richard Borer	R Annunziata	William Donegan	Thomas S Hamilton	. . . .	Harry J Carroll	Arthur C Ferris
Westbrook t (5)	TM 203 399-6236	Paula C Ferrara	Gerda Ziolkowski	Johanna Schneider	Lorraine Cenkus	Patrick Murphy	Paula C Ferrara	John Riggio
Weston t (9)	TM 203 222-2616	(not reporting)						
Westport t (24)	RT 203 226-8311	D Wood	. . . .	J Hyde	D Miklus	R McGuire	W Chiarenzelli	S Edwards
Wethersfield t (26)	CM 203 529-8611	Martin P Gold	Lee C Erdmann	Dorcas McHugh	Joseph Swetcky Jr	John J McAuliffe	John S Karangekis	Lee C Erdmann
Willington t (6)	TM 203 429-5649	Roger Perry	. . . .	Mary Bowen	. . . .	. . . .	. . . .	Elwood Jones
Wilton t (16)	TM 203 834-9200	(not reporting)						
Winchester t (12)	CM 203 379-2713	(not reporting)						
Windham t (22)	MC 203 456-3593	(not reporting)						
Windsor t (28)	CM 203 688-3675	(not reporting)						
Windsor Locks t (12)	CM 203 627-1444	(not reporting)						
Winsted (..)	MC 203 379-4646	(not reporting)						
Wolcott t (14)	MC 203 879-4666	(not reporting)						
Woodbridge t (8)	TM 203 387-6639	Nan Birdwhistell	Richard McGuire	S Ciarleglio	Diane Waldron	Marc Santoro	Dennis Phipps	Joseph Kalson
Woodbury t (8)	TM 203 263-2141	K H Campbell	. . . .	J Sandulli	R Belden	E Kiessling	. . . .	P E Lizauskas
Woodstock t (6)	TM 203 928-0208	Michael J Balch	. . . .	Judy W Cooper	Gale C Garceau	. . . .	. . . .	Sidney E Swenson
DELAWARE (13)								
Bethany Beach t (..)	CM 302 539-5643	Charles Bartlett	Dean S Phillips	Dawn W Lawson	Madalyn Forrest	. . . .	Herbert C Carey	John Ruza
Delmar t (1)	CM 410 896-2777	John F McDonnell	Roberta Ernest	. . . .	. . . .	. . . .	Hal Saylor	Robert Handy
Dover (28)	CM 302 736-7000	(not reporting)						

City, 1990 population figures (000 omitted), form of government	Municipal phone number	Mayor	Appointed administrator	City clerk	Finance officer	Fire chief	Police chief	Public works director
DELAWARE (13) continued								
Elsmere t (6)	CM 302 998-2215	(not reporting)						
Laurel t (3)	MC 302 875-2277	George P Volenik	William S Hitch	. . . .	. . . .	Jeffery Hill	James A Harris	. . . .
Middletown t (4)	MC 302 378-2711	(not reporting)						
Milford (6)	CM 302 422-6616	(not reporting)						
New Castle (5)	CM 302 322-9801	John F Klingmeyer	Anne M Alzapiedi	Mary M Rispoli	. . . .	Grover Ingle	Scott W Rees	. . . .
Newark (25)	CM 302 366-7026	Ronald Gardner	Carl Luft	Susan Lamblack	Patrick McCullar	. . . .	William Hogan	Richard LaPointe
Rehoboth Beach (1)	CM 302 227-6181	(not reporting)						
Seaford (6)	CM 302 629-9173	Guy Longo	Dolores Slatcher	. . . .	. . . .	Daniel Short	Robert Miller	John Hedrick
Smyrna t (5)	CM 302 653-9231	George C Wright	Michael S Jacobs	Carol C McKinney	Andrew P Johnson	. . . .	Donald H McGinty	William E Hamburg
Wilmington (72)	MC 302 571-4011	(not reporting)						
WASHINGTON D.C.								
(607)	MC 202 727-1000	Sharon P Kelly	Robert L Mallet	. . . .	Ellen M O'Connor	Thomas McCaffery	Fred Thomas	Betty Francis
FLORIDA (239)								
Alachua (5)	CM 904 462-1231	. . . .	Charles M Morris	Darlene Bond	Francine Jernigan	. . . .	Freddie Dampier	Paul O'Dea
Altamonte Springs (35)	CM 407 830-3801	(not reporting)						
Apalachicola (3)	MC 904 653-9319	Robert L Howell	. . . .	Betty Taylor Webb	Rose McCoy	Neuman Marshall	Warren Faircloth	Harry Braswell
Apopka (14)	MC 407 889-1743	John H Land	John H Land	Connie V Major	Jack H Douglas	Richard Anderson	Robert Campbell	. . . .
Arcadia (6)	CM 813 494-4114	Eugene Hickson Sr	Edward Strube	Margaret Way	Margaret Way	Tony Messina	Kenneth Carlton	James Bussey
Atlantic Beach (12)	CM 904 247-5800	Wm Gulliford	Kim Leinbach	Maureen King	Kirk Wendland	Ronald Williams	David Thompson	Robert Kosoy
Atlantis (2)	CM 407 965-1744	Clyde F Farmer	Earl Moore	Betty A Yon	Majella Thornton	. . . .	. . . .	Steven Mazuk
Auburndale (9)	CM 813 965-5500	Philip McKinney	Robert R Green	Sandra Jackson	Shirley Conn	Sam Efurd	Dean Longo	Bobby Harbuck
Avon Park (8)	CM 813 452-2221	Gordon R Marshall	V Henderson	V Henderson	V Henderson	Joseph P Trainor	Joseph G Sliva	Bobby Sizemore
Bal Harbour v (3)	MC 305 866-4633	Estelle Stern	Carole S Morris	Jeanette Horton	. . . .	. . . .	Alfred Treppeda	Robert L Wheldon
Bartow (15)	CM 813 533-0911	Charles L Hooks	. . . .	Victoria Troup	John Nickels	Tim Pitts	M L Roy McKinsey	Bill Pickard
Bay Harbor Islands t (5)	CM 305 866-6241	Edward Tavlin	Linda Karlsson	Ellen Umans	Cecil Rash	. . . .	John Ross	Kenneth Cassel
Bay Lake (..)	CM 305 828-2034	(not reporting)						
Belle Glade (16)	CM 407 996-0100	Bill Bailey	Lomax Harrelle	June Boglioli	William Underwood	Tony Tuliano	Mikeal Miller	Frank Green
Belle Isle (3)	MC 407 851-7730	Charles Scott	Linda M Davidson	Linda M Davidson	Linda M Davidson	. . . .	. . . .	. . . .
Belleair t (4)	CM 813 584-7134	Kent R Weible	Stephen J Papalas	Alice Blankenship	Stephen J Papalas	Robin A Millican	Harry F Gwynne	Bill Sliger
Belleair Bluffs (2)	MC 813 584-2151	John E Diller	. . . .	B L Hendrickson	B L Hendrickson	Charles Humiston	James W Mangum	David R Sexsmith
Biscayne Park v (3)	CO 305 893-7490	. . . .	. . . .	Patricia A Cerny	. . . .	. . . .	Barry J Noe	Thomas S Nunn
Blountstown (2)	CM 904 674-5488	(not reporting)						
Boca Raton (61)	CM 407 393-7700	Bill Smith	Rick Witker	C Bridgwater	M Timberlake	Jack Withrow	Peter Petracco	Ronald Laccheo
Bonifay (3)	MC 904 547-4238	James E Sims Jr	. . . .	Shirley F Mitchel	Shirley F Mitchel	Shay McCormick	Dennis Lee	Jack Marell
Boynton Beach (46)	CM 407 734-8111	Edward Harmening	J Scott Miller	Susan Kruse	Grady Swann	Edward Allen	Thomas Dettman	Robert Eichorst
Bradenton (44)	MC 813 748-0800	Bill Evers	. . . .	. . . .	Paul Esquinaldo	Vernon Horne	Vc Badalamenti	Earl Crawley
Brooksville (7)	CM 904 796-4954	F Bernardini	James Malcolm	Karen Phillips	Fred Dean	J Adkins	B Tincher	R Titterington
Bushnell (..)	CM 904 793-2591	Joe P Strickland	Vicente Ruano	Judith C Muller	Judith C Muller	. . . .	James Reed	Ronald Pitts
Callaway (12)	MC 904 872-7780	(not reporting)						
Cape Canaveral (8)	CM 407 868-1200	Joy C Salamone	Bennett C Boucher	Faith G Miller	Deborah Haggerty	. . . .	. . . .	Michael Gluskin
Cape Coral (75)	CM 813 574-0401	J M Mazurkiewicz	M David Sallee	Eula Jorgensen	Howard Kunik	Thomas Kochheiser	. . . .	Greg Olivit
Casselberry (19)	MC 407 831-3551	J Hillebrandt	Jack Schluckebier	Thelma McPherson	Jeffrey Dreier	Paul Algeri	Durbin Gatch	Anthony Segreto
Chattahoochee (4)	MC 904 663-4046	Ken Kimrey	. . . .	Charles Sparks	Charles Sparks	Floyd Pfaedner	David Turnage	Millard Hampton
Chipley (4)	MC 904 638-6350	Tommy McDonald	. . . .	Fred Buchanan	. . . .	Kevan Parker	Robert Pleas	Clyde Land
Clearwater (99)	CM 813 462-6870	Rita Garvey	Michael Wright	Cynthia Goudea	Daniel Deignan	Robert Davidson	Sidney Klein	William Baker
Clermont (7)	CM 904 394-4081	Robert A Pool	David W Saunders	Joseph E Van Zile	Joseph E Van Zile	Carle Bishop	Prentice Tyndal	Elbert P Davis
Clewiston (6)	CO 813 983-9191	(not reporting)						
Cocoa (18)	CM 407 639-7555	Lester Campbell	Stephen Bonczek	Beth Dabrowski	James Holt	F Terry Seawell	Daniel Rettig	Wm Stephenson
Cocoa Beach (12)	CM 407 868-3333	R Lawton	Mark S Eckert	L Kalaghchy	. . . .	. . . .	R Walker	. . . .
Coconut Creek (27)	CM 305 973-6770	Abe Niss	. . . .	Angela A Bender	Harry M Kilgore	. . . .	George L LaFlam	Thomas Lee
Cooper City (21)	CM 305 434-4300	S Fardelmann	Chris Farrell	Susan Bernard	Frank Suozzo	Russell Brown	R Steve Davis	John Flint
Coral Gables (40)	CM 305 446-6800	R J Valdes Fault	H C Eads Jr	Virginia Paul	Donald G Nelson	David H Teems	James H Butler	Aurelio R Linero
Coral Springs (79)	CM 305 344-1150	Jeanne Mills	Tony O'Rourke	Jonda Joseph	David Russek	Bill Fyfe	Roy Arigo	Bob Glenn
Crestview (10)	MC 904 682-6131	Ted Mathis	. . . .	Edward Neal	. . . .	Joseph Traylor	David Carnahan	General Cox
Crystal River (4)	CM 904 795-4216	Curtis A Rich	Merv Waldrop	Shirley L Carroll	George Zoettlein	Brown Dumas	Roger B Krieger	Russell Kreager
Dade City (6)	CM 904 521-1460	Charles McIntosh	Richard R Diamond	James D Class	James D Class	Ronald N McBee	Phillip Thompson	Ronald L Ferguson
Dania (13)	CM 305 921-8700	(not reporting)						
Davenport (..)	CM 813 422-4410	Peter Rust	Wm Drummond	Marge Williams	Paula Munro	Fred Stewart Jr	H B Robinson	Lovit White
Davie t (47)	CM 305 797-1030	James Bush	Irving Rosenbaum	G Reinfeld Jacobs	Chris Wallace	Michael Donati	Jack Mackie	Robert Rawls
Daytona Beach (62)	CM 904 252-6461	Lawrence J Kelly	Howard D Tipton	Gwendolyn Edwards	James C Maniak	. . . .	Paul B Crow	T McClelland
Daytona Beach Shores (2)	CM 904 322-5000	Donald F Large	Charles W McCool	Charles W McCool	John C Yazurlo	. . . .	Frank S Daraio	Carl G Hooper
De Funiak Springs (5)	CM 904 892-8500	John V Lawson	Michael Standley	H Diane Dudley	Sara Wilson	Bill Yearwood	Clinton Hooks	. . . .
De Land (16)	CM 904 738-3900	(not reporting)						
Deerfield Beach (46)	CM 305 480-4200	Albert Capellini	Barry R Evans	Muriel W Rickard	David P Bok	Thomas M Boylston	. . . .	John E Vogel
Delray Beach (47)	CM 407 243-7000	Thomas E Lynch	David T Harden	A M Harty	Joseph M Safford	Kerry Koen	Richard Overman	Richard Corwin
Destin (8)	CM 904 837-4242	Walter Thomas	Philip Cook	Lee Garrett	Philip Cook	. . . .	. . . .	Brice R Nist
Dundee t (..)	CM 813 439-1086	(not reporting)						
Dunedin (34)	CM 813 733-4151	(not reporting)						
Eagle Lake (2)	CM 813 293-4141	Dennis Blanchard	Linda Weldon	Linda Culpepper	. . . .	Frank Kehoe	. . . .	Robert Johnson
Edgewater (15)	CM 904 428-3245	Jack Hayman	George McMahon	Susan Wadsworth	Fred Munoz	Wm Vola	L Schumaker	Hugh Williams
Eustis (13)	CM 904 483-5430	(not reporting)						
Fernandina Beach (9)	CM 904 277-7320	(not reporting)						
Florida City (6)	CM 305 247-8221	Otis T Wallace	Richard Anderson	Sandra Romero	Mara Ben Asher	. . . .	Earnie P Neal	C Liggines
Fort Lauderdale (149)	CM 305 761-5000	(not reporting)						
Fort Meade (5)	CM 813 285-8191	Betty B Johnson	Charles Saddler	Charles Saddler	Charles Saddler	Billy K Gunter	George M Ferris	Bob Carter
Fort Myers (45)	MC 813 332-6775	Wilbur Smith	. . . .	Marie Adams	Ken Hoffman	William Conrod	Donna Hansen	Emmette Waite
Fort Pierce (37)	CM 407 460-2200	W Dannahower	James Powell	Cassandra Steele	George Bergalis	. . . .	Gil Kerlikowske	Robert Morgan
Fort Walton Beach (21)	CM 904 243-3141	Larry Trenary	Reid Silverboard	Helen Spencer	Richard Fort	Richard O Black	Phil Trish	Monty Jackson
Frostproof (3)	CM 813 635-2151	John Durant	Roger A Hood	Lillian Amerson	Roger A Hood	Raymond Chatlos	J Neal Byrd	David F Hand
Fruitland Park (3)	CM 904 787-6089	William R White	Robert D Proctor	Linda I Sparks	. . . .	Thomas Gamble	J M Isom Sr	. . . .
Gainesville (85)	CM 904 334-2011	(not reporting)						
Golden Beach (1)	MC 305 932-0744	(not reporting)						
Graceville (3)	CO 904 263-3250	Patricia Segrest	David C Mitchell	Kathleen B Turner	. . . .	William Stob	Daniel B Ward	. . . .
Green Cove Springs (4)	CM 904 284-5621	Sandra Dunnvant	Robert Paine	Margie Robertson	Sue Heath	Richard Knoff	Gail Russell	Walter Rountree
Greenacres City (19)	CM 407 642-2000	Samuel J Ferreri	David B Farber	Sondra K Hill	David R Miles	. . . .	John T Treanor	Robert R Flemming
Gulf Breeze (6)	CM 904 934-5100	Lane Gilchrist	Edwin Eddy	Marita Rhodes	Nancy Millay	Bob Minshull	John Morgan	Harrold Hatcher
Gulfport (12)	CM 813 321-1158	Michael Yakes	Robert E Lee	Lesley M Demuth	S Jones Boerker	Walter Brooks	G Curt Willocks	Paul Williams
Haines City (12)	CM 813 422-4986	Earnest Vandiver	Ann Toney	Nell Johnson	. . . .	Wayne Walling	Tom Wheeler	Lionel Carroll
Hallandale (31)	CM 305 458-3251	(not reporting)						
Havana t (2)	CM 904 539-6493	T J Davis	Cecil G Trippe	Anne T Bert	Anne T Bert	Don Vickers	Phillip Fusilier	. . . .
Hialeah (188)	MC 305 883-8052	(not reporting)						

Directory 1/9 continued **MUNICIPAL OFFICIALS IN U.S. CITIES OVER 2,500**

City, 1990 population figures (000 omitted), form of government	Municipal phone number	Mayor	Appointed administrator	City clerk	Finance officer	Fire chief	Police chief	Public works director
FLORIDA (239) continued								
Hialeah Gardens (8) MC	305 558-4114	(not reporting)						
Highland Beach t (3) CM	407 278-4548	Arlin Voress	Mary Ann Mariano	Anne Kowals	Michael Seaman	. . . .	William Cecere	Jack Lee
Holly Hill (11) CM	904 252-7631	James M Gaither	Ralph K Hester	Sue W Blackwell	Brenda Gubernator	Robert E Lacy	John P Finn	Marcus E Chattin
Hollywood (122) CM	305 921-3473	Mara Giulianti	Samuel Finz	Martha Lambos	Susan Miller	James Ward	R H Witt	Greg Turek
Holmes Beach (5) MC	813 778-2221	Patrica A Geyer	. . . .	Leslie R Ford	Patrica A Geyer	. . . .	. . . .	John R Fernandez
Homestead (27) CM	305 247-1801	(not reporting)						
Indialantic t (3) CM	407 723-2242	Arthur W Vernon	Edward Gross	C Hazelgrove	C Hazelgrove	Thomas Barker	Roger Skinner	John Eddy
Indian Creek v (..) CM	305 865-4121	(not reporting)						
Indian Harbor Beach (7) CM	407 773-3181	Roland W Denault	Richard G Edgeton	Ruth H Grigsby	Loren L Rueter	Ted Quirk	Fred Fernez	Gil Grignon
Indian River Shores t (2) CM	407 231-1771	Robert Schoen	Joseph Dorsky	Virginia Gilbert	Joseph Dorsky	Thomas Boisvert	Thomas Boisvert	Joseph Dorsky
Indian Rocks Beach (4) CM	813 595-2517	(not reporting)						
Inverness (6) CM	904 726-2611	Orien J Humphries	Bruce D Banning	Marilyn C Jordan	Joseph Levesque	. . . .	Massey W Cook	Daniel Sawyer
Jacksonville (635) MC	904 630-1178	Ed Austin	Lex Hester	Henry Cook	Michael Weinstein	Charles Clark	Jim McMillan	Sam Mousa
Jacksonville Beach (18) CM	904 247-6263	Reid McCormick	Bill Lewis	O Bruce Corbitt	Harry Royal	Gary Brown	Bruce Thomason	Stan Nodland
Jasper (..) CM	904 792-1212	Matthew Hawkins	Ralph O Bowers	Johnnie F Soule	. . . .	Doyle L Grantham	John F Osborn	Walter H Davis Jr
Juno Beach t (..) CM	407 626-1122	Frank W Harris	Gail F Nelson	Deborah S Manzo	Joseph F Lo Bello	. . . .	Mitchell L Tyre	Dennis W Barrett
Jupiter t (25) CM	407 745-5134	Karen J Golonka	Lee R Evett	Sally Boylan	Michael A Simmons	. . . .	Richard Westgate	James C Davis
Jupiter Island t (1) CM	407 546-5011	Russell G Simpson	James R Spurgeon	Antonia M Wickes	. . . .	William G Curry	William G Curry	James D Graham Jr
Kenneth City t (4) MC	813 544-6655	Lester M Eshleman	. . . .	Joan D Musgrave	Lester M Eshleman	John Karpinecz	. . . .	Harold M Paxton
Key Biscayne v (9) CM	305 365-5514	(not reporting)						
Key West (25) CM	305 292-8200	Dennis Wardlow	G Felix Cooper	Josephine Parker	E David Fernandez	Edwin Castro	E R Peterson	P Howanitz
Kissimmee (30) CM	407 847-2821	John Pollet	Mark E Durbin	Sandra L Yeager	Kenneth Killgore	Larry Bell	Frank J Ross	George W Mann Jr
Lady Lake t (..) CM	904 753-2212	Lee W Hokr	Robert K McKee	Ellie L Whigham	Chester Hendricks	. . . .	Richard Colpitts	John F Lang
Lake Alfred (4) CM	813 956-3434	(not reporting)						
Lake Buena Vista (..) CM	407 828-2241	(not reporting)						
Lake City (10) CM	904 752-2031	T Gerald Witt	Charles H Howell	James R Minchin	. . . .	Wayne Roseke	Frank Owens	William T Crews
Lake Clarke Shores t (3) MC	407 964-1515	Gregory W Casey	Stuart Liberman	Joann C Hatton	Stuart Liberman	. . . .	Michael Bruscell	. . . .
Lake Mary (6) CM	407 324-3000	(not reporting)						
Lake Park t (7) CM	407 848-3460	Belinda R Baldwin	George A Long	Barbara Scheihing	Tim W Howard	Jim Boone	Jeffery Lindskoog	Douglas M Poland
Lake Wales (10) CM	813 676-2533	Pat Crosby	Ernest Tyler	Judith Delmar	. . . .	Tom Tucker	Paul G Rumbley	Dale May
Lake Worth (29) CM	407 586-1600	Rodney G Romano	Kerry L Willis	Barbara Forsythe	Charles Powers	Sam Brandsma	Lee Reese	Herbert Lund
Lakeland (71) CM	813 499-6000	Ralph L Fletcher	Eugene Strickland	Paula K Hoffer	Jerry L Reynolds	Jack H Alford	Sam V Baca	Robert M Herr
Lantana t (8) CM	407 582-9094	Robert McDonald	Ron Ferris	Mabel D Weiland	Allan Owens	. . . .	William Carson	Dan Reidy
Largo (66) CM	813 587-6700	Thomas D Feaster	. . . .	Henry P Schubert	Kimball R Adams	Daniel J Fries	Richard A Kistner	Christian Kubala
Lauderdale Lakes (27) MC	305 731-1212	Alfonso A Gereffi	. . . .	Audrey Tolle	. . . .	Cosimo Ricciardi	. . . .	Clifford Goodin
Lauderdale-By-The-Sea t (3) CM	305 776-0576	(not reporting)						
Lauderhill (50) MC	305 730-3010	Ilene Lieberman	. . . .	Muriel Trombley	Donald Giancoli	Charles Faranda	. . . .	John P Clement
Leesburg (15) CM	904 728-9704	Claude R Lovell	Rex Taylor	James A Williams	James A Williams	James G Works	Harlan C Idell	Charles Langley
Lighthouse Point (10) MC	305 943-6500	William Sullivan	Gerald Renuart	Frances Marsh	Gerald Renuart	Jeff Brown	Paul Mannino	Wayne Stambaugh
Live Oak (6) MC	904 362-2276	(not reporting)						
Longboat Key t (6) CM	813 383-3721	James P Brown	Griff H Roberts	Patrizia Arends	Terence Sullivan	Robert Fakelman	Wayne McCammen	Leonard Smally
Longwood (13) CM	407 260-3440	Paul Lovestrand	. . . .	Geraldine Zambri	B Daniel McNutt	Charles Chapman	Gregory Manning	Richard Kornbluh
Lynn Haven (9) CM	904 265-2121	Montel Johnson	Alton Colvin	Alton Colvin	Sharon Hawkins	Jerry Blount	David Messer	Ricky Horst
Macclenny t (4) CM	904 259-6261	T J Raulerson	Gerald Dopson	. . . .	. . . .	Buddy Dagger	. . . .	Wendiell Kirkland
Madeira Beach (4) CM	813 391-9951	Tom DeCesare	John M Mulvihill	Denise M Schlegel	Alan Braithwaite	Brian J Turini	A B Hatcher	Tom S Corbett
Madison (3) CM	904 973-4181	Clarence Ganzy	Joseph J DeLegge	Pearlie M Pearce	Pearlie M Pearce	Raymond F Pinkard	Patrick D Dempsey	Bill B Raines
Maitland (9) CM	407 539-6255	H Darcy Bone	Phyllis Holvey	Donna Williams	William B Jones	Sidney Ballou Jr	Edward Doyle	Anthony Leffin
Manalapan t (..) CM	407 585-9477	Gerald K Shortz	Charles H Helm	Charles H Helm	Beulah G Irwin	. . . .	W W Smith	Mark Hull
Margate (43) CM	305 972-6454	(not reporting)						
Marianna (6) CM	904 482-4353	Paul A Donofro Jr	Julian Laramore	Sharon Hawkins	Sharon Hawkins	Jack Barwick	B L Parmer	John Chelada
Mary Esther t (4) CM	904 243-3566	(not reporting)						
Melbourne (60) CM	407 727-2900	Joe Mullins	Samuel Halter	Zella Gaston	Amy Elliott	Walt Chamberlin	Keith Chandler	. . . .
Melbourne Beach t (3) CM	407 724-5860	James Kelley	William Washburn	Connie J Smith	. . . .	William Roffey	Steven O Walters	. . . .
Miami (359) CM	305 579-6666	Javier Suarez	Cesar H Odio	Matty Hirai	Carlos Garcia	Carlos A Gimenez	Calvin Ross	Waldemar Lee
Miami Beach (93) CM	305 673-7524	Seymour Gelber	Roger Carlton	Richard Brown	Robert Nachlinger	Braniard Dorris	Phillip Huber	Richard Gatti
Miami Shores v (10) CM	305 758-8000	William Heffernan	Tom Benton	Scott W Davis	Patricia Varney	. . . .	Michael Zoovas	Tom Benton
Miami Springs (13) CM	305 885-4581	John A Cavalier	Dodd A Southern	Patricia Cummings	Sheri Shiver	. . . .	Earl C Steffen	William E Godwin
Midway (..) MC	904 574-2355	David M Watson	Christina B Canty	Karen Fitzgerald	Christina B Canty	Donald R Joyner	Morris Thomas	. . . .
Milton (7) MC	904 623-3817	Clyde L Gracey	William R Whitson	Dewitt Nobles	Dewitt Nobles	William Densmore	Robert K Young	. . . .
Miramar (41) CM	305 989-6200	Vicki Coceano	Eric M Soroka	Betty Tarno	Stanley G Hochman	Michael Murphy	George Atkinson	Lawrence Keating
Monticello (3) MC	904 997-3312	(not reporting)						
Mount Dora (7) CM	904 735-7100	P Alexander	Bernice S Brinson	. . . .	James Schuster	Edward Spann	Emory Putman	Rod Stroupe
Mulberry (3) CM	813 425-1125	Frank Satchel Jr	Floyd Woods	Patricia Jackson	Elnora Jackson	Mitch Carmack	John Hunter	D C Henderson
Naples (20) CM	813 434-4610	Paul W Muenzer	Richard Woodruff	Janet L Cason	William Harrison	George T Smith	Paul C Reble Jr	Danny E Mercer
Neptune Beach (7) CM	904 241-3191	John C Kowkabany	James Barrington	Becky Engstrom	Theresa Valentine	William L Brandt	William L Brandt	John Galen
New Port Richey (14) CM	813 841-4520	(not reporting)						
New Smyrna Beach (17) CM	904 427-4166	George E Musson	Frank O Roberts	Lynda Schaidt	William Poling	Mike Kelly	Denver Fleming	Melvin Phillips
Niceville (11) CM	904 729-4000	(not reporting)						
North Bay Village (5) CM	305 756-7171	(not reporting)						
North Lauderdale (27) CM	305 722-0900	(not reporting)						
North Miami (50) CM	305 893-6511	Mike Colodny	Lawrence Casey	Simon Bloom	Thomas Schnieders	. . . .	Kenneth Each	Alfred Signore
North Miami Beach (35) CM	305 947-7581	Jeffrey Mishcon	Michael Roberto	Solomon Odenz	Marilyn Spencer	. . . .	William Berger	Gary Brown
North Palm Beach v (11) CM	407 848-3475	Va Marks	Dennis W Kelly	Kathleen Kelly	Shaukat Dhan	J D Armstrong	Bruce F Sekeres	Charles O'Meilia
North Port (12) CM	813 426-8484	Ben Hardin	Robert L Norris	Doris J Briggs	. . . .	Paul G Kaskey	Victor L Costello	John J Singer
Oakland Park (26) CM	305 561-6250	. . . .	. . . .	Carol Gold	Elbert E Wrains	Mark A Nehiba	Edward Overman	Harry L Wimberly
Ocala (42) CM	904 629-8401	Henry Speight	Scotty Andrews	Mary Jane Milam	Glen Baker	William E Woods	A L McGehee	C H Amerman
Ocean Ridge t (2) CM	407 732-2635	Daniel O'Connell	D Bill Mathis	Karen E Hancsak	Karen E Hancsak	. . . .	Edward G Hillery	. . . .
Ocoee (13) CM	407 656-2322	Scott Vandergrift	Ellis Shapiro	Jean Grafton	Montye Beamer	Ronald Strosnider	John Boyd	Raymond Brenner
Okeechobee (5) CM	813 763-3372	(not reporting)						
Oldsmar (8) MC	813 855-4693	Jerome Provanzano	Bruce Haddock	Cheryl Mortenson	Marguerite Burns	Scott McGuff	. . . .	Fred Schildhauer
Opa-Locka (15) CM	305 688-4611	Robert B Ingram	L Dennis Whitt	Ronetta Taylor	Neva Reed	. . . .	Jimmy R Burke	Harold Little
Orange City (5) CM	904 775-3333	Anthony R Yebba	Robert T Mearns	Alta M Hill	Wilma J Clark	Frank W Snyder	Arthur C Locke	. . . .
Orange Park t (9) CM	904 264-9565	Earl Harrington	John W Bowles	Joyce G Bryan	Dorothy S Mollnow	David L Adams	John C Nelson	William J White
Orlando (165) MC	407 246-2378	Glenda E Hood	Robert C Haven	Grace A Chewning	G Michael Miller	Robert A Bowman	Thomas D Hurlburt	David L Metzker
Ormond Beach (30) CM	904 677-0311	N Fortunado	V Eugene Miller	Marian Maxwell	Paul Lane	Ronald Jacobs	Robert Stewart	Theodore Mac Leod
Oviedo (11) CM	407 366-7000	. . . .	V E Williford	Nancy Cox	Lynda Dennis	. . . .	Dennis Peterson	Charles Smith
Pahokee t (7) CM	407 924-5534	Ramon Horta Jr	Kenneth N Schenck	Debra N Palmer	Glenn T Cline	Gary C Burroughs	Carmen Salvatore	Bruce W Miller
Palatka (10) CM	904 329-0100	(not reporting)						
Palm Bay (63) CM	407 952-3400	Robert Devecki	. . . .	Alice Passmore	James Demming	David Greene	Robert Rossman	Robert Nanni
Palm Beach t (10) CM	407 838-5400	. . . .	Robert Doney	Grace Peters	Marie Crozier	Vincent Elmore	Joseph Terlizzese	Albert Dusey
Palm Beach Gardens (23) CM	407 775-8204	Joseph R Russo	Bobbie Herokavich	Linda V Kosier	. . . .	Edward Arrants	James Fitzgerald	Joseph Blazas
Palm Springs v (10) CM	407 965-4010	Richard H Jette	Patrick D Miller	Irene L Burroughs	Rebecca L Morse	. . . .	E W Hoagland	William A Leasure
Palmetto (9) MC	813 723-4570	J Gordon Dole	. . . .	Linda Stearns	Susan Dann	. . . .	C Mead Britt	Allen Tusing

Directory 1/9 continued — MUNICIPAL OFFICIALS IN U.S. CITIES OVER 2,500

City, 1990 population figures (000 omitted), form of government	Municipal phone number	Mayor	Appointed administrator	City clerk	Finance officer	Fire chief	Police chief	Public works director
FLORIDA (239) continued								
Panama City (34)	CM 904 872-3014	Girard L Clemons	John Baxter	Michael Bush	Doyle Eubanks	Robert Richardson	David Slusser	Joseph Villadsen
Parker (5)	MC 904 871-4104	(not reporting)						
Parkland (4)	CM 305 753-5040	Sal Pagliara	Harry J Mertz	Susan Armstrong	Judith C Kilgore	. . . .	Ronald Bailey	. . . .
Pembroke Park t (5)	CO 305 966-4600	Raymond P Oglesby	Robert A Levy	Robert A Levy	Irwin Lehmann	Dale A Greer	. . . .	Robert Davis
Pembroke Pines (65)	CM 305 431-4505	Charles Flanagan	Charles Dodge	Eileen Tesh	Rene Gonzalez	Vito Splendorio	John Lombardo	Marty Gayeski
Pensacola (58)	CM 904 435-1603	(not reporting)						
Perry (7)	CM 904 584-7161	. . . .	William E Brynes	. . . .	Daniel T Porta	Rodney Lytle	Herman W Putnal	Barney E Johnson
Pinellas Park (43)	CM 813 541-0700	Cecil W Bradbury	Ronald P Forbes	Grace M Kolar	M A McGarrity	Kenneth L Cramer	David C Milchan	Jerry W Halstead
Plant City (23)	CM 813 752-3125	George Collins	Nettie Draughon	Martin Wisgerhof	Martin Wisgerhof	George Contner	Troy Surrency	Steve Cottrell
Plantation (67)	MC 305 797-2200	Frank Veltri	. . . .	Barbara Showalter	Robert Brekelbaum	Robert Pudney	Clarence Sharrett	Joseph Spero
Polk City t (1)	CM 813 984-1375	(not reporting)						
Pompano Beach (72)	CO 305 786-4626	(not reporting)						
Port Orange (35)	CM 904 756-5219	James E Ward	Kenneth W Parker	. . . .	John A Shelley	Michael L Ertz	Robert E Ford	. . . .
Port Richey (3)	MC 813 849-7544	(not reporting)						
Port St. Joe (4)	CM 904 229-8261	. . . .	James R Maloy	. . . .	. . . .	. . . .	. . . .	. . . .
Port St. Lucie (56)	CM 407 878-0097	Robert Minsky	Donald Cooper	Sandra Johnson	Frank Blackwell	. . . .	Charles Reynolds	Cliff Burgess
Punta Gorda (11)	CM 813 575-3302	Rufus C Lazzell	William N Brady	Ellen J Diomedes	Willard R Beck	Edward L Keeler	Ralph R Shoup	Ernest C Miles
Quincy (7)	CM 904 627-7681	(not reporting)						
Riviera Beach (28)	CM 407 845-4000	(not reporting)						
Rockledge (16)	CM 407 690-3978	John J Oates	James P McKnight	Mary E Moist	. . . .	Richard D Nix Jr	Richard R Kallis	Jimmy J Gilliard
Royal Palm Beach v (15)	CM 407 790-5100	Anthony Masilotti	Max Weaver	Mary Anne Gould	. . . .	Karl Combs	Jeff Waites	Chris Stewart
Safety Harbor (15)	CM 813 726-0780	Kent Runnels	Pamela Brangaccio	Bonnie Haynes	Joanne Ryan	William Stout	. . . .	Kurt Peters
Sanford (32)	CM 407 330-5600	Bettye Smith	William Simmons	Janet Donahoe	Carolyn Small	J Thomas Hickson	Ralph W Russell	Robert G Herman
Sanibel (5)	CM 813 472-9615	Mark A Westall	Gary A Price	Gary A Price	Renee M Lynch	. . . .	Richard H Plager	Gates D Castle
Sarasota (51)	CM 813 954-4135	Gene M Pillot	D R Sollenberger	Billy E Robinson	Gibson E Mitchell	Julius E Halas	Gordon R Jolly	Gilbert J Leacock
Satellite Beach (10)	CM 407 773-4407	Linda Tisdale	Michael P Crotty	Mary Terrill	Norma Tetrault	Daniel Rocque	Lionel Cote	Vernon McKinney
Sebastian (10)	CM 407 589-5330	Lonnie R Powell	Robert S McClary	K M O'Halloran	Marilyn Swichkow	. . . .	Earl L Petty	. . . .
Sebring (9)	MC 813 385-0549	Smith Rudasill Jr	. . . .	Shirley Kitchings	Shirley Kitchings	R E DeLoach	Robert Glick	George Fox
Seminole (9)	MC 813 391-0204	Holland G Mangum	S Merrifield	Dorothy Cramer	Holland G Mangum	John R Leahy Jr	Everett S Rice	Mel R Rackett
South Bay (4)	CO 407 996-6751	Clarence Anthony	Lester Baird	Virginia Walker	. . . .	. . . .	Roy Humston Jr	. . . .
South Daytona (12)	CM 904 788-5000	Joe Piggotte	Joseph Yarbrough	Patricia Northrup	Robert Holmquist	. . . .	Gary White	Mark Juliano
South Miami (10)	CM 305 663-6300	(not reporting)						
South Pasadena (6)	CO 813 347-4171	Barbara Gilberg	. . . .	Diane Orloff	D R Perkins	Joseph Novak	. . . .	James Frain
Springfield (9)	MC 904 785-9516	(not reporting)						
St. Augustine (12)	CM 904 825-1013	(not reporting)						
St. Augustine Beach (4)	MC 904 471-2122	(not reporting)						
St. Cloud (12)	CM 407 892-2161	Ernest Gearhart	J Paul Wetzel	. . . .	Michael Turner	Daniel Garaguso	Leo Watko	Mark Luthie
St. Petersburg (239)	CO 813 893-7111	David J Fischer	. . . .	Jane K Brown	Richard L Ashton	Jerry G Knight	Darrel W Stephens	George W Webb
St. Petersburg Beach (9)	CM 813 363-9233	Michael J Horan	Jeffrey B Stone	Jane Ellsworth	Steve Gallaher	Charles Hartman	Tom Lange	Danny Walker
Starke (5)	CO 904 964-5027	(not reporting)						
Stuart (12)	CM 407 288-5300	Susan Hershey	David Collier	Eileen Reeder	Joan Bernola	Louis Papitto	Joan Waldron	William Mathews
Sunrise (64)	CM 305 741-2580	Steve Effman	Patrick Salerno	Dorothy Dunn	Robert Hague	Henry Howard	John Soldenwagner	Paul Callsen
Surfside t (4)	CM 305 861-4863	Paul Novack	Hal Cohen	Jeffrey Naftal	Rina Alfonso	. . . .	Terrill William	Chip Cohen
Sweetwater (14)	MC 305 221-0411	Matilde Aguirre	. . . .	Marie Schmidt	Maria E Denis	Raphael Toledo	Charles Toledo	Manuel Duago
Tallahassee (125)	CM 904 599-8120	. . . .	Daniel A Kleman	Robert B Inzer	Philip F Inglese	Thomas Quillin	Melvin L Tucker	Rhett A Miller
Tamarac (45)	CM 305 722-5900	Harry L Bender	John P Kelly	Carol A Evans	Mary Blasi	James Budzinski	. . . .	Michael R Couzzo
Tampa (280)	MC 813 223-8968	Sandra Freedman	George Pennington	Frances Henriquez	John Harrell	William Austin	Bennie Holder	Jack Morriss
Tarpon Springs (18)	MC 813 942-5602	Anita Protos	Carey Smith	Kathy Alesafis	Dan Katsiyiannis	Alwyn Carr	Mark LeCouris	Stanley Emerson
Tavares (7)	CM 904 742-6220	. . . .	Anthony G Otte	Mary Ann Carney	Donna Watt	C E Sowers	. . . .	Charlene Foster
Temple Terrace (16)	CM 813 989-7100	Robert F Woodard	Thomas J Bonfield	Patricia A Jones	Daniel R Klein	James W Bailey	Tom M Matthews	Robert Fernandez
Tequesta v (4)	CM 407 575-6200	Ron T Mac Kail	Thomas G Bradford	Joann Manganiello	Bill C Kascavelis	Jmaes Weinand	Carl Roderick	Gary Preston
Titusville (39)	CM 407 269-4400	(not reporting)						
Treasure Island (7)	CM 813 360-0811	Walter Stubbs	Peter G Lombardi	Peter G Lombardi	Darren LaFrance	Charles Fant	Joseph Pelkington	Mel Odom
Valparaiso (5)	MC 904 729-5402	John B Arnold Jr	. . . .	Faye B Floyd	Faye B Floyd	Randy Wilke	Lomax Donaldson	Claude Vanderford
Venice (17)	CM 813 485-3311	Katherine Schmidt	George N Hunt	Lori V Stelzer	Michael McPhail	Roy C Williams	Joseph P Slapp	Lawrence A Heath
Vero Beach (17)	CM 407 567-5151	Jay A Smith	. . . .	Phyllis Neuberger	Stephen J Maillet	. . . .	James M Gabbard	Arthur Sargent
Wakulla (14)	CM 904 926-3341	(not reporting)						
Wauchula (3)	MC 813 773-3131	Henry Graham	. . . .	Mavis F Best	Mavis F Best	. . . .	Joey E Brock	Warren E May Jr
West Melbourne (8)	CM 407 727-7700	William A Lane	Mark K Ryan	Janice E Daniels	Charlotte Luikart	. . . .	Brian K Lock	Ray Bullard
West Miami (6)	CM 305 266-1122	C Diaz Padron	Jose A Matas	Yolanda Aguilar	Jose A Matas	. . . .	P O Kiel	George P Kulik
West Palm Beach (68)	CO 407 659-8028	Nancy Graham	. . . .	Agnes Hayhurst	Elizabeth Bloeser	Robert Rehr	Billy R Riggs	Lee Collum
Wildwood (3)	CM 904 748-0302	D Edward Wolf	James R Stevens	Joseph Jacobs	Joseph Jacobs	Thomas L Smart	Don C Clark	R Eugene Kornegay
Wilton Manors (12)	CM 305 390-2100	Sandra J Steen	Wallace A Payne	Angela D Scott	Lisa C Rabon	Richard Rothe	Stephen Kenneth	Wm Joe Moss
Winter Garden (10)	CM 407 656-4111	(not reporting)						
Winter Haven (25)	CM 813 297-4000	Eleanor Threlkel	R Carl Cheatham	Sarah Lee Shumate	Calvin T Bowen	Charles Brown	Ronald S Martin	Dale Smith
Winter Park (22)	CM 407 623-3235	David Johnston	Anthony Barrett	Joyce Swain	Julie Gibson	Dennis Sargent	James Younger	James Williams
Winter Springs (22)	CM 305 327-1800	Philip A Kulbes	John Govoruhk	Mary Norton	Hary Martin	Timothy Lallathin	Charles Sexton	. . . .
Zephyrhills (8)	CM 813 788-2313	James Bailey	Floyd Nichols	Linda Boan	Cathy Familo	William Fenton	William Eiland	Rick Moore
GEORGIA (158)								
Acworth (5)	MC 404 974-3112	(not reporting)						
Adel (5)	CM 912 896-2821	(not reporting)						
Albany (78)	CM 912 431-3214	Paul A Keenan	Roy Lane	Joan P Pope	Herbert N Rushton	Henry L Fields	Washington Long	Russell J Edwards
Alma (4)	CM 912 632-8072	(not reporting)						
Alpharetta (13)	CM 404 475-9566	Jimmy Phillips	J Michael Wilkes	Sue Rainwater	. . . .	William Bates	Gordon Dillon	Foster Cagle
Americus (17)	MC 912 924-4411	Thomas Gailey	Sybil Smith	Charlotte Cotton	. . . .	Bobby Duke	Edwin Williams	Ronny Smith
Ashburn (5)	MC 912 567-3431	(not reporting)						
Athens (46)	CM 404 357-6000	Gwen O'Looney	Russ Crider	Gloria Spratlin	John Culpepper	Wendell Faulkner	Ronnie Chandler	Donald Loomis
Atlanta (394)	MC 404 330-6000	Maynard Jackson	Arthur Cummings	Robert Barger	Michael Bell	David Chamberlin	Eldrin Bell	Douglas Hooker
Augusta (45)	MC 404 821-1790	Charles A Devaney	Charles Dillard	Lena Bonner	Aurelia Epperson	W L Maddox	Austin C McLane	William S Johnson
Austell (4)	MC 404 944-4300	Joe Jerkins	. . . .	Delores Lockridge	Delores Lockridge	Johnny Williams	Clyde Hardin	Clay Hays
Avondale Estates (2)	CM 404 294-5400	John Lawson	A Lee Galloway	Phyllis D Flowers	A Lee Galloway	. . . .	Robert L Maxson	Julius Gresham
Bainbridge (11)	CM 912 246-2150	B K Reynolds	Charles B Tyson	William Lanier	William Lanier	Dennis Mock	Larry Funderburk	Dave Holley
Barnesville (5)	CM 404 358-0181	(not reporting)						
Baxley (4)	CM 912 367-8300	Hilton D Baxley	Jeffrey P Baxley	Jean Spell	. . . .	Mickey Bass	James Godfrey	David Gore
Blackshear (3)	MC 912 449-7000	(not reporting)						
Blakely (6)	MC 912 723-3677	(not reporting)						
Bowdon (2)	MC 706 258-8980	James W Watts	Ted Wadsworth	Betty Cason	. . . .	. . . .	Burl Langley	Jerry Langley
Bremen (4)	MC 404 537-2331	(not reporting)						
Brunswick (16)	CM 912 267-5500	Homer L Wilson	Mark Mitchell	Georgia Marion	Rick Drummond	Lee Stewart	. . . .	Wayne Bullard
Buford (9)	CM 404 945-6761	(not reporting)						
Cairo (9)	CM 912 377-1722	Dan Wells	Thomas Lynn	Martha Faye Lewis	Jimmy Douglas	Jerry Pierce	James Kelly	. . . .
Calhoun (7)	MC 404 629-0151	John Meadows	Kelly Cornwell	Cathy Harrison	Cathy Harrison	Ferell Grizzle	Willie Mitchell	Dean Harris

Directory 1/9 continued   MUNICIPAL OFFICIALS IN U.S. CITIES OVER 2,500

City, 1990 population figures (000 omitted), form of government	Municipal phone number	Mayor	Appointed administrator	City clerk	Finance officer	Fire chief	Police chief	Public works director
GEORGIA (158) continued								
Camilla (5)	CM 912 336-2220	Jimmy Davis	Richard Newbern	Kathy Baker	. . . .	Lazelle McCook	Ray Folsom	Michael Pollock
Canton (5)	CM 404 479-2421	(not reporting)						
Carrollton (16)	MC 404 830-2000	Ray Adams	Danny Mabry	Jewell Mashburn	Danny Mabry	Casey Coleman	Charles Carroll	Stan Brown
Cartersville (12)	CM 404 387-5616	Alex T Dent	Clarence B Walker	Helen W Oglesby	Helen W Oglesby	Malcom Pritchett	James R Willbanks	Ray Southern
Cedartown (8)	CM 706 748-3220	Harold Benefield	Kurt Falkenstein	Emily Shaw	Kurt Falkenstein	Kenneth Roberts	John Dean	Robert McDonald
Centerville (3)	MC 912 953-4734	Maurice Keene Jr	. . . .	Virginia Abbott	Virginia Abbott	Frank Wadsworth	Michael Sullivan	Henry Childs
Chamblee (8)	MC 404 986-5010	(not reporting)						
Clarkston t (5)	MC 404 296-6489	(not reporting)						
Claxton (2)	MC 912 739-1712	Perry L DeLoach	. . . .	Gayle Durrence	. . . .	Larry Rogers	Edward Oglesbee	C W Young
Cochran (4)	MC 912 934-6346	(not reporting)						
College Park (20)	CM 404 767-1537	T Owen Smith	. . . .	Jean C Cress	Jean C Cress	Charles T Dillard	Walter T Sheets	Don E Moore
Columbus-Muscogee (179)	CM 706 571-4700	F K Martin	M B Brown	L H Miller	C S Chronis	W W Collins	W J Wetherington	R W McKee
Commerce (4)	MC 404 335-3164	(not reporting)						
Conyers (7)	CM 404 483-4411	(not reporting)						
Cordele (10)	CM 912 273-3102	. . . .	Jack Miller	. . . .	Steve Fulford	Eugene Stephens	Dwayne Orrick	James Watson
Cornelia (3)	CM 706 778-8585	(not reporting)						
Covington (10)	MC 404 786-5324	William L Dobbs	Frank B Turner	Linda Walden	Faye Huckaby	Whatley E Curtis	Bobby D Moody	Sam Walton
Cuthbert (4)	MC 912 732-3761	(not reporting)						
Dahlonega (3)	MC 404 864-6133	(not reporting)						
Dallas (3)	CM 404 443-8110	Jeffery Miller	Kenneth Elsberry	Helon Wills	. . . .	Gordan McTyre	Mac Author Hicks	Kendall Smith
Dalton (22)	MC 404 278-9500	(not reporting)						
Dawson (5)	CM 912 995-4444	(not reporting)						
Decatur (17)	MC 404 370-4100	Michael Mears	Peggy Merriss	Karen DeSislets	. . . .	. . . .	Sherrard White	Hugh Saxon
Donalsonville (3)	MC 912 524-2118	David B Fain	H M Shingler	Linda Faye Gray	. . . .	Travis Brooks	Mike Thomas	H M Shingler
Doraville (8)	MC 404 451-8745	R Eugene Lively	. . . .	Mary W Grant	. . . .	. . . .	William F Davis	Bobby Pittman
Douglas (10)	MC 912 384-3302	Derward Buchan	W Danny Lewis	Hayvene McFall	Terrell Lott	Freddie Davis	Clyde Purvis	Larry Royal
Douglasville (12)	MC 404 920-3000	Charles Camp	William Osborne	Barbara McCravy	J H Banks	. . . .	Joe L Whisenant	Keith L Williams
Dublin (16)	CM 912 272-1620	Robert J Walker	Kenneth R Hammons	. . . .	Joseph M Kinard	Robert T Drew	Wayne Fuqua	Jimmy D Sawyer
Duluth (9)	MC 404 476-3434	Bobby Williams	Larry Rubenstein	Teresa Lynn	Teresa Lynn	. . . .	Randall Belcher	Red Fowler
East Dublin t (3)	MC 912 272-6883	(not reporting)						
East Point (34)	CM 404 765-1013	(not reporting)						
Eastman (5)	CM 912 374-7721	Juanita B Edwards	James H Wright	Ann S Jones	Ann S Jones	Carl Johnson	Furman Wiggins	Henry T Woodward
Eatonton (5)	MC 404 485-3311	James P Marshall	. . . .	Audrey Hightower	Audrey Hightower	O Vanlandingham	Kent Lawrence	J R Davis
Elberton (6)	CM 706 283-5321	Joe H Fendley Sr	Hayden F Wiley Jr	D Scott Wilson	D Scott Wilson	Niles T Poole	Mike W Seymour	Barney R Taylor
Fairburn (6)	MC 404 964-2244	Betty Hannah	Anthony W Cox	Bobbie C Langston	. . . .	Mike Brown	John T Cameron	Donald Baxter
Fayetteville (6)	MC 404 461-6029	Mike Wheat	Fred Scarborough	Fred Scarborough	Lynn Speir	Henry Argo	Johnny Roberts	Charles Stanley
Fitzgerald (9)	MC 912 423-9827	Gerald H Thompson	Alvie L Dorminy	Louise Guardia	Elaine Poole	Wayne Sherrill	Bill Smallwood	Buck Poole
Forest Park (17)	CM 404 366-4720	Jerome Tomasello	John Parker	. . . .	Sarah Davis	. . . .	Joseph Picard	Otis Berry
Forsyth (4)	MC 912 994-5649	(not reporting)						
Fort Oglethorpe (6)	CM 706 866-2544	John W Norris	William P Magoon	J Harold Silcox	Dottie Haney	Harold Randy Camp	Charles S Dunn Jr	Phillip B Parker
Fort Valley (8)	MC 912 825-8261	C W Peterson	Larry C Smith	Florine Statham	Rachel Douglas	G L Moye	C F Strickland	George Clark
Gainesville (18)	CM 404 535-6860	John W Morrow	J Al Crace	Linda J Shubert	Robert A Loveland	David T Chapman	Fred W Hayes	Edward J Standera
Garden City (7)	MC 912 966-7777	(not reporting)						
Glennville (4)	MC 912 654-2461	Brent B Walker		Jean Bridges	Jean Bridges	Bobby Brannen	Larry Stubbs	Dyril Durrence
Gordon t (2)	MC 912 628-2222	(not reporting)						
Greensboro (3)	MC 706 453-7967	(not reporting)						
Griffin (21)	CM 404 229-6425	Richard Slade	Richard C Crowdis	. . . .	Lee Poolman	Ronald M Ellis	Armand Chapeau	Brant Keller
Grovetown (4)	MC 404 863-4576	(not reporting)						
Hapeville (5)	MC 404 669-2100	(not reporting)						
Hartwell (5)	MC 404 376-4756	Joan H Saliba	Ellis D Foster	Steve Russell	Steve Russell	Terry Vickery	Cecil E Reno	. . . .
Hawkinsville (4)	CM 912 892-3240	Tom Arnold	Clifton Wilkinson	Evelyn Herrington	. . . .	Kenneth Owens	Sam Tripp	Dennis Passmore
Hazlehurst (4)	MC 912 375-6680	Wyatt A Spann	. . . .	Ethelyn S Creech	Ethelyn S Creech	Charles Wasdin	Steven Land	David Hughes
Helen (..)	MC 404 878-3382	Jeff N Ash	Kim A Cox	Janie N Henderson	. . . .	Fred Healan Jr	Frank V Rotondo	Gilbert H Paul
Hinesville (22)	MC 912 876-3564	Allen Brown	Edwards Billy	O Mingledorff	Sara Lumpkin	J Mingledorff	Harlon Deloach	. . . .
Hogansville (3)	CM 706 637-8629	Calvin Turbyfield	Wesley Duffey	Connie Ellis	. . . .	Mike Strickland	Clarence Martin	James Rippy
Homerville (3)	MC 912 487-2375	Carol Chambers	. . . .	William C Vest	William C Vest	Mike Strickland	Truman Lee	. . . .
Jackson (4)	MC 404 775-7535	(not reporting)						
Jesup (9)	CM 912 427-2903	(not reporting)						
Jonesboro (4)	MC 404 478-7407	(not reporting)						
Kennesaw (9)	MC 404 424-8274	J O Stephenson	. . . .	Susan Rackley	Susan Rackley	. . . .	Dwaine L Wilson	Richard Howard
Kingsland (5)	MC 912 729-5613	(not reporting)						
La Fayette (6)	MC 404 638-1272	H Neal Florence	David L Aldrich	Glenna J Thomas	David L Aldrich	Jim T Maffett	C Richardson	James McAlister
La Grange (26)	CM 706 883-2000	Charles C Joseph	James R Hanson	John W Bell	John W Bell	Chris A Smith	George Yates	David Edwa Brown
Lake City (3)	MC 404 366-8080	(not reporting)						
Lawrenceville (17)	MC 404 963-2414	(not reporting)						
Lilburn (9)	MC 404 921-2210	W Calvin Fitchett	. . . .	Jean Cole	. . . .	. . . .	R H Houck	G A Nash
Lithonia (2)	MC 404 482-8136	(not reporting)						
Louisville (2)	CM 912 625-3166	(not reporting)						
Lyons (5)	MC 912 526-6578	(not reporting)						
Macon (107)	MC 912 751-7000	Thomas C Olmstead	Israel G Small	Steven Durden	John D Thompson	Jimmy E Hinson	Milton J Avera	Larry G Brown
Madison (3)	MC 404 342-1251	(not reporting)						
Manchester (4)	CM 404 846-3141	(not reporting)						
Marietta (44)	CM 404 429-4200	Ansley Meaders	William J Buckner	Sheila Hill	Thomas Pellegrino	Kenneth Burris	Ralph Carter	. . . .
Mc Donough (3)	MC 404 957-3915	(not reporting)						
Mc Rae (3)	MC 912 868-6051	(not reporting)						
Metter (4)	MC 912 685-2527	Paul Williams	. . . .	Wanda Leverett	. . . .	James Brantley	Eugene Sherman	. . . .
Milledgeville (18)	MC 912 453-9441	(not reporting)						
Millen (4)	MC 912 982-6100	Robert H Fields	Forrest S Boyer	Marianne Bunn	. . . .	Stan Coleman	Dennis Simmons	Jack Burke
Monroe (10)	MC 404 267-7536	(not reporting)						
Montezuma (5)	MC 912 472-8144	(not reporting)						
Morrow (5)	MC 404 961-4002	(not reporting)						
Moultrie (15)	CM 912 985-1974	William McIntosh	Robert A Rojas	Gary McDaniel	Gary McDaniel	Kenneth Hannon	Richard Crouch	Julian Martin
Nashville (5)	MC 912 686-5527	Dewey Hand		Johnny Hall	. . . .	Earl Powell	Ira L Shealy	Jerry Griner
Newnan (12)	CM 404 253-2682	Clifford B Glover	Richard A Bolin	Peggy Dewberry	Richard A Bolin	. . . .	Jerry C Helton	. . . .
Norcross (6)	MC 404 448-2122	(not reporting)						
Ocilla (3)	MC 404 468-5141	(not reporting)						
Palmetto (3)	CM 404 463-3377	J Clark Boddie	William H Shell	. . . .	. . . .	Roger D Handley	William C Simpson	William F Gaddy
Peachtree City (19)	CM 404 487-7657	Robert L Lenox	Jim Basinger	Frances Meaders	Frances Meaders	Gerald Reed	James V Murray	Colin Halterman
Pelham (4)	MC 912 294-7900	Charles Yates	Johnnie Arnold	Corrinne Davis	. . . .	James Creech	Neal McCormick	Carol Whigham
Perry (9)	CM 912 987-1911	James E Worrall	F Marion Hay	F Marion Hay	Janice Williams	Gary Hamlin	C F Simons	Hugh Sharp
Pooler (4)	MC 912 748-7261	Jack Shearouse	Dennis Baxter	Maribeth Claus	Linda Smith	Jimmy Fields	Clarence Chan	Ralph Phillips
Port Wentworth (4)	MC 912 964-4379	(not reporting)						
Powder Springs (7)	CM 404 943-1666	Richard D Sailors	Wayne P Wright	Betty G Brady	Lynn F Edwards	. . . .	Lester K Guthrie	Bobby C Elliott

City, 1990 population figures (000 omitted), form of government	Municipal phone number	Mayor	Appointed administrator	City clerk	Finance officer	Fire chief	Police chief	Public works director
GEORGIA (158) continued								
Quitman (5)	CM 912 263-4166	(not reporting)						
Rincon t (3)	CM 912 826-5745	(not reporting)						
Riverdale (9)	MC 404 997-8989	Mary Lee	David Abercrombie	Sandra Meyers	. . . .	Alan Shuman	C Wayne Phillips	Ronnie Gossett
Rockmart (3)	CM 706 684-5454	(not reporting)						
Rome (30)	CM 706 236-4400	George Pullen	John Bennett	Joseph Smith	Gary Burkhalter	Bobbie McKenzie	Hubert Smith	W Kirk Milam
Rossville (4)	MC 706 866-1325	Charles Sherrill	. . . .	Bobbie Alexander	Bobbie Alexander	David Hicks	Roger Blackwell	Kennth Whitton
Roswell (48)	MC 404 641-3727	W L Pug Mabry	Bill Johnson	Bill Johnson	John Hunter	Neal Butterworth	Jerry King	Frank Mingledorff
Sandersville (6)	MC 912 552-6006	(not reporting)						
Savannah (138)	CM 912 651-6481	Susan Weiner	Arthur A Mendonsa	Dyanne Reese	Richard Evans	Joseph Hobby	David Gellatly	Billy E Jones
Smyrna (31)	MC 404 434-6600	(not reporting)						
Snellville (12)	MC 404 985-3500	Emmett Clower	. . . .	Sharon Lowery	Sharon Lowery	. . . .	John Hewatt	Alfred Beaver
Social Circle (3)	MC 404 464-2380	Frank W Sherrill	Anne S Peppers	. . . .	. . . .	Steve Shelton	. . . .	Kenny Harper
Soperton (3)	MC 912 529-6173	(not reporting)						
St. Marys (8)	MC 912 882-5516	Jerry Brandon	Michael Mahaney	Gwendolyn Mungin	Michael Fender	Dale Simmons	Ed Wassman	Bennie Smith
Statesboro (16)	MC 912 764-5468	Hal Averitt	Carter Crawford	Susan Mock	Susan Mock	Joe Beasley	Richard Malone	Bobby Colson
Stone Mountain (6)	CM 404 498-8984	Patricia Wheeler	Wayne Johnson	Wayne Johnson	Carla Tuck	. . . .	James Rivers	Henry Shoemake
Sugar Hill (5)	CM 404 945-6716	George O Haggard	Kathy Williamson	Judy Foster	Sandra L Richards	. . . .	. . . .	. . . .
Summerville (5)	MC 404 857-3402	(not reporting)						
Swainsboro (7)	MC 912 237-7025	(not reporting)						
Sylvania (3)	CM 912 564-7411	Sandy Hershey	Roland Stubbs	Mary F Collins	. . . .	H P Brown	W H Black	Dennis Daley
Sylvester (6)	MC 912 776-8505	Thomas Lawhorne	. . . .	Deborah G Bridges	. . . .	Thomas Marchman	Thomas Bozeman	. . . .
Tallapoosa (3)	CM 706 574-2345	(not reporting)						
Thomaston (9)	CM 706 647-6633	Charles E Kersey	James H Nalley Jr	Phillip B Adcock	Phillip B Adcock	Jesse Coogler	Tony E McCard	Jesse Walton
Thomasville (17)	CM 912 228-7673	(not reporting)						
Thomson (7)	MC 706 595-1781	Robert E Knox Jr	Burton D Patrick	Darleen Plunkett	Kenneth J Pittard	Raymond McHatton	John P Hathaway	Harry T Johnson
Thunderbolt t (3)	MC 912 354-5533	(not reporting)						
Tifton (14)	CM 912 382-6231	(not reporting)						
Toccoa (8)	CM 706 886-8451	James A Neal	James A Calvin	Josephine Gleason	James E Shurley	Henry M Thomas	Joseph H Lumpkin	John W Sosebee
Union City (8)	MC 404 964-2288	Fred Etris	Sonya Carter	. . . .	. . . .	Stanley Tarnowski	Bobby Fronebarger	William Landrum
Valdosta (40)	CM 912 333-1804	James H Rainwater	Micahel H Cason	Richard H Hamlen	Richard H Hamlen	C R Williams	Charlie R Spray	. . . .
Vidalia (11)	CM 912 537-7661	(not reporting)						
Vienna (3)	MC 912 268-4744	Willie J Davis	Stanley Gambrell	. . . .	. . . .	Tommy Phillips	Bobby Reed	Larry Allen
Villa Rica (7)	CM 404 459-3957	Teddy Lee	Andy Henshaw	Andy Henshaw	Jean Spiva	. . . .	Mike Gibbs	Don McGill
Warner Robins (44)	MC 912 929-1111	Edward A Martin	. . . .	Clayton P Mays	. . . .	Larry West	George Johnson	Wiley Bowman
Washington (4)	CM 404 678-3277	E B Pope	Warren D Sisson	Michael P Eskew	. . . .	Alan Poss	Roger G Weston	. . . .
Waycross (16)	CM 912 287-2914	Robert Odum	C B Heys	Jerry Grimes	Jerry Grimes	Donald Kovacs	William L Taylor	Gary Bryson
Waynesboro (6)	MC 404 554-8000	J Harold Rowland	T J Brantley	. . . .	T J Brantley	Charles Dickey	H L Ivey	Earl Brown
West Point (4)	MC 404 645-2226	H E Steele Jr	Joel T Wood	Joel T Wood	. . . .	Don K Cagle	David Kerr	. . . .
Winder (7)	MC 404 867-3106	A Lamar Ouzts	E G Graham	E G Graham	Donald Hix	Raymond Mattison	William Stone	. . . .
Woodbine (1)	MC 912 576-3211	W B Clark Jr	Geo L Hannaford	Geo L Hannaford	. . . .	A Keith Kelley	Edwin W Coller	. . . .
Woodstock (4)	CM 404 926-8852	W David Rogers	D Lamar Hamill	Rhonda Bishop	D Lamar Hamill	Robbie Westbrook	Jimmy Mercer	. . . .
Wrightsville (2)	MC 912 864-3303	(not reporting)						
HAWAII (2)								
Hilo (..)	MC 808 961-8361	Stephen Yamashiro	William G Davis	Robin J Yahiku	Harry A Takahashi	Nelson M Tsuji	Victor V Vierra	Donna F Kiyosaki
Honolulu (836)	MC 808 523-4809	Frank F Fasi	Jeremy Harris	Raymond K Pua	Russell W Miyake	Lionel E Camara	Michael Nakamura	C Michael Street
IDAHO (42)								
American Falls (4)	MC 208 226-2569	(not reporting)						
Ammon (5)	MC 208 529-4211	C Bruce Ard	. . . .	Aleen C Jensen	. . . .	Cal Smith	. . . .	David Wadsworth
Blackfoot (10)	MC 208 785-8600	(not reporting)						
Boise City (126)	MC 208 384-3850	(not reporting)						
Bonners Ferry (2)	MC 208 267-3105	Harold Sims	Michael Woodward	Richard Rexford	. . . .	Clifford Kroeger	David Kramer	. . . .
Buhl (4)	MC 208 543-5650	Ted Pence	. . . .	Sharon Sheets	. . . .	Tom Owens	Ron Romero	Gary Winn
Burley (9)	MC 208 678-2224	(not reporting)						
Caldwell (18)	MC 208 455-3000	James R Dakar	Teri L Ottens	Betty Jo Keller	Lisa R Thompson	Bruce Allcott	Robert Sobba	Gordon Law
Chubbuck (8)	MC 208 237-2400	(not reporting)						
Coeur D'Alene (25)	MC 208 667-9533	Ray Stone	Ken Thompson	Susan Weathers	. . . .	Franklin Sexton	David Scates	Rodger Lewerenz
Eagle (3)	MC 208 939-6813	Steve Guerber	B Montgomery	B Montgomery	. . . .	. . . .	. . . .	Jack Dodson
Emmett (5)	MC 208 365-6050	Leroy Campbell	. . . .	Cecile Jensen	. . . .	Orville Wright	Gary Scheihing	Randy Dearden
Garden City (6)	MC 208 377-1831	Jay C Davis	. . . .	Dave O'Leary	. . . .	. . . .	Willard Heaps	Lloyd McLeod
Gooding (3)	MC 208 934-5669	David J Adair	. . . .	Linda Wildman	. . . .	Pat Bishop	Paul Brown	. . . .
Grangeville (3)	MC 208 983-1380	(not reporting)						
Hayden (4)	MC 208 772-4411	(not reporting)						
Heyburn (3)	MC 208 678-8158	Glen J Loveland	. . . .	Ruth Davis	. . . .	. . . .	V Earl Andrew	Roger Denker
Idaho Falls (44)	MC 208 529-1235	(not reporting)						
Jerome (7)	MC 208 324-8189	Gerald M Ostler	Larry Paine	Kathy Miller	John H Yon	Jim Auclaire	Jim Dahl	Larry Paine
Kellogg (3)	MC 208 786-9131	(not reporting)						
Lewiston (28)	CM 208 746-3671	Lovetta R Eisele	Janice Vassar	Rebecca Hubbard	. . . .	Tom Tomberg	Jack Baldwin	Bud Van Stone
Meridian (10)	MC 208 888-4433	(not reporting)						
Montpelier (3)	MC 208 847-0824	(not reporting)						
Moscow (19)	MC 208 882-5553	Paul C Agidius	William A Smith	Elaine Russell	James Wallace	Phillip Gatlin	William Brown Jr	Gary Presol
Mountain Home (8)	MC 208 587-2104	(not reporting)						
Nampa (28)	MC 208 465-2270	Winston Goering	Kendall Harward	Camille Beaubien	. . . .	Douglas Rosin	Marshall Brisbin	Larry Bledsoe
Orofino (3)	MC 208 476-4725	H L Clay	Rick Laam	Virginia T Earl	. . . .	Leonard L Eckman	Ferice B Childers	Floyd Williams
Payette (6)	MC 208 642-6024	(not reporting)						
Pocatello (46)	MC 208 234-6170	Peter Angstadt	. . . .	Pete McDougall	. . . .	Richard Wolfe	James Benham	. . . .
Post Falls (7)	MC 208 773-3517	James C Hammond	. . . .	Christene Pappas	Brentt Ramharter	Lynn Borders	Clifford T Hayes	George E Wilson
Preston (4)	MC 208 852-1817	(not reporting)						
Rexburg (14)	MC 208 359-3020	Nile Boyle	. . . .	Rose Magley	Richad Horner	Rex Larson	Blair K Siepert	Farrell Davidson
Rigby (3)	MC 208 745-8111	Keith Scott	. . . .	A Laree Rainey	. . . .	Leon Guymon	Larry Anderson	Douglas Nelson
Rupert (5)	MC 208 436-9608	(not reporting)						
Salmon (3)	MC 208 756-3214	(not reporting)						
Sandpoint (5)	MC 208 263-3158	Dwight Sheffler	. . . .	Helen M Newton	Larry Chapin	Don Keck	Bill Kice	Kody Van Dyk
Shelley (4)	MC 208 357-3390	Phill Worlton	. . . .	Sandy Hanson	. . . .	. . . .	Alan Dial	Frank Butler
Soda Springs (3)	MC 208 547-2600	Kirk L Hansen	Lee Godfrey	Brenda L Erickson	. . . .	Norm Bjorkman	Blynn B Wilcox	Gary L Jensen
St. Anthony (3)	MC 208 624-3494	Boyd Yancey	. . . .	Rita Morton	. . . .	. . . .	Bryan Fullmer	Woodrow Andersen
St. Maries (2)	MC 208 245-2577	(not reporting)						
Twin Falls (28)	CM 208 736-2271	Howard L Allen	Thomas J Courtney	. . . .	Gary L Evans	. . . .	Paul Dufresne	Bob Van Ostrand
Weiser (5)	MC 208 549-1965	(not reporting)						
ILLINOIS (402)								
Abingdon (4)	MC 309 462-3182	H Jay Sandercock	. . . .	B Joanne Batson	R Boone		Harvey L Meade	Steve Murfin

Directory 1/9 continued

MUNICIPAL OFFICIALS IN U.S. CITIES OVER 2,500

ILLINOIS (402) continued

City, 1990 population figures (000 omitted), form of government	Municipal phone number	Mayor	Appointed administrator	City clerk	Finance officer	Fire chief	Police chief	Public works director
Addison v (32)	MC 708 543-4100	Anthony Russotto	Joseph Block	Lucille Zucchero	Bob G Simpson	....	Melvin Mack	Steven Weinstock
Aledo (4)	MC 309 582-7241	C Wm Stancliff	....	Brian Whitehall	....	....	James Brokaw	Michael Collins
Algonquin v (12)	MC 708 658-4322	Ted Spella	William J Ganek	Gerald Kautz	John R Walde	....	Russell Laine	....
Alsip v (18)	MC 708 385-6902	(not reporting)						
Alton (33)	MC 618 463-3522	Robert Towse	....	Mary Gibson	Mark Bennett	John Sowders	Sylvester Jones	William Moyer
Anna (5)	MC 618 833-8528	(not reporting)						
Antioch v (6)	MC 708 395-1000	(not reporting)						
Arcola (3)	MC 217 268-4966	Lynda Fishel	....	Vickie Dill	....	Mark Faler	Steve Maroon	Jack Logan
Arlington Heights v (75)	CM 708 253-2340	Arlene Mulder	William Dixon	Edwina Corso	Judith Goral	Bruce Rodewald	Rodney Kath	Allen Sander
Auburn (4)	MC 217 438-6151	(not reporting)						
Aurora (100)	MC 708 892-0711	David L Pierce	....	Cheryl Vonhoff	Roger W Cantlin	John Angell	David L Stover	James Nanninga
Barrington v (10)	CM 708 381-2141	(not reporting)						
Barrington Hills v (4)	MC 708 551-3000	(not reporting)						
Bartlett v (19)	MC 708 837-0800	C Melchert	Valerie L Salmons	Linda Gallien	Kevin Lockhart	....	William McHugh	Paul Kuester
Bartonville v (6)	MC 309 697-2323	(not reporting)						
Batavia (17)	MC 708 879-1424	Jeffery Schielke	Ronald Podschweit	Jody Haltenhof	Terry Klein	William Darin	Robert Warner	....
Beardstown (5)	MC 217 323-3110	Robert E Summey	....	Mary L Arenz	....	David Moran	Robert Genseal	Ronald Jones
Beecher v (..)	CM 708 946-2261	Landis Wehling	Robert O Barber	Janett Conner	....	....	Ray Wroblewski	William Merritt
Belleville (43)	MC 618 233-6810	Roger Cook	....	Lois E Hock	Peter Strutynski	Richard Rujawitz	David Brauer	....
Bellwood v (20)	MC 708 547-3500	Donald P Lemm	....	Booker T Brown	I Joseph Lagen	David Stelter	Robert Frascone	John Antonovich
Belvidere (16)	MC 815 544-2612	Rory B Peterson	....	Romell Cunningham	Richard Stegemann	Paul Moses	Charles Burkhart	Craig Lawler
Bensenville v (18)	CM 708 766-8200	(not reporting)						
Benton (7)	CO 618 439-6131	Gale Dawson	....	Michael Malkovich	Harry Stewart	Paul Rogers	Raymond Bain	....
Berkeley v (5)	MC 708 449-8840	(not reporting)						
Berwyn (45)	MC 708 788-2660	(not reporting)						
Bethalto v (10)	MC 618 377-8723	Wm P Stephenson	....	Mary A Meyer	....	John Nolte	Tony Sammis	Joseph Ricci
Bloomingdale v (17)	MC 708 893-7000	Robert Iden	Daniel Wennerholm	Harriet Ford	Gary Szott	....	Gary Schira	Michael Marchi
Bloomington (52)	MC 309 828-7361	Jesse R Smart	Thomas A Hamilton	Earlene M Nelson	Allan W Horsman	Alan R Otto	Timothy M Linskey	Richard I Paulson
Blue Island (21)	MC 708 597-8600	(not reporting)						
Bolingbrook v (41)	MC 708 759-0400	Roger C Claar	William Charnisky	Carol Penning	....	....	Ronald Chruszczyk	Michael Drey
Bourbonnais v (14)	MC 815 937-3570	(not reporting)						
Bradley v (11)	MC 815 933-8533	Ken Hayes	....	William Zajc	....	Albert Wingo	David Greenstreet	James Travis Sr
Braidwood (4)	CO 815 458-2333	(not reporting)						
Breese (4)	MC 618 526-7731	(not reporting)						
Bridge View v (14)	MC 708 594-2525	(not reporting)						
Broadview v (9)	MC 708 681-3600	John R Rodgers	Ruth Mitchell	Michael F Hritz	Michael F Hritz	Donald J Gaertner	Donald M George	Robert Macaluso
Brookfield v (19)	CM 708 485-7344	Thomas A Sequens	James R Mann	Kathleen Markland	George R Turdik	George Zahrobsky	John C Hymel	....
Buffalo Grove v (36)	CM 708 459-2500	Sidney Mathias	William Balling	Janet Sirabian	William Brimm	Thomas Allenspach	Leo McCann	Gregory Boysen
Burbank (28)	MC 708 599-5500	(not reporting)						
Burnham v (4)	MC 708 862-9150	(not reporting)						
Burr Ridge v (8)	CM 708 654-8181	Emil J Coglianese	Steven S Stricker	Patrice Pecora	Hella Tomczak	....	....	Howard Heil
Bushnell (3)	MC 309 772-2521	Jack Promisson	....	Barbara Knott	....	....	Merville Hilliard	....
Cahokia v (18)	MC 618 337-9510	(not reporting)						
Cairo (5)	MC 618 734-4127	(not reporting)						
Calumet City (38)	MC 708 891-8100	(not reporting)						
Calumet Park v (8)	MC 708 389-0850	Buster B Porch	....	Geraldine Galvin	....	T Battistella	Thomas Zielinski	Robert Talaski
Canton (14)	MC 309 647-0020	(not reporting)						
Carbondale (27)	CM 618 549-5302	Neil Dillard	Jeff Doherty	Janet Vaught	Paul Sorgen	Cliff Manis	Don Strom	Ed Reeder
Carlinville (5)	MC 217 854-4076	(not reporting)						
Carlyle (3)	MC 618 594-2468	(not reporting)						
Carmi (6)	MC 618 382-8118	(not reporting)						
Carol Stream v (32)	CM 708 665-7050	Ross Ferraro	Gregory Bielawski	....	Stan Helgerson	....	Gary Konzak	John Turner
Carpentersville v (23)	CM 708 426-3439	John Skillman	Curt Carver	Carol Miller	Donald Mazza	....	Ben Blake	....
Carrollton (3)	MC 217 942-5517	(not reporting)						
Carterville (4)	MC 618 985-2252	Charles W Mausey	....	Joyce A Carney	....	Harry W Treece	William G Davis	Lavern Addison
Cary v (10)	CM 708 639-0003	Sue E McCabe	Carl J Tomaso	Mark Shackelford	Albert L Young	....	Robert J Levitt	Vernon P Keller
Casey (3)	MC 217 932-2700	(not reporting)						
Caseyville v (4)	MC 618 344-1233	George Chance	....	Jack Piesbergen	....	Gerard Scott	Michael Buckner	Gerard Scott
Centralia (14)	CM 618 533-7622	Melvin Hart	Donald E Hahn	Gail Simer	....	Roger Sutherland	Arland Speidel	Donald Copple
Centreville (7)	MC 618 332-1021	John Robinson	....	Clifford Williams	....	....	Mark O'Donnell	Willie L McClain
Champaign (64)	CM 217 351-4458	Dan McCollum	Steve Carter	Marilyn Banks	Richard Schnuer	John Corbly	Don Carter	Jim Carney
Channahon v (4)	MC 815 467-5311	Michael F Rittof	Marian T Gibson	Joi R Walker	....	....	Steve K Admonis	Daniel R Werner
Charleston (20)	CO 217 345-7088	Roscoe M Cougill	....	Patsy J Loew	....	Thomas Watson	H Steidinger	....
Chatham v (6)	MC 217 483-2451	(not reporting)						
Cherry Valley v (2)	MC 815 332-3441	(not reporting)						
Chester (8)	MC 618 826-2326	(not reporting)						
Chicago (2784)	MC 312 744-4000	Richard M Daley	Gery Chico	....	Paul Vallas	Raymond Orozco	Matt L Rodriguez	Joseph Boyle Jr
Chicago Heights (33)	CO 708 756-5300	(not reporting)						
Chicago Ridge v (14)	MC 708 425-7700	Eugene L Siegel	....	Charles E Tokar	....	Randall Grossi	Michael Rio	Peter Chiappetti
Chillicothe (6)	MC 309 274-5056	Sherry L Weis	Denise L Passage	Sharon A Crabel	Richard Eckstein	Gail F Myers	Steven R Maurer	Clyde S Crabel
Christopher (3)	MC 618 724-7648	(not reporting)						
Cicero t (67)	MC 708 656-3600	(not reporting)						
Clarendon Hills v (7)	MC 708 323-3500	(not reporting)						
Clinton (7)	CO 217 935-9438	(not reporting)						
Coal City v (4)	MC 815 634-8608	Thomas McKinney	....	Kim S Walker	Mack McMillin	Harold Holsinger	Dennis M Neary	Jack L Wilson
Coal Valley v (3)	MC 309 799-3604	(not reporting)						
Collinsville (22)	CO 618 344-5252	Fred Dalton	Richard Mays	Louis Jackstadt	Nancy Boeckman	Ken Eichelberger	John Swindle	....
Columbia (6)	MC 618 281-6366	(not reporting)						
Country Club Hills (15)	CM 708 798-2616	Dwight W Welch	Janet R Muchnik	Harriet Scanlan	Mary G Dankowski	....	Robert L Roberts	Edward Meinheit
Countryside (6)	MC 708 354-7270	Carl W Legant	John P McDonald	Denise Likens	....	....	Charles D'Urso	Robert Fullar
Crest Hill v (11)	MC 815 741-5100	(not reporting)						
Crestwood v (11)	MC 708 371-4800	Chester Stranczek	Frank D Gassmere	Nancy C Benedetto	....	A J Kolasinski	John C Hefley	....
Crete v (7)	MC 708 672-5431	Michael S Einhorn	Don Eibling	Mariann E Gemper	....	Lyle Bachert	David L Wallace	Philip Hameister
Creve Coeur v (6)	MC 309 699-6714	(not reporting)						
Crystal Lake (25)	CM 815 459-2020	George Wells	Joseph Misurelli	James Kelley	Bruce Raymond	Richard Nebel	....	Clyde Wakefield
Danville (34)	MC 217 431-2200	Robert E Jones	....	Janet K Cooper	Ron Neufeld	Richard Eaglen	Robert L Dietzen	Thomas Stone Jr
Darien (18)	MC 708 852-5000	Carmen D Soldato	Timothy J Gagen	Joanne Coleman	....	....	Edward Musial	Arthur Benner
De Kalb (35)	CM 815 748-2000	(not reporting)						
Decatur (84)	CM 217 424-2805	Erik Brechnitz	James C Bacon	Phyllis Sands	Beth B Couter	John R Plotner	James L Williams	William B Sands
Deerfield v (17)	CM 708 945-5000	(not reporting)						
Des Plaines (53)	MC 708 391-5300	Ted Sherwood	F Wallace Douthwa	Donna McAllister	Gregory J Peters	David P Clark	John C Storm	....
Dixmoor v (4)	MC 708 389-6121	Zeb Lollis	....	Viviane V Young	....	Richard Gini	Nickolas Graves	Jerry Smith
Dixon (15)	MC 815 288-1485	Donald E Sheets	....	Barbara J Graff	....	James D Hill	Robert L Short	Chris W Hill

Directory 1/9 continued **MUNICIPAL OFFICIALS IN U.S. CITIES OVER 2,500**

City, 1990 population figures (000 omitted), form of government		Municipal phone number	Mayor	Appointed administrator	City clerk	Finance officer	Fire chief	Police chief	Public works director
ILLINOIS (402) continued									
Dolton v (24)	MC	708 849-4000	Donald J Hart	Jerald P Ducay	Judith J Evans	Willard Vanderzee	Robert Kapusta	G Pfotenhauer	Robert Myers
Downers Grove v (47)	CM	708 964-0300	Betty Cheever	Kurt Bressner	Barbara Waldner	. . . .	Lanny Russell	George Graves	Jeff Livergood
Du Quoin (7)	CO	618 542-3841	John Rednour	. . . .	Mell Smigielski	. . . .	Richard Fronek	Ken Dement	. . . .
Dupo v (3)	MC	618 286-3280	(not reporting)						
Dwight v (4)	MC	815 584-3077	Daryl N Holt	Daniel A Allen	Thomas J Slattery	Daniel A Allen	Alex McWilliams	Timothy F Henson	James Dransfeldt
East Alton v (7)	MC	618 259-7714	(not reporting)						
East Dundee v (3)	MC	708 426-2822	Jill A Yucuis	David B Smith	Jane E Theis	Pamela Figolah	. . . .	Ignacio J Pena	R Bockenhauer
East Moline (20)	MC	309 752-1599	William Ward	Steve Verdick	James Hughes	James Hughes	John Long	Adolph Defauw	Mark Demont
East Peoria (21)	CO	309 698-4715	J D Giebelhausen	James D Thompson	Veona I Dinkins	D J Giebelhausen	Jim G Bevard	Jim D Druin	Stephen D Carr
East St. Louis (41)	MC	618 482-6811	(not reporting)						
Edwardsville (15)	MC	618 692-7500	Gary Niebur	. . . .	Nina Baird	. . . .	Dennis Henson	Bennett Dickmann	Bala Kalimuthu
Effingham (12)	CO	217 347-5555	John D Thies	. . . .	Rick J Goeckner	. . . .	Nicholas Althoff	John Lange	Lowell Wines
El Paso (2)	MC	309 527-4005	Ronald D Mool	Richard T Gresham	David Fever	Richard T Gresham	. . . .	Jeffrey L Price	Richard T Gresham
Eldorado (5)	CO	618 273-6566	Walter K Bean	. . . .	Pat Mahoney	. . . .	George Q Wilson	Robert A Briddick	. . . .
Elgin (77)	CM	708 931-5620	G Van DeVoorde	. . . .	Dolonna Mecum	James Nowicki	John Henrici	Charles Gruber	James Kristiansen
Elk Grove Village v (33)	CM	708 439-3900	Dennis Gallitano	Gary Parrin	Patricia Smith	H Ingebrigtsen	Jim Mac Arthur	Fred Engelbrecht	Tom Cech
Elmhurst (42)	CM	708 530-3000	Thomas Marcucci	Thomas Borchert	Janet Edgley	Marilyn Gaston	John Fennell	John Millner	John Wielebnicki
Elmwood Park v (23)	CM	708 452-7300	(not reporting)						
Eureka (4)	MC	309 467-2113	Joe Serangeli	Benny Arbuckle	Robert Watson	Fred Mall	Gary Edwards	G Reinmann	Jim Lehman
Evanston (73)	CM	708 328-2100	Lorraine Morton	Eric Anderson	Kirsten Davis	Robert Shonk	James Hunt	. . . .	David Barber
Evergreen Park v (21)	MC	708 422-1551	Anthony Vacco	. . . .	Ruth Donahue	. . . .	John Hojek	Norbert Smith	Edward Schuth
Fairbury (4)	MC	815 692-2743	Lynn Dameron	. . . .	Brenda Defries	. . . .	Keith Klitzing	Donald Hedrick	Leroy McPherson
Fairfield (5)	MC	618 842-3871	Kenneth E Wood	. . . .	Lea Doty	. . . .	Larry McCoy	Murrel E Day	. . . .
Fairview Heights (14)	MC	618 397-7744	George A Lanxon	. . . .	Harvey Noubarian	James D Jacob	Bernie Rowan	Roger Richards	Robert D Hotz
Farmington (3)	MC	309 245-2011	Dorothy M Cox	Roger Woodcock	R Jeanette Baylor	Roger Woodcock	. . . .	Fred L Smith	Brad Dilts
Flora (5)	CO	618 662-8313	Joetta L Shrum	Marion J Long	Laura O'Donnell	. . . .	Bruce Dickey	Ed McCormick	. . . .
Flossmoor v (9)	CM	708 798-2300	Frank Maher	Peggy A Glassford	Jeanne Gummerson	Brian J Barnes	Greg Berk	Michael Williams	Bruce Ellis
Ford Heights v (4)	MC	708 758-3131	(not reporting)						
Forest Park v (15)	CO	708 366-2323	(not reporting)						
Fox Lake v (7)	MC	708 587-2151	(not reporting)						
Fox River Grove v (4)	MC	708 639-3170	William G Yocius	. . . .	Sylvia Van Dyke	. . . .	. . . .	Robert Polston	Jon Huizinga
Frankfort v (7)	MC	815 469-2177	Raymond Rossi	Bruce Bonebrake	Johanna Mark	. . . .	. . . .	Darrell Sanders	. . . .
Franklin Park v (18)	MC	708 671-4800	Jack B Williams	. . . .	Debra Fiorito	. . . .	Fred Olson	James Bickley	Roy McCampbell
Freeburg v (3)	MC	618 539-5545	(not reporting)						
Freeport (26)	MC	815 235-8200	Richard C Weis	. . . .	Mary J Johnston	. . . .	James Gale	Donald Parker	William Turner
Fulton (4)	CM	815 589-2616	K Ven Huizen	M Joseph Woith	Lavonne Huizenga	Eugene Richter	Terry Bielema	Douglas Krahn	Dale Green
Galena (4)	MC	815 777-1050	Gary R Bartell	Debra Schleicher	Jo Ann Turner	. . . .	Robert Smith	. . . .	. . . .
Galesburg (34)	CM	309 343-4181	Fred Kimble	Robert Knabel	Anita Carlton	Steve Driscoll	Dale May	John Schlaf	Lyman Jensen
Galva (3)	MC	309 932-2555	David E Thomson	Harvey Schmidt	Bonnie Sheahn	. . . .	Jerry Hoxworth	Ray Holman	Sherm Raley Jr
Geneseo (6)	MC	309 944-6419	Thomas P Gorman	. . . .	Tim D Long	. . . .	. . . .	Louis J Bervid	J Vandewoestyne
Geneva (13)	MC	708 232-0854	(not reporting)						
Genoa (3)	MC	815 784-2327	Gene Lawrence	. . . .	Jerry Redden	. . . .	. . . .	Joe Zmick	Dale Schepers
Georgetown (4)	MC	217 662-2525	(not reporting)						
Gibson City (3)	MC	217 784-5872	(not reporting)						
Gillespie (4)	MC	217 839-2919	Michael Mathis	. . . .	Carla Erickson	. . . .	Larry Norville	Kenneth Robertson	James Lafferty
Glen Carbon v (8)	MC	618 288-2100	(not reporting)						
Glen Ellyn v (25)	CM	708 469-5000	John W Demling	Gary L Webster	P O'Connor	Sheryl J Ligon	Stuart Stone	Howard M Thiele	Lynn A Neuhart
Glencoe v (8)	CM	708 835-4111	James O Webb	Peter B Cummins	Ruby Herron	Douglas D Merrill	Paul Harlow	Paul Harlow	Robert W Hogue
Glendale Heights v (28)	MC	708 260-6000	(not reporting)						
Glenview v (37)	CM	708 724-1700	(not reporting)						
Glenwood v (9)	MC	708 758-5150	William Asselborn	Arlene Herkert	Peggy Kozlowski	Nancy Tisza	William Kennedy	Russell Schoeneck	Chuck Michalski
Granite City (33)	MC	618 452-6200	Ron Selph	. . . .	Robert Stevens	K P Mac Taggart	Keith Talley	James Lengyel	Brett Hanke
Grayslake v (7)	MC	708 223-8515	Pat Carey	Michael Ellis	Barb Bacsa	. . . .	. . . .	Edward Wunderle	Roy Wickrsheim
Green Rock (3)	MC	309 792-0571	Terry Van Klavern	. . . .	Lories Graham	Terry Van Klavern	. . . .	C Robert Phillips	C Leroy Kelley
Greenville (5)	CM	618 664-1644	Eldon Tarley	Larry Stoever	Harriet McDonald	. . . .	. . . .	John King	Gary Netzler
Gurnee v (14)	MC	708 623-7650	Richard A Welton	James T Hayner	Norman C Balliet	P Wesolowski	Timothy McGrath	John H Ward	James Repp
Hamilton (3)	MC	217 847-2936	Ken DeYong	. . . .	Diann Means	. . . .	Jim Rackley	Walter Sellens	. . . .
Hanover Park v (33)	CM	708 837-3800	Sonya Crawshaw	Marc Hummel	Sherry Craig	Robert Whyte	. . . .	Gary Altergott	Joseph Atkinson
Harrisburg (9)	MC	618 253-7451	(not reporting)						
Harvard (6)	MC	815 943-6468	William LeFew	David Nelson	Chris Ferguson	. . . .	. . . .	Stanton Stone	James Carbonetti
Harvey (30)	CO	708 210-5300	(not reporting)						
Harwood Heights v (8)	MC	708 867-7200	Ray Willas	. . . .	Eugene J Brutto	. . . .	. . . .	William Bagnole	Thomas Schroeder
Havana (4)	MC	309 543-3411	Allan D McNeil	. . . .	Mary M Howerter	Edward Ray	Rick Trimpe	Robert Huber	. . . .
Hazel Crest v (13)	CM	708 334-9600	Sol J Rocke	Robert L Palmer	Shirley Smith	. . . .	Douglas Chappell	Harold V Moore	Richard W Fish
Henry (3)	MC	309 364-3056	Jay McCracken	. . . .	Almira Clark	. . . .	Daryl Fountain	Virgil Brewer	Thomas Maubach
Herrin (11)	MC	618 942-3175	Edward L Quaglia	. . . .	Marlene Simpson	Margaret Boren	Paul Marlo	Thomas Cundiff	Joe Lapinski
Hickory Hills (13)	MC	708 598-4800	Daniel A Riley	. . . .	Joann Jackson	. . . .	. . . .	George Dulzo	Larry Boettcher
Highland (8)	CM	618 654-9891	Robert W Nagel	Joseph E Frei	Lila Manville	Sharon Rusteberg	Michael Kilgore	William D Pierce	Robert Parker
Highland Park (31)	CM	708 432-0800	Daniel Pierce	David Limardi	David Fairman	David Fairman	Albert Schneider	Daniel Dahlberg	Ronald Kroop
Highwood (5)	MC	708 432-1924	John Sirotti	. . . .	April Powers	Janice Mann	Ron Pieri	George Smith	Jeff Ponsi
Hillsboro (4)	CO	217 532-5566	Bernard C Rappe	. . . .	James R Hart	. . . .	Joe Lyerla	John A Downs	David Booher
Hillside v (8)	MC	708 449-6450	(not reporting)						
Hinsdale v (16)	MC	708 789-7000	Joyce Skoog	Charles Dobbins	Sharon Henderson	David Cook	Stanley Bulat	Robert O'Malley	Ralph Zobjeck
Hoffman Estates v (47)	CM	708 882-9100	Michael O'Malley	Peter T Burchard	Virginia M Hayter	Douglas Ellsworth	Randy R Bruegman	Donald L Condiff	. . . .
Hometown (5)	MC	708 424-7500	Donald L Roberton	. . . .	Joan Dobrowits	. . . .	. . . .	Anthony Wolowicz	Joseph J Madden
Homewood v (19)	CM	708 798-3000	John T Doody Jr	M J Scholefield	Marjory L Dalton	. . . .	Raymond Presnak	Peter Hurst	Chris Wuellner
Hoopeston (6)	MC	217 283-5833	S Robert Ault	. . . .	Donald Dean	. . . .	Chuck Fenwick	Orval Kaag	. . . .
Indian Head Park v (4)	MC	708 246-3080	Werner Perthel	. . . .	Mary Radice	. . . .	. . . .	Thomas Pott	Edward Santen
Inverness v (7)	MC	708 358-7740	Donna L Thomas	William G Grams	Angie Fridono	. . . .	. . . .	Jeff Marquette	. . . .
Itasca v (7)	MC	708 773-0835	Shirley Ketter	. . . .	Carole Schreiber	. . . .	Vince Caravello	Mike McDonald	Alan Anderson
Jacksonville (19)	MC	217 243-3391	Ron Tendick	. . . .	Susan Moreland	. . . .	Jim Hiatt	Tom Weeks	Doug Logan
Jerseyville v (7)	CO	618 498-3312	(not reporting)						
Johnston City (4)	MC	618 983-6651	Vernon Kee	. . . .	Jean Hatfield	. . . .	Dennis Beaumont	Bennie Vick	. . . .
Joliet (77)	CM	815 740-2495	Arthur Schultz	John M Mezera	Nancy M Vallera	Robert D Fraser	Lawrence M Walsh	Joseph P Beazley	Dennis L Duffield
Justice v (11)	MC	708 458-2520	(not reporting)						
Kankakee (28)	MC	815 933-0500	(not reporting)						
Kenilworth v (2)	CM	708 251-1666	James McClamroch	Kenneth A Terlip	William Sethness	. . . .	. . . .	Gary A Wolff	I Fiorentino
Kewanee (13)	CM	309 853-4200	Dewey Colter	John D Kolata	Sandra Murphy	John D Kolata	Don Karau	Jim Kursock	Mike Rapczak
Kildeer v (..)	CM	708 438-6000	B Schwietert	Laurel Schreiber	Sherlyn Good	. . . .	. . . .	Jay Mills	Bill Holmes
Knoxville (3)	MC	309 289-2814	(not reporting)						
La Grange v (15)	CM	708 579-2300	Timothy R Hansen	Marlies Perthel	Robert Milne	Martin Lyons	Walter Mac Dowall	Ray Kaminskas	Clifton E Ferrell
La Grange Park v (13)	CM	708 354-0225	Raymond J Pietrus	Timothy Schuenke	Kerry Brunette	Pierre Garesche	Arthur Tullis	John Dunlop	Jim Schnute
La Salle (10)	MC	815 223-4586	(not reporting)						

Directory 1/9 continued — MUNICIPAL OFFICIALS IN U.S. CITIES OVER 2,500

City, 1990 population figures (000 omitted), form of government		Municipal phone number	Mayor	Appointed administrator	City clerk	Finance officer	Fire chief	Police chief	Public works director
ILLINOIS (402) continued									
Lake Bluff v (6)	CM	708 234-0774	Frederick Wacker	Kent Street	Donald Patton	Susan Griffin	Robert Graham	Fredrick Day	Richard Pelz
Lake Forest (18)	CM	708 234-2600	Rhett W Butler	Robert R Kiely Jr	Barbara S Douglas	Robert D Shaffer	Robert L Wilkins	Robert G Boone	Thomas J Naatz
Lake In The Hills v (6)	MC	708 658-4213	Tina Thornrose	Milton Faurot	Joyce Arient	Russ Nockels	. . . .	James Wales	David Gregoria
Lake Zurich v (15)	MC	708 438-5141	Deborah Vasels	John Dixon	Marcia Reynolds	Richard Ratkowski	T Mastandrea	Herbert Gehrke	Robert Mitchard
Lansing v (28)	MC	708 895-7200	(not reporting)						
Lawrenceville (5)	MC	618 943-4946	Gerald C Harper	. . . .	Helen M Ritchie	. . . .	. . . .	Donald S Foster	Christopher Kelly
Lebanon (4)	MC	618 537-4976	(not reporting)						
Lemont v (7)	MC	708 257-1550	Richard Kwasneski	Steven Jones	Charlene Smollen	. . . .	. . . .	John Bluis	Daniel Fielding
Leroy (3)	MC	309 962-3031	Jerry C Davis	. . . .	Juanita Dagley	. . . .	. . . .	Dennis G Carter	Gary L King
Lewistown (3)	MC	309 547-2113	(not reporting)						
Libertyville v (19)	CM	708 362-2430	Jo Ann Eckmann	Kevin S Bowens	Jane V Curtis	Steven C Noble	John Reitman Sr	W Dan McCormick	Steven R Magnusen
Lincoln (15)	MC	217 735-2815	John Guzzardo	. . . .	Juanita Josserand	. . . .	Wm Haak	Ronald Robbins	Donnie Osborne
Lincolnshire v (5)	CM	708 634-5800	(not reporting)						
Lincolnwood v (11)	MC	708 673-1540	(not reporting)						
Lindenhurst v (8)	MC	708 356-8252	P Baumunk	J Stevens	C Aller	J Stevens	. . . .	J McKeever	W Welsh
Lisle v (20)	MC	708 968-1200	Ronald Ghilardi	Carl Doerr	Melville Handley	Kimberly Schiller	. . . .	Richard Myers	Ray Peterson
Litchfield (7)	MC	217 324-2022	(not reporting)						
Lockport (9)	MC	815 838-0549	Richard C Dystrup	Gordon McCluskey	Paula R Waxweiler	Alan R Janasik	. . . .	James J Antole	Larry McCasland
Lombard v (39)	CM	708 620-5700	William Mueller	William Lichter	Lorraine Gerhardt	Leonard Flood	George Seagraves	Leon Kutzke	Stanley Rickard
Long Grove v (5)	CM	708 634-9440	Lenore J Simmons	D M Cal Doughty	Maria Rodriguez	. . . .	. . . .	. . . .	Ronald Damitz
Loves Park (15)	MC	815 654-5030	Joseph Sinkiawic	. . . .	Lorraine Chaussee	Judith A Bodey	Philip R Foley Jr	Darryl Lindberg	George Brettrager
Lynwood (7)	MC	708 758-6101	(not reporting)						
Lyons v (10)	MC	708 447-8886	(not reporting)						
Machesney Park v (19)	MC	815 877-5432	Frank G Bauer	. . . .	Linda M Vaughn	. . . .	. . . .	. . . .	Brett Coomber
Macomb (20)	MC	309 833-2575	Thomas Carper	Robert Morris	Lucille Gibson	. . . .	Don Bytner	Richard Clark	Lindy Powell
Madison (5)	MC	618 876-6268	John N Bellcoff	Jeanne M Weidner	William Weidner	. . . .	Robert Robbins	Charles Bridick	Robert Robbins
Marengo (5)	MC	815 568-7112	Thomas Siehoff	. . . .	Betty Struckmeier	. . . .	. . . .	Peter Bigalke	C McLaughlin
Marion (15)	MC	618 993-8575	(not reporting)						
Marissa v (2)	MC	618 295-2351	Jerry R Cross	. . . .	Carol Smith	. . . .	. . . .	Michael Kerperien	Danny C Smith
Markham (13)	MC	708 331-4905	(not reporting)						
Marquette Heights (3)	MC	309 382-3455	James F Steele	. . . .	Susan Hoover	. . . .	Dana Dearborn	Robert Quarello	Ronald G Hoyle
Marseilles (5)	CM	815 795-2133	John C Knudson	. . . .	Lucille Sergenti	. . . .	. . . .	Gerald Stevenson	Gary Fleming
Marshall (4)	MC	217 826-2112	(not reporting)						
Mascoutah (6)	CM	618 566-2965	(not reporting)						
Mason City (2)	MC	217 482-3669	Wilbur L Renken	. . . .	Joann E Burris	. . . .	. . . .	David N Coulter	Joe T Burris Jr
Matteson v (11)	MC	708 748-1559	Mark Stricker	Daniel DuBruiel	Donna Brumfield	James Spice	Robert Wilcox	Lawrence Burnson	Frank Denman
Mattoon (18)	CO	217 235-5654	(not reporting)						
Maywood v (27)	CM	708 344-1200	(not reporting)						
Mc Henry (16)	MC	815 363-2100	Steven J Cuda	Gerald R Peterson	Barbara E Gilpin	. . . .	Chris Bennett	Patrick J Joyce	Fredric C Batt
Melrose Park v (21)	MC	708 343-4000	(not reporting)						
Mendota (7)	MC	815 539-7459	(not reporting)						
Metropolis (7)	MC	618 524-4016	(not reporting)						
Midlothian v (14)	MC	708 389-0200	(not reporting)						
Milan v (6)	MC	309 787-8500	Duane Dawson	Steven Seiver	Barbara Lee	. . . .	Ed Handley	Dennis Baraks	Steven Seiver
Millstadt v (3)	MC	618 476-1514	(not reporting)						
Minonk (2)	MC	309 432-2558	William H Herman	David A Shirley	M Samuelson	. . . .	. . . .	Wiliam A Butler	Edward A Shirley
Mokena v (6)	CM	708 479-3900	Ronald Grotovsky	John Downs	Jane McGinn	. . . .	. . . .	Steve Pollak	Craig Heim
Moline (43)	CM	309 797-0463	Stanley F Leach	Alan L Efflandt	Joanne Lambrecht	. . . .	Michael Pierce	F S Etheridge	. . . .
Momence (3)	MC	815 472-2001	(not reporting)						
Monmouth (9)	MC	309 734-2141	David M Sharp	. . . .	Diane Hull	. . . .	Douglas Hoelscher	Michael Sage	Charles W Dowell
Montgomery v (4)	MC	708 896-8080	(not reporting)						
Monticello (5)	MC	217 762-2583	James Avres	Ronald Ivall	Renee Fruendt	Rick Cromwell	Rick Dubson	James Voss	Ronald Ivall
Morris (10)	MC	815 942-4026	(not reporting)						
Morrison (4)	MC	815 772-7657	Robert Atherton	Samuel E Tapson	Nancy Poling	. . . .	. . . .	Robert Snodgrass	Larry Heath
Morton v (14)	MC	309 266-5361	(not reporting)						
Morton Grove v (22)	MC	708 965-4100	Richard P Hohs	Larry N Arft	Wilma Wendt	Spiro Hountalas	Ralph Czerwinski	George Incledon	James Dahm
Mount Carmel (8)	CO	618 262-4822	Rudy L Witsman	Mark A Bader	Mark A Bader	Mick Mollenhauer	Steve Partee	Dan DeWitt	. . . .
Mount Morris v (3)	MC	815 734-6425	Steven Brinker	. . . .	Sandra Blake	Leo Marshall	. . . .	John G Thompson	Greg Unger
Mount Prospect v (53)	CM	708 392-6000	Gerald L Farley	Michael E Janonis	Carol A Fields	David C Jepson	Edward M Cavello	Ronald W Pavlock	Herbert L Weeks
Mount Vernon (17)	CM	618 242-5000	Rolland W Lewis	Craig A Olsen	Karl Powers	John Lunini	Larry Fally	Ron Massey	Dennis Shirley
Mount Zion v (5)	CM	217 864-5424	Harry Ashworth	James F Bowden	Jana L Wood	. . . .	. . . .	Paul D Wood	Steven Simmons
Mundelein v (21)	MC	708 949-3200	Marilyn Sindles	Kenneth Marabella	Colleen Kasting	Mary Kay Hatton	Randy Justus	Raymond Rose	Kenneth Miller
Murphysboro (9)	MC	618 684-4961	(not reporting)						
Naperville (85)	CM	708 420-6111	Samuel Macrane	. . . .	Suzanne Gagner	Julia Carroll	Alan Rohlfs	David Dial	Ned Becker
Nashville (3)	MC	618 327-3058	(not reporting)						
New Lenox v (10)	MC	815 485-6452	John Nowakowski	Russ Loebe	Marjorie Wajchert	Kimberly Newquist	. . . .	Kenneth Oldendorf	Ronald Sly
Newton (3)	MC	618 783-8451	Robert E Burris	. . . .	Jean Ghast	. . . .	. . . .	Michael Swick	. . . .
Niles v (28)	CM	708 967-6100	Nicholas B Blase	Abe Selman	Kathryn Harbison	. . . .	Harry Kinowski	Ray Giovannelli	Teofilo Noriega
Nokomis (3)	MC	217 563-2514	James F Cohan	. . . .	Sherry Finn	John McCall	Jay Heck	James B Herzog	Michael Finn
Normal t (40)	CM	309 454-2444	Kent A Karraker	David S Anderson	Marianne Edwards	Ronald J Hill	George R Cermak	James R Taylor	Ellis G Perl
Norridge v (14)	MC	708 453-0800	Joseph Sieb	. . . .	Irene Gdula	. . . .	. . . .	Ervin F Siemers	Brian M Gaseor
North Aurora v (6)	MC	708 897-8228	Mike Mudry	. . . .	Linda Mitchell	. . . .	Steve Miller	Edward Kelley	James Palmatier
North Chicago (35)	MC	708 578-7750	Bobby Thompson	Evelyn Alexander	Catherine Collins	Keith Bennett	Richard Turner	Ernest Fisher	Willie Mayfield
North Riverside v (6)	MC	708 447-4211	Richard Scheck	Wayne Pesek	Charmaine Kutt	. . . .	Dominic Salvino	George Kratochvil	Kenneth Lange
Northbrook v (32)	CM	708 272-5050	Mark W Damisch	John M Novinson	Lona Louis	David Kowal	John G Julcher	James B Wallace	James M Reynolds
Northfield v (5)	CM	708 446-9200	Richard M Rieser	Mark J Morien	Michael Nystrand	Vivian Perenchio	Michael Nystrand	George A Wagner	Michael Nystrand
Northlake (13)	MC	708 343-8700	(not reporting)						
O'Fallon (16)	MC	618 624-4500	Robert Morton	Don Slazinik	Ben Hamm	. . . .	Bill Henry	Don Slazinik	Jack Nevenner
Oak Brook v (9)	CM	708 990-3000	Karen Bushy	Margaret C Powers	Linda M Gonnella	Margaret C Powers	Robert D Nielsen	James R Fleming	Michael J Meranda
Oak Forest (26)	MC	708 687-4050	James C Richmond	Bernard Kelly	R J Fitzpatrick	Dwayne K Fox	James Berger	David Griffin	Michael Cozzo
Oak Lawn v (56)	CM	708 636-4400	(not reporting)						
Oak Park v (54)	CM	708 383-6400	Larry Christmas	Allen Parker	Sondra Sokol	Nick Narducci	John Davis	Joseph Mendrick	Vincent Akhimie
Oglesby (4)	MC	815 883-3389	(not reporting)						
Olney (9)	CM	618 395-7302	Tom Fehrenbacher	Larry Taylor	Belinda Henton	. . . .	Gary Foster	Elton Wood	. . . .
Olympia Fields v (4)	MC	708 748-8246	(not reporting)						
Oregon (4)	CO	815 732-6321	James L Barnes	. . . .	Julienne Crowley	. . . .	. . . .	Thomas Miller	. . . .
Orland Hills v (6)	MC	708 349-6666	(not reporting)						
Orland Park v (36)	CM	708 403-6100	D McLaughlin	James Smithberg	James Dodge	S Dianne Kallina	. . . .	Charles Rabideau	Richard Dime
Oswego v (4)	MC	708 554-3618	Richard Saletri	Mary McKittrick	Charles Bieber	. . . .	Brad Smith	Robert Wunsch	Jeff Humm
Ottawa (17)	MC	815 433-0161	(not reporting)						
Palatine v (39)	CM	708 358-7500	Rita Mullins	Michael Kadlecik	Margaret Duer	Robert Husselbee	Richard Payne	Jerry Bratcher	Andrew Radetski
Palos Heights (11)	MC	708 361-1800	(not reporting)						
Palos Hills (18)	MC	708 598-3400	(not reporting)						

Directory 1/9 continued — MUNICIPAL OFFICIALS IN U.S. CITIES OVER 2,500

City, 1990 population figures (000 omitted), form of government		Municipal phone number	Mayor	Appointed administrator	City clerk	Finance officer	Fire chief	Police chief	Public works director
ILLINOIS (402) continued									
Palos Park v (4)	CM	708 448-5200	Rosemary Kaptur	Patrica Jones	Annette Mucha	. . . .	. . . .	William Shanley	Fred Froelke
Pana (6)	MC	217 562-3626	Larry J Chaney	. . . .	Terry L Klein	. . . .	Bill Williamson	Michael Harris	. . . .
Paris (9)	CO	217 465-7601	Frank L Clinton	Paul H Ruff	Paul H Ruff	. . . .	James H Kelly	Harold E Ray	. . . .
Park City (5)	MC	708 623-5030	Robert Allen	. . . .	Theresa Oldham	. . . .	. . . .	Robert Williams	Gordon Kosidowski
Park Forest v (25)	CM	708 748-1112	Patrick Kelly	Jack Manahan	Elva Iid	Erica Peterson	Ronald Welch	Robert Maeyama	Benjamin Jordan
Park Ridge (36)	CM	708 318-5200	Ronald W Wietecha	Gerald E Hagman	Betty W Henneman	Diane Lembesis	. . . .	John O Baydek	T A Fredrickson
Pawnee v (2)	MC	217 625-2951	(not reporting)						
Paxton (4)	MC	217 379-4022	James E Kingston	. . . .	Linda Dellerhals	. . . .	Don Jones	Dennis Schneider	John Curtis
Pekin (32)	CO	309 477-2300	Donald Williams	. . . .	James F Kautz	Gloria Fangmeier	John Hamann	Robert Burress	Dennis Kief
Peoria (114)	CM	309 672-8524	James Maloof	Peter Korn	Mary Haynes	Lori Fleming	Lee Daugherty	. . . .	Steve Van Winkle
Peoria Heights v (7)	MC	309 686-2370	(not reporting)						
Peotone v (3)	MC	708 258-3279	Richard Benson	. . . .	Donna Werner	. . . .	. . . .	Gary Bogart	. . . .
Peru (9)	MC	815 223-0061	Donald L Baker	. . . .	Judith A Heuser	. . . .	Donald Nowakowski	Donald Clausen	Donald Kowalczyk
Phoenix v (2)	MC	708 331-2636	Terry Wells	. . . .	Johnnie M Lane	Lester Hemingway	Clarence Elmore	Ronnie Berry	Louis McDaniel
Pinckneyville (3)	CO	618 357-6916	Joseph M Holder	. . . .	Frances I Thomas	Halleck Reese	Jerry Smith	Thomas Denton	Harlan Yeager
Pittsfield (4)	MC	217 285-4484	Rick E Conner	. . . .	Tim Belford	. . . .	Larry Snyder	Bobby Yelliott	Larry Snyder
Plainfield v (5)	MC	815 436-7093	John E Peterson	David Van Vooren	Susan Janik	. . . .	. . . .	Donald E Bennett	. . . .
Plano (5)	MC	708 552-8275	Susan H Nesson	. . . .	Deanna Brown	. . . .	John Dobbs	Steven Eaves	John P McGinnis
Pontiac (11)	MC	815 844-3396	(not reporting)						
Pontoon Beach v (4)	MC	618 931-1982	(not reporting)						
Posen v (4)	MC	708 385-0139	James Adamek	. . . .	Charles White	. . . .	John Krizik	David Torres	William Wilkins
Princeton (7)	CO	815 875-2631	Richard Welte	. . . .	Eugene Wolf	. . . .	Terry Himes	Melvin Hult	Thomas Carr
Prospect Heights (15)	MC	708 398-6070	Edward Rotchford	Kenneth M Bonder	Karen Pedersen	. . . .	. . . .	Robert Bonneville	Duane E Dobner
Quincy (40)	MC	217 228-4500	(not reporting)						
Rantoul v (17)	MC	217 893-1661	Katy Podagrosi	. . . .	Don Frye	Ken Modglin	Richard Quick	Allen Jones	. . . .
Red Bud (3)	MC	618 282-2315	(not reporting)						
Richton Park v (11)	CM	708 481-8950	Rudolph Banovich	David J Niemeyer	. . . .	Timothy P Hammond	Joseph Solick	Richard Labus	Ben Adcock
River Forest v (12)	CM	708 366-8500	Frank M Paris	Charles J Biondo	Emerson K Houser	. . . .	Charles B Henrici	Joseph I Bopp	Gregory W Kramer
River Grove v (10)	MC	708 453-8000	(not reporting)						
Riverdale v (14)	MC	708 841-2200	(not reporting)						
Riverside v (9)	CM	708 447-2700	Joseph DiNatale	Chester Kendzior	Jane Norman	Jim Egeberg	Anthony Bednarz	Donald Doneske	Neil Van Dyke
Riverton v (3)	MC	217 629-9122	Todd E Williams	. . . .	Connie Blissett	. . . .	. . . .	Craig Bangert	. . . .
Riverwoods v (3)	MC	708 945-3990	(not reporting)						
Robbins v (7)	CM	708 385-8940	Irene H Brodie	E Berry Beck	Tyrone Haymore	. . . .	Charles B Lloyd	Johnny L Holmes	Bernard Ward
Robinson (7)	MC	618 544-7616	Gilbert Phillippe	. . . .	Sandra Jared	Gilbert Phillippe	Richard Pearce	Kenneth Watts	. . . .
Rochelle (9)	CO	815 562-6161	Joseph Panozzo	. . . .	Linda Manning	. . . .	Tom McDermott	Al Gorr	Keith Scott
Rock Falls v (10)	MC	815 622-1100	Glen R Kuhlemier	. . . .	Margie C Sommers	. . . .	James W Larsen	Larry G Thoren	. . . .
Rock Island (41)	CM	309 793-3300	Mark W Schwiebert	John C Phillips	Jeann F Paggen	William S Scott	Gary L Mell	Anthony R Scott	Robert T Hawes
Rockford (139)	MC	815 987-5580	Charles E Box	Samuel Schmitz	. . . .	Ronald Malmberg	Bill Robertson	Bill Fitzpatrick	Alan Werner
Rolling Meadows (23)	CM	708 394-8500	Carl Couve	Robert A Beezat	Marylyn Koch	Edward McKee	Philip Burns	Gerald Aponte	Dennis York
Romeoville v (14)	CM	815 886-7200	Sandra K Gulden	. . . .	Judy E Canning	Elvira A Hogan	Carl J Churulo	Andrew J Barto	William Taylor
Roselle v (21)	CM	708 980-2000	Gayle A Smolinski	Robin A Weaver	Linda McDermott	Kathryn M Booth	James E Sunagel	Richard Eddington	Robert O Burns
Rosemont v (4)	MC	708 825-4404	Donald E Stephens	Donald E Stephens	Rosalie Lennstrom	John Hochstettler	Gary Hopkins	Jack Hasselberger	Vito Corriero
Round Lake v (4)	MC	708 546-5400	James Lumber	. . . .	Lillian Frost	Margarete Molidor	. . . .	Joseph Trkovsky	Doug Rowley
Round Lake Beach v (16)	MC	708 546-2351	Ralph E Davis	. . . .	Sharon Fyfe	. . . .	. . . .	Richard Jablonski	Richard Kinzel
Round Lake Park v (4)	MC	708 546-7336	Charlene Beyer	. . . .	Star Southworth	. . . .	. . . .	Gene Kelly	George Johnson
Rushville (3)	MC	217 322-3833	Dennis R Yates	. . . .	Ina J Patterson	. . . .	Tom Acker	William White	. . . .
Salem (7)	CM	618 548-2222	Leonard Ferguson	Roger D Kinney	Jo Chitty	Marilyn Shetley	Jim Raver	John Duncan	Clyde Scott
Sandwich (6)	MC	815 786-9321	Tom Thomas	. . . .	Barbara G Olson	John Korns	. . . .	Frank Spoden	. . . .
Sauk Village v (10)	MC	708 758-3330	Mark Collins	Richard Dieterich	Marjorie L Tuley	Beverly Sterrett	Travis Thornhill	Selvey Grant	Wolfgang Nieft
Savanna (4)	MC	815 273-2251	Eugene T Flack	. . . .	Walter I Shrake	Sheryl L Sipe	Harry R Charneski	Robert F Stretton	Paul E Hartman
Schaumburg v (69)	CM	708 894-4500	Alan Larson	George Longmeyer	Penny M Dietrich	Keith Wendland	Edward M Lacey	Kenneth R Alley	Robert Miller
Schiller Park v (11)	MC	708 678-2550	Anna Montana	John J Gregor Jr	Claudia Irsuto	. . . .	Walter Preiss	Peter J Puleo	. . . .
Shelbyville (5)	CO	217 774-5531	(not reporting)						
Shorewood v (6)	MC	815 725-2150	Bertha J Hofer	Gary C Holmes	Julia A Russell	L Ann Martin	. . . .	Donald R Lattin	Jerry Seil
Silvis (7)	MC	309 792-9181	Bob Steele	. . . .	Barbara J Fox	. . . .	Robert Leibovitz	James Healty	Ronald Hall
Skokie v (59)	CM	708 673-0500	Jacqueline Gorell	Albert J Rigoni	Marlene Williams	Robert J Nowak	James Eaves	William D Miller	Donadl Manak
South Beloit (4)	CO	815 389-3023	Alan J Palmer	. . . .	Marilyn J Hartley	Scott McClellan	Ken C Morse	Jack O Johnson	. . . .
South Chicago Heights v (4)	MC	708 755-1880	(not reporting)						
South Elgin v (7)	MC	708 742-5780	Thomas J Rolando	Mark Isackson	Dale D W Stevens	. . . .	. . . .	James Bobik	Rick Zirk
South Holland v (22)	MC	708 333-0572	(not reporting)						
South Jacksonville v (3)	MC	217 245-4803	Glenda Hazelrigg	. . . .	Jo Ann Lindemann	. . . .	Willard Hickox	Richard Evans	Garry Thomas
Sparta (5)	CO	618 443-2917	Tom Maybell	. . . .	Ronald E Cavalier	. . . .	Bruce Dahlem	Lyndon Thies	Loren D Prest
Spring Valley (5)	MC	815 664-4221	James Narczewski	. . . .	Joseph A Taliano	. . . .	Gene Scheri	Douglas Bernabei	Kevin Sawicki
Springfield (105)	MC	217 789-2446	Ossie Langfelder	Robert Church	Norma Graves	Carl Forn	Russ Steil	. . . .	Ric Lynch
St. Charles (23)	MC	708 377-4446	Fred Norris	. . . .	Jean Conners	Larry Maholland	Larry Swanson	James Roche	Mark Koenen
Staunton (5)	MC	618 635-2233	Wayne Heinemeyer	. . . .	Marilyn Herbeck	. . . .	Ron Dustman	Ron Masinelli	. . . .
Steger v (9)	CM	708 754-3395	Louis Sherman	. . . .	Alvin D Harms	. . . .	Elmer J Joyce	Charles A Tieri	John E Gilkison
Sterling (15)	CM	815 622-2221	William Durham	Stephen Berley	Rosemary Coughlin	Sheila Barton	Arlyn Oetting	Cadet Thorp	Vern Gottel
Stickney v (6)	MC	708 749-4400	(not reporting)						
Stone Park v (4)	MC	708 345-5550	Robert Natale	. . . .	Linda Ruge	Frank Koorasingh	Michael Raetz	Sam Scala	David Webie
Streamwood v (31)	CM	708 837-0200	(not reporting)						
Streator (14)	CM	815 672-2517	Richard Conner	Scot Wrighton	Diane Gaede	Diane Gaede	Henry Araujo	James Dutton	E Jeff Wilson
Sullivan (4)	CO	217 728-4383	(not reporting)						
Summit v (10)	MC	708 563-4800	(not reporting)						
Swansea v (8)	MC	618 234-0044	(not reporting)						
Sycamore (10)	MC	815 895-4515	(not reporting)						
Taylorville (11)	MC	217 824-2101	(not reporting)						
Thornton v (3)	MC	708 877-4456	Jack A Swan	. . . .	Marian A Mikrut	. . . .	James Swan	Peter Belos	Peter Den Hartog
Tinley Park v (37)	MC	708 532-7700	Edward J Zabrocki	Dennis A Kallsen	Frank W German Jr	. . . .	R Bettenhausen	James Wade	Thomas Albright
Trenton (2)	MC	618 224-7323	Virgil E Ripperda	Carol S Metzger	Carol S Metzger	. . . .	. . . .	Timothy J Harris	Roger J Maue
Troy (6)	MC	618 667-6741	Velda Armes	Bud Klaustermeier	Mary Chasteen	David Roady	. . . .	Robert Noonan	Lloyd Wood
Tuscola (4)	MC	217 253-2112	(not reporting)						
University Park v (6)	CM	708 534-6451	Vernon Young	M Grubermann	Irma A Berry	Rita Kueny	M Grubermann	Thomas Leonard	Wesley Scholz
Urbana (36)	MC	217 384-2362	Tod Satterthwaite	Bruce Walden	Phyllis Clark	Ronald Eldridge	Dick Dunn	Bill Schlieter	Bill Gray
Vandalia (6)	MC	618 283-1196	Rich Walker	. . . .	Norma R Croasdale	. . . .	Merle Adermann	. . . .	David Reeter
Venice (4)	MC	618 877-2412	Tyrone Echols	Roseann Koelker	Wilbert Glasper	. . . .	Thomas Brent	James R Bennett	Green Jacks
Vernon Hills v (15)	CM	708 367-3700	Roger L Byrne	Larry Laschen	Kathy Ryg	Larry Nakrin	. . . .	Gary Kupsak	E Laudenslager
Villa Grove (3)	MC	217 832-4721	Ronald H Hunt	Shirley A Howard	Shirley A Howard	. . . .	Chuck Gillins	Dennis W Gire	Lee Closson
Villa Park v (22)	CM	708 834-8500	Rae Rupp Srch	Wayne L Lulay	Mary Murphy	Michael O'Keefe	Richard Davidson	Ronald Ohlson	Vydas Juskelis
Virden (4)	MC	217 965-5805	Susan Rohrer	. . . .	Judy Berry	. . . .	. . . .	Gary Plessa	. . . .
Warrenville (11)	MC	708 393-9427	Vivian Lund	James Connors	Rosemary Tierney	Jean McCabe	. . . .	Robert Ladeur	Dennis Posluszny
Washington (10)	MC	309 444-3196	Donald Gronewold	Dale Claus	Carol Moss	. . . .	. . . .	William Witmer	James B Toon

Directory 1/9
continued

MUNICIPAL OFFICIALS
IN U.S. CITIES OVER 2,500

City, 1990 population figures (000 omitted), form of government	Municipal phone number	Mayor	Appointed administrator	City clerk	Finance officer	Fire chief	Police chief	Public works director
ILLINOIS (402) continued								
Washington Park v (7) .	MC 618 874-2040	Sylvester Jackson	. . . .	Anthony Nesbitt	. . . .	Otis Walker	James Avant	. . . .
Waterloo (5)	MC 618 939-8661	(not reporting)						
Watseka (5)	MC 815 432-2711	(not reporting)						
Wauconda v (6)	MC 708 526-9600	James Eschenbauch	Gerald Sagona	Mary C Taylor	Ila M Reynolds	. . . .	Andrew Mayer	Jeffery Kuester
Waukegan (69)	MC 708 360-9000	William F Durkin	Donald R Weakley	Sam Filippo	Donald L Schultz	Charles Perkey	George Bridges	Robert Johnson
West Chicago (15)	MC 708 293-2200	Steve Lakics	J Donald Foster	Nancy Smith	Warren C Warren	. . . .	Gerald Mourning	Kenneth Dean
West Dundee v (4)	CM 708 551-3800	Calvin Grafelman	Joseph Cavallaro	Barbara Traver	. . . .	Larry McManaman	Allan Demien	Donald Habermehl
West Frankfort (9)	MC 618 932-3262	John Simmons		Barbara Graves	James Ward	. . . .	Lindell Blades	
Westchester v (17)	CM 708 345-0020	John J Sinde	John H Crois	Kathryn Hayes	Michael J Obrien	Thomas Rafferty	Donald R Musker	Robert Mitchard
Western Springs v (12)	CM 708 246-1800	(not reporting)						
Westmont v (21)	CM 708 968-0560	(not reporting)						
Westville v (3)	MC 217 267-2507	(not reporting)						
Wheaton (51)	CM 708 260-2000	(not reporting)						
Wheeling v (30)	CM 708 459-2600	Sheila H Schultz	Craig Anderson	Jeanne Selander	Robert Fialkowski	Keith Mac Isaac	Michael Haeger	Robert Gray
White Hall (3)	MC 217 374-2345	Harold L Brimm	. . . .	Beverly A Howard	. . . .	Weldon Cooper	Robert McMillen	. . . .
Willow Springs v (5) . .	MC 708 839-2701	(not reporting)						
Willowbrook v (9)	MC 708 323-8215	Gary Pretzer	Bernard Oglietti	Patrick Spatafore	Jeffrey Rowitz	. . . .	Raymond Arthurs	Phil Modaff
Wilmette v (27)	MC 708 251-2700	John Jacoby	Heidi J Voorhees	Heidi J Voorhees	Robert Amoruso	Mark J Mitchell	George Carpenter	Richard A Hansen
Wilmington (5)	MC 815 476-2175	Jerry D Hill	. . . .	James C Johnston	Bonita L Hill	Alan Zlomie Jr	Wally D Evans	Fred R Richmond
Winfield v (7)	CM 708 665-1778	Marylou Crane	Bryon Vana	Patrica Stuart	. . . .	. . . .	Doug Riner	Richard Ahrens
Winnetka v (12)	CM 708 501-6000	Paul F Cruikshank	Douglas Williams	Lois C Resnick	Kenneth A Klein	Ronald Colpaert	William Gallagher	Kenneth R Keene
Winthrop Harbor v (6) .	MC 708 872-3846	(not reporting)						
Wood Dale (12)	CM 708 766-4900	Jerry C Greer	Rick O Curneal	Geraldine Jacobs	Peter Stefan	. . . .	Frank Williams	Fred Vogt
Wood River (11)	CM 618 251-3100	Lon A Smith	Barrett H Jones	Jean Bruce	Joey Tolbert	Guy Williams	Charles Nunn	Tim Palermo
Woodridge v (26)	MC 708 852-7000	William Murphy	John Perry	Dorothy Stahl	Laurie Roberts	. . . .	Steven List	Joseph Fennell
Woodstock (14)	CM 815 338-4300	Wm Anderson	Timothy J Clifton	Jean Headley	David Danielson	Phil Parker	Herbert Pitzman	John Isbell
Worth v (11)	MC 708 448-1181	James Bilder		Betty Mattera	. . . .	Steve Twining	Glenn G Rose	Wayne Demonbreun
Yorkville (4)	MC 708 553-4352	Kenneth K Kittoe	Donald E Peck	J Allison	Delene M Drew	. . . .	Anton Graff	J T Johnson
Zion (20)	CO 708 746-4000	Billy McCullough	. . . .	Judy Smith	John Stark	Dave McAdams	Lloyd Detienne	Jim Christensen
INDIANA (159)								
Albany t (2)	MC 317 789-6112	(not reporting)						
Alexandria (6)	MC 317 724-4633	(not reporting)						
Anderson (59)	MC 317 646-9685	(not reporting)						
Angola (6)	MC 219 665-2514	(not reporting)						
Attica (3)	MC 317 762-2467	Harold R Long	. . . .	Tracy R Smith	. . . .	Dave Brown	Timothy Quinn	. . . .
Auburn (9)	MC 219 925-5430	(not reporting)						
Aurora (4)	MC 812 926-1777	Leon Kelly	. . . .	. . . .	. . . .	K Klingelhoffer	Gary L Watts	. . . .
Austin t (4)	MC 812 794-2877	(not reporting)						
Batesville (5)	MC 812 934-2509	(not reporting)						
Bedford (14)	MC 812 279-6555	(not reporting)						
Beech Grove (13)	MC 317 788-4978	J Warner Wiley	. . . .	Marcella L Miceli	. . . .	James Bright	Michael Johnson	Phil Gurganus
Berne (4)	MC 219 589-8526	(not reporting)						
Bicknell (3)	MC 812 735-4636	Jerry Russell	. . . .	Elizabeth Curtis	. . . .	Paul Koenig	John Vendes	Jerry Russell
Bloomington (61)	MC 812 339-2261	Tomilea Allison	Mike Davis	Patricia Williams	Chuck Rockman	Larry Fleener	Steve Sharp	Ted Rhinehart
Bluffton (9)	MC 219 824-1520	Everett Faulkner	. . . .	Nancy Hewitt	. . . .	Gary Markley	Robert Frantz	. . . .
Boonville (7)	MC 812 897-1230	(not reporting)						
Brazil (8)	MC 812 443-2221	Kenneth Crabb	. . . .	Glenna Simons	. . . .	Robert Hayes	John Zuel	Garry Warren
Bremen t (5)	MC 219 546-2471	Thomas Teghtmeyer	Duwaine J Elliott	Joanne Kimmell	. . . .	Jerry Lanning	James Brown	. . . .
Brookville t (3)	CO 317 647-3322	Paul Chaney	. . . .	Alberta Sauerland	. . . .	Daniel Bruns	Thomas Helms	. . . .
Brownsburg t (8)	MC 317 852-1120	. . . .	Mark A White	Jeanette Brickler	. . . .	Glen Bailey	Keith F McCoskey	. . . .
Brownstown t (3)	MC 812 358-5500	Robert Millman	. . . .	. . . .	. . . .	James Renaker	Kenneth Sneed	. . . .
Butler (3)	MC 219 868-5200	Larry Moore	. . . .	C Minehart	. . . .	Rick Husted	Steven A Mosser	Wm Ted Miller
Carmel (25)	MC 317 844-6433	(not reporting)						
Cedar Lake t (9)	CM 219 374-7000	Robert Carnahan	. . . .	Gerry Kortokrax	. . . .	Dennis Wilkening	James Hunley	. . . .
Chandler t (3)	TM 812 925-6882	Wayne A Schuble	Sharon A Gammon	Nicholas Galloway	. . . .	. . . .	Kenneth Musgrave	Robert Hess
Charlestown (6)	MC 812 256-3422	(not reporting)						
Chesterfield t (3)	RT 317 378-3331	Don E Carpenter	. . . .	Patricia Summers	. . . .	Danny Butler	Moses Beemah	. . . .
Chesterton t (9)	RT 219 926-1641	(not reporting)						
Cicero t (3)	MC 317 984-4900	Timothy Schaeffer	. . . .	Max Mosbaugh	. . . .	Billy Scherer	Jerry Cook	. . . .
Clarksville t (20)	CO 812 288-7155	(not reporting)						
Clinton (5)	MC 317 832-9880	(not reporting)						
Columbia City (6)	MC 219 244-5141	(not reporting)						
Columbus (32)	MC 812 376-2500	Robert N Stewart	John M Baughn	. . . .	. . . .	John Breeding	Charles Imel	. . . .
Connersville (16)	MC 317 825-4211	Marion Newhouse	. . . .	H Ripberger	. . . .	Bob Wadle	Ken Faw	Marion Newhouse
Corydon t (3)	MC 812 738-3958	(not reporting)						
Covington (3)	MC 317 793-2331	Eugene Smail	. . . .	Jo Ann Anderson	. . . .	Richard Talbert	Tony Knecht	Eugene Smail
Crawfordsville (14)	MC 317 362-0805	(not reporting)						
Crown Point (18)	MC 219 663-0257	(not reporting)						
Cumberland t (5)	MC 317 894-3580	(not reporting)						
Danville t (4)	CM 317 745-3001	(not reporting)						
De Motte t (2)	MC 219 987-3831	Mark Boer	. . . .	Lois Eakin	. . . .	Michael Orsburn	William Arnold	. . . .
Decatur (9)	MC 219 724-7171	(not reporting)						
Dunkirk (3)	MC 317 768-6565	Grant Fager	. . . .	Judith Garr	. . . .	Steve Fields	Arnold Clevenger	. . . .
Dyer t (11)	MC 219 865-6108	Edward Altgilbers	Glen L Eberly	. . . .	Maryann Brown	John Ozahanic	Charles Thompson	Bobby Thomas
East Chicago (34)	MC 219 392-1600	(not reporting)						
Edinburg t (5)	CM 812 526-2919	(not reporting)						
Elkhart (44)	MC 219 294-5471	James P Perron	. . . .	Sue M Beadle	Maribeth Hicks	Steven Gattman	John J Ivory	Gary Gilot
Ellettsville t (3)	RT 812 876-3860	Herbert Ray	. . . .	. . . .	. . . .	Jim Davis	David Stalcup	Jim Ragle
Elwood (9)	MC 317 552-5078	Denny Robinson	. . . .	Sandra Brewer	. . . .	Milt Gough	Roger Towner	Denny Robinson
Evansville (126)	MC 812 426-5000	Frank McDonald	. . . .	Marsha Abell	Leslie Blenner	Douglas Wilcox	Arthur Gann	Edgar Schletzer
Fairmount t (3)	TM 317 948-4632	John Metzger	. . . .	Michael Burton	Robert McGraw	Doug Jump	Hebert Smith	. . . .
Fort Branch t (2)	CM 812 753-7662	(not reporting)						
Fort Wayne (173)	MC 219 427-1111	W Paul Helmke	. . . .	Sandra Kennedy	Douglas Lehman	Steven Hinton	T Neil Moore	Charles Layton
Fortville t (3)	CM 317 485-4044	. . . .	Jeff Pape	Margie Manship	. . . .	Kit Arnold	Richard Poe	. . . .
Frankfort (15)	MC 317 654-5715	Harold Woodruff	. . . .	Marilyn Chittick	. . . .	Norman Sterling	James Skinner	. . . .
Franklin (13)	MC 317 736-3602	Charles Littleton	. . . .	Lena M McCracken	. . . .	Jack Matthews	N Blankenship	Rick Littleton
Garrett (5)	MC 219 357-3836	(not reporting)						
Gary (117)	MC 219 881-1300	Thomas V Barnes	Arlene Colvin	Katie Hall	Steven B Ash	Benjamin Perry	David Wade	Wilford E Holley
Gas City (6)	MC 317 677-3079	Eugene Linn	. . . .	Anita Smith	. . . .	Joe Miitsch	H Larry Leach	Eugene Linn
Goshen (24)	MC 219 533-8621	(not reporting)						
Greencastle (9)	MC 317 653-3100	Michael Harmless	. . . .	Judith Berry	. . . .	Stever R White	Jack Hanlon	. . . .
Greendale t (4)	CM 812 537-2125	(not reporting)						

City, 1990 population figures (000 omitted), form of government	Municipal phone number	Mayor	Appointed administrator	City clerk	Finance officer	Fire chief	Police chief	Public works director
INDIANA (159) continued								
Greenfield (12)	MC 317 462-8510	(not reporting)						
Greensburg (9)	MC 812 663-8582	Sheldon Smith	. . . .	Lillian June Ryle	Lillian June Ryle	Jerry McGuire	Michael T Riley	Kathryn Crippen
Greenwood (26)	MC 317 888-2100	M McGovern	. . . .	Genevieve Worsham	Genevieve Worsham	Paul Kite	Charles Henderson	. . . .
Griffith t (18)	MC 219 924-7500	L E Owen	. . . .	Ruth E Hopp	. . . .	George Thiel	Karl Grimmer	Ronnie L Cooper
Hammond (84)	MC 219 853-6301	(not reporting)						
Hanover t (4)	MC 812 866-2131	(not reporting)						
Hartford City (7)	MC 317 348-0412	David J Bennett	. . . .	Martha J Funk	Martha J Funk	Gene Henderson	Doug Hall	Alan Bell
Hebron t (3)	MC 219 996-4641	Milton Schroader	. . . .	Marcella Mason	Marcella Mason	David Wilson	H Ray Lockhart	Michael Novac
Highland t (24)	MC 219 838-1080	Lance E Ryskamp	. . . .	Michael W Griffin	Michael W Griffin	William Timmer	Richard Rakoczy	John M Bach
Hobart (22)	MC 219 942-1940	Robert Malizzo	. . . .	Richard L Kobza	. . . .	Thomas Zytko	Russell Kraft	Wayne C Snider
Huntingburg (5)	MC 812 683-2211	Connie K Nass	Sara E Songer	Thomas Ellsworth	Thomas Ellsworth	Glen Kissling	George Lewallen	Connie K Nass
Huntington (16)	MC 219 356-1400	(not reporting)						
Indianapolis-Marion (731)	MC 317 327-5201	Stephen Goldsmith	Anne K Shane	Beverly Rippy	James Steele	Keith D Smith	James D Toler	Michael Stayton
Jasper (10)	MC 812 482-4255	William J Schmitt	. . . .	Iris A Gutgsell	Iris A Gutgsell	William Meyer	Richard Gunselman	. . . .
Jeffersonville (22)	MC 812 283-4451	(not reporting)						
Kendallville (8)	MC 219 347-0352	Jeff Smith	. . . .	Kimberly Forker	. . . .	Larry McGahen	William Forker	. . . .
Knox (4)	MC 219 772-3032	(not reporting)						
Kokomo (45)	MC 317 456-7470	Robert Sargent	Nanette Bowling	Brenda Ott	Lawrence Phillips	Joseph Zuppardo	Lynn Rudolph	Charles R Guge
La Porte (22)	MC 219 362-3175	Elmo Gonzalez	. . . .	. . . .	Constance Ebert	William Smith	Eugene Samuelson	. . . .
Lafayette (44)	MC 317 742-8404	(not reporting)						
Lake Station (14)	MC 219 962-2081	Dewey R Lemley	. . . .	Donna Smelley	. . . .	Robert Janes	Roger Szostek	Joseph Bernardi
Lawrence (27)	MC 317 549-4804	Thomas Schneider	. . . .	Annetta R Sweat	. . . .	Warren W White Jr	Robert A Jones Sr	Billy W Gann
Lawrenceburg (4)	MC 812 537-1676	(not reporting)						
Lebanon (12)	MC 317 482-1218	(not reporting)						
Ligonier (3)	MC 219 894-4113	Glenn Longardner	. . . .	Helen J Gerke	. . . .	Daryl Daniels	John Durham	. . . .
Linton (6)	MC 812 847-4971	(not reporting)						
Logansport (17)	MC 219 753-2551	William A Vernon	Francis J Perrone	Mary Lynn Barnard	Mary Lynn Barnard	Joseph B Casalini	Jerry J Arnold	Donald A Crain
Loogootee (3)	MC 812 295-4770	(not reporting)						
Lowell t (6)	CM 219 696-7794	John Gray	George Gray	Marcia Carlson	. . . .	Dwight Rench	Thomas Felder	. . . .
Madison (12)	MC 812 265-8300	(not reporting)						
Marion (33)	MC 317 668-4462	Ronald Mowery	Saundra Green	Kathleen Kiley	Evelyn Stephenson	Richard Schoolman	David Homer	Owen Gilbert Jr
Martinsville (12)	MC 317 342-6012	Phil R Deckard	Merle McKinney	Kathy D Weddle	. . . .	Roger Laymon	Shannon Buskirk	Merle McKinney
Merrillville (27)	MC 219 769-5711	Roger Chiabai	Thomas Keilman	John E Petalas	John E Petalas	David Dzunda	Daniel Demmon	Daniel Orlich
Michigan City (34)	MC 219 873-1401	Robert Behler	. . . .	Tom Fedder	Charles Oberlie	Mike Marciniak	Larry Kunkel	. . . .
Middletown t (2)	CM 317 354-2268	Jerry Manis	. . . .	. . . .	. . . .	James McIlrath	. . . .	. . . .
Mishawaka (43)	MC 219 258-1622	Robert Beutter	. . . .	Deborah Block	Edwina Kintner	Ronald Watson	George Obren	Philip Miller
Mitchell (5)	MC 812 849-2151	(not reporting)						
Monticello (5)	MC 219 583-9889	(not reporting)						
Mooresville t (6)	RT 317 831-1608	Steven Ballard	. . . .	Ann A Whaley	Ann A Whaley	Darrell Brown	Georg Ditton	Joseph F Beikman
Mount Vernon (7)	MC 812 838-3317	Jackson L Higgins	. . . .	Laura C Bullard	Laura C Bullard	Cecil R Waters	Glenn R Boyster	Steven B Wild
Muncie (71)	MC 317 747-4846	David M Dominick	. . . .	Jack E Donati	Joseph W Chance	Gary L Lucas	Carl D Ent	. . . .
Munster t (20)	CM 219 836-8810	(not reporting)						
Nappanee (6)	MC 219 773-2112	(not reporting)						
New Albany (36)	MC 812 948-5333	(not reporting)						
New Castle (18)	MC 317 529-3502	(not reporting)						
New Chicago t (2)	MC 219 962-1157	(not reporting)						
New Haven (9)	MC 219 749-1911	Lynn H Shaw	. . . .	Caroline Knepp	Caroline R Knepp	George Mason	Geoffrey Robison	Dennis Partridge
New Whiteland t (4)	CM 317 535-9487	Edward J Suding	Maribeth Alspach	. . . .	Maribeth Alspach	Michael Craig	William J Withers	Richard L Abbott
Newburgh t (3)	MC 812 853-3578	Bob Seibert	Mae Mason	Shirley Grzegorek	Shirley Grzegorek	Larry Grimes	Dennis Patton	. . . .
Noblesville (18)	MC 317 773-4614	Mary Sue Rowland	Greg Smallwood	. . . .	Marilyn Conner	Ken Gillam	Tim Garner	. . . .
North Manchester t (6) ...	MC 219 982-6536	Donald Rinearson	James C Taylor	Nancy J Reed	. . . .	Don Kissinger	William McNeeley	John Mugford
North Vernon (5)	MC 812 346-3789	John G Hall	. . . .	. . . .	. . . .	Roger Taylor	Cecil Gerth	. . . .
Oakland City (3)	MC 812 749-3222	Gary L Bise	. . . .	Judy Cochrane	. . . .	Charles Cochren	Tom Rowe	Alfred Cooper
Paoli t (4)	MC 812 723-2739	(not reporting)						
Peru (13)	MC 317 472-2400	David Livengood	. . . .	Marylynn Black	. . . .	William Click	Dennis Hahn	Mark Pyeritz
Petersburg (2)	MC 812 354-8511	(not reporting)						
Plainfield t (10)	MC 317 839-2561	(not reporting)						
Plymouth (8)	MC 219 936-2124	(not reporting)						
Portage (29)	MC 219 762-7784	Sammie L Maletta	. . . .	Felix C Kimbrough	. . . .	Daniel R Thorn	Warren E Lewis	Sammie L Maletta
Porter t (3)	CM 219 926-2771	Brian Dahlin	. . . .	. . . .	. . . .	Lewis Craig	Ed Surgener	. . . .
Portland (6)	MC 219 726-9395	. . . .	Maxine Lewis	Betty Miller	Betty Miller	Douglas Blankenba	Jeffry Harker	Maxine Lewis
Princeton (8)	MC 812 385-4428	(not reporting)						
Rensselaer (5)	MC 219 866-5213	Stephen A Wood	. . . .	. . . .	Susan M Smith	Steven Hoyes	William T Sammons	Stephen A Wood
Richmond (39)	MC 317 983-7200	Roger Cornett	. . . .	Norma Carnes	Dennis Grimes	James Sticco	Dennis Rice	Earnest Jarvis
Rochester (6)	MC 219 223-2510	Edward J Fansler	. . . .	Freda Miller	. . . .	James Cheesman	Richard Roe	Edward J Fansler
Rockville t (3)	MC 317 569-6253	. . . .	. . . .	Imogene Rahn	. . . .	John Malone	Howard D White	. . . .
Rushville (6)	MC 317 932-2672	(not reporting)						
Salem (6)	MC 812 883-4265	(not reporting)						
Schererville t (20)	CM 219 322-4581	John H Fladeland	Stephen Z Kil	. . . .	. . . .	Edward J Kaeser	Jesse W Cook	Kenneth Crocilla
Scottsburg (5)	MC 812 752-4343	William Graham	. . . .	Betty Hayes	. . . .	Raymond Jones	Delbert Meeks	William Graham
Sellersburg t (6)	MC 812 246-3821	(not reporting)						
Seymour (16)	MC 812 522-4020	John S Burkhart	. . . .	Fred M Lewis	. . . .	John D Terry	John J Reinhart	Jerry L Hartsell
Shelbyville (15)	MC 317 398-6624	Robert E Williams	. . . .	Frank Zerr	. . . .	Ken Scott	Kehrt Etherton	Jerry E Bennett
South Bend (106)	MC 219 235-9216	(not reporting)						
Speedway t (13)	MC 317 241-2566	(not reporting)						
Spencer t (3)	MC 812 829-3213	(not reporting)						
St. John t (5)	MC 219 365-8636	Douglas Patterson	. . . .	Judith Companik	Judith Companik	John Geary	Richard Kouder	Clarence Monix
Sullivan (5)	MC 812 268-6077	(not reporting)						
Syracuse t (3)	RT 219 457-3216	Keneth Johnson	Mathew Vigneault	Elgie A Tatman	Elgie A Tatman	Jerry Byrd	Robert Ziller	. . . .
Tell City (8)	MC 812 547-2349	Bill Goffinet	. . . .	Barbara Ewing	. . . .	James Mansfield	Robert Hackel	. . . .
Terre Haute (57)	MC 812 232-9467	P Pete Chalos	. . . .	Charles P Hanley	Tharon S Geckeler	Paul Mason	Raymond Watts	Tharon S Geckeler
Tipton (5)	MC 317 675-7561	David Berkemeier	. . . .	Beth Roach	. . . .	Mark Herron	Robert Sullivan	. . . .
Trail Creek t (2)	MC 219 872-2422	(not reporting)						
Union City (4)	MC 317 964-6534	Perry E Miller	. . . .	Patricia C Hunt	. . . .	Williams Mangas	Monte Poling	. . . .
Upland t (3)	MC 317 998-7439	(not reporting)						
Valparaiso (24)	MC 219 462-1161	(not reporting)						
Vincennes (20)	MC 812 882-7285	(not reporting)						
Wabash (12)	MC 219 563-4171	(not reporting)						
Warsaw (11)	MC 219 267-8894	Jeffrey W Plank	. . . .	Elaine Call	. . . .	Ken Shepherd	Craig Allebach	Kim Leake
Washington (11)	MC 812 254-5575	Charles T Baumert	. . . .	Rita E Ducharme	. . . .	Larry J Turk	Ronald G Perkins	. . . .
West Lafayette (26)	MC 317 463-3571	Sonya L Margerum	Nicole McMillin	Peggy Owens	. . . .	Ronald Ford	Dennis Mitchell	. . . .
Westfield t (3)	MC 317 896-5577	(not reporting)						
Whiting (5)	MC 219 659-3100	Robert J Bercik	. . . .	Margaret Drewniak	. . . .	Mark Kobli	Dennis Weller	Walter Ruzich

Directory 1/9 continued — **MUNICIPAL OFFICIALS IN U.S. CITIES OVER 2,500**

City, 1990 population figures (000 omitted), form of government	Municipal phone number	Mayor	Appointed administrator	City clerk	Finance officer	Fire chief	Police chief	Public works director
INDIANA (159) continued								
Winchester (5)	MC 317 584-6845	Jack L Fowler	. . . .	Marilyn Pash	Marilyn Pash	Leon Leach	Don Hesser	Jack L Fowler
Winona Lake t (4)	CM 219 267-5783	(not reporting)						
Yorktown t (4)	CM 317 759-8521	Paul Cox	David C Stiffler	Kay Sidey	Kay Sidey	Tom Ulmer	Jeff Marlow	. . . .
Zionsville t (5)	MC 317 873-2469	(not reporting)						
IOWA (133)								
Adel (3)	CM 515 993-4525	James F Peters	James P Sanders	. . . .	Vickie Moorhead	Earl Stucker	Bill Hanson	Swede Belgarde
Albia (4)	MC 515 932-2129	Lawrence Bernard	. . . .	Carl Gragg	. . . .	Warren Woollums	Dan Brickner	. . . .
Algona (6)	MC 515 295-2411	Linda Becker	Thomas C Smith	Garlene Schmidt	. . . .	Donald Peterson	Kevin Bangert	Robert C Engstrom
Altoona (7)	MC 515 967-5136	(not reporting)						
Ames (47)	CM 515 239-5199	(not reporting)						
Anamosa (5)	MC 319 462-6055	(not reporting)						
Ankeny (18)	CM 515 965-6400	Ollie J Weigel	Carl M Metzer	Joann Goins	Joann Goins	Thomas Strait	Dennis L Ballard	Richard D Ash
Atlantic (7)	MC 712 243-4810	A Daniel Merrick	Dean Torreson	Debbie Wheatley	. . . .	Kendal Warne	Roger Muri	. . . .
Audubon (3)	MC 712 563-3269	(not reporting)						
Belle Plaine (3)	MC 319 444-2200	Thomas Hollopeter	. . . .	Kaye Buch	. . . .	Dennis Greenlee	Ronald Tippett	Richard Ehlen
Belmond (3)	CM 515 444-3386	(not reporting)						
Bettendorf (28)	MC 319 355-1865	Ann Hutchinson	Decker Ploehn	Decker Ploehn	Carol Barnes	Gerry Voelliger	Phil Redington	Jerry Springer
Bloomfield (3)	MC 515 664-2260	H Nardini Crall	. . . .	M McElderry	. . . .	Robert Hougland	Bernard Gutz	Alan D Johnson
Boone (12)	MC 515 432-4211	George F Maybee	Jeff Kooistra	Audrey Veldhuizen	Audrey Veldhuizen	Ed Knight	Steven Peasley	. . . .
Buffalo (1)	MC 319 381-2226	Betty O Walters	. . . .	Carol A Bernauer	Carol A Bernauer	Terry Adams	Gage D Adams	Ralph E Jewett
Burlington (27)	CM 319 753-8124	Nancy Neafie	M Jane Wood	K Salisbury	D Worden	W Ell	W Patton	. . . .
Camanche (4)	MC 319 259-8342	William G Bradley	. . . .	Carol A Balster	Carol A Balster	William F Rowe	Gerald R Edwards	Dave A Rickertsen
Carlisle t (3)	MC 515 989-3224	Dennis D Rhodes	. . . .	Ethel L Lee	. . . .	Paul Berry	Terry B Hardy	. . . .
Carroll (10)	MC 712 792-1000	(not reporting)						
Carter Lake (3)	MC 712 347-6320	Gerald Waltrip		Patricia Settles	. . . .	Brian Glathar	Robert Warner	James Kyler
Cedar Falls (34)	MC 319 273-8600	Jon T Crews	. . . .	Gary Hesse	Sara Narigon	Arthur Lupkes	Michael Reifsteck	. . . .
Cedar Rapids (109)	CO 319 398-5000	Larry Serbousek	. . . .	Ann Ollinger	Robert McMahan	Joseph Gorman	William Byrne	Wayne Murdock
Centerville (6)	MC 515 437-4339	(not reporting)						
Chariton (5)	CM 515 774-5991	Wm P Marner	Edward W Elam	Ruth A Ryun	. . . .	Steve Irving	Jay A Fisher	. . . .
Charles City (8)	MC 515 228-2631	(not reporting)						
Cherokee (6)	MC 712 225-5749	Lawrence Westphal	Gilbert Bremicker	Debra Taylor	. . . .	Jack Olson	Troy Valentine	. . . .
Clarinda (5)	CM 712 542-2136	Frank Snyder	Robert Bailey	Robert Bailey	Eleanor Moore	Roger Williams	Joseph Newton	. . . .
Clarion (3)	MC 515 532-2847	Bernie Case	Vicky J Fluhrer	Vicky J Fluhrer	Vicky J Fluhrer	Maurice Riley	Steven Hennigar	Jim Redemske
Clear Lake City (8)	MC 515 357-5267	Lois Kotz	Thomas A Lincoln	Thomas A Lincoln	. . . .	John A Simpson	Dan J Jackson	Joseph A Weigel
Clinton (29)	CM 319 242-2144	Elizabeth Snyder	George Langmack	Deborah Neels	Deborah Neels	Russell Luckritz	Gene Beinke	James Haag
Clive (7)	MC 515 223-6220	Robert Brownell	Daniel Olson	Marjorie Roberts	. . . .	Vance Riley	G Dean Dymond	Willard Wray
Coralville (10)	MC 319 351-1266	Michael Kattchee	Kelly Hayworth	Arlys Hannam	. . . .	Gary Kinsinger	Barry Bedford	. . . .
Council Bluffs (54)	CM 712 328-4601	(not reporting)						
Cresco (4)	MC 319 547-3101	Arletta Rose	. . . .	Sharon Smutzler	Sharon Smutzler	Vince Hornberger	Thomas Heath Sr	Gary Lienhard
Creston (8)	MC 515 782-2000	Terry L Donahue	. . . .	Mary Moore	Joseph G Parker	Melford Johnston	Robert Kessler	Tom Myers
Davenport (95)	CM 319 326-7711	Patrick J Gibbs	Cowles B Mallory	Jackie E Ragsdale	Kent R Kolwey	Thomas J Ryan	Donald S Lynn	Diana F Bruemmer
De Witt (5)	MC 319 659-3811	Leo Maynard	Cary Conger	Kay Goddard	. . . .	. . . .	Richard Peasley	Richard Mohr
Decorah (8)	MC 319 382-3651	(not reporting)						
Denison (7)	MC 712 263-3143	Ralph Borcherding	. . . .	Marcia Bretey	. . . .	. . . .	Rod Bradley	. . . .
Des Moines (193)	CM 515 283-4189	John Pat Dorrian	Cy Carney	D Boetel Baker	M Frederickson	. . . .	William Moulder	John Bellizzi
Dubuque (58)	MC 319 589-4110	(not reporting)						
Dyersville (4)	MC 319 875-7724	Robert H Kramer	Gary A Jasper	Susan L Steffen	. . . .	Robert Platz	Allen W Clouse	David J Vorwald
Eagle Grove (4)	CM 515 448-4343	Keith Riley	John Call	John Call	Susan Maier	Gary Lalor	Curt Green	Carl Halverson
Eldora (3)	MC 515 858-2393	A E Shepherd	Roger Tinklenberg	Joyce Lawler	. . . .	John McBride	Ken Collins	Tim Hoskins
Eldridge (3)	MC 319 285-4841	Brian M Roesler	John R Dowd	Jean A Schilling	. . . .	Roger Rigby	Martin Stolmeier	Roger Kirby
Emmetsburg (4)	MC 712 852-4030	Norlyn Stowell	Lee Frederick	Rosie Argabright	. . . .	Virgil Huberty	Eric Hanson	William Dickey
Estherville (7)	MC 712 362-7771	Lyle Hevern	Steven Woodley	Vaughn Brua	. . . .	David Knox	Paul Farber	. . . .
Evansdale (5)	MC 319 232-6683	John W Mardis	. . . .	Carol J Wilson	Carol J Wilson	Peter N Weber	Richard G Lamb	. . . .
Fairfield (10)	MC 515 472-6193	R Rasmussen	J Brown	J Hannam	. . . .	J Cavenee	R Cooksey	. . . .
Forest City (4)	MC 515 582-4597	Paul L Jefson	Paul D Boock	Paul D Boock	. . . .	Douglas Yeager	Douglas Book	. . . .
Fort Dodge (26)	MC 515 576-4551	(not reporting)						
Fort Madison (12)	MC 319 372-7700	Arlene Carlson	John Pick	Judy Clark	. . . .	Steve Etka	Jerry Koerber	. . . .
Garner (3)	MC 515 923-2588	Gus T Erickson	Gerald A Edgar	Carolyn K Martin	Carolyn K Martin	James Jass	David L Martin	. . . .
Glenwood (5)	MC 712 527-4717	(not reporting)						
Graettinger (1)	MC 712 859-3742	Merle Jensen	Brad Bottenfield	Brad Bottenfield	Brad Bottenfield	Mike Flaherty	Ted Helmich	Brad Bottenfield
Grinnell (9)	CM 515 236-2605	Robert E Anderson	Theodore Clausen	Pamela Rupe	. . . .	Jerry Barnes	Darrel Lamb	. . . .
Grundy Center (2)	MC 319 824-6118	Troy Anderson	. . . .	Kenneth Havel	Kenneth Havel	Gerald Hoffman	Bruce Stotser	James Copeman
Guttenberg (2)	CM 319 252-1161	(not reporting)						
Hampton (4)	MC 515 456-4853	W Roger Palmer	Bruce R Slagle	Bruce R Slagle	. . . .	Ronald Weldin	Seldon F Nelson	Montey G Halls
Harlan (5)	MC 712 755-5137	(not reporting)						
Hawarden (2)	MC 712 552-2565	(not reporting)						
Hiawatha (5)	MC 319 393-1515	George H Bowler	. . . .	Roberta A Hamdorf	Roberta A Hamdorf	Mark Powers	David Saari	. . . .
Humboldt (4)	MC 515 332-3435	Jean M Kieve	. . . .	Phyllis Ulk	. . . .	Sherman Silbaugh	Jon Reed	. . . .
Ida Grove (2)	MC 712 364-2428	Ivan A O'Tool	. . . .	Diane F Alborn	. . . .	Mike Collins	. . . .	. . . .
Independence (6)	MC 319 334-2780	Donna K Hansen	N Clark Madison	N Clark Madison	. . . .	Charles M Conklin	Randy Miller	N Clark Madison
Indianola (11)	CM 515 961-9410	George Hladky	Tim Zisoff	Mark Ramthun	. . . .	Dean Hutt	Paul Scranton	Colin Whitley
Iowa City (60)	CM 319 356-5000	. . . .	Stephen J Atkins	Marian Karr	Donald Yucuis	James Pumfrey	Ralph Winkelhake	Charles Schmadeke
Iowa Falls (5)	CM 515 648-2527	(not reporting)						
Jefferson (4)	CM 515 386-3111	Charles F Davis	Tim Moerman	. . . .	Diane M Kennedy	Bill Ecklund	Dan Taylor	. . . .
Johnston (5)	MC 515 278-2344	John R Ver Hoef	R E Hays	Donna K Caylor	Margaret Sharp	Jerry Smeltzer	Bruce K Gaddis	Jerry R Meyers
Keokuk (12)	MC 319 524-2050	Ronald O Bramhall	. . . .	Jack A Finerty	Jack A Finerty	Donald Jenkins	Francis Marlin	William Richards
Knoxville (8)	MC 515 895-0120	Mike Cunningham	Richard Franc	Connie Harsin	Keith Moody	. . . .	Charles Wooldride	. . . .
Lamoni (2)	MC 515 784-6311	Orville Hiles	. . . .	Kirk Bjorland	. . . .	Richard Jackel	M McConnell	. . . .
Le Claire (3)	CM 319 289-5441	(not reporting)						
Le Mars (8)	MC 712 546-7018	Bonnie Dull	David R Schornack	Beverly Langel	. . . .	Wayne Schipper	Casey Stengel	Charlie Eufers
Manchester (5)	MC 319 927-3636	(not reporting)						
Maquoketa (6)	MC 319 652-2485	James Hohnecker	W Azul LaLuz	Vicki Starr	. . . .	Harold Lubben	Mark Brooks	Randy Crouch
Marion (20)	CM 319 377-1581	V L Klopfenstein	Jeff Schott	Wesley A Nelson	Wesley A Nelson	James L Ford	J Mark Diamond	Ervin G Mussman
Marshalltown (25)	CM 515 754-5700	T R Thompson Jr	. . . .	Mary J Skartvedt	. . . .	. . . .	James Wilkinson	Wayne Hartwig
Mason City (29)	MC 515 421-3601	William Schickel	. . . .	A Carlene Davis	Charles B Hammen	Ronald Van Horn	Eugene Kleinow	Victor Potter
Missouri Valley (3)	MC 712 642-3502	Ronald B Reiff	Robert J Alborn	. . . .	. . . .	Kenneth Athay	Austin O'Brien	. . . .
Monticello (4)	MC 319 465-3577	Bernie B Barker	Mark Anderson	Mary Hunt	Mary Hunt	Clarence Goedken	Burton Walters	. . . .
Mount Pleasant (8)	MC 319 385-1470	Stanley E Hill	Scott H Neal	Florence L Olomon	. . . .	Stewart Kinney	Micheal Goldberg	Steve Hoyer
Mount Vernon (4)	MC 319 895-8742	Rick Elliott	Michael R Beimer	Michael R Beimer	Michael R Beimer	Donnie Feaker	Mick Michel	. . . .
Muscatine (23)	CM 319 264-1550	. . . .	A J Johnson	. . . .	David Casstevens	Steve Dalbey	Gary Coderoni	Randy Hill
Nevada (6)	MC 515 382-5466	James Christy	Dennis Henderson	Susan North	Susan North	Steve Herr	Mark See	Harold Mitchell
New Hampton (4)	MC 515 394-5906	A Donald Johnson	. . . .	Shirley E Engel	. . . .	Peter Willadsen	Michael Anderson	Donald J Markle

MUNICIPAL OFFICIALS IN U.S. CITIES OVER 2,500

City, 1990 population figures (000 omitted), form of government	Municipal phone number	Mayor	Appointed administrator	City clerk	Finance officer	Fire chief	Police chief	Public works director
IOWA (133) continued								
Newton (15)	CM 515 792-2787	Alvin E Borchers	Paul Wenbert	Margaret Durbala	Barbara Majerus	Guy Ealey	Michael Quinn	Kenneth Clausen
Nora Springs (2)	CM 515 749-5315	(not reporting)						
Norwalk (6)	MC 515 981-0228	N N Standridge	Mark W Miller	Joyce A Cortum	. . . .	Frank Curtis	M Richardson	Dean C Yordi
Oelwein (6)	CM 319 283-5440	Gene M Vine	Steven H Kendall	Steven H Kendall	. . . .	Wallace Rundle	John Shirkey	. . . .
Onawa (3)	MC 712 423-1181	Dwight Lamb	. . . .	Chris Rustin	. . . .	Jeff Sander	Tom Vaughn	. . . .
Orange City (5)	CM 712 737-4885	Robert M Dunlop	Don Schreur	Don Schreur	Duane Feekes	Ron Koele	Gordon Abels	. . . .
Osage (3)	MC 515 732-3709	Steve Cooper	. . . .	Cathy Penney	. . . .	Robert Frein	Richard Mobley	William Bollinger
Osceola (4)	CM 515 342-2377	(not reporting)						
Oskaloosa (11)	MC 515 673-9431	Harold Kelderman	Donald L Sandor	Marilyn Miller	Marilyn Miller	David Miller	John McGee	. . . .
Ottumwa (24)	MC 515 683-0625	Carl Radovich	Robert Keefe	Ann Cullinan	Michael Heffernan	Dan Thompson	Art Letourneau	Christy Collicott
Pella (9)	MC 515 628-4173	Johnny A Menninga	Douglas A Clark	Beverly J Graves	C Douglas Saubert	George Carson	Gene Vos	Ron Knoke
Perry (7)	MC 515 465-2481	. . . .		Michael Williams		. . . .		
Pleasant Hill (4)	MC 515 262-9368	Phil Hildebrand	Shona Ringgenberg	Shona Ringgenberg	. . . .	Bob Bell	Tom Wilson	Allen Schoemaker
Pocahontas (2)	MC 712 335-4841	Lowell Pedersen	Brian James	Ila Mae Kraus	. . . .	Harry Stoulil	Byron Essing	. . . .
Red Oak (6)	MC 712 623-2507	James A Johnson	Ronald A Crisp	. . . .	. . . .	Rick Askey	Dennis Steffensen	. . . .
Rock Rapids (3)	MC 712 472-2511	C J Gustafson	Judy A Weins	. . . .	. . . .	Gary Hunt	James P Kille	. . . .
Rock Valley (3)	CM 712 476-5707	Kent Eknes	Bill Van Maanen	Bill Van Maanen	. . . .	Jerry Schlodtfeld	Jim Van Berkum	. . . .
Sac City (2)	CM 712 662-7593	E Lynn Minnmann	Gary C Mahannah	. . . .	. . . .	Jack Phillips	John Zimmerman	. . . .
Sanborn (1)	MC 712 729-3842	(not reporting)						
Sheldon (5)	CM 712 324-4651	M Uittenbogaard	Gerald Clausen	Sherlene Krogman	Sherlene Krogman	. . . .	Larry Locke	Eldor Schuerman
Shenandoah (6)	CM 712 246-4411	(not reporting)						
Sibley (3)	MC 712 754-2541	Bert Wille	Scott Pick	Dianne Gruis	. . . .	LeRoy Stevenson	. . . .	. . . .
Sioux Center (5)	MC 712 722-0761	W Dale Den Herder	Brian Gramentz	Brian Gramentz	Eldon Westra	Robert Hamilton	Gary Maas	John Arnold
Sioux City (81)	CM 712 279-6102	James Wharton	Henry Sinda	Shirley Brown	John Meyers	Doug Duncan	Donald R Wolford	Charles L Fisher
Spencer (11)	MC 712 264-7200	Earl D Chapman	Dan L Payne	Donna M Fisher	. . . .	Doug Duncan	Donald R Wolford	Charles L Fisher
Spirit Lake (4)	MC 712 336-1871	(not reporting)						
Storm Lake (9)	MC 712 732-8000	Wilbur L Tucker	Clarence Krepps	Patti Moore	Brian Schaeffer	Ronald C Wilson	Mark A Prosser	Patrick J Kelly
Story City (3)	MC 515 733-2121	Harold A Holm	. . . .	Pat Twedt	. . . .	Jim Beck	Brian Haffner	Jim Skare
Tama (3)	MC 515 484-3822	William Lazar	. . . .	Judy Welch	. . . .	Gary Zigler	Rod McCool	Richard Ervin
Tipton (3)	MC 319 886-6187	(not reporting)						
Urbandale (24)	CM 515 278-3900	E J Giovannetti	Robert Layton	Debra Mains	Sandi Tompkins	Gary Kueter	David Hamlin	David McKay
Vinton (3)	MC 319 472-4707	John Watson	Don Martin	Barbara Smith	Barbara Smith	Bob Downs	Jeff Tilson	. . . .
Washington (7)	MC 319 653-6584	(not reporting)						
Waterloo (66)	MC 319 291-4311	Albert Manning	. . . .	. . . .	. . . .	Stanley Stapella	Bernal Koehrsen	John Meyer
Waukon (4)	MC 319 568-3491	Ralph Grotegut	. . . .	Diane Sweeney	Diane Sweeney	Robert Campbell	Loren Fiet	Francis Kessel
Waverly (9)	MC 319 352-4252	Keith Schuldt	. . . .	Richard Crayne	. . . .	David Nelson	Art Simpson	Tom Goff
Webster City (8)	CM 515 832-5701	Lucien A Wood	John S Rudd	Gerald K Kent	Gerald K Kent	Terry Johnston	Michael Petricca	Greg Malmstrom
West Bend (..)	MC 515 887-2181	Eddie Zinn	Mary J Steil	Laura Montag	. . . .	Mark Laubendhal	Bill Rasmussen	Joe Mikes
West Burlington (3)	MC 319 752-5451	Richard H Logan	David S Plyman	Terrie Simonson	. . . .	Ken Beenblossom	George Rinker	Daniel Shipley
West Des Moines (32)	CM 515 223-3241	Dino Rodish	Arthur E Pizzano	Jody E Smith	Jody E Smith	Randall Bracken	Frederick Carson	Ralph E Speer Jr
West Liberty (3)	CM 319 627-2418	John H Nath	Edward R Stiff	Janet Fulwider	Mary Dreibelbeis	Ken Morrison	Roy Warson	M Joe Stiff
West Point (1)	MC 319 837-6313	(not reporting)						
West Union (2)	MC 319 422-3320	(not reporting)						
Wilton (3)	MC 319 732-2115	(not reporting)						
Windsor Heights (5)	MC 515 279-3662	Donald C Steele	James H Spradling	James H Spradling	. . . .	Albert Hunter	William Hitchcock	John Wiedman
Winterset (4)	MC 515 462-1422	Robert W Howell	Mark Nitchals	. . . .	. . . .	R Truckenbrod	Clyde Klave	. . . .
KANSAS (111)								
Abilene (6)	CM 913 263-2550	Lynda D Scheele	John A Hier	Mildred E Hanson	. . . .	. . . .	James W Davis	Clifford L Gibbs
Andover (4)	MC 316 733-1303	Jack A Finlason	Patricia Stuenkel	Teresa M Sexson	. . . .	. . . .	Thomas Lee Mathes	Leslie E Mangus
Anthony (3)	CO 316 842-5434	Christy L LaRue	Donald F Heidrick	Donald F Heidrick	Donald F Heidrick	Larry Ryan	John H Blevins	Priscilla Goucher
Arkansas City (13)	CM 316 442-0280	Benjamin Givens	Curtis Freeland	Rodney Franz	. . . .	Bill Rowe	William Rice	Ron Parker
Atchison (11)	CM 913 367-5081	(not reporting)						
Augusta (8)	CM 316 775-7671	J David Crum	Warren Porter	Elsie George	Elsie George	David Pate	David Pate	. . . .
Baxter Springs (4)	MC 316 856-2114	Terry L Martin	. . . .	Darla Snook	. . . .	Les Page	Gary Allen	. . . .
Belleville (3)	CM 913 527-2288	Doris Beardsley	Aaron McKee	C Derowitsch	. . . .	Don Slaughter	Ray Smee	Don Danielson
Beloit (4)	MC 913 738-3551	Edward Specht	Eugene S Miles	Charlene Abell	Eugene Miles	Ross Donker	Dave Sutter	Terry Amerine
Bonner Springs (6)	MC 913 422-1020	(not reporting)						
Burlington (3)	MC 316 364-5334	Gene L Merry	. . . .	Daniel K Allen	. . . .	. . . .	Steve E Timmons	. . . .
Chanute (9)	CM 316 431-5200	Leroy Chard	Robert H Walker	James Youngberg	. . . .	Vernon Shultz	Vernon Shultz	Carl Ware
Cheney (2)	MC 316 542-3622	(not reporting)						
Cherryvale (2)	CM 316 336-2776	(not reporting)						
Clay Center (5)	MC 913 632-5454	(not reporting)						
Clearwater (2)	MC 316 584-2311	David T Crews	Yvonne Coon	Debra Shepard	. . . .	Marvin Schauf	Michael Friday	. . . .
Coffeyville (13)	CM 316 252-6100	Perl Schmid	. . . .	Stacey Johnston	Joyce Buckner	J D Spohn	Allen Flowers	Butch Hyatt
Colby (5)	CM 913 462-3973	R V Van Camp	Carolyn Armstrong	Donna Greenlee	Donna Greenlee	Ivan Lee	Randall Jones	Michael Albers
Columbus (3)	MC 316 429-2159	(not reporting)						
Concordia (6)	CM 913 243-2670	Lavern C Robbins	Richard Nienstedt	Verna Ferguson	. . . .	Jack P Graves	Howard S Budreau	Tom Fisher
Council Grove (..)	CM 316 767-5417	(not reporting)						
Derby (15)	CM 316 788-3132	K O Lavergne	Phillip Nelson	Patty Kroll	. . . .	Patrick Swaney	Delbert Fowler	Patrick Cillessen
Dodge City (24)	CM 316 225-8100	Jerry Wilson	Jim Witt	Nannette Lampe	Nannette Lampe	Pat Simpson	Oakley Ralph	Harold Leedom
Edwardsville (4)	MC 913 441-3707	John McTaggart	Edward Dawson	Tammy Stinnett	. . . .	Rox Reed	Larry Boddy	. . . .
El Dorado (12)	CM 316 321-9100	Edward L Blake	Stan B Stewart	Adam R Collins	. . . .	. . . .	Victor Marshall	Oral Taylor
Ellinwood (2)	MC 316 564-3161	Joe Hickel	. . . .	Chris Wornkey	. . . .	Art Huslig	Kevin Pekarek	. . . .
Emporia (26)	CM 316 342-5105	Raymond A Toso	Steven A Commons	Susan A Mendoza	Larry Bucklinger	James Woydziak	Robert Rodriguez	. . . .
Eudora (3)	MC 913 542-2153	James V Hoover	. . . .	Joann Becker	. . . .	Benny Dean	William Long	Gary Malburg
Eureka (3)	CO 316 583-6511	James H Francis	. . . .	Linda Martell	Charles Schneider	Allen D Hall	. . . .	Larry Fritts
Fairway (4)	MC 913 262-0350	(not reporting)						
Fort Scott (8)	CM 316 223-0550	Daryl L Roller	Richard Nienstedt	Kristy J Bolden	Nancy Calkins	Robert L Lowe	Glenn McReynolds	Dennis Kennon
Fredonia (3)	CO 316 378-2231	(not reporting)						
Frontenac (3)	MC 316 231-9210	(not reporting)						
Galena (3)	MC 316 783-5265	(not reporting)						
Garden City (24)	CM 316 276-1175	Michael Scheopner	Robert M Halloran	Jean Solze	Melinda Hitz	Allen Shelton	Roger Schroeder	. . . .
Gardner (..)	MC 913 884-7535	(not reporting)						
Garnett (3)	CM 913 448-5496	Daniel Benjamin	Richard G Doran	Joyce E Martin	Joyce E Martin	Jerry Gettler	Jack Eden	William Garrison
Girard (3)	CO 316 724-8918	(not reporting)						
Goddard (2)	MC 316 794-2441	B J Means	. . . .	Nicki V Vanosdall	. . . .	. . . .	M J Nelson	Larry Padley
Goodland (5)	CM 913 899-2372	. . . .	Ron Thornburg	Mary Antholz	. . . .	Dean Jensen	Anthony Diplacito	Gary Newell
Great Bend (15)	CM 316 793-4111	George Drake	Howard Partington	Debbie Durler	Debbie Durler	Marion Root	Dean Akings	Doyle Webster
Hays (18)	CM 913 625-3465	Eber Phelps	Johann Zacharias	Carol Sue Grabbe	Carol Sue Grabbe	Wayne Schwartz	Lawrence Younger	Leo J Wellbrock
Haysville (8)	MC 316 524-3243	Tom Lindsay	. . . .	Carol McBeath	Beverly Rodgers	. . . .	J E Kitchings	John Eaglin
Herington (3)	CM 913 258-2271	(not reporting)						
Hesston (3)	MC 316 327-4412	John Waltner	John T Wieland	Jean Krehbiel	. . . .	Lyle Bitikofer	Mickey DeHook	. . . .

Directory 1/9 continued

MUNICIPAL OFFICIALS IN U.S. CITIES OVER 2,500

City, 1990 population figures (000 omitted), form of government	Municipal phone number	Mayor	Appointed administrator	City clerk	Finance officer	Fire chief	Police chief	Public works director
KANSAS (111) continued								
Hiawatha (4)	MC 913 742-7417	James Scherer	Gary Weiland	Laurie Neemann	. . . .	Gary Shear	Jim Wolney	. . . .
Hillsboro (3)	MC 316 947-3162	(not reporting)						
Hoisington (3)	CM 316 653-4125	George Rice	Carl Myers	Mary Joan Ray	. . . .	James Sekavec	Daniel L Simpson	Dean A Scott
Holton (3)	MC 913 364-2721	. . . .	Bradley J Mears	Pat McClintock	. . . .	. . . .	Gale Gakle	. . . .
Horton (2)	CM 913 486-2681	Edwin Buser	Ted Hauser	Sheila Gibson	. . . .	Ken Krug	Lamar Shoemaker	. . . .
Hugoton (3)	MC 316 544-8531	Tom L Greenway	Thomas G Hicks	Thomas G Hicks	Thomas G Hicks	. . . .	Donald L Brown	Jerry Leonard
Hutchinson (39)	CM 316 694-2642	Frances Garcia	Joe Palacioz	Vernon Stallman	James Onello	Dallas Jones	James Heitschmidt	Dennis Clennan
Independence (10)	CM 316 331-2500	Mike Seller	Paul A Sasse	Anthony D Royse	. . . .	Dale Rail	Lee A Bynum	Marvin Garner
Iola (6)	CO 316 365-2771	Ray Pershall	Larry Eaton	Carolyn E Dreher	. . . .	Clarence Hydorn	Jay Thyer	. . . .
Junction City (21)	CM 913 238-3103	Robert E Ritter	Blaine R Hinds	. . . .	Rodney D Barnes	Larry E Bruzda	Thomas L Clark	Michael J Fraser
Kansas City (150)	CM 913 573-5000	Joseph Steineger	David Isabell	Tom Roberts	Nancy Zielke	John Bergman	Tom Dailey	Gary Stubbs
Kingman (3)	MC 316 532-3111	Max Mize	. . . .	Cindy A Conrardy	Cindy A Conrardy	Donald G Fischer	Paul S Kalmar	Franklin D Smith
Kinsley (2)	MC 316 659-3611	L L Lancaster	Janet Freel	Marsh Haxton	. . . .	Buford Brodbeck	Doug Murphy	Newt Baker
La Crosse (1)	CM 913 222-2511	James Meder	Robert N Barnhart	Sherri Stevens	. . . .	Armen Ideker	Leroy Penka	. . . .
Lansing (7)	MC 913 727-3233	(not reporting)						
Larned (4)	CM 316 285-2149	Jerry Larson	Donald Gaeddert	Vicki D Gillett	Donald Gaeddert	Ralph Johnson	John Slack	. . . .
Lawrence (66)	CM 913 832-3000	John Nalbandian	H Michael Wildgen	Raymond J Hummert	A Ed Mullins	James McSwain	Wm Ronald Olin	George Williams
Leavenworth (38)	CM 913 682-9201	James K Murphy	W Mark Pentz	Carol S Sadler	Daniel Williamson	James E Meyers	Lemoine Doehring	Michael McDonald
Leawood (20)	MC 913 642-5555	Marcia K Rinehart	Richard Garofano	Martha Heizer	Harry B Malnicof	Jerry Strack	J Stephen Cox	Ronald A Brandt
Lenexa (34)	MC 913 492-8800	(not reporting)						
Liberal (17)	CM 316 626-0101	Larry Koochel	Richard Olson	Debra Giskie	Stanley Wilbers	Jack Taylor	Dariel Hinsdale	. . . .
Lindsborg (3)	MC 913 227-3355	(not reporting)						
Lyons (4)	MC 316 257-3159	Charles E Nichols	Dewey D Breese	Norma A Miller	Norma A Miller	James E Miller	Dennis Luck	David Kendrick
Madison (1)	CO 437-2556	(not reporting)					Rex W Taylor	Richard Pettegrew
Maize (2)	MC 316 722-7561	Stephen Hutchens	Nancy A Scott	Karen S Bailey	. . . .	. . . .	. . . .	Bruce K McCallum
Manhattan (38)	CM 913 537-0056	Roger Maughmer	James R Pearson	Martha P Scott	Curt Wood	Larry D Reese	Bryan Davidson	. . . .
Marysville (3)	MC 913 562-5331	James L Lindeen	Gerald Cooper	Paula Holle	. . . .	Charles Lindeen	. . . .	. . . .
McCracken (..)	MC 913 394-2229	Philena Baus	. . . .	Michelle Moran	Margaret Higgins	Dale Elias	. . . .	. . . .
McPherson (12)	CO 316 241-6300	Vernon L Dossett	. . . .	William J Goering	. . . .	Jack L Hamilton	Waldean F Vincent	Melvin Ferguson
Merriam (12)	MC 913 722-3330	Irene French	Eric Wade	Connie Schmidt	Michael Scanlon	Jerry Montgomery	Kenneth Sissom	Randall Carroll
Mission (10)	MC 913 722-3685	Sylvester Powell	. . . .	Sue A Grosdidier	Sue A Grosdidier	. . . .	Robert Sturm	Stephen L Weeks
Mission Hills (3)	MC 913 362-9620	Betty T Keim	Douglas O Cruce	Dianne R Starcke	. . . .	. . . .	. . . .	. . . .
Mulvane (5)	MC 316 777-1143	(not reporting)						
Neodesha (3)	CM 316 325-2828	Oris Killebrew	Jim McEwen	Jo Vonnah Boecker	. . . .	Charlie Reynolds	Jim Shue	Glen Fuller
Newton (17)	CM 316 284-6000	Bradley D Jantz	Philip A Kloster	Sharon K Petersen	James M Heinicke	James Jackson	Ronald G Jackson	Lon W Walker
Norton (3)	MC 913 877-3355	James L Miller	Allen Loyd	Darla R Ellis	. . . .	Mitch Jones	Lynn Menagh	. . . .
Olathe (63)	CM 913 782-2600	J Michael Haskins	Michael McCurdy	Howard Pevehouse	George Long	Patrick J Couglin	Philip J Major	William A Ramsey
Osage City (3)	MC 913 528-4325	Richard W Prine	. . . .	Nina D Gragg	. . . .	Lawrence Buenger	Douglas Mathey	. . . .
Osawatomie (5)	CM 913 755-2146	Charles R Heckart	Larry L Buchanan	Ann Elmquist	. . . .	James R Maxwell	John D Cragg	Howard O Goodeyon
Oswego (..)	MC 316 795-4433	Philip B Blair	Kris McKechnie	Cheri R Blair	. . . .	M T Bringle	George Elliott	Jeff Strickland
Ottawa (11)	CM 913 242-2190	Richard Jackson	David Warren	Scott Bird	Charles Nichols	Richard Towe	Jeffrey Herrman	Donald Haney
Overland Park (112)	CM 913 381-5252	. . . .	Donald E Pipes	Norma Moffet	Kristy Cannon	. . . .	Myron Scafe	Dennis Garrett
Paola (5)	CM 913 294-2397	Floyd J Grimes	Scott A Botcher	Jill A Holmes	. . . .	Robert T Harris	David E Small	Joseph L Whitaker
Park City (5)	MC 316 744-2026	Jerry L Bressler	Greg A Miles	Carol A Jones	Carol A Jones	. . . .	Ace Van Wey	Ron Crumbliss
Parsons (12)	CM 316 421-7000	Marvin McKnight	James Richardson	Mary Reed	Mary Reed	Gordon Fry	Gary Baldwin	. . . .
Phillipsburg (3)	MC 913 543-5234	Rosalyn Dance	Valerie Lemmie	Benjamin Scott	T Rob Blount	James Patterson	Willie Williams	M Guthrie Smith
Pittsburg (18)	CM 316 231-4100	Edward J Roitz	Larry J Stevens	Karen K Garman	Jon B Garrison	William J Scott	Ralph W Shanks	John D Van Gorden
Prairie Village (23)	MC 913 381-6464	Monroe Taliaferro	Barbara Vernon	. . . .	. . . .	. . . .	Charles Grover	Jerald Robnett
Pratt (7)	CO 316 672-5571	Kurt Heaton	George Anderson	Betsy Koontz	Betsy Koontz	Berkley Miller	Kevin Cavanaugh	Larry Koontz
Roeland Park (8)	MC 913 722-2600	Joan Wendel	Anthony J Pluta	. . . .	. . . .	. . . .	Kenneth Carpenter	Patrick R Mundis
Russell (5)	CM 913 483-6311	(not reporting)						
Sabetha (2)	CO 913 284-2158	(not reporting)						
Salina (42)	CM 913 826-7400	Peter F Brungardt	Dennis Kissinger	Jackie Shiever	Robert K Biles	Thomas C Girard	James D Hill	Frank Weinhold
Scott City (4)	MC 316 872-5322	Carl Kasten	. . . .	Delores Suppes	. . . .	Kenneth Hoover	Alan Stewart	Preston Stewart
Shawnee (38)	CM 913 631-2600	Jim Allen	Gary K Montague	Nancy Hodges	H Lee Meyer	H A Hartley	Tom Hayselden	Ron Freyermuth
St. Marys (2)	CM 913 437-2311	James L Mees	Ross Vander Hamm	Pam Simecka	Sue Martell	Jim Keating	Gary Zinn	Jerry Eichem
Sterling (2)	CM 316 278-3411	. . . .	Randall K Riggs	Sandra Fankhauser	Sandra Fankhauser	. . . .	Ron Groth	Jon Steele
Stockton (2)	CO 913 425-6703	Rusty Hrabe	Myron Chapel	Leta Bouchey	. . . .	Richard Haines	David Ice	Bill Schmitz
Topeka (120)	MC 913 295-3741	(not reporting)						
Ulysses (5)	MC 316 356-4600	Sy Hileman	Gary Burr	Paula Shapland	. . . .	. . . .	Lonnie Lee	Wayne Russett
Valley Center (4)	MC 316 755-7310	Robert Robinson	Robert Finkbiner	Carol Reffner	. . . .	M R Tormey	Kelly Parks	Richard Dunn
Wamego (4)	CM 913 456-9119	(not reporting)						
Wellington (8)	MC 316 326-3631	. . . .	Arthur B Preston	Sandra McCreary	Sandra McCreary	John M Lloyd	Steve L Brown	Rodney Conwell
Westwood (2)	MC 913 362-1550	(not reporting)						
Wichita (304)	CM 316 268-4351	Elma Broadfoot	Chris Cherches	. . . .	Ray Trail	Larry Garcia	Rick Stone	Steve Lackey
Winfield (12)	CM 316 221-3060	Phil Jarvis	Richard E Cotton	Don D Drennan	. . . .	George Gurley	Ron Gould	Russ Tomevi
KENTUCKY (112)								
Alexandria (6)	MC 606 635-4125	Ray Hildebrand	. . . .	Roger Steffen	. . . .	Herbert Steffen	Charles Stein	Robert Bartlett
Ashland (24)	CM 606 327-2000	A Rudy Dunnigan	William H Fisher	Deborah Musser	David D Johnson	Gary Watts	Ronald W McBride	Joseph Harris
Barbourville (4)	MC 606 546-6197	Phillip E Connley	James E Tye	Debbie Hammons	. . . .	James E Tye	Bob Combs	James E Baker
Bardstown (7)	MC 502 348-5947	(not reporting)						
Beaver Dam (3)	CO 502 274-7106	(not reporting)						
Bellevue (7)	MC 606 431-8866	Thomas J Wiethorn	Andrew W Riffe	Mary Scott	. . . .	Ralph Quitter	Rick Sears	Randy Grosch
Benton (4)	MC 502 527-8677	(not reporting)						
Berea (9)	MC 606 986-8528	(not reporting)						
Bowling Green (41)	CM 502 782-2489	Johnny L Webb	Charles W Coates	Linda T Leigh	Kirby L Ramsey	Vindell H Webster	Gary A Raymer	William B Hays
Campbellsville (10)	MC 502 465-7011	Robert L Miller	. . . .	Mary Ann Russell	. . . .	Jimmy Cox	David K Adams	. . . .
Carrollton (4)	MC 502 732-7060	(not reporting)						
Catlettsburg (2)	MC 606 739-5223	(not reporting)						
Central City (5)	CM 502 754-5097	(not reporting)						
Columbia (4)	MC 502 384-2501	Pamela Hoots	. . . .	Jane B Akin	. . . .	Charles V Sparks	Edwin N Taylor	. . . .
Corbin (7)	CM 606 528-0669	Tom Thurston	Dave Hudson	Erin Blount	. . . .	Eugene Rice	J C Mullins	Maurice Ramsey
Covington (43)	CM 606 292-2160	(not reporting)						
Crestview Hills (3)	MC 606 341-7373	Harold A Ries	Joan Weingartner	Lynne Moore	. . . .	Victor Dietz	Fred Anderson	Joan Weingartner
Cumberland (3)	MC 606 589-2106	(not reporting)						
Cynthiana (6)	CO 606 234-7150	Melvin E Hampton	. . . .	Janice F Tolle	. . . .	Greg Lemons	Joe R Barkley	Paul Purcell
Danville (12)	CM 606 238-1200	Bowling	Music	Woolum	Music	Harp	Lamb	Greer
Dawson Springs (3)	MC 502 797-2781	Raymond Thomason	. . . .	Denise Ridley	. . . .	Kenneth Jackson	Barry Boucher	Roger Rose
Dayton (7)	MC 606 491-1600	Bobby Crittendon	Lois Wessling	Helen Lenz	Lois Wessling	Dennis Lynn	Michael Hall	John Creekmore
Douglass Hills (6)	MC 502 245-3600	Warren Walker	. . . .	Faye Tanner	. . . .	. . . .	. . . .	Stan Goetz
Edgewood (8)	MC 606 331-5910	Robert Rademacher	Louis Noll	Nancy Givens	. . . .	. . . .	Charles Dickerson	. . . .
Elizabethtown (18)	MC 502 765-6121	Patricia V Durbin	Charles E Bryant	Wanda W Young	Stephen D Park	Richard A Games	Ruben Gardner	William A Owen

Directory 1/9 continued

MUNICIPAL OFFICIALS IN U.S. CITIES OVER 2,500

City, 1990 population figures (000 omitted), form of government	Municipal phone number	Mayor	Appointed administrator	City clerk	Finance officer	Fire chief	Police chief	Public works director
KENTUCKY (112) continued								
Elsmere (7)	MC 606 342-7911	Al Wermeling	. . . .	Nancy Bowman	Nancy Bowman	Paul Lafontaine	William Hiler	Charles Turner
Erlanger (16)	MC 606 727-2525	Marc T Otto Sr	William L Scheyer	Wilma R Labare	Mary E Egan	Bill Martin	Greg Sandel	David P Hahn
Flatwoods (8)	MC 606 836-9661	(not reporting)						
Flemingsburg (3)	MC 606 845-5951	(not reporting)						
Florence (19)	MC 606 371-5495	Evelyn Kalb	Roger Rolfes	Betsy R Conrad	Ronald Epling	Richard Albers	Charles Callen	Gregory Tindle
Fort Mitchell (7)	CM 606 331-1212	(not reporting)						
Fort Thomas (16)	MC 606 441-1055	Steven Pendery	Jeffrey Earlywine	Dorothy Ivie	Fred Ewald	William Dieckman	Charles Rogers	Thomas Morrison
Fort Wright (7)	MC 606 331-1700	Cindy J Pinto	Joseph E Nienaber	Jody Anderson	. . . .	Ronald Becker	John T Johnson	Timothy J Maloney
Frankfort (26)	CM 502 875-8500	(not reporting)						
Franklin (8)	MC 502 586-4497	Wm H Young Jr	Wm Scott Burklow	Wm Scott Burklow	Wm Scott Burklow	Bobby Turner	Joe Palma	Jerry Munday
Fulton (3)	CM 502 472-1320	(not reporting)						
Georgetown (11)	MC 502 863-9800	Tom Prather	Katherine Tackett	Glenwood Williams	Judy Hynes	Larry Adkins	Craig Birdwhistel	. . . .
Glasgow (12)	MC 502 651-5131	(not reporting)						
Grayson (3)	CO 606 474-6651	George Waggoner	. . . .	Martha Lemaster	. . . .	Norman Felty	Greg Wilburn	. . . .
Greenville (5)	MC 502 338-3966	(not reporting)						
Harlan (3)	MC 606 573-2912	(not reporting)						
Harrodsburg (7)	MC 606 734-2383	(not reporting)						
Hartford (3)	MC 502 298-3612	(not reporting)						
Hazard (5)	CM 606 436-3171	(not reporting)						
Henderson (26)	CM 502 831-1200	William L Newman	Russell R Sights	Joann Roberts	Sharon Phillips	Charles Trodglen	Mack E Brady	X R Royster
Hickman (3)	CM 502 236-2535	Judy Powell	Blake Proctor	Donna Haney	Blake Proctor	Bill Ramsey	Dean Parnel	Alvis Dehart
Highland Heights (4)	MC 606 441-8575	Herbert Kenter	. . . .	Jean A Rauf	. . . .	Brad Derrick	Edgar Hauger	Albert Harris
Hillview (6)	MC 502 957-5280	Richard Terry	Bienda Weber	Bienda Weber	. . . .	. . . .	James Perry	Charlie Owens
Hopkinsville (30)	MC 502 887-4000	W W Bryan Jr	T Mark Withers	T Mark Withers	Windel Wooton	Mike Maxwell	J D Lingenfelter	Rick Deason
Hurstbourne (4)	CO 502 426-7160	Thomas R Dean	J Schweinhart	J Schweinhart	Diana S Isaacs	. . . .	. . . .	W Goodknight
Independence (10)	MC 606 356-5302	James Ellison	. . . .	Linda Carter	. . . .	. . . .	Charles Donaldson	. . . .
Irvine (3)	MC 606 723-2554	W T Williams	. . . .	Rhonda Gould	. . . .	Anthony Murphy	Samuel Tipton	Kelly Morefield
Jackson (2)	MC 606 666-7069	(not reporting)						
Jeffersontown (23)	MC 502 267-8333	Daniel Ruckriegel	Frank Greenwell	Frank Greenwell	. . . .	. . . .	Fred E Roemele	Richard Dunn
Jenkins (3)	MC 606 832-2141	(not reporting)						
La Grange (4)	MC 502 222-1433	John W Black	. . . .	Zella C Smith	. . . .	Harold Whittaker	Jeffrey D Money	Kirby R Miller
Lakeside Park (3)	MC 606 341-6670	Wm Schutte	. . . .	Wanda Wahl	. . . .	. . . .	. . . .	. . . .
Lancaster (3)	MC 606 792-3023	(not reporting)						
Lawrenceburg (6)	MC 502 839-5372	(not reporting)						
Lebanon (6)	MC 502 692-6272	K Blandford	John O Thomas	Joyce A Ford	. . . .	Richard Mattingly	Jimmie D Gribbins	Marvin A Skaggs
Leitchfield (5)	MC 502 259-4034	Sherrill Watson	. . . .	Kerry White	. . . .	Ronald Hudson	Elmer Langdon	Darrell Harrell
Lexington-Fayette (225)	MC 606 258-3030	Pam Miller	. . . .	Liz Damrell	Donna Cantrell	Gary McComas	Larry Walsh	James Street
London (6)	MC 606 864-4169	(not reporting)						
Louisville (269)	MC 502 625-3601	Jerry E Abramson	W E Summers	. . . .	Robert Schwoeppe	Russell E Sanders	Edward D Hamilton	William E Herron
Ludlow (5)	MC 606 491-1233	Gerald Holloway	Brian Haney	Geneva Palmer	. . . .	Terry Keller	Thomas Collins	. . . .
Madisonville (16)	MC 502 824-2100	William M Cox	Lloyd Merrell	Gina Munger	Dahlene Dupree	Glendel Rice	Ronald Hunt	. . . .
Marion (3)	MC 502 965-2266	Mick Alexander	Paul M Story	Melinda Tinsley	. . . .	Red Houton	Kenneth Winn	Wayne James
Mayfield (10)	MC 502 247-1981	(not reporting)						
Maysville (7)	CM 606 564-9411	(not reporting)						
Middlesborough (11)	MC 606 248-5670	(not reporting)						
Monticello (5)	MC 606 348-8473	(not reporting)						
Morehead (8)	MC 606 784-8505	(not reporting)						
Morganfield (4)	MC 502 789-2525	(not reporting)						
Mount Sterling (5)	MC 606 498-8725	Bert May	Bert May	Doris W Baxter	. . . .	. . . .	Bruce Snowden	Robert Hiatt
Mount Washington (5)	MC 502 538-7346	Ralph Lutes	Robert Bush	Robert Bush	Robert Bush	Bobby Grigsby	Leo Oliver	William R Bell
Murray (14)	MC 502 762-0352	(not reporting)						
Newport (19)	CM 606 292-3682	Tom Guidugli	Jim Parsons	Frank Peluso	Phil Ciafardini	Larry Atwell	Tom Fromme	Peter Hesser
Nicholasville (14)	CO 606 885-9473	(not reporting)						
Olive Hill (2)	MC 606 286-5532	(not reporting)						
Owensboro (54)	CM 502 685-8200	David C Adkisson	G Ted Smith	Carol Blake	Ralph Rascoe	John Goins	Arthur Schwartz	. . . .
Paducah (27)	CM 502 444-8530	(not reporting)						
Paintsville (4)	MC 606 789-2600	John D Preston	Robert M Conley	Virgie Castle	Robert M Conley	Bob Dixon	Tom Haney	James Hopson
Paris (9)	CM 606 987-2110	Douglas F Castle	R L Brunner	Cheryl Marsh	. . . .	. . . .	George Boling	. . . .
Park Hills (3)	MC 606 431-6252	Melissa Worstell	. . . .	Evelyn Fogarty	. . . .	James Kaelin	Ronald Heideman	Dennis Finke
Pikeville (6)	CM 606 437-5100	(not reporting)						
Pineville (2)	MC 606 337-2958	(not reporting)						
Prestonsburg (4)	MC 606 886-2335	Ann Latta	Mark Wells	Sue Webb	. . . .	Thomas Blackburn	Gregory A Hall	Mike Meade
Princeton (7)	MC 502 365-9575	(not reporting)						
Providence (4)	MC 502 667-5463	(not reporting)						
Radcliff (20)	MC 502 351-4714	(not reporting)						
Richmond (21)	CM 606 623-1000	Ann L Durham	Ed Worley	Betty Houghton	H D Hurt	William F Lane	Charles Debord	Dave Graham
Russell (4)	MC 606 836-9666	(not reporting)						
Russellville (7)	MC 502 726-5007	Ken Smith	. . . .	Peggy Jenkins	. . . .	J L Williamson	C R Beard	Ernie M Cole
Scottsville (4)	MC 502 237-3238	(not reporting)						
Shelbyville (6)	MC 502 633-1835	Neil S Hackworth	. . . .	Bobbie J Brenner	. . . .	Mike Rodgers	John Miller	Al Minnis
Shepherdsville (5)	MC 502 543-2923	(not reporting)						
Shively (16)	MC 502 449-5000	(not reporting)						
Somerset (11)	MC 606 679-6366	Smith S Vanhook	Sheila C Parkey	David Godsey	. . . .	James Haney Jr	David Gilbert	Jim Fisher
Southgate (3)	MC 606 441-0075	Ronald Blanchet	. . . .	Rose Welscher	Donald Berkemeyer	John Beatsch	Charlie Hazel	Paul Krebs
Springfield (3)	MC 606 336-7739	(not reporting)						
St. Matthews (16)	MC 502 895-9444	(not reporting)						
Stanford (3)	MC 606 365-4500	Jack R Withrow	. . . .	Wanda R Withrow	. . . .	Leeroy Lunsford	Don Young	Dave Rollins
Stanton (3)	MC 606 663-2620	(not reporting)						
Taylor Mill (6)	MC 606 581-3234	Mark Kreimborg	Edwin R Meece	M L Kordenbrock	. . . .	Dennis Haipin	Dennis Bulen	Tom Robke
Tompkinsville (3)	MC 502 487-6776	Veachel Harlan	. . . .	Clarnell Emberton	. . . .	Charles Landrum	Herbert Proffitt	Harold Frazier
Versailles (7)	MC 606 873-5436	(not reporting)						
Villa Hills (8)	MC 606 331-4933	(not reporting)						
Vine Grove (4)	MC 502 877-2422	R Brandenburg	. . . .	Barbara Wilkins	. . . .	Chris Mayhew	Russell Anderson	. . . .
Williamsburg (5)	MC 606 549-6035	(not reporting)						
Williamstown (3)	MC 606 824-3633	A Frances Simpson	Jeffrey W Clemons	Wm D Peddicord	. . . .	Wm F Thelkeld	James G Simpson	. . . .
Wilmore (3)	MC 606 858-4411	Harold L Rainwater	. . . .	C Brandenburg	. . . .	James Anderson	Roger Swallows	Donald Grimes
Winchester (16)	CM 606 744-7017	Clyde Heflin	Edallen Burtner	Marilyn Rowe	Edallen Burtner	Larry W Potter	William M Jackson	Jay Warden
LOUISIANA (98)								
Abbeville t (11)	MC 318 893-8550	R Brady Broussard	. . . .	S Zaunbrecher	. . . .	Nolan Frederick	Mike Hardy	. . . .
Alexandria (49)	MC 318 449-5026	Edward G Randolph	Harold Chambers	Jon W Grafton	Brian Funderburk	Charles Carruth	John Ritchie	D Williamson
Amite City t (4)	MC 504 748-9850	(not reporting)						
Arcadia t (3)	MC 318 263-8455	Ray Dean Smith	. . . .	Jane Pickett	. . . .	Donald Green	Victor Rogers	. . . .

Directory 1/9
continued

MUNICIPAL OFFICIALS
IN U.S. CITIES OVER 2,500

City, 1990 population figures (000 omitted), form of government	Municipal phone number	Mayor	Appointed administrator	City clerk	Finance officer	Fire chief	Police chief	Public works director
LOUISIANA (98) continued								
Baker (13)	MC 504 778-0300	(not reporting)						
Baldwin t (2)	MC 318 923-7523	(not reporting)						
Ball t (3)	MC 318 640-9605	(not reporting)						
Basile t (2)	MC 318 432-6693	(not reporting)						
Bastrop (14)	MC 318 283-0250	(not reporting)						
Baton Rouge (220)	MC 504 389-3100	(not reporting)						
Berwick t (4)	MC 504 384-8858	(not reporting)						
Bogalusa (14)	MC 504 732-6211	Mervin E Taylor	Gerald Bailey	. . . .	. . . .	James Dunaway	Wayne Kemp	Billy Daniels
Bossier City (53)	MC 318 741-8501	George Dement	Lorenz Walker	Helen Thornton	Charles Glover	J T Wallace Jr	Charle Duncan	Mark Hudson
Breaux Bridge (7)	MC 318 332-2171	Louis Kern	. . . .	Pattie Dupuis	. . . .	. . . .	George Menard	Billy Bertrand
Broussard t (3)	MC 318 837-6681	C Langlinais	. . . .	Tina Denais	. . . .	. . . .	Sidney Broussard	Gerald Guilbeau
Bunkie t (5)	MC 318 346-7663	(not reporting)						
Carencro t (5)	MC 318 896-8481	(not reporting)						
Church Point t (5)	MC 318 684-5693	Harold Beaugh	. . . .	Shirley D Kidder		Gene Daigle	Albert Venable	. . . .
Covington (8)	MC 504 892-1811	(not reporting)						
Crowley (14)	MC 318 783-0824	(not reporting)						
De Quincy t (3)	MC 318 786-8241	(not reporting)						
De Ridder (10)	MC 318 462-2461	Gerald Johnson	. . . .	Penny Simmons	Wilbert Curtis	Marvin Whiddon	Arvin Malone	Billy O'Neal
Delhi t (3)	MC 318 878-3792	(not reporting)						
Denham Springs (8)	MC 504 665-8121	James DeLaune	Douglas Hughes	Lerline Barnett	Kenneth Drone	C H Kennedy	Jeffrey Wesley	Willie Rheams
Donaldsonville (8)	CM 504 473-4247	Bernard J Francis	Wilbert Huey	Wilbert Huey	. . . .	Kirk Landry	. . . .	Gerard Joseph
Eunice (11)	MC 318 457-7380	Curtis Joubert	. . . .	Shirley F Vige Sr	. . . .	Gerald E Lejeune	Charles B Manuel	Roy Clavier
Farmerville t (3)	MC 318 368-9242	(not reporting)						
Ferriday t (4)	MC 318 757-3411	(not reporting)						
Franklin (9)	MC 318 828-6316	Sam Jones	Cindy Hebert	Cindy Hebert	Raymond Harris Jr	Timothy Thibodaux	Henry Louviere	Westley Beverly
Franklinton t (4)	MC 318 839-3569	Earle R Brown	. . . .	Faye Boyd	. . . .	Thomas Thiebaud	Lynn Armand	Linwood Corkern
Gonzales (7)	MC 504 647-2841	(not reporting)						
Grambling v (5)	MC 318 247-6120	(not reporting)						
Gramercy t (2)	MC 504 869-4403	Herman Bourgeois	. . . .	Lydia Louque	Tricia Hymel	Tim Jackson	Carl Spizale Sr	. . . .
Gretna (17)	MC 504 363-1500	(not reporting)						
Hammond (16)	MC 504 542-3400	(not reporting)						
Harahan (10)	MC 504 737-6383	(not reporting)						
Haynesville t (3)	MC 318 624-0911	Tom S Crocker	. . . .	Marilyn Bush	. . . .	Tommy Bower	David Mills	Alvin Moss
Homer t (4)	MC 318 927-3555	(not reporting)						
Houma (97)	MC 504 873-6401	Barry Bonvillain	Doug Maier	Paul Labat	Jamie Elfert	Gale Leboeuf	Jack Smith	Al Levron
Jackson t (4)	MC 504 634-7777	(not reporting)						
Jeanerette t (6)	MC 318 256-4587	Darryl A Landry	Edie Harrison	Edie Harrison	. . . .	Robert Grettner	Arthur Kahn	. . . .
Jena t (3)	MC 318 992-2148	Norman Welch	. . . .	Sharon Keel	. . . .	Don Smith	George L King	. . . .
Jennings (11)	MC 318 821-5500	Gregory Marcantel	. . . .	Norman J Cain	. . . .	Thomas Deshotel	Carroll C Morgan	Cyril A Charles
Jonesboro t (4)	MC 318 259-2385	(not reporting)						
Jonesville t (3)	MC 318 339-8596	Billy Edwards	Yolanda McClure	Deborah Savage	Yoland McClure	Ben Adams	Clyde Walker	Billy Edwards
Kaplan (5)	MC 318 643-8602	Bennet Broussard	Carol Perry	Carol Perry	Bennet Broussard	Joseph J Landry	Alton Romero	Wendall David
Kenner (72)	MC 504 468-7200	(not reporting)						
Kentwood t (2)	MC 504 229-3451	Bobby Gill	. . . .	Julia B Forrest	. . . .	Hubert Brown	Sammy Broyles	David Sellers
Kinder t (2)	MC 318 738-2620	Fred A Ashy	. . . .	Dorothy Langley		Alton Baker Jr	Charles R Welch	. . . .
Lafayette (94)	MC 318 261-8200	Kenneth F Bowen	Aros G Mouton	Dee Stanley	Rebecca Fontenot	Robert Benoit	Gary Copes	John Raines
Lake Arthur t (3)	MC 318 774-2211	(not reporting)						
Lake Charles (71)	MC 318 491-1200	(not reporting)						
Lake Providence t (5)	MC 318 559-2288	(not reporting)						
Leesville t (8)	CM 318 239-2444	(not reporting)						
Lutcher t (4)	MC 504 869-5823	Guy J Poche	. . . .	Mary Ann Guidry	. . . .	P J Amato	Brian J Melancon	. . . .
Mamou t (3)	MC 318 468-3272	(not reporting)						
Mandeville (7)	MC 504 626-3144	Paul R Spitzfaden	. . . .	Linda P Barnett	Milton G Stiebing	. . . .	Thomas H Buell	Bryan B Clement
Mansfield (5)	MC 318 872-0406	Harold L Cornett	. . . .	Judy Wilkerson	. . . .	Louie Melton	Don R English	James W Ruffin
Many t (3)	MC 318 256-3651	(not reporting)						
Marksville (6)	MC 318 253-9500	(not reporting)						
Minden (14)	MC 318 377-2144	(not reporting)						
Monroe (55)	MC 318 329-2200	Robert Powell	Billy Pearson	Michelle Williams	Billy Pearson	George Douglas	Joe Stewart	Robert Jefferson
Morgan City (15)	MC 504 385-1770	Timothy Matte	Larry P Bergeron	. . . .	Lorrie Braus	Michael Raymond	Daniel Dossett	George Mikhael
Natchitoches (17)	MC 318 357-3821	Joseph M Sampite	. . . .	Mary Ann Nunley	Charles E Powell	Robert L Hebert	Keith W Thompson	Clifford Walker
New Iberia (32)	MC 318 369-2300	Cliff Aucoin	Grayling Hadnott	Sally Angers	. . . .	Allen Babineaux	Steve Davis	Joe Boles
New Orleans (497)	MC 504 565-6556	(not reporting)						
New Roads t (5)	MC 504 638-7047	(not reporting)						
Oakdale (7)	MC 318 335-3629	(not reporting)						
Opelousas (18)	MC 318 948-2527	John W Joseph	Charles W Ross	Frances C Carron	Mamie C Leach	Robert Trosclair	Larry J Caillier	. . . .
Patterson t (5)	MC 504 395-5205	(not reporting)						
Pineville (12)	MC 318 449-5658	Frederick H Baden	. . . .	Carol Vermillion	Susan M Austin	Gary Morrow	P Oestriecher	Robert G Mickels
Plaquemine t (7)	MC 504 687-3116	(not reporting)						
Ponchatoula (5)	MC 504 386-6484	(not reporting)						
Port Allen (6)	MC 504 348-0441	(not reporting)						
Port Barre t (2)	MC 318 585-7646	(not reporting)						
Rayne (9)	MC 318 334-3121	(not reporting)						
Rayville t (4)	MC 318 728-2011	(not reporting)						
Ruston (20)	MC 318 251-8652	(not reporting)						
Shreveport (199)	MC 318 226-6000	Hazel Beard	Newton Bruce	Arthur Thompson	E Washington	Dale Martin	Stephen Prator	Tom Dark
Slidell (24)	MC 504 646-4300	Salvatore Caruso	Reinhard Dearing	Davis Dautreuil	Dianne Hanephin	. . . .	Ben Morris	Dan Yeates
Springhill (6)	MC 318 539-5681	J Curtis Smith	. . . .	Jimmie N Murph	. . . .	. . . .	Jerry L Stephens	. . . .
St. Martinville (7)	MC 318 394-5591	(not reporting)						
Sulphur (20)	MC 318 527-4500	(not reporting)						
Tallulah (9)	MC 318 574-0964	(not reporting)						
Thibodaux (14)	MC 504 447-3767	Alton Roundtree	. . . .	Thomas Eschete	Kenneth Hoffmann	Michael Oncale	Norman Diaz	Bert Hebert Jr
Vidalia t (5)	MC 318 336-5206	(not reporting)						
Ville Platte t (9)	MC 318 363-2939	(not reporting)						
Vinton t (3)	MC 318 589-7453	Charles Coppels	. . . .	Melba Landry	. . . .	Jerry Merchant	Dennis Drouillard	Raymond Guillory
Vivian t (4)	MC 318 375-3856	(not reporting)						
Walker t (4)	MC 504 664-3123	Mike Grimmer	. . . .	Janet Borne	. . . .	Donald Dedon	Elton Burns	Bert Kelly
Welsh t (3)	MC 318 734-2231	(not reporting)						
West Monroe (14)	MC 318 396-2600	(not reporting)						
Westlake t (5)	MC 318 433-0691	(not reporting)						
Westwego (11)	MC 504 341-3424	(not reporting)						
Winnfield (6)	MC 318 628-3939	Kenneth Henderson	. . . .	Missy Hyman	. . . .	Arthur D Chandler	Ray Shell	Bill Kelley
Winnsboro t (6)	MC 318 435-9087	(not reporting)						
Zachary (9)	MC 504 654-6871	John Womack	R E Amrhein	Merle W Johnston	Nancy Cobb	Douglas Gleason	Johnny Wales	Chris Davezac

Directory 1/9 continued **MUNICIPAL OFFICIALS IN U.S. CITIES OVER 2,500**

City, 1990 population figures (000 omitted), form of government	Municipal phone number	Mayor	Appointed administrator	City clerk	Finance officer	Fire chief	Police chief	Public works director
LOUISIANA (98) continued								
Zwolle t (2)	MC 318 645-6141	Chris Loupe	Larry A Cryer	Brenda Harrison	....	....	Marvin Frazier	....
MAINE (183)								
Amity t (..)	CM	(not reporting)						
Ashland t (2)	CM 207 435-2311	William Beaulier	James E Collins	James E Collins	James E Collins	Ned Labelle	Keith Bishop	Keith Smith
Auburn (24)	CM 207 786-2634	(not reporting)						
Augusta (21)	CM 207 626-2300	William D Burney	Terrence St Peter	Madeline Cyr	Constance Packard	Norman Arbour	Wayne McCamish	John Charest
Baileyville t (2)	TM 207 427-3442	F Doug Jones	Edward M Collins	Edward M Collins	....	Lawrence Gillis	Michael A Coty	William Roehrich
Bangor (33)	CM 207 945-4400	John Bragg	Edward Barrett	Russell McKenna	John Quartararo	John Foley	Randy Harriman	Arthur Stockus
Bar Harbor t (4)	CM 207 288-4098	Jill Goldthwait	Dana J Reed	Jean Barker	....	Royal J Higgins	Nathan W Young	Lyle M Dever
Bath (10)	CM 207 443-8330	Dean Almy	Duncan Ballantyne	Beverly Henrikson	George Sargent	Ronald Clark	Lawrence Dawson	Kenneth Murray
Belfast (6)	CM 207 338-3370	Mary Page Worth	Arlo L Redman	Teresa N Crosby	....	James L Richards	Robert B Keating	Wesley A Richards
Berwick t (6)	CM 207 698-1101	Samuel S Mathews	Christopher Rose	Barbara M Martin	....	Dennis R Plante	Peter C Hussey	Paul Sapierre
Bethel t (2)	TM 207 824-2669	Arthur Gilbert	Madeleine Henley	Merton T Brown Jr	....	James Young	Dale Bellman	Robert Pilgrim
Biddeford (21)	MC 207 284-9307	(not reporting)						
Blaine t (1)	TM 207 425-2611	(not reporting)						
Boothbay t (3)	TM 207 633-2051	Justin C Smith	Carlo M Pilgrim	Joan M Rittall	Carlo M Pilgrim	Stanley W Lewis	....	Carlo M Pilgrim
Boothbay Harbor t (2)	TM 207 633-3671	....	Jeffrey Grossman	....	....	Warren Page	Floyd McDunnah	....
Bowdoinham t (2)	CM 207 666-5531	(not reporting)						
Brewer (9)	CM 207 989-7500	Alan D Whittemore	Harold F Parks	Arthur C Verow	Jane A Warren	Bruce F Kigas	Eugene P Fizell	Gerald P Bowie
Bridgewater t (1)	CM 207 429-9856	(not reporting)						
Bridgton t (4)	TM 207 647-8786	Edward Hatch	James K McMahon	Julie Kimball	Phyllis Taferner	Ronald Smith	Robert Bell	Erald Kilkenny
Brownville t (2)	CM 207 965-2561	(not reporting)						
Brunswick t (21)	CM 207 725-6659	....	Donald H Gerrish	Gail Hodsdon	John S Eldridge	Gary Howard	Jerry A Hinton	John A Foster
Bucksport t (5)	CM 207 469-7368	(not reporting)						
Buxton t (6)	TM 207 929-5191	Gregory A Drew	....	....	....	....	Jody L Thomas	....
Calais (4)	CM 207 454-2521	Harold Clark	Byron E Burke	Theresa M Porter	Tammy L Ginn	Jacob Brocato	Micheal Milburn	Maurice Barnard
Camden t (5)	CM 207 236-3353	Morton Strom	Roger Moody	Carol Rogers	Carol Greenleaf	Robert Oxton	Terry Burgess	Earl Weaver
Cape Elizabeth t (9)	CM 207 799-0881	(not reporting)						
Caribou (9)	CM 207 493-3324	(not reporting)						
Carmel t (2)	TM 207 848-3361	....	Glennis McSorley	....	....	William Crowley	Fred Emerson Jr	....
Castle Hill t (..)	TM 207 764-3755	(not reporting)						
Chelsea t (2)	TM 207 582-4802	(not reporting)						
Cherryfield t (1)	TM 207 546-2376	Peter Duston	James Layton	Mona West	James Layton	Charles Curtis	Robert Grant	Kenneth Perry
China t (4)	TM 207 445-2014	(not reporting)						
Clinton t (3)	TM 207 426-8511	Roger McAllister	Peter Nielsen	Levina McKechnie	Peter Nielsen	Gary Petley	Lee Butler	Dale Bouchard
Corinna t (2)	TM 207 278-4183	N Partridge	G Dorman	B Englehardt	....	J Emerson	....	G Dorman
Corinth t (2)	TM 207 285-3271	(not reporting)						
Crystal t (..)	TM 207 463-2770	Stephen M Porter	Linda B York	Linda M York	....	Jamie Main	....	....
Cumberland t (6)	CM 207 829-5559	E Stephen Murray	Robert Benson	Klara Norton	Melody Main	William Fisher	....	Philip Wentworth
Danforth t (1)	CM 207 448-2321	(not reporting)						
Dexter t (4)	CM 207 924-7351	Roger S Brawn	Stephen Whitesel	Marcia E Delaware	Marilyn A Curtis	Donald Clukey	David A Clukey	Michael Delaware
Dixfield t (3)	CM 207 562-8151	(not reporting)						
Dover-Foxcroft t (5)	TM 207 564-3318	(not reporting)						
Dyer Brook t (..)	TM 207 757-8302	(not reporting)						
Eagle Lake t (1)	CM 207 444-5125	Robert Parent	Paul Blanchette	Linda Allison	Paul Blanchette	Thomas Labbe	....	....
Easton t (1)	TM 207 488-6652	Richard Kneeland	Jackalene Bradley	Cheryl Clark	Jackalene Bradley	Kim White	....	Jackalene Bradley
Eastport (2)	TM 207 853-2332	(not reporting)						
Eliot t (5)	TM 207 439-1813	(not reporting)						
Ellsworth (6)	CM 207 667-2563	Caroline Patten	Timothy J King	Fern Kelley	....	Everett Farnsworth	Albert Carter	....
Exeter t (1)	TM 207 379-2191	(not reporting)						
Fairfield t (7)	CM 207 453-7911	Richard Fortier	Peter A McKenney	Julie Magoon	....	Dale W Sweet	John Pouliot	G Allen Taylor
Falmouth t (8)	TM 207 781-5253	(not reporting)						
Farmingdale t (3)	TM 207 582-2225	Harold Hersom	Phyllis H Weeks	Phyllis H Weeks	....	Eugene Proulx	....	Albert E Barry
Farmington t (7)	CM 207 778-6538	Frances Hardy	Alphonse Dixon	Joan Reed	....	Robert McLeery	Nolan Wilcox	Mitchell Boulette
Fort Fairfield t (4)	TM 207 472-3801	Michael Edmunds	S W Seabury	Susan Levaseur	Lynda Dougherty	Dana McGlaughlin	Neil Saucier	Arnold Fox
Fort Kent t (4)	CM 207 834-3090	(not reporting)						
Freeport t (7)	CM 207 865-4743	....	Dale Olmstead Jr	....	....	....	....	....
Frenchville t (1)	CM 207 543-7301	(not reporting)						
Fryeburg t (3)	TM 207 935-2805	Edward Jones	Nathan Poore	Theresa Shaw	....	Clyde Watson	David Miles	Jay McCluskey
Gardiner (7)	CM 207 582-4200	Brian Rines	Bruce Benwy	Patricia Glidden	Bruce Benway	Larry Bradley	Craig Marshall	Timothy Moody
Garland t (1)	CM 207 924-6615	(not reporting)						
Gorham t (12)	CM 207 839-5041	M Thad Moody	R Paul Weston	D Brenda Caldwell	Shirley Hughes	Robert Lefebvre	Edward T Tolan	James P Plummer
Gray t (6)	CM 207 657-3339	John Welch	Paul Bird	Paul Bird	....	Jon Barton	....	Neal Lavallee
Greenbush t (1)	TM 207 732-3644	Charles Adams	R Littlefield	R Littlefield	....	Edward Haverlock	William Flagg	R Littlefield
Greene t (4)	TM 207 946-5146	(not reporting)						
Greenville t (2)	TM 207 695-2421	(not reporting)						
Guilford t (2)	TM 207 876-2202	William Thompson	R Littlefield	Michelle Nichols	Dorene Graf	David Cookson	....	R Littlefield
Hallowell (3)	CM 207 623-4021	Harmen Harvey	Patrick Gilbert	Deanna Hallett	....	Michael Grant	Rodney Myrick	John Sawyer
Hampden t (6)	CM 207 862-3034	William Romano	Marie Baker	Paula Newcomb	Marie Baker	Robert Bailey	Joseph Rogers	Greg Nash
Harpswell t (5)	TM 207 833-5771	Robert E Webber	....	Laverne Vayo	Anita E Morse	William Beazley	....	....
Hartland t (2)	TM 207 938-4401	(not reporting)						
Haynesville t (..)	TM 207 448-2239	Judith Oliver	Norma Malone	Norma Malone	....	Paul Rouse	....	....
Hermon t (4)	CM 207 848-3485	Robert Yackobitz	Kathryn Ruth	Teresa Mayo	....	John Maynard	....	Kathryn Ruth
Hodgdon t (1)	CM 207 532-6498	(not reporting)						
Holden t (3)	CM 207 843-5151	Michael Legasse	R Larry Varisco	R Larry Varisco	....	Henry Maynard	David Lambert	Bruce Dowling
Hollis t (4)	TM 207 929-8552	(not reporting)						
Houlton t (7)	CM 207 532-7111	M McLaughlin	R Lewis Bone	Cathy J O'Leary	Nedra J Hanson	Milton J Cone	Darrell L Malone	Ralph M Cleale
Island Falls t (1)	TM 207 463-2246	Dwayne M Hartin	Sandra J Lane	Sandra J Lane	....	Guilford P Sirois	....	Cecil R Given
Islesboro t (1)	TM 207 734-2253	(not reporting)						
Jackman t (1)	TM 207 668-2111	(not reporting)						
Jay t (5)	TM 207 897-6785	David McCluskey	Cornell Knight	Ronda Palmer	....	....	Erland Farrington	....
Kennebunk t (8)	TM 207 985-2102	Boyd J Long	Richard A Erb	Ethelyn S Marthia	....	Steven W Nichols	James E Lavalle	....
Kennebunkport t (3)	TM 207 967-4243	(not reporting)						
Kittery t (9)	CM 207 439-1633	Frank L Dennett	Phlip McCarthy	Joanne Lund	Philip McCarthy	George Varney	Edward Strong	Richard Rossiter
Lebanon t (4)	TM 207 457-1171	(not reporting)						
Lewiston (40)	CM 207 784-2951	James P Howaniec	Robert J Mulready	Gerald P Berube	Richard Metivier	Richard R Mailhot	Laurent Gilbert	C Branch
Limestone t (10)	TM 207 325-4704	Florence Young	Troy Brown	Donna Bernier	....	Paul Durepo	Ronnie Sprague	Dale Brooker
Lincoln t (6)	CM 207 794-3372	Deirdra Trask	Clifton Barker	Lisa Goodwin	....	David Rand	Larry Merrithen	David Washburn
Lincolnville t (..)	TM 207 763-3555	E F Littlefield	Joshua T Day	Joshua T Day	....	Maurice Watts	Richard Osgood	....
Linneus t (1)	CM 207 532-6182	A Andrew Brennan	F Hutchinson	F Hutchinson	....	Stephen Bither	....	....
Lisbon Falls t (9)	CM 207 353-5958	(not reporting)						
Litchfield t (3)	TM 207 268-4721	Elton L Wade	Wendi Nesbit	Wendi Nesbit	Wendi Nesbit	Stanley Labbe	W Scott Steitz	Wendi Nesbit
Littleton t (1)	TM 207 538-9862	Gerald E Miller	Roberta Schools	Roberta Schools	....	D Cowperthwaite	....	William Dunbar

Directory 1/9
continued

**MUNICIPAL OFFICIALS
IN U.S. CITIES OVER 2,500**

City, 1990 population figures (000 omitted), form of government	Municipal phone number	Mayor	Appointed administrator	City clerk	Finance officer	Fire chief	Police chief	Public works director
MAINE (183) continued								
Livermore Falls t (3)	CM 207 897-2016	(not reporting)						
Lubec t (2)	CM 207 733-5532	Donald B Hampton	Mark F Decoteau	Jill Mulholland	Mark F Decoteau	Errol Tinker	. . . .	Mark F Decoteau
Ludlow t (..)	CM 207 532-7743	(not reporting)						
Lyman t (3)	TM 207 499-7562	(not reporting)						
Machias t (3)	CM 207 255-6621	S Altmannsberger	C Loughlin	Martha Bagley	C Loughlin	Colby Dennison	Robbie Dirsa	Carlo Coletti
Madawaska t (5)	TM 207 728-6351	(not reporting)						
Madison t (5)	TM 207 696-4689	Jeffery A Lloyd	Richard R Michaud	Lisa F Paine	. . . .	Elwin E Barron	Harley G Dunlap	Philip A Curtis
Mapleton t (2)	TM 207 764-3754	(not reporting)						
Mars Hill t (2)	CM 207 425-3731	. . . .	Raymond Mersereau	Raymond Mersereau	Raymond Mersereau	Barry Dorr	. . . .	. . . .
Masardis t (..)	TM 207 435-2841	John Weeks	Julia Mac Donald	Julia Mac Donald	. . . .	Charles Craig	. . . .	Clive Bragdon
Mechanic Falls t (3)	CM 207 345-2871	Wayne Hackett	Dana K Lee	Sheila Gray	. . . .	Oliver Emery	Jeffrey Goss	Malcolm Sawyer
Merrill t (..)	CM 207 757-8286	(not reporting)						
Mexico t (3)	TM 207 364-7971	(not reporting)						
Milbridge t (1)	TM 207 546-2422	Gary H Willey	Edward J Storey	Marcia G Solomon	. . . .	. . . .	. . . .	Edward J Storey
Millinocket t (7)	CM 207 723-9701	Rodney Daigle	James Kotredes	Dianne Lombard	James Kotredes	Milan Thornton	Wayne Scarano	Robert Lander
Milo t (3)	CM 207 943-2202	Glenn M Ricker	Jane S Jones	Melinda Sherburne	. . . .	David Preble	Todd Lyford	Harold Burton
Monmouth t (3)	TM 207 933-2206	(not reporting)						
Monroe t (1)	TM 207 525-3515	Joseph Lamagna	Marie L Luciani	Valerie Moody	. . . .	Marshall Moody	. . . .	. . . .
Monson t (1)	TM 207 997-3641	Paul Suomi	Jeanne B Reed	Julie S Anderson	. . . .	Patrick Pembroke	. . . .	Brian Turner
Monticello t (1)	TM 207 538-9500	(not reporting)						
Mount Desert t (2)	TM 207 276-5531	Joanne Smith	. . . .	Kimberly Walker	. . . .	. . . .	Edward Mandell	Ernest Coombs
New Canada t (..)	CM 207 834-6673	Danny Watson	Judy Bossie	Judy Bossie	. . . .	. . . .	. . . .	. . . .
New Gloucester t (4)	TM 207 926-4126	(not reporting)						
New Portland t (1)	TM 207 628-4441	(not reporting)						
Newport t (3)	TM 207 368-5575	Al Worden	Arthur Ellingwood	Janet Atkinson	. . . .	Don King	James Ricker	Jack Wilson
Norridgewock t (3)	TM 207 634-2252	(not reporting)						
North Berwick t (4)	TM 207 676-3353	(not reporting)						
Norway t (5)	TM 207 743-6651	(not reporting)						
Oakfield t (1)	TM 207 757-8479	(not reporting)						
Oakland t (6)	CM 207 465-7357	Robert Quinn	Janice Porter	Doug Mather	Charles Pullen	Kevin O'Leary	Jeff Higgins
Ogunquit t (1)	CM 207 646-5139	Dennis E Andrews	Donald C Grant	Madeline D Brown	D Grant	Bruce A Bernard	Michael W Pardue	Jonathan L Webber
Old Orchard Beach t (8)	CM 207 934-5714	Valerie Landry	Jame C Bennett	Maureen O'Leary	. . . .	Philip Laporte	Dana Kelley	Theodore Dydowicz
Old Town (8)	CM 207 827-6148	Roberta Fowler	David Cole	Patricia Ramsey	Constance Murray	Edwin Pollard	Donald Ohalloran	John Ellis
Orono t (11)	CM 207 866-2556	George Gonyar	Gerald Kempen	. . . .	Wanda Thomas	Robert Burke	Daniel Lowe	Calvin Smith
Orrington t (3)	TM 207 825-3340	Joseph Coffin Jr	Candace Guerette	Carole A Hardin	. . . .	Lesley Grover	. . . .	John Hodgins
Oxford t (4)	CM 207 539-4431	(not reporting)						
Paris t (4)	TM 207 743-2501	Arthur Hill Jr	John White	Elizabeth Larson	. . . .	John Bryant	Stephen Cobbett	Galen Curtis
Patten t (1)	TM 207 528-2215	(not reporting)						
Phillips t (1)	TM 207 639-3561	. . . .	Laura Toothaker	Sylvia Adams	. . . .	Daniel Arms	. . . .	Stephen Haines
Pittsfield t (4)	CM 207 487-3136	(not reporting)						
Poland t (4)	TM 207 998-4601	(not reporting)						
Portage Lake t (..)	CM 207 435-4361	(not reporting)						
Portland (64)	CM 207 874-8300	(not reporting)	Thomas R Stevens	Jean Porter	. . . .	James Krysiak	James Ferland	John Carrier
Presque Isle (11)	CM 207 764-4485	Clarence Bell	Thomas R Stevens	Jean Porter	. . . .	James Krysiak	James Ferland	John Carrier
Rangeley t (1)	TM 207 864-3326	(not reporting)						
Reed pl (..)	CM 207 456-7546	(not reporting)						
Richmond t (3)	CM 207 737-4305	Donald Mac Kenzie	Nancy Churchill	. . . .	. . . .	John Carver	John Morris	Richard LaChance
Rockland (8)	CM 207 594-8431	Robert Peabody	Cathy Sleeper	Stuart Sylvester	James Frankowski	Raymond Wooster	Alfred Ockenfels	Greg Blackwell
Rockport t (3)	TM 207 236-9648	Robert Duke	Don Willard Jr	Brenda Richardson	Erica Harriman	Bruce Woodward	Forest Doucette	Steve Beveridge
Rumford t (7)	CM 207 364-4576	James Thibodeau	Robert C Welch	Mary Ann Prue	. . . .	J Arthur Boivin	Dewey Robinson	Robert C Welch
Sabattus t (4)	MC 207 375-4331	(not reporting)						
Saco (15)	CM 207 282-1032	(not reporting)						
Sanford t (20)	RT 207 324-9100	Faith Ballanger	John Webb	Claire Morrison	. . . .	Daniel Hart	Gordon Paul	Richard Wilkins
Sangerville t (1)	TM 207 876-2814	John Flanders	James Catlin	Alice Moulton	James Catlin	John Levesque	. . . .	Brian Wharff
Scarborough t (13)	CM 207 883-4301	Gary Lorfano	Carl Betterley	Laurel Nadeau	Ruth Porter	Robert Carson	Hollis Dixon	William Giguere
Searsport t (3)	TM 207 548-6372	Stetson Hills	Fred T Breslin	Suzan M Cotter	Lee Ann Horowitz	. . . .	James S Gillway	George Parker
Sherman t (1)	TM 207 365-4200	Ernest Elder	Debra J O'Roak	Debra J O'Roak	Debra J O'Roak	Douglas Clark	. . . .	. . . .
Skowhegan t (9)	TM 207 474-6900	(not reporting)						
Smyrna t (..)	CM 207 757-8286	(not reporting)						
South Berwick t (6)	CM 207 384-2263	(not reporting)						
South Portland (23)	CM 207 767-3201	James Soule	Jerre Bryant	Linda Cohen	Ralph St Pierre	John True	Robert Schwartz	Arvin Erskine
Southwest Harbor t (2)	TM 207 244-5404	(not reporting)						
St. Agatha t (1)	TM 207 543-7305	(not reporting)						
St. Albans t (2)	CM 207 938-4568	(not reporting)						
Stacyville t (..)	TM 207 365-4195	(not reporting)						
Standish t (8)	CM 207 642-3461	Eva Tompson	Scott G Cole	Mary E Chapman	Martha S Drew	H Kevin Warren	. . . .	J Richardson
Stockholm t (..)	TM 207 896-5659	Peter B Bossie	Kathleen Lausier	Albertine Dufour	. . . .	John Hotelling	. . . .	. . . .
Stonington t (1)	CM 207 367-2351	. . . .	Roger K Stone	. . . .	. . . .	Daniel Coombs	. . . .	. . . .
Thomaston t (3)	CM 207 354-6107	(not reporting)						
Topsham t (9)	TM 207 725-1718	Alan J Houston	Larry D Cilley	Ruth A Lyons	Priscilla H Hall	Clayton I Baker	Paul J Lessard	Tad A Hunter
Tremont t (1)	CM 207 244-7204	Alison H Price	Gretchen K Strong	Diane E Huff	Gretchen K Strong	Bradley Reed	. . . .	Gretchen K Strong
Turner t (4)	TM 207 225-3416	William P Jones	Kenneth Kokernak	Eva D Leavitt	. . . .	Dana Goodwin	. . . .	Reynard Gilbert
Van Buren t (3)	CM 207 868-2886	(not reporting)						
Vassalboro t (4)	TM 207 872-2826	(not reporting)						
Veazie t (2)	CM 207 947-2781	(not reporting)						
Waldoboro t (5)	TM 207 832-5369	William Blodgett	Lee L Smith	Rebecca Maxwell	Eileen Dondlinger	Robert M Maxcy	Leroy L Jones	Earl C Wallace
Wallagrass t (1)	CM 207 834-5894	(not reporting)						
Warren t (3)	CM 207 273-2421	(not reporting)						
Washburn t (2)	CM 207 455-8485	(not reporting)						
Waterboro t (5)	TM 207 247-5166	(not reporting)						
Waterville (17)	MC 207 873-7131	David E Bernier	Scott Shanley	Lynn Dostie	Carol C P Blier	Darrel Fournier	Bruce Goodman	Kenneth Ryder
Wells t (8)	TM 207 646-5113	(not reporting)						
Westbrook (16)	MC 207 854-9105	Fred C Wescott	Peter L Eckel	William L Clarke	Susan R Rossignol	James F Rulman	Ronald L Allanach	George A Googins
Wilton t (4)	CM 207 645-4961	Clinton Cushman	Richard P Davis	Linda Jellison	Richard P Davis	Theodore Baxter	James C Parker	Kenneth L Vining
Windham t (13)	CM 207 892-1907	Tom Bartell	Glenn Fratto	Rita Bernice	Debra Taber	Charles Hammond	Rick Lewsen	Steve Walker
Winslow t (8)	CM 207 872-2776	Bernard McCaslin	Edward A Gagnon	Roseann Boutin	. . . .	William Page	Ronald Whary	Ernest Baker
Winter Harbor t (1)	TM 207 963-2235	(not reporting)						
Winterport t (3)	TM 207 223-5055	Phillip Pitula	Scott M Tilton	Scott M Tilton	. . . .	Creighton Parker	. . . .	. . . .
Winthrop t (6)	CM 207 377-2286	. . . .	Marshall Hills	Pauline Downes	Jan Tewksbury	Hartley Palleschi	Joseph Young	. . . .
Wiscasset t (3)	TM 207 882-6331	Lawrence R Gordon	. . . .	Anne L Beattie	. . . .	Tim Merry	Michael J Reidy	Roy E Barnes
Yarmouth t (8)	CM 207 846-9036	John Buck	Nathaniel Tupper	Patricia Merrill	. . . .	Carl H Winslow	Richard C Perry	William R Shane
York t (10)	CM 207 363-1000	William Layman	Mark A Green	Mary A Szeniawski	Thomas G Marcoux	. . . .	William R Foster	Leon R Moulton

Directory 1/9 continued

MUNICIPAL OFFICIALS IN U.S. CITIES OVER 2,500

City, 1990 population figures (000 omitted), form of government	Municipal phone number	Mayor	Appointed administrator	City clerk	Finance officer	Fire chief	Police chief	Public works director
MARYLAND (55)								
Aberdeen t (13)	CM 301 272-1600	(not reporting)						
Annapolis (33)	MC 410 263-7997	(not reporting)						
Baltimore (736)	MC 410 396-9939	(not reporting)						
Bel Air t (9)	CM 410 879-2711	Eugene Graybeal	William McFaul	Joyce Oliver	William McFaul	. . . .	Leo Matrangola	Chris Schlehr
Berwyn Heights t (3)	CM 301 474-5000	(not reporting)						
Bladensburg t (8)	MC 301 927-7048	Ben Stephenson	Eric Morsicato	Elsie Morrison	Roy Hicks	. . . .	Robert Zidek	John Parker
Bowie (38)	CM 301 262-6200	Richard J Logue	David J Deutsch	Pamela A Fleming	Robert Patrick	. . . .	. . . .	R James Henrikson
Brentwood t (3)	MC 301 927-3344	George D Denny Jr	Roylene M Roberts	Mary E Reed	. . . .	Leonard Johnson	. . . .	Gregory P Adkins
Brunswick t (5)	MC 301 834-7500	Richard Goodrich	John Kendall	. . . .	Ernestine Phillip	. . . .	Richard Stone	Kevin Brawner
Cambridge (12)	MC 301 228-4020	(not reporting)						
Capitol Heights t (4)	CM 301 336-0626	(not reporting)						
Centreville t (2)	CM 301 758-1180	Sara J Davidson	Denise M Rose	Doris M Payne	Doris M Payne	. . . .	Douglas E Crites	Paul I Roberts
Chestertown t (4)	MC 410 778-0500	Elmer E Horsey	W S Ingersoll	Thelma Legg	. . . .	. . . .	Wayne Bradley	Medford C Capel
Cheverly t (6)	CM 301 773-8360	Larry Beyna	David Warrington	Lenore Lerch	Lenore Lerch	. . . .	Gilbert Jones	Juan Torres
Chevy Chase v (3)	CM 301 654-7300	Margot Anderson	Jerry M Schiro	. . . .	Cheryl A Morgan	. . . .	. . . .	Jerry Lesesne
Chevy Chase t (2)	CM 301 654-7144	Mier Wolf	Susan Robinson	Andi Silverstone				
College Park (22)	CM 301 864-8667	Anna L Owens	Richard N Conti	Miriam P Wolff	John M Markowski	. . . .	. . . .	James C Johnson
Crisfield (3)	MC 301 968-1333	(not reporting)						
Cumberland (24)	MC 301 759-6400	Edward C Athey	Jeffrey Repp	Audrey C Wolford	William Z Burke	Russell Livengood	James R Dick Jr	Dennis McCormick
Delmar t (1)	CM 410 896-2777	Doug Niblett	Roberta Ernest	. . . .	. . . .	. . . .	Hal Saylor	Robert Handy
District Heights t (7)	MC 301 336-1402	Mary A Pumphrey	. . . .	Marie E Gibbs	. . . .	. . . .	Michael W Conboy	Jim McGill
Easton t (9)	MC 301 822-2525	(not reporting)						
Elkton t (9)	CM 301 398-0970	(not reporting)						
Forest Heights t (3)	MC 301 839-1030	Warren F Adams	. . . .	Judith E Renick	Grover E Dare	. . . .	. . . .	. . . .
Frederick (40)	MC 301 694-1440	(not reporting)						
Friendship Heights v (..)	MC 301 656-2797	(not reporting)						
Frostburg (8)	CO 301 689-6000	(not reporting)						
Fruitland (4)	MC 410 548-2800	(not reporting)						
Gaithersburg (40)	CM 301 258-6310	W Edward Bohrer	Sanford W Daily	. . . .	Roger L Anderson	. . . .	Maryann Viverette	James D Arnoult
Glenarden t (5)	CM 301 773-2100	Marvin F Wilson	Norton N Bonapart	. . . .	. . . .	. . . .	Morris A Lewis	Roland Kenner
Greenbelt (21)	CM 301 474-8000	Gil Weidenfeld	Daniel G Hobbs	Dorothy Lauber	. . . .	. . . .	James R Craze	Carl M Hirsch
Hagerstown (35)	CM 301 790-3200	Steven T Sager	Stephen M Feller	Georgiann N Lucas	Alfred E Martin	Gary R Hawbaker	Paul M Wood	Douglas H Stull
Havre De Grace (9)	MC 410 939-1800	Gunther D Hirsch	Robert M Lange	. . . .	Robert M Lange	. . . .	William Lamphere	David L Himes
Hyattsville (14)	MC 301 985-5000	Thomas L Bass	Marge Wolf	Gertrude McCamly	. . . .	. . . .	Robert T Perry	Daniel Jones
Indian Head t (4)	CM 301 743-5511	Dennis Scheessele	Jeffrey Repp	. . . .	Dorothy Smith	. . . .	. . . .	James P Chase
La Plata t (6)	MC 301 870-3377	(not reporting)						
Landover Hills t (2)	MC 301 773-6401	(not reporting)						
Laurel t (19)	MC 301 725-5300	Joseph R Robison	Richard L Grace	Kaye M Sandul	Barbara A Reber	. . . .	Archie H Cook	Martin A Flemion
Mount Rainier (8)	MC 301 927-0104	(not reporting)						
New Carrollton (12)	MC 301 459-6100	(not reporting)						
Ocean City t (5)	CM 410 289-8221	Roland E Powell	Dennis Dare	Carol Jacobs	Martha Bennett	. . . .	David Massey	Hal Adkins
Pocomoke City (4)	CM 301 957-1333	(not reporting)						
Poolesville t (4)	CO 301 428-8927	(not reporting)						
Princess Anne t (2)	CM 410 651-1818	(not reporting)						
Riverdale t (5)	MC 301 927-6381	(not reporting)						
Rockville (45)	CM 301 309-3000	(not reporting)						
Salisbury (21)	MC 410 548-3100	W Paul Martin	Patrick J Fennell	Virginia Crawford	R Baskerville	W Higgins	C Dykes	Thomas Plotts
Seat Pleasant (5)	CM 301 336-2600	Eugene F Kennedy	Samuel Rosser	E Nightengale	Robert L Ashton	. . . .	Ronald Harvey	. . . .
Snow Hill t (2)	MC 410 632-2080	Ray Warren	Lou Volandt	Shirley Calvarese	Jeanne Waters	. . . .	Orlando Blake	Rich Rau
Takoma Park (17)	MC 301 270-1700	Edward F Sharp	Beverly K Habada	C E Sartoph	Linda C McKenzie	. . . .	A Tony Fisher	Richard Knauf
Taneytown (4)	CM 410 751-1100	Henry Reindollar	. . . .	Linda M Hess	. . . .	. . . .	Melvin E Diggs	Bruce P Eyler
Thurmont t (3)	MC 301 271-7313	(not reporting)						
University Park t (2)	MC 301 927-2997	(not reporting)						
Westernport t (2)	MC 301 359-3932	(not reporting)						
Westminster (13)	MC 410 848-9000	(not reporting)						
MASSACHUSETTS (270)								
Abington t (14)	TM 617 878-0805	(not reporting)						
Acton t (18)	TM 508 264-9612	F Dore Hunter	Don P Johnson	Catherine Belbin	W Roy Wetherby	Robert Craig	George W Robinson	Richard Howe
Acushnet t (10)	TM 508 995-1141	Everett Hardy	. . . .	Lillian Garbaciak	. . . .	Paul Cote	Michael Poitras	Richard Provencal
Adams t (9)	RT 413 743-9344	C Solari	James Leitch	Wanda Lebeau	Roland Chaffee	. . . .	Bruce McLaren	Francis Wojtaszek
Agawam t (27)	MC 413 786-0400	C Johnson	. . . .	Richard Theroux	. . . .	Russell Jenks	S Chmielewski	John Stone
Amesbury t (15)	RT 508 388-8100	James N Thivierge	John M Koelsch	Josephine Jacques	Charles Benevento	Arthur Gaudet	Daniel Cleary	Timothy Haskell
Amherst t (35)	RT 413 256-4004	Bryan C Harvey	Barry Delcastilho	Cornelia Como	Nancy Maglione	Victor Zumbruski	Donald N Maia	Noel Ryan
Andover t (29)	TM 508 470-3800	William Downs	R S Stapczynski	Randall Hanson	Anthony Torrisi	Harold Hayes	James Johnson	Robert McQuade
Arlington t (45)	MC 617 646-1000	Donald R Marquis	. . . .	Marge Cabral	. . . .	. . . .	John Carroll	. . . .
Ashburnham t (5)	TM 508 827-5548	(not reporting)						
Ashland t (12)	TM 508 881-0100	Barry M Bresnick	Dexter P Blois	Cindy Watling	. . . .	Frank Karayianes	Robert Gonfrade	Silvio Baruzzi
Athol t (11)	RT 508 249-2368	Joseph F Maga	. . . .	Nita Bates	Charles E Baker	Leon A Lozier	John E Lyons	Paul O Hadsel
Attleboro (38)	MC 508 222-9610	(not reporting)						
Auburn t (15)	RT 508 832-7720	Craig Blais	William A Kennedy	Doris Hill	June Orcutt	Roger Belhumeur	Ronald Miller	. . . .
Avon t (5)	TM 508 588-0414	(not reporting)						
Ayer t (7)	TM 617 772-2072	Stephen M Slarsky	Timothy S Higgins	Ann G Callahan	. . . .	Paul Fillebrown	Arthur J Boisseau	Donald Ouellette
Barnstable t (41)	CM 508 790-6200	. . . .	W J Rutherford	A Cahoon	James Tinsley	. . . .	Neil Nightingale	Thomas Mullen
Barre t (5)	TM 508 355-2504	(not reporting)						
Bedford t (13)	TM 617 275-1111	John McCulloch	Richard T Reed	Doreen Tremblay	Peter Naum	W Kevin O'Toole	. . . .	R Warrington
Belchertown t (11)	TM 413 323-0403	David Fredenburgh	Anne M Alzapiedi	William Barnett	Eleanor W Green	Samuel J Joyal	Robert A Knight	. . . .
Bellingham t (15)	TM 508 966-0040	John Tuttle	Denis Fraine	Kathleen Harvey	Marilyn Mathieu	Richard Ranieri	Richard Boucher	. . . .
Belmont t (25)	RT 617 489-8200	Walter Flewelling	Melvin Kleckner	Ann C Wilson	Stephen Szabo	James Murphy	Ronald Blanchette	Peter Castanino
Berkley t (5)	TM 508 822-3348	George Moitoza	. . . .	Carolyn Awalt	. . . .	Dwight Fournier	Harold Ashley Jr	. . . .
Beverly (38)	MC 508 921-6000	F John Monahan	. . . .	Constance Perron	Donald B Young	Kenneth Pelonzi	John Finnegan	George Zambouras
Billerica t (38)	RT 508 671-0942	Arthur Doyle	Robert A Mercier	Shirley Schult	Ralph McKenna	Anthony Capaldo	John Barretto	Richard Bento
Blackstone t (8)	TM 508 883-7289	. . . .	J Jeffrey Ritter	Susan Mellor	Gerald Levesque	Michael Sweeney	. . . .	Tommy Deulin
Bolton t (3)	TM 617 779-2297	(not reporting)						
Boston-Suffolk (574)	MC 617 725-4000	(not reporting)						
Bourne t (16)	TM 508 759-4486	(not reporting)						
Boxborough t (3)	TM 617 263-1116	(not reporting)						
Boxford t (6)	TM 508 887-8181	Richard W Ulman	Thomas Hauenstein	Patricia Shields	. . . .	Peter Perkins	Gordon Russell Jr	Thomas F Greene
Boylston t (4)	TM 617 869-2234	James Wood	. . . .	Irene Symonds	. . . .	Donald Parker	Frank Sleeper	Donald Parker
Braintree t (34)	RT 617 848-1870	(not reporting)						
Brewster t (8)	TM 508 896-3701	Eric K Rasmussen	Charles L Sumner	Joan Cole	Lisa Souve	Roy Jones	James Ehrhart	Allan Tkaczyk
Bridgewater t (21)	TM 508 697-0919	(not reporting)						
Brockton (93)	MC 508 580-7123	(not reporting)						

Directory 1/9
continued

MUNICIPAL OFFICIALS
IN U.S. CITIES OVER 2,500

City, 1990 population figures (000 omitted), form of government	Municipal phone number	Mayor	Appointed administrator	City clerk	Finance officer	Fire chief	Police chief	Public works director
MASSACHUSETTS (270) continued								
Brookline t (55)	CM 617 730-2210	Michael Merrill	R T Leary	F Halpern	H Beth	R English	H Brackett	A T DeMaio
Burlington t (23)	RT 617 270-1600	Richard C Wilde	David W Owen	Jane L Chew	Patrick J Mullin	Paul Thibault	William Soda	Syamal Chaudhuri
Cambridge (96)	CM 617 349-4000	Kenneth Reeves	Robert Healy	Margaret Drury	James Maloney	Kevin Fitzgerald	Perry Anderson	David Haley
Canton t (19)	TM 617 821-5000	(not reporting)						
Carlisle t (4)	TM 508 369-6136	(not reporting)						
Carver t (11)	TM 617 866-4551	(not reporting)						
Charlton t (10)	TM 508 248-5900	M Wayne Colby	Guy E Helander	Helene Caplette	Evelyn Murkland	Ralph Harris	Philip J Stevens	Kenneth Towle
Chatham t (7)	TM 508 945-2100	Jeffrey E Fryar	. . . .	Beverley E Ricci	. . . .	W K Schwerdtfeger	Barry D Eldredge	G R Borthwick
Chelmsford t (32)	TM 508 250-5201	R DeFreitas	Bernard Lynch	Mary St Hilaire	Charles Mansfield	. . . .	. . . .	James Pearson
Chelsea (29)	MC 617 884-0407	(not reporting)						
Cheshire t (3)	TM 413 743-2826	(not reporting)						
Chicopee (57)	MC 413 594-4711	Joseph J Chessey	. . . .	Nancy A Mulvey	Norman J Ritchott	Robert J Nunes	John F Ferraro Jr	Stanley W Kulig
Clinton t (13)	TM 508 365-4812	(not reporting)						
Cohasset t (7)	TM 617 383-9900	Martha K Gjesteby	Gregory J Doyon	Marion L Douglas	J Michael Buckley	Roger W Lincoln	Brian W Noonan	. . . .
Concord t (17)	TM 617 369-2100	(not reporting)						
Dalton t (7)	TM 413 684-6111	Vivian I Mason	Donna L Boryta	Barbara L Suriner	Richard R Charron	. . . .	Daniel D Filiault	Terry F Young
Danvers t (24)	RT 508 777-0001	(not reporting)						
Dartmouth t (27)	RT 508 999-0700	(not reporting)						
Dedham t (24)	RT 617 326-5770	(not reporting)						
Deerfield t (5)	RT 413 665-4645	(not reporting)						
Dennis t (14)	TM 508 394-8300	Heidi S Schadt	Stephen J Lombard	Elinor E Slade	. . . .	Paul A Tucker	. . . .	Dennis D Hanson
Dighton t (6)	TM 508 669-6431	Armand Gagne	. . . .	Brenda Herbeck	Janice Boucher	Joseph White	Karl Spratt Jr	Paul Demoura
Douglas t (5)	TM 508 476-4000	(not reporting)						
Dover t (5)	TM 508 785-2269	(not reporting)						
Dracut t (26)	TM 508 937-9885	(not reporting)						
Dudley t (10)	TM 617 943-2792	(not reporting)						
Duxbury t (14)	CM 617 934-6586	(not reporting)						
East Bridgewater t (11) ...	TM 508 378-1601	Clifford Williams	Richard J LaFond	Karen Grabau	. . . .	John Parow	John Silva	Leo Trudeau
East Longmeadow t (13) .	TM 413 525-5400	(not reporting)						
Eastham t (4)	TM 508 255-0333	Donald B Sparrow	Sheila Vanderhoef	Lillian Lamperti	Carolyn Gifford	John A Austin	Donald Watson	Steven Douglas
Easthampton t (16)	RT 413 527-0818	(not reporting)						
Easton t (20)	TM 617 238-7951	(not reporting)						
Essex t (3)	TM 508 768-7111	(not reporting)						
Everett (36)	MC 617 389-2100	John R McCarthy	. . . .	John F Hanlon	. . . .	Peter Colameta	James Bonnell	Daniel F Risteen
Fairhaven t (16)	RT 508 992-5416	Ruth Galary	Jeffrey Osuch	Elaine Rocha	Andrew Martin	David Crowley Sr	Stephen Foster Jr	Alfred Raphael
Fall River (93)	MC 508 324-2000	(not reporting)						
Falmouth t (28)	RT 508 548-7611	Nathan Ellis	Peter F Boyer	Carol Martin	. . . .	George Packish	Gene Kulander	William B Owen
Fitchburg (41)	MC 508 345-9550	(not reporting)						
Foxborough t (15)	TM 508 543-1200	James W Evans Jr	Andrew A Gala Jr	Arlene M Crimmins	Todd K Hassett	Hobart H Boswell	Edward T O'Leary	Robert Federico
Framingham t (65)	RT 508 620-4847	(not reporting)						
Franklin t (22)	CM 508 520-4949	(not reporting)						
Freetown t (9)	TM 508 644-2201	(not reporting)						
Gardner (20)	MC 617 632-4350	(not reporting)						
Georgetown t (6)	TM 508 352-5755	(not reporting)						
Gloucester (29)	MC 508 281-9700	(not reporting)						
Grafton t (13)	TM 508 839-5335	(not reporting)						
Granby t (6)	TM 413 467-7177	Bryan Hauschild	Robert Glesmann	Patricia Masiuk	. . . .	David Seiffert	Louis Barry	. . . .
Great Barrington t (8)	MC 413 528-1619	David A Smith Jr	Joseph A Kellogg	Nancy A Crossley	Lauren Sartori	M Fitzpatrick	William Walsh	Donald Chester
Greenfield t (19)	RT 413 774-7441	Peter Ruggeri	Norman Thidemann	Maurine Winseck	Paul Mourzecki	James Mac Kenzie	David McCarthy	John Bean
Groton t (8)	TM 508 448-9818	(not reporting)						
Groveland t (5)	TM 617 372-6861	(not reporting)						
Hadley t (4)	TM 413 586-3354	(not reporting)						
Halifax t (7)	TM 617 293-5761	John N Mulready	. . . .	Ann A Belcher	Marg Fitzgerald	Kenneth P Calvin	Michael Manoogian	Ralph Hayward Jr
Hamilton t (7)	TM 508 468-4455	(not reporting)						
Hampden t (5)	TM 413 566-3713	(not reporting)						
Hanover t (12)	TM 617 826-2261	(not reporting)						
Hanson t (9)	TM 617 293-2131	(not reporting)						
Harvard t (12)	TM 508 456-3995	Virginia Thurston	John Petrin	Nancy Reifenstein	Kent Finkle	Steve Perry	Joseph Picciotti	James Smith
Harwich t (10)	TM 508 430-7513	. . . .	Wayne C Melville	Anita Doucette	M Gallagher	Robert A Peterson	William Greenwood	. . . .
Hatfield t (3)	TM 413 247-9200	(not reporting)						
Haverhill (51)	MC 508 374-2300	(not reporting)						
Hingham t (20)	TM 617 749-1570	Edna S English	Charles Cristello	Thomas P Hall	Allan J Masison	Richard K Wehter	J Ingo Borowski	Brian J Sullivan
Holbrook t (11)	RT 617 767-4312	(not reporting)						
Holden t (15)	CM 508 829-0225	Robert V Johnson	Brian J Bullock	Kathleen Peterson	Marion E Hewson	Edward R Oberg	Charles R Hicks	Alan R Berg
Holliston t (13)	TM 508 429-0608	Carol S Dooling	Paul D Lebeau	Nancy L Norris	Ferdinand Scerra	Raymond Moloney	William George	. . . .
Holyoke (44)	MC 413 534-2176	William Hamilton	. . . .	Susan Egan	Brian Smith	James Pappadellis	Robert Warner	William Fuqua
Hopedale t (6)	TM 508 634-2203	(not reporting)						
Hopkinton t (9)	TM 508 435-2139	John P Hinckley	Theodore D Kozak	. . . .	Stephen Roomian	R Mac Millan	William McRobert	. . . .
Hudson t (17)	TM 508 562-9963	(not reporting)						
Hull t (10)	TM 617 925-2000	James M Tobin	. . . .	Janet Bennett	. . . .	James N Russo	Donald F Brooker	Edward D Parent
Ipswich t (12)	TM 508 356-4848	(not reporting)						
Kingston t (9)	TM 617 585-0500	Ronald Maribett	Doris Haight	Mary Lou Murzyn	Benjamin Husted	Jon Alberghini	Michael DeCapua	Carl Atwood
Lakeville t (8)	TM 617 947-3400	(not reporting)						
Lancaster t (7)	TM 508 365-3326	(not reporting)						
Lanesborough t (3)	TM 413 442-1167	(not reporting)						
Lawrence (70)	MC 508 794-5803	Leonard J Degnan	John McCarthy	James McGravey	Gene R Triplett	Richard Shafer	Joseph St Germain	Raymond DiFore
Lee t (6)	RT 413 243-2100	Martin Deely	Frank Abbondanzio	Patricia Carlino	. . . .	. . . .	Edward Finnegan	Peter Scolford
Leicester t (10)	TM 508 892-8210	(not reporting)						
Lenox t (5)	TM 413 637-0144	W S Pignatelli	John P Musante	Lorita Bosworth	John P Musante	John Stringer	David Berkel	Michael Racicot
Leominster (38)	MC 617 537-6311	(not reporting)						
Lexington t (29)	CM 617 861-2776	. . . .	Richard J White	Bernice H Fallick	John J Ryan	John D Bergeron	. . . .	Richard E Spiers
Lincoln Center t (8)	TM 617 259-8850	R L Denormandie	David W Ramsay	Nancy Zuelke	Betty Lang	D James Arena	D James Arena	Vincent Deamicis
Littleton t (7)	TM 508 952-2311	Paul F Glavey	Mark W Haddad	Mary Crory	. . . .	Alex McCurdy	Thomas W Odea Jr	Eric K Durling
Longmeadow t (15)	TM 413 567-5433	Gerald A Nolet	Patricia A Vinche	Louise W Lines	Paul J Pasterczyk	Stephen N Foley	Richard A Marches	Douglas W Barron
Lowell (103)	CM 508 970-4000	(not reporting)						
Ludlow t (19)	RT 413 589-7511	(not reporting)						
Lunenburg t (9)	TM 508 582-6853	(not reporting)						
Lynn (81)	MC 617 598-4000	(not reporting)						
Lynnfield t (11)	CM 617 334-3180	(not reporting)						
Malden (54)	MC 617 324-6600	(not reporting)						
Manchester t (5)	TM 617 526-1712	(not reporting)						
Manchester-by-the-Sea t (5)	MC 508 526-1712	(not reporting)						
Mansfield t (17)	CM 508 261-7370	Joseph Pasquale	William Williams	. . . .	L Gallagher	Edward Sliney	Arthur O'Neill	Robert Swanson

City, 1990 population figures (000 omitted), form of government	Municipal phone number	Mayor	Appointed administrator	City clerk	Finance officer	Fire chief	Police chief	Public works director
MASSACHUSETTS (270) continued								
Marblehead t (20)	TM 617 631-4056	Thomas McNulty	. . . .	Betty J Brown	George B Snow	Charles Maurais	John B Palmer	. . . .
Marion t (4)	TM 508 748-3500	(not reporting)						
Marlborough (32)	MC 508 460-3700	(not reporting)						
Marshfield t (22)	TM 617 837-5141	(not reporting)						
Mashpee t (8)	MC 508 539-1408	(not reporting)						
Mattapoisett t (6)	TM 508 758-4100	John N Decosta	Carol J Adams	Lois K Ennis	Joseph R Bolton	Ronald E Scott	James F Moran	Wesley N Bowman
Maynard t (10)	TM 508 897-1001	Frank Ignachuck	Michael Gianotis	Judith Peterson	Harry Gannon	Ronald Cassidy	Arner S Tibbetts	Walter Sokolowski
Medfield t (11)	TM 508 359-8505	(not reporting)						
Medford (57)	CM 617 396-5500	(not reporting)						
Medway t (10)	TM 508 533-2013	(not reporting)						
Melrose (28)	MC 617 665-4500	Richard D Lyons	. . . .	Margaret O'Connell	P Dellorusso	Charles Sheridan	Frank Fiandaca	Joseph Mac Kay
Mendon t (4)	TM 508 473-2312	Kevin G Rudden	. . . .	Jean M Bavosi	. . . .	Gioachino DeLuca	Dennis P Grady	Thomas P Guerra
Merrimac t (5)	TM 617 346-8862	(not reporting)						
Methuen t (40)	CM 617 794-3210	. . . .	Donald Desantis	James Maloney	Thomas Kelly	James Clarke	B Mac Dougall	Kenneth Martin
Middleborough t (18)	TM 617 947-0928	Robert Desrosiers	John F Healey	. . . .	Jack Kulian	Carl Reed Sr	William E Warner	Donald Boucher
Middleton t (5)	TM 508 777-3617	Nancy M Jones	Ira S Singer	Sarah B George	. . . .	Henry Michalski	Robert T Peachey	Dennis Roy
Milford t (25)	RT 508 634-2303	D Bartolomeis	Phyllis A Ahearn	Joseph F Arcudi	Barbara A Menna	John A Taddei	Vincent W Liberto	. . . .
Millbury t (12)	TM 508 865-4710	Jude T Cristo	. . . .	Frances Gauthier	. . . .	Philip J Day Jr	Richard Handfield	Joseph Chase
Millis t (8)	TM 508 376-2634	Gregg Guinta	Charles Aspinwall	Roma Curran	. . . .	Robert Volpicelli	Albert Baima	Charles Aspinwall
Milton t (26)	RT 617 698-0100	(not reporting)						
Monson t (8)	TM 413 267-4100	(not reporting)						
Montague t (8)	RT 413 863-4511	Hugh Campbell	Deborah Radway	John Zywna	C Martin	. . . .	Patrick O Bryan	Edward Mleczko Jr
Nahant t (4)	TM 617 581-0088	(not reporting)						
Nantucket t (6)	TM 508 228-7255	Wayne F Holmes	Suzanne K Kennedy	Rebecca J Lohmann	. . . .	Bruce L Watts	Randolph P Norris	Jeffrey Willett
Natick t (31)	RT 508 651-7230	Mel Willens	Fred C Conley	Jane M Hladick	. . . .	Richard Fredette	Dennis R Mannix	Charles Sisitsky
Needham t (28)	RT 617 455-7530	John Marr	Carl Valente	Theodora Eaton	. . . .	Robert DiPoli	William Slowe	Richard Merson
New Bedford (100)	MC 617 999-2931	Rosemary Tierney	Jeanne Mathieu	Janice Davidian	Daniel Patten	Henry Openshaw	Richard Benoit	Lawrence Worden
Newbury t (6)	TM 508 465-9241	(not reporting)						
Newburyport (16)	MC 508 465-4413	(not reporting)						
Newton (83)	MC 617 552-7000	Theodore D Mann	Richard Kelliher	Edward G English	. . . .	Joseph S Daniele	Frank R Gorgone	James L Hickey
Norfolk t (9)	TM 617 528-1408	(not reporting)						
North Adams (17)	MC 413 663-6685	John Barrett	Fred Holmes	Mary Ann Abuisi	. . . .	William Garner	Rodney Prevey	John J Notsley
North Andover t (23)	TM 508 682-6483	Martha J Larson	James P Gordon	Daniel Long	. . . .	William V Dolan	Richard M Stanley	George D Perna
North Attleborough t (25)	RT 508 699-0107	Lynn Gaulin	Sally Melo	Carol Paquette	. . . .	Robert Coleman	John Coyle	Raymond Payson
North Brookfield t (5)	TM 508 867-0200	Richard P Chabot	Melanie A Jenkins	Sheila A Buzzell	Scott Usher	James Black	Nelson Barrett	Raymond Blake
North Reading t (12)	MC 508 664-6010	(not reporting)						
Northampton (29)	MC 413 586-6950	Mary L Ford	. . . .	Christine Skorups	Thomas Hedderick	Lawrence J Jones	Daniel Labato	Samuel Brindis
Northborough t (12)	TM 508 393-5040	William Henries	Charles Kellner	Adele Beatty	Charles Kellner	Brian Duggan	Kenneth Hutchins	John Schunder
Northbridge t (13)	CM 617 234-2095	(not reporting)						
Norton t (14)	TM 508 285-0200	(not reporting)						
Norwell t (9)	TM 617 659-8000	(not reporting)						
Norwood t (29)	CM 617 762-1240	(not reporting)						
Orange t (7)	TM 508 544-2254	(not reporting)						
Orleans t (6)	TM 508 255-0900	(not reporting)						
Oxford t (13)	TM 508 987-6030	Thomas F Spooner	Dennis A Power	F Pansy Kennedy	Donald F Kaminski	Michael Plante	James B Triplett	John A Phillips
Palmer t (12)	TM 413 283-2603	Mark Mac Dougall	Beverly A Lund	Patricia Donovan	Carol Sugrue	. . . .	Howard Case	Phillip Sampson
Paxton t (4)	TM 508 753-2803	(not reporting)						
Peabody (47)	MC 508 532-3000	. . . .	. . . .	Natalie Maga	Patricia Schaffer	Joseph Russell	Robert Champagne	John Seites
Pembroke t (15)	TM 617 293-3844	(not reporting)						
Pepperell t (10)	TM 508 433-6359	(not reporting)						
Pittsfield (49)	MC 413 499-9340	Edward M Reilly	. . . .	. . . .	David Kiley	James W Tobin	Gerald M Lee	William Forestell
Plainville t (7)	TM 508 695-3142	Robert Fennessy	Joseph Fernandes	Kathleen Sandland	Vera Mac Donald	Robert Skinner	Edgar Peavey	Ron Fredrickson
Plymouth t (46)	RT 508 747-1620	William F Nolan	William R Griffin	Laurence Pizer	Michael Daley	Thomas Fugazzi	Robert Pomeroy	Leighton F Peck
Provincetown t (4)	CM 617 487-7000	(not reporting)						
Quincy (85)	MC 617 376-1000	James A Sheets	. . . .	Joseph P Shea	Robert E Foy	Thomas F Gorman	Francis E Mullen	David A Colton
Randolph t (30)	RT 617 963-3212	(not reporting)						
Raynham t (10)	TM 508 824-2700	Marie A Smith	Randall A Buckner	Helen B Lounsbury	Belcher Stanley	George Andrews	Peter King	J Michael Silvia
Reading t (23)	CM 617 942-9001	George Hines	P Hechenbleikner	Cathy Quimby	Elizabeth Klepeis	Donald Wood	Edward Marchand	Edward McIntire
Rehoboth t (9)	TM 508 252-3758	Arthur F Tobin	. . . .	Susan Withers	. . . .	Alan C Bliss	George A Warish	. . . .
Revere (43)	MC 617 284-3600	(not reporting)						
Rochester t (4)	TM 508 763-3871	Lorraine R Hawkes	Shirley Ferreira	Naida L Parker	. . . .	Joseph Clapp	Walter V Denham	. . . .
Rockland t (16)	TM 617 871-1874	(not reporting)						
Rockport t (7)	TM 508 546-6894	Pricilla Garlick	Doris Haris	Fred Frithsen	Roxanne Terri	Russell Anderson	Thomas O'Maley	Donald Atkinson
Rowley t (4)	TM 508 948-2372	David C Petersen	Lawrence Cameron	Jeanne P Grover	Susan W Bailey	Scott McKenzie	Kevin Barry	A Scott Leavitt
Rutland t (5)	TM 508 886-4103	(not reporting)						
Salem (38)	MC 508 745-9595	Neil J Harrington	David Shea	D Burkinshaw	. . . .	Robert Turner	Robert St Pierre	Charles Quigley
Salisbury t (7)	CM 508 462-8232	Barbara S Thomas	Michael W Basque	Wilma Mahoney	. . . .	Robert Cook	Lawrence Streeter	David Keithley
Sandwich t (15)	TM 508 888-4910	Edward Condon	George Dunham	Barbara Walling	Nancy Laffoon	Dennis Newman	Robert Whearty	Patrick Ellis
Saugus t (26)	RT 508 231-4126	Janette Fasano	Edward J Collins	Marcia R Wallace	Richard Cardillo	Walter Newbury	Cornelius Meehan	Joseph Attubato
Scituate t (17)	TM 617 545-6700	(not reporting)						
Seekonk t (13)	RT 508 336-7400	Robert McLintock	Robert Canevazzi	Katherine Tameo	Rudolph Petorelli	David Viera	Dana Beal	Gary Girouard
Sharon t (16)	TM 617 784-6909	Roni Thaler	Benjamin E Puritz	Shirley Davenport	. . . .	James Polito	Joseph Bernstein	John Sulik
Sheffield t (3)	CM 413 229-7000	John James	Robert A Weitz	Natalie Funk	Robert A Weitz	John Ullrich	James McGarry	Ronald Bassett
Sherborn t (4)	TM 508 651-7850	Robert Delaney	Susan Adler	Lucy S Almasian	Kenneth S Crowell	Francis Heffron	Gary B Hendron	Michael Pakstis
Shirley t (6)	TM 508 425-4331	Peter L Fohlin	. . . .	Sylvia Shipton	Eric Cappucci	Alphee Levesque	Paul Thibodeau	Albert Chevrette
Shrewsbury t (24)	CM 508 842-7471	(not reporting)						
Somerset t (18)	TM 508 676-1004	Kenneth S Mello	Arthur Marchand	Patricia Hart	. . . .	Stephen Rivard	James Smith	. . . .
Somerville (76)	MC 617 625-6600	(not reporting)						
South Hadley t (17)	RT 413 538-5017	Linda Young	Normand Cloutier	J Barthelette	Wayne Boulais	. . . .	William Schenker	G Kereakoglow
Southampton t (4)	TM 413 527-4741	(not reporting)						
Southborough t (7)	TM 508 485-0710	Davis O Cowles	Janice C Conlin	Paul J Berry	Dorothy Phaneuf	Peter Phaneuf	William Colleary	John W Boland
Southbridge t (18)	CM 508 764-5405	(not reporting)						
Southwick t (8)	TM 413 569-5995	John M Sinico	Karl J Stinehart	John R Zanolli	. . . .	Donald Morris	Henry LaBombard	Arthur Chevalier
Spencer t (12)	TM 508 885-7500	Robert W Gagne	. . . .	Jean M Ulhall	Norman Pelletier	Walter B Johnson	Thomas P Shamshak	. . . .
Springfield (157)	MC 413 787-6100	(not reporting)						
Sterling t (5)	TM 508 422-8111	(not reporting)						
Stoneham t (22)	TM 617 279-2600	Mark Vaughan	Jeffrey D Nutting	Annamae Arsenault	Ronald Florino	W G McLaughlin	Eugene M Passaro	. . . .
Stoughton t (27)	CM 617 341-1300	(not reporting)						
Stow t (5)	TM 508 897-4515	Leonard H Golder	William J Wrigley	Ann L Allison	. . . .	Douglas V Trefry	Charles C Mayo	Bruce E Fletcher
Sturbridge t (8)	TM 508 347-2500	Charles Blanchard	Patricia Whalen	Susan Blair	George Samia	Leonard Senecal	Kevin Fitzgibbons	Gregory Valiton
Sudbury t (14)	TM 508 443-8891	(not reporting)						
Sunderland t (3)	TM 413 665-4414	Bruce Bennett	Wendy Foxmyn	Rosemary O'Hagan	Gail Weston	Alec Kulessa	Kenneth Heim	Frank Thomas
Sutton t (7)	CM 508 865-5078	Mary K Connor	Dexter P Blois	Ethel M O'Day	Dexter P Blois	John Peterson	John F Annis	Raymond Smith

Directory 1/9
continued

MUNICIPAL OFFICIALS
IN U.S. CITIES OVER 2,500

City, 1990 population figures (000 omitted), form of government	Municipal phone number	Mayor	Appointed administrator	City clerk	Finance officer	Fire chief	Police chief	Public works director
MASSACHUSETTS (270) continued								
Swampscott t (14)	RT 617 596-8850	(not reporting)						
Swansea t (15)	TM 508 678-2981	(not reporting)						
Taunton (50)	MC 508 821-1057	(not reporting)						
Templeton t (6)	TM 508 939-8801	Gladys I Salame	Carol A Skelton	Dana G Putnam	Kevin Flynn	Richard Paine	John Reardon	Richard Kirby
Tewksbury t (27)	TM 617 851-4311	Thomas G Conlon	David G Cressman	Elizabeth Carey	David G Cressman	Thomas Ryan	John Mackey	William Burris
Tisbury t (3)	TM 508 696-4200	(not reporting)						
Topsfield t (6)	TM 617 887-8571	(not reporting)						
Townsend t (8)	TM 508 597-2837	Frederick Darling	Timothy Bragen	M McEachern	. . . .	Donald Hurme	William May	William Felton
Truro t (2)	CM 508 349-3635	(not reporting)						
Tyngsborough t (9)	TM 508 649-7441	John S O'Gorman	Robert P Griffin	. . . .	. . . .	Timothy Madden	Charles Chronopou	Ronald Corcoran
Upton t (5)	TM 617 529-6901	(not reporting)						
Uxbridge t (10)	TM 617 278-2041	(not reporting)						
Wakefield t (25)	TM 617 246-6390	Wayne M Tarr	Thomas P Butler	V Zingarelli	Matthew J Burns	Peter Hubbard	Stephen Doherty	Donald N Onussit
Walpole t (20)	RT 508 660-7294	Joanne Damish	James Merriam	Louis Hoegler	Cynthia Moore	Leonard Anderson	Joseph Betro	Martin Feeney
Waltham (58)	MC 617 893-4040	William F Stanley	. . . .	Peter Koutoujian	Dennis Quinn	Thomas Keough	Stephen Unsworth	John F Snedeker
Ware t (10)	TM 413 967-5289	(not reporting)						
Wareham t (19)	CM 508 291-3100	(not reporting)						
Warren t (4)	TM 413 436-5701	Brian B Baldwin	Jean McCaughey	Beverly B Russell	Milton O Fountain	James R Dolan	Ronald J Syriac	John O'Neill Jr
Watertown (33)	CM 617 972-6465	(not reporting)						
Wayland t (12)	TM 508 358-7701	(not reporting)						
Webster t (16)	TM 617 943-0033	(not reporting)						
Wellesley t (27)	RT 617 431-1019	(not reporting)						
Wellfleet t (2)	TM 508 349-3707	Carolina Kiggins	Julia Enroth	Dawn Rickman	Patricia Eagar	Roger Henson	Richard Rosenthal	. . . .
Wenham t (4)	TM 508 468-5522	William L Shailor	Lucille G Lynch	Frances Y Moscovi	Nancy A Brown	Donald J Killam	Peter L Carnes	Peter J Burnham
West Boylston t (7)	TM 617 835-6091	(not reporting)						
West Bridgewater t (6)	TM 508 588-4820	Judith A Kinney	Elizabeth Faricy	Marion L Leonard	Marilyn Gordon	Leonard T Hunt	Howard Anderson	Donald Newman
West Brookfield t (4)	TM 508 867-6874	Edward Sauer	W Frangiamore	Nancy Korsec	. . . .	Peter Wrobel	John Zabek	Dan Santos
West Newbury t (3)	TM 508 363-5487	R Berkenbush	Marjorie Peterson	Marjorie Peterson	Tracy Blais	Raymond Dower	Jonathon Dennis	. . . .
West Springfield t (28)	RT 413 781-7550	(not reporting)						
Westborough t (14)	TM 508 366-7100	. . . .	Lee Bourgoin	Elizabeth Amoroso	Leah Talbot	James Parker Jr	Harry Shepherd	John Walden
Westfield (38)	MC 413 568-9181	(not reporting)						
Westford t (16)	CM 617 692-5500	John E Wrobel Jr	Robert J Halpin	Elaine V McKenna	Frank Messer	George Rogers	Joseph L Connell	Richard Barrett
Westminster t (6)	TM 508 874-2184	(not reporting)						
Weston t (10)	TM 617 893-7320	Ann G Leibowitz	J Ward Carter	M Elizabeth Nolan	. . . .	John E Thorburn	James J McShane	. . . .
Westport t (14)	TM 508 636-1003	(not reporting)						
Westwood t (13)	TM 617 326-6450	Michael Beaumont	Michael Jaillet	Edith McCracken	Susan Gagner	John Sheehy	Robert Haas	J Timothy Walsh
Weymouth t (54)	RT 617 335-2000	Joseph Piper	Russell J Connor	Franklin Fryer	Donald R Jensen	David M Madden	Thomas J Higgins	Frank Lagroterria
Whitman t (13)	TM 617 447-2561	(not reporting)						
Wilbraham t (13)	TM 413 596-8111	Kevin J Moriarty	William J Fogarty	Mary Iria	Joanne Degray	Daniel P Merritt	Allen M Stratton	Edmond Miga
Williamstown t (8)	CM 413 458-3500	(not reporting)						
Wilmington t (18)	TM 508 658-3311	Chester A Bruce	Michael A Caira	Kathleen Scanlon	Joseph R Peters	Daniel R Stewart	Bobby N Stewart	Robert P Palmer
Winchendon t (9)	TM 508 297-0085	R Clifford Lupien	Richard S Lak	Lois A Regan	Eleanor Black	Richard Williams	Steven Thompson	Michael P Murphy
Winchester t (20)	RT 617 721-7133	Peter T Van Aken	W Chadwick Maurer	Carolyn Ward	. . . .	Charles McNutt	Joseph Perritano	Anthony Celli
Winthrop t (18)	RT 617 846-1077	(not reporting)						
Woburn (36)	MC 617 932-4400	(not reporting)						
Worcester (170)	CM 508 799-1030	(not reporting)						
Wrentham t (9)	TM 508 384-5400	(not reporting)						
Yarmouth t (21)	TM 508 398-2231	Herb Schnitzer	Robt C Lawton Jr	George Barabe	. . . .	David Akin	Robert Chapman	George Allaire
MICHIGAN (270)								
Adrian (22)	CM 517 263-2161	Joseph Wagley	Alden Smith	Marsha Rowley	Larry Opelt	Larry Liedel	David Emerson	Keith Richard
Albion (10)	CM 517 629-5535	Lois McClure	Ralph A Lange	. . . .	James P Bonamy	. . . .	Harold L Hoaglin	William L Rieger
Algonac (5)	CM 313 794-9361	Raymond J Martin	Marilyn S Manning	Mary L Jaros	Marilyn S Manning	Charles Johnson	. . . .	Paul Jarmolowicz
Allegan (5)	CM 616 673-5511	David A Ferber	Aaron Anthony	Aaron Anthony	. . . .	Kevin Blanchard	Edward Cone	Dale Commans
Allen Park (31)	MC 313 928-1400	Gerald N Richards	Richard A Huebler	Bernice Weiss	Daniel P Cassidy	James Cabadas	Leo J Lanctot	Ronald Schmidt
Alma (9)	CM 517 463-8336	Nancy Gallagher	Douglas B Thomas	William Stuckey	Phillip Moore	George Blyton	Robert Lombardi	Ken Feldt
Almont v (2)	CM 313 798-8528	Donald Barker	David M Murphy	Sally McCrea	. . . .	. . . .	Leonard Everitt	Fred Treutle
Alpena (11)	CM 517 354-4158	William LaHaie	Peter Parker	Alan Bakalarski	Alan Bakalarski	. . . .	Roger Anderson	David Nordquist
Ann Arbor (110)	CM 313 994-2700	Elizabeth Brater	Alfred Gatta	W Northcross	Allen Moore	George Markus	Douglas Smith	William Wheeler
Auburn (2)	MC 517 662-6721	John Cimbalik	Jeffery B Lawson	Lucy Wiesenauer	Jeffery B Lawson	Russ Pickelman	James Klann	Roye Burr
Auburn Hills (17)	CM 313 370-9400	(not reporting)						
Bad Axe (3)	CM 517 269-7681	Fred Kalis	Christopher Olson	Kay Goebel	Kay Goebel	David Rapson	Gary Bucholtz	Louis Ligrow
Bangor (2)	CM 616 427-8506	David Rigozzi	Duane Goss	Wanda Rissley	Robert Insidioso	Steve Lowder	. . . .	Roy Hill
Battle Creek (54)	CM 616 966-3300	Thomas Klossa	Rance Leaders	Deborah Owens	Merrill Stanley	Charles Owens	Thomas Pope	Ken Tsuchiyama
Bay City (39)	CM 517 894-8146	(not reporting)						
Belding (6)	CM 616 794-1900	David E Greene	Alan Hartley	Paul J Brake	. . . .	. . . .	D Roger Mason	Gerald Rawlings
Belleville (3)	CM 313 697-9323	Glenn Silvenis	Jeffrey Przygocki	Agnes Frisch	. . . .	Jack Loria	. . . .	. . . .
Benton Harbor (13)	CM 616 927-8400	Emma Hull	Beverly A Brewer	Margaret Adams	Audrey Brodzinski	David Lincoln	David L Walker	Roland Klockow
Berkley (17)	CM 313 546-2410	Jerold Durst	Calvin Teague	Leona Garrett	Michael P Tyler	. . . .	William Rechlin	Richard Shepler
Bessemer (2)	CM 906 663-4311	Joseph Bonovetz	Bruce Carlson	Bruce Carlson	Isabelle Haapoja	. . . .	. . . .	Bruce Carlson
Beverly Hills v (11)	CM 313 646-6404	Andrew Wong	Georg Majoros	Patrick Sullivan	Robert Wisowaty	. . . .	Hugh Cox	. . . .
Big Rapids (13)	CM 616 592-4000	Larry Cox	Steve Stilwell	Roberta R Cline	. . . .	. . . .	Kevin Courtney	Timothy Vogel
Birmingham (20)	CM 313 644-1800	(not reporting)						
Blissfield v (3)	MC 517 486-4347	(not reporting)						
Bloomfield Hills (4)	CM 313 644-1520	. . . .	Charles H Harmon	Charles H Harmon	. . . .	. . . .	David R Piche	. . . .
Boyne City (3)	CM 616 582-6597	Keith Fitzpatrick	W R Frykberg	Sue Hobbs	Carolyn Olsen	Nord Schroeder	Randolph Howard	. . . .
Brighton (6)	CM 313 227-1911	James A Winchel	Dana W Foster	Theresa Swiecicki	David C Gajda	Richard Shinske	Michael Kinaschuk	David C Blackmar
Bronson (2)	CM 517 369-7334	Len Kolcz	Gerald Hollister	Karen Smith	. . . .	Charles Somerlott	Richard Stout	Carl Ransbottom
Brown City (1)	CM 313 346-2325	Virginia Muxlow	Thomas F McCoy	Toni Loutzenhiser	. . . .	Rodger Wood	Fred Maurer	Gary Gorsline
Buchanan (5)	CM 616 695-3844	Deborah Seager	Gregory Buckley	Janet Colip	. . . .	Warren Weaver	Donald Yerrick	Eli Bromley
Buena Vista tp (11)	CM 517 754-6536	(not reporting)						
Burton (28)	MC 313 743-1500	(not reporting)						
Cadillac (10)	CM 616 775-0181	Ronald Blanchard	Robert A Hamilton	Janice Nelson	Dale Walker	. . . .	Robert Denslow	Robert Johnson
Capac v (2)	MC 313 395-4355	(not reporting)						
Carleton v (3)	MC 313 654-6255	(not reporting)						
Caro v (4)	MC 517 673-7671	Wesley Frederick	W Donald Duggar	Charles Spaulding	W Donald Duggar	David Mattlin	Ronald Iseler	W Donald Duggar
Caspian (1)	CM 906 265-2514	Joe Sabol	Rosalie King	. . . .	. . . .	Archie Carlotto	. . . .	. . . .
Cassopolis v (2)	CM 616 445-8648	(not reporting)						
Cedar Springs (3)	CM 616 696-1330	John Teusink	Frank Walsh	Amber Bailey	Kenneth Bailey	Mark Strpko	Marv Weinrich	Gerald Hall
Center Line (9)	CM 313 757-6800	Mary Ann Zielinsk	Ronald Reiterman	Ronald Reiterman	. . . .	. . . .	Gerald M Solai	John J Theisen
Charlevoix (3)	CM 616 547-3260	David Novotny	Michael Wiesner	Jo Anne Patrick	Richard Brandi	Doug Carver	Dennis Halverson	. . . .
Charlotte (8)	CM 517 543-1289	Kathleen Wright	Howard Penrod	Irene Jewett	. . . .	Kevin Fullerton	Tom Potter	James Marry
Cheboygan (5)	CM 616 627-5280	Louis LeBlanc	Scott McNeil	Leona Kwiatkowski	Scott McNeil	Al Bonsecours	Kurt Jones	Scott McNeil

Directory 1/9 continued **MUNICIPAL OFFICIALS IN U.S. CITIES OVER 2,500**

City, 1990 population figures (000 omitted), form of government		Municipal phone number	Mayor	Appointed administrator	City clerk	Finance officer	Fire chief	Police chief	Public works director
MICHIGAN (270) continued									
Chelsea v (4)	MC	313 475-1771	Richard Steele	Jack Myers	Suzanne Morrison	. . . .	. . . .	. . . .	David Bulson
Chesaning v (3)	CM	517 845-3800	William D Adams	Daniel Stasa	Sandra Richardson	. . . .	Jake Fowler	Howard Ormes	. . . .
Clare (3)	CM	517 386-7541	Allen Demarest	Vincent Pastue	Patty Lemm	Vincent Pastue	Robert Bonham	Tony Smolinski	Robert Bonham
Clawson (14)	CM	313 435-4500	Mary F Airriess	D Wayne O'Neal	Carol Kanirie	John Modzinski	Kraig Bouse	Micheal Walsh	Leslie Tinson
Clio (3)	CM	313 686-5850	(not reporting)						
Coldwater (10)	CM	517 279-9501	Louise Wallace	Wiliam Stewart	Gerald Boguth	. . . .	James Thomas	Gary Chester	Thomas Matson
Constantine v (2)	CM	616 435-2085	Robert Coryn	W R Commenator	Hesket Al Kharusy	. . . .	. . . .	Robert Brewer	. . . .
Coopersville (3)	CM	616 837-9731	(not reporting)						
Corunna (3)	MC	517 743-4411	Homer Bennett	Charles Zampich	Lisa Hitchcock	. . . .	David Schaub	Herb Jenkins	Tom Svrcek
Croswell (2)	MC	313 679-2299	Frank Tonge	Jimmie Hanes	April Johnston	Jimmie Hanes	Tom Dickensheets	Jeff Dawson	Harley Wright
Crystal Falls (2)	CM	906 875-6647	Lawrence Hegstrom	Walter E Hagglund	Barbara A Benda	Barbara A Benda	John W Ahola	Jackie L Bicigo	Dennis B Fabrri
Davison (6)	CM	313 653-2191	Dennis D Ryan	Jack N Abernathy	Rosemary Simpson	. . . .	Leland Keeney	Robert D Johnson	Keith Skellenger
De Witt (4)	MC	517 669-2441	Gerald M Nester	Michael J Czymbor	Margie N Lotre	. . . .	Brent Newman	Wendell D Myers	Michael J Czymbor
Dearborn (89)	MC	313 943-2000	(not reporting)						
Dearborn Heights (61)	MC	313 277-7219	Lyle C Van Houten	Brian Hitsky	Helene Sheridan	Donald Barrow	Errol Lewis	Sam DiPrima	John Preston
Delta Charter tp (26)	CM	517 323-8590	Joseph Drolett	Richard Watkins	Janice Vedder	Lawrence Kallio	Victor Hilbert	Richard Wahl	. . . .
Detroit (1028)	MC	313 224-3270	Coleman A Young	Charlie Williams	James H Bradley	Bella I Marshall	Melvin Jefferson	Stanley Knox	Conley Abrams
Dexter v (..)	CM	313 426-8303	Philip Arbour	Dennis J White	Donna Fisher	. . . .	Fred Schmidt	. . . .	Thomas Desmet
Dowagiac (6)	CM	616 782-2195	James Burke	James Palenick	James Snow	David Pilot	Wayne Mattix	Gary Dumeney	Melvin Lyons
Dundee v (3)	CM	313 529-3430	John Williams	Patrick H Burtch	Mary Miller	. . . .	Tom Harwick	. . . .	Dale Goetz
Durand (4)	CM	517 288-3113	Jack Davis	Lynn Markland	Amy Roddy	. . . .	Wayne McGuire	Robert Eldridge	Kevin McDonald
East Grand Rapids (11)	CM	616 949-2110	(not reporting)						
East Lansing (51)	CM	517 337-1731	Liz Schweitzer	Thomas Dority	Susan Donnell	Gary Murphy	Jack Gregg	Lawton Connelly	Peter Eberz
East Tawas (3)	CM	517 362-6161	Robert C Bolen	Ronald J Leslie	Blinda A Baker	. . . .	William Deckett	Dennis Frank	Thomas Lixey
Eastpointe (35)	CM	313 445-5016	Harvey M Curley	Wes McAllister	Wes McAllister	Daniel S Foecking	Ronald J Engle	Lewis L Hunt	Ernest Scheeres
Eaton Rapids (5)	MC	517 663-8118	Larry J Holley	Fabian L Knizacky	Marietta White	. . . .	Richard F Freer	Michael C Seeley	Howard D Hillard
Ecorse (12)	MC	313 386-2344	(not reporting)						
Elk Rapids v (2)	MC	616 264-9274	Joseph Yuchasz	Marc Bergman	Elaine Glowicki	. . . .	. . . .	Jack Blesma	Robert Loper
Escanaba (14)	CM	906 786-9402	Charles Vader	Rosalind Allis	Robert Richards	Michael Dewar	. . . .	Wayne Heikkila	Allen Newman
Essexville (4)	CM	517 893-0772	Winifred Grobbel	Mary Monville	Mary Monville	Mary Monville	. . . .	Terrence Hugo	C Donald Lowe
Evart (..)	CM	616 734-2181	(not reporting)						
Farmington (10)	CM	313 474-5500	William Hartsock	Frank J Lauhoff	Patsy K Cantrell	Patsy K Cantrell	. . . .	Gary M Goss	Earl R Billing
Farmington Hills (75)	CM	313 474-6115	Nancy Bates	William Costick	Kathy Dornan	Charles Rosch	Richard Marinucci	William Dwyer	Dan Rooney
Fenton (8)	CM	313 629-2261	Patricia Lockwood	Michael Schepers	Lucille Little	. . . .	Gerald Palmer	Gerald Cattaneo	Leslie Bland
Ferndale (25)	CM	313 546-2360	Robert McGee	Jess R Soltess	Dorothy L Fuller	Jaynmarie Reddie	Gary M Lohmeier	S Joseph Sullivan	Kenneth G Bautel
Flat Rock (7)	MC	313 782-2455	Richard C Jones	. . . .	. . . .	Carolyn I Beck	Alan J Irwin	Raymond M Hoffman	Bruce Hammond
Flint (141)	MC	313 766-7346	Woodrow Stanley	David Ready	Louis Hawkins	Marc Puckett	Paul Garrison	Clydell Duncan	Fred Watts
Flushing (9)	CM	313 659-3139	John Potbury	Peter Von Drak	Nancy Parks	. . . .	Leon Noack	Fay Peek	Patrick Crighton
Fowlerville v (3)	CM	517 223-3771	(not reporting)						
Frankenmuth (4)	CM	517 652-9901	Gary C Rupprecht	Charles B Graham	Charles B Graham	. . . .	Gene Rittmueller	James R Petteys	Kenneth Knieling
Franklin v (3)	MC	313 626-9666	(not reporting)						
Fraser (14)	CM	313 293-3102	Joseph J Blanke	Frank Rubino	Frank Rubino	. . . .	Ronald Wolber	Ronald Wolber	. . . .
Fremont (4)	CM	616 924-2101	Raymond Rathbun	Chris Yonker	Michael Pohlod	Michael Pohlod	Robin Dawe	Galen Brookens	James Vedders
Garden City (32)	CM	313 525-8800	Jim A Plakas	Steven Aynes	Ronald Showalter	. . . .	Frank Felts	David Kocsis	Richard Lang Jr
Gaylord (3)	CM	517 732-2815	Ernest Grocock	Dave Siegel	Rebecca A Curtis	. . . .	. . . .	John E Jenkins	. . . .
Gibraltar (4)	MC	313 676-3900	(not reporting)						
Gladstone (5)	CM	906 428-2311	Arthur Pickard	Dale Soumis	Linda Gray	Joseph Maki	. . . .	Randall Walter	Michael Albrecht
Gladwin (..)	MC	517 426-9231	Earl Schuster	Robert McConkie	Robert McConkie	. . . .	. . . .	John Simpson	Scott Stanley
Grand Blanc (8)	MC	313 694-1118	Gregory Crane	Randall Byrne	Richard Saathoff	Richard Saathoff	James Harmes	Mark Heidel	Jack Kipp
Grand Haven (12)	CM	616 842-3210	John Nortier	Wm Cargo	Kathryne Olds	Gary Schreiber	Albert Pederico	. . . .	Mark Verberkmoes
Grand Ledge (8)	CM	517 627-2149	Lynda Trinklein	David Rich	Christine Hnatiw	Joanne Flitton	Graydon Briggs	Ronald Flitton	Harold Jolley
Grand Rapids (189)	CM	616 456-3166	John Logie	Kurt Kimball	Sandra Wright	Robert White	Al Conners	William Hegarty	Thomas Ecklund
Grandville (16)	CM	616 531-3030	James R Buck	W David Boehm	Sharon Streelman	. . . .	Harvey Veldhouse	Kenneth Madejczyk	Jerald Postema
Grayling (2)	CM	517 348-2131	Robert Golnick	Jerry Morford	. . . .	. . . .	Russell Strohpaul	Peter Stephan	Thomas Dunham
Greenville (8)	CM	616 754-5645	Jeanne Cunliffe	George Bosanic	David Moore	David Moore	. . . .	Albert Schnepp	Gary Stacey
Grosse Pointe (6)	CM	313 885-5800	Lorenzo Browning	Thomas Kressbach	. . . .	Dennis C Foran	. . . .	Bruce Kennedy	Joe Dube
Grosse Pointe Farms (10)	CM	313 885-6600	(not reporting)						
Grosse Pointe Park (13)	CM	313 822-6200	(not reporting)						
Grosse Pointe Shores v (3)	CM	313 881-6565	John Huetteman	Michael Kenyon	James T Wright	Rhonda Gaskill	. . . .	Dan Healy	Brett Smith
Grosse Pointe Woods (18)	CM	313 343-2440	Robert E Novitke	Peter A Thomas	Louise Warnke	Cliff Maison	. . . .	Jack Patterson	Thomas Whitcher
Hamtramck (18)	MC	313 876-7766	(not reporting)						
Hancock (5)	CM	906 482-2720	Mary Tuisku	Ron Howell	Karen Haischer	Ron Howell	Jim Ahola	Mike Beaudoin	. . . .
Harbor Beach (2)	MC	517 479-9491	(not reporting)						
Harbor Springs (2)	CM	616 526-2104	Jean Jardine	Fred W Geuder	Ronald B McRae	Ronald B McRae	. . . .	Dean Rye	Donald Gregory
Harper Woods (15)	CM	313 343-2505	James R Haley	James E Leidlein	Mickey D Todd	. . . .	Robert Delor	Larry W Semple	Robert Slawinski
Hart (2)	CM	616 873-4381	Kalvin Klotz	Terry Hofmeyer	Terry Hofmeyer	Terry Hofmeyer	. . . .	Daniel Leimback	Robert Green
Hastings (7)	MC	616 945-2468	(not reporting)						
Hazel Park (20)	CM	313 546-4060	(not reporting)						
Highland Park (20)	MC	313 252-0022	(not reporting)						
Hillsdale (8)	MC	517 437-7312	Nicholas L Ferro	Roy D Adams	Herbert H Hine	Tim Vagle	Larry Eichler	C Gutowski	Michael Pilarski
Holland (31)	CM	616 394-1300	Neal Berghoef	Soren Wolff	Jodi Syens	Larry Sandy	Dan Henderson	Charles Lindstrom	Tim Morawski
Holly v (6)	MC	313 634-9571	Ardath Regan	James P Murphy	Alison K Kalcec	Alison K Kalcec	. . . .	Gregory Hansmeier	Kenneth L Poff
Homer v (..)	CM	517 568-4321	(not reporting)						
Houghton (7)	CM	906 482-1700	(not reporting)						
Howell (8)	CM	517 546-3500	Paul B Streng	Michael S Herman	Nancy Roll	. . . .	Jim Reed	Michael Oyler	Terry Wilson
Hudson (3)	CM	517 448-8983	Gerald Blackburn	. . . .	Freda Rodehaver	. . . .	Richard Opsal	Albert Clements	Sheldon Peltier
Hudsonville (6)	CM	616 669-0200	Jim Holtrop	Leon Van Harn	Joan Brouwer	Bob Spaman	Pete Luyk	Richard Honholt	. . . .
Huntington Woods (6)	CM	313 541-4300	Ronald F Gillham	Alex R Allie	Janet M Wayne	Richard Lehmann	. . . .	David Danaher	William Brown
Imlay City (3)	CM	313 724-2135	Rod Dewey	Dennis W Collison	Amy Stryker	Kim Liponoga	Warner Hoeksema	L Dougherty	. . . .
Inkster (31)	CM	313 563-4232	Edward Bivens Jr	S Thomas White	Delphine G Oden	. . . .	Victor Boulanger	Terry Colwell	John Lyons
Ionia (6)	MC	616 527-4170	Dan Balice	Tom Wieczorek	Jean Barker	Robin Marhofer	. . . .	Roger Frazee	Dan Czarnecki
Iron Mountain (9)	CM	906 774-8530	Todd Colenso	James A Urbany	Lou Ann Hagen	James M Brinker	William Rocheleau	David L Lee	Gregory Brown
Iron River (2)	CM	906 265-4719	Dan Stachowicz	Gary Shimun	Peggy Benson	. . . .	. . . .	Russell Westman	Kenneth Rivard
Ironwood (7)	CM	906 933-5050	James A Lorenson	Edward J Bailey	Anita E Zak	Eero J Haukkala	. . . .	Leroy J Johnson	Timothy P Trier
Ishpeming (7)	CM	906 485-1091	James F Tobin	John D Korhonen	Corbin S Hytinen	. . . .	Daniel Gaboury	John A Healey	Richard A Burke
Ithaca (3)	CM	517 875-3200	John Thomas	Troy L Feltman	Todd M Blake	. . . .	Gordon Larry	Lee Schlappi	Neil Allen
Jackson (37)	CM	517 788-4046	Betty Granger	Gary L Dickson	Sandra Price	Phil Hones	Donald Braunreite	Robert L Johnson	. . . .
Jonesville v (..)	MC	517 849-2104	(not reporting)						
Kalamazoo (80)	CM	616 337-8052	(not reporting)						
Kalkaska v (2)	MC	616 258-9191	Edwin Chalker	Virginia Thomas	Virginia Thomas	Scott Yost	. . . .	Melvin Hill	Craig Wood
Keego Harbor (3)	CM	313 682-1930	Arthur Nance	Mike McReynolds	Katy Mann	. . . .	. . . .	William Holloway	. . . .
Kentwood (38)	MC	616 698-9610	Clyde P Hardiman	. . . .	Beverly J Bacon	Thomas P Chase	James Carr	Richard Mattice	John H Heitman
Kingsford (5)	CM	906 774-3526	(not reporting)						

Directory 1/9 continued — MUNICIPAL OFFICIALS IN U.S. CITIES OVER 2,500

City, 1990 population figures (000 omitted), form of government	Municipal phone number	Mayor	Appointed administrator	City clerk	Finance officer	Fire chief	Police chief	Public works director
MICHIGAN (270) continued								
L'Anse v (2) MC	906 524-6116	(not reporting)						
Lake Orion v (3) CM	313 693-8391	(not reporting)						
Lansing (127) MC	517 483-4141	(not reporting)						
Lapeer (8) CM	313 664-5231	Al Gelhausen	George Strand	George Strand	Paul Boucher	Louis Finsterwald	Mike Robinet	Tim O'Neill
Lathrup Village (4) CM	313 557-2600	Marvin Voight	Jeffrey Bremer	Gloria Harr Mason	....	....	David Ford	Cecil Howle
Laurium v (2) CM	906 337-1600	(not reporting)						
Leslie (2) CM	517 589-8236	(not reporting)						
Lincoln Park (42) MC	313 386-1800	Frank Sall	....	Donna Breeding	John Martin	Dave Silvani	Joseph Vagu	Donald Mandernach
Linden (..) MC	313 735-7980	Douglas Wagner	Joseph M Murray	Martha Wills	....	David McDaniel	P Van Driessche	James Letts
Litchfield (1) MC	517 542-2921	Edwin Smith	Clarence Wolfe	Marguerite Dooley	Marguerite Dooley	Richard Wade	John Michelin	Dean Wooden
Livonia (101) MC	313 421-2000	Robert D Bennett	....	Joan McCotter	....	Barney S Knorp	Lee B Grieve	Robert J Beckley
Lowell (4) CM	616 897-8457	James D Maatman	David M Pasquale	David M Pasquale	Davie M Pasquale	Frank W Martin	Barry D Emmons	Art Gall
Ludington (9) MC	616 845-6237	Jack R Scott	James H Miller	Gerry P Klaft	John A Villa	Michael McDonald	Walter Taranko	John H Ver Boam
Mackinaw City v (1) CM	616 436-5351	Paul E Desy	Joseph P Duff	Sandra M Krueger	....	Fred Thompson Jr	Wiliam J Winans	....
Madison Heights (32) CM	313 588-1200	George W Suarez	Jon R Austin	Geraldine A Case	Margaret P Birach	William A Donahue	Ronald F Pearce	Peter J Connors
Manistee (7) CM	616 723-2558	Beth Ann Adams	R Ben Bifoss	Kenneth Oleniczak	Kenneth Oleniczak	Jerry Tabaczka	Robert Hornkohl	John Garber
Manistique (3) CM	906 341-2290	(not reporting)						
Marine City (5) CM	313 765-8830	Ervin LaBuhn	....	Carol Ouellette	....	Justin McCartney	John Kelly	Richard Ames
Marlette (2) CM	517 635-7448	Kenneth L Babich	Robert A Ellisor	Robert E Kiteley	....	....	Steven H Schaub	Robert Foster
Marquette (22) CM	906 228-0435	Charles Coffey	Dale Iman	Norman Gruber	Donna Kohut	....	George Johnson	Steven Lawry
Marquette tp (..) CM	906 228-6220	Max Muelle	George T Lablonde	Kathe Thill	....	Ron E Demarse	....	....
Marshall (7) CM	616 781-5183	Joe Schroeder	Maurice Evans	Sue Kelly Hecht	Sue Kelly Hecht	....	Roger Graves	Tom Tarkiewicz
Marysville (9) CM	313 364-6613	W Deem Boldyreff	Jack M Schumacher	Sharon L Schess	Bradley S Hool	Roger M Bundy	Patrick T O'Boyle	Kenneth Foerster
Mason (7) CM	517 676-9155	Sue Ann Parsons	Patrick Price	Patrick Price	Norman Austin	James Pelton	Roger Fleming	Leslie Bruno Jr
Melvindale (11) MC	313 389-2000	(not reporting)						
Menominee (9) MC	906 863-2656	John B Baker	Anthony D Furton	Anthony D Furton	....	Robert Falkenburg	Harlan Anderson	....
Meridian tp (36) CM	517 349-1200	Alvin E House	Jeffrey H Minor	Virginia L White	....	Phillip Johnson	James Kohl	Bert S Teitzel
Midland (38) CM	517 835-7711	John Coppage	Karl Tomion	....	Bob Fisher	Leo Gay	Jim St Louis	Marty McGuire
Milan (4) CM	313 439-1501	Alan Israel	Patrick McShane	Ann Lindsay	....	Gerald Straits	Herbert Mahony	Timothy Ard
Milford v (6) MC	313 684-1515	R Roy Danley	A L Shufflebarger	Deborah Bridgers	....	....	John Daly	Fred Morin
Monroe (23) MC	313 243-0700	C D Cappucilli	Reid S Charles	Robert Dunbar	John E Sherburne	Raymond W Soleau	Hendrik J Kanavel	Mike Ala
Montrose (2) CM	313 639-6168	Nancy Persons	....	Kathy Parsons	....	....	Ronald Steinhorst	Matthew Fejedelem
Mount Clemens (18) CM	313 469-6804	Quinnie E Cody	Warren D Renando	Frances Pietrzak	William N Ringler	Michael Coyle	William Pringnitz	....
Mount Morris (3) MC	313 686-2160	Robert Slattery	Brian M Bulthuis	Brian M Bulthuis	....	Orville Stephens	Fred Thorsby	David Skornicka
Mount Pleasant (23) CM	517 773-7971	Ken Bovee	Paul Preston	Rick Sanborn	Rick Sanborn	....	Martin Trombley	Duane Ellis
Munising (3) CM	906 387-2095	Glenn E Champagne	Judy Slancik	Betty A Williams	....	Theodore Belfry	Douglas Miron	Eugene Faucette
Muskegon (40) CM	616 724-6724	....	David L Wendtland	Theresa Malik	Timothy Paul	Larry Robbins	Edward Griffen	Robert Kuhn
Muskegon Heights (13) CM	616 733-1331	Robert A Warren	....	....	Craig Loudermill	Ivory B Morris	Johnnie Capehart	Henry Witherspoon
Negaunee (5) CM	906 475-7700	Wil Dompierre	Ken Huber	Joan DuShane	....	Tom Gordyko	Paul Waters	Bob Johnson
New Baltimore (6) MC	313 725-2151	Greg Bayer	Lauren Wood	Ann Billock	....	Larry Marcero	Leo Parrott	Ed Santo
New Buffalo (2) CM	616 469-1500	(not reporting)						
Newaygo (1) CM	616 652-1657	(not reporting)						
Niles (12) MC	616 683-4700	Dan Excleshymer	Bernard Vanosdale	Ruth Harte	Susan Coulston	Richard Davidson	Myron Galchut	Brian Day
North Muskegon (4) CM	616 744-1621	Sabina Freeman	Dennis W Stepke	Margaret Kivinski	Kristi Mattson	Jay Kersman	Marvin Wegner	Bruce Moore
Northville (6) CM	313 349-1300	Chris J Johnson	Gary L Word	Delphine Dudick	Mark Christiansen	James Allen	Rodney A Cannon	Ted Mapes
Norton Shores (22) CM	616 798-4391	(not reporting)						
Norway (3) CM	906 563-8015	(not reporting)						
Novi (33) CM	313 347-0460	Matthew Quinn	Edward Kriewall	Gerry Stipp	Les Gibson	Art Lenaghan	Doug Shaeffer	Tony Nowicki
Oak Park (30) CM	313 547-1331	(not reporting)						
Ontonagon v (2) CM	906 884-2305	Kurt Giesau	Glenn Anderson	Joan Nygard	....	....	Timothy Guzek	....
Ortonville v (1) MC	313 627-4976	Susan Bess	Harvey Fletcher	Cindy Van Megroet	....	....	....	Melvin T Baker
Otisville v (..) CM	313 631-4680	(not reporting)						
Otsego (4) CM	616 692-3391	Russell Hover	Curtis Holt	Paula Baker	Matthew Storbeck	Gerald Seibert	Elton Goswick	Darl Gilliland
Owosso (16) CM	517 723-8844	Michael Dvorak	Gregg Guetschow	Gail Wickenhiser	Richard Williams	John Kenney	Nelson Gates	Stanley Jelinek
Oxford v (3) CM	313 628-2543	Peter C Burke	Darwin D Parks	Kevin J Rulkowski	....	Fred R Gill	John H Leroy	Darwin D Parks
Parchment (2) CM	616 349-3785	John H Bultje	Richard J Rice	Curt Flowers	....	Tim Bourgeois	Ralph G Herrick	Carl Flamm
Paw Paw v (3) CM	616 657-3148	(not reporting)						
Petoskey (6) CM	616 347-2500	Joe Kilborn	George Korthauer	Alan Terry	Alan Terry	....	Tom Postelnick	Walt Goodwin
Pinconning (1) CM	517 879-2360	Michael Duranczyk	Bradley Noeldner	Karen Waterman	....	Harold Schumann	Arthur Hopp	Timothy Stalker
Plainwell (4) CM	616 685-6821	Lori K Snyder	Richard G Runnels	Ruth A King	....	....	Frank E Post	Thomas R Seymour
Pleasant Ridge (3) CM	313 541-2900	(not reporting)						
Plymouth (10) CM	313 453-1234	Robert L Jones	Steven Walters	Linda Langmesser	William Graham	Alan Matthews	Robert Scoggins	Paul Sincock
Pontiac (71) MC	313 857-7601	(not reporting)						
Port Huron (34) CM	313 987-6000	Alicia Sancheq	Gerald R Bouchard	Pauline Madler	Bruce A Seymore	Robert Carmichael	William J Corbett	Larry A Osborn
Portage (41) CM	616 329-4400	(not reporting)						
Portland (4) CM	517 647-7531	Joseph V Tichuon	Rex Wambaugh	Kathleen Smith	....	Jon Hyland	Richard White	....
Reed City (2) CM	616 832-2245	Gregory Hornbaker	Phillip Rathbun	Judith Utrup	....	Ralph Westerburg	....	Kevin Rambadt
Richland tp (..) MC	517 642-2097	Frederick L Clark	David D McKeage	David H Schafer	....	Gary H Wade	David D McKeage	Timothy Rohn
Richmond (4) CM	313 727-7571	Joseph Maniaci	Gerald Williams	Karen Stagl	....	Marvin Spens	Thomas Needham	Paul Fejedelem
River Rouge (11) MC	313 842-0801	(not reporting)						
Riverview (14) MC	313 281-4201	P Rotteveel	Robert Elliott	Marilyn Girardin	C Abercrombie	Robert C Hale	James A Bartus	Gerald N Perry
Rochester (7) CM	313 651-9061	Thomas L Werth	Kenneth A Johnson	Nancy D Miller	Charles Ogler	William Gray	Ted Glynn	Carl R Renius
Rockford (4) CM	616 866-1537	Betty Combs	Daryl J Delabbio	Daryl J Delabbio	John L Strauss	Robert Vandermex	John V Porter	Michal R Chesher
Rockwood (3) MC	313 379-9496	(not reporting)						
Rogers City (4) CM	517 734-2191	Fred W Lewis	Terry L Ross	Theresa A Heinzel	Terry L Ross	Keith Froelich	Garnet Robinson	Vernon Langlois
Romeo v (4) MC	313 752-3565	Paul Hansen	M McLaughlin	M McLaughlin	....	C Richardson	Larry Howell	Barry Trowsse
Romulus (23) MC	313 942-7571	(not reporting)						
Roosevelt Park (4) CM	616 755-3721	M Sherry White	William K Gleason	Barbara L Smith	....	....	Alan J Ortquist	Terry A Sladick
Roseville (51) CM	313 445-5410	Jeanne Riesterer	Thomas Van Damme	Charles LaGrant	John Knapp	Morley Ireland	William Lucas	Larry Snelling
Royal Oak (65) CM	313 546-1000	Patricia Paruch	William Baldridge	Mary C Haverty	John L Dagiau	William Crouch	John H Ball	James T Perry
Saginaw (70) CM	517 759-1400	Henry Nickleberry	J Marvin Baldwin	Bevelyn Bradley	Jon Bayless	Donald Couturier	Alex Perez	James Gallagher
Saginaw tp (38) MC	517 791-9800	George L Olson	Ronald Lee	Tim Braun	V Gottschalk	Richard Powell	Kenneth Ott	Gerald Francis
Saline (7) MC	313 429-4907	Patrick J Little	David M White	Dianne S Hill	David M White	R Weisenreder	James Douglas	George Danneffel
Sault Ste. Marie (15) CM	906 635-5261	William Lynn	Spencer R Nebel	Lori J Clarke	Elmer Adams	Ken Eagle	Scott Fitzgerald	....
Scottville (1) CM	616 757-4729	Duane Slagle	....	Bob Peterson	....	Rick Gleason	Larry Nichols	Charles Smith
South Haven (6) CM	616 637-0700	Dave Paull	Alan Vanderberg	Gary Simpson	Gary Simpson	....	Rod Somerlott	Robert Stickland
South Lyon (6) CM	313 437-1735	Jeffrey L Potter	Rodney L Cook	Julie Zemke	....	Chuck Buers	Gerald Smith	Linden Beebe
Southfield (76) CM	313 354-1000	Donald Fracassi	Robert Block	Mary Bonner	James Scharret	Walter Chapman	Joseph Thomas	Thomas Vukonich
Southgate (31) MC	313 246-1305	(not reporting)						
Sparta v (4) MC	616 887-8251	(not reporting)						
Spring Lake v (3) CM	616 842-1393	Victoria Verplank	Eric R DeLong	Robert G Lucking	J L Van Bemmelen	....	William Kaufman	John Hansen
Springfield (6) CM	616 965-2354	Richard A Fleming	Bernard Guida	Marilyn Calladine	....	....	James Jenkins	Rod McKee
St. Charles v (2) CM	517 865-8287	Richard C Hoerner	....	Robert J Grnak	....	....	David J Sickle	Hal Mead

Directory 1/9
continued

MUNICIPAL OFFICIALS IN U.S. CITIES OVER 2,500

City, 1990 population figures (000 omitted), form of government	Municipal phone number	Mayor	Appointed administrator	City clerk	Finance officer	Fire chief	Police chief	Public works director
MICHIGAN (270) continued								
St. Clair (5)	CM 313 329-7121	Bernard E Kuhn	Patrick G Greve	Janice DiGiusto	. . . .	William A Beaudua	Wayne R Goralski	. . . .
St. Clair Shores (68)	CM 313 445-5240	Ted Wahby	Mark Wollenweber	Jack Fields	Tim Haney	Frank Turner	Larry Germain	. . . .
St. Ignace (3)	CM 906 643-8545	Bruce J Dodson	Gary L Heckman	Larry E Morris	Larry E Morris	John Robinson	Timothy S Matelsk	Gary L Heckman
St. Johns (7)	CM 517 224-8944	(not reporting)						
St. Joseph (9)	CM 616 983-5541	Jeffrey Richards	William Sinclair	Ronald S Momany	. . . .	Elwood Munson	Francis Fleisher	
St. Louis (4)	CM 517 681-2137	George Kubin	Larry Wernette	Nancy L Roehrs	. . . .	Larry Parsons	Howard Teed	James Pavlik
Stambaugh (1)	CM 906 265-4213	(not reporting)						
Standish (1)	CM 517 846-9588	Curtis Hillman	Douglas Terry	Peggy Burtch	. . . .	Dick Linton	Doug Terry	John Dubiel
Sterling Heights (118)	CM 313 977-6123	Stephen Rice	Steve Duchane	Mary Zander	Virginia Fette	Kenneth Durham	Thomas Derocha	Ray Filipchuk
Sturgis (10)	CM 616 651-2321	Carl Holsinger	Jerome Kisscorni	Carol F Rambadt	Michael L Vance	Paul Trinka	Eugene Alli	. . . .
Swartz Creek (5)	CM 313 635-4464	Donna McCoy	Thomas L Hundley	Terri C Nurkala	. . . .	Ron Mills	Raymond Adams	Michael Shumaker
Sylvan Lake (2)	CM 313 682-1440	Richard B Farms	John P Martin	Dennise Clippert	Dennise Clippert	William Brown	Marvin McTavish	John P Martin
Tawas City (2)	CM 517 362-8688	(not reporting)						
Taylor (71)	MC 313 374-1460	(not reporting)						
Tecumseh (7)	CM 517 423-2107	Vera Gardner	Frank L Crosby	Laura Caterina	. . . .	Joseph Tuckey	L Van Alstine	Dave Williams
Three Rivers (7)	CM 616 273-1075	Kathy Gieber	David Richards	Barbara Redford	Kelly Clark	Steven Sullivan	Kenneth Baker	Mark Glessner
Tittabawassee tp (5)	CM 517 695-9512	Ken Kasper	George A Brown	Robert Ducharme	Jo Ella Krantz	William Kirchner	Robert Harken	Kenneth Hoff
Traverse City (15)	CM 616 922-4481	Linda Johnson	Richard Lewis	Debbra Curtiss	W Twietmeyer	. . . .	Ralph Soffredine	Michael Slater
Trenton (21)	MC 313 675-6500	Thomas W Boritzki	Larry W Fitch	Kyle F Stack	Ralph E Lesko	Glenn D Spry	Gerald R Brown	Larry Dusincki
Troy (73)	MC 313 524-3300	Jeanne M Stine	F Gerstenecker	Kenneth Courtney	Kenneth Courtney	James L Halsey	Lawrence R Carey	Michael Culpepper
Utica (5)	MC 313 739-1600	Jacqueline Noonan	. . . .	M C McGrail	. . . .	Robert Beck	Bruce Bissonnette	Joseph Francis
Vassar (3)	CM 517 823-8517	Charles Whitney	William Lefevere	Dianne Johnston	Edna Eastham	Raymond Hess	John Horwath	Raymond Hess
Vicksburg v (2)	CM 616 649-3733	Robert J Philipp	Donald R Flanders	Mercer D Mynn	Donald R Flanders	William Sillaman	M Deschengau	Roy Hodgman
Wakefield (2)	CM 906 229-5132	(not reporting)						
Walker (17)	MC 616 453-6311	Norman Dole	Joseph Fendt	Linda Wiser	Bill Vantuinen	William Schmidt	Walter Sprenger	John Kinney
Walled Lake (6)	CM 313 624-4847	William T Roberts	Phillip S Vawter	M Cornelius	. . . .	Bill Friar	Ken Borieo	Ralph Smith
Warren (145)	MC 313 574-4670	(not reporting)						
Wayland (3)	CM 616 792-2265	Linden Anderson	H A Stull	H A Stull	Karen Doyle	Hugh DeWeerd	Daniel Miller	John Noordyke
Wayne (20)	MC 313 722-2000	Kenneth Warfield	John J Zech	Doris A Nall	Thomas Norwood	Wayne Bennett	John Colligan	. . . .
West Branch (2)	CM 517 345-0500	Todd Thompson	Patrick McGinnis	Jane Tennant	Debra Heisler	. . . .	Howard Hanft	Thomas Brindley
Westland (85)	MC 313 467-3200	(not reporting)						
Whitehall (3)	CM 616 894-4048	Wallace Weesies	Gerald Homminga	Scott Huebler	Laurie Audo	Gary Bohling	James Bartholomew	Jack Van Geison
Williamston (3)	CM 517 655-2774	(not reporting)						
Wixom (9)	CM 313 624-0885	(not reporting)						
Wolverine Lake v (5)	CM 313 624-1710	Jimmy R Allen	Michael Cain	Sharon A Miller	Frances A Barber	. . . .	James Davis	Michael Cain
Woodhaven (12)	MC 313 675-4925	Richard C Withey	David W Flaten	Karen M Mazo	David W Flaten	Dennis M Andrew	Richard C Foster	Charles A Horn Jr
Wyandotte (31)	MC 313 246-4500	James R DeSana	. . . .	William K Griggs	David Sabuda	Ralph Savage	Charles Brown	Robert Jagiello
Wyoming (64)	CM 616 530-7241	Jack Magnuson	Donald Mason	Charles Gress	Joseph Bommarito	James Austin	Lowell Henline	Gerald Snyder
Ypsilanti (25)	CM 313 483-1100	(not reporting)						
Zeeland (5)	MC 616 772-6400	Lester Hoogland	. . . .	John D Leisenring	. . . .	William Gruppen	Robert Metzger	David R Walters
Zilwaukee (2)	CM 517 755-0931	James J Darland	Rolland C Spencer	C E Langschwager	. . . .	Douglas Luplow	Joel J Dobis	M F Langschwager
MINNESOTA (204)								
Afton (3)	MC 612 436-5090	Jon Kroschel	Alex Wikstrom	Anna Nordin	. . . .	. . . .	. . . .	. . . .
Albert Lea (18)	CM 507 377-4300	Marvin E Wangen	Paul T Sparks	Sandi Behrens	Don Rippentrop	Orrion Roisen	Clarence Ayers	David Olson
Alexandria (8)	MC 612 763-6678	Karl Glade	Arlan E Johnson	Arlan E Johnson	Daryl Sulander	Pat Ellingson	Charles Nettestad	David Nelson
Andover (15)	MC 612 755-5100	J E McKelvey	James Schrantz	Victoria Volk	Daryl Sulander	Dale Mashuga	. . . .	James Schrantz
Annandale (2)	CM 612 274-3055	Daryl D Gunnarson	Garrison L Hale	Ronita A Walburn	Sylvia J Onstad	Chris J Strand	Myron A Morris	Wm D McNellis
Anoka (17)	CM 612 421-6630	Peter Beborg	Mark Nagel	. . . .	James Knutson	Ronald Bickford	Andy Revering	Ray Schultz
Apple Valley (35)	MC 612 431-8800	Willis E Branning	Thomas M Melena	Mary E Mueller	George Ballenger	Richard Tuthill	Lloyd Rivers	John Gretz
Arden Hills v (9)	MC 612 633-5676	Thomas R Sather	Dorothy A Person		Terrance R Post	. . . .	. . . .	Daniel A Winkel
Aurora v (2)	MC 218 229-2614	Alan Hodnik	. . . .	Linda Cazin	. . . .	. . . .	. . . .	Walter Brune
Austin (22)	MC 507 437-7671	. . . .	Patrick McGarvey	Lucy Johnson	Richard Benzkofer	Daniel Wilson	Paul Philipp	Jon Erichson
Baxter (4)	MC 218 829-7161	Jon L Main	Donald C Lorsung	Donald C Lorsung	. . . .	. . . .	Robbi J Gallant	Earle Johnson
Bayport (3)	MC 612 439-2530	Beverly H Schultz	Kenneth H Hartung	. . . .	. . . .	Charles Schwartz	Peter Vollmer	John Burkhart
Becker (2)	CM 612 261-4302	Norman Jensen	Joe Rudberg	Janet Boettcher	. . . .	. . . .	Kevin Rieland	James Boettcher
Belle Plaine (3)	MC 612 873-5553	Gerald J Meyer	David R Iverson	David R Iverson	David R Iverson	Terry Gregory	Steve Rost	Robert Kruse
Bemidji (11)	CM 218 759-3560	Douglas Peterson	Philip Shealy	Shirley Kubian	Dale Page	. . . .	Robert Tell	Michael Barclay
Benson (3)	CM 612 843-4775	Robert Christiasn	Chuck Whiting	. . . .	Glen Pederson	Greg Lee	Jeff Stewart	Brian Flynn
Biwabik (1)	CM 218 865-4183	Bob Woods	Jan Huizing	Pamela Berts	. . . .	Ed Holmstrom	Kathleen Beise	Charles Licari
Blaine (39)	CM 612 784-6700	Elwyn Tinklenberg	Donald G Poss	Joyce Twistol	William Stawarski	. . . .	Ron Nicholas	Kev Irvin
Bloomington (86)	MC 612 881-5811	Neil Peterson	Mark Bernhardson	Evelyn Woulfe	Lyle Olson	Ulysses Seal	Robert Lutz	Charles Honchell
Blue Earth (4)	MC 507 526-7336	(not reporting)						
Brainerd (12)	MC 218 828-2307	Bonnie Cumberland	Daniel J Vogt	Daniel J Vogt	Daniel J Vogt	Ron Johnson	Frank Ball	Walt Sjolund
Branch (..)	MC 612 674-7401	(not reporting)						
Breckenridge (4)	MC 218 643-1431	(not reporting)						
Brooklyn Center (29)	CM 612 569-3300	Todd Paulson	Gerald G Splinter	. . . .	Charles Hansen	Ron Boman	Trevor Hampton	Sy Knapp
Brooklyn Park (56)	MC 612 493-8000	Jesse Ventura	Craig R Rapp	Myrna Maikkula	Peter Hames	James Driste	Donald Davis	Jon Thiel
Buffalo (7)	CM 612 682-1181	Fred Naaktgeboren	Merton Auger	Merton Auger	Merton Auger	Brian Loberg	Robert Fix	Gary Mattson
Burnsville (51)	CM 612 895-4400	(not reporting)						
Caledonia (3)	MC 507 724-3450	Robert H Burns	. . . .	Robert L Nelson	Robert L Nelson	Anthony J Klug	Duane L St Mary	. . . .
Cambridge v (5)	CM 612 689-3211	(not reporting)						
Cannon Falls (3)	MC 507 263-3954	Leon Hanson	Dallas Larson	. . . .	. . . .	Ray Rapp	William Schultz	Dennis Neva
Champlin (17)	CM 612 421-8100	Steven Boynton	Kurtis Ulrich	Joanne Brown	P Boedigheimer	Ron Bickford	. . . .	Bret Heitkamp
Chanhassen (12)	CM 612 937-1900	(not reporting)						
Chaska (11)	CM 612 448-2851	(not reporting)						
Chisholm (5)	MC 218 254-3353	(not reporting)						
Circle Pines (5)	MC 612 784-5898	Marshall Dahl	James Keinath	. . . .	Peggy Link	Milo Bennet	Dave Van Burkleo	Bert Caverson
Cloquet (11)	MC 218 879-3347	(not reporting)						
Cokato (2)	MC 612 286-5505	(not reporting)						
Columbia Heights (19)	CM 612 782-2800	Donald Murzyn Jr	Patrick Hentges	William Elrite	William Elrite	Charles Kewatt	David Mawhorter	Mark Winsom
Coon Rapids (53)	CM 612 755-2880	William Thompson	Robert Svehla	Betty Backes	Lyle Haney	Richard Mowan	Steven Ahrens	William Ottensman
Corcoran (5)	MC 612 420-2288	Frank Larkin	Robert Derus	Cynthia Patnode	. . . .	Carl Sorensen	Daniel Brotzler
Cottage Grove (23)	MC 612 458-2800	. . . .	Kevin Frazell	Carol Stransky	. . . .	Denis Erickson	Dennis Cusick	Les Burshten
Crookston (8)	MC 218 281-1232	Douglas Oman	Raymond Ecklund	Allen Chesley	. . . .	George Jacobs	Paul Monteen	Pat Kelly
Crystal (24)	CM 612 537-8421	Peter Meintsma	Jerry Dulgar	Darlene George	. . . .	Kevin McGinty	James Mossey	William Monk
Dawson (2)	MC 612 769-4615	Richard Pollei	David A Bovee	Melva Larson	. . . .	Larry Stangeland	Bill Stock	Brent Powers
Dayton (4)	MC 612 427-4589	(not reporting)						
Deephaven (4)	MC 612 474-4755	R Engebretson	. . . .	Sandra Langley	. . . .	. . . .	James Anderson	Raymond Williams
Delano (3)	MC 612 972-3213	Dwight A Poss	. . . .	Marlene E Kittock	. . . .	. . . .	. . . .	Dan Alger
Detroit Lakes (7)	MC 218 847-5658	(not reporting)						
Dilworth (3)	MC 218 287-2313	(not reporting)						
Duluth (85)	MC 218 723-3291	Gary Doty	Karl Nollenberger	Jeff Cox	Elaine Hansen	Larry Bushey	Scott Lyons	Richard Larson

Directory 1/9 continued **MUNICIPAL OFFICIALS IN U.S. CITIES OVER 2,500**

City, 1990 population figures (000 omitted), form of government		Municipal phone number	Mayor	Appointed administrator	City clerk	Finance officer	Fire chief	Police chief	Public works director
MINNESOTA (204) continued									
Eagan (47)	CM	612 681-4600	Thomas Egan	Thomas L Hedges	E J Van Overbeke	E J Van Overbeke	Dale Nelson	Patrick Geagan	Thomas A Colbert
East Bethel (8)	MC	612 434-9569	Jeff Hintz	. . . .	Sherri Anderson	. . . .	Ardie Anderson	Anoka Sheriff	Richard Hass
East Grand Forks (9)	MC	218 773-2483	(not reporting)						
Eden Prairie (39)	CM	612 937-2262	Douglas Tenpas	Carl J Jullie	. . . .	John D Frane	Conrad	James G Clark	Eugene A Dietz
Edina (46)	CM	612 927-8861	Fred Richards	Ken Rosland	Marc Daehn	John Wallin	Ted Paulfranz	Bill Bernhjelm	Francis Hoffman
Elk River (11)	MC	612 441-7420	Henry Duitsman	Patrick Klaers	Sandra Thackeray	L Johnson Warner	Russell Anderson	Thomas Zerwas	Philip Hals
Ely (4)	MC	218 365-3224	Michael Forsman	. . . .	Lee Tessier	Robert Hedloff	Gary Klun	John Manning	Richard Mattila
Eveleth (4)	MC	218 744-2501	Wm Tom Coombe Jr	. . . .	Raymond J Eck	Raymond J Eck	. . . .	James Bozicevich	John J Palo
Excelsior (2)	CM	612 474-5233	John E Anderson	Carl Zieman	Marlin H Amundson	. . . .	. . . .	. . . .	Carl Zieman
Eyota (..)	MC	507 545-2135	(not reporting)						
Fairmont (11)	CM	507 238-9461	Marlin Gratz	. . . .	Lois J Cairns	James Zarling	Roger Carlson	Erwin Butch Thiel	Larry Read
Falcon Heights (5)	MC	612 644-5050	Tom Baldwin	Susan Hoyt	Shirley Chenoweth	Tom Kelly	Clem Kurhajetz	. . . .	Vince Wright
Faribault (17)	CM	507 334-2222	Jeanette Hammond	Timothy Madigan	. . . .	Dale Martinson	Micheal Monge	William Weishaar	Brian Wagstrom
Farmington (6)	MC	612 463-7111	Eugene Kuchera	Larry Thompson	. . . .	Wayne Henneke	. . . .	Dan Siebenaler	Thomas Kaldunski
Fergus Falls (12)	MC	218 739-2251	Calvin Ferber	James L Nitchals	. . . .	Gary M Nelson	Burke Schultz	John Wagner	Donald Eisenhuth
Forest Lake (6)	MC	612 464-3550	James C Crawford	Robert R Houle	Robert R Houle	Robert R Houle	Gary Sigfrenius	David Schwartz	Arthur E Jensen
Franklin (..)	MC	507 557-2259	Ronald Degner	. . . .	Laurie Sherman	. . . .	Ronald Zempel	Roger Degner	Kevin Kokesch
Fridley (28)	CM	612 571-3450	William J Nee	William W Burns	William A Champa	Richard D Pribyl	Charles McKusick	James P Hill	John G Flora
Gilbert (2)	MC	218 741-9443	Karl Oberstar Jr	Gary Mackley	. . . .	. . . .	Michael Bradach	. . . .	Kenneth Kuitunen
Glencoe (5)	CM	612 864-5586	(not reporting)						
Golden Valley (21)	CM	612 593-8000	Larry A Bakken	William S Joynes	Shirley A Nelson	Donald Taylor	Mark Kuhnly	Dean Mooney	Fred Salsbury
Goodview (3)	MC	507 452-1630	John Weimerskirch	. . . .	. . . .	Daryl Zimmer	Robert Matzke	Reed Schmidt	Greg Volkart
Grand Rapids (8)	MC	218 327-2807	James Hoolihan	Craig J Mattson	Karlene Gale	Jean Lane	Greg Taylor	Harvey Dahline	Jeff Davies
Granite Falls (3)	CM	612 564-3011	Roy E Lenzen	William P Lavin	Marj Bottge	Mark Jensen	Michael Ohliger	Donald Ericson	Paul Krogstad
Ham Lake (9)	MC	612 434-9555	(not reporting)						
Hastings (15)	MC	612 437-4127	Mike Werner	Dave Osberg	Barb Thompson	Lori Webster	Don Latch	Nick Wasylik	Tom Montgomery
Hermantown (7)	MC	218 729-6331	Wallace R Loberg	Lynn A Lander	Nancy A Sirois	. . . .	. . . .	T Gulshafer	James H Olson
Hibbing (18)	CM	218 262-3486	(not reporting)						
Hopkins (17)	CM	612 935-8474	(not reporting)						
Hoyt Lakes (2)	RT	218 225-2344	Ronald Nemanic	Richard Bradford	. . . .	. . . .	Thomas Ferris	Steven Stoks	Paul Forlan
Hugo (4)	CM	612 429-6676	Walter Stoltzman	Robert Museus	Mary Ann Creager	Ronald Otkin	Ron Istvanovich	. . . .	. . . .
Hutchinson (12)	CM	612 587-5151	Paul L Ackland	Gary D Plotz	. . . .	Kenneth B Merrill	. . . .	Steven C Madson	. . . .
Independence (3)	MC	612 479-0527	(not reporting)						
International Falls (8)	MC	218 283-9484	(not reporting)						
Inver Grove Heights (22)	CM	612 457-2111	Joseph Atkins	James Willis	Loretta Garrity	Daniel Maiers	James Karels	Stanley Trover	Gary Johnson
Isanti (2)	MC	612 444-5512	Ken Kahle	Michael Robertson	Michael Robertson	Michael Robertson	Lester Peterson	Norris Sorenson	Harlen Stecker
Jackson (4)	MC	507 847-4410	David Fell	Dean Albrecht	. . . .	Marilyn Ailts	Albert Winrich	Richard Seim	. . . .
Janesville (..)	MC	507 234-6265	Frank Morrill	S Schwenck Salter	Julie Redmann	. . . .	Steve Schroeder	Matt Peters	David Wheelock
Jordan (3)	MC	612 492-2535	Ronald Jabs	D Kay Kuhlman	Coralee Fox	Kathy Lapic	William Busch	Alvin Erickson	David Bendzick
Kasson (4)	MC	507 634-7071	Folmer Carlsen	Dolores Meyer	Dolores Meyer	. . . .	Randy Fjerstad	David Johnson	Burt Fjerstad
Kenyon (2)	MC	507 789-6415	John Cole	Duane Hebert	Duane Hebert	Duane Hebert	Gary Pavek	Bob Vanderheiden	. . . .
La Crescent (4)	MC	507 895-2595	Richard Wieser	. . . .	Marlene Butzman	. . . .	. . . .	Vern Yolton	Haffis Waller
Lake City (4)	MC	612 345-5383	Donald Larson	Richard Abraham	. . . .	Bruce Schumacher	Duane Sprick	Robert Schmidt	John Brandt
Lake Elmo (6)	MC	612 777-5510	Wyn John	Mary Kueffner	Mary Kueffner	Marilyn Banister	Richard Sachs	. . . .	Daniel Olinger
Lakeville (25)	CM	612 469-4431	Duane R Zaun	Robert A Erickson	Charlene Friedges	Dennis D Feller	Barry Christensen	Donald Gudmundson	James A Robinette
Le Sueur (4)	CM	612 665-6401	John K King	Richard Almich	K Johannsen	. . . .	Daniel LaBelle	Harry Thorau	Dean Kunze
Lino Lakes (9)	MC	612 464-5562	(not reporting)						
Litchfield (6)	CM	612 693-7201	Ron Ebnet	Bruce Miller	Betty Anderson	. . . .	Gale Smith	Bruce Dicke	. . . .
Little Canada (9)	CM	612 484-2177	Raymond Hanson	Joel Hanson	. . . .	. . . .	. . . .	. . . .	David Harris
Little Falls (7)	CM	612 632-2341	Ron Hinnenkamp	Richard N Carlson	Susan G Haugen	. . . .	Fred Tabatt	Michael J Pender	Gerald M Lochner
Long Prairie (3)	CM	612 732-2167	(not reporting)						
Luverne (4)	CM	507 283-2388	William V Weber	Douglas Bunkers	Marianne Ouverson	Barbara Berghorst	Jim Johannsen	Keith Aanenson	Darrell Huiskes
Madison (2)	CM	612 598-7373	Norma Larsen	David Huseman	David Huseman	. . . .	Bob Buer	. . . .	Harold L Hodge
Mahtomedi (6)	CM	612 426-3344	(not reporting)						
Mankato (31)	CM	507 387-8600	Stan Christ	William A Bassett	Sandra Paulson	Harley Mohr	. . . .	Glenn Gabriel	Paul Baker
Maple Grove (39)	CM	612 420-4000	James Deane	Jon Elam	Jon Elam	Fred Christianson	Scott Anderson	Sherman Otto	Gerry Butcher
Maplewood (31)	CM	612 770-4500	Gary Bastian	Michael McGuire	Lucille Aurelius	Daniel Faust	. . . .	Ken Collins	Ken Haider
Marshall (12)	MC	507 537-6763	Robert Byrnes	Duane Aden	. . . .	T Muelebroeck	David Marks	Marvin Bahn	Richard Herigon
Medina v (3)	MC	612 473-4643	Anne E Theis	. . . .	Jeffrey E Karlson	. . . .	. . . .	Richard Rabenort	James Dillman
Mendota Heights (9)	CM	612 452-1850	C Mertensotto	Thomas Lawell	Kathleen Swanson	. . . .	John Maczko	Dennis Delmont	James Danielson
Milaca (2)	CM	612 983-3141	(not reporting)						
Minneapolis (368)	MC	612 673-3000	Donald M Fraser	James F Wright	Merry Keefe	John Moir	Thomas Dickinson	John Laux	Richard Straub
Minnetonka (48)	CM	612 939-8200	Timothy Bergsted	David Childs	Elizabeth Norton	Dale Eggenberger	Daniel Hargarten	Richard Setter	Lloyd Pauly
Minnetrista (3)	MC	612 446-1660	(not reporting)						
Montevideo (5)	CM	612 269-6575	K John Jones	Stephen P King	LaVonne Sundlee	Jan Flaherty	Haven Larson	Tim Taylor	John Donahue
Monticello (5)	CM	612 295-2711	Kenneth Maus	Rick Wolfsteller	Rick Wolfsteller	Rick Wolfsteller	Jerry Wein	. . . .	John Simoca
Moorhead (32)	CM	218 299-5179	Morris L Lanning	James W Antonen	Kaye Buchholz	Gerald H Sorenson	Gary Schulz	Leslie Sharrock	Robert Martin
Mora (3)	CM	612 679-1511	Mary Schwartz	Steven C Jones	D McCallum	. . . .	Gene Anderson	Gary Gronos	. . . .
Morris (6)	CM	612 589-3141	Lee Swanson	Edward Larson	. . . .	Gene Krosschell	Ron Sharstrom	Curt Wiese	Bill Storck
Mound (10)	CM	612 472-0600	Skip Johnson	Ed Shukle	Fran Clark	Gino Businaro	Don Bryce	Len Harrell	. . . .
Mounds View (13)	MC	612 784-3055	Jerry Linke	Samantha Orduno	Michele Severson	Donald Brager	. . . .	Timothy Ramacher	Mike Ulrich
Mountain Iron (3)	MC	218 735-8267	William Mattila	Peter Abbey	Jill Forseen	. . . .	Tom Cvar	. . . .	Don Kleinschmidt
New Brighton (22)	CM	612 633-1533	Robert J Benke	. . . .	Margaret A Egan	Margaret A Egan	Mark Frieden	John C Kelley	Leslie J Proper
New Hope (22)	CM	612 531-5100	Edward Erickson	Daniel Donahue	Valerie Leone	Larry Watts	Doug Smith	Colin Kastanos	Roger Paulson
New Prague (4)	MC	612 758-4401	Terry Flicek	Jerry Bohnsack	Kathy Novotny	. . . .	Joseph Vaughn	Dennis Rohloff	Robert Vohnoutka
New Ulm (13)	CM	507 359-8233	Carl Wyczawski	Richard Salvati	. . . .	Bruce Kessel	Dave Clancy	Richard Gulden	Lance Lundsten
Newport (4)	MC	612 459-5677	(not reporting)						
North Branch (2)	CM	612 674-8113	Ellis Johnson	Thomas Johnson	Thomas Johnson	. . . .	Don Brown	Douglas Brown	Gary Schaefer
North Mankato (10)	CM	507 625-4141	David L Dehen	Bob Ringhofer	Marlene Peters	Wendell Sande	Arlo Zander	Les Ennis	. . . .
North Oaks (3)	MC	612 484-5777	(not reporting)						
North St. Paul (12)	CM	612 770-4450	W Sandberg	R Gatti	. . . .	A Mahlum	D Zick	D Scott	. . . .
Northfield (15)	MC	507 645-8833	(not reporting)						
Oak Park Heights (3)	CM	612 439-4439	Barbara O'Neal	Lavonne Wilson	Lavonne Wilson	Judy Holst	. . . .	Lindy Swanson	Roger G Benson
Oakdale (18)	CM	612 739-5086	Ted Bearth	Craig Waldron	Susan Barry	Suzanne Warren	. . . .	William Sullivan	Roland Harrington
Olivia (3)	MC	612 523-2361	(not reporting)						
Orono (7)	MC	612 473-7357	Edward Callahan	Ronald Moorse	Dorothy Hallin	Thomas Kuehn	. . . .	Stephen Sullivan	John Gerhardson
Ortonville (2)	MC	612 839-3428	Paul Taffe	Maureen Laughlin	. . . .	. . . .	Steve Barr	Robert Meyer	Roger Anderson
Osseo (3)	MC	612 425-2624	(not reporting)						
Owatonna (19)	MC	507 451-4540	Klinkhammer	Hierstein	. . . .	Moeckly	Rosendahl	Brown	Putnam
Park Rapids (3)	MC	218 732-3163	(not reporting)						
Perham (2)	CM	218 346-4455	Marlin Zitzow	Robert Louiseau	. . . .	Linda Bjelland	Thomas Hammers	Terry Shannon	Dwight Lundgren
Pine City (..)	MC	612 629-2575	(not reporting)						
Pine Island (2)	MC	507 356-4591	Gerald Vettel	Terry J Berg	. . . .	. . . .	Howard Klennert	. . . .	Mark Swarthout

Directory 1/9
continued

MUNICIPAL OFFICIALS IN U.S. CITIES OVER 2,500

City, 1990 population figures (000 omitted), form of government	Municipal phone number	Mayor	Appointed administrator	City clerk	Finance officer	Fire chief	Police chief	Public works director
MINNESOTA (204) continued								
Pipestone (5)	MC 507 825-3324	(not reporting)						
Plymouth (51)	CM 612 550-5000	Kim Bergman	Dwight Johnson	Laurie Ravenhorst	Dale Hahn	....	Craig Gerdes	Fred Moore
Princeton (4)	CM 612 389-2040	Gregory Furzland	William Schimmel	William Schimmel	Steven Jackson	Gerald Bieringer	David Warneke	Thomas Mismash
Prior Lake (11)	CM 612 447-4230	Lydia Andren	Frank Boyles	....	Ralph Teschner	Alan Borchardt	Dick Powell	Larry Anderson
Proctor (3)	MC 218 624-3641	(not reporting)						
Ramsey (12)	MC 612 427-1410	James Gilbertson	Ryan Schroeder	Ryan Schroeder	Jessie Hart	David Griffin	Michael Auspos	Steven Jankowski
Red Wing (15)	MC 612 388-6734	Romeo C Cyr	Steven L Perkins	Burton C Will	Burton C Will	Richard Kosec	Edward Krause	Thomas W Drake
Redwood Falls (5)	MC 507 637-5755	(not reporting)						
Renville (1)	CM 612 329-8366	(not reporting)						
Richfield (36)	CM 612 861-9700	Martin J Kirsch	James D Prosser	Thomas P Ferber	Steven L Devich	....	John D Erskine	Donald A Fondrick
Robbinsdale (14)	CM 612 537-4534	Joy Robb	Francis D Hagen	Terri Johnson	R Gangelhoff	Tom Sipe	John Spetch	Francis D Hagen
Rochester (71)	MC 507 285-8082	Charles Hazama	Stevan Kvenvold	Carole Grimm	Paul Utesch	Larry Eischen	Patrick Farrell	Roger Plumb
Rosemount (9)	CM 612 423-4411	(not reporting)						
Roseville (33)	CM 612 490-2200	Vern Johnson	Steve Sarkozy	....	Ed Burrell	Joel Hewitt	Jim Zelinsky	Steve Gatlin
Rush City (1)	CM 612 358-4743	Mike Skalsky	Mike Thompson	Lynne Laakso	....	Curt Burda	Floyd Pinotti	Leon Kruse
Sandstone (2)	MC 612 245-5241	John A Wright	Douglas J Schulze	Douglas J Schulze	Douglas J Schulze	Chris Thorvig	....	....
Sartell (5)	MC 612 253-2171	(not reporting)						
Sauk Centre (4)	MC 612 352-3467	Robert Polipnick	....	Joseph Heinen	....	Virgil Marthaler	G Trierweiler	Harold Wessel
Sauk Rapids (8)	MC 612 251-1022	Thomas Braun	Robert Haarman	....	Julie Braun	Andrew Hovanes	John Welsh	Richard Gronau
Savage (10)	CM 612 890-1045	Donald Egan	Mark McNeill	Janis Saarela	....	Alan McColl	Gordon Vlasak	Bruce Bullert
Shakopee (12)	MC 612 445-3650	(not reporting)						
Shoreview (25)	CM 612 490-4600	James Chalmers	Terry C Schwerm	Terry C Schwerm	Jeanne Haapala	Daniel Winkel	Jerry Bergeron	Karl Keel
Shorewood (6)	MC 612 474-3236	Barbara Brancel	James C Hurm	Jamesc Hurm	Alan J Rolek	....	....	Donald Zdrazil
Silver Bay (2)	MC 218 226-4408	(not reporting)						
Sleepy Eye (4)	MC 507 794-3731	James J Broich	....	Edwin V Treml	....	Robert Zinniel	Ronald Ellevold	....
South Internatl Falls (..)	MC 218 283-9461	(not reporting)						
South St. Paul (20)	MC 612 450-8700	Kathleen Gaylord	Douglas Reeder	Christy Wilcox	Kathleen McBride	James Cosgrove	Craig Kinney	Gerald Goers
Spring Lake Park v (7)	MC 612 784-6491	Harley Wells	....	Donald Busch	Donald Busch	Richard Johnson	Bruce Porter	Gary Peterson
Spring Valley v (2)	MC 507 346-7367	(not reporting)						
St. Anthony (8)	CM 612 789-8881	Clarence Ranallo	Thomas Burt	Connie Kroeplin	Roger Larson Sr	W Graham	Richard Engstrom	Lawrence Hamer
St. Cloud (49)	MC 612 255-7217	C Winkelman	C Hagelie	G Engdahl	J Norman	Bill Carstensen	D O'Keefe	J Dolentz
St. James (4)	CM 507 375-3241	Bob Kline	Mark Sievert	Roy Trullinger	....	....	Don Mickelson	....
St. Joseph (3)	MC 612 363-7201	Donald Bud Reber	....	Rachel Stapleton	....	Richard Taufen	Bradley Lindgren	Richard Taufen
St. Louis Park (44)	CM 612 924-2500	(not reporting)						
St. Paul (272)	MC 612 298-4221	James Scheibel	Thomas Welna	Molly O'Rourke	Richard Gehrman	Timothy Fuller	William Finney	Thomas Eggum
St. Paul Park (5)	CM 612 459-9785	Donald Mullan	Barry Sittlow	Barry Sittlow	....	Stan Kulbitski	Duwayne Rydberg	H Schnegelberger
St. Peter (9)	MC 507 931-4840	Ellery Peterson	Daniel Jordet	....	....	Arthur Zuhlsdorf	Bradley Kollmann	Lewis Giesking
Staples (3)	MC 218 894-2550	(not reporting)						
Stewartville (5)	MC 507 533-4745	Larry Gray	Larry Hansen	....	....	Joe Himmer	....	Kenneth Kraft
Stillwater (14)	MC 612 439-6121	Charles M Hooley	Nile L Kriesel	Mary Lou Johnson	Diane K Deblon	Gordon C Seim	Donald L Beberg	David C Junker
Thief River Falls (8)	MC 218 681-2943	Bob Reeve	....	Gerald Wigness	Roger DeLap	David Bjorkman	Ken Froschheiser	....
Tracy (2)	MC 507 629-3460	(not reporting)						
Two Harbors (4)	CM 218 834-5631	Wayne Sletten	Roger Simonson	....	Lee Klein	Robert Sellman	Richard Hogenson	Robert Soderstrom
Vadnais Heights (11)	MC 612 429-5343	Mark Haider	Gerald Urban	....	....	....	....	Joseph Momsen
Virginia (9)	CM 218 741-3890	Elmer Metsa	Nick Dragisich	Susan Lemieux	Susan Lemieux	Ed Clark	Tom Yarick	Robert Manzoline
Waconia (3)	MC 612 442-2184	(not reporting)						
Wadena (4)	MC 218 631-2383	James N Lundquist	Bradley A Swenson	Bradley A Swenson	Bradley A Swenson	Tom Reger	Lane Waldahl	Mark Petsche
Waite Park v (5)	MC 612 252-6822	(not reporting)						
Waseca (8)	CM 507 835-3840	Steven E Manthe	Michael McCauley	Robert Jellum	Julie Linnihan	Robert Johnson	Jim Staloch	....
Watertown (2)	MC 612 955-2681	Norman A Bauer	Michael A Ericson	Marilyn Paschka	....	Hubert D Widmer	....	K Gulbrandson
Waterville (2)	MC 507 362-8300	Lawrence Meskan	Nickie Roberge	Maria Stoering	....	Steve Anderson	Arlie Bluhm	Rick Vollbrecht
Wayzata (4)	CM 612 473-0234	(not reporting)						
Wells (2)	MC 507 553-6371	Dave Jacobson	Dolly Schultz	Dolly Schultz	Dolly Schultz	Jack Horntasch	Gary Robbins	Ray Wigern
West St. Paul (19)	CM 612 552-4100	Michael Bisanz	William Craig	Dianne Krogh	John Remkus	Richard Krogh	....	Philip Stefaniak
White Bear Lake (25)	CM 612 429-8526	(not reporting)						
Willmar (18)	CM 612 235-4913	(not reporting)						
Windom (4)	CM 507 831-2363	(not reporting)						
Winona (25)	CM 507 457-8200	(not reporting)						
Woodbury (20)	CM 612 739-5972	Kenneth Mahle Jr	Barry P Johnson	....	Thomas C Wright	Kenneth Southorn	Gregory T Orth	David R Jessup
Worthington (10)	MC 507 372-8600	(not reporting)						
Young America (1)	MC 612 467-2603	(not reporting)						
MISSISSIPPI (88)								
Aberdeen (7)	MC 601 369-4165	(not reporting)						
Amory (7)	MC 601 256-5635	(not reporting)						
Baldwyn t (3)	MC 601 365-2383	(not reporting)						
Batesville (6)	MC 601 563-4576	Bobby Baker	....	Barbara L Broome	Barbara L Broome	Tim Taylor	R D Vanlandingham	Wayne Darby
Bay St. Louis (8)	MC 601 467-9092	Edward A Favre	....	Michael Cuevas	L Kay Johnson	Andrew Lizana	Frank McNeil	Ronald Vanney
Belzoni (3)	MC 601 247-1343	(not reporting)						
Biloxi (46)	MC 601 435-6300	A J Holloway	....	Brenda Johnston	Bill Lanham	Floyd Thibodoux	Frank Duggan	Jerry Morgan
Booneville t (8)	MC 601 728-6810	(not reporting)						
Brandon (11)	MC 601 825-5021	(not reporting)						
Brookhaven (10)	MC 601 833-2362	M D Sullivan	....	Iris C Rudman	....	Paul Cartwright	Fred C McKee	Lanny C Dickey
Canton (10)	MC 601 859-4331	(not reporting)						
Carthage t (4)	MC 601 267-8322	(not reporting)						
Charleston (2)	MC 601 647-5841	(not reporting)						
Clarksdale (20)	CO 601 627-8400	Henry Espy	....	Sylvia H Burton	....	Thomas B Davis	Danny L Vick	....
Cleveland (15)	MC 601 846-1471	(not reporting)						
Clinton (22)	MC 601 924-5462	Rosemary Aultman	Nelson Byrd	Nelson Byrd	Lois McKay	Jeffrey Landrum	Donald Byington	Harold Alderman
Columbia (7)	MC 601 736-8201	Harold Bryant	....	Don Martin	....	Ted Thompson	Joe Sanders	Bob Kearschner
Columbus (24)	MC 601 328-7021	Fred M Hayslett	....	Dorothy Pridmore	Dorothy Pridmore	James L Massey	Edward H Bowen	....
Corinth (12)	MC 601 286-6644	(not reporting)						
Crystal Springs (6)	MC 601 892-1212	(not reporting)						
Drew (2)	MC 601 745-8556	Eugene Wakham	....	Bettie T Dickey	....	Ricky Jenkins	Burner Smith	Mac Benson
Durant (3)	MC 601 653-3221	(not reporting)						
Ellisville (4)	MC 601 477-3323	Ernest P Todd	....	Kathy Brewer	....	Stan Kinmon	R L Jenkins	Howell Beech
Forest (5)	MC 601 469-2921	(not reporting)						
Fulton t (3)	MC 601 862-4929	Jack Creely	....	Betty Pearson	....	Charles Grimes	Ray Barrett	Dan Pate
Gautier (10)	CM 601 497-2332	Charles A Keith	Ronald Waller	Pearl B Mercer	....	Ernest Brimacombe	Allen Johnson	....
Greenville (45)	MC 601 378-1500	(not reporting)						
Greenwood (19)	MC 601 453-2246	(not reporting)						
Grenada (11)	CM 601 227-3440	L D Boone Jr	L R Kegley	....	....	Eugene Doss	Ben Simmons	J Kenneth Mixon
Gulfport (41)	MC 601 868-5831	(not reporting)						

Directory 1/9 **MUNICIPAL OFFICIALS**
continued **IN U.S. CITIES OVER 2,500**

City, 1990 population figures (000 omitted), form of government	Municipal phone number	Mayor	Appointed administrator	City clerk	Finance officer	Fire chief	Police chief	Public works director
MISSISSIPPI (88) continued								
Hattiesburg (42)	MC 601 545-4572	J Ed Morgan	. . . .	Clarice Wansley	Joe Townsend	George Herrington	Mark McCarver	Bennie Sellers
Hazlehurst (4)	MC 601 894-3131	(not reporting)						
Hernando (3)	MC 601 429-9092	(not reporting)						
Hollandale (4)	MC 601 827-2241	(not reporting)						
Holly Springs (7)	MC 601 252-4280	(not reporting)						
Horn Lake (9)	MC 601 393-6178	Mike Thomas	. . . .	Diane Stewart	. . . .	J Larry Newton	Darryl Whaley	James McKell
Houston (4)	MC 601 456-2328	(not reporting)						
Indianola (12)	MC 601 887-3101	(not reporting)						
Itta Bena t (2)	MC 601 254-7231	(not reporting)						
Iuka (3)	MC 601 423-3781	(not reporting)						
Jackson (197)	MC 601 960-1005	John Kane Ditto	Jean Shaw	Gay Huff	Lee Dumbauld	Joseph Donovan	Jimmy Wilson	Theodore Somers
Kosciusko (7)	MC 601 289-1226	George E Lewis	. . . .	Janet P Baird	Janet P Baird	Roy Frazier	Dirk Thayer	Lavown Pope
Laurel (19)	CO 601 428-6424	Susan B Vincent	Tinnon G Myrick	Jolyn Sellers	Don K Bullock	Marvin Overstreet	James E Bush	Roy Jones
Leland (6)	MC 601 686-4136	Sam Thomas	. . . .	Michael Fratesi	. . . .	Junior Walker	Michael Dees	. . . .
Lexington (2)	MC 601 834-1261	Richard Spencer	. . . .	Pamela Williams	. . . .	Jessie Joiner	Jessie Joiner	James Keith
Long Beach (16)	MC 601 863-1556	(not reporting)						
Louisville (7)	MC 601 773-9201	(not reporting)						
Magee t (4)	MC 601 849-3344	(not reporting)						
Mc Comb (12)	MC 601 684-4000	Ronald Wilkinson	Sam Mims	Donna Ladner	Donna Ladner	Richard Coghlan	Lee Barkdull	Ronnie Lindsey
Mendenhall t (2)	MC 601 847-1212	(not reporting)						
Meridian (41)	MC 601 485-1926	John Robert Smith	Donald H Farrar	Ed Skipper	. . . .	Joseph S Taylor	William D Sollie	Benny Wolfe
Moorhead t (2)	CM 601 246-5461	Betty Fowler	James Griffin	Joyce Walker	. . . .	Danny McCraney	Henry Manuel	. . . .
Morton (3)	MC 601 732-8609	Charles Steadman	. . . .	C Hollingshead	. . . .	Clell Harrell	Oscar Tadlock
Moss Point (18)	MC 601 475-0300	Ira S Polk	Kay Toncrey	. . . .	Terrence Williams	Ed Hudson	Charles Barber	Jimmy Miles
Mound Bayou (2)	MC 601 741-2193	(not reporting)						
Natchez (19)	MC 601 446-6641	Larry L Brown Sr	. . . .	Frances Trosclair	. . . .	Gary Winborne	Willie Huff	Richard Burke
New Albany (7)	MC 601 534-1010	Thomas R Cooper	. . . .	Anne D Neal	. . . .	William Dovell	David Grisham	Wayne Treadaway
Newton (4)	MC 601 683-6181	Preston H Beatty	Geraldine M Seal	Geraldine M Seal	. . . .	Charles Vance	Joe R Mowdy	Daryl Ford
Ocean Springs (15)	MC 601 875-4236	Kevin V Alves Sr	. . . .	Sandra F Jenkins	. . . .	James Murray	Carolyn Frayser	Robert Powell
Okolona (3)	MC 601 447-5461	(not reporting)						
Oxford (10)	MC 601 236-1310	John Leslie	. . . .	V Chrestman	. . . .	Terry McDonald	Billy White	
Pascagoula (26)	CM 601 762-1020	Wayne S Savell	. . . .	Brenda Reed	Kenneth McKeown	Jewell McMillian	Michael Whitmore	Garland Lear
Pass Christian (6)	MC 601 452-3310	(not reporting)						
Pearl (20)	MC 601 932-2262	Mitch Childre	. . . .	Shirley Rogers	. . . .	Mike Burns	Bill Slade	John Grant
Petal (8)	MC 601 545-1776	Jack Gay	. . . .	Priscilla Daniel	. . . .	Leonard A Evans	Billy W Murphy	Charles Z Stevens
Philadelphia (7)	MC 601 656-3612	Harlan P Majure	. . . .	. . . .	. . . .	Kenneth Coleman	James A Gentry	. . . .
Picayune (11)	CM 601 798-9770	Woody Spiers	James M Young	. . . .	Jackie Booth	Jackie Mitchell	Freddy Drennan	Raymond Pearson
Pontotoc (5)	MC 601 489-4321	(not reporting)						
Poplarville (3)	MC 601 795-8161	Billy W Spiers	. . . .	Brenda T Burge	. . . .	Bobby Strahan	Joe Stuart	John Davis
Quitman t (3)	MC 601 776-3728	(not reporting)						
Richland (4)	MC 601 932-3000	(not reporting)						
Ridgeland (12)	MC 601 856-7113	(not reporting)						
Ripley (5)	MC 601 837-8578	(not reporting)						
Rolling Fork (2)	MC 601 873-2814	John Pippin Jr	. . . .	Dorothy K Pearson	. . . .	Larry Harris	Charles McPhail	Billy Johnson
Ruleville (3)	MC 601 756-2791	Harvey Springer	. . . .	Annell R Weed	. . . .	. . . .	Ronnie Houston	John Downs
Senatobia (5)	MC 601 562-4474	(not reporting)						
Shelby (3)	MC 601 398-5156	(not reporting)						
Southaven (18)	MC 601 393-5931	Joseph A Cates	. . . .	Marlene Sprinkle	. . . .	Vernon McCammon	Tom Long	Michael Forsythe
Starkville (18)	CM 601 324-4011	Jesse Greer	. . . .	Vivian Collier	. . . .	Willie Johnson	H B Maxey	H W Webb
Tupelo (31)	MC 601 841-6487	Jack L Marshall	. . . .	William L Norris	William L Norris	. . . .	Billy V White	George Walsh
Vicksburg (21)	CO 601 636-3411	(not reporting)						
Water Valley (4)	MC 601 473-2431	Larry G Hart	. . . .	Doris B Cox	. . . .	Robert Ward	Michael W King	Harry Womble
Waveland (4)	MC 601 467-4134	Stella Frilot	Michael Barnes	Betsy Phillips	Michael Barnes	David Garcia	James Varnell	John Woodall
Waynesboro t (5)	MC 601 735-4874	Craig L Ezell	. . . .	Allene Rigney	. . . .	C L Westover	J C Denham	Joe C Walley
West Point (8)	MC 601 494-2573	Kenny Dill	Dewel Brasher	. . . .	. . . .	Caradine Young	Bill Ladd	. . . .
Wiggins t (3)	MC 601 928-7221	(not reporting)						
Winona (6)	MC 601 283-1232	(not reporting)						
Yazoo City (12)	MC 601 746-1401	(not reporting)						
MISSOURI (185)								
Arnold (19)	MC 314 296-2100	Marion Becker	Eric G Knoll	Diane Bast	John Brazeal	Ron Fiala	B J Nelson	Robert Eade
Aurora (6)	CM 417 678-5121	Junior McKinley	. . . .	Juli A Baldridge	. . . .	Alan Abel	Bill Merritt	. . . .
Ava (3)	MC 417 683-4122	(not reporting)						
Ballwin (22)	CM 314 227-8580	Richard G Andrews	Robert Kuntz	. . . .	Donette Johnson	. . . .	Donald Loehr	. . . .
Bel-Ridge v (3)	MC 314 429-2878	(not reporting)						
Bellefontaine Neighbors (11)	MC 314 867-0076	Marty Rudloff	Mae McKay	. . . .	Lawrence Abeln	. . . .	Dave Erker	Lou Roth
Belton (18)	CM 816 331-4331	Steve Farmer	Ron Trivitt	Alice Strathman	Leon Ellis	Kirt Denkler	James Person	. . . .
Berkeley (12)	CM 314 524-3313	William Miller	Arbon Hairston	Lorraine Batton	. . . .	Roosevelt Sims	Robert Stewart	Thomas Manning
Bethany (3)	MC 816 425-3511	(not reporting)						
Black Jack (6)	MC 314 355-0400	(not reporting)						
Blue Springs (40)	CM 816 228-0138	Gregory Grounds	Frederick R Siems	Dianne Gardner	Isabel Stoecklein	. . . .	Howard Brown	. . . .
Bolivar (7)	MC 417 326-5298	(not reporting)						
Bonne Terre (4)	CM 314 358-2254	Wayne Weber	Terrance Rickard	Sandra Wells	. . . .	David Pratte	Gene Archer	Butch Keen
Boonville (7)	CM 816 882-2332	(not reporting)						
Bowling Green (3)	MC 314 324-5451	(not reporting)						
Branson (4)	MC 417 334-3345	Wade Meadows	Samuel E Grove	Sandra Williams	. . . .	Ernie Braswell	Steve Mefford	Larry Van Gilder
Breckenridge Hills v (5)	MC 314 427-6868	Archie Ledbetter	Pamela Price	. . . .	. . . .	. . . .	Donald Kaley	Fred Green
Brentwood (8)	MC 314 962-4800	Mark E Kurtz	Chris Seemayer	Chris Seemayer	Susan Zimmer	Robert Niemeyer	William Karabas	Willie Wright
Bridgeton (18)	MC 314 344-0600	Conrad W Bowers	. . . .	Carole Stahlhut	Dennis Rainey	. . . .	Warren Runge	Richard Houchin
Brookfield (5)	CM 816 258-3377	Jack Forbes	Stan Kasiske	Dana Tarpening	. . . .	Walter Gordon	David Hane	. . . .
Buckner (3)	MC 816 249-3191	Ben Whited	Judy Buttress	Kelly Gilgour	. . . .	Robert Pottberg	C Michael Seibert	Carl Williams
Butler (4)	MC 816 679-4013	(not reporting)						
Cabool (2)	MC 417 962-3136	Ed Hardy	Mike Mac Pherson	Tracy Upton	. . . .	Jerry Miller	Lynn Jones	. . . .
California (3)	MC 314 796-2500	Carol Rackers	Edmund Martin	Sue A Kuhn	. . . .	Allen Smith	Jerry McCarty	Gary Wells
Camdenton (..)	MC 314 346-3600	(not reporting)						
Cameron (5)	CM 816 632-2177	. . . .	Phil Lammers	Barbara O'Connor	. . . .	Glenn Sherman	Harold Riddle	James Roach
Cape Girardeau (34) ...	MC 314 334-1212	Francis E Rhodes	J Ronald Fischer	Mary F Thompson	Alvin M Stoverink	Robert Ridgeway	Howard Boyd Jr	Douglas K Leslie
Carl Junction (4)	MC 417 649-7237	(not reporting)						
Carrollton (4)	MC 816 542-1414	(not reporting)						
Carthage (11)	MC 417 358-5904	Herbert Casteel	Mike Randall	Barbara Welch	Barbara Welch	Don Simmons	Edward Ellefsen	Wayne Weber
Caruthersville (7)	CM 314 333-2142	(not reporting)						
Centralia (3)	MC 314 682-2139	Deanna Richman	Lynn P Behrns	Ruby McDonald	. . . .	Lannie Patton	Gerald Goins	. . . .
Chaffee (3)	MC 314 887-3558	Ronald Moyers	. . . .	Diane Eftink	. . . .	Steve Graham	Jerry Bledsoe	John Martin

Directory 1/9 continued

MUNICIPAL OFFICIALS IN U.S. CITIES OVER 2,500

City, 1990 population figures (000 omitted), form of government	Municipal phone number	Mayor	Appointed administrator	City clerk	Finance officer	Fire chief	Police chief	Public works director
MISSOURI (185) continued								
Charleston (5)	CM 314 683-3325	Fred Gordon	Brian Donovan	Marsha Hart	Brian Donovan	Robert Ritchey	Robert Ritchey	David Teeters
Chesterfield (38)	MC 816 537-4000	Jack Leonard	Michael Herring	Marty Demay	Jan Hawn	. . . .	Ray Johnson	Bill Hawn
Chillicothe (9)	MC 816 646-2267	Dana Ringberg	Mark Adcock	Janet Price	Diane Deringer	Joseph Rinehart	Tom Black	. . . .
Clayton (14)	CM 314 727-8100	B Uchitelle	Steven Hoffner	Linda Huffman	Dale Dickmann	Richard Morris	Richard Morris	Bryan Pearl
Clinton (9)	MC 816 885-6121	(not reporting)						
Columbia (69)	CM 314 874-7111	M McCollum	Raymond Beck	Launa Daniel	Harold Boldt	William Margraf	Ernest Barbee	Lowell Patterson
Crestwood (11)	CM 314 957-4790	Patricia Killoren	D Kent Leichliter	Carol Schneiderhahn	Robert L Wuebbels	William J Kramer	Donald E Greer	. . . .
Creve Coeur (12)	CM 314 432-6000	Sue Baum	T M McDowell	Laverne Collins	Jeffrey Steiner	. . . .	Richard Schnarr	Vijay K Bhasin
Crystal City (4)	MC 314 937-4614	(not reporting)						
De Soto (6)	CM 314 586-3326	Bruce King	David Greene	Arlene Burt	Evelyn Lewis	John Wood	Lloyd Davis	. . . .
Dellwood (5)	MC 314 521-4339	David Bardgett	Tom Zak	. . . .	. . . .	. . . .	Dan Chapman	. . . .
Des Peres (8)	MC 314 966-4600	(not reporting)						
Desloge (4)	MC 314 431-3700	Earl E Hoehn	Herman Skaggs	Linda Aubuchon	. . . .	J D Hodge	Fred Meagher	. . . .
Dexter (8)	MC 314 624-5959	Willis Conner	. . . .	Joann Steinbrueck	. . . .	Al Banken	Rick Walker	Randy Robinson
East Prairie (3)	MC 314 649-3057	(not reporting)						
El Dorado Springs (4)	CM 417 876-2521	(not reporting)						
Eldon (4)	CM 314 392-3638	Dwight E Smittle	. . . .	LaVerne Belk	James A Link	Charles Wilson	Thomas Russell	. . . .
Ellisville (8)	CM 314 227-9660	Dennis N Smith	Stephen A Arbo	Catherine Demeter	. . . .	. . . .	B Wayne Prince	Terry Keran
Eureka (5)	MC 314 938-5233	Otis Nelson	. . . .	Ralph Lindsey	Ralph Lindsey	. . . .	Michael Wiegand	Michael Schlereth
Excelsior Springs (10)	CM 816 637-0752	Charles Asberry	Craig Hubler	Frances Smith	Ralph Hockman Jr	William Stewart	John McGovern	Rex Brinker
Farmington (12)	MC 314 756-1701	Gay Wilkinson	Roger Hoehn	Phyllis Hartrup	. . . .	Phillip Johnson	Robert Oder	Duane Johnson
Fayette (3)	MC 816 248-5246	John Holtzclaw	Michael P Brown	Robin Overstreet	. . . .	Benjie Conrow	Bryan Kunze	. . . .
Ferguson (22)	CM 314 521-7721	Michael James	Michael Miller	Dorris Carter	Joann Bordeleau	Don Parrotte	James Carter	Dan Fain
Festus (8)	MC 314 937-4694	John A Graham	Richard T Turley	Charlene I Byers	Gordon Russell	Donald D DeClue	Ronald J Scaggs	. . . .
Flat River (5)	CM 314 431-3577	(not reporting)						
Florissant (51)	MC 314 921-5700	(not reporting)						
Fredericktown (4)	MC 314 783-3683	W Laplant	. . . .	L Stevens	. . . .	D Asher	R Roberts	. . . .
Frontenac (3)	MC 314 994-3200	Newell A Baker	Wayne A Neal	. . . .	. . . .	Charles Rinne	Benjamin Branch	Donald J Rohlfing
Fulton (10)	MC 314 642-6826	(not reporting)						
Gladstone (26)	CM 816 436-2200	Roger Norris	James H Norris	Marilyn Ahnefeld	E Sue Henning	. . . .	William Adamo	Gerald Menefee
Glendale (6)	MC 314 965-3600	Anthony Monaco	Michael Pounds	Shirley Richter	Barbara Senn	Gilyette Soffner	Richard Black	Edward Veazey
Grain Valley (2)	CM 816 229-6275	Michael King	Joseph Murray	Jere Chieppo	. . . .	. . . .	Skipper Hedges	. . . .
Grandview (25)	CM 816 763-3900	Harry O Wilson	Cory L Smith	Ruth K Gray	Kevin C Watson	. . . .	Robert M Beckers	Lawrence N Creek
Hannibal (18)	MC 314 221-0111	Richard Schwartz	. . . .	Carol McGee	. . . .	Roy Hark	John Waldschlager	Robert Williamson
Harrisonville (8)	MC 816 884-3285	William Mills	Damon Bartles	Cheri Powell	Vernon Chalfant	Joe Gerke	Norman Schnorf	Dan Powell
Hayti (3)	MC 314 359-0632	H R Euell	. . . .	Teresa Merrell	. . . .	Milford Chism	Barry McKay	Leonard Plunkett
Hazelwood (15)	CM 314 839-3700	David Farquharson	Edwin G Carlstrom	Norma Caldwell	Donnie Bryant	Jim Matthies	Carl Wolf	Jose Hernandez
Hermann (3)	MC 314 486-5400	John G Bartel	Terry L Helton	D Grannemann	. . . .	Melvin Speckhals	Robert O Sitton	. . . .
Higginsville (5)	MC 816 584-2106	(not reporting)						
Holts Summit (2)	MC 314 896-5600	R C Miller	. . . .	Linda Batye	. . . .	. . . .	Andrew Goldman	. . . .
Houston (2)	MC 417 967-3348	(not reporting)						
Independence (112)	CM 816 836-8300	William Carpenter	Larry N Blick	Bruce E Lowrey	Frank Muser	Larry B Hodge	. . . .	Howard B Penrod
Jackson (9)	MC 314 243-3568	Paul Sander	Carl Talley	Mary Lowry	. . . .	Gary Niswonger	Larry Koenig	. . . .
Jefferson City (35)	MC 314 634-6300	(not reporting)						
Jennings (16)	MC 314 388-1164	William D Tharp	. . . .	Cheryl Balke	Beverly Roche	James Sutphin	James Trentham	Richard Perry
Joplin (41)	CM 417 624-0820	Bernie Johnson	Leonard Martin	Mary Davis	Linda Sharp	Harry Guinn	David Niebur	Harold McCoy
Kansas City (435)	CM 816 274-2000	. . . .	Larry Brown	. . . .	. . . .	. . . .	. . . .	. . . .
Kearney (2)	CM 816 635-4142	David Pence	Jim Eldridge	. . . .	. . . .	. . . .	Tom Carey	. . . .
Kennett (11)	CM 314 888-9001	Charles B Brown	. . . .	Leverna S Moore	. . . .	John H Mallott	Michael E Damron	. . . .
Kinloch (3)	MC 314 521-3335	(not reporting)						
Kirksville (17)	CM 816 627-1224	Sondra Murray	Robert Irvin	Vickie Parrish	Kathy Rogers	Ron Stewart	Dave Pingel	Mark Gaugh
Kirkwood (27)	CM 314 822-5802	(not reporting)						
Knob Noster (..)	MC 816 563-2595	B E Carr	Rodney W Avery	Diane Clemons	. . . .	Rick Johnson	Joseph Thering	. . . .
La Plata (1)	MC 816 332-7166	(not reporting)						
Ladue (9)	MC 314 993-3439	(not reporting)						
Lake Saint Louis (7)	CM 314 625-1200	Edward Hajek Jr	Ronald A Nelson	Mary L Von Blohn	Jean McDonough	. . . .	Michael Force	Freddy Williams
Lamar (4)	MC 417 682-5554	Gerald Gilkey	Lynn Calton	Carolyn Taffner	. . . .	Bill Rawlings	Ron Hager	. . . .
Lawson (..)	CM 816 296-3217	(not reporting)						
Lebanon (10)	MC 417 532-2157	(not reporting)						
Lee's Summit (46)	CM 816 251-2301	Marvin Ensworth	Kenneth R Murray	Denise Chisum	Conrad Lamb	Richard Dyer	D Greg Henderson	W Stockhausen
Lexington (5)	MC 816 259-4633	Cindy Dickmeyer	Abigail W Tempel	Carla Gniselberti	Abigail W Tempel	Scott Wandell	. . . .	. . . .
Liberty (20)	CM 816 781-7100	Robert J Saunders	Gary W Jackson	Donna L Holloway	Arthur H Dewitt	Richard J Lehmann	Bruce W Davis	. . . .
Louisiana (4)	MC 314 754-4132	(not reporting)						
Macon (6)	MC 816 385-6421	Dale Whitley	. . . .	Vicky McLeland	Cathay Swan	Raymond Blomberg	Floyd Leathers	Gary Quick
Malden (5)	MC 314 276-4502	(not reporting)						
Manchester (7)	CM 314 227-1385	Frank J McGuire	Michael B Leavitt	. . . .	Diana M Madrid	. . . .	John T Quinn	Edwin M Blattner
Maplewood (10)	CM 314 645-3600	Jane Moeller	Martin J Corcoran	Charlotte First	Martin J Corcoran	Mervin Feick	. . . .	Michael Doi
Marceline (3)	MC 314 376-3528	Brian McGlothlin	William R Johnson	Elizabeth Cupp	William R Johnson	Larry Ervie	Robert Schmitt	Charles Tomlinson
Marshall (13)	MC 816 886-2226	Mitchel Geisler	Charles Tryban	Janet French	Debbie Boyd	John Rieves	Jim Simmerman	Paul Jensen
Marshfield (4)	MC 417 468-2310	(not reporting)						
Maryland Heights (25)	MC 314 291-6650	John T Saffa Jr	Mark M Levin	Carol Turner	David Watson	. . . .	Neil Kurlander	Marty Macke
Maryville (11)	MC 816 562-2811	Gerald Henggeler	William Galletly	Jo E Gill	Bill Blankenship	. . . .	Keith Woods	Ronald Franz
Mexico (11)	CM 314 581-2100	Tim Williams	Daniel Parrott	Donna M Barnes	Joseph M Kernell	. . . .	Donald J Bolli	Glenn P Phillips
Moberly (13)	CM 816 263-4420	Larry Noel	Don Tuley	Carole Kehoe	Nick Burton	David Lacy	Michael Garbulski	Ron Wilson
Moline Acres (3)	MC 314 868-2533	(not reporting)						
Monett (7)	CO 417 235-3763	H C Beckwith	. . . .	Doris Meyer	. . . .	Kenneth Smalley	Larry Zimmerman	Peter C Rauch
Monroe City (3)	MC 314 735-4585	Danny Porter	. . . .	Gary Osbourne	. . . .	Gary McElroy	Monzell Sharp	. . . .
Montgomery City (2)	MC 314 564-3160	John J O'Fallon	James K Koshmider	James K Koshmider	James K Koshmider	Thomas J O'Keefe	Gary W Hemby	Emory Gerken
Mount Vernon (4)	MC 417 466-2122	(not reporting)						
Mountain Grove (4)	MC 417 926-4162	Delbert Crewse	Joe Rodery	Judy Kjellberg	Joe Rodery	Norman Jarrett	Tommy Gaddis	Joe Rodery
Neosho (9)	CM 417 451-8050	Howard Birdsong	Jim Cole	James E Haddock	Cheryl Mosby	Wayne Blauert	Terry Herron	Malcolm Mosby
Nevada (9)	CM 417 667-7894	George Washburn	A Wayne Neal	Falena Vittetoe E	Ronald Chandler	William Gillette	Larry Moore	. . . .
New Madrid (3)	MC 314 748-2458	(not reporting)						
Nixa (5)	CM 417 725-3785	Jack B Payne	Jan M Blase	Coralee M Patrick	. . . .	. . . .	John Burdick	. . . .
Normandy (4)	MC 314 385-3300	Betty Houlihan	. . . .	Jackie Iocca	Jackie Iocca	. . . .	Jerome Burke	John Hutchison
North Kansas City (4)	MC 816 274-6000	Elizabeth Short	George DeFrench	Virginia Viar	Frank Henderson	Frank Smith	Wm Biggerstaff	Carl Elshire
Northwoods (5)	MC 314 385-8000	(not reporting)						
O'Fallon (19)	CM 314 272-6244	. . . .	Patrick A Nasi	Sandra Stokes	Juli Schmidt	. . . .	Michael Kernan	John G Griesenaur
Oak Grove (5)	MC 816 625-4012	Audrey Griffin	Thomas Schaefer	Linda Majors	. . . .	. . . .	. . . .	Mark Schaufler
Odessa (4)	MC 816 633-5577	(not reporting)						
Olivette (8)	CM 314 993-0444	Charles Feldman	Jerome Feldman	James Hoke	Jerome Feldman	Al Wedel	Robert Cole	Gene Kunzie
Osage Beach (3)	MC 314 348-3151	Gary Martin	Pat McCourt	Diann Warner	Brett Vuagniaux	. . . .	Roland Trautman	Pat McCourt
Overland (18)	MC 314 428-4321	Frank Munsch	. . . .	Gail Waggoner	. . . .	. . . .	Eddy Williams	Charles Karam

Directory 1/9
continued

MUNICIPAL OFFICIALS
IN U.S. CITIES OVER 2,500

City, 1990 population figures (000 omitted), form of government	Municipal phone number	Mayor	Appointed administrator	City clerk	Finance officer	Fire chief	Police chief	Public works director
MISSOURI (185) continued								
Ozark (4)	MC 417 485-2407	(not reporting)						
Pacific (4)	MC 314 257-7200	(not reporting)						
Pagedale (4)	MC 314 726-1200	(not reporting)						
Palmyra (3)	MC 314 769-2223	William Huffman	. . . .	Shirley J Nix	. . . .	Charles Hoehne	James Beadle	Raymond Houston
Perryville (7)	MC 314 547-2594	Robert J Miget	Craig M Lindsley	Marilyn Dobbelare	. . . .	Wayne Walker	Eugene Besand	Melvin Niswonger
Pevely (3)	MC 314 479-4452	(not reporting)						
Pine Lawn (5)	MC 314 261-5500	Linda S Givins	. . . .	Janet S Wright	Pervais Butt	. . . .	John P Morgan	Jimmie Wilder
Pleasant Hill (4)	CM 816 987-3135	Terry C Wilson	Mark R Randall	Sandi F Beatty	Sandi F Beatty	. . . .	Thomas D Bass	Jerry D Barbarick
Poplar Bluff (17)	CM 314 785-7474	Betty Absheer	Thomas J Lawson	William Pettet	. . . .	Gerald Garrett	Dennis Long	. . . .
Portageville (3)	MC 314 379-5789	Donald Rone Jr	. . . .	Vella B Moody	. . . .	Bob Duggins	Ronnie Adams	. . . .
Potosi (3)	MC 314 438-2767	P R Dessieux	. . . .	C D McCourtney	P R Dessieux	. . . .	Donald Cooksey	. . . .
Raymore (6)	MC 816 331-0488	(not reporting)						
Raytown (31)	MC 816 737-6000	Willard Ross	. . . .	R A Reis	R A Reis	Dale Collins	Kris Turnbow	Eugene Yeokum
Republic (6)	MC 417 732-6065	Harold Tindell	. . . .	Karen Cline	Jane Medlin	Don Murray	Sam Hartsell	Ronnie Smith
Richland (2)	MC 314 765-4421	. . . .	D DuRossette	Clarice Payne	. . . .	Ricky Hobbs	John Abbott	. . . .
Richmond (6)	MC 816 776-5304	Monroe Evert	Rick Outersky	Jean Elliston	. . . .	Lonnie Quick	Doug Porter	Allen D Minnick
Richmond Heights (10)	CM 314 645-0404	B W LaTourette	Carl L Schwing	M R Khamlaksana	Carl L Schwing	William P O'Neal	Ronald F Pfeiffer	Byrl J Engel
Riverside (3)	MC 816 741-3993	(not reporting)						
Riverview v (3)	CM 314 868-0700	(not reporting)						
Rock Hill (5)	MC 314 968-1410	(not reporting)						
Rolla (14)	MC 314 364-1835	Floyd D Ferrell	Merle L Strouse	Carol Daniels	Daniel Murphy	William Oliver	Michael Snavely	Steve Hargis
Salem (4)	CM 314 729-4811	C Clar Leonard	Mark J Girth	Nadine Victor	. . . .	. . . .	Micheal Allgire	Larry Major
Savannah (4)	MC 816 324-3315	David Ingersoll	. . . .	Janice Hatcher	. . . .	James Edwards	George Birdsong	Kenny Lance
Scott City (4)	MC 314 264-2157	(not reporting)						
Sedalia (20)	MC 816 827-3000	Jane A Gray	Irl Tessendorf	Shirley Collins	Pat Allen	Michael Ditzfeld	Phillip T Bue	Gary Johnson
Shrewsbury (6)	MC 314 647-5795	(not reporting)						
Sikeston (18)	CM 314 471-2511	Charles Leible	S Borgsmiller	Carroll Couch	. . . .	. . . .	James W Leist	K Doug Friend
Slater (2)	MC 816 529-2271	Andree Petersen	. . . .	Russell Griffith	. . . .	David Butler	Melvin Mullins	Tim Riesch
Smithville (3)	MC 816 532-0500	(not reporting)						
Springfield (140)	CM 417 864-1000	(not reporting)						
St. Ann (14)	MC 314 427-8009	(not reporting)						
St. Charles (55)	MC 314 949-3200	Grace M Nichols	Allan T Williams	Linda Medlock	Karen McDermott	Edward Underwood	David King	Cliff Baber
St. Clair (4)	MC 314 629-0333	James A Barns	Marvin S Harman	Darlene Coons	. . . .	. . . .	Tom Yoder	Harley Kamper
St. James (3)	MC 314 265-7011	Nelson A Hart	. . . .	Marilyn Linke	. . . .	B H Green	Richad Woolsey	Kenneth A Young
St. John (7)	CM 314 427-8700	(not reporting)						
St. Joseph (72)	CM 816 271-4610	(not reporting)						
St. Louis (397)	MC 314 622-4000	Freeman Bosley Jr	Lloyd Jordan	. . . .	Virvus Jones	Neil Svetanics	Clarence Harmon	James Shea
St. Peters (46)	MC 314 928-3800	Thomas W Brown	Robert R Irvin	Janice D Simmons	Timothy Wilkinson	. . . .	Ronald S Neubauer	Dale L Houdeshell
Ste. Genevieve (4)	CM 314 883-5400	(not reporting)						
Sugar Creek (4)	MC 816 252-4400	(not reporting)						
Sullivan (6)	MC 314 468-4612	Elmer E Cowan	John D Butz	Janice Nolie	. . . .	. . . .	George R Counts	. . . .
Sunset Hills (5)	MC 314 849-3400	(not reporting)						
Town And Country (10)	MC 314 432-6606	Peggy Symes	James Robinson	Joan Klinghammer	Betty Cotner	. . . .	Salvador Delmar	Douglas Hopkins
Trenton (6)	MC 816 359-4310	Nick McHarque	Brian Paulsen	Cindy Simpson	Cindy Simpson	Bill Vaughn	Ed Koenig	Buddy Bennett
Union (6)	MC 314 583-3600	(not reporting)						
University City (40)	CM 314 862-6767	Janet Majerus	Frank Ollendorff	Dolores A Miller	Willie Norfleet	Bob Metcalf	Stanley Topper	Allan Dieckgraefe
Valley Park (4)	MC 314 225-5171	Fred L Palmer Jr	. . . .	M Wilburn	. . . .	. . . .	David Brown	Gerald Martin
Vandalia (3)	CM 314 594-6186	Ramon Barnes	Bret Jones	Kim Wood	Sharon Myers	Ramon Barnes	George Hannaford	Roger Woodward
Warrensburg (15)	CM 816 747-9131	Ann B Houx	Roger L Nelson	Nancy Anderson	. . . .	Philip D Schlup	Gene L Burden	Robert S Crumb
Warrenton (4)	MC 314 456-3535	Greg Costello	. . . .	Eileen Boehm	Anita Koelling	. . . .	Ray Clark	Denneth Schwerdt
Washington (11)	MC 314 390-1006	Stephen Reust	James Briggs	Dolly Gerstenkorn	Janet Braun	Bill Halmich	Dan Rowden	Gary Thornhill
Waynesville (3)	MC 314 774-6171	Bill Ransdall	John T Tinsley	Barbara Stinson	. . . .	Danny Fry	John Mellan	. . . .
Webb City (7)	MC 417 673-4651	Sterling Gant	. . . .	Lorinda Southard	. . . .	Larry Horine	Emmett McFarland	. . . .
Webster Groves (23)	CM 314 961-4100	Glenn J Sheffield	Carl E Ramey	Lynne N Greene	Carl E Ramey	Jack R Buechler	Gene A Young	Dennis L Wells
Wellston (4)	MC 314 385-1015	(not reporting)						
Wentzville (5)	MC 314 327-5101	Darrel B Lackey	H Joe McReynolds	Lou Ann Wibe	Dennis Walsh	. . . .	Loyde K Davidson	Roger Cox
West Plains (9)	CO 417 256-7176	Harry Kelly	Gerald Elmore	Constance Shelton	Constance Shelton	Hubert Redburn	James Boze	Jim Davidson
Windsor (3)	MC 816 647-3512	(not reporting)						
Woodson Terrace (4)	MC 314 427-2600	John L Brown	Robert J Gereaux	Dorothy E Rickard	. . . .	. . . .	Thomas A McKay	Stephen G Wipfler
MONTANA (29)								
Anaconda-Deer Lodge (10)	CM 406 563-8421	. . . .	Cheryl S Beatty	Tracey Sweeney	. . . .	Thomas Shagina	James Connors	. . . .
Billings (81)	CM 406 657-8200	Richard L Larsen	Mark S Watson	Marita R Herold	Nathan R Tubergen	Lorren L Ballard	Wayne R Inman	Kenneth L Haag
Bozeman (23)	CM 406 586-3321	Tim Swanson	Jim Wysocki	Pat Estey	Miral Gamradt	Aaron Holst	Dick Boyer	Phillip Forbes
Butte-Silver Bow (33)	MC 406 723-8262	Jack Lynch	. . . .	Barbara Sullivan	Gary Rowe	Bob Armstrong	John McPherson	Jim Johnston
Columbia Falls (3)	MC 406 892-4391	Edwin H Toren	. . . .	Connie Konopatzke	. . . .	Donald Barnhart	Dale Stone	Claude Tesmer
Conrad (3)	MC 406 278-3623	T Hammerbacker	. . . .	M Eve	. . . .	J Williams	G Dent	S Ruhd
Cut Bank (3)	MC 406 873-5526	Bryan Buchanan	. . . .	Marie Mitch	. . . .	James Taylor	Joseph Gauthier	Lorin Lowry
Deer Lodge (3)	MC 406 846-3649	(not reporting)						
Dillon (4)	MC 406 683-4245	(not reporting)						
Forsyth (2)	MC 406 356-2521	Warren J Becker	Daniel D Watson	Daniel D Watson				Joseph G Foran
Glasgow (4)	MC 406 228-2476	(not reporting)						
Glendive (5)	MC 406 365-3318	(not reporting)						
Great Falls (55)	CM 406 727-5881	Gayle Morris	John Lawton	Peggy Lamberson	Timothy Magee	Richard Meisinger	Robert Jones	Erling Tufte
Hamilton (3)	MC 406 363-2101	Laurel Hegstad	Don Williamson	L Higginbotham	. . . .	Buzz Greenup	Allan Auch	. . . .
Hardin (3)	MC 406 665-2113	(not reporting)						
Havre (10)	MC 406 265-6719	Donald Driscoll	. . . .	Lowell Swenson	. . . .	Jerry Benbrooks	Mike Shortell	Gerald Grabofsky
Helena (25)	CM 406 447-8404	Kay H McKenna	William J Verwolf	Debbie Lesmeister	Shelly A Laine	Don Hurni	William J Ware	Richard Nisbet
Kalispell (12)	CM 406 752-6600	Douglas Rauthe	Bruce Williams	. . . .	Amy Robertson	Ted Waggener	Addison Clark	Robert Babb
Laurel (6)	MC 406 628-8791	Chuck Rodgers	. . . .	Don Hackmann	. . . .	. . . .	Mike Atkinson	. . . .
Lewistown (6)	MC 406 538-2302	Lloyd Johnson	. . . .	Sue Glenn	. . . .	Terry Phillips	Russel Dunnington	William Shaw
Libby (3)	MC 406 293-2731	Fred A Brown	. . . .	Kim D Shaver	. . . .	Kenneth Preston	. . . .	William A Kemp
Livingston (7)	CM 406 222-6120	Bill Dennis	Kenton G Griffin	Julianne Blakely	James Christiaens	David Fredrick	Lynn H Gillett	Clint Tinsley
Miles City (8)	CM 406 232-3462	George Kurkowski	. . . .	Patricia D Huss	. . . .	Leonard F Smith	Wade N Schmidt	Patrick L Rogers
Missoula (43)	MC 406 523-4700	Daniel Kemmis	Mary Walsh	Charles Stearns	Charles Stearns	Charles Gibson	James Oberhofer	Joseph Aldegarie
Polson (3)	MC 406 883-2131	(not reporting)						
Shelby (3)	MC 406 434-5222	Larry J Bonderud	. . . .	Jo Ann Wright	. . . .	. . . .	. . . .	Jack Boettcher
Sidney (5)	MC 406 482-2809	Harold Mercer	. . . .	Ethel Sobolik	. . . .	Gail Peterson	Frank DiFonzo	Terry Meldahl
Whitefish (4)	CM 406 862-2640	(not reporting)						
Wolf Point (3)	MC 406 653-1852	Delmar J Olsen	. . . .	Marlene R Mahlum	. . . .	Clark Johnson	. . . .	Charles L Worley

Directory 1/9
continued

MUNICIPAL OFFICIALS
IN U.S. CITIES OVER 2,500

City, 1990 population figures (000 omitted), form of government	Municipal phone number	Mayor	Appointed administrator	City clerk	Finance officer	Fire chief	Police chief	Public works director
NEBRASKA (56)								
Alliance (10)	CM 308 762-5400	Mike Dafney	. . . .	Linda S Jines	Leah J King	Howard Taylor Jr	Robert Jatczak	. . . .
Auburn (3)	MC 402 274-3420	Gary Volkmer	. . . .	Sherry Heskett	Harvey Bergmann	Dale Thomas	Dennis Hogue	James Dietz
Aurora (4)	MC 402 694-6992	Kenneth Harter	Michael Bair	Erma Luth	Erma Luth	Harlan Schaefer	Wm Gage	Bill Vandeman
Beatrice (12)	MC 402 223-3569	David I Maurstad	James W Bauer	Gwen Grabouski	. . . .	Darrell Eastin	Bruce Lang	James W Bauer
Bellevue (31)	MC 402 293-3000	Inez M Boyd	S P Benson	Beverly J Hrdy	. . . .	. . . .	Hines G Smith	Dennis D Hilfiker
Blair (7)	MC 402 426-4191	Jerome Jenny	Rodney Storm	Alice Diedrichsen	. . . .	. . . .	Marvin Doeden	Warren Whitaker
Broken Bow (4)	MC 308 872-5831	(not reporting)						
Central City (3)	MC 308 946-3806	(not reporting)						
Chadron (6)	CM 308 432-4444	Cliff Hanson	Carl Dierks	Donna Rust	Carl Dierks	Robert Geister	Theodore Vastine	Milo Rust
Columbus (19)	MC 402 564-8584	A F Wertz	Robert Freson	Linda Walters	Jim Heck	Dean Hefti	David Purdy	. . . .
Cozad (4)	MC 308 784-3907	Catherine Walters	. . . .	Carl York	. . . .	Craig Brestel	Bill Stevenson	. . . .
Crete (5)	MC 402 826-4311	(not reporting)						
Dakota City (1)	MC 402 987-3448	Ronald Brunton	Linda Gagnon	Linda Gagnon	. . . .	Jon Norris	. . . .	Danny Rager
David City (3)	MC 402 367-3135	Stephen Smith	Douglas C Rix	Joan E Kovar	. . . .	Mike Hiatt	Stephen Sunday	. . . .
Fairbury (4)	MC 402 729-2476	Lewis J Mason	. . . .	Lila Hannappel	. . . .	Ronald Southwick	Rick Carmichael	Michael Beachler
Falls City (5)	MC 402 245-2707	Stephen P Kottich	Martin R Gist	Martin R Gist	Martin R Gist	Alan L Romine	Norman Hemmerling	Larry R Merz
Fremont (24)	MC 402 727-2630	(not reporting)						
Fullerton (1)	MC 308 536-2893	(not reporting)						
Geneva (2)	MC 402 759-3109	Gaylord Songster	Robert Higel	Barbara Whitley	. . . .	Robert Hofferber	Robert Taylor	Robert Higel
Gering (8)	MC 308 436-5096	Bob Unzicker	Don W Baird	Pamela Richter	Larry Gion	James Templar	Melvin Griggs	Brian Sweeney
Gordon (2)	CM 308 282-0837	Thomas H Morris	Fred E Hlava	Toni Siders	. . . .	Vereen Forster	Ronald D Ehlers	Michael D Winter
Gothenburg (3)	MC 308 537-3677	Richard L Blase	Bruce Clymer	Connie Stull	. . . .	Dale Franzen	Randell Olson	William Crouch
Grand Island (39)	MC 308 381-5451	Ernest Dobesh	Zachary Zoul	Cindy Cartwright	Chuck Haase	Jimmy Rowell	Eugene Watson	Wayne Bennett
Hastings (23)	MC 402 461-2309	J Phillip Odom	Barbara Bramblett	Connie Hartman	. . . .	James Mitera	James Ruberson	Dave Wacker
Holdrege (6)	MC 308 995-2774	James Van Marter	Norman J Melton	Norman J Melton	. . . .	Jim Wagner	Ken Jackson	Larry Duval
Kearney (24)	CM 308 237-5133	Ron Larsen	Gary Greer	Michaelle Trembly	Wendall Wessels	. . . .	Steven Lamken	Thomas Murry
Kimball (3)	CM 308 235-3639	Thomas Wilson	Bruce Smith	Julie Schnell	. . . .	Art Schindler	Billy Shank	. . . .
La Vista (10)	MC 402 331-6116	Harold Anderson	Donald B Eikmeier	Dorothy McGinnis	Judy Nemetz	Pat Archibald	John Packett	C Ed McGinnis
Lexington (7)	CM 308 324-2341	John Wightman	Wm Podraza	Leon Malzahn	Neldene Skwarek	. . . .	Charles Clark	. . . .
Lincoln (192)	MC 402 471-7171	Michael Johanns	Polly McMullen	Paul Malzer	Jamie Warner	Michael Merwick	Allen Curtis	Richard Erixson
Madison (2)	MC 402 454-3412	Wayne Glasser	Don Barnhart	George Moehnert	. . . .	Raymond Keifer	Michael Hagley	Jim Lewis
Mc Cook (8)	CM 308 345-2022	Philip P Lyons	John E Carter	Kathryn D Casper	. . . .	Clifford Clapp	Richard Brunswick	Jack G Lytle
Minden (3)	MC 308 832-1820	Peter M Jensen	Brent Lewis	Dick Young	Dick Young	Raph Layton	Jim Huff	Rick Bienhoff
Nebraska City (7)	CO 402 873-5515	Larry Rawlings	. . . .	Kay Dammast	Kay Dammast	Charles Swanson	Kent Roumpf	William Brockley
Norfolk (21)	MC 402 644-8720	Harley Rector	Michael Nolan	Betty Bonac	Randy Gates	Bill Malone	Bill Mizner	Dennis Smith
North Platte (23)	MC 308 534-2610	(not reporting)						
O'Neill (4)	MC 402 336-3640	Dennis Shannahan	. . . .	James Schwartz	. . . .	Scott Menish	Gary Smith	Larry Peters
Ogallala (5)	CM 308 284-6001	Mary Lou Heelan	Gary Rimington	Louis H Kinnan	. . . .	Darrell Bassett	Joe Humphrey	. . . .
Omaha (336)	MC 402 444-5000	(not reporting)						
Ord (2)	MC 308 728-5791	(not reporting)						
Papillion (10)	MC 402 339-3376	(not reporting)						
Plainview (1)	MC 402 582-4928	M Bernecker	Mark Kober	J Gentzler	M Kober	D Nissen	G Umberger	. . . .
Plattsmouth (6)	MC 402 296-2522	(not reporting)						
Ralston (6)	MC 402 331-6677	(not reporting)						
Scottsbluff (14)	CM 308 632-4136	Donald Overman	Keith Jantz	Lynn Gibb	Margaret Elder	Roger Wheeler	Jim Livingston	. . . .
Seward (6)	MC 402 643-2928	Roger E Glawatz	Daniel Berlowitz	Debra Schaefer	. . . .	Terry Kamprath	C Marlin Sturgis	. . . .
Sidney (6)	CM 308 254-5300	Robert Van Vleet	Marlan V Ferguson	G F Anthony	. . . .	Keith Stone	Richard T Willis	Lawrence Heinrich
South Sioux City (10)	MC 402 494-7500	Vernie A Larson	Lance A Hedquist	Brenda S Basquin	. . . .	Jerry Stolze	Scot Ford	Jeffrey Harcum
Superior (2)	MC 402 879-4713	Lloyd Rust	. . . .	Dewayne L Aberg	. . . .	Michael Fenimore	Robert Allgood	Richard Elliott
Sutton (..)	MC 402 773-4225	Virgil D Ulmer	Malcolm Tilberg	Sherrie Klein	. . . .	Pat Merrick	Richard Fringer	Kevin Finnegan
Valentine (3)	CM 402 376-2323	Donn Petersen	Rick Medema	John Hanzlicek	John Hanzlicek	Al Brott	Jim Lutter	Rick Medema
Wahoo (4)	MC 402 443-3222	Donald Virgl	. . . .	Phyllis Nozicka	. . . .	Rodney Kuss	John Kolterman	. . . .
Wakefield (1)	MC 402 287-2080	Merlyn E Olson	Lowell D Johnson	Jean V Fischer	Jean V Fischer	Dean Ulrich	Daniel Gustafson	Laverle Obermeyer
Wayne (5)	MC 402 375-1733	Robert Carhart	Joe Salitros	Betty McGuire	. . . .	Ken Sitzman	Vern Fairchild	Vern Schulz
West Point (3)	MC 402 372-2468	E M Mueller	. . . .	May Dee Stoltzman	. . . .	Paul Sharp	Patrick Ell	. . . .
York (8)	MC 402 362-4407	Ken Kunze	Jack R Kidder	C Jean Thiele	Jack R Kidder	Mark M Grosshans	Donald D Kluge	Orville Davidson
NEVADA (12)								
Boulder City (13)	CM 702 293-9202	. . . .	George D Forbes	Vicki G Bergdale	Robert E Boyer	Dean F Molburg	David R Mullin	Alan F Gove
Carson City-Ormsby (40)	CM 702 887-2103	Marv Teixeira	John Berkich	Kiyoshi Nishikawa	Mary C Walker	Lou Buckley	Paul McGrath	Dan O'Brien
Elko (15)	CM 702 738-5176	Jim Polkinghorne	Lorry Lipparelli	Giuliana Murphy	. . . .	O P Cash	Robert L Songer	Charles Williams
Ely (5)	MC 702 289-2430	Joann Malone	. . . .	. . . .	. . . .	. . . .	. . . .	Max Vigil
Fallon (6)	MC 702 423-5107	Robert Erickson	. . . .	Gary Cordes	. . . .	. . . .	Louis Fetherholf	Larry White
Henderson (65)	MC 702 565-2080	Robert Groesbeck	Philip Speight	Colleen Bell	Steve Hanson	Olien Haskett	Jim Goff	Mark Calhoun
Las Vegas (258)	CM 702 386-6011	Janis L Jones	William J Noonan	Kathy M Tighe	Steven P Houchens	Clell A West	. . . .	Richard D Goecke
North Las Vegas (48)	CM 702 649-5811	James K Seastrand	Michael H Dyal	Eileen M Sevigny	Vytas Vaitkus	Michael A Massey	Ronald E Lusch	Gary W Holler
Reno (134)	CM 702 334-2000	Pete Sferrazza	Clay Holstine	Don Cook	Bruce Brooks	Marty Richard	Richard Kirkland	. . . .
Sparks (53)	CM 702 353-2345	Bruce Breslow	Terry Reynolds	Deborine Peebles	Terri Thomas	Ronald Irwin	John Dotson	Shaun Carey
Wells (1)	MC 702 752-3355	(not reporting)						
Winnemucca (6)	MC 702 623-6339	Paul Vesco	Steve West	Mary Echeverria	. . . .	Walter Johnstone	Roger Peterson	Geno Bernardi
NEW HAMPSHIRE (84)								
Allenstown t (5)	TM 603 485-4276	(not reporting)						
Amherst t (9)	TM 603 673-6041	William Overholt	Dana G Crowell	. . . .	. . . .	John Bachman	Gary D Mac Guire	. . . .
Atkinson t (5)	TM 603 362-5266	(not reporting)						
Auburn t (4)	TM 603 483-5052	(not reporting)						
Barrington t (6)	TM 603 664-5179	(not reporting)						
Bedford t (13)	CM 603 472-5242	Richard Stoner	Artie Robersen	Edith Schmidtchen	Anthony Plante	Robert Fabich	David Bailey	Edward Kelly
Belmont t (6)	TM 603 267-8300	Ward R Peterson	Frederick W Welch	Doralyn M Harper	. . . .	Albert Akerstrom	Michael McCarty	Luther M Brown
Berlin (12)	CM 603 752-7532	Leo G Ouellet	M A Berkowitz	Lise Malia	Aline Boucher	Paul Fortier	Alan Tardiff	Maurice Wheeler
Boscawen t (4)	RT 603 796-2426	Thomas Danko	Sherlene Fisher	Barbara Holmes	Patricia Knight	Roland Bartlett	Mark Pepler	Richard Hollins
Bow t (6)	MC 603 228-1187	Richard F Bean	Albert R St Cyr	C Batchelder	Albert R St Cyr	H Dana Abbott	Peter A Cheney	Leighton Cleverly
Candia t (4)	TM 603 483-8101	Gary W Work	. . . .	Christine Dupere	. . . .	Leonard Wilson	S Agrafiotis	Ronald Severino
Charlestown t (5)	RT 603 826-4400	Gary W Bigelow	Susan S Spaulding	. . . .	. . . .	Robert W Burns	Fredrick Domini	. . . .
Chesterfield t (3)	TM 603 363-4624	(not reporting)						
Claremont (14)	CM 603 542-6262	Alan Whipple	Robert W Jackson	Doris Nelson	Jeannine Perry	Thomas Ford	Michael Prozzo Jr	Peter Goewey
Concord (36)	CM 603 225-8570	Wm Veroneau	Julia M Griffin	Eliz Campbell	James R Howard	John M Dionne	David G Walchak	Michael Bobinsky
Conway t (8)	TM 603 447-3811	(not reporting)						
Derry t (30)	MC 603 432-6100	Arthur McLean	William Jackson	Pauline Myers	Grace Collette	. . . .	Edward Garone	Alan Swan
Dover (25)	CM 603 743-6023	(not reporting)						
Durham t (12)	CM 603 868-5571	William Healy Jr	Larry R Wood	Linda Ekdahl	Clara Varney	Robert Wood	Paul Gowen	Joseph Grady
Enfield t (4)	TM 603 632-4201	Nickolas Coupis	S DeMontigny	Ilene Reed	. . . .	Donald Crate	Peter Giese	Gerald Lashua
Epping t (5)	TM 603 679-5441	Kim Sullivan	Philip Munck	Linda Foley	Janet LaPlante	Richard Marcotte	Gregory Dodge	Kevin Hammond

**Directory 1/9
continued**

MUNICIPAL OFFICIALS
IN U.S. CITIES OVER 2,500

City, 1990 population figures (000 omitted), form of government	Municipal phone number	Mayor	Appointed administrator	City clerk	Finance officer	Fire chief	Police chief	Public works director
NEW HAMPSHIRE (84) continued								
Epsom t (4)	TM 603 736-9002	John F Hickey	Gloria J Reeves	Merilee Ellsworth	. . . .	Paul E Lavoie	Cameron Harbison	. . . .
Exeter t (12)	TM 603 778-0591	(not reporting)						
Farmington t (6)	TM 603 755-2208	(not reporting)						
Franklin (8)	MC 603 934-3900	Brenda J Elias	James C Pitts	Elaine S Rayno	James Fenn	Scott Clarenbach	Douglas Boyd	Alfred Elliott
Gilford t (6)	RT 603 524-7438	Russell Dumais	David R Caron	Debra Eastman	Geoffrey Ruggles	Michael Mooney	Evans Juris	Sheldon C Morgan
Goffstown t (15)	TM 603 497-3616	John Sarette	John Scruton	Marlene Gamans	Twila Barss	Richard Fletcher	Steven Monier	Donald Hambidge
Gorham t (3)	TM 603 466-5591	(not reporting)						
Hampstead t (7)	TM 603 329-5011	Joseph A Guthrie	P R Lindquist	Nancy H Watson	. . . .	Paul S Wentworth	William LeToile	Proctor Wentworth
Hampton t (12)	TM 603 926-6766	Arthur J Moody	Hunter Rieseberg	Jane Kelley	. . . .	William Sullivan	Robert Mark	John Hangen
Hanover t (9)	TM 603 643-4123	Marilyn Black	Clifford Vermilya	Elizabeth Banks	B Michael Gilbar	Roger Bradley	Kurt Schimke	Richard Hauger
Haverhill t (4)	TM 603 747-3318	Richard G Kinder		Helen M Smith	. . . .	. . . .	Walter R George	
Henniker t (4)	RT 603 428-3221	W Belanger	E Wojnowski	K Johnson	. . . .	B Ayer	T Russell	T Woodley
Hillsborough t (4)	TM 603 464-3877	(not reporting)						
Hinsdale t (4)	RT 603 336-5401	(not reporting)						
Hollis t (6)	RT 603 465-2209	(not reporting)						
Hooksett t (9)	TM 603 485-8471	William Lyon	Gerald Cottrell	Leslie Nepveu	Matthew Shevenell	Raymond O'Brien	James Oliver	James McColl
Hopkinton t (5)	TM 603 746-3170	(not reporting)						
Hudson t (20)	CO 603 886-6024	Ralph Scott	. . . .	Cecile Nichols	Lydia Angell	Brian Mason	. . . .	Mark Devine
Jaffrey t (5)	CM 603 532-7445	Peter Davis	Jonathan Sistare	Maria Chamberlain	Pamela Bernier	John White	Gary Phillips	Floyd Roberts
Keene (22)	CM 603 357-9804	(not reporting)						
Kingston t (6)	TM 603 642-3342	(not reporting)						
Laconia (16)	CM 603 524-1520	Paul Fitzgerald	Daniel McKeever	Ann Dearborn	Carol Trottier	Richard Judkins	Robert Babineau	Franklin Tilton
Lancaster t (4)	TM 603 788-3391	Michael W Beattie	Pamela L Andrade	Jean E Oleson	Michael W Nadeau	Samuel F Evans	Edward Samson Jr	Peter E Kulbacki
Lebanon (12)	CM 603 448-1720	David Jescavage	Steven Smith	Dorothy Doyle	Leonard Jarvi	Stephen Allen	Edward Laurie	George Gline
Lincoln t (1)	CM 603 745-2757	Duncan Riley	Kalene H Roberts	Sandra A Dovholuk	. . . .	Clifton Dauphine	Craig R Ohlson	Clifton Dauphine
Litchfield t (6)	TM 603 424-4045	(not reporting)						
Littleton t (6)	TM 603 444-3996	Michael F Farrell		Faye White	Melodie Hodgdon	Fred Whitcomb	Louis Babin	Larry Jackson
Londonderry t (20)	TM 603 432-1126	Daniel Vecchione	. . . .	Alice Taylor	Peter J Curro	Alan J Sypek	Richard J Bannon	. . . .
Manchester (100)	MC 603 624-6500	(not reporting)						
Meredith t (5)	TM 603 279-4538	Edith B Mongo	Peter G Russell	Pauline Fournier	Joyce M Bavis	Frederic Copp	John Curran	Barry Cotton
Merrimack t (22)	TM 603 424-2331	Richard E Dumont	Richard S Borden	. . . .	Robert T Levan	Charles Q Hall	Joseph R Devine	Earle M Chesley
Milford t (12)	TM 603 673-2257	Peter R Leishman	Lee F Mayhew	Wilfred Leduc	K Chambers	R Tortorelli	Steven Sexton	Robert E Courage
Nashua (80)	MC 603 880-3300	(not reporting)						
New London t (3)	TM 603 526-4821	Sally K Fifield	. . . .	Lois Marshall	. . . .	Walt Partridge	Stuart Sidmore	. . . .
Newmarket t (7)	CM 603 659-3617	Richard Wilson	Frank Edmunds	. . . .	. . . .	Charles Clark	Kerryl L Clement	David Walker
Newport t (6)	TM 603 863-1877	Henry Rodeschin	Daniel O'Neill	Karlene Stoddard	Paul Brown	John Marcotte	David Hoyt	Larry Wiggins
Newton t (3)	TM 603 382-4405	(not reporting)						
North Hampton t (4)	TM 603 964-8087	. . . .	Beverley Frenette	Deloras Chase	. . . .	Richard Pauley	Frank Beliveau	Bob Strout
Northfield t (4)	TM 603 286-7039	(not reporting)						
Northumberland t (2)	CM 603 636-1450	John Normand	Frances S Rich	. . . .	. . . .	James Sanborn	Harry L Rice Jr	David McMann
Pelham t (9)	RT 603 635-8233	Paul R Scott	Peter R Flynn	Linda M Lavallee	Doris S Mannies	E David Fisher	David F Rowell	. . . .
Pembroke t (7)	TM 603 485-4747	Larry W Young Sr	David L Stack	James F Goff	. . . .	Richard Chase	Lucien Bouffard	Henry Malo
Peterborough t (5)	TM 603 924-3201	Gordon Kemp	John Isham	Robert Lambert	. . . .	Stephen Black	Quentin Estey Jr	John Isham
Pittsfield t (4)	TM 603 435-6773	Dean E Whittier	David F Barker	Elizabeth A Hast	. . . .	John S Kidder	John P Charron	George Bachelder
Plaistow t (7)	CM 603 382-5200	Lawrence W Gil	Donald W Whitman	Barbara Tavitian	. . . .	Donald Petzold	Stephen C Savage	. . . .
Plymouth t (6)	RT 603 536-1731	(not reporting)						
Portsmouth (26)	CM 603 431-2000	(not reporting)						
Raymond t (9)	TM 603 895-4735	Edward C Varney	Martha St Amand	Gloria E Carney	L Wikstrom	Kevin Pratt	Richard E Dolan	Dennis McCarthy
Rindge t (5)	TM 603 899-5181	Redvers G White	Jeanne Cunningham	Amy Raymond	. . . .	Robert Lapointe	David Collum	Peter Anderson
Rochester (27)	CM 603 332-3110	Roland Roberge	Ricard Stenhouse	Gail Varney	R Larochelle	Mark Dellner	Donald Vittum	Bert George
Rye t (5)	TM 603 964-5523	Joseph G Mills Jr	Janet C Thompson	Jane Ireland	. . . .	Ronald Lima	Bradley B Loomis	Cornelius Moynahan
Salem t (26)	TM 603 893-5731	George P Jones	Barry M Brenner	Barbara Lessard	Francis Bernard	John Nadeau	James Ross	George Sealy
Seabrook t (7)	RT 603 474-3311	Asa H Knowles Jr	E Russell Bailey	Virgina L Small	. . . .	Jerry W Brown	Paul J Cronin	Veron G Dow
Somersworth (11)	CM 603 692-4262	Jim McLin	Douglas R Elliott	Nancy Liebson	Eileen Cabanel	Paul Vallee	Patrick Cote	Gregory Mack
Stratham t (5)	TM 603 772-4741	(not reporting)						
Swanzey t (6)	RT 603 352-7411	(not reporting)						
Tilton t (3)	TM 603 286-4521	William Joscelyn	Betty J Pierce	F Gayle Twombly	. . . .	Harold Harbour	Charles B Chase	David Wadleigh
Walpole t (3)	TM 603 756-3672	Roger Santaw	. . . .	Sandra Smith	. . . .	. . . .	Carl Baird	. . . .
Weare t (6)	TM 603 529-7525	(not reporting)						
Wilton t (3)	TM 603 654-9451	(not reporting)						
Winchester t (4)	RT 603 239-4951	Vernon A Jones	Erica Sands Ryll	Marjorie M Austin	. . . .	Richard Lapoint	James E Harrison	Dale R Gray
Windham t (9)	RT 603 432-7732	(not reporting)						
Wolfeboro t (5)	TM 603 569-3900	Shirley Ganem	James McSweeney	Patricia Waterman	Carroll Piper	Michael Howard	Stanley Stevens	Marty Bilafer
NEW JERSEY (357)								
Aberdeen tp (17)	CM 908 583-4200	David Lipman	James Cox	Ann T Barker	Robert Daetsch	. . . .	Brian Dougherty	James Lauro
Absecon (7)	MC 609 641-0663	(not reporting)						
Allendale b (6)	MC 201 818-4400	Albert H Klomburg	Thomas F Carroll	Lorraine E Stark	Paula E Favata	Steven Forbes	Robert Herndon	George Higbie
Alpha b (3)	MC 908 454-0088	(not reporting)						
Andover tp (5)	MC 201 383-8299	John Denick Jr	Marie Goble	Mae Bauerlein	Marie Goble	Barry Holland	George Smith	Dave Mosner
Asbury Park (17)	CM 201 775-2100	(not reporting)						
Atlantic City (38)	MC 609 347-5300	(not reporting)						
Atlantic Highlands b (5)	MC 908 291-1444	(not reporting)						
Audubon b (9)	CO 609 547-0710	Alfred W Murray	. . . .	Lee C Daniels	Margaret Meekins	Paul Hartstein	William V Taulane	Anthony Pugliese
Barrington b (7)	MC 609 547-0706	(not reporting)						
Bayonne (61)	MC 201 858-6010	(not reporting)						
Beachwood b (9)	MC 201 286-6000	(not reporting)						
Belleville tp (34)	CM 201 450-3300	(not reporting)						
Bellmawr b (13)	MC 609 933-1313	(not reporting)						
Belmar b (6)	MC 908 681-1176	Kenneth E Pringle	J Ascione	Charles Ormsbee	Charles Ormsbee	. . . .	Harold Allen	Paul Greco
Bergenfield b (24)	CM 201 387-4055	Charles McDowell	Gerard V Leary	Gerald V Leary	Norman L Gust	John Fuhrman	Richard Baroch	Robert Bartley
Berkeley Heights tp (12)	MC 908 464-2700	Janet Prince	Joseph Cara	Gertrude Gonnelli	Angela Rica	Dominick Imbimbo	Theodore Rica	Frederick Miller
Berlin b (6)	MC 609 767-7777	(not reporting)						
Bernards tp (17)	MC 908 766-2510	Robert P Haycock	H Steven Wood	Rita Osborne	Dorothy J Stikna	. . . .	C Fortenbacher	Michael Beale
Bernardsville b (7)	MC 908 766-3000	Peter S Palmer	Ralph A Maresca	Sandra G Jones	Ralph A Maresca	. . . .	Thomas Sciaretta	Allan Rome
Beverly (3)	MC 609 387-0205	(not reporting)						
Bloomfield tp (45)	MC 201 680-4000	(not reporting)						
Bloomingdale b (8)	MC 201 838-0778	William Hulme	Thomas Zangara	Jane Febbi	Robert Hammer	Richard Boud	Edward Fletcher	Kenneth Barrett
Bogota b (8)	MC 201 342-1736	(not reporting)						
Boonton t (8)	MC 201 335-2400	Robert Depue	Terry McCue	Ann Marie Fitch	Terry McCue	Ray Reyerson	Robert Banks	Stephen Koval
Bordentown (4)	CO 609 298-0604	Zigmont Targonski	. . . .	Patricia D Ryan	Patricia D Ryan	Steve McGowan	Philip Castagna	Joseph R Malone
Bound Brook b (9)	MC 908 356-0833	Brian S Jannone	Thomas R Brodbeck	Thomas R Brodbeck	Roger Pribush	Timothy Braden	Anthony Cimino	Mark Cassebaum
Bradley Beach b (4)	CO 908 776-2999	Stephen Schueler	Phyllis Quixley	Phyllis Quixley	Charles Ormsbee	Daniel Flood	Robert Denardo	S Galassetti

Directory 1/9 continued

MUNICIPAL OFFICIALS IN U.S. CITIES OVER 2,500

City, 1990 population figures (000 omitted), form of government	Municipal phone number	Mayor	Appointed administrator	City clerk	Finance officer	Fire chief	Police chief	Public works director
NEW JERSEY (357) continued								
Branchburg tp (11)	MC 908 526-1300	Denise M Coyle	Donato J Nieman	. . . .	Patrick Vitale	. . . .	Brian Fitzgerald	Joseph Stala
Bridgeton (19)	MC 609 455-3230	Donald H Rainear	Elaine V Mitchell	Darlene Richmond	Teresa C Delp	Gerald Kimble	John Bondi	Albert Fralinger
Bridgewater tp (33)	MC 201 725-6300	James T Dowden	William O'Neill	Bette B Nuse	Peter P Sepelya	. . . .	Richard Voorhees	Hugh McCluskey
Brielle b (4)	MC 908 528-6600	Thomas B Nicol	Thomas F Nolan	Thomas F Nolan	Karen S Brisben	Kristen Hauge	Harry Whelan	William Burkhardt
Brigantine (11)	CM 609 266-7600	(not reporting)						
Buena b (4)	MC 609 697-1780	(not reporting)						
Burlington (10)	MC 609 386-0316	(not reporting)						
Butler b (7)	MC 201 838-7200	Romano Assante	Gary Webb	Carol Whritenour	Matthew M Luther	. . . .	Gerald Napoleone	. . . .
Byram tp (8)	CM 201 347-2500	Richard A Bowe	Ronald F Gatti	Mary Johnson	Joan Cardin	Richard Mach	Eskil Danielson	Gary Stevens
Caldwell tp (8)	MC 201 226-6100	Irene Gibbons	Kathryn Kitchener	Lorraine Billings	Louise Cetrangolo	Anthony Grenci	Joseph Durr	George Krueger
Camden (87)	MC 609 757-7200	Aaron A Thompson	Patrick J Keating	Dorothy Burley	Richard Cinaglia	Kenneth Penn	George D Pugh	James Chalmus
Cape May (5)	CM 609 884-9525	Robert W Elwell	J Fred Coldren	Virginia Petersen	John H Jansen Jr	Wister Dougherty	Robert Boyd	Jerome Inderwies
Carlstadt b (6)	MC 201 939-2850	Dominick Presto	. . . .	Claire Foy	D Giancaspro	Dennis Monks	John Occhiuzzo	Thomas DeLeasa
Carteret b (19)	MC 908 541-3800	Peter J Sica	. . . .	Kathleen Barney	Patrick Deblasio	Richard Greenberg	Joseph F Sica	Theodore Surick
Cedar Grove tp (12)	CM 201 239-1410	Kevin O'Toole	Joseph DiGiacomo	Evelyn Huey	William M Homa	James Reilly	William Schneider	. . . .
Chatham b (8)	MC 201 635-0674	Barbara L Hall	Henry M Underhill	Henry M Underhill	Dorothy L Klein	Greg Henrich	Donald C Cardinal	Thomas Zilinek
Cherry Hill tp (69)	MC 609 488-7800	(not reporting)						
Cinnaminson tp (15)	MC 609 829-6000	. . . .	John M Ostrowski	Grace Z Campbell	. . . .	. . . .	Edmund DeLussey	. . . .
Clark tp (15)	MC 908 388-3600	Robert Ellenport	Edward Pomerantz	Kathleen Leonard	Jeanne Decker	Chris Buccarelli	Anton Danco	Robert Gable
Clayton b (6)	MC 609 881-2882	(not reporting)						
Clementon b (6)	MC 609 783-0284	(not reporting)						
Cliffside Park b (20)	MC 201 945-3456	(not reporting)						
Clifton (72)	CM 201 470-5800	(not reporting)						
Clinton tp (11)	MC 908 735-5328	Thomas L Ogden	Richard J Sheola	Carol A Piazza	Arthur E Johnson	Robert Emery	Richard J Sheola	George Piazza
Closter b (8)	MC 201 784-0756	Edward T Rogan	Robert J Anderson	Loretta Castano	Christine Cauvet	Alphonso Young Jr	John Rose	Harry Lampman
Collingswood b (15)	CO 609 854-0720	Frank F Law Jr	Jean DiGennaro	Joanne McCormack	Sandra Leahy	Robert Eckert	John Spavlik	Bradford Stokes
Colts Neck t (9)	MC 908 462-5470	(not reporting)						
Cranford tp (23)	CM 201 709-7200	Dnaiel Aschenbach	John F Laezza	Arlene M Gigon	Thomas J Grady	Arthur A Kiamie	Harry W Wilde	Robert Maiberger
Cresskill b (8)	MC 201 569-5400	John Bergamini	. . . .	Dorothy M Giguere	Robert Camasto	Robert Ahearn	Frank Tino Jr	Gerald Crum
Delran tp (13)	MC 609 461-7734	(not reporting)						
Demarest b (5)	MC 201 768-0167	Richard Schooler	. . . .	Carol A Kroepke	Ann Marie Mancuso	Richard Motta	James Powderley	Fred Shaffer
Denville tp (14)	MC 201 627-1234	James F Dyer	Ellen M Sandman	Donna I Costello	John J Doherty	Robert C Matschke	Howard C Shaw	Joseph Lowell
Deptford tp (24)	CM 609 845-5300	(not reporting)						
Dover t (15)	MC 201 366-2200	(not reporting)						
Dumont b (17)	MC 201 387-5023	Donald Winant	Marvin Katz	Beth Schaffer	Marvin Katz	Robert Stevens	Michael Affrunti	John Cook
Dunellen b (7)	MC 201 968-3033	(not reporting)						
East Brunswick tp (44)	MC 201 390-6760	Ira Oskowsky	Raymond Stone	Elizabeth Kiss	Leon M Neely	. . . .	John Cross	Michael Opaleski
East Hanover tp (10)	MC 201 887-5454	(not reporting)						
East Orange (74)	MC 201 266-5100	Cardell Cooper	Leroy J Jones Jr	Constance Newton	Linda Munro	Eliott Peterkin	Harry Harman	. . . .
East Rutherford b (8)	MC 201 933-3444	James L Plosia	. . . .	Darlene A Sawicki	Anthony Bianchi	Colin Swift	Gilbert Logatto	Thomas Miller
East Windsor tp (22)	CM 609 443-4000	Ralph L Bradley	Barry Larson	Elizabeth G Nolan	John P Milano	. . . .	Barry G Barlow	Robert W DiMarco
Eastampton tp (5)	CM 609 267-5723	(not reporting)						
Eatontown b (14)	MC 908 389-7600	(not reporting)						
Edgewater b (5)	MC 201 943-1700	(not reporting)						
Edison tp (89)	MC 201 282-0900	Samuel V Convery	Paul A Abati	Adelaide Searfoss	G Ross Bobal	Albert Lamkie	Edward Costello	Robert Heck
Egg Harbor tp (..)	MC 609 926-4088	Maria Bohle	Peter Miller	P Indrieri	Charlene Canale	. . . .	Alfred Lisicki	N Ciarlante
Egg Harbor City (5)	MC 609 965-0081	(not reporting)						
Elizabeth (110)	MC 908 820-4000	J Chris Bollwage	Myrna M Rivera	Anthony R Pillo	Joseph B Mularz	Edward J Sisk	Mary F Rabadeau	Blaise E Lapolla
Elmwood Park b (18)	MC 201 796-1457	(not reporting)						
Emerson b (7)	MC 201 262-6086	Harvey Truppi	Arlene Raymond	Arlene Raymond	Ann Burns	Joseph Solimando	Peter Mazzeo	Raymond Donnelly
Englewood (25)	CM 201 871-6658	Donald Aronson	Jack Drakeford	Jack Drakeford	Robert Benecke	Douglas Baker	William Luciano	Bettina Rance
Englewood Cliffs b (6)	MC 201 569-5252	Joseph C Parisi	Joseph Favaro	Joseph Favaro	Joseph Iannaconi	James Radcliffe	Patrick Farley	Rodney Bialko
Essex Fells tp (2)	MC 201 226-3400	D McWilliams	Robert Ditommaso	Robert Ditommaso	William Homa	James Egan	George Haydu	Robert Gervasi
Evesham tp (35)	CM 609 983-2900	Augustus Tamburro	Florence Ricci	Florence Ricci	Thomas Tontarski	Thaddeus Lowden	Nicholas Matteo	. . . .
Ewing tp (34)	MC 609 883-2900	. . . .	Fred R Walters	Ted M Yim	Ronald Zilinski	. . . .	Edward Schaller	. . . .
Fair Haven b (5)	MC 908 747-0241	T David Hinton	Michael Pellechio	Michael Pellechio	Michael Pellechio	Stewart Watson	Richard Towler	John Riley
Fair Lawn b (31)	CM 201 796-1700	John Keith	Bertrand Kendall	. . . .	Barry Eccleston	Walter Demeraski	William Gormanns	William Davidson
Fairfield tp (8)	MC 201 882-2700	(not reporting)						
Fairview b (11)	MC 201 943-3300	Joseph Scala	Angelo Checki	Victor Graziano	Joseph Rutch	Ralph Salemme	John Booth	. . . .
Fanwood b (7)	MC 908 322-8236	Linda D Stender	Eleanor McGovern	Eleanor McGovern	Llewyellen Fisher	Thomas Rose	Anthony Parenti	Raymond Manfra
Flemington b (4)	MC 201 782-8840	(not reporting)						
Florham Park b (9)	MC 201 377-5800	(not reporting)						
Fort Lee b (32)	MC 201 592-3670	Jack Alter	Carol Kohout	Gladys Brunell	Joseph Iannaconi	James Piccirillo	John Orso	Daniel Kingcaid
Franklin tp (43)	CM 908 873-2500	Helen Reilly	John C Lovell	Jean Pellicane	George Ramsey	. . . .	Jonn Blazakis	C Andy Twiford
Franklin b (5)	MC 201 827-9280	(not reporting)						
Franklin Lakes b (10)	MC 201 891-0048	(not reporting)						
Freehold b (11)	MC 908 462-1410	(not reporting)						
Freehold tp (25)	CM 908 294-2000	William Williams	Frederick E Jahn	Romeo Cascaes	Debrah Dedeo	. . . .	John D Willis	Richard A Warren
Galloway tp (23)	CM 609 652-3700	(not reporting)						
Garfield (27)	CM 201 340-2001	(not reporting)						
Garwood b (4)	MC 201 789-0710	(not reporting)						
Gibbsboro b (2)	MC 609 783-6655	(not reporting)						
Glassboro b (16)	MC 609 881-9230	(not reporting)						
Glen Ridge tp (7)	MC 201 748-8400	Carolyn W Bourne	V A Belluscio	V A Belluscio	V A Belluscio	. . . .	Thomas P Dugan	M L Modin
Glen Rock b (11)	MC 201 670-3956	Jacqueline Kort	R Freudenrich	Jean Malone	Lenora Benjamin	Alvin Siebold	Steven Cherry	Roy Nordstrand
Gloucester tp (54)	MC 609 228-4000	(not reporting)						
Gloucester City (13)	MC 609 456-0205	Walter W Jost	Edward F Doczy	Mary A Moran	Jeffrey Coles	William Glassman	Theodore Howarth	James J Johnson
Guttenberg t (8)	MC 201 868-2315	(not reporting)						
Hackensack (37)	CM 201 646-3901	John F Zisa	James S Lacava	Doris L Dukes	Raymond Carnevale	Ronald Freeman	John Aletta	Jesse D'Amore
Hackettstown t (8)	MC 908 852-3130	John DiMaio	William W Kuster	William W Kuster	Donna M Palmieri	John W Zellars	Leonard Kunz Jr	Theodore Lake
Haddon tp (15)	CO 609 854-1176	William J Park Jr	. . . .	Denise P White	Joanne Schaefer	. . . .	Charles E Gooley	. . . .
Haddon Heights b (8)	MC 609 547-7164	R J Battersby	. . . .	Joan Young	Ernest J Merlino	Edward Zwaska	Donald G Wilson	James Young
Haddonfield b (12)	CM 609 429-4700	John J Tarditi Jr	Richard B Schwab	Janet G Betley	Richard B Schwab	George R Cox	William Ostrander	Letitia G Colombi
Haledon b (7)	MC 201 595-7766	(not reporting)						
Hamilton tp (87)	MC 609 890-3500	John K Rafferty	Joseph Bellina	Christina Wilder	Paul Kramer	. . . .	Richard Taylor	Harry Bonacci
Hammonton t (12)	MC 609 567-4300	(not reporting)						
Hardyston tp (5)	CM 201 697-4987	. . . .	John Eskilson	Laure Lyons	Margery Brown	Edward Zinck	Peter Carson	. . . .
Harrington Park b (5)	MC 201 768-1700	(not reporting)						
Harrison t (13)	MC 201 268-2425	(not reporting)						
Hasbrouck Heights b (11)	MC 201 288-0195	(not reporting)						
Haworth b (3)	MC 201 384-4785	John D DeRienzo	Ann E Fay	Ann E Fay	Christine Villani	Ronald Green	Donald Galgano	Martin Mahon
Hawthorne b (17)	MC 201 427-1167	(not reporting)						
Hazlet tp (22)	MC 908 264-1700	(not reporting)						

Directory 1/9
continued

MUNICIPAL OFFICIALS
IN U.S. CITIES OVER 2,500

City, 1990 population figures (000 omitted), form of government	Municipal phone number	Mayor	Appointed administrator	City clerk	Finance officer	Fire chief	Police chief	Public works director
NEW JERSEY (357) continued								
High Bridge b (4)	MC 908 638-6455	Carl J Lewis	. . . .	Claire R Knapp	. . . .	Jeffrey Smith	Joseph M Lacey	Mark Banks
Highland Park b (13)	MC 908 572-3400	H James Polos	Evelyn Sedehi	Valerie Thompson	Jose Agosto	Vince Murphy	Ronald Haskins	Lloyd Young
Highlands b (5)	MC 201 872-1515	Richard Schwartz	Michael Balzarano	Nina L Flannery	Stephen Pfeffer	Matthew Kane	James T Davis	Michael Balzarano
Hightstown b (5)	MC 604 490-5100	(not reporting)						
Hillsdale b (10)	MC 201 666-4800	Douglas A Groner	Joseph S Rompala	Elizabeth F Rotar	Joseph S Rompala	James Fisher	Ronald Schramm	Keith I Durie
Hillside tp (21)	MC 201 926-3000	Peter D Corvelli	. . . .	C Defilippo	Rosemary McClave	James Dill	Frank Desanto	Scott Anderson
Hoboken (33)	MC 201 420-2084	Anthony Russo	George W Crimmins	James Farina	. . . .	R Tremeiditi	Carmen LaBruno	Timothy Calligy
Hohokus b (4)	MC 201 652-4400	Richard M Sayers	Cathern Henderson	Judith Odo	Cathern Henderson	Richard Keeley	Russell J Berke	Thomas J Dawson
Holmdel tp (12)	MC 908 946-8685	Ernest Cote	Carol Williams	Sheila Van Winkle	Joseph Annecharic	Ron Pontrelli	Robert Phillips	James Allocco
Hopatcong b (16)	MC 201 770-1200	(not reporting)						
Hopewell tp (12)	MC 609 737-0638	William J Nunan	Robert Pellegrino	Annette Bielawski	Robert Pellegrino	. . . .	Robert J Ferrarin	Gary Crossland
Irvington tp (61)	MC 201 399-8111	(not reporting)						
Jackson tp (33)	CO 908 928-1200	Peter Carlson	William Santos	David Miller Sr	William Antonides	. . . .	Richard Chinery	John Smatusik Jr
Jamesburg b (5)	MC 201 521-2222	(not reporting)						
Jefferson tp (18)	MC 201 697-1500	Frances Slayton	Robert A Cutter	June Cetro	John Katilas	. . . .	George Stamer	Thomas Lemanowicz
Jersey City (229)	MC 201 547-5000	Bret Schundler	Robert Lombard	Robert Byrne	Jane Feigenbaum	F Constantinoble	Robert Sabo	Charlotte H Mizzi
Keansburg b (11)	CM 201 787-0215	(not reporting)						
Kearny t (35)	MC 201 991-2700	(not reporting)						
Kenilworth b (8)	MC 908 276-9090	Joseph J Rego	. . . .	Margaret Adler	Dianne Kurutza	John Fugett	Brent David	Frank Plummer
Keyport b (8)	MC 908 739-3900	John J Merla	John P Wadington	Judith L Poling	John P Wadington	Roy J Cadoo	Raymond G Lee	Arthur S Rooke
Kinnelon b (8)	MC 201 838-5401	(not reporting)						
Lakehurst b (3)	CM 908 657-4141	Alton H Tilton	Robert J Morris	Robert J Morris	Philip Del Turco	Robert J Morris	Norbert Mac Lean	Mark Hartnett
Lakewood tp (45)	CM 908 364-2500	Jose Alonso	G Fehrenbach	Bernadette Work	Carl A Inniss	. . . .	Michael Prisco	Larry Branch
Lambertville (4)	MC 609 397-0110	(not reporting)						
Lawnside b (3)	MC 609 573-6200	(not reporting)						
Lawrence tp (26)	CM 609 896-9400	Gloria S Teti	William J Guhl	D Simonelli	Joseph P Monzo	. . . .	John H Prettyman	Joseph H Maher
Leonia b (8)	MC 201 592-5743	F Berenbroick	Calvin G Weaver	Anne G Williams	Theodoracopoulos	Robert Moran	Robert F Vodde	Jose Alvarez
Lincoln Park b (11)	MC 201 694-6100	Lorelei N Mottese	William E Close	Annette Maida Smi	. . . .	George Gilliland	John C Gibbons	. . . .
Linden (37)	MC 908 474-8495	John T Gregorio	. . . .	Val D Imbriaco	Joseph Suliga	William J Konecny	John E Miliano	John Brozana
Lindenwold b (19)	MC 609 783-2121	Thomas J Horner	. . . .	Barbara L Dolchan	Bruce Finkle	. . . .	Francis McHenry	Robert Lodovici
Linwood (7)	MC 609 927-4108	D Vass	. . . .	. . . .	F B Tiemann	. . . .	A J Ferguson	J Hutchins
Little Falls tp (11)	MC 201 256-0170	(not reporting)						
Little Ferry b (10)	MC 201 641-9234	(not reporting)						
Little Silver b (6)	TM 201 842-2400	(not reporting)						
Livingston tp (27)	CM 201 992-5000	(not reporting)						
Lodi b (22)	MC 201 365-4005	Philip V Toronto	Charles S Cuccia	John L Barrachina	. . . .	Arthur Woods	Edward Kukalski	. . . .
Long Branch (29)	MC 908 222-7000	(not reporting)						
Lower tp (21)	CM 609 886-2005	(not reporting)						
Lyndhurst tp (18)	CO 201 804-2457	Louis J Stellato	. . . .	Josephine Oleske	Deborah Ferrato	Richard Pizzuti	John Scalese	John P Beirne
Madison b (16)	MC 201 593-3000	(not reporting)						
Magnolia b (5)	MC 609 783-1520	(not reporting)						
Mahwah tp (18)	MC 201 529-5757	(not reporting)						
Manalapan tp (27)	MC 908 446-3200	Howard Bachman	Fred C Kniesler	Rose Ann Weeden	John Omalley	. . . .	Jimmie Potts	Anthony Braica
Manasquan b (5)	MC 201 223-0544	(not reporting)						
Manville b (11)	MC 908 725-9478	(not reporting)						
Maple Shade tp (19)	CM 609 779-9610	(not reporting)						
Maplewood tp (22)	MC 201 762-8120	Robert H Grasmere	W David Carew	Elizabeth Fritzen	Joseph Bonin	Sam Santucci	R Richardella	W Michael Bishop
Margate City (8)	CO 609 822-2605	(not reporting)						
Matawan b (9)	MC 201 566-3898	(not reporting)						
Maywood b (9)	MC 201 845-6343	John A Steuert Jr	. . . .	Mary A Rampolla	Charles Cuccia	Peter Casamento	Andrew Costa	Sam Pernetti
Medford tp (21)	CM 609 654-2608	Dominic Grosso	Constance Lauffer	Jean Lobach	N Janet Cooper	. . . .	E John Foulk	John Crafchun
Medford Lakes b (4)	CM 609 654-8898	David D Wasson	Paul E Thomas Jr	Paul E Thomas Jr	Paul E Thomas Jr	Clarence Wingert	Roger N Smith	P McCorriston
Mendham b (5)	MC 201 543-7152	C W Steelman	Victor L Woodhull	Denise V Fuchs	Susan Giordano	Thomas Porter	George Vanderbush	C David Crotsley
Merchantville b (4)	MC 609 662-2474	(not reporting)						
Metuchen b (13)	MC 908 632-8540	Susan Marshall	William E Boerth	Alison Barrella	Lori Majeski	James M Ratcliffe	Frederick Hall	Chester Dilorenzo
Middlesex b (13)	MC 908 356-7400	Ronald S Dobies	. . . .	Ruth Yambor	A Collins	. . . .	James Benson	Jerry Schaefer
Middletown tp (68)	CM 908 615-2000	Anthony Musella	Joseph P Leo	Elaine M Wallace	Robert Roth	Thomas Amato	William Fowlie	Paul Linder
Midland Park b (7)	MC 201 445-5720	(not reporting)						
Millburn tp (19)	CM 201 564-7073	(not reporting)						
Milltown b (7)	MC 908 828-2100	(not reporting)						
Millville (26)	CO 609 825-7000	Robert J Shannon	Lewis N Thompson	Lewis N Thompson	R Charlesworth	Gary Wallen	Wm Herman	Vicki Marshall
Monmouth Beach b (3)	CO 201 229-2204	(not reporting)						
Montclair tp (38)	CM 201 509-4939	(not reporting)						
Montgomery tp (10)	CM 908 359-8211	(not reporting)						
Montvale b (7)	MC 201 391-5700	David Metlitz	. . . .	Margaret Palella	. . . .	Kevin Krazit	Joseph Marigliani	Alvin Walters
Montville tp (16)	MC 201 334-2370	Robert E Purnell	Edward J Pullan	Gladys C Jarombek	F L Vanderhoof	. . . .	Carl DeBacco	Robert A Cook
Moonachie b (3)	MC 201 641-1813	Frederick Dressel	Paul Hansen	Jean Finch	Paul Hansen	Ignatius Tullo	Michael McGahn	Henry Van Saders
Moorestown tp (16)	CM 609 235-0912	Walter T Maahs	John T Terry	Margie P Murphy	John Schoenberg	. . . .	W Wesolowski	John Lallier
Morris Plains b (5)	MC 201 538-2224	Frank J Druetzler	. . . .	Ruth C Mills	David E Banks	Mark Van Orden	William E Pierson	Robert Sturtevant
Morristown t (16)	MC 201 292-6600	Norman Bloch	Terence Reidy	William Chambers	Sandra Flower	James Egbert	Joseph Varro	Richard McFadden
Mount Arlington b (4)	MC 201 398-6832	Dolores Rivinius	. . . .	Mary Secola	Morris Perugini	Douglas Zoldak	William Morgan	. . . .
Mount Ephraim b (5)	CO 609 931-1546	Joseph E Wolk	. . . .	Catherine Pepe	C Humphreville	Richard Holmes	. . . .	J Blocklinger
Mount Holly tp (11)	CM 609 267-0170	Lauri Sheppard	. . . .	Joan L Boas	Chris Chambers	Joe Gaskill	James Hansen	. . . .
Mount Laurel tp (30)	CM 609 234-0001	G Nardello	W Binder	P Halbe	J Bakos	. . . .	S Weinstein	E Johnson
Mount Olive tp (22)	MC 201 691-0900	James E Schiess	L V Corea Jr	Lisa Lashway	Randy Carter	. . . .	Edward A Kane	. . . .
Mountain Lakes b (4)	CM 201 334-3131	Glenn Tippy	Ricky Prill	Alison Wood	Robert Kapral	Donald McNeill	Charles McCoy	Carl Danser
Mountainside b (7)	MC 201 232-2400	Robert Viglianti	Kathleen Toland	Judith E Osty	Michelle Swisher	Jim Sanford	William Alder	Robert Wyckoff
National Park b (3)	MC 201 845-3891	(not reporting)						
Neptune tp (28)	CO 908 988-5200	John O Gross	Alayne M Shepler	Richard Cuttrell	Michael J Bascom	. . . .	Anthony Paduano	Willard Clarkson
Neptune City b (5)	MC 908 776-7224	Ted Wardell	. . . .	Joel Popkin	Charles Ormsbee	Robert Reynolds	James Johnson	Gerrit Devos
Netcong b (3)	MC 201 347-0252	(not reporting)						
New Brunswick (42)	MC 908 745-5004	James M Cahill	Thomas A Loughlin	Ludwig Previte	. . . .	Horace Jordan	M Beltranena	Steven Zarecki
New Hanover tp (10)	CO 609 758-7149	(not reporting)						
New Milford b (16)	MC 201 967-5044	Theresa M King	Richard N Shuss	Dianne Rothweiler	Richard N Shuss	William Pessler	J R Costello	Robert Chester
New Providence b (11)	MC 908 665-1400	Harold Weideli	Edward Bien	Wendi Barry	Richard Burr	Kevin Kennedy	James Venezia Jr	John Meyer
Newark (275)	MC 201 733-3780	(not reporting)						
Newton t (8)	CM 201 383-3521	Arthur C Frisbie	Camille Furgiuele	Douglas L Cummins	Camille Furgiuele	Peter Kays	James J Kilduff	Christopher Bond
North Arlington b (14)	MC 201 955-5660	Leonard R Kaiser	Robert Landolphi	Constance Meehan	Anthony Blasi	Michael Guarino	Joseph Zadroga	Ronald Rossmell
North Bergen tp (48)	CO 201 392-2000	(not reporting)						
North Brunswick tp (31)	MC 908 247-0922	Paul J Matacera	J Paul Keller	Nancy Troichuk	Kurt A Cherry	. . . .	George Lepre	Douglas Robertson
North Caldwell tp (7)	MC 201 228-4444	(not reporting)						
North Haledon b (8)	MC 201 427-7793	Renate Lampe	Robert J Pacca	Lucille B Debiak	Rosalie Tebbs	A J Ricciardi	Edward Dombroski	William Graham
North Plainfield b (19)	MC 908 769-2902	(not reporting)						

MUNICIPAL OFFICIALS IN U.S. CITIES OVER 2,500

City, 1990 population figures (000 omitted), form of government	Municipal phone number	Mayor	Appointed administrator	City clerk	Finance officer	Fire chief	Police chief	Public works director
NEW JERSEY (357) continued								
North Wildwood (5)	MC 609 522-2030	Lewis G Vinci	D Robert Heal	Jane Parson	James G Nicola	Willam Callahan	Anthony Sittineri	Timothy O'Leary
Northfield (7)	MC 609 641-2832	(not reporting)						
Northvale b (5)	MC 201 767-3330	(not reporting)						
Norwood b (5)	MC 201 767-7200	(not reporting)						
Nutley tp (27)	CO 201 284-4961	(not reporting)						
Oakland b (12)	MC 201 337-8111	J Peter Kendall	Robert P Hammer	Jeannine Hickey	Steven Schwager	Roy Bauberger	James O'Connor	N David Fagerlund
Oaklyn b (4)	MC 609 858-2457	Vincent Scriboni	. . . .	Marie Hawkins	John Bruno	Curt Hudson	Ronald Frumento	W Koppleberger
Ocean tp (25)	CM 908 531-5000	T Weldon	D Kochel	V Bergeron	H Kushner	. . . .	W Koch	W Taylor
Ocean City (16)	MC 609 399-6111	Henry S Knight	Richard W Deabet	Angela H Pileggi	John J Hansen	Todd E Bower	Dominick Longo	Howard Dill
Oceanport b (6)	MC 201 222-8221	(not reporting)						
Ogdensburg b (3)	MC 201 827-3444	A J Rutkowski	. . . .	J Dickson	M Alfano	. . . .	J Duke	R Search
Old Bridge tp (56)	MC 908 721-5600	Barbara L Cannon	John J Coughlin	R Saracino	Himanshu Shah	. . . .	Jerry V Palumbo	Rocco Donatelli
Old Tappan b (4)	MC 201 664-1849	Edward Gallagher	. . . .	Marie Koehler	Christine Cauvet	Charles Anders	John Kramer	George Pomponio
Oradell b (8)	MC 201 261-8200	(not reporting)						
Orange Township (30) ...	MC 201 266-4200	Robert L Brown	Thomas J Morrison	Dwight Mitchell	John W Kelly	John Gamba	Charles Cobbertt	Arlene Kemp
Palisades Park b (15) ...	MC 201 585-4100	(not reporting)						
Palmyra b (7)	MC 609 829-6100	(not reporting)						
Paramus b (25)	MC 201 265-2100	(not reporting)						
Park Ridge b (8)	MC 201 573-1800	(not reporting)						
Parsippany-Troy Hills tp (48)	MC 201 263-4350	Frank Priore	Gregory Hill	Judy Silver	Robert Griffith	. . . .	M Filippello	Jerry Rhodes
Passaic (58)	MC 201 365-5500	Margie Semler	. . . .	S Fiorellino	Edward Routel	Louis Imparato	Victor Jacalone	Bernard Geminder
Paterson (141)	MC 201 881-3343	(not reporting)						
Paulsboro b (7)	MC 609 423-1500	(not reporting)						
Pemberton tp (31)	MC 609 894-8201	Thalia C Kay	Michael Spurgeon	Charlotte Newhart	Douglas B Ayrer	Craig Augustoni	William C Hann	Paul D Leary Sr
Penns Grove b (5)	MC 609 299-0098	(not reporting)						
Pennsauken tp (35) ...	CM 609 665-1000	(not reporting)						
Pequannock tp (13) ...	CM 201 835-5700	Ruth E Spellman	Thomas F Kane	Elizabeth D Eley	Thomas F Kane	James Schneider	John Reeves	Anthony Barile Jr
Perth Amboy (42)	MC 908 826-0290	(not reporting)						
Phillipsburg t (16)	MC 908 454-5500	Gloria A Decker	Frank J Tolotta	Michele Broubalow	Joseph Hriczak	Richard A Hay	James F Macaulay	Frank J Tolotta
Pine Hill b (10)	MC 609 783-0374	Curtis H Noe	. . . .	Joan A Schneebele	George McDermott	Richard Wright	Otis Booker	Nicolas Hrynenko
Piscataway tp (47)	MC 908 562-2300	Ted Light	Harold Klein	Ann Nolan	Michael F Conti	. . . .	Pat Larocca	. . . .
Pitman b (9)	MC 609 589-3522	Bruce Ware	Jay P Todd	Jay P Todd	Earl J Kelly	Clarence Brown	Robert F Leach	Edward T Lewis
Plainfield (47)	CM 908 753-3000	Harold W Mitchell	J Thompson Chin	Laddie Wyatt	Jerome Reddy	Henry Lariccia	John Waldron	David Ervin
Plainsboro tp (14)	MC 609 799-0909	Peter Cantu	Patrick Guilfoyle	Patricia Hullfish	Jayne McGuigan	Ken Wilson	Clifford Maurer	Jeff Cramer
Pleasantville (16)	MC 609 484-3600	Ralph Peterson	Andrew Salerno	Alice Foster	Theodore Freedman	Leroy Borden	Hubert Hill	Leroy Stephens
Point Pleasant b (18) ..	MC 908 892-3434	(not reporting)						
Point Pleasant Beach b (5)	MC 908 892-1118	(not reporting)						
Pompton Lakes b (11) ...	MC 201 835-0143	(not reporting)						
Princeton b (12)	MC 609 924-3118	Marvin R Reed	Thomas B Shannon	P Edwards Carter	Decimus Marsh	Raymond Bianco	Thomas B Michaud	Carl E Peters
Princeton tp (13)	CM 609 924-5704	Laurence Glasberg	James Pascale	Patricia Shuss	. . . .	. . . .	Anthony Gaylord	. . . .
Prospect Park b (5)	MC 201 790-7903	(not reporting)						
Rahway (25)	MC 908 381-8000	(not reporting)						
Ramsey b (13)	MC 201 825-3400	John L Scerbo	Nicholas C Saros	Nancy M Ecke	Richard Mathieson	E Cohn	R Franceschi	William Horton
Randolph tp (20)	CM 201 989-7100	Kevin Creter	J Peter Braun	Frances Bertrand	Michael Soccio	. . . .	James McLagan	Ken Hauptvogel
Raritan tp (6)	MC 908 806-6100	Wilson Jones	Allan D Pietrefes	Dorothy Gooditis	Allan D Pietrefes	. . . .	William Meytrott	Robert Kling
Raritan b (6)	MC 908 231-1300	Anthony DeCicco	Daniel Jaxel	Louise Salerno	Jackson Hurst	Stephen Krachun	Joseph Sferra	DiGuiseppantonio
Red Bank b (11)	MC 908 530-2740	Edward McKenna	Sally Levine	Carol Vivona	Bruce Loversidge	Peter Defazio	Robert Clayton	J Bonnacquista
Ridgefield b (10)	MC 201 943-5215	(not reporting)						
Ridgefield Park v (12)	CO 201 641-4950	(not reporting)						
Ridgewood v (24)	CM 201 670-5534	Patrick Mancuso	Rodney Irwin	Heather Mailander	James Ten Hoeve	Robert Missel	L J Mader	William Cooke Jr
Ringwood b (13)	CM 201 962-7002	(not reporting)						
River Edge b (11)	MC 201 599-6300	James Kirk	Alan P Negreann	Grace Gutekunst	Alan P Negreann	Mark Mitchel	Kenneth Quinn	John Pusterla
River Vale tp (9)	MC 201 664-2346	Walter V Jones	Roy S Blumenthal	Corinne Verhille	Ann Olivarius	. . . .	Vincent Lally	Peter Wayne
Riverdale b (2)	MC 201 835-4060	(not reporting)						
Riverside tp (8)	CO 609 461-0284	(not reporting)						
Riverton b (3)	MC 609 829-0120	Anna L Cannon	. . . .	Mary Longbottom	Joachim H Jung	. . . .	Thomas R Gilbert	Charles Bishop
Rochelle Park tp (6) ...	CO 201 587-7729	Joseph Scarpa	Joseph Manzella	Virginia DeMaria	Joseph Manzella	Craig Schneider	William Betten	John Tanucilli
Rockaway tp (20)	MC 201 627-7200	David N Fischer	A P Guadagnino	Almira Salvesen	Charles Wood Jr	James Henderson	Steven Dachisen	Gerald Kunkel
Rockaway b (6)	MC 201 627-2000	(not reporting)						
Roseland b (5)	MC 201 226-8080	(not reporting)						
Roselle b (20)	MC 908 245-5600	Joseph F Safaryn	John Florentino	Johanna Breden	John Florentino	Donn Dwyer	Kenneth Hagamann	. . . .
Roselle Park b (13)	MC 908 245-2300	(not reporting)						
Roxbury tp (20)	CM 201 927-2000	William Silcox	James Zouvelekis	B Johannesen	Gary Rieth	Spencer Kinkle	Mark Noll	. . . .
Rumson b (7)	MC 908 842-3300	(not reporting)						
Runnemede b (9)	MC 609 939-5161	Anthony Beatrice	. . . .	Joyce Pinto	David J Watson	Michael Cox	James Leason	J Frank Gunn
Rutherford b (18)	MC 201 939-0020	(not reporting)						
Saddle Brook tp (13) ...	MC 201 843-7100	R Santalucia	. . . .	P Manichetti	Freda Brett	Floyd Henderson	Paul Jacob	Charles Cerone
Saddle River b (3)	MC 201 327-2609	(not reporting)						
Salem (7)	MC 609 935-0372	(not reporting)						
Sayreville b (35)	MC 201 390-7000	John B McCormack	Joseph Dominic	Gladys Rzepka	Wayne Kronowski	John Gorman	Douglas Sprague	A Eugene Crummy
Scotch Plains tp (21) ...	CM 201 322-6700	(not reporting)						
Sea Girt b (2)	MC 908 449-9433	(not reporting)						
Sea Isle City (3)	CO 609 263-4461	(not reporting)						
Secaucus t (14)	MC 201 330-2007	(not reporting)						
Shrewsbury b (3)	MC 908 741-4200	(not reporting)						
Somerdale b (5)	MC 609 783-6320	(not reporting)						
Somers Point (11)	MC 609 927-8938	Charles A Parker	Judson Moore Jr	Carol DeGrassi	Judson Moore Jr	Andrew Hawn	Orville Mathis	Richard Gray
Somerville b (12)	MC 201 725-2300	(not reporting)						
South Amboy (8)	MC 201 727-4600	(not reporting)						
South Bound Brook b (4)	MC 908 356-0258	Russ Reynolds	. . . .	Donald E Kazar	Catherine Hoats	Mike Kelly	Ronald Henry	. . . .
South Brunswick tp (26) ..	CO 908 329-4000	Roger Craig	Louis C Goetting	Kathleen Thorpe	Ralph Palmieri	. . . .	Franklin College	Thomas Evans
South Orange Village tp (16)	CO 201 378-7715	(not reporting)						
South Plainfield b (20) .	MC 908 754-9000	(not reporting)						
South River b (14)	MC 201 257-1999	(not reporting)						
South Toms River b (4)	MC 908 349-0403	(not reporting)						
Sparta tp (15)	CM 201 729-8485	Dolores Blackburn	David J Ferguson	Miriam Tower	Nicholas Lella	. . . .	Frederick Geffken	Charles Ryan
Spotswood b (8)	MC 908 251-3378	(not reporting)						
Spring Lake b (3)	MC 908 449-0800	(not reporting)						
Spring Lake Heights b (5)	MC 908 449-3500	Frank E Adams	. . . .	Claire Barrett	Claire Barrett	Harvey Hogan	Vernon Henderson	James Costigan
Springfield tp (13)	RT 201 912-2200	Philip Kurnos	Helen E Keyworth	Helen E Keyworth	Jeanne Decker	William Gras	William Chisholm	S Boettcher
Stanhope b (3)	MC 201 347-0159	Michael Bender	John Arntz	Audrey Dressel	Alan Dickinson	Harry Peterson	Douglas Waldron	James Floyd

Directory 1/9 continued

MUNICIPAL OFFICIALS IN U.S. CITIES OVER 2,500

City, 1990 population figures (000 omitted), form of government	Municipal phone number	Mayor	Appointed administrator	City clerk	Finance officer	Fire chief	Police chief	Public works director
NEW JERSEY (357) continued								
Stratford b (8)	MC 609 783-0600	(not reporting)						
Summit (20)	MC 908 273-6400	Janet L Whitman	Reagan Burkholder	David L Hughes	Ronald J Angelo	John Gerity	Lonnie Davis	Michael F Luciano
Teaneck tp (38)	CM 201 837-4807	John Abraham	Gary A Saage	E O'Brien	Sandra L Kaye	Wm Hillermeier	Donald Giannone	....
Tenafly b (13)	MC 201 568-6100	W W Hemberger	Robert P Miller	Nancy Hatten	Anita Diamond	Harvey Eisner	Allen Layne	Brooks Bodecker
Tinton Falls b (12)	MC 908 542-3400	Ann Y McNamara	Anthony Muscillo	Karen Mount	Stephen G Pfeffer	....	Wayne White	Louis Buono
Totowa b (10)	MC 201 956-1000	Jack Masklee	....	Joseph Wassel	Andrew Carioti	Allen Del Vecchio	Thomas Clifton	Douglas Wright
Trenton (89)	MC 609 989-3030	(not reporting)						
Union tp (50)	MC 908 688-2800	Anthony Russo	Louis Giacona	Nancy Issenman	....	....	James Trohe	George Salzmann
Union Beach b (6)	MC 201 264-2277	(not reporting)						
Union City (58)	CO 201 348-5754	(not reporting)						
Upper Saddle River b (7)	MC 201 327-2196	Francis J Grout	....	Rita M Hagen	Roy A Rossow	Stephen Pink	Theodore Preusch	Craig Rossiter
Ventnor City (11)	CO 609 823-7900	Ted M Bergman	Charles F Beirne	Sandra M Biagi	William M Johnson	Daniel J Cahill	Gerald J Schaffer	David Smith
Verona tp (14)	MC 201 239-3220	James Treffinger	Vincent DiMauro	Vincent DiMauro	Dorothy Trimmer	Charles Magatti	William Wilks	James Helb
Vineland (55)	MC 609 794-4000	Joseph E Romano	Linda Dechen	Dolores Lopergold	Edward Rochetti	Biaggio Ciulla	Mario R Brunetta	William Rich
Waldwick b (10)	MC 201 652-5070	Rick Vander Wende	Gary Kratz	Paula Jaegge	Mary Ann Viviani	James O'Connell	Daniel Lupo	Ray Schmidt
Wall tp (20)	MC 908 449-8444	Wesley Jost	Joseph Verruni	Beatrice Gassner	Stephen Mayer	....	....	James White
Wallington b (11)	MC 201 779-4879	(not reporting)						
Wanaque b (10)	MC 201 839-3000	(not reporting)						
Warren tp (11)	RT 908 753-8000	Frank Salvato	Mark Krane	Doris Lortie	Carolyn J Gara	James R Herlich	Michael G Lach	Ewald Friedrich
Washington b (6)	CM 908 689-3600	Ronald Kaplowitz	Alan M Fisher	Linda Hendershot	Bernadette Tuttle	Harold Radcliff	Stephen B Speirs	....
Washington (Bergen) tp (9)	MC 201 664-4404	(not reporting)						
Washington (Glcstr) tp (42)	MC 609 589-0520	Gerald J Luongo	Douglas Chastain	Charlotte Cella	Douglas Chastain	....	Richard Moore	James McKeever
Washington (Morris) tp (16)	MC 908 876-3315	(not reporting)						
Washington (Warren) tp (5)	MC 908 689-7200	Michael A Kovacs	....	Judith M Hanke	Catherine Gangawa	William Duryea	John F Corrigan	Jeff Hoser
Watchung b (5)	MC 201 756-0080	Anthony Addario	Lyn A Evers	Adele Widin	Catherine Schley	Robert Pittenger	George King	Donald Scotti
Wayne tp (47)	MC 201 694-1800	Newton Miller	Neal Bellet	John O'Brien	John Aitken	....	Donald Pavlak	Anthony Buzzoni
Weehawken tp (12)	CO 201 867-1707	(not reporting)						
West Caldwell tp (10)	MC 201 226-2300	Robert Reiher	B F Martorana	B F Martorana	Russell Jarger	Jock Watkins	Harry Jensen	Kenneth Mathews
West Deptford tp (19)	CM 609 845-4004	(not reporting)						
West Long Branch b (8)	MC 908 229-1756	(not reporting)						
West Milford tp (25)	CM 201 728-7000	Cral Richko	Kevin J Byrnes	Kevin J Byrnes	Theresa V Benack	....	James Breslin	Gerald Storms
West New York t (38)	CO 201 861-7000	(not reporting)						
West Orange tp (39)	MC 201 325-4050	(not reporting)						
West Paterson b (11)	MC 201 345-8100	Mary B Zaccaria	William E Wilk	William E Wilk	Andrew Carioti	John Wittig	Joseph Renne	George Galbraith
West Windsor tp (16)	MC 609 799-2400	Thomas Fracella	Robert Bruschi	Barbara Evans	Joanne Louth	....	Frank Cox	George Spille
Westfield t (29)	MC 908 789-4230	(not reporting)						
Westville b (5)	MC 609 456-0030	(not reporting)						
Westwood b (10)	MC 201 664-7100	Henry G Geier	Victor Lapychak	Teresa Massood	Rebecca Overgaard	John Woods	Robert Burroughs	Robert Woods
Wharton b (5)	MC 201 361-8444	Harry R Shupe	Edward M Griffin	Susan R Best	Jean Mench	....	Anthony Fernandez	Arnold Boyer
Wildwood (4)	MC 609 522-2444	(not reporting)						
Wildwood Crest b (4)	CO 609 522-7788	(not reporting)						
Willingboro tp (36)	CM 609 877-2200	Paul Stephenson	Sadie Johnson	Lenore Stern	Joanne Diggs	Anthony Burnett	Gary Owens	Harry McFarland
Wood-Lynne b (3)	MC 609 962-8300	J Drew Coyle	....	....	Donna Condo	Ken Steward	John Ragan	Richard Dadamo
Wood-Ridge b (8)	MC 201 939-0202	Paul Calocino	Janet L Lynds	Janet L Lynds	Doris A Marek	Robert Concato	John Frank	John Sabia
Woodbine b (3)	MC 609 861-2153	William Pikolycky	Frances P Pettit	Frances P Pettit	....	Anthony Mayshura	....	Clarence Ryan
Woodbridge tp (93)	MC 908 634-4500	James McGreevey	James M Davy	Philip M Cerria	John E McCormac	....	William G Trenery	Timothy J Dacey
Woodbury (11)	MC 609 845-1300	(not reporting)						
Woodbury Heights b (3)	MC 609 848-2832	(not reporting)						
Woodcliff Lake b (5)	MC 201 391-4977	Bernard Kettler	John T Doyle	John T Doyle	John T Doyle	Bruce Mautz	Dennis Winters	Edward Barboni
Woodstown b (3)	MC 609 769-2200	(not reporting)						
Wrightstown b (4)	MC 609 723-4450	(not reporting)						
Wyckoff tp (15)	MC 201 891-7000	R Van Hassel	Robert J Shannon	Theresa M Moffa	Robert J Shannon	Wayne P Remo	John W Ydo	....
NEW MEXICO (43)								
Alamogordo (28)	CM 505 437-4530	Dan King	Robert Stockwell	Angie Rahn	Maurice Gutirezz	....	Truman Nix	Jose Miramontes
Albuquerque (385)	MC 505 768-3705	Louis Saavedra	Arthur Blumenfeld	Karen Aceves	....	Thomas Montoya	Bob Stover	Robert Gurule
Angel Fire v (..)	MC 505 377-3232	(not reporting)						
Artesia (11)	MC 505 746-4612	Ernest Thompson	....	Shirley Clark	....	Ray Castleberry	Ernest Chavez	Tommy Howell
Aztec (5)	CM 505 334-9456	(not reporting)						
Bayard v (3)	MC 505 537-3327	(not reporting)						
Belen t (7)	CM 505 864-8221	(not reporting)						
Bernalillo t (6)	MC 505 867-3311	(not reporting)						
Bloomfield (5)	MC 505 632-8096	Arthur C Kittell	Albert Keller	Carol S Miller	Shirley K Ross	George T Duncan	Bill R Goodman	James A Moore
Bosque Farms v (4)	MC 505 869-2358	Carl R Allen	M Sue Padilla	M Sue Padilla	....	Walter Shoemaker	Hastings Hutchins	James Vaughan
Carlsbad (25)	CM 505 887-1191	Bob Forrest	Jon R Tully	Pearlene Bradshaw	Eli T Rivera	....	James C Koch	James M Harrison
Clayton t (2)	MC 505 374-8331	Lee Shields	Bill Freeman	Jane May	Jane May	Dwayne Massey	James Atkins	Bill Freeman
Clovis (31)	CM 505 769-2384	James B Moss	Donald E Clifton	....	Terri McCully	Billy Morey	Harry Boden	Joe Thomas
Corrales v (5)	MC 505 897-0502	Gary Kanin	Phillip Rios	Tina Dominguez	Phillip Rios	Bob Bone	Michael Tarter	Tony Tafoya
Deming (11)	MC 505 546-8848	Sam D Baca	John G Strand	....	....	Fred Rossiter	Mike Carillo	Louis Jenkins
Espanola (8)	MC 505 753-2377	Richard L Lucero	Fred J Rivera	Alice Lucero	Lillian Brooks	Manuel Vigil	Richard Guillen	Jim Farmer
Eunice (3)	MC 505 394-2576	(not reporting)						
Farmington (34)	CM 505 327-7701	Thomas C Taylor	Daniel R Dible	Mary L Banks	Hilary Parker	Carl J Peskor	Richard G Melton	....
Gallup t (19)	CM 505 863-1202	George Galanis	David H Ruiz	Ruth Ruiz	Lynne Thompson	Michael Lovato	Danny Ross	Joshua Richardson
Grants (9)	MC 505 287-7927	Jackie A Fisher	Willie R Alire	Brenda Lucero	Robert Horacek	Jasper A Mace	Fred Radosevich	....
Hobbs (29)	CM 505 397-9200	Robert L Love	Robert Gallagher	Joyce Edmiston	Lawrence Jones	Mike Gray	Marshal Newman	....
Jal (2)	MC 505 395-2222	(not reporting)						
Las Cruces (62)	CM 505 526-0000	Ruben A Smith	Bruno Zaldo	Karen P Stevens	Barbara E Willis	John Toledo	William P Hampton	James Erickson
Las Vegas (15)	CM 505 454-1401	Tony Martinez Jr	Les Montoya	Carmen Gonzales	Carmen Tafoya	Robert Gonzales	John Perea	Benny Romero
Lordsburg (3)	MC 505 542-3421	Salvador Diaz Jr	....	Irene Galvan	Ted Castillo	John Hill	John McDonald	Alex Delagarza
Los Lunas v (6)	MC 505 865-9689	Louis F Huning	Phillip Jaramillo	....	Viv Santistevan	Atilano Chavez	Nick Balido	J Eddie Saiz
Los Ranchos de Albuqrq v (4)	MC 505 344-6582	John S O'Connor	....	Annabelle Martine	Sylvia M Pesce	Jose Jaramillo	....	Jose Jaramillo
Lovington (9)	CM 505 396-2884	Troy J Harris	Bob G Carter	Kristi Mannan	Kristi Mannan	Jack Davis	Archie Cunningham	Bob G Carter
Milan v (2)	MC 505 285-6694	(not reporting)						
Portales (11)	MC 505 356-6662	(not reporting)						
Raton (7)	CM 505 445-9551	(not reporting)						
Rio Rancho (33)	MC 505 892-6704	Pat D'Arco	Harold Donovan	Tina Gonzales	Eugene Waite	....	Dencil Haycox	Jerry Fossenier
Roswell (45)	MC 505 624-6700	(not reporting)						
Ruidoso (5)	MC 505 258-4014	Jerry Shaw	Ronald Wicker	Tammie Maddox	Leeana Bosewell	Virgil Reynolds	Richard Swenor	....
Santa Fe (56)	MC 505 984-6500	Samuel Pick	Isaac Pino	Frances Romero	David Sena	George Quintana	Robert Lucero	James Traxler
Santa Rosa (2)	MC 505 472-3404	(not reporting)						
Silver City t (11)	CM 505 538-3731	(not reporting)						

Directory 1/9 continued

MUNICIPAL OFFICIALS IN U.S. CITIES OVER 2,500

City, 1990 population figures (000 omitted), form of government	Municipal phone number	Mayor	Appointed administrator	City clerk	Finance officer	Fire chief	Police chief	Public works director
NEW MEXICO (43) continued								
Socorro (8)	MC 505 835-0240	(not reporting)		Concha Medina	Concha Medina	Benito Hernandez	Eduardo Medina	Kurt Moffatt
Sunland Park (8)	MC 505 589-7565	Irene Aguirre		Lorraine Gallegos	Orlando Marquez	Jim Fambro	Neil Curran	Walter Vigil
Taos t (4)	MC 505 751-2000	Eloy A Jeantete	Gustavo Cordova	Lorraine Gallegos	Sharon L Roberts	Mike Tooley	Beatrice Walsmith	Gene E Hoskinson
Truth Or Consequences (6)	CM 505 894-6673	Freddie J Torres	Walter C Armijo	Evelyn B Renfro	Marty Garcia	Mike Cherry	Steven Rabi	Richard Quintana
Tucumcari (7)	CM 505 461-3451	David Hale	Bernadetta Moya	Rachel Dominguez		Fernando Leal	Eynaldo Guilez	T P Guilez
Tularosa v (3)	MC 505 585-2771	Mary R Stanfill		Margaret Gonzales				
NEW YORK (275)								
Akron v (3)	MC 716 542-9636	Michael F Charles		Raymond J Carlo		Daniel R Kowalik		Daniel R Huff
Albany (101)	MC 518 434-5100	Thomas M Whalen		Pamela Alley	Robert J Kukla	James Larson	John Dale	George E Nealon
Albion v (6)	MC 716 589-9176	David C Albanese		Kathleen Ludwick		Andrew Eibl	Donald Hinman	Jose Palacios
Alfred v (5)	MC 607 587-9188	(not reporting)						
Amityville v (9)	MC 516 264-6000	Emil G Pavlik Jr	Bruce E Mac Gill	Bruce E Mac Gill	Anne Mackin	Dennis James	Kenneth Greguski	Kendall W Muncy
Amsterdam (21)	MC 518 841-4329	(not reporting)						
Ardsley v (4)	CM 914 693-1550	E John Morehouse	George F Calvi	Mary Kamens	Marion Demaio	Robert Reid	Louis Daliso	Louis Pascone
Attica v (3)	MC 716 591-0898	Dale L Slocum	Donadl Kellner	Kathleen Sennott	Kathleen Sennott	Robert Willard	Daniel Norcross	Donald Kellner
Auburn (31)	CM 315 255-4146	Guy Cosentino	James E Malone	Paul C Norman	Beatrice O'Hora	Frank Calarco	John E Ecklund	Francis J DeOrio
Avon v (3)	MC 716 226-8118	John C Whitney	Michael McGinnis	Robyn Harris	Joseph Prinzi		John Braisington	John Barrett
Babylon v (12)	MC 516 669-1212	(not reporting)						
Baldwinsville v (7)	MC 315 635-3521	(not reporting)						
Ballston Spa v (5)	MC 518 885-5711	James L Capasso	Patricia Bowers	Patricia Bowers	Martin Glastetter			Martin Glastetter
Batavia (16)	CM 716 343-8180	Steven L Dworzack	William Reemtsen	Rebecca Swanson	William Reemtsen	Keith Hunt		Dennis Larson
Batavia t (..)	MC 716 343-1729	June Vukman	Francis Repicci	Rubie Levins	June Vukman			
Bath v (6)	MC 607 776-3811	(not reporting)						
Bayville v (7)	MC 516 628-1439	Edward J Esposito	Diane Symanski	Anita Clark				Stanley Symanski
Beacon (13)	MC 914 831-0302	Clara Lou Gould	Joseph H Braun	Helen Nuccitelli	Linda Greenough	Steven Van Buren	John E Johnson	Randy Casale
Bellport v (3)	MC 516 286-0327	Frank C Trotta		Stephen J Yacubch				Louis Cardamone
Binghamton (53)	MC 607 772-7000	(not reporting)						
Blasdell v (3)	MC 716 822-1921	(not reporting)						
Briarcliff Manor v (7)	CM 914 941-4800	Freda Delton	Lynn M McCrum	Susan P Gaffney		Timothy Reilly	Ronald N Trainham	Robert L Ferreira
Brighton t (34)	MC 716 473-8800	(not reporting)						
Brightwaters v (3)	MC 516 665-1280	(not reporting)						
Brockport v (9)	MC 716 637-5300	(not reporting)						
Bronxville v (6)	CM 914 337-6500	Nancy D Hand			Robert J Fels		A DiVernieri	Peter J Woodcock
Brookville v (4)	MC 516 626-1792	(not reporting)						
Buffalo (328)	MC 716 851-4841	(not reporting)						
Camden v (3)	MC 315 245-0560	(not reporting)						
Canandaigua (11)	CM 716 396-5000	Ellen Polimeni	William Bridgeo	Joseph Del Forte		James Farrell	Patrick McCarthy	Louis Loy
Canastota v (5)	MC 315 697-7559	(not reporting)						
Canisteo v (2)	MC 607 698-4553	(not reporting)						
Canton v (6)	MC 315 386-2871	David T Button		Marlene Thompson		Dale Gardner	David Sullivan	Charles A Carvel
Carthage v (4)	CO 315 493-1060	(not reporting)						
Catskill v (5)	MC 518 943-3830	(not reporting)						
Cayuga Heights v (3)	MC 607 257-1238	Ronald E Anderson		Anne M Krohto		Gary Leonhardt	David Wall	John B Rogers
Cazenovia v (3)	MC 315 655-3041	John W Ryan		Patricia Costello		William Emerson	Robert B Young	James A Brady
Cedarhurst v (6)	MC 516 295-5770	(not reporting)						
Chestnut Ridge v (8)	MC 914 425-2805	Jerome Kobre	Harriet L Slater	Harriet L Slater	Harriet L Slater			
Chittenango v (5)	MC 315 687-3936	(not reporting)						
Cobleskill v (5)	MC 518 234-3891	(not reporting)						
Cohoes (17)	MC 518 237-7811	Robert Signoracci		M Archambeault	Michael Gagnon	Andrew Gisondi	Michael Robich	John Stackrow
Colonie v (8)	MC 518 869-7562	(not reporting)						
Corinth v (3)	MC 518 654-2012	(not reporting)						
Corning (12)	MC 607 962-0721	(not reporting)						
Cornwall-On-Hudson v (3)	MC 914 534-4200	Edward C Moulton		Roberta Hirsch	Edward C Moulton	James Bryan	Richard Douglass	Robert Gilmore
Cortland (20)	MC 607 756-7312	(not reporting)						
Coxsackie v (3)	MC 518 731-2718	Margaret Chaloner		Angela D Wilsey		Robert Frank	Gary Grigalus	John Halsted
Croton-On-Hudson v (7)	CM 914 271-4781	Robert W Elliott	Richard F Herbek	Richard F Herbek		Frank Streany	Dennis J Coxen	Lawrence Black
Dannemora v (4)	MC 518 492-7000	Charles E Layhee		Donna D Taylor		Byron Wing		Wilmer Barber
Dansville v (5)	MC 716 335-5330	(not reporting)						
Delhi v (3)	MC 607 746-2258	(not reporting)						
Depew v (18)	MC 716 683-1400	Michael J Rusniak		Joyce M Rauker		Kenneth Balzer	John Maccarone	John S Wojcik
Dobbs Ferry v (10)	MC 914 693-2203	(not reporting)						
Dolgeville v (2)	MC 315 429-3112	Philip G Dahlia		Donna L Cammann		Richard Levonski	Douglas Murphy	Robert R Sheppard
Dunkirk (14)	MC 716 366-1600	Margarte Wuerstle		Susan Pupenbroke	Charles Herron	Michael Edwards	Wade Weatherlow	David Manzella
East Aurora v (7)	CM 716 652-6000	John Pagliaccio	Jerry C Hiller	Jerry C Hiller	Jerry C Hiller	David Meyer	William Nye	Robert Urban
East Hills v (7)	MC 516 621-4251	Lawrence Aaronson		Marlene Bettman				Angelo DeCurtis
East Rochester v (7)	CM 716 586-3553	(not reporting)						
East Rockaway v (10)	MC 516 599-1211	Irving F Shaw		Phyllis J Rand		Robert M Walker		John H Conklin
East Syracuse v (3)	MC 315 437-3541	(not reporting)						
East Williston v (3)	MC 516 746-0782	Anthony J Casella		Joane A Lauman		Ronald Rico		James J Daw
Ellenville v (4)	CM 914 647-7080	Elliott Auerbach	Michael Mills	Ann Bowler	Linda Polkoski		Richard Basile	
Elmira (34)	CM 607 737-5646	James Hare		Dorothy Terris		Donald Harrison	Joseph Michalko	Steven White
Elmira Heights v (4)	MC 607 734-7156	Allen L Rice		Mary T Phillips	Allen L Rice	Thomas E Pesesky	Robert N Hauptan	Jean Cazorla
Elmsford v (4)	MC 914 592-6555	(not reporting)						
Endicott v (14)	MC 607 757-2421	(not reporting)						
Fairport v (6)	MC 716 223-0313	Clark T King	Kenneth W Moore	Nancy E Loughney	Kenneth W Moore	Michael Kenney	Brian T Page	Kenneth W Moore
Falconer v (3)	MC 716 665-4400	(not reporting)						
Fallsburg t (11)	CM 914 434-8810	Nat Kagan	Robert Robinson	Patricia Haaf	Robert V Robinson		Robert Robinson	David D Meckes
Farmingdale v (8)	MC 516 249-0093	(not reporting)						
Fayetteville v (4)	MC 315 637-9864	Marian S Loosmann		Martin E Lynch		James Craw		Robert Grevelding
Floral Park v (16)	MC 516 326-6300	(not reporting)						
Flower Hill v (4)	MC 516 627-2253	John W Walter		Barbara W Errett	Barbara W Errett			
Fort Edward v (4)	MC 518 747-4023	(not reporting)						
Fort Plain v (2)	MC 518 993-4271	Albert T Nalli		Susanne Mahn		David Bowman	Harold Wilday Jr	Raymond Pedrick
Frankfort v (3)	MC 315 894-8811	(not reporting)						
Fredonia v (10)	MC 716 673-1325	Louis C Mancuso	James M Sedota	James M Sedota	James M Sedota	Julius Leone	Daniel Johnson	Richard Lascola
Freeport v (40)	MC 516 378-4000	Arthur W Thompson	Michael Williams	Karen Navin	Andrew Ludwick	Timothy Seaman	Joseph W King Jr	David R Lovejoy
Fulton (13)	MC 315 592-7330	George Valette		Joseph Tetro	James Laboda	Marvin Jensen	Michael Stafford	Raymond Graham
Garden City v (22)	MC 516 742-5800	Allen S Mathers	Robert L Schoelle	Robert L Schoelle	Robert L Schoelle	Donald P Jenkins	Ernest J Cipullo	Edward W Purcell
Gates t (29)	TM 716 247-6100	Ralph J Esposito		Richard Warner	Christopher Russo		Thomas J Roche	John O Lathrop
Geneseo v (7)	MC 716 243-1177	Richard B Hathawa		Mark E Schnitzler	Mark E Schnitzler	Craig Moses	Joseph Guarino	
Geneva (14)	CM 315 789-2603	Frank J Cecere Jr	Sanford I Miller	Margaret A Cass	David M Stowell	Ralph E DeBolt	Frank T Pane Jr	John Berry

Directory 1/9 continued

MUNICIPAL OFFICIALS IN U.S. CITIES OVER 2,500

City, 1990 population figures (000 omitted), form of government	Municipal phone number	Mayor	Appointed administrator	City clerk	Finance officer	Fire chief	Police chief	Public works director
NEW YORK (275) continued								
Glen Cove (24)	MC 516 676-2000	(not reporting)						
Glens Falls (15)	MC 518 761-3800	Francis X O'Keefe	. . . .	Carol Barlow	Edward Bethel	Ronald Cote	Carl Carlton	Robert Schiavoni
Gloversville (17)	MC 518 773-4500	(not reporting)						
Goshen v (5)	MC 914 294-6750	(not reporting)						
Gouverneur v (5)	MC 315 287-1720	. . . .	Scott A Hudson	Sheryl E Simmons	. . . .	Dale A Johnson	David C Whitton	Ronald D Cochrane
Gowanda v (3)	MC 716 532-3353	(not reporting)						
Granville v (3)	MC 518 642-2640	(not reporting)						
Great Neck v (9)	MC 516 482-0019	Isabel Varlotta		Thomas F Albanese	. . . .	. . . .	. . . .	Lawrence Dunn
Great Neck Estates v (3) . .	MC 516 482-8283	Howard S Weitzman	. . . .	Kathleen Santelli	Howard S Weitzman	. . . .	Joseph J Meade	Frank Marcellino
Great Neck Plaza v (6) . . .	MC 516 482-4500	(not reporting)						
Green Island v (2)	MC 518 273-2201	(not reporting)						
Greenwood Lake v (3) . . .	MC 914 477-9215	Gilbert Shapiro	. . . .	Doris Hawkins	Robert Langan	. . . .	Ed Baldesweiler	George Kluwe
Hamburg v (10)	MC 716 649-0200	(not reporting)						
Hamilton v (4)	MC 315 824-1111	Lawrence Baker	. . . .	Paul Kogut	Paul Kogut	. . . .	James Tilbe	. . . .
Harrison (23)	MC 914 835-2000	Charles Balancia	. . . .	Joan Walsh	Eleanor McDonald	. . . .	Albert Klein	Benedict Cutrone
Hastings-On-Hudson v (8)	CM 914 478-3400	Wm Lee Kinnally	Neil P Hess	Mary Callas		. . . .	Joseph Marsic	Marco Gennarelli
Haverstraw v (9)	MC 914 429-0300	Thomas L Watson	. . . .	Deborah P Smith	. . . .	Robert Sullivan	John J Reilly	Andrew M Connors
Hempstead v (49)	MC 516 489-3400	James A Garner	. . . .	Audrey D Tourt	Sal Lombardi	Robert Grams	James Russo	Harry Dickenson
Herkimer v (8)	MC 315 866-3303	(not reporting)						
Highland Falls v (4)	MC 914 446-3400	(not reporting)						
Hilton v (5)	MC 716 392-4144	(not reporting)						
Homer v (3)	MC 607 749-3322	Mary A Bellardini	. . . .	Joanne B Williams	. . . .	James S Reif	David V Sampson	. . . .
Hoosick v (3)	MC 518 686-7072	Donald E Bogardus	John Dwyer	Denise McMahon	Ann M Bornt	. . . .	Royal Howard	Timothy Stratton
Hornell (10)	MC 607 324-7421	(not reporting)						
Horseheads v (7)	CM 607 739-5691	Patricia Gross	Chris Lawrick	S Cunningham	. . . .	Richard Sullivan	R Craig Banfield	James Stevens
Hudson (8)	MC 518 828-1030	(not reporting)						
Hudson Falls v (8)	MC 518 747-5426	(not reporting)						
Ilion v (9)	MC 315 895-7449	Stephen Canipe	Marilyn Slaughter	Gale Hatch	. . . .	Karl Tripple	Lloyd Wadsworth	James Rowland
Irondequoit t (52)	MC 716 467-8840	Fredrick Lapple	. . . .	E Ann Long	. . . .	. . . .	William Frey	Edward Purdell
Irvington v (6)	MC 914 591-7070	(not reporting)						
Island Park v (5)	MC 516 431-0600	(not reporting)						
Islandia v (3)	MC 516 348-1133	(not reporting)						
Ithaca (30)	MC 607 272-1713	Benjamin Nichols	. . . .	C Paolangeli	D Cafferillo	Brian H Wilbur	Harlin R McEwen	William J Gray
Jamestown (35)	MC 716 483-7610	(not reporting)						
Johnson City v (17)	MC 607 798-7861	(not reporting)						
Johnstown (9)	MC 518 762-3911	Francis W Reed	. . . .	Marilyn H Muzzi	Frank S Kovarik	James L Cook	Edward W Heberer	. . . .
Kenmore v (17)	MC 716 873-5700	John W Beaumont	Edmund J O'Grady	. . . .	. . . .	Felix Coniglio	Elmer Arnet	John Neiss
Kings Point v (5)	MC 516 482-7872	(not reporting)						
Kingston (23)	MC 914 331-0080	John A Amarello	. . . .	Margaret M Phelan	. . . .	John E Reinhardt	James K Riggins	Jay Hogan
Lackawanna (21)	MC 716 827-6464	K Staniszewski	A Swygert	D Wojcik	R Marciniak	S Kaminski	J Deren	. . . .
Lake Grove v (10)	MC 516 585-2000	Lillian B Griffin	. . . .	Mary C Brady	. . . .	. . . .	. . . .	Douglas J Colino
Lake Success v (2)	MC 516 482-4411	Albert Zimbalist	Roberta Penchina	Roberta Penchina	Roberta Penchina	. . . .	William Roberts	. . . .
Lakewood v (4)	MC 716 763-8557	(not reporting)						
Lancaster v (12)	MC 716 683-2105	William Cansdale	. . . .	B Depasquale	B W Depasquale	Paul Murawski	Gary Stoldt	Wm R Natalzia
Lansing v (3)	MC 607 257-0424	Theodore Wixom	. . . .	Sylvia Smith	. . . .	. . . .	. . . .	Dennis Reinhart
Larchmont v (6)	MC 914 834-6202	Cheryl Lewy	. . . .	Eileen Finn	. . . .	Eric Verhave	William Keresey	. . . .
Lawrence v (7)	MC 516 239-4600	(not reporting)						
Le Roy v (5)	CM 716 768-2527	Floyd E Lee	. . . .	Jeffrey R Smith	. . . .	David Ehrhart	Samuel C Steffeni	Roger Lander
Lewiston v (3)	MC 716 754-8271	(not reporting)						
Liberty v (4)	CM 914 292-2250	Ron F Gozza	Janet Salamon	Judy Zurawski	Patrick Galloway	Donald Nichols	Michael Ward	Marvin Cox
Lindenhurst v (27)	MC 516 957-7500	(not reporting)						
Little Falls (6)	MC 315 823-2400	(not reporting)						
Liverpool v (3)	MC 315 457-3441	F Bobenhausen	. . . .	N O'Brien	. . . .	R Cussens	G Neri	P Babcock
Lloyd Harbor v (3)	MC 516 423-9044	(not reporting)						
Lockport (24)	MC 716 439-6665	Thomas Rotondo	. . . .	Richard Mullaney	. . . .	Thomas Darroch	Henry Newman	John Claypool
Long Beach (34)	CM 516 431-1000	(not reporting)						
Lowville v (4)	MC 315 376-6711	Carl L Kellogg	. . . .	Eleanor L Field	. . . .	Donald Kraeger	John J Youngs	Brian M Bush
Lynbrook v (19)	MC 516 599-8300	(not reporting)						
Lyons v (4)	MC 315 946-4531	Gabriel Vardabash	. . . .	Corrine Kleisle	Corrine Kleisle	Arthur Witt	John Lese	Charles R Bowers
Malone v (7)	MC 518 483-4570	James Feeley	. . . .	E Bessette	. . . .	. . . .	James Phillips	Ralph Jesmer
Malverne v (9)	MC 516 599-1200	Joseph J Hennessy	. . . .	Carolyn E Knauer	. . . .	Robert Kutcher	Raymond Garrigan	Vincent Gebbia
Mamaroneck t (17)	CM 914 381-7810	(not reporting)						
Manlius v (5)	MC 315 682-9171	(not reporting)						
Manorhaven v (6)	MC 516 883-7000	(not reporting)						
Massapequa Park v (18) . .	MC 516 798-0244	George Nussbaum	M Capobianco	M Capobianco	. . . .	. . . .	. . . .	William Colfer
Massena v (12)	MC 315 769-8625	Charles Boots	. . . .	Sandra Smith	. . . .	Thomas Lacomb	Paul King	Hassan Fayad
Mechanicville (5)	CO 518 664-9884	Patrick Hildeth	. . . .	Clara Pitcheralle	Thomas J Higgins	Raymond Lorenzo	John Wallace	Michael Rinaldi
Medina v (7)	MC 716 798-0710	(not reporting)						
Menands v (4)	MC 518 434-2922	(not reporting)						
Middletown (24)	MC 914 343-4189	Gertrude Mokotoff	. . . .	. . . .	Nancy Carrington	Mark Davis	Thomas Lopez	Alfred Fusco
Mineola v (19)	MC 516 746-0750	(not reporting)						
Minoa v (4)	MC 315 656-3100	(not reporting)						
Mohawk v (3)	MC 315 866-4312	(not reporting)						
Monroe v (7)	MC 914 782-8341	(not reporting)						
Montebello v (..)	MC 914 368-2211	(not reporting)						
Monticello v (7)	CM 914 794-6130	Robert Friedland	James J Malloy	Edith Schop	James J Malloy	Vince Price	Michael Brennan	George Panchyshyn
Morrisville v (3)	MC 315 684-3214	(not reporting)						
Mount Kisco v (9)	CM 914 241-0500	Richard Roth	John Pierpont	John Pierpont	. . . .	. . . .	Robert Martini	John Appedu
Mount Morris v (3)	MC 716 658-4160	(not reporting)						
Mount Vernon (67)	MC 914 665-2300	(not reporting)						
Munsey Park v (3)	MC 516 365-7790	(not reporting)						
Muttontown v (3)	MC 516 364-2240	(not reporting)						
New Hempstead v (4)	MC 914 354-8100	(not reporting)						
New Hyde Park v (10) . . .	MC 516 354-0022	(not reporting)						
New Paltz v (5)	MC 914 255-0130	(not reporting)						
New Rochelle (67)	CM 914 654-2000	Timothy Idoni	C Indelicato	Gwen Byrd	Howard Rattner	Raymond Kiernan	John Carboni	. . . .
New York City (7323)	MC 212 566-5700	(not reporting)						
New York Mills v (4)	MC 315 736-9212	(not reporting)						
Newark v (10)	MC 315 331-4770	Fred J Pirelli	. . . .	Steven H Brumm	Steven H Brumm	Albert Mels	Edward Hethcoat	. . . .
Newburgh (26)	CM 914 565-3333	Audrey Carey	Harold Porr	Nancy D'Addio	Harry Patel	James Barry	Chris Gershel	James Politi
Niagara Falls (62)	CM 716 286-4300	Jacob A Pilillo	Thomas C Lizardo	Elsie M Paradise	Patrick D Brown	John Gabriele	Thomas Zwelling	Richard Lucinski
North Syracuse v (7)	MC 315 458-0900	James Hotchkiss	. . . .	Jane Visell	. . . .	Paul Linnertz	Duane Foster	Michael Abruzzese
North Tarrytown v (8)	MC 914 631-1440	Sean Treacy	William T Regan	William T Regan	. . . .	. . . .	James Bropy	Joseph DeFeo

Directory 1/9
continued

**MUNICIPAL OFFICIALS
IN U.S. CITIES OVER 2,500**

City, 1990 population figures (000 omitted), form of government	Municipal phone number	Mayor	Appointed administrator	City clerk	Finance officer	Fire chief	Police chief	Public works director
NEW YORK (275) continued								
North Tonawanda (35) ...	MC 716 695-8555	James A McGinnis	. . . .	John W Wylucki	David Jakubaszek	David A Rogge	Lloyd C Graves	Gary J Franklin
Northport v (8)	MC 516 261-7502	Peter J Nolan	. . . .	Judith Zahm	. . . .	Chris Hughes	Robert Howard	Joseph Correia
Norwich (8)	MC 607 334-1200	M Chomyzsak	. . . .	Jody Zakrevsky	Harold Hutton	Timothy Ashcraft	Richard Whiting	Joseph Loscavio
Nyack v (7)	MC 914 358-0548	(not reporting)						
Ocean Beach v (..)	MC 516 583-5940	(not reporting)						
Ogdensburg (14)	CM 315 393-6100	Richard Lockwood	John Krol	Rebecca Claxton	Philip Cosmo	Albert Livingston	Lorne Fairbairn	James Farrell
Old Westbury v (4)	MC 516 626-0800	(not reporting)						
Olean (17)	MC 716 372-2200	(not reporting)						
Oneida (11)	MC 315 363-4800	A Carinci	. . . .	G Perretta	J Cukierski	E Smith	J McClellan	J Bacher
Oneonta (14)	MC 607 432-0670	(not reporting)						
Orchard Park v (3)	MC 716 662-9327	(not reporting)						
Ossining v (23)	CM 914 941-3554	Maryann Roberts	Gennaru J Faiella	Marie Fuesy	Pat D'Imperio	Louis DiLoreto	Joseph Burton	Michael Sterlacci
Oswego (19)	MC 315 342-8160	(not reporting)						
Owego v (4)	MC 607 687-3555	William F Franz	Karen Richardson	Lynne Mieczkowski	Lynne Mieczkowski	Ken Easton	Robert Williams	Charles Lohmeyer
Palmyra v (4)	MC 315 597-4849	James G Elliott	. . . .	Bonnie J Hays	Darlene Matteson	Ronald Hickman	David M Dalton	. . . .
Patchogue v (11)	MC 516 475-4300	F S Leavandosky	. . . .	Rosemarie Berger	Gerard R Nocita	Joseph Galletelli	. . . .	Joseph Tusso
Peekskill (20)	CM 914 737-3400	Vincent Vesce	Joseph Seymour	Pamela Beach	W Winstanley	Robert Ferris	Edward Hayes	James Madaffari
Pelham v (6)	MC 914 738-2015	Joseph E Durnin	Michael S Delong	Lisa Stiefvater	Michael S Delong	Robert Glover	Joseph Benefico	Harry Pallett
Pelham Manor v (5)	MC 914 738-8820	Valentine Taubner	Richard Blessing	Richard Blessing	Richard Blessing	Archelle Petrucci	Dennis Carroll	. . . .
Penn Yan v (5)	MC 315 536-3015	Floyd Paddock	. . . .	. . . .	Joyce E Benedict	Jens Jensen	. . . .	. . . .
Perry v (4)	MC 716 237-5278	(not reporting)						
Plattsburgh (21)	MC 518 563-7702	(not reporting)						
Pleasantville v (7)	CM 914 769-1900	M Gail Grimaldi	Patricia Dwyer	Judith Weintraub	. . . .	. . . .	A Chiarlitti	Steven Johnson
Port Chester v (25)	CM 914 939-2200	John Branca	Michael Graessle	Richard Falanka	Robert Reardon	Michael Dileo	Carl Verrastro	William Summa
Port Jefferson v (7)	MC 516 473-4724	(not reporting)						
Port Jervis (9)	MC 914 858-4014	R Michael Worden	. . . .	. . . .	James J Hinkley	James Rohner	William Wagner	Vincent Lopez
Port Washington North v (3)	MC 516 883-5900	(not reporting)						
Potsdam v (10)	MC 315 265-7480	(not reporting)						
Poughkeepsie (29)	CM 914 451-4200	Paul Buccellato	Joseph Chiseri	Barbara Schelin	Joseph Chiseri	Dennis McComb	. . . .	Michael Murphy
Ravena v (4)	MC 518 756-8233	(not reporting)						
Rensselaer (8)	MC 518 462-9511	Joseph E Harrigan	. . . .	Maureen Nardacci	. . . .	Philip B Smith	James W Stark	James M Crouch
Rhinebeck v (3)	MC 914 876-7015	(not reporting)						
Rochester (232)	MC 716 428-7115	Thomas P Ryan	Chris Lindley	Ellen Clifford	Vincent Carfagna	Charles Ippolito	Roy Irving	Edward Doherty
Rockville Centre v (25) .	MC 516 678-9300	(not reporting)						
Rome (44)	MC 315 336-6000	Joseph A Griffo	. . . .	Jeanette Denton	William Glasso	Ronald Swinney	Merino Ciccone	Robert Comis
Rye (15)	CM 914 967-5400	Warren R Ross	Frank J Culross	Alice K Conrad	Chris E Martino	George Ballantoni	Anthony Schembri	Joseph M Carlucci
Rye Brook (8)	CM 914 939-1121	S Cresenzi	Christopher Russo	Christopher Russo	Christopher Russo	. . . .	Robert Santoro	Rocco Circosta
Sag Harbor v (2)	MC 516 725-0222	Pierce W Hance	. . . .	R Winchell	. . . .	Kevin O'Brien	Joseph Ialacci	James Early
Salamanca (7)	MC 716 945-4620	Jerry Lockwood	. . . .	A Vecchiarella	Linda Rychcik	John McClune	Edward Gimbrone	A Pascarella
Sands Point v (2)	MC 516 883-3044	(not reporting)						
Saranac Lake v (5)	CM 518 891-4150	William Madden	J Pat Fitzgerald	Marilyn Clement	J Pat Fitzgerald	Robert Girard Jr	Steven Farmer	Steven Natoli
Saratoga Springs (25) .	CO 518 587-3550	(not reporting)						
Saugerties v (4)	MC 914 246-2321	Anthi Chorvas	. . . .	Jean Turner	. . . .	. . . .	William Kimble	John Kolano
Scarsdale v (17)	CM 914 723-5591	Walter Handelman	Lowell Tooley	Lowell Tooley	David Coldrick	Walter Felice	Donald Ferraro	. . . .
Schenectady (66)	MC 518 382-5000	(not reporting)						
Scotia v (7)	MC 518 374-1071	(not reporting)						
Sea Cliff v (5)	MC 516 671-0080	(not reporting)						
Seneca Falls v (7)	MC 315 568-8107	Robert G Freeland	Scott A Smith	. . . .	. . . .	James Wood	Frederick Capozzi	Richard H Lapp
Sherrill (3)	CM 315 363-2440	Dwight Evans	Gordon Silsby	Michael Holmes	Michael Holmes	Bill Vineall	Francis Broski	Gary Onyan
Sidney v (5)	MC 607 563-3571	(not reporting)						
Silver Creek v (3)	MC 716 934-3240	E Turzillo	. . . .	Cynthia M Klocko	. . . .	James Graf	John M Yannie	John L Burt
Skaneateles v (3)	MC 315 685-3440	Martin L Hubbard	. . . .	Sally L Sheehan	. . . .	Dave Card	Mack McNeil	John O Abbott
Sloan v (4)	MC 716 897-1560	Adeline Sicignano	Patricia Krzemien	Patricia Krzemien	Patricia Krzemien	Joseph Coffta	. . . .	Anthony H Sisti
Sloatsburg v (3)	MC 914 753-2727	(not reporting)						
Solvay v (7)	MC 315 468-1679	M C DeSantis	. . . .	Phyllis DiFlorio	Robert M Prowak	John Fall	Rocco C Femano	Norman Nicolini
South Glens Falls v (4)	MC 518 793-1455	Robert Phinney	. . . .	Karin Blood	. . . .	Joseph Reynolds	Kevin Judd	John Dixon
South Nyack v (3)	MC 914 358-0287	Charles Cross	. . . .	Mary G Martini	Wallace B Martini	Champ D Knecht	Alan B Colsey	George W Abrams
Southampton v (4)	MC 516 283-0247	(not reporting)						
Spencerport v (4)	MC 716 352-4771	Clyde W Carter	Roy G Hill	Gina M Tojek	Gary R Boughter	John Galligan	. . . .	Richard F Gosnell
Spring Valley v (22) ...	MC 914 352-1100	(not reporting)						
Springville v (4)	MC 716 592-4936	Craig R Helms	Gail M Riggs	Gail M Riggs	Gail M Riggs	Paul Smith	. . . .	Karl R Lux
Suffern v (11)	MC 914 357-2600	George Parenss	. . . .	V Menschner	. . . .	John Keegan	Frank Finch	Donald Grosso
Syracuse (164)	MC 315 448-8077	(not reporting)						
Tarrytown v (11)	MC 914 631-1405	Eileen Pilla	Michael Blau	Louise Camilliere	Gerald Barbelet	James Lennox	James Weaver	B Salanitro
Thomaston v (3)	MC 516 482-3110	Bryan Holzberg	. . . .	Susan Blaeser	. . . .	. . . .	. . . .	Patrick Knowles
Ticonderoga v (3)	MC 518 585-7404	Michael Diskin	. . . .	W Kay Otley	June Borho	. . . .	. . . .	Scott Tierney
Tonawanda (17)	MC 716 695-1800	Alice Roth	. . . .	James Coogan	. . . .	Thomas Miller	Edward Ringler	David Derrick
Troy (54)	CM 518 270-4401	(not reporting)						
Tuckahoe v (6)	MC 914 961-3662	Philip A White	. . . .	Susan Ciamarra	. . . .	. . . .	Gerald Mignone	Anthony Cacciola
Tupper Lake v (4)	MC 518 359-3341	Mark Arsenault	. . . .	P Littlefield	. . . .	Kenneth Gravlin	Robert Degrace	Ronald Martin
Union t (60)	MC 607 754-2102	(not reporting)						
Utica (69)	MC 315 792-0300	(not reporting)						
Valley Stream v (34) ...	MC 516 825-4200	George A Donley	Vincent W Ang	Vincent W Ang	Nunzio Columbo	Mark Watenberg	. . . .	Robert Gunther
Voorheesville v (3)	MC 518 765-2692	(not reporting)						
Walden v (6)	CM 914 778-2177	Andrew Uszenski	John Kelly	Nancy Mitchell	Jan Weiner	Kenneth Kruehne	Jeffrey Holmes	Walter Sweed
Walton v (3)	MC 607 865-4358	John J Kelly	. . . .	Virginia O'Dell	Virginia O'Dell	. . . .	Melvin Woodin	Jeffrey Francisco
Wappingers Falls v (5) .	MC 914 297-8773	(not reporting)						
Warsaw v (4)	MC 716 786-2120	Daniel W Moran	. . . .	C Eccleston	. . . .	. . . .	William C Blythe	Gilbert B Stearns
Warwick v (6)	MC 914 986-2031	(not reporting)						
Waterloo v (5)	MC 315 539-9131	(not reporting)						
Watertown (29)	CM 315 785-7730	Jeffrey E Graham	Karl R Amylon	Donna M Dutton	James M McCauley	Ronald Chisamore	Michael Hennegan	Gene Hayes
Watervliet (11)	CM 518 270-3810	J Leo O'Brien	Paul S Murphy	Bruce A Hidley	Robert A Fahr	M Wayne Ellis	Francis Landrigan	Nick Ostapkovich
Waverly v (5)	MC 607 565-8106	Daniel F Leary	. . . .	Sondra Casterline	. . . .	. . . .	Larry K Preston	Gordon North
Webster v (5)	MC 716 265-3770	(not reporting)						
Wellsville v (5)	MC 716 593-1121	(not reporting)						
Wesley Hills v (..)	MC 914 354-0400	Robert H Frankl	. . . .	Dorothy L France	. . . .	. . . .	. . . .	. . . .
West Haverstraw v (9) .	MC 914 947-2800	Edward P Zugibe	. . . .	O Fred Miller	. . . .	John Zajac	. . . .	George E Wargo Sr
West Seneca t (48)	MC 716 674-5600	(not reporting)						
Westbury v (13)	MC 516 334-1700	(not reporting)						
Westfield v (3)	MC 716 326-4961	(not reporting)						
White Plains (49)	MC 914 422-1257	A Del Vecchio	. . . .	Janice Minieri	Dorothy Erard	John Cullen	James Bradley	Joseph Nicoletti
Whitehall v (3)	MC 518 499-0871	(not reporting)						
Whitesboro v (4)	MC 315 736-1613	(not reporting)						

Directory 1/9 continued

MUNICIPAL OFFICIALS IN U.S. CITIES OVER 2,500

City, 1990 population figures (000 omitted), form of government	Municipal phone number	Mayor	Appointed administrator	City clerk	Finance officer	Fire chief	Police chief	Public works director
NEW YORK (275) continued								
Williamsville v (6)	MC 716 632-4120	Ronald Daniels	Theresa Cummins	Theresa Cummins	Theresa Cummins	James Zymanek	. . . .	David Laubisch
Williston Park v (8)	MC 516 746-2193	(not reporting)						
Woodridge v (1)	CM 914 434-7447	(not reporting)						
Yonkers (188)	MC 914 377-6000	Terence Zaleski	Hector Rivera	Joan Deierlein	Andrew Maniglia	Neil Curry	Robert Olson	Joseph Green
Yorkville v (3)	MC 315 736-0263	Leo S Malecki	. . . .	Helen Petruccione	. . . .	George Farley	John J Cerino	Conrad Chaya
NORTH CAROLINA (171)								
Ahoskie t (4)	CM 919 332-5146	Jame W Hutcherson	W Russell Overman	Edith Merritt	. . . .	Kenneth Dilday	Barry S Hoggard	Terry Padgett
Albemarle (15)	CM 704 982-0131	Roger F Snyder	Raymond I Allen	Raymond I Allen	Robert N Stewart	G E McDaniel	Charles McManus	James C Coble
Angier tp (2)	CO 919 639-2071	Jack Marley	John W Moore	Jean J Matthews	Leslie Flood	S Teffteller	Leslie Halpin	Emory Brooks
Apex t (5)	CM 919 362-8661	Everette Edwards	William Sutton	Georgia Parker	Sonja Lumley	Bill Stevenson	Ronnie Hearn	Larry Thomas
Archdale (7)	CM 919 431-9141	Donald Hancock	Carl Howie	Maxine Renn	Carl Howie	. . . .	Larry Allen	Shelton Bradshaw
Asheboro (16)	CM 919 626-1200	W Joseph Trogdon	David B Leonard	Carol J Cole	. . . .	James W Smith	James C Finch Jr	Dumont Bunker
Asheville (62)	CM 704 259-5691	Ken Michalove	. . . .	Wm Wolcott	Larry Fisher	John Rukavina	Gerald Beavers	Jim Ewing
Ayden t (5)	CM 919 746-4152	(not reporting)						
Beaufort t (4)	CM 919 728-2141	Kathryn Cloud	Gordon Davis	. . . .	. . . .	John Young	Charles McDonald	Curtis Perry
Beech Mountain t (..)	CM 704 387-4236	Enrico Miller	Alfred Greene	Barbara Mooradian	Sally Rominger	. . . .	Marvin Jay Hefner	Joe Perry
Belhaven t (2)	CM 919 943-3055	(not reporting)						
Belmont (8)	CM 704 825-5586	Kevin B Loftin	Mitchell B Moore	M Lingafeldt	Mitchell B Moore	Jimmy Austin	Charlie Flowers	. . . .
Benson t (3)	MC 919 894-3553	(not reporting)						
Bessemer City (5)	CM 704 629-5542	John Clark Jr	Ralph S Messera	Janice M Costner	Mary Ann Hook	David Ford	Ken Hunsucker	Eddie Sykes
Biltmore Forest t (1)	CM 704 274-0824	E Glenn Kelly	Nelson E Smith	Nelson E Smith	Nelson E Smith	Randy Plemmons	Fred Rickman	Swain Ballard
Black Mountain t (5)	CM 704 669-9102	Carl R Bartlett	Albert Richardson	Suzanne S Turner	Albert Richardson	Gary D Bartlett	C E Slagle Jr	Joseph L Melton
Boone t (13)	CM 704 262-4530	Velma Burnley	Greg Young	Freida Vanallen	Joyce Watson	Reginald Hassler	Zane Tester	Blake Brown
Brevard (5)	CM 704 884-4123	K Anderson	Dee Freeman	Glenda Sansosti	Dot Angel	. . . .	Lud Vaughan	Don Owen
Burlington (39)	CM 919 227-3603	James Gerow	William Baker	. . . .	Billy Truett	Frank Andrews	John Glenn	Randall Kornegay
Canton t (4)	CM 704 648-2363	Robert M Phillips	William G Stamey	Jimmy L Flynn	William G Stamey	Phillip Smathers	William M Guillet	Roger M Lyda
Carolina Beach t (4)	MC 919 458-2992	(not reporting)						
Carrboro t (12)	CM 919 942-8541	Eleanor Kinnaird	Robert Morgan	Sarah Williamson	William Gibson Jr	. . . .	Benjamin Callahan	Monty Peterson
Cary t (44)	CM 919 469-4000	Koka Booth	James Westbrook	Sue Rowland	Karen Mills	Ned Perry	David Fortson	Kim Fisher
Chadbourn t (2)	CM 919 654-4146	(not reporting)						
Chapel Hill t (39)	CM 919 968-2700	Kenneth Broun	W Calvin Horton	Peter Richardson	James Baker	Daniel Jones	Ralph Pendergraph	Bruce Heflin
Charlotte (396)	CM 704 336-2241	Richard A Vinroot	D Wendell White	Brenda Freeze	Richard Martin	Luther Fincher	D R Stone	. . . .
Cherryville (5)	CM 704 435-4184	J Ralph Beam Jr	Janice Hovis	Jean Beam	Janice Hovis	Jeffery Cash	Johnny Wehunt	Ted Mace
Claremont (1)	CM 704 459-7009	Joseph M Chandler	Marion McGinnis	Patricia C Miller	Patricia C Miller	Gary Sigmon	Gerald R Tolbert	Billy L Henson
Clayton t (5)	CM 919 553-5866	Douglas McCormac	Robert Hyatt	Jessica Coutu	Marc Jones	Lee Barbee	Paul Keen	Edward Whaley
Clinton t (8)	CM 919 592-1961	A E Kennedy Jr	Tommy M Combs	Elizabeth Fortner	Peggy B Wiggins	Leonard Edge	Alton Hunter	Wayne Hollowell
Concord (27)	CM 704 786-6161	Bernie E Edwards	Leonard Sossamon	Vickie Weant	Joyce A Allman	Randy Holloway	Robert E Cansler	Bill Barringer
Conover (5)	CM 704 464-1191	Bruce R Eckard	L B Beasley Jr	Frances L Kincaid	Vickie K Yandle	J Reid Poovey Jr	Dale C Stewart	Jimmy A Clark
Cornelius t (3)	CM 704 892-6031	(not reporting)						
Dallas t (3)	MC 704 922-3176	Coleen Cloninger	. . . .	N E Vlaservich	N E Vlaservich	David Calahan	Harold Guffey	John Ferguson
Davidson t (4)	MC 704 892-7591	Russell B Knox	Leamon B Brice	Peggy W Smith	. . . .	Robert Gurley	Henry McKiernan	Tommy Treadaway
Drexel t (2)	CM 704 437-7421	Richard Propst	Morris Baker	Sherri Bradshaw	Morris Baker	Benny Orders	Terry Yount	Bill Dowdle
Dunn (8)	CM 919 892-2633	Oscar N Harris	Carl G Dean	Joyce Valley	Teresa Haney	Allan Cain	. . . .	Ronald Autry
Durham (137)	CM 919 560-4214	Harry Rodenhizer	Orville W Powell	Margaret M Bowers	John G Pedersen	N L Thompson	Jackie W McNeil	Anthony T Rolan
Eden (15)	CM 919 623-9707	Lawrence Cox	Steven Routh	Mary Lambert	. . . .	. . . .	Gary Benthin	Richard Sexton
Edenton t (5)	CM 919 482-2155	Roy L Harrell	Anne Marie Kelly	. . . .	Janet P Hines	Lynn C Perry	Charles Williams	William C Skinner
Elizabeth City (14)	CM 919 338-3981	James Harrington	Ralph Clark	Dianne Pierce	Sarah Blanchard	Tedd Melvin	Hermon Bunch	Ray Rogerson
Elizabethtown t (4)	MC 919 862-3979	Wallace Leinwand	Jim Freeman	Marion Morrisey	Marion Morrisey	Timmy Sessoms	Michael Royston	Carey Ayres
Elkin t (4)	CM 919 835-9800	Thomas M Gwyn	Joseph R Huffman	Joe C Layell	Joe C Layell	Tommy Wheeler	Steve Hampton	Tim Darnell
Elon College t (4)	CM 919 584-3601	Jerry R Tolley	Michael A Dula	Sabrina M Oliver	Michael A Dula	Walter E King Jr	Dan W Ingle	Donald Wagoner
Enfield t (3)	CM 919 445-3146	Kai Hardaway	William Emmerich	Julius G Woody	Julius G Woody	James P Ellen	Theodore H Mayer	Bobby E Davis
Erwin t (4)	MC 919 897-5140	George R Joseph	Charles S Simmons	Ramona D Warren	. . . .	. . . .	Thomas Chandler	Mark W Byrd
Fairmont t (2)	CM 919 628-9768	(not reporting)						
Farmville t (4)	CM 919 753-5774	S H Aycock Jr	Richard N Hicks	Michelle Creech	Michelle Creech	John Baker	Robert A Smith	W R Oakley
Fayetteville (76)	CM 919 433-1990	J L Dawkins	John P Smith	Bobbie Joyner	Kai Nelson	Duke Piner	Ronald Hanson	. . . .
Forest City t (7)	CM 704 245-0148	Charles E Butler	Charles R Summey	Sandra P Mause	F Pruett Walden	L Mark McCurry	Thomas McDevitt	Herbert R Toms Jr
Franklin t (3)	MC 704 524-2516	David E Henson	James Williamson	Janet A Anderson	Janet A Anderson	William Jamison	Ernest C Wright	Alvin L Ledford
Franklinton t (2)	CM 919 494-2520	Charles Draughn	Seth Lawless	Kim Worley	. . . .	. . . .	Ray Gilliam	Raymond Bragg
Fuquay-Varina t (5)	CM 919 552-3178	Alfred M Johnson	Laurice W Bennett	Rachel B Turner	Rachel B Turner	. . . .	Alvis S Pleasant	Thomas O'Connell
Gamewell (3)	MC 704 754-1991	John Wootton Jr	. . . .	Carolyn K Warren	Jack Roberts	. . . .	. . . .	. . . .
Garner t (15)	CM 919 772-4688	F D Rohrbaugh	Peter G Bine	Mary Lou Rand	Richard L Smiley	Phil Mitchell	Thomas M Moss	Daniel W Rudy
Gastonia (55)	MC 704 866-6719	James B Garland	Danny O Crew	Susan C Kluttz	John A Philyaw	Robert L Murray	Jackie S Postell	Donald Carmichael
Gibsonville t (3)	CM 919 449-4144	William Moricle	Deleno Flynn	. . . .	Connie Woody	James Thomas	Morris McPherson	Coy May
Goldsboro (41)	CM 919 580-4357	Hal K Plonk	Richard Slozak	Lura Ray	Richard E Durham	Willard Herring	Chester Hill	C R Southerland
Graham (10)	CM 919 228-8362	Troy W Woodard	Ray Fogleman	Eydie C May	. . . .	Kenneth Evans	Gary Young	Donnie Braxton Jr
Granite Falls t (3)	CM 704 396-3131	A W Huffman Jr	Linda K Story	Judy L Mackie	. . . .	Thomas Laws	Jerry Bumgarner	Bill Hamilton
Greensboro (184)	CM 919 373-2065	V M Nussbaum Jr	W H Carstarphen	Nancy J McPeak	Richard L Lusk	R K Flowers	S Daughtry Jr	. . . .
Greenville (45)	CM 919 830-4492	Nancy M Jenkins	Ronald R Kimble	Wanda T Elks	Bernita W Demery	Raymond L Carney	Charles E Hinman	Thomas N Tysinger
Hamlet (6)	CM 919 582-2651	Abbie Covington	Lee Matthews	Lisa Blue	Michael Deese	David Fuller	Terry Moore	Charlie Utter
Havelock (20)	CM 919 444-6402	Donald Beaver	H Ralph Kennedy	Kathleen Townsend	Diane Scarborough	Michael Green	Michael Campbell	Robert Collins
Henderson (16)	CM 919 492-6111	Robert Young Jr	Eric Williams	Dianne White	Jerry Moss	Thomas Wilkerson	Steve Kincheloe	James Morgan
Hendersonville (7)	MC 704 697-3000	(not reporting)						
Hickory (28)	CM 704 323-7421	William McDonald	B Gary McGee	Patricia Williams	Julie McCollum	Herman R Bishop	Floyd W Lucas Jr	G Cecil Clark
High Point (69)	CM 919 883-3259	Rebecca Smothers	H Lewis Price	Patricia Simmons	William A Gear	Stephen D Hudson	James F Hoyng	Carl D Wills
Hillsborough t (4)	CM 919 732-2104	(not reporting)						
Holden Beach t (1)	CM 919 842-6488	(not reporting)						
Hope Mills t (8)	CM 919 424-4513	(not reporting)						
Hudson t (3)	CM 704 728-8272	Bill J Beane	M Alan Thornton	Rebecca M Bentley	Rebecca M Bentley	. . . .	Tony D Coluard	Carl V Henderson
Jacksonville (30)	CM 919 455-2600	George Jones	Jerry A Bittner	S McMurtrey	Debra Bailey	Franklin Barger	Roger Halbert	Michael Ellzey
Kannapolis (30)	MC 704 938-5131	Bachman S Brown	R Gene McCombs	B L Laws	Michael W Shinn	Larry C Phillips	Paul D Brown	Melvin W Rape
Kenly t (2)	MC 919 284-2116	James I Baker	Edison E Temple	Sharon E Evans	Sharon A Bailey	Steve Brinchek	Larry Carter	Terry Strickland
Kernersville t (11)	CM 919 996-3121	Thomas W Prince	Randy E McCaslin	Betty B Teague	John W Cater	Jimmy L Barrow	Grady C Stockton	Charles Hamilton
Kill Devil Hills t (4)	CM 919 441-2531	Joseph G Deneke	Debora P Diaz	Mary E Quidley	Teresa Pickrel	William E Gard	James H Gradeless	C A Smith
King (4)	CM 919 983-8265	Joel B New	R Randy Martin	. . . .	Christine Whicker	. . . .	Timothy A Patrick	Thomas F New
Kings Mountain (9)	CM 704 734-0333	G Scott Neisler	George A Wood	Marilyn H Sellers	Jeffrey S Rosencr	Clyde F Burns	C Warren Goforth	Karl R Moss
Kinston (25)	CM 919 559-4200	Buddy Ritch	Stephen W Raper	Peggy Boone	Ed Pierce	Tony Kelly	John Wolford	J T Pratt
La Grange t (3)	MC 919 566-3186	Randolph Pridgen	Mike Taylor	Phyllis Harrison	Mike Taylor	Richard C Hinson	Robert Pelletier	Thomas Monsees
Lake Lure t (..)	CM 704 625-9983	(not reporting)						
Laurinburg (12)	CM 919 276-8324	William R Purcell	Peter Vandenberg	Betty R Childress	Phillip Robey	. . . .	Robert Malloy	Harold Smith
Lenoir (14)	CM 704 757-2200	Robert A Gibbons	James H Hipp	Lynn P Martin	Elizabeth Wilson	Bobby H Coffey	Jack F Warlick	Graham K Gilley
Lewisville t (..)	CM 919 998-6683	(not reporting)						
Lexington (17)	CM 704 243-2489	Vernon Price Jr	Duke Whisenant	Martha Hoffman	Richard Ratcliff	William Deal	Leroy Pearson	Jeffrey Edmonds

Directory 1/9 continued — MUNICIPAL OFFICIALS IN U.S. CITIES OVER 2,500

City, 1990 population figures (000 omitted), form of government	Municipal phone number	Mayor	Appointed administrator	City clerk	Finance officer	Fire chief	Police chief	Public works director
NORTH CAROLINA (171) continued								
Lincolnton t (7)	CM 704 732-2281	Jerry Campbell	David E Lowe	Kay B Polhill	George E Heavner	Donald Wise	Terry Burgin	Stephen H Peeler
Long Beach t (4)	CM 919 278-5011	Joan P Altman	Tim M Johnson	Patricia Brunell	Cathy B Harvell	Timothy Pittman	Danny L Laughren	Charles P Derrick
Long View t (3)	CM 704 322-3921	Norman E Cook	E Bruce Morgan	Amy Hall	Brenda Hill	Ernest Riley	David Turner	Teddy Franklin
Louisburg t (3)	MC 919 496-4145	Lucy T Allen	C L Gobble	Elmar Holmes	Elmar Holmes	Timmy Smith	Tommy Leonard	Lee Smith
Lowell (3)	MC 704 824-3518	(not reporting)						
Lumberton (19)	CM 919 671-3800	Ray B Pennington	Robert W Hites	Janie Revels	Timothy Inch	Ronald Parker	Harry P Dolan	Dixon Ivey
Madison t (2)	CM 919 427-0221	(not reporting)						
Maiden t (3)	CM 704 428-5000	Robert L Smyre	Doris C Bumgarner	Sharon S Sipe	. . . .	Rick Cansler	D Ray Walker	Billy R Price
Marion (5)	CM 704 652-3551	A Everette Clark	J Earl Daniels	J Earl Daniels	J Earl Daniels	Thomas S Milligan	Thomas B Pruett	Glen Sherlin
Maxton t (2)	MC 919 844-5231	Robert W Fisher	Paul G Davis	Terry S Jones	Paul G Davis	James R Driggers	Ronald L Wagner	Sheldon McNair
Mayodan t (2)	CM 919 427-0241	Jeffrey G Bullins	Jerry R Carlton	Debra E Cardwell	Debra E Cardwell	Donald H Case	Lawrence Shelton	. . . .
Mebane t (5)	CM 919 563-5901	G Stephenson	Robert Wilson	Elaine J Hicks	Elaine J Hicks	James A Jobe	Gary Bumgarner	Jimmy Jobe
Mint Hill t (12)	MC 704 545-9726	Joseph V Hamilton	James F Owens	Beth Q Hamrick	William H Sirakos	Paul Campbell	. . . .	. . . .
Mocksville t (3)	CM 704 634-2259	(not reporting)						
Monroe (16)	CM 704 282-4500	Lewis Fisher	Jerry E Cox	. . . .	F Craig Meadows	. . . .	Bobby G Kilgore	J Ronald Griffin
Mooresville t (9)	CM 704 663-3800	Joe V Knox	Richard A McLean	B B Whittington	Kenneth Kistler	Doug Nantz	Joe Puett	Frankie White
Morehead City t (6)	MC 919 726-6848	Nick Galantis	David Walker	Joanne Spencer	Ellen Sewell	Jerry Leonard	Sammie Turner	David McCabe
Morganton (15)	CM 704 437-8863	Mel L Cohen	Michael C Cronk	Debbie B Ogle	Sally W Sandy	. . . .	Robert W Williams	John D Cannon
Morrisville t (1)	CM 919 469-1426	Ernest Lumley	John Crumpton	Evelyn Lumley	Julia Powell	Tony Chiotakis	Bruce Newnam	Steve Lawrence
Mount Airy (7)	CM 919 786-3501	Wm Beamer	Ronald Niland	Dorothy Boyles	John Overton	Bill Joe Woodruff	Leo Shores	Elmer Dawson
Mount Holly (8)	CM 704 827-3931	Charles B Black	Phillip G Ponder	Phillip G Ponder	Phillip G Ponder	Ray Massey	Jerry Bishop	Winton Nichols
Mount Olive t (5)	CM 919 658-9536	Louis M Pate Jr	M Thomas Barnes	Arlene G Talton	Arlene G Talton	C R Witherington	John J Wilson	R Lloyd Warren
Murfreesboro t (3)	MC 919 398-5904	(not reporting)						
Nags Head t (2)	CM 919 441-5508	Renee Cahoon	J Webb Fuller	Constance Hardee	. . . .	Douglas Remaley	Lonnie Dickens	Harry Lange
Nashville t (4)	CM 919 459-4511	Warren Evans	Tony Robertson	Gail Thomas	Barbara Woodall	Ross Strickland	Donald Skinner	Edward White
New Bern (17)	MC 919 636-4000	Leandor Morgan	Walter Hartman Jr	Vickie Johnson	Mary Bratcher	Robert Aster	Kenneth Bumgarner	Danny Meadows
Newton (9)	CM 704 465-7400	Hugh R Gaither	Radford Thomas	Rita K Williams	Dorothy Bumgarner	Charles Doty	James Masters	Dwight E Wilson
North Wilkesboro t (3)	CM 919 667-7129	Neil G Cashion Jr	Chris A Carter	Gail M Harris	Gail M Harris	Conley Call	Barry Brown	Charles Billings
Oxford t (8)	CM 919 693-2195	Allie Ellington	H T Ragland Jr	Ann S Parrott	Kelway L Howard	John B Norris	James H Waugh	Jimmy D Crews
Pembroke t (2)	CM 919 521-9758	Milton R Hunt	M Cummings	Jo Ann Neville	Leavira Chavis	Ray Hunt	Larry T Roberts	James H Locklear
Pinehurst v (5)	CM 919 295-1900	Albert L Bethel	Andrew Wilkison	Mary McGraw	Marie Hunt	Robert S Viall	Ernest Hooker	James T Ritter
Pineville t (3)	MC 704 889-2291	(not reporting)						
Pittsboro t (1)	MC 919 542-4621	(not reporting)						
Plymouth t (4)	CM 919 793-9101	(not reporting)						
Princeville t (2)	CM 919 823-1057	Glenni Matthewson	Joseph E Cate	Patrica Woodard	Joseph E Cate	. . . .	Jesse Ransom	Danny White
Raeford (3)	CM 919 875-8161	Bob M Gentry	Thomas A Phillips	Betty S Smith	Helen H Huffman	Crawford L Thomas	James E Murdock	James M McNeill
Raleigh (208)	CM 919 890-3315	Avery Upchurch	Dempsey Benton Jr	Gail Smith	Z B Hill	Sherman Pickard	F K Heineman	William L Baird
Red Springs t (4)	CM 919 843-5241	George T Paris	Thomas W Horne	Regenia Humphrey	Regenia Humphrey	William McPhaul	Olin Levi Powers	Cleveland Parker
Reidsville (12)	CM 919 349-1030	Benton Gooch	D Kelly Almond	Ann Bradsher	Bernice Phillips	Charlie King	James Festerman	Jerry Rothrock
Roanoke Rapids (16)	CM 919 535-2031	J Lloyd Andrews	Victor H Denton	Lisa B Vincent	Phyllis P Lee	Kenneth R Carawan	Drewery N Beale	J Richard Parnell
Rockingham (9)	CM 919 895-9088	G R Kindley Jr	Monty R Crump	William Reynolds	Monty R Crump	Charles D Trotter	Eddie R Martin	. . . .
Rocky Mount (49)	CM 919 972-1111	Fred Turnage	William Batchelor	Jean Bailey	Craig Kivett	John Hawkins	Joseph Brown	Douglas Roberson
Roxboro (7)	CM 919 599-3116	Donald J Waldo	Thomas G Hogg	Dorothy Harris	Bertha Thomas	Roy W Hall	Terry Hill	James P Whitfield
Rutherfordton t (4)	MC 704 287-3520	W Fred Williams	Karen E Andrews	Karen E Andrews	Janet Nix	Jim Hall	Randy Greenway	Glenn Cash
Salisbury (23)	CM 704 638-5229	Margaret H Kluttz	David W Treme	Virginia P Petrea	John A Sofley Jr	Samuel I Brady	Jeffrey M Jacobs	Vernon E Sherrill
Sanford (14)	CM 919 775-8200	Rex McLeod	Tom Spivey	Lois Oldham	Glenda Tomlinson	Floyd Caviness	Ronnie Yarborough	Larry Thomas
Scotland Neck t (3)	MC 919 826-3152	Ferd L Harrison	W Scott Buffkin	Patsy A Faithful	. . . .	Bruce Josey	John Hodnett	Doug Braddy
Selma t (5)	CM 919 965-9841	J A Creech	Bruce Radford	Fran Davis	Debbie Holloman	Joe Price	Roy Godwin	Terry Keen
Seven Devils t (..)	CM 704 963-5343	Harold F Wolf	Chess C Hill	Joanna L Cates	Barbara Presnell	Dennis K Cook	Joe R Buchanan	Gary C Fox
Shelby (15)	CM 704 482-3457	George W Clay Jr	David M Wilkison	Steph Carouthers	E Warren Newton	Anthony Boyd	Charles Cochran	Roy Wellmon
Siler City t (5)	CM 919 742-4733	Earl B Fitts	Leonard Barefoot	Wanda Ingold	Wanda Ingold	Billy Scott	Lewis S Phillips	Joel J Brower
Smithfield t (8)	CM 919 934-2116	Norwood Worley	Ronald W Owens	Debbie W Pierce	Robert Plowman	Norman Johnson	J R Peterson	Jimmy C Clapp
Southern Pines t (9)	CM 919 692-7021	Alex Bowness	Kyle Sonnenberg	Eleanore Ogletree	Melissa Miller	Peter Rapatas	Gerald Galloway	Bobby Teague
Southern Shores t (..)	CM 919 261-2394	(not reporting)						
Southport (2)	CM 919 457-7900	Norman R Holden	Robert S Gandy	. . . .	S H Butterworth	Gregory Cumbee	Robert N Gray	Ed Honeycutt
Spencer (3)	CM 704 633-2231	Buddy Gettys	Steve Leary	Lisa Perdue	. . . .	Jody Everhart	Steve Schenk	Scott Benfield
Spindale t (4)	CM 704 286-3466	Ray Wilson	Chuck Nance	Sheila Gibson	Ruthe Henderson	John Horne	Jack Conner	Mike Brooks
Spring Lake t (8)	MC 919 436-0241	Vernon Hobson	Richard Higgins	Cora Nunes	. . . .	Pat Stevens	Gil Campbell	Rudie Dickerson
Statesville (18)	CM 704 878-3570	(not reporting)						
Stoneville t (1)	MC 919 573-9393	(not reporting)						
Sugar Mountain v (..)	MC 704 898-9292	(not reporting)						
Tabor City t (2)	CM 919 653-3458	(not reporting)						
Tarboro t (11)	CM 919 641-4200	Moses A Ray	Samuel W Noble	William L Corbett	William L Corbett	George Cherry	Danny D Hayes	John H Chapman
Thomasville (16)	CM 919 475-4229	Hubert Leonard	Mike Moore	Mary G Hill	Tony Jarrett	C R Cranford	Don Truell	Layton Paul
Topsail Beach t (..)	CM 919 328-5841	Milton Oppegaard	Eric J Peterson	S Rivenbark	. . . .	Bob Humphrey	Rickey Smith	Frank Ricks
Troy t (3)	CM 919 572-3661	Roy Maness	Matt Bernhardt	Cathy Maness	Cathy Maness	Joe Huntley	E J Phillips Jr	Bill Curlee
Tryon t (2)	CM 704 859-6654	Robert Neely	Matthew Dolge	Judy Foy	Matthew Dolge	James Lankford	Benny Cook Jr	Roy Williams
Valdese t (4)	CM 704 879-2116	Jim Draughn	Jeff Morse	Frances Hildebran	Bill Chapman	Ernest Bertlot	John Clark	Jim Stockton
Wadesboro t (4)	CM 704 694-5171	Joe E Gaddy	William Chewning	Nancy Huntley	. . . .	Eddie Pope	Robert F Kendall	Harold Carpenter
Wake Forest t (6)	CM 919 556-2024	John G Mills	Mark S Williams	. . . .	Aileen J Staples	. . . .	. . . .	Rose O'Donnell
Wallace t (3)	CM 919 285-4136	Arnold Duncan	Douglas Drymon	Douglas Drymon	Douglas Drymon	Thomas Townsend	Bobby Maready	Darret Ezzell
Warrenton t (1)	MC 919 257-3315	(not reporting)						
Warsaw t (3)	MC 919 293-7814	(not reporting)						
Washington (9)	CM 919 946-1033	Floyd Brothers	Ed Burchins	Rita Thompson	Carol Williams	Hugh Sterling	John Crone	Russell Waters
Waynesville t (7)	CM 704 456-3515	Henry B Foy	John H Siler	Phyllis McClure	Edward Caldwell	William Fowler	Coleman Moody	Fred Baker
Weaverville t (2)	CM 704 645-7116	(not reporting)						
Wendell t (3)	CM 919 365-4444	Lucius Jones	Ira C Fuller	. . . .	. . . .	. . . .	Joe A Privette	Donnie Ayscue
Whiteville (5)	CM 919 642-8046	Horace B Whitley	Jeff Emory	Susan D Rhodes	Jean Babson	Terry R McCall	Randall Aragon	Stancil Davis
Williamston t (6)	MC 919 792-5142	Thomas B Brandon	John T Boykin Jr	Mary P Jackson	Ronnie R Wilson	James B Peele	Richard Holloman	Willie M Long Jr
Wilmington (56)	CM 919 341-7840	Donald H Betz	Mary M Gornto	Agnes P Spicer Si	William B McAbee	Samuel C Hill Sr	Robert C Wadman	. . . .
Wilson (37)	CM 919 291-8111	Bruce Rose	Edward Wyatt	Ana Heder	Gordon Baker	Donald Oliver	Thomas Younce	Charles Pittman
Winston-Salem (143)	CM 919 727-2123	Martha Woods	Bryce Stuart	Marie Matthews	Loris Colclough	F E Harless	George Sweat	Paschal Swann
Woodfin t (3)	MC 704 253-4887	Coy F Rice	P A Honeycutt	Cheryl W Mears	P A Honeycutt	. . . .	Eugene F Rice	Ernest W Rice
Wrightsville Beach t (3)	CM 919 256-2245	Frances L Russ	Anthony N Caudle	Linda Askew	Linda Askew	Everett K Ward Jr	George M Antley	John T Nesbitt
Zebulon t (3)	CM 919 269-7455	W Thurston Debnam	Charles R Horne	Charles R Horne	Carla Stephens	Sidney C Perry	J Wayne Medlin	Deck Shaver Jr
NORTH DAKOTA (18)								
Beulah (3)	MC 701 873-4637	Darold Benz	Robert Wendel	Doris Tonneson	Robert Wendel	. . . .	Dave Paetz	Gordon Schmidt
Bismarck (49)	CO 701 222-6471	Bill Sorensen	Dan Dahlgren	. . . .	. . . .	Jack Hegedus	Bob Matzke	Bob Gausvik
Bottineau (3)	MC 701 228-3232	(not reporting)						
Carrington (2)	MC 701 652-2911	Samuel B Law	Vicky L Triplett	. . . .	. . . .	Peter Kautzman	Carson L Helton	Dale Townsend
Devils Lake (8)	CO 701 662-7600	Fred Bott	. . . .	. . . .	Todd E Dalziel	William Oehlke	Bruce Kemmet	Glenn J Olson
Dickinson (16)	CO 701 225-6765	Henry Schank	Tobias Miller	Tobias Miller	Tobias Miller	Joe Boespflug	Duane Wolf	. . . .

Directory 1/9 continued — MUNICIPAL OFFICIALS IN U.S. CITIES OVER 2,500

City, 1990 population figures (000 omitted), form of government	Municipal phone number	Mayor	Appointed administrator	City clerk	Finance officer	Fire chief	Police chief	Public works director
NORTH DAKOTA (18) continued								
Fargo (74)	MC 701 241-1300	(not reporting)						
Grafton (5)	MC 701 352-1561	(not reporting)						
Grand Forks (49)	MC 701 746-2607	Micheal Polovitz	. . . .	Alice Fontaine	Donald Tingum	Richard Aulich	Chester Paschke	Mark Lambrecht
Harvey (2)	MC 701 324-2000	Alfred Weisser	. . . .	Corey Leintz	. . . .	Gary Keller	Larry Hoffer	Robert Weninger
Jamestown (16)	MC 701 252-5900	Frank Chase	. . . .	. . . .	Jeff Fuchs	Bert Gray	David Donegan	. . . .
Mandan (15)	CO 701 667-3210	Robert Dykshoorn	Kevin Christ	. . . .	Greg Welch	Pete Gartner	Dennis Rohr	Peter Snider
Minot (35)	CM 701 857-4756	G Christiensen	Robert Schempp	. . . .	Robert Frantsvog	Duwayne Ward	Carroll Erickson	Alan Walter
Rugby (3)	MC 701 776-5630	Curtis L Teigen	Howard O Burns	Judy M Heintz	Howard O Burns	Tim Bonn	Boyd Eagleson	Jerome W Voeller
Valley City (7)	CO 701 845-1700	(not reporting)						
Wahpeton (9)	MC 701 642-8448	Warren Schuett	. . . .	Arden Anderson	. . . .	Jim Wegener	Delano Lotzer	Jerry C Lein
West Fargo (12)	CO 701 282-3843	(not reporting)						
Williston (13)	CO 701 572-8161	(not reporting)						
OHIO (355)								
Ada v (5)	MC 419 634-4045	Donald L Traxler	James Meyer	. . . .	Kathryn J Gulbis	. . . .	Wayne Seely	. . . .
Akron (223)	MC 216 375-2780	D Plusquellic	. . . .	. . . .	Richard Merolla	Thomas Alexander	Larry Givens	William Mullen
Alliance (23)	MC 216 821-3110	(not reporting)						
Amberley v (3)	CM 513 531-8675	Dean Fite	Bernard Boraten	Evelyn Dumont	Ada Keller	John Monahan	John Monahan	John Platter
Amherst (10)	MC 216 988-4380	(not reporting)						
Archbold v (3)	CM 419 445-4726	Chuck Rychener	Nolan Tuckerman	Gladys Winzeler	. . . .	Richard Erbskorn	Martin Schmidt	. . . .
Ashland (20)	MC 419 289-8622	(not reporting)						
Ashtabula (22)	MC 216 992-7103	Joseph Varckette	. . . .	Michael Zullo	Michael Zullo	Norman Jepson	David Colucci	Dennis Johnson
Athens (21)	MC 614 592-3338	(not reporting)						
Aurora (9)	MC 216 562-6131	(not reporting)						
Avon (7)	MC 216 934-1200	Pearl Olearcik	. . . .	Patricia Vierkorn	Mary Ann Nowak	Frank Root Jr	John Vilagi	Donald Mac Donald
Avon Lake (15)	MC 216 933-6141	(not reporting)						
Baltimore v (3)	MC 614 862-4491	Dennis R Keller	Hugh O Schaffner	. . . .	. . . .	. . . .	David Wolfel	. . . .
Barberton (28)	MC 216 753-6611	(not reporting)						
Barnesville v (4)	MC 614 425-1880	Thomas Michelli	John R McCort	. . . .	Marie McCrate	Harold Arnold	Chris Ditto	. . . .
Bay Village (17)	MC 216 871-2200	(not reporting)						
Beachwood (11)	MC 216 464-1070	(not reporting)						
Beavercreek (34)	CM 513 427-5500	Gerald Petrak	Stephen Stapleton	Lucia Ball	Jon Stoops	. . . .	Warner Huston	. . . .
Bedford (15)	CM 216 232-1600	D Grossenbaugh	Vilas S Gamble	Gayle C Pastor	Frank C Gambosi	Jeffrey L Duber	Robert R Reid	Clinton E Bellar
Bedford Heights (12)	MC 216 439-1600	(not reporting)						
Bellaire (6)	MC 614 676-6538	Tino Esposito	. . . .	Mary C Nixon	Lawrence Gress	Michael Wallace	Robert Wallace	Vince DiFabrizio
Bellbrook (7)	CM 513 848-4666	(not reporting)						
Bellefontaine (12)	MC 513 592-4376	Richard J Vicario	. . . .	Ardythe Predmore	. . . .	James Furby	Bradley Kunze	Philip D Beasley
Bellevue (8)	MC 419 483-4560	George J Branco	R C Salkowitz	Vickie K Dauch	Ethel R Foti	Sherrard D Barr	Ronald D Zerman	. . . .
Belpre (7)	MC 614 423-7592	(not reporting)						
Berea (19)	MC 216 826-5800	(not reporting)						
Bexley (13)	MC 614 235-8694	David H Madison	. . . .	. . . .	John W Hornberger	. . . .	Thomas W Tobin Jr	Dorothy Pritchard
Blanchester v (4)	MC 513 783-2431	Lee Miller	. . . .	Bernice Hoggatt	. . . .	. . . .	Richard Payton	Donald Walker
Blue Ash (12)	CM 513 745-8500	Walter L Reuszer	Marvin D Thompson	Mary Malone	Nancy Hennel	Glen Ross	Michael W Allen	Woody Cauble
Bluffton v (3)	MC 419 358-2066	Roger Edwards	Larry R Core	David R Steiner	David R Steiner	Dan Bowden	Howard R Foust	. . . .
Bowling Green (28)	MC 419 354-6200	Wesley H Hoffman	Colleen Smith	Kay Scherreik	Charles E Kerr	Joseph Burns	Galen Ash	William N Blair
Brecksville (12)	MC 216 526-4351	Jerry N Hruby	. . . .	. . . .	Dolores A Wood	Russell Clark	Dennis Kancler	John J Smith
Bridgeport v (2)	MC 614 635-2424	Charles W Furbee	. . . .	Betty Riley	Betty Riley	Mark Subasic	Carl R Smith	Robert Trautman
Broadview Heights (12)	MC 216 526-4357	Leo H Bender	. . . .	Eileen R Matia	Linda M Pertz	Lee D Ippolito	Fred Carmichael	Raymond E Mack
Brook Park (23)	MC 216 433-1300	Thomas J Coyne Jr	Eileen McNamara	Mary Ann Skiba	Shelby Lawhun	Neal Donnelly	Thomas A Dease	Brian Higgins
Brooklyn (12)	MC 216 351-2133	John M Coyne	. . . .	Frank P Scarano	. . . .	Dennis Corrigan	James F Maloney	Kenneth Patton
Brookville v (5)	CM 513 833-2135	(not reporting)						
Brunswick (28)	CM 216 225-9144	J Beadell Rapp	Robert A Trimble	Betty Taller	M J Thesling	Tex Combs	Patrick Beyer	Gregory Crane
Bryan (8)	MC 419 636-4232	Runkle	. . . .	Hoffman	Hoffman	Robinson	Mock	Tarntz
Buckeye Lake v (3)	MC 614 928-7100	(not reporting)						
Bucyrus (13)	MC 419 562-6767	Robert Whitmeyer	Karl F Dilley	S M Assenheimer	Carol A Wagner	Dallis Easterday	Joseph Beran	. . . .
Byesville v (2)	MC 614 685-5901	(not reporting)						
Cadiz v (3)	MC 614 942-8844	(not reporting)						
Cambridge (12)	MC 614 439-1050	C Charles Schaub	Richard D Giroux	Sharron Cassler	Donna Gander	Ermal Shimp	Frank Stroud	Jerry Williams
Campbell (10)	MC 216 755-1451	Dominic J Medina	John S Judin	Judith Clement	John A Jeren	Vincent Leone	Frank Phillips	John S Judin
Canal Fulton v (4)	MC 216 854-2225	Thomas E Cihon	Robert Wilkinson	Thomas E Andes	. . . .	John Locke	Michael McNeely	. . . .
Canal Winchester v (3)	MC 614 837-7493	Russell Arledge	. . . .	. . . .	. . . .	. . . .	. . . .	Kevin Harper
Canfield (5)	CM 216 533-1101	T McLaughlin	C Tieche	P Matevich	S Mayberry	. . . .	D Blystone	R Wiant
Canton (84)	MC 216 489-3378	(not reporting)						
Carey v (4)	MC 419 396-7681	(not reporting)						
Carlisle v (5)	CM 513 746-0555	Patrick D Long	Matthew W Coppler	Flo Cracraft	Daniel Muldowney	Robert Miller	Gary A Long	. . . .
Carrollton v (3)	MC 216 627-2411	Harold Laizure Jr	. . . .	Betty Davis	. . . .	Robert Herron	Ronald Yeager	. . . .
Cedarville v (3)	MC 513 766-2911	(not reporting)						
Celina (10)	MC 419 586-6464	(not reporting)						
Centerville (21)	CM 513 433-7151	Shirley Heintz	Gregory Horn	Marilyn McLaughlin	William Bettcher	. . . .	William Lickert	. . . .
Chagrin Falls v (4)	MC 216 247-5050	(not reporting)						
Chardon v (4)	CM 216 285-3585	John G Reid	David A Lelko	Jeffrey L Smock	Jeffrey L Smock	Ed Brick	David J Hyslop	Gayland Moore
Cheviot (10)	MC 513 661-2700	(not reporting)						
Chillicothe (22)	MC 614 774-1185	(not reporting)						
Cincinnati (364)	CM 513 352-3000	Dwight Tillery	. . . .	Sandy Sherman	Frank Dawson	Thomas Steidel	Michael Snowden	John Hamner
Circleville (12)	MC 614 477-2551	Thomas Royster	. . . .	Patricia Fouch	Madeline Sanders	Wayne Malott	Francis Smallwood	Patrick Altvater
Cleveland (506)	MC 216 664-2000	Michael R White	Darlene E McCoy	Benny Bonanno	Stephen Strnisha	Walter V Zimmerer	Edward P Kovacic	Michael G Konicek
Cleveland Heights (54)	CM 216 291-4444	(not reporting)						
Clyde (6)	MC 419 547-0575	Kenneth Winke	Dennis E Albrinck	Virginia Cullen	Dennis Tuck	Dave Moyer	Daniel Weaver	. . . .
Coal Grove v (2)	MC 614 532-7447	(not reporting)						
Coldwater v (4)	MC 419 678-4881	Walter C Weigel	. . . .	J M Billerman	. . . .	John Moorman	Donald Adams	Fred Thees
Colerain Township t (..)	MC 513 385-7500	Joseph Wolterman	David Foglesong	Kathy Mohr	. . . .	G Bruce Smith	Edmund Phillips	Dennis Chapman
Columbiana v (5)	CM 216 482-2173	Richard G Simpson	Keith Chamberlin	Cindy Souder	Marylouise Dicken	Charles Flohr	Mark Shaffer	Keith Chamberlin
Columbus (633)	MC 614 645-7671	Gregory Lashutka	Ronald Poole	Tim McSweeney	Wyatt Kingseed	Harmon Dutko	James Jackson	Joyce James
Conneaut (13)	MC 216 593-4357	Judith Parlongo	Robert Herron	Norma Sass	Julie Sanger	Bim Orrenmaa	Darrell Thomas	George Adams
Cortland v (6)	MC 216 637-3916	Robert Moyers	. . . .	Donna Lyden	Frances Moyer	. . . .	Gary Mink	. . . .
Coshocton (12)	MC 614 622-1373	Charles Turner	Ray T Miskimens	Marlene Griffith	Louis Murphy	Chuck Turner	. . . .	Mike Hamilton
Covington v (3)	MC 513 473-2102	(not reporting)						
Crestline (5)	MC 419 683-3800	(not reporting)						
Crooksville v (3)	MC 614 982-2656	(not reporting)						
Cuyahoga Falls (49)	MC 216 923-9921	Don L Robart	. . . .	Kenneth Lahn	Vic Nogalo	Robert Leonard	Donald S Smith	Gerald L Pursley
Dayton (182)	CM 513 443-4000	Richard C Dixon	Richard B Helwig	James L Francis	Timothy H Riordan	Raymond Hughes	James E Newby	Clarence Williams
Deer Park (6)	MC 513 791-1081	Francis R Healy	David A O'Leary	Michael Brune	John C Applegate	Thomas Camp	Donald J Lally	. . . .
Defiance (17)	MC 419 784-2101	Rita A Kissner	Joel Daniels	. . . .	Jeffery S Leonard	Robert Marihugh	James Scheirer	. . . .

Directory 1/9 continued

MUNICIPAL OFFICIALS IN U.S. CITIES OVER 2,500

City, 1990 population figures (000 omitted), form of government	Municipal phone number	Mayor	Appointed administrator	City clerk	Finance officer	Fire chief	Police chief	Public works director
OHIO (355) continued								
Delaware (20)	CM 614 363-1965	(not reporting)						
Delhi tp (30)	MC 513 922-3111	Hal Franke	Joseph R Morency	Robert Bedinghaus	Robert Bedinghaus	Harold E Edwards	Howard R Makin	Robert W Bass
Delphos (7)	MC 419 695-4010	John E Sheeter	G Roland Williams	Marsha Mueller	T Jettinghoff	L Wayne Suever	Dennis Kimmet	. . . .
Delta v (3)	CM 419 822-3190	(not reporting)						
Dennison v (3)	MC 614 922-4072	(not reporting)						
Dover (11)	MC 216 343-7725	R P Homrighausen	Matthew D Kline	. . . .	Zoe Ann Kelley	Fred Nixon	Ronald Johnson	. . . .
Dublin (16)	CM 614 761-6500	. . . .	Tim Hansley	Anne Clarke	Marsha Grigsby	. . . .	Ron Ferrell	. . . .
East Cleveland (33)	CM 216 681-5020	Wallace D Davis	. . . .	. . . .	Sharon A Dumas	Paul Blockson	Mitchell Guyton	. . . .
East Liverpool (14)	MC 216 385-3381	James F Scafide	. . . .	. . . .	Angeline M Frank	Edward A Croxall	Charles B Coen	Robert W Disch
East Palestine (5)	MC 216 426-4367	Mark L Rhodes	John K Francis	Cindy Stonemetz	Connie Robinson	Merle Stewart	Gary Clark	Richard Pillsbury
Eastlake (21)	MC 216 951-1416	(not reporting)						
Eaton (7)	CM 513 456-4125	Gary Russell	Martin D Gabbard	Betty L Sowder	Betty L Sowder	John J Stover	James P Dearth	Gary Wagner
Elmwood Place v (3)	MC 513 242-2578	(not reporting)						
Elyria (57)	MC 216 322-1829	(not reporting)						
Englewood (11)	CM 513 836-5106	Edward S Kemper	Eric A Smith	Karen E Sodders	Mark B Brownfield	. . . .	Michael J Dickey	. . . .
Enon v (3)	MC 513 864-7870	(not reporting)						
Euclid (55)	MC 216 289-2700	(not reporting)						
Fairborn (31)	CM 513 879-1730	(not reporting)						
Fairfield (40)	CM 513 867-5300	Sterling R Uhler	Cheryl A Hilvert	Dena Morsch	James A Hanson	Donald Bennett	Gary Rednour	David Bock
Fairfield tp (49)	MC 513 863-5414	(not reporting)						
Fairlawn (6)	MC 216 666-8875	(not reporting)						
Fairport v (3)	MC 216 352-3620	(not reporting)						
Fairview Park (18)	MC 216 333-2200	(not reporting)						
Findlay (36)	MC 419 424-7137	Keith Romick	David J Wobser	Rebecca A Greeno	Janet R Wobser	Roy A Devore	Daniel Routzon	. . . .
Forest Park (19)	CM 513 595-5200	Joseph Ragase	Ray Hodges	Kathy Lives	Alfred Watterson	Dan Anderson	Steve Vollmar	Dave Stenger
Fort Shawnee v (4)	MC 419 991-2015	Douglas C Harris	. . . .	Diane L Barnes	Diane L Barnes	. . . .	M A Harnishfeger	. . . .
Fostoria (15)	MC 419 435-8282	(not reporting)						
Franklin (11)	CM 513 746-9921	. . . .	Samuel Coxson	Dorothy McGee	Sandra Morgan	Hugh Depew	Don Fry	Howard Lewis
Fremont (18)	MC 419 334-5900	Terry M Overmyer	. . . .	Linda F Swartz	Fred Recktenwald	Daniel Devanna	Robert Dorsey	Kenneth Myers
Gahanna (28)	MC 614 471-2563	James McGregor	. . . .	Peg Cunningham	W Jerome Isler	. . . .	Robert Kelley	Wayne Murphy
Galion (12)	MC 419 468-1857	(not reporting)						
Gallipolis (5)	CM 614 446-2489	Carol P O'Rourke	Glenn A Smith	Deborah L Hughes	Deborah L Hughes	Silas Hamilton	Joe Owen	. . . .
Garfield Heights (32)	MC 216 475-7234	(not reporting)						
Geneva (7)	CM 216 466-4675	Ronald Marchewka	Charles B Bowman	Nancy J Bowdler	Nancy J Bowdler	Gary J Farley	James Pearson	Charles V Bowman
Georgetown v (4)	MC 513 378-6395	Joseph O Rose	Delmar Pullins	Idella Bauer	. . . .	Joseph Brookbank	Harry Lee Graves	. . . .
Germantown (5)	CM 513 855-6567	Mary Arnold	Ed Schwaberow	Karen Epperson	Robyn Charlton	Gary Nesslage	James Desch	Ed Schwaberow
Girard (11)	MC 216 545-3879	(not reporting)						
Golf Manor (5)	MC 513 531-7491	Dennis J Puthoff	Stephen A Tilley	John Mitchell	. . . .	Gregory Ballman	George P Olvey	Stephen A Tilley
Grandview Heights (7)	MC 614 488-3159	John R Leutz	Julie A Gafford	. . . .	J Mikal Townsley	Henry K Kauffman	Ronald C Treon	Sam Troiano
Granville v (4)	CM 614 587-0707	Arnold Eisenberg	Douglas Plunkett	Carie Miller	Shirley Robertson	. . . .	Steven Cartnal	. . . .
Green tp (53)	MC 513 574-4848	Stephen E Grote	Thomas R Maley	Marilyn Wagner	. . . .	Robert J Weitzel	James L Suder	Adam B Goetzman
Greenfield (5)	MC 513 981-3500	(not reporting)						
Greenhills v (4)	MC 513 825-2100	Oscar A Hoffmann	David B Moore	. . . .	Kathryn L Brokaw	Thomas P Eberle	Donald Slaughter	. . . .
Greenville (13)	MC 513 548-1819	Richard A Rehmert	Terry Emery	Marvella Fletcher	Marvella Fletcher	Steve Birt	Eric Hughes	. . . .
Grove City (20)	MC 614 875-6368	Richard L Stage	Charles W Boso Jr	Tami K Kelly	Robert E Behlen	. . . .	James R McKean	James M Blackburn
Groveport v (3)	MC 614 836-5301	(not reporting)						
Hamilton (61)	CM 513 868-5891	Adolf Olivas	Hal Shepherd	Linda Landi	. . . .	Ronald Johnson	Simon Fluckiger	Michael Samoviski
Harrison v (8)	MC 513 598-6650	(not reporting)						
Heath (7)	MC 614 522-1420	John C Geller	. . . .	Lynn Hunt	Carolyn J Broyles	Richard Padar	. . . .	. . . .
Hicksville v (4)	MC 419 542-6138	(not reporting)						
Highland Heights (6)	MC 216 461-2440	(not reporting)						
Hilliard (12)	MC 614 876-7361	Roger A Reynolds	. . . .	Deborah Wells	Lynn A Skeels	. . . .	Rodney Garnett	Robert L Tucker
Hillsboro (6)	MC 513 393-5219	(not reporting)						
Hubbard (8)	MC 216 534-3090	(not reporting)						
Huber Heights (39)	CM 513 233-1423	Sherwin Eisman	James W Pierce	Margaret Stivers	Catherine Shannon	Thomas J Grice	Michael D'Amico	Steve Overholser
Hudson v (5)	CM 216 650-1799	Harold L Bayless	S S Schweikert	Mary Ann George	. . . .	. . . .	James Brown	. . . .
Huron (7)	MC 419 433-5268	George Sheard	. . . .	Phyllis Wassner	Michael E Tann	John A Zimmerman	Randy L Glovinsky	. . . .
Independence (7)	MC 216 524-4131	Gregory Kurtz	. . . .	E Hackett	George Spilker	Carl Frimel	A Appenzeller	Walter Ellert
Indian Hill v (5)	CM 513 561-6500	Donald P Klekamp	Michael W Burns	Paul C Riordan	Paul C Riordan	Robert Coy	William C Wiebold	David M Couch
Ironton (13)	MC 614 532-3833	(not reporting)						
Jackson (6)	MC 614 286-3224	(not reporting)						
Jefferson v (3)	MC 614 576-3941	(not reporting)						
Jefferson (Madison) v (5)	MC 614 879-7363	Jim Miles	. . . .	Charles Mauger	Charles Mauger	. . . .	Frank Cox	Ron Collins
Johnstown v (3)	MC 614 967-3177	(not reporting)						
Kent (29)	CM 216 678-8100	Kathleen Chandler	P Blanchard	Linda Mauck	Barbara Rissland	Barry Blankenship	William C Lillich	Michael Sepi
Kenton (8)	MC 419 674-4850	Clay Flinn	. . . .	Brenda Keckler	Robert Brown	Arnold Downey	Reginald Slack	Byron J Pfeiffer
Kettering (61)	CM 513 296-2400	(not reporting)						
Kirtland (6)	MC 216 256-3332	Mario V Marcopoli	. . . .	Valerie A Beres	Keith W Martinet	Richard Martincic	Dennis Yarborough	James F Jacobs
Lakemore v (3)	MC 216 733-6125	(not reporting)						
Lakewood (60)	MC 216 521-7580	David R Harbarger	. . . .	. . . .	Gale Fisk	Lawrence Mroz	Matthew Biscotti	David Coyle
Lancaster (35)	MC 614 687-6600	(not reporting)						
Lebanon (10)	CM 513 932-3060	Jackson Hedges	Richard Hayward	Debbie Biggs	Debbie Biggs	Mike Hannigan	Ken Burns	Bill Marshall
Leipsic v (2)	MC 419 943-2009	Judith Crawford	James Russell	Jeanne Baumeier	Jeanne Baumeier	David Herring	Ed Long	James Russell
Lexington v (4)	MC 419 884-0765	(not reporting)						
Lima (46)	MC 419 228-5462	(not reporting)						
Lincoln Heights (5)	MC 513 733-5900	(not reporting)						
Lisbon v (3)	MC 216 424-5503	Willis Coleman	. . . .	Kelli Rose	. . . .	Harold Adams	Charles Carlisle	. . . .
Lockland v (4)	MC 513 761-1124	(not reporting)						
Lodi v (3)	MC 216 948-2040	Russell A Bell	Annette Geissman	Annette Geissman	Annette Geissman	Carl Stewart	Steve Sivard	Donald Eaken
Logan (7)	MC 614 385-8310	(not reporting)						
London (8)	MC 614 852-3243	David Eades	Elmer Olsen	Arlene Duffey	Kathy McClelland	Richard Minner	Ronald Cooper	Paul Maddux
Lorain (71)	MC 216 244-2237	(not reporting)						
Lordstown v (3)	MC 216 824-2507	Arno A Hill	. . . .	Judith A Hall	Judith A Hall	Robert Hoffman	William Catlin	Lee A Davis
Loudonville v (3)	MC 419 994-3214	Thomas R Miller	. . . .	Susan R Kern	. . . .	C Ronald Hans	William Porter	Calvin Keene
Louisville (8)	CM 216 875-3321	Thomas Zwick	Stephen Townley	Peggy Brazelton	Robert Miller	Denny Myers	Ross Riggs	Walt Metzger
Loveland (10)	CM 513 683-0150	Roland Boike	Wayne Barfels	Linda Cox	Bill Taphorn	. . . .	Howard Espelage	Joe Geers
Lyndhurst (16)	MC 216 442-5777	Leonard M Creary	. . . .	. . . .	Joseph G Mirtel	Joseph A Sweeney	Sherwood Eldredge	William M Moviel
Macedonia (8)	MC 216 468-1300	Joseph Migliorini	. . . .	. . . .	Tom DiLellio	Daniel Gagliardi	James Popovich	Earl Rizzo
Madeira (9)	CM 513 561-7228	Richard Staubach	Thomas W Moeller	Donna Goens	Sharon King	Robert Coy	Gerald Beckman	Floyd Poppenhouse
Mansfield (51)	MC 419 755-9626	Lydia Reid	. . . .	. . . .	Sandy Converse	Richard Krizan	Lawrence Harper	Francis Fisher
Maple Heights (27)	MC 216 662-6000	Santo T Incorvaia	. . . .	Linda Sigado	Prashant Shah	James Castelucci	M Dale Canter	Robert Girardi
Mariemont v (3)	MC 513 271-3246	Donald L Shanks	. . . .	Stanley L Bahler	Stanley L Bahler	Thomas A Driggers	Richard A Pope	. . . .

Directory 1/9 continued — **MUNICIPAL OFFICIALS IN U.S. CITIES OVER 2,500**

City, 1990 population figures (000 omitted), form of government	Municipal phone number	Mayor	Appointed administrator	City clerk	Finance officer	Fire chief	Police chief	Public works director
OHIO (355) continued								
Marietta (15)	MC 614 373-1387	(not reporting)						
Marion (34)	MC 614 382-2020	Jack Kellogg	. . . .	Marsha Adams	Robert Cramer	Robert Varner	Frank Arnold	Tracy Mercer
Martins Ferry (8)	MC 614 633-2876	(not reporting)						
Marysville (10)	MC 513 642-6015	Thomas Kruse	Kenneth M Kraus	Lois Reese	Ivan L Schrock	John F Collins	Rick Coutts	. . . .
Mason (11)	CM 513 398-8010	(not reporting)						
Massillon (31)	MC 216 830-1700	(not reporting)						
Maumee (16)	MC 419 893-8751	(not reporting)						
Mayfield v (3)	MC 216 461-2210	(not reporting)						
Mayfield Heights (20)	MC 216 442-2626	Ross C DeJohn	Robert G Tribby	. . . .	Robert G Tribby	Michael J Forte	Thomas J Slivers	Andrew D Fornaro
Mc Donald v (4)	MC 216 530-5472	Thomas J Hannon	Virginia Evans	Barbara J Urban	. . . .	Michael Badila	Jimmy Tyree	E Domitrovich
Medina (19)	MC 216 725-8861	(not reporting)						
Mentor (47)	CM 216 255-1100	James Struna	Julian Suso	Maureen Russo	John Aten	John Preuer	Richard Amiott	. . . .
Mentor-On-The-Lake (8)	MC 216 257-7216	John S Crocker	Kip L Molenaar	J Peggy Guinn	. . . .	Robert J Mahoney	Edward P Wild	. . . .
Miami tp (28)	MC 513 248-3725	Joseph W Uecker	David D Duckworth	Eric C Ferry	Eric C Ferry	James H Whitworth	Harry C Snyder	Walter D Fischer
Miamisburg (18)	CM 513 866-3303	Richard C Church	John K Weithofer	Judith E Barney	George S Perrine	Robert L Bobbitt	Thomas R Schenck	John K Weithofer
Middleburg Heights (15)	MC 216 234-8811	Gary Starr	. . . .	Mary Ann Beaune	Timothy Pope	James McCarthy	John Maddox	Frank Castelli
Middleport v (3)	MC 614 992-6424	(not reporting)						
Middletown (46)	CM 513 425-7766	Paul D Nenni	Ronald L Olson	Bettie J Arthur	John T Lyons	John J Sauter	Earl R Smith Jr	Preston M Combs
Milford (6)	CM 513 831-4192	Fred Getch	David L Spinney	. . . .	Stephen J Wagner	John Cooper	Stanley Doughman	Elmer Weigel
Millersburg v (3)	CM 216 674-1886	(not reporting)						
Minerva v (4)	CM 216 868-7705	James Waller	David Harp	Rhea Cochran	J M Chuckalovchak	Gary Chilson	Richard Taff	. . . .
Mingo Junction v (4)	MC 614 535-1511	John A Corrigan	Russ Hyde	Richard Crugnale	Richard Crugnale	John McGuire	James Thompson	. . . .
Minster v (3)	MC 419 628-3497	(not reporting)						
Mogadore v (4)	MC 216 628-4896	Fred Farina	. . . .	Juliann McCulley	. . . .	Don Adams	Marvin Wilmoth	. . . .
Monroe v (4)	CM 513 539-7374	E R Tannreuther	A Seth Johnston	Linda Egelston	Frank C Pahr	Mark A Neu	Ernest Howard	. . . .
Montgomery (10)	CM 513 891-2424	Ivan Silverman	Jon Bormet	Susam Hamm	Terri Mayle	. . . .	Don McGlothlin	. . . .
Montpelier v (4)	MC 419 485-5543	William Shatzer	John Bitler	Kelly Hephner	. . . .	Dail Fritsch	William Noethan	. . . .
Moraine (6)	CM 513 299-7312	Harold Johnson	J R Harville	Rita Caton	Marty Brown	Harold Sigler	Dan Chilton	. . . .
Moreland Hills v (3)	MC 216 248-1188	Osborne C Dodson	. . . .	Claudette E Pesti	. . . .	. . . .	Frank Swanek	. . . .
Mount Gilead v (3)	MC 419 946-3926	(not reporting)						
Mount Healthy (8)	MC 513 931-8840	(not reporting)						
Mount Vernon (15)	MC 614 393-9517	(not reporting)						
Munroe Falls v (5)	MC 216 688-7491	(not reporting)						
Napoleon (9)	CM 419 592-4010	Steven Lankenau	Terry Dunn	. . . .	R Scheinhagen	Scott Highley	George Schmidt	. . . .
Nelsonville (5)	MC 614 753-1314	Reginald Levering	Gary Campbell	Margaret Steenrod	Patricia Monk	Kevin Canter	David Valkinburg	. . . .
New Boston (3)	MC 614 456-4103	Charles L Ottney	Raymond C Gulley	Constance Gulley	Constance Gulley	Richard E Mershon	Gary L Stone	. . . .
New Carlisle (6)	CM 513 845-9492	. . . .	Madge Shellhaas	Clair Miller	Constance Barney	. . . .	. . . .	Hank Taynor
New Lebanon v (4)	MC 513 687-1341	Paul E Shock	Ron J Singel	Carol D Ratcliffe	Carol D Ratcliffe	David G Falldorf	Ronald J Carbaugh	. . . .
New Lexington (5)	MC 614 342-1633	(not reporting)						
New Miami v (3)	MC 513 896-7337	Eugene Rogers	. . . .	Virginia Hensley	Virginia Hensley	Gerald Cook	Danny J Schultz	Leroy Jackson
New Philadelphia (16)	MC 216 364-4491	Tim A Hurst	. . . .	. . . .	Betty L Gleitsman	Charles Caton	Thomas Staggers	. . . .
New Richmond v (2)	MC 513 553-4146	(not reporting)						
Newark (44)	MC 614 349-6600	Frank L Stare	. . . .	Dianna Eshelman	G L Feightner	Earl Whittington	Paul Green	Tim Matheny
Newburgh Heights v (2)	MC 216 641-4650	Kathleen Edwards	. . . .	B Bizon	. . . .	J Martin	C Voland	. . . .
Newcomerstown v (4)	MC 614 498-6313	(not reporting)						
Newton Falls (5)	CM 216 872-0806	Patrick Layshock	Dennis L Kirkland	Cindy L Magargle	Cheryl B Bucy	Kenneth Whetzel	Robert T Carlson	Harry J Shaver
Niles (21)	MC 216 652-3415	(not reporting)						
North Baltimore v (3)	MC 419 257-2394	Donald L Hendren	. . . .	Faith K Gallant	. . . .	Donald Baltz	Gerald E Perry	Robert J Lulfs
North Canton (15)	MC 216 499-8223	Willam R Hines	John M Boyjian	Marion Wilsonbarr	V M Loretto	Dale R Hardgrove	David L Lindower	. . . .
North College Hill (11)	MC 513 521-7413	Dan Brooks	Jerry Thamann	Miriam Tucker	George Snyder	Mike Lotz	Pete Zappulla	. . . .
North Kingsville v (3)	MC 216 224-0091	Carl D Oxley	. . . .	Barbara Lambert	. . . .	Edwin Kampii	Charles Hitzel	. . . .
North Olmsted (34)	MC 216 777-8000	Ed Boyle	. . . .	Barba Seman	James Burns	Roger Osterhouse	Dennis Sefcek	Ralph Bohlmann
North Ridgeville (22)	MC 216 353-0811	(not reporting)						
North Royalton (23)	MC 216 237-5686	Gary Skorepa	. . . .	Laura Haller	Christine I May	Michael Fabish	Paul Bican	Leone Darby
Northfield v (4)	MC 216 467-7130	(not reporting)						
Northwood (6)	MC 419 693-9320	John Donegan	Daniel E Hiskey	Lynn Richey	Marsha Kurek	William St Claire	Douglas Breno	Jerry Amrhein
Norton (11)	MC 216 825-7815	Terry Jones	John R Morgan	James Mitchell	Joseph Betkoski	M Antoniotti	. . . .	Barry Moore
Norwalk (15)	MC 419 663-6740	John Borgia	Larry Silcox	. . . .	Mary Lou Noftz	Robert Bores	Michael Ruggles	Ralph Seward
Norwood (24)	MC 513 396-8106	(not reporting)						
Oak Harbor v (3)	MC 419 898-5561	(not reporting)						
Oakwood (9)	CM 513 298-0600	Jeffrey Ireland	Michael J Kelly	Cathy Blum	Callie M Rehrig	. . . .	John Hohensee	John C Chain
Oakwood v (3)	MC 216 232-9988	(not reporting)						
Oberlin (8)	CM 216 775-1531	Gary Goddard	. . . .	. . . .	Kelly Clark	Doyle Jones	Robert Jones	Mike Sigg
Obetz v (3)	MC 614 491-1080	(not reporting)						
Olmsted Falls (7)	MC 216 235-5550	Tom Jones	. . . .	Susan J Prehoda	Dan M Patrick	Bill Fisher	Richard Krusinski	Chuck McManus
Ontario v (4)	MC 419 529-3723	Robert E Urwin	Frederick Shrader	Shirley A Bowman	. . . .	. . . .	Timothy McClaran	. . . .
Oregon (18)	MC 419 698-7045	Michael Dansack	. . . .	Sandy Bihn	Sandy Bihn	Raymond Walendzak	Mark Venia	Donald Surface
Orrville (8)	MC 216 684-5000	Howard Wade	William Stocker	Julia Leathers	Charles Horst	Robert Ballentine	Wesley Morris	Robert Nichols
Ottawa v (4)	MC 419 523-5020	Kenneth Maag	John Williams	Harold Schierloh	. . . .	Eugene Diemer	John Kottenbrock	. . . .
Ottawa Hills v (5)	CM 419 536-1111	Jean Youngen	Marc Thompson	Gay Mac Arthur	Karen Urbanik	Donald Farley	Ronald Tornd	Tom Griesinger
Oxford (19)	CM 513 523-2171	William Snavely	James C Collard	Donna Gross	. . . .	Len Endress	Stephan Schwein	Mark Tate
Painesville (16)	CM 216 352-9301	. . . .	Lester N Nero	Shirley Onderisin	David D Miller	Jack A Martin	Jerry T White	Raymond L Dray
Parma (88)	MC 216 885-8000	(not reporting)						
Parma Heights (21)	MC 216 884-9600	Paul W Cassidy	. . . .	. . . .	Terrence B Hickey	John Diamond	Kenneth Schlacht	M Kronenberger
Paulding v (3)	MC 419 399-4011	Vera M Miles	Harry Wiebe	Janice K Phlipot	. . . .	Roscoe Waters	Paul Keeler	. . . .
Pepper Pike (6)	MC 216 831-8500	(not reporting)						
Perrysburg (13)	MC 419 872-8010	R D Cotner	James Bagdonas	Wayne Tuckerman	Wayne Tuckerman	Merlin Artz	William Dhondt	Douglas Dariano
Pickerington v (6)	CO 614 759-4100	Lee Gray	Joyce Bushman	Susan Sheikh	Linda Fersch	. . . .	Don Pruden	. . . .
Piqua (21)	CM 513 778-2051	Lucinda L Fess	Frank Patrizio Jr	Rebecca J Cool	Robert N Slagle	Gregory L Fashner	Philip K Potter	Thomas R Zechman
Plain tp (34)	MC 216 492-4689	John Baker	Thomas Leach	Michael Cirelli	. . . .	Clarence Snyder	. . . .	. . . .
Poland v (3)	MC 216 757-2112	Ruth Z Wilkes	. . . .	Linda M Srnec	. . . .	. . . .	Russell Beatty	. . . .
Pomeroy v (2)	MC 614 992-2246	Bruce J Reed	John A Anderson	Kathy A Hysell	. . . .	Danny S Zirkle	Gerald Rought	. . . .
Port Clinton (7)	MC 419 734-5522	(not reporting)						
Portsmouth (23)	MC 614 354-8807	Franklin Gerlach	. . . .	Jo Ann Aeh	Pat Jenkins	Robert Storey	Thomas Bihl	William Rush
Powell v (2)	CM 614 885-5380	Jane Van Fossen	Robt Schaumleffel	Tracey Pyles	Donna Waggener	. . . .	Harold Yinger	Robert Schutz
Ravenna (12)	MC 216 296-9629	Donald J Kainrad	. . . .	Timothy Thomas	Ronald E Hartley	Larry Shafer	Michael Swartout	. . . .
Reading (12)	MC 513 733-3725	Frank R Carnevale	Frank V Sherman	Midge Brown	Don Dawdy	Robert Hollmeyer	Robert Huelsman	Jerry Glaser
Reynoldsburg (26)	MC 614 866-6391	Robert McPherson	. . . .	. . . .	. . . .	. . . .	Jess Moore	Mel Clemens
Richfield v (3)	MC 216 659-9201	(not reporting)						
Richmond Heights (10)	MC 216 486-2474	(not reporting)						
Rittman (6)	CM 216 925-2045	(not reporting)						
Rocky River (20)	MC 216 331-0600	Earl Martin	. . . .	. . . .	Susan Wollenzier	Jack Gerson	Bernard Barrett	Don Umerley
Rossford (6)	MC 419 666-0210	Mark G Zuchowski	Vincent Langevin	. . . .	Vincent Langevin	Tony Jackson	Richard N Caro	Milan L Vavrik

City, 1990 population figures (000 omitted), form of government	Municipal phone number	Mayor	Appointed administrator	City clerk	Finance officer	Fire chief	Police chief	Public works director
OHIO (355) continued								
Sabina v (3)	MC 513 584-2123	(not reporting)						
Salem (12)	MC 216 332-4482	Alvahn Mondell	. . . .	Stacey Darner	Frances Dickey	Dwight Stacy	John Sommers	Larry Dejane
Sandusky (30)	CM 419 627-5844	(not reporting)						
Sebring (5)	CM 216 938-9340	Michael Pinkerton	Kent Bell	Judy Frasher	Kent Bell	James Cannell	Paul Freer	Gary Eberling
Seven Hills (12)	MC 614 524-4421	(not reporting)						
Shadyside (4)	MC 614 676-5972	(not reporting)						
Shaker Heights (31)	MC 216 491-1400	Patricia Mearns	Wm Schuchart	Wm Schuchart	Wm Schuchart	. . . .	Walter A Ugrinic	Randall Devaul
Sharonville (13)	MC 513 563-1144	(not reporting)						
Sheffield Lake (10)	MC 216 949-7141	Charles H Kelly	William Andersen	Ruth Bukowski	William Andersen	Eugene Rouse	Thomas Schmidt	Francis E Schremp
Shelby (10)	MC 419 347-5131	James E Henkel	. . . .	. . . .	John R DeVito	Phillip Curren	John Vanwagner	Roger Merriman
Sidney (19)	CM 513 492-4080	Doris Blackston	William Barlow	Tanyce Lang	Michael Puckett	Stanley Crosley	Steven Wearly	Richard Hohman
Silver Lake v (3)	MC 216 923-5233	Ann W Thudium	. . . .	Frank J Sherman	Frank J Sherman	. . . .	Gary DeMoss	Richard Fenwick
Silverton (6)	MC 513 793-7980	Richard F Hunter	. . . .	Willam M Kuhr	Willan M Kuhr	Paul J Steman	Dennis P Race	Paul J Steman
Solon (19)	MC 216 248-1155	Paulson		Bartoshek	Tellep	Zugan	Bruckner	McDaries
South Charleston v (2)	MC 513 462-8888	Theresa Siejack	Sarah Wildman	Bonnie White	. . . .	Jeff Ervin	Beryl McCloud	. . . .
South Euclid (24)	MC 216 381-0400	John T Kocevar	. . . .	Celeste DiCillo	Celeste DiCillo	Larry Huston	James Farrell	. . . .
South Lebanon v (3)	MC 513 494-2296	Albert E Shepherd	Vance Jacobs Jr	Debra L Humston	Debra L Humston	. . . .	Lester Kilburn	
South Point v (4)	MC 614 377-4838	(not reporting)						
South Russell v (3)	MC 216 338-7843	(not reporting)						
Springboro (7)	CM 513 748-1041	Earl West	William R Covell	Gayle Bennett	Sam Steadman	. . . .	R Hochstrasser	George Brackney
Springdale (11)	MC 513 671-0885	Ronald L Pitman	Cecil W Osborn	Doyle H Webster	Doyle H Webster	Robert Posega	James Freland	Robert N Sears
Springfield (70)	CM 513 324-7700	Warren Copeland	Matthew J Kridler	Connie Chappell	Sandra Gaier	Donald J Lee	Roger Evans	Leonard Hartoog
St. Bernard (5)	MC 513 242-7770	Barbara C Siegel	Raymond P Schrand	Carolyn Ungruhe	C Vondermeulen	Orin Kreyenhagen	Allen B Rusche	. . . .
St. Clairsville (5)	MC 614 695-1324	(not reporting)						
St. Marys (8)	MC 419 394-3303	William Sell	Michael L Weadock	Betty A Wehrman	Pamela J Edgar	Mark Freer	William Applegate	. . . .
Steubenville (22)	CM 614 283-6133		Gary DuFour		Robert Corabi	Richard Blair	Jerry McCartney	
Stow (28)	MC 216 688-8206	Donald J Coughlin	. . . .	Bonnie J Emahiser	Robert J Swanson	Robert E Dauchy	Robert E Tilton	Gerald R Dolson
Streetsboro (10)	MC 216 626-4942	(not reporting)						
Strongsville (35)	MC 216 238-5720	(not reporting)						
Struthers (12)	MC 216 755-2181	Daniel C Mamula	John P Sveda	Toni Constantino	Mary Ellen Jones	Harold Milligan	Robert Norris	. . . .
Swanton v (4)	CM 419 826-9515	Richard Ueberroth	John Syx	Ardys Slaninka	Nancy Spaulding	Lewis Taylor	Homer Chapa	Lewis Taylor
Sycamore tp (20)	MC 513 791-8447	Richard C Kent	Timothy A Shearer	Robert C Porter	. . . .	Fred Benz	. . . .	
Sylvania (17)	MC 419 885-8932	James E Seney	. . . .	Mragaret T Rauch	John W Plock	. . . .	Gerald A Sobb	Jeffrey P Ballmer
Tallmadge (15)	MC 216 633-0857	Paul Warzinski	Jack Cooper	Karen Morgan	Jill Stritch	Dennis Crossen	Gale Gault	Bill Ward
Tiffin (19)	MC 419 447-3440	(not reporting)						
Tipp City (6)	CM 513 667-8425	Carl Suerdieck	William Nelson Jr	Neva B Hufford	Richard Drennen	David Imler	Thomas Davidson	Milton Eichman
Toledo (333)	CO 419 245-1000	John McHugh	Thomas Hoover	Larry Brewer	William Werner	Michael Bell	Marti Felker	. . . .
Toronto (6)	MC 614 537-3743	John F Geddis	. . . .	. . . .	. . . .	. . . .	Dan Mosti	. . . .
Trenton (5)	CM 513 988-6304	Roy Wilham	Melvin Ruder	Katherine Richard	Gregory S Watson	Kenneth Achberger	Joe Richard	Freelen Whitt
Trotwood (9)	CM 513 837-7771	(not reporting)						
Troy (19)	MC 513 335-1725	Peter Jenkins	N Lawrence Wolke	J Sue Knight	. . . .	Robert M Counts	Charles W Frank	Steven Weaver
Twinsburg (10)	MC 216 425-7161	James Karabec	. . . .	Cynthia Kaderle	Joanne Terry	Daniel Simecek	Anthony Frank	. . . .
Uhrichsville (6)	MC 614 922-1242	(not reporting)						
Union tp (33)	CM 513 752-1741	(not reporting)						
Union tp (40)	CM 513 777-5900	Gary Cates	David Gully	Patricia Williams	. . . .	James Detherage	Lynn Brown	. . . .
Union (6)	CM 513 836-8624	Robert Packard	John P Applegate	Denise Winemiller	Denise Winemiller	. . . .	Dan Gessner	. . . .
University Heights (15)	MC 216 932-7800	Beryl Rothschild	. . . .	Nancy Moore	Anthony L Ianiro	Richard Kosmerl	Charles Lobello	Christopher Vild
Upper Arlington (34)	CM 614 457-5080	Virginia Barney	Richard King	Margie Halk	Pete Rose	Michael Gibbons	Thomas Kulp	Larry Helscel
Upper Sandusky (6)	MC 419 294-3862	(not reporting)						
Urbana (11)	MC 513 653-3812	Thomas Crowley	John Kane	. . . .	Dale Miller	James McIntosh	Billy Lingrell	Arthur Baer
Van Wert (11)	MC 419 238-6976	(not reporting)						
Vandalia (14)	CM 513 898-5891	Joy Clark	Bruce Sycher	. . . .	William Hoffman	Robert Trieber	Douglas Knight	Theodore Rusen
Vermilion (11)	MC 216 967-0123	(not reporting)						
Versailles v (2)	CM 513 526-3294	Larry J Subler	James L Wierville	Mary Ann Reed	. . . .	Dick Gigandet	. . . .	. . . .
Wadsworth (16)	MC 216 335-1521	John Hanna	William J Lyren	. . . .	Lynda Carrino	Richard Hontert	Michael King	William J Lyren
Walbridge v (3)	MC 419 666-1830	(not reporting)						
Wapakoneta (9)	MC 419 738-3011	Donald R Wittwer	R Katterheinrich	Carlene S Koch	Karen S Poplar	S McClintock	David L Harrison	. . . .
Warren (51)	MC 216 841-2610	Daniel J Sferra	Herbert Laukhart	. . . .	Anthony Iannucci	Kent Fusselman	Thomas Hutson	. . . .
Warrensville Heights (16)	MC 216 587-6500	(not reporting)						
Washington (13)	CM 614 335-5720	Gordon Davis	R Mark Rohr	Jack Stackhouse	Jack Stackhouse	Dan Fowler	Larry Walker	. . . .
Washington tp (8)	CM 513 433-0152	(not reporting)						
Waterville v (5)	CM 419 878-8107	Charles P Duck	Thomas L Mattis	Claudia L Guimond	Thomas L Mattis	Keith McCullough	Lance W Martin	Kenneth B Blair
Wauseon (6)	MC 419 335-9022	Jerry G Matheny	. . . .	Judy F Schlosser	Wayne J Badenhop	James E Gamber	Paul A Arruda	John R Sanderson
Waverly (4)	MC 614 947-5162	H Blaine Beekman	. . . .	R Dawn Hutchison	Max W Way	R R Armbruster	Michael D Corwin	. . . .
Wellington v (4)	MC 216 647-4626	Roland K Handley	. . . .	Karen Webb	. . . .	Robert Walker	Morris Furcron	. . . .
Wellston (6)	MC 614 384-2725	(not reporting)						
Wellsville (5)	MC 216 532-2524	Wayne Elliott	Perry Daniels	Thomas Lascola	Thomas Lascola	Dave Lloyd	Keith Thorn Jr	. . . .
West Carrollton (14)	CM 513 859-5181	Maxine Gilman	G Tracy Williams	Roberta Donaldson	Roberta Donaldson	Bill Ennis	Bill Przybylek	Donald Hill
West Milton v (4)	CM 513 698-4191	Donald Hamann Sr	Bradley C Vath	Linda Cantrell	Donna R Clark	Rodger Hurley	David Mote	Robert Sowers
West Union v (3)	MC 513 544-5326	Donald N Kirker	. . . .	Dorothy W Davis	. . . .	John C Bradford	Ray A Pendell	. . . .
Westerville (30)	CM 614 890-8542	John Parimuha	G David Lindimore	Sharon L Hahn	John P Winkel	Richard Morrison	James J Whitney	Karl Craven
Westlake (27)	MC 216 871-3300	Dennis M Clough	. . . .	Nora T Hill	. . . .	Robert Anderson	John Kreps	John Lehlbach
Whitehall (21)	MC 614 237-8611	(not reporting)						
Whitehouse v (3)	MC 419 877-5383	Diane McGilvery	James C Fox	Louann Artiaga	Linda Snyder	Kenneth Rupp	. . . .	Mark G Weber
Wickliffe (15)	MC 216 943-7117	Robert Aufuldish	. . . .	C Theophylactos	Joseph Unetic	David Geosano	Robert Dion	Darryl Crossman
Willard (6)	CM 419 933-2591	Stanley Ware	Christian Morris	Joann Jones	Anne Fritz	George Painter	David Sattig	Raymond Ryman
Willoughby (21)	MC 216 951-2800	David Anderson	. . . .	Loretta Radebaugh	Chalmers Glover	Melvin House	Conrad Straube	Dean Keller
Willoughby Hills (8)	MC 216 946-1234	John J Zur	Steven Toth	Susan V Biello	Steven Toth	William J Heckler	George N Malec	. . . .
Willowick (15)	MC 216 585-3700	A Fitzgerald	Roberta Savastano	James Teknipp	James Teknipp	Harley Rudersdorf	John Germ	Douglas Metzung
Wilmington (11)	MC 513 382-5458	Clifford Eveland	L S Eichelberger	L S Eichelberger	D Hollingsworth	Joseph Spicer	Michael Hatten	Robert W Holmes
Windham v (3)	MC 216 326-2622	Michael D Archon	. . . .	Rachel W Barertt	. . . .	Donald Miller	Thomas E Denvir	. . . .
Wintersville v (4)	MC 614 264-5533	(not reporting)						
Woodlawn v (3)	MC 513 771-6130	(not reporting)						
Woodsfield v (3)	MC 614 472-0418	L William Bolon	. . . .	Phyllis Monahan	. . . .	Mark Masters	Manifred Keylor	. . . .
Wooster (22)	MC 216 263-5200	J Clyde Breneman	. . . .	Sheila Stanley	James Pyers	Vic Haugh	Robert Merillat	Robert Holland
Worthington (15)	CM 614 436-3100	John P Coleman	David B Elder	Janice Yarrington	Barry A Brooks	. . . .	Wayne I McCoy	David W Groth
Wyoming (8)	CM 513 821-7600	David J Savage	Shari S Haldeman	Susan Geruie	Mary Ann Engel	John Wirtz	Timothy World	John Wirtz
Xenia (25)	CM 513 376-7273	Patricia Felton	David Spahr	James Freeman	James Freeman	David Price	Claude Lyons	. . . .
Yellow Springs v (4)	CM 513 767-7202	(not reporting)						
Youngstown (96)	MC 216 742-8700	(not reporting)						
Zanesville (27)	MC 614 455-0600	Marilyn Swope	Dale Raines	Joan Ziemer	Margo Moyer	. . . .	John Fenton	Dave Zulandt

**Directory 1/9
continued**

**MUNICIPAL OFFICIALS
IN U.S. CITIES OVER 2,500**

City, 1990 population figures (000 omitted), form of government	Municipal phone number	Mayor	Appointed administrator	City clerk	Finance officer	Fire chief	Police chief	Public works director
OKLAHOMA (129)								
Ada (16)	CM 405 436-6300	Ray L Stout	Patrick Copeland	Joe Ann Dean	Donna Doolen	John Ryan	Wayne McElhannon	David Hathcoat
Altus (22)	MC 405 481-2216	Boozie McMahan	Charles Martin	C Richardson	Chuck Reagan	Kenneth Tyra	Jim Hughes	....
Alva (5)	MC 405 327-1340	(not reporting)						
Anadarko (7)	CM 405 247-2481	(not reporting)						
Antlers t (3)	MC 405 298-3756	(not reporting)						
Ardmore (23)	CM 405 223-2933	Milton Cooper	Kevin P Evans	Penny Long	Penny Long	Wayne Phelps	Bill Culley	Joe G Elles
Atoka (3)	CM 405 889-3341	Bill Miller	Martha Yates	Sharon Lang	....	Royce Blaker	John Smithart	Stephen Smith
Bartlesville (34)	CM 918 336-0000	Harvey Little	Robert Metzinger	....	George Jones	O Harrington	....	....
Bethany (20)	CM 405 789-2146	(not reporting)						
Bixby (10)	CM 918 366-4430	(not reporting)						
Blackwell (8)	CM 405 363-5490	(not reporting)						
Bristow (4)	MC 918 367-6233	Tom Elias	....	Sharie Campbell	Linda Tate	Bob Grant	Perry Low	Bennie Raiston
Broken Arrow (58)	CM 918 251-5311	James C Reynolds	John T Vinson	Brenda Rinehart	Thomas Caldwell	Melvin Mashburn	James R Stover	David Wooden
Broken Bow (4)	CM 405 584-2282	Charles E Darby	Mark G Guthrie	Lisa G Glass	....	Robert Peavy	Dan Phillips	Gary Swift
Chandler (3)	CM 405 258-3200	Jim Bullock	Perry Beck	Tonya Jarvis	....	Dave Hoover	Mel Roberts	Tom Gatlin
Checotah (3)	MC 918 473-5411	(not reporting)						
Cherokee (2)	CM 405 596-3326	(not reporting)						
Chickasha (15)	CM 405 222-6020	Harold Jackson	Larry Shelton	Sharon Chapman	....	John Clift	Dany Sterling	Larry Fuchs
Choctaw (9)	CM 405 390-8198	Ruth Ann Luke	Robert L Floyd	Aneata R McBride	Robert L Floyd	David Newby	John Whetsel	Bernard Nauheimer
Claremore (13)	MC 918 341-1325	Tom Pool	....	Carlene Webber	....	Chris Neal	Mickey Perry	Noal Brown
Cleveland (3)	CM 918 358-3506	Jim King	Bill L Rowton	Virginia Grantham	....	Jerry L Keller	Bill E Jordan	Floyd E Johnson
Clinton (9)	CM 405 323-0217	Ron Rodolph	Dan Galloway	Glendene Goucher	....	Leon Kinder	Bill Weedon	Alvin Knauf
Coalgate (2)	CM 405 927-2241	(not reporting)						
Collinsville (4)	MC 918 371-2811	K Michael Sheehan	....	Fern Young	....	Russell L Young	Don Abel	Frank Morland
Comanche (2)	CM 405 439-8868	Larry Jones	James E Beene	Janice Willis	Linda Courtright	Austin Martin	George Newton	....
Commerce (2)	MC 918 675-4373	(not reporting)						
Coweta (6)	CM 918 486-2189	Vertis Watkins	Steven C Whitlock	Joyce Terry	....	Bill Osburn	Dale Bradley	John Kirkpatrick
Crescent (1)	CM 405 969-2538	James E Lowe	Milo C Johnson	Bill Fillmore	....	Joe Kegin	Steve Mize	Clinton Wallace
Cushing (7)	CM 918 225-2394	(not reporting)						
Davis (3)	CM 405 369-2323	Delford Fox	Buck Wilson	Sandra Webb	....	Norman Shiplett	General Smith Jr	Ralph Thomasson
Del City (24)	CM 405 677-5741	Joe Nichols	Bill J Dashner	Reba Basinger	Reba Basinger	Tom Tollison	Leon Rippee	Steve Beck
Dewey (3)	CM 918 534-2272	(not reporting)						
Drumright (3)	CM 918 352-2610	Earl Miner	Sandra Brock	Janice Holland	....	Jerry Slane	Loren Guyer	Rick Dillard
Duncan (22)	CM 405 252-0250	(not reporting)						
Durant (13)	CM 405 924-7200	(not reporting)						
Edmond (52)	CM 405 348-8830	Randel C Shadid	C Max Speegle	Nancy C Nichols	Roy L Moeller	Dwight L Maker	....	....
El Reno (15)	CM 405 262-4070	Phil Todd	Lawrence C Palmer	John P Wiewel	John P Wiewel	Ronald G Martin	Lloyd D Blaine	Donald R Goucher
Elk City (10)	CM 405 225-3230	(not reporting)						
Enid (45)	CM 405 234-0400	(not reporting)						
Eufaula (3)	MC 918 689-2532	(not reporting)						
Fairview (3)	CM 405 227-4416	(not reporting)						
Frederick (5)	CM 405 335-7551	Leo J Fallon	Robert B Johnston	Yvonne Rector	....	Louis Hickerson	Jack Whitson	....
Glenpool (7)	CM 918 322-5409	Donald Bahnmaier	Daniel Gibson	Patricia Morris	Daniel Gibson	Orville Lugo Jr	Larry Bible	Tom Laust
Grandfield (1)	CM 405 479-5215	(not reporting)						
Grove (4)	CM 918 786-6107	Charles Perry	Richard Ball	Ivonne Buzzard	....	Gene Wheat	Raymond Johnson	....
Guthrie (11)	CM 405 282-0493	....	Patsy L Sandefur	....	....	....	....	....
Guymon (9)	CM 405 338-3396	Jess Nelson	Wayne Hill	Marcy D Twyman	....	Quinten Smith	Duane Boren	Nolan Bowers
Harrah t (4)	CM 405 454-2951	Kevin Spaeth	Robert P Sherry	Bill C Knox	....	Sammy Martin	Richard J Reier	Gregory Hill
Healdton (3)	CM 405 229-1283	(not reporting)						
Heavener (3)	CM 918 653-2217	Dale Elliott	Paul Evans	Gail Wagner	....	Bobby Carter	Gerald Branam	Johnny Woodral
Henryetta (6)	CM 918 652-3348	(not reporting)						
Hobart (4)	MC 405 726-3100	Herb Henderson	....	Charlene Pulley	....	Billy Robbins	Joe McCall	Herb Henderson
Holdenville (5)	MC 405 379-3397	Jack Barrett	....	Frenola Janes	....	Orville Reid	Robert Horton	Renola Janes
Hollis (3)	CM 405 688-2167	(not reporting)						
Hominy (2)	CM 918 885-2164	(not reporting)						
Hugo (6)	MC 405 326-2722	(not reporting)						
Idabel (7)	MC 405 286-7608	(not reporting)						
Jenks (8)	CM 918 299-5883	Mike Tinker	V R Ewing	Kenda Rice	Kenda Rice	Bob Douglas	Lloyd Ruddell	Leon Earp
Kingfisher (4)	CM 405 375-3705	(not reporting)						
Konawa (2)	CM 405 925-3775	M P Bullington	Max Dye	Wanda Lowry	....	Richard Thomas	Mark Thomas	Max Dye
Lawton (81)	CM 405 581-3500	Ted Marley	Robert Hopkins	Brenda Smith	Steve Livingston	Mike Carter	Michael Wightman	J B Howle
Lindsay (3)	CM 405 756-2019	Willie Rushing Jr	Janice Cain	Linda Newby	....	Bob Shelton	Gene Jones	....
Lone Grove (4)	CM 405 657-3111	Clayton Redding	Ron Holt	Vonnie Updike	Peggy Thomason	Leo Potts	Gary Wilson	....
Madill (3)	CM 405 795-3378	(not reporting)						
Mangum (3)	CM 405 782-2256	(not reporting)						
Marlow (4)	CM 405 658-5401	(not reporting)						
Mc Alester (16)	CM 918 423-9300	Tim Wynn	Randy Green	Bobbie Lanz	Carolyn Hearod	Larry Ketchum	Dale Nave	George Marcangeli
Mc Loud t (2)	MC 405 964-5264	(not reporting)						
Medford (1)	CM 405 395-2875	Louise McGregor	Warren A Beggs	Frances Mark	Frances Mark	Dennis Brittain	Alan Kunzman	Dennis Brittain
Miami (13)	MC 918 542-6685	Louis E Mathia	Alton Rivers	....	Charles A Tomlin	Wm Pete Cooper Jr	Bill G Melton	....
Midwest City (52)	CM 405 739-1235	Eddie Reed	Charles Johnson	Tommy Melton	Tommy Melton	Mike Bower	Clovis Davis	Tom Canfield
Moore (40)	CM 405 793-5000	Debe Homer	....	Michael Drea	Michael Drea	Johnny Knight	Bruce Storm	Bruce Taylor
Muldrow t (3)	MC 918 427-3226	(not reporting)						
Muskogee (38)	CM 918 682-6602	(not reporting)						
Mustang (10)	CM 405 376-4521	Richard Riley	....	Trish Thomas	Janet Isaacs	Tom Strother	Ron Lewis	....
New Cordell (3)	MC 405 832-3825	Max Cunningham	....	....	....	Tommy Merrill	Gary Coburn	....
Newcastle (4)	CM 405 387-4427	....	Stan Patty	Loycie Kerr	....	....	Jim Greene	Virgil Fielding
Newkirk (2)	MC 405 362-2117	(not reporting)						
Nichols Hills (4)	CM 405 843-6637	Warren Felton	Douglas Henley	Douglas Henley	Douglas Henley	Keith Bryan	James Stoddard	Russ Fields
Nicoma Park t (2)	MC 405 769-5673	(not reporting)						
Noble t (5)	CM 405 872-9251	Harlen Fipps	Harry Hill	James Hunt	James Hunt	James Stufflebean	Paul Boyd	Elza Harris
Norman (80)	CM 405 366-5482	(not reporting)						
Nowata (4)	CM 918 273-3538	(not reporting)						
Okemah (3)	CM 918 623-1050	Jerry Smith	Leland Scrimshire	Ann Rutland	Rhonda Jones	Vance Vanhoozer	Edward Smith	David Swayze
Oklahoma City (445)	CM 405 297-2345	Ronald Norick	Donald Bown	Thomas Hurley	Glenn Deck	Gary Marrs	Sam Gonzales	Paul Brum
Okmulgee (13)	CM 918 756-4060	Carlisle W Mabrey	David Harris	Judith Milroy	Judith Milroy	Terry Ballard	Chester Hodge	Robert Morrow
Owasso (11)	CM 918 272-2251	(not reporting)						
Pauls Valley (6)	CM 405 238-3308	(not reporting)						
Pawhuska (4)	CM 918 287-3576	Preston Landrum	Bruce Decker	Lucile Smith	....	Uriah Sholl	John Boone	Dean Branson
Perry (5)	MC 405 336-9360	(not reporting)						
Pocola t (4)	MC 918 436-2388	(not reporting)						
Ponca City (26)	CM 405 767-0300	Marilyn Andrews	Jay Johnson	....	....	Martin Smith	Raymond Ham	Gary Martin
Poteau (7)	MC 918 647-4191	(not reporting)						

Directory 1/9
continued

MUNICIPAL OFFICIALS IN U.S. CITIES OVER 2,500

City, 1990 population figures (000 omitted), form of government	Municipal phone number	Mayor	Appointed administrator	City clerk	Finance officer	Fire chief	Police chief	Public works director
OKLAHOMA (129) continued								
Prague (2)	CM 405 567-2270	J Ted McBride	Nancy Ellis	Nancy Ellis	. . . .	Mike Grissom	Jim Bartlett	Louis Devereaux
Pryor (8)	MC 918 825-0888	Lucy B Schultz	. . . .	Patricia Morgan	. . . .	David Harrison	Dennis Nichols	. . . .
Purcell (5)	CM 405 527-6561	Tony Baird	Robert H Collings	Robert B Lambert	Robert B Lambert	Alton Clifton	Darrell Moring	Robert Shea
Sallisaw (7)	CM 918 775-6241	George Glenn	James R Hudgens	E W Rogers	. . . .	Gus Fullbright	Wayne Craghead	. . . .
Sand Springs (15)	CM 918 245-8751	Charles P Garner	Loy E Calhoun	Mary Sue Overbey	Mary Sue Overbey	Fred D Shawger	Tom Lewallen	Kenneth E Hill
Sapulpa (18)	CM 918 224-3040	J D Marketic	Mark B Roath	Shirley Burzio	Mary Wesson	James R Yeager	Ron Sole	Glenn Gregory
Sayre (3)	MC 405 928-2260	(not reporting)						
Seminole (7)	CM 405 382-4330	M McCreight	Thomas DeArman	Diane Johnson	. . . .	Howard Allen	Steve Williams	. . . .
Shawnee (26)	CM 405 273-1250	(not reporting)						
Skiatook t (5)	MC 918 396-2767	Richard E Barnes	Lee Wert	Darlene Bricker	. . . .	Scott Hilton	Richard Davis	Lee Wert
Spencer (4)	CM 405 771-3226	(not reporting)						
Stigler (3)	CM 918 967-2164	(not reporting)						
Stillwater (37)	CM 405 372-0025	Terry Miller	Carl Weinaug	. . . .	Marcy Alexander	Jim Smith	Norman McNickle	Jeff Hough
Stroud (3)	CM 918 968-2571	(not reporting)						
Sulphur (5)	MC 405 622-5096	(not reporting)						
Tahlequah (10)	MC 918 456-0651	Eunice B Ross	Jerry Latty	Jo Ann Bradley	. . . .	Robert Frank	Norman Fisher	. . . .
Tecumseh (6)	CM 405 598-2188	Phil Hartoon	Randy Swinson	Joanne Reed	. . . .	Jimmy Stokes	Richard Holland	Jim Amerson
The Village (10)	CM 405 751-8861	(not reporting)						
Tishomingo (3)	MC 405 371-2369	(not reporting)						
Tonkawa (3)	CM 405 628-2508	Jerry A Legg	Edward Richardson	John C Ramey	. . . .	Roland Jones	David Rogers	. . . .
Tulsa (367)	MC 918 596-7440	M Susan Savage	Robert Lemons	Hettie Green	. . . .	Thomas Baker	Ronald Palmer	Charles Hardt
Tuttle t (3)	CM 405 381-2335	(not reporting)						
Vinita (6)	MC 918 256-6468	(not reporting)						
Wagoner (7)	MC 918 485-2554	Kenneth Peters	Alva Smith	Linda Gaylor	. . . .	Ray Ferguson	Jim Parker	. . . .
Walters (3)	CM 405 875-3337	Glen Smith	Buddy Vetema	Jackie Ray	. . . .	Richard Lewallen	Dave Perkins	Buddy Veltema
Warr Acres (9)	MC 405 789-2892	(not reporting)						
Watonga (3)	MC 405 623-4669	(not reporting)						
Waurika (2)	CM 405 228-2713	Darvin R Bates	Nolan Combs	Donna Brown	Kathy Deaton	Greg Henderson	Fred Haragan	Ken Ferreira
Weatherford (10)	MC 405 772-7451	(not reporting)						
Wetumka (1)	CM 405 452-3251	(not reporting)						
Wewoka (4)	CM 405 257-2413	(not reporting)						
Wilburton (3)	MC 918 465-2262	Earl Jeffrey	. . . .	Phyllis Wilson	. . . .	Danny Baldwin	Ronald Massey	. . . .
Woodward (12)	CM 405 256-2280	George Goetzinger	Gary L Lyon	Harry Sever	. . . .	Ronald Waggoner	Harvey Rutherford	Harry Sever
Wynnewood (2)	CM 405 665-2307	(not reporting)						
Yale (1)	CM 918 387-2405	Tom Lilly	Carl W Hensley	Sharon Crisjohn	Carl W Hensley	Richard Adsit	Hogart Simpson	Wes Thurman
Yukon (21)	CM 405 354-1895	Ray Wright	Stan Greil	Mary Huckaba	Mary Huckaba	Robert Noll	James Huffman	. . . .
OREGON (92)								
Albany (29)	CM 503 967-4300	Eugene Belhumeur	Steve Bryant	. . . .	D Gary Holliday	Darrel Tedisch	Pat Merina	Mark Yeager
Ashland (16)	MC 503 482-3211	Cathy Golden	Brian Almquist	. . . .	Jill Turner	Keith Woodley	Gary Brown	Steve Hall
Astoria (10)	CM 503 325-5821	(not reporting)						
Baker City (9)	CM 503 523-6541	Lawrence Griffith	Arthur F Reiff	. . . .	Roland C Campbell	Donald Everson	Douglas Humphress	James L Adamson
Bandon (2)	MC 503 347-2437	Judith Densmore	Ben M McMakin	. . . .	. . . .	Lanny R Boston	Richard E Lewis	. . . .
Beaverton (53)	MC 503 526-2222	(not reporting)						
Bend (20)	CM 503 388-5505	Terry Blackwell	Larry Patterson	James W Kerfoot	James W Kerfoot	. . . .	R David Malkin	Thomas Gellner
Boardman (1)	MC 503 481-9252	(not reporting)						
Brookings (4)	CM 503 469-2163	Tom Davis	Dennis Cluff	Beverly Shields	Beverly Shields	William Sharp	Kent Owens	Dennis Barlow
Brownsville (1)	CM 503 466-5666	Robert L Campbell	Diane J Rinks	Sandra L Jensen	Diane J Rinks	. . . .	. . . .	Jody L Anthony
Burns (3)	MC 503 573-5255	Joe Hayse	Harvey Barnes	Norma Hill	Harvey Barnes	Chris Briels	Aaron Richardson	David Cullens
Canby (9)	CM 503 266-4021	Scott Taylor	Michael Jordan	Marilyn Perkett	Virginia Biddle	. . . .	Jerry Giger	. . . .
Cannon Beach (1)	CM 503 436-1581	(not reporting)						
Cascade Locks (1)	CM 503 374-8484	Ken Lambert	George R Lewis	Kate Mast	. . . .	Neil McCormick	. . . .	Richard McCulley
Central Point (8)	CM 503 664-3321	(not reporting)						
Clatskanie (2)	CM 503 728-2622	Addison Harrison	William McDonald	Arlene Long	William McDonald	William Mellinger	David Nelson	David True
Coos Bay (15)	CM 503 269-1181	Joanne Verger	Jim Watson	. . . .	Gail George	Cliff Vaniman	Marc Adams	. . . .
Coquille (4)	CM 503 396-2115	Mike Swindall	Joseph G Wolf	Shirley Patterson	Shirley Patterson	Jerry McCue	David Knapp	John Higgins
Cornelius (6)	CM 503 357-9112	Neal Knight	Jerald P Taylor	. . . .	. . . .	Chris Asanovic	Charles Standley	Frank J Neys
Corvallis (45)	CM 503 757-6900	Charles Vars	Jon Nelson	M Sue Mariner	Debra Edgington	. . . .	Pam Roskowski	Rolland Baxter
Cottage Grove (7)	CM 503 942-5501	Jean Sinclair	Jeffrey Towery	. . . .	Linda Gardner	Stephen Allen	Michael Grover	Robert Sisson
Dallas (9)	CM 503 623-2338	G Van Den Bosch	Roger Jordan	. . . .	Del Funk	Mark Stevens	Jim Harper	Dave Shea
Eagle Point (3)	MC 503 826-4212	Walter B Barker	. . . .	Nita Gosnell	Nita Gosnell	Dennis Jordan	Leon C Sherman	Jim Robertson
Estacada (2)	CM 503 630-6813	Dave Vail	Shelley Jones	Denise Carey	Shelley Jones	. . . .	. . . .	William Strawn
Eugene (113)	CM 503 687-5010	(not reporting)						
Florence (5)	MC 503 997-3436	(not reporting)						
Forest Grove (14)	CM 503 359-3200	Richard G Kidd	. . . .	Cathy Jansen	Ivan M Burnett	Bob Davis	Tom Lowther	John Burdett
Gladstone (10)	CM 503 656-5225	Wade Byers	Ronald Partch	Verna Howell	Verna Howell	Wayne Hauck	Robert King	. . . .
Gold Beach (2)	CM 503 247-7029	Marlyn Schafer	Bill Curtis	Norma Rath	Bill Curtis	Bruce Floyd	Bruce Ladd	Rich Eccleston
Grants Pass (17)	CM 503 474-6360	Gordon Anderson	William Peterson	Joanne Stumpf	Joanne Stumpf	. . . .	Eric Mellgren	. . . .
Gresham (68)	CM 503 661-3000	Gussie McRobert	Bonnie Kraft	. . . .	Roy Wall	Joe Parrott	Art Knori	. . . .
Hermiston (10)	MC 503 567-5521	Frank Harkenrider	Ed Brookshier	Robert Irby	Robert Irby	James Stearns	Grant Asher	. . . .
Hillsboro (38)	CM 503 681-6100	Gordon Faber	Tim Erwert	. . . .	Robert Massar	Dayton Arruda	Ronald Louie	Roy Gibson
Hood River (5)	MC 503 386-1488	Glenn P Taylor	Charlie L Warren	Jay C Reynolds	Steve Everroad	Roy Irwin	Rich Younkins	Doug Clement
Independence (4)	MC 503 838-1212	Marion Rossi	Erik V Kvarsten	. . . .	Martha Wildfang	Richard Hopkins	Vernon T Wells	Douglas Linville
Junction City (4)	MC 503 998-2153	John W Peterson	James D Minard	. . . .	Roberta L Likens	David Harlacher	Michael J Cahill	Robert L Fountain
Keizer (22)	CM 503 390-3700	Dennis Koho	Dotty Tryk	Tracy Davis	Paul Frykberg	. . . .	Charles Tull	Wally Mull
Klamath Falls (18)	CM 503 883-5317	Todd Kellstrom	James Keller	Elisa Fritz	George Jacobs	. . . .	Dan Tofell	Raymond Bidegary
La Grande (12)	CM 503 962-1301	D Larsen Hill	Larry Dalrymple	. . . .	Eldon Slippy	Doug Perry	John Courtney	Ron Gross
Lake Oswego (31)	CM 503 635-0270	Alice Schlenker	Douglas Schmitz	Kris Hitchcock	Bruce Griswold	Phil Sample	Les Youngbar	Jerry Baker
Lakeview t (3)	MC 503 947-2029	Donald R Alger	Sherry Grisel	Linda Nelson	. . . .	Del Lepley	John Bush	Ron Wilkie
Lebanon (11)	MC 503 451-7422	Robert Smith	Joseph A Windell	. . . .	Judith Wendland	. . . .	Walter Richmond	Jim P Ruef
Lincoln City (6)	CM 503 996-2151	Sam Cribbs	Kathleen Stockton	D W Works	D W Works	. . . .	Michael Holden	John McKevitt
Mc Minnville (18)	CM 503 472-9371	Edward Gormley	Kent Taylor	Caole Benedict	. . . .	Bruce Caldwell	Rod Brown	Donald Schut
Medford (47)	CM 503 770-4432	Jerry Lausmann	Harold Anderson	Kathleen Ishiara	Jonathan Jalali	David Bierwiler	Oscar Shipley	Donald Walker
Milton-Freewater (6)	CM 503 938-5531	Mary Nicholson	James A Swayne	. . . .	Linda K Carter	Bill Saager	Don Witt	Howard Moss
Milwaukie (19)	CM 503 659-5171	Craig Lomnicki	Dan Bartlett	Patricia DuVal	Angus Anderson	Daniel Olsen	Charles Mansfield	R Timothy Corbett
Molalla (4)	CM 503 829-6855	Richard Lefever	Stacy Reeves	Melanie Helmig	Chris Culver	. . . .	Robert Elkins	Jack Dunn
Monmouth (6)	CM 503 838-0722	Marc Nelson	Stanley Kenyon	Joan Howard	Joan Howard	. . . .	Richard Brungardt	Gary Wilson
Mt. Angel (3)	MC 503 845-9291	(not reporting)						
Myrtle Creek (3)	CM 503 863-3171	Robert Cotterell	Leroy Blodgett	Charity Hays	Jeanne Babcock	Bill Leming	David Oelrich	Steven Johnson
Myrtle Point (3)	CM 503 572-2626	Edward Cook	Richard Meyers	Richard Meyers	Richard Meyers	Mitch Myers	Ed Tyner	Bill Floyd
Newberg (13)	MC 503 538-9421	Donna Proctor	Duane R Cole	. . . .	Katherine Tri	Michael Sherman	Robert Tardiff	Greg Scoles
Newport (8)	CM 503 265-5331	Mark Collson	Sam I Sasaki	. . . .	Patricia Bearden	Donald Rowley	James Rivers	Larry Crisler
North Bend (10)	CM 503 756-0405	Timm Slator	Jim C Allan	Terri Turi	Carol Bender	. . . .	Gil Zaccaro	Ron Stillmaker

Directory 1/9
continued

MUNICIPAL OFFICIALS
IN U.S. CITIES OVER 2,500

City, 1990 population figures (000 omitted), form of government	Municipal phone number	Mayor	Appointed administrator	City clerk	Finance officer	Fire chief	Police chief	Public works director
OREGON (92) continued								
Nyssa (3)	MC 503 372-2264	J R Shuster	Gordon Zimmerman	Hilda Contreras	Gordon Zimmerman	Jim Farmer	Terry Thompson	Ray Page
Oakridge (3)	MC 503 782-2258	R Culbertson	R Wes Hare	Sharon S O'Brien	Sharon S O'Brien	James R Archer	Michael W Reaves	Jerald A Shanbeck
Ontario (9)	CM 503 889-7684	Ray Kenney	Al Brown	. . . .	Roger Dexter	Michael Sopkis	Mitchell Lawson	William Critz
Oregon City (15)	CM 503 657-0891	(not reporting)						
Pendleton (15)	CM 503 276-1811	Robert E Ramig	Larry L Lehman	. . . .	Carol A James	Richard D Hopper	Edwin S Taber	Jerry Odman
Philomath (3)	CM 503 929-6148	Van Hunsaker	Hal Million	Terri Phillips	Phyllis Beggs	. . . .	Richard Raleigh	Dick Clark
Pilot Rock (1)	MC 503 443-2811	John Standley	. . . .	Amanda Howard	Jackie Carey	. . . .	Ronnie Layton	Steve Draper
Portland (437)	CO 503 823-4352	Vera Katz	. . . .	Barbara Clark	Steve Bauer	. . . .	Charles Moose	Felicia Trader
Prineville (5)	CM 503 447-5627	(not reporting)						
Redmond (7)	CM 503 548-2148	Jerry C Thackery	Joe Hannan	. . . .	David Reeves	Robert Garrison	James Carlton	Stanley Stevenson
Reedsport (5)	CM 503 271-3603	Steven W Wilson	Nolan K Young	. . . .	Sandra K Hanson	Zack Turner	John D Smart	Jeff L McIlvenna
Roseburg (17)	CM 503 672-7701	Jeri Kimmel	Randy Wetmore	Sheila Murphy	C Lance Colley	Ford Swauger	John Hodgson	Chris Berquist
Salem (108)	CM 503 588-6255	Anderson Wyckoff	Larry Wacker	. . . .	. . . .	James Bone	Brian Riley	Frank Mauldin
Sandy (4)	CM 503 668-5533	Mark Mullins	Scott Lazenby	. . . .	June Peterson	. . . .	Fred Punzel	Mike Walker
Scappoose (4)	CM 503 543-7146	. . . .	Jill Monley	Lenore Akerson	Lenore Akerson	. . . .	Scott Woods	. . . .
Seaside (5)	CM 503 738-5511	(not reporting)						
Sheridan (4)	CM 503 843-2347	(not reporting)	Lonnie Hinchcliff					
Sherwood (3)	CM 503 625-5522	Walter Hitchcock	James Rapp	P Blankenbaker	P Blankenbaker	. . . .	Larry Laws	Tad Milburn
Silverton (6)	CM 503 873-5321	Ken Hector	Michael J Scott	. . . .	Suzanne Studer	. . . .	Randall Lunsford	Richard Barstad
Springfield (45)	CM 503 726-3704	Bill Morrisette	Mike Kelly	Eileen Stein	. . . .	Dennis Murphy	. . . .	Dan Brown
St. Helens (8)	MC 503 397-6272	Donald L Kallberg	Rosaline Mallory	Rosaline Mallory	Marilyn Peterson	. . . .	Roger Roth	. . . .
Stayton (5)	MC 503 769-3425	Willmer Van Vleet	David W Kinney	. . . .	Elaine Fisk	. . . .	. . . .	Craig Johns
Sutherlin (5)	CM 503 459-2856	Stan McKnight	John Bruce Long	. . . .	Roy M Stulken	Tom Wells	Richard Schwartz	Don Moore
Sweet Home (7)	CM 503 367-5128	Craig Fentiman	Dan Dean	. . . .	Patricia Gray	Joseph Mengore	Gary David	David Sypher
Talent (3)	CM 503 535-1566	Leo Lomski	Tony C Paxton	Tony C Paxton	Tony C Paxton	Jim Flynn	Dale Kinnan	Timothy Connolly
The Dalles (11)	CM 503 296-5481	L D Cochenour	William Elliott	Julie Krueger	Donald Gower	Robert Palmer	Darrell Hill	William Keyser
Tigard (29)	CM 503 639-4171	Gerald R Edwards	Patrick J Reilly	Catherine Wheatly	R Wayne Lowry	. . . .	Ronald Goodpaster	. . . .
Tillamook (4)	CM 503 842-2472	J R McPheeters	Michael Mahoney	Joanne D Boggs	Michael Mahoney	Tom Weber Jr	Roy S White	Michael Mahoney
Toledo (3)	CM 503 336-2247	Floyd D Ferguson	Jim Landon	Renee Ballinger	. . . .	David Simmons	Jerry Pryor	Lance Burke
Troutdale (8)	CM 503 665-5175	Paul Thalhofer	Pamelia Christian	Valerie Raglione	Robert Gazewood	. . . .	Brent Collier	Jim Galloway
Tualatin (15)	CM 503 692-2000	Steven L Stolze	Stephen A Rhodes	. . . .	Marilyn Matthias	. . . .	Steve Winegar	Dan Boss
Umatilla (3)	MC 503 922-3226	George Hash	Bonnie Parker	Linda Gettmann	Shannon Vannett	Don Drayton	Eldon Olson	Roger Frances
Warrenton (3)	CM 503 861-2233	Leslie Newton	Gilbert Gramson	Kathi Smith	. . . .	Duane Mullins	Daniel Kneale	David Haskell
West Linn (16)	CM 503 657-0331	Robert P Liddell	John Atkins	. . . .	Willie Gin	Terry Hart	Terry Hart	David Monson
Wilsonville (7)	CM 503 682-1011	Gerald A Kurmmel	Arlene Loble	. . . .	Tom Jowaiszas	. . . .	. . . .	Steve Starner
Winston (4)	CM 503 679-6739	James McClellan	Bruce Kelly	Margo Moore	. . . .	. . . .	Bruce Justis	Eric Wilson
Woodburn (13)	CM 503 982-5210	Len Kelley	C Childs	Mary Tennant	Nancy Gritta	. . . .	Kenneth Wright	G S Tiwari
PENNSYLVANIA (555)								
Abington tp (56)	MC 215 884-5000	Richard E Fluge	Burton T Conway	Burton T Conway	Allyn R Larash	Robert G Stahl Jr	William J Kelly	Ed Micciolo
Abington tp (2)	MC 717 586-0111	Henry Belin	Ronald G Bray	. . . .	Henry Belin	. . . .	Daniel J Mooney	Harry F Derr Jr
Akron b (4)	MC 717 859-1600	(not reporting)						
Aldan b (5)	MC 215 626-3553	(not reporting)						
Aliquippa b (13)	CO 412 375-5188	Daniel Britza	. . . .	Rodna Casto	R Marksteiner	Oresto Costanza	William Alston	. . . .
Allentown (105)	MC 215 437-7523	Joseph Daddona	Karl Kercher	Michael Hanlon	Barbara Bigelow	David Novosat	Wayne Stephens	Neal Kern
Altoona (52)	CM 814 949-2408	Daniel Milliron	Robert F Hagemann	Michael F Hubert	Richard J Peo	Reynold D Santone	John J Reilly	Robert C McPhee
Ambler b (7)	MC 215 646-1000	(not reporting)						
Ambridge b (8)	CM 412 266-4070	Walter Panek	Alfred P Vennare	. . . .	Alfred P Vennare	Orlando Gagliardi	Frank Kamalich	Robert Hare
Amity tp (6)	CM 215 689-9415	(not reporting)						
Archbald b (6)	MC 717 876-1800	(not reporting)						
Arnold (6)	MC 412 337-4441	William Demao	Oscar Doutt Jr	Pamela Moses	Elias Moses	. . . .	Ronald Hopkins	. . . .
Ashland b (4)	MC 717 875-2411	June P Gressens	Thomas W Joyce	. . . .	. . . .	Thomas P Towers	Adam Bernodin	. . . .
Ashley b (3)	MC 717 824-1364	(not reporting)						
Aspinwall b (3)	MC 412 781-0213	(not reporting)						
Aston (15)	MC 215 494-1636	James H Persing	Richard D Lehr	Carol Thompson	Joan L Brunner	. . . .	James McCarthy	Richard Lehr Jr
Athens b (3)	MC 717 888-2120	(not reporting)						
Avalon b (6)	CM 412 761-5820	Nicholas Grande	Joan Welsh	Pat O'Neill	John Hahn	William Carney	Robert Howie	Joseph Zabawsky
Avoca b (3)	MC 717 457-4011	Thomas Durkin	Ann Baclasky	Steve Yokimishyn	Jos Satkowski	C Van Luvender	Wm Thomas	James McGlynn
Baden b (5)	MC 412 869-3700	Louis F Marsilio	Susan A Blum	. . . .	. . . .	David Trzcianka	Frank Tavern Jr	Jack McKenna
Baldwin b (22)	MC 412 882-9600	Michael Romanus	Shirley Kuchta	. . . .	. . . .	. . . .	Christopher Kelly	. . . .
Bally b (1)	MC 215 845-2351	(not reporting)						
Bangor b (5)	MC 215 588-2216	Carol Cuono	Linda Rousset	. . . .	. . . .	Robert Owens	Donald Gillingham	. . . .
Barnesboro b (3)	MC 814 948-8230	(not reporting)						
Beaver b (5)	MC 412 773-6700	(not reporting)						
Beaver Falls (11)	CO 412 847-2803	James C Reynolds	Perry C Wayne Jr	. . . .	. . . .	Robert Butler	Donald Burdine	Bruno Gratteri
Beavertown b (1)	MC 717 658-2505	(not reporting)						
Bedford b (3)	MC 814 623-8192	James Edwards	John Montgomery	Lisa Merritt	. . . .	Jay Speicher	Earl Packer	Earl Horne
Bellefonte b (6)	CM 814 355-1501	(not reporting)						
Bellevue b (9)	CM 412 766-6164	Rosemary Heflin	Robert Grimm	. . . .	. . . .	. . . .	Michael Bookser	Larry Guerriero
Bensalem tp (57)	CM 215 639-2500	Edward F Burns	James R White	Bill C Morey	James R White	Robert Ludwig	Frank Friel	James Nolan
Bentleyville b (3)	MC 412 239-2112	(not reporting)						
Benzinger tp (9)	MC 814 781-1274	Robert Mohr	Thomas Fleming	Mary A Hasselman	. . . .	Michael Bauer	Gary Eckert	Steve Samick
Berwick b (11)	CM 717 752-2723	Lou Biacchi	Matthew Kulhanek	. . . .	Matthew Kulhanek	Charles East	James Comstock	James Gavitt
Bethel Park (34)	CM 412 831-6800	Reno Virgili	William J Spagnol	William J Spagnol	Timothy A Babik	Daniel Moore	Joseph Kletch	Marshall Scurlock
Bethlehem (71)	MC 215 865-7100	Kenneth R Smith	Robert C Wilkins	C Biendenkopf	Robert C Wilkins	Carmen J Oliver	Thomas P Murphy	Wendell S Sherman
Bethlehem tp (16)	CM 215 865-5563	(not reporting)						
Big Beaver b (2)	MC 412 827-2416	Donald Wachter	Joseph R Lindsay	. . . .	. . . .	Jeff Pinkerton	J Diffenbacher	. . . .
Birdsboro b (4)	MC 215 582-6030	Pamela Hawman	Ronald M Ewing	. . . .	. . . .	Craig Seidel	Robert Rothharpt	. . . .
Blairsville b (4)	CM 412 459-9100	Harry W Adkins	B Edward Smith	Mary J Brown	B Edward Smith	Robert Thompson	Joseph Cameron	. . . .
Blakely b (7)	MC 717 383-3340	Robert Klinko	Harold McCusker	. . . .	Dennis Corvo	Dana Deleo	Thomas Dubas	Joseph Cirba
Bloomsburg t (12)	MC 717 784-7703	(not reporting)						
Blossburg b (2)	MC 717 638-2452	(not reporting)						
Boyertown b (4)	CM 215 367-2688	(not reporting)						
Brackenridge b (4)	MC 412 224-0800	William Beale	. . . .	Carol Jones	. . . .	Dan Brestensky	Guy Gula	Joseph Chifulini
Braddock b (5)	MC 412 271-1018	(not reporting)						
Braddock Hills b (2)	MC 412 241-5080	(not reporting)						
Bradford (10)	CM 814 368-3232	Arvid A Nelson	. . . .	Joseph Roslinski	Maxwell Moore	Frank Frontino	Richard Cavallero	Joseph Roslinski
Brentwood b (11)	MC 412 884-1500	(not reporting)						
Bridgeport b (4)	MC 215 272-1811	(not reporting)						
Bridgeville b (5)	CM 412 221-6012	(not reporting)						
Brighton tp (7)	MC 412 774-4803	Roy E Harden	Bryan K Dehart	Robert Flick	. . . .	John Curtaccio	Jack Erath	. . . .
Bristol tp (57)	MC 215 785-5884	(not reporting)						
Bristol b (10)	MC 215 788-3828	(not reporting)						

City, 1990 population figures (000 omitted), form of government	Municipal phone number	Mayor	Appointed administrator	City clerk	Finance officer	Fire chief	Police chief	Public works director
PENNSYLVANIA (555) continued								
Brookhaven b (9)	MC 215 874-2557	(not reporting)						
Brookville b (4)	MC 814 849-5325	(not reporting)						
Brownsville b (3)	MC 412 785-5761	Robert W Bakewell	. . . .	. . . .	. . . .	. . . .	Richard A Gordon	. . . .
Buckingham tp (9)	CM 215 794-8834	George M Collie	Beverly J Curtin	Annemarie T Lusen	Nancy L Saxe	Gary L Cosner	Steven P Daniels	Donald G Naylor
Butler (16)	CO 412 285-4124	Marian L Taylor	Glenn P Crytzer	. . . .	Glenn P Crytzer	Don Acquaviva	Paul Cornibe	Pete Zissi
Butler tp (17)	MC 412 283-3430	(not reporting)						
California b (6)	MC 412 938-8878	(not reporting)						
Callimont b (..)	MC	(not reporting)						
Caln tp (12)	MC 215 384-0600	(not reporting)						
Cambridge Springs b (2)	CM 814 398-2311	(not reporting)						
Camp Hill b (8)	CM 717 737-3456	Stephen M Urban	E J Knittel	. . . .	. . . .	. . . .	Gregory Ammons	C Zettlemoyer
Canonsburg b (9)	CM 412 745-1800	Daniel Caruso	. . . .	. . . .	Charles Bergensky	. . . .	R T Bell	Chester Osiecki
Carbondale (11)	MC 717 282-4110	(not reporting)						
Carlisle b (18)	CM 717 249-4422	Kirk R Wilson	Allen L Loomis Jr	. . . .	R H Fahnestock	David A Boyles	Stephen Margeson	Michael T Keiser
Carnegie b (9)	MC 412 276-1414	Albert Falcioni	Paul McKenna	. . . .	. . . .	. . . .	Heff Harbin	John Kandracs
Carroll Valley b (1)	MC 717 642-8269	Grady H Edwards	Virginia Ciliotta	Barbara M Hertz	. . . .	. . . .	. . . .	. . . .
Castle Shannon b (9)	CM 412 561-9200	Thomas O'Malley	E R McFadden	. . . .	. . . .	James F O'Brien	Harold C Lane	George Fuss
Catasauqua b (7)	CM 215 264-0571	Robert C Boyer	Eugene Goldfeder	. . . .	. . . .	Samuel W Burrows	Wayne W Muffley	Joseph I Nicklas
Center tp (11)	MC 412 774-0271	(not reporting)						
Centerville b (4)	MC 412 757-6307	(not reporting)						
Chalfont b (3)	MC 215 822-0991	(not reporting)						
Chambersburg b (17)	CM 717 264-5151	Robert P Morris	Julio D Lecuona	Tanya Mickey	C Forrester	William Sheppard	Michael T Defrank	Robert Wagner
Charleroi b (5)	MC 412 483-6011	(not reporting)						
Cheltenham tp (35)	CM 215 887-1000	Herbert Wile	David G Kraynik	. . . .	Rosemary Poppert	Michael Moonblatt	Stephen Ott	. . . .
Chester (42)	MC 215 447-7700	(not reporting)						
Chippewa tp (7)	CM 412 843-8177	Thomas A Roberts	Stephan L Johnson	. . . .	Stephen L Johnson	Richard Lamey	C Robt Berchtold	. . . .
Churchill b (4)	MC 412 241-7113	William Richards	L Bruwelheide	Anna C Sekela	. . . .	L Bruwelheide	Richard H James	. . . .
Clairton (10)	CM 412 233-8113	(not reporting)						
Clarion b (6)	CM 814 226-7707	(not reporting)						
Clarks Summit b (5)	CM 717 586-9316	(not reporting)						
Clearfield b (7)	MC 814 765-7817	(not reporting)						
Clifton Heights b (7)	MC 215 623-1000	Mary Natale	Deborah Bebko	. . . .	. . . .	Edward Volante	Ronald Berry	. . . .
Coaldale b (3)	RT 717 645-7986	(not reporting)						
Coatesville (11)	CM 215 384-0300	Mary Frances John	Jeff Braun	. . . .	Lewis J Gay	Francis Pilotti	Dennis Alexander	David Gay
College tp (7)	CM 814 234-7200	Fred E Smith	C Thomas Lechner	Linda S Caswell	Denise L Elbell	. . . .	. . . .	. . . .
Collegeville b (4)	MC 215 489-9208	(not reporting)						
Collingdale b (9)	MC 215 586-0500	(not reporting)						
Columbia b (11)	CM 717 684-2468	(not reporting)						
Colwyn b (3)	MC 215 461-2000	Thomas Kilian	Daniel McEnhill	Mary Martin	. . . .	D Ciancaglione	. . . .	. . . .
Concord tp (7)	CM 215 459-8911	John S Kemper	John W Cornell	. . . .	. . . .	Steve Cooper	. . . .	Harry T Shinn
Connellsville (9)	MC 412 628-2020	(not reporting)						
Conshohocken b (8)	MC 215 828-1092	(not reporting)						
Conway b (2)	MC 412 869-5550	(not reporting)						
Coopersburg b (3)	MC 215 282-3307	Thelma M Kiess	Roberta M Shelly	Carol A Anderson	. . . .	Calvin Sharrer	James M Lawrence	Harvey A Heaps
Coplay b (3)	MC 215 262-6088	J Shemanski	Carol Schleder	Carol Schleder	. . . .	Jay Ambearle	Donald Hill	Richard Bundra
Coraopolis b (7)	MC 412 264-3002	(not reporting)						
Cornwall b (3)	MC 717 274-3436	(not reporting)						
Corry (7)	CO 814 663-7041	(not reporting)						
Coudersport b (3)	MC 814 274-9776	(not reporting)						
Crafton b (7)	MC 412 921-0752	(not reporting)						
Cranberry tp (15)	CM 412 776-4806	(not reporting)						
Cumru tp (13)	CO 215 777-1343	(not reporting)						
Curwensville b (3)	MC 814 236-1840	(not reporting)						
Dallas b (3)	MC 717 675-1389	Paul Labar	Milton Lutsey	Barbara Zimniski	. . . .	Robert Besecker	John Fowler	Ralph Parsons
Dallastown b (4)	MC 717 244-6626	(not reporting)						
Danville b (5)	MC 717 275-3091	(not reporting)						
Darby b (11)	MC 215 586-1100	(not reporting)						
Darby tp (11)	CO 215 586-1514	L Patterson	John B Ryan Jr	Donna Mollichella	Michael Dipaolo	. . . .	Robert Thompson	Charles Joyner
Derry tp (18)	CM 717 533-2057	Lawrence F Clark	. . . .	. . . .	. . . .	Richard Lenker	James N Negley	Lane R Painter
Derry b (3)	MC 412 694-2030	D M McWherter Sr	. . . .	Mary Jane Geary	. . . .	. . . .	Lawrence Brodrick	. . . .
Dickson City b (6)	MC 717 489-5758	V Wiercinski	Kenneth Novack	Nancy Anderson	Albert J Frekey	Joseph Chowanec	W Stadnitski	John Lukasik
Dillsburg b (2)	CM 717 432-9969	(not reporting)						
Donora b (6)	MC 412 379-6600	(not reporting)						
Dormont b (10)	MC 412 561-8900	Thomas A Morrone	Deborah J Grass	. . . .	. . . .	Donald James	Russell McKibben	Dio Sciulli
Dover tp (16)	CM 717 292-3634	(not reporting)						
Downingtown b (8)	MC 215 269-0344	(not reporting)						
Doylestown tp (15)	MC 215 348-9915	Joe Conti	David R Jones	. . . .	William Whightman	Robert Lanetti	Stephen J White	Richard John
Doylestown b (9)	CM 215 345-4140	William E Neis	Benjamin W Jones	. . . .	Caroline Brinker	Steve Walther	Paul P Brady	John H Davis
Dravosburg b (2)	MC 412 466-5200	R McKelvey	B Honick	D Stockett	. . . .	R Vezzani Jr	K Holland	. . . .
Du Bois (8)	CM 814 371-2000	William H Reay	Patrick A Nuzzo	J Lamarr Adamson	. . . .	. . . .	Darrel Clark	. . . .
Duncannon b (1)	CM 717 834-4311	(not reporting)						
Dunmore b (15)	CM 717 343-7611	Helen M Domnick	Richard F Carr	. . . .	. . . .	Carmen Magnotta	. . . .	Joseph Straub
Dupont b (3)	MC 717 655-6216	Ann M O'Malley	A J Dubeck	Julie Jendrey	. . . .	Fred Betterly	Anthony DeMark	David Powell
Duquesne (9)	MC 412 469-3770	(not reporting)						
Duryea b (5)	MC 717 457-6784	(not reporting)						
East Caln tp (3)	CM 215 269-1989	. . . .	Edwin R Hill	Barbara M Kelly	. . . .	. . . .	. . . .	. . . .
East Goshen tp (15)	CM 215 692-7171	. . . .	Louis F Smith Jr	Diane L Degnan	. . . .	. . . .	C W Mac Intyre	Mark S Miller
East Lampeter tp (..)	CM 717 393-1567	James C Nolt	Ralph M Hutchison	. . . .	. . . .	. . . .	Jacob Glick	. . . .
East Lansdowne b (3)	MC 215 623-7131	Robert L Dimond	. . . .	. . . .	James Bonner	James Carr	Thomas Pearlingi	. . . .
East Mc Keesport b (3)	MC 412 824-2531	C Thomas Hall	Rosemarie Mazur	June Kohl	Rita Lavella	Paul Marcoz	Robert R Morgan	Samuel E Pack
East Norriton tp (13)	MC 215 275-2800	(not reporting)						
East Pennsboro tp (15)	CO 717 732-0711	(not reporting)						
East Petersburg b (4)	MC 717 569-9282	(not reporting)						
East Stroudsburg b (9)	CM 717 421-8200	Irving Sommer	Kenneth R Brown	. . . .	. . . .	William L Miller	Charles McDonald	Thomas Sekula
East Whiteland tp (8)	CM 215 648-0600	Charles DiSipio	J Reimenschneider	. . . .	J Reimenschneider	Darin Fitzgerald	Robert Redzig	Edward Galante
Easton (26)	MC 215 250-6600	(not reporting)						
Easttown tp (10)	MC 215 644-9000	(not reporting)						
Ebensburg b (4)	MC 814 472-8930	(not reporting)						
Economy b (10)	MC 412 869-4779	(not reporting)						
Eddystone b (2)	MC 215 874-9325	(not reporting)						
Edgewood b (4)	MC 412 242-4824	R Pickering	P Messina	M Bowen	R Walter	T Hale	P Messina	R Christensen
Edgeworth b (2)	CM 412 741-2866	William M Kelly	B D Slaugenhaupt	D Frischmann	B D Slaugenhaupt	H J Lauderbaugh	James E Creese	Eugene A Kunkel
Edinboro b (8)	CM 814 734-1812	(not reporting)						

Directory 1/9
continued

MUNICIPAL OFFICIALS
IN U.S. CITIES OVER 2,500

City, 1990 population figures (000 omitted), form of government	Municipal phone number	Mayor	Appointed administrator	City clerk	Finance officer	Fire chief	Police chief	Public works director
PENNSYLVANIA (555) continued								
Edwardsville b (5)	MC 717 288-6484	Joseph Stochla	Paul Keating	Anne Williams	. . . .	Raymond King	Rowland Roberts	Donald Kulick
Elizabethtown b (10)	CM 717 367-1700	John Buch	Nick Viscome	. . . .	. . . .	. . . .	Robert Ardner	Wayne DeVan
Ellwood City b (9)	CM 412 758-5576	(not reporting)						
Emmaus b (11)	MC 215 965-9292	Ray Erb	Bruce E Fosselman	. . . .	. . . .	Robert Reiss	Frank Taylor	Dan Delong
Emporium b (3)	CM 814 486-0768	David McManigle	David J Greene	. . . .	. . . .	Raymond Housler	Allen H Neyman	. . . .
Emsworth b (3)	MC 412 761-1161	(not reporting)						
Ephrata b (12)	CM 717 738-9232	(not reporting)						
Erie (109)	MC 814 870-1200	Joyce Savocchio		James Klemm	John Bachman	Richard Robb	Paul DeDionisio	John Barzano
Etna b (4)	MC 412 781-0569	William Dougherty	Mary E Cavlovic	. . . .	. . . .	Robert Ettmyer	Ronal C Harris	Joseph D Ferraro
Exeter tp (17)	MC 215 779-5660	(not reporting)						
Exeter b (6)	MC 717 654-3001	Andrew Mauriello	. . . .	. . . .	Maryjo Cumbo	Doug Roberts	John McNeil	Joseph Venetz
Fairview tp (13)	CM 717 774-3190	(not reporting)						
Falls tp (35)	CM 215 736-5308	Walter Almond	James J Dillon	. . . .	Elaine Gibbs	Raymond Forestal	James Kettler	Charles Mazenko
Farrell (7)	CM 412 983-2700	(not reporting)						
Ferguson tp (9)	CM 814 238-4651	Dan R Harner	Mark A Kunkle	. . . .	. . . .	. . . .	Edward J Connor	Ronald A Seybert
Fleetwood b (3)	MC 215 944-8220	Samuel G Borrell	. . . .	Sandra A Harding	J Aulenbach	. . . .	Ray A Nester	Floyd M Rhodes
Folcroft b (8)	MC 215 522-1305	(not reporting)						
Ford City b (3)	MC 412 763-3081	Gregory D Dinko	M J Markilinski	Lisa Bittner	. . . .	Ronald Wojcik	Jan Lysakowski	Henry Fijal
Forest Hills b (7)	CM 412 351-7330	Elmer Incheck	Richard J Branzel	. . . .	Marian Horsmon	Raymond Heller	Domenic Brusco	Richard J Branzel
Forty Fort b (5)	MC 717 287-8586	(not reporting)						
Foster tp (5)	CO 814 362-4656	. . . .	. . . .	Sally McGuire	. . . .	. . . .	Richard Gaertner	. . . .
Fountain Hill b (5)	MC 215 867-0301	(not reporting)						
Fox Chapel b (5)	CM 412 963-1100	(not reporting)						
Frackville b (5)	MC 717 874-3860	(not reporting)						
Franconia tp (7)	CM 215 723-1137	(not reporting)						
Franklin (7)	CM 814 437-1485	Jack C Sanford	E William Gabrys	E William Gabrys	Cheryl A Carson	James E Guyton	Lynn D McMasters	Robert E Heller
Franklin Park b (10)	CM 412 364-4115	(not reporting)						
Freeland b (4)	MC 717 636-0111	(not reporting)						
Geistown b (3)	MC 814 266-8313	(not reporting)						
Gettysburg b (7)	MC 717 334-1160	(not reporting)						
Girard b (3)	CM 814 774-9683	Robert Orr	Richard C Higley	. . . .	. . . .	Jay Ball	Daniel Bucho	. . . .
Glassport b (6)	MC 412 672-7400	Thomas Urbanski	Nancy M Piazza	Terry Woytovich	Anthony Pepe	Dan Kolick	Bernard Dworek	Dan Kunf
Glenolden b (7)	MC 215 583-3221	(not reporting)						
Green Tree b (5)	CM 412 921-1110	John McManus	Howard J Bednar	Audrey Henn	Howard J Bednar	Dan Walsh	Timothy Logue	Joseph Seibel
Greencastle b (4)	CM 717 597-7143	John F Benchoff	Kenneth E Myers	. . . .	. . . .	. . . .	Terry L Sanders	David W Nichols
Greensburg (16)	MC 412 838-4323	Daniel J Fajt	R Edward Jackson	. . . .	John R Finfrock	Edward Hutchinson	R Attenberger	Emil Peterinelli
Greenville b (7)	CM 412 588-4193	Robert S Gargasz	Marie H Julian	. . . .	. . . .	Walter C Saney	Barry W Williams	Paul D Boyer
Grove City b (8)	CM 412 458-7060	(not reporting)						
Hamburg b (4)	CM 215 562-7821	William Dengler	Lynda Albright	Denise Prutzman	. . . .	. . . .	Gene Schappell	Donald Homm
Hampden tp (20)	CO 717 761-0119	M Finkelstein	John E Bradley Jr	. . . .	. . . .	Richard Wertz	Kenneth Fetrow	Steven Campbell
Hampton tp (16)	CM 412 486-0400	Gloria J Newman	W C Lochner	Susan Bernet	Irene Reaghard	. . . .	Chester J Kline	Edward Berzonski
Hanover b (14)	CM 717 637-3877	(not reporting)						
Hanover tp (2)	CM 215 264-1069	Eleanore Hayden	Sandra Pudliner	Vicky Roth	Sandra Pudliner	Ray Henry	. . . .	Bruce Pudliner
Harmony b (4)	CO 412 266-1910	(not reporting)						
Harris tp (4)	CM 814 466-6228	Joseph Carroll	Thomas Miller	. . . .	Linda Carter	. . . .	. . . .	Allen Klinger
Harrisburg (52)	MC 717 255-3011	Stephen R Reed	Napoleon Saunders	Oscar Douglas	Robert F Kroboth	Donald H Konkle	Richard S Shaffer	James M Close
Harrison tp (12)	CO 412 226-1393	Craig A Negley Sr	Faith A Payne	Susan K Motosicky	. . . .	John Desicki	Fred L Phillippi	Harry B Gourley
Hatboro b (7)	MC 215 443-9100	Thomas McMackin	Albert L Herrmann	. . . .	. . . .	. . . .	Frank L Campbell	W Robert Stauch
Hatfield tp (15)	CM 215 855-0900	John F Norman	S W Seitzinger Jr	. . . .	. . . .	. . . .	W Robert Stanley	Fred R Leister
Hatfield b (3)	MC 215 855-0781	S DeLisio	Mark A Curfman	. . . .	Lola K Bridi	Ralph Rehrig	. . . .	Robert F Hickson
Haverford tp (50)	CM 215 446-1000	Fred C Moran	Thomas J Bannar	. . . .	Timothy L Sander	. . . .	Gary Hoover	Al Digirolamo
Hazleton (25)	MC 717 459-4960	John Quigley	Samuel Monticello	Carol Destefano	. . . .	John Andeara	James Joseph	Agenlo Cusatis
Hellertown b (6)	CM 215 838-7041	Donald Zimpfer	James W Sigworth	Janice Unangst	D Campanella	Gerald Malone	Allen W Stiles	Lorrain L Cawley
Hempfield tp (43)	CO 412 834-7232	Samuel Testa	Donald Denezza	Gerald Answine	. . . .	. . . .	. . . .	Joe Svetkovich
Hermitage (15)	MC 412 981-0800	Dean Alexander	Terry S Fedorchak	Terry S Fedorchak	Terry S Fedorchak	Robert S Goeltz	John A Marriott	Peter V D'Orazip
Highspire b (3)	CM 717 939-3303	James Baker	C Montgomery	Patricia Julian	. . . .	. . . .	Timothy Roth	. . . .
Hollidaysburg b (6)	CM 814 695-7543	James L Shoemaker	Thomas Fountaine	Ann M Andrews	Robert Kuntz	Robert E Kerns	Edward L Plowman	Kenneth Holsinger
Homer City b (2)	CM 412 479-8005	Casper Tartalone	Judith Nipps	Peggy Citeroni	. . . .	Joseph Iezi	Louis Saceo	. . . .
Homestead b (4)	MC 412 461-1340	Betty Esper	John Cornelius	Lynette Mariner	. . . .	Robert Stuart	Ellsworth Ford	Daniel Kelly
Honesdale b (5)	MC 717 253-0731	(not reporting)						
Hopewell b (13)	CO 412 378-1460	(not reporting)						
Horsham tp (22)	CM 215 643-3131	. . . .	Michael J McGee	. . . .	. . . .	. . . .	John L Donovan Jr	Stanley J Mroz
Hughesville b (2)	CM 717 584-5272	P Montgomery	Rebecca Jo Fought	. . . .	. . . .	Steven Stiger	John Rechel	Dale Cahn
Hummelstown b (4)	MC 717 566-2555	Marion Alexander	Michael O'Keefe	. . . .	. . . .	. . . .	Gary Gingrich	Richard Engle
Huntingdon b (7)	CM 814 643-3966	(not reporting)						
Indiana b (15)	MC 412 465-6691	(not reporting)						
Indiana tp (6)	CM 412 767-5333	(not reporting)						
Ingram b (4)	CM 412 921-3625	Charles Mitsch Jr	Cynthia L Baccaro	. . . .	. . . .	Roy McGee	Robert B Clark	Ray Cato
Irwin b (5)	CM 412 864-3100	Daniel T Rose	Joseph R Plues	Mary L Benko	. . . .	Harry Neil	John R Karasek	Art C Youngstead
Jeannette (11)	MC 412 527-4000	(not reporting)						
Jefferson b (10)	CM 412 655-7735	Wm Chamberlin	Richard Clark	Saundra Walsh	. . . .	. . . .	John Maple	. . . .
Jenkintown b (5)	MC 215 885-0700	(not reporting)						
Jersey Shore b (4)	MC 717 398-0104	(not reporting)						
Jessup b (5)	MC 717 489-0411	(not reporting)						
Jim Thorpe b (5)	MC 717 325-3025	Thomas J Wildoner	Charlotte Malchon	. . . .	. . . .	Patrick McGinley	Thomas L Mase	John R Marks
Johnsonburg b (3)	CM 814 965-5682	(not reporting)						
Johnstown (28)	MC 814 533-2001	Herbert Pfuhl	. . . .	John Williams	Joseph W Bunk	George Shiley	Robert Huntley	George Avarmis
Kane b (4)	CM 814 837-9240	Edgar James	Dennis Fiscus	Suzanne O'Rourke	. . . .	Jim Greville	William Osmer	Mike Walter
Kenhorst b (3)	CM 215 777-7327	(not reporting)						
Kennett Square b (5)	CM 215 444-4590	(not reporting)						
Kingston (15)	MC 717 288-4576	Francis Sorochak	James Phillips	. . . .	Linda S Suponcic	Raymond Novitski	Gerald O'Donnell	Daniel Thomas
Kingston tp (7)	CM 717 696-3809	Dan Wisnieski	Jeffrey K Box	Carole Loberg	Jeffrey K Box	. . . .	James Balavage	Robert Chamberlan
Kittanning b (5)	MC 412 543-2091	(not reporting)						
Kulpmont b (3)	MC 717 373-1521	(not reporting)						
Kutztown b (5)	MC 215 683-6131	(not reporting)						
Lancaster (56)	MC 717 291-4720	Janice C Stork	. . . .	Janet E Spleen	Robert I Bolton	Charles Welcomer	Walter E Goeke	Richard B Nissley
Lancaster tp (13)	MC 717 291-1213	(not reporting)						
Lansdale b (16)	CM 215 368-1691	Michael Dinunzio	F Lee Mangan	. . . .	Frank Celona	Jay Daveler	Frank Heinze	Wayne Williams
Lansdowne b (12)	CM 215 623-7300	(not reporting)						
Lansford b (5)	MC 717 645-3900	(not reporting)						
Larksville b (5)	MC 717 288-6619	(not reporting)						
Latrobe b (9)	MC 412 539-8548	Oland Canterna	Robert L Barto	. . . .	. . . .	John G Orzehowski	John J Smetanka	David H Williams
Laureldale b (4)	MC 215 929-8700	(not reporting)						

City, 1990 population figures (000 omitted), form of government	Municipal phone number	Mayor	Appointed administrator	City clerk	Finance officer	Fire chief	Police chief	Public works director
PENNSYLVANIA (555) continued								
Lebanon (25)	CO 717 273-6711	Betty J Eiceman	Debra J Gates	Debra J Gates	Rhoda K Lauver	Matthias Arnt	Bernard P Reilly	Edward M Keener
Leechburg b (3)	MC 412 842-8511	(not reporting)						
Lehighton b (6)	CM 215 377-4002	Wilbur Bauchspies	John F Hanosek		John F Hanosek	Wayne Nothstein	Fred Scott	Evor Williams
Lemoyne b (4)	CM 717 737-6843	(not reporting)						
Lewisburg b (6)	MC 717 523-3614	(not reporting)						
Lewistown (9)	CM 717 248-1361	Joseph Fiore	David J Frey		Fleta Magen	Robert McCaa	James Wagner Jr	Burle Fisher
Liberty b (3)	MC 717 324-3461	(not reporting)						
Limerick tp (7)	CM 215 495-6432	Edward Noa	Lee B Gregory				W Douglas Weaver	Ed Fink
Lititz b (8)	MC 717 626-2044	John Petty	Sue Ann Barry		Sue Ann Barry		James Fritz	Nevin Koch
Littlestown b (3)	MC 717 359-5101	Charles Bridinger	Richard Selby	Samuel B Michael		M Sneeringer	Donald F Baker	Michel Dillman
Lock Haven (9)	CM 717 893-5900	R A Edmonston	Paul K Cornell	Paul K Cornell	C G Beers	Lewis L Summers	C E Shoemaker	Richard C Ardner
Logan tp (12)	MC 814 944-5340	(not reporting)						
Lower Allen tp (15)	CM 717 737-8681	Robert B Roth	Ronald J Mull		Thomas Vernau	James Polly	Raymond Rhodes	
Lower Burrell (12)	MC 412 335-9875	Dennis L Kowalski	Edward A Kirkwood				Willian Newell	George Vasilopus
Lower Gwynedd tp (10)	MC 215 646-5302	Edward Brandt	Edward Clifford		Ruth Dunn		Edward Hancock	Robert Pierson
Lower Makefield tp (25)	CM 215 493-3646	Michael Quinn			Elizabeth Sell	William Winslade	Charles Ronaldo	James Coyne
Lower Merion tp (58)	CM 215 649-4000	(not reporting)						
Lower Moreland tp (12)	MC 215 947-3100	(not reporting)						
Lower Paxton tp (39)	CM 717 657-5600	H Michael Liptak	George S Wolfe		Donna G Speakman		Stanley Holsinger	Glen L Farling
Lower Pottsgrove tp (9)	MC 215 323-0436	Gerald Richards	Gregory Prowant	Patricia Mazeski		R Sierocinski	Richard Lengel	Richard Yoder
Lower Providence tp (19)	CM 215 539-8020	Ernest Gaugler	Rick Schnaedter		Alva Stead	Robert Keyser	Thomas P Rogers	David H Shaffer
Lower Saucon tp (8)	CM 215 865-3291		James McCann		Martha Chase		Guy Lesser	Charles Senich
Lower Southampton tp (20)	CO 215 357-7300	Dan Fraley	Kathleen Goldhahn		Joseph P Stangl	Rich J Noon	Edward J Donnelly	John F Murhy
Lower Swatara tp (7)	CM 717 939-9377	Franklin Linn Sr	David Clouser	Jean Arroyo	Mary Lou Rittner	John F Rubinic	Richard H Malwitz	Keith Condran
Luzerne b (3)	MC 717 287-7633	Walter Yablonski	Bonnie Arnone	Linda Ziegenfus		David White	Charles Urban	
Mahanoy City b (5)	MC 717 773-2150	Michael DiBaggio	David I Weisberg			Randall Kalce	John W Lewis	
Malvern b (3)	MC 215 644-2602	....	Patrick McGuigan	Mary A Morelli	Patrick McGuigan	Gerald R Vaughn	John C Rychlak Jr	Ira Dutter Jr
Manchester tp (8)	CM 717 764-4646	Tim L Horner	David A Raver		David A Raver	Richard R Shank	W Ronald Smeal	Larry E Gross
Manheim tp (29)	CM 717 569-6408	(not reporting)						
Manheim b (5)	CM 717 665-2463	Ralph B Martin	James W Williams			Rick Carpenter	John C Winters	Robert J Maul
Mansfield b (4)	CM 717 662-2315	(not reporting)						
Marcus Hook b (3)	MC 215 485-1341	James F Jackson	Bruce A Dorbian	Dolores Kowac		Lawrence Walgand	Theodore McGrath	Patsy Aulisa
Marietta b (3)	MC 717 426-4143	(not reporting)						
Marple tp (23)	MC 215 356-4040	(not reporting)						
Marysville b (2)	CM 717 957-3110	Russel L Sponsler	Larry N Wilfong	Anita E Wilfong	Larry N Wilfong	Kenneth B Seitz	Leonard Lotrick	
Masontown b (4)	MC 412 583-7731	(not reporting)						
McAdoo b (2)	MC 717 929-1182	(not reporting)						
McCandless t (29)	CM 412 364-0616	Robert J Powers	Tobias M Cordek		Edith M Liguori	Allen W Baldwin	Ralph J LeDonne	Mark E Sabina
McDonald b (2)	MC 412 926-8711	Lyman L Bellaire		Gloria J Stroop		Douglas Cooper	Mark E Dorsey	
Mc Kees Rocks b (8)	MC 412 331-2498	David Thomas	William C Beck	Charlotte Myers		Nicholas Radoycis	Robert Martineau	Richard Naughton
McKeesport (26)	MC 412 675-5050	Lou Washowich	James Humanic			Richard Dellepwna	Duane Senay	Darryl Segina
Mc Sherrystown b (3)	MC 717 637-1838	(not reporting)						
Meadville (14)	CM 814 724-6000	A Petruso	G Knowles	R Rushton	T Groves	L Hedrick	H Tubbs	J Chriest
Mechanicsburg b (9)	CM 717 691-3310	Harold V Hertzler	Scott R Eppley	Nancy C Hanlon			Rodney Whitcomb	
Media b (6)	MC 215 566-5210	Robert A McMahon	H G Grimditch		Francis Marabella	Edward Gibson	Martin Wusinich	
Mercer b (2)	MC 412 662-3980	(not reporting)						
Mercersburg b (2)	CM 717 328-3116	James W Smith	Judith R Chambers	Betty Ensminger			Larry Thomas	Leeroy Beck
Meyersdale b (3)	CM 814 634-5110	(not reporting)						
Middletown tp (43)	CM 215 943-0300	Raymond Mongillo	John Burke		Nancie Vaihinger	Lyle Winters	Frank McKenna	Joseph Giacomuzzi
Middletown tp (5)	CM 215 525-2700	Lawrence Hartley	W Bruce Clark		Celeste Dunion	John McKeown		Arthur Rothe
Middletown b (9)	CM 717 948-3051	Robert G Reid	Jack Hadge		James C Harper	Richard Leisey	George M Miller	
Midland b (3)	CM 412 643-4170	William F Shovlin	Daisy Vucinich	Erma Direnzo		Jack Balser	Morris Vaughn	Lewis Steele
Mifflinburg b (3)	CM 717 966-1013	Thomas Muchler	George Steese	Doris Guffey	Margaret Metzger		Douglas Lauver	
Millcreek tp (47)	MC 814 833-1111	(not reporting)						
Millersburg b (3)	MC 717 692-4713	Robert A Stoner	H Randall Dilling	Edra Carvell	Edra Carvell		H Randall Dilling	H Randall Dilling
Millersville b (8)	MC 717 872-4645	Joseph W Hipple	Michael H Morris		Michael H Morris	James D Eshleman	Richard L McCue	
Millvale b (4)	MC 412 821-2777	(not reporting)						
Milton b (7)	CM 717 742-8759	(not reporting)						
Minersville b (5)	MC 717 544-2149	(not reporting)						
Monaca b (7)	CM 412 774-9600	John A Antoline	Thomas A Stoner	Sandy Puhalla		Garry Venn	Lawrence Conti	Dennis Marinkovic
Monessen (10)	MC 412 684-9712	(not reporting)						
Monongahela (5)	MC 412 258-5500	John Moreschi		Carole Foglia		Chris Bartkus	David Jaynes	
Monroeville (29)	CM 412 856-1000	Thomas Schuerger	Mary Ann Nau	Dara Barnett	Susan E Weksman		Walter Luniewski	Eugene Mezeivtch
Montgomery tp (12)	CM 215 855-1771	(not reporting)						
Montgomery b (2)	CM 717 547-1671	George Smith	Fred Pfeiffer	Andrea Rowe			Terry Lynn	John Lynch
Montoursville b (5)	MC 717 368-2486	....	Eugene E Boyles	Claire Ann Sharp			Brian L Aldinger	Frank R Tallman
Moon tp (20)	CM 412 262-1700	(not reporting)						
Moosic b (5)	MC 717 457-5480	(not reporting)						
Morrisville b (10)	CM 215 295-8181	(not reporting)						
Mount Carmel b (7)	CM 717 339-4486	(not reporting)						
Mount Joy b (6)	CM 717 653-2300	H Staley Wills	Daniel Zimmerman		Jane Maxwell		John Sweigart	Amos Hershey
Mount Joy tp (..)	CM 717 367-8917	(not reporting)						
Mount Oliver b (4)	MC 412 431-8107	....	Joanne M Malloy		Walter P Herold	James Cassidy	John V Hindmarch	Donold Froehlich
Mount Penn b (3)	MC 215 779-5151	Regina Skrincosky	....			Barry Vogt	Clifford Barcliff	
Mount Pleasant b (5)	MC 412 547-6745	Gerald D Lucia				Gerald D Lucia	Gregory S Smolka	
Mount Union b (3)	MC 814 542-4051	(not reporting)						
Mt. Lebanon (33)	CM 412 343-3400	John Fernsler	Wilmer Baldwin		G David Egler	Steve Darcangelo	Frank Brown	James Harrod
Muncy b (3)	MC 717 546-3952	(not reporting)						
Munhall b (13)	MC 412 464-7310	(not reporting)						
Murrysville (17)	MC 412 327-2100	Dorothy Pack	James Morrison		Diane Hemming		Craig Thompson	Bruce Light
Myerstown b (3)	MC 717 866-5038	Glenn E Miller	Edward H Treat	John S Brown		Frederick L Shaak	Phillip W Stark	Randall L Brown
Nanticoke (12)	MC 717 735-2200	(not reporting)						
Nanty-Glo b (3)	MC 814 749-0331	Arthur C Price Sr	James P Bracken	Dorothy Kozlovac		Thomas Waltz	Ronald Brown	Gerald Lightcap
Narberth b (4)	CM 215 664-2840	Denise J Sharkey	William J Martin			John Thomas		
Nazareth b (6)	MC 215 759-0202	(not reporting)						
Nesquehoning b (3)	MC 717 669-6635	Isabel Zickler	Joseph G Greco Jr	Suzanne Nothstein		Michael Kravelk	Joseph Tout	
Nether Providence tp (13)	CO 215 566-4516	(not reporting)						
New Brighton b (7)	CM 412 846-1870	(not reporting)						
New Britain tp (9)	CM 215 822-1391	(not reporting)						
New Britain t (2)	CM 215 348-4586	Robert Snavely	John K Wolff	Robin E Trymbiski			David Sempowski	Edward Deschamps
New Castle (28)	MC 412 656-3500	R Christofer	Anthony Cialella	Elaine McEwing		Dean Boak	Lou Pisetelli	Frank Pipro
New Cumberland b (8)	CM 717 774-0404	Robert Henning	S C Sultzaberger			Walter Sral	Oren Kauffman	

**Directory 1/9
continued**

**MUNICIPAL OFFICIALS
IN U.S. CITIES OVER 2,500**

City, 1990 population figures (000 omitted), form of government	Municipal phone number	Mayor	Appointed administrator	City clerk	Finance officer	Fire chief	Police chief	Public works director
PENNSYLVANIA (555) continued								
New Eagle b (2)	MC 412 258-4477	(not reporting)						
New Hanover tp (6) ...	MC 215 323-1008	. . . .	Anita B Turner	Maria Hitchens	Janice Keyser	William C Moyer	Michael A Dykie	C Ray Batchelder
New Holland b (4)	CM 717 354-4567	W Frank Simmers	J Richard Fulcher	. . . .	. . . .	Larry Usner	Edward L Sprecher	Barry G Eitnier
New Hope b (1)	CM 215 862-3347	James Magill	. . . .	. . . .	. . . .	Thomas Markey	Robert Brobson	Russell Vender
New Kensington (16) ..	CO 412 337-4523	(not reporting)						
New Stanton b (2)	MC 412 925-9700	Dick W Rhea	. . . .	Faith Thomas	. . . .	Paul Todd	. . . .	Harry C Kauffman
New Wilmington b (3) .	MC 412 946-8167	(not reporting)						
Newtown tp (11)	CM 215 356-0200	(not reporting)						
Newtown b (3)	MC 215 968-2109	Harold A Smith	Frank B Fabian Jr	Lois B Saurman	. . . .	Dennis Forsyth	John H Feeney	. . . .
Norristown b (31)	MC 215 272-8080	W DeAngelis	Joseph Charlton	. . . .	Anthony Biondi	Jim Mullane	. . . .	Joseph Picard
North Braddock b (7) ..	CM 412 271-1306	George Choma	Edward Calabria	. . . .	. . . .	. . . .	Henry J Wiehagen	Frank Ruffalo
North Catasauqua b (3)	MC 215 264-1504	(not reporting)						
North Coventry tp (8) ..	MC 215 323-1694	William R Deegan	Robert Layman	. . . .	. . . .	Rich Beideman	Michael A Benyo	James R Batdorf
North East b (5)	MC 814 725-8611	(not reporting)						
North Huntingdon tp (28)	CM 412 863-3806	(not reporting)						
North Londonderry tp (6)	MC 717 838-1373	R Fouche	P Garber	. . . .	. . . .	. . . .	R Carpenter	. . . .
North Middleton tp (10)	MC 717 243-8550	(not reporting)						
North Strabane b (8) ..	CM 412 745-4880	Charlotte Courie	Frank R Siffrinn	Margaret Householder	. . . .	Gary Zimak	Dan Strimel	Walter Klamut
North Versailles tp (12)	MC 412 823-6602	(not reporting)						
North Wales b (4)	MC 215 699-4424	Frank Hartman	Susan Patton	Ann Marie Unger	. . . .	William Goltz	Kenneth C Veit	Thomas Costella
Northampton tp (35) ...	CM 215 357-6800	Pete Palestina	D Bruce Townsend	. . . .	Vicki Dworak	. . . .	William Feeney	Pasquale Giradi
Northampton b (9)	MC 215 262-2576	Robert Hantz	Gene Zarayko	. . . .	V Kostenbader	M Holtzman	R Fenstermacker	David Marsh
Northumberland b (4) ..	MC 717 473-3414	(not reporting)						
Norwood b (6)	MC 215 586-5800	(not reporting)						
O'Hara tp (9)	CM 412 782-1400	. . . .	Douglas Arndt	. . . .	Susan Hockenberry	. . . .	Raymond Schafer	Charles Clinton
Oakmont b (7)	CM 412 828-3232	(not reporting)						
Ohio tp (2)	CO 412 364-6321	. . . .	John L Sullivan	D Wintermantel	. . . .	. . . .	Scott Kording	Frank Chappel
Ohioville b (4)	MC 412 643-1920	Darryl R Michael	Thomas R Wamsley	. . . .	. . . .	Clarence R Dawson	Ronald H Lutton	. . . .
Oil City (12)	CM 814 678-3012	Barbara F Davison	Thomas Rockovich	. . . .	C Marshall	James Stack	Fredrick Weaver	James Hicks
Old Forge b (9)	MC 717 457-8852	(not reporting)						
Olyphant b (5)	MC 717 489-2135	Michael Chekansky	Michael Wargo Jr	Patricia Angradi	. . . .	Joseph Kranick	James F Foley	. . . .
Orwigsburg b (3)	MC 717 366-3103	(not reporting)						
Oxford b (4)	MC 215 932-2500	Glenn Elters	Jon Walker	Virginia Holt	. . . .	Jim Prettyman	Noel Roy	Tom Hindman
Palmerton b (5)	CM 215 826-2505	(not reporting)						
Palmyra b (7)	MC 717 838-6361	(not reporting)						
Parkesburg b (3)	MC 215 857-2616	(not reporting)						
Patton tp (10)	MC 814 234-0271	Philip Park	Thomas Kurtz	Connie Thomas	Cindy Rollins	. . . .	Gary Davenport	John Miknis
Pen Argyl b (3)	MC 215 863-4119	(not reporting)						
Penbrook b (3)	MC 717 232-3733	(not reporting)						
Penn b (12)	CM 717 632-7366	Frederick W Stine	Jeffrey R Garvick	Karen M Little	. . . .	Jan Cromer	Joseph H Maddox	. . . .
Penn Hills (51)	CM 412 798-2100	. . . .	Harry R McIndoe	Harry R McIndoe	Ed Schrecengost	. . . .	Kenneth Sechoka	Daniel Farabaugh
Penndel b (3)	MC 215 757-5152	(not reporting)						
Perkasie b (8)	MC 215 257-5065	Jay Godshall	Paul A Leonard	. . . .	. . . .	Eugene Hunsberger	Paul T Dickinson	Neil Fosbenner
Peters tp (14)	CM 412 941-4180	O Forrest Morgan	Michael Silvestri	. . . .	. . . .	Daniel Coyle	Harry Fruecht	Peter Overcashier
Philadelphia (1586)	MC 215 686-1776	Edward G Rendell	. . . .	. . . .	Ben Hallger	Harold B Hairston	Richard Neal	Kumar Kishinchand
Philipsburg b (3)	MC 814 342-3440	(not reporting)						
Phoenixville b (15)	CM 215 933-8801	Michael J Basca	William McCauley	. . . .	Steven Wiesner	. . . .	Louis Farnell	Norman Milnes
Pine tp (4)	CM 412 625-1591	John S Mayberry	Gary J Koehler	Joni L Preston	. . . .	Kenneth M Young	Rudolph A Vojtko	Jack C Fasick
Pitcairn b (4)	MC 412 372-6500	(not reporting)						
Pittsburgh (370)	MC 412 255-2100	(not reporting)						
Pittston (9)	CO 717 654-0513	Thomas A Walsh	Wilfrid E Toole	. . . .	. . . .	Lou Calabrese	Ed Doran	Don Cawley
Pleasant tp (3)	MC 814 723-5240	(not reporting)						
Pleasant Hills b (9)	MC 412 655-3300	(not reporting)						
Plum b (26)	CM 412 795-6800	Alfed J Franci	Martha L Perego	. . . .	. . . .	. . . .	Terry L Focareta	John E Walters
Plymouth tp (16)	CM 215 277-4100	Thomas J Speers	Joan M Mower	. . . .	Carol L Clopp	. . . .	Joseph R Cross	Timothy A Boyd
Plymouth b (7)	MC 717 779-1011	(not reporting)						
Port Allegany b (2)	CM 814 642-2526	(not reporting)						
Port Carbon b (2)	MC 717 622-2255	Francis Lubinsky	. . . .	Sandra Honse	. . . .	Scott Krater	. . . .	. . . .
Port Vue b (5)	MC 412 664-9323	(not reporting)						
Portage b (3)	MC 814 736-4330	Merle Thomas	Joyce French	. . . .	. . . .	. . . .	Donald Kehn	Raymond Bowman
Pottstown b (22)	CM 215 970-6500	Jim Smale	Thomas J Harwood	. . . .	Helene Foley	. . . .	Chris Carlile	Doug Yerger
Pottsville (17)	CO 717 622-1234	(not reporting)						
Prospect Park b (7) ...	MC 215 532-1007	(not reporting)						
Punxsutawney b (7) ...	CM 814 938-4480	(not reporting)						
Quakertown b (9)	CM 215 536-5001	Dennis Hallman	David Woglom	. . . .	. . . .	Ray Stever	James McFadden	Rick Hostvedt
Radnor tp (29)	CM 215 688-5600	Clinton Stuntbeck	Robert M Crofford	C R Clayton	David A Bashore	Joseph Maguire	Henry P Jansen	Daniel E Malloy
Rankin b (3)	MC 412 271-1027	(not reporting)						
Red Lion b (6)	CM 717 244-3475	(not reporting)						
Reynoldsville b (3)	MC 814 653-2110	(not reporting)						
Richland tp (..)	CM 215 536-4066	(not reporting)						
Richland tp (9)	MC 412 443-5921	(not reporting)						
Ridgway b (5)	CM 814 776-1125	(not reporting)						
Ridley tp (31)	CM 215 534-4800	. . . .	Anne E Howanski	. . . .	. . . .	. . . .	Richard Herrow	Louis Depietro
Ridley Park b (8)	MC 215 532-2100	(not reporting)						
Roaring Spring b (3) ...	MC 814 224-4814	Paul I Holsinger	Barbara Wagner	. . . .	. . . .	. . . .	Kenneth Bathurst	. . . .
Robinson tp (11)	CO 412 788-8120	William Blumling	Bernard Dudash	Mildred Cvengros	. . . .	. . . .	James Felt	. . . .
Rochester b (4)	MC 412 775-1200	(not reporting)						
Ross tp (33)	MC 412 931-7055	J Robert McAfee	Thomas D Lavorini	Linda Gillespie	Sarah A Scharding	Frank Stright	Carl M Zotter	Gary Gorajewski
Royersford b (4)	MC 215 948-3737	(not reporting)						
Salisbury tp (13)	CM 215 797-4000	Janet Keim	. . . .	. . . .	Janice Walz	Jack Kelly	Charles Durner	Ronald Gantert
Sayre b (6)	CM 717 888-7739	Nicholas Chacona	Richard J Biery	. . . .	. . . .	. . . .	. . . .	. . . .
Schuylkill Haven b (6) .	MC 717 385-2841	Paul Donmoyer	D Satterfield	. . . .	. . . .	. . . .	Thomas Smith	. . . .
Scott tp (17)	CO 412 276-5300	Gerald McNamara	Gary Williard	. . . .	. . . .	. . . .	Stanley Butkus	Lewis Dellano
Scottdale b (5)	CM 412 887-8220	Eugene J Beran	Barry D Whoric	. . . .	. . . .	Chuck Connors	Tony J Martin	. . . .
Scranton (82)	MC 717 348-4100	James P Connors	John Cawley	Frank Naughton	. . . .	Richard Pica	George Murphy	Joseph Loughney
Selinsgrove b (5)	CM 717 374-2311	Richard Norman	George Kinney	Ann Wochley	. . . .	. . . .	James Hartley	Gary Klingler
Sellersville b (4)	CM 215 257-5075	(not reporting)						
Sewickley b (4)	MC 412 741-4015	S D George	. . . .	. . . .	. . . .	George Edel	John Mook	Ray Wolfgang
Sewickley Heights b (1)	CM 412 741-5111	(not reporting)						
Shaler tp (31)	MC 412 486-9700	Joe Gally	Timothy J Rogers	. . . .	Judith Kording	. . . .	Leo T Kandzer	Wayne Shomaker
Shamokin (9)	MC 717 644-0876	Harvey M Boyer Sr	. . . .	William Strausser	. . . .	Charles Carpenter	William F Grow	Gerard W Waugh
Sharon (17)	MC 412 983-3220	Robert T Price	. . . .	Mary Beth Fragle	Gary M Gulla	Arthur Scarmack	David O Ryan	Gary R Douglas
Sharon Hill b (6)	MC 215 586-8200	Joseph Kelly	William Scott	. . . .	. . . .	William Scott	William Hanna	William Scott

Directory 1/9
continued

MUNICIPAL OFFICIALS
IN U.S. CITIES OVER 2,500

City, 1990 population figures (000 omitted), form of government	Municipal phone number	Mayor	Appointed administrator	City clerk	Finance officer	Fire chief	Police chief	Public works director
PENNSYLVANIA (555) continued								
Sharpsburg b (4)	MC 412 781-0546	(not reporting)						
Sharpsville b (5)	CM 412 962-7896	Louis Dejulia	Michael Wilson	. . . .	. . . .	. . . .	Willard Thompson	Dale Bocher
Shenandoah b (6)	MC 717 462-1918	(not reporting)						
Shillington b (5)	CM 215 777-1338	(not reporting)						
Shippensburg b (5)	CM 717 532-2147	(not reporting)						
Shrewsbury b (3)	MC 717 235-4371	(not reporting)						
Silver Spring tp (8) ...	MC 717 766-0178	Jan LeBlanc	John E Freilino	Karen S Dunlevy	. . . .	. . . .	John H Toomey	Harold Rudy
Sinking Spring b (2) ...	MC 215 678-4903	Clarence Noecker	Larry Meglathery	Elaine Lascomb	Ronald Dentzer	Richard Good	Joseph Orlando	. . . .
Slatington b (5)	CM 215 767-2131	Timothy I Kern	Stephen Sechriest	. . . .	. . . .	Ronald Hausman	Arthur Kistler	. . . .
Slippery Rock b (3) ...	MC 412 794-6391	(not reporting)						
Somerset b (6)	CM 814 443-2661	Terry Dwyer	Ben G Vinzani Jr	Mathilda Brown	. . . .	. . . .	Ronald Stern	Elwood Hutzel
Souderton b (6)	CM 215 723-4371	(not reporting)						
South Fayette tp (10) ..	MC 412 221-8700	Al Iagnemma	Richard Kasmer	Claudia Smelko	Marion Thomas	. . . .	Ted Villani	Steve Zeman
South Greensburg b (2)	MC 412 837-8858	James Ciarimboli	Lee Kunkle	. . . .	. . . .	Randy Jabara	Maurice Rabusseau	. . . .
South Hanover tp (5) ..	MC 717 566-0224	Robert E Cassel	Edna I Young	Kay F Stare	. . . .	. . . .	. . . .	. . . .
South Lebanon tp (7) ..	MC 717 274-0481	(not reporting)						
South Park tp (14)	CM 412 831-7000	(not reporting)						
South Strabane tp (8) .	MC 412 225-1786	William H Orndoff	John J Stickle	. . . .	. . . .	. . . .	Donald M Zofchak	D Reed Mankey
South Whitehall tp (18)	CO 215 398-0401	Martha P Nolan	Gerald J Gasda	. . . .	Ronnie J Rice	. . . .	D Mac Connell	Ralph H Kocher
South Williamsport b (6)	CM 717 322-0158	(not reporting)						
Southmont b (2)	MC 814 255-3104	(not reporting)						
Southwest Greensburg b (2)	MC 412 834-0360	(not reporting)						
Spring tp (19)	MC 215 678-5393	(not reporting)						
Spring City b (3)	CM 215 948-3660	Harold Keppen	D Rittenhouse	. . . .	. . . .	. . . .	Clarence Collopy	. . . .
Spring Garden tp (11) .	CM 717 848-2858	Joseph Bath	William Conn	Glenda Alwine	. . . .	Joseph Barron	Spurgeon Lehman	Edward Salabsky
Springdale b (4)	MC 412 274-8366	(not reporting)						
Springettsbury tp (22) .	CM 717 757-3521	. . . .	Samuel J Lynch Jr	. . . .	Samuel J Lynch Jr	Glenn O Kline	Harold D Kessler	Charles H Lauer
Springfield tp (24)	CM 215 544-1300	(not reporting)						
Springfield tp (20)	CM 215 836-7600	Joseph Gerber	Donald Berger	Carol Holcomb	. . . .	Earl Hopkins	John Connor	John Connor
St. Clair b (4)	MC 717 429-0640	Richard Tomko	. . . .	Roland Price	. . . .	Robert Shellhamer	Robert Wapinski	. . . .
St. Marys b (6)	CM 814 781-1718	(not reporting)						
State College b (39) ...	CM 814 234-7100	Arnold Addison	Peter S Marshall	Barbara J Natalie	Michael S Groff	. . . .	Thomas R King	Lee L Lowry
Steelton b (5)	MC 717 939-9842	Michael L Rozman	Michael G Musser	Jill Perez	Michael G Musser	David Hughes	Kenneth J Tindal	Joseph Conjar
Stowe tp (8)	CO 412 331-4050	(not reporting)						
Stroudsburg b (5)	CM 717 421-5444	. . . .	Pamela S Caskie	. . . .	. . . .	Clement Kochanski	Kevin M Kelly	. . . .
Sugar Creek b (6)	CM 814 432-4717	(not reporting)						
Summit Hill b (3)	MC 717 645-2305	(not reporting)						
Sunbury (12)	CO 717 286-7820	(not reporting)						
Susquehanna tp (19) ..	MC 717 545-4751	(not reporting)						
Swarthmore b (6)	MC 215 543-4599	G Guy Smith	Jane C Billings	. . . .	David Bowler	Chris Hansen	Donald H Lee	Charles Rowles
Swatara tp (20)	MC 717 564-2551	Anthony Spagnolo	James Brokenshire	. . . .	. . . .	George Bittinger	Ronald Mellott	Harlow Emerick
Swissvale b (11)	MC 412 271-7101	(not reporting)						
Swoyersville b (6)	MC 717 288-6581	Vincent T Dennis	Eugene Breznay	Shirley Gavlick	Eugene Breznay	. . . .	John Shemo	Edward Volack
Tamaqua b (8)	CM 717 668-0300	Jerome P Knowles	Donald Matalavage	Joan D Snyder	. . . .	Arthur Connely Jr	Donald Gerber	Robert Delay
Tarentum b (6)	MC 412 224-1818	James Wolfe	Joe Dicaro	. . . .	. . . .	. . . .	Frank Prazenica	David Hilliard
Taylor b (7)	MC 717 562-1400	(not reporting)						
Telford b (4)	CM 215 723-5000	Jay R Stover	Charles Feindler	Charles Feindler	Erma Slemmer	Joseph Rausch	Douglas E Bickel	Donald F Beck
Throop b (4)	MC 717 489-8311	(not reporting)						
Titusville (6)	CM 814 827-9651	(not reporting)						
Tobyhanna (4)	CM 717 646-1212	Alfred A Kerrick	Richard Manfredi	. . . .	. . . .	John E Kerrick	Henry E Bockelman	. . . .
Towamencin tp (14) ...	CM 215 368-7602	Robert N Rau Jr	John A Granger	Helen L Riccardi	Beth F Diprete	Chris Bohmueller	Joseph Kirschner	John Reinhart
Towanda b (3)	CM 717 265-2696	(not reporting)						
Trafford b (3)	MC 412 372-6559	(not reporting)						
Tredyffrin tp (28)	CM 215 644-1400	Stephen Aichele	Joseph Janasik	Joan Woods	Harry D Marrone	. . . .	Paul Pennypacker	Frank Kelley
Troy b (1)	CM 717 297-2966	(not reporting)						
Turtle Creek b (7)	MC 412 824-2500	(not reporting)						
Tyrone b (6)	CM 814 684-1330	(not reporting)						
Union tp (3)	MC 717 935-2890	(not reporting)						
Union City b (4)	CM 814 438-2331	George Ainsworth	Cheryl R Capela	. . . .	Louie Johnson	Edward Eastman	Marvin Tubbs	Jeanne Vallimont
Uniontown (12)	MC 412 430-2900	Charles Macheskey	. . . .	Grace Giachetti	Odilia A John	William Sneddon	Ronald Macheskey	Charles A Ellis
Upland b (3)	MC 215 874-7317	(not reporting)						
Upper Allen tp (13)	CM 717 766-0756	Ray Trimmer	Robert Sabatini	. . . .	. . . .	Karl Kunkle	Richard Hammon	George Anderson
Upper Chichester tp (..)	MC 215 855-5881	(not reporting)						
Upper Darby tp (81) ...	MC 215 352-4100	Margaret Murcoch	F Raymond Shay	Anthony L Milone	James D Smith	Edward A Cubler	Anthony Celia	Joseph W Vasturia
Upper Dublin tp (24) ..	CM 215 643-1600	(not reporting)						
Upper Gwynedd tp (12)	MC 215 699-7777	James A Santi	Leonard T Perrone	. . . .	. . . .	R Kenneth Nolan	Wayne A Cassel	Willard W Troxel
Upper Merion tp (26) ..	CM 215 265-2600	Edward J Wilkes	Ronald Wagenmann	. . . .	Kenneth Pennoyer	. . . .	Clement G Reedel	Roman M Pronczak
Upper Moreland tp (25)	CM 215 659-3100	Brian L Mook	. . . .	. . . .	Patricia Burns	Thomas M Sullivan	Edward O Stauch	Jack Snyder
Upper Providence tp (10)	CM 215 933-9179	(not reporting)						
Upper Providence tp (10)	CM 215 565-4944	N Lippincott	Elizabeth Crane	C Tatasciore	Maxine Burkholder	. . . .	Thomas Davis	. . . .
Upper Saucon tp (10) ..	CM 215 282-1171	Philip Spaeth	Bernard A Rodgers	. . . .	. . . .	Glen Scholl	Robert Coyle	. . . .
Upper Southampton tp (16)	MC 215 322-9700	Franz Kautz	Paul G Janssen Jr	. . . .	Awoop Tolant	. . . .	David Schultz	Wayne Crompton
Upper St. Clair tp (20) .	CM 412 831-9000	(not reporting)						
Upper Yoder tp (5)	CM 814 255-5243	. . . .	Robert Amistadi	. . . .	. . . .	. . . .	Theodore Clites	. . . .
Uwchlan tp (13)	MC 215 363-9450	John J Pribanic	Douglass D Hanley	Lorna Minahan	. . . .	Richard Ruth	George Harmansky	Martin Sorensen
Vandergrift b (6)	CM 412 567-7818	(not reporting)						
Verona b (3)	MC 412 828-8080	(not reporting)						
Warminster tp (33)	MC 215 443-5414	(not reporting)						
Warren b (11)	CM 814 723-6300	(not reporting)						
Warrington tp (12)	CM 215 822-1318	(not reporting)						
Warwick tp (12)	CM 717 626-8900	Michael Brubaker	Robert C Smith	Barbara J Kreider	Robert C Smith	. . . .	Alfred O Olsen	Karl J Schmidt
Washington (16)	MC 412 223-4200	Francis L King	. . . .	Cathy B Voytek	Susanne E Gomez	John A Manning	Ronald Rossi	Robert Nicolella
Watsontown b (2)	MC 717 538-1000	(not reporting)						
Waynesboro b (10)	CM 717 762-2101	Louis M Barlup	Lloyd R Hamberger	Sonia Medevich	. . . .	Donald Ringer	Glenn Phenicie	Paul Doub
Waynesburg b (4)	MC 412 627-8111	Charles Berryhill	. . . .	Bonnie L Baily	Cynthia S Varner	Larry Marshall	Timothy Hawfield	. . . .
Weatherly b (3)	MC 717 427-8640	(not reporting)						
Wellsboro b (3)	CM 717 724-3186	(not reporting)						
Wesleyville b (4)	MC 814 899-9124	E Paul Johnson	Cindy Smith	Pat Jerioski	. . . .	Bryan Sanderson	Leonard Sallot	. . . .
West Bradford tp (10) .	CM 215 269-4174	Mark Blair	Jack M Hines Jr	. . . .	. . . .	John Carbo	. . . .	. . . .
West Caln tp (6)	CM 215 384-5643	(not reporting)						
West Chester b (18) ...	CM 215 692-7574	(not reporting)						
West Goshen tp (18) ..	CM 215 696-5266	. . . .	Patricia Guernsey	L Joan Rivell	. . . .	. . . .	Michael Carroll	. . . .
West Hazleton b (4) ...	MC 717 455-3694	(not reporting)						

Directory 1/9 **MUNICIPAL OFFICIALS**
continued **IN U.S. CITIES OVER 2,500**

City, 1990 population figures (000 omitted), form of government	Municipal phone number	Mayor	Appointed administrator	City clerk	Finance officer	Fire chief	Police chief	Public works director
PENNSYLVANIA (555) continued								
West Homestead b (2) .	MC 412 461-1844	(not reporting)						
West Manchester tp (14)	CM 717 792-3505	Bradley C Jacobs	Jan R Dell	. . . .	Betty L Keller	John J Bierling	Robert D March	Bill Bollinger
West Mifflin b (24)	CM 412 461-4469	Robert L Hess	Paul W Amic	. . . .	Paul W Amic		Frank Defazio	Donald Finney
West Newton b (3)	MC 412 872-6860	(not reporting)						
West Norriton tp (15) ..	CO 215 631-0450	(not reporting)						
West Pittston b (6)	MC 717 654-6567	Merle Bainbridge	. . . .	. . . .	. . . .	John Janczewski	Richard Simonson	Robert Dovin
West Pottsgrove b (4) .	MC 215 323-7717	(not reporting)						
West Reading b (4)	CM 215 374-8273	(not reporting)						
West View b (8)	MC 412 931-2800	(not reporting)						
West Whiteland tp (12)	CM 215 363-9525	David Bortner	Patricia Refford	C McKenney	. . . .	David Jones	Robert Bitter	Joseph Roscioli
West Wyoming b (3) ..	MC 717 693-1311	(not reporting)						
West York b (4)	MC 717 846-8889	(not reporting)						
Westmont b (6)	MC 814 255-3865	(not reporting)						
White Oak b (9)	CM 412 672-9727	Robert Massie	Paul L Kreckel	. . . .	. . . .	. . . .	John Salopek	. . . .
Whitehall b (14)	MC 412 884-0505	(not reporting)						
Whitehall tp (23)	MC 215 437-5524	(not reporting)						
Whitemarsh tp (15) ...	CM 215 825-3535	John P McCarthy	Lawrence J Gregan	. . . .	Thomas Mullin	Calvin Bonenberge	Richard A Zolko	. . . .
Whitpain tp (16)	CM 215 277-2400	(not reporting)						
Wilkes-Barre (48)	MC 717 826-8222	Lee Namey	Richard Muessig	Bill Brace	John Rollman	George Soltis	Joseph Coyne	Al Clocker
Wilkins tp (8)	CM 412 824-6650	(not reporting)						
Wilkinsburg b (21)	CM 412 244-2900	(not reporting)						
Williamsport (32)	MC 717 327-7500	Phillip Preziosi	. . . .	Diane Ellis	James Crossley	Randy Goodbrod	Anthony Evans	John Grado
Willistown tp (9)	CM 215 647-5300	D Mancini	W Rosenberry	. . . .	. . . .	. . . .	Charles O Bennett	John Dimascio
Wilson b (8)	MC 215 258-6142	(not reporting)						
Wind Gap b (3)	MC 215 863-7288	(not reporting)						
Windber b (5)	CM 814 467-9014	(not reporting)						
Windsor b (2)	CM 717 244-3512	H B Sprenkle	Marlene Workinger	Jennifer Gunnet	. . . .	. . . .	Earle K Shenk	Larry Keller
Wormleysburg b (3) ...	MC 717 763-4483	George Sellers	Gary Berresford	Barbara Harlacher	. . . .	Ronald Frank	Russell Lukens	Robert Chiolo
Wyoming b (3)	MC 717 693-0291	(not reporting)						
Wyomissing b (7)	CM 215 376-7481	(not reporting)						
Yardley b (2)	MC 215 493-6832	(not reporting)						
Yeadon b (12)	MC 215 284-1606	(not reporting)						
York (42)	MC 717 849-2301	William J Althaus	Bernard L Frick	Miriam Neff	Joseph A Robinson	George E Kroll	William E Smith	Charles E Strehl
York tp (19)	MC 717 741-3861	(not reporting)						
Youngsville b (2)	CM 814 563-4604	Robert P Williams	William L Slocum	Alice Harlan	William L Slocum	Kenneth Roberts	. . . .	Martin Filla
Youngwood b (3)	MC 412 925-3660	(not reporting)						
Zelienople b (4)	MC 412 452-6610	(not reporting)						
RHODE ISLAND (39)								
Barrington t (16)	CM 401 247-1900	. . . .	Dennis M Phelan	Lorraine A Derois	David B Okun	Edward Carey	Charles Brule	Peter DeAngelis
Bristol t (22)	TM 401 253-7000	. . . .	Halsey Herreshoff	Diane C Mederos	. . . .	David Sylvaria	Thomas Moffatt	Paul E Romano
Burrillville t (16)	CM 401 568-4300	Leo Lafreniere	Thomas Bercher	Robert E Potter	John P Mainville	. . . .	Wallace F Lees	R St Sauveur
Central Falls (18)	MC 401 724-4500	(not reporting)						
Charlestown t (6)	CM 401 364-1235	. . . .	George C Hibbard	Marcia D Carsten	. . . .	. . . .	Michael T Brady	Alan A Arsenault
Coventry t (31)	CM 401 822-9100	James Kiley	Francis Frobel	Roberta Johnson	Barry Yeaw	. . . .	Roger Laliberte	Sheila Patnode
Cranston (76)	MC 401 461-1000	(not reporting)						
Cumberland t (29)	MC 401 728-2400	(not reporting)						
East Greenwich t (12)	CM 401 886-8665	Judith H Bailey	William Sequino	Avis B Gardiner	David P Faucher	Kenneth Ross Jr	Lawrence Campion	John K Cook
East Providence (50) ..	CM 401 434-3311	Roland Grant	Paul B Lemont	Valerie Perry	James McDonald	Ken Marcotrigiano	Carl Winquist	Julie Forgue
Exeter t (5)	RT 401 294-3891	William Devanney	. . . .	Cheryl Chorney	. . . .	. . . .	. . . .	Harold Gifford
Foster t (4)	RT 401 392-9200	Marjorie Borders	. . . .	Maureen Comerford	. . . .	. . . .	Donald Kettelle	Walter May
Glocester t (9)	MC 401 568-6206	Patricia Hayward	. . . .	Barbara Robertson	John Driscoll	. . . .	Joseph Green	Paul Bilsky
Hopkinton t (7)	TM 401 377-2220	Linda Perra	. . . .	Jenarita Aldrich	Bailey Blanchette	. . . .	George Weeden	Charles Niles
Jamestown t (5)	CM 401 423-0444	Fred Pease	Frances H Shocket	Theresa Donovan	Maryanne Crawford	Joseph Texeria	Thomas Tighe	Steven Goslee
Johnston t (27)	MC 401 351-6618	Ralph Arusso	. . . .	Anthony Querceto	Dennis Quaranta	Alan Zambarano	William P Tocco	Ralph Arusso
Lincoln t (18)	MC 401 333-1100	Burton Stallwood	. . . .	Sue Sheppard	Claudette Paine	. . . .	William P Strain	Robert Schultz
Little Compton t (3) ...	MC 401 635-4658	(not reporting)						
Middletown t (19)	CM 401 849-2898	(not reporting)						
Narragansett t (15) ...	CM 401 789-1044	(not reporting)						
New Shoreham t (1) ...	CM 401 466-3200	Edward McGovern	David C Holt	Susan Shea	Mary Jane Balser	R Batchelder	William McCombe	. . . .
Newport (28)	CM 401 846-9600	Robert McKenna	Francis Edwards	Jane McManus	Joel Johnson	Garrett Sullivan	Steven Weaver	Susan Cooper
North Kingstown t (24)	CM 401 294-3331	(not reporting)						
North Providence t (32)	MC 401 232-0900	(not reporting)						
North Smithfield t (10) .	MC 401 767-2202	(not reporting)						
Pawtucket (73)	MC 401 728-0500	Robert E Metivier	William Noonan	Richard Goldstein	John Rahill	Joseph Burns	Richard DeLyon	F Ihenacho
Portsmouth t (17)	MC 401 683-2101	. . . .	Robert G Driscoll	Carol Zinno	Donna A Barker	Ronald L Chace	Madison A Bailey	Neil St Laurent
Providence (161)	MC 401 421-7740	(not reporting)						
Richmond t (5)	RT 401 539-2497	(not reporting)						
Scituate t (10)	MC 401 647-2822	(not reporting)						
Smithfield t (19)	MC 401 233-1012	(not reporting)						
South Kingstown t (25)	CM 401 789-9331	. . . .	Stephen Alfred	Dale Holberton	Alan Lord	. . . .	Vincent Vespia	Alfred Curnow
Tiverton t (14)	TM 401 625-5323	(not reporting)						
Warren t (11)	TM 401 245-7340	(not reporting)						
Warwick (85)	MC 401 738-2000	Lincoln Chafee	Burke Sarno	Marie Bennett	Peder Schaefer	George Noble	Wesley Blanchard	Charles Sheahan
West Greenwich t (3) ..	TM 401 397-5016	Kevin A Breene	. . . .	Janet E Olsson	. . . .	. . . .	Robert J Andrews	David P Andrews
West Warwick t (29) ..	TM 401 822-9219	Kathryn O'Hare	Don Centracchio	Frank Conti	Rosemarie Davis	Don Centracchio	Cyrille Cote	James Andruchow
Westerly t (22)	CM 401 596-0341	(not reporting)						
Woonsocket (44)	MC 401 762-6400	Francis L Lanctot	Vincent P Ward	Pauline S Payeur	John P Kuzmiski	Henry A Renaud	Rodney C Remblad	Ilidio Azinheira
SOUTH CAROLINA (94)								
Abbeville (6)	CM 803 459-5017	(not reporting)						
Aiken (20)	CM 803 642-7654	Fred Cavanaugh	Steven Thompson	Sara Ridout	Anita Lilly	. . . .	James C Busbee	Roger Leduc
Allendale t (4)	MC 803 584-4619	William Holmes	Wilbur Cave	. . . .	Dwight Williams	Marshall Lawson	James Grant	. . . .
Anderson (26)	CM 803 231-2200	(not reporting)						
Andrews t (3)	MC 803 264-8666	(not reporting)						
Bamberg t (3)	MC 803 245-5128	(not reporting)						
Barnwell (5)	MC 803 259-3266	(not reporting)						
Batesburg t (4)	MC 803 532-9231	(not reporting)						
Beaufort (10)	CM 803 525-7241	David M Taub	Gary M Cannon	Beverly W Gay	Ross A Jones	Wendell D Wilburn	William R Neill	Clayton H Cooler
Belton (5)	MC 803 338-7773	(not reporting)						
Bennettsville (9)	CM 803 479-9001	(not reporting)						
Bishopville t (4)	MC 803 484-9418	(not reporting)						
Blackville t (3)	MC 803 284-2444	(not reporting)						

City, 1990 population figures (000 omitted), form of government	Municipal phone number	Mayor	Appointed administrator	City clerk	Finance officer	Fire chief	Police chief	Public works director
SOUTH CAROLINA (94) continued								
Camden (7)	CM 803 432-2421	Philip Minges	Gilbert F Broom	Monica Sheorn	Phillip W Jackson	Robert Parnell	Jack Cobb	James K Parnelle
Cayce (11)	MC 803 796-9020	(not reporting)						
Charleston (80)	MC 803 577-6970	Joseph P Riley Jr	....	Mary Wrixon	James Etheredge	Russell Thomas Jr	Reuben Greenberg	Douglas Smits
Cheraw t (6)	MC 803 537-8400	C H McBride	J William Taylor	Helen Funderburk	....	Donald Baker	Harry Drakeford	Tommy Lewis Jr
Chester (7)	CM 803 581-2123	(not reporting)						
Clemson (11)	MC 803 653-2030	(not reporting)						
Clinton (8)	CM 803 833-7505	H Francis Blalock	Steven L Harrell	Barbara Haggray	....	Troy N Bentley	C L Richards	C Litchfield
Clover t (3)	MC 802 222-9495	John M Smith	....	Betty R Ferguson	....	Mack E McCarter	David P Milligan	Mack E McCarter
Columbia (98)	CM 803 733-8268	Robert Coble	Miles B Hadley	Zenda Leaks	Susan Busbice	John D Jansen	Charles P Austin	Mark McCain
Conway (10)	MC 803 248-7351	Ike G Long Jr	Stephen J Sobers	Carolyn C Stevens	J Larry Lewis	Tony Hendrick	Larry Barnhill	Freddie Dubose
Darlington (7)	MC 803 393-5838	(not reporting)						
Denmark t (4)	MC 803 793-3734	(not reporting)						
Dillon (7)	CM 803 774-0040	Howard T Cutler	....	....	Rebecca D Coleman	Billy W Caines	....	Troy Price
Easley (15)	MC 803 859-3890	(not reporting)						
Edgefield t (3)	MC 803 637-3935	(not reporting)						
Florence (30)	CM 803 665-3158	Haigh Porter	Thomas W Edwards	....	David Williams	Gerald Welch	Waymon Mumford	Robert C Holland
Folly Beach (1)	MC 803 588-2447	(not reporting)						
Forest Acres (7)	MC 803 782-9475	(not reporting)						
Fort Mill t (5)	MC 803 547-2034	Charles Powers	Sanford W Griffin	Sherry Stegall	Libby Gibson	....	Robert Kimbrell	Waddell Gibson
Fountain Inn t (4)	MC 803 862-4221	(not reporting)						
Gaffney (13)	MC 803 487-8505	Vernon L Sanders	John C McDonough	....	....	Don Parris	Jimmy Scates	....
Georgetown (10)	MC 803 546-2556	Thomas J Rubillo	J M Sizemore	Joseph C Steen	R Cobb Bell	Kenneth E Gaiser	Roger C Haddix	Elder B Holmes
Goose Creek (25)	MC 803 797-6220	Michael Heitzler	Dennis C Harmon	Sherry Ferguson	L Lee Moulder	Barfield Holland	Harvey Becker	Johnny Askins
Great Falls t (2)	MC 803 482-2055	James R Baker	....	Rose B Alexander	....	James T Evans	John Brown Sr	....
Greenville (58)	CM 803 240-4530	(not reporting)						
Greenwood (21)	CM 803 942-8400	John T Nave	Steven J Brown	Mary E Edwards	....	Harold G Hinton	Gerald L Brooks	Danny Polatty
Greer (10)	CM 803 877-9061	(not reporting)						
Hampton t (3)	MC 803 943-2951	(not reporting)						
Hanahan (13)	MC 803 554-4221	Larry Cobb	Fenton Miller Jr	Deborah E Lewis	Berlino D Veloso	David B Peterson	Melvin C Bellew	Jerry W Stegall
Hardeeville t (..)	MC 803 784-2231	Thornton A Butler	Julian L Jackson	Jeanie P Bennett	Jeanie P Bennett	Donald L Hubbard	R J Fialskowski	Stephen W Murdock
Hartsville (8)	CM 803 383-3015	Flora C Hopkins	William F Bruton	Sherron L Skipper	Pam P Sansbury	Tommy Livingston	R Terry Swett	Mike A Welch
Hemingway t (1)	MC 803 558-2824	Jeffrey Lawrimore	....	Brenda Barnhill	....	George Sutton	R Carmichael	Kenneth Laster
Hilton Head Island t (24)	CM 803 681-9440	Harvey Ewing	Mike O'Neill	Sandy Santaniello	Shirley Freeman	David Mac Lellan	....	....
Honea Path t (4)	CM 803 369-2466	(not reporting)						
Irmo t (11)	CM 803 781-7050	John Gibbons	P McMahon	Terri Saxon	P McMahon	....	Everett Howard	....
Isle Of Palms (4)	MC 803 886-6428	Carmen R Bunch	Mark M Williams	Nellie McDuffie	....	....	James B Arnold	Andrew J Parrish
Johnston t (3)	MC 803 275-2488	F Charles Lucas	Bernard Welborn	Frances Quarles	....	Howard Wates	Lelex Easler	Joe Easler
Kershaw t (2)	MC 803 475-6065	Bill Clyburn	....	Phyllis Dorman	....	Mike Gardner	Emerson Coates	C Todd Knight
Kingstree t (4)	MC 803 354-7484	(not reporting)						
Lake City (7)	MC 803 394-5421	William J Sebnick	Adalia A Sova	Cherline L Miles	Ann H Locke	Walter L Moody	Michael Brumbles	Donald M Parrott
Lancaster (9)	MC 803 283-8426	Joe Shaw	Paul Paskoff	....	....	Dennis Cole	William Sumner	Charles Pardue
Laurens (10)	MC 803 984-0144	Bob Dominick	Julie Thomas	Patricia Beeks	....	Bootsie Cox	Joseph Floyd	Oscar Tribble
Liberty t (3)	MC 803 843-6011	Marvin Kelley	....	Elizabeth Roper	....	Pat Turner	Robert Moore	Robert Chappell
Manning (4)	MC 803 435-8477	(not reporting)						
Marion t (8)	MC 803 423-5962	(not reporting)						
Mauldin (12)	MC 803 288-4910	L S Green	David Bates	Blanche Dayberry	....	James Moore	Harold Sherbert	....
Mc Coll t (3)	MC 803 523-5341	(not reporting)						
Moncks Corner t (6)	MC 803 761-6650	John S West	Marion T Graham	Marilyn Baker	....	....	Gregory Hoover	....
Mount Pleasant t (30)	MC 803 884-8517	C Woods Flowers	R Mac Burdette	Carol Hunter	Jan Bunton	Frederick Tetor	Thomas Sexton	Furman Reynolds
Mullins t (6)	MC 803 464-9583	(not reporting)						
Myrtle Beach (25)	CM 803 626-7645	Robert M Grissom	Thomas E Leath	Joan Grove	Maria E Baisden	Lynwood O Womack	Samuel H Killman	Larry S Kerr
Newberry (11)	CM 803 276-4193	T E Kyzer	W A Harvey	Tina P Wicker	....	L E Lee	L J Swindler	A D Hiller
North Augusta (15)	MC 803 279-0333	Thomas W Greene	Charles B Martin	Leona J Lewis	John P Potter	....	Walter E Newman	Gary D Dernlan
North Charleston (70)	MC 803 554-5700	W Robert Kinard	Louise K Miller	Amelia Greer	Harley Henderson	Alvar Rissanen	Michael Whatley	Gregg S Varner
North Myrtle Beach (9)	MC 803 280-5555	Philip Tilghman	William Moss	Beverly Franz	Randy Wright	....	Johnny Causey	Jerry Pierce
Orangeburg (14)	CM 803 533-6000	Martin C Cheatham	John H Yow	Sharon G Fanning	Sharon G Fanning	....	....	B Reese Earley
Pageland t (3)	MC 803 672-7292	James L Kirk	Robert C Kimrey	Virginia Outen	....	Bruce E Rivers	Johnny Sowell	Ronny Cato
Pendleton t (3)	MC 803 646-3622	H B Durham	....	Joyce Elrod	....	David Crenshaw	James Cleveland	Richard Bork
Pickens t (3)	MC 803 878-6421	(not reporting)						
Port Royal t (3)	MC 803 524-5125	(not reporting)						
Ridgeland t (1)	MC 803 726-3351	Joseph N Malphrus	Carl F Lehmann	Penelope B Daley	Sharon W Boyles	Thomas Jenkins	Harry D Dibiase	....
Rock Hill (42)	CM 803 329-7000	Elizabeth Rhea	Russell Allen	....	Gerry Schapiro	Dickie Hoffman	Clyde Long	Nick Stegall
Saluda t (3)	MC 803 445-3522	(not reporting)						
Seneca t (8)	MC 803 885-2700	Devoe Blackston	Tommy Grant	Walter Smith	Walter Smith	Richard Timms	Theodore Davis	Benny Burrell
Simpsonville t (12)	MC 803 963-3461	(not reporting)						
Spartanburg (43)	CM 803 596-2000	James E Talley	Wayne Bowers	Mandy Merck	L Gray Brewton	Thomas Ivey	W C Bain Jr	Michael Garrett
Springdale t (3)	CM 803 794-0408	(not reporting)						
Summerville t (23)	MC 803 871-6000	Berlin G Myers	....	Gracie L Smith	....	Richard G Waring	Ray Nash	James H Avant
Sumter (42)	CM 803 773-3371	Stephen M Creech	Talmadge Tobias	Sherry Evans	Julia Muldrow	Eli Parnell	Harold Johnson	Ed Davis
Surfside Beach t (4)	MC 803 238-2590	Dick M Johnson	H Neil Ferguson	Elaine K Cowart	Sharon Cashion	Dan Thomas	John M Lloyd	Ron E Peaks
Travelers Rest (3)	CM 803 834-8740	(not reporting)						
Union (10)	MC 803 429-1700	....	Charles Potts	Patricia Hicks	Walker Gallman	Phillip Moore	Russell Roark	Albert Dill
Walhalla t (4)	MC 803 638-2529	J Stoudemire	....	V Satterfield	....	J McMahan	B Albertson	G Milam
Walterboro (5)	CM 803 549-2545	W Harry Cone	Chriswell Bickley	Augustine Brown	Brenda Colson	Ashton Syfrett	Thomas McJunkin	Charlie Chewning
West Columbia (11)	MC 803 791-1880	(not reporting)						
Westminster t (3)	MC 803 647-5071	Ted N Phillips	....	....	Dorothy L Bibb	Bobby Williams	....	Gary G Cobb
Williamston t (4)	MC 803 847-7473	(not reporting)						
Williston t (3)	MC 803 266-7015	Thomas B Brady	....	Nell Nix	Nell Nix	Calvin Melton	Roger W Kaney	Robert Augustine
Winnsboro t (3)	CM 803 635-4943	(not reporting)						
Woodruff (4)	CM 803 476-8154	Guy S Blakely Sr	....	Beverley Maddox	....	T Westmoreland	Ralph Alverson	Gerald Bailey
York (7)	CM 803 684-2341	W Rodney Connolly	Karen S Carter	Nelle J Helms	....	Domenico M Manera	C David Morton	Charles G Helms
SOUTH DAKOTA (24)								
Aberdeen (25)	CO 605 622-7000	(not reporting)						
Belle Fourche (4)	MC 605 892-2494	Willard Pummel	....	....	William S Noziska	Curtis Gillette	....	Chuck Snoozy
Box Elder (3)	MC 605 923-1403	Glenn R Baldwin	....	....	Kevin J Dukart	Thomas Baumker	Robert W Sanders	Vincent Finkhouse
Brandon (4)	MC 605 582-6515	D Kleinvachter	D Olson	E Henriksen	....	A Rothenbuehler	Phil Youngdale	Leo Narum
Brookings (16)	CO 605 692-6281	Wayne A Hauschild	....	....	Theodore Kryger	Curtis Jensen	Dennis Falken	Andy Jensen
Canton (3)	CO 605 987-2881	David Gard	....	Karen Leffler	Daniel Amert	Norris Ekle	Dennis Johnson	Palmer Erickson
Hot Springs (4)	MC 605 745-3135	(not reporting)						
Huron (12)	CO 605 352-6791	(not reporting)						
Lead (4)	CO 605 584-1401	Dennis J York	....	....	Harley Lux	Dave Tesch	Steve Palmer	Clifford Rook
Madison (6)	CO 605 256-4586	Gene Borchardt	....	....	Jeff Heinemeyer	Dan Millard	Gary Gile	....

Directory 1/9
continued

**MUNICIPAL OFFICIALS
IN U.S. CITIES OVER 2,500**

City, 1990 population figures (000 omitted), form of government	Municipal phone number	Mayor	Appointed administrator	City clerk	Finance officer	Fire chief	Police chief	Public works director
SOUTH DAKOTA (24) continued								
Milbank (4)	MC 605 432-9575	Rudolph A Nef	Craig Wellnitz	Cynthia Schultz	Craig Wellnitz	Gene Johnsen	Robert Eide	Dave Zinter
Mitchell (14)	MC 605 996-6452	Leonard Williams	. . . .	. . . .	Michele Franey	Robert Miller	Douglas Kirkus	Tim McGannon
Mobridge (4)	MC 605 845-3509	(not reporting)						
Pierre (13)	CO 605 224-5921	Gary L Drewes	Kenneth L Hericks	. . . .	Kenneth L Hericks	Stan Mikkonen	Bill Abernathy	David Padgett
Rapid City (55)	MC 605 394-4136	Ed McLaughlin	. . . .	. . . .	Richard Wahlstrom	Owen Hibbard	Thomas Hennies	
Redfield (3)	MC 605 472-0660	Duane Sanger	. . . .	. . . .	Sharon Jungwirth	Gordon Schroeder		Royce Bush Jr
Sioux Falls (101)	CO 605 339-7200	Jack White	. . . .	Dianne Metlie	Manfred Szameit	Kirk Anderson	Terri Satterlee	. . . .
Sisseton (2)	CM 605 698-3391	(not reporting)						
Spearfish (7)	MC 605 642-7775	Fred W Romkema	. . . .	. . . .	Elizabeth Benning	. . . .	Rick Mowell	Ted Vore
Sturgis (5)	MC 605 347-4422	(not reporting)						
Vermillion (10)	CM 605 624-5641	Grant Sammelson	Jeffrey Pederson	. . . .	Michael D Carlson	Doug Brunick	Gary Wright	. . . .
Watertown (18)	MC 605 886-4057	Howard Hopper	. . . .	. . . .	. . . .	Al Satter	Laverne McPeek	. . . .
Winner (3)	MC 605 842-2606	(not reporting)						
Yankton (13)	MC 605 665-4501	Terrence Crandall	William R Ross	. . . .	Jerald J Knodel	Patrick C Smith	Leon J Cantin	Eugene G Hoag
TENNESSEE (134)								
Adams t (1)	MC 615 696-2593	Omer G Brooksher	. . . .	Rachel Nolen	. . . .	Ray Brown		
Alamo t (2)	MC 901 696-4515	(not reporting)						
Alcoa (6)	CM 615 981-4100	Donald R Mull	Carl L Overman	. . . .	Ray E Richesin	Larry L Graves	Wayne M Chodak	Kenneth D Wiggins
Athens (12)	CM 615 745-3140	L A Roseberry	Melvin Barker	Kaye Burton	Jackie Jenkins	Robert Miller	Charles Ziegler	Mark Miller
Bartlett t (27)	MC 901 385-6400	(not reporting)						
Beersheba Springs t (1)	CO 615 692-3508	(not reporting)						
Belle Meade (3)	CM 615 297-6041	T S Fillebrown	William D Brinton	. . . .	. . . .	. . . .	Vince Perry Jr	George Bartlett
Berry Hill (1)	CM 615 292-5531	Charles McKelvey	Glenn H Delzell	. . . .	Glenn H Delzell	. . . .	Herman Jett	
Bolivar t (6)	MC 901 658-2020	(not reporting)						
Brentwood (16)	CM 615 371-0060	Joe Sweeney	Michael W Walker	. . . .	Randy Sanders	Kenneth Lane	Howard Buttrey	Louis J Baltz
Bristol (23)	CM 615 989-5500	Patrick W Hickle	Frank W Clifton	Nancy J Sparger	Nancy J Sparger	Phil W Vinson	David E Wampler	Charles Robinette
Brownsville t (10)	MC 901 772-1212	Jimmy Halbrook	. . . .	Jerry Taylor	. . . .	Jimmy White	Lucion English	. . . .
Camden t (4)	MC 901 584-4656	Wendel Oglesby	. . . .	Phyllis Woodard	. . . .	Tom Bordonaro	William S Terry	. . . .
Carthage (2)	MC 615 735-1881	David H Bowman	Joyce M Rash	Brenda McKinley	Joyce M Rash	Edward Stallings	Scotty L Lewis	Charle E Hunt
Centerville t (4)	MC 615 729-4246	. . . .	Kenneth R Wright	. . . .	. . . .	Kenneth Thompson	Roger T Livengood	. . . .
Charleston t (1)	CM 615 336-1483	Walter Goode	Caroline Geren	Geraldine Turner	. . . .	Dave Thompson	Freddie Jones	Joe Kimpson
Chattanooga (152)	CO 615 757-5200	Gene Roberts	. . . .	Carol O'Neal	James Boney	Jerry Evans	Ralph Cothran	Jack Marcellis
Church Hill t (5)	MC 615 357-6161	(not reporting)						
Clarksville (75)	MC 615 645-7451	Don Trotter	. . . .	Sylvia Smith	Wilbur Berry	Eugene Keel	Johnny Rosson	Denzil Biter
Cleveland (30)	CO 615 472-4551	John T Rowland	. . . .	Janice Casteel	. . . .	David W May Jr	Wesley B Snyder	Richard T Lyles
Clifton City t (1)	CM 615 676-3370	(not reporting)						
Clinton t (9)	MC 615 457-0424	Frank L Diggs	Steve R Queener	. . . .	. . . .	Steve Payne	Clifton Melton	Gene Stewart
Collegedale (5)	CM 615 396-3135	(not reporting)						
Collierville t (14)	MC 901 853-3200	Herman W Cox Jr	Steven H Schertel	Mary Lee Burley	Jane Bevill	Ben F Wilson	Dennis E Joyner	Wilbur M Betty
Collinwood (1)	CM 615 724-9107	James A Dicus	William Thompson	Sherry A Gallien	. . . .	. . . .	Jerry A Benedict	. . . .
Columbia (29)	CM 615 388-5432	Barbara McIntyre	William E Gentner	. . . .	Betty R Modrall	H Wayne Hickman	James B Boyd	. . . .
Cookeville (22)	CM 615 526-9591	(not reporting)						
Covington (7)	MC 901 476-9531	Russell B Bailey	. . . .	Jere H Hadley	. . . .	Jerry W Craig	Ronald J Gagnon	Robert D Stockman
Crossville (7)	CM 615 484-5113	Earl Dean	C M Tabor	Sally Oglesby	. . . .	Mike Turner	Robert Foutch	Lesley Sherrill
Dayton (6)	CM 615 775-1818	(not reporting)						
Dickson t (9)	MC 615 441-9503	(not reporting)						
Dunlap (4)	MC 615 949-2115	George Wagner	. . . .	Mary Phipps	Larry Hixson	Norman Walker	Roger Snyder	. . . .
Dyersburg (16)	MC 901 286-7607	(not reporting)						
East Ridge t (21)	CO 615 867-7711	Jack Sharp	Michael Nettles	Evelyn Keith	. . . .	Eddie Phillips	Bill Muse	Clifford Ackerson
Elizabethton (12)	CM 615 543-3551	H Lingerfelt	R Collins	. . . .	S Cox	B Carter	R Deal	K McElyea
Erwin t (5)	MC 615 743-6231	Russell Brackins	Doris D Hensley	Lisa Saylor	Doris D Hensley	Larry Ayers	James H Hicks	Paul D Griffith
Etowah t (4)	CM 615 263-2202	E Burke Garwood	Richard Whitehead	Yvonne Derreberry	Jean B James	. . . .	Marty Aderhold	Larry Lanning
Fairview (4)	CM 615 799-2484	J T King	Asa Stewart	K Daugherty	K Daugherty	Paul Runk	Terry Harris	Asa Stewart
Farragut t (13)	CM 615 966-7057	W Edward Ford	Jack S Hamlett	. . . .	Mary Lou Koepp	. . . .	. . . .	William McKelvey
Fayetteville t (7)	MC 615 433-6154	(not reporting)						
Forest Hills (4)	CO 615 383-8447	James J Wert	James T Balthrop	. . . .	. . . .	. . . .	. . . .	. . . .
Franklin (20)	MC 615 794-4572	Jerry Sharber	. . . .	. . . .	Judy Kennedy	Samuel Liggett	M Fred Wisdom	. . . .
Gallatin (19)	MC 615 452-5400	Tom Garrott	Joyce Savage	Robert Langford	Peggy Vantrease	Joe Womack	Wayne Womack	Lynn Patillo
Gatlinburg (3)	CM 615 436-1400	Charles K Bradley	Cindy C Ogle	. . . .	David Beeler	Terry Reagan	Harry Montgomery	. . . .
Germantown (33)	MC 901 757-7200	Charles Salvaggio	Patrick Lawton	Judy Simerson	John Dluhos	James R Smith	Eddie Boatwright	Sam Beach
Goodlettsville (11)	CM 615 859-4078	(not reporting)						
Greenbrier t (3)	MC 615 643-4531	Tommy Overby	. . . .	Sherry Corlew	. . . .	. . . .	Norman Mayo	William Maitland
Greeneville t (14)	MC 615 639-7105	G Thomas Love	James L Warner	. . . .	. . . .	James Parman	Charles Kinser	Robert Bird
Harriman (7)	MC 615 882-3960	(not reporting)						
Hartsville (2)	MC 615 374-3074	(not reporting)						
Henderson (5)	MC 901 989-4628	Charles Patterson	. . . .	Jim E Garland	. . . .	Prince Bukkeen	Jerome Hurst	Jerry L King
Hendersonville (32)	MC 615 822-1000	Roland J Thompson	. . . .	William Brinton	William Brinton	Charles L Black	David L Key	Bob K Freudenthal
Hohenwald (4)	MC 615 796-2231	(not reporting)						
Humboldt (10)	MC 901 784-2511	(not reporting)						
Huntingdon t (4)	MC 901 986-8211	(not reporting)						
Jackson (49)	MC 901 425-8252	Charles H Farmer	. . . .	. . . .	Russell Truell	Owen Collins	Richard S Staples	Claude Martin
Jasper t (3)	MC 615 942-3180	(not reporting)						
Jefferson City (5)	CM 615 475-9071	Bill Bales	Don Darden	Florence Denton	. . . .	Bob Kinder	Will Clark	Mike Jones
Jellico (2)	MC 615 784-6351	(not reporting)						
Johnson City (49)	CM 615 929-9171	Jeff Anderson	John Campbell	. . . .	Jim Crumley	Doug Buckles	Ron Street	Phil Pindzola
Jonesborough t (3)	CM 615 753-6128	Kevin B McKinney	Robert E Browning	. . . .	Laura Hamilton	Ed McKee	Craig Ford	. . . .
Kingsport (36)	CM 615 229-9400	Hunter Wright	Peter T Connet	. . . .	Arthur L Doggett	Conner L Caldwell	James F Keesling	B R Wilkerson
Kingston (5)	CM 615 376-6584	Don Woody	Edwin Smith	Eleanor Neal	Carolyn Brewer	Robert Scruggs	Gary Humpherys	Gid McEachern
Knoxville (165)	MC 615 521-2000	Victor Ashe	. . . .	. . . .	Randy Vineyard	Bruce Cureton	Phil Keith	Robert Whetsel
La Follette (7)	CM 615 562-4961	Clifford Jennings	Cade Sexton	Debbie Pierce	Terry Sweat	Wayne Gregg	Steve Carson	Max Robinson
La Vergne (7)	MC 615 793-6295	(not reporting)						
Lafayette (4)	MC 615 666-2194	Ben Holder	Ruby Flowers	Linda Goodman	. . . .	Loryn Atwell	Buford Wix	. . . .
Lake City t (2)	CO 615 426-2838	G Lovely	. . . .	Margie Golden	. . . .	Ronnie Spitzer	James Shetterly	. . . .
Lakewood (2)	CM 615 847-2187	(not reporting)						
Lawrenceburg (10)	CO 615 762-4459	Lindsey Garner	. . . .	J Ralph Cross	. . . .	Roy Holloway	Bid Lindsey	
Lebanon (15)	MC 615 443-2839	(not reporting)						
Lenoir City (6)	MC 615 986-2715	Charles T Eblen	Harold E Proaps	. . . .	. . . .	David P Denton	Jake Chapman	. . . .
Lewisburg (10)	CM 615 359-1544	Jamie Bone	Eddie Derryberry	. . . .	A C Sweeney	John Redd	Ray Green	Bill Wheat
Lexington (6)	MC 901 968-6657	(not reporting)						
Livingston t (4)	MC 615 823-1269	(not reporting)						
Loudon (4)	MC 615 458-2033	Bernie Swiney	. . . .	S Putkonen	. . . .	Rondel Branam	Bill Grimes	Bill Fagg
Madisonville t (3)	MC 615 442-9416	Frances Maxwell	Ted Cagle	. . . .	. . . .	. . . .	Danny Russell	Donnie Chambers

City, 1990 population figures (000 omitted), form of government	Municipal phone number	Mayor	Appointed administrator	City clerk	Finance officer	Fire chief	Police chief	Public works director
TENNESSEE (134) continued								
Manchester (8)	MC 615 728-4652	Lonnie J Norman	. . . .	. . . .	Nina H Moffitt	J Sam Miller	Ross Rimmons	Ed Anderson
Martin (9)	MC 901 587-3126	Larry W Taylor	Richard L Tidwell	. . . .	. . . .	N B Williams	Jackie Moore	Jim Crocker
Maryville (19)	CM 615 981-1300	Stanley Shields	Gary H Hensley	. . . .	Mark L Johnson	Kenneth G Abbott	Terry L Nichols	Richard Whaley
Maynardville (1)	CM 615 992-3821	. . . .	Edgar Cook	. . . .	. . . .	Jeffery Chesney	Edgar Cook	
Mc Kenzie (5)	MC 901 352-2292	(not reporting)						
Mc Minnville (11)	MC 615 473-1200	Norman W Rone	Thomas M Sprowl	. . . .	. . . .	William H Baker	Dickie Kesey	William Brock
Memphis (610)	MC 901 576-6571	(not reporting)						
Milan t (8)	MC 901 686-3301	Don Farmer	Alan Deck	. . . .	. . . .	James Beasley	James Bratton	Billie West
Millington (18)	MC 901 872-2211	George Harvell	. . . .	Carolyn Madill	James Knipple	Charles Carter	Jon Hall	Jack Huffman
Monterey t (3)	MC 615 839-2323	Jack Phillips	Debbie Stephens	Jo Nelda Stamps	. . . .	Richard Milligan	Bruce Breedlove	A C McCowan
Morristown (21)	CM 615 581-0100	John R Johnson	Keith Jackson	Keith Jackson	Michael W Lutche	Rick Reynolds	Joel K Seal	Carl Gilbert
Mount Carmel t (4)	MC 615 357-7311	(not reporting)						
Mount Juliet (5)	CM 615 754-2552	David J Waynick	Danny C Farmer	. . . .	Sheila S Luckett	. . . .	Charles McCrary	James Evetts
Mount Pleasant (4)	MC 615 379-7717	William H Boyd	Robert A Murray	Carolyn Douglas	. . . .	W H Massey	Harlan McKissick	Larry Holden
Murfreesboro (45)	CM 615 893-5210	Joe B Jackson	Roger A Haley	. . . .	Jim B Penner	David Baxter	Billy Lee Jones	Rick Cantrell
Nashville-Davidson (511)	MC 615 862-6000	Philip Bredesen	. . . .	Marilyn Swing	Gene Nolan	Martin Coleman	Robert E Kirchner	William M Keel
Newbern (3)	MC 901 627-3221	Joe Adams	. . . .	Judy Steelman	. . . .	Bill Berry	Harold Dunivant	Jerry Wiley
Newport t (7)	CM 615 623-7323	(not reporting)						
Norris (1)	CM 615 494-7645	George R Dyer	. . . .	Darlene Buckner	. . . .	. . . .	. . . .	Marian W Pointer
Oak Hill (4)	CM 615 371-8291	Warren Wilkerson	George W Morris	Beatrice James	George W Morris	. . . .	. . . .	. . . .
Oak Ridge (27)	CM 615 482-8464	Edmund A Nephew	Jeffrey Broughton	Jacquelyn Bernard	Steven W Jenkins	W Mack Bailey	Timothy A Braaten	Gary M Cinder
Oliver Springs t (3)	MC 615 435-7722	(not reporting)						
Oneida t (4)	MC 615 569-4295	(not reporting)						
Paris (9)	CM 901 642-1215	John T Van Dyck	Carl Holder Jr	. . . .	Evonne J Phifer	George Atkins	Richard H Dunlap	. . . .
Pigeon Forge (3)	CM 615 453-9061	Ralph Chance	Earlene M Teaster	Mable O Ellis	Elsie Cole	. . . .	Jack H Baldwin	Garland C Harmon
Portland t (5)	MC 615 325-6776	(not reporting)						
Pulaski (8)	CM 615 363-2516	(not reporting)						
Red Bank (12)	CM 615 877-1103	. . . .	Jerry Robinson	. . . .	. . . .	Mark Mathews	Ronnie Dodd	Gary Jackson
Ripley (6)	MC 901 635-4000	Richard Douglas	. . . .	. . . .	. . . .	Ronnie Crawford	Dennis King	Leamon Pennington
Rockwood (5)	CO 615 354-0163	(not reporting)						
Rogersville t (4)	MC 615 272-7497	Jim Sells	William H Lyons	. . . .	. . . .	Hal Price Jr	Larry Lawson	
Samburg t (..)	CM 901 538-2735	(not reporting)						
Savannah (7)	CM 901 925-3300	Jack D Cherry Jr	Robert F Polk	. . . .	William P Fox Jr	James A Berry	Donald B Cannon	Warren G Higgins
Selmer t (4)	MC 901 645-3242	(not reporting)						
Sevierville (7)	CM 615 453-5504	(not reporting)						
Shelbyville (14)	CM 615 684-2691	Henry Feldhaus	Thomas Christie	. . . .	. . . .	Garland King	Austin Swing	William Sullivan
Signal Mountain t (7)	CM 615 886-2177	R Phil Corker	Rick Sonnenburg	. . . .	. . . .	. . . .	Larry P Eddings	Randall Wilson
Smithville t (4)	MC 615 597-4745	(not reporting)						
Smyrna t (14)	CM 615 459-2553	Knox Ridley	Mike Woods	Mike Woods	. . . .	Bill Culbertson	Charles Vance	Ben Andrews
Soddy-Daisy (8)	CM 615 332-5323	Leroy Grant	Edward E West	. . . .	Sara Burris	Steve Grant	Douglas M Everett	Jack Parker
South Fulton (3)	CM 901 479-2151	Kent Greer	Larry Eaton	Debra Beadles	. . . .	Tommy Smith	. . . .	Roy Coley
South Pittsburg (3)	CM 615 837-7511	(not reporting)						
Sparta (5)	MC 615 836-3248	(not reporting)						
Spring City t (2)	CM 615 365-6441	(not reporting)						
Springfield (11)	CM 615 382-2200	Billy P Carneal	Doug Bishop	Janice Frey	Bobby Lehman	David Greer	Mike Wilhoit	Allan Ellis
St. Joseph (1)	CM 615 845-4141	Chuck Kizer	Robert B Russ	Jean Hill	. . . .	Walter Shelton	Dennis Daniel	Wayne Shaw
Sweetwater (5)	MC 615 337-6979	Billy Ridenour	. . . .	Shannon Creasman	Charlotte Starnes	Lynn Phillips	Mike Jenkins	Roy Inman
Tennessee Ridge t (1)	CM 615 721-3385	(not reporting)						
Trenton (5)	MC 901 855-2013	(not reporting)						
Tullahoma (17)	CM 615 455-2648	(not reporting)						
Tusculum (2)	MC 615 638-6211	. . . .	. . . .	B A Fitzgerald	. . . .	. . . .	. . . .	. . . .
Union City (11)	CM 901 885-1341	Terry Hailey	Don Thornton	Mildred Roberts	. . . .	Dale Burgess	Lawrence J Garner	Bobby Grimes
Watauga (..)	CM 615 928-3490	(not reporting)						
Waverly t (4)	MC 615 296-2101	(not reporting)						
Waynesboro (2)	MC 615 722-5458	Bruce Howell	Steve Collie	Darlene Skelton	Flora E Lacher	Doug Gobbell	Thomas E Seitz	Howard Riley
Whitwell (2)	CM 615 658-5151	(not reporting)						
Winchester t (6)	MC 615 967-4771	(not reporting)						
TEXAS (427)								
Abernathy (3)	CM 806 298-2546	(not reporting)						
Abilene (107)	CM 915 676-6249	Gary McCaleb	Jim C Blagg	Jo A Moore	David M Wright	J Deloss Edwards	Dwain T Pyburn	Marva Pritchett
Addison (9)	CM 214 450-7000	Rich Beckert	Ronald Whitehead	. . . .	Randolph Moravec	R Wallingford	James McLaughlin	John Baumgartner
Alamo (8)	MC 512 787-0006	Marcelino Medina	H G Lumbreras	. . . .	Lydia Aleman	Harold Nunn	Noe Garza	P Barrientes
Alamo Heights (7)	CM 512 822-3331	William Balthrope	Susan Hennessy	Susan Hennessy	Susan Hennessy	W E Renken	Jack Summey	Steve Steinmetz
Alice (20)	CM 512 668-7200	(not reporting)						
Allen (18)	CM 214 727-0100	(not reporting)						
Alpine t (6)	MC 915 837-3301	Paul Weyerts	Jerry Carvajal	Annabel Holguin	Tomi McDaniel	Paul Loeffler	Tom Moring	Ted Scown
Alton (3)	CM 512 581-2733	(not reporting)						
Alvarado (3)	MC 817 783-3351	Amon T Adcock	Frances Johnson	Marla King	Linda Lewis	R Van Winkle	Roger Carroll	Terry Reynolds
Alvin (19)	CM 713 388-4235	Elmer Dezso	Greg Harrison	Wynette Stoner	Fred Mendoza	Donald Eernisse	Micheal Merkel	Douglas Wilson
Amarillo (158)	CM 806 378-3000	Kel Seliger	John Q Ward	Donna Deright	Dean Frigo	Curtis Richards	Jerry Neal	Mike Kennedy
Andrews (11)	CM 915 523-4820	Greg Sweeney	Len L Wilson	. . . .	Kitty F Bristow	Tim Boren	Dolphus Bud Jones	Larry D Fleming
Angleton (17)	CM 409 849-4364	(not reporting)						
Anson (3)	MC 915 823-2411	Thurman Simmons	David Fenwick	Sue Willis	. . . .	Bill Cromeens	Gary Bouton	Freddie Elkins
Anthony (3)	MC 915 886-3944	Art Franco	Nila J Stillwell	. . . .	Keith Puhlman	. . . .	Hal B Caldwell	. . . .
Aransas Pass (7)	CM 512 758-2908	Billy St Clair	Rick Ewaniszyk	Natalia Smith	. . . .	Gilbert Ritz	Melvin Shedd	Allen Berna
Arlington (262)	CM 817 275-3271	(not reporting)						
Athens (11)	CM 903 675-5131	(not reporting)						
Atlanta (6)	CM 903 796-7153	Peyton Childs	Andre Wimer	Sylvia Combest	Andre Wimer	David Burden	Mike Scott	Jeff Buzbee
Austin (466)	CM 512 499-2000	Bruce Todd	Camille Barnett	Elden Aldridge	Betty Dunkerley	Bill Roberts	Elizabeth Watson	Bill Stockton
Azle (9)	CM 817 444-2541	C Y Rone	Harry H Dulin Jr	Kim Shelton	Robert Horton	Robert E Fowler	Marvin L Ivy	Darrell Riding
Balch Springs (17)	CM 214 557-6070	David Haas	Aniela J Warner	. . . .	Edith L Cates	Michael F Cooper	Edward M Leach Jr	D James Glover
Balcones Heights (3)	MC 512 735-9148	(not reporting)						
Ballinger (4)	MC 915 365-5437	Daniel Morelock	. . . .	Bonita F Shields	. . . .	Timothy Kresta	W Paul Buggess	Tommy New
Bastrop (4)	MC 512 321-3941	David Lock	Mike Talbot	Shawnda Sanders	Jo Ann Wilcoxen	Mike Fisher	Ronnie Duncan	Marvin Patterson
Bay City (18)	CM 409 245-2137	(not reporting)						
Baytown (64)	CM 713 422-8281	Pete Alfaro	Bobby Rountree	Eileen Hall	Monte Mercer	Robert Leiper	Charles Shaffer	Herbert Thomas
Beaumont (114)	CM 409 880-3700	(not reporting)						
Bedford (44)	CM 817 952-2100	Rick R Barton	James Walker	Rita Frick	Charles Gardner	E Bilger	Jimmy Simpson	Don Burns
Beeville (14)	CM 512 358-4641	(not reporting)						
Bellaire (14)	CM 713 662-8229	Betty Janicek	Lea Dunn	Roena Loftin	Norma Quinn	Rufus Summers	Jerry H Loftin	Richard Larsen
Bellmead (8)	CM 817 799-2436	Robert Hawkins	S G Radcliffe	. . . .	Elizabeth Dieterh	James Karl	Bob Harold	Mike Willis
Bellville (3)	MC 409 865-3136	(not reporting)						

Directory 1/9
continued

**MUNICIPAL OFFICIALS
IN U.S. CITIES OVER 2,500**

City, 1990 population figures (000 omitted), form of government	Municipal phone number	Mayor	Appointed administrator	City clerk	Finance officer	Fire chief	Police chief	Public works director
TEXAS (427) continued								
Belton (12)	CM 817 939-5851	Charley Powell	Jeff Holberg	Connie Torres	Cristy Daniell	Michael Foegelle	Roy Kneese	Louis Griffin
Benbrook (20)	CM 817 249-3000	Jerry Dunn	Kennith Neystel	Joanna King	David Ragsdale	Billie Ostrom	Sam Horan	Chuck Rogers
Big Lake t (4)	MC 915 884-2511	H F Ritchie	Lee Kane	Lee Kane	Lee Kane	Doc Robertson	. . . .	Jerry Floyd
Big Spring (23)	CM 915 263-8311	Tim Blackshear	Lanny Lambert	Maurine Pittman	Tom Ferguson	Frank Anderson	Joe Cook	Tom Decell
Bishop t (3)	CM 512 584-2567	Austin C Abshier	Georgina Ybarra	Rebecca Rodriguez	Georgina Ybarra	Fred Shieble	Lester Mayberry	Juan Puente
Boerne (4)	MC 512 249-9511	Patrick R Heath	Ronald C Bowman	Bernell Norton	Ronald C Bowman	. . . .	Gary Miller	John Moring
Bonham (7)	CM 903 583-7555	Bobby McCraw	Jim Stiff	Janell Whited	Jim Stiff	. . . .	Mike Bankston	Ronny Ford
Borger (16)	CM 806 273-2881	Judy Flanders	Alyn Rogers	Wanda Klause	Glynn Carlock	W G McWilliams	Michael Smith	Henry Veach
Bowie (5)	CM 817 872-1114	Bert Cunningham	James Cantwell	Linda Shelton	Sue Fitzgerald		Mike Gentry	. . . .
Brady (6)	MC 915 597-2152	H L Gober Jr	T H Jack Caffall	Lina R Cruz	Lindell L Estes	Garon L Salter	James D Ledford	Gary L Broz
Brazoria (3)	CM 409 798-9131	William V James	K C Timmermann	Betty M Wilson	Ken Timmermann	Marcus Rabren	Theresa Guidry	William Humphrey
Breckenridge (6)	CM 817 559-8287	(not reporting)						
Brenham (12)	MC 409 836-7911	Robert Appel Jr	Kent Van Eman	Doris Seilheimer	Randall Patterson	Don Hoffman	Wm Kenneth Carnes	Ronald Bottoms
Bridge City (8)	CM 409 735-6801	(not reporting)						
Bridgeport (4)	MC 812 683-5906	(not reporting)						
Brownfield (10)	CM 806 637-4547	(not reporting)						
Brownsville (99)	CM 512 548-6000	(not reporting)						
Brownwood (18)	CM 915 646-6056	Bert V Massey	Gary T Butts	. . . .	. . . .	Kenneth W Taylor	Joe H Robbins	Donald R Hatcher
Bryan (55)	CM 409 361-3600	Marvin Tate	Michael Conduff	Mary L Galloway	Mary Kaye Moore	James Bland	Lee Freeman	Ed Ilschner
Bunker Hill Village (3)	MC 713 467-9762	G G Stubblefield	David F Eby	Gloria Drabek	Eileen O'Leary	. . . .	. . . .	James L Williams
Burkburnett (10)	CM 817 569-2263	Pat Norriss	Gary Bean	Tamara Burchett	. . . .	. . . .	Curtis Salyer	John Brookman
Burleson (16)	CM 817 295-1113	Rick Roper	Kay Godbey	Jean Phillips	Charlie Harris	Stacy Singleton	. . . .	Bill Davison
Burnet t (3)	CM 512 756-6093	(not reporting)						
Caldwell (3)	CM 409 567-3271	Bernard E Rychlik	William Broaddus	. . . .	William Broaddus	Douglas Beavers	Willie J Kovar	William Broaddus
Cameron (6)	MC 817 697-6646	(not reporting)						
Canadian t (2)	CM 806 323-6473	(not reporting)						
Canton (3)	CM 903 567-2826	(not reporting)						
Canyon (11)	CM 806 655-5000	Lois Rice	Glen Metcalf	James Glenn	Howard Morris	Robert Rice	Bobby Griffin	Mark Clark
Carrizo Springs (6)	CM 512 876-2476	Rufus Lozano Jr	Richard Cantu	Mario A Martinez	. . . .	Jose Rodriquez	. . . .	. . . .
Carrollton (82)	CM 214 466-3090	Milburn Gravley	Daniel Johnson	. . . .	Bob Scott	Bruce Varner	Vernon Campbell	Bobby Atteberry
Carthage (6)	CM 903 693-3868	(not reporting)						
Castle Hills (4)	MC 512 342-2341	(not reporting)						
Cedar Hill (20)	CM 214 291-5100	(not reporting)						
Cedar Park (5)	CM 512 258-4121	Dorthey Duckett	Daron Butler	Nancy Faulkner	Wesley Vela	. . . .	Robert Young	Sam Roberts
Center (5)	CM 409 598-2941	(not reporting)						
Childress (5)	CM 817 937-3684	(not reporting)						
Cisco (4)	CM 817 442-2111	Joe Wheatley	Michael D Moore	Ginger Johnson	Maryann Perry	W T Eaton	Douglas Fairbanks	Leon Boles
Clarksville (4)	CM 903 427-3834	J R Lewis	Wilt Brown	Melissa Gibson	. . . .	Keith Crockett	Wilt Brown	. . . .
Cleburne (22)	CM 817 641-3321	Katherine Raines	Joel Victory	Jean Hamilton	Thomas G Wilmore	Lloyd McVicker	Thomas D Cowan	Larry R Barkman
Cleveland (7)	CM 711 592-2667	Lloyd Meadows	W N Petropolis	Barbara Burns	Kandy Littrell	Steve Wheeler	Ike Hines	Al Alford
Clifton (3)	MC 817 675-8337	(not reporting)						
Clute (9)	MC 713 265-2541	Billy R Harlan	Barbara Hester	Sarah Jo Oakes	Marcia Herring	Bill Rickey	Mark Wicker	Roy D Fairbanks
Clyde t (3)	MC 915 893-4234	Robert J Gwilt	. . . .	C Jean Gilmore	. . . .	Rick Gilmore	Ronald L Young	Norman Smith
Cockrell Hill (4)	MC 214 330-6333	Tony Hinojosa Jr	. . . .	Elizabeth White	. . . .	Randy Franklin	Micheal Jones	Rodolfo Carrillo
Coleman (5)	CM 915 625-5114	Woodrow J Maddox	Roy E McCorkle	David S Sooter	Roy E McCorkle	Mark Beard	Larry Titsworth	James Hammonds
College Station (52)	CM 409 764-3500	Larry Ringer	Ron Ragland	Connie Hooks	Glenn Schroeder	William Kennedy	Edgar Feldman	Joe LaBeau
Colleyville (13)	CM 817 281-4044	(not reporting)						
Colorado City (5)	CM 915 728-3464	(not reporting)						
Columbus (3)	MC 409 732-2366	Dwain Dungen	John Brasher	Earline Drumm	Jill Ready	Robert C Walla	Robert E Connor	Milton Wavra
Comanche (4)	MC 915 356-2616	(not reporting)						
Commerce (7)	CM 214 886-2105	Marna Martinez	Roger McKinney	Camille Poteet	Sue Porter	. . . .	. . . .	Billy Turney
Conroe (28)	MC 409 539-4431	Carter Moore	Craig Lonon	Marla Porter	Hattie Weisinger	Dave Miller	Harold Goodwin	Dean Towery
Converse (9)	CM 512 658-5356	Rick Maas	John L Klaiber	Gracie Beane	. . . .	Jack Doughtery	Mark E D'Spain	Keith Dickerson
Coppell (17)	CM 214 462-0022	Tom Morton	. . . .	. . . .	. . . .	Clay Phillips	Neil McKinney	Steve Goram
Copperas Cove (24)	CM 817 547-4221	James Schmitz	Johnny P Smith	Rose E Mansfield	Sheila L Creek	Ray E Ashcraft	Stephen J Klempa	Daniel McIntyre
Corpus Christi (257)	CM 512 880-3000	(not reporting)						
Corsicana (23)	CM 903 654-4803	(not reporting)						
Cotulla (4)	MC 512 879-2367	(not reporting)						
Crane (4)	MC 915 558-3563	(not reporting)						
Crockett (7)	CM 409 544-5156	C Von Doenhoff	Ann McNabb	Ann McNabb	Ann McNabb	David Williamson	Jimmy Fisher	Vernon Miner
Crowley (6)	MC 817 297-2201	Nancy Behrens	K M Waterstreet	Debbie Byrd	K M Waterstreet	Jeff Stubbs	Armen Tamakian	Jim McDonald
Crystal City (8)	CM 512 374-3477	Maria Sanchez Rivera	Felix Benavides	. . . .	Marie C Abrego	Delwin Hale	Luis Contreras	. . . .
Cuero (7)	CM 512 275-6114	John Post	John M Trayhan	Corlis Riedesel	. . . .	Eldred Schultz	W T Allen Jr	. . . .
Daingerfield (3)	CM 903 645-3906	William L Thorne	Margie J Hargrove	Margie J Hargrove	. . . .	Tony Hall	Scott Sartain	Marion D Clayton
Dalhart (6)	MC 806 249-5511	(not reporting)						
Dallas (1007)	CM 214 670-3563	. . . .	John L Ware	. . . .	. . . .	. . . .	. . . .	. . . .
Dayton t (5)	CM 409 258-2642	Guy L Harris	Clarence P Cowart	Terri Dryden	. . . .	Earl Heider	Buddy Bean	Terry Key
De Soto (31)	CM 214 223-4120	David Doyle	Mark Sowa	Jean Garner	Joe Barrett	Johnnie Bowmann	Bob Hayes	Gordon Mayer
Decatur (4)	MC 817 627-2741	Bobby Wilson	Brett Shannon	Brett Shannon	Brett Shannon	Kevin Burns	Rex Hoskins	Robert Gage
Deer Park (28)	CM 713 479-2394	Jimmy Burke	Ronald Crabtree	Sandra Watkins	Glenn Windsor	. . . .	Donald Little	Paul Pondish
Del Rio (31)	CM 512 774-8552	Alfredo Gutierrez	Florencio Sauceda	Jayne Douglas	Yvonne Gomez	Howard Baughman	Charles Bruce	Robert Sifuentez
Denison (22)	CM 903 465-2720	Ben Munson	Larry Cruise	Barbara Forrest	Andy Wilkins	Bill Taylor	Jimmy Lovell	Jerry White
Denton (66)	CM 817 566-8200	Bob Castleberry	Lloyd Harrell	Joseph Portugal	John McGrane	John Cook	Michael Jez	Bill Angelo
Denver City t (5)	MC 806 592-5426	(not reporting)						
Devine (4)	MC 512 663-2804	(not reporting)						
Diboll (4)	MC 409 829-4757	(not reporting)						
Dickinson v (9)	MC 713 337-2489	Veta L Winick	Don E Taylor	. . . .	Debra Winnagel	. . . .	Wayne T Broussard	. . . .
Dilley t (3)	MC 512 965-1624	(not reporting)						
Dimmitt t (4)	MC 512 478-6601	Wayne Collins	Reeford Burrous	Dolores Baldridge	Reeford Burrous	Randy Griffit	Gary Thurman	James Killough
Donna (13)	CM 512 464-3314	(not reporting)						
Dublin (3)	MC 817 445-3331	(not reporting)						
Dumas (13)	MC 806 935-4101	(not reporting)						
Duncanville (36)	CM 214 780-5017	James Tow	Dan Savage	Pam Schmidt	Jerry Striplin	Jackie Walton	Michael Courville	Dennis Schwartz
Eagle Lake (4)	CM 409 234-2640	Donald N Bendy	Ronald W Holland	Lucille Perry	Lucille Perry	Darrell Gertson	. . . .	Harry Supak
Eagle Pass (21)	CM 512 773-1111	Arturo Garcia	Guadalupe Cardona	. . . .	Manuel Contreras	Guadalupe Cardona	Leonardo Santoya	Hector Chavez
Early (2)	CM 915 643-5451	Richard Bean	Ken Thomas	Deloris Walker	Ken Thomas	Bryan Chambers	Charles Thomas	Raymond Edwards
Eastland (4)	CM 817 629-8321	C W Hoffmann Jr	Paul Catoe	Karen Moore	Juanita Grisham	. . . .	Cecil Funderburgh	Steve Jameson
Edcouch t (3)	CM 512 262-2140	(not reporting)						
Edgecliff Village t (3)	MC 817 293-4313	Bill Sherman	Rebecca Stark	Yolanda Trevino	Yolanda Trevino	Tom Dransfield	. . . .	Mike Duehring
Edinburg (30)	CM 512 383-5661	Joe Ochoa	John R Milford	Maria M Corona	Jose H Gonzalez	Johnny Economedes	Raul C Garza	Arnold Vera
Edna (5)	CM 512 782-3122	(not reporting)						
El Campo (11)	CM 409 543-5361	(not reporting)						
El Lago (3)	MC 713 326-1951	(not reporting)						

MUNICIPAL OFFICIALS IN U.S. CITIES OVER 2,500

City, 1990 population figures (000 omitted), form of government	Municipal phone number	Mayor	Appointed administrator	City clerk	Finance officer	Fire chief	Police chief	Public works director
TEXAS (427) continued								
El Paso (515)	MC 915 541-4000	Larry Francis	Kenneth E Beasley	Carole A Hunter	William A Chapman	Andrew F Mehl	John E Scagno Jr	David W Harned
Electra (3)	CM 817 495-2146	Ted Miller	David Vestal	. . . .	Bob Meeks	. . . .	J W Mayfield	Ed Helton
Elgin (5)	MC 512 285-5721	Jan Schroeder	Jack Harzke	. . . .	Loren Mayfield	Wilford Alexander	Bill Smith	Gary N Cooke
Elsa (5)	CM 512 262-2127	(not reporting)						
Ennis (14)	CM 214 875-1234	Bill Lewis	Steve Howerton	Wynell Rose	Rose Wynell	David Hopkins	Dale Holt	Roy Callahan
Euless (38)	CM 817 685-1400	Mary Lib Saleh	Tom Hart	Susan Crim	Debra B Forte	Lee Koontz	K B Fuller	Randy Byers
Everman (6)	MC 817 293-0525	(not reporting)						
Fairfield (3)	MC 214 389-2633	(not reporting)						
Falfurrias (5)	CO 512 325-2420	Jimmie Dunn	Aurora Rodriguez	Aurora Rodriguez	. . . .	Gonzalo Benavidez	Baldemar Rivera	Kenneth V Martin
Farmers Branch (24)	CM 214 247-3131	(not reporting)						
Farmersville (3)	CM 214 782-6151	George G Crump	Randall E Holly	Susan Martin	Randall E Holly	John Cooper	Gregory Gorden	Alan Hein
Flatonia t (1)	CM 512 865-3548	(not reporting)						
Floresville (5)	MC 512 393-3105	Raymond M Ramirez	Sam R Hughes	Barbara A Brown	. . . .	Donald Stevens	Daniel Martinez	Larry Mac Host
Flower Mound t (16)	CM 214 539-8511	Larry W Lipscomb	Van R James	Ruth DeShaw	Linda Truitt	Eric Metzger	G Paul Griffith	Robert Stengele
Floydada t (4)	CM 806 983-2834	Hulon Carthel	Gary Brown	S Quisenberry	. . . .	. . . .	James L Hale	Jimmy Green
Forest Hill (11)	CM 817 568-3000	Donald Walker	Edward Badgett	Juanita Willman	Cecil Berry	Paul Philbin	Douglas Wright	. . . .
Fort Stockton (9)	CM 915 336-8525	(not reporting)						
Fort Worth (448)	CM 817 871-8900	Kay Granger	Robert Terrell	Alice Church	Charles Boswell	Howard McMillen	Thomas Windham	Gary Santerre
Fredericksburg t (7)	MC 512 997-7521	(not reporting)						
Freeport (11)	CM 409 233-3526	(not reporting)						
Freer (3)	MC 512 394-6612	Malloy Hamilton	. . . .	Hilda Rosales	. . . .	. . . .	George Gomez Jr	. . . .
Friendswood (23)	CM 713 482-3323	M Newman	. . . .	L Vance	L Bucher	B Brown	J Stout	M Meinecke
Friona (4)	CM 806 247-2761	(not reporting)						
Frisco (6)	MC 214 377-2161	(not reporting)						
Fritch (2)	CM 806 857-3143	(not reporting)						
Gainesville (14)	CM 817 665-4323	Jim Hatcher	Lyle Dresher	. . . .	Phill Conner	Steve Boone	Carl Dunlap	Jim Gray
Galena Park (10)	MC 713 672-2556	(not reporting)						
Galveston (59)	CM 409 766-2113	Barbara Crews	Douglas Matthews	Anna Lee	Robert Richardson	Willie Wisko	Dale Rogers	Kathi Flowers
Garland (181)	CM 214 205-2000	. . . .	Ronald Holifield	Ranette Boyd	James Hager Jr	Daniel Grammer	Terry Hensley	. . . .
Gatesville (11)	CM 817 865-8951	Wyllis H Ament	Bob Stevens	. . . .	Evelyn Thomas	Billy Vaden	Carroll Duke	Robert Patterson
George West (3)	CM 512 449-1556	(not reporting)						
Georgetown (15)	CM 512 869-3636	(not reporting)						
Giddings (4)	CM 409 542-2311	Lavonne D Morrow	James E Dover	Dianne Schneider	. . . .	Don Schulz	Dennis R Oltmann	Serapio Garza
Gilmer (5)	CM 214 843-2553	Roy Owens	. . . .	Peggy J Smith	. . . .	Mike Waller	A L McAllister	Donnie Bond
Gladewater (6)	CM 903 845-2196	Jackie D Wood	Sharon G Johnson	Barbara Kennedy	Sharon G Johnson	. . . .	James R Keene	Roy Perryman
Gonzales (7)	CM 512 672-2815	(not reporting)						
Graham (9)	CM 817 549-3324	Ed M Hinson	Larry M Fields	H Rogers Nancy	H Rogers Nanny	Rudy Dye	Jim Nance	Chester Smith
Granbury (4)	CM 817 573-1114	Rick Frye	Robert D Brockman	Dee Arcos	Mike W Easley	Jerry Campbell	Randy Jaquess	Greg Reynolds
Grand Prairie (100)	CM 214 660-8000	Charles England	Gary Gwyn	Sue Shawver	Wayne Usry	David McCarty	Harry Crum	Jim McMeans
Grand Saline (3)	MC 903 962-1322	Larry W Martin Sr	Sam Beeler	Nancy Thatcher	. . . .	Walt Bryant	Charles S Tull	. . . .
Grapevine (29)	CM 817 481-0404	William D Tate	Trent Petty	Linda Huff	Larry Koonce	Bill Powers	Tom Martin	Jerry L Hodge
Greenville (23)	CM 903 457-3100	Everett Gladding	Edward Thatcher	Patricia Merrell	Lee Maness	Robert Wood	Barry Paris	Massoud Ebrahim
Gregory (2)	MC 512 643-6562	(not reporting)						
Groesbeck (3)	MC 817 729-3293	Jim Longbotham	. . . .	Martha Stanton	. . . .	Dwain Funderburk	Charles Walker	Keith Tilley
Groves (17)	CM 409 962-4471	(not reporting)						
Hallettsville (3)	MC 512 798-3681	Don R Jones	Maxine Mikulenka	Betty Woytek	Sharon Rose	Anthony Ludwig	Elmo Grant	Bill Cardiff
Haltom City (33)	CM 817 834-7341	Trae Fowler	William Eisen	Jan Kaase	Patrick Elfrink	Jerry McEntire	. . . .	Kenneth Slovak
Hamilton (3)	MC 817 386-8116	(not reporting)						
Hamlin (3)	MC 915 576-2711	Melvin J Scott	Jenny White	Oletha Waldrop	. . . .	Claude Scifres	Ronnie Hill	Gerald Barnett
Harker Heights (13)	CM 817 699-2301	Stewart Meyer	Gary Jackson	Patricia Brunson	Alberta Barrett	. . . .	John Drake	Stephen Cast
Harlingen (49)	CM 512 427-8800	H William Card Jr	. . . .	Debra A Ritchie	Jerry Dale	Sigfredo Cantu	James Scheopner	Ruben Diaz
Haskell (3)	MC 817 864-2355	Pat Henry	. . . .	Loretta Gray	. . . .	James Reynolds	Tom Bassett	Dave Miller
Hearne (5)	CM 409 279-3461	Thomas Mathews	Loyd Hafley	Dorothy Cooper	Verna Rachui	Horace Mathews	James Jones	Willard Johnson
Hedwig Village (3)	MC 713 465-6009	Robert I Goehrs	Lana Rizzuto	Lana Rizzuto	Lana Rizzuto	Anthony Calagna	William G Rush	Paul Addington
Hempstead (4)	MC 409 826-2486	(not reporting)						
Henderson (11)	CM 214 657-6551	Brad Holmes	Earl Heath	Patsy Farley	Nancy Jackson	Dwayne Pirtle	Randall Freeman	Connie Monk
Henrietta t (3)	CM 817 538-4316	C S Catlin	Joe Pence	Betty Thorn	. . . .	Ricky Langford	. . . .	. . . .
Hereford (15)	CM 806 364-2123	Bob Josserand	Chester Nolen	. . . .	Mike Hatley	Jay Spain	David Wagner	. . . .
Hewitt (9)	CM 817 666-6171	Louis P Mexia	Dennis H Woodard	Betty A Orton	. . . .	Tom Lucenay	Jack Caswell	Paul Holroyd Jr
Highland Park t (9)	CM 214 521-4161	(not reporting)						
Highland Village (7)	CM 214 317-2558	Kay T Stephens	Robert McDaniel	. . . .	Alan Dickerson	T Glen Harris	David Farrar	Chris Curry
Hillsboro (7)	CM 817 582-3271	Henry Moore	C Gene Cravens	. . . .	Frankie Lahr	Jackie Halbert	Jackie Halbert	Terry Hafer
Hitchcock (6)	MC 409 986-5591	(not reporting)						
Hollywood Park (3)	MC 512 494-2023	(not reporting)						
Hondo (6)	CM 512 426-3378	Mary J Lopez	Scott L Wall	Vangie Pimentel	. . . .	. . . .	Joe Aynesworth	. . . .
Houston (1631)	MC 713 247-1000	Robert Lanier	Richard Lewis	Anna Russell	. . . .	Edward Corral	Samuel M Nuchia	J Schindewolf
Humble (12)	MC 713 446-3061	Haden E McKay	James P Baker	Georgia B Fields	James P Baker	Max W Cullum	Donald R Maddox	Raymond C Dreyer
Hunters Creek Village (4)	MC 713 465-2150	(not reporting)						
Huntsville (28)	CM 409 295-6471	William Hodges	Gene Pipes	Danna Welter	Patricia Allen	Joe French	Hank Eckhardt	Boyd Wilder
Hurst (34)	CM 817 281-6160	(not reporting)						
Hutchins (3)	MC 214 225-6121	(not reporting)						
Ingleside (6)	CM 512 776-2517	(not reporting)						
Iowa Park (6)	MC 817 592-2131	(not reporting)						
Irving (155)	CM 214 721-2600	Bobby J Raper	S W McCullough	Lester G Ford	Ralph Ellis	Richard A Knopf	Benny M Newman	Lewis W Patrick
Jacinto City (9)	CM 713 674-8424	David Gongre	Joann Griggs	Joyce Raines	. . . .	Roland Hobbs	Joseph T Clark	John L Coope
Jacksboro (3)	CM 817 567-6321	Jerry Craft	Leroy Lane	Oneta Teague	. . . .	. . . .	Arthur Reaves	John Ash
Jacksonville (13)	CM 903 586-3510	Larry K Durrett	Jim D Dunaway	Shine Chancellor	Dewey Jones	Rodney Kelley	Floyd Stiefer	Jim Anderson
Jasper (7)	CM 409 384-4651	Frank R Lindsey	Kerry M Lacy	Betty Glenn	Ben F Griffin	Jimmy Dougharty	Harlan Alexander	Joe Matthews
Jefferson (2)	MC 214 665-3922	(not reporting)						
Jersey Village (5)	CM 713 466-6159	(not reporting)						
Jones Creek v (2)	MC 409 233-2700	Wayne Dubose	Tamie Schmidt	Bella Ortiz	. . . .	Thomas Grissett	Howard Rape	. . . .
Jourdanton (3)	CM 512 769-3589	(not reporting)						
Junction (3)	CO 915 446-2622	(not reporting)						
Karnes City t (3)	MC 512 780-3422	Don Tymrak	Retta Sides	. . . .	. . . .	Charles Malik	Nolan Jonas	Michael Therot
Katy (8)	MC 713 391-9181	Jonas W Conner	Dion O Miller	Virginia Maddox	Diana Ulbig	Charles Hooper	Pat Adams	Danny Harris
Kaufman (5)	CM 214 932-2216	Jess M Murrell	R Scott Magee	Jo Ann Talbot	Karen Waddle	Eddie Brown	Johnny Riggins	. . . .
Keene (4)	MC 817 641-3336	(not reporting)						
Keller (14)	MC 817 431-1517	John Buchanan	Allen Bogard	. . . .	Beverly Queen	Kelly King	Bill Griffith	Mike Barnes
Kenedy (4)	MC 512 583-2230	Ruhman C Franklin	Joe E Ponish	Janie Rodriguez	. . . .	Robert Alexander	Dennis Fenner	Gary Wegner
Kennedale (4)	CM 817 478-5418	Bill Abbott	Ted Rowe	Linda Gress	Vicki Thompson	Jerry Kirkpatrick	David Geeslin	Joey Highfill
Kermit (7)	CM 915 586-3460	(not reporting)						
Kerrville (17)	CM 512 257-8000	. . . .	Glenn Brown	Sheila Brand	Dane Tune	Raymond Holloway	Chuck Dickerson	George Kerr
Kilgore (11)	CM 903 984-5081	Bob Barbee	Ronald Stephens	Karen Brock	Ronald Stephens	. . . .	Ronnie Moore	Chuck Overbeck

Directory 1/9 continued — MUNICIPAL OFFICIALS IN U.S. CITIES OVER 2,500

TEXAS (427) continued

City, 1990 population figures (000 omitted), form of government		Municipal phone number	Mayor	Appointed administrator	City clerk	Finance officer	Fire chief	Police chief	Public works director
Killeen (64)	CM	817 634-2191	Raul Villaronga	June E Lykes	Paula A Miller	Connie Green	. . . .	F L Giacomozzi	Bennie Hedden
Kingsville (25)	CM	512 595-8018	. . . .	Carlos Lerma	Diana Ramirez	Hector Hinojosa	Juan A Torres	Felipe Garza	Meg Conner
Kirby (8)	CM	512 661-3198	Jerry R Kneupper	Ricardo T Cortes	Zina Tedford	. . . .	Kevin Riedel	B Riemenschneider	Carl Griffith
Kountze (2)	MC	409 246-3463	Charles Bilal	. . . .	Sonya Wilson	. . . .	Dale Williford	. . . .	Chet Deaver
La Feria (4)	MC	512 797-2261	(not reporting)						
La Grange (4)	CM	409 968-5805	Don Chovanec	Shawn Raborn	Violet Zbranek	Frances Wied	Werner Willrich	Eugene Ulbrich	Gary Becher
La Marque (14)	CM	409 938-7201	Pete W Rygaard	Nicholas Finan	. . . .	Terry Knudsen	Clark Cofer	Larry Crow	Rick Malbrough
La Porte (28)	CM	713 471-5020	(not reporting)						
Lacy-Lakeview (4)	MC	817 799-2458	C W Doherty	. . . .	B Cook	J Perkins	T Fiene	. . . .	J Powell
Lake Dallas (4)	MC	817 497-2226	Jerry McCutcheon	Donna Hamilton	. . . .	. . . .	. . . .	Nick Ristago	Johnny Webber
Lake Jackson (23)	CM	409 297-2481	Doris Williams	William Yenne	Charles Smith	Pam Eaves	Steve Shultz	P C Miller	Dyson Campbell
Lake Worth Village (5)	MC	817 237-1211	(not reporting)						
Lamesa (11)	CM	806 872-2124	Bill Gerber	Paul Feazelle	. . . .	Linda Scott	Royce Dyess	G M Cox	. . . .
Lampasas (6)	CM	512 556-6831	(not reporting)						
Lancaster (22)	CM	214 227-2111	Margie Waldrop	William Gaither	Jacqueline Denman	Pauline Hodges	Donald McMullan	Malcolm McGuire	Robert Foster
Laredo (123)	CM	512 791-7300	Saul N Ramirez	Peter H Vargas	Gustavo Guevara	Diana L Arredondo	Michael Perez	Jose L Martinez	Jose Guerra
League City (30)	MC	713 332-3431	(not reporting)						
Leon Valley (10)	MC	512 684-1391	Irene Baldridge	Henry Brummett	Gretchen Black	Henry Brummett	Curtis Dunn	Willard Stannard	James Malone
Levelland (14)	CM	806 894-0113	Raymond Dennis	Greg Ingham	Chris Wade	Judy Stephens	Thurman Davis	Ted Holder	. . . .
Lewisville (47)	CM	214 219-3400	Bobbie Mitchell	Charles Owens	Martie Hendrix	. . . .	Randy Corbin	Steve McFadden	Steven Bacchus
Liberty (8)	CM	409 336-3684	C Scott Parker	Roy N Bennett	Beth Staton	Beth Staton	Jamie Galloway	Billy Tidwell	. . . .
Littlefield (6)	CM	806 385-5161	Ray G Keeling	Martin Mangum	Amalia A Martinez	. . . .	Don Huckabey	Gary Lightfoot	Jimmy Durham
Live Oak (10)	CM	512 653-9140	Ray Hilderbrand	Douglas G Faseler	Marian Elbel	. . . .	Brian D Elbel	Mark S Jackley	Mark A Wagster
Livingston (5)	CM	409 327-4311	Ben R Ogletree Jr	Sam Gordon	Marilyn Sutton	Marilyn Sutton	Corky Cochran	Dennis Clifton	Richard Walker
Llano (3)	MC	915 247-4158	Jeffrey Hopf	Tom Donaldson	. . . .	Lynda Kuder	Beverly Harden	Stacey Nobles	Don Stewart
Lockhart (9)	CM	512 398-3461	M Louis Cisneros	Joe A Michie	Gwen Barrett	James P Blystone	John Walters	Mark Hinnenkamp	Ralph Gerald
Longview (70)	CM	903 237-1220	Tom Hayes	James B Baugh	Lois G McCaleb	Al L Milligan Jr	Tommie McMaster	Johnny W Upton	Wayne A Johnston
Lubbock (186)	CM	806 767-2315	(not reporting)						
Lufkin (30)	CM	409 634-8881	Louis Bronaugh	C G Maclin	Atha Stokes	Molly Hicks	Fenton Prewitt	Edwin Collins	Ronald Wesch
Luling (5)	CM	512 875-2481	Martin Weiner	Harold Watts	Ruby White	Pat Jackson	Paul Stahl	Travis Thomas	Sam Jernigan
Madisonville (4)	CM	409 348-2748	(not reporting)						
Mansfield (16)	CM	817 473-9371	Tom Corbin	Clayton Chandler	Judy Howard	Tommie Johnson	Bobby Looney	Coy Martin	. . . .
Manvel (4)	MC	713 489-0630	Doyle Fenn	. . . .	. . . .	. . . .	. . . .	John Rose	. . . .
Marble Falls t (4)	CM	512 693-3615	(not reporting)						
Marlin (6)	MC	817 883-5542	Tom Black	Sue Philley	Margaret Moore	Sue Philley	Clifford Webster	Clifford Webster	Bud Moore
Marshall (24)	CM	903 935-4416	(not reporting)						
Mathis (5)	MC	512 547-3343	(not reporting)						
McAllen (84)	CM	512 686-6551	Othal E Brand	Mike R Perez	Letty Vacek	Guillermo Seguin	Everett Derr	A Longoria	Alvaro Gonzalez
Mc Gregor (5)	CM	817 840-3688	Kathleen Anglin	Bill Dake	Christine Otter	Bill Dake	Junior Fisher	Mike Cook	Dave Faubion
McKinney (21)	CM	214 542-2675	John Gay	Donald E Paschal	Jennifer Smith	Beverly N Lange	Robert Hultkrantz	Ken Walker	. . . .
Meadows (5)	MC	806 539-2377	Dale Wylie	. . . .	Jerry Blair	. . . .	Joe Perez	. . . .	. . . .
Memphis (2)	MC	806 259-3001	Homer Tucker	Nelwyn Ward	Nelwyn Ward	Nelwyn Ward	Wilie Davis	Robert McGuire	Jack Scott
Menard (2)	CM	915 396-4616	(not reporting)						
Mercedes (13)	CM	512 565-3114	Miguel Castillo	Alan Kamasaki	Arcelia L Felix	Janie Gonzales	Rudy Garza	Jose H Flores	Albert Zavala
Mesquite (101)	CM	214 288-7711	Cathye Ray	James A Prugel Jr	Gay L Prugel	Donald W Simons	Donald R Nelson	Travis L Hass	Morris Bishop
Mexia (7)	CM	817 562-5385	Stanley Cotton	Gerald Yarbrough	Cloyce Tyner	Gerald Yarbrough	Aaron Thompson	Rodger Cotton	Robert Vaughan
Midland (89)	CM	915 685-7100	(not reporting)						
Midlothian (5)	CM	214 775-3481	Maurice Osborn	Robert Powers	. . . .	Jimmie McClure	David Schrodt	Roy Vaughn	Duane Hill
Mineola (4)	MC	214 569-6183	Ralph Bruner	Thomas R Taylor	Patsy R Brott	Thomas R Taylor	Red Humphreys	Joe Dell Bevill	Richard E Harbuck
Mineral Wells (15)	CM	817 328-1211	(not reporting)						
Mission (29)	CM	512 580-8661	Richard Perez	. . . .	Ramona Martinez	J R Gonzalez	Armando Ocana	Patrick D Dalager	Juan A Barrera
Missouri City (36)	CM	713 261-4260	(not reporting)						
Monahans (8)	CM	915 943-4343	David Cutbirth	David Mills	Sheri Lord	Shirlan Turner	Billy Riley	David Watts	Bobby Sinclair
Morton t (3)	MC	806 266-8850	Ray Lewis	Mitch Grant	. . . .	. . . .	Jerry Arthur	. . . .	. . . .
Mount Pleasant (12)	CM	903 572-3412	Jim Blanchard	. . . .	. . . .	Brenda Reynolds	Larry McRae	Conrad Mars	Pete Donnelly
Muleshoe (5)	CM	806 272-4528	Robert Montgomery	Dave Marr Jr	Mary Hicks	. . . .	Donald Harrison	Wayne Holmes	Cleve Bland
Nacogdoches (31)	CM	409 564-4693	(not reporting)						
Nassau Bay (4)	CM	713 333-4211	G Allen	D Stall	N Sweningson	. . . .	J McGee	R Holden	P Briscoe
Navasota (6)	CM	409 825-6475	Bill Miller Jr	Harold Underwood	. . . .	Geraldine Binford	Tommy Dedmon	Chris Siracusa	Gary E Johnson
Nederland (16)	CM	409 727-2711	Carl N Leblanc	Damaso E Sosa	Ladonna Floyd	Cheryl Dowden	Mike Lovelady	Billy Neal	Steve Hamilton
New Boston t (5)	MC	903 628-5596	John H McCoy	. . . .	Carol Ensey	. . . .	Billy House	Kerry Pinkham	R C Thomas
New Braunfels (27)	CM	512 625-3425	Rudy Seidel	Hector M Tamayo	Veronica Sarkozi	D Sollberger	Phillip Baker	C R Headen	. . . .
Nocona (3)	MC	817 825-3281	John Gibbs	Melvin Adams	Minnie Walker	. . . .	. . . .	Bill Bratcher	Sam Williams
North Richland Hills (46)	MC	817 581-5500	Tommy Brown	Rodger Line	Jeanette Rewis	Larry Cunningham	Stanley Gertz	Jerry McGlasson	Greg Dickens
Oak Ridge North (2)	MC	713 292-4648	Gary A Louie	Richard E Derr	Susan Hensley	. . . .	. . . .	George Biernesser	. . . .
Odessa (90)	CM	915 337-7381	Lorraine Perryman	Jerry McGuire	Jerri Sullivan	Peggy Hetzler	James Wiggs	James Jenkins	Matt Squyres
Olmos Park (2)	CM	512 824-3281	(not reporting)						
Olney (4)	MC	817 564-2102	Jeff McClatchy	Jack R Northrup	Lee Ann Campbell	Jean Clifton	Garry Keeter	Cliff Blackstock	Ronnie Stroud
Orange (19)	CM	409 886-3611	Dan Cochran	Charles W Pinto	Judy Davis	Gail English	Jerry Wimberley	Sam Kittrell	James Foyle
Palacios (4)	MC	512 972-3605	Beverly Watson	Charles Winfield	Jane Mower	Charles Winfield	Sammy Davidson	Emil Sliva	. . . .
Palestine (18)	CM	903 729-2181	(not reporting)						
Pampa (20)	CM	806 669-5700	(not reporting)						
Panhandle (2)	CM	806 537-3517	Jack Miller	Thomas J Blazek	Amy Wright	. . . .	Richard Robinson	Kenneth J Rogers	Lenro L Jennings
Pantego t (2)	CM	817 274-1381	Robert D Surratt	Larry W Smith	Tracy B Norr	Larry W Smith	. . . .	Doug Davis	Ronnie Gibson
Paris (25)	CM	903 785-7511	(not reporting)						
Pasadena (119)	MC	713 477-1511	Johnny Isbell	. . . .	Pan Ramey	Wayne Long Jr	Jimmy Cameron	Floyd Daigle	Edward B Simmons
Pearland (19)	CM	713 485-2411	Vic Coppinger	Paul Grohman	Pat Jones	Janet Eastburn	Larry Steed	Mike Hogg	Richard Burdine
Pearsall (7)	MC	512 334-3676	(not reporting)						
Pecos (12)	CM	915 445-2421	(not reporting)						
Perryton (8)	MC	806 435-4014	David Hale	David Landis	Janice Henson	Don Jennings	C B Luther	Joe Hannon	Ted B Dodd
Pharr (33)	CO	512 787-2703	(not reporting)						
Pinehurst (3)	CM	409 886-2221	(not reporting)						
Piney Point Village (3)	MC	713 782-0271	(not reporting)						
Pittsburg (4)	MC	903 856-3621	D H Abernathy	Ned C Muse	Sue Sharp	. . . .	. . . .	Weldon Reynolds	Wayne Hadderton
Plainview (22)	CM	806 296-1100	Gene Ridlehuber	. . . .	Katherina Ellena	Norman Huggins	Bruce Watson	Roy Osborne	William Hogge
Plano (129)	CM	214 424-6531	James B Muns	T Muehlenbeck	Jackie Blakely	James D Forte	William Peterson	Bruce Glasscock	James R Hogan
Pleasanton (8)	CM	512 569-3867	Bob Hurley	Larry Pippen	Kathy McMullen	. . . .	. . . .	Keith Blair	William Lamb
Port Aransas (2)	CM	512 749-4111	(not reporting)						
Port Arthur (59)	CM	409 983-8100	Mary Summerlin	Cornelius Boganey	Carolyn Dixon	Walter Thomas	Clifford Barbay	Melbourne Gorris	E J Romero
Port Isabel (4)	CM	512 943-2682	Calvin Byrd	Manuel Hinajosa	Luisa Gonzalez	Loretta Streif	Robert Harris	Charles Londrie	Eduardo Holland
Port Lavaca (11)	CM	512 552-9795	Tiney Browning	C J Webster	. . . .	John Iles	C R Stringham	Dave Brungardt	Bob Coen
Port Neches (13)	CM	409 727-2181	Gary C Graham Sr	James Harrington	Nancy Goodwin	Caryl Richardson	Ken D Doise	C R Bennefield	Leon Rhame
Portland (12)	CM	512 643-6501	Billy G Webb	Patrick Conner	Norma S Lockhart	Sarah Murphy	James Bishop	Harrold White	Kim Parker

City, 1990 population figures (000 omitted), form of government	Municipal phone number	Mayor	Appointed administrator	City clerk	Finance officer	Fire chief	Police chief	Public works director
TEXAS (427) continued								
Post (4)	MC 806 495-2811	(not reporting)						
Poteet (3)	MC 512 742-3574	(not reporting)						
Prairie View (4)	MC 409 857-3711	(not reporting)						
Premont (3)	MC 512 348-2022	(not reporting)						
Princeton t (2)	MC 214 736-2416	B Caldwell				Mike Woody	Allen Gibson	
Quanah (3)	MC 817 663-5336	Weldon Dickerson	Joel M Epps	Billie Duncan	Dena Jo Daniel	Paul Converse		
Ranger (3)	CO 817 647-3522	Ronnie Ainsworth	Barbara Wheat	Joyanne Hathcock	Leroy Hoerner	Darrell Fox	Elton McCoy	Samuel Sanchez
Raymondville (9)	CM 512 689-2443	C M Crowell	Jose L Lopez	Jose L Lopez	Jose L Lopez	Fred Ramirez	Rene R Martin	Octavio A Correa
Refugio (3)	MC 512 526-5361	(not reporting)						
Richardson (75)	CM 214 238-4100	Gary Slagel	Bob Hughey	Ina Garber	Daniel Parker	Bobby Holley	Ken Yarbrough	Marshall Haney
Richland Hills t (8)	CM 817 595-6600	C F Kelley	Stephen D Hughes			Greg Tucker	Barbara Childress	Robert Osborn
Richmond t (10)	CM 713 342-5456	Hilmar Moore	Glen Gilmoore	A Villalobez		Stephen Noto	Charles Gore	Mark Zgabay
Richwood (3)	MC 409 265-2082	James M Vera		Karen B Schrom	Karen B Schrom	Rick Cary	Glenn Patton	Mike Harper
River Oaks (7)	MC 817 626-5421	(not reporting)						
Robinson (7)	MC 817 662-1425	(not reporting)						
Robstown (13)	MC 512 387-4589	Manuel B Lopez Jr	Osvaldo Romero	Norma Nunez	Osvaldo Romero	Julio M Flores	Rene DeAlejandro	Roy L Gutierrez
Rockdale (5)	MC 512 446-2511	Bill T Avrett	Sue Foster			Mike Korenek	R D Wilmeth	George Patterson
Rockport (5)	CM 512 729-2213	(not reporting)						
Rockwall (10)	CM 214 771-7700	Alma Williams	Julie Couch		Mike Phemister	Mark Poindexter	Bill Watkins	Rick Crowley
Roma (8)	CM 512 849-1411	(not reporting)						
Rosebud (2)	CM 817 583-7926	Charles Ratenke	Wanda Fischer	Shelle Ohlendorf	Wanda Fischer	Mike Bell	Richard Elifrits	Robert Blakley
Rosenberg (20)	MC 713 342-3850	(not reporting)						
Round Rock (31)	CM 512 255-3612	Charles Culpepper	Bob Bennett		David Kautz	Lynn Bizzell	Wes Wolff	Jim Nose
Rowlett (23)	CM 214 475-3841	Mike McCallum	Michael Gibson		Ronnie Hutchison	Joe Howard	Randy Posey	Nathan Stewart
Rusk t (4)	CM 214 683-2213	(not reporting)						
Sachse (5)	CM 214 495-1212	Larry Holden	Lloyd Henderson	Jo Ann London	Erik Andersen	M Jack Yates	Tom Fenley	Daniel Martin
Saginaw (9)	CM 817 232-4640	(not reporting)						
San Angelo (84)	CM 915 657-4241	(not reporting)						
San Antonio (936)	CM 512 299-8360	Nelson Wolff	Alexander Briseno	Norma S Rodriguez	Nora W Chavez	Robert Ojeda	William O Gibson	John Loren German
San Augustine t (2)	MC 409 275-2121	Curt Goetz	Alton B Shaw	Amelia Jeanes		Raymond Neal	John M Cartwright	
San Benito (20)	CM 512 399-5344	Charles Weekley	Richard Torres	Lupita Passement	Mark Yates	Armando Lucio	Richard Clark	Hector Jalomo
San Diego (5)	MC 512 279-3341	(not reporting)						
San Juan (11)	CM 512 787-9923	Arturo Guajardo	Gilbert A Hernand	Vicki Ramirez	Pete Maldonado		Jorge Arcaute	Ted Trevino
San Marcos (29)	CM 512 353-4444	Kathy Morris	Larry D Gilley	Janis Womack	William White	Daniel O'Leary	James L Kendrick	George Boeker
Sanger (4)	MC 817 458-7930	Nel Armstrong	John Hamilton			Bill Murrell		Chuck Tucker
Sansom Park Village (4)	MC 817 626-3791	(not reporting)						
Santa Fe (8)	CM 409 925-6412	George Willoughby	Vince DiPiazza	Janet Davis			Michael Barry	Richard Anderson
Schertz (11)	CM 512 658-7477	Earl W Sawyer	Kerry R Sweatt	June G Krause	Debra L Kline	Johnny J Woodward	Norman W Agee Sr	John Bierschwale
Seabrook (7)	CM 713 474-3201	Larry King		Evelyn Purswell	Pam Lab		Robert Kerber	Gary Jones
Seagoville (9)	CM 214 287-2050	Neal Wooley		Ruth Sorrells	Linnie Weaver	David Maroney	I D Smith	Mike Hitt
Seagraves (2)	MC 806 546-2593	Patrick L McAdoo		Catherin Mitchell	Catherin Mitchell		Dale Alwan	James W Fischer
Sealy (5)	CM 409 885-3511	Betty Reinbeck	Roger Carlisle	Pauline Small	Roger Carlisle	Charles Wendt		John Maresh
Seguin (19)	CM 512 379-3212	Edward Gotthardt	Jake Krauskopf		Leann Piatt	Terry Mayfield	Gary Hopper	
Selma (1)	MC 512 651-6661	Kenneth R Fleenor	Margie Lubianski	Margie Lubianski		Scott Lee	Mark Riffe	Scott Lee
Seminole (6)	CM 915 758-3676	Wayne Mixon	Tommy Phillips	Sharon Wilson	Anna Smith	Jerry Mutschler	Michael Browne	Gary Duncan
Seymour (3)	MC 817 888-3148	Dick Wirz	Gary R Jones	Judy S Gilbert	Judy S Gilbert	Gene Robinson	Floyd Burke	Carl Parker
Shamrock (2)	CM 806 256-3281	R L Roberts	Johnny Rhodes	Linda Amos	Johnny Rhodes	Randy Tallant	Art Taylor	Bill Bonner
Sherman (32)	CM 903 892-4545	Harry Reynolds	Jim Andrews	Helen Friend	Giles Brown	Jackie Mayfield	Stephen Pilant	David Gattis
Silsbee (6)	CM 409 385-2863	Wesley C Latham	Ronald Hickerson	Edna E Brown	Cesar Dominguez	Bo Welborn	Dennis M Allen	
Sinton t (6)	CM 512 364-2381	Jose A Gutierrez	Ron Garrison	Betty Wood	Dennis Lindeman	Dennis Lindeman	Joe Schumann	Ruben Fonseca
Slaton (6)	MC 806 828-6505	Don Kendrick	Jim Estes	Kay E Bruedigam	Jim Estes	Bob Kern	Barbara Fowler	Doyce Field
Smithville (3)	CM 512 237-3282	(not reporting)						
Snyder (12)	CM 915 573-4957	Paul Zeck	John W Gayle	Jeanne Johnson	Jeanne Johnson	Terry McDowell	Lannie Lee	
Sonora (3)	MC 915 387-2558	(not reporting)						
South Houston t (14)	MC 713 947-7700	Dennis Cordray			Young Lorfing	Jim Sybert	Paul Brookover	Bennie Romero
South Padre Island t (2)	CM 512 761-6456	Peggy Trahan	James Chisholm	Joyce Arp	Richard Middleton	Clifford Rowell	Edward Sanders	Arturo Garcia Jr
Southlake (7)	MC 817 481-5581	Gary Fickes	Curtis E Hawk	Sandra L Legrand	Lou Ann Heath		Billy Campbell	Robert Whitehead
Spearman (3)	CM 806 659-2524	Burl Buchanan	Kelvin Knauf	Cheryl Gibson	Kelvin Knauf	Ron Antalek	Joe Raper	
Spring Valley (3)	MC 713 465-9308	(not reporting)						
Stafford t (8)	MC 713 499-4537	(not reporting)						
Stamford (4)	CM 915 773-2591	(not reporting)						
Stephenville (14)	MC 817 965-7887	(not reporting)						
Sugar Land (25)	CM 713 242-3176	(not reporting)						
Sulphur Springs (14)	CM 903 885-7541		Olen Petty	Sharon Ricketson	Wendell Sapaugh	Charles Bolding	Donnie Lewis	Bill Farler
Sundown (2)	MC 806 229-3131	Joe Craddock	Dorothy Dominguez			Doug Barry	Larry Bradley	Frank Hernandez
Sunray (2)	CM 806 948-4111	(not reporting)						
Sweeny t (3)	MC 409 548-3321	Larry Piper	Exa Mae Keller	Tina Bernshausen		Benny Hock	Jerry Murphy	Tim Moss
Sweetwater (12)	CM 915 236-6313	(not reporting)						
Taft (3)	MC 512 528-3512	(not reporting)						
Tahoka (3)	CM 806 998-4211	(not reporting)						
Taylor (11)	CM 512 352-3675	Wallace Brueckner	Ken Taylor	Donna Seaholm	David Weber	Haywood Stanford	Fred Stansbury	Kenneth Jirasek
Taylor Lake Village (3)	MC 713 474-2843	(not reporting)						
Teague (3)	MC 817 739-2547	(not reporting)						
Temple (46)	CM 817 770-5561	J W Perry	David Taylor		Sam Huey	Eddy Clanton	Thomas Vannoy	Leonard Henry
Terrell (12)	CM 214 551-6600	Don L Lindsey	Jim Mullins		Bobby Bishop	Michael Roscoe	Geoffrey Whitt	Steve Rogers
Terrell Hills (5)	CM 512 824-7401	Barbara Christian	Cal D Johnson	Edyth E Warren	Cal D Johnson	Arnold G Rose	Barney R Flowers	Juan D Camacho
Texarkana (32)	CM 903 794-0912	John Jarvis	G Shackelford	Geri Haddock	John Hackleman	George Chamblee	Gary Adams	Philip Ball
Texas City (41)	MC 409 948-3111	Charles T Doyle		Thomas E Pedersen	Charles T Doyle	Gerald J Grimm	Jerry D Purdon	Thomas E Kessler
The Colony (22)	CM 214 625-1756	William Manning	William Hall	Patti Hicks	James England	Van Morrison	Bruce Stewart	Tom Cravens
Tomball t (6)	CM 713 351-5484	H G Harrington	Warren Driver	Anna Kreger	Joe Stegall	Jesse Arnold	Paul Michna	Robert Johnson
Tulia (5)	CM 806 995-3547	David Edwards	Bryan Easum	Barbara Cabe	Bryan Easum	Wayne Nevins	Jimmy McCaslin	Foy Campbell
Tyler (75)	CM 214 531-1100	S P Reynolds	E R Clark	A A Lanier	H V Bryan	P C White	L W Robinson	
Universal City (13)	CM 512 659-0333	(not reporting)						
University Park (22)	CM 214 363-1644	Barb Hitzelberger	Bob Livingston	Bobbie Sharp	Bob Hicks	Robert Dixon	Robert Dixon	Gene Smallwood
Uvalde (15)	CM 512 278-3315	(not reporting)						
Van Horn (3)	MC 915 283-2050	(not reporting)						
Vernon (12)	CM 817 552-2581	(not reporting)						
Victoria (55)	CM 512 573-2401	Ted Reed	James Miller	Virginia Yeater	Charles Windwehen	Henry Juenke	Ronald Perkins	John J Byrum
Vidor (11)	MC 409 769-5473	(not reporting)						
Waco (104)	CM 817 750-5600	J Robert Sheehy	James Holgersson	Nana L Cornwell	Robert H Salter	Robert W Mercer	Gilbert E Miller	Comer W Dickens
Wake Village (5)	MC 903 838-0515	Mike Huddleston	Bob Long	Maxine Orr		Tommy Seale	Tony Estes	Dwight Smith
Watauga (20)	CM 817 281-8047	(not reporting)						
Waxahachie (18)	CM 214 937-7330	Pat McElroy	Bob Sokoll	Nancy Ross	Carl Wessels	David Hudgins	Allwin Barrow	Frank Davis

Directory 1/9 continued — **MUNICIPAL OFFICIALS IN U.S. CITIES OVER 2,500**

City, 1990 population figures (000 omitted), form of government	Municipal phone number	Mayor	Appointed administrator	City clerk	Finance officer	Fire chief	Police chief	Public works director
TEXAS (427) continued								
Weatherford (15)	CM 817 594-5441	(not reporting)						
Weimar (2)	CM 409 725-8554	Bennie Kosler	Francis E Parks	Evelyn Theumler	. . . .	Frank Mac Aulay	Charles Coulter	Frankie Vana
Wellington (2)	CM 806 447-2544	(not reporting)						
Weslaco (22)	CM 512 968-3181	Eugene A Braught	Wai Lin Lam	Amanda Elizondo	Enrique Guzman	Tony Abrigo	William Roach	Juan Flores
West Columbia (4)	CM 409 345-3123	Robert R Dixon	Max Pitts	Debbie Sutherland	. . . .	Charley Tindol	Don Fairrel	Chuck Tielke
West Orange (4)	MC 409 883-3468	Carl K Thibodeaux	Walter Schexnyder	Linda Morvant	. . . .	Tommy Aven	Bruce Simpson	Alex Caswell
West University Place (13)	CM 713 668-4441	(not reporting)						
Westworth Village (2)	MC 817 738-3673	(not reporting)						
Wharton (9)	CM 409 532-2491	Garland S Novosad	R A Miller	Lou Ann Rumfield	Karl S Schwartz	Jim Wendel	Tim Guin	Phillip M Bush
White Oak t (5)	MC 903 759-3936	(not reporting)						
White Settlement (15)	CM 817 246-4971	(not reporting)						
Whitesboro t (3)	MC 214 564-3311	(not reporting)						
Wichita Falls (96)	CM 817 761-7611	Michael Lam	James Berzina	. . . .	Fred Werner	Ronnie James	Curtis Harrelson	George Bonnett
Wills Point (3)	CM 214 873-2578	Bobby Mitchell	Wilson Read	Lillian Samples	Wilson Read	C C Girdley	Richard Koonce	Scott Drake
Windcrest (5)	MC 512 655-0022	(not reporting)						
Winnsboro (3)	MC 903 342-3654	Jerry Hopper	Jerry Poe	Pamela Mangum	. . . .	Kenneth Russell	Gary Lile	. . . .
Winters (3)	CM 915 754-4424	Joe Gerhart	Aref Hassan	Donna Donica	. . . .	Johnny Merrill	Carey Balentine	Charles Grenwelge
Woodville t (3)	MC 409 283-2234	Billy Rose	Donald W Shaw	. . . .	. . . .	Alva Cook	Scott Yosko	. . . .
Woodway (9)	CM 817 772-4480	. . . .	Marvin P Norwood	Margie Barker	Linda Sansom	. . . .	Yousry Zakhary	Dean Conner
Wylie (9)	CM 214 442-2236	John W Akin	Steven P Norwood	Mary Nichols	Brady Snellgrove	Jimmy M Lynch	Harvey Hightower	. . . .
Yoakum (6)	CM 512 293-6321	(not reporting)						
UTAH (67)								
Alpine (3)	MC 801 756-6347	Don Christiansen	. . . .	Eleanor Jenks	. . . .	John Pool	Daniel Jones	William H Devey
American Fork (16)	MC 801 756-3571	(not reporting)						
Blanding (3)	CM 801 678-2791	(not reporting)						
Bountiful (37)	MC 801 298-6140	(not reporting)						
Brian Head t (..)	MC 801 677-2029	(not reporting)						
Brigham City (16)	MC 801 734-2001	Clark N Davis	Roger K Handy	Dennis Sheffield	Dennis Sheffield	Rod Romer	Charles G Earl	E Bruce Leonard
Cedar City (13)	MC 801 586-2950	Harold Shirley	Joe Melling	Bonnie Moritz	. . . .	David Bently	Pete Hansen	. . . .
Centerville (12)	MC 801 295-3477	(not reporting)						
Clearfield (21)	CM 801 774-7200	(not reporting)						
Clinton (8)	CM 801 825-5098	Steven Weller	Patrick Sorensen	Carla Parsons	. . . .	Floyd Peterson	Bill Chilson	Mel Wood
Draper (7)	MC 801 571-4121	Kumen B Davis	David C Campbell	Barbara Sadler	David C Campbell	Boyd Johnson	. . . .	Trey Eppley
Ephraim (3)	MC 801 283-4631	(not reporting)						
Farmington (9)	CM 801 451-2383	Robert W Arbuckle	Max Forbush	Dona Scharp	Dona Scharp	David F White	Jeff Jacobson	Walt Hokanson
Fruit Heights (4)	MC 801 546-0861	(not reporting)						
Grantsville (5)	MC 801 884-3411	Howard Murray	Jerry Medina	Monica Giffing	Jerry Medina	Brent Marshall	Danny Johnson	Joel Kertamus
Heber (5)	MC 801 654-0757	S Wright	M Anderson	. . . .	. . . .	. . . .	J J Matthews	L Higgs
Helper (2)	MC 801 472-5391	(not reporting)						
Hyrum (5)	MC 801 245-6033	(not reporting)						
Kaysville (14)	CM 801 546-1235	Brit Howard	Linda Ross	Dean Storey	. . . .	David Helquist	. . . .	. . . .
Layton (42)	MC 801 546-8500	James Layton	Alex R Jensen	. . . .	Steven Ashby	Allan Peek	Doyle Talbot	Terry Coburn
Lehi (8)	MC 801 768-8467	(not reporting)						
Lindon (4)	MC 801 785-5043	Noal T Greenwood	E Ray Brown	C Inger Cordner	. . . .	. . . .	. . . .	Don C Peterson
Logan (33)	MC 801 750-9812	(not reporting)						
Mapleton (4)	MC 801 489-5655	Everet Predmore	Lois Murdock	Dianne Wittusen	Lori Brierley	Alan Bisj	Bret Barney	Kent Wheeler
Midvale (12)	MC 801 561-1418	(not reporting)						
Moab (4)	MC 801 259-5121	(not reporting)						
Monticello (2)	MC 801 587-2271	Jack N Young	Richard C Terry	Dan Shoemaker	Richard C Terry	Joe Slade	Kent Adair	Clyde Christensen
Murray (31)	MC 801 264-2656	Lynn Pett	. . . .	. . . .	Don Whetzel	Wendell Coombs	Ken Killian	Charles Clay
Nephi (4)	MC 801 623-0822	Robert L Steele	J Randy McKnight	J Corrine Garrett	R Blair Painter	Harold Parkin	Chad M Bowles	Gary Howarth
North Ogden (12)	MC 801 782-7211	(not reporting)						
North Salt Lake (6)	MC 801 298-3877	Dewayne Simmons	Collin H Wood	Terry Curtis	. . . .	. . . .	Val Wilson	Rodney Wood
Ogden City (64)	MC 801 629-8737	(not reporting)						
Orem (68)	CM 801 224-7070	Stella Welsh	Daryl Berlin	. . . .	Phillip Goodrich	. . . .	Ted Peacock	Richard Manning
Panquitch (1)	MC 801 676-2311	Maloy Dodds	Allen K Henrie	Shirley Chidester	Allen K Henrie	Russel Buckley	Martin Nay	David Owens
Park City (4)	MC 801 645-5000	Bradley Olch	Toby Ross	Anita Sheldon	Kent Parker	. . . .	Francis Bell	Jerry Gibbs
Payson (10)	MC 801 465-9226	Richard Harmer	Keith Morey	Sheila Anderson	J Callaway	Ron Gordon	James E Box	. . . .
Pleasant Grove (13)	MC 801 785-5045	(not reporting)						
Pleasant View (4)	MC 801 782-8529	(not reporting)						
Price (9)	MC 801 637-5010	(not reporting)						
Providence (3)	MC 801 752-9441	Gary K Millburn	Brent Speth	Kathleen H Gale	. . . .	. . . .	. . . .	Dee Barnes
Provo (87)	MC 801 379-6000	Michael R Hill	Thomas Martin	Marilyn Perry	George J Karlsven	Rodney C Jones	Swen C Nielsen	Merril L Bingham
Richfield (6)	MC 801 896-6439	(not reporting)						
Riverdale (6)	MC 801 394-5541	L Leon Poulsen	V Dean Steel	Glenna Stump	Lynn Fortie	Steve Carter	Wayne Hoaldridge	Lynn Moulding
Riverton (11)	MC 801 254-0704	(not reporting)						
Roosevelt (4)	MC 801 722-5001	Leonard Ferguson	D Brad Hancock	Carolyn Krissman	Ralph T Hill Jr	Robert Yack	Cecil Gurr	Roger Eschler
Roy (25)	CM 801 774-1000	Kathleen Browning	Randy Sant	Laurel Dalton	Gail Hill	Noel Padden	M Jr Hammon	Mike Mansfield
Salem (2)	MC 801 423-2770	(not reporting)						
Salt Lake City (160)	MC 801 535-7704	(not reporting)						
Sandy City (75)	MC 801 566-1561	Lawrence P Smith	Byron Jorgenson	Patricia Davis	Arthur D Hunter	Jacob G Nielson	Gary J Leonard	Darrel M Scow
Smithfield (6)	MC 801 563-6226	J Kenneth Webb	. . . .	Mary Ann Barkdull	James P Gass	Robert Richardson	. . . .	Joel Downs
South Jordan (12)	MC 801 254-3742	Theron Hutchings	Anthony Murphy	. . . .	Anthony Murphy	Gary Whatcott	John Parker	Alden Winters
South Ogden (12)	MC 801 399-4413	(not reporting)						
South Salt Lake (10)	MC 801 483-6000	(not reporting)						
Spanish Fork (11)	CM 801 798-3568	Marie W Huff	David A Oyler	. . . .	Kent R Clark	Lloyd L Miller	Dee Rosenbaum	Richard J Hemp
Springville (14)	MC 801 489-2700	Delora Bertelsen	J Douglas Bird	. . . .	. . . .	Philip Whitney	Leland Bowers	. . . .
St. George (29)	MC 801 634-5800	(not reporting)						
Sunset (5)	MC 801 825-1628	(not reporting)						
Syracuse (5)	MC 801 825-1477	(not reporting)						
Tooele (14)	MC 801 882-0110	(not reporting)						
Tremonton (4)	MC 801 257-3324	(not reporting)						
Vernal (7)	MC 801 789-2255	Leonard Heeney	Kenneth L Bassett	Kenneth L Bassett	Harley Hales	Dale Slaugh	Michael Hamner	. . . .
Washington (4)	CM 801 628-1666	(not reporting)						
Washington Terrace (8)	MC 801 393-8681	(not reporting)						
West Bountiful (4)	MC 801 292-4486	Carl M Johnson	Wendell W Wild	Laverne Greaves	. . . .	. . . .	Wayne A Jeppson	. . . .
West Jordan (43)	CM 801 561-1463	(not reporting)						
West Valley City (87)	CM 801 966-3600	Brent Anderson	John Patterson	Karen Leftwich	Russell Sanderson	John Williams	Dennis Nordfelt	R Willardson
Woods Cross (5)	CM 801 292-4421	(not reporting)						
VERMONT (70)								
Barre (9)	CM 802 476-5246	Harry S Monti	Michael A Welch	James F Milne	. . . .	Douglas Brent	Edward Fish	Reginald T Abare

Directory 1/9
continued

**MUNICIPAL OFFICIALS
IN U.S. CITIES OVER 2,500**

City, 1990 population figures (000 omitted), form of government	Municipal phone number	Mayor	Appointed administrator	City clerk	Finance officer	Fire chief	Police chief	Public works director
VERMONT (70) continued								
Barre t (7)	CM 802 479-9331	David L Roberts	Carl R Rogers	Ruth A Finn	Carl R Rogers	Rene Larouche	Michael Stevens	. . . .
Barton t (3)	TM 802 525-6222	(not reporting)						
Bellows Falls v (3)	CM 802 463-3964	Tom Mac Phee	Paul McGinley	Doreen Aldrich	. . . .	. . . .	Gary Derosia	Maurice Kelly
Bennington t (16)	TM 802 447-1037	. . . .	Stuart A Hurd	. . . .	. . . .	. . . .	. . . .	. . . .
Bethel t (2)	TM 802 234-9876	John Washburn	Geneva Gaiko	Jean Burnham	. . . .	Robert Dean	Wendell Wills	Gary Slack
Brandon t (4)	CM 802 247-3635	Bill Heath	Brannon Godfrey	Wilda Harris	. . . .	. . . .	Joseph Arduca	Bruce Rounds
Brattleboro t (12)	CM 802 254-4541	Martha O'Connor	Glenn E Hill	Annette Cappy	David Fredenburgh	David Emery	Bruce Campbell	Jerome Remillard
Bristol t (4)	CM 802 453-2410	Doug Corkins	Robert Bernstein	Penny Sherwood	. . . .	. . . .	. . . .	. . . .
Bristol v (2)	CM 802 453-2410	George M Tighe	. . . .	Penny Sherwood	Penny Sherwood	Mark Bouvier	Kevin Gibbs	A Scott Powell
Burlington (39)	MC 802 658-9300	Peter Brownell	. . . .	Ruth Stokes	Brendan Keleher	Richard Desautels	Kevin Scully	Scott Johnstone
Castleton t (4)	CM 802 468-5319	(not reporting)						
Cavendish t (1)	CM 802 226-7292	Thomas Lazetera	Richard Svec	Ronald Butler	. . . .	. . . .	. . . .	Richard Svec
Charlotte t (3)	TM 802 425-3071	Wendy Schroeder	. . . .	Terry Silva	. . . .	Gary Therrien	. . . .	. . . .
Chester t (3)	TM 802 875-2173	(not reporting)						
Colchester t (15)	CM 802 655-0811	(not reporting)						
Derby t (4)	TM 802 766-4906	(not reporting)						
Dorset t (2)	CM 802 362-4571	John P Stannard	Vernon Squiers	Denise Hebert	Vernon Squiers	Thomas Beebe	. . . .	. . . .
Essex t (16)	TM 802 879-0413	Martin Myers	Patrick Scheidel	Rosalee Crewdson	Douglas Fisher	Larry Ransom	John Terry	Dennis Lutz
Essex Junction v (8)	CM 802 878-6944	George Dunbar Sr	William Dugan	Cathy Jones	. . . .	Steve Miller	. . . .	Craig Cushing
Fair Haven t (3)	TM 802 265-3010	Robert Richards	Patricia Paolillo	Suzanne Ruest	Patricia Paolillo	H Kenneth Allen	Andrew Brown	Richard Reid
Hardwick t (3)	TM 802 472-6120	(not reporting)						
Hartford t (9)	CM 802 295-9353	Richard Carbrello	Ralph W Lehman	Deborah Adams	Evelyn Stevens	John G Wood Jr	Joseph Estey	. . . .
Hartland t (3)	TM 802 436-2236	Patricia B Peat	Hiram E Allen	Mary W Davis	. . . .	Mark Cote	. . . .	Hiram E Allen
Hinesburg t (4)	TM 802 482-2281	Lynn Gardner	Kathleen Ramsay	Mary Zuber	. . . .	Bernard Giroux	Allen Fortin	. . . .
Jericho t (4)	TM 802 899-4936	John C Stewart	. . . .	Judith Pitcher	. . . .	David Tillotson	. . . .	. . . .
Johnson t (3)	TM 802 635-2611	(not reporting)						
Ludlow t (2)	CM 802 228-2841	(not reporting)						
Ludlow v (1)	TM 802 228-2841	(not reporting)						
Lyndon t (5)	TM 802 626-5785	(not reporting)						
Manchester t (4)	CM 802 362-1313	Ivan Beattie	Jeffrey D Wilson	Barbara Cross	Ruth Skuse	Thomas Ouellette	Manfred Wessner	Jeffrey Williams
Middlebury t (8)	TM 802 388-4041	Tim Buskey	Betty Wheeler	Richard Goodro	Pauline Singley	Roger Young	Tom Hanley	William Hageman
Milton t (8)	TM 802 893-6655	(not reporting)						
Montpelier (8)	CM 802 223-9502	Ann E Cummings	Ryan D Cotton	Charlotte L Hoyt	John R Kroll	. . . .	Dougla S Hoyt	Stephen A Gray
Morristown t (5)	TM 802 888-3534	(not reporting)						
Newport (4)	CM 802 334-5136	K Zisselsberger	Craig Whitehead	Charles Blake	. . . .	Leo Parenteau	William Hughes	Keith Southworth
North Troy v (1)	CM 802 988-2663	(not reporting)						
Northfield t (6)	TM 802 485-6121	(not reporting)						
Northfield v (2)	CM 802 485-6121	(not reporting)						
Poultney t (3)	CM 802 287-9751	(not reporting)						
Poultney v (2)	CM 802 287-4003	Orba Beer	Paul H Hermann	Barbara Betit	. . . .	. . . .	. . . .	. . . .
Pownal t (3)	TM 802 823-7757	(not reporting)						
Randolph t (5)	CM 802 728-5433	Mitchell Harrness	. . . .	Doris M Bowman	. . . .	Larry Thurston	Philip F Mollitor	H Ruppertsberger
Richmond t (4)	TM 802 434-2221	Wright Preston	Ronald Rodjenski	Velma E Godfrey	. . . .	Tom Levesque	John O'Hara	Kendall Chamberla
Rockingham t (5)	CM 802 463-3964	N Lincoln Divoll	Paul McGinley	Rita Bruce	Lynn Dunn	. . . .	. . . .	Maurice Kelly
Rutland (18)	MC 802 773-1800	(not reporting)						
Rutland t (4)	TM 802 773-2528	Rodney Gallipo	Joseph Zingale Jr	R Del Bianco	. . . .	Tim Perry	. . . .	. . . .
Shaftsbury t (3)	TM 802 442-4038	(not reporting)						
Shelburne t (6)	CM 802 985-2342	Alice Winn	William Finger	Colleen Haag	William Finger	Craig Wooster	James Warden	. . . .
Sherburne t (1)	CM 802 422-3241	(not reporting)						
South Burlington (13)	CM 802 658-7953	(not reporting)						
Springfield t (10)	CM 802 885-2104	(not reporting)						
St. Albans (7)	CM 802 524-1500	(not reporting)						
St. Albans t (5)	CM 802 524-2415	(not reporting)						
St. Johnsbury t (8)	CM 802 748-3926	(not reporting)						
Stowe t (3)	TM 802 253-7350	Theodore Teffner	Greg Federspiel	Marie Betterley	Karla Spaulding	Wendall Mansfield	. . . .	. . . .
Swanton t (6)	TM 802 868-4421	(not reporting)						
Swanton v (2)	CM 802 868-3397	Leon Babbie	George Lague	Carol Winchester	. . . .	Al Kinzinger	Michael McCarthy	Michael Menard
Troy t (2)	TM 802 988-2663	(not reporting)						
Waterbury t (5)	TM 802 244-7033	Edward Steele	William Shepeluk	Edward Finn	. . . .	Edward Eldredge	Wayne Sourdiff	. . . .
Weathersfield t (3)	CM 802 674-2626	Neil Daniels	C Peter Cole	Carol Daniels	. . . .	Rodney Spaulding	Richard Poland	. . . .
West Rutland t (2)	TM 802 438-2263	Paul Kulig	Thomas Yennerell	Jayne Pratt	. . . .	. . . .	. . . .	Thomas Yennerell
Westminster t (3)	CM 802 722-4255	William A Noyes	William O'Connor	Janette Holton	. . . .	. . . .	. . . .	Mark C Lund
Williamstown t (3)	TM 802 433-6671	William Graham	J Leo Donahue	Doreen Townsend	. . . .	Edward Eaton	. . . .	Everett Hurlburt
Williston t (5)	TM 802 878-5121	Ronald Blair	Bert S Moffatt	Arlene H Degree	Susan E Sieg	H P Lunderville	Osburn C Glidden	Neil H Boyden
Wilmington t (2)	TM 802 464-8591	(not reporting)						
Windsor t (4)	CM 802 674-6786	William Hochstin	David Battistoni	Gloria Tansey	. . . .	Lewis O Gage	Patrick Foley	. . . .
Winooski (7)	CM 802 655-6410	William Norful	Michael D Letcher	Pauline Schmoll	. . . .	David Bergeron	Walter Nieliwocki	Steve Woodworth
Woodstock t (3)	TM 802 457-3456	(not reporting)						
Woodstock v (1)	CM 802 457-3456	(not reporting)						
VIRGINIA (93)								
Abingdon t (7)	CM 703 628-3167	Joe T Phipps	G M Newman	G M Newman	Mark W Godbey	H M McCormick Jr	Cecil Kelly	C M Vernon Jr
Alexandria (111)	CM 703 838-4699	Patricia S Ticer	Vola Lawson	Beverly Jett	Daniel Neckel	Thomas Hawkins Jr	Charles Samarra	Thomas O'Kane Jr
Altavista t (4)	CM 804 369-5001	J R Burgess	Stanley Goldsmith	Myra M Chism	. . . .	Haywood Belvin	T L Neal	Clarence E Dawson
Appalachia t (2)	CM 703 565-3900	Gary A Bush	Bobby L Dorton	Mary D Reece	Bobby L Dorton	Robert Anderson	Roy L Munsey	Bobby G Reynolds
Appomattox t (2)	MC 804 352-8268	Ronald C Spiggle	Bobbie H Mullins	. . . .	. . . .	. . . .	. . . .	David T Garrett
Arlington (171)	CM 703 358-3000	(not reporting)						
Ashland t (6)	CM 804 798-9219	Stephen E Merritt	David Reynal	Eliz C Kennon	. . . .	. . . .	John D Rochat	Michael A Davis
Bedford (6)	CM 703 586-7102	G Michael Shelton	Jack A Gross	Teresa W Hatcher	Barry W Thompson	Michael Burnette	Milton H Grahame	C H Broesamle
Berryville t (3)	MC 703 955-1099	R Sponseller	John Hogan	Nancy Tinsman	Desiree Ellmore	. . . .	Elden Nesselrodt	James O'Brien
Big Stone Gap t (5)	CM 703 523-0115	Patrick Murphy	George R Polly	Joyce M Page	George R Polly	W R Mumpower	Larry R Mohn	George R Polly
Blacksburg t (35)	CM 703 961-1000	Roger Hedgepeth	Ronald A Secrist	Donna B Caldwell	Mary C Kemp	B Keith Bolte	Donald L Carey	Adele P Schirmer
Blackstone t (3)	CM 804 292-7251	(not reporting)						
Bluefield t (5)	CM 703 322-4626	Cecile Barrett	Art Mead	Art Mead	Art Mead	Edward Honaker	Jack Asbury	James Mayo
Bridgewater t (4)	CM 703 828-3390	(not reporting)						
Bristol (18)	CM 703 466-2221	Jerry A Wolfe	Paul D Spangler	Daniel L Johnson	Paul D Spangler	Charles W Denton	William H Price	W A Dennison Jr
Brookneal t (1)	MC 804 376-3124	(not reporting)						
Buena Vista (6)	CM 703 261-6121	(not reporting)						
Cape Charles t (1)	CM 804 331-3259	Alice B Brown	Richard Barton	Ruth A McNamara	. . . .	William Powell	William Lewis	Norman C Bell
Charlottesville (40)	CM 804 971-3490	(not reporting)						
Chase City t (2)	CM 804 372-5136	Charles Duckworth	Rickey G Reese	Cynthia Gordon	. . . .	Winthy Hatcher Jr	Fred A Parsons	Stanley Duckworth
Chatham t (1)	MC 804 432-8153	J Haywood Crider	. . . .	Catherine Miller	. . . .	Landon Worsham	. . . .	Craig C Motley
Chesapeake (152)	CM 804 547-6166	William Ward	James Rein	Betty Callaway	Joseph Sibley	Michale Bolal	Ian Shipley Jr	John O'Connor

Directory 1/9 continued — **MUNICIPAL OFFICIALS IN U.S. CITIES OVER 2,500**

City, 1990 population figures (000 omitted), form of government	Municipal phone number	Mayor	Appointed administrator	City clerk	Finance officer	Fire chief	Police chief	Public works director
VIRGINIA (93) continued								
Christiansburg t (15) CM	703 382-6128	Harold G Linkous	John E Lemley	Imogene Brumfield	....	James W Epperly	Ronald L Lemons	Robert Gearheart
Clarksville t (1) MC	804 374-8177	Kathleen N Walker	Greg Ailsworth	Karlotta Young	....	Raymond Hite	Ricky Wilkinson	Terry Hite
Clifton Forge (5) CM	703 863-2500	Johnny S Wright	Stephen A Carter	Craig Hudson	....	Thomas Fitch	Barry G Balser	Brandon Nicely
Coeburn t (2) CM	703 395-3323	Harold L Ringley	Terry L Gibson	Sherry B Bise	Terry L Gibson	Clinton Hawkins	F Harold Markham	Danny Jordan
Colonial Heights (16) CM	804 520-9265	James B McNeer	Robert E Taylor	Rita C Schiff	William Johnson	Allan G Moore	Steve Sheffield	Kurt E Ankrom
Covington (7) CM	703 965-6300	James L Jamison	David H Dew	Edith S Wood	....	Roscoe Humphries	Jeffrey S Brown	Jack C Munsey Jr
Crewe t (2) CM	804 645-9453	(not reporting)						
Culpeper t (9) CM	703 825-1120	Waller Jones	Griff Griffin	Donna Foster	Roger Mitchell	....	Charles Jones	Tommie Beales
Danville (53) CM	804 799-5100	....	A Ray Griffin Jr	....	Aubrey Dodson	David Lampley	Neal Morris	Ric Drazenovich
Dumfries t (4) MC	703 221-3400	Samuel W Bauckman	Thomas E Harris	Retta S Ladd	Thomas E Harris	....	James K Habern	Charles Sakowicz
Emporia (5) CM	804 634-3332	(not reporting)						
Fairfax (20) CM	703 385-7855	J Mason	....	J Henderson	J Cawley	G Mesaris	J Skinner	J Veneziano
Falls Church (10) CM	703 241-5003	Brian O'Connor	David R Lasso	Elizabeth Shawen	Douglas B Scott	....	Stanley K Johnson	Richard J Durgin
Farmville t (6) CM	804 392-5686	J David Crute	Gerald J Spates	Robert Hazelwood	Robert Hazelwood	Phillip Gay	Otto S Overton	Eugene M Philbeck
Franklin (8) CM	804 562-8508	C Elliott Cobb Jr	John J Jackson	John J Jackson	John J Jackson	James M Wagenbach	Robert K Eubanks	William W Fleming
Fredericksburg (19) CM	703 372-1010	Lawrence Davies	....	Beverly Cameron	Clarence Robinson	Denny Kelly	James Powers	Tim Slaydon
Front Royal t (12) CM	703 635-7799	Stan W Brooks Jr	M Lyle Lacy III	Rhonda S North	John B O'Neill	Elmer D McIntosh	Larry W Daniel	Eugene T Tewalt
Galax (7) CM	703 236-3441	(not reporting)						
Glasgow t (1) CM	703 258-2246	Sam H Blackburn	William S Knick	William S Knick	....	Richard Spangler	Richard Hostetter	....
Grundy t (1) MC	703 935-2551	(not reporting)						
Hampton (134) CM	804 727-6407	(not reporting)						
Harrisonburg (31) CM	703 434-6776	(not reporting)						
Herndon t (16) CM	703 435-6800	Thomas Davis Rust	Robert A Stalzer	....	Leonard C Parks	....	George E Kranda	John E Moore
Hopewell (23) CM	804 541-2245	D Paul Karnes	Clinton H Strong	Mary Frances Pito	Elesteen Hager	Steve Brown	Wilbur R Clarke	Henry Wilde
Lebanon t (3) MC	703 889-7200	(not reporting)						
Leesburg t (16) CM	703 777-2420	James E Clem	Steven C Brown	Barbara Messinger	Paul E York	....	James M Kidwell	Thomas Mason
Lexington (7) CM	703 463-7133	H E Derrick Jr	T Jon Ellestad	Georgiana M Vita	Keith L Holland	Kenneth L Hall Jr	Bruce M Beard	David A Woody
Luray t (5) CM	703 743-5511	(not reporting)						
Lynchburg (66) CM	804 847-1400	Julian Adams	Charles F Church	Patricia Kost	Michael W Hill	William Anderson	Joseph M Seiffert	Raymond A Booth
Manassas (28) CM	703 257-8200	Robert L Browne	John G Cartwright	Linda A Hawley	M Joy Ringler	....	Christopher Tutko	....
Manassas Park (7) CM	703 335-8800	Ernest Evans	James Norlund	Lana Conner	Brett Shorter	Gerald Grove	William Kiefer	Frank McDonough
Marion t (7) CM	703 783-4113	Marshall Guy	Henry Booker	Dixie Sheets	Dixie Sheets	Stuart Buchanan	Charles Overbay	Dale Richardson
Martinsville (16) CM	703 638-3971	Allan McClain	Earl B Reynolds	Lance G Heater	Richard D Fitts	W Lewis Reeves	Terry L Roop	Leon Towarnicki
Middleburg t (1) CM	703 687-5152	(not reporting)						
Narrows t (2) CM	703 726-2423	Donald Richardson	Robert P Mercure	Catherine T Lloyd	Rob Mercure	Jerry D Duncan	William H Clemons	Glenn J Duncan
Newport News (175) MC	804 247-8444	Barry E Duval	Edgar E Maroney	Bernice I Berry	Kamal C Doshi	Larry L Orie	Jay A Carey	Max T Palmer
Norfolk (261) CM	804 441-2549	Mason C Andrews	James B Oliver Jr	Robert Daughtrey	Sterling Chearham	Ronald T Wakeham	Melvin C High	John M Keifer
Norton (4) CM	703 679-1160	B Robert Raines	E W Ward	Mary D Brown	E W Ward	Danny G Still	Samuel A Mongle	James L Hall
Orange t (3) CM	703 672-1020	William Chewning	Donald A Smith	Donald A Smith	....	Bert Roby	Alexander Clary	William Smith
Pearisburg t (2) CM	703 921-3208	Frank Winston	Kenneth Vittum	Judy Harrell	....	Daryl Scott	William Whitsett	Steve Stafford
Petersburg (38) CM	804 733-2324	(not reporting)						
Poquoson (11) CM	804 868-7181	L Cornell Burcher	Robert M Murphy	Judy F Wiggins	Carol O Davis	C E Ward	John T White	J L Montgomery
Portsmouth (104) CM	804 393-8626	(not reporting)						
Pulaski t (10) CM	703 980-1000	Gary C Hancock	Thomas Combiths	Ruth Harrell	Mildred Bolen	Jeff Hall	E J Williams	Mike Jenkins
Purcellville t (2) MC	703 338-7421	(not reporting)						
Radford (16) CM	703 731-3603	Thomas L Starnes	Robert P Asbury	Roy I Lloyd Jr	Jess Cantline	Martin R Roberts	Alvin C Earles	James H Hurt Jr
Richlands t (4) CM	703 964-2566	John Willis	Timothy Taylor	Elva Lee Van Dyke	....	Drew Puckett	Jack Young	Donald Van Dyke
Richmond (203) CM	804 780-7000	Walter T Kenney	Robert C Bobb	Edna Williams	Max Bohnstedt	Ronald Lewis	Marty Tapscott	Jerry Ellett
Roanoke (96) CM	703 981-2000	David A Bowers	W Robert Herbert	Mary Parker	James Grisso	Rawleigh Quarles	M David Hooper	William F Clark
Rocky Mount t (4) CM	703 483-7660	Broaddus Shively	Mark R Henne	Patricia H Hooke	Don E Fecher	Posey W Dillon	R B Jenkins	Cecil R Mason
Salem (24) CM	703 375-3060	James Taliaferro	Randolph M Smith	Forest G Jones	Frank P Turk	Danny W Hall	Harry T Haskins	....
Smithfield t (5) CM	804 357-3247	James Chapman	Kenneth McLawhon	Suzzann Pittman	....	I N Jones Jr	Mark A Marshall	W R Batten
South Boston (7) CM	804 575-4200	Raynell G Lantor	Gary F Christie	Gary F Christie	....	William E Murray	John V Simmons	G C Carrington
South Hill t (4) CM	804 447-3191	Earl O Horne	G Morris Wells Jr	....	....	James E Crowder	Norman Hudson	Clarence Ezell
Staunton (24) CM	703 332-3825	(not reporting)						
Strasburg t (4) CM	703 465-9197	Harry Applegate	Kevin Fauber	Mary Price	Mary Price	William Walton	James Hall	John Rhodes
Suffolk (52) CM	804 934-3111	S Chris Jones	Richard L Hedrick	Henry L Murden	Carroll L Acors	J Samuel Carter	Gilbert F Jackson	Thomas G Hines
Tappahannock t (2) CM	804 443-3336	Edward L Hammond	G G Belfield Jr	Beverley Corrieri	G G Belfield Jr	William Ellis III	....	Thomas P Wyatt
Tazewell t (4) CM	703 988-2501	Jerry Wood	Doyle Frye	Linda Griffith	....	A D Buchanan	Jim Higginbotham	Flint McAmis
Victoria t (2) MC	804 696-2343	(not reporting)						
Vienna t (15) CM	703 255-6300	Charles Robinson	John Schoeberlein	Carol Orndorff	Philip Grant	....	Daniel Kerr	John Stockton
Vinton t (8) CM	703 983-0607	Charles R Hill	B Clayton Goodman	Carolyn S Ross	Joan B Furbish	Barry L Fuqua	R R Foutz	Cecil W Stacy
Virginia Beach (393) CM	804 427-4242	(not reporting)						
Warrenton t (5) CM	703 347-1101	(not reporting)						
Waynesboro (19) CM	703 942-6600	(not reporting)						
West Point t (3) MC	804 843-3330	R Tyler Bland	Watson M Allen	Watson M Allen	Watson M Allen	Stephen Ogg	W Wayne Healy	Edward L Haurand
Williamsburg (12) CM	804 229-4821	Trist McConnell	Jackson C Tuttle	Lois S Bodie	Raymond Adams	T K Weiler	Larry Vardell	Dan Clayton
Winchester (22) CM	703 667-1815	(not reporting)						
Wise t (3) CM	703 328-6013	Caynor Smith Jr	Beverly Collins	Robin Bryant	....	Conley Holbrook	Anthony Bates	....
Woodstock t (3) CM	703 459-3621	J Timothy Dalke	Larry D Bradford	Michelle M Lohr	....	Gary Yew	Jerry P Miller	Robert L Neff
Wytheville t (8) CM	703 228-3111	Trenton G Crewe	C Wayne Sutherland	Sharon Cassell	....	James Waller	Robert A Doyle	Dennis Hackler
WASHINGTON (103)								
Aberdeen (17) MC	206 533-4100	Chuck Gurrad	....	Fred J Thurman	Fred J Thurman	Lowell Killen	William G Ellis	Robert A Salmon
Anacortes (11) MC	206 293-5131	(not reporting)						
Arlington (4) MC	206 435-5785	Robert Kraski	Thomas Myers	Kathy Peterson	....	Dean Olsen	Steve Robinson	Terry Castle
Auburn (33) MC	206 931-3000	(not reporting)						
Battle Ground (4) MC	206 687-7131	Frank DeShirlia	....	Judie Kastner	....	....	Ron Johnson	Frank Hodgson
Bellevue (87) CM	206 455-6838	(not reporting)						
Bellingham (52) MC	206 676-6960	(not reporting)						
Blaine (2) CM	206 332-8311	(not reporting)						
Bonney Lake (7) MC	206 862-8602	Vern Strong	....	Kathleen Clayton	Kathleen Clayton	Alden Dobson	Donald Frazier	Richard Meuschke
Bothell (12) CM	206 489-3437	Paul O Cowles	Anne L Pflug	Terry A Briscoe	Nancy A Crossley	Richard O Duncan	Mark Ericks	Warren Gray
Bremerton (38) MC	206 478-5290	Louis Mentor	....	Kathy McCluskey	....	Michael McKinley	Delbert McNeal	Eddy Chu
Brier (6) MC	206 775-5440	Wayne E Kaske	Norma Wilds	Norma Wilds	....	....	Jim Palmer	Alan Hammerquist
Buckley (4) MC	206 829-1921	Kathleen Sandor	Merlin Reynolds	....	Sheila Hulett	....	Arthur McGehee	Mike Brendel
Burlington (4) MC	206 755-0531	Raymond C Henery	Phillip M Messina	....	Richard A Patrick	Glen H Staheli	Edward M Goodman	Rodney D Garrett
Camas (6) MC	206 834-2462	Dean E Dossett	Lloyd N Halverson	....	Dale E Scarbrough	David G Artz	Michael C Slyter	Douglas A Quinn
Centralia (12) CM	206 736-4992	William Mason	Bill R Davee	Carol Lee Neely	Mark Griffin	Charles Newbury	Toni Breckel	Terry Calkins
Chehalis (7) CM	206 748-6664	Robert Spahr	David Campbll	Jo Ann Hakola	Jo Ann Hakola	....	Randy Hamilton	Barry Heid
Chelan (3) MC	509 682-4037	Joyce Stewart	John Greiner	Robert Daykin	....	William Greenway	Edwin Bush	William Greenway
Cheney (8) MC	509 235-7211	Allen Ogden	James Reinbold	Grant Murie	Grant Murie	John Montague	Jerry Gardner	Paul Schmidt
Clarkston (7) MC	509 758-5541	Howard Clovis	....	Vickie Storey	....	Robert Berreman	....	....

Directory 1/9 continued

MUNICIPAL OFFICIALS IN U.S. CITIES OVER 2,500

City, 1990 population figures (000 omitted), form of government	Municipal phone number	Mayor	Appointed administrator	City clerk	Finance officer	Fire chief	Police chief	Public works director
WASHINGTON (103) continued								
Clyde Hill t (3)	MC 206 453-7800	Philip Rourke	Mitch Wasserman	Mitch Wasserman	. . . .	. . . .	William Wehmeyer	Samuel Schille
Colfax (3)	MC 509 397-3861	(not reporting)						
College Place (6)	MC 509 529-1200	(not reporting)						
Colville (4)	MC 509 684-5094	Duane Scott	. . . .	Lynne Somerville	. . . .	Rick Naff	Damond Meshishnek	. . . .
Connell (2)	MC 509 234-2701	Jim Klindworth	Jeff Bishop	Carol Seachriest	Joan Eckman	. . . .	Rick Rochleau	John Klein
Dayton (2)	MC 509 382-2361	Greg Lewis	Don Avery	. . . .	. . . .	Larry Munden	Larry Groom	Gus Hawks
Des Moines (17)	CM 206 878-4595	Richard T Kennedy	Greg Prothman	Denis Staab	Gene Logas	. . . .	Martin Pratt	Dale Schroeder
Edmonds (31)	MC 206 775-2525	(not reporting)						
Ellensburg (12)	CM 509 962-7220	Ray Stanley	Cynthia M Curreri	Darlene Arnold	. . . .	Steven A Alder	Hal A Rees	Thomas M Chini
Elma t (3)	MC 206 482-2212	William Bilsland	. . . .	Ingrid Daniels	. . . .	P Craig Nelson	Leslie Bonfield	C Quentin Boyer
Enumclaw (7)	MC 206 825-3591	Keith Blackburn	Michael Quinn	Lynn Shephard	Scott J Richard	Joseph Kolisch	Richard Williams	Mark Bayer
Ephrata (5)	MC 509 754-4601	(not reporting)						
Everett (70)	MC 206 259-8701	Pete Kinch	Carlton Gipson	Donna Rider	William Cushman	Terry Ollis	Michael Campbell	Ken Housden
Federal Way (..)	CM 206 941-1696	Robert Stead	J Brent McFall	Maureen Swaney	Deborah Larson	. . . .	. . . .	Philip Keightley
Ferndale (5)	CM 206 384-4302	Madelyn Waslohn	Stanley Strebel	Roland Signett	Roland Signett	. . . .	Dale Baker	John Eley
Fircrest t (5)	CM 206 564-8900	Stephen R Shelton	Jill Monley	Susan Clough	Pam Gardner	Jan L Chamberland	Ronald F Ames	. . . .
Forks t (3)	MC 206 374-5412	Richard Haberman	R Daniel Leinan	R Daniel Leinan	. . . .	Phil Arbieter	Vern Johnson	Dave Zellar
Gig Harbor (3)	MC 206 851-8136	Grethen Wilbert	Mark Hoppen	Mark Hoppen	Tom Enlow	. . . .	Dennis Richards	Ben Yazici
Goldendale (3)	CM 509 773-3771	James Grimes	Ehman Sheldon	Betty Smith	Betty Smith	John Halm	David Charvet	Ehman Sheldon
Grandview (7)	MC 509 882-9200	Jesse S Palacios	C J Sewell	Jean Wallar	. . . .	Jerry Donaldson	David Charvet	Cus Arteaga
Hoquiam (9)	MC 206 532-9330	Phyllis Shrauger	Peter Wall	Joann Stover	Joann Stover	Lance Talley	Scott Finlayson	Kathy Sellman
Issaquah (8)	MC 206 391-1000	(not reporting)						
Kelso (12)	CM 206 423-0900	Don Gregory	Doug Robinson	Veryl Anderson	Veryl Anderson	. . . .	Tony Stoutt	Robert Gregory
Kennewick (42)	CM 509 586-4181	Bob Quay	Robert M Kelly	Marge Price	Robert F Noland	Bob Kirk	Robert C Farnkoff	Roy Cross
Kent (38)	MC 206 859-3300	Daniel P Kelleher	Tony McCarthy	Brenda Jacober	. . . .	Norman Angelo	Edward Crawford	Don Wickstrom
Kirkland (40)	CM 206 828-1100	Terrence Ellis	Tara Adams	Tom J Anderson	. . . .	Eric Shields	Tom Fieldstead	Gary Sund
Lacey (19)	CM 206 491-3214	Jon Halvorson	Greg Cuoio	Charlotte Taylor	Martin Blaine	. . . .	John Mansfield	Brian Barnett
Longview (31)	CM 206 577-3300	Mark E Hoehne	Edwin R Ivey	C Sue Marsh	Nelson Graham	Ron Spreadborough	Jan Duke	Leroy Gower
Lynden (6)	MC 206 354-4270	Egbert Maas	. . . .	J Halderman	. . . .	Jim Top	Jack Foster	Terry Klimpel
Lynnwood (29)	MC 206 775-1971	M J Hrolicka	Michael Caldwell	Robert Noack	Robert Noack	Robert Meador	Larry Kalsbeek	Loren Sand
Marysville (10)	MC 206 659-8477	David Weiser	David Zabell	Mary Swenson	Steven Wilson	. . . .	Robert Dyer	Kenneth Winckler
Medical Lake (4)	MC 509 299-7712	(not reporting)						
Medina (3)	CM 206 454-9222	Ray Cory	Joyce Papke	Lynn Batchelor	. . . .	. . . .	Joseph Race	Anne Weigle
Mercer Island (21)	CM 206 236-5300	Eliott Newman	Paul Lanspery	Deb Symmonds	Joanne Sylvis	. . . .	Jan Deveny	. . . .
Mill Creek (3)	CM 206 745-1891	Pam Pruitt	John Sims Jr	Michele Schutz	Michele Schutz	. . . .	John Klei	Michael Monken
Milton t (5)	MC 206 922-8733	Leonard Sanderson	. . . .	Deborah Orosier	G Van Amberg	Richard Wall	Stan Jack	Darwin Myers
Monroe (4)	MC 206 794-7400	Gordon Tjerne	Douglas Jacobson	Betty King	Carol Grey	Kirk Stickels	Colleen Wilson	Douglas Jacobson
Montesano (3)	MC 206 249-3021	A L Jack Frost	. . . .	Sharon Morgan	. . . .	Don Bradshaw	W Brookshire	Robert Manley
Moses Lake (11)	CM 509 766-9210	R Wayne Rimple	Joseph Gavinski	. . . .	Walter Fry	Elvis Swisher	Fred Haynes	Gary Harer
Mount Vernon (18)	MC 206 336-6207	(not reporting)						
Mountlake Terrace (19)	CM 206 776-1161	Roger J Bergh	Walter R Fehst	Ron Swanson	Ron Swanson	Pat Vollandt	John H Turner	. . . .
Mukilteo (..)	MC 206 355-4151	Brian Sullivan	Jerald Osterman	Linda Miller	Linda Miller	William Scheller	Jon Walters	Larry Harmon
Normandy Park (7)	CM 206 248-7603	Stuart Creighton	James T Murphy	Brenda J Trent	Brenda J Trent	. . . .	Alfred J Teeples	Chuck Heit
Oak Harbor (17)	MC 206 679-5551	Al Koetje	Pat Nevins	Rosemary Morrison	Brad E Nelson	Mark Soptich	Tom Miller	. . . .
Ocean Shores (2)	CM 206 289-2488	Bruce Wolgemuth	Michael L Pence	. . . .	Gregory A Young	David H Cowardin	Michael F Wilson	John L Gow
Olympia (34)	CM 206 753-8447	Bob Jacobs	Richard C Cushing	. . . .	Jane Kirkemo	Jimmy Rambo	John Wurner	Art O'Neal
Omak (4)	MC 509 826-1170	E Walt Smith	. . . .	Trish Sieker	. . . .	Cal Bowling	Ron Bailey	Fred Sheldon
Othello (5)	MC 509 488-5686	(not reporting)						
Pasco (20)	CM 509 545-3408	Joyce Defelice	Gary Crutchfield	Dan Underwood	Dan Underwood	Larry Dickinson	Donald Francis	James Ajax
Port Angeles (18)	CM 206 457-0411	James Hallett	Jeffrey Pomeranz	Becky Upton	Katherine Godbey	Larry Glenn	Steve Ilk	Jack Pittis
Port Orchard (5)	MC 206 876-4407	Leslie Weatherill	. . . .	Patricia Hower	. . . .	Joseph Snow	Joseph Mathews	Lawrence Curles
Port Townsend (7)	MC 206 385-3000	(not reporting)						
Poulsbo (5)	MC 206 779-3901	R Mitchusson	. . . .	Karol Jones	. . . .	James Shields	Jeffrey Doran	John Cannon
Prosser (4)	MC 509 786-2332	(not reporting)						
Pullman (23)	MC 509 334-4555	Alfred Halvorson	John F Sherman	. . . .	John D Tonkovich	Patrick Wilkins	William Weatherly	James J Hudak
Puyallup (24)	CM 206 841-4321	Jack Parrish	Bob Jean	Barbara Price	Karen Clements	Merle Frank	Lockheed Reader	Tom Heinecke
Quincy t (4)	MC 509 787-3523	Debra A Adams	Donald D Rose	Linda B Mead	. . . .	Skip Simmons	Merle S Wilson	Peter M Smith
Raymond (3)	CO 206 942-3451	Leon P Lead	. . . .	Ronald L Hatfield	. . . .	Tom Betrozoff	Michael Kandoll	. . . .
Redmond (36)	MC 206 556-2120	Rosemarie Ives	Linda Herzog	Doris Schaible	Lenda Crawford	Rand Scott Coggan	Steve Harris	Carol Osborne
Renton (42)	MC 206 235-2556	Earl Clymer	Jay Covington	Marilyn Petersen	Victoria Runkle	A Lee Wheeler	Allan Wallis	Lynn Guttmann
Richland (32)	CM 509 943-7396	Craig Buchanan	Joseph C King	Leslie A Smith	Ron D Musson	Robert T Panuccio	Dave Lewis	William R Gilbert
Seattle (516)	MC 206 684-4000	(not reporting)						
Sedro-Woolley (6)	MC 206 855-1661	William Stendal	James Neher	Robin Hertlein	Robin Hertlein	Dean Klinger	David Cooper	. . . .
Selah (5)	MC 509 697-7215	John Sweesy	Frank Sweet	. . . .	. . . .	John Soden	Steve Robertson	Dale Nobel
Sequim (4)	MC 206 683-4139	Edward Beggs	. . . .	Lonna L Muirhead	. . . .	. . . .	Russell Barnes	Richard Parker
Shelton (7)	CO 206 426-4491	Joyce Jaros	Michael McCarty	Dennis Colvin	. . . .	Dan Ward	Samuel Johnston	Gary Rhoades
Snohomish (6)	CM 206 568-3115	Stephen Dana	Kelly Robinson	. . . .	. . . .	. . . .	Patrick Murphy	Lawrence Waters
Spokane (177)	MC 206 625-6267	Sheri Barnard	Roger Crum	M Montgomery	Pete Fortin	Bobby Williams	Terry Mangan	Irv Reed
Stanwood (2)	MC 206 629-2181	Robert N Larson	. . . .	Donald L Glancy	. . . .	Walter G Hood	. . . .	Gary A Armstrong
Steilacoom t (6)	MC 206 581-1900	Janda Volkmer	David Moseley	Susan Wilson	Paul Menter	Michael Campbell	Michael Campbell	Jim Richards
Sumner (6)	MC 206 863-8300	(not reporting)						
Sunnyside (11)	CM 509 837-3997	. . . .	Leo S Fancey	. . . .	Hugo R Schatz	Gary L Cole	Wallace Anderson	Gary F Potter
Tacoma (177)	CM 206 591-5130	Karen Viaile	Ray Corpuz	Genelle Birk	Peter Luttropp	Richard Moore	Raymond Fjetland	. . . .
Toppenish (7)	MC 509 865-5000	Gilbert Alaniz	James Southworth	LuHumphrey	. . . .	William Sharp	James Andrews	Jo Miles
Tukwila (12)	MC 206 433-1831	John W Rants	John McFarland	Jane E Cantu	Alan Doerschel	Tom Keefe	Ron Waldner	Ross Earnst
Union Gap (3)	MC 509 248-0432	(not reporting)						
Vancouver (46)	CM 206 696-8121	Bruce Hagensen	John Fischbach	Kent Shorthill	Kent Shorthill	Harold Steele	Rod Frederiksen	John Ostrowski
Walla Walla (26)	CM 509 527-4522	(not reporting)						
Wapato (4)	MC 509 877-2334	Richard Calahan	. . . .	Pauline Groth	. . . .	Tom Kehm	Lonnie James	Don Groth
Washougal (5)	MC 206 835-8501	(not reporting)						
Wenatchee (22)	CO 509 663-0551	(not reporting)						
West Richland (4)	MC 509 967-3431	Alvin C Metz	Paul A Chasco	Grace E Higgins	. . . .	. . . .	Michael W Noski	. . . .
Yakima (55)	CM 509 575-6090	. . . .	Richard Zais	Karen Roberts	John Hanson	Gerald Beeson	Pleas Green	Jerry Copeland
WEST VIRGINIA (59)								
Barboursville v (3)	MC 304 736-8994	(not reporting)						
Beckley (18)	MC 304 256-1768	(not reporting)						
Bethlehem v (3)	MC 304 242-4180	(not reporting)						
Bluefield (13)	CM 304 327-2401	Joe Long	William H Looney	Beverly Tresch	Charles Stahl	Richard Poe	Mike Poe	Al Werner
Bridgeport t (7)	MC 304 842-8229	Carl E Furbee Jr	. . . .	Judith S Lawson	. . . .	Kelly L Blackwell	Jack A Clayton	Mason W Steele
Buckhannon (6)	MC 304 472-1651	(not reporting)						
Charles Town (3)	MC 304 725-2311	Rufus W Park	J Patrick Holcomb	C Strosnider	. . . .	. . . .	. . . .	Herbert McDaniel
Charleston (57)	MC 304 348-8033	Kent Strange Hall	Curtis D Voth	C Critchfield	Robert Ruckle	Carl Beaver	Dallas Staples	Richard Carvell

Directory 1/9
continued

**MUNICIPAL OFFICIALS
IN U.S. CITIES OVER 2,500**

City, 1990 population figures (000 omitted), form of government	Municipal phone number	Mayor	Appointed administrator	City clerk	Finance officer	Fire chief	Police chief	Public works director
WEST VIRGINIA (59) continued								
Chester (3)	MC 304 387-2820	(not reporting)						
Clarksburg (18)	CM 304 624-1677	Louis Iquinto	Paul Shives	Pat D'Anselmi	Frank Ferarri	Bill Spencer	Thomas Durett	Frank Scarcelli
Dunbar (9)	MC 304 766-0222	(not reporting)						
Elkins (7)	MC 304 636-1414	Jimmy Hammond	. . . .	Philip J Graziani	. . . .	Roger Bolyard	Dale Kelley	. . . .
Fairmont (20)	CM 304 366-6211	Wayne A Stutler	Edwin J Thorne	Janet Keller	Fred Thompson	David Wimer	Ted Offutt	Micheal Demary
Fayetteville t (2)	MC 304 574-0101	(not reporting)						
Follansbee (3)	MC 304 527-1330	(not reporting)						
Grafton (6)	CM 304 265-1412	Carole F Klepfel	Carl R Clay Jr	Margaret A Cox	Larry M Richman	William M Roy	Thomas Broadstock	Gerald T Weber Jr
Hinton (3)	CM 304 466-3255	James A Lesli	Cynthia S Cooper	. . . .	. . . .	Ray Pivont	. . . .	Ralph Trout Jr
Huntington (55)	MC 304 696-5978	Jean Dean	David Harrington	Ann Shaye	Glenn White	Jerald Cremeans	Gary Wade	George Burgess
Hurricane v (4)	MC 304 562-5896	(not reporting)						
Kenova (4)	MC 304 453-1571	(not reporting)						
Keyser (6)	MC 304 788-1511	(not reporting)						
Kingwood t (3)	MC 304 329-1225	(not reporting)						
Lewisburg (4)	MC 304 645-2080	James Matheny	. . . .	Pat Pennington	. . . .	Wayne Pennington	Richard Weikel	Herb Montgomery
Logan t (2)	MC 304 752-4044	(not reporting)						
Madison (3)	MC 304 369-2762	(not reporting)						
Mannington t (2)	MC 304 986-2700	(not reporting)						
Martinsburg (14)	CM 304 263-0805	(not reporting)						
Montgomery t (2)	MC 304 442-5181	Ben Carson	. . . .	Jean Lorea	. . . .	Larry Robinson	Dave Stephenson	. . . .
Morgantown (26)	MC 304 284-7405	. . . .	Dan Boroff	Patricia Campbell	Donna Frum	Larry Rose	James McCabe	. . . .
Moundsville (11)	CM 304 845-3394	W McConnell	Thomas B Smyser	Judy Hunt	Dianne Menard	Don Wise	Allen Hendershot	Cecil Blake
Mullens t (2)	MC 304 294-7132	(not reporting)						
New Martinsville (7)	MC 304 455-9120	(not reporting)						
Nitro t (7)	MC 304 755-0701	(not reporting)						
Oak Hill (7)	CM 304 469-9541	(not reporting)						
Paden City t (3)	MC 304 337-2295	Eileen Smittle	Bernidene Culp	Peggy Nicholson	. . . .	James Richmond	John Lyons	Clifford Duke
Parkersburg (34)	MC 304 424-8400	Helen G Albright	. . . .	Connie S Shaffer	Randall H Craig	David Blasingame	Russell H Miller	Robert Eschbacher
Philippi (3)	CM 304 457-3700	Don Baughman	Joe Mattaliano	Doris Mundy	. . . .	John Green	Gerald Gaynor	Mike Scott
Point Pleasant (5)	MC 304 675-2360	Russell Holland	. . . .	Etta Gheen	Russell Holland	. . . .	John Sallaz	Dan Rodgers
Princeton (7)	CM 304 487-5020	Jo Anna Fredeking	Richard J Shakman	Kelly F Davis	Richard J Shakman	John W Howell	Charles A Kassay	Wayne C Shumate
Ranson (3)	MC 304 725-1010	(not reporting)						
Ravenswood (4)	CM 304 273-2621	John Alderson	. . . .	Joan Turner	. . . .	. . . .	Edward Speece	Thomas Carter
Richwood (3)	MC 304 846-2596	Jimmy Gladwell	. . . .	Dixie Cornell	Millie Stinnett	John Greer	Larry Tinney	B Shuttlesworth
Ripley (3)	MC 304 372-3482	(not reporting)						
Shinnston (3)	MC 304 592-5631	James H Jackson	. . . .	Patricia Andrews	Kenneth E Yost	Robert Burnett Jr	Donald W Book	Salvatore Ayers
South Charleston (14)	MC 304 744-5301	Richard A Robb	. . . .	Jack Wooline	. . . .	Claud Sigman	Alfred Leavitt	Franklin Mullin
Spencer (2)	MC 304 927-1640	(not reporting)						
St. Albans (11)	MC 304 722-3391	A Eddie Bassitt	. . . .	Bennett Burgess	. . . .	Dwight Pettry	Homer Clark	Donald Cheek
St. Marys (2)	MC 304 684-2401	(not reporting)						
Summersville t (3)	MC 304 872-1211	(not reporting)						
Vienna (11)	MC 304 295-4541	(not reporting)						
Weirton (22)	MC 304 797-8500	(not reporting)						
Welch (3)	CM 304 436-3113	(not reporting)						
Wellsburg (3)	CM 304 737-2104	Ernest Jack	Mark S Baldwin	Kathleen Traubert	Mark S Baldwin	Dick Kins	Larry Teeters	Don Birkett
Weston (5)	MC 304 269-6141	John C Burkhart	. . . .	Joyce A Brown	. . . .	Edward Griffin	George E Blake	. . . .
Westover (4)	MC 304 296-6860	Joseph C Janco	. . . .	Linda K Rose	. . . .	Brad Wilson	David Harris	. . . .
Wheeling (35)	CM 304 234-3617	Jack W Lipphardt	Jimmy E Curnes	Marilyn A Weidle	Thomas J Beatty	Cliff Sligar	Edward D Long	Russell J Jebbia
White Sulphur Springs (3)	MC 304 536-1454	(not reporting)						
Williamson (3)	MC 304 235-1510	Sam G Kapourales	. . . .	Frances K Frye	. . . .	Grover C Phillips	Roby Pope Jr	Dewey L Dingess
Williamstown (3)	MC 304 375-7761	(not reporting)						
WISCONSIN (174)								
Algoma (3)	MC 414 487-2163	(not reporting)						
Allouez v (..)	MC 414 448-2800	Audrey S Murphy	David Waffle	Susan L Foxworthy	. . . .	Jeff Roemer		
Altoona (6)	CM 715 839-6092	(not reporting)						
Amery (3)	MC 715 268-7486	Jerome Wittstock	J Riemenschneider	J Riemenschneider	. . . .	Rick Van Blaricom	Michael Holmes	John Frisco
Antigo (8)	MC 715 623-3033	Miles Stanke	Gary G Rogers Jr	Eleanor Hoerman	. . . .	. . . .	Robert Brehm	Pat Vanderleest
Appleton (66)	MC 414 832-6425	(not reporting)						
Ashland (9)	MC 715 682-7071	Russell Korpela	. . . .	Carol Larson	. . . .	Keith Tveit	Gordon Gilbertson	Steven Stadler
Ashwaubenon v (16)	MC 414 435-3751	(not reporting)						
Baraboo (9)	MC 608 356-8361	Dean D Steinhorst	. . . .	Patricia Seaberg	. . . .	Allyn P Swayze	Thomas J Lobe	. . . .
Barron (3)	MC 715 537-5631	(not reporting)						
Bayside v (5)	CM 414 351-8811	Francine Press	Joseph A Tanski	Joseph A Tanski	Joseph A Tanski	. . . .	Gary Mikolec	Harold Hohmann
Beaver Dam (14)	MC 414 885-5541	(not reporting)						
Beloit (36)	CM 608 364-6610	. . . .	Daniel T Kelley	Diane Henry	Hank Schreve	Gerald Buckley	Terry Fell	Richard Freese
Berlin (5)	CM 414 361-0800	Harold Klassa	Mark Rohloff	Louise Sedarski	Mark Rohloff	John Stetter	James Dobson	Mark Rohloff
Black River Falls (3)	MC 715 284-2315	Louis J Perry	. . . .	William R Arndt	. . . .	Jeffrey R Amo	Danny L Gomer	Carroll Zillmer
Bloomer (3)	MC 715 568-3032	Randy Summerfield	. . . .	Desiree Roth	. . . .	Rod Schmidt	Wayne Geist	. . . .
Boscobel (3)	MC 608 375-5001	Stephen Wetter	. . . .	John DuCharme	. . . .	Albert Mezera	Gerald Staskal	Michael Reynolds
Brillion (3)	CM 414 756-2250	(not reporting)						
Brodhead (3)	MC 608 897-4018	Allan Herrington	. . . .	Nancy Schoeller	. . . .	Philip McManus	David Wickstrum	Randy Rosheisen
Brookfield (35)	MC 414 782-9650	K Bloomberg	. . . .	G Rasmussen	A Wesner	J Mehring	G Wolff	W Muth
Brown Deer v (12)	CM 414 357-0100	(not reporting)						
Burlington (9)	MC 414 763-3717	Jeannie Hefty	Mark S Fitzgerald	Christine Kerkman	. . . .	R Vandesande	Ronald V Patla	. . . .
Butler v (2)	MC 414 783-2525	Richard Ensslin	Charles Erickson	Charles Erickson	. . . .	Robert Zoulek	Ernie Rosenthal	Charles Schaffer
Cedarburg (10)	MC 414 375-7600	John P Kuerschner	Clinton P Gridley	Jacquelyn Dekker	. . . .	R Van Dinter	George Rees	Robert Dreblow
Chilton (3)	MC 414 849-2451	(not reporting)						
Chippewa Falls (13)	MC 715 726-2719	(not reporting)						
Clintonville (4)	MC 715 823-6584	Allen Mahnke	Wallace C Thiel	C Vollrath	. . . .	John Krubsack	Gerald Bartelt	. . . .
Columbus (4)	MC 414 623-5900	(not reporting)						
Combined Locks v (2)	MC 414 788-2059	(not reporting)						
Cudahy (19)	MC 414 769-2200	(not reporting)						
De Forest v (5)	CM 608 846-6751	Rex Yankee	Duane Gau	Duane Gau	. . . .	Joel Rider	James Culbertson	. . . .
De Pere (17)	CM 414 339-4050	(not reporting)						
Delafield (5)	MC 414 646-3395	(not reporting)						
Delavan (6)	MC 414 728-5585	Peter F Dantone	Timothy Freitag	Betty L Wassel	. . . .	Neill Flood	Lawrence Malsch	Lyle Smith
Dodgeville (4)	MC 608 935-5228	(not reporting)						
Eau Claire (57)	CM 715 839-4902	Mark D Lewis	Don Norrell	Carol Schumacher	Rebecca Noland	Ron Brown	Dave Malone	William Bittner
Edgerton (4)	MC 608 884-3341	T Roenneburg	R Schultz	. . . .	. . . .	. . . .	K Burdick	S Strandlie
Elkhorn (5)	MC 414 723-2219	Paul Ormson	Edward Geick	Phyllis Patek	Lyle Peterson	Dennis Hommen	John Giese	. . . .
Elm Grove v (6)	CM 414 782-6700	Thomas E Vavra	Edmund M Henschel	James J Pellowski	Edmund M Henschel	William Selzer	Jeffrey W Haig	Kenneth Blaedow
Evansville (3)	MC 608 882-4424	Harlin Miller	. . . .	R Poffenberger	. . . .	Edd McCaffrey	Charles DiPiazza	David Milbrandt

City, 1990 population figures (000 omitted), form of government	Municipal phone number	Mayor	Appointed administrator	City clerk	Finance officer	Fire chief	Police chief	Public works director
WISCONSIN (174) continued								
Fitchburg t (16)	MC 608 275-7141	Doug Morrissette	Dan Elsass	Virginia Zugich	Dan Elsass	Larry Huber	Terry Askey	Paul Woodard
Fond Du Lac (38)	CM 414 929-3322	. . . .	Jack Howley	Thomas Lehman	G A Rebensburg	David Flagstad	Daniel J Bord	J William Roemer
Fort Atkinson (10)	CM 414 563-7760	Keneth Pattow	Robert C Martin	John Wilmett	John Wilmett	Steve Mode	Greg Gilbert	Jeff Woods
Fox Point v (7)	CM 414 351-8900	Mark Pollack	Allan Medoff	Constance McHugh	Louise M Haddon	. . . .	Mark Hayes	Michael Lynett
Franklin (22)	MC 414 425-7500	Frederich Klimetz	James C Payne	James C Payne	. . . .	David Bublitz	Norman Pollman	John M Bennett
Germantown v (14)	CM 414 251-1211	Charles J Hargan	Steven S Kubacki	Jane A Wilms	Hal Wortman	Gary Pollpeter	Gerald Blum	Lloyd Turner
Glendale (14)	MC 414 228-1700	(not reporting)						
Grafton v (9)	MC 414 375-5300	Rodney Schroeder	Darrell Hofland	Teri Dylak	. . . .	Rich Bulgrin	Howard Thiede	Mark Gottlieb
Green Bay (96)	MC 414 448-3147	Samuel J Halloin	. . . .	Paul G Janquart	Richard L Wessel	John L Troeger	Robert J Langan	Richard D Hall
Greendale v (15)	CM 414 423-2100	Bernard Schroedl	Frank Pascarella	Dianne Robertson	Frank Pascarella	Arnold Heling	David Leack	Nick Paulos
Greenfield (33)	MC 414 543-5500	James Besson	. . . .	Donna Rynders	John Possell	Roland Poppy	. . . .	Richard Andersen
Hales Corners v (8)	CM 414 529-6161	James R Ryan	Kristine Hinrichs	Kristine Hinrichs	. . . .	Richard Demien	Duwayne Dzibinski	Ronald J Romeis
Hartford (8)	MC 414 673-8204	James H Core	Matthew S Fulton	John C Spielmann	. . . .	Robert Baus	Thomas Jones	Lucian Darin
Hartland v (7)	CM 414 367-2714	David Lamerand	. . . .	Karen Compton	. . . .	Allen Wilde	Morton Hetznecker	James Wilson
Horicon (4)	MC 414 485-3500	R Greshay	. . . .	D Pasewald	. . . .	G Schwartz	D Glamann	S Bogenschneider
Hortonville v (2)	MC 414 779-6011	Alfred Handrich	M Schiedermayer	Joan Dockter	. . . .	Lyle Otto	Kenneth Hansen	Robert Henrickson
Howard v (10)	CM 414 434-4640	George Speaker	Kevin Anderson	Kevin Anderson	. . . .	John O'Connor	. . . .	Bruce Boykin
Hudson (6)	MC 715 386-5821	Thomas H Redner	. . . .	Gerald P Berning	. . . .	Dean Rossing	Randy Morrisette	Henry M Paulson
Janesville (52)	CM 608 755-3080	. . . .	Steven Sheiffer	Jean A Wulf	Herbert Stinski	Larry J Grorud	Ray A Voelker	Thomas O Rogers
Jefferson (6)	MC 414 674-3443	William R Brandel	Karl P Frantz	Karl P Frantz	. . . .	Donald Wegner	Michael P Besel	Reuben F Schulz
Kaukauna (12)	MC 414 766-6300	(not reporting)						
Kenosha (80)	MC 414 656-8124	John Antaramian	Donald Holland	Gail Procarione	Nickolas Arnold	Richard Thomas	Gerald Schuetz	Frederick Haerter
Kewaskum v (3)	MC 414 626-8484	Robert G Wagner	Daniel S Schmidt	Daniel S Schmidt	. . . .	Mark R Groeschel	Richard L Knoebel	Jerry E Gilles
Kewaunee (3)	MC 414 388-5000	(not reporting)						
Kiel (3)	MC 414 894-2909	(not reporting)						
Kimberly v (5)	CM 414 734-9441	James J Siebers	Rick J Hermus	Nancy Stuyvenberg	. . . .	Eugene Vandenberg	Dennis Jansen	D Vanden Boogaard
La Crosse (51)	MC 608 789-7579	Patrick Zielke	. . . .	Teri Lehrke	Eugene Pfaff	Howard Johnson	Ed Kondracki	Bob Schroeder
Ladysmith (4)	MC 715 532-2600	(not reporting)						
Lake Geneva (6)	MC 414 248-3673	(not reporting)						
Lake Mills (4)	CM 414 648-2344	. . . .	Vernon Johnson	James Heilman	. . . .	Richard Heinz	Ronald Klick	. . . .
Lancaster (4)	MC 608 723-4246	Jo Pebworth	. . . .	Vanda Vorwald	. . . .	Gary Reuter	Rodger Janssen	David Holmes
Little Chute v (9)	CM 414 788-7380	(not reporting)						
Madison (191)	MC 608 266-4671	Paul R Soglin	. . . .	Ray Fisher	Paul Reilly	Earle Roberts	David Couper	Herbert Hellen
Manitowoc (33)	MC 414 683-4440	. . . .	. . . .	. . . .	. . . .	. . . .	. . . .	. . . .
Maple Bluff v (..)	CM 608 244-3048	Robert A Cooper	Andrea S Crawford	Andrea S Crawford	. . . .	Richard W Reiter	Randolph Swingen	Edward M Koval
Marinette (12)	MC 715 735-7427	(not reporting)						
Marshfield (19)	MC 715 384-2919	Marvin J Duerr	Randall L Allen	Carolyn Kautzer	Michael Brehm	Gregg Cleveland	Clem Spencer	David Patek
Mauston (3)	MC 608 847-6676	Larry M Taylor	Joan Boyer	Joan Boyer	Joan Boyer	. . . .	O J Foster	Pat Geisendorfer
Mayville (4)	MC 414 387-7900	(not reporting)						
Mc Farland v (5)	MC 608 838-3153	(not reporting)						
Medford (4)	MC 715 748-4321	Dolores Meyer	. . . .	Donna Goodman	. . . .	Pat Doyle	Jack Kay	William Tylka
Menasha (15)	MC 414 751-5100	Joseph Laux	. . . .	Raymond Zielinski	Tom Stoffel	Tom Miller	Robert Stanke	Mark Radtke
Menomonee Falls v (27)	CM 414 255-8300	Joseph Greco	R Farrenkoph	Patricia Struve	Diane Conrad	John Fulcher	David Steingraber	Max Vogt
Menomonie (14)	MC 715 232-2180	Charles E Stokke	Lowell R Prange	Jo Ann L Kadinger	. . . .	Charles Vind	Dennis Beety	. . . .
Mequon (19)	MC 414 242-3100	James Moriarty	Harry Kollman	L Rzentkowski	Douglas Bates	Curtis Witzlib	Patrick Call	Jon Garms
Merrill (10)	MC 715 536-5594	(not reporting)						
Middleton (13)	MC 608 836-7481	(not reporting)						
Milton (4)	MC 608 868-6900	Richard Dabson	. . . .	Doris Viney	. . . .	. . . .	Terry Hawkins	Howard Robinson
Milwaukee (628)	MC 414 278-2002	John Norquist	David Webster	Ronald Leonhardt	W Martin Morics	August Erdmann	Philip Arreola	James Kaminski
Mondovi (2)	MC 715 926-3866	Allen R Whelan	. . . .	Daniel Lauersdorf	. . . .	Dennis Brion	Terry M Pittman	Gary D Risen
Monona (9)	CM 608 222-2525	Tom Metcalfe	Kevin M Brunner	Manette Ursino	. . . .	Everetet Pettey	Paul Welch	Richard Vela
Monroe (10)	MC 608 325-4101	(not reporting)						
Mosinee (4)	MC 715 693-2275	James B Jacobson	Larry Saeger	Marcella B Sitko	Larry Saeger	B Rheinschmidt	M Grzadzielewski	Kevin Briet
Mount Horeb v (4)	MC 608 437-3084	(not reporting)						
Mount Pleasant t (20)	RT 414 554-8750	Thomas Melzer	Michael F Weber	Joann Kovac	Joanne Tuinstra	Ric Marlatt	James Majdoch	Donald Hallowell
Mukwonago v (4)	MC 414 363-4081	(not reporting)						
Muskego (17)	MC 414 679-4100	David Deangelis	. . . .	Jean Marenda	. . . .	. . . .	John Johnson	John Loughney
Neenah (23)	MC 414 751-4604	(not reporting)						
Neillsville (3)	MC 715 743-2105	Robert F Lulloff	. . . .	Rex Roehl	. . . .	Duane Peterson	Thomas Woods	Frederick Seelow
Nekoosa (3)	MC 715 886-3811	(not reporting)						
New Berlin (34)	MC 414 786-8610	(not reporting)						
New Holstein (3)	MC 414 898-5766	(not reporting)						
New London (7)	MC 414 982-8500	Gregory Mathewson	L Steinbrecher	James Villiesse	James Villiesse	Wayne Wilfuer	David Neumann	Christopher Zoppa
New Richmond (5)	MC 715 246-4268	(not reporting)						
North Fond Du Lac v (4)	CM 414 929-3765	(not reporting)						
Oak Creek (20)	MC 414 768-6500	Dale Richards	Robert L Kufrin	Beverly Buretta	. . . .	Lyle Brossman	Michael Younglove	. . . .
Oconomowoc (11)	MC 414 569-2175	M Schumacher	Richard Mercier	Ardyce Senfleben	L Wandschneider	. . . .	Hugh Martin	George Langohr
Oconto (4)	MC 414 834-7711	William Bake	. . . .	Linda M Belongia	. . . .	Michael Hoppe	Oren Woodworth	Robert Mommaerts
Omro (3)	MC 414 685-5693	Raymond Hoeft	Janet Schettl	Janet Schettl	. . . .	David Treleven	John Vonderloh	Mike Domke
Onalaska (11)	MC 608 783-5666	(not reporting)						
Oregon v (5)	MC 608 835-3118	(not reporting)						
Oshkosh (55)	CM 414 236-5000	Richard Wollangk	William Frueh	Donna Serwas	Edward Nokes	Stanley Tadych	James Thome	Gerald Konrad
Park Falls (3)	MC 715 762-2436	(not reporting)						
Peshtigo (3)	MC 715 582-3041	J F Dale Berman	. . . .	Mary Ann Rodgers	Joseph R Race	Steven R Anderson	Thomas F Strouf	Steven A Cota
Pewaukee v (5)	MC 414 691-5660	John Laimon	Frank M Paulus	E Williams	Frank M Paulus	James Babe	Edward Baumann	Louis Thibault
Platteville (10)	CM 608 348-9741	. . . .	Rosemary E Kulow	Annette M Dutcher	. . . .	Bob Leighty	James Enfelt	. . . .
Pleasant Prairie v (..)	MC 414 694-1400	Thomas Terwall	Michael Pollocoff	Carol Lamminen	Teresa Matheny	Paul Guilbert Jr	James Horvath	Michael Foran
Plover v (8)	MC 715 345-5250	Daniel Schlutter	Mark Arentsen	Lee Emmajane	. . . .	Joe Radomski	Roger Zebro	William Konkol
Plymouth (7)	MC 414 892-4474	William B Kiley	. . . .	Daryl M Lemke	. . . .	Ronald Nicolaus	Norman Sorenson	William Immich
Port Washington (9)	MC 414 284-5585	Mark Dybdahl	Mark Grams	. . . .	. . . .	Marc Eernisse	Edward Rudolph	. . . .
Portage (9)	MC 608 742-2176	(not reporting)						
Prairie Du Chien (6)	MC 608 326-6406	William Farnum	Gary Koch	. . . .	. . . .	Michael Demuth	Gary Knickerbocke	Roger Grunow
Prescott (3)	CM 715 262-5544	Lane E Danielzuk	Janet S Huppert	. . . .	. . . .	Don A Johnson	William Cook	Jeff J Kittleson
Racine (84)	MC 414 636-9101	(not reporting)						
Reedsburg (6)	MC 608 524-6404	I Wayne Farber	. . . .	Caroline R Held	. . . .	Donald Lichte	Wilbur Abel	William Meyer
Rhinelander (7)	MC 715 369-1657	(not reporting)						
Rice Lake (8)	MC 715 234-7088	John P Vaughn	Curtis E Snyder	Kathleen V Morse	. . . .	James C Resac	Bradley E Beffa	. . . .
Richland Center (5)	MC 608 647-3466	(not reporting)						
Ripon (7)	MC 414 748-7771	(not reporting)						
River Falls (11)	MC 715 425-0900	Duane Pederson	Neil Ruddy	Dorothy Frederick	Julie Bergstrom	Dan Reis	Roger Leque	. . . .
River Hills v (2)	CM 414 352-8213	(not reporting)						
Rothschild v (3)	MC 715 359-3660	Neal C Torney	. . . .	Sheila Pudelko	. . . .	Jeffrey Hanson	Joseph E Toth	Merlin Owen
Sauk City v (3)	CM 608 643-3932	Maurice Schaefer	Vicki Breunig	. . . .	. . . .	. . . .	R Rentmeester	Don Moen

Directory 1/9 continued **MUNICIPAL OFFICIALS IN U.S. CITIES OVER 2,500**

City, 1990 population figures (000 omitted), form of government	Municipal phone number	Mayor	Appointed administrator	City clerk	Finance officer	Fire chief	Police chief	Public works director
WISCONSIN (174) continued								
Saukville v (4)	CM 414 284-9423	Jeffery P Knight	Christopher Lear	Christopher Lear	. . . .	Glenn B Dickmann	William B Meloy	. . . .
Seymour (3)	MC 414 833-2209	Judith Schuette	. . . .	Susan Garsow	. . . .	Tom Seidl	Don Raymakers	Michael Pepin
Shawano (8)	MC 715 526-6138	Lee M Schrader	. . . .	Marlene I Brath	. . . .	Doug Knope	Don Thaves	Rick J Stautz
Sheboygan (50)	MC 414 459-3373	(not reporting)						
Sheboygan Falls (6)	MC 414 459-3191	(not reporting)						
Shorewood v (14)	CM 414 963-6990	Michael R Schulte	Edward C Madere	Robert W Ries	. . . .	. . . .	Alvin J Berndt	James F Bartnicki
Shorewood Hills v (2)	CM 608 266-4781	Gard Strother	Tom Popp	Tom Popp	. . . .	Tom Reiter	Terry Ninneman	Denny Lybeck
South Milwaukee (21)	MC 414 762-2222	(not reporting)						
Sparta (8)	MC 608 269-4340	Milo D Seubert	Stephen J Gunty	Janice E Foss	. . . .	Scott G Lindemann	Ray G Harris	Larry K Brown
St. Francis (9)	MC 414 481-2300	(not reporting)						
Stevens Point (23)	MC 715 346-1571	W Scott Schultz	. . . .	Barbara Kranig	. . . .	Peter Ugorek	Robert Kreisa	Jon Van Alstine
Stoughton (9)	MC 608 873-6677	Helen J Johnson	. . . .	Judy A Kinning	. . . .	Odean Teigen	Patrick O'Connor	Robert Kardasz
Sturgeon Bay (9)	MC 414 746-2900	N D Schachtner	Dennis E Jordan	Paul C Bellin	Paul C Bellin	Gary G Drexler	Michael C Nordin	John P Kolodziej
Sturtevant v (4)	MC 414 886-7200	Clay Morgan	. . . .	Barbara Pauls	. . . .	Rick Schenkenberg	Ronald R Kittel	Rex O Parsons
Sun Prairie (15)	MC 608 837-2511	Jo Ann C Orfan	Patrick A Cannon	Edna Markstahler	. . . .	Robert Krause	Frank Sleeter	Larry Herman
Superior (27)	MC 715 394-0212	Herbert Bergson	. . . .	Margaret Ciccone	Timothy Nelson	Stephen Gotelaere	Doyle Barker	Jeffrey Vito
Sussex v (5)	CM 414 246-5200	John Tews	Chris Swartz	Susan Freiheit	Chris Swartz	Robert Schlei		
Thiensville v (3)	CO 414 242-3720	Roy Wetzel	Jack C Haney	John R Gibbons	Jack C Haney	William F Rausch	Richard W Preston	Jack C Haney
Tomah (8)	MC 608 372-5948	John F Graf	David Berner	Phillis Zimmerman	. . . .	Thomas Flock	Steven Rinzel	Kenneth Patterson
Tomahawk (3)	MC 715 453-4040	Richard Bierlich	. . . .	Paul Garner	. . . .	John Peeters	John DuPlayee	. . . .
Twin Lakes v (4)	MC 414 877-2858	John Staudemeyer	. . . .	Dorothy E Sandona	. . . .	Wayne Trongeau	Dale Crichton	. . . .
Two Rivers (13)	CM 414 793-5528	Gregory Erickson	Stephen Nenonen	Anthony Roach	Anthony Roach	Kenneth Swade	Michael Lien	Mike Lewis
Union Grove v (4)	MC 414 878-1818	(not reporting)						
Verona (5)	MC 608 845-6495	Arthur R Cresson	Bevery J Beyer	Bevery J Beyer	. . . .	. . . .	Edward E Moffett	Ronald R Rieder
Viroqua (4)	MC 608 637-7154	Charles Dahl	. . . .	Patrick Griffin	. . . .	John Thompson	John Thompson	Thomas Henry
Washington t (6)	CM 715 834-3257	Webster Hart	Micheal Peterson	Pamela D Hicks	. . . .	. . . .	. . . .	. . . .
Watertown (19)	MC 414 261-4500	Frederick Smith	. . . .	Mike Hoppenrath	. . . .	Ronald Weavel	Charles McGee	Joseph Radocay
Waukesha (57)	MC 414 524-3500	Paul Vrakas	. . . .	Thomas Neill	Bruce Hutchins	Robert Stedman	Thomas Stigler	R Vanden Noven
Waunakee v (6)	MC 608 849-5626	. . . .	Paul Brandenburg	. . . .	. . . .	. . . .	. . . .	. . . .
Waupaca (5)	MC 715 258-2044	James Boyer	. . . .	Beverly Sather	. . . .	. . . .	Douglas Prust	Gene Sorensen
Waupun (8)	MC 414 324-7900	Harold Nummerdorf	. . . .	Kyle J Clark	. . . .	Norman Lenz	Thomas Winscher	Bruce Zellner
Wausau (37)	MC 715 843-1000	John Hess	. . . .	Gary Klingbeil	Carla Manthe	Ken Szeklinski	Bill Brandimore	David Koch
Wauwatosa (49)	MC 414 471-8400	Maricolette Walsh	James Grassman	Janice Simonsen	Ronald Braier	Donald Pekel	Barry Weber	Howard Young
West Allis (63)	MC 414 256-8400	Joyce Ann Radtke	Paul M Ziehler	Eldon Rinka	Paul M Ziehler	Raymond Schrader	John Butorac	Michael Pertmer
West Bend (24)	MC 414 335-5100	Michael R Miller	Dennis W Melvin	Barbara Barringer	. . . .	Brian R Mayer	James W Skidmore	Terry Kiekhaefer
West Milwaukee v (4)	MC 414 645-1530	Ronald Hayward	Thomas Tollaksen	Jadell Ferge	. . . .	. . . .	Eugene Oldenburg	Jack Russell
West Salem v (4)	MC 608 786-1858	(not reporting)						
Whitefish Bay v (14)	CM 414 962-6690	James H Gormley	Edmund M Henschel	Barbara C Patin	. . . .	. . . .	. . . .	. . . .
Whitewater (13)	CM 414 473-0502	. . . .	Gary W Boden	Wava Jean Nelson	Wava Jean Nelson	C T Coe	James Coan	Dean Fischer
Wisconsin Dells (2)	MC 608 254-2012	(not reporting)						
Wisconsin Rapids (18)	MC 715 421-8214	Carl Greeneway	. . . .	Vernon Borth	. . . .	Kenneth Huettl	Robert Ziegert	James Borski
WYOMING (25)								
Buffalo t (3)	MC 307 684-5566	(not reporting)						
Casper (47)	CM 307 235-8400	(not reporting)						
Cheyenne (50)	CM 307 637-6200	(not reporting)						
Cody (8)	MC 307 527-7511	Jack T Skates	. . . .	James S Smiley	. . . .	. . . .	Dan Kelsey	. . . .
Douglas (5)	CM 307 358-3462	Ray Haskins	. . . .	Janet Dahmke	V H McDonald	. . . .	Lawrence Majerus	Steve Bennett
Evanston (11)	MC 307 789-9690	Dennis J Ottley	. . . .	Don U Welling	Stephen D Widmer	. . . .	Dennis Harvey	Brian Honey
Evansville t (1)	MC 307 234-6530	(not reporting)						
Gillette (18)	CM 307 686-5203	E J Collins	John C Darrington	Mildred Huravitch	. . . .	. . . .	Jeff Pfau	Bill Carson
Glenrock t (2)	MC 307 436-9294	(not reporting)						
Green River (13)	MC 307 875-5000	George A Eckman	James J Hauser Jr	Marna Grubb	James J Hauser Jr	Glenn Hill	Greg Gillen	Robert Edwards
Jackson t (4)	MC 307 733-3932	(not reporting)						
Kemmerer (3)	CM 307 877-9007	Jim Carroll	Steven B Golnar	Glenda R Young	. . . .	. . . .	Wayne T Wright	. . . .
Lander (7)	MC 307 332-2870	Arland Carlson	. . . .	Paul J Freese	. . . .	. . . .	Richard Currah	Laurence Ashdown
Laramie (27)	CM 307 721-5228	Amber Travsky	F McConnaughey	Sue Vosseller	Bill Morrison	Jim Noel	Mark Bridgmon	. . . .
Lyman t (2)	MC 307 786-4898	(not reporting)						
Newcastle (3)	MC 307 746-3535	(not reporting)						
Powell (5)	CM 307 754-5106	Janna Harkrider	Duane F Wroe	Ardyce Busboom	A Thorington	. . . .	John Cox	Robert Brock
Rawlins (9)	CM 307 328-4500	(not reporting)						
Riverton (9)	MC 307 856-2227	Albert T Brown	. . . .	Marie Burkhalter	Marie Burkhalter	. . . .	Mike Hays	Harry C Labonde
Rock Springs (19)	MC 307 362-3911	Paul S Oblock	. . . .	Marlene E Kudar	Lisa M Tarufelli	Harvey Cozad	Matthew Bider	Glenn Sugano
Sheridan (14)	MC 307 674-6483	Della Herbst	. . . .	Arthur W Elkins	Arthur W Elkins	James Wenzel	Charles Hendren	Tony Pelesky Jr
Thermopolis t (3)	MC 307 864-9285	Mike Mortimore	. . . .	Sharon Basse	. . . .	Marvin Andreen	Steven Shay	William DeRomedi
Torrington t (6)	MC 307 532-5666	Ed Jolovich	. . . .	Sandy Pittman	Larry Miskimins	Cactus Covello	Billy Janes	John Tucker
Wheatland t (3)	MC 307 322-2962	(not reporting)						
Worland (6)	MC 307 347-2486	(not reporting)						

Directory 1/10 **COUNTY OFFICIALS IN ALL U.S. COUNTIES**

The data for the directory of county officials were collected by ICMA in the summer of 1993 through a mail survey. The 3,107 counties surveyed include all counties with populations of 2,500 and over and those under 2,500 that are recognized by ICMA as providing for a professional management position.

In addition to the names of officials (and the county phone number), data on race and sex were collected for the county board chairman, judge or president, the appointed administrator, clerk to the governing board, chief financial officer, county health officer, planning director, county engineer, director of welfare/human services, chief law enforcement officer, purchasing director, and personnel director. The positions of planning director, director of welfare, purchasing director, health officer, and engineer are not shown in the individual county directory that follows. All data collected other than the names and phone numbers are treated with complete confidentiality, and only aggregate data are presented below.

Sex and Race of County Officials. Tables 1/10/a and 1/10/b present a breakdown of each sex by race and ethnicity for the county officials.

Given the level of detail shown, it is possible to reaggregate these data for other displays that would show race and sex characteristics of the total number of officials reporting.

The Directory. For convenience, the directory shows the names of counties in alphabetical order within each state. Other items indicated in the directory for each county-type government are the population and county phone number.

Table 1/10/a   MALE COUNTY OFFICIALS BY RACE AND ETHNICITY

Position	Total reporting (A)	Total males No. (B)	Total males % of (A)	White No.	White % of (B)	Black No.	Black % of (B)	American Indian No.	American Indian % of (B)	Asian No.	Asian % of (B)	Other No.	Other % of (B)	Race not reported No.	Race not reported % of (B)	Hispanic No.	Hispanic % of (B)
Board chairman	1,583	1,422	89.8	1,320	92.8	42	3.0	9	0.6	2	0.1	3	0.2	46	3.2	19	1.3
Chief appointed administrative officer	735	605	82.3	561	92.7	16	2.6	2	0.3	3	0.5	4	0.7	19	3.1	10	1.7
Clerk to the governing board	1,486	471	31.7	425	90.2	9	1.9	2	0.4	5	1.1	2	0.4	28	5.9	12	2.5
Chief financial officer	1,250	696	55.7	636	91.4	9	1.3	4	0.6	6	0.9	2	0.3	39	5.6	13	1.9
County health officer	990	613	61.9	551	89.9	10	1.6	2	0.3	6	1.0	9	1.5	35	5.7	8	1.3
Planning director	810	686	84.7	636	92.7	6	0.9	6	0.9	2	0.3	1	0.1	35	5.1	4	0.6
County engineer	829	821	99.0	773	94.2	4	0.5	3	0.4	4	0.5	4	0.5	33	4.0	11	1.3
Director health/human services	857	493	57.5	439	89.0	16	3.2	2	0.4	3	0.6	2	0.4	31	6.3	17	3.4
Chief law enforcement official	1,582	1,572	99.4	1,458	92.7	19	1.2	6	0.4	3	0.2	7	0.4	79	5.0	37	2.4
Purchasing director	622	388	62.4	349	89.9	17	4.4	5	1.3	3	0.8	2	0.5	12	3.1	10	2.6
Personnel director	763	410	53.7	359	87.6	23	5.6	2	0.5	6	1.5	3	0.7	17	4.1	7	1.7

Table 1/10/b   FEMALE COUNTY OFFICIALS BY RACE AND ETHNICITY

Position	Total reporting (A)	Total females No. (B)	Total females % of (A)	White No.	White % of (B)	Black No.	Black % of (B)	American Indian No.	American Indian % of (B)	Asian No.	Asian % of (B)	Other No.	Other % of (B)	Race not reported No.	Race not reported % of (B)	Hispanic No.	Hispanic % of (B)
Board chairman	1,583	161	10.2	151	93.8	6	3.7	1	0.6	1	0.6	0	0.0	2	1.2	2	1.2
Chief appointed administrative officer	735	130	17.7	125	96.2	3	2.3	0	0.0	0	0.0	0	0.0	2	1.5	8	6.2
Clerk to the governing board	1,486	1,015	68.3	954	94.0	22	2.2	11	1.1	0	0.0	4	0.4	24	2.4	25	2.5
Chief financial officer	1,250	554	44.3	537	96.9	6	1.1	4	0.7	0	0.0	3	0.5	4	0.7	8	1.4
County health officer	990	377	38.1	355	94.2	7	1.9	2	0.5	3	0.8	3	0.8	7	1.9	3	0.8
Planning director	810	124	15.3	119	96.0	3	2.4	0	0.0	1	0.8	0	0.0	1	0.8	0	0.0
County engineer	829	8	1.0	7	87.5	0	0.0	0	0.0	1	12.5	0	0.0	0	0.0	0	0.0
Director welfare/human services	857	364	42.5	336	92.3	18	4.9	2	0.5	1	0.3	1	0.3	6	1.6	9	2.5
Chief law enforcement official	1,582	10	0.6	7	70.0	2	20.0	0	0.0	0	0.0	0	0.0	1	10.0	0	0.0
Purchasing director	622	234	37.6	210	89.7	13	5.6	3	1.3	1	0.4	0	0.0	7	3.0	3	1.3
Personnel director	763	353	46.3	320	90.7	24	6.8	2	0.6	0	0.0	0	0.0	7	2.0	10	2.8

Directory 1/10 OFFICIALS IN U.S. COUNTIES
continued

County designation
c   City-county consolidation
i   Independent city
b   Borough
p   Parish

Population
Note: The only jurisdictions under 2,500 in population that are listed are those recognized by ICMA.
Population figures are not rounded up; 14,500 will appear as 14.
(..) Less than 500 population

Other codes
. . . . Data not reported or not applicable

County, county seat, 1990 population figures (000 omitted)	County telephone number	Board chairman	Appointed administrator	Clerk to the governing board	Chief financial officer	Personnel director	Chief law enforcement official
ALABAMA (67)							
Autauga (Prattville) (34)	205 361-3701	Leroy F Jones	Shirley Wallace	Shirley Wallace	Leroy F Jones	. . . .	James Johnson
Baldwin (Bay Minette) (98)	205 937-0380	Don Koontz	Jim Zumwalt	Locke Williams	Locke Williams	Byron Calhoun	James Johnson
Barbour (Clayton) (25)	205 775-3203	(not reporting)					
Bibb (Centreville) (17)	205 926-4823	(not reporting)					
Blount (Oneonta) (39)	205 274-9111	(not reporting)					
Bullock (Union Springs) (11)	205 738-3883	(not reporting)					
Butler (Greenville) (22)	205 382-3512	(not reporting)					
Calhoun (Anniston) (116)	205 236-3521	(not reporting)					
Chambers (Lafayette) (37)	205 864-8823	(not reporting)					
Cherokee (Centre) (20)	205 927-3668	Phillip W Jordan	R L McCleskey	R L McCleskey	R L McCleskey	R L McCleskey	Roy Wynn
Chilton (Clanton) (32)	205 755-1551	Bobby Agee	Sharon Sumrall	Sharon Sumrall	Sharon Sumrall	Cathy Martin	Neeley Strength
Choctaw (Butler) (16)	205 459-2417	Charles V Ford	Alice C Smith	Alice C Smith	Alice C Smith	. . . .	Donald H Lolley
Clarke (Grove Hill) (27)	205 275-3251	(not reporting)					
Clay (Ashland) (13)	205 354-2198	(not reporting)					
Cleburne (Heflin) (13)	205 463-2951	(not reporting)					
Coffee (Elba) (40)	205 987-5430	(not reporting)					
Colbert (Tuscumbia) (52)	205 383-4981	(not reporting)					
Conecuh (Evergreen) (14)	205 578-2095	(not reporting)					
Coosa (Rockford) (11)	205 377-2420	(not reporting)					
Covington (Andalusia) (36)	205 222-3613	(not reporting)					
Crenshaw (Luverne) (14)	205 335-6568	(not reporting)					
Cullman (Cullman) (68)	205 739-3530	(not reporting)					
Dale (Ozark) (50)	205 774-6262	(not reporting)					
Dallas (Selma) (48)	205 875-4401	(not reporting)					
De Kalb (Fort Payne) (55)	205 845-0541	(not reporting)					
Elmore (Wetumpka) (49)	205 567-2571	(not reporting)					
Escambia (Brewton) (36)	205 867-6261	William C America	Kenneth Taylor	Kenneth Taylor	Kenneth Taylor	. . . .	Timothy A Hawsey
Etowah (Gadsden) (100)	205 549-5313	(not reporting)					
Fayette (Fayette) (18)	205 932-4510	(not reporting)					
Franklin (Russellville) (28)	205 332-3814	(not reporting)					
Geneva (Geneva) (24)	205 684-2276	(not reporting)					
Greene (Eutaw) (10)	205 372-3349	(not reporting)					
Hale (Greensboro) (15)	205 624-4257	Riley Lucas	Nell McMillan	Nell McMillan	Nell McMillan	. . . .	Larry Johnson
Henry (Abbeville) (15)	205 585-2753	(not reporting)					
Houston (Dothan) (81)	205 677-4700	(not reporting)					
Jackson (Scottsboro) (48)	205 259-6617	(not reporting)					
Jefferson (Birmingham) (652)	205 325-5311	Mary Buckelew	. . . .	Howard Brooks	Steve Sayler	Diane Clark	Mel Bailey
Lamar (Vernon) (16)	205 695-7333	Ted Boyett	. . . .	Rita Taylor	Rita Taylor	Kim McAdams	Terry Perkins
Lauderdale (Florence) (80)	205 760-5750	(not reporting)					
Lawrence (Moulton) (32)	205 974-0663	(not reporting)					
Lee (Opelika) (87)	205 745-6471	(not reporting)					
Limestone (Athens) (54)	205 232-1320	John C Black	. . . .	Bonnie J Strain	. . . .	. . . .	Michael Blakely
Lowndes (Haynesville) (13)	205 548-2331	(not reporting)					
Macon (Tuskegee) (25)	205 727-5120	(not reporting)					
Madison (Huntsville) (239)	205 532-3492	(not reporting)					
Marengo (Linden) (23)	205 295-2200	(not reporting)					
Marion (Hamilton) (30)	205 921-3172	Don Barnwell	. . . .	Gearldean Lindsey	. . . .	. . . .	J Max Brasher
Marshall (Guntersville) (71)	205 571-7701	(not reporting)					
Mobile (Mobile) (379)	205 470-7727	(not reporting)					
Monroe (Monroeville) (24)	205 743-3782	(not reporting)					
Montgomery (Montgomery) (209)	205 832-4950	William F Joseph	David T Stochman	David T Stockman	Donnie L Mims	Barbara Montoya	James D Jones
Morgan (Decatur) (100)	205 351-4737	(not reporting)					
Perry (Marion) (13)	205 683-6886	Johnny L Flowers	. . . .	Walta Mae Kennie	. . . .	. . . .	James Hood
Pickens (Carrollton) (21)	205 367-8179	(not reporting)					
Pike (Troy) (28)	205 566-6374	Ronald M Morgan	Britt Thomas	Britt Thomas	Britt Thomas	Britt Thomas	Harold Anderson
Randolph (Wedowee) (20)	205 357-4551	(not reporting)					
Russell (Phenix City) (47)	205 298-0516	(not reporting)					
Shelby (Columbiana) (99)	205 669-3741	(not reporting)					
St. Clair (Ashville) (50)	205 594-3641	(not reporting)					
Sumter (Livingston) (16)	205 652-2731	(not reporting)					
Talladega (Talladega) (74)	205 362-2112	(not reporting)					
Tallapoosa (Dadeville) (39)	205 825-4268	(not reporting)					
Tuscaloosa (Tuscaloosa) (151)	205 349-3870	W Hardy McCollum	. . . .	Robert H Johnston	William M Lamb	Melvin L Vines Jr	Edward M Sexton
Walker (Jasper) (68)	205 221-4994	(not reporting)					
Washington (Chatom) (17)	205 847-2208	(not reporting)					
Wilcox (Camden) (14)	205 682-9112	(not reporting)					
Winston (Double Springs) (22)	205 489-5026	(not reporting)					
ALASKA (12)							
Anchorage (Anchorage) c (226)	907 343-4425	(not reporting)					
Bristol Bay (Naknek) b (1)	907 246-4224	Fred Pike	Ed Pefferman	Betty Bonin	Eben Hopson	Ed Pefferman	Floyd Steele
Fairbanks North Star (Fairbanks) b (78)	907 459-1000	. . . .	. . . .	. . . .	Judith Salter	Diane Thalker	
Haines (Haines) b (2)	907 766-2711	(not reporting)					
Juneau (Juneau) c (27)	907 586-5240	Jamie Parsons	Mark Palesh	Patricia A Polley	Craig W Duncan	Kenneth L Kareen	Richard Gummow
Kenai Peninsula (Soldotna) b (41)	907 262-4441	. . . .	. . . .	Gaye Vaughan	Ross Kinney	Richard Campbell	. . . .
Ketchikan Gateway (Ketchikan) b (14)	907 228-6625	. . . .	Micheal D Rody	G Zimmerle	Alvin Hall	Micheal D Rody	. . . .

Directory 1/10   **OFFICIALS IN U.S. COUNTIES**
continued

County, county seat, 1990 population figures (000 omitted)	County telephone number	Board chairman	Appointed administrator	Clerk to the governing board	Chief financial officer	Personnel director	Chief law enforcement official
ALASKA (12) continued							
Kodiak Island (Kodiak) b (13)	907 486-9301	Jerome Selby	. . . .	Donna Smith	Karleton Short	Rachael Miller	. . . .
Matanuska Susitna (Palmer) b (40)	907 745-4801	Ernest W Brannon	Donald L Moore	Linda Dahl	R Desmond Mayo	Ann K Stokes	. . . .
North Slope (Barrow) b (6)	907 852-2611	Jeslie Kaleak	Joe Upicksoun	Evelyn Donovan	Dan Fauske	Dorcas Thompson	James Christensen
Northwest Arctic (Kotzebue) b (6)	907 442-2500	Reggie Cleveland	. . . .	Paulette Lambert	Judy Hassinger	Linda Joule	. . . .
Sitka (Sitka) c (9)	907 747-3294	(not reporting)					
ARIZONA (15)							
Apache (St. Johns) (62)	602 337-4364	(not reporting)					
Cochise (Bisbee) (98)	602 432-9200	Mike Palmer	Jody Klein	Nadine Parkhurst	. . . .	Morry Gilbert	John Pintek
Coconino (Flagstaff) (97)	602 779-6690	Paul J Babbitt Jr	James R Keene Jr	Ethel G Ulibarri	Holly M Lindfors	Donna P Patterson	Joe D Richards
Gila (Globe) (40)	602 425-3231	Cruz Salas	Daniel Field	Daniel Field	Daniel Field	Susan Mitchell	Joe Rodriquez
Graham (Safford) (27)	602 428-3250	(not reporting)					
Greenlee (Clifton) (8)	602 865-2072	Donald R Stacey	Robert K Stokes	Deborah K Gale	Robert K Stokes	Robert K Stokes	Allen Williams
La Paz (Parker) (14)	602 669-6115	Gene Fisher	. . . .	Eileen Thompson	Sandra Dodge	Sandra Dodge	Marvin Hare
Maricopa (Phoenix) (2122)	602 506-3011	James D Bruner	Roy R Pederson	Frances McCarrol	Frank Abeyta	Paul G Ahler	Joseph Arpalo
Mohave (Kingman) (93)	602 753-0736	Samuel Standerfer	David J Grisez	Patsy Chastain	Robert Kenney	Joyce Clifton	Joe Cook
Navajo (Holbrook) (78)	602 524-6161	Larry A Layton	Edward J Koury	S Keenewright	Clinton O Shreeve	Gilbert Gonzales	Gary H Butler
Pima (Tucson) (667)	602 740-8661	Ed Moore	Manoj N Vyas	Jane S Williams	Carl Remus	. . . .	Clarence Dupnik
Pinal (Florence) (116)	602 868-5801	Jimmie Kerr	Stanley D Griffis	Stanley D Griffis	Terry L Doolittle	Robert L Keiser	Frank R Reyes
Santa Cruz (Nogales) (30)	602 281-4695	(not reporting)					
Yavapai (Prescott) (108)	602 771-3252	Gheral Brownlow	James Holst	Ann Lawrie Aisa	Michael Danowski	Carol Berra	George Buchanan
Yuma (Yuma) (107)	602 329-2104	Kathryn Prochaska	James R Stahle	. . . .	Donald P Wicks	Cherlene Penilla	Ralph Ogden
ARKANSAS (75)							
Arkansas (Stuttgart) (22)	501 673-3181	(not reporting)					
Ashley (Hamburg) (24)	501 853-5144	(not reporting)					
Baxter (Mountain Home) (31) ...	501 425-2755	(not reporting)					
Benton (Bentonville) (97)	501 271-1000	Bruce Rutherford	. . . .	. . . .	Gloria Peterson	Linda Patrick	Andrew Lee
Boone (Harrison) (28)	501 741-5760	Dale Wagner	. . . .	David Witty	Benjamin Dodson	. . . .	Kenneth Foley
Bradley (Warren) (12)	501 226-3853	(not reporting)					
Calhoun (Hampton) (6)	501 798-2042	(not reporting)					
Carroll (Berryville) (19)	501 423-2967	Phil Jackson	. . . .	. . . .	. . . .	. . . .	Lonnie Nichols
Chicot (Lake Village) (16)	501 265-2208	(not reporting)					
Clark (Arkadelphia) (21)	501 246-4491	James Fisher	. . . .	. . . .	. . . .	. . . .	Troy Tucker
Clay (Piggott) (18)	501 598-2667	Travis Boyd	. . . .	. . . .	. . . .	. . . .	Darvin Stow
Cleburne (Heber Springs) (19) ..	501 362-8141	(not reporting)					
Cleveland (Rison) (8)	501 325-6214	(not reporting)					
Columbia (Magnolia) (26)	501 234-4194	Barney H Reeves	. . . .	. . . .	. . . .	. . . .	Terry Bolton
Conway (Morrilton) (19)	501 354-9640	D H Pettingill	Linda McNeal	Beverly Paladino	Roy B Bain	. . . .	Carl Poteete
Craighead (Jonesboro) (69)	501 933-4520	(not reporting)					
Crawford (Van Buren) (42)	501 474-1312	(not reporting)					
Crittenden (Marion) (50)	501 739-3383	(not reporting)					
Cross (Wynne) (19)	501 238-3373	(not reporting)					
Dallas (Fordyce) (10)	501 352-2307	(not reporting)					
Desha (Arkansas City) (17)	501 877-2426	(not reporting)					
Drew (Monticello) (17)	501 367-3574	Dale L Hughes	. . . .	. . . .	. . . .	. . . .	Tommy C Free
Faulkner (Conway) (60)	501 450-4900	John Wayne Carter	. . . .	Melinda Reynolds	Kathy Barrett	Rick Whitaker	Bob Blankenship
Franklin (Ozark) (15)	501 667-3607	Joe Powell	Laura Rudolph	Mary Williams	Jane Ferguson	Jeo Powell	Kenneth Ross
Fulton (Salem) (10)	501 895-3310	(not reporting)					
Garland (Hot Springs) (73)	501 321-2819	Bud Williams	. . . .	Nancy Johnson	Jo West Taylor	. . . .	Larry Selig
Grant (Sheridan) (14)	501 942-2551	(not reporting)					
Greene (Paragould) (32)	501 239-6300	(not reporting)					
Hempstead (Hope) (22)	501 777-6164	(not reporting)					
Hot Spring (Malvern) (26)	501 332-2261	(not reporting)					
Howard (Nashville) (14)	501 845-7500	(not reporting)					
Independence (Batesville) (31) ..	501 793-8829	(not reporting)					
Izard (Melbourne) (11)	501 368-4328	(not reporting)					
Jackson (Newport) (19)	501 523-6152	Jerry Carlew	Mary Hohn	Geneva White	Donna Lewis	. . . .	Donald Ray
Jefferson (Pine Bluff) (85)	501 541-5360	Jack Jones	. . . .	. . . .	. . . .	. . . .	W C Dub Brassell
Johnson (Clarksville) (18)	501 754-2175	(not reporting)					
Lafayette (Lewisville) (10)	501 921-4858	(not reporting)					
Lawrence (Walnut Ridge) (17) ..	501 886-2167	(not reporting)					
Lee (Marianna) (13)	501 295-2339	(not reporting)					
Lincoln (Star City) (14)	501 628-4147	(not reporting)					
Little River (Ashdown) (14)	501 898-5021	(not reporting)					
Logan (Paris) (21)	501 963-3601	(not reporting)					
Lonoke (Lonoke) (39)	501 676-2368	(not reporting)					
Madison (Huntsville) (12)	501 738-6721	(not reporting)					
Marion (Yellville) (12)	501 449-6231	(not reporting)					
Miller (Texarkana) (38)	501 774-1301	(not reporting)					
Mississippi (Blytheville) (58) ...	501 763-3212	(not reporting)					
Monroe (Clarendon) (11)	501 747-3632	(not reporting)					
Montgomery (Mount Ida) (8) ...	501 867-3114	(not reporting)					
Nevada (Prescott) (10)	501 887-3115	John Henry	. . . .	Julie Stockton	Sydney DuCharme	. . . .	William A Morman
Newton (Jasper) (8)	501 446-5127	(not reporting)					
Ouachita (Camden) (31)	501 836-4116	(not reporting)					
Perry (Perryville) (8)	501 889-5126	(not reporting)					
Phillips (Helena) (29)	501 338-5500	Kenneth Stoner	Virginia Cooper	Kay Benz	Ray Culver	. . . .	Kenneth Winfrey
Pike (Murfreesboro) (10)	501 285-2231	(not reporting)					
Poinsett (Harrisburg) (25)	501 578-5333	Steve Ryan	. . . .	Ida Bettis	. . . .	. . . .	Jimmy Carter
Polk (Mena) (17)	501 394-4945	(not reporting)					
Pope (Russellville) (46)	501 968-6064	(not reporting)					
Prairie (Des Arc) (10)	501 256-3741	Guyman DeVore	. . . .	Nancy Guthrie	Dorothy Flanagan	. . . .	Dale Madden
Pulaski (Little Rock) (350)	501 372-8305	(not reporting)					
Randolph (Pocahontas) (17)	501 892-5264	(not reporting)					
Saline (Benton) (64)	501 776-5600	(not reporting)					
Scott (Waldron) (10)	501 637-2155	(not reporting)					
Searcy (Marshall) (8)	501 448-3554	(not reporting)					
Sebastian (Fort Smith) (100)	501 783-6139	W R Harper	David O Hudson	. . . .	Marsline Porter	David O Hudson	Gary Grimes
Sevier (De Queen) (14)	501 642-2425	O H Durham	. . . .	Sandra Dunn	. . . .	. . . .	John Partain
Sharp (Ash Flat) (14)	501 994-7338	Frank Arnold	. . . .	Tommy Estes	Norman Girtman	. . . .	T J Sonny Powell
St. Francis (Forrest City) (28) ...	501 633-8640	Gazzola Vaccaro	. . . .	Dick Krablin	. . . .	. . . .	Dave Parkman

Directory 1/10
continued
OFFICIALS IN U.S. COUNTIES

County, county seat, 1990 population figures (000 omitted)	County telephone number	Board chairman	Appointed administrator	Clerk to the governing board	Chief financial officer	Personnel director	Chief law enforcement official
ARKANSAS (75) continued							
Stone (Mountain View) (10)	501 269-3106	(not reporting)					
Union (El Dorado) (47)	501 863-5244	(not reporting)					
Van Buren (Clinton) (14)	501 745-2443	Dale U Lynch	Ron Bennett	Rickey Whillock	Roy Dean Dempsey	....	Mike Bridges
Washington (Fayetteville) (113) .	501 521-8400	Charles A Johnson	Roger Haney	....	Joan Perry	Naomi Mitchell	Kenneth McKee
White (Searcy) (55)	501 268-2950	(not reporting)					
Woodruff (Augusta) (10)	501 347-2871	John Davis	....	William Rives	....	....	....
Yell (Danville) (18)	501 495-2414	Gary M Moore	....	Carolyn Morris	Dorothy Keathley	....	Loyd Maughn
CALIFORNIA (58)							
Alameda (Oakland) (1279)	510 272-6984	Edward Campbell	Steven Szalay	William Mehrwein	Patrick O'Connell	Naomi Burns	Charles Plummer
Alpine (Markleeville) (1)	916 694-2287	Eric Jung	Jeanne Lear	Karen Keebaugh	Barbara Ryan	Jeanne Lear	Henry Veatch
Amador (Jackson) (30)	209 223-6470	(not reporting)					
Butte (Oroville) (182)	916 538-7651	Mary Ann Houx	John Blacklock	Candace Grubbs	Dave Houser	Steve Harman	Mick Grey
Calaveras (San Andreas) (32) ...	209 754-6303	Tom Tryon	Brent Harrington	Mary Jane Giuffra	Clay Hawkins	Jalynne Tobias	Bill Nuttall
Colusa (Colusa) (16)	916 458-2101	Kay K Nordyke	Jack Lawrence	Kathleen Moran	Robert Kessinger	Jack Lawrence	Jerry Shadinger
Contra Costa (Martinez) (804) ...	510 646-4064	(not reporting)					
Del Norte (Crescent City) (23) ..	707 464-7204	Clarke Moore	Ronald S Holden	Karen L Walsh	Lois Standley	Ronald S Holden	Mike Ross
El Dorado (Placerville) (126)	916 621-5575	William Center	Paul McIntosh	Dixie Foote	Larry Klaus	Kathy Libicki	Don McDonald
Fresno (Fresno) (667)	209 488-1721	Stan Oken	William Randolph	Shari Greenwood	Gary W Peterson	....	Steve Magarian
Glenn (Willows) (25)	916 934-6400	Dick Mudd	....	Carollyn Davis	Joe Sites	John Greco	Roger Roberts
Humboldt (Eureka) (119)	707 445-7509	Julie Fulkerson	Chris Arnold	Chris Arnold	Neil Prince	D McClelland	David Renner
Imperial (El Centro) (109)	619 339-4488	W Van DeGraaff	Richard Inman	Linda Weaver	Raymond Comstock	Hoyl Belt	Oren Fox
Inyo (Independence) (18)	619 878-2411	(not reporting)					
Kern (Bakersfield) (543)	805 861-2111	Roy Ashburn	Joseph E Drew Jr	Tonya S Pickett	James A Rhoades	Kay F Madden	C L Sparks
Kings (Hanford) (101)	209 582-3211	Nick Kinney	....	Rose Martinez	Darrell Warnock	Dennis Berry	Tom Clark
Lake (Lakeport) (51)	707 263-2213	(not reporting)					
Lassen (Susanville) (28)	916 257-8311	(not reporting)					
Los Angeles (Los Angeles) (8863)	213 974-1101	Edmund D Edelman	Harry L Hufford	Larry F Monteilh	....	Harry L Hufford	Sherman Block
Madera (Madera) (88)	209 675-7703	Gail McIntyre	Stell Manfredi	Wanda Gavello	Robert DeWall	Earl Eckert	Glenn Seymour
Marin (San Rafael) (230)	415 499-7331	(not reporting)					
Mariposa (Mariposa) (14)	209 966-3222	Eric J Erickson	Mike Coffield	Margie Williams	Evelyn Billings	Nancy J Kyle	Roger Matlock
Mendocino (Ukiah) (80)	707 463-4261	James Eddie	Michael Scannell	Joyce Beard	Dennis Huey	Steven Smith	James Tuso
Merced (Merced) (178)	209 385-7682	Mike Bogna	Clark Channing	Kenneth L Randol	James L Ball	Marvin J Bolling	Tom Sawyer
Modoc (Alturas) (10)	916 233-6413	(not reporting)					
Mono (Bridgeport) (10)	619 932-5228	Andrea Lawrence	William Mayer	Nancy Wells	Annika Wilkes	William Mayer	Martin Strelneck
Monterey (Salinas) (356)	408 755-5115	(not reporting)					
Napa (Napa) (111)	707 253-4303	Vince Ferriole	Jay Hull	....	Pam Kindig	Bill Carden	Gary Simpson
Nevada (Nevada City) (79)	916 265-1480	Willard Schultz	H Douglas Latimer	Cathy Thompson	Bruce Bielefelt	Lori Walsh	William Heafey
Orange (Santa Ana) (2411)	714 834-5315	Harriett Wieder	Ernie Schneider	Phyllis Henderson	Steve Lewis	Russ Patton	Brad Gates
Placer (Auburn) (173)	916 889-4000	(not reporting)					
Plumas (Quincy) (20)	916 283-6246	(not reporting)					
Riverside (Riverside) (1170)	714 275-1000	Patricia Larson	Larry Parrish	Gerald Maloney	Tom Courbat	Dennis Morris	Cois Byrd
Sacramento (Sacramento) (1041)	916 440-7097	Grantland Jonnson	Bob Smith	Bev Williams	John Dark	Roger Fong	Glen Craig
San Benito (Hollister) (37)	408 637-6550	Ruth Kesler	David Edge	John Hodges	John Hodges	David Edge	Harvey Nyland
San Bernardino (San Bernardino) (1418)	714 387-5563	(not reporting)					
San Diego (San Diego) (2498) ..	619 694-3900	(not reporting)					
San Francisco c (724)	415 558-6161	Frank Jordan	R Nothenberg	John Taylor	Edward Harrington	Wendell Pryor	Michael Hennessey
San Joaquin (Stockton) (481) ...	209 468-3370	William N Sousa	Mel Wingett	Joretta Hayde	Adrian Van Houten	Trish Pechan	Baxter Dunn
San Luis Obispo (San Luis Obispo) (217)	805 549-5959	Harry Ovitt	Robert Hendrix	Francis M Cooney	Gere Sibbach	Robert W Conen	Edward Williams
San Mateo (Redwood City) (650)	415 363-4000	Mary Griffin	John Maltbie	Richard Silver	....	Mary Welch	Donald Horsley
Santa Barbara (Santa Barbara) (370)	805 681-4200	(not reporting)					
Santa Clara (San Jose) (1498) ..	408 299-2011	(not reporting)					
Santa Cruz (Santa Cruz) (230) ..	408 425-2171	(not reporting)					
Shasta (Redding) (147)	916 225-5557	(not reporting)					
Sierra (Downieville) (3)	916 289-3295	(not reporting)					
Siskiyou (Yreka) (44)	916 842-8005	Ivan Young	Michael B Hanford	Lisa Chandler	David Elledge	Darby Hayes	Charles Byrd
Solano (Fairfield) (340)	707 421-6170	Sam Caddle	Michael Johnson	Linda Terra	William Ricciardi	Susan Harrington	Al Cardoza
Sonoma (Santa Rosa) (388)	707 527-2331	(not reporting)					
Stanislaus (Modesto) (371)	209 525-6333	Nick W Blom	Reagan M Wilson	Christine Ferraro	Byron Bystrom	....	Les Weidman
Sutter (Yuba City) (64)	916 741-7100	(not reporting)					
Tehama (Red Bluff) (50)	916 527-4655	(not reporting)					
Trinity (Weaverville) (13)	916 623-1217	Matthew Leffler	Donald Benedetti	....	John Larkin	Jeanne Gravette	Paul Schmidt
Tulare (Visalia) (312)	209 733-6531	(not reporting)					
Tuolumne (Sonora) (48)	209 533-5511	Larry Rotelli	Mark A Mitton	Edna Bowcutt	Tim Johnson	Mark A Mitton	Richard Nutting
Ventura (Ventura) (669)	805 654-5000	Susan Lacey	R Wittenberg	Richard Dean	Thomas Mahon	Ron Komers	Larry Carpenter
Yolo (Woodland) (141)	916 666-8055	(not reporting)					
Yuba (Marysville) (58)	916 741-6281	Joan Saunders	Fred Morawcznski	Fred Morawcznski	....	Roger Carey	Gary Tindel
COLORADO (63)							
Adams (Brighton) (265)	303 659-2120	Harold E Kite	John M Bramble	....	Terry Funderburk	....	Edward J Camp
Alamosa (Alamosa) (14)	719 589-3841	Robert Zimmerman	Harold E Andrews	Holly Z Lowder	Harold E Andrews	Peggy R Curto	James Drury
Arapahoe (Littleton) (392)	303 795-4400	(not reporting)					
Archuleta (Pagosa Springs) (5) ..	303 264-2536	(not reporting)					
Baca (Springfield) (5)	303 523-4521	Don E Self	Dana L Christie	Sheila Ingle	Dana L Christie	Dana Christie	Willard E Goff
Bent (Las Animas) (5)	719 456-2223	Harrell Ridley	Virley Burkhalter	Patti Nickel	Virley Burkhalter	....	Greg Trujillo
Boulder (Boulder) (225)	303 441-3131	(not reporting)					
Chaffee (Salida) (13)	719 539-2218	Thomas Eve	Frank M Thomas	Mary Ellen Belmar	Helen Argys	....	George Chavez
Cheyenne (Cheyenne Wells) (2) .	303 767-5685	Floyd McEwen	....	Rita Holthus	....	....	James L Blain
Clear Creek (Georgetown) (8) ...	303 569-3251	Nelson Fugate	Jack Benson	Roberta Hawkes	Carl Small	Gail Buckley	Robert Cahill
Conejos (Conejos) (7)	303 376-5772	Leroy Velasquez	Miguel Lujan	Andrew Perea	Tressesa Martinez	....	Gerald Rivera
Costilla (San Luis) (3)	303 672-3962	(not reporting)					
Crowley (Ordway) (4)	719 267-3248	(not reporting)					
Custer (Westcliffe) (2)	719 783-2552	(not reporting)					
Delta (Delta) (21)	303 874-7595	Jim D Ventrello	Susan Hansen	Josephine Gore	....	....	William Blair
Denver (Denver) c (468)	303 640-2721	(not reporting)					
Dolores (Dove Creek) (2)	303 677-2383	(not reporting)					
Douglas (Castle Rock) (60)	303 660-7400	Michael Maag	....	....	Barbara Krohta	Ken Milano	Stephen Zotos
Eagle (Eagle) (22)	303 328-8600	George Bud Gates	Jack D Lewis	Sara Fisher	Allen Sartin	Chris Armstead	A J Johnson
El Paso (Colorado Springs) (397)	303 520-6400	(not reporting)					
Elbert (Kiowa) (10)	303 621-2348	(not reporting)					

Directory 1/10   **OFFICIALS IN U.S. COUNTIES**
continued

County, county seat, 1990 population figures (000 omitted)	County telephone number	Board chairman	Appointed administrator	Clerk to the governing board	Chief financial officer	Personnel director	Chief law enforcement official
COLORADO (63) continued							
Fremont (Canon City) (32)	719 275-1515	(not reporting)					
Garfield (Glenwood Springs) (30)	303 945-1377	Buckey Arbaney	Charles Deschenes	Mildred Alsdorf	Charles Deschenes	Charles Deschenes	Vern Soucie
Gilpin (Central City) (3)	303 582-5214	(not reporting)					
Grand (Hot Sulphur Springs) (8)	303 725-3347	R L Thompson	R Howard Moody	Sara Rosene	Bob Nilsson	. . . .	Jim Bartels
Gunnison (Gunnison) (10)	303 641-2203	Fred Field	Gary Tomsic	Judy Goodman	John McBride		Richard Murdie
Hinsdale (Lake City) (..)	303 944-2225	James Lewis	Donald Van Wormer	Oleta Bebout	Donald Van Wormer	Donald Van Wormer	Frank Wilcox
Huerfano (Walsenburg) (6)	303 738-2370	William Reiners	Andrew P Nigrini	Albert P Vigil	Andrew P Nigrini	. . . .	Harold Martinez
Jackson (Walden) (2)	303 723-4334	Robert Carlstrom	Wm Kent Crowder	Sherry Wofford	Mildred C Potter	. . . .	Gary L Cure
Jefferson (Golden) (438)	303 271-8676	. . . .		Lori O'Neall	. . . .	Joanne Norte	Ron Beckham
Kiowa (Eads) (2)	719 438-5810	Cardon Berry	Gloria Peck	Betty V Crow	Gloria Peck	Gloria Peck	Gary Rehm
Kit Carson (Burlington) (7)	719 346-8638	LeRoy Herndon	. . . .	Della Calhoon		Nancy Baker	James Hetland
La Plata (Durango) (32)	303 259-4000	Fred Klatt	Bob Brooks	Nancy Sofka	Wayne Bedor	Karen Malouff	Bill Gardner
Lake (Leadville) (6)	719 486-1410	James E Martin	Nancy Hilleary	June Ossman	Nancy Hilleary	Nancy Hilleary	David Duarte
Larimer (Fort Collins) (186)	303 498-7000	(not reporting)					
Las Animas (Trinidad) (14)	303 846-3314	Eugene D Lujan	Margie Herrera	Bernard Gonzales	Eugene D Lujan	. . . .	Lou Girodo
Lincoln (Hugo) (5)	719 743-2444	Charles Covington	. . . .	Roxana Devers	James Covington	. . . .	Leroy Yowell
Logan (Sterling) (18)	303 522-0888	Jerry Montague	. . . .	Charlene Craddock	. . . .	Richard Snook	Don Bollish
Mesa (Grand Junction) (93)	303 244-1800	. . . .	. . . .	M Jean Hawk	William Voss	Nancie Flenaro	Riecke Claussen
Mineral (Creede) (1)	719 658-2331	Robert A Boppe	Kent Hager	Chloe Rogers	Dick Kolisch	. . . .	Phil Leggitt
Moffat (Craig) (11)	303 824-5517	(not reporting)					
Montezuma (Cortez) (19)	303 565-8317	(not reporting)					
Montrose (Montrose) (24)	303 249-7755	Robert D Corey	. . . .	Patricia Vernon	Patricia Morris	Julie A Gowen	Thomas Gilmore
Morgan (Fort Morgan) (22)	303 867-8202	Cynthia L Erker	. . . .	Fay A Johnson	. . . .	Susan Wiegel	W Gale Davey
Otero (La Junta) (20)	719 384-7785	Robert Bauserman	Barry Shioshita	Stella Sedillo	Barry Shioshita	. . . .	John Eberly
Ouray (Ouray) (2)	303 325-4961	(not reporting)					
Park (Fairplay) (7)	719 836-2771	Ajmes D Coggin Jr	. . . .	Harriet Anderson	Frances E Greene	. . . .	Robert K Harrison
Phillips (Holyoke) (4)	303 854-3778	Keith Sharpe	Randy Schafer	Mary Evans	Linda Statz	. . . .	Richard Potter
Pitkin (Aspen) (13)	303 920-5200	William E Tuite	Reid J Haughey	Silvia Davis	Thomas C Oken	Cheryl Cumnock	Robert C Braudis
Prowers (Lamar) (13)	303 336-9001	Robert R Tempel	Carl F Winsor	. . . .	. . . .	. . . .	James L Hamilton
Pueblo (Pueblo) (123)	719 546-6000	Kathy Farley	. . . .	Lucille Wilson	Dorothy Hewitt	Jeanette O' Quin	Dan Corsentino
Rio Blanco (Meeker) (6)	303 878-5001	David Smith	. . . .	Nancy Amick	Joann Findlay	Rob Munger	Ron Hilkey
Rio Grande (Del Norte) (11)	719 657-2744	Vern Rominger	Suzanne Benton	Lela Ann Bennett	. . . .	. . . .	J Desi Medina
Routt (Steamboat Springs) (14) .	303 879-0108	L Dennis Fisher	. . . .	Dorothy L Mariano	Daniel L Strnad	L Kelly Udall	Edgar F Burch
Saguache (Saguache) (5)	719 655-2231	Rod Hines	Brad Jones	Mary Moore	Brad Jones	Shirley Anderson	Dan Pacheco
San Juan (Silverton) (1)	303 387-5671	(not reporting)					
San Miguel (Telluride) (4)	303 728-3844	William Wenger	Darlene Frieman	Paula MacMillan	Gordon Glockson	. . . .	William Masters
Sedgwick (Julesburg) (3)	303 474-3346	Charles E Powell	Maedine Nelson	Maedine Nelson	Dan Pederson	. . . .	M Gene Mikelson
Summit (Breckenridge) (13)	303 453-2561	Joe Sands	Bob Taylor	Dori J Webb	Linda Trausch	Debbie Jackman	Delbert Ewoldt
Teller (Cripple Creek) (12)	719 689-2988	Frank M Ricard	Gregory M Winkler	Constance Joiner	Laurie M Litwin	. . . .	Gary D Shoemaker
Washington (Akron) (5)	303 345-2701	John B Howlett	. . . .	Garland M Wahl	. . . .	. . . .	Bill Wood
Weld (Greeley) (132)	303 356-4000	Constance Harbert	Donald Warden	Donald Warden	Claud Hanes	David Worden	L Jordan
Yuma (Wray) (9)	303 332-5796	(not reporting)					
DELAWARE (3)							
Kent (Dover) (111)	302 736-2040	Ronald Smith	Bob McLeod	Edith Hemphill	Stephen Cimo	. . . .	Carl Wright
New Castle (Wilmington) (442) . .	302 571-7500	(not reporting)					
Sussex (Georgetown) (113)	302 855-7741	(not reporting)					
WASHINGTON D.C. (1) i (607)	202 727-1000	(not reporting)					
FLORIDA (66)							
Alachua (Gainesville) (182)	904 374-5210	P Wheat	R Fernandez	J Irby	S Carr	C Hayes	S Oelrich
Baker (Macclenny) (18)	904 259-3613	Clifton Barton	Josie L Davis	Harry Richardson	. . . .	. . . .	Murray Richardson
Bay (Panama City) (127)	904 784-4013	Danny Sparks	Dan Duda	Harold Bazzel	Joseph Rogers	Joy Bates	Guy Tunnell
Bradford (Starke) (23)	904 964-6280	(not reporting)					
Brevard (Melbourne) (399)	407 633-2031	(not reporting)					
Broward (Fort Lauderdale) (1255)	305 357-6044	Gerald F Thompson	B Jack Osterholt	. . . .	Phillip C Allen	Phil Rosenberg	Ron Cochran
Calhoun (Blountstown) (11)	904 674-4545	Pack Bowden	. . . .	Willie D Wise	Willie D Wise	. . . .	William G Smith
Charlotte (Port Charlotte) (111) .	813 743-1200	(not reporting)					
Citrus (Inverness) (94)	904 637-9400	Gary Bartell	Anthony Shoemaker	Betty Strifler	Gary Herndon	Dwight Small	Charles Dean
Clay (Green Cove Springs) (106)	904 284-6300	Dale Wilson	Robert Wilson	John Keene	John Keene	. . . .	Scott Lancaster
Collier (Naples) (152)	813 774-8999	Burt Saunders	W Neil Dorrill	Dwight Brock	John Yonkosky	T Whitecotton	Donald Hunter
Columbia (Lake City) (43)	904 755-4100	James W Knox	Dale Williams	P Dewitt Cason	P Dewitt Cason	Dale Williams	Thomas Tramel
Dade (Miami) (1937)	305 375-5311	Arthur E Teele Jr	Joaquin G Avino	Harvey Ruvin	Ed Marquez	Grace Poley	Frederick Taylor
De Soto (Arcadia) (24)	813 993-4800	(not reporting)					
Dixie (Cross City) (11)	904 498-5806	Jerry W Hill	Winnie Hicks	Joe Hubert Allen	Joe Hubert Allen	Elaine Pridgeon	Larry E Edmonds
Escambia (Pensacola) (263)	904 444-8610	Steve Del Gallo	Robert W Koncar	Joe A Flowers	Joe A Flowers	A L Maltby	Jim Lowman
Flagler (Bunnell) (29)	904 437-7414	James A Darby	Stan Denison	Syd Crosby	. . . .	. . . .	Robert McCarthy
Franklin (Apalachicola) (9)	904 653-8861	(not reporting)					
Gadsden (Quincy) (41)	904 875-8650	Anthony Powell	James Carter	Nicholas Thomas	Nicholas Thomas	Arthur Lawson	W A Woodham
Gilchrist (Trenton) (10)	904 463-2341	(not reporting)					
Glades (Moore Haven) (8)	813 946-0949	Franklin Simmons	. . . .	Jerry L Beck	Jerry L Beck	. . . .	Barry Walbourn
Gulf (Port Saint Joe) (12)	904 229-6113	(not reporting)					
Hamilton (Jasper) (11)	904 792-1288	Wendall Wynn	. . . .	Elaine Rozier	Elaine Rozier	Elaine Rozier	J Harrell Reid
Hardee (Wauchula) (19)	813 773-6952	(not reporting)					
Hendry (La Belle) (26)	813 675-5217	Cecil O Akin	Lionel E Beatty	Christine Pratt	Christine Pratt	Sue Moss	Thomas Vaughan
Hernando (Brooksville) (101)	904 754-4013	Anthony Mosca Jr	Charles Hetrick	Karen Nicolai	Robert Simpson	Y Jennene Norman	Thomas Mylander
Highlands (Sebring) (68)	813 385-2581	(not reporting)					
Hillsborough (Tampa) (834)	813 272-5750	Ed Turanchik	Fred Karl	Richard Ake	Richard Ake	Gene Gardner	Cal Henderson
Holmes (Bonifay) (16)	904 547-5055	(not reporting)					
Indian River (Vero Beach) (90) . .	407 567-8000	Dick Bird	James Chandler	Jeff Barton	. . . .	Jack Price	Gary Wheeler
Jackson (Marianna) (41)	904 482-9633	Chuck Lockey	Leon Foster	Daun Crews	Larry Spivey	John Mader	John McDaniel
Jacksonville-Duval -(Jacksonville) c (635)	904 630-1178	Donald R Moran	Lex Hester	Henry Cook	Michael Weinstein	C W Marshall	Jim McMillan
Jefferson (Monticello) (11)	904 997-3596	(not reporting)					
Lafayette (Mayo) (6)	904 294-1600	(not reporting)					
Lake (Tavares) (152)	904 343-9888	Richard Swartz	Peter Wahl	James Watkins	Barbara Lehman	Lois Martin	George Knupp
Lee (Fort Myers) (335)	813 335-2245	John Manning	Donald Stilwell	Charlie Green	Bruce Loucks	George Bradley	John McDougall
Leon (Tallahassee) (192)	904 487-2220	(not reporting)					
Levy (Bronson) (26)	904 486-4311	(not reporting)					
Liberty (Bristol) (6)	904 643-5404	John T Sanders	. . . .	Vernon Ross	Vernon Ross	Vernon Ross	William L Burke
Madison (Madison) (17)	904 973-3179	Marybelle James	Cohen Bond	Tim Sanders	Tim Sanders	. . . .	Joe Peavey

Directory 1/10 **OFFICIALS IN U.S. COUNTIES**
continued

County, county seat, 1990 population figures (000 omitted)	County telephone number	Board chairman	Appointed administrator	Clerk to the governing board	Chief financial officer	Personnel director	Chief law enforcement official
FLORIDA (66) continued							
Manatee (Bradenton) (212)	813 748-4501	(not reporting)					
Marion (Ocala) (195)	904 620-3307	Norm Perry	Joseph L Cone	Frances E Thigpin	Frances E Thigpin	Sarah McCarroll	Ken Ergle
Martin (Stuart) (101)	407 288-5437	Jeff Krauskopf	....	Marsha Stiller	Daniel Hudson	Stephen Novak	Robert Crowder
Monroe (Key West) (78)	305 294-4641	Jack London	Thomas Brown	Danny Kolhage	Sandy Carlile	Paula Rodriquez	Rick Roth
Nassau (Fernandina Beach) (44) .	904 261-6127	James E Testone	....	T J Greeson	T J Greeson	T J Greeson	Ray Geiger
Okaloosa (Crestview) (144)	904 689-5000	(not reporting)					
Okeechobee (Okeechobee) (30) .	813 763-6441	(not reporting)					
Orange (Orlando) (677)	407 836-7370	(not reporting)					
Osceola (Kissimmee) (108)	407 847-1200	Larry Whaley	William Goaziou	Mel Wills Jr	T J Allen	....	Charles Croft
Palm Beach (West Palm Beach) (864)	407 355-2040	Mary McCarty	Robert Weisman	....	....	Brad Merriman	....
Pasco (Newport Richey) (281) ..	813 847-2411	Ann Wildebrand	John J Gallagher	Joseph E Pittman	Joseph E Pittman	....	Lee Cannon
Pinellas (Clearwater) (852)	813 462-3367	Charles Rainey	Fred Marquis	Karleen DeBlaker	C Ricard Short	Jack Houk	Everett Rice
Polk (Bartow) (405)	813 534-6030	Daniel J Costello	C R Jackson	E D Dixon	....	F M Bell	L M Crowe
Putnam (Palatka) (65)	904 329-0212	Kevin R Durscher	Gary D Adams	Edward L Brooks	Robert D Moore	Donna L Gunn	C Taylor Douglas
Santa Rosa (Milton) (82)	904 623-0135	(not reporting)					
Sarasota (Sarasota) (278)	813 951-5261	Wayne L Derr	John Wesley White	Karen E Rushing	Peter H Ramsden	H Skeet Surrency	Geoff Monge
Seminole (Sanford) (288)	407 321-1130	Robert J Sturm	Ron H Rabun	Maryanne Morse	Bob Wilson	German Romero	Donald Eslinger
St. Johns (St. Augustine) (84) ..	904 824-8131	Linda Balsavage	Nicholas Meiszer	Carl Markel	Michael Givens	Karen Van Volkinb	Neil Perry
St. Lucie (Fort Pierce) (150) ...	407 466-1100	Judy Culpepper	Thomas Kindred	Joann Holman	Linda Childress	Patricia Clute	Robert Knowles
Sumter (Bushnell) (32)	904 793-0200	John Stephens	Bernard Dew	Sara Mason	Sara Mason	....	James L Adams
Suwannee (Live Oak) (27)	904 362-4002	(not reporting)					
Taylor (Perry) (17)	904 584-6413	(not reporting)					
Union (Lake Butler) (10)	904 496-3711	(not reporting)					
Vclusia (De Land) (371)	904 736-5951	Robert Tuttle	Thomas Kelly	Diane Matousek	Albert Gault	Michael Lary	Robert Vogel Jr
Walton (De Funiak Springs) (28)	904 892-3137	(not reporting)					
Washington (Chipley) (17)	904 638-6200	Lenzy Corbin	Roger D Hagan	Earnestine Miller	Earnestine Miller	....	Danny Hasty
GEORGIA (159)							
Appling (Baxley) (16)	912 367-8100	William L Leggett	Mike Cleland	Ann Jones	Mike Cleland	Mike Cleland	Lewis Parker
Atkinson (Pearson) (6)	912 422-3391	(not reporting)					
Bacon (Alma) (10)	912 632-5214	Virgil Taylor	....	Mary Edna Wheeler	....	....	Johnny Hayes
Baker (Newton) (4)	912 734-5294	(not reporting)					
Baldwin (Milledgeville) (40)	912 453-4007	(not reporting)					
Banks (Homer) (10)	404 677-2320	Milton Patterson	....	Avis Lewallen	Avis Lewallen	....	Allen Venable
Barrow (Winder) (30)	404 867-7581	(not reporting)					
Bartow (Cartersville) (56)	404 382-4766	Clarence Brown	Steve Bradley	Lane McMillan	Evelyn Rhyne	Sandra Southern	Don Thurman
Ben Hill (Fitzgerald) (16)	912 423-2455	(not reporting)					
Berrien (Nashville) (14)	912 686-5421	(not reporting)					
Bibb (Macon) (150)	912 749-6343	Larry G Justice	....	Barbara Yocum	William C Vaughn	W Leo Wright Jr	Robbie Johnson
Bleckley (Cochran) (10)	912 934-3200	(not reporting)					
Brantley (Nahunta) (11)	912 462-5256	(not reporting)					
Brooks (Quitman) (15)	912 263-5561	(not reporting)					
Bryan (Pembroke) (15)	912 653-4681	(not reporting)					
Bulloch (Statesboro) (43)	912 764-6245	Raybon Anderson	E Scott Wood	Evelyn Wilson	....	....	Arnold Akins
Burke (Waynesboro) (21)	706 554-2324	Ellis Godbee	C W Hopper Jr	C W Hopper Jr	C W Hopper Jr	C W Hopper Jr	Gregory T Coursey
Butts (Jackson) (15)	404 775-8200	Robert W Haley	H Thomas Williams	Jackie R Cavender	Jackie R Cavender	Dianne Holloway	Joseph E Pope
Calhoun (Morgan) (5)	912 849-4835	Calvin Schramm	....	Dawn Scarborough	Dawn Scarborough	Dawn Scarborough	Charles Cheney
Camden (Woodbine) (30)	912 576-5601	(not reporting)					
Candler (Metter) (8)	912 685-2835	(not reporting)					
Carroll (Carrollton) (71)	706 830-5800	Horrie B Duncan	....	Lillie L Jones	Kathy Chapman	Sam Price	Jack Bell
Catoosa (Ringgold) (42)	404 935-4047	(not reporting)					
Charlton (Folkston) (8)	912 496-2549	William J Carter	....	Rosa Mae Brooks	Rosa Mae Brooks	....	Ernest H Conner
Chatham (Savannah) (217)	912 652-7174	Joseph E Mahany	Russell E Abolt	Sybil Tillman	David Persaud	Beverly Whitehead	Al St Lawrence
Chattahoochee (Cusseta) (17) ..	706 989-3602	Walter F Rosso	....	Annelle D Harp	....	....	Glynn Cooper
Chattooga (Summerville) (22) ...	706 857-4021	Jim Parker	....	Martha A Latta	Jim Parker	....	Ralph Kellett
Cherokee (Canton) (90)	404 479-0400	(not reporting)					
Clarke (Athens) (88)	706 613-3020	Gwen Oloooney	H Russ Crider	Gloria Spratlin	John Culpepper	James H Alford Jr	Jerry L Massey
Clay (Fort Gaines) (3)	912 768-2631	(not reporting)					
Clayton (Jonesboro) (182)	404 477-3208	(not reporting)					
Clinch (Homerville) (6)	912 487-2667	(not reporting)					
Cobb (Marietta) (448)	404 429-3000	Bill Byrne	David Hankerson	Carol Myers	Virgil Moon	Shelia Buckner	Bill Hutson
Coffee (Douglas) (30)	912 384-4799	(not reporting)					
Colquitt (Moultrie) (37)	912 985-6859	Joe G Clark	Robert M Cobb	Deborah Cox	Robert M Cobb	Robert M Cobb	Billy Howell
Columbia (Evans) (66)	706 868-3300	(not reporting)					
Columbus-Muscogee (Columbus) c (179)	404 571-4740	F K Martin	M B Brown	L H Miller	C S Chronis	....	W J Wetherington
Cook (Adel) (13)	912 896-2266	(not reporting)					
Coweta (Newnan) (54)	404 254-2601	Diane Dawson	Theron Gay	Roxie Clark	Eva Wagner	....	Michael Yeager
Crawford (Knoxville) (9)	912 836-3328	(not reporting)					
Crisp (Cordele) (20)	912 276-2672	J Reginald Berry	W D Goff Jr	....	....	....	Donald Haralson
Dade (Trenton) (13)	706 657-4625	Bill Wallin	J D Kirby	Ronda Gold	....	....	Philip Street
Dawson (Dawsonville) (9)	404 265-3164	(not reporting)					
De Kalb (Decatur) (546)	404 371-2881	(not reporting)					
Decatur (Bainbridge) (26)	912 248-3030	(not reporting)					
Dodge (Eastman) (18)	912 374-4361	J Don McCranie	....	Glenda G Williams	....	....	Jackson Jones
Dooly (Vienna) (10)	912 268-4228	(not reporting)					
Dougherty (Albany) (96)	912 431-2121	Gil Barrett	W Alan Reddish	W Alan Reddish	Gail W Kohler	A Gosseer Jenkins	G Jamil Saba
Douglas (Douglasville) (71)	404 920-7266	Rita Rainwater	Samuel J Durden	Aida L Tullis	....	Gloria Turner	Tommy Waldrop
Early (Blakely) (12)	912 723-4304	(not reporting)					
Echols (Statenville) (2)	912 559-6538	(not reporting)					
Effingham (Springfield) (26)	912 754-6071	(not reporting)					
Elbert (Elberton) (19)	404 283-4702	(not reporting)					
Emanuel (Swainsboro) (21)	912 237-8911	(not reporting)					
Evans (Claxton) (9)	912 739-1141	(not reporting)					
Fannin (Blue Ridge) (16)	404 632-2039	(not reporting)					
Fayette (Fayetteville) (62)	404 461-6041	Steve Wallace	Billy P Beckett	Billy P Beckett	Emory McHugh	Connie L Boehnke	Randall Johnson
Floyd (Rome) (81)	404 291-5110	(not reporting)					
Forsyth (Cumming) (44)	404 781-2100	Michael Bennett	Donald Major	Betty Shadburn	....	Jim Masaschi	Wesley Walraven
Franklin (Carnesville) (17)	706 384-2483	(not reporting)					
Fulton (Atlanta) (649)	404 730-4000	Michael L Lomax	John H Stanford	Avarita L Hanson	Peter Cunningham	Robert O Brandes	Jacquelyn Barrett
Gilmer (Ellijay) (13)	404 635-4361	Robert Holden	Doug Griffin	Kimberly Rogers	Charles Fowler	Deborah Cochran	Billy Bernhardt
Glascock (Gibson) (2)	404 598-2671	Joe Dean Usry	....	Denise L Kent	....	....	James L English

Directory 1/10 **OFFICIALS IN U.S. COUNTIES**
continued

County, county seat, 1990 population figures (000 omitted)	County telephone number	Board chairman	Appointed administrator	Clerk to the governing board	Chief financial officer	Personnel director	Chief law enforcement official
GEORGIA (159) continued							
Glynn (Brunswick) (62)	912 267-5600	Robert H Boyne	Richard L Gilmour	Martha D Dominey	Charles R Lewis	David A Bandy	Carl H Alexander
Gordon (Calhoun) (35)	706 629-3795	Joe Powell	T McDearis	Pat James	Linda D Dunlap	Garah L Childers	William S Roberts
Grady (Cairo) (20)	912 377-1512	Jack C Drew	Mike Stephenson	Ann W Mobley	Bonnie H Amdahl	. . . .	Sydney Turner
Greene (Greensboro) (12)	404 453-7716	(not reporting)					
Gwinnett (Lawrenceville) (353)	404 822-8000	(not reporting)					
Habersham (Clarkesville) (28)	706 754-6264	Dewey H Tench	F Lewis Canup	Ruby S Fulbright	. . . .	. . . .	Harrison Nix
Hall (Gainesville) (95)	404 531-7000	Brenda W Branch	Harry W Hayes	. . . .	Arlin W Pitts	Phil H Sutton	Robert G Vass
Hancock (Sparta) (9)	404 444-5746	(not reporting)					
Haralson (Buchanan) (22)	706 646-2002	Jim McBrayer	. . . .	Charlene Smith	. . . .	. . . .	Kenneth Spearman
Harris (Hamilton) (18)	706 628-4958	George E Elmore	Marian T Young	Carol A Silva	Carol A Silva	. . . .	Mike Jolley
Hart (Hartwell) (20)	404 376-2024	(not reporting)					
Heard (Franklin) (9)	706 675-3821	(not reporting)					
Henry (Mc Donough) (59)	404 957-1538	(not reporting)					
Houston (Perry) (89)	912 542-2115	Sherrill Stafford	Steve Engle	Steve Engle	Sandra Stalnaker	Harold Wilson	Cullen Talton
Irwin (Ocilla) (9)	912 468-9441	(not reporting)					
Jackson (Jefferson) (30)	404 367-9838	(not reporting)					
Jasper (Monticello) (8)	404 468-2812	(not reporting)					
Jeff Davis (Hazlehurst) (12)	912 375-6611	Lonnie Waters	Lonnie V Roberts	Lonnie V Roberts	Lonnie V Roberts	Lonnie V Roberts	Jimmy Boatright
Jefferson (Louisville) (17)	912 625-3332	Frank A Gordy	Carl Flowers	Mary H Lamb	. . . .	. . . .	Gary Hutchins
Jenkins (Millen) (8)	912 982-2563	Charles F Bragg	. . . .	Al Knight	. . . .	. . . .	Bobby Womack
Johnson (Wrightsville) (8)	912 864-3388	(not reporting)					
Jones (Gray) (21)	912 986-6405	(not reporting)					
Lamar (Barnesville) (13)	706 358-5146	Bobby Burnette	. . . .	Patty Johnston	. . . .	. . . .	Frank Monaghan
Lanier (Lakeland) (6)	912 482-2088	(not reporting)					
Laurens (Dublin) (40)	912 272-4755	Mike Wolfe	Will McDonald	. . . .	C Strickland	Will McDonald	Kenny Webb
Lee (Leesburg) (16)	912 759-6000	Robert H Reid	William R Dean	Carolyn Bowers	Esther R Griffith	William R Dean	Harold Breeden
Liberty (Hinesville) (53)	912 876-2164	(not reporting)					
Lincoln (Lincolnton) (7)	404 359-4444	(not reporting)					
Long (Ludowici) (6)	912 545-2143	Randall T Wilson	. . . .	Mary Ann Odum	Mary Ann Odum	. . . .	Cecil Nobles
Lowndes (Valdosta) (76)	912 333-5116	G Norman Bennett	. . . .	Inez Pendleton	Marcus Campbell	Michael Tillman	Ashley Paulk
Lumpkin (Dahlonega) (15)	404 864-3742	J B Jones	Ruth Bohac	Ellen Holbrook	. . . .	. . . .	Jimmy L Berry
Macon (Oglethorpe) (13)	912 472-7021	(not reporting)					
Madison (Danielsville) (21)	404 795-3351	William C Madden	. . . .	Junne B Temple	. . . .	. . . .	Jack D Fortson
Marion (Buena Vista) (6)	912 649-2603	(not reporting)					
Mc Duffie (Thomson) (20)	404 595-2100	(not reporting)					
Mc Intosh (Darien) (9)	912 437-6671	(not reporting)					
Meriwether (Greenville) (22)	404 672-1314	(not reporting)					
Miller (Colquitt) (6)	912 758-4104	(not reporting)					
Mitchell (Camilla) (20)	912 336-2000	Benjamin Hayward	Bennett W Adams	Shelia H Cannon	Bennett W Adams	Bennett W Adams	W J Bozeman
Monroe (Forsyth) (17)	912 994-7000	(not reporting)					
Montgomery (Mount Vernon) (7)	912 583-4401	(not reporting)					
Morgan (Madison) (13)	706 342-0725	Henry Carson	C Rosebrough	Doris Harris	Doris Harris	C Rosebrough	Ken Pritchet
Murray (Chatsworth) (26)	404 695-2413	Jimmie Witherow	Stephen North	Arlene Gibson	. . . .	Marla Bearden	Howard Ensley
Newton (Covington) (42)	404 784-2000	Davis Morgan	. . . .	Mildred Johnson	. . . .	Jesse L Knight	Gerald Malcom
Oconee (Watkinsville) (18)	706 769-5120	Wendell Dawson	Peter Mallory	Gina Lindsey	. . . .	Malinda Smith	Scott Berry
Oglethorpe (Lexington) (10)	404 743-5270	(not reporting)					
Paulding (Dallas) (42)	404 445-6668	Bobby H Hollis	. . . .	Pat C Brannum	Pat C Brannum	Lillian T Norton	Bruce Harris
Peach (Fort Valley) (21)	912 825-2535	Charles Bartlett	. . . .	Thomas J Franklin	. . . .	Thomas J Franklin	Johnnie V Becham
Pickens (Jasper) (14)	404 692-2121	W Don Mullinax	I Layne Arnold	Lorie P Fleming	. . . .	I Layne Arnold	Billy P Wofford
Pierce (Blackshear) (13)	912 449-2022	Robert Howard	. . . .	Nicole Y Carter	. . . .	. . . .	Richard King
Pike (Zebulon) (10)	404 567-3406	(not reporting)					
Polk (Cedartown) (34)	404 748-1305	(not reporting)					
Pulaski (Hawkinsville) (8)	912 783-1911	Pat Nelson	. . . .	Barbara Bell	. . . .	. . . .	Jerry Lancaster
Putnam (Eatonton) (14)	404 485-5826	(not reporting)					
Quitman (Georgetown) (2)	912 334-2159	(not reporting)					
Rabun (Clayton) (12)	404 782-5271	(not reporting)					
Randolph (Cuthbert) (8)	912 732-6440	(not reporting)					
Richmond (Augusta) (190)	706 821-2300	Hobson Chavous	Linda Beazley	. . . .	Albert McKie	. . . .	Charles Webster
Rockdale (Conyers) (54)	404 929-4000	Randolph Poynter	Jean F Hambrick	. . . .	Sarah Alexander	John B Meyers	J Guy Norman
Schley (Ellaville) (4)	912 937-2101	(not reporting)					
Screven (Sylvania) (14)	912 564-7535	(not reporting)					
Seminole (Donalsonville) (9)	912 524-2878	Dan E Ponder Jr	Ray Pridgeon	Leah G Miller	. . . .	. . . .	Jerry Godby
Spalding (Griffin) (54)	404 228-9900	Martha McDaniel	Michael M Ruffin	Maureen C Jackson	William Wilson Jr	Elaine M Bonds	Richard Cantrell
Stephens (Toccoa) (23)	706 886-9491	(not reporting)					
Stewart (Lumpkin) (6)	912 838-6769	(not reporting)					
Sumter (Americus) (30)	912 924-6725	J Wade Halstead	Barbara McCarty	Marcia L Royal	Barbara McCarty	Barbara McCarty	Randy Howard
Talbot (Talbotton) (7)	404 665-3220	(not reporting)					
Taliaferro (Crawfordville) (2)	706 456-2494	Jesse L Brown	. . . .	Ruby Harper	. . . .	. . . .	James M Leslie
Tattnall (Reidsville) (18)	912 557-4335	(not reporting)					
Taylor (Butler) (8)	912 862-3336	(not reporting)					
Telfair (Mc Rae) (11)	912 868-5688	(not reporting)					
Terrell (Dawson) (11)	912 995-4476	Wilbur Gamble Jr	. . . .	Deborah Crawford	. . . .	. . . .	John Bowens
Thomas (Thomasville) (39)	912 225-4100	John Bulloch	J Rick Morrison	Ruth M Jones	. . . .	. . . .	R Carlton Powell
Tift (Tifton) (35)	912 386-7850	Charles Kent	Hunter Walker	Imogene Register	. . . .	. . . .	Edd Walker
Toombs (Lyons) (24)	912 526-3311	James A Thompson	. . . .	Barbara Dismuke	. . . .	. . . .	Charles Durst
Towns (Hiawassee) (7)	706 896-2276	Jack Dayton	. . . .	Wilma Youngblood	Jack Dayton	. . . .	Rudy Roach
Treutlen (Soperton) (6)	912 529-3664	Jim L Gillis Jr	. . . .	Sylvia Norris	. . . .	. . . .	Wayne Hooks
Troup (La Grange) (56)	404 883-1610	(not reporting)					
Turner (Ashburn) (9)	912 567-4313	(not reporting)					
Twiggs (Jeffersonville) (10)	912 945-3629	William E Hamrick	. . . .	Robin N McGuffin	. . . .	. . . .	Doyle Stone Jr
Union (Blairsville) (12)	404 745-9655	(not reporting)					
Upson (Thomaston) (26)	706 647-7012	J Irvin Hendricks	. . . .	Lakeitha Reeves	. . . .	Lakeitha Reeves	Mountain Greene
Walker (La Fayette) (58)	404 638-1437	Roy E Parrish Jr	. . . .	Bebe A Heiskell	. . . .	Bebe A Heiskell	Albert D Millard
Walton (Monroe) (39)	404 267-4571	(not reporting)					
Ware (Waycross) (35)	912 287-4300	Roger Strickland	Michael J Stewart	Gail C Barron	Jim Johnson	. . . .	Herbert E Bond
Warren (Warrenton) (6)	706 465-2171	Bobby W Johnson	. . . .	Lynette Johnson	. . . .	. . . .	Joseph Peebles
Washington (Sandersville) (19)	912 552-2325	(not reporting)					
Wayne (Jesup) (22)	912 427-5900	Richard Madray	Nancy Jones	Nancy Jones	. . . .	. . . .	David Herrin
Webster (Preston) (2)	912 828-5775	Lucius Black	. . . .	Vivian Bankston	Janice Storey	. . . .	Tony Kennedy
Wheeler (Alamo) (5)	912 568-7137	(not reporting)					
White (Cleveland) (13)	706 865-2235	(not reporting)					
Whitfield (Dalton) (72)	400 275-7500	(not reporting)					
Wilcox (Abbeville) (7)	912 467-2737	H L Conner	. . . .	Hazel Keen	. . . .	. . . .	C E Bloodsworth

Directory 1/10 **OFFICIALS IN U.S. COUNTIES**
continued

County, county seat, 1990 population figures (000 omitted)	County telephone number	Board chairman	Appointed administrator	Clerk to the governing board	Chief financial officer	Personnel director	Chief law enforcement official
GEORGIA (159) continued							
Wilkes (Washington) (11)	404 678-2511	(not reporting)					
Wilkinson (Irwinton) (10)	912 946-2236	J M Howell	. . . .	Charlene Stuckey	. . . .	Charlene Stuckey	T Lloyd Gibbs
Worth (Sylvester) (20)	912 776-8200	(not reporting)					
HAWAII (4)							
Hawaii (Hilo) (120)	808 961-8361	Spencer K Schutte	William G Davis	Robin J Yahiku	Harry A Takahashi	Michael R Ben	Victor V Vierra
Honolulu (Honolulu) c (836)	808 523-4005	Frank F Fasi	Jeremy Harris	Raymond K Pua	Russell W Miyake	Cynthia M Bond	Michael Nakamura
Kauai (Lihue) (51)	808 245-3385	Joann Yukimura	Thomas Batey	Jerome Hew	Michael Veith	Allan Tanigawa	Calvin Fujita
Maui (Wailuku) (100)	808 243-7711	Goro Hokama	Richard Haake	Daryl T Yamamoto	Travis Thompson	Raymond Kokubun	Howard Tagomori
IDAHO (44)							
Ada (Boise) (206)	208 383-4429	Vern Bisterfeldt	. . . .	J David Navarro	Barbara Baur	Terry L Johnson	Vaughn Killeen
Adams (Council) (3)	208 253-4561	(not reporting)					
Bannock (Pocatello) (66)	208 236-7211	Tom Katsilometes	. . . .	Larry Ghan	Pat Wilson	Bill Lloyd	William Lynn
Bear Lake (Paris) (6)	208 945-2212	(not reporting)					
Benewah (St. Maries) (8)	208 245-3212	(not reporting)					
Bingham (Blackfoot) (38)	208 785-5005	(not reporting)					
Blaine (Hailey) (14)	208 788-5505	Tom Blanchard	Pam Smith	Mary Green	. . . .		Jerry Femling
Boise (Idaho City) (4)	208 392-4431	Margaret Drake	. . . .	Arlene C Kolar	. . . .	Kathie Brady	Michael Butler
Bonner (Sandpoint) (27)	208 265-1438	Eugene Brown	. . . .	Marie Scott	Karen Weldon	Jan Morrison	Evan Roos
Bonneville (Idaho Falls) (72)	208 529-1100	Clifford V Long	. . . .	Ronald Longmore	Ronald Longmore	Daniel D Byron	Byron Stommel
Boundary (Bonners Ferry) (8) ...	208 267-2242	(not reporting)					
Butte (Arco) (3)	208 527-3021	James O Andreason	. . . .	Judith R Bailey	. . . .	. . . .	. . . .
Camas (Fairfield) (1)	208 764-2242	Jack Renfrow	. . . .	Rollie Bennett	Rollie Bennett	Rollie Bennett	Harold Lee
Canyon (Caldwell) (90)	208 454-7300	George Vance	. . . .	Ned Kerr	Ned Kerr	James Scherer	George Nourse
Caribou (Soda Springs) (7)	208 547-4342	(not reporting)					
Cassia (Burley) (20)	208 678-7302	John Adams	Timothy Hurst	Frank Kearns	Timothy Hurst	. . . .	Billy Crystal
Clark (Dubois) (1)	208 374-5304	Charles R Vadnais	. . . .	Jo Ann S Tavenner	Bonnie G Burns	. . . .	Craig King
Clearwater (Orofino) (9)	208 476-3615	V James Wilson	. . . .	. . . .	Robin Christensen	. . . .	Nick Albers
Custer (Challis) (4)	208 879-2360	(not reporting)					
Elmore (Mountain Home) (21) ...	208 587-2130	M A Riddle	. . . .	Dolores Robison	. . . .	. . . .	Ricky Layher
Franklin (Preston) (9)	208 852-1090	Jeff Olson		. . . .	. . . .		Don Beckstead
Fremont (St. Anthony) (11)	208 624-7332	(not reporting)					
Gem (Emmett) (12)	208 365-4561	Rick Welch	. . . .	Thelma Kolodziej	Edith Sawyer	. . . .	James H Wood
Gooding (Gooding) (12)	208 934-4841	Phil Becker	. . . .	John Myers	John Myers		Jim Jax
Idaho (Grangeville) (14)	208 983-2751	George Enneking	. . . .	Rose E Gehring	Rose E Gehring		Gene Meinen
Jefferson (Rigby) (17)	208 745-7756	Paul D Walker	. . . .	Connie M Keller	Margaret Treasure		Blair Olsen
Jerome (Jerome) (15)	208 324-8811	Jerry Ridley	. . . .	Chery M Watts	. . . .		George Silver
Kootenai (Coeur D'Alene) (70) ..	208 769-4400	(not reporting)					
Latah (Moscow) (31)	208 882-8580	Dana Magnusen	. . . .	Susan R Petersen	Susan R Petersen	Susan R Petersen	Joseph Overstreet
Lemhi (Salmon) (7)	208 756-2815	(not reporting)					
Lewis (Nezperce) (4)	208 937-2661	Joe A Leitch	. . . .	Cathy Larson	Cathy Larson	. . . .	Don Fortney
Lincoln (Shoshone) (3)	208 886-7641	(not reporting)					
Madison (Rexburg) (24)	208 356-3662	M Dell Barney	. . . .	Beth B Reese	Jayne Green	. . . .	Greg Moffat
Minidoka (Rupert) (19)	208 436-9511	(not reporting)					
Nez Perce (Lewiston) (34)	208 799-3020	(not reporting)					
Oneida (Malad City) (3)	208 766-4116	(not reporting)					
Owyhee (Murphy) (8)	208 495-2421	Richard Bass	. . . .	Barbara Jayo	. . . .	. . . .	Tim Nettleton
Payette (Payette) (16)	208 642-9371	(not reporting)					
Power (American Falls) (7)	208 226-7611	Ralph Wheeler	. . . .	Carol Schreiber	. . . .	. . . .	Howard Sprague
Shoshone (Wallace) (14)	208 752-3331	(not reporting)					
Teton (Driggs) (3)	208 354-2501	Keith J Kunz	. . . .	Asa J Drake	Asa J Drake	Keith J Kunz	Kim Cooke
Twin Falls (Twin Falls) (54)	208 736-4074	James Fraley	. . . .	Robert Fort	. . . .	Renee Robbins	Wayne Tousley
Valley (Cascade) (6)	208 382-4297	Tom N Olson	. . . .	Leland G Heinrich	. . . .	. . . .	Lewis E Pratt
Washington (Weiser) (9)	208 549-2092	Don Stephens	. . . .	Mary Kautz	Patricia Harberd	. . . .	Mike Wadley
ILLINOIS (102)							
Adams (Quincy) (66)	217 223-6300	(not reporting)					
Alexander (Cairo) (11)	618 734-7000	(not reporting)					
Bond (Greenville) (15)	618 664-1966	Hollie Willmann	. . . .	Eldon Roe	. . . .	. . . .	Earl Bare
Boone (Belvidere) (31)	815 547-4770	(not reporting)					
Brown (Mount Sterling) (6)	217 773-3110	Robert E Koch	. . . .	Judy J Woodworth	George Clark	. . . .	Michael B Myers
Bureau (Princeton) (36)	815 875-2014	Arnold Clayton	. . . .	Tom Velon	Madge Noble		Jack Narczewski
Calhoun (Hardin) (5)	618 576-2351	(not reporting)					
Carroll (Mount Carroll) (17)	815 244-9171	(not reporting)					
Cass (Virginia) (13)	217 452-7201	(not reporting)					
Champaign (Urbana) (173)	217 384-3772	Lyle E Shields	Jacquelin A White	Dennis R Bing	Geraldine Parr	Lyle E Shields	David J Madigan
Christian (Taylorville) (34)	217 824-4969	William C Curtin	. . . .	Terry E Ryan	Colleen Hadley	. . . .	Richard E Mahan
Clark (Marshall) (16)	217 826-8311	David Schiver	. . . .	Bill Downey	Carol A Cornwell		Dan Crumrin
Clay (Louisville) (14)	618 665-3626	(not reporting)					
Clinton (Carlyle) (34)	618 594-2464	(not reporting)					
Coles (Charleston) (52)	217 348-0501	Eli Sidwell Jr	. . . .	Betty Coffrin	Bill Grimes	. . . .	Jim Kimball
Cook (Chicago) (5105)	312 443-5500	(not reporting)					
Crawford (Robinson) (19)	618 546-1212	Bob Waldrop	. . . .	Ruth E Knoblett	Doris Gill	. . . .	Tom W Weger
Cumberland (Toledo) (11)	217 849-2631	(not reporting)					
De Kalb (Sycamore) (78)	815 895-7189	(not reporting)					
De Witt (Clinton) (17)	217 935-2119	(not reporting)					
Douglas (Tuscola) (19)	217 253-2411	Russell S Ghere	. . . .	James A Ingram	Rick Hackler	. . . .	Charles L Talbott
Du Page (Wheaton) (782)	708 682-7000	Aldo E Botti	Clarence Maxwell	Gary A King	George K Kouba	. . . .	Richard Doria
Edgar (Paris) (20)	217 465-4151	Jim McCulloch	. . . .	Rebecca R Kraemer	Linda Robertson	. . . .	Karl E Farnham
Edwards (Albion) (7)	618 445-2115	(not reporting)					
Effingham (Effingham) (32)	217 342-4990	J Pat Green	. . . .	Robert Behrman	Joseph Green	. . . .	Art Kinkelaar
Fayette (Vandalia) (21)	618 283-5000	Jean B Finley	. . . .	Isabelle B Brandt	David C Marty		Michael Kleinik
Ford (Paxton) (14)	217 379-2721	Howard E Haley	. . . .	Ronald A Rasmus	Nancy L Krumwiede		Ralph E Henson
Franklin (Benton) (40)	618 438-3221	(not reporting)					
Fulton (Lewistown) (38)	309 547-3041	(not reporting)					
Gallatin (Shawneetown) (7)	618 269-3025	Ronald Abell	. . . .	. . . .	. . . .		Raymond Martin
Greene (Carrollton) (15)	217 942-5443	Jeffrey Gilbert	. . . .	Deborah Banghart	. . . .		Mike Fry
Grundy (Morris) (32)	815 942-9024	(not reporting)					
Hamilton (Mc Leansboro) (8) ...	618 643-2721	(not reporting)					
Hancock (Carthage) (21)	217 357-3911	(not reporting)					
Hardin (Elizabethtown) (5)	618 287-2251	Ronald Armstrong	. . . .	Sue McMaster	David Humphrey	. . . .	Lowell D Lasater
Henderson (Oquawka) (8)	309 867-2911	Larry Dowell		Joyce Meloan	. . . .	. . . .	Daryl Thompson

Directory 1/10   OFFICIALS IN U.S. COUNTIES
continued

County, county seat, 1990 population figures (000 omitted)	County telephone number	Board chairman	Appointed administrator	Clerk to the governing board	Chief financial officer	Personnel director	Chief law enforcement official
ILLINOIS (102) continued							
Henry (Cambridge) (51)	309 937-5192	Tom Nicholson	Dick Erickson	Martha Sawyer	Chuck Clacys	. . . .	Gib Cady
Iroquois (Watseka) (31)	815 432-6955	D Widholm	. . . .	John M Kuntz	Shelby J Townsend	. . . .	Joseph V Mathy
Jackson (Murphysboro) (61)	618 684-2157	David E Conrad	. . . .	Robert B Harrell	Shirley D Booker	. . . .	William Kilquist
Jasper (Newton) (11)	618 783-3124	(not reporting)					
Jefferson (Mount Vernon) (37)	618 244-8000	(not reporting)					
Jersey (Jerseyville) (21)	618 498-5571	(not reporting)					
Jo Daviess (Galena) (22)	815 777-0161	William McFadden	. . . .	Pam Miller	Carol Soat	. . . .	Steven Allendorf
Johnson (Vienna) (11)	618 658-3611	Max Ray	. . . .	Jerry R Simmons	. . . .	. . . .	Elry Faulkner
Kane (Geneva) (317)	708 232-3400	Warren Kammerer	. . . .	Lorraine Sava	Thomas Walter	Carol Moyer	F John Randall
Kankakee (Kankakee) (96)	815 937-2910	(not reporting)					
Kendall (Yorkville) (39)	708 553-4205	James S Boan	Jay D Young	Paul Anderson	Thomas Holbrook	. . . .	Richard Randall
Knox (Galesburg) (56)	309 343-3121	Richard D Allen	. . . .	Yvonne Tabb	Carolyn Griffith	. . . .	Mark J Shearer
La Salle (Ottawa) (107)	815 434-8242	(not reporting)					
Lake (Waukegan) (516)	708 360-6600	Robert Depke	Dwight Magalis	Linda Ianuzi Hess	Raymond Amadei	Cliff Van Dyke	Clinton Grinnell
Lawrence (Lawrenceville) (16)	618 943-2346	Harold Benson	. . . .	Will Gibson	Larry Umfleet	. . . .	Eddie Ryan
Lee (Dixon) (34)	815 288-5676	Ronald Conderman	. . . .	Nancy Nelson	. . . .	. . . .	Tim K Bivins
Livingston (Pontiac) (39)	815 844-5166	Charles M Brady	. . . .	Arnold E Natzke	. . . .	. . . .	Don M Wall
Logan (Lincoln) (31)	217 732-6400	(not reporting)					
Macon (Decatur) (117)	217 424-1470	Robert M Owen	Marily A Riley	Stephen M Bean	Julie A Curry	. . . .	H Lee Holsapple
Macoupin (Carlinville) (48)	217 854-3214	(not reporting)					
Madison (Edwardsville) (249)	618 692-6200	Nelson Hagnauer	James K Monday	Evelyn Bowles	Frederick Bathon	Chris Aldridge	Bob Churchich
Marion (Salem) (42)	618 548-3400	(not reporting)					
Marshall (Lacon) (13)	309 246-6325	Andrew L Placher	. . . .	Marjorie Rossetti	Nedra Junker	. . . .	James E Frawley
Mason (Havana) (16)	309 543-6661	Henry W Imlg	. . . .	Willim R Blessman	. . . .	. . . .	Richard E Walker
Massac (Metropolis) (15)	618 524-5213	Dale Cougill	. . . .	John D Taylor	. . . .	. . . .	Sam Dunning
Mc Donough (Macomb) (35)	309 837-2308	Charles C Gilbert	. . . .	Janet Hurtgen	Pat Waggoner	. . . .	John Bliven
Mc Henry (Woodstock) (183)	815 338-2040	Dianne Klemm	William Morefield	Katherine Schultz	Albert Jourdan	Evelyn Frazier	George Hendle
Mc Lean (Bloomington) (129)	309 888-5110	Gary C Riss	John M Zeunik	Jeanette Barrett	James E Boylan	. . . .	Steven R Brienen
Menard (Petersburg) (11)	217 632-2415	(not reporting)					
Mercer (Aledo) (17)	309 582-7021	Wayne Anderson	. . . .	Thomas Hanson	Verla Thompson	. . . .	Larry Glancey
Monroe (Waterloo) (22)	618 939-8681	R Rippelmeyer	. . . .	Richard Trost	Merrill Prange	. . . .	Dan Kelley
Montgomery (Hillsboro) (31)	217 532-2552	(not reporting)					
Morgan (Jacksonville) (36)	217 245-4619	(not reporting)					
Moultrie (Sullivan) (14)	217 728-4389	Kerry L Pate	. . . .	Richard Purdeu	Johna L Sims	Steven Mayberry	Russell Moore
Ogle (Oregon) (46)	815 732-3201	Jerry Daws	. . . .	Jean Wolfe	. . . .	. . . .	Mel Messer
Peoria (Peoria) (183)	309 672-6056	Sharon Kennedy	Lawrence A Asaro	Mary E Harkrader	Edward O'Connor	John A Saxton	Alan H Misener
Perry (Pinckneyville) (21)	618 357-5116	Leonard Heisner	. . . .	Don Hirsch	Frank Mangin	. . . .	Samuel D Hiller
Piatt (Monticello) (16)	217 762-9487	(not reporting)					
Pike (Pittsfield) (18)	217 285-6812	Don Apps Sr	. . . .	Carrol K Hoover	. . . .	. . . .	Mike Lord
Pope (Golconda) (4)	618 683-8101	Johnny Climer	. . . .	Evelyn Hogg	. . . .	. . . .	John Crabb
Pulaski (Mound City) (8)	618 748-9360	Travis Rose Jr	. . . .	C E Pete Windings	Edna Kerr	. . . .	Gene Dixon
Putnam (Hennepin) (6)	815 925-7129	William G Urnikis	. . . .	Gudmund Jessen Jr	. . . .	. . . .	Donald J A Maggi
Randolph (Chester) (35)	618 826-2510	Daniel Reitz	. . . .	William Rabe	. . . .	. . . .	Ben Picou
Richland (Olney) (17)	618 392-3111	Dan Sulsberger	. . . .	Mike Buss	D George Rumsey	. . . .	Randy Stevenson
Rock Island (Rock Island) (149)	309 786-4451	(not reporting)					
Saline (Harrisburg) (27)	618 252-6905	Eric Gregg	. . . .	Jim Fowler	Jay D Williams	. . . .	George Henley
Sangamon (Springfield) (178)	217 753-6600	Larry K Bomke	. . . .	Joseph T Aiello	Joseph Bonefeste	. . . .	J William Demarco
Schuyler (Rushville) (7)	217 322-4734	(not reporting)					
Scott (Winchester) (6)	217 742-3178	(not reporting)					
Shelby (Shelbyville) (22)	217 774-4421	(not reporting)					
St. Clair (Belleville) (263)	618 277-6600	(not reporting)					
Stark (Toulon) (7)	309 286-5901	E Musselman	. . . .	L Pyell	P Becket	. . . .	L Dennison
Stephenson (Freeport) (48)	815 235-8289	F Dean Danner	Russell J Mulnix	Dean W Amendt	Edith M Dadez	. . . .	Samuel J Volkert
Tazewell (Pekin) (124)	309 477-2274	George Saal Jr	David A Nelson	Duane Gray	Christy Webb	. . . .	Jim Donahue
Union (Jonesboro) (18)	618 833-5711	(not reporting)					
Vermilion (Danville) (88)	217 431-2550	Max Call	. . . .	Lynn Foster	Herbert Hales Jr	Edythe M Hesser	William Hartshorn
Wabash (Mount Carmel) (13)	618 262-4561	(not reporting)					
Warren (Monmouth) (19)	309 734-8592	William L Reichow	. . . .	Janet M Rutledge	Mary Jane Darrah	. . . .	Gary R Higbee
Washington (Nashville) (15)	618 327-8314	(not reporting)					
Wayne (Fairfield) (17)	618 842-5182	Donnie Barnard	. . . .	Georgia Isle	. . . .	. . . .	Benie Suddarth
White (Carmi) (17)	618 382-7211	(not reporting)					
Whiteside (Morrison) (60)	815 772-5100	Tony Arduini	J R Gallagher Jr	Dan Heusinkveld	Karen Mulnix	J R Gallagher Jr	Roger Schipper
Will (Joliet) (357)	815 722-5515	(not reporting)					
Williamson (Marion) (58)	618 997-1301	Sam Shemwell	. . . .	Barney R Boren	Bruce A Troutman	. . . .	Russell Oxford
Winnebago (Rockford) (253)	815 987-3000	Eugene Quinn	Steven M Chapman	Gloria Lind	. . . .	Donna R Bennett	Donald Gasparini
Woodford (Eureka) (33)	309 467-2822	Gary Jones	. . . .	Peggy S Rapp	Patricia Eckhoff	. . . .	William L Myers
INDIANA (92)							
Adams (Decatur) (31)	219 724-2600	William F Baker	. . . .	. . . .	James K Hill	. . . .	Thomas Coolman
Allen (Fort Wayne) (301)	219 428-7555	(not reporting)					
Bartholomew (Columbus) (64)	812 379-1515	Juanita Harden	. . . .	Sue R Paris	Sue R Paris	. . . .	David Mann
Benton (Fowler) (9)	317 884-0760	(not reporting)					
Blackford (Hartford City) (14)	317 348-1620	Rex Chaney	. . . .	David Troyer	. . . .	Jackie Ruble	Jerry Brown
Boone (Lebanon) (38)	317 482-2940	. . . .	. . . .	. . . .	Maryln Smith	. . . .	Ern Hudson
Brown (Nashville) (14)	812 988-5486	Jerry Floyd	Robert Melton	. . . .	. . . .	. . . .	David Anderson
Carroll (Delphi) (19)	317 564-3172	William E Duff	. . . .	Kenneth I Red Elk	Kenneth I Red Elk	. . . .	Lee Hoard
Cass (Logansport) (38)	219 753-7720	Merlyn Raikes	. . . .	Keneta Musall	Charlene Gibson	. . . .	Ron Woolley
Clark (Jeffersonville) (88)	812 283-4451	(not reporting)					
Clay (Brazil) (25)	812 448-8044	(not reporting)					
Clinton (Frankfort) (31)	317 659-6309	(not reporting)					
Crawford (English) (10)	812 338-2601	Herbert Newton	. . . .	Donald Childers	Donald Childers	. . . .	Alvin Crecelius
Daviess (Washington) (28)	812 254-1090	(not reporting)					
De Kalb (Auburn) (35)	219 925-2362	(not reporting)					
Dearborn (Lawrenceburg) (39)	812 537-1040	Rodney Dennerline	Louis J Meyer	Jackie Stutz	. . . .	Louis J Meyer	R Cunningham
Decatur (Greensburg) (24)	812 663-2546	Paul Menefee	. . . .	Mary M Doggett	. . . .	. . . .	Larry Snyder
Delaware (Muncie) (120)	317 747-7730	(not reporting)					
Dubois (Jasper) (37)	812 482-6545	. . . .	. . . .	. . . .	Marge Gadlage	. . . .	Terry Tanner
Elkhart (Goshen) (156)	219 534-3541	. . . .	Dick Bowman	Joyce Rowe	Charles Miller	Kathy Brewton	Randall Yohn
Fayette (Connersville) (26)	317 825-8987	(not reporting)					
Floyd (New Albany) (64)	812 948-5491	Larrison Denison	. . . .	Lela L McBarron	William Jenks	. . . .	Leland Watson
Fountain (Covington) (18)	317 793-2243	Vincent F Grogg	. . . .	Debra Goodson	Donna Burgner	Suzette Burgner	Teryl Martin
Franklin (Brookville) (20)	317 647-4631	Eugene Stewart	. . . .	Catherine Pelsor	Janice Kuntz	. . . .	Lee Davidson
Fulton (Rochester) (19)	219 223-2912	Stephen Hartzler	. . . .	Judith A Reed	Melvin Myers Jr	. . . .	Bruce Bauer

Directory 1/10   **OFFICIALS IN U.S. COUNTIES**
continued

County, county seat, 1990 population figures (000 omitted)	County telephone number	Board chairman	Appointed administrator	Clerk to the governing board	Chief financial officer	Personnel director	Chief law enforcement official
INDIANA (92) continued							
Gibson (Princeton) (32)	812 386-8401	. . . .	. . . .	. . . .	. . . .	. . . .	Bruce McClellan
Grant (Marion) (74)	317 668-8871	(not reporting)					
Greene (Bloomfield) (30)	812 384-3537	David Johnson	. . . .	Rae Della Cravens	Mary Jo Smith	. . . .	Thomas Franklin
Hamilton (Noblesville) (109)	317 776-9600	(not reporting)					
Hancock (Greenfield) (46)	317 462-1105	James Kerkhof	. . . .	Marilyn Counter	Marilyn Counter	. . . .	James Bradbury
Harrison (Corydon) (30)	812 738-8241	Terry Miller	. . . .	Barbara J Mathes	. . . .	. . . .	Edward L Davis Jr
Hendricks (Danville) (76)	317 745-9341	John D Clampitt	. . . .	Marthalyn Pearcy	. . . .	Susan Fair	Thomas Underwood
Henry (New Castle) (48)	317 529-4705	(not reporting)					
Howard (Kokomo) (81)	317 456-2215	James Shearer	Melissa K Shafer	Marilyn M Cook	Marilyn M Cook	Tamaria N Chester	J D Beatty
Huntington (Huntington) (35)	219 356-0692	(not reporting)					
Indianapolis-Marion (Indianapolis) c (731)	317 236-3200	(not reporting)					
Jackson (Brownstown) (38)	812 358-6122	Gary Darlage	. . . .	Max Pearcy	Brian Tidd	. . . .	Herschel Baughman
Jasper (Rensselaer) (25)	219 866-4930	Willis R Pettet	. . . .	Carol A Spall	Carol A Spall		Steve Reames
Jay (Portland) (22)	219 726-9575	(not reporting)					
Jefferson (Madison) (30)	812 265-8900	(not reporting)					
Jennings (Vernon) (24)	812 346-2131	(not reporting)					
Johnson (Franklin) (88)	317 736-5000	(not reporting)					
Knox (Vincennes) (40)	812 743-2552	(not reporting)					
Kosciusko (Warsaw) (65)	219 267-4444	James Jarrette	. . . .	Marsha McSherry	Patricia Brown	. . . .	Al Rovenstine
La Porte (La Porte) (107)	219 326-6808	(not reporting)					
Lagrange (Lagrange) (29)	219 463-7801	(not reporting)					
Lake (Crown Point) (476)	219 755-3000	(not reporting)					
Lawrence (Bedford) (43)	812 275-3111	. . . .	. . . .	. . . .	. . . .	. . . .	Chester Hall
Madison (Anderson) (131)	317 641-9470	(not reporting)					
Marshall (Plymouth) (42)	219 935-8555	Raymond Borggren	. . . .	Mary Lou Leavell	Mary Lou Leavell	. . . .	Ed Criswell
Martin (Shoals) (10)	812 247-3731	(not reporting)					
Miami (Peru) (37)	317 472-3901	(not reporting)					
Monroe (Bloomington) (109)	812 333-3550	(not reporting)					
Montgomery (Crawfordsville) (34)	317 364-6400	James M Kirtley	. . . .	Nelda J Hester	. . . .	. . . .	Dennis Rice
Morgan (Martinsville) (56)	317 342-1001	Tommy J Goss	. . . .	Karen Brummett	. . . .	. . . .	Charles Beaver
Newton (Kentland) (14)	219 474-6081	Russell Collins	. . . .	. . . .	. . . .	. . . .	Charles Mulligan
Noble (Albion) (38)	219 636-2658	Samuel W Patton	. . . .	Anita Huff	. . . .	. . . .	Gary Dial
Ohio (Rising Sun) (5)	812 438-2062	(not reporting)					
Orange (Paoli) (18)	812 723-3600	(not reporting)					
Owen (Spencer) (17)	812 829-2260	Dwight Dunigan	Wiley Truesdel	Lois Bixler	Margaret Tucker	. . . .	Steve Cradick
Parke (Rockville) (15)	317 569-3422	Josiah Gene Jones	. . . .	Catherine Lewis	Dale Gerrish	. . . .	Mark Bridge
Perry (Cannelton) (19)	812 547-2758	Donald Etienne	Lori Cassidy	. . . .	Marietta Dauby	. . . .	Oscar Ballis Jr
Pike (Petersburg) (13)	812 354-8448	Arvel Grubb	. . . .	Gayle Bradfield	. . . .	. . . .	William Scales
Porter (Valparaiso) (129)	219 465-3440	(not reporting)					
Posey (Mount Vernon) (26)	812 838-1300	(not reporting)					
Pulaski (Winamac) (13)	219 946-3653	(not reporting)					
Putnam (Greencastle) (30)	317 653-4603	(not reporting)					
Randolph (Winchester) (27)	317 584-7070	Jan Chalfant	. . . .	Shirley A Wright	Evard Thompson	. . . .	Ralph E Harris
Ripley (Versailles) (25)	812 689-6311	Kenneth Copeland	. . . .	Virginia Busching	Virginia Busching	. . . .	Steven Lovins
Rush (Rushville) (18)	317 932-2077	(not reporting)					
Scott (Scottsburg) (21)	812 752-4745	(not reporting)					
Shelby (Shelbyville) (40)	317 392-6310	(not reporting)					
Spencer (Rockport) (19)	812 649-4376	(not reporting)					
St. Joseph (South Bend) (247)	219 235-9547	Richard Jasinski	. . . .	M Rzeszewski	Beverly Crone	Thomas Borowski	Joseph Nagy
Starke (Knox) (23)	219 772-9101	(not reporting)					
Steuben (Angola) (27)	219 665-3014	Dale Hughes	Rodney Wells	Linda Hansen	Cheryl Beck	. . . .	L McClelland
Sullivan (Sullivan) (19)	812 268-4491	(not reporting)					
Switzerland (Vevay) (8)	812 427-3302	Robert P Bovard	. . . .	. . . .	. . . .	. . . .	Lonny Harris
Tippecanoe (Lafayette) (131)	317 423-9215	Nola Gentry	Vickie Rhine	Betty Michael	S Ruth Davidson	Frank Cederquist	. . . .
Tipton (Tipton) (16)	317 675-2795	(not reporting)					
Union (Liberty) (7)	317 458-5464	Jay Ewing	. . . .	. . . .	. . . .	. . . .	Charles Marcum
Vanderburgh (Evansville) (165)	812 426-5241	(not reporting)					
Vermillion (Newport) (17)	317 492-3570	James R Young	. . . .	Phyllis Orman	Ruth A Swinford	. . . .	Larry Jones
Vigo (Terre Haute) (106)	812 462-3000	(not reporting)					
Wabash (Wabash) (35)	219 563-0661	Dean Eppley	. . . .	. . . .	Jean Gilbert	. . . .	Bill Wheatley
Warren (Williamsport) (8)	317 762-3275	(not reporting)					
Warrick (Boonville) (45)	812 897-6120	(not reporting)					
Washington (Salem) (24)	812 883-4805	(not reporting)					
Wayne (Richmond) (72)	317 973-9200	Roy Werking	. . . .	Joseph Kaiser	Joseph Kaiser	June Clements	Dennis Andrews
Wells (Bluffton) (26)	219 824-6470	(not reporting)					
White (Monticello) (23)	219 583-5761	(not reporting)					
Whitley (Columbia City) (28)	219 248-3101	(not reporting)					
IOWA (99)							
Adair (Greenfield) (8)	515 743-2546	Cora McClain	. . . .	Jenice Wallace	Constance Sheriff	. . . .	Fred Skellenger
Adams (Corning) (5)	515 322-3340	Donald E Wolf Sr	. . . .	Donna L West	. . . .	. . . .	Merlin Dixon
Allamakee (Waukon) (14)	319 568-3522	David D Snitker	. . . .	Bill Roe Jr Elsa Hager	. . . .	Neil Becker	
Appanoose (Centerville) (14)	515 856-6191	John Broshar	. . . .	Linda Demry	. . . .	. . . .	Gerald Banks
Audubon (Audubon) (7)	712 563-2584	Laverne Deist	. . . .	Duane Deist	K W Slothouber	. . . .	Bill Shaw
Benton (Vinton) (22)	319 472-2365	Dell Hanson	. . . .	Jill Marlow	Warren E Richart	. . . .	K Popenhagen
Black Hawk (Waterloo) (124)	319 291-2422	Jack Roehr	. . . .	Julie Priest	. . . .	Thomas Pounds	Michael Kubik
Boone (Boone) (25)	515 432-1122	Robert Whitmore	. . . .	Philippe Meier	. . . .	. . . .	Ronald Fehr
Bremer (Waverly) (23)	319 352-5040	Evelyn Koepke	. . . .	Kathy J Thoms	John Devries	Kathy J Thoms	W Westendorf
Buchanan (Independence) (21)	319 334-3578	(not reporting)					
Buena Vista (Storm Lake) (20)	712 749-2542	Bob Rehnstrom	. . . .	. . . .	Karen Strawn	. . . .	Chuck Eddie
Butler (Allison) (16)	319 267-2670	Vern Echelberger	. . . .	Donald G Johnson	Henry Groeneveld	. . . .	Timothy A Junker
Calhoun (Rockwell City) (12)	712 297-7741	Larry Hood	. . . .	Judy Howrey	Joyce Toms	. . . .	Wm Davis
Carroll (Carroll) (21)	712 792-9802	Neil Trobak	. . . .	Paul Fricke	. . . .	. . . .	Doug Bass
Cass (Atlantic) (15)	712 243-4570	Duane P Becker	. . . .	Dale E Sunderman	Dale E Sunderman	. . . .	Larry G Jones
Cedar (Tipton) (17)	319 886-3168	(not reporting)					
Cerro Gordo (Mason City) (47)	515 421-3046	Chris Nannenga	. . . .	Sandy Sievers	Ken Kline	Larry Phearman	Robert Balek
Cherokee (Cherokee) (14)	712 225-4890	William G Hurd	. . . .	Barbara Huey	Barbara Huey	. . . .	Larry Simon
Chickasaw (New Hampton) (13)	515 394-2100	Arnold J Boge	. . . .	Gloria Hauser	Gloria Hauser	. . . .	Thomas Bernatz
Clarke (Osceola) (8)	515 342-3315	Dennis Chaney	. . . .	Anita Chandler	Anita Chandler	. . . .	Mark Addison
Clay (Spencer) (18)	712 262-1569	Sylvia D Schoer	. . . .	Philip L Hurst	Lavon Montgomery	. . . .	L Stanislav
Clayton (Elkader) (19)	319 245-1106	Robert Walke	. . . .	Dennis Freitag	Dorothy Samuelson	. . . .	Verdean Dietrich
Clinton (Clinton) (51)	319 243-6210	Gene T Burke	. . . .	Chas A Sheridan	Ken L Weaver	. . . .	Gary R Mulholland

Directory 1/10   OFFICIALS IN U.S. COUNTIES
continued

County, county seat, 1990 population figures (000 omitted)	County telephone number	Board chairman	Appointed administrator	Clerk to the governing board	Chief financial officer	Personnel director	Chief law enforcement official
IOWA (99) continued							
Crawford (Denison) (17)	712 263-3045	Leroy Hansohn	. . . .	. . . .	. . . .	. . . .	Thomas Hogan
Dallas (Adel) (30)	515 993-3687	(not reporting)					
Davis (Bloomfield) (8)	515 664-2101	Max Leyda	. . . .				D Wayne Rogers
Decatur (Leon) (8)	515 446-4323	Miles Leeper	. . . .	Douglas Akers	Goldie Martin	. . . .	Fred Buckingham
Delaware (Manchester) (18)	319 927-2515	Bob Clemen	. . . .	Sharon McCrabb	Sharon McCrabb	. . . .	Ronald Wilhelm
Des Moines (Burlington) (43)	319 753-8232	Stephen Ritter	. . . .	J V Leonard	Patricia Bean	. . . .	Joel Behne
Dickinson (Spirit Lake) (15)	712 336-3356	(not reporting)					
Dubuque (Dubuque) (86)	319 589-4440	Donna L Smith	Jan Hess	Denise M Dolan	Denise M Dolan	Jan Hess	Leo J Kennedy
Emmet (Estherville) (12)	712 362-4261	Roland Jasper	. . . .	Beverly Juhl	Betty Anderson	. . . .	Larry Lamack
Fayette (West Union) (22)	319 422-6061	Marilyn Rubner	. . . .	Larry Popenhagen	. . . .	. . . .	E Dietzenbach
Floyd (Charles City) (17)	515 257-6131	Arlin Enabnit	. . . .	Bret Stowe	Frank Rottinghaus	. . . .	William Cavanaugh
Franklin (Hampton) (11)	515 456-5622	William Jurgens	. . . .	Bob Davies Jr	Jane Lubkeman	. . . .	Duane Payne
Fremont (Sidney) (8)	712 374-2031	(not reporting)					
Greene (Jefferson) (10)	515 386-2552	(not reporting)					
Grundy (Grundy Center) (12)	319 824-5813	Donald Schildroth	. . . .	Mary L Schmidt	Susan K Kitzman	. . . .	Rick Penning
Guthrie (Guthrie Center) (11)	515 747-3619	Jay W Coffman	. . . .	Darwin Hall	Darwin Hall	. . . .	Stuart Stringham
Hamilton (Webster City) (16)	515 832-1771	Miles L Butler	. . . .	Mary Shultz	Deborah Leksell	. . . .	Scott Anderson
Hancock (Garner) (13)	515 923-3163	(not reporting)					
Hardin (Eldora) (19)	515 858-3461	Mildred Lloyd	. . . .	Renee McClellan	. . . .	Renee McClellan	Loren Goodknight
Harrison (Logan) (15)	712 644-2401	(not reporting)					
Henry (Mount Pleasant) (19)	319 385-0756	Roger Tweedy	. . . .	Carol McCulley	Marjorie Burden	Shelly Barber	Terry Morrow
Howard (Cresco) (10)	319 547-2880	Michael W Mahr	. . . .	. . . .	. . . .	. . . .	Gary Cleveland
Humboldt (Dakota City) (11)	515 332-1571	Gary Kuehnast	. . . .	Jerry C Diedrick	Pat Albrecht	. . . .	Marvin Andersen
Ida (Ida Grove) (8)	712 364-2626	Robert Bumann	. . . .	Joy Sharkey	Shirley Palm	. . . .	Donald Bremer
Iowa (Marengo) (15)	319 642-3923	. . . .	. . . .	Linda Griggs	. . . .	. . . .	James Slockett
Jackson (Maquoketa) (20)	319 652-3144	John C Engel	. . . .	T M Cotton	Alfred Tebbe Jr	. . . .	Robert P Lyons
Jasper (Newton) (35)	515 792-9808	Howard Peters Jr	. . . .	Linda Gifford	Linda Gifford	. . . .	Jim Verwers
Jefferson (Fairfield) (16)	515 472-2851	(not reporting)					
Johnson (Iowa City) (96)	319 356-6000	Patricia Meade	Carol Peters	. . . .	. . . .	. . . .	Robert Carpenter
Jones (Anamosa) (19)	319 462-2282	Steven Strang	. . . .	Michael S Albers	Michael S Albers	. . . .	John W Cook
Keokuk (Sigourney) (12)	515 622-2320	Maryl Grove	. . . .	Marilyn Wells	Arlene Nilles	. . . .	Ron George
Kossuth (Algona) (19)	515 295-2718	Lennon Brandt	. . . .	D Thilges Dodds	D Thilges Dodds	. . . .	Kevin Otterloo
Lee (Fort Madison) (39)	319 372-6557	(not reporting)					
Linn (Cedar Rapids) (169)	319 398-3958	Jean E Oxley	. . . .	Linda Langenberg	Stephen B Tucker	Trude J Elliott	Dennis H Blome
Louisa (Wapello) (12)	319 523-3371	Jack Estle	. . . .	. . . .	Kay Skipton	. . . .	Herbert Eutsler
Lucas (Chariton) (9)	515 774-4512	John D Hardie	. . . .	Linda Reed	G Patterson	. . . .	James Swarthout
Lyon (Rock Rapids) (12)	712 472-3713	(not reporting)					
Madison (Winterset) (12)	515 462-3914	(not reporting)					
Mahaska (Oskaloosa) (22)	515 673-7148	Albert Stewart	. . . .	Kay Swanson	Kay Swanson	Kay Swanson	Charles Van Toorn
Marion (Knoxville) (30)	515 828-2217	William Shepherd	. . . .	Delores Devries	. . . .	. . . .	M Van Haaften
Marshall (Marshalltown) (38)	515 754-6300	Matthew A Edel	. . . .	M Grimes Knutson	Deane Adams	. . . .	Ted Kamatchus
Mills (Glenwood) (13)	712 527-3146	Robert E Honig	. . . .	Cheryll Ross	. . . .	. . . .	Mack G Taylor
Mitchell (Osage) (11)	515 732-5861	(not reporting)					
Monona (Onawa) (10)	712 423-2191	Lawrence Collins	. . . .	Benita J Davis	Roger Blatchford	. . . .	Dennis K Smith
Monroe (Albia) (8)	515 932-7706	Dennis Ryan	. . . .	C Brothers	. . . .	. . . .	Wayne Messamaker
Montgomery (Red Oak) (12)	712 623-5127	Bernard Palmquist	. . . .	Donnamae Smith	Anita Walker	. . . .	Jeffrey H Smith
Muscatine (Muscatine) (40)	319 263-5821	Chad James	. . . .	Richard Crooks	. . . .	. . . .	Ronald Hazen
O'Brien (Primghar) (15)	712 757-3225	Rudolf Riessen	. . . .	. . . .	Barb Kreibaum	. . . .	Michael Anderson
Osceola (Sibley) (7)	712 754-2241	Fred Year	. . . .	Duane Vandehoef	Linda Carter	. . . .	Mitchell Watters
Page (Clarinda) (17)	712 542-3219	Maurice Reavis	. . . .	Judy Clark	Donna Wheeler	. . . .	Bob Rank
Palo Alto (Emmetsburg) (11)	712 852-2924	Mary Greene	. . . .	Gary Leonard	Kathleen Thompson	. . . .	Russell Jergens
Plymouth (Le Mars) (23)	712 546-6100	Donald G Law	. . . .	K Kae Meyer	Norman G Kehrberg	K Kae Meyer	Mike Van Otterloo
Pocahontas (Pocahontas) (10)	712 335-3361	Vincent L Triggs	. . . .	Margene A Bunda	Shirley Dense	. . . .	Richard R Jergens
Polk (Des Moines) (327)	515 286-3000	(not reporting)					
Pottawattamie (Council Bluffs) (83)	712 328-5700	(not reporting)					
Poweshiek (Montezuma) (19)	515 623-5443	Robert M Sutfin	Jo Wray	Jo Wray	Jo Wray	. . . .	Max Allen
Ringgold (Mount Ayr) (5)	515 464-3244	Kenneth Quick	. . . .	. . . .	Eloise Brown	. . . .	Lyle Minnick
Sac (Sac City) (12)	712 662-7401	(not reporting)					
Scott (Davenport) (151)	319 326-8611	Edwin G Winborn	F Glen Erickson	Karen Fitzsimmons	C Ray Wierson	David C Whan	Mike Bladel
Shelby (Harlan) (13)	712 755-3831	Gayle B Petersen	. . . .	. . . .	. . . .	. . . .	Gene Cavenaugh
Sioux (Orange City) (30)	712 737-2216	(not reporting)					
Story (Nevada) (74)	515 382-6581	Larry Larson	. . . .	Judy Emmons	Doris Samson	Sherry Howard	Paul Fitzgerald
Tama (Toledo) (17)	515 484-2740	Ferdinand Kvidera	. . . .	John A Adams	Sandra Fowler	. . . .	Mike Richardson
Taylor (Bedford) (7)	712 523-2280	David Nally	. . . .	Carole Noer	Wanda Campbell	. . . .	David Holben
Union (Creston) (13)	515 782-7218	Michael J King	. . . .	Donald M Krings	. . . .	. . . .	John Coulter
Van Buren (Keosauqua) (8)	319 293-3129	R Reynols Knight	. . . .	Jon P Finney	. . . .	. . . .	Hugh H Hardin
Wapello (Ottumwa) (36)	515 683-0025	Harold D Giltner	. . . .	Mary A Gaskill	Dianne L Kiefer	. . . .	Buddy C Erwin
Warren (Indianola) (36)	515 961-1001	(not reporting)					
Washington (Washington) (20)	319 653-7715	(not reporting)					
Wayne (Corydon) (7)	515 872-2242	Jerry O'Dell	. . . .	Sue Ruble	Dean Besco	. . . .	Gilbert Sanders
Webster (Fort Dodge) (40)	515 573-7175	Jill Kirkberg	. . . .	. . . .	. . . .	. . . .	
Winnebago (Forest City) (12)	515 582-3412	Vernon Hogard	. . . .	Robert D Paulson	Ruth Bachman	. . . .	Thomas Lillquist
Winneshiek (Decorah) (21)	319 382-5085	Linus Rothmeyer	. . . .	G Schweinefus	. . . .	. . . .	Floyd Ashbacher
Woodbury (Sioux City) (98)	712 279-6525	(not reporting)					
Worth (Northwood) (8)	515 324-2316	(not reporting)					
Wright (Clarion) (14)	515 532-3262	Larry E Olson	. . . .	Gladys Riley	Bernice Valley	. . . .	Vernon R Elston
KANSAS (105)							
Allen (Iola) (15)	316 365-7491	(not reporting)					
Anderson (Garnett) (8)	913 448-6841	Dudley Feuerborn	. . . .	Phyllis Nolan	. . . .	. . . .	David Vaughan
Atchison (Atchison) (17)	913 367-1653	(not reporting)					
Barber (Medicine Lodge) (6)	316 886-3961	Mike Mills	. . . .	Linda S McGuire	. . . .	. . . .	Tommy Tomson
Barton (Great Bend) (29)	316 793-1800	James Nolte	Mike Leighton	Coleen Murphy	Mike Leighton	Mike Leighton	James Daily
Bourbon (Fort Scott) (15)	316 223-3800	Carey Lockwood	. . . .	Barbara Wood	Opal Hess	Doylene Kennedy	Harold Coleman
Brown (Hiawatha) (11)	913 742-2581	Luther Pederson	. . . .	Grace L Miller	Judy Grathwohl	. . . .	Rob Hendricks
Butler (El Dorado) (51)	316 321-1960	Leon White	. . . .	Ernest Sifford	. . . .	. . . .	Dave Williams
Chase (Cottonwood Falls) (3)	316 273-6423	(not reporting)					
Chautauqua (Sedan) (4)	316 725-5389	Charles D Bowen	. . . .	Lori E Martin	Peggy McAfee	. . . .	Harry Williams
Cherokee (Columbus) (21)	316 429-2042	(not reporting)					
Cheyenne (St. Francis) (3)	913 332-2401	William Leach	. . . .	Elaine Kehlbeck	. . . .	. . . .	Ray Lee
Clark (Ashland) (2)	316 635-2813	Mike Myatt	. . . .	Rebecca Mishler	. . . .	. . . .	Brad Harris
Clay (Clay Center) (9)	913 632-2552	W H Pfizenmaier	. . . .	Mary Brown	. . . .	. . . .	Gary Caldwell

Directory 1/10 **OFFICIALS IN U.S. COUNTIES**
continued

County, county seat, 1990 population figures (000 omitted)	County telephone number	Board chairman	Appointed administrator	Clerk to the governing board	Chief financial officer	Personnel director	Chief law enforcement official
KANSAS (105) continued							
Cloud (Concordia) (11)	913 243-8110	(not reporting)					
Coffey (Burlington) (8)	316 364-2191	Johnnie Sleezer	. . . .	Vernon Birk	. . . .	. . . .	Warren Ganlock Sr
Comanche (Coldwater) (2)	316 582-2361	Dennis Swayze	. . . .	Alice Smith	. . . .		Jene Allen
Cowley (Winfield) (37)	316 221-4066	Dick Bonfy	. . . .	H Joe Gaston	. . . .	H Joe Gaston	Robert Odell
Crawford (Girard) (36)	316 724-6117	(not reporting)					
Decatur (Oberlin) (4)	913 475-2132	(not reporting)					
Dickinson (Abilene) (19)	913 263-7157	(not reporting)					
Doniphan (Troy) (8)	913 985-3513	Dana Foley	. . . .	Bev Schoenfelder	Jacqueline Linck	. . . .	Mark Long
Douglas (Lawrence) (82)	913 841-7700	(not reporting)					
Edwards (Kinsley) (4)	316 659-3121	(not reporting)					
Elk (Howard) (3)	316 374-2490	(not reporting)					
Ellis (Hays) (26)	913 628-9410	Guy Windholz	. . . .	Peggy McCullick	Mike Billinger Jr	. . . .	Frank Reese
Ellsworth (Ellsworth) (7)	913 472-4161	(not reporting)					
Finney (Garden City) (33)	316 272-3500	Gary Dick	Pete Olson	Carol Brown	. . . .		Grover Craig
Ford (Dodge City) (27)	316 227-4550	(not reporting)					
Franklin (Ottawa) (22)	913 242-1471	Gardner Hayden	. . . .		. . . .	. . . .	Rex Bowling
Geary (Junction City) (30)	913 238-3912	Eldon L Hoyle	. . . .	Joyce Bielefeld	. . . .		William L Deppish
Gove (Gove) (3)	913 938-2300	(not reporting)					
Graham (Hill City) (4)	913 674-3453	Alvin Denk	. . . .	Darlene Riggs	Jerilyn Keith		Don Scott
Grant (Ulysses) (7)	316 356-1335	(not reporting)					
Gray (Cimarron) (5)	316 855-3618	(not reporting)					
Greeley (Tribune) (2)	316 376-4256	Paul J Shafer	. . . .	Linda K Firner	Joy A Sawyer		Steve A Schmidt
Greenwood (Eureka) (8)	316 583-7421	(not reporting)					
Hamilton (Syracuse) (2)	316 384-5629	Terryi Spiker	. . . .	Beverly Holdren	. . . .	. . . .	Daniel Levens
Harper (Anthony) (7)	316 842-5555	Sandra Gates	. . . .	Tanis L Lieurance	Carmen Alldritt		Terry G Bane
Harvey (Newton) (31)	316 283-6810	Eugene Wendling	Craig Simons	Margaret Wright	Craig Simons	Evelyn Reimer	Byron Motter
Haskell (Sublette) (4)	316 675-2263	(not reporting)					
Hodgeman (Jetmore) (2)	316 357-6421	(not reporting)					
Jackson (Holton) (12)	913 364-2891	Dorothy J Lewis	. . . .	Kathy L Mick	. . . .	Kathy L Mick	Philip McManigal
Jefferson (Oskaloosa) (16)	913 863-2272	William K Rhodes	. . . .	Shirley Walbridge	. . . .	Shirley Walbridge	Roy Dunnaway
Jewell (Mankato) (4)	913 378-3121	Gene Barrett	. . . .	Wes Moore	. . . .		John Owen
Johnson (Olathe) (355)	913 782-5000	S Weltner	E H Denton	B Baker	R Cousino	C Leichliter	F Allenbrand
Kearny (Lakin) (4)	316 355-6422	(not reporting)					
Kingman (Kingman) (8)	316 532-2521	Joe Dirks	. . . .	Donna R Brown	. . . .	. . . .	Robert M Bayack
Kiowa (Greensburg) (4)	316 723-3366	Harvey Ulmer	. . . .	Evelyn Grimm	. . . .	. . . .	Thomas Boman
Labette (Oswego) (24)	316 795-2138	Cecil L Fish	. . . .	Linda Schreppel	Barbara Goodnight	Bonnie Wilson	M T Bringle
Lane (Dighton) (2)	316 397-2802	Edwin A Habiger	. . . .	. . . .	. . . .	. . . .	Donald L Wilson
Leavenworth (Leavenworth) (64)	913 684-0400	Louis Klemp	. . . .		Linda Sheer	Esther Kasper	Herbert Nye
Lincoln (Lincoln) (4)	913 524-4757	Alfred W Wallace	. . . .	Doris White	Donna L West	. . . .	Anne Branda
Linn (Mound City) (8)	913 795-2668	Frank Gable	. . . .	Donald L Proffitt	Patricia E Davey	. . . .	Richard O' Bryant
Logan (Oakley) (3)	913 672-4244	Robert K Scott	. . . .	Patricia M Miller	. . . .	. . . .	Ronald Keith
Lyon (Emporia) (35)	316 342-4950	Myron Van Gundy	. . . .	Karen Harbenbower	Dora Hartig	. . . .	Cliff Hacker
Marion (Marion) (13)	316 382-2185	Linda Peterson	. . . .	Marquetta Eilerts	Verden A Harms	. . . .	Edward Davies
Marshall (Marysville) (12)	913 562-5361	(not reporting)					
Mc Pherson (Mc Pherson) (27)	316 241-8149	Duane Patrick	Richard Whitte	Susan Henson	Richard Whitte	Marilyn Widler	Larry Powell
Meade (Meade) (4)	316 873-2581	(not reporting)					
Miami (Paola) (23)	913 294-3976	Joseph W Towne	. . . .	Kathy Peckman	. . . .	. . . .	Dan Morgan
Mitchell (Beloit) (7)	913 738-3652	Lyle McPeak	. . . .	Joleen Walker	Carol Emmot		Douglas Daugherty
Montgomery (Independence) (39)	316 331-2710	(not reporting)					
Morris (Council Grove) (6)	316 767-5518	Robert Mark Jr	. . . .	Michelle Garrett	Patty Carson		Gary Carrier
Morton (Elkhart) (3)	316 697-2157	(not reporting)					
Nemaha (Seneca) (10)	913 336-2170	(not reporting)					
Neosho (Erie) (17)	316 244-3293	Hugo Spieker	. . . .	Linda S Powers	Wayne B Gibson Jr	. . . .	Rick L Wingate
Ness (Ness City) (4)	913 798-2401	Paul D Pavlu	. . . .	Ramona Meis	. . . .	. . . .	Gary W O' Brien
Norton (Norton) (6)	913 877-2363	Dean Esslinger	. . . .	Dorothy Shearer	Sally Breiner	. . . .	Myron Cochran
Osage (Lyndon) (15)	913 828-4812	(not reporting)					
Osborne (Osborne) (5)	913 346-2431	Donald S Kiper	. . . .	Gloria B Wood	Gloria B Wood	Gloria B Wood	Curtis L Miner
Ottawa (Minneapolis) (6)	913 392-2279	(not reporting)					
Pawnee (Larned) (8)	316 285-3721	Kathy Bowman	. . . .	Ruth Searight	. . . .	. . . .	Charles Shearrer
Phillips (Phillipsburg) (7)	913 543-5513	Foster Matteson	. . . .	Linda McDowell	. . . .	. . . .	Leroy Stephen
Pottawatomie (Westmoreland) (16)	913 457-3314	(not reporting)					
Pratt (Pratt) (10)	316 672-5181	(not reporting)					
Rawlins (Atwood) (3)	913 626-3351	Charles E Unger	. . . .	Meredith Hrnchir	Cheryl Wederski	. . . .	Jack Maris
Reno (Hutchinson) (62)	316 694-2929	David Holmes	. . . .	Roxanne Wheatley	Larry Tucker	Monica Holtsclaw	Larry Leslie
Republic (Belleville) (6)	913 527-5691	(not reporting)					
Rice (Lyons) (11)	316 257-2232	Mary Bolton	. . . .	Joan Davison	Rosemary Schmidt	. . . .	Jeff Baker
Riley (Manhattan) (67)	913 537-0700	Wilton Thomas	. . . .	Ilene Colbert	Eileen King	Janee Roche	Alvin Johnson
Rooks (Stockton) (6)	913 425-6391	Normand Hrabe	. . . .	Clara Strutt	. . . .	. . . .	David Denton
Rush (La Crosse) (4)	913 222-2731	Mary C Brening	. . . .	Linda M Bott	. . . .	. . . .	Jack Mendenhall
Russell (Russell) (8)	913 483-4641	(not reporting)					
Saline (Salina) (49)	913 827-1961	Michael J White	Dana H Morse	Shirley J Jacques	Charles K Lily	Rita A Deister	Darrell L Wilson
Scott (Scott City) (5)	316 872-2420	(not reporting)					
Sedgwick (Wichita) (404)	316 383-7166	Mark F Schroeder	William Buchanan	S Crockett Spoon	Terry Coltrain	Mary Ann Mamoth	Michael D Hill
Seward (Liberal) (19)	316 626-3200	Anna F Harrison	. . . .	Paul W Hoag	Paul W Hoag	Paul W Hoag	Billy McBryde
Shawnee (Topeka) (161)	913 291-4149	(not reporting)					
Sheridan (Hoxie) (3)	913 675-3361	(not reporting)					
Sherman (Goodland) (7)	913 899-6125	(not reporting)					
Smith (Smith Center) (5)	913 282-6832	(not reporting)					
Stafford (St. John) (5)	316 549-3509	(not reporting)					
Stanton (Johnson) (2)	316 492-2140	Melvin Winger	. . . .	Sharon Dimitt	Phyllis Kistler	. . . .	James R Garrison
Stevens (Hugoton) (5)	316 545-2541	Laurence Brower	. . . .	Opal Hall	Belva Hickey	. . . .	Russ DeWitt
Sumner (Wellington) (26)	316 326-3395	Elmer C Dill	. . . .	Sibyl P Whipple	. . . .	. . . .	Tony Schwabauer
Thomas (Colby) (8)	913 462-2561	John Bremenkamp	. . . .	Rosalie Seemann	. . . .	. . . .	Thomas W Jones
Trego (Wakeeney) (4)	913 743-2114	Gleyn A Lowe	. . . .	Kathleen Conness	Gary Watson	. . . .	Jerry White
Wabaunsee (Alma) (7)	913 765-3414	Stephen Anderson	. . . .	Ruth Diepenbrock	. . . .	. . . .	Michael Watson
Wallace (Sharon Springs) (2)	913 852-4282	Doris Harrison	Jacalyn Mai	Jacalyn Mai	. . . .	. . . .	
Washington (Washington) (7)	913 325-2974	Dwain Compton	. . . .	LaVon Hornbostel	. . . .	. . . .	J Wiley Kerr
Wichita (Leoti) (3)	316 375-2731	(not reporting)					
Wilson (Fredonia) (10)	316 378-2186	Glenn Jones	. . . .	Maurine R Burns	Rita Githens	. . . .	Paul Ammann
Woodson (Yates Center) (4)	316 625-2179	Glay Yoho	. . . .	Sondra Solander	. . . .	. . . .	Mark Brilke
Wyandotte (Kansas City) (162)	913 573-2800	Verdis Robinson	. . . .	Edward Mayfield	Robert Brown		Bill Dillon

Directory 1/10   OFFICIALS IN U.S. COUNTIES
continued

County, county seat, 1990 population figures (000 omitted)	County telephone number	Board chairman	Appointed administrator	Clerk to the governing board	Chief financial officer	Personnel director	Chief law enforcement official
KENTUCKY (120)							
Adair (Columbia) (15)	502 384-4703	Richard L Walker	. . . .	Joyce C Rodgers	Lynn B McLean	. . . .	Bob Willis
Allen (Scottsville) (15)	502 237-3631	(not reporting)					
Anderson (Lawrenceburg) (15) ..	502 839-3041	(not reporting)					
Ballard (Wickliffe) (8)	502 335-5177	(not reporting)					
Barren (Glasgow) (34)	502 651-3338	(not reporting)					
Bath (Owingsville) (10)	606 674-6346	(not reporting)					
Bell (Pineville) (32)	606 337-3076	(not reporting)					
Boone (Burlington) (58)	606 334-2100	Kenneth R Lucas	James H Collins	Carol Rudicill	M Vaughn Rogers	M K Kruempelman	Thomas Schwartz
Bourbon (Paris) (19)	606 987-3010	Charles R Hinkle	. . . .	Betty Jo Heick	Mary Allen Hedges	. . . .	John Ransdell
Boyd (Catlettsburg) (51)	606 739-4134	(not reporting)					
Boyle (Danville) (26)	606 238-1100	(not reporting)					
Bracken (Brooksville) (8)	606 735-2300	Dwayne Jett	. . . .	Mary Bauer	. . . .	. . . .	Michael Nelson
Breathitt (Jackson) (16)	606 666-2818	(not reporting)					
Breckinridge (Hardinsburg) (16) .	502 756-2269	(not reporting)					
Bullitt (Shepherdsville) (48)	502 543-2262	(not reporting)					
Butler (Morgantown) (11)	502 526-3433	(not reporting)					
Caldwell (Princeton) (13)	502 365-6660	J D Jones	Molly Rogers	B Van Hooser	Toni Watson	J D Jones	James Dorroh
Calloway (Murray) (31)	502 753-2920	(not reporting)					
Campbell (Newport) (84)	606 292-3838	(not reporting)					
Carlisle (Bardwell) (5)	502 628-5451	(not reporting)					
Carroll (Carrollton) (9)	502 732-4426	(not reporting)					
Carter (Grayson) (24)	606 474-5366	Joe D Kitchen	. . . .	Hugh R McDavid	Joy C Nolan	Joe D Kitchen	Coleman Binion
Casey (Liberty) (14)	606 787-6154	(not reporting)					
Christian (Hopkinsville) (69)	502 887-4100	(not reporting)					
Clark (Winchester) (29)	606 745-0200	(not reporting)					
Clay (Manchester) (22)	606 598-2071	Carl E Sizemore	Debra K Parks	Bessie C Mitchell	Diane Roberts	Carl E Sizemore	Ed Jordan
Clinton (Albany) (9)	606 387-5234	(not reporting)					
Crittenden (Marion) (9)	502 965-5251	(not reporting)					
Cumberland (Burkesville) (7)	502 864-3444	(not reporting)					
Daviess (Owensboro) (87)	502 685-8424	(not reporting)					
Edmonson (Brownsville) (10) ..	502 597-2819	Donald Houchin	. . . .	Richard Sanders	Sharon French	. . . .	Eddie Railey
Elliott (Sandy Hook) (6)	606 738-5335	David Blair	. . . .	Melanie Blair	Melanie Blair	. . . .	C Pennington
Estill (Irvine) (15)	606 723-7524	Donnie Watson	. . . .	Dora N Henry	Wesley Farley	. . . .	Glendle Flynn
Fleming (Flemingsburg) (12)	606 845-8461	(not reporting)					
Floyd (Prestonsburg) (44)	606 886-9193	(not reporting)					
Franklin (Frankfort) (44)	502 875-8751	(not reporting)					
Fulton (Hickman) (8)	502 236-2594	Harold Garrison	Karen Argo	Lesia Larue	Bethel E Choate	Karen Argo	N D Hill
Gallatin (Warsaw) (5)	606 567-5691	Clarence Davis	. . . .	Cathy Adams	Opaline Moore	. . . .	Delmar Alexander
Garrard (Lancaster) (12)	606 792-3531	(not reporting)					
Grant (Williamstown) (16)	606 823-7561	Carol L Woodyard	. . . .	Evalene Davis	Katsia J Baird	. . . .	Charles Hudson
Graves (Mayfield) (34)	502 247-3626	(not reporting)					
Grayson (Leitchfield) (21)	502 259-3159	(not reporting)					
Green (Greensburg) (10)	502 932-4024	(not reporting)					
Greenup (Greenup) (37)	606 473-3151	(not reporting)					
Hancock (Hawesville) (8)	502 927-8137	(not reporting)					
Hardin (Elizabethtown) (89)	502 765-2350	Glen D Dalton	. . . .	David L Logsdon	Margie Ree Oliver	. . . .	Charles Logsdon
Harlan (Harlan) (37)	606 573-2600	(not reporting)					
Harrison (Cynthiana) (16)	606 234-7136	C Swinford	. . . .	. . . .	. . . .	. . . .	B Hampton
Hart (Munfordville) (15)	502 524-9474	Vince Lang	. . . .	. . . .	Tammie Gray	Anna Hogan	Charles Lisenby
Henderson (Henderson) (43)	502 826-3971	(not reporting)					
Henry (New Castle) (13)	502 845-2891	(not reporting)					
Hickman (Clinton) (6)	502 653-4369	(not reporting)					
Hopkins (Madisonville) (46)	502 821-7361	(not reporting)					
Jackson (Mc Kee) (12)	606 287-8562	William O Smith	Patricia Gabbard	Jerry Dean	. . . .	. . . .	Hershel Lynch
Jefferson (Louisville) (665)	502 625-6161	David L Armstrong	Wendell P Wright	Mary W Bolton	Steve J Rowland	Patricia M Childs	Leon E Jones Sr
Jessamine (Nicholasville) (31) ..	606 885-4500	(not reporting)					
Johnson (Paintsville) (23)	606 789-2550	(not reporting)					
Kenton (Covington) (142)	606 491-2800	Clyde Middleton	George Neack	Carol Brockell	Ivan Frye	Ralph Bailey	Jeffrey Butler
Knott (Hindman) (18)	606 785-5592	(not reporting)					
Knox (Barbourville) (30)	606 546-6192	(not reporting)					
Larue (Hodgenville) (12)	502 358-4400	(not reporting)					
Laurel (London) (43)	606 864-5158	(not reporting)					
Lawrence (Louisa) (14)	606 638-4108	(not reporting)					
Lee (Beattyville) (7)	606 464-3678	(not reporting)					
Leslie (Hyden) (14)	606 672-3200	(not reporting)					
Letcher (Whitesburg) (27)	606 633-2129	(not reporting)					
Lewis (Vanceburg) (13)	606 796-2722	(not reporting)					
Lexington-Fayette (Lexington) c (225)	606 258-3030	(not reporting)					
Lincoln (Stanford) (20)	606 365-2534	John Sims	Patricia L Young	. . . .	Teresa Padgett	Patricia L Young	Earl D McWhorter
Livingston (Smithland) (9)	502 928-4522	Ralph Smith	. . . .	James Jones	Eileen Chesnut	. . . .	. . . .
Logan (Russellville) (24)	502 726-3116	John H Guion	Karen Taylor	Brenda Hoots	Doris McMillen	John H Guion	Dannie Blick
Lyon (Eddyville) (7)	502 388-7311	(not reporting)					
Madison (Richmond) (58)	606 624-4700	(not reporting)					
Magoffin (Salyersville) (13)	606 349-2313	(not reporting)					
Marion (Lebanon) (16)	502 692-3451	(not reporting)					
Marshall (Benton) (27)	502 527-3388	(not reporting)					
Martin (Inez) (13)	606 298-2800	(not reporting)					
Mason (Maysville) (17)	606 564-6706	(not reporting)					
Mc Cracken (Paducah) (63)	502 444-4707	Gary L Hovekamp	M Annet Lofton	Martha N Bradford	Mary M Hoffman	Gary L Hovekamp	Howard Walker
Mc Creary (Whitley City) (16) ...	606 376-2413	Jimmie W Greene	Bruce Murphy	Jo Kidd	John A Crabtree	Sue K Kidd	Roger Stephens
Mc Lean (Calhoun) (10)	502 273-3082	(not reporting)					
Meade (Brandenburg) (24)	502 422-3967	(not reporting)					
Menifee (Frenchburg) (5)	606 768-3482	Henry Ratliff	. . . .	. . . .	. . . .	. . . .	Sam Swartz
Mercer (Harrodsburg) (19)	606 734-5135	(not reporting)					
Metcalfe (Edmonton) (9)	502 432-4821	(not reporting)					
Monroe (Tompkinsville) (11)	502 487-5505	Mitchell Page	. . . .	. . . .	. . . .	. . . .	B McClendon
Montgomery (Mount Sterling) (20)	606 498-1992	William E Johnson	Brenda L Jackson	Judy L Witt	Brenda J Mapel	Brenda L Jackson	Dewey Compton
Morgan (West Liberty) (12)	606 743-3949	(not reporting)					
Muhlenberg (Greenville) (31) ...	502 338-2520	(not reporting)					
Nelson (Bardstown) (30)	502 348-5941	(not reporting)					
Nicholas (Carlisle) (7)	606 289-2404	(not reporting)					
Ohio (Hartford) (21)	502 298-7629	(not reporting)					

Directory 1/10 **OFFICIALS IN U.S. COUNTIES**
continued

County, county seat, 1990 population figures (000 omitted)	County telephone number	Board chairman	Appointed administrator	Clerk to the governing board	Chief financial officer	Personnel director	Chief law enforcement official
KENTUCKY (120) continued							
Oldham (La Grange) (33)	502 222-9311	(not reporting)					
Owen (Owenton) (9)	502 484-3405	Horace D West	. . . .	Eugene Young	Cynthia Ellis	. . . .	Glenn Waldrop
Owsley (Booneville) (5)	606 593-6202	(not reporting)					
Pendleton (Falmouth) (12)	606 654-4321	(not reporting)					
Perry (Hazard) (30)	606 436-4513	(not reporting)					
Pike (Pikeville) (73)	606 432-6247	(not reporting)					
Powell (Stanton) (12)	606 663-2834	Forest Meadows	. . . .	Sherry Bowen	Judith Hale	. . . .	James Congleton
Pulaski (Somerset) (49)	606 678-4853	Darrell Beshears	Dexter Thompson	Willard Hansford	Arlene Phelps	. . . .	Samuel W Catron
Robertson (Mount Olivet) (2)	606 724-5615	G Wayne Buckler	. . . .	S Hendricks	Janet England	. . . .	Randy Insko
Rockcastle (Mount Vernon) (15)	606 256-2856	Roland D Mullins	. . . .	Anna R Mullins	Joseph Clontz	. . . .	Shirley Smith
Rowan (Morehead) (20)	606 784-5151	Clyde A Thomas	. . . .	Jean W Bailey	Dana T Baldridge	. . . .	Jack Carter
Russell (Jamestown) (15)	502 343-2112	(not reporting)					
Scott (Georgetown) (24)	502 863-7875	George Lusby	Don Olver	Martha Neclevio	Robert W Ward	George Lusby	Mike Leaverton
Shelby (Shelbyville) (25)	502 633-1220	Bobby Stratton	. . . .	Sue C Perry	Mary Jo Wiley	Bobby Stratton	Harold Tingle
Simpson (Franklin) (15)	502 586-7184	(not reporting)					
Spencer (Taylorsville) (7)	502 477-8127	(not reporting)					
Taylor (Campbellsville) (21)	502 465-7729	Fred L Waddle	. . . .	Randall Phillips	Everette Lee	. . . .	Eddie Marcum
Todd (Elkton) (11)	502 265-2363	(not reporting)					
Trigg (Cadiz) (10)	502 522-8459	Zelner Cossey	. . . .	Wanda Thomas	Elsie Tinsley	. . . .	Randy Clark
Trimble (Bedford) (6)	502 255-7196	Jack F Couch	. . . .	Lavaughn Clark	. . . .	. . . .	Howard Long
Union (Morganfield) (17)	502 389-1081	(not reporting)					
Warren (Bowling Green) (77)	502 843-4146	(not reporting)					
Washington (Springfield) (10)	606 336-5410	Bobby Brady	Mary Lou McRay	A H Robertson Sr	Sheila Curtsinger	Sheila Curtsinger	Donnie Barr
Wayne (Monticello) (17)	606 348-4241	(not reporting)					
Webster (Dixon) (14)	502 639-5042	(not reporting)					
Whitley (Williamsburg) (33)	606 549-1330	(not reporting)					
Wolfe (Campton) (7)	606 668-3040	(not reporting)					
Woodford (Versailles) (20)	606 873-4139	(not reporting)					
LOUISIANA (64)							
Acadia (Crowley) p (56)	318 783-0953	(not reporting)					
Allen (Oberlin) p (21)	318 639-4376	(not reporting)					
Ascension (Donaldsonville) p (58)	504 473-9866	(not reporting)					
Assumption (Napoleonville) p (23)	504 369-7435	Martin Triche	Bettie Monson	Lawrence Bergeron	Bettie Monson	Calvin James	Thomas Mabile
Avoyelles (Marksville) p (39)	318 253-9208	Gene Britton	Allison Dauzat	Allison Dauzat	Janice Brevelle	Matt Bordelon	. . . .
Baton Rouge (Baton Rouge) c (220)	504 389-3141	(not reporting)					
Beauregard (De Ridder) p (30)	318 463-7019	Wayne Hall	Thomas W Smith	. . . .	. . . .	Willie Vincent Jr	
Bienville (Arcadia) p (16)	318 263-2019	(not reporting)					
Bossier (Benton) p (86)	318 965-2329	(not reporting)					
Caddo (Shreveport) p (248)	318 226-6780	(not reporting)					
Calcasieu (Lake Charles) p (168)	318 437-3500	(not reporting)					
Caldwell (Columbia) p (10)	318 649-2273	(not reporting)					
Cameron (Cameron) p (9)	318 775-5718	George Leboeuf	Earnestine Horn	Debbie Theriot	Bonnie Conner	. . . .	James Savoie
Catahoula (Harrisonburg) p (11)	318 744-5435	H C Peck Jr	Emmett R Book	Emmett R Book	Emmett R Book	Emmett R Book	Joe Tom Trunzler
Claiborne (Homer) p (17)	318 927-9601	(not reporting)					
Concordia (Vidalia) p (21)	318 336-7151	Fred Falkenheiner	Robbie Shirley	Clyde Webber	Cathy Darden	Don Glynn	Randy Maxwell
De Soto (Mansfield) p (25)	318 872-0738	Persley White Jr	. . . .	Shirley C Wheless	Betty A Woods	Dewayne Mitchell	Hugh Bennett Jr
East Carroll (Lake Providence) p (10)	318 559-2256	(not reporting)					
East Feliciana (Clinton) p (19)	504 683-8577	James F Hunt	Clarence Payne	Judith G Kelly	Judith G Kelly	. . . .	T R Maglone
Evangeline (Ville Platte) p (33)	318 363-5651	(not reporting)					
Franklin (Winnsboro) p (22)	318 435-9429	Ray Young	. . . .	Kaye Cupp	Colleen Hammons	. . . .	Eugene Parker
Grant (Colfax) p (18)	318 627-9907	(not reporting)					
Iberia (New Iberia) p (68)	318 365-8246	(not reporting)					
Iberville (Plaquemine) p (31)	504 687-5190	(not reporting)					
Jackson (Jonesboro) p (16)	318 259-2795	(not reporting)					
Jefferson (Gretna) p (448)	504 736-6400	(not reporting)					
Jefferson Davis (Jennings) p (31)	318 824-4792	(not reporting)					
La Salle (Jena) p (14)	318 992-2158	(not reporting)					
Lafayette (Lafayette) p (165)	318 233-6220	Walter Comeaux	John Warner Smith	Lloyd Rochon	James Dorton	Rudolph Bourg	Donald Breaux
Lafourche (Thibodaux) p (86)	504 446-8427	Steven D Wilson	Marie Fertitta	Sheila Boudreaux	. . . .	Jackie W Jackson	Craig Webre
Lincoln (Ruston) p (42)	318 251-5150	H F Delony	Richarf I Durrett	Sue Sanderson	Jerry Smith	Annie Hamlin	Wayne Houck
Livingston (Livingston) p (71)	504 686-2266	Pat Scivicque	. . . .	Robbie C Hill	Melissa St Pierre	. . . .	Odom Graves
Madison (Tallulah) p (12)	318 574-3451	(not reporting)					
Morehouse (Bastrop) p (32)	318 281-3343	(not reporting)					
Natchitoches (Natchitoches) p (37)	318 352-2714	(not reporting)					
New Orleans (New Orleans) c (497)	504 565-6000	Dorothy Taylor	Leonard D Simmons	Emma Williams	Etta R Morris	J Michael Doyle	Joseph Orticke
Ouachita (Monroe) p (142)	318 323-5188	Abe E Pierce	Cecil Willis	Cecil Willis	Cecil Willis	LaQuita S Danna	Laymon Godwin
Plaquemines (Pointe a la Hache) p (26)	504 682-0081	(not reporting)					
Pointe Coupee (New Roads) p (23)	504 638-9596	Clement Guidroz	Joseph H Jarreau	Gerrie Patin	. . . .	. . . .	Preston Chustz
Rapides (Alexandria) p (132)	318 473-6660	(not reporting)					
Red River (Coushatta) p (9)	318 932-5719	(not reporting)					
Richland (Rayville) p (21)	318 728-2061	(not reporting)					
Sabine (Many) p (23)	318 256-5637	(not reporting)					
St. Bernard (Chalmette) p (67)	504 278-4200	Lynn Dean	John Carney	Myra Kattengell	Lewis Heston	Eleanor LeFebvre	Jack Stephens
St. Charles (Hahnville) p (42)	504 783-5000	(not reporting)					
St. Helena (Greensburg) p (10)	504 222-4549	(not reporting)					
St. James (Convent) p (21)	504 562-2387	D J Hymel	J A Lubrano	G J Schexnayder	A J Laiche	S J Oubre	. . . .
St. John the Baptist (Laplace) p (40)	504 652-9569	(not reporting)					
St. Landry (Opelousas) p (80)	318 948-3688	(not reporting)					
St. Martin (St. Martinville) p (44)	318 394-3711	(not reporting)					
St. Mary (Franklin) p (58)	318 828-4100	Oray P Rogers	Connie M Fournet	Kim Pusateri	Sue Carter	Tammy C Migues	. . . .
St. Tammany (Covington) p (145)	504 898-2360	. . . .	Allan Cartier	Diane Hueschen	Lynn W Cox	Lynn W Cox	. . . .
Tangipahoa (Amite) p (86)	504 748-3211	(not reporting)					
Tensas (St. Joseph) p (7)	318 766-3542	Hoyt Arnold	Ronnie W Hopkins	Ronnie W Hopkins	Ronnie W Hopkins	. . . .	Jeff Britt
Terrebonne (Houma) c (..)	504 873-6401	Barry Bonvillain	Doug Maier	Paul A Labat	Jamie Elfert	Lawrence Robinson	Jerry Carpenter
Union (Farmerville) p (21)	318 368-8687	Don Acree	Patty Allen	. . . .	. . . .	. . . .	. . . .

Directory 1/10   **OFFICIALS IN U.S. COUNTIES**
continued

County, county seat, 1990 population figures (000 omitted)	County telephone number	Board chairman	Appointed administrator	Clerk to the governing board	Chief financial officer	Personnel director	Chief law enforcement official
LOUISIANA (64) continued							
Vermilion (Abbeville) p (50)	318 898-4300	(not reporting)					
Vernon (Leesville) p (62)	318 239-2444	(not reporting)					
Washington (Franklinton) p (43) .	504 839-4582	(not reporting)					
Webster (Minden) p (42)	318 377-2144	(not reporting)					
West Baton Rouge (Port Allen) p (19)	504 383-4755	Ted Blanchard	Ted Denstel	Ted Denstel	Curtis Dupuy	....	....
West Carroll (Oak Grove) p (12) .	318 428-3390	Dianne Sistrunk	Martha Stephens	....	Martha Stephens	Jackie McBride	Gary Bennett
West Feliciana (St. Francisville) p (13)	504 635-3794	(not reporting)					
Winn (Winnfield) p (16)	318 628-5824	Loyd E Vines	Thelma Jarnagin	Thelma Jarnagin	Thelma Jarnagin	....	James E Jordan
MAINE (16)							
Androscoggin (Auburn) (105) ...	207 784-8390	Carol S Boyce	....	Patricia Fournier	Richard Fournier	Patricia Fournier	Ronald B Gagnon
Aroostook (Caribou) (87)	207 493-3318	Norman L Fournier	Roland D Martin	Roland D Martin	James McBreairty	....	Edgar M Wheeler
Cumberland (Portland) (243) ...	207 871-8380	(not reporting)					
Franklin (Farmington) (29)	207 778-6614	Gary T McGrane	Marie A Andrews	Marie A Andrews	William Woodside	Marie A Andrews	Donald P Richards
Hancock (Ellsworth) (47)	207 667-9542	Walter L Bunker	....	Eugenia L Labelle	Robert F Lakin	....	William F Clark
Kennebec (Augusta) (116)	207 622-0971	(not reporting)					
Knox (Rockland) (36)	207 594-0420	Gene M Kenniston	....	Virginia Lindsey	Pauline S Curtis	....	Daniel G Davey
Lincoln (Wiscasset) (30)	207 882-6311	M Robert Barter	....	Ann M Merry	Rupert Neily Sr	....	William C Carter
Oxford (South Paris) (53)	207 743-6359	(not reporting)					
Penobscot (Bangor) (147)	207 942-8535	Peter K Baldacci	....	Donna L Keim	....	....	Edward J Reynolds
Piscataquis (Dover-Foxcroft) (19)	207 564-2161	Eben G Dewitt	....	Carolyn K Doore	Philip E Warren	....	John J Goggin
Sagadahoc (Bath) (34)	207 443-8200	John D Chapman	....	Barry M Sturgeon	Gloria P Barnes	....	Mark A Westrum
Somerset (Skowhegan) (50)	207 474-9861	Charles Carpenter	Cynthia Pomerleau	Cynthia Pomerleau	Ruth Poland	....	Spencer Havey
Waldo (Belfast) (33)	207 338-3282	(not reporting)					
Washington (Machias) (35)	207 255-3127	(not reporting)					
York (Alfred) (165)	207 324-1571	(not reporting)					
MARYLAND (24)							
Allegany (Cumberland) (75)	301 777-5911	John W Stotler	Daniel McMullen	Carol A Gaffney	Jerry L Frantz	....	Gary W Simpson
Anne Arundel (Annapolis) (427) .	410 222-7000	David G Boschert	Dennis Parkinson	Judith C Holmes	Steven E Welkos	Donald Tynes Sr	Robert P Russell
Baltimore (Baltimore) i (736) ...	410 396-9939	Kurt Schmoke	Lynnette Young	Leonard F Wright	William R Brown	Jesse E Hoskins	Edward Woods
Baltimore (Towson) (692)	410 887-3139	....	Merreen E Kelly	....	James Gibson	Richard Holloway	Cornelius Behan
Calvert (Prince Frederick) (51) ..	301 535-1600	Hagner R Mister	Richard L Holler	Mary S Watson	James J Allman	G Davis Bourdon	Lawrence Stinnett
Caroline (Denton) (27)	301 479-0660	Margaret R Myers	Edwin G Richards	K Leigh Sands	Dorsey L Wooters	Edwin G Richards	Louis C Andrew
Carroll (Westminster) (123)	410 848-4500	Donald I Dell	Robert A Bair	Shawn D Reese	Eugene C Curfman	Jimmie L Saylor	John H Brown
Cecil (Elkton) (71)	410 996-5200	Edwin Cole	Edward Sealover	Christine Main	Brian Shivery	Toni Shivery	Rodney Kennedy
Charles (La Plata) (101)	301 645-0500	Thomas Middleton	Thomas Fritz	Shirley Gore	Richard Winkler	Susan Hathaway	James Gartland
Dorchester (Cambridge) (30)	410 228-1700	(not reporting)					
Frederick (Frederick) (150)	301 694-1100	(not reporting)					
Garrett (Oakland) (28)	301 334-8970	Elwood L Groves	....	Robert J Fousek	....	....	Martin Van Evans
Harford (Bel Air) (182)	301 838-6000	Jeffrey D Wilson	Larry W Klimovitz	Doris Poulsen	James M Jewell	Randall J Schultz	Robert E Comes
Howard (Ellicott City) (187)	410 313-2033	Charles I Ecker	Raquel Sanudo	Beverly Wilhide	Raymond Servary	Joanne Nelson	James Robey
Kent (Chestertown) (18)	410 778-7435	William S Sutton	Charles Mac Leod	Janice F Fletcher	....	....	William T Bright
Montgomery (Rockville) (757) ..	301 217-1000	Marilyn Praisner	William Hussmann	....	Timothy Firestine	William P Garrett	Clarence Edwards
Prince Georges (Upper Marlboro) (729)	301 952-3000	P Glendening	Major Riddick	Joyce T Sweeney	Eric M Tucker	Michael J Knapp	David B Mitchell
Queen Annes (Centreville) (34) .	410 758-0322	William V Riggs	Robert O Sallitt	Lynda H Palmatary	Joseph Zimmerman	Robert D Sallitt	Charles Crossley
Somerset (Princess Anne) (23) ..	410 651-0320	Phillip L Gerald	Charles E Massey	Charles E Massey	Charles L Muir	....	Robert N Jones
St. Marys (Leonardtown) (76) ...	301 475-5621	Carl M Loffler	Edward V Cox	....	Charles H Wade	George A Foster	Wayne L Pettit
Talbot (Easton) (31)	410 822-2401	Clinton S Bradley	Blenda Armistead	Patricia Rasinski	Blenda Armistead	Blenda Armistead	John J Ellerbusch
Washington (Hagerstown) (121) .	301 791-3090	Richard Roulette	Barry A Teach	Joni L Bittner	James A Young	Alan J Davis	Charles Mades
Wicomico (Salisbury) (74)	301 548-4800	Henry Parker	Matthew Creamer	....	Joseph Schiller	Karl J Petersen	R Hunter Nelms
Worcester (Now Hill) (35)	410 632-1194	....	John A Yankus	....	Gerald T Mason	Matthew Azzolini	G D McAllister
MASSACHUSETTS (14)							
Barnstable (Barnstable) (187) ...	508 362-2511	(not reporting)					
Berkshire (Pittsfield) (139)	413 448-8424	(not reporting)					
Boston-Suffolk (Boston) c (574) .	617 725-4000	(not reporting)					
Bristol (Taunton) (506)	617 824-9681	Maria F Lopes	....	Marc J Santos	P Harrington	....	David R Nelson
Dukes (Edgartown) (12)	617 627-5535	(not reporting)					
Essex (Salem) (670)	617 741-0201	Marguerite P Kane	Janis Simard	James D Leary	K O' Leary	....	Charles Reardon
Franklin (Greenfield) (70)	413 774-3167	Margaret Striebel	Jay Dipucchio	Leah Kowalski	Margaret Sullivan	....	Red Mac Donald
Hampden (Springfield) (456)	413 781-8100	(not reporting)					
Hampshire (Northampton) (147) .	413 584-0557	(not reporting)					
Middlesex (East Cambridge) (1398)	617 494-4000	(not reporting)					
Nantucket (Nantucket) c (6)	617 228-0790	Wayne F Holmes	Suzanne K Kennedy	Patricia Church	Peter Lamb	Libby Girson	Henry Clute
Norfolk (Dedham) (616)	617 461-6100	(not reporting)					
Plymouth (Plymouth) (435)	508 830-9100	Patricia A Lawton	....	Francis R Powers	John F McLellan	....	Peter Y Flynn
Worcester (Worcester) (710)	508 798-7700	John R Sharry	James P Purcell	Loring Lamoureux	Michael Donoghue	....	John M Flynn
MICHIGAN (83)							
Alcona (Harrisville) (10)	517 724-6807	John F Gray	....	Gayle E Simmons	John F Gray	John F Gray	Douglas Ellinger
Alger (Munising) (9)	906 387-2076	(not reporting)					
Allegan (Allegan) (91)	616 673-8471	David Babbitt	Joanne Jones	Joyce Watts	P Birkholtz	Christine Jurkas	David Haverdink
Alpena (Alpena) (31)	517 356-0930	Gerald F Newhouse	Gary A Roussin	B Smolinski	Howard Maze	R Donakowski	Thomas Male
Antrim (Bellaire) (18)	616 533-8607	Gale Murphy	....	....	....	....	Dale Roggenbeck
Arenac (Standish) (15)	501 673-3181	(not reporting)					
Baraga (L'Anse) (8)	906 524-6183	Roland Sweeney	....	Nelda J Robillard	....	....	Bob Teddy
Barry (Hastings) (50)	616 948-4891	Orvin H Moore	Judith A Peterson	Nancy L Boersma	....	....	David O Wood
Bay (Bay City) (112)	517 892-5536	Edward L Rivet	Thomas L Hickner	Barbara Albertson	Michael Regulski	....	Gerald P Vanalst
Benzie (Beulah) (12)	616 882-9671	(not reporting)					
Berrien (St. Joseph) (161)	616 983-7111	R J Burkholz	J M Henry	M L Stine	....	....	R Kimmerly
Branch (Coldwater) (42)	517 279-8411	John T Swanson	John C Dean	Judy Elliott	Sandra Thatcher	....	Ted Gordon
Calhoun (Marshall) (136)	616 781-0910	Michael Nofs	Peter Herlofsky	Anne Norlander	Peter Herlofsky	Roger Likkel	James Roberts
Cass (Cassopolis) (49)	616 445-8621	R James Guse	Terry L Proctor	Ann Simmons	Sharon K Hansell	....	Joseph Underwood
Charlevoix (Charlevoix) (21)	616 547-7200	Donald R Smith	....	Jane E Brannon	Jane E Brannon	....	George T Lasater
Cheboygan (Cheboygan) (21) ...	616 627-8808	....	....	Joanne Spray	Clayton J Cannis	Brenda Pollex	John A Grabowski
Chippewa (Sault Ste. Marie) (35)	906 635-6300	(not reporting)					
Clare (Harrison) (25)	517 539-7131	Ed Howland	....	Donna M Carr	....	....	Howard Haskin
Clinton (St. Johns) (58)	517 224-5100	Robert Ditmer	David Benda	Jane Swanchara	David Benda	Jeanette Smith	Donald Hengesh

Directory 1/10 OFFICIALS IN U.S. COUNTIES continued

County, county seat, 1990 population figures (000 omitted)	County telephone number	Board chairman	Appointed administrator	Clerk to the governing board	Chief financial officer	Personnel director	Chief law enforcement official
MICHIGAN (83) continued							
Crawford (Grayling) (12)	517 348-2841	Dennis Long	....	Elizabeth Wieland	....	....	David G Lovely
Delta (Escanaba) (38)	906 786-2237	Douglas R Bovin	....	Wallace C Thorsen	Thomas J Boyne	Nora Viau	Gary R Carlson
Dickinson (Iron Mountain) (27)	906 774-2573	Vertin Rock	William Marchetti	Dolly Cook	Joanne Johnson	....	Don Charlevoix
Eaton (Charlotte) (93)	517 543-7500	(not reporting)					
Emmet (Petoskey) (25)	616 347-2801	James E Tamlyn	Lyn E Johnson	Irene D Granger	Martin J Krupa	Lyn E Johnson	Jeffrey P Bodzick
Genesee (Flint) (430)	313 257-3020	Debbie Cherry	....	Dan Harrell	Leonard Smorch	Steve Stratton	Joe Wilson
Gladwin (Gladwin) (22)	517 426-4821	(not reporting)					
Gogebic (Bessemer) (18)	906 667-0411	V Melvin Jacobson	Juliane Giackino	Richard Brown	Sharon Hallberg	Juliane Giackino	Donald B Pezzetti
Grand Traverse (Traverse City) (64)	616 922-4700	Antony Buday	K Ross Childs	Virginia Watson	Glenn Peroceschi	Marilyn Brown	Harold Barr
Gratiot (Ithaca) (39)	517 875-3343	Floyd Demott	....	Pauline Merchant	Mary L Sullivan	....	Michael T Vetter
Hillsdale (Hillsdale) (43)	517 437-3932	Olin Hinkle	....	Thomas C Mohr	Gary A Leininger	....	Gerald M Hicks
Houghton (Houghton) (35)	906 482-8307	Jackie A Niemi	Glenn H Pyhtila	Nancy A Fenili	....	....	James Ruotsala
Huron (Bad Axe) (35)	517 269-8242	(not reporting)					
Ingham (Lansing) (282)	517 887-4327	Jean McDonald	Gerald Ambrose	Lingg Brewer	Mary Barnes	Harold Hailey	G Wriggelsworth
Ionia (Ionia) (57)	616 527-5300	(not reporting)					
Iosco (Tawas City) (30)	517 362-4212	Clyde L Soucie	....	Michael A Welsch	....	....	Craig Herriman
Iron (Crystal Falls) (13)	906 875-3301	Thomas A Korpi	Daniel A Kaepp	Klaryce Bilski	Arthur G Hibbard	Daniel A Kaepp	Robert Remondini
Isabella (Mount Pleasant) (55)	517 772-0911	Sandy Caul	Diane Block	Betty Prout	Steve Pickens	....	Barry DeLau
Jackson (Jackson) (150)	517 788-4333	James Shotwell	Randy Terronez	Mickey Mortimer	Janet Rochefort	Phyllis Way	Henry Zavislak
Kalamazoo (Kalamazoo) (223)	616 384-8111	Richard Kleiman	Wesley K Freeland	James O Youngs	William L Dundon	Richard L Kinas	Thomas N Edmonds
Kalkaska (Kalkaska) (13)	616 258-3304	Melvin F Hill	....	Patricia Rodgers	Frank Wright	Frank Wright	Nelson J Cannon
Kent (Grand Rapids) (501)	616 774-3679	(not reporting)					
Keweenaw (Eagle River) (2)	906 337-2229	Nancy Pintar	....	Marilyn Winquist	....	....	Ronald Lahti
Lake (Baldwin) (9)	616 745-4641	M F Doug Deman	....	Lucinda K Dechow	....	....	Robert Hilts
Lapeer (Lapeer) (75)	313 667-0366	Richard Blonde	John Biscoe	Marlene Bruns	Craig Horton	....	Ron Kalanquin
Leelanau (Leland) (17)	616 256-9711	G N Henshaw	D C Beard	D Wunderlich	J Blackburn	D C Beard	C A Johnson
Lenawee (Adrian) (91)	517 263-8831	Charles Lockwood	William Bacon	Lou Ann Bluntschl	Harold Baily	....	Richard Germond
Livingston (Howell) (116)	517 546-3520	(not reporting)					
Luce (Newberry) (6)	906 293-5521	Elmer Hetrick	....	Kathy Mahar	Lois Fighter	....	Kevin Erickson
Mackinac (St. Ignace) (11)	906 643-7300	Dale P Webber	Mary K Tamlyn	Mary K Tamlyn	....	....	Lawrence Leveille
Macomb (Mount Clemens) (717)	313 469-5100	Mark A Steenbergh	....	Carmella Sabaugh	David M Diegel	William M Israel	William Hackel
Manistee (Manistee) (21)	616 723-3331	Carl Rutske	Thomas Kaminski	Dorlene Schudlich	Alan Verheek	Thomas Kaminski	Edward Haik
Marquette (Marquette) (71)	906 228-1501	Gerald Corkin	Dennis Aloia	David Roberts	Gary Yoder	Randell Girard	Gary Walker
Mason (Ludington) (26)	616 843-8202	(not reporting)					
Mecosta (Big Rapids) (37)	616 796-2505	John E Todd	Charles Randolph	Ruth Hess	....	....	Henry Wayer
Menominee (Menominee) (25)	906 863-9648	Len Therriault	Kevin Hamann	Barbara Morrison	Kevin Hamann	Kevin Hamann	Dennis Kenney
Midland (Midland) (76)	517 832-6780	(not reporting)					
Missaukee (Lake City) (12)	616 839-4967	Gary Birgy	....	Carolyn Flore	Carolyn Flore	Carolyn Flore	James Bosscher
Monroe (Monroe) (134)	313 243-7053	Raymond Noble	....	Geraldine Allen	Charles Curtis	Peggy Howard	Carl Van Wert
Montcalm (Stanton) (53)	517 831-5226	Mark Stevens	Nancy Hansing	Joyce Ehle	John Chapin	Nancy Hansing	Donald Godell
Montmorency (Atlanta) (9)	517 785-3358	(not reporting)					
Muskegon (Muskegon) (159)	616 724-6211	Kenneth Hulka	Frank Bednarek	Ruth Stevens	....	James Delaney	Robert Carter
Newaygo (White Cloud) (38)	616 689-7200	Larry M Hansen	Kurt W Humphrey	Morey L Butler	Amber A Snow	....	Roger G Altena
Oakland (Pontiac) (1084)	313 858-1000	Larry Crake	L B Patterson	Lynn D Allen	Robert Daddow	Vince Luzi	John Nichols
Oceana (Hart) (22)	616 873-4835	Loyd Vansickle	Paul E Inglis	Phyllis J Schlee	Paul E Inglis	Paul E Inglis	Fred S Korb
Ogemaw (West Branch) (19)	517 345-0215	(not reporting)					
Ontonagon (Ontonagon) (9)	906 884-4255	(not reporting)					
Osceola (Reed City) (20)	616 832-3261	(not reporting)					
Oscoda (Mio) (8)	517 826-3241	(not reporting)					
Otsego (Gaylord) (18)	517 732-6484	Roland Chavey	Lambert Chard	Evelyn Pratt	Erma Backenstose	....	Donald Anderson
Ottawa (Grand Haven) (188)	616 846-8295	(not reporting)					
Presque Isle (Rogers City) (14)	517 734-3288	Charles A Rhode	....	Robert J Urlaub	....	....	Terry Flewelling
Roscommon (Roscommon) (20)	517 275-5923	Richard Kobman	....	Robert W Smith	Joyce M Webber	....	Thomas McKindles
Saginaw (Saginaw) (212)	517 790-5200	James Gaertner	Fred Todd	Kaye Schultz	Michael Thompson	Larry Polk	Thomas McIntyre
Sanilac (Sandusky) (40)	313 648-2933	Helen Takacs	Richard F Lessner	Linda I Kozfkay	....	....	Virgil Strickler
Schoolcraft (Manistique) (8)	906 341-5532	Louis L Lauzon	....	Sigrid I Doyle	Sigrid I Doyle	Sigrid I Doyle	Gary L Maddox
Shiawassee (Corunna) (70)	517 743-2279	(not reporting)					
St. Clair (Port Huron) (146)	313 985-2001	Mary Mechtenberg	Donald Dodge	....	....	Terry Pettee	Daniel Lane
St. Joseph (Centreville) (59)	616 467-6361	Cameron Brown	J Patrick Yoder	Pattie Bender	Brad Whaley	....	Matthew Lori
Tuscola (Caro) (55)	517 673-5999	Norma Bates	Michael Hoagland	Margie White	....	Juliana Dillon	Thomas Kern
Van Buren (Paw Paw) (70)	616 657-5581	Daniel J Ruzick	Douglas S Cultra	Shirley K Jackson	Wayne D Nelson	....	Cal Rosema
Washtenaw (Ann Arbor) (283)	313 994-2400	Mary Egnor	....	Peggy Haines	Peter Ballios	Verna McDaniel	Ron Schibel
Wayne (Detroit) (2112)	313 224-5900	(not reporting)					
Wexford (Cadillac) (26)	616 779-9453	Larry Rogers	Larry Huebner	Donald Linn	Larry Huebner	Larry Huebner	Gary Finstrom
MINNESOTA (87)							
Aitkin (Aitkin) (12)	218 927-7276	Mary Haug	Peter Schutte	Pam Solsvig	Tom Palmer	Peter Schutte	Rick Passer
Anoka (Anoka) (244)	612 421-4760	Dan Erhart	Jay McLinden	....	Terry L Johnson	Ronald B Welde	Ken Wilkinson
Becker (Detroit Lakes) (28)	218 846-7301	Jack Murray	....	Kieth Brekken	Rita Thompson	Daniel Dougherty	Clarance Paurus
Beltrami (Bemidji) (34)	218 759-4156	Richard Florhaug	Gregory Lewis	Gregory Lewis	Christine Patten	Marilyn Nelson	Dwight Stewart
Benton (Foley) (30)	612 968-6254	Mike Moulzolf	....	William Scott	....	Roxanne Casper	Frank Wippier
Big Stone (Ortonville) (6)	612 839-2525	(not reporting)					
Blue Earth (Mankato) (54)	507 389-8100	(not reporting)					
Brown (New Ulm) (27)	507 359-7900	Richard Petersen	Jerome Bentz	Jerome Bentz	Marlin Helget	Leah Crabtree	Larry Pederson
Carlton (Carlton) (29)	218 384-4281	Patty Murto	....	....	Paul Gassert	Michael Stafford	Dave Seboe
Carver (Chaska) (48)	612 448-3435	Earl Gnan	Richard Stolz	....	Frederic Boethin	M Dailey Fischer	Allen Wallin
Cass (Walker) (22)	218 547-3300	Jim Demgen	T Dudgeon	S Anderson	Sharon Anderson	....	Dowson
Chippewa (Montevideo) (13)	612 269-7447	G Vanbinsbergen	Byron Zurn	Byron Zurn	Jon Clauson	....	Michael Dann
Chisago (Center City) (31)	612 257-1300	(not reporting)					
Clay (Moorhead) (50)	218 299-5002	Dewey Possehl	Vijay Sethi	Vijay Sethi	....	Terry Jacobson	Larry Costello
Clearwater (Bagley) (8)	218 694-6177	(not reporting)					
Cook (Grand Marais) (4)	218 387-2282	Chet Linoskog	....	Janet Iverson	Carol Gresczyk	Janet Iverson	John Lyght
Cottonwood (Windom) (13)	507 831-1905	Bruce Gross	....	Bill Mielke	Bill Mielke	....	Glen Ward
Crow Wing (Brainerd) (44)	218 828-2932	Mary Koep	....	Theresa Flannigan	Roy Luukkonen	Siegfried Stier	Dick Ross
Dakota (Hastings) (275)	612 437-3191	Steven G Loeding	Brandt Richardson	Joan Kendall	Richard Neumann	Will Volk	Rodney Boyd
Dodge (Mantorville) (16)	507 635-2321	(not reporting)					
Douglas (Alexandria) (29)	612 762-2381	Roland Kronberg	....	Harvey Tewes	A C Olsen	K LeBrasseur	Wm Ingebrigtsen
Faribault (Blue Earth) (17)	507 526-6225	Loren Lein	....	Nan Crary	John Thompson	Nan Crary	Scott Campbell
Fillmore (Preston) (21)	507 765-4701	Robert Thompson	....	Richard Stensgard	Philip Burkholder	Karen Brown	James Connolly
Freeborn (Albert Lea) (33)	507 377-5116	Arnold Biedermann	Eugene Smith	Eugene Smith	Harold Olson	Eugene Smith	Donald Nolander
Goodhue (Red Wing) (41)	612 385-3001	Lowell Peterson	Stephen Bloom	Stephen Bloom	Jeff Cole	Stephen Bloom	Forest Wipperling
Grant (Elbow Lake) (6)	218 685-4520	Vernell Wagner	....	Patricia Shearer	Pat Soberg	Patricia Shearer	Greg Schelin

Directory 1/10 **OFFICIALS IN U.S. COUNTIES**
continued

County, county seat, 1990 population figures (000 omitted)	County telephone number	Board chairman	Appointed administrator	Clerk to the governing board	Chief financial officer	Personnel director	Chief law enforcement official
MINNESOTA (87) continued							
Hennepin (Minneapolis) (1032) ..	612 348-3000	Mark Andrew	James M Bourey	Kay Mitchell	Richard Schultz	Charles Sprafka	Donald Omodt
Houston (Caledonia) (18)	507 724-5803	Nels Gulbranson	. . . .	A Peter Johnson	A Peter Johnson	. . . .	Dennis Swedberg
Hubbard (Park Rapids) (15)	218 732-3196	(not reporting)					
Isanti (Cambridge) (26)	612 689-3859	Frank Weisbrod	Robyn Sykes	Robyn Sykes	Lyle Myren	Robyn Sykes	Larry Southerland
Itasca (Grand Rapids) (41)	218 327-2847	(not reporting)					
Jackson (Jackson) (12)	507 847-2763	Edward G Yonker	. . . .	Luther F Glaser	Clayton E Olson	. . . .	Peter Eggimann
Kanabec (Mora) (13)	612 679-1030	(not reporting)					
Kandiyohi (Willmar) (39)	612 231-6215	H A Christiansen	Wayne Thompson	Sam Modderman	Sam Modderman	Wayne Thompson	Larry Kleinhuizen
Kittson (Hallock) (6)	218 843-2655	Joseph Bouvette	. . . .	Marilyn Gustafson	Marilyn Gustafson	. . . .	Raymond Hunt
Koochiching (International Falls) (16)	218 283-6252	Charles Lepper	. . . .	Darlene Olsen	. . . .	. . . .	Bill Elliott
Lac Qui Parle (Madison) (9)	612 598-7444	Arvid Gollnick	. . . .	Stan Bjorgan	Stan Bjorgan	Stan Bjorgan	Graylen Carlson
Lake (Two Harbors) (10)	218 834-8300	(not reporting)					
Lake Of the Woods (Baudette) (4)	218 634-2836	Robert Sutherland	. . . .	Ellen Larson	Ellen Larson	Ellen Larson	Robert Paulseth
Le Sueur (Le Center) (23)	612 357-2251	Robert Culhane	. . . .	. . . .	Terry Overn	. . . .	Pat Smith Jr
Lincoln (Ivanhoe) (7)	507 694-1529	(not reporting)					
Lyon (Marshall) (25)	507 537-6728	Bill Cole	. . . .	C Sheffield	. . . .	C Sheffield	Donald Stokke
Mahnomen (Mahnomen) (5)	218 935-5669	(not reporting)					
Marshall (Warren) (11)	218 745-4851	(not reporting)					
Martin (Fairmont) (23)	507 235-3261	(not reporting)					
Mc Leod (Glencoe) (32)	612 864-5551	(not reporting)					
Meeker (Litchfield) (21)	612 693-6329	Dale Smolnisky	Paul Virnig	D Groskreutz	D Groskreutz	Paul Virnig	Mike Hirman
Mille Lacs (Milaca) (19)	612 983-2561	(not reporting)					
Morrison (Little Falls) (30)	612 632-2941	Don Meyer	. . . .	Russ Nygren	S Messerscmidt	Paul Froncak	Paul Tschida
Mower (Austin) (37)	507 437-9535	Donald Johnson	. . . .	Craig Oscarson	. . . .	. . . .	Wayne Goodnature
Murray (Slayton) (10)	507 836-6163	(not reporting)					
Nicollet (St. Peter) (28)	507 931-6800	William Schimmel	Robert Podhradsky	Robert Podhradsky	Robert Bruns	Robert Podhradsky	Richard Witty
Nobles (Worthington) (20)	507 372-8231	Marv Baumgaard	Ken Roberts	Ken Roberts	Ken Roberts	Alan Peterson	Dale Peters
Norman (Ada) (8)	218 784-2101	Herb Mauritson	. . . .	Jack A Deitz	. . . .	. . . .	Larry Miller
Olmsted (Rochester) (106)	507 285-8115	(not reporting)					
Otter Tail (Fergus Falls) (51)	218 739-2271	(not reporting)					
Pennington (Thief River Falls) (13)	218 681-4011	Oliver Swanson	Kenneth Olson	Kenneth Olson	Kenneth Olson	. . . .	Gerald Moe
Pine (Pine City) (21)	612 629-6781	Everetet Koecher	. . . .	L Perreault	L Perreault	. . . .	Donald Faulkner
Pipestone (Pipestone) (10)	507 825-4494	Leroy Stensgaard	. . . .	Godon Baden	Steven Weets	Judith Oldemeyer	Ronald Smidt
Polk (Crookston) (32)	218 281-5408	Don Bakken	John Schmalenberg	John Schmalenberg	. . . .	. . . .	Douglas Qualley
Pope (Glenwood) (11)	612 634-5301	(not reporting)					
Ramsey (St. Paul) (486)	612 298-4145	Hal Norgard	Terry Schutten	Bonnie Jackelen	James Van Houdt	Richard Brainerd	Charles Zacharias
Red Lake (Red Lake Falls) (5) ...	218 253-4281	(not reporting)					
Redwood (Redwood Falls) (17) .	507 637-3207	Joan Miska	Cheryl M Hanson	Cheryl M Hanson	Larry L Bunting	Cheryl M Hanson	Jerry Luttman
Renville (Olivia) (18)	612 523-2071	Raymond Knudson	. . . .	Jim Tersteeg	Jim Tersteeg	Jim Tersteeg	Jerry Agre
Rice (Faribault) (49)	507 332-6100	Gerald Pineur	Steve O' Malley	Sandi Roush	Fran Windschitl	Thomas Barnett	Dave Schweisthal
Rock (Luverne) (10)	507 283-9165	(not reporting)					
Roseau (Roseau) (15)	218 463-2541	(not reporting)					
Scott (Shakopee) (58)	612 496-8100	Dick Underferth	Clifford McCann	Clifford McCann	Thomas E Muelken	Thomas J Longmire	William J Nevin
Sherburne (Elk River) (42)	612 241-2700	Leslie Schumacher	. . . .	David Loch	. . . .	. . . .	Richard Witschen
Sibley (Gaylord) (14)	612 237-2369	John Bach	. . . .	Gene Solmonson	Waldo Reckdahl	Roseann Nagel	Roger Graham
St. Louis (Duluth) (198)	218 726-2000	Marilyn Krueger	. . . .	Karen Erickson	Russell Peterson	Anthony Bruno	Gary Waller
Stearns (St. Cloud) (119)	612 656-3600	Leigh Lenzmeier	George Rindelaub	Henry Kohorst	Thomas Winter	Irene Koski	James Kostreba
Steele (Owatonna) (31)	507 451-8040	(not reporting)					
Stevens (Morris) (11)	612 589-7417	Gerald Loher	Gene Wiegand	Gene Wiegand	Richard Bluth	Gene Wiegand	Larry Sayre
Swift (Benson) (11)	612 843-4069	Orville Rudningen	. . . .	Byron L Giese	Ron Vadnais	. . . .	Ken Hanson
Todd (Long Prairie) (23)	612 732-4469	L Greenwaldt	. . . .	J Rosenow	K Gresser	J Rosenow	D Asmus
Traverse (Wheaton) (4)	612 563-4242	(not reporting)					
Wabasha (Wabasha) (20)	612 565-2648	(not reporting)					
Wadena (Wadena) (13)	218 631-2425	Lyle Freer	. . . .	Robert Fort	. . . .	. . . .	H Michael Carr
Waseca (Waseca) (18)	507 835-0630	George V Doyle	Bruce M Boyce	Joan M Manthe	Roderick Joyce	Bruce M Boyce	Edward F Kubat
Washington (Stillwater) (146) ...	612 439-3220	(not reporting)					
Watonwan (St. James) (12)	507 375-3341	Milo Holland	. . . .	Donald Kuhlman	Donald Kuhlman	Donald Kuhlman	Jack Keech
Wilkin (Breckenridge) (8)	218 643-4981	Robert Perry	. . . .	C Ellingson	C Ellingson	C Ellingson	Thomas Matejka
Winona (Winona) (48)	507 457-6350	Lester Ladewig	P Blaisdell	. . . .	Cherie Mac Lennan	Colleen Schultz	Richard Johnson
Wright (Buffalo) (69)	612 682-7377	Pat Sawatzke	Richard Norman	Richard Norman	Darla Groshens	Richard Norman	Donald Hozempa
Yellow Medicine (Granite Falls) (12)	612 564-3132	(not reporting)					
MISSISSIPPI (82)							
Adams (Natchez) (35)	601 446-6684	(not reporting)					
Alcorn (Corinth) (32)	601 286-6265	(not reporting)					
Amite (Liberty) (13)	601 657-8022	(not reporting)					
Attala (Kosciusko) (18)	601 289-2921	(not reporting)					
Benton (Ashland) (8)	601 224-6611	(not reporting)					
Bolivar (Cleveland) (42)	601 843-9413	(not reporting)					
Calhoun (Pittsboro) (15)	601 983-3117	(not reporting)					
Carroll (Carrollton) (9)	601 237-9274	(not reporting)					
Chickasaw (Houston) (18)	601 456-2513	K Funderburk	David Thomas	David Thomas	David Thomas	David Thomas	James T Simmons
Choctaw (Ackerman) (9)	601 285-6329	(not reporting)					
Claiborne (Port Gibson) (11)	601 437-4992	(not reporting)					
Clarke (Quitman) (17) ...	601 776-2126	(not reporting)					
Clay (West Point) (21)	601 494-3124	(not reporting)					
Coahoma (Clarksdale) (32)	601 624-3000	(not reporting)					
Copiah (Hazlehurst) (28)	601 894-3011	(not reporting)					
Covington (Collins) (17)	601 765-4242	(not reporting)					
De Soto (Hernando) (68)	601 429-1315	James D Pearson	Kenneth Murphree	William E Davis	William E Davis	Ginger K Allison	James A Riley
Forrest (Hattiesburg) (68)	601 545-6000	(not reporting)					
Franklin (Meadville) (8)	601 384-2330	(not reporting)					
George (Lucedale) (17)	601 947-7506	Larry A Havard	. . . .	Jerry Ray Harvey	. . . .	. . . .	Eugene Howell
Greene (Leakesville) (10)	601 394-2377	(not reporting)					
Grenada (Grenada) (22)	601 226-1821	(not reporting)					
Hancock (Bay St. Louis) (32) ...	601 467-5404	(not reporting)					
Harrison (Gulfport) (165)	601 865-4194	(not reporting)					
Hinds (Jackson) (254)	601 968-6501	George S Smith	Roy DeBerry	Alice James	Joseph P Griffin	James L Terry	Malcolm McMillin
Holmes (Lexington) (22)	601 834-2508	William D Green	. . . .	Jamie T Moore	. . . .	. . . .	Willie March
Humphreys (Belzoni) (12)	601 247-1740	(not reporting)					
Issaquena (Mayersville) (2)	601 873-2761	W E Fleeman Jr	. . . .	Erline Fortner	. . . .	. . . .	Arthur Lawler

Directory 1/10 continued   OFFICIALS IN U.S. COUNTIES

County, county seat, 1990 population figures (000 omitted)	County telephone number	Board chairman	Appointed administrator	Clerk to the governing board	Chief financial officer	Personnel director	Chief law enforcement official
MISSISSIPPI (82) continued							
Itawamba (Fulton) (20)	601 862-3421	Danny Holley	Gary Franks	Jim Witt	Jim Witt	Gary Franks	Leon Hayes
Jackson (Pascagoula) (115)	601 769-3089	(not reporting)					
Jasper (Bay Springs) (17)	601 764-3368	(not reporting)					
Jefferson (Fayette) (9)	601 786-3021	(not reporting)					
Jefferson Davis (Prentiss) (14)	601 792-4204	J E O'Connell					
Jones (Laurel) (62)	601 428-0527	Jerome Wyatt	Charles Miller	Jack D Berry	Jack D Berry	Faye Bedwell	Hal Magee
Kemper (De Kalb) (10)	601 743-2460	Mike Luke	Bobbie M Harbour	Roy Boutwell	. . . .	. . . .	Maurice Hooks
Lafayette (Oxford) (32)	601 234-2131	(not reporting)		Shelby Kilpatrick	. . . .	. . . .	Joe Sciples
Lamar (Purvis) (30)	601 794-8504	(not reporting)					
Lauderdale (Meridian) (76)	601 482-9701	(not reporting)					
Lawrence (Monticello) (12)	601 587-7351	(not reporting)					
Leake (Carthage) (18)	601 267-8002	(not reporting)					
Lee (Tupelo) (66)	601 841-9110	(not reporting)					
Leflore (Greenwood) (37)	601 453-1041	(not reporting)					
Lincoln (Brookhaven) (30)	601 833-4911	(not reporting)					
Lowndes (Columbus) (59)	601 327-7880	(not reporting)					
Madison (Canton) (54)	601 859-1177	(not reporting)					
Marion (Columbia) (26)	601 736-2691	(not reporting)					
Marshall (Holly Springs) (30)	601 252-4431	(not reporting)					
Monroe (Aberdeen) (37)	601 369-8143	(not reporting)					
Montgomery (Winona) (12)	601 283-2333	(not reporting)					
Neshoba (Philadelphia) (25)	601 656-3581	(not reporting)					
Newton (Decatur) (20)	601 683-6181	Walter Gardner	. . . .	Janice Nelson	. . . .	. . . .	James Hanna
Noxubee (Macon) (13)	601 726-4243	(not reporting)					
Oktibbeha (Starkville) (38)	601 323-5834	(not reporting)					
Panola (Batesville) (30)	601 563-3171	(not reporting)					
Pearl River (Poplarville) (39)	601 795-4539	(not reporting)					
Perry (New Augusta) (11)	601 964-8398	(not reporting)					
Pike (Magnolia) (37)	601 783-5289	Theodore Bullock	Chuck E Lambert	Joel R Barr	. . . .		C V Glennis
Pontotoc (Pontotoc) (22)	601 489-3451	(not reporting)					
Prentiss (Booneville) (23)	601 728-8151	(not reporting)					
Quitman (Marks) (10)	601 326-2661	(not reporting)					
Rankin (Rankin) (87)	601 825-2217	(not reporting)					
Scott (Forest) (24)	601 469-1922	(not reporting)					
Sharkey (Rolling Fork) (7)	601 873-2755	Joe F Carson					
Simpson (Mendenhall) (24)	601 847-1418	(not reporting)	. . . .	Sandra Oxner	. . . .	Sandra Oxner	Joe W Ford
Smith (Raleigh) (15)	601 782-4463	Benjie K Ford	. . . .	C Gary Crumpton	C Gary Crumpton	Dennis R Robinson	Keith Bounds
Stone (Wiggins) (11)	601 928-5266	(not reporting)					
Sunflower (Indianola) (33)	601 887-4703	(not reporting)					
Tallahatchie (Charleston) (15)	601 647-5551	(not reporting)					
Tate (Senatobia) (21)	601 562-5661	(not reporting)					
Tippah (Ripley) (20)	601 837-7374	(not reporting)					
Tishomingo (Iuka) (18)	601 423-6021	Ricky Cummings	. . . .	Richard H Ables	. . . .	. . . .	Johnny S Nunley
Tunica (Tunica) (8)	601 363-1465	(not reporting)					
Union (New Albany) (22)	601 534-5284	(not reporting)					
Walthall (Tylertown) (14)	601 876-3553	(not reporting)					
Warren (Vicksburg) (48)	601 636-4415	(not reporting)					
Washington (Greenville) (68)	601 332-1595	(not reporting)					
Wayne (Waynesboro) (20)	601 735-6223	Chester Andrews	. . . .	H H Hardee	Sylvia Chancellor	. . . .	Marvin Farrior
Webster (Walthall) (10)	601 258-4131	Jack Knight	. . . .	Lady H Doolittle	. . . .	. . . .	John Bowen
Wilkinson (Woodville) (10)	601 888-4381	(not reporting)					
Winston (Louisville) (19)	601 773-3319	(not reporting)					
Yalobusha (Water Valley) (12)	601 473-2091	Butch Surrette	. . . .	Bob Chandler	. . . .	Bob Chandler	Lloyd Defer
Yazoo (Yazoo City) (26)	601 746-2661	(not reporting)					
MISSOURI (115)							
Adair (Kirksville) (25)	816 665-2283	Bill Novinger	. . . .	Joan Elmore	Clara Wheeler	. . . .	Randy Forquer
Andrew (Savannah) (15)	816 324-3624	Wilton H Adkins	. . . .	Rose Latham	. . . .	. . . .	Gary Howard
Atchison (Rockport) (7)	816 744-6214	Marlin L Logan	. . . .	Dale E Faulkner	Dale E Faulkner	. . . .	Dennis Martin
Audrain (Mexico) (24)	314 581-8211	(not reporting)					
Barry (Cassville) (28)	417 847-2561	(not reporting)					
Barton (Lamar) (11)	417 682-3529	Gary Frieden	. . . .	Bonda Rawlings	Frances Cato	. . . .	William Griffitt
Bates (Butler) (15)	816 679-3371	(not reporting)					
Benton (Warsaw) (14)	816 438-7326	Duane Brodersen	. . . .	. . . .	. . . .	. . . .	Robert Breshears
Bollinger (Marble Hill) (11)	314 238-2126	(not reporting)					
Boone (Columbia) (112)	313 874-7515	Don Stamper	. . . .	Wendy Noven	June Pitchford	. . . .	Ted Boehm
Buchanan (St. Joseph) (83)	816 271-1412	(not reporting)					
Butler (Poplar Bluff) (39)	314 686-8050	(not reporting)					
Caldwell (Kingston) (8)	816 586-2571	Dale Hartley	. . . .	Shari Lee	. . . .	. . . .	Wayne Adkison
Callaway (Fulton) (33)	314 642-0730	Rodney Garnett	. . . .	Linda Love	Rosemary Gannaway	. . . .	Harry Lee
Camden (Camdenton) (27)	314 346-4440	(not reporting)					
Cape Girardeau (Jackson) (62)	314 243-1052	(not reporting)					
Carroll (Carrollton) (11)	816 542-0615	(not reporting)					
Carter (Van Buren) (6)	314 323-4527	James Grassham	. . . .	Rebecca Simpson	Rebecca Simpson	Rebecca Simpson	Jerry Reynolds
Cass (Harrisonville) (64)	816 884-5165	(not reporting)					
Cedar (Stockton) (12)	417 276-3514	(not reporting)					
Chariton (Keytesville) (9)	816 288-3273	(not reporting)					
Christian (Ozark) (33)	417 485-6360	(not reporting)					
Clark (Kahoka) (8)	816 727-3283	Wayne J Blum	. . . .	Leih Ann Hayden	Leih Ann Hayden	. . . .	Barry Donald
Clay (Liberty) (153)	816 792-7600	(not reporting)					
Clinton (Plattsburg) (17)	816 539-3713	Terry Houghton	. . . .	Mary Taylor	. . . .	. . . .	Dan Jones
Cole (Jefferson City) (64)	314 634-9100	Donald C Stockman	. . . .	William J Deeken	L Steinkuehler	L Steinkuehler	John C Hemeyer
Cooper (Boonville) (15)	816 882-2114	(not reporting)					
Crawford (Steelville) (19)	314 775-2376	(not reporting)					
Dade (Greenfield) (7)	417 637-2724	(not reporting)					
Dallas (Buffalo) (13)	417 345-2632	(not reporting)					
Daviess (Gallatin) (8)	816 663-2641	(not reporting)					
De Kalb (Maysville) (10)	816 449-5402	Jerry Popplewell	. . . .	Mary Berry	. . . .	. . . .	Jerry Smith
Dent (Salem) (14)	314 729-4144	S T Anderson	. . . .	Paul Hagler Jr	. . . .	. . . .	Robert D Wofford
Douglas (Ava) (12)	417 683-4714	J G Heinlein	. . . .	Bill Merritt	Kathlen Potter	. . . .	Roldan Turner
Dunklin (Kennett) (33)	314 888-2796	(not reporting)					
Franklin (Union) (81)	314 583-6355	Tom Fenner	. . . .	Tom Herbst			
Gasconade (Hermann) (14)	314 486-5427	(not reporting)					Gary Toelke

Directory 1/10 continued — OFFICIALS IN U.S. COUNTIES

County, county seat, 1990 population figures (000 omitted)	County telephone number	Board chairman	Appointed administrator	Clerk to the governing board	Chief financial officer	Personnel director	Chief law enforcement official
MISSOURI (115) continued							
Gentry (Albany) (7)	816 726-3525	(not reporting)		R Struckhoff	Ernest Frisch		John T Pierpont
Greene (Springfield) (208)	417 868-4000	H C Compton	....	L D Gibson	....	....	Greg Coon
Grundy (Trenton) (11)	816 359-6305	Dwaine Meservey	....	Barbara J Gates	Julia A Alexander	....	George W Martz
Harrison (Bethany) (8)	816 425-6424	Harold W Flint	....				
Henry (Clinton) (20)	816 885-6963	(not reporting)					
Hickory (Hermitage) (7)	417 745-6450	(not reporting)		Jim Luce	....	....	Bernie Delany
Holt (Oregon) (6)	816 446-3303	....					Bill Shephard
Howard (Fayette) (10)	816 248-2284	(not reporting)		Dennis Von Allmen			
Howell (West Plains) (31)	417 256-2591	Dean Proffitt	....				James Anderson
Iron (Ironton) (11)	314 546-2912	(not reporting)					
Jackson (Kansas City) (633)	816 881-3000	Marsha Murphy	Leon Brownfield	Mary Jo Brogoto	Susan Sweeney	Joanne Mossie	
Jasper (Carthage) (90)	417 358-0416	(not reporting)		Wendell Davis	C Kay Dolan	C Kay Dolan	Charles Norman
Jefferson (Hillsboro) (171)	314 789-3911	(not reporting)					
Johnson (Warrensburg) (43)	816 747-2112	Ray Maring	....				
Knox (Edina) (4)	816 397-2104	(not reporting)					
Laclede (Lebanon) (27)	417 532-5471	(not reporting)					B Lavern Whitaker
Lafayette (Lexington) (31)	816 259-4315	(not reporting)		Sharon Schlager	Sharon Schlager	....	
Lawrence (Mount Vernon) (30)	417 466-3666	Dennis McCutchan	....				
Lewis (Monticello) (10)	314 767-5205	(not reporting)		Kathleen N Jones	Robert C Walgren	....	
Lincoln (Troy) (29)	314 528-4415	Buck Farrenkopf	....				....
Linn (Linneus) (14)	816 895-5417	(not reporting)		Pat Clarke	....	Pat Clarke	Robert Dawson
Livingston (Chillicothe) (15)	816 646-2293	Roger P Kohl	....				
Macon (Macon) (15)	816 385-2913	(not reporting)					
Madison (Fredericktown) (11)	314 783-2176	(not reporting)					
Maries (Vienna) (8)	314 422-3388	(not reporting)					
Marion (Palmyra) (28)	314 769-2549	(not reporting)		Jane Lowrey	Ray Woodward	....	Duane Hobbs
Mc Donald (Pineville) (17)	417 223-4717	Russell Hobbs	....				
Mercer (Princeton) (4)	816 748-3425	(not reporting)		Hubert Delay Jr	Hubert Delay Jr	Hubert Delay Jr	Larry Turley
Miller (Tuscumbia) (21)	314 369-2317	Fred Defield					
Mississippi (Charleston) (14)	314 683-2146	(not reporting)		Sandra Carter	....	....	Gary Tawney
Moniteau (California) (12)	314 796-4661	(not reporting)					
Monroe (Paris) (9)	816 327-5817	David Utterback	....				
Montgomery (Montgomery City) (11)	314 564-3357	(not reporting)					
Morgan (Versailles) (16)	314 378-4644	(not reporting)					
New Madrid (New Madrid) (21)	314 748-2524	(not reporting)		Robert Bridges	Robert Bridges	....	Ron Doerge
Newton (Neosho) (44)	417 451-4540	Jerry Owen	....	John W Zimmerman	Mary L Noel	....	Ben Espey
Nodaway (Maryville) (22)	816 582-2251	Lester Keith	....				
Oregon (Alton) (9)	417 778-7475	(not reporting)					
Osage (Linn) (12)	314 897-2139	(not reporting)					
Ozark (Gainesville) (9)	417 679-3516	(not reporting)					
Pemiscot (Caruthersville) (22)	314 333-4203	(not reporting)		Randy Taylor	Karl J Klaus	Randy Taylor	Gary Schaff
Perry (Perryville) (17)	314 547-4242	Karl J Klaus	....				
Pettis (Sedalia) (35)	816 826-4892	(not reporting)					
Phelps (Rolla) (35)	314 364-1891	(not reporting)		Jim Ford	....	....	Jim Wells
Pike (Bowling Green) (16)	314 324-2412	Robert Turpin	....	Doris V Gerner	Bob Griffith	....	Tom Thomas
Platte (Platte City) (58)	816 464-3966	Carol Tomb	John Sandridge				
Polk (Bolivar) (22)	417 326-4031	(not reporting)					
Pulaski (Waynesville) (41)	314 774-2241	(not reporting)					
Putnam (Unionville) (5)	816 947-2674	(not reporting)					
Ralls (New London) (8)	314 985-7111	(not reporting)					
Randolph (Huntsville) (24)	816 277-4717	(not reporting)					
Ray (Richmond) (22)	816 776-3184	(not reporting)					
Reynolds (Centerville) (7)	314 648-2494	(not reporting)					
Ripley (Doniphan) (12)	314 996-3215	(not reporting)					
Saline (Marshall) (24)	816 886-3331	(not reporting)					
Schuyler (Lancaster) (4)	816 457-3842	(not reporting)					
Scotland (Memphis) (5)	816 465-7027	(not reporting)		Bob Kielhofner	H J Holyfield		Bill Ferrell
Scott (Benton) (39)	314 545-3549	Durward Dover	....				
Shannon (Eminence) (8)	314 226-3414	(not reporting)					
Shelby (Shelbyville) (7)	314 633-2181	(not reporting)					
St. Charles (St. Charles) (213)	314 947-2624	Gene Schwendemann	Jim O' Loughlin	Jim Primm	Jim Hodges	William Kauffman	Raymond Runyon
St. Clair (Osceola) (8)	417 646-2315	(not reporting)					
St. Francois (Farmington) (49)	314 756-4551	(not reporting)		John A Grellner	Glenn Pearl	Sandra J Edwards	Ronald Battelle
St. Louis (Clayton) (994)	314 889-2000	Buzz Westfall	James E Baker	....	Virgus Jones	William Duffe	Clarence Harmon
St. Louis (St. Louis) i (397)	314 622-4000	Freeman Bosley Jr	Lloyd Jordan	....			
Ste. Genevieve (Ste. Genevieve) (16)	314 883-5589	(not reporting)					
Stoddard (Bloomfield) (29)	314 568-3339	(not reporting)					
Stone (Galena) (19)	417 357-6127	(not reporting)					
Sullivan (Milan) (6)	816 265-3786	(not reporting)		Ronald D Houseman	....	....	Theron Jenkins
Taney (Forsyth) (26)	417 546-2241	John Strahan Jr	....				
Texas (Houston) (21)	417 967-2112	(not reporting)		Wava Halcomb	....	....	Ted Thomas
Vernon (Nevada) (19)	417 448-2500	Jime Earnest		Janis Meyer	....	....	Michael Baker
Warren (Warrenton) (20)	314 456-3331	Leon Stonebarger	....				
Washington (Potosi) (20)	314 438-4901	(not reporting)					
Wayne (Greenville) (12)	314 224-3513	(not reporting)		Lois Minor	Lois Minor	....	C E Wells
Webster (Marshfield) (24)	417 468-2223	Don Rost	....				
Worth (Grant City) (2)	816 564-2219	(not reporting)					
Wright (Hartville) (17)	417 741-6661	(not reporting)					
MONTANA (56)							
Anaconda-Deer Lodge (Anaconda) c (10)	406 563-8421	(not reporting)		R B Richardson	Kathy Allard		Harold Forsman
Beaverhead (Dillon) (8)	406 683-2642	Randall Tommerup	....				
Big Horn (Hardin) (11)	406 665-1506	(not reporting)		Lucille T Oehmcke	....	....	Jack Harrington
Blaine (Chinook) (7)	406 357-3250	Arthur Kleinjan	....	Elaine Graveley	....	....	Richard Thompson
Broadwater (Townsend) (3)	406 266-3443	Robert L Davis	....				
Butte-Silver Bow (Butte) c (33)	406 723-8262	(not reporting)					
Carbon (Red Lodge) (8)	406 446-1595	(not reporting)					
Carter (Ekalaka) (2)	406 775-8749	(not reporting)					Barry Michelotti
Cascade (Great Falls) (78)	406 761-6700	Harry B Mitchel	Judy Guisti	Robert Bateman	Tom Meech	....	
Chouteau (Fort Benton) (5)	406 622-5151	(not reporting)					

Directory 1/10
continued

OFFICIALS IN U.S. COUNTIES

County, county seat, 1990 population figures (000 omitted)	County telephone number	Board chairman	Appointed administrator	Clerk to the governing board	Chief financial officer	Personnel director	Chief law enforcement official
MONTANA (56) continued							
Custer (Miles City) (12)	406 232-7800	(not reporting)					
Daniels (Scobey) (2)	406 487-5561	C William Tande	....	Carol Malone	Lorraine Jerome	....	James P Kramer
Dawson (Glendive) (10)	406 365-3058	Judy Reddig	....	Patricia Boje	....	....	James George
Fallon (Baker) (3)	406 778-2883	Donald Rieger	....	Mary Lee Dietz	Faye Koenig		Leland Gundlach
Fergus (Lewistown) (12)	406 538-5119	(not reporting)					
Flathead (Kalispell) (59)	406 752-5300	(not reporting)					
Gallatin (Bozeman) (50)	406 585-1400	(not reporting)					
Garfield (Jordan) (2)	406 557-2760	(not reporting)					
Glacier (Cut Bank) (12)	406 873-5063	Fred Pambrun	Reagan McClure	Clara Henderson	Phyllis Withers	....	Gary Bjorklund
Golden Valley (Ryegate) (1)	406 568-2231	Edgar E Lewis	....	Aileen Mattheis	....	....	Richard Zaharko
Granite (Philipsburg) (3)	400 859-3771	Frank Waldbillig		Jo Bayer			Don Dee Kennedy
Hill (Havre) (18)	406 265-5481	Kathy Bessette	....	Diane Mellem	Diane Mellem	Donna Ahlert	Tim Solomon
Jefferson (Boulder) (8)	406 225-4251	(not reporting)					
Judith Basin (Stanford) (2)	406 566-2301	(not reporting)					
Lake (Polson) (21)	406 883-6211	(not reporting)					
Lewis And Clark (Helena) (47)	406 447-8304	L Stoll Anderson	Duane Johnson	Paulette DeHart	Ed Blackman	Sheila Cozzie	Charles O Reilly
Liberty (Chester) (2)	406 759-5365	(not reporting)					
Lincoln (Libby) (17)	406 293-7781	Noel E Williams	....	Coral M Cummings	Geri A Miller	....	Ray Nixon
Madison (Virginia City) (6)	406 843-5392	(not reporting)					
Mc Cone (Circle) (2)	406 485-3505	Connie Eissinger	....	Leanne Switzer	Janet McCabe		Robert Jensen
Meagher (White Sulphur Springs) (2)	406 547-3612	(not reporting)					
Mineral (Superior) (3)	406 822-4541	(not reporting)					
Missoula (Missoula) (79)	406 721-5700	(not reporting)					
Musselshell (Roundup) (4)	406 323-1104	Sue M Olson	....	Jane E Mang	Mary C Nelson	....	G Paul Smith
Park (Livingston) (15)	406 222-6120	Carlo Cieri	....	B Dean Holmes	D Bayles Frazer		Charlie Johnson
Petroleum (Winnett) (1)	406 429-5551	(not reporting)					
Phillips (Malta) (5)	406 654-2423	Eugene E Cowan		Laurel N Hines			Gene Peigneux
Pondera (Conrad) (6)	406 278-7681	Bill Rappold	Gordon Bechard	Elsie Lamma	Marlene Fischer	....	Leon Simpson
Powder River (Broadus) (2)	406 436-2657	Ted Fletcher	....	Karen Amende	Nancy Klapmeier	....	Ken Rogge
Powell (Deer Lodge) (7)	406 846-3680	Don F Valiton	....	Dorothy Benson	Dalice M Rogers		Gerald Fiske
Prairie (Terry) (1)	406 637-5575	(not reporting)					
Ravalli (Hamilton) (25)	406 363-4790	(not reporting)					
Richland (Sidney) (11)	406 482-1708	(not reporting)					
Roosevelt (Wolf Point) (11)	406 653-1590	(not reporting)					
Rosebud (Forsyth) (11)	406 356-7318	(not reporting)					
Sanders (Thompson Falls) (9)	406 827-4391	(not reporting)					
Sheridan (Plentywood) (5)	406 765-2310	C S Holje	....	Milt Hovland	....		Dave Christman
Stillwater (Columbus) (7)	406 322-4546	Fred J Weiler	....	Janet R Parkins	Carol Rice	....	Cliff Brophy
Sweet Grass (Big Timber) (3)	405 932-5152	(not reporting)					
Teton (Choteau) (6)	406 466-2151	Arnold Gettel	Gigi Mathis	Joan Pierce	Diane Ameline	Gigi Mathis	George Anderson
Toole (Shelby) (5)	406 434-2232	John A Alstad	Melodee A Robins	Melodee A Robins	Melodee A Robins	Jewel Moritz	Vern Anderson
Treasure (Hysham) (1)	406 342-5547	Ole Redland	....	Lavon Adair	Kathleen Thomas	....	Bill W Hedges
Valley (Glasgow) (8)	406 228-8221	Eleanor D Pratt	....	Mary Lou Eide	....		Daniel Taylor
Wheatland (Harlowton) (2)	406 632-4891	David Miller	....	Carol Clark	....		Richard Egebakken
Wibaux (Wibaux) (1)	406 795-2481	(not reporting)					
Yellowstone (Billings) (113)	406 256-2701	(not reporting)					
NEBRASKA (93)							
Adams (Hastings) (30)	402 461-7104	M B Ellerbee	....	Phyllis Newell	....	....	Gregg Magee
Antelope (Neligh) (8)	402 887-4410	Gordon Baker	....	Eleanor Holm	....	....	Ralph Black
Arthur (Arthur) (..)	308 764-2203	(not reporting)					
Banner (Harrisburg) (1)	308 436-5265	Klayton Johnson					
Blaine (Brewster) (1)	308 547-2222	Dennis Wyckoff	....	Barbara Stoddard	Betty Hughbanks		K Patrick Mooney
Boone (Albion) (7)	402 395-2055	Merlin Buettner	....	Edna D Spencer	....		Tim Sierks
Box Butte (Alliance) (13)	308 772-6565	(not reporting)		Robert Zoucha			Gerald Benne
Boyd (Butte) (3)	402 775-2391	(not reporting)					
Brown (Ainsworth) (4)	402 387-2705	(not reporting)					
Buffalo (Kearney) (37)	308 236-1200	(not reporting)					
Burt (Tekamah) (8)	402 374-1955	(not reporting)					
Butler (David City) (9)	402 367-3091	(not reporting)					
Cass (Plattsmouth) (21)	402 296-2164	(not reporting)					
Cedar (Hartington) (10)	402 254-7411	(not reporting)					
Chase (Imperial) (4)	308 882-5266	(not reporting)					
Cherry (Valentine) (6)	402 376-2420	(not reporting)					
Cheyenne (Sidney) (9)	308 254-2141	Frank Rauner	....	Dianne Cook	....	....	Darrell Johnson
Clay (Clay Center) (7)	402 762-3463	Lawrence Griess	....	Janet Hajny	....	....	Richard Marsh
Colfax (Schuyler) (9)	402 352-3434	Don Trojan	....	Lamar J Broicko	....	....	Lynn Blum
Cuming (West Point) (10)	402 372-2144	(not reporting)					
Custer (Broken Bow) (12)	308 872-5701	(not reporting)					
Dakota (Dakota City) (17)	402 987-2126	Jackie Hartnett	....	Theodore A Piepho	....	....	James Wagner
Dawes (Chadron) (9)	308 432-2863	Thomas Brown	....	Florence Mikesell	....		....
Dawson (Lexington) (20)	308 324-2127	Wendell Atchison	....	Donna M Linn	Kermit O Pearson	....	Lawrence Mandelko
Deuel (Chappell) (2)	308 874-3308	(not reporting)					
Dixon (Ponca) (6)	402 755-2208	(not reporting)					
Dodge (Fremont) (35)	402 727-2767	Dean Lux					
Douglas (Omaha) (416)	402 444-7000	Mike Albert	Dean Sykes	Thomas Cavanaugh	Louis Pantano	John Taylor	Danny Weddle
Dundy (Benkelman) (3)	308 423-2058	Boyd Blair Jr	....	....	....		Richard Roth
Fillmore (Geneva) (7)	402 759-4931	Albert Simacek		Carol Vejraska	M Christiancy		Robert Bellamy
Franklin (Franklin) (4)	308 425-6202	Claudette Russell	....	Marcia Volk	....		William Burgess
Frontier (Stockville) (3)	308 367-8641	(not reporting)					Timothy Moninger
Furnas (Beaver City) (6)	308 268-4145	(not reporting)					
Gage (Beatrice) (23)	402 223-1300	Bruce Carsten	....	Calvin Gullion	....	....	....
Garden (Oshkosh) (2)	308 772-3924	(not reporting)					Jerry Dewitt
Garfield (Burwell) (2)	308 346-4161	(not reporting)					
Gosper (Elwood) (2)	308 785-2611	(not reporting)					
Grant (Hyannis) (1)	308 458-2488	Lewis A Anderson	....	Delores M Blakey	....		
Greeley (Greeley Center) (3)	308 428-3625	B J Meyer	....	....	....	....	Kenneth B McCune
Hall (Grand Island) (49)	308 381-5083	(not reporting)					
Hamilton (Aurora) (9)	402 694-3443	Paul M Kemling	....	Becky A Richter	Elmer C Obermeier		Kirk W Handrup
Harlan (Alma) (4)	308 928-2173	Richard D Heft	....	Verdeen L Leopold	Diane M Grotfeld		Chris N Becker
Hayes (Hayes Center) (1)	308 286-3413	(not reporting)					
Hitchcock (Trenton) (4)	308 334-5646	James M Loibl	....	Cindy Williamson	....	....	D Bryan Leggott

Directory 1/10 OFFICIALS IN U.S. COUNTIES
continued

County, county seat, 1990 population figures (000 omitted)	County telephone number	Board chairman	Appointed administrator	Clerk to the governing board	Chief financial officer	Personnel director	Chief law enforcement official
NEBRASKA (93) continued							
Holt (O'Neill) (13)	402 336-1762	(not reporting)					
Hooker (Mullen) (1)	308 546-2244	(not reporting)					
Howard (St. Paul) (6)	308 754-4343	(not reporting)					
Jefferson (Fairbury) (9)	402 729-2323	James Weichel	. . . .	Sandra Stelling	Alice Nelson	. . . .	Rex E Southwick
Johnson (Tecumseh) (5)	402 335-3246	Howard Wilkinson	. . . .	Kathleen Nieveen	. . . .		Vernon Pike
Kearney (Minden) (7)	308 832-1155	Ross Wright	. . . .	Patricia Osterbuh	Marcele Schmidt	. . . .	Marshall Nelson
Keith (Ogallala) (9)	308 284-4726	Clifford Welsh	. . . .	. . . .	. . . .	. . . .	. . . .
Keya Paha (Springview) (1)	402 497-3791	(not reporting)					
Kimball (Kimball) (4)	308 235-2241	Vernon Bourlier	. . . .	Elaine Sandridge	Diana L Quicke		John J Thacker Jr
Knox (Center) (10)	402 288-4282	(not reporting)					
Lancaster (Lincoln) (214)	402 471-7447	Marcia Malone	Kerry Eagan	. . . .	David Kroeker	. . . .	Thomas Casady
Lincoln (North Platte) (33)	308 534-4350	(not reporting)					
Logan (Stapleton) (1)	308 636-2311	(not reporting)					
Loup (Taylor) (1)	308 942-3135	(not reporting)					
Madison (Madison) (33)	402 454-3311	Louis F Barry	. . . .	Nacy Scheer	Donna J Primrose	. . . .	Vernon J Hjorth
Mc Pherson (Tryon) (1)	308 587-2363	(not reporting)					
Merrick (Central City) (8)	308 946-2881	. . . .	. . . .	Ellen M Palser	. . . .	. . . .	D Schneiderheinz
Morrill (Bridgeport) (5)	308 262-0860	Peggy J Golden	. . . .	Dorothy P Lanik	. . . .	. . . .	John D Edens
Nance (Fullerton) (4)	308 536-2331	Vernon Olson	. . . .	Dianne Carter	. . . .	. . . .	Sam King
Nemaha (Auburn) (8)	402 274-4213	(not reporting)					
Nuckolls (Nelson) (6)	402 225-4361	(not reporting)					
Otoe (Nebraska City) (14)	402 873-3586	John J Hodges	. . . .	Marcina Cody	Jacqueline Smith	. . . .	James M Gress
Pawnee (Pawnee City) (3)	402 852-2962	(not reporting)					
Perkins (Grant) (3)	308 352-4643	James A Deaver	. . . .	Mary Buss	. . . .		David A Deaver
Phelps (Holdrege) (10)	308 995-4469	Willard Peterson	. . . .	Lois E Young	Sharon Rupe		Dwayne Newman
Pierce (Pierce) (8)	402 329-4225	(not reporting)					
Platte (Columbus) (30)	402 563-4904	B Brandenburgh	. . . .	Diane C Pinger	. . . .	. . . .	Jon Zavadil
Polk (Osceola) (6)	402 747-5431	Norman Leach	. . . .	Ruth N Stromberg	Coral R Boden	. . . .	Steven L Cherry
Red Willow (Mc Cook) (12)	308 345-1552	(not reporting)					
Richardson (Falls City) (10)	402 245-2911	(not reporting)					
Rock (Bassett) (2)	402 684-3933	(not reporting)					
Saline (Wilber) (13)	402 821-2374	Phil F Weber	. . . .	Norma K Ripa	. . . .	. . . .	Byron R Buzek
Sarpy (Papillion) (103)	402 593-2346	Ron Woodle	Mark Wayne	Debra Houtaling	Brian Hanson	. . . .	Patrick Thomas
Saunders (Wahoo) (18)	402 443-4335	(not reporting)					
Scotts Bluff (Gering) (36)	308 436-6600	(not reporting)					
Seward (Seward) (15)	402 643-2883	(not reporting)					
Sheridan (Rushville) (7)	308 327-2633	(not reporting)					
Sherman (Loup City) (4)	308 745-1513	(not reporting)					
Sioux (Harrison) (2)	308 668-2443	Harold Keener	. . . .	M Wasserburger	. . . .	. . . .	James Robertson
Stanton (Stanton) (6)	402 439-2222	(not reporting)					
Thayer (Hebron) (7)	402 768-6126	Milton C Eickman	. . . .	Marilyn K Free	. . . .	. . . .	Gary R Young
Thomas (Thedford) (1)	308 645-2261	Wayne Rodocker	. . . .	Marilyn Maseberg	. . . .	. . . .	Stephen Petersen
Thurston (Pender) (7)	402 385-2343	Mark E Casey	. . . .	Pat Higgins	. . . .	. . . .	Harold Obermeyer
Valley (Ord) (5)	308 728-3700	(not reporting)					
Washington (Blair) (17)	402 426-6822	John Lutz	. . . .	C Petersen	Kay Erwin	. . . .	DeWayne Flora
Wayne (Wayne) (9)	402 375-2288	(not reporting)					
Webster (Red Cloud) (4)	402 746-2716	(not reporting)					
Wheeler (Bartlett) (1)	308 654-3235	(not reporting)					
York (York) (14)	402 362-7759	Dean D Buller	. . . .	P Bredenkamp	. . . .	. . . .	Steve A Rediger
NEVADA (17)							
Carson City-Ormsby (Carson City) c (40)	702 887-2100	Marv Teixeira	John Berkich	Kiyoshi Nishikawa	Mary C Walker	Judie Fisher	Paul McGrath
Churchill (Fallon) (18)	702 423-5136	Bjorn Selinder	. . . .	. . . .	Alan F Kalt	. . . .	William L Lawry
Clark (Las Vegas) (741)	702 455-3530	Jay Bingham	Donald L Shalmy	Loretta Bowman	Guy Hobbs	Cheryl Miller	John Moran
Douglas (Minden) (28)	702 782-9860	David Pumphrey	. . . .	Barbara Reed	. . . .	Neldon Demke	Jerry Maple
Elko (Elko) (34)	702 738-5398	R Llee Chapman	George Boucher	Karen Vasquez	Linda P Ritter	Linda P Ritter	Neil Harris
Esmeralda (Goldfield) (1)	702 485-3406	(not reporting)					
Eureka (Eureka) (2)	702 237-5262	(not reporting)					
Humboldt (Winnemucca) (13) ...	702 623-6300	Tom Fransway	Kerry L Hawkins	Susan Harrer	Belle Bundy	Kerry L Hawkins	Gene Hill
Lander (Austin) (6)	702 964-2447	(not reporting)					
Lincoln (Pioche) (4)	702 962-5495	(not reporting)					
Lyon County (Yerington) (20) ...	702 463-3341	Chet Hillyard	Stephen Snyder	Marion Pinkerton	Rita Evasovic	Rita Evasovic	Sid Smith
Mineral (Hawthorne) (6)	702 945-2446	Herman F Staat	. . . .	Marlene S Bunch	Patricia Fisk	. . . .	John H Leonhardt
Nye (Tonopah) (18)	702 482-8191	Cameron McRae	William Offutt	Juanita Robb	Geneva Neuhauser	Debra Jeffrey	Wade Lieseke
Pershing (Lovelock) (4)	702 273-2208	(not reporting)					
Storey (Virginia City) (3)	702 847-0577	(not reporting)					
Washoe (Reno) (255)	702 328-2000	Larry Beck	John Mac Intyre	Judi Bailey	Robert Jasper	Joanne Ray	Vince Swinney
White Pine (Ely) (9)	702 289-4567	(not reporting)					
NEW HAMPSHIRE (10)							
Belknap (Laconia) (49)	603 524-3579	Norman C Marsh	Philip P Daigneau	Mark E Thurston	Robert T Corbin	. . . .	Stephen G Hodges
Carroll (Ossipee) (35)	603 539-7751	Brenda M Presby	. . . .	. . . .	. . . .	. . . .	Roy H Larson Jr
Cheshire (Keene) (70)	603 352-8215	(not reporting)					
Coos (Berlin) (35)	603 752-2144	(not reporting)					
Grafton (Woodsville) (75)	603 787-6941	Betty Jo Taffe	Evelyn I Smith	Raymond S Burton	Kathleen W Ward		Charles Barry
Hillsborough (Manchester) (336)	603 627-5600	(not reporting)					
Merrimack (Concord) (120)	603 228-0331	Stuart Trachy	Carol Haessly	Larry Boucher	Charles Carroll	Barry Cox	Chester Jordan
Rockingham (Epping) (246)	603 679-2256	Ernest P Barka	. . . .	Warren Henderson	Theresa Young	Roy E Morrisette	Wayne Vetter
Strafford (Dover) (104)	603 742-1458	(not reporting)					
Sullivan (Newport) (39)	603 863-2560	(not reporting)					
NEW JERSEY (21)							
Atlantic (Atlantic City) (224)	609 345-6700	Richard Squires	Helen Walsh	Thomas Somers	William Tate	Joyce Ross	Jeff Blitz
Bergen (Hackensack) (825)	201 646-2000	(not reporting)					
Burlington (Mount Holly) (395) ..	609 265-5000	Francis L Bodine	Frederick F Galdo	Frederick F Galdo	Arthur J Collins	Frederick F Galdo	Edward A Cummings
Camden (Camden) (503)	609 757-8000	(not reporting)					
Cape May (Cape May Court House) (95)	609 465-1060	(not reporting)					
Cumberland (Bridgeton) (138) ..	609 453-2121	John Reinard	David Gray	Clair Miller Jr	Gary Simmerman	Ralph Brownlee	James Forcinito
Essex (Newark) (778)	201 621-4977	Sara Bost	Donald Biase	Adrianne Davis	Vincent Foti	Brenda Possumato	Armando Fontoura
Gloucester (Woodbury) (230) ...	609 853-3200	(not reporting)					
Hudson (Jersey City) (553)	201 795-6255	R Janiszewski	Geoffrey Perselay	Jean Byrnes	Abraham Anton	L Henderson	Edward Webster

Directory 1/10   OFFICIALS IN U.S. COUNTIES
continued

County, county seat, 1990 population figures (000 omitted)	County telephone number	Board chairman	Appointed administrator	Clerk to the governing board	Chief financial officer	Personnel director	Chief law enforcement official
NEW JERSEY (21) continued							
Hunterdon (Flemington) (108) ..	908 788-1102	Frank J Fuzo	Dorothy K Bertany	Denise B Doolan	Charles Balogh Jr	. . . .	James Marino
Mercer (Trenton) (326)	609 989-6517	Robert Prunetti	John F Ricci	C DiCostanzo	Steven Zielinski	Lewis Goldstein	Samuel Plumeri
Middlesex (New Brunswick) (672)	908 745-3000	(not reporting)					
Monmouth (Freehold) (553)	201 431-7384	(not reporting)					
Morris (Morristown) (421)	201 285-6000	Edward Tamm	James J Rosenberg	Ilene St John	Robert Natoli	Herman Hoopes	W Michael Murphy
Ocean (Toms River) (433)	908 929-2128	Joseph H Vicari	A Paul King	Daniel J Hennessy	James J Mullins	Keith J Goetting	William Polhemus
Passaic (Paterson) (453)	201 881-4405	(not reporting)					
Salem (Salem) (65)	609 935-7510	(not reporting)					
Somerset (Somerville) (240)	908 231-7000	. . . .	Richard Williams	. . . .	. . . .	. . . .	. . . .
Sussex (Newton) (131)	201 579-0350	John Warren	Thomas P Bellucci	Elaine A Morgan	Doris Bush	Connie J Sutton	Robert Untig
Union (Elizabeth) (494)	201 527-4200	. . . .	Ann M Baran	. . . .	. . . .	Gregory Hardoby	. . . .
Warren (Belvidere) (92)	908 475-6500	Kenneth Miller	Melinda Carlton	Melinda Carlton	Robert Leupo	Dorothy Neith	John O' Reilly
NEW MEXICO (33)							
Bernalillo (Albuquerque) (481) ..	505 768-4000	(not reporting)					
Catron (Reserve) (3)	505 533-6423	(not reporting)					
Chaves (Roswell) (58)	505 624-6600	Joe Velasquez	Curtis Woolf	Rhoda Goodloe	Marylou Rodriguez	Curtis Woolf	Terrell Tucker
Cibola (Grants) (24)	505 287-9431	(not reporting)					
Colfax (Raton) (13)	505 445-2906	Frank Cimino	Whitney O Hite	Barbara Castillo	Susie A Apodaca	. . . .	Jim Maldonado
Curry (Clovis) (42)	505 763-6016	Paul D Barnes	Geneva Cooper	Coni Lyman	Geneva Cooper	Geneva Cooper	James M Jackson
De Baca (Fort Sumner) (2)	505 355-2601	Frank McRee	. . . .	Shana Kenyon	Lahonda Fox	Shana Kenyon	Champ E Landrum
Dona Ana (Las Cruces) (136) ...	505 525-6600	Everardo L Chavez	Don Brooks	Rita Torres	Delia Barncastle	Don Brooks	William Storment
Eddy (Carlsbad) (49)	505 887-9511	Fred T Alvarez	Stephen D Massey	Karen Davis	Louise Greene	. . . .	Jack Childress
Grant (Silver City) (28)	505 538-3338	(not reporting)					
Guadalupe (Santa Rosa) (4)	505 472-3306	(not reporting)					
Harding (Mosquero) (1)	505 673-2927	Michael E Lewis	Arlene Aragon	E Martinez	. . . .	. . . .	Raymond Gutierrez
Hidalgo (Lordsburg) (6)	505 542-9213	(not reporting)					
Lea (Lovington) (56)	505 396-8521	(not reporting)					
Lincoln (Carrizozo) (12)	505 648-2385	Monroey Montes	Andrew C Wynham	Martha M Proctor	Charlene Schlarb	Martha Guevara	James McSwane
Los Alamos (Los Alamos) (18) ..	505 662-8040	James Greenwood	James M Flint	Bettie Kerr	Max Baker	Karen Willis	Allen Kirk
Luna (Deming) (18)	505 546-0494	(not reporting)					
Mc Kinley (Gallup) (61)	505 722-3868	Harry Mendoza	Teodolo Arellano	Milton Gabaldon	Steven Baumgardt	Pat Holloway	Frank Gonzales
Mora (Mora) (4)	505 387-5279	Henry Sanchez	Gilbert R Valdez	Margarat Lujan	Gilbert R Valdez	Gilbert R Valdez	Nazario Montoya
Otero (Alamogordo) (52)	505 437-7427	Robert Bishop	David Weitzel	Mary Quintana	David Weitzel	Jeanette L Abney	John A Lee
Quay (Tucumcari) (11)	505 461-2112	Glen Briscoe	Sandra P Garley	J Maddaford	Nadine Angel	Sandra P Garley	James Knight
Rio Arriba (Tierra Amarilla) (34) .	505 588-7255	Alfrero L Montoya	Arthur Rodarte	David S Chavez	Livia Olguin	Arthur Rodarte	Nelson E Cordova
Roosevelt (Portales) (17)	505 356-8562	Blonnie Rea	. . . .	Maudene Haragan	. . . .	. . . .	Bobby W Dodgin
San Juan (Aztec) (92)	505 334-9481	John A Dean Jr	Tony Atkinson	Carol Bandy	Patricia Wood	James Smith	Roger Lasater
San Miguel (Las Vegas) (26) ...	505 425-9333	Edmund Joe Lang	Debbie Hays	Sally Padilla	Leroy Arquero	Robert Schneider	Bert Delara
Sandoval (Bernalillo) (63)	505 867-2341	Edmund Joe Lang	Debbie Hays	Sally Padilla	Leroy Arquero	Robert Schneider	Bert Delara
Santa Fe (Santa Fe) (99)	505 984-5000	Raymond Chavez	Gilbert Tercero	Jona Armijo	Peter Garcia	Paul O' Donoghue	Benjamin Montano
Sierra (Truth Or Consequences) (10)	505 894-6215	Ralph Gooding	. . . .	Lupe Carrejo	Sandi Chatfield	Ella Elston	Ronald Brown
Socorro (Socorro) (15)	505 835-0589	(not reporting)					
Taos (Taos) (23)	505 758-8834	(not reporting)					
Torrance (Estancia) (10)	505 384-2418	Bill Williams	Larry S Jones	Carla Clayton	Ruben Miranda	Paula Rodriguez	Robert Chavez
Union (Clayton) (4)	505 374-9491	D E Carter	Della Wetsel	Freida Birdwell	. . . .	. . . .	Jess Yeargain
Valencia (Los Lunas) (45)	505 866-2003	(not reporting)					
NEW YORK (58)							
Albany (Albany) (293)	518 447-7040	(not reporting)					
Allegany (Belmont) (50)	716 268-7612	(not reporting)					
Broome (Binghamton) (212)	607 778-2185	Timothy M Grippen	. . . .	Richard Blythe	Jerome Knebel	Michael Klein	Geno DeAngelo
Cattaraugus (Little Valley) (84) ..	716 938-9111	Joseph Eade	Donald Furman	Donald Furman	Joseph Keller	Howard Peterson	Jerry Burrell
Cayuga (Auburn) (82)	315 253-1011	(not reporting)					
Chautauqua (Mayville) (142)	716 753-7111	Ward John	R Gilbert Randell	Robert White	Robert Beckman	Robert M Laughlin	John Bentley
Chemung (Elmira) (95)	607 737-2918	John Flory	G Thomas Tranter	Linda Palmer	Steven Hoover	Michael Krusen	Charles Houper
Chenango (Norwich) (52)	607 335-4500	Clifford Crouch	. . . .	Thomas Whittaker	William Evans	Bonnie Carrier	Thomas Loughren
Clinton (Plattsburgh) (86)	518 565-4600	Jay Lepage	William Bingel	William Bingel	Janet Duprey	Carol Wallett	Russell Trombly
Columbia (Hudson) (63)	518 828-1527	(not reporting)					
Cortland (Cortland) (49)	607 753-5052	Richard Tupper	. . . .	Deanna Lincoln	Alex Fumarola	Bethany O' Rourke	Duane Whiteman
Delaware (Delhi) (47)	607 746-2603	(not reporting)					
Dutchess (Poughkeepsie) (259) ..	914 431-2169	(not reporting)					
Erie (Buffalo) (969)	716 846-8500	(not reporting)					
Essex (Elizabethtown) (37)	518 873-6301	Joseph E Boone	Kim A Higgs	Peter R Mends	S Egglefield	Peter R Mends	Robert Lavigne
Franklin (Malone) (47)	518 483-6767	(not reporting)					
Fulton (Johnstown) (54)	518 762-0540	(not reporting)					
Genesee (Batavia) (60)	716 344-2550	Carl J Perkowski	Jay A Gsell	Carolyn P Pratt	Richard Seibert	Martha A Standish	Gary Maha
Greene (Catskill) (45)	518 943-3080	(not reporting)					
Hamilton (Lake Pleasant) (5)	518 548-6651	Robert L Morrison	. . . .	Natalie Williams	Nancy Rhodes	Zereda Lane	Douglas Parker
Herkimer (Herkimer) (66)	315 867-1002	(not reporting)					
Jefferson (Watertown) (111)	315 785-3147	Wm H Fulkerson	John V Hartzell	John V Hartzell	Jane T Jenkins	Stephen R Miller	Donald F Newberry
Lewis (Lowville) (27)	315 376-5325	(not reporting)					
Livingston (Geneseo) (62)	716 243-7000	James Steele	Dominic Mazza	Virginia Amico	Arlene Johnston	Elizabeth Sliker	John York
Madison (Wampsville) (69)	315 366-2201	(not reporting)					
Monroe (Rochester) (714)	716 428-5301	Robert L King	Irene Matichyn	Patricia Knapp	Gerald Mecca	Richard Mackey	Andrew Meloni
Montgomery (Fonda) (52)	518 853-3431	John Vankersen	Wayne Allen	Richard Healey	Norma Palmer	Richard Baia	Ronald Emery
Nassau (Mineola) (1287)	516 535-3131	(not reporting)					
New York City (New York) c (7323)	212 566-5700	(not reporting)					
Niagara (Lockport) (221)	716 439-6194	(not reporting)					
Oneida (Utica) (251)	315 798-5790	John J Williams	. . . .	Susan Crabtree	Blake Ford	Mary Lou Berie	Gerald Washburn
Onondaga (Syracuse) (469)	315 435-2222	Nicholas Pirro	Edward Kochian	Jerry Hayes	Michael Sullivan	Elaine Walter	John Dillon
Ontario (Canandaigua) (95)	716 396-4465	(not reporting)					
Orange (Goshen) (308)	914 294-5151	Mary McPhillips	J Daniel Bloomer	Gail Sicina	Ruth McMorrow	Joseph M Dwyer	James Garvey
Orleans (Albion) (42)	716 589-7053	(not reporting)					
Oswego (Oswego) (122)	315 349-8230	Hollis Iselin	Arthur Ospelt	M Lincoln	William Brouse	Peter Seipel	Charles Nellis
Otsego (Cooperstown) (61)	607 547-4202	(not reporting)					
Putnam (Carmel) (84)	914 628-6868	James Gordan	. . . .	Jean Lepere	William Carlin	Paul Eldridge	Robert Thoubboron
Rensselaer (Troy) (154)	518 270-2700	Marilyn Douglas	. . . .	Larry Quinn	Philip Wood	Felix Pugliese	Daniel Keating
Rockland (New City) (265)	914 638-5000	John T Grant	. . . .	Richard Menocker	Harold Peterson	Patsy Prendergast	James Kralik
Saratoga (Ballston Spa) (181) ...	518 885-5381	(not reporting)					
Schenectady (Schenectady) (149)	518 388-4270	M Buhrmaster	Robert McEvoy	Joseph Parillo Jr	George Davidson	James Edgar	William Barnes

Directory 1/10 **OFFICIALS IN U.S. COUNTIES**
continued

County, county seat, 1990 population figures (000 omitted)	County telephone number	Board chairman	Appointed administrator	Clerk to the governing board	Chief financial officer	Personnel director	Chief law enforcement official
NEW YORK (58) continued							
Schoharie (Schoharie) (32)	518 295-8347	David Handy	....	Carl Barbic	Lawrence Tague	Craig Mausler	Harvey Stoddard
Schuyler (Watkins Glen) (19)	607 535-2051	Angeline Franzese	....	Doris Craig	Nancy Peters	Margaret Jensen	Michael Maloney
Seneca (Waterloo) (34)	315 539-5655	(not reporting)					
St. Lawrence (Canton) (112)	315 379-2276	(not reporting)					
Steuben (Bath) (99)	607 776-9631	(not reporting)					
Suffolk (Hauppauge) (1322)	516 853-4000	Robert J Gaffney	D Blydenburgh	Elisabeth Taibbi	Joseph Caputo	Alan Schneider	Peter Cosgrove
Sullivan (Monticello) (69)	914 794-3000	Walter Sipple	L Green Decarlo	....	Damiel Briggs	Richard L Green	Joseph Wasser
Tioga (Owego) (52)	607 687-0100	(not reporting)					
Tompkins (Ithaca) (94)	607 274-5551	Robert Watros	Scott Heyman	Cathy Covert	David Squires	Anita Fitzpatrick	Emery Quest
Ulster (Kingston) (165)	914 331-9300	(not reporting)					
Warren (Lake George) (59)	518 761-6535	(not reporting)					
Washington (Fort Edward) (59)	518 747-4260	R Harry Booth	Kevin Hayes	Helen Longdaue	Phyllis Cooper	Margaret Wright	Robert Endee
Wayne (Lyons) (89)	315 946-5400	Marvin E Decker	....	Helen Maddock	Thomas Warnick	Peter S Stirpe	Richard Pisciotti
Westchester (White Plains) (875)	914 285-2000	Andrew O' Rourke	Neil DeLuca	Patricia Gorski	Joseph Phelan	Anthony Giambruno	Ernest Colaneri
Wyoming (Warsaw) (43)	716 786-8800	(not reporting)					
Yates (Penn Yan) (23)	315 536-5150	David K Ingram	Amy G Manley	Martha K Lattin	Daniel Taylor	....	Ronald Spike
NORTH CAROLINA (100)							
Alamance (Graham) (108)	919 228-1312	W B Teague Jr	Robert Smith	S C Kitchen	David Cheek	Joanne Garner	Richard Frye
Alexander (Taylorsville) (28)	704 632-9332	(not reporting)					
Alleghany (Sparta) (10)	919 372-4179	John A Hampton	Daniel McMillan	....	Wanda S Edwards	....	John Caudill
Anson (Wadesboro) (23)	704 694-2796	Herman K Little	Steven Carpenter	Bonnie M Huntley	Dorothy V Tyson	....	Thomas W Allen Jr
Ashe (Jefferson) (22)	919 246-8841	Jerry D Powers	Wm Jeff Miller	Sandra Richardson	Patricia Fowler	....	James C Hartley
Avery (Newland) (15)	704 733-8201	Susan Pittman	Randall Fletcher	Nancy Cook	James Buchanan	....	Edward Gwyn
Beaufort (Washington) (42)	919 946-0079	Granville Lilley	Donald Davenport	Sharon Singleton	Donald Davenport	....	Nelson Sheppard
Bertie (Windsor) (20)	919 794-5300	Joseph W Spruill	John E Whitehurst	John E Whitehurst	Lydia M Hoggard	John E Whitehurst	James W Perry
Bladen (Elizabethtown) (29)	919 862-6700	Lewis C Tatum	Alexis H Jones	Alexis H Jones	Ann A Weeks	Phoebe McGavock	Earl Storms
Brunswick (Bolivia) (51)	919 253-4331	(not reporting)					
Buncombe (Asheville) (175)	704 255-5702	Gene Rainey	William McElrath	Kathy Hughes	James Roach	Robert Thornberry	Charles Long
Burke (Morganton) (76)	704 433-4000	Larry A Huffman	Thomas B Robinson	Frances McKinney	W Paul Ijames	Jacqueline Kanipe	Ralph E Johnson
Cabarrus (Concord) (99)	704 788-8100	Carolyn Carpenter	John Witherspoon	Frankie F Bonds	Blair Bennett	Donald J Moorhead	Robert Canaday
Caldwell (Lenoir) (71)	704 757-1300	Jane Greene	David T Flaherty	Betty Blankenship	Robert R Query Jr	David Hill	Roger L Hutchings
Camden (Camden) (6)	919 338-1919	(not reporting)					
Carteret (Beaufort) (53)	919 728-8400	(not reporting)					
Caswell (Yanceyville) (21)	919 694-4193	(not reporting)					
Catawba (Newton) (118)	704 465-8200	Robert Hibbitts	J Thomas Lundy	Virginia Sobotken	Michael Talbert	Janith Huffman	David Huffman
Chatham (Pittsboro) (39)	919 542-8200	Henry H Dunlap Jr	Ben Shivar	Sandra B Cape	Vicki McConnell	....	Don Whitt
Cherokee (Murphy) (20)	704 837-5527	(not reporting)					
Chowan (Edenton) (14)	919 482-8431	(not reporting)					
Clay (Hayesville) (7)	704 389-6301	(not reporting)					
Cleveland (Shelby) (85)	704 484-4800	Cecil D Dickson	Lane Alexander	Wanda C Sisk	David C Dear	Jeff Richardson	Buddy R McKinney
Columbus (Whiteville) (50)	919 642-5700	Samuel G Koonce	Roy L Lowe	Ida Long Smith	Gayle B Godwin	Roy L Lowe	Harold Lee Rains
Craven (New Bern) (82)	919 636-6600	Edward Armstrong	....	Gwendolyn Bryan	Richard Hemphill	Ray H Moser	Calton Bland
Cumberland (Fayetteville) (275)	919 678-7653	Thomas Bacote	C Strassenburg	Marsha Fogle	John Nalepa	Pat Jones	Morris Bedsole
Currituck (Currituck) (14)	919 232-2075	B U Evans	W S Richardson	Gwendolyn H Tatem	Daniel Scanlon	Barbara C Long	William N Newbern
Dare (Manteo) (23)	919 473-1101	Robert V Owens	Terry L Wheeler	Frances W Harris	J David Clawson	Shawn R Murphey	Albert L Austin
Davidson (Lexington) (127)	704 242-2000	Kenny L Moore	L Norman Shronce	Garry Frank	William Bryan Jr	Virginia Lou May	Jimmy E Johnson
Davie (Mocksville) (28)	704 634-5513	Carl Boon	Kenneth Windley	Brenda Hunter	James Stockert	Kenneth Windley	Bill Wooten
Duplin (Kenansville) (40)	919 296-1200	T Elwood Revelle	Ralph Cottle	Ralph Cottle	Russell Tucker	Ralph Cottle	George E Garner
Durham (Durham) (182)	919 560-7900	William V Bell	George H Williams	Garry E Umstead	Linwood C Jones	Jackye Knight	Albert L Hight
Edgecombe (Tarboro) (57)	919 641-7832	(not reporting)					
Forsyth (Winston-Salem) (266)	919 727-2851	Wayne G Willard	Graham Pervier	Jane F Cole	Paul L Fulton Jr	Dwight D Defee	Ronald N Barker
Franklin (Louisburg) (36)	919 496-5994	James G Hardy	David P Hodgkins	Jean P Gordon	Michael C Sumner	David P Hodgkins	Robert G Redmond
Gaston (Gastonia) (175)	704 866-3100	Porter L McAteer	Philip L Hinely	Martha M Jordan	Ronald L Courtney	Elean W McCarley	....
Gates (Gatesville) (9)	919 357-1240	(not reporting)					
Graham (Robbinsville) (7)	704 479-3361	William H Jenkins	Pat S Irons	Janet C Lequire	Sharon F Crisp	....	Melvin E Howell
Granville (Oxford) (38)	999 693-5240	Robert E Strother	Harold J Blizzard	Bobbie R Wilson	Phyllis R Vick	Harold J Blizzard	Marion Grissom
Greene (Snow Hill) (15)	919 747-3446	(not reporting)					
Guilford (Greensboro) (347)	919 373-3383	Wallace Harrelson	John W Shore	Norma H Bodsford	Brenda L Jones	Iris W Roberson	Walter A Burch Jr
Halifax (Halifax) (56)	919 583-1131	(not reporting)					
Harnett (Lillington) (68)	919 893-7555	H L Sorrell Jr	Neil Emory	Vanessa W Young	Vanessa W Young	....	Lewis Rosser Jr
Haywood (Waynesville) (47)	704 452-6625	Edwin Russell	C Jack Horton	Gwen Chambers	Nancy A Brooks	C Jack Horton	Tom Alexander
Henderson (Hendersonville) (69)	704 697-4747	Vollie G Good	David F Thompson	Elizabeth W Corn	Peter Molleur	Mona W Quinn	Albert Jackson
Hertford (Winton) (23)	919 358-7805	Vernice B Howard	Donald C Craft	Patricia M Weaver	Robbin Stephenson	Patricia M Weaver	Winfred Hardy Jr
Hoke (Raeford) (23)	919 875-8751	L E McLaughlin	Michael Wood	Oleta K Lopez	Chrales A Davis	Michael Wood	Wayne Byrd
Hyde (Swanquarter) (5)	919 926-5711	Troy L Mayo	Cliff Swindell	Linda M Basnight	Emily C Thomas	Cliff Swindell	David Mason
Iredell (Statesville) (93)	704 878-3056	Sara Haire	Joel Mashburn	Alice Fortner	Susan Blumenstein	Carolyn Harris	Clyde Lloyd
Jackson (Sylva) (27)	704 586-4055	T Wayne Hooper	....	Darlene T Fox	Darlene T Fox	T Wayne Hooper	Robert L Allen
Johnston (Smithfield) (81)	919 989-5100	....	Richard B Self	Joyce H Ennis	John R Massey	Jan M Whitley	Freddy Narron
Jones (Trenton) (9)	919 448-7571	Nolan B Jones	Larry P Meadows	Cora Davenport	Judy Smith	Larry P Meadows	Ralph W Mallard
Lee (Sanford) (41)	919 774-8403	William Stafford	William K Cowan	Gaynell M Beal	....	Patsy E Rogers	William A Bryant
Lenoir (Kinston) (57)	919 527-6231	George Graham	Bob Snapp	Pamela McLawhorn	Nola Tyndall	....	William Smith
Lincoln (Lincolnton) (50)	704 732-9000	C Harry Huss	Richard L French	H Lineberger	J Leon Harmon	Jackie L Moore	Joe L Kiser
Macon (Franklin) (23)	704 524-6421	Cecil Poindexter	Richard Honeycutt	Richard Honeycutt	Evelyn Southard	....	Homer Holbrook
Madison (Marshall) (17)	704 649-2521	James T Ledford	....	Larry B Leake	Michael K Worley	....	James D Brown
Martin (Williamston) (25)	919 792-1901	William H Manson	Donnie H Pittman	Ramon T Revilla	Danette B Carter	....	George W Ayers
Mc Dowell (Marion) (36)	704 652-7121	Jack A Wood	Charles Abernathy	Carrie Padgett	Alison Morgan	Lesa Gragg	Bob R Haynes
Mecklenburg (Charlotte) (511)	704 336-2931	H Parks Helms	Gerald G Fox	Janice Paige	J Harry Weatherly	Susan B Hutchins	C W Kidd
Mitchell (Bakersville) (14)	704 688-2139	(not reporting)					
Montgomery (Troy) (23)	919 576-4221	D T Scarborough	Gary S McCaskill	Sally Morris	Janice G Shaw	Gary S McCaskill	Waynn Wooten
Moore (Carthage) (59)	919 947-6362	David M Harris	W David McNeill	Allison Dandar	Michael Griffin	Linda Clark	James Wise
Nash (Nashville) (77)	919 459-4141	Claude Mayo	J Wayne Deal	Wayne Moore	Daphne Daughtry	Wayne Moore	Frank Brown
New Hanover (Wilmington) (120)	919 341-7178	Robert G Greer	M Allen O' Neal	Lucie F Harrell	Andrew J Atkinson	Andre R Mallette	Joseph McQueen
Northampton (Jackson) (21)	919 534-2501	Jasper Eley	W E Daniels	Rose R Sumner	W E Daniels	W E Daniels	John Wood
Onslow (Jacksonville) (150)	919 347-4717	Larry Fitzpatrick	Rick G Leary	Pamela Bunch	Alvin W Barrett	Sara H Straughan	Edward E Brown
Orange (Hillsborough) (94)	919 732-8181	Moses Carey	John Link	Beverly Blythe	Ken Chavious	Elaine Holmes	Lindy Pendegrass
Pamlico (Bayboro) (11)	919 745-3133	Johnnie Tripp	William R Rice	William R Rice	William R Rice	William B Rice	Daniel A Miller
Pasquotank (Elizabeth City) (31)	919 335-0865	W C Witherspoon	Randy Keaton	Karen Jennings	Hilda Ward	....	Davis Sawyer
Pender (Burgaw) (29)	919 259-1200	John K Swann	John A Bauer	John A Bauer	Barbara McClure	John A Bauer	Michael H Harvell
Perquimans (Hertford) (10)	919 426-8484	Leo A Higgins	N Paul Gregory	Sharon S Ward	N Paul Gregory	N Paul Gregory	Joseph L Lothian
Person (Roxboro) (30)	919 597-5120	H G Stonbraker	Barry J Reed	Faye T Fuller	Andrew Davenport	Barry J Reed	Dennis Oakley
Pitt (Greenville) (108)	919 830-6317	F Moore	T B Robinson	S J Banks	M M Roberts	V J Stanley	B L Vandiford
Polk (Columbus) (14)	704 894-3301	Benny Smith	Wm Lane Bailey	Wm Lane Bailey	Wm Lane Bailey	Wm Lane Bailey	Boyce Carswell

Directory 1/10   **OFFICIALS IN U.S. COUNTIES**
continued

County, county seat, 1990 population figures (000 omitted)	County telephone number	Board chairman	Appointed administrator	Clerk to the governing board	Chief financial officer	Personnel director	Chief law enforcement official
NORTH CAROLINA (100) continued							
Randolph (Asheboro) (107)	919 629-2131	(not reporting)					
Richmond (Rockingham) (45) ...	919 997-8200	(not reporting)					
Robeson (Lumberton) (105)	919 671-3022	Bobby D Locklear	James E Martin	Linda A Hedgpath	Leo Hunt	Cynthia G Neloms	Hubert Stone
Rockingham (Reidsville) (86) ...	919 342-8101	James A Collins	Jerry D Myers	Pamela M Robertso	Michael W Apple	Ben L Neal	Clinton D Vernon
Rowan (Salisbury) (111)	704 636-1658	J Newton Cohen Sr	Baron T Russell	. . . .	Brady R Frick	Keen E Deal	Robert G Martin
Rutherford (Rutherfordton) (57) .	704 287-6045	Franklin Goode	John Condrey	Hazel Haynes	Stella Womack	Joe L Swing	Daniel J Good
Sampson (Clinton) (47)	919 592-6308	Kermit Williamson	Jerry Hobbs	. . . .	Sylvia Robichaud		O L McUllen
Scotland (Laurinburg) (34)	919 277-2406	J D Willis Jr	Jack DiSarno	Annie J Kohnen	Charles Williams	Susan Butler	Wayne Bryant
Stanly (Albemarle) (52)	704 982-7200	W Dwight Smith	Gary L Page	Joyce M Mauldin	Steven M Walters	Gary L Page	Joseph E Lowder
Stokes (Danbury) (37)	919 593-2811	Robert Robertson	W Craig Greer	W Craig Greer	Julia E Edwards	. . . .	. . . .
Surry (Dobson) (62)	919 386-9201	(not reporting)					
Swain (Bryson City) (11)	704 488-9273	(not reporting)					
Transylvania (Brevard) (26)	704 884-3100	John Smart	Arthur C Wilson	Sandra Jamison	Archie Cal Cooper	Sheila Cozart	Milton Whitmire
Tyrrell (Columbia) (4)	919 796-1371	(not reporting)					
Union (Monroe) (84)	704 283-3810	Leroy Pittman	John C Munn	Barbara W Moore	H Michael Wilson	. . . .	Frank McGuirt
Vance (Henderson) (39)	919 492-2141	J Timothy Pegram	Jerry L Ayscue	Sandra Catherwood	Jerry L Tucker	Jerry L Ayscue	R T Breedlove
Wake (Raleigh) (423)	919 856-6090	(not reporting)					
Warren (Warrenton) (17)	919 257-3115	Lucious Hawkins		Loria D Williams	Susan W Brown	. . . .	Theodore Williams
Washington (Plymouth) (14)	919 793-5823	Andy Allen	Lee Smith	Lois C Askew	Gayle T Critcher	Lee Smith	Jim Whitehurst
Watauga (Boone) (37)	704 264-1300	(not reporting)					
Wayne (Goldsboro) (105)	919 731-1435	(not reporting)					
Wilkes (Wilkesboro) (59)	919 651-7300	John A Garwood	Cecil E Wood	Alene E Faw	Edward Bowers	. . . .	Dane Mastin
Wilson (Wilson) (66)	919 237-6600	(not reporting)					
Yadkin (Yadkinville) (30)	919 679-4200	Michael D Crouse	Jimmy M Varner	Jimmy M Varner	Geraldine V Nance	. . . .	Jackie Henderson
Yancey (Burnsville) (15)	704 682-3971	Keith Presnell	Earl N Tipton	Earl N Tipton	Jean Buchanan	Robin York	Kermit Banks
NORTH DAKOTA (53)							
Adams (Hettinger) (3)	701 567-4363	(not reporting)					
Barnes (Valley City) (13)	701 845-0881	(not reporting)					
Benson (Minnewaukan) (7)	701 473-5340	(not reporting)					
Billings (Medora) (1)	701 623-4491	(not reporting)					
Bottineau (Bottineau) (8)	701 228-2225	(not reporting)					
Bowman (Bowman) (4)	701 523-5421	(not reporting)					
Burke (Bowbells) (3)	701 377-2861	LaVern Chrest	. . . .	Ranae Ehlke	Hazel Herman	. . . .	Fred Marquardt
Burleigh (Bismarck) (60)	701 222-6718	(not reporting)					
Cass (Fargo) (103)	701 241-5720	(not reporting)					
Cavalier (Langdon) (6)	701 256-2229	Neil H Romfo	. . . .	Jerome P Dosmann	Jerome P Dosmann	. . . .	David J Zeis
Dickey (Ellendale) (6)	701 349-3249	Gene Young	. . . .	Lawrence Hoffman	. . . .	Hoffman	Jim Bohannon
Divide (Crosby) (3)	701 965-6351	(not reporting)					
Dunn (Manning) (4)	701 573-4448	Orris M Bang	. . . .	Reinhard Hauck	Reinhard Hauck	. . . .	Larry Boepple
Eddy (New Rockford) (3)	701 947-2434	Dick Turcotte	. . . .	Wanda Lee Kurtz	. . . .	Wanda Lee Kurtz	Lawrence Schagunn
Emmons (Linton) (5)	701 254-4807	(not reporting)					
Foster (Carrington) (4)	701 652-2441	John Murphy	. . . .	Shearn Hirsch	Dorothy Peterson	. . . .	John Statema
Golden Valley (Beach) (2)	701 872-3243	George Hildebrant	. . . .	Cecilia Stedman	Cecilia Stedman	. . . .	Larry Fischer
Grand Forks (Grand Forks) (71) .	701 780-8200	(not reporting)					
Grant (Carson) (4)	701 622-3275	Dawson Wendal	. . . .	E H Schatz	E H Schatz	. . . .	Darwin D Roth
Griggs (Cooperstown) (3)	701 797-3117	Edward Urness	. . . .	Walter F Kerbaugh	. . . .	. . . .	Paul Hendrickson
Hettinger (Mott) (3)	701 824-2515	Patrick Candrian	. . . .	Roy J Steiner	. . . .	. . . .	Robert D Norton
Kidder (Steele) (3)	701 475-2632	(not reporting)					
La Moure (La Moure) (5)	701 883-5301	Orville Ogren	. . . .	Michial Johnson	Michial Johnson	. . . .	Robert Marke
Logan (Napoleon) (3)	701 754-2425	(not reporting)					
Mc Henry (Towner) (7)	701 537-5724	Paul Swedlund	Renae Linstrom	Renae Linstrom	. . . .	. . . .	Rod Finck
Mc Intosh (Ashley) (4)	701 288-3347	Edgar R Jast	. . . .	LuElla Blumhardt	LuElla Blumhardt	. . . .	Milton O Wiest
Mc Kenzie (Watford City) (6)	701 842-3616	Morris Cross	. . . .	. . . .	Frances Olson	. . . .	Paul Larson
Mc Lean (Washburn) (10)	701 462-8541	(not reporting)					
Mercer (Stanton) (10)	701 745-3292	Robert E Albers	. . . .	Leora R Retterath	Leora R Retterath	. . . .	Ronald Kessler
Morton (Mandan) (24)	701 667-3300	. . . .	. . . .	Paul E Trauger	Paul E Trauger	Paul E Trauger	Leo Snider
Mountrail (Stanley) (7)	701 628-2145	Kenneth Lystad	. . . .	Karen Eliason	Karen Eliason	Karen Eliason	Kenneth Halvorson
Nelson (Lakota) (4)	701 247-2463	Noel Lofthus	. . . .	W J Davidson	W J Davidson	. . . .	Arthur Varty
Oliver (Center) (2)	701 794-8777	Donald Albers	. . . .	Leland Ogden	Leland Ogden	. . . .	Gordon Albers
Pembina (Cavalier) (9)	701 265-4231	(not reporting)					
Pierce (Rugby) (5)	701 776-6161	(not reporting)					
Ramsey (Devils Lake) (13)	701 662-7007	Gary Krantz	. . . .	Byrdia Spidahl	Byrdia Spidahl	. . . .	Perry Horner
Ransom (Lisbon) (6)	701 683-5823	Judy Tanger	. . . .	. . . .	. . . .	. . . .	Conrad Steinhaus
Renville (Mohall) (3)	701 756-6301	Charles Routledge	. . . .	Susan A Ritter	. . . .	. . . .	Robert F Thomas
Richland (Wahpeton) (18)	701 642-7700	Beverly Stone	. . . .	Marilyn Nisja	Marilyn Nisja	. . . .	Harlan Muehler
Rolette (Rolla) (13)	701 477-3816	(not reporting)					
Sargent (Forman) (5)	701 724-6241	(not reporting)					
Sheridan (Mc Clusky) (2)	701 363-2205	Armin Erdmann	. . . .	Shirley A Murray	Shirley A Murray	. . . .	Arlen Schatz
Sioux (Fort Yates) (4)	701 854-3481	(not reporting)					
Slope (Amidon) (1)	701 879-6276	Ralph Urlacher	. . . .	. . . .	Robert Strommen	. . . .	Pat Lorge
Stark (Dickinson) (23)	701 264-7630	(not reporting)					
Steele (Finley) (2)	701 524-2110	Dale Gulson	Ruth Gullicks	Ruth Gullicks	Ruth Gullicks	. . . .	Gilman Johnson
Stutsman (Jamestown) (22)	701 252-9035	Harold Herseth	. . . .	Lary J Olson	Lary J Olson	. . . .	David F Orr
Towner (Cando) (4)	701 968-4340	Darwin Baerwald	. . . .	Verna M Martz	. . . .	. . . .	Howard Soderberg
Traill (Hillsboro) (9)	701 436-4458	Larry Linneman	. . . .	Joanne Haugen	Joanne Haugen	. . . .	Merle Haisley
Walsh (Grafton) (14)	701 352-2851	(not reporting)					
Ward (Minot) (58)	701 857-6499	(not reporting)					
Wells (Fessenden) (6)	701 547-3521	(not reporting)					
Williams (Williston) (21)	701 572-1700	Don Arnson	. . . .	Marie Guderjohn	. . . .	. . . .	Stan Lyson
OHIO (88)							
Adams (West Union) (25)	513 544-3286	Paul W Rothwell	. . . .	Linda Mendenhall	Carroll E Newman	. . . .	Robert Johnston
Allen (Lima) (110)	419 228-3700	Alberta M Lee	Fred D Eldridge	Kelli A Singhaus	H Dean French	. . . .	Daniel Beck
Ashland (Ashland) (48)	419 289-0000	Robert Valentine	. . . .	Susan Norris	Stanley E Ryland	. . . .	Larry Overholt
Ashtabula (Jefferson) (100)	216 576-9090	Duane Feher	Brian Condron	Julie Chelciu	Daniel Ross	. . . .	William Johnson
Athens (Athens) (60)	614 592-3219	(not reporting)					
Auglaize (Wapakoneta) (45)	419 738-3612	(not reporting)					
Belmont (St. Clairsville) (71)	614 695-2121	Jim Hepe		P Bittengle	Joseph A Pappano		Thomas C McCort
Brown (Georgetown) (35)	513 378-3956	(not reporting)					
Butler (Hamilton) (291)	513 887-3247	(not reporting)					
Carroll (Carrollton) (27)	216 627-4869	William Martin	. . . .	Dorothy Peterson	E Leroy Van Horne	. . . .	Wm Offenberger
Champaign (Urbana) (36)	513 653-2701	Daniel Rooney	. . . .	Carolyn Poe	Bonnie M Warman	. . . .	Paul D Williams

OFFICIALS IN U.S. COUNTIES

County, county seat, 1990 population figures (000 omitted)	County telephone number	Board chairman	Appointed administrator	Clerk to the governing board	Chief financial officer	Personnel director	Chief law enforcement official
OHIO (88) continued							
Clark (Springfield) (148)	513 328-2400	Gordon R Flax	W Darrell Howard	Rochelle White	George Sodders	J Kevin Sellards	Gene A Kelly
Clermont (Batavia) (150)	513 732-7300	Martha Dorsey	Steve Wharton	Judith Kocica	Gary Vogelgsang	Kathleen Gilliam	John Vancamp
Clinton (Wilmington) (35)	513 382-2250	(not reporting)					
Columbiana (Lisbon) (108)	216 424-9511	(not reporting)					
Coshocton (Coshocton) (35)	614 622-1753	Harold F Turner		M Jean Clark	Richard Tompkins	. . . .	David Corbett
Crawford (Bucyrus) (48)	419 562-5876	(not reporting)					
Cuyahoga (Cleveland) (1412) . . .	216 443-7190	(not reporting)					
Darke (Greenville) (54)	513 548-2035	(not reporting)					
Defiance (Defiance) (39)	419 782-4761	(not reporting)					
Delaware (Delaware) (67)	614 368-1820	(not reporting)					
Erie (Sandusky) (77)	419 627-7682	William P Scheid	Michael J Bixler	Carolyn S Spayd	James W McKeen	Wayne T Taylor	John E Magnuson
Fairfield (Lancaster) (103)	614 687-7190	Lisa M Kessler	. . . .	Mary K Webb	Jon Slater	. . . .	Gary Demastry
Fayette (Washington Ct Hse) (27) . .	614 335-0720	(not reporting)					
Franklin (Columbus) (961)	614 462-3322	(not reporting)					
Fulton (Wauseon) (38)	419 337-9255	Lowell F Rupp	. . . .	Mary Behnfeldt	. . . .	. . . .	Darrell Merillat
				Joan Davis	Ronald K Canaday		James Taylor
Gallia (Gallipolis) (31)	614 446-4612	. . . .	. . . .	B McGunnigle	Richard Makowski	Stephen R Popp	George Simmons
Geauga (Chardon) (81)	216 285-2222	Neil C Hofstetter	John B Murray	Judy K Cremeans	Luwanna Delaney	M Jordan Smart	Jerry W Erwin
Greene (Xenia) (137)	513 376-5002	W Reed Madden	Ralph C Harper				
Guernsey (Cambridge) (39)	614 432-9200						
Hamilton (Cincinnati) (866)	513 632-8841	John Dowlin	David Krings	C Spencer Barkley	Dusty Rhodes	James Gibson Jr	Simon Leis Jr
Hancock (Findlay) (66)	419 424-7044	(not reporting)					
Hardin (Kenton) (31)	419 674-2205	(not reporting)					
Harrison (Cadiz) (16)	614 942-8861	Ken Mallernee	. . . .	Cynthia Heisler	Patrick Moore	. . . .	Richard Rensi
Henry (Napoleon) (29)	419 592-4876	(not reporting)					
Highland (Hillsboro) (36)	513 393-1911	Rich Graves	. . . .	Doris Edgington	Bill Fawley	. . . .	Tom Horst
							James P Jones
Hocking (Logan) (26)	614 385-5195	. . . .	. . . .	. . . .	. . . .	. . . .	Tim Zimmerly
Holmes (Millersburg) (33)	216 674-0286	Thomas White	. . . .	. . . .	Richard A Graven		Dick Sutherland
Huron (Norwalk) (56)	419 668-3092	Thomas Kilbane	. . . .	Ann Winters	John Elmlinger		
Jackson (Jackson) (30)	614 286-3301	(not reporting)					
Jefferson (Steubenville) (80)	614 283-4111	(not reporting)					
Knox (Mount Vernon) (47)	614 393-6703	Richard K Mavis	. . . .	Joan Dailey	Robert L Jones	. . . .	David Barber
Lake (Painesville) (215)	216 357-2745	Mildred Teuscher	Ken R Gauntner Jr	Philip Dolan	Dale O Langbehn	. . . .	Daniel Dunlap
Lawrence (Ironton) (62)	614 533-4300	(not reporting)					
Licking (Newark) (128)	614 349-6066	Phil Shipley	. . . .	Glen K Porter	George D Buchanan	. . . .	Gerry Billy
Logan (Bellefontaine) (42)	513 599-7283	(not reporting)					
Lorain (Elyria) (271)	216 329-5000	Elizabeth Blair	Virgil J Muntean	Roxann Blair	Daniel J Talarek	. . . .	Martin J Mahony
Lucas (Toledo) (462)	419 245-4500	Sandy Isenberg	Edward J Ciecka	Herbert O Hoehing	Larry Kaczala	Barbara J Walker	James Telb
Madison (London) (37)	614 852-2972	(not reporting)					
Mahoning (Youngstown) (265) . .	216 740-2130	(not reporting)					
Marion (Marion) (64)	614 387-5871	John Watkins	. . . .	Gloria Dickason	Michele Pearson	Tina Carper	John Butterworth
Medina (Medina) (122)	216 723-3641	(not reporting)					
Meigs (Pomeroy) (23)	614 992-2895	(not reporting)					
Mercer (Celina) (39)	419 586-3178	Ronald Puthoff	. . . .	Joan Bollenbacher	R Schwieterman	. . . .	Carl Eichlar
Miami (Troy) (93)	513 332-6800	(not reporting)					
Monroe (Woodsfield) (15)	614 472-0873	(not reporting)					
Montgomery (Dayton) (574)	513 225-4690	Donna Moon	Donald Vermillion	Juanita Hunn	Bertha Henry	Leon Walker	. . . .
Morgan (Mc Connelsville) (14) . .	614 962-4752	(not reporting)					
Morrow (Mount Gilead) (28)	419 947-4085	(not reporting)					
Muskingum (Zanesville) (82)	614 455-7100	Charles Elson	. . . .	Rebecca Cooper	Norma Bowman	. . . .	Bernard Gibson
Noble (Caldwell) (11)	614 732-2969	(not reporting)					
Ottawa (Port Clinton) (40)	419 734-6700	Steven Arndt	Jere Witt	Barbara Hermes	James Snider	John Mahr	Craig Emahiser
Paulding (Paulding) (20)	419 399-3786	(not reporting)					
Perry (New Lexington) (32)	614 342-2045	William Crane	. . . .	Judith Snider	Joann N Hankinson	. . . .	William R Barker
Pickaway (Circleville) (48)	614 474-6093	Harley Evans	Carol L Brown	Carol L Brown	Beverly Crawford	. . . .	Dwight Radcliff
Pike (Waverly) (24)	614 947-4817	(not reporting)					
Portage (Ravenna) (143)	216 296-6466	(not reporting)					
Preble (Eaton) (40)	513 456-8143	(not reporting)					
Putnam (Ottawa) (34)	419 523-3656	(not reporting)					
Richland (Mansfield) (126)	419 755-5500	(not reporting)					
Ross (Chillicothe) (69)	614 773-5115	James M Caldwell	James L Kennard	Letitia S Dobbins	. . . .	Sherry Hamman	William Knott
Sandusky (Fremont) (62)	419 332-6411	(not reporting)					
Scioto (Portsmouth) (80)	614 355-8313	Vernal G Riffe	. . . .	Inez Bloomfield	Dorothy K Deemer	. . . .	James Sutterfield
Seneca (Tiffin) (60)	419 447-4550	Timothy Rook	. . . .	Sandra K Phipps	Rick Smith		Larry Stephens
Shelby (Sidney) (45)	513 498-7226	(not reporting)					
Stark (Canton) (368)	216 438-0371	(not reporting)					
Summit (Akron) (515)	216 379-2500	Tim Davis	William Hartung	Peggy A Spraggins	John A Donofrio	Nancy L Wilson	David W Troutman
Trumbull (Warren) (228)	216 841-0400	(not reporting)					
Tuscarawas (New Philadelphia) (84)	216 364-8811	(not reporting)					
Union (Marysville) (32)	513 642-4601	(not reporting)					
Van Wert (Van Wert) (30)	419 238-1022	(not reporting)					
Vinton (Mc Arthur) (11)	614 596-4571	Jerry M Fee	. . . .	Barbara Radekin	Barbara Radekin	. . . .	Donald Peters
Warren (Lebanon) (114)	513 933-1250	C Michael Kilburn	Robert Price	Tina Davis	Nick Nelson	Sandra Stevens	Tom Ariss
Washington (Marietta) (62)	614 373-6623	(not reporting)					
Wayne (Wooster) (101)	216 263-1111	(not reporting)					
Williams (Bryan) (37)	419 636-2059	(not reporting)					
Wood (Bowling Green) (113) . . .	419 354-9000	Marilyn R Baker	Linda M Amos	Kristy Muir	Harold Bateson	Linda M Amos	John Kohl
Wyandot (Upper Sandusky) (22)	419 294-3836	Carl E Turnbell	. . . .	M Sue Shrider	Jeffrey McClain	. . . .	Michael R Hetzel
OKLAHOMA (77)							
Adair (Stillwell) (18)	918 696-7198	(not reporting)					
Alfalfa (Cherokee) (6)	405 596-2392	(not reporting)					
Atoka (Atoka) (13)	405 889-2643	(not reporting)					
Beaver (Beaver) (6)	405 625-3151	(not reporting)					
Beckham (Sayre) (19)	405 928-2457	Purcy D Walker	. . . .	Elena Roper	. . . .	. . . .	Terry Poff
Blaine (Watonga) (11)	405 623-5890	George Bisel	. . . .	Sharon R Gates	Carol L Foley		Delmar L Scoville
Bryan (Durant) (32)	405 924-2202	(not reporting)					
Caddo (Anadarko) (30)	405 247-6609	(not reporting)					
Canadian (El Reno) (74)	405 262-1070	(not reporting)					
Carter (Ardmore) (43)	405 223-8414	(not reporting)					
Cherokee (Tahlequah) (34)	918 456-3171	(not reporting)					
Choctaw (Hugo) (15)	405 326-5331	Gene Honeycutt	. . . .	Emily Van Worth	. . . .	. . . .	J W Trapp
Cimarron (Boise City) (3)	405 544-2251	John W Twyman	. . . .	Dwilene Holbert	. . . .	. . . .	Ken C Miller

Directory 1/10 **OFFICIALS IN U.S. COUNTIES**
continued

County, county seat, 1990 population figures (000 omitted)	County telephone number	Board chairman	Appointed administrator	Clerk to the governing board	Chief financial officer	Personnel director	Chief law enforcement official
OKLAHOMA (77) continued							
Cleveland (Norman) (174)	405 366-0200	....	....	Pat Dodson	....	Dorinda Harvey	Dewayne Beggs
Coal (Coalgate) (6)	405 927-3122	(not reporting)					
Comanche (Lawton) (111)	405 353-3717	Frank Walker	....	Charley Maguire	....	....	Kenny Stradley
Cotton (Walters) (7)	405 875-3026	(not reporting)					
Craig (Vinita) (14)	918 256-3564	(not reporting)					
Creek (Sapulpa) (61)	918 224-4084	(not reporting)					
Custer (Arapaho) (27)	405 323-4420	(not reporting)					
Delaware (Jay) (28)	918 253-4432	(not reporting)					
Dewey (Taloga) (6)	405 328-5361	W C Baker	....	Patricia Riley	Cindy Farris	....	Ivan Evans
Ellis (Arnett) (4)	405 885-7301	(not reporting)					
Garfield (Enid) (57)	405 237-0225	(not reporting)					
Garvin (Pauls Valley) (27)	405 238-2772	(not reporting)					
Grady (Chickasha) (42)	405 224-7388	Doyle A Pendley	....	Betty Ballard	....		Ronald J Taylor
Grant (Medford) (6)	405 395-2214	(not reporting)					
Greer (Mangum) (7)	405 782-3664	(not reporting)					
Harmon (Hollis) (4)	405 688-3658	(not reporting)					
Harper (Buffalo) (4)	405 735-2870	(not reporting)					
Haskell (Stigler) (11)	918 967-2107	(not reporting)					
Hughes (Holdenville) (13)	405 379-2746	(not reporting)					
Jackson (Altus) (29)	405 482-4420	Ricky Crouch	....	Bobbie Reynolds	....	....	Jerry Schuster
Jefferson (Waurika) (7)	405 228-2029	Kenny Wall	....	Doris Pilgreen			Don Allen
Johnston (Tishomingo) (10)	405 371-3184	(not reporting)					
Kay (Newkirk) (48)	405 362-2537	(not reporting)					
Kingfisher (Kingfisher) (13)	405 375-3887	Henry Senn	....	Jane Hightower	....	....	Danny Graham
Kiowa (Hobart) (11)	405 726-3377	Wayne Barker	....	Geanea Watson	Deanna Beamon	Geanea Watson	Tommy Denton
Latimer (Wilburton) (10)	918 465-3543	(not reporting)					
Le Flore (Poteau) (43)	918 647-2527	(not reporting)					
Lincoln (Chandler) (29)	405 258-1264	Riley Miller Jr	....	Sharon K Turk	Don E Sporleder	....	A T Brixey Jr
Logan (Guthrie) (29)	405 282-2124	(not reporting)					
Love (Marietta) (8)	405 276-3059	Clifford Harris	....	Dora Jackson	Langdon Spivey	....	Wessley Liddell
Major (Fairview) (8)	405 227-4732	Skip Wood	....	Janie Cravens	Harry Martens	....	John C Davis
Marshall (Madill) (11)	405 795-3165	(not reporting)					
Mayes (Pryor) (33)	918 825-0639	(not reporting)					
Mc Clain (Purcell) (23)	405 527-3117	Wayne Chapman	....	Phyllis Bennett	....	....	Dwayne Anderson
Mc Curtain (Idabel) (33)	405 286-2370	(not reporting)					
Mc Intosh (Eufaula) (17)	918 689-2741	(not reporting)					
Murray (Sulphur) (12)	405 622-3920	(not reporting)					
Muskogee (Muskogee) (68)	918 682-9601	(not reporting)					
Noble (Perry) (11)	405 336-2141	(not reporting)					
Nowata (Nowata) (10)	918 273-2480	Phillip W Moore	....	Teresa Jackson	Helen Jo Baldwin	....	Lewis R Arnold
Okfuskee (Okemah) (12)	918 623-0939	(not reporting)					
Oklahoma (Oklahoma City) (600)	405 278-1500	(not reporting)					
Okmulgee (Okmulgee) (36)	918 756-0788	(not reporting)					
Osage (Pawhuska) (42)	918 287-2615	(not reporting)					
Ottawa (Miami) (31)	918 542-3332	James E Leake	....	Carol J Randall	Brenda Conner	....	James Ed Walker
Pawnee (Pawnee) (16)	918 762-3741	(not reporting)					
Payne (Stillwater) (62)	405 624-9300	Bernice Mitchell	....	Sherri Schieffer	Bonita Stadler	....	Carl Hiner
Pittsburg (Mc Alester) (41)	918 423-6865	Oben Weeks	....	Debbie Lenox	....	....	Don Hass
Pontotoc (Ada) (34)	405 332-1425	(not reporting)					
Pottawatomie (Shawnee) (59)	405 273-4305	(not reporting)					
Pushmataha (Antlers) (11)	405 298-2512	(not reporting)					
Roger Mills (Cheyenne) (4)	405 497-3365	(not reporting)					
Rogers (Claremore) (55)	918 341-2518	(not reporting)					
Seminole (Wewoka) (25)	405 257-2450	(not reporting)					
Sequoyah (Sallisaw) (33)	918 775-5539	Hoyet Philpot	....	Donna Jamison	Jerry Trotter		Teddy Eubanks
Stephens (Duncan) (42)	405 255-8460	(not reporting)					
Texas (Guymon) (16)	405 338-3233	Ray Depuy	....	Linda Bowman	Anne Scott	....	Arnold Peoples
Tillman (Frederick) (10)	405 335-3421	Johnnie Carpenter	....	Delores Haynie	....	....	Billy Hanes
Tulsa (Tulsa) (503)	918 596-5000	....	....	....	....	Terry Tallent	Stanley Glanz
Wagoner (Wagoner) (48)	918 485-2216	(not reporting)					
Washington (Bartlesville) (48)	918 336-0330	(not reporting)					
Washita (Cordell) (11)	405 832-2284	(not reporting)					
Woods (Alva) (9)	405 327-0998	(not reporting)					
Woodward (Woodward) (19)	405 256-8097	(not reporting)					
OREGON (36)							
Baker (Baker) (15)	503 523-8200	Steve M Bogart	....	Julia Woods	Peggy L Vernholm	Sherry L Jurd	Terry Speelman
Benton (Corvallis) (71)	503 757-6802	John Dilworth	Neil Richardson	....	Clark Ruggles	Frank Dieu	David Coor
Clackamas (Oregon City) (279)	503 655-8011	Darlene Hooley	Mike Swanson	Penny Morrison	Nancy McClain	Mike Webby	Riz Bradshaw
Clatsop (Astoria) (33)	503 325-1000	Eric Olsen	William Barrons	Lori Davidson	Keith Moes	....	John Raichl
Columbia (St. Helens) (38)	503 397-3796	Micheal Sykes	Jan Greenhalgh	Elizabeth Huser	Gerilyn Johnson	....	Bruce Oester
Coos (Coquille) (60)	503 396-3121	Gordon Ross	....	Mary Ann Wilson	Mary Barton	Janis Silveus	Michael Cook
Crook (Prineville) (14)	503 447-4160	Fred Rodgers	....	Della Harrison	Mary Johnson	....	Rodd Clark
Curry (Gold Beach) (19)	503 247-7011	Terry C Hanscam	....	Renee Kolen	Kathy Bell	Kathy Bell	Charles Denney
Deschutes (Bend) (75)	503 388-6570	(not reporting)					
Douglas (Roseburg) (95)	503 440-4405	Joyce Morgan	....	Debby Mendenhall	Tom Eckerd	Jim Bruce	John Dardon
Gilliam (Condon) (2)	503 384-2311	Laura Pryor	....	Rena Kennedy	....	....	Paul Barnett
Grant (Canyon City) (8)	503 575-0059	(not reporting)					
Harney (Burns) (7)	503 573-6356	Dale White	....	Dolores Swisher	....	LaDene Hurd	Dave Glerup
Hood River (Hood River) (17)	503 386-3970	Jerry Routson	James F Azumano	Donna Layman	Dan Chamness	James F Azumano	Joe Wampler
Jackson (Medford) (146)	503 776-7248	(not reporting)					
Jefferson (Madras) (14)	503 475-2449	Daniel J Ahern	....	Elaine Henderson	Bonnie Namenuk	....	Mike Throop
Josephine (Grants Pass) (63)	503 474-5100	Fred Borngasser	....	Harlene Darkins	V Alan Hudson	David Dickman	Daniel Calvert
Klamath (Klamath Falls) (58)	503 883-4296	Edwin Kentner	....	Evelyn Biehn	Michael Long	Dennis Engelhard	Carl Burkhart
Lake (Lakeview) (7)	503 947-6004	Robert M Pardue	Ray Simms	Karen O'Connor	Theresa Molthan	Ray Simms	Charles Withers
Lane (Eugene) (283)	503 687-4171	(not reporting)					
Lincoln (Newport) (39)	503 265-6611	Nancy Leonard	....	Dana Jenkins	Glen Morris	Bob Huddleston	Larry Spencer
Linn (Albany) (91)	503 967-3825	Richard Stach	Ralph E Wyatt	S Druckenmiller	Shannon Willard	....	Art Martinak
Malheur (Vale) (26)	503 473-5183	Russell F Hursh	Nancy D Moore	Deborah DeLong	....	....	Ronald K Mallea
Marion (Salem) (228)	503 588-5212	Randall E Franke	Kenneth Roudybush	Alan H Davidson	Kenneth Roudybush	Randy G Curtis	Robert J Prinslow
Morrow (Heppner) (8)	503 676-9061	Louis Carlson	Andrea Denton	Barb Bloodsworth	Lisanne Currin	Andrea Denton	Roy Drago
Multnomah (Portland) (584)	503 248-3511	....	....	....	David Boyer	Curtis Smith	Robert Skipper
Polk (Dallas) (50)	503 623-8173	Ron Dodge	John K Anderson	....	Kenneth Gallaway	Andrew Nelson	R E Steele

Directory 1/10 **OFFICIALS IN U.S. COUNTIES**
continued

County, county seat, 1990 population figures (000 omitted)	County telephone number	Board chairman	Appointed administrator	Clerk to the governing board	Chief financial officer	Personnel director	Chief law enforcement official
OREGON (36) continued							
Sherman (Moro) (2)	503 565-3606	Mike McArthur	. . . .	Linda Cornie	Nancy McCoy	. . . .	Gerald Lohrey
Tillamook (Tillamook) (22)	503 842-3403	Ken Burdick	. . . .	Jo Veltri	Karen Richards	Darlene Cherry	Tom Dye
Umatilla (Pendleton) (59)	503 276-7111	Emile Holeman		Thomas Groat	Bruce Peet	Bob Small	James Carey
Union (La Grande) (24)	503 963-1001	John Howard	Marlene Perkins	. . . .		Marlene Perkins	Steve Oliver
Wallowa (Enterprise) (7)	503 426-4543	Arleigh G Isley	. . . .	Charlotte McIver	Ginger K Goebel	Marcia M Bird	Roger Decker
Wasco (The Dalles) (22)	503 296-2207	(not reporting)					
Washington (Hillsboro) (312)	503 648-8681	(not reporting)					
Wheeler (Fossil) (1)	503 763-2400	Lee Hoover		. . . .	Howard McGee	Howard McGee	Otho Caldera
Yamhill (Mc Minnville) (66)	503 472-9371	Debi Owens	John Krawczyk	. . . .	. . . .	Steven Mikami	Lionel Vasquez
PENNSYLVANIA (67)							
Adams (Gettysburg) (78)	717 334-6781	(not reporting)					
Allegheny (Pittsburgh) (1336)	412 355-5300	(not reporting)					
Armstrong (Kittanning) (73)	412 543-2500	(not reporting)					
Beaver (Beaver) (186)	412 728-5700	Robert C Reed	. . . .	Robert W Cyphert	Richard Towcimak	William P Greer	Frank Policaro Jr
Bedford (Bedford) (48)	814 623-4807	Dick M Rice	Tammy B Kendall	Tammy B Kendall	Barry A Crawford	Barry A Crawford	. . . .
Berks (Reading) (337)	215 378-8000	(not reporting)					
Blair (Hollidaysburg) (131)	814 695-5541	(not reporting)					
Bradford (Towanda) (61)	717 265-5700	(not reporting)					
Bucks (Doylestown) (541)	215 348-6000	(not reporting)					
Butler (Butler) (152)	412 285-4731	James A Green	. . . .	W O' Donnell	Arthur Shuker Jr	Eileen R McCue	Dennis Rickard
Cambria (Ebensburg) (163)	814 472-5440	(not reporting)					
Cameron (Emporium) (6)	814 486-2315	(not reporting)					
Carbon (Jim Thorpe) (57)	717 325-3611	Dean D W Delong	Mortimer Smedley	Marie A Midas	. . . .	Mary L Kelshaw	Peter P Hoherchak
Centre (Bellefonte) (124)	814 355-6700	Vicki L Wedler	Evan B Smith	. . . .	Donald Asendorf	Oliver Goodman	Dennis Nau
Chester (West Chester) (376)	215 344-6100	(not reporting)					
Clarion (Clarion) (42)	814 226-4000	David Black	. . . .	Donna Hartle	Nancy Murray	Peter Sysyn	Vern Smith
Clearfield (Clearfield) (78)	814 765-2641	(not reporting)					
Clinton (Lock Haven) (37)	717 893-4000	(not reporting)					
Columbia (Bloomsburg) (63)	717 389-5600	William Soberick	Gail Kipp	Gail Kipp	Gail Kipp	Janet Weeks	Harry Roadarmel
Crawford (Meadville) (86)	814 336-1151	Morris W Waid	William E Harry	William E Harry	Robyn Sye	William E Harry	Robert Stevens
Cumberland (Carlisle) (195)	717 240-6100	Earl Keller	Wm Dennis	Joanne Burkhart	Al Whitcomb	Dan Hartnett	Tom Kline
Dauphin (Harrisburg) (238)	717 255-2741	Russell Sheaffer	Jeffrey T Haste	Jeffrey T Haste	Charles E Henery	Jeffrey T Haste	Wm H Livingston
Delaware (Media) (548)	215 891-4000	Mary Ann Arty	Edwin B Erickson	Joyce A Lamont	Edwin B Erickson	Leonard J Maloney	Ann Osborne
Elk (Ridgway) (35)	814 776-1161	(not reporting)					
Erie (Erie) (276)	814 451-6000	Judith M Lynch	Barry T Drew	Florindo Fabrizio	Ronald Komorek	Frank N Scalise	Robert N Michael
Fayette (Uniontown) (145)	412 437-4525	Fred L Lebder	. . . .	Joseph P Korona	Harry J Fike	. . . .	Norma J Santore
Forest (Tionesta) (5)	811 755-3537	Samuel J Wagner	. . . .	Virginia M Call	Pamela Millin	. . . .	Harry E Tucker
Franklin (Chambersburg) (121)	717 264-4125	(not reporting)					
Fulton (Mc Connellsburg) (14)	717 485-4212	(not reporting)					
Greene (Waynesburg) (40)	412 852-1171	(not reporting)					
Huntingdon (Huntingdon) (44)	814 643-3091	(not reporting)					
Indiana (Indiana) (90)	412 465-3800	Thomas Coyne	Helen C Hill	Helen C Hill	. . . .	Margaret J Karp	Donald Beckwith
Jefferson (Brookville) (46)	814 849-8031	Lugene Inzana	. . . .	Julie Coleman	Paul Corbin	. . . .	Harry Dunkle
Juniata (Mifflintown) (21)	717 436-8991	(not reporting)					
Lackawanna (Scranton) (219)	717 963-6800	Ray Alberigi	Gerald Stanvitch	. . . .	Steve Barcoski	Anthony Bernardi	John Szymanski
Lancaster (Lancaster) (423)	717 299-8310	(not reporting)					
Lawrence (New Castle) (96)	412 658-2541	(not reporting)				Gary B Robson	Michael Deleo
Lebanon (Lebanon) (114)	717 274-2801	John Walter	Donald J Rhine	. . . .	. . . .	Charles H Dorn Jr	Ronald W Rossi
Lehigh (Allentown) (291)	215 820-3306	David K Bausch	John J Kachmar Jr	Robert E Korp	Thomas J Lazorik	Eugene R Klein	Frank Jagodinski
Luzerne (Wilkes-Barre) (328)	717 825-1500	Frank P Crossin	Eugene R Klein	Eugene R Klein	Eugene R Klein	Ann M Gehret	Charlie Brewer
Lycoming (Williamsport) (119)	717 327-2314	Henry F Frey	David D Winterle	David D Winterle	Orrie Brown	. . . .	Donald Morey
Mc Kean (Smethport) (47)	814 887-5571	Harrijane Hannon	Audrey Irons	Audrey Irons	Connie Eaton	Ambrose Rocco	William Romine
Mercer (Mercer) (121)	412 662-3800	Joseph Fragle	. . . .	Freida Eakman	Nettie Pantall		
Mifflin (Lewistown) (46)	717 248-6733	(not reporting)					
Monroe (Stroudsburg) (96)	717 424-5100	Janet Weidensaul	Zenia Citsay	. . . .	Donald Chase	Richard Bielat	Forrest Sebring
Montgomery (Norristown) (678)	215 278-3000	(not reporting)					
Montour (Danville) (18)	717 271-3000	Darla J Gill	Susan M Kauwell	Susan M Kauwell	Luther L Cooke	. . . .	Fred R Shepperson
Northampton (Easton) (247)	215 559-3000	(not reporting)					
Northumberland (Sunbury) (97)	717 988-4100	(not reporting)					
Perry (New Bloomfield) (41)	717 582-2131	Keith B Quigley	Mark E Brungard	Mark E Brungard	Bonnie L Delancey	Mark E Brungard	G W Frownfelter
Philadelphia (Philadelphia) c (1586)	215 686-1776	(not reporting)					
Pike (Milford) (28)	717 296-7613	Sally Thomson	. . . .	Centa T Quinn	Robert C Phillips	. . . .	Harry L Geiger
Potter (Coudersport) (17)	814 274-8290	(not reporting)					
Schuylkill (Pottsville) (153)	717 622-5570	(not reporting)					
Snyder (Middleburg) (37)	717 837-0691	(not reporting)					
Somerset (Somerset) (78)	814 443-1434	Robert J Will	Kay F Slope	. . . .	Donna Schmitt	. . . .	Ronald J Delano
Sullivan (Laporte) (6)	717 946-5201	Pamela K Arthur	. . . .	Lynne A Stabryla	. . . .	. . . .	Burton R Adams
Susquehanna (Montrose) (40)	717 278-4600	Warren Williams	. . . .	Jerry Myers	. . . .	. . . .	. . . .
Tioga (Wellsboro) (41)	717 724-1906	(not reporting)					
Union (Lewisburg) (36)	717 524-8634	Ruth Zimmerman	Diana Robinson	Diana Robinson	Diana Robinson	Diana Robinson	Donald Everitt
Venango (Franklin) (59)	814 437-6871	(not reporting)					
Warren (Warren) (45)	814 723-7550	Richard Campbell	. . . .	Eunice Herrington	Robert Hansen	Clare Morrison	Larry Kopko
Washington (Washington) (205)	412 228-6738	Frank R Mascara	Lou Lignelli	Tina Dallatore	Roger Metcalfe	Katherine Emery	James Pazzoni
Wayne (Honesdale) (40)	717 253-5970	(not reporting)					
Westmoreland (Greensburg) (370)	412 830-3786	(not reporting)					
Wyoming (Tunkhannock) (28)	717 836-3200	Willard Baker	William Gaylord	. . . .	Carl Smith	. . . .	Robert Truesdale
York (York) (340)	717 771-9614	George Trout	Allan Dameshek	. . . .	Michael Gingerich	Patrick McFadden	Kenneth Markel
SOUTH CAROLINA (46)							
Abbeville (Abbeville) (24)	803 459-5312	(not reporting)					
Aiken (Aiken) (121)	803 642-2013	Carrol Warner	William Shepherd	Tamara Sullivan	Richard Starks	Tony Brown	Howard Sellers
Allendale (Allendale) (12)	803 584-3438	(not reporting)					
Anderson (Anderson) (145)	803 260-4000	James M Holden	Gary A Smoak	Linda N Gilstrap	George J Hunter	Nancy O Baxter	Gordon E Taylor
Bamberg (Bamberg) (17)	803 245-5191	William Nimmons	Mark David Baskin	Rose Shepherd	Booker Patrick	Susan Hiers	Edward Darnell
Barnwell (Barnwell) (20)	803 259-3464	Danny Black	Robert Boland	Jane O Bradley	Elaine D Bryan	Alice L Martin	Joseph Zorn
Beaufort (Beaufort) (86)	803 525-7100	Thomas C Taylor	Michael G Bryant	Suzanne M Rainey	Thomas Henrikson	Marie S Smalls	David J Lucas Jr
Berkeley (Moncks Corner) (129)	803 761-6900	. . . .	. . . .	Betty Lou Hanna	Betty Jo Fondren	Bryan O Sorensen	Raymond O Isgett
Calhoun (St. Matthews) (13)	803 874-2435	(not reporting)					
Charleston (Charleston) (295)	803 723-6716	R Keith Summey	Ernest E Fava	Beverly T Craven	Harold Bisbee	Barbara D Demarco	James A Cannon Jr
Cherokee (Gaffney) (45)	803 487-2560	(not reporting)					
Chester (Chester) (32)	803 385-5133	(not reporting)					

Directory 1/10　　OFFICIALS IN U.S. COUNTIES
continued

County, county seat, 1990 population figures (000 omitted)	County telephone number	Board chairman	Appointed administrator	Clerk to the governing board	Chief financial officer	Personnel director	Chief law enforcement official
SOUTH CAROLINA (46) continued							
Chesterfield (Chesterfield) (39) ..	803 623-2535	Andrew R Ingram	J Chappell Hurst	. . . .	John W Sowell	Peggy E Miller	Ralph C Freeman
Clarendon (Manning) (28)	803 435-8424	Betty Roper	W Ray Brown	Thomas L Harvin	. . . .	Linda J Taylor	Hoyt Collins
Colleton (Walterboro) (34)	803 549-1725	Floyd Buckner	Henry B Veleker	J Holmes	Bette R Fralick	Henry B Veleker	Cecil Chasteen
Darlington (Darlington) (62)	803 398-4100	James Stone	James Schafer	Janet Blow	Phyllis Griffits	Brenda Broach	Glenn Campbell
Dillon (Dillon) (29)	803 774-1400	(not reporting)					
Dorchester (St. George) (83) . . .	803 821-0425	Ben C Cole	Jack C Langston	Myrtle Barten	Anthony Oglietti	Anne S Ayer	John Southerland
Edgefield (Edgefield) (18)	803 637-4000	C Monroe Kneece	T C McCain	T C McCain	James W McCord	T C McCain	R Billy Parker
Fairfield (Winnsboro) (22)	803 635-1415	(not reporting)					
Florence (Florence) (114)	803 665-3099	(not reporting)					
Georgetown (Georgetown) (46) .	803 546-4189	James Nichols	Gordon Hartwig	Jacquelyn Owens	David Parks Jr	Mary Graham	Alton Cribb
Greenville (Greenville) (320) . . .	803 240-7200	C Wade Cleveland	. . . .	Elizabeth Hanzey	John F Hansley	Beverly R Pruitt	Johnny Mack Brown
Greenwood (Greenwood) (60) . . .	803 942-8502	(not reporting)					
Hampton (Hampton) (18)	803 943-4951	Lee S Bowers	Rose D Winn	Aline Newton	Edna L Smith	. . . .	. . . .
Horry (Conway) (144)	803 248-1207	Paul E Creel	Douglas E Freeman	Gladys A Allenet Allen	Shirley Barnhill	Bert L Brown Jr	J Gordon Harris
Jasper (Ridgeland) (15)	803 726-3173	(not reporting)					
Kershaw (Camden) (44)	803 425-1500	(not reporting)					
Lancaster (Lancaster) (55)	803 285-1565	Ray E Gardner	. . . .	Irene L Plyler	Jerry Witherspoon	. . . .	Williford Faile
Laurens (Laurens) (58)	803 984-5214	A Eugene Madden	Ernest B Segars	Betty A Walsh	. . . .	Columbus Stephens	James Moore
Lee (Bishopville) (18)	803 484-5341	(not reporting)					
Lexington (Lexington) (168)	803 359-8000	Lowell C Spires	Edward M Parler	Dorothy K Black	Larry M Porth	Charles W Shealy	James R Metts
Marion (Marion) (34)	803 423-3904	Jasper Eaddy	Claude W Graham	Landis H Baxley	Claude W Graham	Cheryl S Rogers	L C Richardson
Marlboro (Bennettsville) (29) . . .	803 479-4462	George McIntyre	Richard Burnette	. . . .	Dennis Cox	Shirley Covington	Charles Foley
Mc Cormick (Mc Cormick) (9) . . .	803 465-2231	Alonzo Harrison	Paul H Bjorkman	Mary Beckwith	Ferrel Percival	. . . .	George Reid
Newberry (Newberry) (33)	803 321-2100	(not reporting)					
Oconee (Walhalla) (57)	803 638-4242	Sandra B Orr	Norman D Crain	Opal O Green	George Hunnicutt	Merle P Orr	James Singleton
Orangeburg (Orangeburg) (85) . .	803 533-1000	Vernon Ott	Donnie Hilliard	Susan Matthews	Robert Crout	Bill Clark	Cameron Smith
Pickens (Pickens) (94)	803 898-5900	(not reporting)					
Richland (Columbia) (286)	803 748-4616	(not reporting)					
Saluda (Saluda) (16)	803 445-2635	(not reporting)					
Spartanburg (Spartanburg) (227)	803 596-2522	David Dennis	Roland Windham	Carolyn Parris	Alfred Rickett	Bonnie Hammond	William Coffey
Sumter (Sumter) (103)	803 773-1581	Joseph B Davis Jr	William T Noonan	Mary W Lewis	William Houser	Martin E Rogers	Thomas Mims
Union (Union) (30)	803 429-1600	(not reporting)					
Williamsburg (Kingstree) (37) . . .	803 354-9321	(not reporting)					
York (York) (131)	803 684-8511	Carl Gullick	Clay Killian	Nancy Moore	Anne Bunton	David Larson	Joseph Mitchell
SOUTH DAKOTA (66)							
Aurora (Plankinton) (3)	605 942-7752	Darrel E Johnson	. . . .	Darlene Haines	Brenda Anderson	. . . .	David E Fink
Beadle (Huron) (18)	605 352-2655	(not reporting)					
Bennett (Martin) (3)	605 685-6969	James Slattery	. . . .	Susan Williams	Darleen DeKay	Susan Williams	Arnold Beem
Bon Homme (Tyndall) (7)	605 589-3391	Allen Sternhagen	. . . .	. . . .	Kathy Horacek	. . . .	Lyle O' Donnell
Brookings (Brookings) (25)	605 692-6284	Lloyd Sterud	. . . .	Sara Kneip	Debra Hanson	. . . .	Gordon Ribstein
Brown (Aberdeen) (36)	605 622-7110	Dennis Feickert	Dennis Biegler	Maxine Taylor	. . . .	. . . .	Steve Oakes
Brule (Chamberlain) (5)	605 734-6521	Ronald W Bairey	. . . .	Bette A Shields	Bette A Shields	. . . .	Darrell Miller
Buffalo (Gannvalley) (2)	605 293-3217	Joe Collins	. . . .	Elaine J Wulff	Janice Von Eye	Elaine J Wulff	Wayne Willman
Butte (Belle Fourche) (8)	605 892-4485	Kenny Kudlock	. . . .	Lorraine Schmidt	. . . .	. . . .	Richard Davis
Campbell (Mound City) (2)	605 955-3366	(not reporting)					
Charles Mix (Lake Andes) (9) . . .	605 487-7131	Bruce Bakken	. . . .	. . . .	Norman E Cihak	. . . .	Ray Westendorf
Clark (Clark) (4)	605 532-5921	(not reporting)					
Clay (Vermillion) (13)	605 624-2281	(not reporting)					
Codington (Watertown) (23)	605 886-8497	(not reporting)					
Corson (Mc Intosh) (4)	605 273-4229	George Seiler Jr	. . . .	Zella Lemer	Joan Bauer	. . . .	Keith Gall
Custer (Custer) (6)	605 673-4815	(not reporting)					
Davison (Mitchell) (18)	605 996-2474	Dan Cunningham	. . . .	John Oster	John Oster	. . . .	Lyle W Swenson
Day (Webster) (7)	605 345-3102	(not reporting)					
Deuel (Clear Lake) (5)	605 874-2330	(not reporting)					
Dewey (Timber Lake) (6)	605 865-3672	Bob Berndt	. . . .	Adele Enright	Adele Enright	. . . .	Jim Fisher
Douglas (Armour) (4)	605 724-2423	(not reporting)					
Edmunds (Ipswich) (4)	605 426-6762	(not reporting)					
Fall River (Hot Springs) (7)	605 745-5130	Frank Birkholt	. . . .	Sherrill A Dryden	Shirley Green	. . . .	Leo W Bray
Faulk (Faulkton) (3)	605 598-6224	(not reporting)					
Grant (Milbank) (8)	605 432-6711	Guy E Mann	. . . .	Karen M Layher	Maureen Dinter	. . . .	Michael McKernan
Gregory (Burke) (5)	605 775-2664	(not reporting)					
Haakon (Philip) (3)	605 859-2800	(not reporting)					
Hamlin (Hayti) (5)	605 783-3201	(not reporting)					
Hand (Miller) (4)	605 853-2182	Delmar B Gerdes	. . . .	Betty Morford	Betty Morford	. . . .	Jerry Miller
Hanson (Alexandria) (3)	605 239-4714	Chester McManus	. . . .	Janet Ibis	Janet Ibis	. . . .	Robert Brown
Harding (Buffalo) (2)	605 375-3313	(not reporting)					
Hughes (Pierre) (15)	605 224-2181	Kenneth Stewart	. . . .	Shellie Baker	Maggie Oliva	. . . .	Arlo Mortimer
Hutchinson (Olivet) (8)	605 387-2835	Luverne Locken	. . . .	Jerome Hoff	Darlene Schoon	. . . .	Raymond Zeeb
Hyde (Highmore) (2)	605 852-2519	Lane Zeigler	. . . .	Connie Konrad	Sandra Blair	. . . .	Charles Wortman
Jackson (Kadoka) (3)	605 837-2422	Larry Byrd	. . . .	Vicki D Wilson	Vicki D Wilson	. . . .	Arlo B Madsen
Jerauld (Wessington Springs) (2)	605 539-1202	(not reporting)					
Jones (Murdo) (1)	605 669-2242	(not reporting)					
Kingsbury (De Smet) (6)	605 854-3832	William Cronkhite	. . . .	Audrey Penney	Audrey Penney	. . . .	Norman Lee
Lake (Madison) (11)	605 256-2068	Shirlee Leighton	. . . .	Kay A Schmidt	Kay A Schmidt	. . . .	Herb Lurz
Lawrence (Deadwood) (21)	605 578-1941	Gerald F Apa	. . . .	Marlene Barrett	Connie Hopkins	. . . .	Charles Crotty
Lincoln (Canton) (15)	605 987-2581	Richard Fossum	. . . .	Helen Nelson	Carol Mulder	. . . .	Kenneth Albers
Lyman (Kennebec) (4)	605 869-2247	Richard Reuer	. . . .	Joan Brinckmeyer	Adelia B Olsen	. . . .	John H Michalek
Marshall (Britton) (5)	605 448-2401	Maurice Erickson	. . . .	C Christianson	. . . .	. . . .	Dale Elsen
Mc Cook (Salem) (6)	605 425-2791	Tony Nugteren	. . . .	Geralyn Sherman	Joan Matthaei	. . . .	Eugene Taylor
Mc Pherson (Leola) (3)	605 439-3314	Harley Neuharth	. . . .	Steve Serr	Sylvia Arioso	. . . .	Keith Kunz
Meade (Sturgis) (22)	605 347-4513	(not reporting)					
Mellette (White River) (2)	605 259-3291	(not reporting)					
Miner (Howard) (3)	605 772-4671	Thomas Dold	. . . .	Cindy Callies	Debra Eggert	. . . .	Tim Reisch
Minnehaha (Sioux Falls) (124) . .	605 335-4206	Carol Twedt	Ken McFarland	Sue Roust	Sue Roust	Nora Buckman	Les Hawkey
Moody (Flandreau) (7)	605 997-3161	(not reporting)					
Pennington (Rapid City) (81)	605 394-2153	(not reporting)					
Perkins (Bison) (4)	605 244-5624	Robert Jangula	. . . .	Fern Brockel	Dolores Chapman	. . . .	Kelly Serr
Potter (Gettysburg) (3)	605 765-9408	(not reporting)					
Roberts (Sisseton) (10)	605 698-7336	(not reporting)					
Sanborn (Woonsocket) (3)	605 796-4513	(not reporting)					
Shannon (Hot Springs) (10)	605 745-5130	C Whirlwind Horse	. . . .	Sherrill A Dryden	Shirley Green	. . . .	Leo W Bray
Spink (Redfield) (8)	605 472-1825	Richard Mueller	. . . .	Rosemary Parker	Janet Morrison	Rosemary Parker	Gary Newman

County, county seat, 1990 population figures (000 omitted)	County telephone number	Board chairman	Appointed administrator	Clerk to the governing board	Chief financial officer	Personnel director	Chief law enforcement official
SOUTH DAKOTA (66) continued							
Stanley (Fort Pierre) (2)	605 223-2673	Robert Wilcox	....	Phyllis Kenzy	Rose M Nelson	Phyllis Kenzy	Bradley J Rathbun
Sully (Onida) (2)	605 258-2541	William Floyd	....	Patty McGee	Edna Brunmeier	Patty McGee	Bill Stahl
Todd (Winner) (8)	605 856-2646	Harold W Whiting	....	Kathleen Flakus	Donna D Trego	....	Larry Christensen
Tripp (Winner) (7)	605 842-3727	Louis Polasky	....	Kathleen Flakus	Donna D Trego	....	C Schroeder
Turner (Parker) (9)	605 297-3153	Luverne Langerock	....	Sheila Hagemann	Marlys Andersen	....	Paul Morehouse
Union (Elk Point) (10)	605 356-2101	M C Bak	....	Carol Klumper	....	....	Dan Limoges
Walworth (Selby) (6)	605 649-7878	Gerhard Schlomer	....	Mary L Bucklin	Julie Lundquist	Mary L Bucklin	James A Spiry
Yankton (Yankton) (19)	605 665-2143	(not reporting)					
Ziebach (Dupree) (2)	605 365-5157	Clinton Farlee	....	Cindy Longbrake	Cindy Longbrake	Cindy Longbrake	Robert Menzel
TENNESSEE (95)							
Anderson (Clinton) (68)	615 457-5400	David O Bolling	....	Jack Keeney	Dale C Isabell	....	Thomas Edwards
Bedford (Shelbyville) (30)	615 684-1921	(not reporting)					
Benton (Camden) (15)	901 584-6011	(not reporting)					
Bledsoe (Pikeville) (10)	615 447-6855	(not reporting)					
Blount (Maryville) (86)	615 982-1302	James Kyker	William A Crisp	Roy Crawford Jr	John Troyer	....	James Berrong
Bradley (Cleveland) (74)	615 476-0600	(not reporting)					
Campbell (Jacksboro) (35)	615 562-2526	Tommy C Stiner	Ralph Grant	Don Nance	Jeff Marlow	Tommy C Stiner	Ron McClellan
Cannon (Woodbury) (10)	615 563-2320	Harold Patrick	....	Robert P Smith	Joe Rogers	....	Robert Simpson
Carroll (Huntingdon) (28)	901 986-3762	(not reporting)					
Carter (Elizabethton) (52)	615 542-1801	(not reporting)					
Cheatham (Ashland City) (27)	615 792-4316	(not reporting)					
Chester (Henderson) (13)	901 989-5672	(not reporting)					
Claiborne (Tazewell) (26)	615 626-5236	(not reporting)					
Clay (Celina) (7)	615 243-2161	Coell Hickman	....	Pat Hix	Coell Hickman	Donna Rich	Jerry Rhoton
Cocke (Newport) (29)	615 623-8791	(not reporting)					
Coffee (Manchester) (40)	615 723-5100	James R Wilhelm	....	Charles E Wells	Barbara W Arp	....	Freddie L Conn
Crockett (Alamo) (13)	901 696-5451	(not reporting)					
Cumberland (Crossville) (35)	615 484-6165	(not reporting)					
De Kalb (Smithville) (14)	615 597-5177	(not reporting)					
Decatur (Decaturville) (10)	901 852-2131	(not reporting)					
Dickson (Charlotte) (35)	615 789-4171	(not reporting)					
Dyer (Dyersburg) (35)	901 286-7800	(not reporting)					
Fayette (Somerville) (26)	901 465-2461	(not reporting)					
Fentress (Jamestown) (15)	615 879-7713	(not reporting)					
Franklin (Winchester) (35)	615 967-2905	(not reporting)					
Gibson (Trenton) (46)	901 855-4550	(not reporting)					
Giles (Pulaski) (26)	615 363-5300	(not reporting)					
Grainger (Rutledge) (17)	615 828-3513	(not reporting)					
Greene (Greeneville) (56)	615 638-8118	(not reporting)					
Grundy (Altamount) (13)	615 692-3455	(not reporting)					
Hamblen (Morristown) (50)	615 586-1931	Stancil Ford	....	Wilburn Beck	Paul Bruce	Sonia Miller	Charles Long
Hamilton (Chattanooga) (286)	615 757-2496	(not reporting)					
Hancock (Sneedville) (7)	615 733-4341	(not reporting)					
Hardeman (Bolivar) (23)	901 658-3266	(not reporting)					
Hardin (Savannah) (23)	901 925-9078	(not reporting)					
Hawkins (Rogersville) (45)	615 272-7359	(not reporting)					
Haywood (Brownsville) (19)	901 772-1432	Franklin Smith	....	Ann D Medford	Franklin Smith	....	Raymond Russell
Henderson (Lexington) (22)	901 968-7141	(not reporting)					
Henry (Paris) (28)	901 642-5212	Herman Jackson	....	Jerry Bomar	Herman Jackson	....	Tom Jenkins
Hickman (Centerville) (17)	615 729-2492	Steve Gregory	....	Lamar Chessor	Scott Powers	Steve Gregory	Frank Adkinson
Houston (Erin) (7)	615 289-3633	(not reporting)					
Humphreys (Waverly) (16)	615 296-7795	(not reporting)					
Jackson (Gainesboro) (9)	615 268-9888	(not reporting)					
Jefferson (Dandridge) (33)	615 397-3800	Gary W Holiway	....	R E Farrar	Gary W Holiway	....	Doug Quarles
Johnson (Mountain City) (14)	615 727-9696	(not reporting)					
Knox (Knoxville) (336)	615 521-2005	Dwight Kessel	Patsy Miller	Mike Padgett	Kathy Hamilton	Joe Hamby	Tim Hutchison
Lake (Tiptonville) (7)	901 253-7382	(not reporting)					
Lauderdale (Ripley) (23)	901 635-3500	(not reporting)					
Lawrence (Lawrenceburg) (35)	615 762-7700	Marty Dunkin	Robin A Roberts	Kenneth Weathers	Robin A Roberts	Robin A Roberts	Bruce Durham
Lewis (Hohenwald) (9)	615 796-3378	(not reporting)					
Lincoln (Fayetteville) (28)	615 433-3045	(not reporting)					
Loudon (Loudon) (31)	615 458-4663	(not reporting)					
Macon (Lafayette) (16)	615 666-2363	(not reporting)					
Madison (Jackson) (78)	901 423-6020	(not reporting)					
Marion (Jasper) (25)	615 942-2552	(not reporting)					
Marshall (Lewisburg) (22)	615 359-1279	(not reporting)					
Maury (Columbia) (55)	615 381-3690	Sam Kennedy	....	Nancy Thompson	A C Howell	....	Wade Matheny
Mc Minn (Athens) (42)	615 745-7634	Ronald L Banks	....	Helen Haskins	Ed J Fiegle	....	....
Mc Nairy (Selmer) (22)	901 645-3511	(not reporting)					
Meigs (Decatur) (8)	615 334-5850	(not reporting)					
Monroe (Madisonville) (31)	615 442-3981	(not reporting)					
Montgomery (Clarksville) (100)	615 648-5787	(not reporting)					
Moore (Lynchburg) (..)	615 759-7076	(not reporting)					
Morgan (Wartburg) (17)	615 346-6288	(not reporting)					
Nashville-Davidson (Nashville) c (511)	615 862-5000	Phil Bredesen	....	Marilyn Swing	Gene Nolan	John W Lynch	Robert Kirchner
Obion (Union City) (32)	901 885-9611	(not reporting)					
Overton (Livingston) (18)	615 823-5638	(not reporting)					
Perry (Linden) (7)	615 589-2216	(not reporting)					
Pickett (Byrdstown) (5)	615 864-3798	(not reporting)					
Polk (Benton) (14)	615 338-2841	(not reporting)					
Putnam (Cookeville) (51)	615 526-6321	(not reporting)					
Rhea (Dayton) (24)	615 775-7803	(not reporting)					
Roane (Kingston) (47)	615 376-5578	Ken Yager	....	Dorothy Marshall	Ronald Woody	....	Arnold Clower
Robertson (Springfield) (41)	615 384-2476	Emerson Meggs	....	....	Larry Morris	....	Taylor T Emery
Rutherford (Murfreesboro) (119)	615 898-7745	(not reporting)					
Scott (Huntsville) (18)	615 663-2355	(not reporting)					
Sequatchie (Dunlap) (9)	615 949-3479	(not reporting)					
Sevier (Sevierville) (51)	615 453-6136	(not reporting)					
Shelby (Memphis) (826)	901 576-4500	(not reporting)					
Smith (Carthage) (14)	615 735-2294	C E Hackett	....	James B Norris	....	....	Johnny C Bane
Stewart (Dover) (9)	615 232-5371	(not reporting)					

Directory 1/10   **OFFICIALS IN U.S. COUNTIES**
continued

County, county seat, 1990 population figures (000 omitted)	County telephone number	Board chairman	Appointed administrator	Clerk to the governing board	Chief financial officer	Personnel director	Chief law enforcement official
TENNESSEE (95) continued							
Sullivan (Blountville) (144)	615 323-6417	Johny McKamey	....	....	Harry P Trent	....	Keith Carr
Sumner (Gallatin) (103)	615 452-4282	Bethel Brown		William Kemp	Dennis Petty		Richard Sutton
Tipton (Covington) (38)	901 476-2604	(not reporting)					
Trousdale (Hartsville) (6)	615 374-2461	(not reporting)					
Unicoi (Erwin) (17)	615 743-9391	Paul C Monk	....	....	....	....	Bob Whitson
Union (Maynardville) (14)	615 992-3061	Gerald E Simmons	Glenn Coppock	Roy Carter	James Phillips	....	Thomas Keaton
Van Buren (Spencer) (5)	615 946-2314	(not reporting)					
Warren (Mc Minnville) (33)	615 473-2505	(not reporting)					
Washington (Jonesborough) (92)	615 753-1666	(not reporting)					
Wayne (Waynesboro) (14)	615 722-3653	James C Anderson	....	Jimmy Dixon	Perlis Brison Jr	....	Leon Nutt
Weakley (Dresden) (32)	901 364-5413	(not reporting)					
White (Sparta) (20)	615 836-3203	(not reporting)					
Williamson (Franklin) (81)	615 790-5700	Robert A Ring	....	Charlie Fox Jr	Bill Giddens	....	Lance Saylor
Wilson (Lebanon) (68)	615 444-1383	(not reporting)					
TEXAS (254)							
Anderson (Palestine) (48)	214 723-7428	(not reporting)					
Andrews (Andrews) (14)	915 523-3062	(not reporting)					
Angelina (Lufkin) (70)	409 634-5413	Joe Berry	....	Pauline Grisham	E H Bush Jr	....	Michael Lawrence
Aransas (Rockport) (18)	512 790-0100	Agnes A Harden	....	Val Jean Eaton	Stanley Svehla	Stanley Svehla	David Petrusaitis
Archer (Archer City) (8)	817 574-4811	(not reporting)					
Armstrong (Claude) (2)	806 226-3221	(not reporting)					
Atascosa (Jourdanton) (31)	512 769-3093	(not reporting)					
Austin (Bellville) (20)	409 865-5911	J Lee Dittert Jr	....	Dorothy Himly	Betty Krueger	....	Vernon Brzozowski
Bailey (Muleshoe) (7)	806 272-3077	Marilyn Cox	....	Barbara McCamish	Dorothy Turner	....	Jerry N Hicks
Bandera (Bandera) (11)	512 796-3781	Ray F Mauer	....	Bernice Bates	Elizabeth James	....	James Mac Millan
Bastrop (Bastrop) (38)	512 321-2579	(not reporting)					
Baylor (Seymour) (4)	817 888-3322	Joe Dickson		Doris Rushing	Pat Coker		Jerry Barton
Bee (Beeville) (25)	512 358-1394	Jay Kimbrough		Julia V Torres	Bonnie M White	....	Robert L Horn
Bell (Belton) (191)	817 939-3521	John Garth		Vada Sutton	Bert Liles	Bert Liles	Dan Smith
Bexar (San Antonio) (1185)	512 220-2626	Cyndi T Krier	....	....	Marcus Jahns	M Vargas McCabe	Ralph Lopez
Blanco (Johnson City) (6)	512 868-4266	(not reporting)					
Borden (Gail) (1)	806 756-4391	(not reporting)					
Bosque (Meridian) (15)	817 435-2382	(not reporting)					
Bowie (New Boston) (82)	903 628-2571	James M Carlow	....	Marylene Megason	Pansy L Baird	....	Mary Choate
Brazoria (Angleton) (192)	409 849-5711	(not reporting)					
Brazos (Bryan) (122)	409 775-7400	(not reporting)					
Brewster (Alpine) (9)	915 837-2412	(not reporting)					
Briscoe (Silverton) (2)	806 823-2131	(not reporting)					
Brooks (Falfurrias) (8)	512 325-5604	Homer Mora	Gloria Perez	Ruben Castellano	Ninfa G Ogdee	....	Ruben Longoria
Brown (Brownwood) (34)	915 643-2828	(not reporting)					
Burleson (Caldwell) (14)	409 567-4161	Woods A Caperton	....	....	....	....	Ronald Rubanovsky
Burnet (Burnet) (23)	512 756-5420	Martin McLean	....	Janet Parker	Katy Gilmore	Katy Gilmore	Joe Pollock
Caldwell (Lockhart) (26)	512 398-1809	(not reporting)					
Calhoun (Port Lavaca) (19)	512 553-4600	(not reporting)					
Callahan (Baird) (12)	915 854-1155	(not reporting)					
Cameron (Brownsville) (260)	512 544-0830	(not reporting)					
Camp (Pittsburg) (10)	214 856-3845	(not reporting)					
Carson (Panhandle) (7)	806 537-3622	(not reporting)					
Cass (Linden) (30)	903 756-5181	Tommy Kessler	....	Wilma O' Rand	Carol Cox	....	Paul Boone
Castro (Dimmitt) (9)	806 647-5534	(not reporting)					
Chambers (Anahuac) (20)	409 267-3671	(not reporting)					
Cherokee (Rusk) (41)	214 683-2324	(not reporting)					
Childress (Childress) (6)	817 937-2221	(not reporting)					
Clay (Henrietta) (10)	817 538-7408	Billy Ray Nobles	....	Kay Hutchison	Sue Sims Brock	Sue Sims Brock	Paul Bevering
Cochran (Morton) (4)	806 266-5508	Robert Yeary	....	Rita Tyson	Betty Hudson	....	Royce Fred
Coke (Robert Lee) (3)	915 453-2641	Royce Lee	Stover Taylor	Ettie Hubbard	Stover Taylor	Royce Lee	Marshall Millican
Coleman (Coleman) (10)	915 625-4218	(not reporting)					
Collin (Mc Kinney) (264)	214 548-4100	(not reporting)					
Collingsworth (Wellington) (4)	806 447-5408	Zook Thomas	....	Karen Coleman	Yvone Brewer	....	Dale Tarver
Colorado (Columbus) (18)	409 732-2604	(not reporting)					
Comal (New Braunfels) (52)	512 620-5501	Carter Casteel	Tom N Corlette	....	H Bate Bond	....	John G Bremer
Comanche (Comanche) (13)	915 356-2466	John M Weaver	....	....	....	....	Billy J Works
Concho (Paint Rock) (3)	915 732-4321	Charles Dankworth	....	Margaret T Taylor	D R Kirkpatrick	....	....
Cooke (Gainesville) (31)	817 668-5435	(not reporting)					
Coryell (Gatesville) (64)	817 865-5911	(not reporting)					
Cottle (Paducah) (2)	806 492-3613	(not reporting)					
Crane (Crane) (5)	915 558-3581	(not reporting)					
Crockett (Ozona) (4)	915 392-2022	(not reporting)					
Crosby (Crosbyton) (7)	806 675-2011	(not reporting)					
Culberson (Van Horn) (3)	915 283-2059	John Conoly	....	Linda Urias	Francisco Gomez	....	Placido Nunez
Dallam (Dalhart) (5)	806 249-2450	David D Field	....	LuAnn Taylor	Jiggs Payne	....	E H Little
Dallas (Dallas) (1853)	214 653-7668	(not reporting)					
Dawson (Lamesa) (14)	806 872-7544	Charles Arthur	Don Stephens	Gloria Vera	Gene Defee	....	Terry Brown
De Witt (Cuero) (19)	512 275-2116	Ben E Prause	....	Ann Drehr	Phyllis Massey	....	A Wayne Mills
Deaf Smith (Hereford) (19)	806 364-1451	(not reporting)					
Delta (Cooper) (5)	903 395-2611	John I Hickman	....	Patsy P Barton	Dawn Curtis	....	Bill L Allen
Denton (Denton) (274)	817 565-8500	(not reporting)					
Dickens (Dickens) (3)	806 623-5532	(not reporting)					
Dimmit (Carrizo Springs) (10)	512 876-2323	(not reporting)					
Donley (Clarendon) (4)	806 874-3625	W R Christal	....	Fay Vargas	Wanda Smith	....	Jimmy Thompson
Duval (San Diego) (13)	512 279-3322	(not reporting)					
Eastland (Eastland) (18)	817 629-1583	(not reporting)					
Ector (Odessa) (119)	915 335-3025	Jim T Jordan	....	Barbara Bedford	Bill D Hicks	Pat Mac Allister	O A Brookshire
Edwards (Rocksprings) (2)	512 683-2235	(not reporting)					
El Paso (El Paso) (592)	915 546-2218	Alicia R Chacon	Lisa Colquitt	Hector Enriquez	Steve E Seely	Nita Corral Nava	Leo Samaniego
Ellis (Waxahachie) (85)	214 937-8620	Penny Redington	....	Cindy Polley	Yvonne Odom	Mark Price	John Gage
Erath (Stephenville) (28)	817 965-4310	(not reporting)					
Falls (Marlin) (18)	817 883-2961	(not reporting)					
Fannin (Bonham) (25)	903 583-7451	Jimmy L Doyle	....	Margaret Gilbert	Kathleen M Moss	....	Talmage Moore
Fayette (La Grange) (20)	409 968-3055	Edward Janecka	....	Irene Pratka	Dan Von Rosenberg	....	Richard Vandel Sr
Fisher (Roby) (5)	915 776-2443	(not reporting)					
Floyd (Floydada) (8)	806 983-2244	William D Hardin	....	Margaret Collier	Glenna Orman	....	C L Overstreet

County, county seat, 1990 population figures (000 omitted)	County telephone number	Board chairman	Appointed administrator	Clerk to the governing board	Chief financial officer	Personnel director	Chief law enforcement official
TEXAS (254) continued							
Foard (Crowell) (2)	817 684-1424	Charlie Bell	. . . .	Janis Everson	Jan Bond	. . . .	Bobby Bond
Fort Bend (Richmond) (225)	713 342-3411	. . . .	. . . .			Richard Selleh	
Franklin (Mount Vernon) (8)	214 537-2342	Wayne Foster	. . . .	Wanda Johnson	Sue Ann Harper	. . . .	Charles White
Freestone (Fairfield) (16)	214 389-2635	(not reporting)					
Frio (Pearsall) (13)	512 334-2154	(not reporting)					
Gaines (Seminole) (14)	915 758-3521	(not reporting)					
Galveston (Galveston) (217)	713 762-8621	(not reporting)					
Garza (Post) (5)	806 495-2521	Giles W Dalby	. . . .	L E Gossett Jr	Ruth Ann Young	Ruth Ann Young	Kenneth Ratke
Gillespie (Fredericksburg) (17)	512 997-7502	Jay Weinheimer	. . . .	Doris Lange	Jeanie Crenweige	. . . .	Milton Jung
Glasscock (Garden City) (1)	915 354-2415	W E Bednar	. . . .	Betty Pate	Judy Kingston	. . . .	Royce Pruit
Goliad (Goliad) (6)	512 645-3337	John Barnhill	. . . .	Gail Turley	Lauren Henry	Lauren Henry	J K McMahan
Gonzales (Gonzales) (17)	512 672-2327	(not reporting)					
Gray (Pampa) (24)	806 669-8004	(not reporting)					
Grayson (Sherman) (95)	214 868-9515	(not reporting)					
Gregg (Longview) (105)	214 758-6181	(not reporting)					
Grimes (Anderson) (19)	409 873-2111	Larry Snook	Paul Yount	David Pasket	Alvina Schroeder	Alvina Schroeder	William Foster
Guadalupe (Seguin) (65)	512 379-4188	James E Sagebiel	. . . .	Davene Ball	Lamar Schulz	. . . .	Melvin L Harborth
Hale (Plainview) (35)	806 293-8488	(not reporting)					
Hall (Memphis) (4)	806 259-2511	Kenneth Dale	. . . .	Dean Cochran	Marion Bownds	. . . .	Kenny Schull
Hamilton (Hamilton) (8)	817 386-3815	(not reporting)					
Hansford (Spearman) (6)	806 659-2626	Jim D Brown	. . . .	Amelia C Johnson	Norma Jean Mackie	. . . .	R L McFarlin Jr
Hardeman (Quanah) (5)	817 663-2911	Kenneth McNabb	. . . .	Judy Cokendolpher	Van R White	. . . .	Randy Akers
Hardin (Kountze) (41)	409 246-3371	(not reporting)					
Harris (Houston) (2818)	713 755-5000	Jon Lindsay	. . . .	Molly Pryor	Richard Raycraft	Janie Reyes	J Klevenhagen
Harrison (Marshall) (57)	903 938-4805	(not reporting)					
Hartley (Channing) (4)	806 235-3442	(not reporting)					
Haskell (Haskell) (7)	817 864-2451	(not reporting)		Ronald Dannelley	William Herzog	. . . .	Paul Hastings
Hays (San Marcos) (66)	512 392-4858	Eddy Etheredge	. . . .	Gwen Moffeit	Winston Duke	. . . .	Slick Alfred
Hemphill (Canadian) (4)	806 323-6521	Tommy Smith	. . . .				
Henderson (Athens) (59)	214 675-6120	Tommy Smith	. . . .	Ruth Pelham	Jewel Burton	. . . .	Brent Button
Hidalgo (Edinburg) (384)	512 383-2751	(not reporting)					
Hill (Hillsboro) (27)	817 582-2371	Tommy J Walker	. . . .	Anjanette Ables	Don Cleveland	Reva Hendrix	Rodney Jeanis
Hockley (Levelland) (24)	806 894-6856	(not reporting)					
Hood (Granbury) (29)	817 573-1767	Don Cleveland	. . . .	Nancy Huff	Patricia Sims		James Rains
Hopkins (Sulphur Springs) (29)	214 885-3926	(not reporting)					
Houston (Crockett) (21)	409 544-3255	John E Musgrove	. . . .				
Howard (Big Spring) (32)	915 263-7132	(not reporting)					
Hudspeth (Sierra Blanca) (3)	915 369-2321	(not reporting)					
Hunt (Greenville) (64)	214 455-4504	(not reporting)					
Hutchinson (Stinnett) (26)	806 878-2171	(not reporting)		Jane Ethridge	Betty Dennis	. . . .	Jimmy Martin
Irion (Mertzon) (2)	915 835-4361	Jim Westfall	. . . .	Martha Knapp	Caroline Pitzer	Marcell Maresh	Kelly R Janica
Jack (Jacksboro) (7)	817 567-2241	(not reporting)					
Jackson (Edna) (13)	512 782-2352	Harrison Stafford	. . . .				
Jasper (Jasper) (31)	713 384-2632	(not reporting)					
Jeff Davis (Fort Davis) (2)	915 426-3968	(not reporting)					
Jefferson (Beaumont) (239)	409 835-3741	(not reporting)					
Jim Hogg (Hebbronville) (5)	512 527-3015	(not reporting)					
Jim Wells (Alice) (38)	512 668-5706	(not reporting)					
Johnson (Cleburne) (97)	817 645-2292	(not reporting)					
Jones (Anson) (16)	915 823-3741	(not reporting)					
Karnes (Karnes City) (12)	512 780-3732	(not reporting)					
Kaufman (Kaufman) (52)	214 932-4331	(not reporting)		Darlene Herrin	Barbara J Schwope	. . . .	Lee D' Spain Jr
Kendall (Boerne) (15)	512 249-9343	James Gooden	. . . .				
Kenedy (Sarita) (..)	512 294-5224	(not reporting)					
Kent (Jayton) (1)	806 237-3373	(not reporting)					
Kerr (Kerrville) (36)	512 257-6711	(not reporting)					
Kimble (Junction) (4)	915 446-2724	(not reporting)		Dolores Raney	Tim Ward	. . . .	Norman H Hooten
King (Guthrie) (..)	806 596-4411	(not reporting)					
Kinney (Brackettville) (3)	512 563-2521	Tim Ward	. . . .				
Kleberg (Kingsville) (30)	512 592-2411	(not reporting)					
Knox (Benjamin) (5)	817 454-2191	(not reporting)					
La Salle (Cotulla) (5)	512 879-3033	(not reporting)		Kathy Poole	Kevin Parsons	Kevin Parson	Billy Joe McCoy
Lamar (Paris) (44)	903 737-2417	Deane Loughmiller	. . . .				
Lamb (Littlefield) (15)	806 385-4222	(not reporting)		Connie Hartmann	Jack Clark	. . . .	Gordon Morris
Lampasas (Lampasas) (14)	512 556-8271	Norris Monroe	. . . .				
Lavaca (Hallettsville) (19)	512 798-2301	(not reporting)					
Lee (Giddings) (13)	713 542-3178	(not reporting)					
Leon (Centerville) (13)	214 536-2352	(not reporting)					
Liberty (Liberty) (53)	409 336-8071	(not reporting)					
Limestone (Groesbeck) (21)	817 729-3810	(not reporting)					
Lipscomb (Lipscomb) (3)	806 862-4131	(not reporting)					
Live Oak (George West) (10)	512 449-2733	(not reporting)					
Llano (Llano) (12)	915 247-5054	(not reporting)		Juanita E Busby	Jaime A Jones	. . . .	Richard N Putnam
Loving (Mentone) (..)	915 377-2362	Donald C Creager	Clay P Hueister				
Lubbock (Lubbock) (223)	806 767-1004	(not reporting)					
Lynn (Tahoka) (7)	806 998-4222	(not reporting)		Joyce M Coleman	Judy Weathers	. . . .	Travis Neeley
Madison (Madisonville) (11)	409 348-2670	James R Fite	Mary A Turner				
Marion (Jefferson) (10)	214 665-3971	(not reporting)		Virginia James	H D Howard	H D Howard	C M Welling
Martin (Stanton) (5)	915 756-3631	Bob Deavenport	. . . .	Bea Langehennig	Jane Hoerster	. . . .	Don Grote
Mason (Mason) (3)	915 347-5556	Fritz E Landers	. . . .				
Matagorda (Bay City) (37)	409 244-7611	(not reporting)					
Maverick (Eagle Pass) (36)	512 773-3824	(not reporting)		Rose M Luttrell	Norma Holloway	. . . .	Dwain Hensley
Mc Culloch (Brady) (9)	915 597-0733	Randy Young	. . . .	Rosalie Miller	Weldon Wells	Linda Lewis	Jack Harwell
Mc Lennan (Waco) (189)	857 757-5000	James Lewis	Lynne Salyards				
Mc Mullen (Tilden) (1)	512 274-3215	(not reporting)					
Medina (Hondo) (27)	512 426-5381	(not reporting)					
Menard (Menard) (2)	915 396-4682	(not reporting)					
Midland (Midland) (107)	915 688-1000	(not reporting)		Laverne Soefje	M Michalka	. . . .	Leroy Broadus
Milam (Cameron) (23)	817 697-2932	Roger Hashem	. . . .				
Mills (Goldthwaite) (5)	915 648-2222	(not reporting)					
Mitchell (Colorado City) (8)	915 728-8439	(not reporting)					
Montague (Montague) (17)	817 894-2131	(not reporting)		Roy Harris	Martha Gustavsen	Diane J Bass	Guy L Williams
Montgomery (Conroe) (182)	409 756-0571	Alan B Sadler	. . . .				

OFFICIALS IN U.S. COUNTIES

County, county seat, 1990 population figures (000 omitted)	County telephone number	Board chairman	Appointed administrator	Clerk to the governing board	Chief financial officer	Personnel director	Chief law enforcement official
TEXAS (254) continued							
Moore (Dumas) (18)	806 935-5588	(not reporting)					
Morris (Daingerfield) (13)	214 645-3691	(not reporting)					
Motley (Matador) (2)	806 347-2334	(not reporting)					
Nacogdoches (Nacogdoches) (55)	409 560-7755	(not reporting)					
Navarro (Corsicana) (40)	903 654-3090	(not reporting)					
Newton (Newton) (14)	409 379-5691	(not reporting)					
Nolan (Sweetwater) (17)	915 235-2263	(not reporting)					
Nueces (Corpus Christi) (291)	512 888-0580	Robert N Barnes	. . . .	Ernest M Briones	Margaret L Hayes	John D Falcon	J P Luby
Ochiltree (Perryton) (9)	806 435-8075	J Kenny Morris	Jeffrey L Lowery	Jane Hammerbeck	Ginger Hays	. . . .	Joe Hataway
Oldham (Vega) (2)	806 267-2607	(not reporting)					
Orange (Orange) (81)	409 883-7740	John C McDonald	. . . .	Molly Theriot	W Tod Mixson	J Masciarelli	Huel Fontenot
Palo Pinto (Palo Pinto) (25)	817 659-1253	(not reporting)					
Panola (Carthage) (22)	214 693-0391	John Cordray	. . . .	Joyce Burgess	Sidney Burns	. . . .	Jack Ellett
Parker (Weatherford) (65)	817 599-6591	(not reporting)					
Parmer (Farwell) (10)	806 481-3383	(not reporting)					
Pecos (Fort Stockton) (15)	915 336-2792	(not reporting)					
Polk (Livingston) (31)	409 327-8113	John P Thompson	. . . .	Jo Anne Hopkins	Dianne Bass	Betty Rundell	Billy Ray Nelson
Potter (Amarillo) (98)	806 379-2400	Arthur Ware	. . . .	Sue Daniel	Gerald Joy	L Youngblood	Jimmy D Boydston
Presidio (Marfa) (7)	915 729-4452	(not reporting)					
Rains (Emory) (7)	214 473-2461	(not reporting)					
Randall (Canyon) (90)	806 655-6256	C W McMenamy	. . . .	Leroy Hutton	. . . .	Geneva Bagwell	Harold Hooks
Reagan (Big Lake) (5)	915 884-2665	(not reporting)					
Real (Leakey) (2)	512 232-5304	G W Twilligear	. . . .	Rosemary Brice	Kathy Brooks	Kathy Brooks	James Brice
Red River (Clarksville) (14)	214 427-2680	L D Williamson	. . . .	Mary Hausler	Shirley Anderson	. . . .	Bob Edrington
Reeves (Pecos) (16)	915 445-5418	(not reporting)					
Refugio (Refugio) (8)	512 526-2245	Charles S Stone	. . . .	Janelle Morgan	Ernest Guerrero	. . . .	Jim D Hodges
Roberts (Miami) (1)	806 868-3721	Vernon H Cook	. . . .	Jackie M Jackson	Sarah E Gill	. . . .	Billy Britton
Robertson (Franklin) (16)	409 828-3542	(not reporting)					
Rockwall (Rockwall) (26)	214 771-5152	(not reporting)					
Runnels (Ballinger) (11)	915 365-2720	(not reporting)					
Rusk (Henderson) (44)	214 657-5584	(not reporting)					
Sabine (Hemphill) (10)	409 787-3543	(not reporting)					
San Augustine (San Augustine) (8)	409 275-2762	Jack B Nichols	. . . .	Geraldine Smith	Carol Vaughn	. . . .	Charles Bryan
San Jacinto (Coldspring) (16)	409 653-2353	(not reporting)					
San Patricio (Sinton) (59)	512 364-1120	Josephine Miller	. . . .	Dorothea Maley	David W Wendel	Norma J Gonzales	Charles L Moody
San Saba (San Saba) (5)	915 372-3635	(not reporting)					
Schleicher (Eldorado) (3)	915 853-2833	(not reporting)					
Scurry (Snyder) (19)	915 573-8576	Bob Doolittle	Eddie R McHaney	F Billingsley	Charlie Bell	Charlie Bell	Keith Collier
Shackelford (Albany) (3)	915 762-2232	(not reporting)					
Shelby (Center) (22)	409 598-3863	Floyd A Watson	. . . .	Peaches Conway	. . . .	Wanda J Smith	Carl N Shofner
Sherman (Stratford) (3)	806 396-5551	W C Fesler	. . . .	M L Albert	L R Keener	. . . .	J Haile
Smith (Tyler) (151)	903 535-0500	Larry Craig	. . . .	. . . .	Nancy Braswell	James McConnell	J B Smith
Somervell (Glen Rose) (5)	817 897-2322	(not reporting)					
Starr (Rio Grande City) (41)	512 487-2014	Jose M Martinez	. . . .	Omar J Garza	Joaquin Gutierrez	Eliza Barerra	Eugenio Falcon Jr
Stephens (Breckenridge) (9)	817 559-3700	(not reporting)					
Sterling (Sterling City) (1)	915 378-5191	Robert L Browne	. . . .	. . . .	Beth Kilpatrick	. . . .	Lloyd J Brown
Stonewall (Aspermont) (2)	817 989-3393	(not reporting)					
Sutton (Sonora) (4)	915 387-2711	Carla Garner	. . . .	. . . .	Charles Graves	. . . .	William Webster
Swisher (Tulia) (8)	806 995-3294	(not reporting)					
Tarrant (Fort Worth) (1170)	817 884-1188	Tom Vandergriff	G K Maenius	. . . .	. . . .	Gerald Wright	David Williams
Taylor (Abilene) (120)	915 674-1235	(not reporting)					
Terrell (Sanderson) (1)	915 345-2391	Dudley Harrison	. . . .	Martha Allen	Ginette Litton	. . . .	Y E Duarte
Terry (Brownfield) (13)	806 637-6421	Douglas Ryburn	. . . .	Ann Willis	. . . .	. . . .	Jerry Johnson
Throckmorton (Throckmorton) (2)	817 849-3081	(not reporting)					
Titus (Mount Pleasant) (24)	214 572-8891	(not reporting)					
Tom Green (San Angelo) (98)	915 659-6508	William R Moore	. . . .	. . . .	Billie McDaniel	Ginger Merrill	Ule Pete Skains
Travis (Austin) (576)	512 473-9555	(not reporting)					
Trinity (Groveton) (11)	409 642-1443	(not reporting)					
Tyler (Woodville) (17)	409 283-3652	Jerome P Owens Jr	Joyce Moore	Donece Gregory	Joyce Moore	Jean Phillips	Gary Hennigan
Upshur (Gilmer) (31)	903 843-3083	(not reporting)					
Upton (Rankin) (4)	915 693-2321	(not reporting)					
Uvalde (Uvalde) (23)	512 278-3216	(not reporting)					
Val Verde (Del Rio) (39)	512 774-7500	Val Cadena	Oscar San Miguel	Emma Mansfield	Frank Lowe	Gloria Villarreal	James R Koog
Van Zandt (Canton) (38)	214 567-2551	Truett Mayo	. . . .	Elizabeth Everitt	Shirley Morgan	Shirley Morgan	Pat Jordan
Victoria (Victoria) (74)	512 575-4558	Helen R Walker	. . . .	Val D Huvar	Cathy Bailey	. . . .	Michael Ratcliff
Walker (Huntsville) (51)	409 291-9500	Frank J Robinson	. . . .	James D Patton	Dan C Clower	. . . .	Dale Myers
Waller (Hempstead) (23)	713 826-3357	(not reporting)					
Ward (Monahans) (13)	915 943-3209	(not reporting)					
Washington (Brenham) (26)	409 836-9374	Dorothy Morgan	. . . .	Gertrude Lehrmann	A Q Plummer	. . . .	J W Jankowski
Webb (Laredo) (133)	512 721-2500	Mercurio Martinez	. . . .	Henry Flores	. . . .	. . . .	Juan Garza
Wharton (Wharton) (40)	409 532-4612	I J Irvin	. . . .	Delfin Marek	Wilton Niemier	Gus Wessels Jr	Jess Howell
Wheeler (Wheeler) (6)	806 826-5544	(not reporting)					
Wichita (Wichita Falls) (122)	817 766-8100	(not reporting)					
Wilbarger (Vernon) (15)	817 552-5486	(not reporting)					
Willacy (Raymondville) (18)	512 689-2710	Eustolio Gonzales	. . . .	Terry Flores	Eleazar Garcia Jr	. . . .	Larry Spence
Williamson (Georgetown) (140)	512 863-3585	(not reporting)					
Wilson (Floresville) (23)	512 393-7303	(not reporting)					
Winkler (Kermit) (9)	915 586-2526	(not reporting)					
Wise (Decatur) (35)	817 627-3540	(not reporting)					
Wood (Quitman) (29)	903 763-4186	Lee Williams	Barbara Statser	Brenda Taylor	June Robinson	. . . .	Frank L White
Yoakum (Plains) (9)	806 456-2721	(not reporting)					
Young (Graham) (18)	817 549-2030	(not reporting)					
Zapata (Zapata) (9)	512 765-9920	Jose L Guevara	Esther L Gallegos	Arnoldo Flores	Alejandro Ramirez	Sylvia R Mendoza	Romeo R Ramirez
Zavala (Crystal City) (12)	512 374-3810	Pablo Avila	. . . .	Teresa P Flores	. . . .	Susis Perez	Jose Serna
UTAH (29)							
Beaver (Beaver) (5)	801 438-2352	(not reporting)					
Box Elder (Brigham City) (36)	801 734-2031	R Lee Allen	. . . .	Marie G Korth	Carlla J Secrist	Peggy C Madsen	Robert E Limb
Cache (Logan) (70)	801 752-5935	Chris S Coray	Seth S Allen	Stephen Erickson	Tamra Stones	M Lynn Lemon	Sidney P Groll
Carbon (Price) (20)	801 637-4700	William Krompel	. . . .	Norman Prichard	Norman Prichard	Dennis Dooley	James Robertson
Daggett (Manila) (1)	801 784-3154	(not reporting)					
Davis (Farmington) (188)	801 451-3200	Gayle A Stevenson	. . . .	Margene Isom	. . . .	G Steven Baker	Glenn Clary
Duchesne (Duchesne) (13)	801 738-2435	(not reporting)					

Directory 1/10 **OFFICIALS IN U.S. COUNTIES**
continued

County, county seat, 1990 population figures (000 omitted)	County telephone number	Board chairman	Appointed administrator	Clerk to the governing board	Chief financial officer	Personnel director	Chief law enforcement official
UTAH (29) continued							
Emery (Castle Dale) (10)	801 381-2119	(not reporting)					
Garfield (Panguitch) (4)	801 676-8826	(not reporting)					
Grand (Moab) (7)	801 259-5645	(not reporting)					
Iron (Parowan) (21)	801 477-3375	James C Robinson		David I Yardley	Merna H Mitchell	Dennis A Lowder	Ira M Schoppman
Juab (Nephi) (6)	801 623-0271	J Morris Lunt	Randy Freston	Pat P Greenwood	Joyce C Pay		David H Carter
Kane (Kanab) (5)	801 644-2551	F Kirk Heaton		Karla Johnson			Maxwell Jackson
Millard (Fillmore) (11)	801 743-6223	(not reporting)					
Morgan (Morgan) (6)	801 829-6811	(not reporting)					
Piute (Junction) (1)	801 577-2840	(not reporting)					
Rich (Randolph) (2)	801 793-2415	Kenneth R Brown		Pamela Shaul	Pamela Shaul		Farren Floyd
Salt Lake (Salt Lake City) (726)	801 468-3000	E James Bradley	Anthony Mitchell	Sherrie Swensen	Craig Sorensen	James D Johnson	Aaron Kennard
San Juan (Monticello) (13)	801 587-3223	Ty Lewis	Richard M Bailey	Gail M Northern	Marian Bayles		Claude Lacy
Sanpete (Manti) (16)	801 835-2131	(not reporting)					
Sevier (Richfield) (15)	801 896-9262	(not reporting)					
Summit (Coalville) (16)	801 336-4451	(not reporting)					
Tooele (Tooele) (27)	801 882-5557	Leland J Hogan		Dennis Ewing	Glenn Caldwell	Pamela Loth	Donald Proctor
Uintah (Vernal) (22)	801 781-0770	Max D Adams		Pat S McNeill	Michael Wilkins	Joyce Robbins	Lloyd D Meacham
Utah (Provo) (264)	801 373-5510	(not reporting)					
Wasatch (Heber City) (10)	801 654-3211	Moroni Besendorer		Sherry Bond			Michael Spanos
Washington (St. George) (49)	801 634-5700	Gayle M Aldred		E R Christenian	Alis M Ritz	Alis M Ritz	G Humphries
Wayne (Loa) (2)	801 836-2731	(not reporting)					
Weber (Ogden) (158)	801 399-8401	Joan D Hellstrom		Greg W Haws	Greg W Haws	Douglas H Dieu	Craig L Dearden
VERMONT (14)							
Addison (Middlebury) (33)	802 388-7741	(not reporting)					
Bennington (Bennington) (36)	802 442-8528	(not reporting)					
Caledonia (St. Johnsbury) (28)	802 748-3813	(not reporting)					
Chittenden (Burlington) (132)	802 863-3467	(not reporting)					
Essex (Guildhall) (6)	802 254-6857	(not reporting)					
Franklin (St. Albans) (40)	802 524-3863	. . . .	. . . .	Roger N Lumeau	. . . .	. . . .	Dale Messier
Grand Isle (North Hero) (5)	802 372-8350	. . . .	. . . .	Sherry L Little			John S Lawrence
Lamoille (Hyde Park) (20)	802 888-2207	(not reporting)					
Orange (Chelsea) (26)	802 685-4610	(not reporting)					
Orleans (Newport) (24)	802 334-2711	(not reporting)					
Rutland (Rutland) (62)	802 775-4394	(not reporting)					
Washington (Montpelier) (55)	802 223-7066	(not reporting)					
Windham (Newfane) (42)	802 254-4994	(not reporting)					
Windsor (Woodstock) (54)	802 457-2121	(not reporting)					
VIRGINIA (135)							
Accomack (Accomac) (32)	804 787-4289	(not reporting)					
Albemarle (Charlottesville) (68)	804 296-5841	David Bowerman	Robert Tucker	Lettie Neher	Melvin Breeden	Carole Hastings	John Miller
Alexandria (Alexandria) i (111)	703 838-4699	Patricia S Ticer	Vola Lawson	Beverly Jett	Daniel Neckel	Douglas Fertig	Charles Samarra
Alleghany (Covington) (13)	703 965-1600	Clarence Farmer	Eston Burge	Melissa Meadows	Anna Fox	Eston Burge	Thomas Warlitner
Amelia (Amelia Court House) (9)	804 561-3039	Edward T Hurley	John R Wallace	John R Wallace	John R Wallace	John R Wallace	Jimmy E Weaver
Amherst (Amherst) (29)	804 946-9400	Stanley C Harris	Stewart E Shaner	Stewart E Shaner	Donald T Wood	. . . .	Michael E Cox
Appomattox (Appomattox) (12)	804 352-2637	W E Jamerson	. . . .	. . . .	. . . .	. . . .	James Richardson
Arlington (Arlington) (171)	703 358-3000	James B Hunter	Anton S Gardner	Janice C Nisbet	Mark B Jinks	Alan Christenson	William K Stover
Augusta (Verona) (55)	703 245-5600	(not reporting)					
Bath (Warm Springs) (5)	703 839-7221	Douglas P Hirsh	Claire A Collins	Claire A Collins	Claire A Collins	Claire A Collins	James W Bryan Jr
Bedford (Bedford) (46)	703 586-7601	E Anthony Ware	William C Rolfe	William C Rolfe	Norma M Edwards	Kathleen D Guzi	Carol H Wells
Bedford (Bedford) i (6)	703 586-7102	(not reporting)					
Bland (Bland) (7)	703 688-4622	(not reporting)					
Botetourt (Fincastle) (25)	703 473-8220	Robert E Layman	Gerald A Burgess	Gerald A Burgess	C Benton Bolton	. . . .	B Reed Kelly
Bristol i (18)	703 466-5252	. . . .	Paul D Spangler	Daniel L Johnson	Paul D Spangler	Lola G Greer	Howard E Barnes
Brunswick (Lawrenceville) (16)	804 848-3107	(not reporting)					
Buchanan (Grundy) (31)	703 935-2745	(not reporting)					
Buckingham (Buckingham) (13)	804 969-4242	Bobby H Bryan	. . . .	David V Moorman	. . . .	. . . .	Garnett Shumaker
Buena Vista (Buena Vista) i (6)	703 261-6121	(not reporting)					
Campbell (Rustburg) (48)	804 332-5161	J M Davidson	E F Talbert Jr	E F Talbert Jr	Barbara T Farmer	. . . .	Robert E Maxey Jr
Caroline (Bowling Green) (19)	804 633-5380	(not reporting)					
Carroll (Hillsville) (27)	703 728-3331	(not reporting)					
Charles City (Charles City) (6)	804 829-2401	Gilbert A Smith	Gail P Clayton	Gail P Clayton	J Wallace	J Wallace	James H Bowman
Charlotte (Charlotte Crt House) (12)	804 542-5117	(not reporting)					
Charlottesville (Charlottesville) i (40)	804 971-3490	(not reporting)					
Chesapeake (Chesapeake) i (152)	804 547-6166	William Ward	James Rein	Betty Callaway	Joseph Sibley	Carolyn Darden	Ian Shipley Jr
Chesterfield (Chesterfield) (209)	804 748-1000	Art Warren	Lane Ramsey	Theresa Pitts	Jay Stegmaier	Frederick Willis	Joseph Pittman Jr
Clarke (Berryville) (12)	703 955-3269	(not reporting)					
Clifton Forge (Clifton Forge) i (5)	703 863-5091	(not reporting)					
Colonial Heights (Colonial Heights) i (16)	804 520-9265	James B McNeer	Robert E Taylor	Rita C Schiff	William Johnson	Robert E Taylor	Steve Sheffield
Covington (Covington) i (7)	703 965-6300	(not reporting)					
Craig (New Castle) (4)	703 864-5010	Zane M Jones	Richard C Flora	Richard C Flora	Richard C Flora	. . . .	Billy McPherson
Culpeper (Culpeper) (28)	703 825-3035	Jack E Fincham	Steven B Miner	Steven B Miner	Ronald L Mabry	Steven B Miner	Robert E Peters
Cumberland (Cumberland) (8)	804 492-3625	Robert L Rigsby	Thomas C Foley	Thomas C Foley	. . . .	. . . .	Marshall S Smith
Danville (Danville) i (53)	804 799-5100	. . . .	A Ray Griffin Jr	. . . .	Aubrey Dodson	Lundy Shackelford	Neal Morris
Dickenson (Clintwood) (18)	703 926-1679	Paul Buchanan	Vicki B Garrett	Vicki B Garrett	Gary M Artrid	Betty R Hill	F Childress
Dinwiddie (Dinwiddie) (21)	804 469-4500	Aubrey Clay	Wendy Weber	Wendy Weber	Glenice Townsend	. . . .	Bennie Heath
Emporia (Emporia) i (5)	804 634-3332	(not reporting)					
Essex (Tappahannock) (9)	804 443-4331	James F Moore	R Gary Allen	Linda E Lumpkin	. . . .	Paul L Baldino	Damon E Davis
Fairfax (Fairfax) (819)	703 324-2000	Thomas M Davis	W J Leidinger	Nancy Vehrs	Susan S Planchon		Michael N Young
Fairfax (Fairfax) i (20)	703 385-7855	. . . .	. . . .	J Henderson	J Cawley	D Sudduth	J Skinner
Falls Church (Falls Church) i (10)	703 241-5001	(not reporting)					
Fauquier (Warrenton) (49)	703 347-8699	Georgia Herbert	G Robert Lee	D Gouldthorpe	Dennis Hunsberger	Deborah Johnson	Joe Higgs
Floyd (Floyd) (12)	703 745-9300	William Whitlock	Randal E Arno	Randal E Arno	Randal E Arno	Randal E Arno	Charles T Higgins
Fluvanna (Palmyra) (12)	804 589-3138	Ryland C Watts	Charles W Burgess	Charles W Burgess	Charles W Burgess	Charles W Burgess	Gordon Richardson
Franklin (Rocky Mount) (40)	703 483-3030	W Wayne Angell	Macon C Sammons	Sharon F Keatts	Elaine H Chitwood	. . . .	W Q Overton
Franklin (Franklin) i (8)	804 562-8508	G Elliott Cobb	John J Jackson	John J Jackson	John J Jackson	Baucom Hinson	Robert K Eubanks
Frederick (Winchester) (46)	703 665-5600	Richard G Dick	John R Riley Jr	John R Riley Jr	Cheryl B Shiffler	Ann K Kelican	Robert Williamson
Fredericksburg (Fredericksburg) i (19)	703 372-1010	. . . .	Marvin Bolinger	. . . .	Clarence Robinson	Melissa B Webb	Roland Oates
Galax (Galax) i (7)	703 236-3441	(not reporting)					

Directory 1/10   **OFFICIALS IN U.S. COUNTIES**
continued

County, county seat, 1990 population figures (000 omitted)	County telephone number	Board chairman	Appointed administrator	Clerk to the governing board	Chief financial officer	Personnel director	Chief law enforcement official
VIRGINIA (135) continued							
Giles (Pearisburg) (16)	703 921-2525	(not reporting)					
Gloucester (Gloucester) (30)	804 693-4042	Benjamin Seawell	William H Whitley	William H Whitley	R Edward Brown	William H Whitley	Robin P Stanaway
Goochland (Goochland) (14)	804 556-5300	(not reporting)					
Grayson (Independence) (16) . . .	703 773-2471	Raymond L Carico	Donald G Young	Donald G Young	. . . .	. . . .	Herbert McKnight
Greene (Stanardsville) (10)	804 985-5299	James A Henshaw	Julius L Morris	Julius L Morris	Mary E Garth	Julius L Morris	William L Morris
Greensville (Emporia) (9)	804 348-4205	Peggy R Wiley	. . . .	David Whittington	. . . .	. . . .	Earl D Sasser
Halifax (Halifax) (29)	804 476-2141	Fulton C Conner	William D Sleeper	William D Sleeper	Linda S Foster	Julia A Moss	Eugene G Shortt
Hampton (Hampton) i (134)	804 727-6407	James L Eason	Robert J O' Neill	Diana T Hughes	James A Peterson	Tharon Greene	. . . .
Hanover (Hanover) (63)	804 730-8000	(not reporting)					
Harrisonburg (Harrisonburg) i (31)	703 434-6776	(not reporting)					
Henrico (Richmond) (218)	804 672-4000	John A Waldrop Jr	Virgil R Hazelett	Betty C Taylor	Dennis W Kerns	George H Cauble	Richard G Engels
Henry (Collinsville) (57)	703 638-5311	R J Frye	Robert Lawler Jr	. . . .	Jimmie L Wright	. . . .	Harold F Cassell
Highland (Monterey) (3)	703 468-2447	(not reporting)					
Hopewell (Hopewell) i (23)	804 541-2200	(not reporting)					
Isle Of Wight (Isle Of Wight) (25)	804 357-3191	(not reporting)					
James City (Williamsburg) (35) .	804 253-6605	Judy Knudson	David Norman	David Norman	John McDonald	Carol Luckam	Robert Key
King and Queen (King & Queen Ct. Hse.) (6)	804 785-7955	(not reporting)					
King George (King George) (14) .	703 775-9181	Cedell Brooks Jr	L Eldon James Jr	L Eldon James Jr	Lisa M Baxter	. . . .	C W Dobson
King William (King William) (11)	804 769-3011	L T McAllister	David S Whitlow	David S Whitlow	Terri E Hale	David S Whitlow	W Wayne Healy
Lancaster (Lancaster) (11)	804 462-5129	Betty Barrack	William H Pennell	William H Pennell	William H Pennell	William H Pennell	Ronald D Crockett
Lee (Jonesville) (24)	703 346-7714	. . . .	Phillip F Gay	. . . .	Helen Duncan	. . . .	Robert V Chadwell
Lexington (Lexington) i (7)	703 463-7133	H E Derrick Jr	T Jon Ellestad	Georgiana M Vita	Keith L Holland	T Jon Ellestad	Bruce M Beard
Loudoun (Leesburg) (86)	703 777-0200	George Barton	Kirby Bowers	. . . .	M E Poole	Candice DeButts	John Isom
Louisa (Louisa) (20)	703 967-0401	John J Purcell	William C Porter	William C Porter	William E Johnson	. . . .	Henry A Kennon
Lunenburg (Lunenburg) (11)	804 696-2142	(not reporting)					
Lynchburg (Lynchburg) i (66) . . .	804 847-1315	(not reporting)					
Madison (Madison) (12)	703 948-6102	David C Jones	. . . .	Stephen L Utz	Corrie M Smith	. . . .	Robert C Russell
Manassas (Manassas) i (28)	703 257-8200	(not reporting)					
Manassas Park (Manassas Park) i (7)	703 361-0124	(not reporting)					
Martinsville (Martinsville) i (18) . .	703 638-3971	(not reporting)					
Mathews (Mathews) (8)	804 725-7172	(not reporting)					
Mecklenburg (Boydton) (29)	804 738-6191	(not reporting)					
Middlesex (Saluda) (9)	804 758-4330	(not reporting)					
Montgomery (Christiansburg) (74)	703 382-5700	Ira D Long	Betty S Thomas	. . . .	J J Lunsford	E Randall Wertz	Kennard L Phipps
Nelson (Lovingston) (13)	804 263-4873	Heywood Greenberg	R H Moore	R H Moore	J Marvin Davis	. . . .	Ronald Wood
New Kent (New Kent) (10)	804 966-9861	Michael D Salmon	H G Hart	H G Hart	Betty J Burrell	Alease Christian	Farrar W Howard
Newport News (Newport News) i (175)	804 247-8444	(not reporting)					
Norfolk i (261)	804 441-2000	(not reporting)					
Northampton (Eastville) (13)	804 678-5148	John W White Sr	Thomas E Harris	Thomas E Harris	E B Savage	. . . .	W Wayne Bradford
Northumberland (Heathsville) (11)	804 580-7666	(not reporting)					
Norton (Norton) i (4)	703 679-1160	B Robert Raines	E W Ward	Mary D Brown	E W Ward	E W Ward	Samuel A Mongle
Nottoway (Nottoway) (15)	804 645-8696	Sherman C Vaughn	Ronald E Roark	Ronald E Roark	Barbara L Senger	Ronald E Roark	Larry J Parrish
Orange (Orange) (21)	703 672-3313	R Duff Green	A T Baskerville	. . . .	. . . .	Janice C Crockett	William Spence
Page (Luray) (22)	703 743-4142	Raymond Kite	Ron Wilson	Ron Wilson	Gerald Judd	Geraldine Cubbage	Edward Sedwick
Patrick (Stuart) (17)	703 694-6094	Ewell Harold	David R Hoback	David R Hoback	N Louise Harris	. . . .	Jay E Gregory
Petersburg i (38)	804 733-2324	Rosalyn Dance	Valerie Lemmie	Barbara Moore	T Rob Blount	M Angela White	Willie Williams
Pittsylvania (Chatham) (56)	804 432-2041	(not reporting)					
Poquoson (Poquoson) i (11)	804 868-7181	L Cornell Burcher	Robert M Murphy	Judy F Wiggins	Carol O Davis	. . . .	John T White
Portsmouth (Portsmouth) i (104) .	804 393-8000	Gloria Webb	V Wayne Orton	Sheila Pittman	J Peter Teig	C Fletcher	Leslie Martinez
Powhatan (Powhatan) (15)	804 598-5600	Robert R Cosby	Stephen F Owen	Stephen F Owen	Ruth N Heath	. . . .	Shirley Reynolds
Prince Edward (Farmville) (17) . .	804 392-8837	Hugh E Carwile Jr	Mildred B Hampton	Mildred B Hampton	Mable Shanaberger	Mildred B Hampton	Gene A Southall
Prince George (Prince George) (27) .	804 733-2600	Marion B Williams	John G Kines Jr	John G Kines Jr	Jean M Barker	John G Kines Jr	Perry A Lewis
Prince William (Woodbridge) (216) .	703 792-6640	Kathryn Seefeldt	James Mullen	James Agbayani	John Wenderski	Cleil Fitzwater	Charlie Deane
Pulaski (Pulaski) (34)	703 980-7705	Jerry D White	Joseph N Morgan	. . . .	Rose Marie Tickle	Nancy M Burchett	Ralph Dobbins
Radford (Radford) i (16)	703 731-3603	Thomas Starnes	Robert Asbury Jr	Roy Lloyd Jr	Jess Cantline	Robert Asbury Jr	A C Earles
Rappahannock (Washington) (7)	703 675-3342	Hubert S Gilkey	John W McCarthy	. . . .	. . . .	. . . .	John H Woodward
Richmond (Richmond) i (203) . .	804 780-7000	Walter T Kenney	Robert C Bobb	Edna Williams	Max Bohnstedt	Johnel Bracey	Marty Tapscott
Richmond (Warsaw) (7)	804 333-3415	(not reporting)					
Roanoke (Roanoke) (79)	703 772-2018	Harold O Mannix	Elmer C Hodge	Mary Allen	Diane D Hyatt	D Keith Cook	John H Cease
Rockbridge (Lexington) (18)	703 463-4361	(not reporting)					
Rockingham (Harrisonburg) (57)	703 564-3000	James V Couch	William O' Brien	William O' Brien	Cecil L Wampler	William O' Brien	G W Weatherholtz
Russell (Lebanon) (29)	703 889-2372	(not reporting)					
Salem (Salem) i (24)	703 375-3060	James Taliaferro	Randolph M Smith	Forest G Jones	Frank P Turk	Carolyn H Barrett	Harry T Haskins
Scott (Gate City) (23)	703 386-6521	Frank Sarge Reed	Patrick L Loggans	Patrick L Loggans	Martha H Bledsoe	Patrick L Loggans	Jerry Broadwater
Shenandoah (Woodstock) (32) . .	703 459-2195	Dennis M Morris	John D Cutlip	John D Cutlip	Cindy A George	. . . .	Marshall Robinson
Smyth (Marion) (32)	703 783-3298	M Jay Hubble	Kenneth C Noble	Kenneth C Noble	Ruth D Albert	Kenneth C Noble	John H Grubb Jr
South Boston (South Boston) i (7)	804 575-4200	(not reporting)					
Southampton (Courtland) (18) . .	804 653-3015	A M Felts	R L Taylor	R L Taylor	R L Taylor	R L Taylor	V W Francis Jr
Spotsylvania (Spotsylvania) (57)	703 582-7000	Jean W Jones	L Kimball Payne	Linda Johnson	Tammy D Petrie	Susan B Reynolds	T C Waddy Jr
Stafford (Stafford) (61)	703 659-8603	Lyle R Smith	C M Williams Jr	C M Williams Jr	James M K Reid	Robert W Clark	Ralph M Williams
Staunton (24)	703 332-3825	. . . .	Bernard J Murphy	Deborah L Sutton	Jeanne R Colvin	John W Cutsinger	Grafton L Wells
Suffolk (Suffolk) i (52)	804 934-3111	S Chris Jones	Richard L Hedrick	Henry L Murden	Carroll L Acors	. . . .	Gilbert F Jackson
Surry (Surry) (6)	804 294-5271	Ray D Peace	Terry D Lewis	Terry D Lewis	. . . .	Terry D Lewis	Harold D Brown
Sussex (Sussex) (10)	804 246-7000	Glover W Pegram	George N Walker	George N Walker	. . . .	George N Walker	E Stuart Kitchen
Tazewell (Tazewell) (46)	703 988-7541	James Jones	Lavern Bechtel	Lavern Bechtel	Norman Cook	Patricia Green	D J Joe Johnson
Virginia Beach (Virginia Beach) i (393)	804 427-4242	(not reporting)					
Warren (Front Royal) (26)	703 636-4600	Staige F Miller	J Ronald George	J Ronald George	Doris D Miller	. . . .	Lynn C Armentrout
Washington (Abingdon) (46)	703 628-2983	Joe W Derting	Bruce E Bentley	Bruce E Bentley	Mark Seamon	Rebecca K Patrick	Joe D Mitchell
Waynesboro i (19)	703 942-6600	(not reporting)					
Westmoreland (Montross) (15) . .	804 493-8911	. . . .	Norman Risavi	. . . .	. . . .	. . . .	. . . .
Williamsburg (Williamsburg) i (12)	804 220-6100	(not reporting)					
Winchester (Winchester) i (22) . .	703 667-1815	Gary Chrisman	Edwin C Daley	Bonnie McCurry	Bill M Ewing	Sharen E Gromling	Floyd A Barley
Wise (Wise) (40)	703 328-2321	(not reporting)					
Wythe (Wytheville) (25)	703 223-6020	(not reporting)					
York (Yorktown) (42)	804 890-3690	Jere M Mills	Daniel M Stuck	Daniel M Stuck	James McReynolds	Peter A Iannl	Preston Williams
WASHINGTON (39)							
Adams (Ritzville) (14)	509 659-0090	Bill Wills	. . . .	Linda Reimer	Leon Long	. . . .	Ron Snowden
Asotin (Asotin) (18)	509 243-4160	Harley Williams	. . . .	Kathie Dahlin	Doug Mattoon	Kathie Dahlin	Donald Steele

Directory 1/10
continued

OFFICIALS IN U.S. COUNTIES

County, county seat, 1990 population figures (000 omitted)	County telephone number	Board chairman	Appointed administrator	Clerk to the governing board	Chief financial officer	Personnel director	Chief law enforcement official
WASHINGTON (39) continued							
Benton (Prosser) (113)	509 786-5600	(not reporting)					
Chelan (Wenatchee) (52)	509 663-1147	Ronald W Myers	Paul F Dunning	Evelyn L Arnold	Allen Martin	. . . .	Dan Breda
Clallam (Port Angeles) (56)	206 452-7831	Dave Cameron	Jim Rumpeltes	Karen Flores	. . . .	Marge Uphamrood	Joe Hawe
Clark (Vancouver) (238)	206 699-2000	(not reporting)					
Columbia (Dayton) (4)	509 382-4542	Jon W McFarland	. . . .	Tairy J Lembcke	Betty A Fletcher	. . . .	Jim Latour
Cowlitz (Kelso) (82)	206 577-3020	(not reporting)					
Douglas (Waterville) (26)	509 745-8527	Jay P Weber	. . . .	Marilyn Northrup	Laurie Evenhus	. . . .	Dan Laroche
Ferry (Republic) (6)	509 775-5200	Ed F Windsor	. . . .	Shilah Moores	Kathryn Almquist	. . . .	Richard E Baldwin
Franklin (Pasco) (37)	509 545-3535	(not reporting)					
Garfield (Pomeroy) (2)	509 843-1391	Ronald E Crawford	. . . .	Donna J Deal	. . . .	. . . .	William C Taylor
Grant (Ephrata) (55)	509 754-2011	Helen Fancher	. . . .	Peggy Grigg	Bill Varney	. . . .	Bill Wiester
Grays Harbor (Montesano) (64) .	206 249-3731	(not reporting)					
Island (Coupeville) (60)	206 679-7300	(not reporting)					
Jefferson (Port Townsend) (20) ..	206 385-9100	Richard E Wojt	. . . .	Lorna L Delaney	. . . .	David Goldsmith	Mel Mefford
King (Seattle) (1507)	206 296-0100	(not reporting)					
Kitsap (Port Orchard) (190)	206 876-7053	Win Granlund	Deborah Broughton	Holly Anderson	Sharon Shrader	Bert Furuta	Pat Jones
Kittitas (Ellensburg) (27)	509 962-7508	Ray Owens	. . . .	. . . .	Bev Allenbaugh	. . . .	Bob McBride
Klickitat (Goldendale) (17)	509 773-4612	Joan Frey	. . . .	Nancy Evans	Robert Niemela	. . . .	James Gleason
Lewis (Chehalis) (59)	206 748-9121	(not reporting)					
Lincoln (Davenport) (9)	509 725-3031	Robert Wyborney	. . . .	Shelly Johnston	Doris Hein	. . . .	Dan Berry
Mason (Shelton) (38)	206 427-9670	William O Hunter	. . . .	Rebecca S Rogers	. . . .	. . . .	Robert Shepherd
Okanogan (Okanogan) (33)	509 422-3521	Ronald V Weeks	. . . .	Brenda J White	. . . .	. . . .	James K Weed
Pacific (South Bend) (19)	206 875-9337	(not reporting)					
Pend Oreille (Newport) (9)	509 447-4119	Michael D Keogh	. . . .	Alice Mitchell	. . . .	. . . .	Doug Malby
Pierce (Tacoma) (586)	206 591-7480	(not reporting)					
San Juan (Friday Harbor) (10) ..	206 378-2898	(not reporting)					
Skagit (Mount Vernon) (80)	206 336-9300	Robert Hart	Robert Taylor	Connie Carter	Mike Woodmansee	. . . .	Gary Frazier
Skamania (Stevenson) (8)	509 427-5141	Dean Evans	Marilyn Breckel	Gary Olsen	. . . .	. . . .	Ray Blaisdell
Snohomish (Everett) (466)	206 388-3411	(not reporting)					
Spokane (Spokane) (361)	509 456-2265	(not reporting)					
Stevens (Colville) (31)	509 684-3751	(not reporting)					
Thurston (Olympia) (161)	206 754-3800	Diane Oberquell	T Fitzsimmons	Bonita Bowmar	John Bartz	M Wright Dohrn	Gary Edwards
Wahkiakum (Cathlamet) (3)	206 795-3219	. . . .	. . . .	Rhonda Hiewer	. . . .	. . . .	. . . .
Walla Walla (Walla Walla) (48) ..	509 525-6161	Charles A Maiden	. . . .	Connie R Vinti	. . . .	. . . .	Billy H Jackson
Whatcom (Bellingham) (128) ...	206 676-6690	(not reporting)					
Whitman (Colfax) (39)	509 397-4622	William A Scmick	. . . .	Louise Burgess	Richard Brown	Jean M Conger	Steve Tomson
Yakima (Yakima) (189)	509 575-4061	Charles Klarich	Dema Harris	Sylvia Hinojosa	Craig Warner	Dema Harris	Doug Blair
WEST VIRGINIA (55)							
Barbour (Philippi) (16)	304 457-2232	(not reporting)					
Berkeley (Martinsburg) (59)	304 267-3000	William Kisner	Daniel O'Donnell	John Small	John Small	Daniel O' Donnell	Preston Gooden
Boone (Madison) (26)	304 369-3925	(not reporting)					
Braxton (Sutton) (13)	304 765-2833	(not reporting)					
Brooke (Wellsburg) (27)	304 737-3661	Daniel Gilchrist		Sylvia Benzo	Michael Allman		Michael Allman
Cabell (Huntington) (97)	304 525-7754	(not reporting)					
Calhoun (Grantsville) (8)	304 354-6725	(not reporting)					
Clay (Clay) (10)	304 587-4259	(not reporting)					
Doddridge (West Union) (7)	304 873-2631	(not reporting)					
Fayette (Fayetteville) (48)	304 574-1200	Gene Carte Jr	Charlotte Holly	Kelvin Holliday	William Laird		William Laird
Gilmer (Glenville) (8)	304 462-7641	(not reporting)					
Grant (Petersburg) (10)	304 257-4422	(not reporting)					
Greenbrier (Lewisburg) (35)	304 645-2373	(not reporting)					
Hampshire (Romney) (16)	304 822-5112	(not reporting)					
Hancock (New Cumberland) (35) .	304 564-3311	(not reporting)					
Hardy (Moorefield) (11)	304 538-2929	(not reporting)					
Harrison (Clarksburg) (69)	304 624-8500	(not reporting)					
Jackson (Ripley) (26)	304 372-2011	(not reporting)					
Jefferson (Charles Town) (36) ..	304 725-9761	Edgar Ridgeway	Leslie D Smith	John Ott	. . . .	. . . .	William Senseney
Kanawha (Charleston) (208)	304 357-0101	William J Reese	Carl R Clay Jr	Alma Y King	Michael Greenleaf		Art Ashley
Lewis (Weston) (17)	304 269-8200	(not reporting)					
Lincoln (Hamlin) (21)	304 824-3336	Jay M Hoke	. . . .	Donald C Whitten	Greg Stowers	. . . .	Jackie Cooper
Logan (Logan) (43)	304 752-2000	(not reporting)					
Marion (Fairmont) (57)	304 367-5400	(not reporting)					
Marshall (Moundsville) (37)	304 845-1220	Malcolm M Shimp	. . . .	Norma Glover Sine	Robert L Lightner	. . . .	Robert L Lightner
Mason (Point Pleasant) (25)	304 675-1110	(not reporting)					
Mc Dowell (Welch) (35)	304 436-8344	(not reporting)					
Mercer (Princeton) (65)	304 487-8311	John K Rapp	Herbert Tate	Rudolph Jennings	Don B Meadows	. . . .	Don B Meadows
Mineral (Keyser) (27)	304 788-5921	Robert D Harman	Michael C Bland	Ruby L Staggs	. . . .	. . . .	Patrick L Nield
Mingo (Williamson) (34)	304 235-1638	(not reporting)					
Monongalia (Morgantown) (76) .	304 291-7257	John W Pyles	Diane F DeMedici	Thelma J Gibson	Joseph C Bartolo		Joseph C Bartolo
Monroe (Union) (12)	304 772-3096	(not reporting)					
Morgan (Berkeley Springs) (12) .	304 258-2774	Glen R Stotler	William Clark	Ralph N Shambaugh	Debra Kesecker	. . . .	Kermit M Ambrose
Nicholas (Summersville) (27) ...	304 872-3630	Gary Johnson	. . . .	John Greer	. . . .	. . . .	Tom Blankship
Ohio (Wheeling) (51)	304 234-3628	(not reporting)					
Pendleton (Franklin) (8)	304 358-7573	(not reporting)					
Pleasants (St. Marys) (8)	304 684-3513	(not reporting)					
Pocahontas (Marlinton) (9)	304 799-4604	(not reporting)					
Preston (Kingwood) (29)	304 329-1805	(not reporting)					
Putnam (Winfield) (43)	304 586-9036	(not reporting)					
Raleigh (Beckley) (77)	304 255-9146	(not reporting)					
Randolph (Elkins) (28)	304 636-0543	(not reporting)					
Ritchie (Harrisville) (10)	304 643-2164	(not reporting)					
Roane (Spencer) (15)	304 927-2860	(not reporting)					
Summers (Hinton) (14)	304 466-4235	(not reporting)					
Taylor (Grafton) (15)	304 265-1401	(not reporting)					
Tucker (Parsons) (8)	304 478-2606	(not reporting)					
Tyler (Middlebourne) (10)	304 758-2102	Robert D Wable	. . . .	Donna J Thomas	. . . .	. . . .	Michael Griffin
Upshur (Buckhannon) (23)	304 472-0535	Thomas H Keadle	William A Parker	Teresa C Beer	William A Parker	Debbie T Wilfong	Virgil D Miller
Wayne (Wayne) (42)	304 272-5101	(not reporting)					
Webster (Webster Springs) (11) .	304 847-2508	(not reporting)					
Wetzel (New Martinsville) (19) ..	304 455-1390	Shirley Michael	. . . .	Mary Riggenbach	. . . .	. . . .	N E Higginbotham
Wirt (Elizabeth) (5)	304 275-4222	(not reporting)					
Wood (Parkersburg) (87)	304 424-1984	Holmes R Shaver	Mary R Rader	Jamie Six	Jamie Six	. . . .	Ken Merritt
Wyoming (Pineville) (28)	304 732-8000	(not reporting)					
WISCONSIN (72)							
Adams (Friendship) (16)	608 339-4200	George Dixon	. . . .	Beverly Ward	Sharlene Klicko	Michael McKenna	Robert Farber

Directory 1/10 **OFFICIALS IN U.S. COUNTIES**
continued

County, county seat, 1990 population figures (000 omitted)	County telephone number	Board chairman	Appointed administrator	Clerk to the governing board	Chief financial officer	Personnel director	Chief law enforcement official
WISCONSIN (72) continued							
Ashland (Ashland) (16)	715 682-7000	Michael Ellias	Thomas Kieweg	Elaine Stibbe	Tracey Hoglund	. . . .	John Kovach
Barron (Barron) (41)	715 537-3212	Arnold Ellison	. . . .	Judith Genereau	Marla Thompson	. . . .	Jerry Johnson
Bayfield (Washburn) (14)	715 373-6100	(not reporting)					
Brown (Green Bay) (195)	414 448-4067	(not reporting)					
Buffalo (Alma) (14)	608 685-4940	(not reporting)					
Burnett (Siren) (13)	715 349-2181	Milt Stellrecht	Myron Schuster	Helen Steffen	Julie Johnson	. . . .	Donald Taylor
Calumet (Chilton) (34)	414 849-2361	(not reporting)					
Chippewa (Chippewa Falls) (52) .	715 723-1831	(not reporting)					
Clark (Neillsville) (32)	715 743-5148	(not reporting)					
Columbia (Portage) (45)	608 742-2191	John Tramberg	. . . .	Cathy Lathrop	Lois Schwepp	Jim Aiello	Jim Smith
Crawford (Prairie Du Chien) (16)	608 326-0200	(not reporting)					
Dane (Madison) (367)	608 266-4114	(not reporting)					
Dodge (Juneau) (77)	414 386-3690	(not reporting)					
Door (Sturgeon Bay) (26)	414 743-5511	Lyle Hill	. . . .	Nancy Bemmann	. . . .	James Jetzke	Charles Brann
Douglas (Superior) (42)	715 394-0429	David Dumke	. . . .	Ray Sommerville	Larry Kroll	John Mulder	Marvin Arneson
Dunn (Menomonie) (36)	715 232-2429	(not reporting)					
Eau Claire (Eau Claire) (85)	715 839-4711	C W Chatterson	Ronald Wampler	Joanne Lester	Richard Roe	Marvin Niese	Richard Hewitt
Florence (Florence) (5)	715 528-3201	(not reporting)					
Fond Du Lac (Fond Du Lac) (90) .	414 929-3000	G Stanchfield	Dick Celichowski	Joyce Buechel	Karen Kuehl	Rich Brzozowski	Jim Gilmore
Forest (Crandon) (9)	715 478-2422	(not reporting)					
Grant (Lancaster) (49)	608 723-2675	(not reporting)					
Green (Monroe) (30)	608 328-9430	(not reporting)					
Green Lake (Green Lake) (19) ...	414 294-6581	Herbert A Dahlke	. . . .	Marge Bostelmann	. . . .	. . . .	Lance Buchholtz
Iowa (Dodgeville) (20)	608 935-5445	(not reporting)					
Iron (Hurley) (6)	715 561-3375	(not reporting)					
Jackson (Black River Falls) (17) .	715 284-7441	(not reporting)					
Jefferson (Jefferson) (68)	414 674-7100	Wendell Wilson	Willard Hausen	Barbara Geyer	. . . .	Willard Hausen	Orval Quamme
Juneau (Mauston) (22)	608 847-9300	James C Barrett	. . . .	Carl E Wilke	Lori L Chipman	Nancy Krueger	Richard McCurdy
Kenosha (Kenosha) (128)	414 653-6422	Leonard Johnson	John Collins	Nancy Principe	David Geertsen	Brooke Koons	Alan Kehl
Kewaunee (Kewaunee) (19)	414 388-3580	(not reporting)					
La Crosse (La Crosse) (98)	608 785-9640	James A Ehrsam	Paul B Webber	Sharon M Lemke	Gerald Seubert	Robert B Taunt	Karl W Halverson
Lafayette (Darlington) (16)	608 776-4850	(not reporting)					
Langlade (Antigo) (20)	715 627-6200	Judy Rustick	. . . .	Norman Cejka	Jeff Mundinger	. . . .	David Steger
Lincoln (Merrill) (27)	715 536-0312	Robert Sumnicht	. . . .	Marlene Fox	. . . .	Daniel Mundt Jr	. . . .
Manitowoc (Manitowoc) (80) ...	414 683-4000	Don Markwart	Bam Peterson	Daniel Fischer	Todd Reckelburg	. . . .	Thomas Kocourek
Marathon (Wausau) (115)	715 847-5000	Ted Telleckson	Mort McBain	Louann Fenhaus	Bryon Karow	Brad Karger	Gerald Kittel
Marinette (Marinette) (41)	715 732-7400	Claryce Maedke	Steve Fredericks	Don Phillips	Roger DeGroot	. . . .	James Kanikula
Marquette (Montello) (12)	608 297-9114	(not reporting)					
Menominee (Keshena) (4)	715 799-3311	(not reporting)					
Milwaukee (Milwaukee) (959) ...	414 278-4148	Robert Jackson Jr	. . . .	Rod Lanser	Earl Hawkins Jr	Federico Zaragoza	Richard Artison
Monroe (Sparta) (37)	608 269-8719	Harv Simmons	. . . .	David Hering	Annette Erickson	Ken Kittleson	Dale Trowbridge
Oconto (Oconto) (30)	414 834-5322	(not reporting)					
Oneida (Rhinelander) (32)	715 369-6154	Tony Lorbetske	. . . .	Robert Bruso	Marge Coffen	Carey Jackson	Charles Crofoot
Outagamie (Appleton) (141)	414 832-5051	(not reporting)					
Ozaukee (Port Washington) (73) .	414 284-9411	Leroy Bley	. . . .	Harold Dobberphul	Karen Makoutz	Michael J Puksich	Michael Milas
Pepin (Durand) (7)	715 672-8857	Bernard Milliren	. . . .	Carol M Forster	. . . .	Lawrence Krcmar	John C Andrews
Pierce (Ellsworth) (33)	715 273-5272	Richard Wilhelm	David Sorenson	David Sorenson	June Olson	Sandra Langer	James Hines
Polk (Balsam Lake) (35)	715 485-3161	Stanley Anderson	. . . .	Sharon Schiebel	. . . .	Thomas Wishman	Craig Benware
Portage (Stevens Point) (61)	715 346-1351	Clarence Hintz	. . . .	Roger Wrycza	Jerry Glad	Gerald Lang	Ronald Borski
Price (Phillips) (16)	715 339-3325	(not reporting)					
Racine (Racine) (175)	414 636-3118	(not reporting)					
Richland (Richland Center) (18) .	608 647-2197	(not reporting)					
Rock (Janesville) (140)	608 757-5510	Donald Upson	Craig Knutson	Kay O'Connell	Jeff Smith	James Bryant	F Joseph Black
Rusk (Ladysmith) (15)	715 532-2100	(not reporting)					
Sauk (Baraboo) (47)	608 356-5581	Roger Shanks	Thomas McCarty	Beverly Mielke	Deborah Gaffney	Michael Wolfe	Virgil Steinhorst
Sawyer (Hayward) (14)	715 634-4866	(not reporting)					
Shawano (Shawano) (37)	715 526-9135	(not reporting)					
Sheboygan (Sheboygan) (104) ..	414 459-3000	Corby Felsher	. . . .	Patricia Meyer	Robert Danforth	Louella Conway	Wm D Spelshaus
St. Croix (Hudson) (50)	715 386-4610	Richard Peterson	John Krizek	Sue Nelson	Richard Loney	Debra Kathan	Ralph Bader
Taylor (Medford) (19)	715 748-3131	Edwin H Ahlers	. . . .	Roger L Emmerich	Roger L Emmerich	. . . .	William Breneman
Trempealeau (Whitehall) (25) ...	715 538-2311	Peter Speerstra	. . . .	Paul Syverson	. . . .	. . . .	R Weisenberger
Vernon (Viroqua) (26)	608 637-3569	(not reporting)					
Vilas (Eagle River) (18)	715 479-6469	(not reporting)					
Walworth (Elkhorn) (75)	414 741-2593	Gerald Byrnes	. . . .	Carol Krauklis	Nicole Andersen	Janice St John	Dean McKenzie
Washburn (Shell Lake) (14)	715 468-7808	(not reporting)					
Washington (West Bend) (95) ...	414 338-4400	Reuben Schmahl	. . . .	Arthur G Degnitz	Susan Haag	Gary G Moschea	Robert Schulteis
Waukesha (Waukesha) (305) ...	414 548-7194	James Luebke	. . . .	Patricia Madden	Norman Cummings	Allan C Walsch	Arnold Moncada
Waupaca (Waupaca) (46)	715 258-6200	Duane R Brown	Mary A Robbins	Mary A Robbins	James W Goeser	Laura A Langman	William E Mork
Waushara (Wautoma) (19)	414 787-4631	George Sorenson	Debra Behringer	. . . .	. . . .	Debra Behringer	Patrick Fox
Winnebago (Oshkosh) (140)	414 236-4747	Jack Steinhilber	. . . .	Linda Wolfe	Charles Orenstein	William Wagner	Robert Kraus
Wood (Wisconsin Rapids) (74) ..	715 421-8400	Al A Reynolds	. . . .	Anthony Ruesch	David M Goetz	Douglass F Maurer	Brian Illlngworth
WYOMING (23)							
Albany (Laramie) (31)	307 721-2541	Pat Gabriel	. . . .	Jackie R Gonzales	. . . .	. . . .	Gary L Puls
Big Horn (Basin) (11)	307 568-2357	Donald M Russell	. . . .	Ellen Whipps	George H Hoffman	. . . .	Gary Anders
Campbell (Gillette) (29)	307 682-7283	Willis Chrans	. . . .	Vivian E Addison	. . . .	. . . .	Byron Oedekoven
Carbon (Rawlins) (17)	307 328-2699	Artlin Zeiger	. . . .	W E Harshman	W E Harshman	. . . .	Chet Engstrom
Converse (Douglas) (11)	307 358-2244	(not reporting)					
Crook (Sundance) (5)	307 283-1323	(not reporting)					
Fremont (Lander) (34)	307 332-2405	Tom Satterfield	. . . .	Alma Nicol	H S Harnsberger	. . . .	Joe Lucero
Goshen (Torrington) (12)	307 532-4051	(not reporting)					
Hot Springs (Thermopolis) (5) ..	307 864-3515	Darvin Longwell	. . . .	M Christofferson	. . . .	. . . .	John P Lumley
Johnson (Buffalo) (6)	307 684-7272	(not reporting)					
Laramie (Cheyenne) (73)	307 638-4260	Byron Rookstool	. . . .	Janet Whitehead	. . . .	Emily Smith	Rudy Restivo
Lincoln (Kemmerer) (13)	307 877-9056	(not reporting)					
Natrona (Casper) (61)	307 235-9200	Bill R Brauer	. . . .	Mary Ann Collins	. . . .	. . . .	David Dovala
Niobrara (Lusk) (2)	307 334-2211	Richard L James	. . . .	Suzanne R Sturman	Teresa Poage	. . . .	Eldon R Alexander
Park (Cody) (23)	307 587-2204	Jack J Winninger	. . . .	. . . .	. . . .	. . . .	Bill J Brewer
Platte (Wheatland) (8)	307 322-2315	Chuck Frederick	. . . .	Jerry G Orr	Linda Poe Bowen	. . . .	William Letcher
Sheridan (Sheridan) (24)	307 674-6722	Ken Kerns	. . . .	Ronald Dailey	Janet Lewis	. . . .	Robert Shelley
Sublette (Pinedale) (5)	307 367-4372	Monte B Skinner	. . . .	Mary L Lankford	. . . .	. . . .	Jack Cain
Sweetwater (Green River) (39) ..	307 875-7602	Linda Taliaferro	. . . .	Albert Vesco	Robb Slaughtery	Robert Walters	Gary Bailiff
Teton (Jackson) (11)	307 733-4430	(not reporting)					
Uinta (Evanston) (19)	307 789-1780	Paul R Barnard	. . . .	Lynne D Fox	Terry Brimhall	. . . .	Forrest Bright
Washakie (Worland) (8)	307 347-3131	Alice E Lass	. . . .	Janice Wake	Janice Wake	. . . .	Ralph Seghetti
Weston (Newcastle) (7)	307 746-4225	(not reporting)					

Professional, Special Assistance and Educational Organizations Serving Local and State Governments

This article briefly describes 75 organizations that provide services of particular importance to cities, counties, and other local and state governments. Most of the organizations are membership groups for school administrators, health officers, city planners, city managers, public works directors, city attorneys, and other administrators who are appointed rather than elected. Several are general service and representational organizations for states, cities, counties, and administrators and citizens. Some organizations provide distinctive research, technological, consulting, and educational programs on a cost-of-service basis and have been established to meet specific needs of state and local governments. The others support educational activities in urban affairs or government administration and conduct research and other educational activities in urban affairs or government administration and conduct research and other educational activities thereby indirectly strengthening professionalism in government administration.

Included are (1) a listing of the 75 organizations with name, address, telephone number, name of executive director or other administrator, major publications, purpose of the organization, and date established; and (2) Table 2/1 with information on these 75 organizations with respect to membership, number of chapters, services, conferences, staff, and expenditures.

The assistance available through the secretariats of these national organizations provides an excellent method of obtaining expert advice and actual information on specific problems. The information secured in this way enables local and state officials to improve administrative practices, organization, and methods and thus to improve the quality of services rendered to the people. Many of these organizations also are active in raising the professional standards of their members through inservice training, special conferences and seminars, and other kinds of professional development.

Research on current problems is a continuing activity of many of these groups, and all issue a variety of publications ranging from a newsletter and occasional bulletins to diversified books, monographs, research papers, conference proceedings, and regular and special reports.

These organizations provide many of the services that in other countries would be the responsibility of the national government. They arrange annual conferences, publish newsletters and magazines, answer inquiries, provide inservice training and other kinds of professional development, provide placement services for members, and develop service and cost standards for various activities.

Most of the organizations in Table 2/1 have individual memberships, and several also have agency or institutional memberships. Some of these organizations have service memberships that may be based on the population of the jurisdiction, the annual revenue of the jurisdiction or agency, or other criteria that roughly measure the costs of providing service.

In addition to these kinds of membership fees, some of the organizations provide specialized consulting, training, and information services both by annual subscription and by charges for specific projects.

LISTING OF ORGANIZATIONS

Academy for State and Local Government, 444 North Capitol Street, N.W., Room 345, Washington, D.C. 20001. (202) 434-4850 Director: Enid Beaumont. Major publications: Publications list available on request. Purpose: To serve as the research, training, and policy center for joint projects and programs of Council of State Governments, International City/County Management Association, National Association of Counties, National Conference of State Legislatures, National Governors' Association, National League of Cities, and U.S. Conference of Mayors. An arm of the Academy, the State and Local Legal Center, is devoted to the interests of state and local governments in the Supreme Court. The Academy's International Center facilitates the exchange of people and ideas between the international community and state and local governments. Established 1971.

Airports Association Council International-North America, 1220 19th Street, N.W., Suite 200, Washington, D.C. 20036. (202) 293-8500; Fax (202) 331-1362. President: George Howard. Major publications: *Airport Highlights*, studies, surveys, and reports. Purpose: To promote sound policies dealing with financing, construction, management, operations, and development of airports; to provide reference and resource facilities and information for airport operators; and to act as the "voice" of airports to governmental agencies, officials, and the public on the problems and solutions concerning airport operations. Established 1948.

American Association of Airport Executives, 4212 King Street, Alexandria, Virginia 22302. (703) 824-0500. President: Charles M. Barclay. Major publications: *Airport Report*; *Airport Magazine*. Purpose: To assist the airport managers in performing their complex and diverse responsibilities for the airport and community through an airport management reference library; a consulting service; publications containing technical, administrative, legal, and operational information; an electronic bulletin board system; a professional accreditation program for airport executives; and a private satellite broadcast network, Aviation News and Training Network (ANTN), for airport employee training and news. Established 1928.

American Association of Port Authorities, 1010 Duke Street, Alexandria, Virginia 22314. (703) 684-5700. President: Erik Stromberg. Purpose: To exchange information relative to port construction, maintenance, operation, organization, administration, and management; to standardize and establish uniformity in operation, construction, and management of port facilities; and to promote the concept and interests of port authorities and the development and encouragement of waterborne transportation. Established 1912.

American Association of School Administrators, 1801 North Moore Street, Arlington, Virginia 22209. (703) 528-0700. Executive Director: Richard D. Miller. Major publications: *The School Administrator*; *Leadership News*; Critical Issues Series. Purpose: To develop qualified educational leaders and support excellence in educational administration; to initiate and support laws, policies, research, and practice that will improve education; to promote programs and activities that focus on leadership for learning and excellence in education; and to cultivate a climate in which quality education can thrive. Established 1865.

American College of Healthcare Executives, 840 North Lake Shore Drive, Chicago, Illinois 60611. (312) 943-0544. President/CEO: Thomas C. Dolan, Ph.D., FACHE. Major publications: *Hospital & Health Services Administration*; *Healthcare Executive, Frontiers, Directory* (biennial); and miscellaneous task force, committee, and seminar reports.

Purpose: The mission of the American College of Healthcare Executives is to be the professional membership society for healthcare executives; to meet its affiliates' professional, educational, and leadership needs; to increase the effectiveness of healthcare management; and to advance healthcare management excellence.

American Institute of Architects, 1735 New York Avenue, N.W., Washington, D.C. 20006. (202) 626-7300. Executive Vice President/CEO: James P. Cramer, Hon. AIA. Major publications: *AIA Memo*. Purpose: The objectives of the American Institute of Architects shall be to organize and unite in fellowship the members of the architectural profession of the United States of America; to promote the aesthetic, scientific, and practical efficiency of the profession; to advance the science and art of planning and building by advancing the standards of architectural education, training, and practice; to coordinate the building industry and the profession of architecture to ensure the advancement of the living standards of people through their improved environment; and to make the profession of ever-increasing service to society.

American Library Association, 50 East Huron Street, Chicago, Illinois 60611. (312) 944-6780. Executive Director: Peggy Sullivan. Major publications: *American Libraries*; *Booklist*; *Choice*. Purpose: To assist libraries and librarians in promoting and improving library service and librarianship. Established 1876.

American Planning Association, Including the American Institute of Certified Planners (AICP). 1776 Massachusetts Avenue, N.W., Washington, D.C. 20036. (202) 872-0611. With an office also at 1313 East 60th Street, Chicago, Illinois 60637. (312) 955-9100. Executive Director: Israel Stollman. Major publications: *Journal of the APA*; *Planning*; *Planning Advisory Service Reports*; *Land-Use Law & Zoning Digest*; *Zoning News*; *Environment & Development*. Purpose: To advance the art and science of urban and regional planning; to promote effective techniques for development in cities, regions, and states; to provide research for planners and information on new developments; and to bring together the professional planner, citizen, elected official, developer, and private practitioner. AICP provides an examination for certification, promotes professional continuing education, establishes ethical standards, and sponsors accreditation of university planning programs. Established 1909.

American Public Gas Association, Suite 102, 11094-D Lee Highway, Fairfax, Virginia 22030. (703) 352-3890. Executive Director: Robert S. Cave. Major publications; *Newsletter*; *Publicly Owned Natural Gas System Directory* (annual). Purpose: To provide professional assistance to publicly owned natural gas systems. Established 1961.

American Public Health Association, 1015 15th Street, N.W., Washington, D.C. 20005. (202) 789-5600. Executive Director: William H. McBeath, M.D., M.P.H. Major publications:

American Journal of Public Health; *The Nation's Health*. Purpose: To protect the health of the public through the maintenance of standards for scientific procedures, legislative education, and practical application of innovative health programs. Established 1872.

American Public Power Association, 2301 M Street, N.W., Washington, D.C. 20037. (202) 467-2900. Executive Director: Larry Hobart. Major publications: *Public Power*; *Weekly Newsletter*. Purpose: To promote the efficiency of publicly owned electric systems; to achieve greater cooperation among public systems; to protect the interest of publicly owned utilities; and to provide services in the fields of management and operation, energy conservation, consumer services, public relations, engineering, design, construction, research and accounting practice. Established 1940.

American Public Transit Association, 1201 New York Avenue, N.W., Washington, D.C. 20005. (202) 898-4000. Executive Vice President: Jack R. Gilstrap. Major publications: *Passenger Transport*; *Transit Factbook*. Purpose: To represent the operators of and suppliers to public transit; to provide a medium for exchange of experiences, discussion, and comparative study of industry affairs; to research and investigate methods to improve public transit; to provide assistance in dealing with special issues; and to collect, compile, and make available data and information relative to public transit. Established 1882.

American Public Welfare Association, 810 First Street, N.E., Washington, D.C. 20002. (202) 682-0100. Executive Director: A. Sidney Johnson, III. Major publications: *Public Welfare*; *Public Welfare Directory*; *This Week in Washington*; *W-Memo*; *APWA News*. Purpose: To work for more effective federal policy in human services, including income assistance, social services, health care, and employment services, and to promote the professional development of persons working in the field of public welfare. Established 1930.

American Public Works Association, 106 W. Eleventh Street, Suite 1800, Kansas City, Missouri 64105-1806. Executive Director: William J. Bertera. Major publications: *APWA Reporter* (monthly); research reports; technical publications and manuals. Purpose: To advance the theory and practice of all aspects of public works facilities and services; to disseminate information on improved practices; to encourage high professional standards; and to promote cooperation in the field of public works. Established 1894.

American Society for Public Administration, 1120 G Street, N.W., Suite 700, Washington, D.C. 20005. (202) 393-7878. Executive Director: John P. Thomas. Major publications: *Public Administration Review*; *PA Times*. Purpose: To improve the management of public service at all levels of government; to advocate on behalf of public service; to advance the science, processes, and art of public administration; and to disseminate information and facilitate the exchange of knowledge

among persons interested in the practice or teaching of public administration. Established 1939.

American Water Works Association, 6666 West Quincy Avenue, Denver, Colorado 80235. (303) 794-7711. Executive Director: J. B. Mannion. Major publications: *Journal AWWA*; *MainStream*; *OpFlow*; *WaterWeek*. Purpose: To promote public health, safety, and welfare through the improvement of the quality and quantity of drinking water for the public. Established 1881.

Building Officials and Code Administrators International, 4051 West Flossmoor Road, Country Club Hills, Illinois 60478-5795. (708) 799-2300. Chief Executive Officer: Paul K. Heilstedt, P.E. Major publications: National Code Series; *The Building Official and Code Administrator*; *BOCA Bulletin*; Research Reports; Professional Development Series. Publications catalog available on request. Purpose: To promulgate a complete package of performance model codes; to assist the user through training and educational services; and to provide technical services such as plan reviews, product evaluations, inspections, and administrative and management reviews. Established 1915.

Cable Television Information Center, 1700 Shaker Church Road, N.W., Olympia, Washington 98502. (206) 866-2080. President: Harold E. Horn. Purpose: To help local officials make informed decisions about cable television; to provide a centralized cable resource and information center to local governments across the country; to provide information, valuable contacts, and suggestions to local governments; and to represent local government interests in the formation of cable policy at the federal level. Established 1972.

Canadian Association of Municipal Administrators, 24 Clarence Street, Ottawa, Ontario K1N 5P3 Canada. (613) 563-2590. Executive Director: Marja Hughes. Purpose: To achieve greater communication and cooperation between municipal administrators across Canada and to focus the talents of its members on the preservation and advancement of local government through enhancing the quality of municipal management and administration in Canada. Established 1972. An affiliate, the Canadian Municipal Personnel Association, serves as a major resource group in the area of personnel administration in municipal government and labor relations. Established 1975.

Council of State Community Development Agencies, 444 North Capitol Street, Room 224, Washington, D.C. 20001. (202) 393-6435. Executive Director: John Sidor. Major publications: *The State Line*; *The National Line*; *Put Up or Give Way: States, Economic Competitiveness and Poverty*; *Linking Housing and Human Services: Guide to Completing a CHAS*; *1990 Compendium of State Housing Initiatives*; *Role of CDBG Funds in Rural Development*; *Assisting Rural Development*; and others. Purpose: To help state agencies keep abreast of state and federal initiatives in community and economic devel-

opment, housing, public facilities, and local assistance and to improve state programs through interstate coordination. Established 1974.

Council of State Governments. Iron Works Pike, P.O. Box 11910, Lexington, Kentucky 40578. (606) 231-1939. Executive Director: Dan Sprague. Major publications: *Book of the States*; *SPECTRAM: The Journal of State Government*; *State Government News*. Purpose: To strengthen state government and preserve its role in the federal system via research, information, and leadership programs; to assist states in improving their legislative, administrative, and judicial practices; to promote state, local, regional, and interstate cooperation; and to facilitate state-federal relations. Established 1933.

Federation of Canadian Municipalities, 24 Clarence Street, Ottawa, Ontario KIN 5P3, Canada. (613) 237-5221. FAX (613) 237-2965. Executive Director: James W. Knight. Purpose: To represent the national interest of local governments in Canada and to act as a spokesman for Canadian local governments and as a clearinghouse for the collection, exchange, and dissemination of statistical data and information on Canadian municipal practices and procedures. Major publications: *FCM Forum* (newsletter); two reports on the physical condition of Canada's municipal infrastructure; *Urban Infrastructure Conference Proceedings* (1987, 1989); *FCM Policy Development*; *At Your Service: In Both Official Languages*; *Consolidated Response to Policy Statements and Resolutions* (Task Force Reports and Resolutions); *FCM: 50 Years of Making History* (1987), briefs on goods and services tax, municipal infrastructure, federal payment of property taxes (grants in lieu of taxes), social housing, transportation, municipal liability insurance, race relations, tax reform, radio license fees, etc., presented to federal government departments and agencies; Municipal Economic Development Publications: *Management and Planning Capabilities in Small Communities*; *Community Crossroads*; "How to . . ." manuals; *A FCM International Program Aid and Trade: New Municipal Roles in International Development*; *Gateways*; *Meeting the Challenge: Urban Development in the Third World*; *A Practical Guide to Municipal Twinning*; A-C-T brochures (Affordability and Choice Today-housing initiatives); Race Relations Series. Established 1937.

Government Finance Officers Association, 180 North Michigan Avenue, Suite 800, Chicago, Illinois 60601. (312) 977-9700. With an office at 1750 K Street, N.W., Suite 650. Washington, D.C. 20006. (202) 429-2750. Executive Director: Jeffrey L. Esser. Major publications: *GFOA Newsletter*; *Government Finance Review Magazine*; *Public Investor*; *GAAFR Review*; *Cash Management for Small Governments*; *An Elected Official's Guide to Government Finance*; *Public Employee Retirement Series*: *Guides for Trustees and Administrators*. Purpose: To enhance and promote the professional management of governmental financial resources by identifying, developing, and advancing fiscal strategies, policies, and practices for the public benefit. Established 1906.

Governmental Accounting Standards Board, 401 Merritt 7, P.O. Box 5116, Norwalk, Connecticut 06856-5116. (203) 847-0700. Chairman: James Antonio. The Governmental Accounting Standards Board was organized by the Financial Accounting Foundation to establish standards of financial accounting and reporting for state and local governmental entities. Its standards guide the preparation of external financial reports of those entities. Interested parties are invited to read and comment on discussion documents of proposed standards. One copy of a discussion document can be obtained free of charge by calling the order department during the comment period. For automatic mailings of discussion and final documents, contact the order department to subscribe. Established 1984.

Governmental Research Association, 315 Samford Hall, Birmingham, Alabama 35229. (205) 870-2482. President: Donald C. Berno. Major publications: *GRA Directory*; *GRA Reporter*. Purpose: To promote and coordinate the activities of governmental research agencies; to encourage the development of effective organization and methods for the administration and operation of government; to encourage the development of common standards for the appraisal of results; to facilitate the exchange of ideas and experiences; and to serve as a clearinghouse. Established 1914.

ICMA, 777 North Capitol Street, N.E., Washington, D.C. 20002-4201. (202) 289-4262. FAX (202) 962-3500. Executive Director: William H. Hansell, Jr. Major publications: *Public Management*; *ICMA Newsletter*; *Municipal Management Series*; *Municipal Yearbook*; Baseline Data Reports; Management Information Service Reports; Practical Management Series; *Compensation*. Purpose: To enhance the quality of local government through professional management; to support and assist professional local government managers internationally. Provides training and development programs and publications for local government professionals that improve their skills, increase their knowledge of local government, and strengthen their commitment to the ethics, values, and ideals of the profession. Serves as a clearinghouse for the collection, analysis, and dissemination of local government information and data to enhance current practices and serve as a resource to public interest groups in the formulation of public policy. Established 1914.

ICMA Retirement Corporation, 777 North Capitol Street, N.E., Washington, D.C. 20002. President: Girard Miller. (800) 669-7400. Purpose: To provide and administer retirement plans as aids to units of government in their overall management benefits programs. Included are qualified and deferred compensation programs for all personnel, plus investment management services for employers. Established 1972.

Institute of Internal Auditors, Inc., 249 Maitland Avenue, Altamonte Springs, Florida 32701-4201. (407) 830-7600. President: William G. Bishop III. Major publication: *Internal Auditor*. Purpose: To provide comprehensive professional development activities and the standards for the practice of internal auditing and to research, disseminate, and promote knowledge and information about internal auditing and internal control. Of special interest to government auditors are the Institute's activities in governmental and public affairs. Established 1941.

Institute of Public Administration, 55 West 44th Street, New York, New York 10036. (212) 730-5480. President: Dwight Ink. Director, Government Programs: Howard N. Mantel. Director, Human Resource Programs: Ted Thomas. Director, International Urban Studies: David Mammen. Luther H. Gulick Scholar in Residence: Annmarie H. Walsh. Library Director: Steven Unger. Major publications: list of publications available on request. Purpose: To provide research, training, education, consulting, and advisory services in the United States and abroad in areas of public policy, government structure, public policy, government structure, public authorities, public enterprises, government procurement, personnel management and training, public-private sector improvements, economic development, charter revision, local government legislative bodies, planning and management, intergovernmental program responsibilities and relationships, and public ethics. Operates Gulick Center for Citizenship and Ethics. Established 1906.

Institute of Transportation Engineers (formerly Institute of Traffic Engineers), 525 School Street, S.W., Washington, D.C. 20024. (202) 554-8050. Executive Director: Thomas W. Brahms. Major publications: *ITE Journal*; Transportation Training Series; *Transportation and Traffic Engineering Handbook*; *Manual of Traffic Signal Design*; *Manual of Transportation Engineering Studies*; *Trip Generation*; *Parking Generation*. Purpose: To promote professional development in the field through support and encouragement of education, research, development of public awareness, and exchange of information. Established 1930.

International Association of Assessing Officers, 130 East Randolph Street, Chicago, Illinois 60601. (312) 819-6100. Executive Director: John Eckenrod. Major publications: *Assessment Digest*; *Property Tax Journal*; *Improving Real Property Assessment: A Reference Manual*; *Property Appraisal and Assessment Administration*; Bibliographic Series; Research and Information Series; Assessment Standards. Purpose: To provide leadership in accurate property valuation, property tax administration, and property tax policy throughout the world. Established 1934.

International Association of Auditorium Managers, 4425 W. Airport Freeway, Suite 590,

Irving, Texas 75062-5835. (214) 255-8020. FAX: (214) 255-9582. Executive Director: John Swinburn. Major publications: *Facility Manager*; *IAAM Guide to Members and Services*; *IAAM News*. Purpose: To promote professional development in the public assembly field and provide assistance to members. Membership consists of the managers of arenas, convention centers, auditoriums, exhibit halls, amphitheaters, and stadiums. Established 1924.

International Association of Chiefs of Police, 515 N. Washington Street, Alexandria, Virginia 22314-2357. (703) 836-6767. Executive Director: Dan Rosenblatt. Major publications: *Police Chief*; *Training Keys*. Purpose: To advance the art of police science through development and dissemination of improved administrative, technical, and operational practices and to promote their use in police work; to foster police cooperation and exchange of information and experience among police administrators; to recruit and train qualified persons; and to encourage adherence of all police officers to high professional standards of performance and conduct. Established 1893.

International Association of Fire Chiefs, 4025 Fair Ridge Drive, Fairfax, Virginia 22033-2868. (703) 273-0911. Executive Director: Gary L. Briese, C.A.E. Major publications: *On Scene* (twice-monthly newsletter). Purpose: To provide information and assistance to those charged with the task of administering fire prevention, protection and suppression efforts, and emergency medical services in the United States, Canada, and abroad. Established 1873.

Operation Life Safety is an affiliate organization. It is a consortium of public, government, and private sector agencies that promote life safety from fire through public awareness and education, use of smoke detector and alarm systems, installation of quick response residential fire sprinklers, and development of community programs to support these objectives.

International Association of Public-Safety Communications Officers, Inc., 2040 S. Ridgewood Avenue, South Daytona, Florida 32119. (904) 322-2500. Executive Director: Ronnie Rand. Major publications: *APCO BULLETIN*; *The Journal of Public Safety Communications*; *APCO Reports Newsletter*; *Public Safety Operating Procedures Manual*; *APCO Training Courses*. Purpose: To promote the development and progress of public safety telecommunications through research, planning, and training; to promote cooperation among public safety agencies; to perform frequency coordination for radio services administered by the Federal Communications Commission; and to act as a liaison with federal regulatory bodies. Established 1935.

International Conference of Building Officials, 5360 South Workman Mill Road, Whittier, California 90601-2258. (310) 699-0541. President: John S. Traw, P.E. Major publications: Uniform Building Code and related codes, mechanical, plumbing, housing, signs, dangerous buildings, and fire prevention; textbooks on building department administration, building inspection, building code community, plan review, mechanical inspection, concrete inspection; instructor guides and student workbooks on fire protection, building department administration, all phases of building inspection; video training films; *Building Standards* magazine; and newsletter. Purpose: To develop and maintain uniform codes for the benefit of member city, county, and state agencies; to provide through its subsidiary, ICBO Evaluation Service, Inc., an evaluation service on new building products and systems; to develop educational programs and seminars and certification programs for inspectors; to provide management studies of building department operations; and to provide engineering consultative services on code matters, including plan review and interpretation and application of code requirements. Established 1922.

International Institute of Municipal Clerks, 160 North Altadena Drive, Pasadena, California 91107. (818) 795-6153. Executive Director: John Devine. Major publications: *IIMC News Digest*; Case Study Packets; *Consent Agenda*; *Meeting Administration Handbook*; *The Language of Local Government*; *Role Call*: *Strategy for a Professional Clerk*. Purpose: To improve administration of state, provincial, county, and local government through the position of clerk, secretary, or recorder— by maintaining central facilities for study and research devoted to improvement of methods and procedures relating to the municipal clerk's duties; by sponsoring professional career development institutes in 39 universities; by maintaining an Academy for Advanced Education with seminars at 32 universities; by offering a home study course in supervision; and by administering a professional certification program. Established 1947.

International Personnel Management Association—United States, 1617 Duke Street, Alexandria, Virginia 22314. (703) 549-7100. Executive Director: Donald K. Tichenor. Major publications: *Public Personnel Management*; *Agency Issues*; *IPMA News*; Public Employee Relations Library (PERL) Series. Purpose: To improve service to the public by promoting quality human resource management in the public sector. Established 1973.

League of Women Voters. 1730 M Street, N.W., Washington, D.C. 20036. (202) 429-1965. President: Becky Cain. Executive Director: Gracia Hillman. Purpose: The League of Women Voters of the United States is a nonpartisan, political organization that encourages the informed and active participation of citizens in government and influences public policy through education and advocacy. The League's current advocacy priorities are voter registration and campaign finance reform, environmental issues, reproductive choice, and health care. Major publications: *The National Voter*, *Report from the Hill*. Established 1920.

The League of Women Voters Education Fund, a separate but complementary organization, provides research and citizen education services to League members and to the public to encourage and enable citizen participation in government. Current citizen education programs involve health care, the environment, the right of privacy in reproductive choices, electoral participation, and emerging democracies. Major publications: *Getting into Issues*; *VOTE, the First Steps*; *Pick a Candidate*; *Getting out the Vote*; *Plastics in the Municipal Waste Stream*; *Garbage: A Citizen's Guide to Service Reduction and Solid Waste Management*; and *The Nuclear Waste Primer*. Established 1957.

Maritime Municipal Training and Development Board, 6100 University Avenue, Halifax, Nova Scotia B3H 3J5 Canada. (902) 494-3712. FAX: (902) 494-1961. Executive Director: A. Donald Smeltzer. The Maritime Municipal Training and Development Board (MMTDB) was established in 1974 as an agency of the Council of Maritime Premiers. Its mission is to *assist municipalities, provinces and all bodies and organizations in the Maritime region concerned with local government operations; and to improve municipal government capability through training, education, and development in order to bring about more efficient and effective local government administration, management, and decision-making operations and processes.*

The MMTDB is a coordinator, a facilitator, and is a catalyst for positive change. The organization and activity of this agency are unique to Canada and have helped to establish the Maritime region as a pioneer and leader in municipal management training and development.

Among its many activities, the MMTDB acts as a clearinghouse for training and development information; provides a forum for discussion of important issues; convenes problem-solving meetings; initiates and coordinates training; encourages the use of new technology of benefit to local government; undertakes research; develops and publishes needed resources; and provides assistance and counsel to municipal officials on matters falling within its mandate.

Municipal Treasurers Association, 1229 19th Street, N.W., Washington, D.C. 20036. (202) 833-1017. Executive Director: Stacey L. Crane. Major publications: *Technical Topics*; *Treasury Notes*. Purpose: To enhance local treasury management by providing educational training, technical assistance, legislative services, and a forum for treasurers to exchange ideas and develop policy papers and positions.

National Animal Control Association, 806 S. New York, Liberal, Kansas 67901. (800) 828-6474. Executive Director: Mike Burgwin. Major publications: *The NACA News*, newsletter; *The NACA Training Guide*. Purpose: To provide training for animal control personnel; to provide consultation and guidance for local governments on animal control ordinances, animal shelter design, budget and

program planning, and staff training; and to provide public education. Established in 1978.

National Association of Counties, 440 First Street, N.W., Washington, D.C. 20001. (202) 393-6226. Executive Director: Larry Naake. Major publication: *County News.* Purpose: To serve as the voice of county government at the national level; to improve county government; to serve as a liaison between county and other levels of government; to achieve public understanding of the role of counties in the intergovernmental system; to provide information and analysis of data. Two-thirds of the nation's counties are members of NACo and its 25 affiliated organizations. Established 1935. Through the National Association of Counties Research Foundation, Inc. (NACoR, Inc.), NACo undertakes grant and contract funded research and maintains expertise in major problems and programs of county government.

National Association of Housing and Redevelopment Officials, 1320 18th Street, N.W., Suite 500, Washington, D.C. 20036. (202) 429-2960. FAX: (202) 429-9684. Executive Director: Richard Y. Nelson, Jr. Major publications: *Journal of Housing; NAHRO Monitor; Directory of Local Agencies; Commissioners Dictionary; Commissioners Handbook.* Purpose: To serve as a professional membership organization representing local housing authorities, community development agencies, and individual professionals in the housing, community development, and redevelopment fields. Divided into 8 regions and 43 chapters, NAHRO works to provide safe, decent, and affordable housing for low- and moderate-income persons. NAHRO provides its 9,000 members with information on federal policy, legislation, regulations, and funding. NAHRO also provides professional development and training programs in all phases of agency operations, including management, maintenance, and procurement. Established 1933.

National Association of Regional Councils, 1700 K Street, N.W., Washington, D.C. 20006. (202) 457-0710. FAX: (202) 296-9352. Executive Director: John W. Epling. Major publications: *Directory of Regional Councils; The Regional Reporter.* Purpose: To promote the development and understanding of regional councils; to provide up-to-date information and technical assistance to councils; to assist in the expansion of regional council program opportunities; to develop and communicate national policy proposals on issues of regional impact; and to act as a liaison with federal and state agencies in order to promote the use of regional councils and present their needs. Established 1967.

National Association of Schools of Public Affairs and Administration, Suite 730, 1120 G Street, N.W., Washington, D.C. 20005. (202) 628-8965. FAX: (202) 626-4978. Executive Director: Alfred M. Zuck. Major publications: *Directory of Programs in Public Af-* *fairs and Administration 1992; Newsletter; MPA Standards; Doctoral Policy Statement; Guidelines/Standards for Undergraduate Programs; MPA Career Brochure; Peer Review and Accreditation* documents. Purpose: To serve as a national center for information about programs and developments in the area of public affairs and administration; to foster goals and standards of educational excellence; to represent members' concerns and interests in the formulation and support of national, state, and local policies for education and research; and to serve as a specialized accrediting agency for MPA degrees. Established 1970.

National Association of State Information Resource Executives, Iron Works Pike, P.O. Box 11910, Lexington, Kentucky 40578-1910. (606) 231-1905. Research Associate: Rhonda Wheeler. Major publications: *NASIRE Exchange* (newsletter); *NASIRE Biennial Report.* Purpose: To strengthen state government through the application of information systems technology; to act as a liaison with federal agencies; to promote the development and transferral of information systems technology between states. Established 1969.

National Association of Towns and Townships, 1522 K Street, N.W., Suite 600, Washington, D.C. 20005. (202) 737-5200. Executive Director: Jeffrey H. Schiff. Major publication: *NATaT's Reporter.* Purpose: To offer technical assistance, educational services, and public policy support to local government officials from towns, townships, and other small communities across the country; through its National Center for Small Communities to conduct research and to develop public policy recommendations scaled to the unique needs and nature of rural governments and small towns; to keep local officials abreast of decisions and actions of national import. Established 1963.

National Civic League, 1445 Market Street, Suite 300, Denver, Colorado 80202. (303) 571-4343. FAX: (303) 571-4404. President: John Parr. Major publications: *NATIONAL CIVIC REVIEW; Civic Action.* Purpose: To promote citizen participation in local governance through consensus-based decision making and collaborative problem solving; to provide visioning and problem-solving technical assistance to communities; to provide guides, model charters, and research on government structures; to recognize collaborative problem solving through the All-American City Award Program. Will celebrate 100th anniversary in 1994.

National Conference of State Legislatures, 1560 Broadway, Suite 700, Denver, Colorado 80202. (303) 830-2200. Executive Director: William Pound. Major publication: *State Legislatures.* Purpose: To improve the quality and effectiveness of state legislatures; to assure states a strong, cohesive voice in the federal decision-making process; and to foster interstate communication and cooperation. Established 1975. The Conference's Office of State-Federal Relations, 444 North Capitol Street, Suite 515, Washington, D.C. 20001 (202) 624-5400, produces *Federal Update* and *Mandate Monitor.*

National Council for Urban Economic Development, 1730 K Street, N.W., Suite 915, Washington, D.C. 20006. (202) 223-4735. Executive Director: Jeffrey A. Finkle. Major publications: *Urban Economic Developments; Economic Development Commentary; Economic Development Abroad;* and *Legislative Report.* Purpose: To serve public and private participants in economic development across the United States and in international settings; to provide information to its members, who build local economies through job creation, attraction, and retention and who include public economic development directors, chamber of commerce staff, utility executives, academicians, and many other professionals. Established 1967.

National Environmental Health Association, 720 South Colorado Boulevard, Suite 970, South Tower, Denver, Colorado 80222. (303) 756-9090. FAX: (303) 691-9490. Executive Director: Nelson E. Fabian. Major publications: *Journal of Environmental Health* and more than 170 other publications. Purpose: To advance the professional who works in the environmental field by promoting and encouraging research, education, professional meetings, and the dissemination of information; to publish information relating to environmental health and protection; and to promote professionalism in the field. Established 1937.

National Fire Protection Association, Batterymarch Park, P.O. Box 9101, Quincy, Massachusetts 02269-9101. (617) 770-3000. President: George D. Miller. Major publications: *National Electrical Code®; National Fire Codes®; Fire Protection Handbook; Life Safety Code®; NFPA Journal; Fire Technology;* textbooks, manuals, training packages, detailed analyses of important fires, fire officers guides, and others. Purpose: To safeguard people and their environment from destructive fire using scientific and engineering techniques and education; to develop and publish consensus standards intended to minimize the possibility and effects of fire; and to educate the public in ways to avoid loss of life and property from fire by making fire safety habits a way of life. Established 1896.

National Governors' Association, Hall of the States, 444 North Capitol Street, Suite 267, Washington, D.C. 20001-1572. (202) 624-5300. Executive Director: Raymond C. Scheppach. Major publications: *Governors' Bulletin; Fiscal Survey of the States; Directory of Governors; Governors' Staff Directory;* reports on a wide range of state issues. Purpose: To act as a liaison between the states and the federal government and to serve as a clearinghouse for information and ideas on state and national issues. Established 1908.

National Housing Conference, 815 15th Street, N.W., Suite 601, Washington, D.C. 20005. (202) 393-5772. Executive Director: Robert

J. Reid. Major publications: *NHC Reports from Washington*. Purpose: To promote better communities and housing for Americans through legislative action. Established 1931.

National Institute of Governmental Purchasing, 115 Hillwood Avenue, Suite 201, Falls Church, Virginia 22046. (703) 533-7300. FAX: (703) 532-0915. Executive Vice President: J. E. Brinkman, CPPO. Major publications: *NIGP Letter Service Bulletin*; *NIGP Technical Bulletin*; *Dictionary of Purchasing Guide*; *General Public Purchasing*; *Public Purchasing and Materials Management*; *Public Procurement Management, Parts 1 and 2*; *Annual Governmental Procurement Research Survey*; *Annual Survey of In-State (Buy Local), Buy American Practices, and Recycle Preferences*; *Commodity Service Code Index (A Numbering System)*. Seminars on the foregoing, plus: Competitive Sealed Proposals/Competitive Negotiation seminar; Standardization and Specification Writing. Also, in-site technical and consulting services; research projects and reports; NGIP Commodity/Service Coding System (2 Parts: Class-Item Code and Detailed Item Description Code); Certification for Public Purchasing Personnel. Purpose: To raise the standards of the public purchasing profession through the interchange of information and ideas. Established 1944.

National Institute of Municipal Law Officers, 1000 Connecticut Avenue, N.W., Suite 902, Washington, D.C. 20036. (202) 466-5424. FAX: (202) 785-0152. General Counsel: Benjamin L. Brown. Major publication: *The Municipal Attorney*. Purpose: To provide an organization for cooperation on litigation of nationwide municipal concern, law information, research, library services, and publications on law information to municipal attorneys of member municipalities. Established 1935.

National League of Cities, 1301 Pennsylvania Avenue, N.W., Washington, D.C. 20004. (202) 626-3000. Executive Director: Donald J. Borut. Major publications: *Nation's Cities Weekly*; *Issues and Options*; guide books, directories, and research reports. Purpose: To serve as an advocate for its members in Washington in the legislative, administrative, and judicial processes that affect them; to develop and pursue a national urban policy that meets the present and future needs of the nation's urban communities and the people who live in them; to offer training, technical assistance, and information to local government and state league officials to help them improve the quality of local government in our urban nation; and to undertake research and analysis on policy issues of importance to urban America. Established 1924.

National Public Employer Labor Relations Association, 1620 Eye Street, N.W., 4th Floor, Washington, D.C. 20006. (202) 296-2230. President: Dema Harris. Executive Director: Roger E. Dahl. Major publications: *NPELRA Newsletter*; contract clause reference manual; strike contingency planning manual; family and medical leave guide; health care cost containment guide; labor relations supervisor's training manual; and drug testing and AIDS monographs. Purpose: To further the professional interests of federal, state, county, school/special district, and municipal government managers in the area of labor relations through training programs and the dissemination and exchange of information and policy pertaining to all areas of public sector labor relations; and to promote cooperation among members and professional standards in the field. Established 1971.

National Recreation and Park Association, 2775 South Quincy Street, Arlington, Virginia 22206-2204. (703) 820-4940. Executive Director: R. Dean Tice, Major publications: *Parks & Recreation*; *Journal of Leisure Research*; *Therapeutic Recreation Journal*; *Recreation & Parks Law Reporter*; *Park Practice Program*; *Dateline: NRPA* (newsletter); *Programmers Information Network, Recreation . . . Access in the 90s*. Worldwide NRPA/SCHOLE™ computer network. Purpose: To improve and expand park and recreation systems and leisure services for the public through assisting park and recreation officials in the development and administration of physical, human, and financial resources. Parent organization established 1898.

National School Boards Association, 1680 Duke Street, Alexandria, Virginia 22314. (703) 838-6722. FAX: (703) 683-7590. Executive Director: Thomas A. Shannon. Major publications: *The American School Board Journal*; *The Executive Educator*; *The School Administrator's Policy Portfolio*; *Leadership Reports*; *School Board News*. Purpose: To work with and through all of its federation members to foster excellence and equity in public education through school board leadership. Established 1940.

National Society for Experiential Education. 3509 Haworth Drive, Suite 207, Raleigh, North Carolina 27609. (919) 787-3263. Executive Director: Allen J. Wutzdorff. Major publications: *NSEE Quarterly*; *The National Directory in Internships*; *Strengthening Experiential Education within Your Institution*; *The Experienced Hand: A Student Manual for Making the Most of an Internship*; *Combining Service and Learning: A Resource Book for Community and Public Service*; *A Guide to Environmental Internships: How Environmental Organizations Can Utilize Internships Effectively*; Resource papers on issues of quality program design and administration. Purpose: As a community of individuals, institutions, and organizations, NSEE is committed to fostering the effective use of experience as an integral part of education, in order to empower learners and promote the common good. Established 1971.

Police Foundation, 1001 22nd Street, N.W., Washington, D.C. 20037. (202) 833-1460. President: Hubert Williams. Major publications: research and technical assistance reports on a wide range of issues related to law enforcement and public safety; list of publications available upon request. Purpose: To improve policing in America through research and technical assistance. The foundation offers state and local governments assistance in such areas as community policing, strategic planning, civil disorder preparedness, operational and administrative review, program evaluation, community and race relations, illegal drug control, and police chief selection. Created and operates the National Center for the Study of Police and Civil Disorder. Established 1970.

Public Administration Service, 8301 Greensboro Drive, Suite 420, McLean, Virginia 22102. (703) 734-8970. President and Executive Director: Theodore Sitkoff. Purpose: To provide management and specialized consulting services and conduct research for public jurisdictions and public managers—domestic and international—in order to improve the quality and delivery of public services. Consulting and research services provided include the development and installation of modern management systems, methods, techniques, and practices in many different functional fields such as local, state, and federal organization and reorganization; human resource administration; criminal justice; public works; intergovernmental relations; telecommunications; data processing and office automation; and public sector productivity and responsiveness and privatization. Nonprofit organization. Established 1933.

Public Risk Management Association, 1117 N. 19th St., Suite 900, Arlington, Virginia 22209. (703) 528-7701. Executive Director: Dennis Kirschbaum. Major publications: *Public Risk magazine*; *Riskwatch newsletter*; *Public Sector Risk Management manual*; *Tort Liability Today*; *Public Official Liability Decisions in Federal Courts* (subscription series); *Risk Management Behind the Blue Curtain: A Primer on Law Enforcement Liability*. Special Reports: *State of the Profession Survey*; *Employee Assistance Programs: Strategies for Local Government Workplaces*; *1991–92 Risk Financing Survey*; *Workers' Compensation Cases: Local Government*. Purpose: To increase the proficiency of risk management in local government by providing an information network between government officials and employees involved in risk management, by assisting in the establishment of effective risk-management programs, and by conducting research projects and training programs to aid in the development of more effective techniques. Established 1978.

Public Technology, Inc., 1301 Pennsylvania Avenue, N.W., Washington, D.C. 20004. (202) 626-2400. FAX: (202) 626-2. President: Costis Toregas. Purpose: With ICMA, NLC, and NACO as sponsors, PTI works with 150 progressive member cities and counties to identify and create technologies and management approaches for providing the best possible services to citizens and business communities. Three priorities of PTI are 1) to make communities 'well-connected' by

advancing communication capabilities, 2) to develop tools and processes for wise decision-making, and 3) to create approaches to ensure a balance between economic development and a clean, quality environment. A research and development program combined with a strong Public Enterprise program are the means by which PTI priorities are carried forward. The PTI member program provides a local government executive information service including LEX (an electronic information and communications system), AN-SWER (a research service), publications, executive briefings, and an extensive consultation service. Recent major publications: *The Enterprising Government: Improving Services and Generating Revenues*; *Solutions for Technology Sharing Networks* (annual); *The Local Government Guide to Geographic Information Systems*. The Public Enterprise Program integrates three elements to help member cities and counties create new revenues: a how-to guide and training for local leaders, expert business planning assistance, and access to venture capital for the PTI Investment Fund and other capital sources. Established 1971.

Solid Waste Association of North America, P.O. Box 7219, Silver Spring, Maryland 20910. (301) 585-2898. Executive Director: H. Lanier Hickman, Jr., PE, DEE. Purpose: To advance the practice of environmentally and economically sound municipal solid waste management in North America. Established 1961.

Southern Building Code Congress International, Inc., 900 Montclair Road, Birmingham, Alabama 35213. (205) 591-1853. Chief Executive Officer: William J. Tangye, P.E. Major publications: *The Standard Codes*; *A Directory of Services* listing other publications and services and a membership directory are available on request. Purpose: To provide a forum for governments, design professionals, and industry to join together to democratically promulgate and maintain a set of model regulatory construction codes. Established 1940.

Special Libraries Association, 1700 18th Street, N.W., Washington, D.C. 20009-2508. (202) 234-4700. Executive Director: David R. Bender. Major publications: *Special Libraries*; *SpeciaList*; publications catalog available on request. Purpose: To provide an association of individuals and organizations having a professional, scientific, or technical interest in library and information science, especially as these are applied in the recording, retrieval, and dissemination of knowledge and information in areas such as the physical, biological, technical and social sciences, the humanities, and business; and to promote and improve the communication, dissemination, and use of such information and knowledge for the benefit of libraries or other educational organizations. Established 1909; membership 14,000.

Town Affiliation Association of the United States (Sister Cities International), 120 S. Payne Street, Alexandria, Virginia 22314. (703) 836-3535. Executive Vice President: Thomas W. Gittins. Major publications: *Your City and the World*; *A Sister City Handbook*; *Sister City News*; *Directory of Sister Cities by State and Country*. Purpose: To provide a national forum for the interchange of ideas and resources to help local communities further their international programs. Established 1956.

United States Conference of Mayors, 1620 Eye Street, N.W., Washington, D.C. 20006. (202) 293-7330. Executive Director: J. Thomas Cochran. Major publications: *U.S. Mayor*; *Mayors of America's Principal Cities*. Purpose: To act as the official nonpartisan organization of cities with populations of 30,000 or more; to aid the development of effective national urban policy; to serve as a legislative action force in federal-city relations; to ensure that federal policy meets urban needs; and to provide mayors with leadership and management tools of value in their cities. Each city is represented in the Conference by its chief elected official, the mayor. Established 1932.

Urban Affairs Association, University of Delaware, Newark, Delaware 19716. (302) 831-1681. Executive Director: Mary Helen Callahan. Major publications: *Urban Affairs*; *Journal of Urban Affairs*; *Directory of University Urban Programs*; selected papers of annual meetings; other special studies and reports. Purpose: To encourage the dissemination of information and research findings about urbanism and urbanization; to support the development of university education, research, and service programs in urban affairs; and to foster the development of urban affairs as a professional and academic field. Established 1969.

The Urban Institute, 2100 M Street, N.W., Washington, D.C. 20037. (202) 833-7200. President: William Gorham. Major publication: *Policy and Research Report*; publication catalog and annual report available on request. Purpose: To respond to needs for objective analyses and basic information regarding social and economic problems confronting the nation and government policies and programs designed to alleviate such problems. Established 1968.

Water Environment Federation, 601 Wythe Street, Alexandria, Virginia 22314. (703) 684-2400. Executive Director: Quincalee Brown. Major publications: *Water Environment Research*; *Water Environment and Technology*; *Operations Forum*; *Industrial Wastewater*; *Water Environment Regulation Watch*; series of Manuals of Practice. Purpose: To develop and disseminate technical information concerning the nature, collection, treatment, and disposal of domestic and industrial wastewater. The Federation has held as an integral component of its mandate the pledge to act as a source of education to the general public as well as to individuals engaged in the field of water pollution control. Established 1928.

Table 2/1   PROFESSIONAL ORGANIZATIONS SERVING LOCAL AND STATE GOVERNMENTS

Data for 75 professional organizations are presented in this table, based on a survey conducted in August 1993.

Membership services
1 Advisory or information services
2 Annual conference report
3 Directory
4 On-site technical assistance
5 Journal
6 Newsletter
7 Personnel placement service
8 Special service reports
9 Training
10 Yearbook
11 Legislative representation
12 Professional accreditation
13 Research projects

Services available to other than membership
1 Advisory or information services
2 Annual conference report
3 Directory
4 On-site technical assistance
5 Journal
6 Newsletter
7 Personnel placement service
8 Special service reports
9 Training
10 Yearbook
11 Legislative representation
12 Professional accreditation
13 Research projects

Organization	No. of individual members	No. of agency members	No. of state or regional chapters	Membership services	Nonmembership services	Conferences: national-state or regional	No. of full-time staff	Operating expenditures ($000)
Academy for State and Local Government	...	7	...	1,3,6,13	3,6,13	...	8	1,000
Airports Association Council International-North America[1]	250	...	...	1,2,3,6,8,11,13	2,3,6,8	Yes-Yes	27	4,000
American Association of Airport Executives	4,000	...	6	1,2,3,4,5,6,7,8,9,11,12,13	1,2,3,5,6,7,9,13	Yes-Yes	24	5,000
American Association of Port Authorities	25	126	...	1,2,3,4,6,11,13	1,2,4,13	Yes-Yes	12	...
American Association of School Administrators	18,000	...	...	1,2,5,6,8,9,10	5,6,9,11,13	Yes-Yes	62	9,000
American College of Healthcare Executives	27,000	...	...	1,3,5,6,8,9,11,12,13	1,5,8,9,11,12	Yes-No	99	12,000
American Institute of Architects	57,000	...	301	1,2,3,5,6,8,9,11,13	3,5,6,8,10	Yes-Yes	200	34,000
American Library Association	51,645	3,090	52	1,3,5,6,7,8,9,10,11,12,13	1,3,5,6,7,8,9,10,11,12,13	Yes-Yes	245	25,000
American Planning Association	27,000	...	46	1,3,5,6,7,9,11,12,13	1,5,6,9,13	Yes-Yes	69	7,900
American Public Gas Association	450	150	...	1,3,4,6,9,11	...	Yes-Yes	3	500
American Public Health Association	30,926	215	50	5,6,7,11	5,6	Yes-No	56	5,320
American Public Power Association	1,700	...	50	1,3,6,8,9,11,13	...	Yes-Yes	57	7,600
American Public Transit Association	...	1,040	...	1,3,4,6,8,9,10,11,13	6,8	Yes-Yes	60	...
American Public Welfare Association	4,000	800	...	5,6	...	Yes-Yes	50	...
American Public Works Association	27,000	...	64	1,6,9,12,13	1,9,13	Yes-Yes	65	7,444
American Society for Public Administration	12,000	200	126	1,2,5,6,7,9,13	1,2,5,6,7,9,13	Yes-Yes	15	1,750
American Water Works Association	49,000	3,800	43	1–13	1,2,4,5,7,9,12,13	Yes-Yes	...	18,500
Building Officials and Code Administrators International, Inc.	15,000	...	61	1,2,3,4,5,6,9,12,13	1,5,6,9	Yes-Yes	67	7,000
Cable Television Information Center	...	...	...	1,4,8,9,13	1,4,8,9,13	No-Yes	6	...
Canadian Association of Municipal Administrators	320	...	...	1,2,3,6	1,2,6	Yes-No	1	...
Council of State Community Development Agencies	10	47	...	1,3,4,6,8,9,11,13	3,6	Yes-Yes	6	580
Council of State Governments	...	56	5	1,2,3,4,5,6,8,9,11,12,13	1,2,3,5,6	Yes-Yes	160	5,000
Federation of Canadian Municipalities	...	...	17	1,3,6,8,13	...	...-Yes	21	...
Governmental Accounting Standards Board	11,000	...	...	1,6,13	13	No-No	16	3,000
Government Finance Officers Association	12,500	...	...	1,4,5,6,8,9,11,13	1,4,5,6,8,9,13	Yes-Yes	75	7,500
Governmental Research Association	150	...	...	3,6	3,6	Yes-No	...	8
ICMA	7,443	...	47	1,2,3,6,8,9,10,13	1,2,3,6,8,10,13	Yes-No	67	7,200
ICMA Retirement Corporation	180,000	4,800	...	1,4,6,8,9,11,13	1,4,8,13	...	310	28,000
Institute of Internal Auditors, Inc.	50,000	...	182	1,2,3,5,6,7,9,12,13	5,9,12,13	Yes-Yes	73	8,000
Institute of Public Administration	...	...	...	...	1,4,8,9,13	No-No	15	2,000
Institute of Transportation Engineers	12,000	...	68	1,2,3,5,7,9,10,13	1,2,3,5,7,9,10,13	Yes-Yes	14	2,800
International Association of Assessing Officers	8,380	40	32	1,2,3,4,5,6,7,8,9,12,13	1,2,3,4,5,6,7,8,9,13	Yes-Yes	32	4,000
International Association of Auditorium Managers	1,284	259	7	1,3,5,6,8,9,12,13	1,3,5,6,8,9,12,13	Yes-Yes	11	1,500
International Association of Chiefs of Police	13,000	...	...	1,3,4,6,8,9,10,11,13	1,3,4,6,8,9,10	Yes-Yes	50	6,000
International Association of Fire Chiefs	9,500	500	...	1,2,4,6,8,9,11,12,13	1,2,6,8,9,13	Yes-Yes	30	2,500
International Association of Public-Safety Communications Officers, Inc.	10,000	...	44	1–13	1–13	Yes-Yes	40	...
International Conference of Building Officials	12,000	2,600	89	1,2,3,4,5,6,7,8,9,12,13	1,2,3,4,5,6,7,8,9,12,13	Yes-Yes	135	16,000
International Institute of Municipal Clerks	10,000	...	...	1,2,3,6,9,11,12,13	1,6,13	Yes-Yes	7	...
International Personnel Management Association	4,625	1,415	55	1,3,5,6,7,8,9,11,13	6,7	No-Yes	16	2,400
League of Women Voters/League of Women Voters Education Fund	100,000	...	1,150	1,2,3,4,5,6,8,9,11,13	5	Yes-Yes	50	4,700
Maritime Municipal Training and Development Board	...	...	...	...	1,5,9,13	...	4	400
Municipal Treasurers Association	1,500	...	12	1,2,3,6,8,9,11,12	1,2,3,6	Yes-Yes	3	340
National Animal Control Association	3,000	81	39	1,2,3,6,7,9,12	1,2,3,4,6,7,9,12	Yes-Yes	3	...
National Association of Counties	1,700	...	...	1,4,6,8,9,11,13	1,6,8,13	Yes-Yes	70	12,000
National Association of Housing and Redevelopment Officials	6,336	2,511	51	1,2,3,4,5,6,7,8,9,11,12,13	1,3,5,9,12,13	Yes-Yes	36	5,000
National Association of Regional Councils	240	40	...	1,2,3,5,6,8,9,11,12,13	2,3,6,9,12	Yes-...	14	1,800
National Association of Schools of Public Affairs and Administration	...	220	...	1,2,3,4,6,8,12,13	...	Yes-No	5	...
National Association of State Information Resource Executives	500	...	...	1,2,3,4,6,8,9,13	2,3,9	Yes-Yes	3	250
National Association of Towns and Townships	12,000	...	11	1,4,6,8,9,11,12	6,8,11,13	Yes-No	10	800
National Civic League	1,000	...	...	1,3,4,5,6,8,9,13	1,4,5,6,8,9,13	Yes-No	20	2,000
National Conference of State Legislatures	56	...	...	1,3,4,6,8,9,13	3,6	Yes-Yes	145	13,000
National Council for Urban Economic Development	1,200	...	7	1,3,4,5,6,8,11,13	4,5,8,13	Yes-Yes	7	900
National Environmental Health Association	5,700	...	50	1,3,5,6,7,9,12,13	1,5,6,7,9,12,13	Yes-Yes	14	1,500
National Fire Protection Association	60,971	1,092	...	1,3,5,6,13	1,9,12,13	Yes-Yes	237	50,000
National Governors' Association	55	...	2	1,3,4,6,8,11,13	1,3,6,8	Yes-Yes	100	11,000
National Housing Conference	500	...	6	1,2,3,6,11	...	Yes-No	4	300
National Institute of Governmental Purchasing	230	1,467	65	1,2,3,4,6,7,8,9,12,13	2,3,4,6,13	Yes-No	16	1,300

Table 2/1
continued

PROFESSIONAL ORGANIZATIONS SERVING LOCAL AND STATE GOVERNMENTS

Organization	No. of individual members	No. of agency members	No. of state or regional chapters	Membership services	Nonmembership services	Conferences: national-state or regional	No. of full-time staff	Operating expenditures ($000)
National Institute of Municipal Law Officers	1,600	45	...	1,2,3,4,5,9,12,13	1,5,13	Yes-Yes	13	1,200
National League of Cities	...	1,500	49	1,3,4,6,8,9,11,13	3,6,8,9,11	Yes-Yes	75	9,800
National Public Employer Labor Relations Association	2,200	...	16	1,2,3,6,11	2,6,11	Yes-Yes	4	500
National Recreation and Park Association	20,435	1,823	56	1,2,4,5,6,8,9,11,12,13	1,2,4,5,8,9,11,12,13	Yes-Yes	41	6,000
National School Boards Association	...	...	53	1,3,4,5,6,8,9,11,13	1,5,6	Yes-Yes	120	16,000
National Society for Experiential Education	1,300	800	...	1,2,4,6	1	Yes-Yes	8	331
Police Foundation	...	...	...	...	1,4,9,11	...-No	17	2,300
Public Administration Service	16	...	...	...	1,4,13	No-No	25	3,000
Public Risk Management Association	...	2,100	32	1,3,5,6,8,11,13	1,5,6,8,13	Yes-Yes	14	1,600
Public Technology, Inc.	...	150	...	1,3,4,6,8,9,13	6,13	No-Yes	30	5,000
Solid Waste Association of North America	5,600	1,500	38	1,2,3,4,6,9,11,12,13	1,2,3,9	Yes-Yes	17	...
Southern Building Code Congress International	6,600	...	90	1,3,4,5,6,9,12	1,3,4,5,6,9,12	Yes-Yes	56	...
Special Libraries Association	14,000	...	58	1,2,3,4,5,6,7,9,10,11,13	1,2,3,5,6,9,11,13	Yes-No	34	...
Town Affiliation Association of the U.S. (Sister Cities International)	...	450	...	1,2,3,4,6,8,9,13	6	Yes-Yes	13	1,500
U.S. Conference of Mayors	...	...	...	1,2,3,4,6,8,11,13	3,6,13	Yes-No	52	...
Urban Affairs Association	300	75	...	1,3,4,5,6,8,9,13	1,3,8,9,13	Yes-Yes	2	100
The Urban Institute	...	...	...	...	1,4,6,13	Yes-No	220	21,000
Water Environment Federation	40,500	...	64	1,3,5,6,8,10,11,13	1,5,10,13	Yes-Yes	110	14,500

Leaders (. . .) indicate not applicable or data not reported.
¹Formerly the Airport Operators Council International.

E References

1
Sources of Information

Sources of Information

Eleanor Ferrall
Librarian Emerita
Arizona State University

The following reference listings are compiled primarily for urban administrators, staff members of government or research bureaus and other research and service organizations, and staff members of state and federal government agencies directly involved in urban affairs.

This edition's basic and functional area references have been compiled by Eleanor Ferrall, librarian emerita of Hayden Library at Arizona State University. The "Basic Statistical Resources Section" was prepared by Grace Waibel, information analyst at the U.S. Bureau of the Census.

Few sources listed in the 1994 *Municipal Year Book* were included in preceding editions. Nearly all sources listed have been published since January 1991. For a complete picture of publications issued during the past several years in this field, use this edition in conjunction with the Sources of Information in the preceding editions of *The Municipal Year Book*.

This updated bibliography includes a section on Basic References and another on Basic Statistical Resources, followed by 15 functional area subject headings. Under each subject are three sections: the first includes books, reports, monographs, bibliographies, and reference works and is intended to keep the urban administrator informed of the latest thinking in various fields. Annotations appear as necessary. The second section lists periodicals and includes magazines, journals, and newsletters. Frequency of publication is indicated as follows: (W) weekly, (BW) biweekly, (M) monthly, (BM) bi-

monthly, (Q) quarterly, (SM) semimonthly, (SA) semiannually, (BA) biannually, (IRR) irregularly. A third section lists databases.

Local Exchange (LEX) is the International City/County Management Association's (ICMA) official electronic network, bulletin board, and database service.

Many references listed here are written and published by well-known public interest groups or professional associations. In these cases, the name of the organization is not written in full. An abbreviation of the organization's name is used. For example, APA refers to the American Planning Association; IPMA refers to the International Personnel Management Association, etc. All abbreviations are included in the publishers' list at the end of this bibliography. Where they appear, they precede the full name of the organization and are followed by the word *see*. The publishers' list also provides the full names and addresses of other publishers whose publications have been listed in the bibliography.

The publications are not available from ICMA unless so noted in the entry or unless ICMA is the publisher.

Many ICMA publications are included in this bibliography. The notation BDR refers to Baseline Data Reports. MIS refers to the reports of the Management Information Service. These reports are available by subscription and by individual copy. Information on how to order ICMA reports may be obtained by telephoning 1-800-745-8780.

Subject headings (2 basic reference headings followed by 15 functional area headings) used in this bibliography are

Basic References
Basic Statistical Resources
Emergency Management
Environment and Energy
Fire Protection
Housing
Human Resources and Services
Information Technologies
Intergovernmental Relations
Law Enforcement and Criminal Justice
Local Government Organization and
    Management
Personnel and Labor Relations
Planning and Development
Public Finance
Public Works and Utilities
Recreation and Leisure
Transportation and Roads

BASIC REFERENCES

Eleanor Ferrall
Librarian Emerita
Arizona State University

BOOKS, REPORTS, MONOGRAPHS, BIBLIOGRAPHIES, AND REFERENCE SOURCES

Acronyms and Abbreviations of Computer Technology and Telecommunications. Dekker. 1993. 291p. One listing of definitions of over 7,000 combinations used in the fields of computer software, communications, and general technological methodology.

Almanac of the Fifty States: Basic Data Profiles with Comparative Tables. Edith R. Horner, ed. Information Publications. 1993. 447p. Profiles of each state, the District of Columbia, and a U.S. summary are organized into 13 categories including governmental finance, housing and construction, communication, energy, and transportation. Includes 54 comparative tables for selected characteristics.

Business Organizations, Agencies and Publications Directory. 7th ed. Michael B. Huellmantel, ed. Gale. 1993. 1,838p. Expansion to 30,000 entries with directory and textual information on organizations, both U.S. and international, government agencies and programs, facilities and services, research and educational facilities, and publications and information services.

Catalog of Federal Domestic Assistance, 1993. GPO. 1993. 600p. Published in June and updated in December, the *Catalog* describes 1,308 assistance programs administered by 51 federal agencies. Indexed by agency, function, subject, eligibility, and deadline. Entries set forth the provisions of the assistance program, the application and award process, requirements, and financial information. Cross references to related programs are provided. The staff provides for-pay computer access to this information through its Federal Assistance Programs Retrieval Systems (FAPRS).

CD-ROM Finder. James H. Shelton, ed. Learned Information. 1993. 550p. Lists CD-ROMs alphabetically and indexes them by publisher and application. Entry information includes title, publisher, source and type of information, format description, frequency of updates, computer configuration requirements, price, disk drive manufacturers, and search requirements.

Chemical Hazard Communication Guidebook: OSHA, EPA, and DOT Requirements. 2d ed. Andrew B. Waldo, Richard deC. Hinds. McGraw-Hill. 1993. 583p. Covers compliance with hazard communication requirements, reporting responsibilities involving emergency planning divisions, community right to know, and transporting restrictions of hazardous substances and materials.

Condition of Education, 1993. Nabeel Alsalam, *et al.* National Center for Education Statistics. GPO. 1993. 486p. Sixty indicators, divided into six major divisions, are presented on a double page spread with survey results and charts showing the implication of the in-

dicator. Divisions include access, participation, and progress; achievement, attainment, and curriculum; and climate, classrooms, and diversity in educational institutions, such as time spent doing homework and crime in schools. A glossary defines terms.

Congressional Quarterly's Politics in America, 1994: The 103rd Congress. Phil Duncan, ed. CQ. 1993. 1,746p. For each state, general information is followed by narrative accounts of each congressional delegate, including committee membership, campaign finances, key voting record, and elections. Representatives from Guam, Virgin Islands, American Samoa, District of Columbia, and Puerto Rico are pictured with brief personal information.

Congressional Quarterly's Washington Information Directory: 1993–1994. CQ. 1993. In its 18 chapters, arranged by function, this directory provides current access to key agencies, congressional offices and nongovernmental organizations, many of which are nonprofits. Fourteen recently independent states are added to the foreign embassies list. Name and subject indexes enhance the value of this tool.

Consultants and Consulting Organizations Directory. 2v. 13th ed. Janice McLean, ed. Gale. 1993. 2,804p. 18,000 consultants and consulting firms are classified into 14 major areas of expertise. Information includes contact details, service with the government or nonprofit organizations, publications, owner status, and technological experience. Volume 2 is used exclusively for indexes: geographic, consulting activities, personal name, and consulting firms index.

Dictionary of Architecture and Construction. 2d ed. Cyril M. Harris, ed. McGraw-Hill. 1993. 736p. Updated, revised, and well-illustrated, this edition comprehensively covers the terms of architecture and construction.

Dictionary of Statistics and Methodology: A Non-Technical Guide for the Social Sciences. W. Paul Vogt. Sage. 1993. 256p. To his definitions, which emphasize concept over calculations, Vogt adds examples.

Dollars and Cents of Shopping Centers, 1993. 12th ed. ULI. 1993. This real estate reference tool proves useful to community leaders in economic development planning, in understanding shopping center needs for realistic zoning rules, and in evaluating a center's financial benefit to the community through sales taxes and property taxes. The comparative data on receipts and operating expenses in this annual study covers 900 centers in the U.S. and Canada.

Encyclopedia of Governmental Advisory Organizations, 1994–95. 9th ed. Donna Batten, ed. Gale. 1993. 1,529p. Advisory Committees may be presidential, ad hoc, White House, departmental, agency, congressional, public, or interagency. They are arranged here under subject areas such as agriculture, education and social welfare, environment and natural resources, government, law, and transportation. Names, addresses, and telephone numbers are followed by brief references to

history and authority, program, findings and recommendations, membership, and publications. Five separate indexes create easy access to information.

Encyclopedia of Women's Associations Worldwide. Gale. 1993. 550p. A spin-off from *Encyclopedia of Associations*, this directory provides information on 3,000 organizations concerned with women's issues. Details include directory information, size, a brief history, and publications issued by the organization. Indexes are by name, keyword, and geographical location.

Federal Personnel Guide: 1993. Kenneth D. Whitehead, ed. Key Communications. 1993. 176p. Summary of current laws and regulations affecting civilian employees of the U.S. government and postal service. Covers RIFs and current pay charts.

Gale Directory of Databases: v.1. Kathleen Young Marcaccio, ed. Gale. 1993. 1,352p. Comprehensive, clear descriptions provide easy access to over 5,200 online databases, database producers, and online services. A master index follows geographic and subject ones. The companion volume 2 (829p.) provides the same information for CD-ROM, diskette, magnetic tape, handheld and batch access database products. These volumes resulted from the merger of several information resources and do a difficult job extremely well.

Geographic Reference Report, 1993. 7th ed. BTA Economic Research Institute. 1993. 292p. Covering U.S. and Canadian metropolitan areas, the institute provides data on costs, wages, salaries, and human services such as housing and health care.

Government Assistance Almanac: 1993–94. 7th ed. J. Robert Dumouchel. Omnigraphics. 1993. 843p. Among the 1,288 domestic programs described in this book are a number for which cities and rural areas qualify. Help is available in such areas as housing, community development, and public health. A reformatting of selective *Catalog of Federal Domestic Assistance* information, the book details each program, states the level of funding, the administering agencies, and directory information for field offices. Includes an index.

Greenpeace Guide to Anti-Environmental Organizations. Carl Deal. Odonian. 1993. 110p. Greenpeace seeks to list those organizations, corporate front groups, and charities that appear to support the green movement, but do not. Includes history of the organization and officers and financial backers. Presents one view of a controversial subject.

Hispanic-American Almanac: A Reference Work on Hispanics in the United States. Gale. 1993. 780p. Both historical and current information presents a broad picture of Hispanic culture.

Illustrated Computer Graphics Dictionary. Donald D. Spencer. Camelot. 1993. 305p. As more governmental units use graphics software to produce their own brochures, flyers, and annual reports, knowledge of computer

graphics terminology is necessary. These definitions based on Macintosh computers but applicable to the broader field, are easily understood.

Information Finding and the Research Process: A Guide to Sources and Methods for Public Administration and the Policy Sciences. Anthony E. Simpson. Greenwood. 1993. Simpson, a New York academic librarian, analyzes the design of the research process. He reveals primary and secondary sources, suggesting in which format each is the most accessible.

The Municipal Year Book 1993. Evelina R. Moulder, ed. ICMA. 1993. 394p. Ethics, pay-for-performance, and state-local relations are among the current article topics. Data on personnel and expenditures are followed by directories of local officials and public administration organizations.

Municipal Yellow Book: Who's Who in the Leading City and County Governments and Local Authorities. Monitor Leadership Directories. 1993. 700p. Issued semiannually, this directory lists names, addresses, telephone and FAX numbers of policy shapers at the municipal level. Included is an index of cities and counties by population, allowing the user to find units comparable in size. Monitor also publishes quarterly *State Yellow Book* (1,000p.) with similar information on both the executive and legislative branches of state government.

Networking Directory. Carol L. Eyler. Phillips. 1993. 400p. Eyler lists over 2,000 manufacturers of computer networking products, including LAN hardware and operating systems software, applications software, security systems, telecommunications equipment, and diagnostic and test equipment. Entries are arranged by type of group, then alphabetical.

National Directory of Addresses and Telephone Numbers: The Business-to-Business Book That Covers the Entire U.S.A.: 1993. Steven A. Miles, ed. Omnigraphics. 1992. 1,557p. This enhanced phone book profiles major U.S. cities and lists numbers for hotels, travel, goods and services, restaurants, media and local attractions, and special events. Also lists address, phone, fax, and toll free numbers for the most important corporations, organizations, government offices, and institutions in the U.S. The classified section subscribes to SIC codes heading with subdivisions.

National Directory of Children, Youth and Families Services, 1993–94: The Professionals' Reference. 9th ed. National Directory of Children, Youth and Families Services. 1993. 781p. Part 1 identifies human services/social service agencies, health and mental health services, juvenile justice/youth services, and special service agencies for states, counties, and major cities. Part 2 is a who's who of persons in government, resource centers, national agencies, runaway centers, etc. Part 3 is a buyers' guide for specialized services such as publications, shelters, and treatment centers.

1993 County and City Extra: Annual Metro, City, and County Data Book. Courtenay M. Slater, George E. Hall, eds. Bernan. 1993. Various paging. Reprints and regroups for easier usage the tables and maps from various U.S. census documents.

Official Export Guide: 1993 Version. 11th ed. North American. 1993. Various paging. Presents country profiles and notes the most recent export opportunities, trade and finance data, key contacts, and shipping information. Export know-how, information sources, and a service directory of international air cargo carriers, ocean carriers, and financial services are included along with export administration regulations.

Older Volunteer: An Annotated Bibliography. C. Neil Bull, Nancy D. Levine, eds. Greenwood. 1993. 111p. This bibliography selects 400 American journal articles dealing with the older person as an active volunteer.

Prentice-Hall Encyclopedic Dictionary of English Usage. 2d ed. N. H. Mager, S. K. Major. Rev. by John Domini. Prentice Hall. 1993. 427p. Easy to use, this volume's 15,000 entries provide answers to grammatical questions, problem spellings, and pronunciations.

Sexuality and the Law: An Encyclopedia of Major Legal Cases. Arthur S. Leonard. Garland. 1993. 709p. Not specifically geared to sexual harassment, this reference deals with the wider fields of free speech and discrimination, and provides a basic understanding of legal cases involving sexuality from 1970 on. A table of cases and an index ease access to the material.

Software Encyclopedia, 1993: A Guide for Personal, Professional and Business Users. 8th ed. 2v. Bowker. 1993. 2,203p. Software program entries are arranged alphabetically by both title and by system/application; publishers are listed by name. Over 16,000 programs from 3,000 producers are described and indexed by title and systems application.

Software Reference Guide, 1993. Christine Ulrich. ICMA. 1993. 472p. This guide cites 900 software programs that are especially useful in government work. It also suggests appropriate databases, publications, and organizations.

State Elective Officials and the Legislatures. Council of State Governments. 1993. 165p.

State Legislative Leadership, Committees, and Staff. Council of State Governments. 1993. 280p.

State Administrative Officials Classified by Function. Council of State Governments. 1993. 280p. These three guides are published during odd-numbered years to complement information found in *Book of the States.* Directory information is provided for states and territories of the U.S.

State Legislative Sourcebook: A Resource Guide to Legislative Information in the 50 States. Lynn Hellebust, ed. Government Research Services. 1993. 545p. Arranged geographically, this resource records legislative informational sources such as publishers, hotlines, and tracking and monitoring services within the states. Appendixes list legislative bill status and phone numbers to call for bill information.

Statistical Record of Native North Americans. Marlita A. Reddy, ed. Gale. 1993. 1,661p. The editor notes the source of the information on each table in twelve chapters covering such topics as demographics, the family, education, health and healthcare, business and industry, and land and water management. Canadian subjects are included. Gale published companion statistical volumes on Hispanics in 1993 and Black America in 1990.

U.S. Government Datafiles for Mainframes and Microcomputers, 1993. NTIS. 1993. Various paging. Updated datafiles and software from more than 100 federal agencies are described and arranged by title under the broad subject areas of economics, social studies, and science and technology. Purchase information is provided. Indexes are by subject and by agency. A separate publication lists available software.

Webster's New World Dictionary of Computer Terms. 4th ed. Donald Spencer, comp. Prentice Hall. 1993. 458p. The 5,000 terms defined in this dictionary cover the computer field efficiently with well-chosen, understandable definitions.

Work-Family Policy Implementation Handbook. Joseph A. Brislin. Thompson. 1993. Various paging. This handbook suggests the planning stages and considerations involved in establishing family-friendly employment policies. Available by annual subscription, the package includes quarterly newsletters on trends and policies and quarterly replacement pages to maintain currency of handbook information.

PERIODICALS

Administration and Society. (Q) Sage.
Baseline Data Report. (BM) ICMA.
COGEL Guardian. (BM) Council on Governmental Ethics Laws.
Congressional Quarterly Service Weekly Report. (W) CQ.
Governing. (M) CQ.
Government Executive. (M) National Journal.
Index to Current Urban Documents. (Q) Greenwood.
Management Information Service. (M) ICMA.
National Civic Review. (Q) National Civic League.
National Journal. (W) National Journal.
PAIS International in Print. (M) PAIS.
Planning. (M) APA.
Political Woman. (M) Political Woman.
Public Administration Review. (BM) ASPA.
Public Affairs Quarterly. (Q) Bowling Green State University. Philosophy Documentation Center.
Public Management. (M) ICMA.
Public Productivity and Management Review. (Q) Jossey-Bass.
Sage Urban Studies Abstracts. (Q) Sage.
Social Sciences Index. (Q) H. W. Wilson.
Urban Affairs Abstracts. (W) NLC.
Urban Affairs Quarterly. (Q) Sage.

Urban Land. (M) ULI.

Urban Lawyer. (Q) Urban, State and Local Government Law Section. American Bar Association.

DATABASE RESOURCES

Local Exchange (LEX)

Type: Bibliographic, referral, full text, bulletin board, electronic mail.

Coverage: LEX is a database established and maintained through a partnership of public sector service organizations such as ICMA, National League of Cities, GTE Education Services, National Association of Counties, National Association of Housing and Redevelopment Officials, and the U.S. Environmental Protection Agency. Specialized information unique to local governments is made available to subscribers via research in databases, electronic mail services, bulletin boards, and question and answer services.

Scope: Current.

Producer: Public Technology.

Available: Producer.

Local Government Information Network (LOGIN)

Type: Directory, full text.

Coverage: An information exchange service, LOGIN offers local government experience and expertise, technical data, how-to instructions, and information sources. Emphasis is on innovation and efficiency. Bibliographic citations are pertinent to local government.

Scope: Updated daily. 1979—.

Producer: Login Services Corporation.

Available: Producer.

Management Information Service (MIS)

Type: Reference.

Coverage: ICMA offers this fee-based annual subscription service to local governments. In addition to receiving selected ICMA publications, users may borrow documents or utilize Inquiry Service, in which answers to specific research requests are provided from a database of 12,000 documents.

Scope: Current.

Producer: ICMA.

Available: Producer.

BASIC STATISTICAL RESOURCES

Grace Waibel
Population Division
U.S. Bureau of the Census

BOOKS, REPORTS, MONOGRAPHS, BIBLIOGRAPHIES, AND REFERENCE SOURCES

ICMA often receives requests from urban administrators concerning the availability of data sources. In response to these requests, we have compiled the following list of selected publications of the U.S. Departments of Commerce and Labor. The publications are divided into Employment, Finance, Population, and Housing, followed by the 1992 Census of Governments with descriptions of each volume and number. Other basic data sources are included at the end of this list. All publications that appear in this section of the *Year Book* are available from the GPO.

EMPLOYMENT

U.S. Department of Labor
Bureau of Labor Statistics

Analysis of Work Stoppages. Annual statistical analysis.

Current Wage Developments. Monthly report summarizing wage and benefit changes in major collective bargaining situations. Compiled primarily from newspapers and other secondary sources.

National Survey of Professional, Administrative, Technical, and Clerical Pay. Annual bulletin summarizing the bureau's annual survey of selected professional, administrative, technical, and clerical pay in industry.

State and Local Government Employment and Payrolls. Monthly publication.

Work Stoppages. Preliminary statistical estimates of work stoppages for the entire year.

U.S. Department of Commerce
Bureau of the Census

City Employment in (year). National and population size group statistics on October employment and payrolls of municipal governments, by function, with individual figures for about 460 cities and selected townships that have 50,000 population or more. GE (yr), No. 2.

Public Employment in (year). National totals on October employment and payrolls of all governments (including the federal government), by function, and by type of government. GE (yr), No. 1.

Survey of Governments, (year). Annual employment statistics. (Available from Customer Services, Census Bureau.)

FINANCE

U.S. Department of Labor
Bureau of Labor Statistics

The Consumer Price Index. Monthly report on consumer price movements. Includes statistical tables and technical notes.

U.S. Department of Commerce
Bureau of the Census

City Government Finances in (year). National and size-group totals of municipal government finances, with comparative totals for previous years. Supplies financial statistics for each of the approximately 460 cities and selected townships having 50,000 population or more, and additional detail for each of the 50 largest cities having 300,000 population or more. GF (yr), No. 4.

Finances of Employee-Retirement Systems of State and Local Governments in (year). Figures for the nation, by states, and for major individual systems, on the receipts, payments, and financial assets of employee-retirement systems administered by state and local governments. GF (yr), No. 2.

Government Finances in (year). National totals of revenue, expenditure, indebtedness, and assets covering all governments—federal, state, and local—with comparative summary data for previous years, and statistics for state and local governments, by states. GF (yr), No. 5.

Quarterly Summary of Federal, State, and Local Tax Revenue (quarter). These reports provide nationwide figures on tax revenue by level of government and type of tax, data on property tax collections for county areas with a population of 200,000 or more, and data for individual state governments of selected major taxes. GT (qr), Nos. 1–4.

POPULATION

U.S. Department of Commerce
Bureau of the Census

1990 Census

Public Law 94-171, the Legislative Redistricting Program. Selected population and housing unit counts for all states and the District of Columbia by geographic areas, ranging from states to Census blocs. Provided to all state legislatures and governors for legislative redistricting. P.L. 94-171 tapes, listings, and maps available for purchase; data also released on CD-ROM.

1990 Census of Population and Housing

Printed Reports

Summary Population and Housing Characteristics. (1990 CPH-1). Provides total population and housing unit counts, as well as summary statistics on age, sex, and race. Provides Hispanic origin, household relationship, units in structure, value and rent, number of rooms, tenure, and vacancy characteristics for local governments, including American Indian and Alaska Native areas.

Population and Housing Unit Counts. (1990 CPH-2 Series). Provides total population and housing unit counts for 1990 and previous censuses. Counts provided for most geographic units.

Population and Housing Characteristics for Census Tracts and Block Numbering Areas. (1990 CPH-3 Series). Statistics on 100 percent and sample population and housing subjects.

Population and Housing Characteristics for Congressional Districts of the 103rd Congress. (1990 CPH-4 Series). One report for each state and the District of Columbia show-

ing population and housing data for Congressional districts, as well as other geographic units.

Summary Social, Economic, and Housing Characteristics. (1990 CPH-5 Series). These reports provide sample population and housing data for local governments, including American Indian and Alaska Native areas.

Computer Tape Files

STF 1. Includes 100 percent population and housing counts and characteristics similar in subject content to the 1980 STF 1 but with expanded detail.

STF 2. Contains 100 percent population and housing characteristics similar to the 1980 STF 2 but with expanded detail.

STF 3. Includes sample population and housing characteristics similar in subject to the 1980 STF 3 but with expanded detail.

STF 4. Contains sample population and housing characteristics similar in content to 1980 STF 4 but with more subject detail than STF 3.

1990 Census of Population

General Population Characteristics. (1990 CP-1 Series). Detailed statistics on age, sex, race, Hispanic origin, marital status, and household relationship characteristics for various geographic areas, including states, counties, place of 1,000 or more inhabitants, and other geographic areas. Separate reports issued for each state and the United States.

General Population Characteristics for American Indian and Alaska Native Areas. (1990 CP-1-1A).

General Population Characteristics for Metropolitan Areas. (1990 CP-1-1B).

General Population Characteristics for Urbanized Areas. (1990 CP-1-1C).

Social and Economic Characteristics. (1990 CP-2 Series). These reports, one for each state and the U.S. summary, focus on the population subjects collected on a sample basis in 1990. Data shown for states, counties, and other geographic areas.

Social and Economic Characteristics for American Indian and Alaska Native Areas. (1990 CP-2-1A).

Social and Economic Characteristics for Metropolitan Areas. (1990 CP-2-1B).

Social and Economic Characteristics for Urbanized Areas. (1990 CP-2-1C).

Population Subject Reports. (1990 CP-3 Series). More than twenty reports (in print or tape or both) are planned covering population subjects and subgroups, including migration, income, and the older population.

(1990 CPH-L-Selected population and housing data paper listings). A series of works in progress. Listings compiled to meet needs of potential users. Covers various geographic areas and subjects; may include rankings, changes, etc. Available from Statistical Information Staff, Population Division, Bureau of the Census, Washington, DC 20233; (301) 763-5002.

Current Population Reports

In addition to the findings of the Census of Population conducted every ten years, the Bureau of the Census publishes continuing and up-to-date statistics on population counts, characteristics, and other special studies on the American people (described below). All issued under the general title *Current Population Reports.*

Local Population Estimates. (P-26 Series). Population estimates for counties and metropolitan areas for selected states. Figures prepared by a state agency as part of the Federal-State Cooperative Program for Local Population Estimates.

Population Characteristics. (P-20 Series). Current national and, in some cases, regional data on geographic residence and mobility, fertility, education, school enrollment, marital status, numbers, and characteristics of households and families.

Population Estimates and Projections. (P-25 Series). Monthly estimates of the total population of the United States. Annual midyear state population estimates. Projections of the future population of the United States and individual states.

Special Censuses. (P-28 Series). Summary of population censuses generally taken at the request and expense of city or other local governments. Data are also available in Current Populations Survey Data Files. Subjects include personal and labor force data, estimates of after-tax money income, and non-cash benefit value. For complete description and list, see the *Census Catalog and Guide, 1992.*

Special Studies. (P-23 Series). Studies on methods, concepts, and specialized data. Includes occasional reports on the black population and other categories.

HOUSING

U.S. Department of Commerce
Bureau of the Census

1990 Census of Housing

General Housing Characteristics. (1990 CH-1 Series). Presents detailed statistics on units in structure, value and rent, number of rooms, tenure, and vacancy characteristics for states, counties, and other geographic areas.

General Housing Characteristics for American Indian and Alaska Native Areas. (1990 CH 1-1A).

General Housing Characteristics for Metropolitan Areas. (1990 CH-1-1B).

General Housing Characteristics for Urbanized Areas. (1990 CH-1-1C).

Detailed Housing Characteristics. (1990 CH-2 Series). These reports will focus on the housing subjects collected on a sample basis in 1990. Data will be shown for states, counties, and other geographic areas.

Detailed Housing Characteristics for American Indian and Alaska Native Areas. (1990 CH-2-1A).

Detailed Housing Characteristics for Metropolitan Areas. (1990 CH-2-1B).

Detailed Housing Characteristics for Urbanized Areas. (1990 CH-2-1C).

Housing Subject Reports. (1990 CH-3 Series). Ten housing subject reports are planned for items such as structural characteristics and space utilization. Geographic areas shown in the report generally will include the United States, regions, and divisions.

Products of the 1990 Census have been issued since 1991 with PL 94-171 reports. More complete descriptions of the reports as published can be found in the annual *Census Catalog and Guide* and the Monthly Report Announcement, issued by the Bureau of the Census and for sale by the Superintendent of Documents. For more information, call or write Customer Services, Bureau of the Census, Washington, DC 20233, or see these publications from the Bureau of the Census:

1990 Census of Population and Tabulation and Publication Program. A free report describing 1990 Census products, comparing 1990 with those of 1980, and more. Request from Customer Services, Bureau of the Census.

Census '90 Basics. A free booklet covering how 1990 Census data were collected and processed, data products, and more, available from Customer Services, Bureau of the Census.

AMERICAN HOUSING SURVEY

The American Housing Survey, published every other year in odd-numbered years, continues the Annual Housing Survey published annually until 1984. It provides current information on (1) size and composition of the housing inventory, (2) characteristics of its occupants, (3) changes in the inventory resulting from new construction, (4) indicators of housing and neighborhood quality, and (5) characteristics of recent movers.

1992 CENSUS OF GOVERNMENTS

U.S. Department of Commerce
Bureau of the Census

The 1992 Census of Governments, similar to those taken every 5 years since 1957, covers four major subject fields relating to state and local governments—government organization, taxable property values, public employment, and government finances.

The results are issued in six volumes, described below. Publication of individual reports/volumes is announced in the *Monthly Product Announcement,* issued by the Bureau of the Census. Publications order forms for specific reports may be obtained from any Department of Commerce district office or from Customer Services (publications), Bureau of the Census, Washington, DC 20233.

The 1992 Census of Governments begins publication in 1993. For details, see the *Monthly Product Announcement* issued by the Data User

Services Division, Bureau of the Census, Washington, DC 20233, or call Customer Services, (301) 763-4100.

Vol. 1. Government Organization.

No. 1. Government Organization. Data for the nation and by states on county, municipal, and township governments by size classes; on public school systems by size of enrollment, grades provided, and number of schools provided; and on special district governments by function and by amount of outstanding debt. Also shown is the number of local governments, by type, in each county area in the nation. This report also includes a description of local government structure in each state.

Vol. 2. Taxable Property Values.

Figures for the nation, states, counties, and selected cities having a population of 25,000 or more, on numbers of realty parcels and amounts of assessed value distributed by major property use categories.

Vol. 3. Public Employment.

No. 1. Employment of Major Local Governments. Statistics on October 1992 employment and payrolls for all county governments; municipalities and northeast townships having 10,000 or more population; school systems having 5,000 or more enrollment; and special district governments having 100 or more full-time employees.

No. 2. Compendium of Public Employment. Employment and payroll data are shown by government function for the nation, by states, and by type of government. Local government employment and payrolls are also summarized by county area.

No. 3. Labor-Management Relations. National and state-by-state statistics on the number of employees belonging to an employee organization; contractual agreements and employees covered; and employee bargaining units.

No. 4. Government Costs for Employee Benefits. A report providing statistics on state and local government costs for providing selected employee benefits. Data are presented by type of employee benefit, by state, and by type of government. Selected benefits include federal Social Security, retirement, unemployment insurance, disability insurance, life insurance, hospital/medical insurance, uniform and equipment allowances, bonuses and cash awards, and other benefits. The report also includes information on the number of current state and local government employees determined by federal Social Security.

Vol. 4. Government Finances.

No. 1. Finances Public School Systems. Statistics on revenue, expenditure, debt, and financial assets of school systems, presented for the nation, for states, and for school systems having 5,000 or more enrollment.

No. 2. Finances of Special Districts. Statistics on finances of special district governments by states and for selected large districts.

No. 3. Finances of County Governments. Statistics on revenue, expenditure, debt, and financial assets of county governments in summary for the nation, by size group and state, and for all individual county governments.

No. 4. Finances of Municipal and Township Governments. Statistics on revenue, expenditure, debt, and financial assets of municipalities and townships in summary for the nation, by size and state, and for all individual municipalities and northeast townships with a population of 10,000 or more.

No. 5. Compendium of Government Finances. A summary of census findings on government finances for federal, state, and local governments including derived data on per capita amounts and percentage distributions. Data are presented for the nation, for state areas by type of government, and local governments in each individual county area.

No. 6. Employee Retirement Systems of State and Local Governments. Membership, receipts, expenditure, number of beneficiaries, and financial assets of state and local government employee-retirement systems. Data are shown for the nation, for states, and for individual retirement systems having 200 or more members.

Vol. 6. Guide to the 1992 Census of Governments. A compilation of samples of tables published in the 1992 Census of Governments report series.

OTHER BASIC DATA SOURCES

U.S. Department of Commerce Bureau of the Census

County and City Data Book, 1988. Statistical data for counties, states, regions, divisions, and cities.

Guide to Recurrent and Special Governmental Statistics. Summarizes the tabular presentations produced as part of the Census Bureau's program of state and local government statistics. Covers governmental finances, public employment, city employment, etc. Includes tabular presentation of summary statistics on a wide variety of subjects.

State and Local Government Special Studies. Irregular series of publications based on data collected through the Census Bureau's program of state and local government statistics.

State and Metropolitan Area Data Book, 1991. Presents a variety of statistical information for states and metropolitan areas, including population, vital statistics, education, labor, employment and earnings, business enterprises, and various economic data. Includes state, metropolitan, and area ranking tables.

Statistical Abstract of the United States. Annual. National data book and guide to sources. Standard summary of statistics on social, political, and economic organizations of the United States.

FUNCTIONAL AREAS

Eleanor Ferrall
Librarian Emerita
Arizona State University

EMERGENCY MANAGEMENT

BOOKS, REPORTS, MONOGRAPHS, BIBLIOGRAPHIES, AND REFERENCE SOURCES

Biological Hazards and Emergency Management. Janet K. Bradford, *et al.* NHRAIC. 1993. 20p. This handbook for risk managers looks at the potential for toxicological emergencies in the context of existing disaster planning and suggests specific applications and courses of action.

Building Performance: Hurricane Andrew in Florida: Observations, Recommendations, and Technical Guidance. FEMA. 1992. 93p. Site survey by an eight-member team investigating the structural system of damaged homes forms the basis for recommendations on building materials, construction techniques, code compliance, quality of construction, plan review inspection, and reconstruction/retrofit activities designed to reduce future hurricane damage.

Citizens' Guide to Geologic Hazards. Edward B. Nuhfer, *et al.* American Institute of Professional Geologists. 1993. 144p. This guide for planners and policymakers allows users to understand geologic hazards and risks and evaluate their threat to property.

City in Crisis: A Report. 2v. Special Advisor to the Board of Police Commissioners on the Civil Disorder in Los Angeles. Police Foundation. 1992. Various paging.

Coping with Catastrophe: Building an Emergency Management System to Meet People's Needs in Natural and Manmade Disasters. National Academy of Public Administration. 1993. 138p. This Congress-mandated study examines the evolution of emergency management, the extensive interplay of federal, state, and local governments and the need for bold action to bring about a high-performance, high-reliability coordinating agency for emergency management.

Disaster and After: Social Work in the Aftermath of Disaster. Tim Newburn. Taylor & Francis. 1993. 160p.

Emergency Response. American Red Cross Staff. Mosby-Year Book. 1993. 320p.

Environment as Hazard. 2d ed. Ian Burton, Robert W. Kates, Gilbert F. White. Guilford. 1993. 290p. Rapid social change may actually contribute to the increase in loss of life and property from natural hazards, according to the authors. Updating and citing of newer research enhance this edition.

Federal Emergency Management Agency (FEMA) and the Army: Emerging Missions for Emergency Management. Arthur L. Bradshaw. NTIS. 1993. 29p. (AD-A251 401). Bradshaw explores support, current regulations, and trends of military contribution to

disaster management, including recommendations for the future.

Great Earthquake Experiment: Risk Communication and Public Action. Dennis S. Mileti, Colleen Fitzpatrick. Westview. 1993. 149p.

Hazardous Chemicals Desk Reference. 3d ed. Richard J. Lewis, Sr. Van Nostrand Reinhold. 1993. 1,742p. Nine hundred new entries and extensive revisions to the 6,000-plus chemicals with hazardous properties listed provide quick reference for the emergency manager.

Hazardous Substances Resource Guide. Richard B. Pohanish, Stanley A. Greene, eds. Gale. 1993. 632p. In addition to a clear description of each substance, this volume notes the danger associated with it, proper storage, first aid treatment, and a directory of organizations for further consultation.

Lessons from Disaster. Trevor Kletz. Gulf. 1993. 180p. Kletz considers industrial accidents, especially those in the chemical industry.

Living Conditions, Disasters and Development: An Approach to Cross-cultural Comparisons. Frederick L. Bates, Walter G. Peacock. University of Georgia. 1993. 159p. Using the Domestic Assets Scale, the authors investigate the impact of physical events on households in Italy, Mexico, Peru, Turkey, Yugoslavia, and the U.S.

Organizing Neighborhoods for Earthquake Preparedness. Association of Bay Area Governments. 1993. 65p. This guide tells how neighborhoods may mitigate earthquake damage by advance forming of emergency response groups.

Partnerships for Community Preparedness. David F. Gillespie, *et al.* NHRAIC. 1993. 150p. Disaster response can be significantly improved if diverse participating agencies that react to emergencies develop a network of organizational planning.

Prehospital Documentation: A Systematic Approach. Armando S. Bevelacqua. Brady. 1992. 144p. Sample reports guide the user in accurate report preparation while the text assures quality documentation.

Proceedings: 1993 National Earthquake Conference. 2v. CUSEC. 1993. v.1, 716p; v.2, 720p. Volume I addresses hazard potential, preparedness, and policy while volume II looks at buildings and infrastructure.

Psycheresponse: Psychological Skills for Optimal Performance by Emergency Responders. Michael J. Asken. Prentice Hall. 1993. 172p. Asken addresses the emotional impact of emergency work and advocates self-assessment, concentration, and relaxation techniques.

Reducing Earthquake Hazards in the United States. Robert B. Olshansky, Paul Hanley. CUSEC. 1993. Various paging. Advice on ways to minimize losses due to earthquakes through education and preparation. Seven separately published monographs are entitled *Nonstructural Hazards, Seismic Hazard Mapping, Education of Architects and Engineers, State Seismic Safety Advisory Committees, Critical Facilities, Historic Resources,* and *Seismic Building Codes.*

Reporting on Risk: How the Mass Media Portray Accidents, Diseases, Disasters, and Other Hazards. Eleanor Singer, Phyllis M. Endreny. Russell Sage Foundation. 1993. 288p. The authors investigate the depth and length of risk coverage as well as the accuracy of information and the sources of hazard reports.

Seismic Safety of Federal and Federally Assisted, Leased, or Regulated New Building Construction. 2v. FEMA. 1993. v.1, 28p; v.2, 340p. FEMA relates the progress made in response to Executive Order 12699.

Socioeconomic Impacts. CUSEC. 1993. 254p. This volume caps a five-title series emanating from the steering committee of the 1993 National Earthquake Conference. The set details seismic concerns from preactivity assessment to aftermath effects and activities. Available as a unit, the other four titles are *Hazard Assessment; Mitigation of Damage to the Built Environment; Preparedness, Awareness and Public Education;* and *Emergency Response and Recovery.*

Tales of the Earth: Paroxysms and Perturbations of the Blue Planet. Charles Office, Jake Page. Oxford. 1993. 226p. The authors discuss natural and man-induced catastrophes in the context of social causes such as depletion of resources and population problems.

Targeted: The Anatomy of an Animal Rights Attack. Lorenz O. Lutherer, Margaret S. Simon. University of Oklahoma. 1992. 170p. Research institutions, targets for break-ins, are advised of crisis management tactics, security, legal, and other appropriate responses.

Total Contingency Planning for Disaster: Managing Risk, Minimizing Loss. Kenneth N. Myers. Wiley. 1993. 270p.

Toward a New Damage Assessment Architecture: Adapting Nuclear Effects Reporting for Comprehensive Disaster Support. John Y. Schrader, *et al.* Rand. 1993. 130p. (R-4176-ONA).

Variable Resolution Approach to Modeling Command and Control in Disaster Relief Operations. Walt L. Perry, John Y. Schrader, Barry M. Wilson. Rand. 1993. 37p. (P 7804).

PERIODICALS

Aware: Warning Coordination and Hazard Awareness Report. (Q) National Oceanic and Atmospheric Administration.

CRICOM: The Crisis Communications Report. (10/yr) CRICOM, PASE, Inc.

Disaster Management. (Q) Joint Assistance Centre.

Disasters: The Journal of Disaster Relief and Management. (Q) Basil Blackwell.

Earthquake Spectra. (Q) Earthquake Engineering Research Institute.

Earthquakes and Volcanos. (BM) U.S. Geological Survey. GPO.

Emergency Preparedness Digest. (Q) Emergency Preparedness Canada.

Emergency Preparedness News. (BW) Business Publishers.

Hazard. (10/yr) EIS International.

Hazard/Disaster Research Update. (Q) Claire B. Rubin & Associates.

Hazardous Materials Control. (BM) Hazardous Materials Control Resources Institute.

Hazardous Materials Newsletter. (BM) Hazardous Materials Publishing.

Hazardous Waste News. (W) Business Publishers.

Journal of Civil Defense. (Q) American Civil Defense Association.

Natural Hazards. (Q) Kluwer.

Natural Hazards Observer. (BM) NHRAIC.

NCCEM's Official Monthly Newsletter. (M) National Coordinating Council on Emergency Management.

Phenomenal News. (Q) Natural Phenomena Hazards Project.

Press On! (Q) NIUSR.

Rescue. (BM) JEMS.

Response! The Journal of Search, Rescue, and Emergency Response. (Q) National Association of Search and Rescue Headquarters.

SARScene: The Canadian Search and Rescue Newsletter. (Q) National Search and Rescue Secretariat.

Watermarks. (2/yr) FEMA, Federal Insurance Administration.

DATABASE RESOURCES

Disaster Management Information System (DMIS)
Type: Reference, directory.
Coverage: The Federal Emergency Management Agency (FEMA) creates a series of files under this rubric. Included are the Automated Disaster Reporting System, Counties Files (those eligible for disaster relief based on declared disasters), Damage Survey Report, Disaster Field Office/Disaster Assistance Center, Disbursements File, Duplication of Benefits, Federal Information Processing Standards, Individual and Family Grants, Notice of Interest, Obligations File, and Projects File.
Scope: English language. Most files are updated daily or when changes occur.
Producer: Federal Emergency Management Agency, Office of Information Resources Management.
Available: FEMA.

Emergency Management Information Center (EMIC)
Type: Loan program.
Coverage: The National Emergency Training Center provides a loan service of case studies, both print and audiovisual, that document specific natural or man-made disasters, including floods, hurricanes, tornadoes, earthquakes, urban fires, and transportation accidents.
Available: National Emergency Training Center. FEMA.

National Earthquake Information Center (NEIC)
Type: Digital and analog data.
Coverage: The Center compiles, computes, and distributes digital and analog data on earthquakes that have occurred around the world. Information includes time, location, depth, magnitude, and other characteristics.
Scope: Updated as events occur.
Producer: U.S. Geological Survey, Denver, CO.
Available: Producer.

National Emergency Training Center. Learning Resource Center. FEMA
Type: Reference.
Coverage: A library rather than a database itself, the Learning Resource Center provides personnel who will answer subject inquiries, perform literature searches, compile bibliographies and, within the confines of copyright restrictions and length, provide documentation.
Available: National Emergency Training Center, Learning Resource Center.

National Fire Incident Reporting System (NFIRS)
Type: Statistical.
Coverage: NFIRS is compiled by the U.S. Fire Administration to assist state and local governments in developing their own fire data systems. Data proves useful in determining magnitude and characteristics of fire problems and in decision making.
Scope: U.S. 1982—
Producer: FEMA
Available: Producer. Magnetic tape.

Urban Search and Rescue Database
Type: Directory.
Coverage: Names and addresses of persons and organizations involved with heavy collapse search and rescue operations following a disaster.
Scope: Current information.
Producer: NIUSR.
Available: Labels available for purchase from producer.

ENVIRONMENT AND ENERGY

BOOKS, REPORTS, MONOGRAPHS, BIBLIOGRAPHIES, AND REFERENCE SOURCES

Cars and Climate Change. OECD. 1993. 236p. This title examines the effects of air pollution, greenhouse gases, and developing governmental policies on the environment.

Cleaning Up the Mess: Implementation Strategies in Superfund. Thomas W. Church, Robert T. Nakamura. Brookings. 1993. 209p. By means of case studies at six Superfund cleanup sites, the authors examine the fund's strategies of prosecution, accommodation, and public works. They make recommendations for organizational changes and liability procedures for reauthorization of the program.

Community Associations and the Environment. Ken Budd, ed. Community Association Institute Research Foundation. 1993. 112p.

Confronting Environmental Racism: Voices from the Grass Roots. Robert D. Bullard, ed. South End. 1993. 259p. Environmental justice is questioned as these writers examine populations whose neighborhoods are chosen as likely sites for unpopular environmental projects.

Cost-Benefit Analysis of Environmental Change. Per-Olov Johansson. Cambridge. 1993. 256p.

Earth Follies: Coming to Feminist Terms with the Global Environmental Crisis. Joni Seager. Routledge. 1993. 332p. Seager argues that environmental problems present both social and technological issues, and it is therefore necessary for humanists as well as scientists to be involved in their solution.

"Earth Summit" Agreements: A Guide and Assessment. Michael Grubb, *et al.* Brookings. 1993. 208p. Key elements of the agreements reached at the Rio Earth Summit are explained, along with an analysis of the conference achievements, failures, and implications.

Ecological Assessment of Hazardous Waste Sites. James T. Maughan. Van Nostrand Reinhold. 1993. 352p.

Energy Politics. 4th ed. David Howard Davis. University of Toledo. 1992. 336p. Davis adds to his study of standard fuels such sources as solar, geothermal, waste, and wind, always observing their relationship to public policy.

Environment of Oil. Richard J. Gilbert, ed. Kluwer. 1993. 307p. Gilbert involves both the environmental and economic aspects of the petroleum industry in his consideration of energy policy.

Environmental Protection at the State Level: Politics and Progress in Controlling Pollution. Evan J. Ringquist. Sharpe. 1993. 256p. The author compares pollution control activities and their impacts among various states.

Environmental Risk, Environmental Values, and Political Choices: Beyond Efficiency Trade-offs in Public Policy Analysis. John M. Gillroy, ed. Westview. 1993. 189p.

Expert Systems in Environmental Planning. J. R. Wright, *et al.* Springer-Verlag. 1993. 311p. Wright involves facility planning, geographic information systems, groundwater, hazardous waste sites, and transportation in his application of expert systems.

Fierce Green Fire: The American Environmental Movement. Philip Shabecoff. Hill and Wang. 1993. 352p. Journalist Shabecoff balances the needs of human welfare and environmental interest in his observations and history of the environmental movement.

Grand Theft and Petty Larceny: Property Rights in America. Mark L. Pollot. Pacific Research Institute for Public Policy. 1993. 222p. One of a growing number of titles that show concern about the government's right to take private property, the focus of recent court decisions, and environmental activities.

Hollow Core: Private Interests in National Policy Making. John P. Heinz, *et al.* Harvard. 1993. 450p. Heinz deals with decisionmaking of consequence to energy policy.

Indoor Air: Quality and Control. Anthony L. Hines, *et al.* PTR Prentice Hall. 1993. 340p. The authors assess the risks of indoor pollution, cite sources and their control, and explain absorption and adsorption processes.

Mass Media and Environmental Issues. Anders Hansen, ed. St. Martin's. 1993. 256p.

Natural Gas in the Internal Market: A Review

of Energy Policy. Ernst J. Mestmacker, ed. Graham & Trotman. 1993. 274p.

New Resource Wars: Native and Environmental Struggles Against Multinational Corporations. Al Gedicks. South End. 1993. 250p. An environmental activist, Gedicks highlights the use of coalitions and sophisticated political action by native peoples to protect their territories.

Park Waters in Peril. Terri Martin, William J. Lockhart. National Parks & Conservation Association. 1993. 126p.

Pesticide Question: Environment, Economics, and Ethics. David Pimental, Hugh Lehman, eds. Chapman and Hall. 1993. 441p. Both benefits and dangers of pesticide use are examined, with recommendations for policies to protect people and the environment.

Practical Handbook for Wetland Identification and Delineation. John G. Lyon. Lewis. 1993. 157p.

Regulating Toxic Substances: A Philosophy of Science and the Law. Carl F. Cranor. Oxford. 1993. 252p. Focusing on carcinogens as the toxic substance for consideration, Cranor discusses the relationships among scientific evidence, risk assessment, tort law, and regulatory agencies.

Renewable Energy: Sources for Fuel and Electricity. Thomas B. Johansson, *et al.*, eds. Island. 1993. 1,160p. Internationally prepared, this volume responds to a United Nations resolution for a comprehensive and analytical study on new and renewable sources of energy.

Role of Natural Gas in Environmental Policy. Stephen L. MacDonald, ed. University of Texas at Austin, Bureau of Business Research. 1993. 120p.

Solar Florida: A Sustainable Energy Future. John O. Blackburn. Florida Conservation Foundation Books. 1993. 237p.

Victim: Caught in the Environmental Web. Bruce G. Siminoff. Glenbridge. 1993. 264p. Based on experiences in New Jersey, this book challenges environmental laws, which the author believes extract unreasonable damage fees and employ unfair inspection policies.

Wetlands and Coastal Zone Regulation and Compliance. Steven M. Silverberg, Mark Dennison. Wiley. 1993. Various paging.

World Without End: Economics, Environment, and Sustainable Development. David W. Pearce, Jeremy J. Warford. Oxford. 1993. 440p.

PERIODICALS

Air and Waste: Journal of the Air and Waste Management Association. (M) Air and Waste Management Association.

Buzzworm: The Environmental Journal. (6/yr) Buzzworm.

Coastal Management: An International Journal of Marine Environment, Resources, Law and Society. (Q) Taylor and Francis.

Environmental Viewpoints (A) Gale.

From the State Capitals: Waste Disposal and Pollution Control. (W) Wakeman/Walworth.

Garbage: The Practical Journal for the Environment. (6/yr) Old House Journal.

International Journal of Environment and Pollution. (Q) Interscience Enterprises.

Journal of Energy and Development. (SA) International Research Center for Energy and Economic Development.

Journal of Environmental Engineering. (BM) American Society of Civil Engineers.

Land Economics. (Q) University of Wisconsin-Madison.

Resources, Conservation and Recycling. (8/yr) Pergamon Press.

Wasteline. (Q) New York State Department of Environmental Conservation.

DATABASE RESOURCES

Energy, Science, and Technology
Type: Bibliographic.
Coverage: The U.S. Department of Energy produces this source of over two million references to all aspects of energy and related topics. Coverage includes nuclear, wind, fossil, geothermal, tidal, and solar energy.
Scope: Updated biweekly. 1974—.
Producer: U.S. Department of Energy.
Available: Dialog, STN International.

Energyline
Type: Bibliographic.
Coverage: Also available in print as *Energy Information Abstracts*, this source covers energy issues and problems discussed in books, journals, Congressional committee prints, conference proceedings, speeches, and statistics.
Scope: Updated monthly. 1971—.
Producer: Bowker A&I Publishing.
Available: Data-Star, Dialog, ESA-IRS, ORBIT. CD-ROM, magnetic tape.

Enviroline
Type: Bibliographic.
Coverage: Comprehensive, interdisciplinary, and worldwide, this file includes periodicals, government documents, industry reports, proceedings, newspaper articles, films and monographs. Environmentally related materials are noted as well as rulings from the *Federal Register* and patents from the *Official Gazette*.
Scope: Updated monthly. 1971—.
Producer: Bowker A&I Publishing.
Available: Data-Star, Dialog, DIMDI, ESA-IRS, LifeScience Network, ORBIT. CD-ROM, magnetic tape.

Hazardous Waste News
Type: Full text.
Coverage: Legislative, regulatory, and judicial decisions at both federal and state levels relating to the field of hazardous waste management are included.
Scope: English language. Updated weekly. 1982—.
Producer: Business Publishers.
Available: NewsNet.

Pollution Abstracts
Type: Bibliographic.
Coverage: This environmental database contains over 175,000 citations to worldwide technical and nontechnical literature on pollution research sources and controls. Covered are air, water, land, thermal, noise and radiological pollution; pesticides; sewage and waste treatment; environmental action; and toxicology and health.
Scope: Updated bimonthly. 1970—.
Producer: Cambridge Scientific Abstracts.
Available: BRS, Data-Star, Dialog, ESA-IRS, Life Science Network. CD-ROM, magnetic tape.

RecycleLine
Type: Bulletin Board.
Coverage: This is a directory of current information on upcoming events in the recycling field, markets, prices, and recycled products.
Scope: Current.
Producer: American Recycling Market.
Available: Producer.

Water Resources Abstracts
Type: Bibliographic.
Coverage: This database contains about 214,000 citations, with abstracts, to scientific and technical literature on all aspects of water including quality, quantity, conservation, control, use, and management of water resources.
Scope: Updated monthly. 1968—.
Producer: U.S. Geological Survey. Water Resources Scientific Information Center.
Available: Dialog. CD-ROM, magnetic tape.

FIRE PROTECTION

BOOKS, REPORTS, MONOGRAPHS, BIBLIOGRAPHIES, AND REFERENCE SOURCES

American Volunteer Firetrucks. Don Wood, Wayne Sorensen. Krause. 1993. 300p.

Annual Book of ASTM Standards, 1993, v. 04.07: Building Seals and Sealants; Fire Standards; Building Constructions. ASTM. 1993. 1222p.

Art of EKG Interpretation: A Self-Instructional Text, With Special Sections on Antiarrhythmic and Thrombolitic Drug Therapy, 3d ed. Karen S. Ehrat. Kendall/Hunt. 1993. 403p. Ehrat uses humor to help train rescue personnel in a critical technique.

Benchmarking: Achieving Superior Performance in Fire and Emergency Medical Services. ICMA. 1993. 15p. (MIS). Describes ways to perform ongoing comparisons between a division's services and those considered the best in the field.

Cardiopulmonary Resuscitation. David V. Skinner, Richard I. Vincent. Oxford. 1993. 214p.

CFAST: The Consolidated Model of Fire Growth and Smoke Transport. R. D. Peacock et al. NTIS 1993. 245p. (PB 97-174902/GAR). CFAST is a zone model used for predicting the environment in a multicompart-

ment structure under fire. It calculates the spread time of smoke and fire gases and the temperature throughout the building.

Effectiveness of Hand-Held Fire Extinguishers on Cargo Container Fires. L. Dickerson, D. Blake. NTIS. 1993. 21p. (N 93-21821/2/GAR).

Emergency Dispatching: A Medical Communicator's Guide. Susi B. Steele. Prentice Hall. 1993. 254p. In addition to methods for building an EMS system, the author presents sample conversations illustrating methods of voice control and calming techniques.

Emergency, 1993: A Coding and Reimbursement Guide for Emergency Services. Trudy Whitehead, Paula Fassett. Med-Index. 1993. 160p.

Emergency Services Sourcebook. 3d ed. 2v. Specialized. 1993. 1200p. Updated, expanded, and revised, this reference tool apprises fire and EMS personnel of courses and training programs available and serves as a directory to supportive associations, information centers, government agencies, books, periodicals, audiovisuals, and computer software.

EMT: Prehospital Care. Mark C. Henry, Edward R. Stapleton. W. B. Saunders. 1992. 860p. Advanced airway maneuvers, defibrillation, and trauma are among the comprehensive entries keyed to DOT guidelines.

Fighting the Close Fight with Fires: An Operational Analysis of the Brigade Support Paradigm. H. W. Stratman. NTIS. 1993. 44p. (AD-A263 919/3/GAR). This study examines the brigade support paradigm and recommends changes that increase effectiveness of fire support and simplify synchronization of fire and maneuver.

Fire and Explosion Protection Systems: A Design Professional's Introduction. Michael R. Lindeburg. Professional. 1993. 73p.

Fire and Vegetation Dynamics: Studies from the North American Boreal Forest. Edward A. Johnson. Cambridge. 1992. 129p.

Fire Chief Remembers: Tales of the FDNY. Edwin F. Schneider. Fire Buff House. 1992. 144p.

Fire Suppression and Detection Systems. 3d ed. John L. Bryan. Maxwell Macmillan. 1993. 518p. Bryan updates his title with advanced information on fire extinguishers, foam, and halogenated systems, and improved flame detection devices.

Firefighters Hazardous Materials Reference Book and Index. 2d ed. Daniel J. Davis, Julie A. Davis, Grant T. Christianson. Van Nostrand Reinhold. 1993. 1333p. As first responders these authors found a need for this information compiled into one source. A page is devoted to each material with information on the chemical; its physical description; chemical properties; health, fire, reactivity, corrosivity, radioactivity, and shipping container hazards; and recommended protection of response personnel.

Management of Mass Burn Casualties and Fire Disasters. M. Masellis, ed. Kluwer. 1993. 339p.

NFPA Codes and Standards, 1993. NFPA. 1993.

Various paging. Among new or revised codes appearing in 1993 are *Water Tanks for Private Fire Protection*, NFPA 24, 66p.; *Health Care Facilities*, NFPA 99, 248p.; *Emergency and Standby Power Systems*, NFPA 110, 30p.; *Professional Qualifications for Fire Investigator*, NFPA 1033, 11p.; and *Master Planning Airport Water Supply Systems for Fire Protection*, NFPA 419, 12p.

9-1-1 Trainer Guide: The How To Book: Methods, Ideas, and Tips. Sue Pivetta. Professional Pride. 1992. 120p.

Offshore Fire Safety. Tony Paterson. PennWell. 1993. 232p. Paterson outlines the offshore oil industry, explains its unique firefighting needs, and stresses fire precautions.

Programmer's Reference Guide to FDMS File Formats. R. W. Porter. NTIS. 1993. 45p. (PB 93-182038/GAR). Fire Data Management System is a computer database designed to store and retrieve fire test results.

Smoke Spread Experiments in Large Rooms: Experimental Results and Numerical Simulations. J. Soederbom. NTIS. 1993. 35p. (PB 93-197804/GAR). More powerful computers now make it possible to simulate compartment fire and smoke spread models for practical commercial use. More effective evaluation of numerical simulations is the result.

Trauma Update for the Emergency Medical Technician. Kimball I. Maull, Jackie Kirby, Dennis Rowe, eds. Brady. 1992. 222p.

Young Men and Fire. Norman Maclean. University of Chicago. 1992. 301p. Twelve of the 15 young, elite sky jumpers sent into Montana's Mann Gulch fire in 1949 died within two hours of their descent. Maclean identifies the "screwups" with the poignant, realistic dignity you expect from this master storyteller.

PERIODICALS

American Fire Journal. (M) Fire Publications.
Chief Fire Executive. (BM) PTN Publishing.
Codewatch. (Q) National Fire Sprinkler Association.
Emergency. (M) Hare.
Emergency Medical Services. (M) Creative Age.
Fire and Arson Investigator. (Q) International Association of Arson Investigators.
Fire and Police Personnel Reporter. (M) Public Safety Personnel Research Institute.
Fire Chief. (M) Communications Channels.
Fire Command. (BM) NFPA.
Fire Engineering. (M) PennWell, NJ.
Fire Surveyor. (BM) Paramount Publishing, U.K.
Fire Technology. (Q) NFPA.
Firehouse. (M) PTN Publishing.
HOTSHEET. (Q) International Association of Wildland Fire.
International Bulletin of Wildland Fire. (M) International Association of Wildland Fire.
JEMS: A Journal of Emergency Medical Services. (M) JEMS Publishing.
Journal of Fire Protection Engineering. (Q) Society of Fire Protection Engineers.

Journal of Fire Sciences. (BM) Technomic.
NFPA Journal. (BM) NFPA.
NFPA National Fire Codes. (A) NFPA.
Sprinkler Age. (M) American Fire Sprinkler Association.
Sprinkler Quarterly. (Q) National Fire Sprinkler Association.
Wildfire News and Notes. (5/yr) NFPA.

DATABASE RESOURCES

Applied Science and Technology Index
Type: Bibliographic.
Coverage: Fire prevention is an area covered in this basic index to 335 science and technology journals.
Scope: Updated twice weekly. Oct 1983—.
Producer: H. W. Wilson.
Available: BRS, Wilsonline. CD-ROM, magnetic tape.

BRIX/FLAIR
Type: Bibliographic.
Coverage: Citations, with abstracts, are available to the worldwide literature of books, journals, and reports on construction and fire science. The FLAIR file covers fire detection, ignition, growth, extinction and suppression, special fire hazards in industries and materials, structural aspects of fire in buildings, firefighting, and fire statistics.
Scope: English language, international. Updated monthly. 1950—.
Producer: Great Britain Department of the Environment.
Available: ESA-IRS.

Fire Research Computer bulletin board
Type: Computer bulletin board.
Coverage: This public access computer bulletin board notes computer programs developed by the Center for Fire Research, its activities, information about FIREDOC, and simulation programs. No fee or password is needed, but telephone costs are paid by user.
Scope: Center for Fire Research Activities. Current.
Producer: U.S. National Institute of Standards and Technology. Center for Fire Research.
Available: Producer.

FIREDOC
Type: Bibliographic.
Coverage: FIREDOC accesses reports, articles, books, conference proceedings, and audiovisual materials held by the Fire Research Information Service. Over 20,000 citations are included.
Scope: Updated daily. 1974—.
Producer: U.S. National Institute of Standards and Technology. Building and Fire Research Laboratory.
Available: Producer.

FIREfacts
Type: Computer bulletin board.
Coverage: FIREfacts extracts information from NFPA's *Fire News*, and includes notices of meetings and public education materials.
Scope: Current.

Producer: NFPA.
Available: Accessed via Connect and Connect software.

ICHIEFS
Type: Computer bulletin board.
Coverage: Segments include a master calendar of events and conferences; *Fire Flash* which is news and studies of local incidents; the ICHIEF library; hazardous materials information; and discussions, issues, drills, product support, and troubleshooting tips for Computer-Aided Management of Emergency Operations (CAMEO).
Scope: Current.
Producer: IAFC.
Available: Accessed via Connect and Connect software.

HOUSING

BOOKS, REPORTS, MONOGRAPHS, BIBLIOGRAPHIES, AND REFERENCE SOURCES

American Dream Foreclosed: Strategies for an Affordable Housing Revival. Peter Dreier. Bywood. 1993.

Breaking New Ground: Developing Innovative AIDS Care Residences. Betsy Lieberman, Donald Chamberlain. AIDS Housing of Washington. 1993. 250p. The gamut of activities from initial planning through construction activities to management and maintenance of HIV/AIDS housing is thoroughly covered.

Building Performance: Hurricane Andrew in Florida: Observations, Recommendations, and Technical Guidance. FEMA. 1992. 93p. This study cites obvious examples of poor construction in its discussion of postdisaster mitigation.

Building the Future: A Blueprint for Change, "By Our Homes You Will Know Us." GPO. 1992. 121p. This final report of a national commission on housing for American Indians, Native Alaskans, and Hawaiians makes "policy recommendations for development, management, and modernization of safe and affordable housing for Native Americans."

Comparing Housing Systems: Housing Performance and Housing Policy in the United States and Britain. Valerie Karn, Harold Wolman. Oxford. 1992. 274p.

Development Regulation and Housing Affordability. Ira S. Lowry, Bruce W. Ferguson. ULI. 1992. 180p. Controls may vary from permit rationing to impact fees to zoning moratoria to environmental regulation—any or all of which affect housing availability and cost.

Element of Risk: The Politics of Radon. Leonard A. Cole. American Association for the Advancement of Science. 1993. 250p.

Energy Conservation in Housing for the Homeless: A Guide for Providers. DOE, HUD. 1993. 30p. Within its five sections, the guide offers advice on planning and implementing

programs of housing renovation and maintenance that lead to cost effective energy usage.

Forced to Move: Housing Displacement in the United States. Margo P. Koss. Garland. 1993. 127p. The author concludes from her study that displacement will continue to be a danger for low-income families with children. She suggests that governments must provide a more adequate supply of affordable housing and financial assistance to renters facing housing loss due to a monetary crisis.

Housing: Enabling Markets to Work (with Technical Supplements). S. K. Mayo, S. Angel, A. Imhoff. NTIS. 1993. 167p. (PB 93-201820/GAR). The World Bank urges governments and institutions to change from producing houses to managing the housing sector as a whole.

Housing and Community Development Issues. GAO. GPO. 1993. 29p. (GAO-OCG-93-22). The report discusses affordable housing and HUD management and also addresses cost exposure due to insurance losses and the abatement of lead paint exposure in federal housing inventories.

Housing Markets and Residential Mobility. G. Thomas Kingsley, Margery A. Turner, eds. Urban Institute. 1993. 315p. Mobility for the poor and for minorities is limited by racial segregation and high cost of housing.

HUD Compendium: A Compilation of Processing Directories, DE Updates, Policy Memoranda & CHUMS Updates. Mortgage Bankers Association of America. 1993. 110p.

Keeping to the Marketplace: The Evolution of Canadian Housing Policy. John C. Bacher. McGill-Queens University. 1993. 327p.

Malign Neglect: Homelessness in an American City. Jennifer Wolch, Michael Dear. Jossey-Bass. 1993. 375p. After examining the origins of homelessness, the authors note the lack of public policy and local responses, ending with accounts of life in the homeless arena.

New Approach to Homelessness: A Guide for Local Governments. ICMA. 1993. Small and midsize communities will benefit from these plans to create services among private, public, and intergovernment sources to alleviate homelessness.

New Neighbors: A Case Study of Cooperative Housing. Matthew Cooper, Margaret Critchlow Rodman. University of Toronto. 1992. 326p. Diversity of incomes, backgrounds, ethnicity, and physical abilities characterize the occupants of these cooperative housing ventures in urban Toronto. The authors investigate the results of resident involvement and democratic control in co-ops.

Ownership, Control and the Future of Housing Policy. R. Allen Hays, ed. Greenwood. 1993. 257p. An overview of various national programs, issues, trends, and policies in Canada, Great Britain, Russia, and the U.S.

Public Housing: Index of New Information with Authors, Subjects & Bibliography. Lester W. Wakefield. ABBE Publishers Association of Washington, DC. 1993. 180p. (GAO/T-RCED-93-54).

Public Housing: Low Income Tax Credit as an Alternative Development Method. GAO. GPO. 1993. 48p. (GAO/RCED-93-31).

Radon-Resistant Construction Techniques for New Residential Construction: Technical Guidance. Mike Clarkin, Terry Brennan. Diane. 1993. 52p.

Removing Regulatory Barriers to Affordable Housing: How States and Localities are Moving Ahead. Carol T. Robbins. HUD. 1992. 84p. As a followup study to its *Not in My Backyard*, the Advisory Commission on Regulatory Barriers to Affordable Housing cites numerous state and local programs that have successfully diffused such regulatory barriers.

Shelter Poverty: New Ideas on Housing Affordability. Michael E. Stone. Temple. 1993. 423p. Detailed, creative solutions are proposed for solving the housing affordability problem.

Tower Block: Modern Public Housing in England, Scotland, Wales, and Northern Ireland. Stefan Muthesius, Miles Glendinning. Yale. 1993. 288p.

Unhealthy Housing: Research, Remedies, and Reform. Roger Burridge, David Ormandy. Routledge. 1993. 443p.

PERIODICALS

Architecture. (M) BPI Communications.

Builder. (M) NAHB.

Building Official and Code Administrator. (BM) BOCA.

Current Construction Reports. (Q,M) U.S. Bureau of the Census.

Current Housing Reports. (Q) U.S. Bureau of the Census.

Historic Preservation. (BM) National Trust for Historic Preservation.

Housing and Development Reporter. (BW) Warren, Gorham & Lamont.

Journal of Housing. (BM) NAHRO.

Journal of Preservation Technology—The Bulletin. (Q) Association for Preservation Technology International.

NAHRO Monitor. (SM) NAHRO.

Town and Country Planning. (M) Town and Country Planning Association, England.

DATABASE RESOURCES

CENDATA
Type: Statistical, full text.
Coverage: U.S. population and demographic figures are reflected in this database that provides text from reports and summary data from all programs conducted by the U.S. Bureau of the Census, including housing.
Scope: Updated daily. 1980—.
Producer: U.S. Bureau of the Census. Data Users Services Division.
Available: CompuServe, Dialog.

DRI Housing Forecast
Type: Numeric.
Coverage: This database contains projections of new and existing single-family homes in the U.S. Thirteen quarterly historical and forecast time series show housing sales and prices.
Scope: Updated quarterly. 1970—.
Producer: DRI/McGraw-Hill. Data Products Division.
Available: DRI/McGraw Hill.

State Housing and Construction
Type: Time series.
Coverage: Contains 36,000 weekly, monthly, quarterly, and annual time series data for U.S., states, and regions. Housing, demographics, financial data, economic data, and construction expenditures.
Scope: U.S. Time and updating vary by series.
Producer: WEFA Group.
Available: Producer. Diskette, magnetic tape.

HUMAN RESOURCES AND SERVICES

BOOKS, REPORTS, MONOGRAPHS, BIBLIOGRAPHIES, AND REFERENCE SOURCES

Aging in Place with Dignity: International Solutions Relating to the Low-Income and Frail Elderly. Leonard F. Heumann, Duncan P. Boldy. Praeger. 1993. 193p.

At Risk in America: The Health and Health Care Needs of Vulnerable Populations in the United States. Lu Ann Aday. Jossey-Bass. 1993. 375p.

Behavior Modification in the Human Services: A Systematic Introduction to Concepts and Applications. 3d ed. Sandra S. Sundel, Martin Sundel. Sage. 1993. 346p.

Caught in the Mix: An Oral Portrait of Homelessness. Philip Michael Bulman. Auburn House. 1993. 211p. Problems of homeless women, teens, crime victims, jobless, and addicts are addressed through interviews with persons living on the streets or in shelters.

Children at Risk in America: History, Concepts, and Public Policy. Roberta Wollens, ed. SUNY. 1993. 310p. Contributors suggest that the concept of risk has changed over time and that difficulties arise in reconciling policy with practice as new problems are discovered.

Client Socialization: The Achilles Heal of the Helping Professions. James A. Jones, Abraham Alcabes. Auburn House. 1993. 200p. This indepth analysis of helper/help-seeker relations determines that seekers must become involved in their own rehabilitation.

Costing Community Care: Theory and Practice. Ann Netten, Jeni Beecham. Ashgate. 1993. 180p.

Current Issues in the Economics of Welfare. Nicholas Barr, David Whynes. St. Martin's. 1993. 257p.

Effectively Managing Human Service Organizations. Ralph Brody. Sage. 1993. 271p. Both theoretical and practical advice are offered by an experienced director in the human services field. The author discusses standard manage-

ment and personnel interrelationships, as well as sexual harassment, stress, and cultural diversity.

Emerging Policies for Biomedical Research. William N. Kelley, Marion Osterweis, Elaine R. Rubin. Association of Academic Health Centers. 1993. 250p. Discussions of such subjects as research integrity, ethical use of genetic findings, societal goals, and funding for biomedical research will be of interest to policymakers.

Ethnic Elderly and Long-term Care. Charles M. Barresi, Donald E. Stull, eds. Springer. 1993. 289p.

Homeless Families: Causes, Effects, and Recommendations. Meredith van Ry. Garland. 1993. 122p. The author, whose research in Seattle concentrates on the homeless with children, recommends prehomeless assistance, job aid, and a more effective and functional welfare system.

Implementing the Americans with Disabilities Act: Rights and Responsibilities of All Americans. Lawrence O. Gostin, Henry A. Beyer, eds. Brookes. 1993. 331p.

International Handbook of Child Care Policies and Programs. Moncrieff Cochran. Greenwood. 1993. 688p. A cross-national comparison, this study examines 29 countries, citing causal factors, mediating influences, and the policy and program emphases that result.

Kindness of Strangers: Adult Mentors, Urban Youth and the New Voluntarism. Marc Freedman. Jossey-Bass. 1993. 160p. While Freedman recognizes there may be limits to the successes of mentoring, he stresses its benefits for children caught in the abyss of poverty and neighborhood violence.

Leadership and Management of Volunteer Programs: A Guide for Volunteer Administrators. James C. Fisher, Kathleen M. Cole. Jossey-Bass. 1993. 228p. Not just city hospitals, but police departments, libraries, and parks departments are utilizing more and more volunteers. This title exposes the competencies needed for volunteer programs administration as determined by certification standards of the Association for Volunteer Administration.

Nation in Denial: The Truth About Homelessness. Alice S. Baum, Donald W. Burnes. Westview. 1993. 247p. Baum and Burnes examine the roles of alcohol, drugs, and mental illness among the homeless and suggest appropriate avenues of action, including recognition, not denial, of the problems.

Politics of Parenthood: Child Care, Women's Rights, and the Myth of the Good Mother. Mary Frances Berry. Viking. 1993. 303p. Berry traces the history of the mother as primary care giver, challenges to that theory during the 20th century, and an agenda for the future.

Power and Illness: The Failure and Future of American Health Policy. Daniel M. Fox. University of California. 1993. 210p. Fox advocates a shift from emphasis on acute health conditions to prevention and management of chronic illness.

Remainder of Their Days: Domestic Policy and

Older Families in the United States and Canada. John Hendricks, Carolyn J. Rosenthal. Garland. 1993. 232p.

Technology in People Services: Research, Theory, and Applications. Marcus Leiderman, *et al.* Haworth. 1993. 519p.

Total Quality Management in Human Service Organizations. Lawrence L. Martin. Sage. 1993. 112p.

Transferring Technology in the Personal Social Services. Emilia E. Martinez-Brawley, ed. NASW. 1993. 210p. A call for innovative thinking in the organization of service delivery at the state and local level through decentralization, community-oriented social work, and locality-based services.

Turning Promises into Performances: The Management Challenge of Implementing Workfare. Richard P. Nathan. Columbia. 1993. 161p. Workfare consists of a combination of social service programs including education, child care, and job training. Nathan presents some practical methods for changing welfare concepts.

Utilizing Community Resources: An Overview of Human Services. William Crimando, T. F. Riggar. Paul M. Deutsch. 1993. 370p.

Welfare Costs of Income Uncertainty: A Nonparametric Analysis of Households in the United States and Western Germany. Edward J. Bird. Westview. 1993. 207p.

Women and Children in Health Care: An Unequal Majority. Mary B. Mahowald. Oxford. 1993. 281p.

PERIODICALS

Administration in Social Work. (Q) Haworth.

Aging. (Q) U.S. Administration on Aging, GPO.

Aging Research and Training News. (BW) Business Publishers.

American Journal of Hospice Care. (BM) Prime National Publishing.

Child Abuse and Neglect. (6/yr) Pergamon.

Child Protection Report. (BW) Business Publishers.

Child Welfare. (BM) Child Welfare League of America.

Families in Society. (10/yr) Family Service America.

Journal of Human Resources. (Q) Industrial Relations Research Institute.

Journal of Rehabilitation. (Q) National Rehabilitation Association.

Journal of Social Service Research. (Q) Haworth.

New England Journal of Human Services. (Q) Osiris.

Nutrition Week. (W) Community Nutrition Institute.

Public Welfare. (Q) American Public Welfare Association.

Social Service Review. (Q) University of Chicago.

Social Work Research and Abstracts. (Q) National Association of Social Workers.

DATABASE RESOURCES

AgeLine

Type: Bibliographic.

Coverage: Social gerontology is the focus of AgeLine, with particular emphasis on the delivery of health care to older citizens. Public policy for all concerns of seniors is stressed. Citations, with abstracts, are from journals, books, book chapters, and reports.

Scope: Updated bimonthly. 1978—, with selected coverage back to 1960.

Producer: American Association of Retired Persons.

Available: BRS, Dialog.

PAIS International

Type: Bibliographic.

Coverage: PAIS is an index to the public policy literature of business, economics, finance, law, international relations, government, political science, and other social sciences. International in scope, it cites journal articles, books, government documents at all levels, pamphlets, and reports.

Scope: Updated monthly. 1976—.

Producer: Public Affairs Information Service.

Available: BRS, Data-Star, Dialog. CD-ROM, magnetic tape.

Social Work Abstracts

Type: Bibliographic.

Coverage: These abstracts cover social work, services, conditions and policy. The database contains over 25,000 citations to journal articles, doctoral dissertations, and other materials.

Scope: International. Updated quarterly. July 1977—.

Producer: National Association of Social Workers.

Available: BRS. CD-ROM.

Sociological Abstracts

Type: Bibliographic.

Coverage: Abstracts accompany 330,000 citations to articles in the field of sociology and related areas of the social and behavioral sciences. Coverage is equivalent to the printed versions of *Sociological Abstracts* and *Social Planning, Policy and Development Abstracts*. Both titles include citations on social welfare, planning, policy and development, both urban and rural.

Scope: English. 1963—. Updated 5 × year.

Producer: Sociological Abstracts.

Available: BRS, Dialog, Data-Star, DIMDI, OCLC. CD-ROM, magnetic tape.

INFORMATION TECHNOLOGIES

BOOKS, REPORTS, MONOGRAPHS, BIBLIOGRAPHIES, AND REFERENCE SOURCES

Burwell Directory of Information Brokers, 1993. 10th ed. Helen P. Burwell, ed. Burwell.

1993. 524p. Covering U.S. and 47 other countries, the directory lists for-hire companies and individuals skilled in information retrieval.

Decision Support in Public Administration. 1993. 200p. *Local Area Network Application.* 1993. 272p. *Information Development Process.* 1993. 337p. *Human, Organizational and Social Dimensions of Systems Development.* 1993. 496. North-Holland published each of the above titles, products of an IFIP data processing congress held in the Netherlands, May 1993.

Dynamics of the Computer Industry: Modeling the Supply of Workstations and Their Components. Walid R. Touma. Kluwer. 1993. 213p.

Future Trends in Telecommunications. R. J. Horrocks, R. W. Scarr. Wiley. 1993. 452p.

Intelligent Workstations for Professionals. A. H. Rubenstein, H. Schwartzel, eds. Springer-Verlag. 1993. 286p. A joint symposium of Siemans AG and Northwestern University produced these proceedings on microcomputer work stations and expert systems.

Local and Metropolitan Area Networks. 4th ed. William Stallings. Maxwell Macmillan. 1993. 550p.

Managing the Future of Information Services. Barbara H. Peters, James L. Peters, eds. Conference Board. 1993. 38p. (Report no. 1020). Issues such as partnerships, organizational design, outsourcing, and information services are discussed.

McGraw-Hill Telecommunications Factbook. Joseph A. Pecar, Roger J. O'Connor, David A. Garbin. McGraw-Hill. 1993. 373p. Clear and copious illustrations add to the usefulness of this easily understood perspective of telecommunication systems and technologies.

Multiple Access Communications: Foundations for Emerging Technologies. Norman Abramson, ed. IEEE. 1993. 519p.

Narrowband Land-Mobile Radio Networks. Jean-Paul Linnartz. Artech House. 1993. 445p. Linnartz studies the performance of mobile radio systems with narrowband radio channels. Equations and graphs illustrate this technical study.

National Innovation Systems: A Comparative Analysis. Richard R. Nelson. Oxford. 1993. 541p.

National Issues in Science and Technology, 1993. National Academy. 1993. 88p.

Networking with Windows for Workgroups. Cheryl Currid. Sybex. 1993. 437p.

Professional Communication: The Social Perspective. Nancy R. Blyler, Charlotte Thralls, eds. Sage. 1993. 292p. In addition to discussing the social aspects of communication in science and technology, the editors cover technical and report writing.

Reinventing Public Television: Task Force on the Future of Public Television. Richard Somerset-Ward. Brookings. 1993. 144p.

Secret Science: Federal Control of American Science and Technology. Herbert N. Foerstal. Praeger. 1993. 227p. Foerstal questions the increasing government supervision, classifi-

cation, and control of technological research and information.

Softwars: The Legal Battles for Control of the Global Software Industry. Anthony L. Clapes. Quorum. 1993. 325p. Layman-readable, this title interprets the influences of hackers, clones, patents, and copyrights on the software industry and discusses litigation over reverse engineering of software and the intellectual property law/software technology variance.

Stephen Cobb Complete Book of PC and LAN Security. Stephen Cobb. Windcrest. 1992. 556p. Cobb covers software and procedures ensuring security and discusses software piracy and viruses.

Steps for Implementing Local Area Networks: A Business Guide. Peter Cauchi, Suzanne Dennison. Wiley. 1993. 313p.

Techniques for Technical Communicators. Carol M. Barnum, Saul Carliner. Maxwell Macmillan. 1993. 368p.

Telecommunications: Systems and Applications. William Mitchell, Robert Hendricks, Leonard Sterry. Paradigm. 1993. 240p.

United States-Japan Trade in Communications: Conflict and Compromise. Meheroo Jusswalla, ed. Greenwood. 1993. 190p. Authors in this study consider the impact in both countries of domestic relations, political activity, sociocultural factors, and foreign trade regulations upon trade in communications.

Usage Indicators: A New Foundation for Information Technology Policies. OECD. 1993. 127p. OECD has issued a pioneer cross-national survey of reports and current activities in IT usage, relating IT investment and employment to total investment and employment.

Value of Convenience: A Genealogy of Technical Culture. Thomas F. Tierney. SUNY. 1993. 281p. Tierney looks at the philosophy of technological culture, the fetishistic attitudes toward technology, and the modern consumption of ease, which he describes as convenience.

Voice Networking Systems. Datapro. 1993. Various paging. General information on the field and on specific systems is released and updated monthly.

Whole Internet: Users Guide and Catalog. Ed Krol. O'Reilly and Associates. 1993. 376p. Krol explores the variety of files available in the world's largest network, explaining how to access it and how to use the electronic mail mode.

Windows Networking and Connectivity Guide: How to Survive in a World of Windows, Netware, and DOS. Ralph Davis. Addison-Wesley. 1993. 562p.

Writing Disaster Recovery Plans for Telecommunications Networks and LANs. Leo A. Wrobel. Artech House. 1993. 138p.

PERIODICALS

Annual Review of Information Science & Technology. (IRR) Elsevier (The Netherlands).

ARMA Records Management Quarterly. (Q)

Association of Records Managers and Administrators.

Artificial Intelligence. (18/yr) Elsevier (The Netherlands).

Business Communications Review. (M) BCR Enterprises.

Byte. (M) McGraw-Hill Information Services.

CIO: The Magazine for Information Executives. (18/yr) CIO.

Communications News. (M) Nelson.

Communicationsweek. (W) CMP.

Computer Design. (M) PennWell, MA.

Computer Graphics World. (M) PennWell, MA.

Computers and Security. (8/yr) Elsevier (Essex, England).

Computerworld: The Newsweekly for Information Systems Management. (W) IDG Communications.

Computing Reviews. (M) Association for Computing Machinery.

Data Based Advisor. (M) Data Based Solutions.

Data Communications. (M) McGraw-Hill.

Datamation. (SM) Cahners, MA.

Government Computer News. (BW) Cahners, MD.

Information Today. (11/yr) Learned Information.

Information Week. (W) CMP.

Infoworld. (W) Infoworld.

Journal of the Association for Computing Machinery. (Q) Association for Computing Machinery.

Manage IT. (Q) CAUSE.

MicroSoftware News. (M) ICMA.

Office. (M) Office Publications.

Office Automation Report. (M) Automated Office.

Online: The Magazine of On-Line Information Systems. (BM) Online.

PC Week. (W) Ziff-Davis, MA.

PC World. (M) PCW Communications.

Rural Telecommunications. (BM) National Telephone Cooperative Association.

Software Digest Ratings Report. (15/yr) National Software Testing Laboratories.

State Telephone Regulation Report. (BW) Capitol.

Telecommunications. (M) Horizon House.

Trends in Communications Policy. (M) Economics and Technology.

Urban Data Service. (3/yr) ICMA.

DATABASE RESOURCES

ABI/INFORM

Type: Bibliographic.

Coverage: With its inclusion of public administration and information technology, this database can be accessed via multiple sources. It contains more than 500,000 citations, with abstracts, to 1200 international journals.

Scope: International. Updated weekly or monthly, depending upon online service schedules. 1971—.

Producer: UMI/DataCourier.

Available: BRS, Data-Star, Dialog, ESA-IRS, HRIN, Mead Data Central, NEXIS, OCLC, ORBIT. CD-ROM, magnetic tape.

Business Software Database
Type: Referral, bibliographic.
Coverage: This database describes over 38,000 software packages that are available for micro-, mini-, and mainframe computers.
Scope: Primarily U.S. Updated monthly or quarterly depending upon online service schedules. Currently available software.
Producer: Information Sources.
Available: BRS, DATA-STAR, Dialog, ESA-IRS, HRIN.

Computer Database
Type: Bibliographic.
Coverage: In this database over 510,000 citations note articles on computers, electronics, telecommunications, and the computer industry. Full text of 70 of the journals included is available in Computer ASAP.
Scope: International. Updated weekly. 1983—.
Producer: Information Access Company.
Available: CompuServe, Data-Star, Dialog. CD-ROM, magnetic tape.

FCC Report
Type: Full text.
Coverage: This weekly newsletter available online covers regulatory activities of information-related governmental units, including the Federal Communications Commission, Congress, U.S. Departments of Justice and of Commerce.
Scope: U.S. Updated biweekly. 1985—.
Producer: Capitol Publications, Telecom Publishing Group.
Available: NewsNet.

ICCA Directory
Type: Referral.
Coverage: This directory refers user to member firms of the Independent Computer Consultants Association, with information on their hardware, software, and subject specializations.
Scope: U.S. and Canada. Current. Updated monthly.
Producer: Independent Computer Consultants Association.
Available: CompuServe.

The Information Report
Type: Referral, full text.
Coverage: Sources are listed to obtain free or inexpensive government and private publications, including federal, state, local, international, professional, and trade information.
Scope: U.S. Updated monthly. 1985—.
Producer: Washington Researchers.
Available: NewsNet.

Management Information Service (MIS)
Type: Bibliographic.
Coverage: MIS is not a database per se. It is both a customized database search service of 13,000 documents held by ICMA, plus a loan service to members of documents on successful programs and ideas.
Producer: ICMA.
Available: ICMA by subscription.

Microcomputer Index
Type: Bibliographic.
Coverage: About 142,500 citations, with abstracts, refer users to reviews and commentaries on the use and applications of microcomputers and software. Full text book reviews are retrievable.
Scope: Australia, U.K., U.S. Updated monthly. 1981—.
Producer: Learned Information.
Available: Dialog. Magnetic tape.

Online Today Daily Edition
Type: Referral, full text.
Coverage: The first file in this database contains the full text of *Online Today*, a monthly periodical covering the computer, videotext, and information industry. The second concentrates on legislation pertaining to computers and the computer industry.
Scope: Primarily U.S. Updated 6 times daily or, with legislation, as available. Current.
Producer: CompuServe.
Available: Producer.

PTS PROMT
Type: Bibliographic, full text.
Coverage: PROMT Predicasts Overview of Markets and Technology—cites over 2.8 million items, with abstracts and selected full texts, from business literature.
Scope: International. Updated daily or weekly depending upon online service schedules.
Producer: Predicasts.
Available: Data-Star, Dialog, NEXIS.

Social SciSearch
Type: Bibliographic.
Coverage: International coverage of 1,500 social science journals and books and 3,000 science journals makes this a viable source for information technology material that will prove useful for networking among authors with similar subject expertise.
Scope: Updated weekly. 1972—.
Producer: Institute for Scientific Information.
Available: BRS, Data-Star, Dialog, DIMDI. CD-ROM, magnetic tape.

INTERGOVERNMENTAL RELATIONS

BOOKS, REPORTS, MONOGRAPHS, BIBLIOGRAPHIES, AND REFERENCE SOURCES

American Intergovernmental Relations: Foundations, Perspectives and Issues. 2d ed. Lawrence J. O'Toole, Jr., ed. CQ. 1993. 430p.
Bill of Rights in Modern America: After 200 Years. David J. Bodenhamer, James W. Ely, Jr., eds. Indiana University. 1993. 246p. New federalism, state-law revolution, and increasing emphasis upon state constitutions exemplify changing relationships among governmental units.
Cities Without Suburbs. David Rusk. Johns Hopkins. 1993. 147p. Rusk advocates the creation of metropolitan area-wide governments or state required metro-wide actions by local governments to offset racial segregation and creation of an urban underclass.

County and City Extra, 1993: Annual Metro, City, and County Databank. 2d ed. Courtenay M. Slater, George E. Hall, eds. Bernan. 1993. 1,034p.
Economic Development Strategies for State and Local Governments. Robert P. McGowan, Edward J. Ottensmeyer, eds. Nelson-Hall. 1993. 194p.
Federal Policymaking and the Poor: National Goals, Local Choices, and Distributional Outcomes. Michael J. Rich. Princeton. 1993. 424p.
Federal Regulation of State and Local Governments: The Mixed Record of the 1980s. ACIR. 1993. 140p. Reform of intergovernmental regulation, examination of new rules, and Supreme Court interpretations as they affect intergovernmental relations are explored.
Government that Works: Innovation in State and Local Government. Edward T. Wheeler. McFarland. 1993. 208p. Wheeler believes governments can develop creative programs if their content, management, organization, clients, and funding are carefully planned and executed.
Grassroots Tyranny: The Limits of Federalism. Clint Bolick. Cato. 1993. 195p. According to the author, federalism has come to represent the tyranny of local government. He proposes a return to federalism as a source of protection of individual liberty.
Guide to Reinventing Government in Oregon: A Do-It-Yourself Handbook for Cities, Counties, School District, State and Local Government Employees, Civic and Fraternal Organizations, Elected Officials, and Concerned Citizens. James Garder. Oregon Historical Society. 1993. 250p.
Knowledge Revolution for All Americans: Competing in Our Global Economy: Empowering Federal Education Programs for Our Children. Kent Lloyd, Sven Groennings, Diane Ramsey. Knowledge Network for All Americans. 1993. 1,000p. An integrated approach to education reform; recommended changes; and involvement of state and local governments, families, and organizations—all are key units in this policy evaluation of education and training programs.
Lesson-Drawing in Public Policy. Richard Rose. Chatham House. 1993. 176p. Rose cites both the potentials and pitfalls of transferring public policy across governmental jurisdictions.
Metropolitan Governance: American-Canadian Intergovernmental Perspectives. Donald N. Rothblatt, Andrew Sancton, eds. University of California, Institute of Governmental Studies. 1993. 469p.
Metropolitan Reorganization: A Response to Urban Fragmentation. Roger K. Hedrick. CPL. 1993. 45p. (CPL Bibliography No. 291).
Moving the Earth: Cooperative Federalism and Implementation of the Surface Mining Act. Uday Desai, ed. Greenwood. 1993. 256p. Using the Surface Mining Control and Reclamation Act as a case study, Desai offers an in-depth look at policy implementation and the intergovernmental relationships involved.

Multijurisdictional Drug Law Enforcement Strategies: Reducing Supply and Demand. Jan M. Chaiken, Marcia Chaiken, Clifford Karchmer. Diane. 1993. 127p.

National Guard: Defending the Nation and the States. ACIR. 1993. 60p. As part of both the nation's defense system and the states' emergency corps, the functions of the Guard are subject to dual administration.

Pollution Prevention: A Practical Guide for State and Local Government. David T. Wigglesworth. Lewis. 1993. 200p.

Power/Resistance: Local Politics and the Chaotic State. Andrew Kirby. Indiana. 1993. 179p.

Role of General Government Elected Officials in Criminal Justice. ACIR. 1993. 220p. Policy, management, and intergovernmental issues challenge the elected official dealing with the criminal justice system. Valuable information for decision making is included. Also helpful is ACIR's 56-page *Guide to the Criminal Justice System for General Government Elected Officials* (1993).

Significant Features of Fiscal Federalism, 1993; v.1: Budget Processes and Tax Systems. ACIR. 1993. 188p. This annual looks at federal and state budget actions, with a view of federal, state, and local taxes and fees.

State and Local Government and Politics: Essential Readings. Harry A. Bailey, Jay M. Shafritz, eds. Peacock. 1993. 360p.

State and Local Politics: Government by the People. 7th ed. James M. Burns *et al.* Prentice-Hall. 1993. 320p.

State Government and Economic Performance. Paul Brace. Johns Hopkins. 1993. 152p. Using four case studies, Brace proposes a model for evaluating the economic impact of state activities and policies as national economic activities slow.

State Laws Governing Local Government Structure and Administration. ACIR. 1993. 124p. State laws and constitutional provisions impact local and county governments in areas such as boundary alterations, financial and personnel management, local elections, and form of government.

States and the Economy: Policymaking and Decentralization. Robert H. Wilson. Praeger. 1993. 290p. Recognizing that economic and political decentralization are changing functions and programs of the states, Wilson uses case studies to illustrate the states' emerging roles as economic development program provider, economic regulator, and social infrastructure provider.

Welfare System Reform: Coordinating Federal, State, and Local Public Assistance Programs. Edward T. Jennings, Jr., Neal S. Zank, eds. Greenwood. 1993. 249p. Practical reforms are proposed by a blue-ribbon national commission.

PERIODICALS

Government Finance. (SM) GFOA.
Intergovernmental Issues. (M) Illinois Commission on Intergovernmental Cooperation.
Intergovernmental Perspective. (Q) ACIR.
National Journal. (W) National Journal.
Nation's Cities Weekly. (W) National League of Cities.
State and Local Government Review. (3/yr) University of Georgia, Carl Vinson Institute of Government.
State Legislatures. (M) National Conference of State Legislatures.

DATABASE RESOURCES

PAIS International
Type: Bibliographic.
Coverage: PAIS uses a number of subject headings valuable for finding information on intergovernmental affairs, such as intergovernmental relations, federal and local government relations, state and local government relations, and state and municipal relations. Books, journal articles, and government publications at all levels and reports are covered.
Scope: International. Updated monthly. 1972—.
Producer: Public Affairs Information Service.
Available: Dialog, Data-Star. CD-ROM, magnetic tape.

Urban Data Service (UDS)
Type: Statistical.
Coverage: Survey data, including salaries of officials, police, and fire personnel, encompasses incorporated cities of more than 2500 city-manager cities, counties, and regional councils.
Scope: 1964—.
Producer: ICMA.
Available: Producer.

Washington Post
Type: Full text.
Coverage: This newspaper database provides in-depth coverage of governmental affairs.
Scope: Updated daily. 1989—.
Producer: Washington Post News Library.
Available: CompuServe, Dialog, Dow Jones News/Retrieval, VU/TEXT. CD-ROM.

LAW ENFORCEMENT AND CRIMINAL JUSTICE

BOOKS, REPORTS, MONOGRAPHS, BIBLIOGRAPHIES, AND REFERENCE SOURCES

Call to Action: An Analysis and Overview of the United States Criminal Justice System, with Recommendations. Linda M. Thurston, ed. Third World. 1993. 102p. The independent National Commission on Crime and Justice was formed under the sponsorship of the American Friends Service Committee in 1990. The African American, Latino, Asian/Pacific, and Native American members of the commission stress community action in their recommendations on the criminal justice system.

Confessions in the Courtroom. Lawrence S. Wrightsman, Saul M. Kassin. Sage. 1993. 164p. The authors cover coerced and voluntary confessions, the role of the police, and the reactions of jurors.

Crime in the Making: Pathways and Turning Points Through Life. Robert J. Sampson, John H. Laub. Harvard. 1993. 309p. A reexamination of the longitudinal data done by Sheldon and Eleanor Glueck in the context of crime and deviance during the lifetimes of individuals involved in the criminal justice system.

Crimes of Style: Urban Graffiti and the Politics of Criminality. Jeff Ferrell. Garland. 1993. 236p.

Criminal and Civil Investigation Handbook. 2d ed. Joseph J. Grau. McGraw-Hill, NY. 1993. Various paging.

Drug Treatment and Criminal Justice. James A. Inciardi, ed. Sage. 1993. 271p. Contributors to this volume appraise current innovative drug treatment programs, including TASC and those aimed at incarcerated women and children.

Failure of the Criminal Procedure Revolution. Craig M. Bradley. University of Pennsylvania. 1993. 264p. Bradley examines U.S. Supreme Court decisions during the 1960s that revolutionized state criminal procedures, why they failed, and what needs to be done.

Hate Crimes: The Rising Tide of Bigotry and Bloodshed. Jack Levin, Jack McDevitt. Plenum. 1993. 287p. The authors suggest that citizens, police, and legislators must face domestic terrorism with effective hate crime legislation, effective help to vulnerable groups, and coalitions of diverse groups.

How to Stop Crime. Anthony V. Bouza. Plenum. 1993. 435p. Former Minneapolis Police Chief Bouza charges *all* Americans to recognize complicity in violence, not just the ''under class.'' He cites problems and suggests both short-term and long-term answers.

Inside the Juror: The Psychology of Juror Decision Making. Reid Hastie, ed.. Cambridge. 1993. 277p. After discussing juror bias, the author tests social and behavior models to show how jurors arrive at verdicts.

Judicial Reform in the States. Anthony Champagne, Judith Haydel, eds. University Press of America. 1993. 198p. An examination of judicial reform in seven states. With competition increasing over both selection method and the candidates, the editors foresee further politicization of judicial selection.

Justice Under Pressure: A Comparison of Recidivism Patterns among Four Successive Parolee Cohorts. Sheldon Ekland-Olson, William R. Kelly. Springer-Verlag. 1993. 141p.

Management of Correctional Institutions. Marilyn D. McShane, Frank P. Williams III. Garland. 1993. 340p. Three-fourths of this title is devoted to literature sources and detailed abstracts of materials dealing with correctional units.

Mental Disorder in the Criminal Process: Stan Stress and the Vietnam/Sports Conspiracy.

Grant H. Morris, Allen C. Snyder. Greenwood. 1993. 305p. The authors, using a case history, confront the issues of law and psychiatry in the context of the justice process.

Police Under Pressure: Resolving Disputes. Robert Coulson. Greenwood. 1993. 164p. Coulson, an arbitration authority, cites real cases to show how grievances against police should be solved through arbitration.

Power and the Police Chief: An Institutional and Organizational Analysis. Raymond G. Hunt, John M. Magenau. Sage. 1993. 163p. Police chiefs, subject to societal and institutional changes, are moving more into political arenas according to the authors.

Prevention and Control of Juvenile Delinquency. 2d ed. Richard J. Lundman. Oxford. 1993. 279p.

Principles of Good Policing: Avoiding Violence between Police and Citizens. GPO. 1993. 197p.

Professional Law Enforcement Codes: A Documentary Collection. John Kleinig. Greenwood. 1993. 273p. The first compilation of ethical codes dealing with law enforcement.

Psychology of Criminal Conduct: Theory, Research, and Practice. Ronald Blackburn. Wiley. 1993. 496p.

Responsible Judge: Readings in Judicial Ethics. John T. Noonan, Jr., Kenneth I. Winston, eds. Praeger. 1993. Personal attributes, external influences, and judicial independence and accountability are discussed in relation to judicial ethics.

Taming the System: The Control of Discretion in Criminal Justice, 1950–1990. Samuel Walker. Oxford. 1993. 191p.

Thinking Cop—Feeling Cop: A Study in Police Personalities. Rev. ed. Stephen M. Hennessy. Leadership. 1993. 135p.

Unlocking the Files of the FBI: A Guide to Its Records and Classification System. Gerald K. Haines, David A. Langbart. Scholarly Resources. 1993. 348p.

U.S. Criminal Justice Interest Groups: Institutional Profiles. Michael A. Hallett, Dennis J. Palumbo. Greenwood. 1993. 130p.

Verbal Judo: The Gentle Art of Persuasion. George J. Thompson, Jerry B. Jenkins. Morrow. 1993. 222p.

Verdict: Assessing the Civil Jury System. Robert E. Litan. Brookings. 1993. 600p. Outgrowth of a Brookings/ABA litigation section conference, this book examines the civil jury system and makes both policy and procedure recommendations geared to alter and improve the system.

Victims Still: The Political Manipulation of Crime Victims. Robert Elias. Sage. 1993. 177p.

Women After Prison. Mary Eaton. Taylor & Francis. 1993. 168p.

Women in Control: The Role of Women in Law Enforcement. Frances Heidensohn. Oxford. 1993. 283p. Heidensohn looks at the history of women in both U.S. and British law enforcement and concludes that women are not in control, but they are currently freer, have greater economic and political clout, and are infiltrating key positions.

PERIODICALS

BJS National Update. (Q) U.S. Bureau of Justice Statistics.

Corrections Today. (BM) ACA.

Crime and Delinquency. (Q) Sage.

Criminal Justice and Behavior. (Q) Sage.

Criminal Justice Review. (SA) Georgia State University.

Criminology. (Q) American Society of Criminology.

Federal Probation. (Q) Administrative Office of United States Courts. GPO.

From the State Capitals: Justice Policies. (W) Wakeman/Walworth.

Journal of Criminal Justice. (6/yr) Pergamon.

Journal of Criminal Law and Criminology. (Q) Northwestern University School of Law.

Journal of Police Science and Administration. (Q) IACP.

Journal of Research in Crime and Delinquency. (Q) Sage.

Judicature. (BM) American Judicature Society.

Justice Quarterly. (Q) Academy of Criminal Justice Sciences.

Juvenile and Family Court Journal. (Q) National Council of Juvenile and Family Court Judges.

Police Chief. (M) IACP.

Prison Journal. (Q) Sage.

DATABASE RESOURCES

Criminal Justice Abstracts
Type: Bibliographic.
Coverage: This database, the online, full-text format of *Criminal Justice Abstracts,* provides citations, with abstracts, to books, journal articles, reports, dissertations, and newspapers dealing with crime and criminal justice. The 1968 to 1976 volumes were issued as *Crime and Delinquency Literature.*
Scope: U.S. Updated quarterly. 1968—.
Producer: Willow Tree.
Available: WESTLAW. CD-ROM.

Criminal Justice Periodical Index
Type: Bibliographic.
Coverage: This online counterpart to the printed index of the same name covers the administration of justice and law enforcement, including penology, criminal law, environmental and industrial crime, and security management.
Scope: U.S., Canada, and U.K. Updated monthly. 1975—.
Producer: University Microfilms International.
Available: Dialog.

Law Enforcement and Criminal Justice Information Database
Type: Bibliographic, full text.
Coverage: This is a merged database of sources drawn from journal articles, reports, projects, standards, dissertations, and other databases. Criminal justice systems, criminology, equip-

ment, forensics, and crime prevention are subject areas covered.
Scope: International. Updated quarterly. 1954—.
Producer: International Research and Evaluation.
Available: Producer. CD-ROM.

NCJRS (National Criminal Justice Reference Service)
Type: Bibliographic, directory.
Coverage: Both print and nonprint materials are cited on all aspects of law enforcement, crime prevention, security, criminal justice, and juvenile justice. Entries reflect NCJRS holdings and include books, journals, audiovisual materials, theses, and dissertations. The database is particularly valuable for access to fugitive materials not readily available elsewhere.
Scope: International. Updated monthly. 1972—.
Producer: U.S. National Institute of Justice.
Available: Dialog, producer.

WESTLAW Criminal Justice Library
Type: Full text.
Coverage: In addition to full text of articles and documents relating to federal criminal justice, this database presents federal sentencing guidelines from the *U.S. Code, Code of Federal Regulations,* and *Federal Register.*
Scope: U.S. Updating and time varies by sources used.
Producer: West.
Available: WESTLAW.

WESTLAW Topical Highlights Data Base
Type: Bibliographic, full text.
Coverage: Summaries of significant state and federal criminal justice cases and summaries of relevant statutes, administrative rules, and news items are included. Database also covers other subject areas.
Scope: U.S. Current. Updated daily.
Producer: West.
Available: WESTLAW.

LOCAL GOVERNMENT ORGANIZATION AND MANAGEMENT

BOOKS, REPORTS, MONOGRAPHS, BIBLIOGRAPHIES, AND REFERENCE SOURCES

Applied Statistics for Public Administration. 3d ed. Kenneth Meier, Jeffrey Brudney. Wadsworth. 1993. 448p. Expanded coverage of probability, measurement and research design, and interrupted time series mark this new edition stressing use of statistics as a tool for effective management.

Careers in City Politics: The Case for Urban Democracy. Timothy Bledsoe. University of Pittsburgh. 1993. 231p.

Cities Without Suburbs. David Rusk. Johns Hopkins. 1993. 147p.

County Governments in an Era of Change. David R. Berman, ed. Greenwood. 1993. 167p. This description and history of county

government captures the changing relationships between county governments and state and national jurisdictions.

Drama of Leadership. Robert J. Starratt. Taylor and Francis. 1993. 175p. Starratt has been involved for 30 years in public life and teaching about the nature of leadership.

Effective Local Government Manager. 2d ed. Charldean Newell, ed. ICMA. 1993. 320p. The role and the responsibilities of the local government manager are explored and related to real-world experiences.

Egos and Eggshells: Managing for Success in Today's Workplace. Margot Robinson. Stanton & Harper. 1993. 209p.

Ethics and Public Administration. H. George Frederickson, ed. Sharpe. 1993. 269p. Attitudinal studies accompany topics such as whistle blowing, corruption, and the moral obligations of those in public administration.

Ethics in Public Administration: A Philosophical Approach. Patrick J. Sheeran. Praeger. 1993. 166p. Sheeran supports an ethic concept rooted in philosophy, not theology, and suggests public administrators take responsibility for their actions.

Facing the Bureaucracy: Living and Dying in a Public Agency. Gerald Garvey. Jossey-Bass. 1993. 240p. Garvey looks at effective personnel, legislative relations, and outside influences using the Federal Energy Regulatory Commission as a case study in organizational change.

Governing the Postindustrial City. Marcus D. Pohlman. Longman. 1993. 399p. Pohlman discusses the influences of postindustrialism on city political power, the relationship of the city to both the suburbs and the federal government, and the role of minority politics in urban governance.

Guide to Reinventing Government in Oregon: A Do-It-Yourself Handbook for Cities, Counties, School District, State and Local Government Employees, Civic and Fraternal Organizations, Elected Officials and Concerned Citizens. James Garder. Oregon Historical Society. 1993. 250p.

Handbook of Organizational Behavior. Robert T. Golembiewski, ed. Dekker. 1993. 528p. This collection by organizational behavior experts focuses on primary themes in organization, recent issues, current findings, and the role of values in research.

Managing Fast Growing Cities: New Approaches to Urban Planning and Management in the Developing World. Nick Devas, Carole Rakodi. Wiley. 1993. 337p.

Managing the Public Sector. 4th ed. Grover Starling. Wadsworth. 1993. 632p. Cases, profiles, and examples reflect the cultural diversity of today's society and the management techniques needed for effective leadership.

Political World of a Small Town: A Mirror Image of American Politics. Nelson Wikstrom. Greenwood. 1993. 207p. The author presents West Point, Virginia, as a mirror image of American politics, noting the general rise of executive-centered government, community political indifference, core of political activ-

ists, and growing attention to intergovernmental relations.

Principle-Centered Leadership. Stephen R. Covey. ICMA. 1993. 334p. This treatise proposes that leadership should focus on values and building trust.

Public Management: The State of the Art. Barry Bozeman, ed. Jossey-Bass. 1993. 424p. According to these authors, public management is placing its emphasis upon strategy, interorganizational relations, the implications of innovation and technology, and policy design.

Public Opinion and Policy Leadership in the American States. Phillip W. Roeder. University of Alabama. 1993. 248p. State activism, innovation, and federal assignment of domestic affairs to the states have elevated state governments to leadership in domestic policy making.

Pursuit of Significance: Strategies for Managerial Success in Public Organizations. Robert B. Denhardt. Wadsworth. 1993. 300p. Denhardt crosses geographical boundaries to find newer, nontraditional approaches to public management. He proposes a five-point model to bring about effective management.

Rebirth of Urban Democracy. Jeffrey M. Berry, Kent E. Portney, Ken Thomson. Brookings. 1993. 326p. The authors conclude that neighborhood-driven community decision making leads to better urban policies. They base their conclusions on surveys and interviews in five core cities.

Responsive Local Government Package. ICMA. 1993. Various paging. Articles, brochures and monographs in a packet show citizens how the council-manager plan works.

State and Local Government. 2d ed. Ann O'M. Bowman, Richard C. Kearney. Houghton Mifflin. 1993. 529p.

Strategic Planning for Local Government. Gerald L. Gordon. ICMA. 1993. 119p.

Strategic Planning for Local Government: A Handbook for Officials and Citizens. Roger L. Kemp, ed. McFarland. 1993. 310p.

Strategic Planning for Public Service and Non-Profit Organizations. John M. Bryson, ed. Pergamon. 1993. 137p. Explains how strategic planning differs from other types of planning and how it can be adapted to various needs.

Total Quality Management: Strategies for Local Government. ICMA. 1993. Various paging. Total Quality Management seeks to meet citizens' demands with ever-improving quality services in spite of diminishing resources. This training package consists of a handbook on TQM and a leader's guide to structured learning experiences, case studies, and role play.

Total Quality Management in Government: A Practical Guide for the Real World. Steven Cohen, Ronald Brand. Jossey-Bass. 1993. 228p. Government agency success stories with TQM dot these pages as the authors explain the concept and its implementation.

Urban Policy in Twentieth Century America. Arnold R. Hirsch, Raymond A. Mohl, eds. Rutgers. 1993. 238p.

PERIODICALS

American City and County. (M) Communication Channels.
City and State. (BW) Crain Communications.
City Hall Digest. (M) City Hall Communications.
County News. (BW) National Association of Counties.
Current Municipal Problems. (Q) Callaghan.
Downtown Idea Exchange. (SM) Alexander Research & Communications.
Guide to Management Improvement Projects in Local Government. (Q) ICMA.
Journal of State Government. (Q) Council of State Governments.
The Mayor. (SM) USCM.
NATaT's Reporter (M) National Association of Towns and Townships.
Nation's Cities Weekly. (W) National League of Cities.
Public Management. (M) ICMA.
State Government News. (M) Council of State Governments.
State Legislatures. (M) National Conference of State Legislatures.
State and Local Government Review. (3/yr) Carl Vinson Institute of Government.

DATABASE RESOURCES

CIVITEX (Civic Information and Techniques Exchange)
Type: Information, Referral.
Coverage: Local problem-solving projects and their results are highlighted in this database designed to foster inter-community communication among citizens engaged in local activities.
Scope: Updated continually. 1983—.
Producer: National Civic League.
Available: Producer.

Computer Fraud and Security Bulletin
Type: Full text.
Coverage: The monthly newsletter of the same name spotlights computer crime, prevention methods, and related commercial products.
Scope: U.S. Updated daily or weekly. 1988—.
Producer: Elsevier Advanced Technology.
Available: Data-Star, Dialog.

Local Government Information Network (LOGIN)
Type: Bibliographic, directory.
Coverage: An information exchange system, LOGIN offers local government experiences and expertise, technical data, how-to instructions, and information sources. Emphasis is on innovation and efficiency. Bibliographic citations are pertinent to local government.
Scope: Updated daily. 1979—.
Producer: Login Services Corp.
Available: Producer.

Privatization Center
Type: Directory.
Coverage: A division of the Reason Foundation, PC produces the online *Privatization Database* listing privatized public services in the

U.S. and the *Directory of Private Service Providers.* The Center also amasses material on privatization.

Scope: Current.
Producer: Privatization Center.
Available: Producer.

Urban Data Service (UDS)
Type: Bibliographic, statistical.
Coverage: ICMA provides a subscription service package at cost that includes three *Special Data Issues* each year with responses to survey data, three *Baseline Data Reports,* and *The Municipal Year Book.*
Scope: 1964—.
Producer: ICMA.
Available: Producer.

PERSONNEL AND LABOR RELATIONS

BOOKS, REPORTS, MONOGRAPHS, BIBLIOGRAPHIES, AND REFERENCE SOURCES

As the Workforce Ages: Costs, Benefits, and Policy Challenges. Olivia S. Mitchell, ed. ILR. 1993. 280p.

Complying with the Americans with Disabilities Act: A Guidebook for Management and People with Disabilities. Don Fersh, Peter W. Thomas. Quorum. 1993. 261p. Reviewing the background of this law critical for 22.7 million Americans with disabilities, the authors clarify the employment and accessibility regulations.

Education and Training for Work in the Fifty States: A Compendium of State Policies. Lorraine McDonnell. Rand. 1993. 251p. (N-3560-NCRVE/UCB).

EEO Law and Personnel Practices. Arthur Gutman. Sage. 1993. 320p. Gutman considers legislation relative to the personnel process and the case law interpreting the rulings.

Employee Benefits: Valuation, Analysis and Strategies. Steven G. Vernon. Wiley. 1993. 556p.

Ethics for Government Employees. Charles Lickson. Crisp. 1993. 113p.

Fractured Marketplace for Standardized Testing. Walter M. Haney, George F. Madaus, Robert Lyons. Kluwer. 1993. 347p.

Gender Images in Public Administration: Legitimacy and the Administrative State. Camilla Stivers. Sage. 1993. 164p. Stivers states that the images of expertise, leadership, and virtue defining public administration powers contain gender problems. She urges a closer look at the dilemmas these images pose for women.

Handbook of Training and Development for the Public Sector: A Comprehensive Resource. Montgomery Van Wart, N. Joseph Cayer, Steve Cook. Jossey-Bass. 1993. 385p. New or experienced public managers at all levels will find useful the real-world examples and the overall survey of current training methods and teaching technology.

Incomparable Worth: Pay Equity Meets the Market. Steven E. Rhoads. Cambridge. 1993. 296p. Rhoads attacks the use of the comparable worth practice as being irreconcilable with a market-driven economy.

Job Evaluation: The Myth of Equitable Assessment. Mauve Quaid. University of Toronto. 1993. 277p. Quaid challenges the ability of job evaluations to solve the pay equity problem. The author uses a case study to support the theory.

Job-Hunting Handbook for the Local Government Professional. ICMA. 1993. (40196).

Justice in the Workplace: Approaching Fairness in Human Resources Management. Russell Cropanzano, ed. Erlbaum. 1993. 298p.

Local Government Labor Relations: A Guide for Public Administrators. Joan E. Pynes, Joan M. Lafferty. Quorum. 1993. 242p.

Managing Mavericks: How to Lead Your Staff to Think Like Einstein, Create Like Da Vinci, and Invent Like Edison. IPMA. 1992. 225p.

Private Pay for Public Work: Performance-Related Pay for Public Sector Management. OECD. 1993. 199p. The popularity of performance-related pay at present is outstripping current methodologies for assessment. This study, based on procedures in Australia, Canada, United Kingdom, and the United States, concludes that such pay offers the possibility of improving public sector efficiency.

The Promise and Paradox of Civil Service Reform. Patricia W. Ingraham, David H. Rosenbloom, eds. University of Pittsburgh. 1992. 384p. Contributors discuss the design of change, agencies involved with civil service reform, processes and procedures of the reform act, and lessons and evaluations of results.

Public Employer's Guide. Ronald S. Cooper, Leslie A. Blackmon, Cynthia M. Pols. ICMA. 1993. 542p. In addition to recommendations for compliance with changes in the Fair Labor Standards Act due to court decisions, the authors clarify for cities the 1985 amendments and the DOL regulations.

Public Personnel Administration. Dennis D. Riley. Harper Collins. 1993. 331p. Riley includes discussions of sexual harassment and comparable worth in this consideration of the role of personnel policy in achieving responsible, citizen-oriented government.

Public Personnel Systems. 3d ed. Robert D. Lee. Aspen. 1993. 450p. Revised and updated, this title contains discussions of patronage and merit, total quality management, test administration and validity, collective bargaining, and employee accountability.

Rights at Work: Employment Relations in the Post-Union Era. Richard Edwards. Brookings. 1993. 300p. Edwards proposes innovative public policies that will protect workers' rights and also allow employers to compete in the global market.

Sexual Harassment in the Workplace: A Guide to the Law and a Research Overview for Employers and Employees. Titus Aaron, Judith A. Isaksen. McFarland. 1993. 215p.

Stern's Sourcefinder: Human Resource Management, 1993–1994. Michael Daniels. 1993. 512p. Stern's is compiled to serve all administrative levels of persons dealing with personnel management. Printed and electronic information sources, bibliographies, and directories of involved persons and associations are included in the 3,500 entries covering 8,000 HR topics.

Strategic Human Resource Management. William P. Anthony, Pamela L. Perrewe. Dryden. 1993. 791p.

Supervising Employees with Disabilities: Beyond ADA Compliance. Mary Dickson. Crisp. 1993. 124p.

Training Enhancement in Government Organizations. Ronald R. Sims. Quorum. 1993. 233p.

PERIODICALS

Benefits Law Journal. (Q) Executive Enterprises.

Compensation. (A) ICMA.

Creative Training Techniques. (M) Lakewood.

Federal Labor Relations Reporter. (BA) Labor Relations Press.

From the State Capitals: Public Employee Policy. (W) Wakeman/Walworth.

Government Employee Relations Report. (W) Bureau of National Affairs.

HR Report. (M) ICMA.

Journal of Collective Negotiations in the Public Sector. (Q) Baywood.

Journal of Individual Employment Rights. (Q) Baywood.

Labor and Employment Law Anthology. (A) International Library.

Labor Arbitration in Government. (M) American Arbitration Association.

Monthly Labor Review. (M) U.S. Bureau of Labor Statistics.

Personnel Journal. (M) A.C.C. Communications.

Public Administration Review. (BM) ASPA.

Public Management. (M) ICMA.

Public Personnel Management. (Q) IPMA.

Public Productivity and Management Review. (Q) Jossey-Bass.

SAM Focus on Management. (Q) Society for Advancement of Management.

DATABASE RESOURCES

ABI/INFORM
Type: Bibliographic.
Coverage: Intended to meet the needs of the business executive, ABI/INFORM covers all phases of business management, including human resources and labor relations. Abstracts accompany citations to periodical literature.
Scope: Updated weekly or monthly. 1971—.
Producer: UMI/Data Courier.
Available: BRS, Data-Star, Dialog, ESA/IRS, HRIN, NEXIS, ORBIT, STN International. CD-ROM, magnetic tape.

Business Periodicals Index (BPI)
Type: Bibliographic.

Coverage: A general index to periodical literature in all areas of business, BPI notes personnel administration articles found in trade and business research journals. Over 345 periodicals are scanned.
Scope: Updated twice weekly. 1982—.
Producer: H. W. Wilson.
Available: BRS, OCLC. CD-ROM, magnetic tape.

Employee Benefits Infosource (EBIS)
Type: Bibliographic.
Coverage: EBIS provides online citations, with abstracts, to literature dealing with all facets of employee benefit plans. The citations are extracted from periodicals, newspapers, newsletters, books, research reports, news releases, and proceedings.
Scope: Updated monthly. 1986—.
Producer: International Foundation of Employee Benefit Plans.
Available: Dialog, WESTLAW.

Government Manager
Type: Full text.
Coverage: This online text of *The Government Manager* provides advice to federal government supervisors on handling all aspects of personnel management. Included are court and National Labor Relations Board rulings.
Scope: Updated biweekly. 1985—.
Producer: Bureau of National Affairs.
Available: HRIN.

Human Resources Information Network (HRIN)
Type: Online service. Bibliographic, referral.
Coverage: HRIN is an online service that groups many different current awareness and information sources together under three access points: HRIN Announcements Database (current information updated daily); HRIN Daily Developments Database (updated daily); and HRIN Special Reports Library (updated as needed). All cover subjects of interest to human resources and/or personnel managers.
Scope: Updating varies. Years vary.
Producer: Executive Telecom System International (ETSI).
Available: Producer.

LABORLAW II
Type: Bibliographic.
Coverage: Each U.S. federal, state, and administrative agency decision pertaining to labor relations is entered as a separate record with supportive details and summaries by BNA attorney/editors.
Scope: U.S. Updated monthly. 1980—. LABORLAW I, a closed file, covers 1938–1987.
Producer: Bureau of National Affairs.
Available: Dialog, HRIN.

Management Contents
Type: Bibliographic.
Coverage: Labor relations, management,and personnel are subjects covered by the 300,000 citations to 130 international, English language business journals, newsletters, and tabloids indexed here.

Scope: Updated monthly. 1974—.
Producer: Information Access.
Available: Data-Star, Dialog.

PLANNING AND DEVELOPMENT

BOOKS, REPORTS, MONOGRAPHS, BIBLIOGRAPHIES, AND REFERENCE SOURCES

American Town Plans: A Comparative Timeline. Keller Easterling. Princeton Architectural. 1993. 119p.
Citistates: How Urban America Can Prosper in a Competitive World. Neal Peirce. Seven Locks. 1993. 359p.
City Planning in America: Between Promise and Despair. Mary Hommann. Greenwood. 1993. 155p. The author condemns the lack of federal support for amelioration of central city decline and targets the need for a strong, legally empowered city planning profession.
Community Economic Development: Policy Formation in the U.S. and U.K. David Fasenfest, ed. St. Martin's. 1993. 241p. Contributors stress citizen participation in urban and regional development.
Comparative Studies in Local Economic Development: Problems in Policy Implementation. Peter B. Meyer, ed. Greenwood. 1993. 202p. Innovative programs in the United States, United Kingdom, and Germany are compared and discussed.
Development Policy and Public Action. Marc Wuyts, Maureen Mackintosh, Tom Hewitt, eds. Oxford. 1993. 304p.
Economics for the Built Environment. Marcus Warren, Milton Keynes. Butterworth-Heinemann. 1993. 267p.
Enterprise Culture and the Inner City. Nicholas Deakin, John Edwards. Routledge. 1993. 273p. Urban Development Corporations in England have generated favorable publicity, but the authors choose to take a hard look, through case studies, at the enterprise solution and its results in the inner city.
Fail-Safe Society: Community Defiance and the End of American Technological Optimism. Charles Piller. University of California. 1993. 240p.
From Redlining to Reinvestment: Community Responses to Urban Disinvestment. Gregory D. Squires. Temple. 1992. 288p. Struggles to promote community reinvestment in major cities across America are described by community and academic activists.
Great Streets. Allan B. Jacobs. MIT. 1993. 331p.
Growth Management: The Planning Challenge of the 1990s. Jay M. Stein, ed. Sage. 1993. 238p. Stein discusses the use of government regulation to create a balance between economic protections and environmental protection.
Land and the City: Patterns and Processes of

Urban Change. Philip Kivell. Routledge. 1993. 223p. After studying the allocation, the measuring and monitoring, and the changing patterns of urban land, Kivell discusses land ownership, land policy, and vacant and derelict land.
Managing Community Growth: Policies, Techniques, and Impacts. Eric Damian Kelly. Praeger. 1993. 248p. Kelly places urban growth in the contexts of urban form, natural environment, public services, cost and availability, and housing opportunities. He includes a chapter on state involvement.
Metropolis 2000: Planning, Poverty and Politics. Thomas Angotti. Routledge. 1993. 276p. Metropolitanization and economic development go hand-in-hand in the twentieth century according to the author, and must lead to a more humane approach to city planning.
Minor League Baseball and Local Economic Development. Arthur T. Johnson. University of Illinois. 1993. 273p. Johnson covers the political process of stadium decisions, the role of development policy to guide the decision, and the value of a minor league team and its stadium to a community. He concludes that a stadium must serve the community's nonbaseball recreation and entertainment needs if it is to play an important role in economic development.
New York Approach: Robert Moses, Urban Liberals, and Redevelopment of the Inner City. Joel Schwartz. Ohio State University. 1993. 375p. This book takes a backward look at Title I, the role of City Planning Commissioner Robert Moses, and redevelopment gone awry in New York City.
Next American Metropolis: Ecology, Communities, and the American Dream. Peter Calthorpe. Princeton Architectural. 1993. 160p.
Property Rights and the Constitution: Shaping Society Through Land Use Regulation. Dennis J. Coyle. SUNY. 1993. 382p. The court appears reluctant to rule on legislative economic judgments and Coyle examines this phenomenon in light of present and future land use and property rights.
Recent Publications in Planning. 3v. Dennis Jenks. CPL. 1993. Various paging. Jenks cites sources on infrastructure, planning, public works, and transportation. He includes lists of periodicals and publishers.
Right Place: Shared Responsibility and the Location of Public Facilities. Bryan H. Massam. Halsted. 1993. 231p. Locations for schools, toxic waste dumps, and parks sites are considered in light of equity, economy, and service.
Setting Priorities for Land Conservation. National Research Council. National Academy. 1993. 262p.
Social Justice and Local Development Policy. Robert Mier. Sage. 1993. 256p. Mier chooses to tell the Chicago story as he highlights an equity-based approach to local development.
Street Trees: A Manual for Municipalities. Richard D. Schein. TreeWorks. 1993. 398p. Professional botanist provides a comprehensive look, both theoretical and practical, at

street trees. He goes from a master plan to ordering to planting, with all steps in between.

Urban Waterside Regeneration: Problems and Prospects. K. N. White, *et al.*, eds. Ellis Horword. 1993. 422p.

Winning Community Support for Land Use Projects. Debra Stein. ULI. 1992. 172p. Preparation, sound planning, and negotiation are significant factors in generating public support.

PERIODICALS

American Real Estate and Urban Economics Association Journal. (Q) AREUEA.

City and State. (BW) Crain Communications.

Economic Development and Law Center Report. (Q) National Economic Development and Law Center.

Economic Development Review. (Q) American Economic Development Council.

Entrepreneurial Economy Review. (Q) Corporation for Enterprise Development.

Journal of Architectural and Planning Research. (Q) Locke Science.

Journal of Planning Literature. (Q) Sage.

Journal of the American Planning Association. (Q) APA.

Journal of Urban and Contemporary Law. (SA) Washington University.

Journal of Urban Planning and Development. (2–3/yr) American Society of Civil Engineers.

Land Use Digest. (M) ULI.

Land Use Law and Zoning Digest. (M) APA.

Planning. (M) APA.

Planning and Zoning News. (M) Planning and Zoning Center.

Project Reference File. (Q) ULI.

Quality Cities. (M) Florida League of Cities.

Urban Affairs Abstracts. (W) NLC.

Urban Land. (M) ULI.

Zoning and Planning Law Report. (M) Clark Boardman.

Zoning News. (M) APA.

DATABASE RESOURCES

Avery Index to Architectural Periodicals
Type: Bibliographic.
Coverage: City planning, environmental studies, landscape architecture, and historic preservation are included in the 100,000 plus citations to items appearing in the *Avery Index*.
Scope: International. English. 1979—. Updating varies.
Producer: Columbia University, Avery Architectural and Fine Arts Library.
Available: RLIN, Dialog.

Civil Engineering Database
Type: Bibliographic.
Coverage: One division of this database is devoted to urban planning and development, with citations to journal papers, discussions, feature articles, or books produced by the American Society of Civil Engineers.

Scope: Updated bimonthly. 1975—.
Producer: American Society of Civil Engineers.
Available: STN International.

Social Sciences Index
Type: Bibliographic.
Coverage: Among general social science subjects covered in 240,000 citations from 350 English-language journals are planning at all levels, economic development, geography, and environmental sciences.
Scope: International. Updated semiweekly. 1983—.
Producer: H.W. Wilson.
Available: Wilsonline, BRS, OCLC-EPIC. CD-ROM, magnetic tape.

PUBLIC FINANCE

BOOKS, REPORTS, MONOGRAPHS, BIBLIOGRAPHIES, AND REFERENCE SOURCES

Balanced Budget Requirements: State Experiences and Implications for the Federal Government. GAO. GPO. 1993. 48p. Definitions of balance differ among the 48 states with mandated balanced budgets. Raising taxes and cutting spending may not by themselves balance the budget at the federal level.

Best of Budgeting: A Guide to Preparing Budget Documents. GFOA. 1993.

Catalog of Public Fees and Charges. Dennis Strachota, Bruce Engelbrekt. GFOA. 1992. 245p. The compilers record detailed information on 1,500 user fees and charges used by 178 governments in 38 states and four provinces.

City Finances, City Futures. John Mikesell. National League of Cities. 1993. 100p. Mikesell cites the city, not the state or federal government, as its own saviour in fiscal affairs. He suggests creative funding and tapping of area resources.

Community Development Institutions: Hearings. GPO. 1993. 680p. This in-depth report studies development banks and cooperative banks and their impact on community development.

Credit Where It's Due: Development Banking for Communities. Julia Ann Parzen, Michael Hall Kieschnick. Temple. 1992. 275p. Public administrators can ease the economic needs of their communities by understanding and encouraging the work of community development banks.

Debt, Deficit, and Economic Performance. Mario Baldassarri, Robert Mundell, John McCallum, eds. St. Martin's. 1993. 480p.

Economic Report of the President: Transmitted to Congress. GPO. Annual. 1994. Various paging.

Elected Official's Guide to Debt Issuance. J. B. Kurish, Patricia Tigue. GFOA. 1993. 77p. Instructions run the gamut from developing financing plans and debt policies, to bond

issuance and sale, to the subsequent management of debt.

Handbook of Comparative Public Budgeting and Financial Management. Thomas D. Lynch, Lawrence L. Martin, eds. Dekker. 1993. 330p. Four hundred bibliographic citations supplement budgeting and financial management information for local, state, and cross-national areas.

Handbook of Governmental Accounting and Finance. Nicholas G. Apostolou, D. Larry Crumbley, eds. Wiley. 1993. Various paging. PhDs and CPAs contribute to this benchmark study of governmental procedures.

Highway Taxes and Fees: How They Are Collected and Distributed. FHWA. 1993. 126p. Detailed statistical and tabular information deals with state fees and taxes and state laws that impact highway activities. The involvement of federal agencies and funds is also documented.

Impact of Declining Property Values on Local Government Finances. John E. Peterson, Kimberly K. Edwards. ULI. 1993. 68p.

Industrial Development Bonds: Achievement of Public Benefits is Unclear. GAO. GPO. 1993. 30p. GAO takes a critical look at state and local tax exempt bonds issued for financing manufacturing facilities. GAO found it difficult to substantiate the claimed benefits of job creation and depressed areas improvement.

Information Systems Development. Michael A. Brown, et al. GFOA. 1993. 50p. System development, implementation, operation, and maintenance are covered for a data system useful for public employment retirement plans.

Local Government Infrastructure Financing. Evelina R. Moulder. ICMA. 1993. 39p. This Special Data Issue (40800) emanates from a survey of over 5,000 U.S. cities. Noted are types of impact fees charged developers, cost shifting methods, forms of financing, and short-term financing mechanisms used by governmental units.

Making Ends Meet: Congressional Budgeting in the Age of Deficits. Daniel P. Franklin. CQ. 1993. 254p. Tracing a single year's budget, Franklin contends that budget procedures and outcomes reflect American consensus and compromise. He concludes the budget deficit and national debt are not as formidable as commonly perceived.

No Pain, No Gain: Taxes, Productivity, and Economic Growth. Louis A. Ferlegar, Jay R. Mandle. Brookings. 1993. 61p. Aversion to taxes by the American people and the relationship between tax burden and productivity growth are studied.

Performance Budgeting: State Experiences and Implications for the Federal Government. GAO. GPO. 1993. 16p. GAO presents a study of performance budgeting in the states with carry-over possibilities for the federal government.

Politics of Public Budgeting: Getting and Spending, Borrowing and Balancing. 2d ed. Irene S. Rubin. Chatham House. 1992. 284p. Rubin shows how politics affects what she

terms the five clusters of budgeting at the federal, state, and local government levels: the revenue, budget process, expenditure, balance, and implementation clusters.

Practical Exercises in Local Government Finance: Concepts and Practices. John E. Peterson, Dennis R. Strachota, eds. GFOA. 1993. 183p.

Private Interests, Public Spending: Balanced Budget Conservatism and the Fiscal Crisis. William E. Scheuerman, Sidney Plotkin. South End. 1993. 160p. The authors contrast efficiency with equity in fiscal policy and demonstrate the impact of budget cuts and tax policy on human needs.

State and Local Government Deferred Compensation Programs. Kathleen Jenks Harm. GFOA. 1993. 89p. A joint venture of GFOA and the ICMA Retirement Corporation, the book includes plan benefits, elective and nonelective deferrals, and plan implementation.

Tax Rebates and Tax Differentials: Issues and Alternatives. ICMA. 1993. 42p. (Clearinghouse Report 40788). Four formulas were devised to measure the value of municipal operations in Oakland, MD, to Garrett County, MD, in order to negotiate a tax rebate or tax differential. Supporting expenditures and revenues are in the appendices.

Understanding Nonprofit Funding: Managing Revenues in Social Services and Community Development. Kirsten A. Gronbjerg. Jossey-Bass. 1993. 375p.

Urban Finance under Siege. Thomas R. Swartz, Frank J. Bonello. Sharpe. 1993. 192p.

User Fees: Current Practice. Donald Levitan, Adam D. Silverman. ICMA. 1992. 21p.

Who Bears the Lifetime Tax Burden? Don Fullerton, Diane Lim Rogers. Brookings. 1993. 246p. The authors develop a general equilibrium model to calculate the distribution of each current tax. The model can simulate the economic effect of any change in major U.S. federal, state, or local taxes.

PERIODICALS

City and State. (BW) Crain Communications.
Financing Local Government. (BM) Government Information Services.
Fiscal Letter. (BM) NCSL.
From the State Capitals: Taxation and Revenue Policies. (W) Wakeman/Walworth.
Government Executive. (M) National Journal.
Government Finance Review. (BM) GFOA.
Journal of Finance. (5/yr) American Finance Association.
Muniweek. (W) American Banker/Bond Buyer.
National Tax Journal. (Q) National Tax Association.
Property Tax Journal. (Q) IAAO.
Public Budgeting and Finance. (Q) Transaction.
Public Budgeting and Financial Management. (3/yr) Marcel Dekker.
Public Finance Quarterly. (Q) Sage.
Public Finance/Washington Watch. (W) Thomas Publishing.
Public Investor. (M) GFOA.

State and Local Government Review. (3/yr) University of Georgia, Carl Vinson Institute of Government.
Tax Notes. (W) Tax Analysts.

DATABASE RESOURCES

Financial Indicators Database
Type: Statistical.
Coverage: Critical data elements from comprehensive, award-winning annual financial reports are made available to governments for comparative purposes. Reports are issued by municipalities, counties, and school districts.
Scope: U.S. 1989—.
Producer: GFOA.
Available: Producer. Diskette.

Grants
Type: Directory.
Coverage: Oryx merges its directories of subject-oriented grants into this file which references grants offered by local, state, and federal governments; commercial sources; private foundations; and associations.
Scope: Updated monthly. Current.
Producer: Oryx.
Available: Dialog, Life Science Network. CD-ROM.

Municipal Debt Database
Type: Numeric.
Coverage: Information on new issues of municipal debt, including public, limited, and private, is descriptive. Corresponds to *Monthly Survey of Municipal Debt.*
Scope: Updated daily. 1980—.
Producer: Securities Data.
Available: Producer.

MUNIWEEK
Type: Full text.
Coverage: Commentary and analyses of major issues of the municipal market appear in this online counterpart of *Muniweek.* Information covers finance, economic indicators, government legislation, and debt problems of state and local government.
Scope: Updated weekly. 1989—.
Producer: American Banker/Bond Buyer.
Available: Online as part of *The Bond Buyer* full text.

Public Finance New Issues
Type: Directory, numeric.
Coverage: Detailed information is given on more than 130,000 new issues in all amounts and maturities. The database corresponds in part to the *Monthly Deal List.*
Scope: Updated weekly. 1966—.
Producer: IDD Information Services.
Available: Producer.

Public Finance/Washington Watch
Type: Full text.
Coverage: Like its print counterpart, this database covers developments in the federal government that affect state and local finance, especially government bonds.
Scope: Updated weekly. 1989—.
Producer: American Banker/Bond Buyer.

Available: NewsNet.

PUBLIC WORKS AND UTILITIES

BOOKS, REPORTS, MONOGRAPHS, BIBLIOGRAPHIES, AND REFERENCE SOURCES

Airport Landside Planning and Operations. Transportation Research Board. 1993. 45p.

Assessment and Control of VOC Emissions from Waste Treatment and Disposal Facilities. Thomas T. Shen, Charles E. Schmidt, Thomas R. Card. Van Nostrand Reinhold. 1993. 220p.

Autostress Design of Highway Bridges. Transportation Research Board. 1993. 49p.

Biotreatment of Industrial and Hazardous Waste. Morris Levin, Michael A. Gealt, eds. McGraw-Hill. 1993. 331p.

Demand-Side Management Planning. Clark H. Gellings, John H. Chamberlin. Prentice-Hall. 1993. 452p. All components of the DSM program for utilization of electric power are covered, including load management, forecasting, pricing, and promotion of end-use technologies. The authors have also published the second edition of their *Demand Side Management: Concepts and Methods* (Fairmont. 1993. 451p.).

Economics of Solid Waste Reduction: The Impact of User Fees. Robin R. Jenkins. E. Elgar. 1993. 150p. After detailed modeling to determine the quantity and the demand for solid waste services, Jenkins proposes that establishing residential and commercial user fees will reduce the demand for solid waste services.

Effective and Safe Waste Management: Interfacing Sciences and Engineering with Monitoring and Risk Analysis. Robert L. Jolley, Rhoda G. M. Wang. Lewis. 1993. 387p.

Electrical Power Engineering. Henslay W. Kabisama. McGraw-Hill. 1993. 292p.

Electrical Power Systems Safety Handbook. John Cadick. McGraw-Hill. 1993. 509p.

Emerging Technologies in Hazardous Waste Management III. D. William Tedder, Frederick G. Pohland, eds. American Chemical Society. 1993. 466p. These 22 chapters were selected from 84 manuscripts dealing with the treatment of the increasing quantity and toxicity of hazardous waste.

Federal Public Works Infrastructure R&D: A New Perspective. Civil Engineering Research Foundation Staff. American Society of Civil Engineers. 1993.

Geotechnical Practice in Dam Rehabilitation: Proceedings of the Specialty Conference. Loren R. Anderson, ed. ASCE. 1993. 1,078p. Papers from a 1993 conference on dam rehabilitation include information on dam safety as well as maintenance and repair.

Hazardous Waste Cost Control. Richard A. Selg. Dekker. 1993. 276p.

In Defense of Garbage. Judd H. Alexander. Praeger. 1993. 288p. Judd asserts that waste contributes to the national economy. He dispels some myths about garbage quantity and handling and suggests a solution to the management of local solid waste.

Integrated Solid Waste Management: Engineering Principles and Management Issues. George Tchobanoglous, Hilary Theisen, Samuel Vigil. McGraw-Hill. 1993. 978p.

Interior Lighting for Environmental Designers. 3d ed. Gary Goodman, James Nuckolls. Wiley. 1993. 407p. Well illustrated, the text covers basic terms, materials, and techniques.

Issues in Underground Storage Tank Management: Tank Closure and Financial Assistance. Janet E. Robinson, *et al.* Lewis. 1993. 298p. Governments as well as service stations and private citizens must deal with the myriad of regulations overseeing underground storage tanks. The authors provide information about close tank systems and include a useful section on federal financial assurance requirements.

Lighting Handbook: Reference and Application. 8th ed. Mark S. Rea, ed. IESNA. 1993. 989p. Among topics found in this comprehensive reference tool are lighting engineering, design and application; energy management; and software designed for lighting calculations.

Making Less Garbage: A Planning Guide for Communities. Bette K. Fishbein, Caroline Gelb. INFORM. 1993. 192p. Local governments seeking to reduce the costs of waste management will find detailed examples of possible actions. Packaging and ''cash for trash'' are two of the programs included.

McGraw-Hill Recycling Handbook. Herbert F. Lund. McGraw-Hill. 1993. Various paging. A general overview, details of major recyclable materials, facilities and equipment, and implementation and management of a program are addressed in this detailed reference source.

Mercury and Arsenic Wastes: Removal, Recovery, Treatment, and Disposal. EPA. Noyes Data. 1993.

Municipal Sludge Use in Land Reclamation. William E. Sopper. Lewis. 1993. 163p.

Municipal Wastewater Treatment Technology: Recent Developments. EPA. Noyes Data. 1993. 250p.

1993 Manual of Concrete Practice. American Concrete Institute. 1993. Various paging. City engineers concerned with infrastructure will reference this source for standards, for inspection information, and for the latest advances in concrete technology.

Public Works Inspector's Manual. 4th ed. Silas B. Birch, Jr. BNI. 1993.

Public Works Manual. James Kircher, *et al.* Public Works Journal. 1993. Primarily devoted to technical articles on public works topics, this manual lists about 4,000 manufacturers and distributors of equipment, materials, services, and computers used in relation to streets and highways, water systems, wastewater and solid wastes, and recreation areas. The manual is produced annually.

RCRA Policy Documents: Finding Your Way Through the Maze of EPA Guidance and Solid and Hazardous Waste. Theodore L. Garrett, Joshua D. Sarnoff, eds. ABA. 1993.

Recycling Equipment and Technology for Municipal Solid Waste: Material Recovery Facilities. Joseph T. Swartzbaugh, *et al.* Noyes Data. 1993. 150p.

Recycling Solid Waste: The First Choice for Private and Public Sector Management. Thomas E. Duston. Quorum. 1993. 204p. Incineration and landfill quantities could be reduced by recovering and recycling most of the waste. Practical ways to do so are suggested.

Service Opportunities for Electric Utilities: Creating Differentiated Products. Shmuel S. Oren, Stephen A. Smith. Kluwer. 1993. 330p.

Standard Handbook for Electrical Engineers. 13th ed. Donald G. Fink, H. Wayne Beaty, eds. McGraw-Hill. 1993. Various paging. Information on changes in the field accompanies basic electrical engineering information. Computer technology for power industry management is covered.

Water Quality and Availability: A Reference Handbook. E. Willard Miller. ABC-CLIO. 1992. 430p. An overview of the spectrum of water availability, distribution, contamination, regulation, and management is augmented by a directory of involved organizations and a bibliography of reference works.

PERIODICALS

AASHTO Quarterly. (Q) AASHTO.

American City and County. (M) Communication Channels.

APWA Reporter. (M) APWA.

AWWA Journal. (M) AWWA.

Civic Public Works. (M) MacLean Hunter, Ltd.

Civil Engineering. (M) ASCE.

ENR. (W) McGraw-Hill.

Facilities Manager. (Q) Association of Physical Plant Administrators of Universities and Colleges.

Fleet Equipment. (M) Maple.

From the State Capitals: Waste Disposal and Pollution Control. (W) Wakeman/Walworth.

From the State Capitals: Public Utilities. (W) Wakeman/Walworth.

Garbage. (6/yr) Old House Journal.

Gas Industries Magazine. (M) Gas Industries.

Journal of Water Resources Planning and Management. (BM) ASCE.

Management of World Wastes. (M) Communication Channels.

Public Power. (BM) American Public Power Association.

Public Works. (M) Public Works Journal.

Research Journal: Water Pollution Control Federation. (M) Water Pollution Control Federation.

Solid Waste and Power. (BM) H.C.I. Publications.

Waste Age. (M) National Solid Wastes Management Association.

DATABASE RESOURCES

Applied Science and Technology Index
Type: Bibliographic.
Coverage: A basic index to 335 science and technology journals, this database includes entries on construction, waste disposal, water distribution, pollution control, recycling, and the various fields of engineering.
Scope: Updated twice weekly. October 1983—.
Producer: H. W. Wilson.
Available: BRS. CD-ROM, magnetic tape.

COMPENDEX (Computerized Engineering Index)
Type: Bibliographic.
Coverage: Entries, with abstracts, number over 2.1 million in this worldwide source to all aspects of engineering. Topics of use here include civil, sanitary, and waste engineering; water and waterworks; construction; and materials testing.
Scope: International. Updated monthly. Years covered vary with services.
Producer: Engineering Information.
Available: ESA-IRS. As COMPENDEX*PLUS on Data-Star, Dialog, ORBIT, STN International. CD-ROM, magnetic tape.

Local Government Information Network (LOGIN)
Type: Directory, full text.
Coverage: An information exchange service, LOGIN offers local government experiences and expertise, technical data, how-to instructions, and information sources. Emphasis is on innovation and efficiency. Bibliographic citations are pertinent to local government.
Scope: Updated daily. 1979—.
Producer: Login Services Corporation.
Available: Producer.

Public Utilities Reports
Type: Full text.
Coverage: The complete text of *Public Utilities Fortnightly* available in this database covers the public utilities and energy industry. Problems, trends, finance, policy, legislation, and case decisions are featured.
Scope: Updated continually. 1953—.
Producer: Public Utilities Reports, Inc.
Available: WESTLAW.

WasteInfo
Type: Bibliographic, directory.
Coverage: Dealing with nonradioactive waste management, *WasteInfo* includes public policy, legislation, management guidelines, environmental aspects, recycling, disposal, and treatment.
Scope: Updated monthly. 1973—.
Producer: Waste Management Information Bureau.
Available: ORBIT. CD-ROM.

Water Resources Abstracts
Type: Bibliographic.
Coverage: This comprehensive database, which corresponds to *Selected Water Resources Abstracts*, discusses all aspects of water, including cycles, supply, augmentation, management of quantity and quality, planning, and related engineering activities.

Scope: Updated monthly. 1968—.
Producer: U.S. Geological Survey. Water Resources Scientific Information Center.
Available: Dialog. CD-ROM, magnetic tape.

RECREATION AND LEISURE

BOOKS, REPORTS, MONOGRAPHS, BIBLIOGRAPHIES, AND REFERENCE SOURCES

American Art Directory, 1993–94. 54th ed. Bowker. 1993. 780p. The directory surveys more than 7,000 art institutions, noting collections, funding, exhibitions, and key personnel.

America's Ancient Treasures: A Guide to Archeological Sites and Museums in the United States and Canada. Mary E. Folsom, Frank Folsom. University of New Mexico. 1993. 420p.

Art of Teaching Dance Technique. Joan Schlaich, Betty DuPont. AAHPERD. 1993. 112p.

Dance, Gender, and Culture. Helen Thomas, ed. St. Martin's. 1993. 272p. Thomas examines social aspects and sexual differences in this study of dancing.

Facility Planning for Physical Education, Recreation, and Athletics. Richard B. Flynn, ed. AAHPERD. 1993. 251p. Noted authorities in recreational facilities planning contributed to this book, which covers not only the planning of indoor and outdoor facilities but also risk management and current trends.

Identity in Ethnic Leisure Pursuits. Dorceta E. Taylor. Mellen Research University. 1992. 306p. Taylor breaks new ground in her comparative study of race and ethnic leisure participation. Surveying the use of parks by African Americans, Jamaicans, Italians, and other whites, she concludes the delivery of recreational services needs to be studied in a sociological context.

Integrated Public Lands Management: Principles and Applications to National Forests, Parks, Wildlife Refuges, and BLM Lands. John B. Loomis. Columbia. 1993.

Law in Plain English for Art and Craft Galleries. Leonard DuBoff. Interweave. 1993. 156p.

Law in Plain English for Craftspeople. 3d ed. Leonard DuBoff. Interweave. 1993. 148p. Both titles explain U.S. law and define the legal status of galleries and artisans.

Leisure and Family Fun. Mary Attebury-Rogers. Venture. 1993. 96p. A therapeutic recreation specialist describes her work with chemically dependent adolescents in single or multifamily recreational sessions. Each of the 16 sessions focuses on a treatment issue such as communication, self esteem, or cooperation.

Leisure and the Environment: Essays in Honour of Professor J. Allan Patmore. Halsted. 1993. 311p. Essays deal with outdoor recreation and the social aspects of leisure planning.

Leisure Environment. Marcus Colquhoun. Trans-Atlantic. 1993. 208p.

Leisure in a Changing America: A Multicultural Perspective. Richard Kraus. Macmillan. 1993. 416p.

Leisure in the 1990s: Rolling Back the Welfare State. J. Sugden, C. Knox. LSA. 1992. 288p. Although these conference papers are centered on Ireland and Great Britain, the problems and trends are universal. Attendees examine the future role of the public sector in community play, sport, and recreation.

Leisure Programming: Concepts, Trends, and Professional Practice. 2d ed. E. Edgington, C. J. Hanson, S. R. Edgington. Brown. 1992. 479p. Customer/leader interactions join program planning and organization and program management as key elements in meaningful leisure activities.

Museum Design: Planning and Building for Arts. Joan Darragh, James S. Snyder. Oxford. 1993. 319p. The authors cover museum design planning both before and after involving an architect. They go on to explain bidding, contracting, construction, and completion activities and offer advice on moving in and on maintenance.

Museums and the Appropriation of Culture. Susan Pearce, ed. Humanities. 1993. 256p.

Of Time, Work, and Leisure. Sebastian De Grazia. Vintage. 1993.

Official Museum Directory, 1993. American Association of Museums. 1993. 1,732p. Entries include art, science, history, children's museums, aquariums, zoos, botanical gardens, and historical houses and sites.

Politics of Leisure Policy. Ian P. Henry. Macmillan (London). 1993. 235p. The author presents an economic rationale for state involvement in sports, recreation, and cultural activities.

Practical Handbook for the Historic House Museum. Sherry Butcher-Younghans. Oxford. 1993. 240p.

Recreation, Leisure and Chronic Illness: Therapeutic Rehabilitation as Intervention in Health Care. Miriam P. Lahey, *et al.* Haworth. 1993. 130p. Published as volume 6, number 4 of *Loss, Grief and Care,* the chapters examine the field of therapeutic rehabilitation and its relationship to the elderly, the injured, the disabled, the dying, and practitioners themselves.

Science and Technology Museums. Stella V. F. Butler. Leicester University. 1992. 149p.

Stern's Performing Arts Directory, 1994. Rev. ed. Allen E. McCormack, ed. Dance Magazine. 1993. 406p.

Time and Money: The Making of Consumerist Modernity. Gary Cross. Routledge. 1993. 294p. The author presents cross-cultural studies in economic consumption and leisure.

Tourism and Heritage Attractions. Richard Prentice. Routledge. 1993. 253p. Prentice investigates tourism to historic places in a marketing context, noting user characteristics, the variety of attractions, and the benefits to the visitor.

Urban Tourism: Attracting Visitors to Large Cities. Christopher M. Law. Cassell. 1993. 224p.

PERIODICALS

Cardozo Arts and Entertainment Law Journal. (SA) Cardozo School of Law.

Coastal Management. (Q) Taylor and Francis.

Curator. (Q) American Museum of Natural History.

Journal of Leisure Research. (Q) NRPA.

Journal of Park and Recreation Administration. (Q) Sagamore.

Journal of Physical Education, Recreation and Dance. (M) AAHPERD.

Landmark. (BM) Pendragon.

Leisure Sciences. (Q) Taylor and Francis.

National Parks. (BM) National Parks and Conservation Association.

Park and Grounds Management. (M) Madisen.

Parks and Recreation. (M) NRPA.

Public Art Review. (SA) Forecast.

Recreation and Parks Law Reporter. (Q) NRPA.

Recreation Canada. (5/yr) Canadian Parksreation Association.

Research Quarterly for Exercise and Sport. (Q) AAHPERD.

Waterfront World. (5/yr) Waterfront Center.

DATABASE RESOURCES

CAB: Leisure, Recreation and Tourism
Type: Bibliographic.
Coverage: *Leisure, Recreation and Tourism* is a subset of *CAB Abstracts* and is available from selected online services as a separate unit. Monographs and journals are indexed and abstracted.
Scope: Updated quarterly, monthly. Time span varies with online service.
Producer: C.A.B. International.
Available: Data-Star, DIMDI. Magnetic tape.

Schole
Type: Referral, full text.
Coverage: *Schole* offers full text retrieval from *Disability Advocates Bulletin, Recreation and Parks Law Reporter,* and *Fitness and Disability Handbook,* along with general news items, travel writings, parks and recreation works, and references to the National Recreation and Parks Association publications.
Scope: Updating varies. Current.
Producer: Boston University, School of Education.
Available: DELPHI.

SPORT (SIRC)
Type: Bibliographic.
Coverage: More than 275,000 citations, some with abstracts, cover the worldwide scientific and practical literature in the areas of individual and team sports, sports medicine, physical fitness, and education.
Scope: Updated monthly. 1949—.
Producer: Sport Information Research Centre.
Available: BRS, CAN/OLE, Data-Star, Dialog, DIMDI, Knowledge Index, Life Science Network. CD-ROM.

Sports Illustrated
Type: Full text.

Coverage: Database is online counterpart of *Sports Illustrated*, a weekly magazine covering current sports events and trends in recreation and leisure.

Scope: Updated weekly. U.S., some international. 1982—.

Producer: Time, Inc.

Available: NEXIS, Magazine ASAP.

TRANSPORTATION AND ROADS

BOOKS, REPORTS, MONOGRAPHS, BIBLIOGRAPHIES, AND REFERENCE SOURCES

Accepting the Challenge: Global Aviation for the 21st Century. FAA. 1993. Unpaged. This FAA publication focuses on international cooperation to improve the global air transport arena. Photos in color illustrate research and development in communication, navigation, surveillance, air traffic, weather, and security and safety.

Accident Reconstruction: Technology and Animation III. SAE. 1993. 305p. (SP-946). With the dwindling of federal safety research funds, reconstruction studies such as these 24 papers assume even greater importance in the improvement of highway safety.

Bicycle and City Traffic: Principles and Practice. Hugh McClintock, ed. Halsted. 1993. 217p. Contributors point out factors that encourage or inhibit cycling and the role of city planning in providing for bicycle travel.

Commitment, Communication, Cooperation: Traffic Safety and Public Health Working Together to Prevent Traffic Injury. DOT. 1993. 99p. Recognizing the increasing role of health care professionals in injury reduction as well as injury treatment, this treatise recommends methods to reduce traffic injuries and death.

Electric and Hydrogen Vehicles: Transportation Technologies for the Twenty-First Century. James J. MacKenzie. World Resources Institute. 1993. 75p.

Estimating Capital and Operating Costs in Urban Transportation Planning. Aurilio Menendez. Praeger. 1993. 197p. A discussion of alternative ways to estimate capital, operating, financing, maintenance, and repair costs.

Geometric Design Projects for Highways: An Introduction. John G. Schoon. ASCE. 1993. 136p.

Going Private: The International Experience with Transport Privatization. José A. Gomez-Ibanez, John R. Meyer. Brookings. 1993. 300p. Emphasis is on highway and bus privatization with some carryover to urban rail transport and airports. The authors suggest that political and social factors accompany economic factors during consideration for privatization.

Hazardous Materials Shipment Information for

Emergency Response. National Research Council. 1993. 222p. (Special Report Series No. 239).

High Speed Ground Transportation Systems I—Planning and Engineering: Proceedings of the First International Conference on High Speed Ground Transportation (HSGT) Systems. Murthy V. Bondada, Roger L. Wayson, eds. ASCE. 1993. 798p.

Information Technology on the Move: Technical and Behavioral Evaluations of Mobile Telecommunications. Geoffrey Underwood, *et al.* Wiley. 1993. 250p. The authors look toward European research and design of intelligent vehicle highway systems.

Interaction between Heavy Vehicles and Roads: The Thirty-Ninth L. Ray Buckendale Lecture. David Cebon. SAE. 1993. 81p. Cebon concludes that introduction of ''road friendly'' heavy goods haulers, results in lower costs for freight charges and for road construction and maintenance.

Jane's World Railways, 1992–93. 34th ed. Geoffrey Freeman Allen. Jane's Information Group. 1992. 826p. Photos, sketches, and tables accompany text describing railway components, manufacturers, systems, and underground railways.

Moving America through Innovative Technology. FHWA. 1993. 24p. At the federal level, the Office of Technology Applications coordinates highway technology transfer among international, state, regional, and local governmental units. Its programs are explored and regional offices listed in this colorful brochure.

NETS: Four Seasons Guide for Saving Lives. Network of Employers for Traffic Safety. DOT. 1992. Various paging. NETS is a public sector/private corporation program to develop effective highway safety programs for the workforce. Incentives and publicity play major roles.

Paving the Way to Natural Gas Vehicles. James S. Cannon. INFORM. 1993. 182p. Regarded by many as a viable alternative to pollutants spewing from standard gasoline and diesel fuels, NGVs are investigated in terms of their current development, fueling possibilities, and government incentives for implementation.

Pedestrian and City Traffic. Carmen Hass-Klau. Halsted. 1993. 284p.

Pilot's Air Traffic Control Handbook. 2d ed. Paul E. Illman. TAB. 1993. 221p.

Privatizing Los Angeles International Airport: Analyzing the Alternatives. Robert W. Poole, Jr., Bryan E. Snyder. Reason Foundation. 1993. 40p. Privatization can encompass total sale, partial sale, leasing out, or long-term leases for development. This study states that the net present value to LA would be highest with a 30-year lease, followed by outright sale, with city operation the least profitable option.

Public Transit Economics and Deregulation Policy. Joseph Berechman. Elsevier Science NY. 1993. 341p.

Roadway Lighting Fundamentals Course. IESNA. 1993. 300p. Twelve lessons in this

updated resource cover the most commonly encountered roadway applications. Example problems illustrate calculations for both luminance and illuminance.

Supertrains: Solutions to America's Transportation Gridlock. Joseph Vranich. St. Martin's. 1993. 432p.

Transportation of Hazardous Materials: Issues in Law, Social Science, and Engineering Series. Leon N. Moses, Dan Lindstrom, eds. Kluwer. 1993. 323p.

Transportation Planning, Programming, Land Use, and Applications of Geographic Information Systems. National Research Council. 1993. 201p. (Transportation Research Record Series No. 1364.)

Vanpooling: A Handbook to Help You Set Up a Program at Your Company. Computer Transportation Services. DOT. GPO. 1993. 54p. City officials working with the private sector to reduce automobile traffic will find these clear cut, detailed instructions for setting up vanpools a strong asset to their efforts.

PERIODICALS

Airport Services Management. (M) Lakewood.

Aviation Week & Space Technology. (W) McGraw-Hill.

Bus Ride. (8/yr) Friendship.

Business and Commercial Aviation. (M) McGraw-Hill.

Electric Vehicle Progress. (SM) Alexander Research and Communications.

Fleet Owner. (M) INTERTEC.

ITE Journal. (M) Institute of Transportation Engineers.

Journal of Transportation Engineering. (BM) ASCE.

Mass Transit. (M) PTN Publishing.

Passenger Transport. (W) American Public Transit Association.

Public Roads. (Q) U.S. Federal Highway Administration. GPO.

Railway Age. (M) Simmons-Boardman.

School Bus Fleet. (BM) Bobit.

TR News. (BM) TRB.

Traffic World. (W) Journal of Commerce.

Transport Topics. (W) American Trucking Association.

Transportation Journal. (Q) American Society of Transportation and Logistics.

Transportation Quarterly. (Q) Eno Foundation for Transportation.

Transportation Research. Part A: General; Part B: Methodological. (BM) Pergamon.

DATABASE RESOURCES

Business Publishers

Type: Full text.

Coverage: Business Publishers publishes more than 50 newsletters, many of which are available online in merged databases. Among the publications are the biweekly *Toxic Materials News* (information on laws and regulation concerning transportation of hazardous ma-

terials), biweekly *U.S. Rail News* (railroad industry), and biweekly *Urban Transport News* (government and industry developments affecting public transportation).

Scope: Varies with title.

Producer: Business Publishers.

Available: NewsNet, PTS Newsletter Database.

DRI/McGraw-Hill. Data Products Division.

Type: Statistical.

Coverage: This is not a database *per se*, but a service in which DRI provides, for a variety of topics, information such as economic data, analyses, forecasts, and simulation models. In the area of transportation, this information covers the automotive, truck, and transportation industries.

Scope: Varies with sources.

Producer: DRI/McGraw-Hill.

Available: Producer.

TRIS (Transportation Research Information Services)

Type: Bibliographic.

Coverage: Materials from government agencies and private transportation organizations are cited and abstracted in this database devoted to air, highway, rail, maritime, pipeline, and mass transportation. Research in progress is also noted. Policy, planning, administration, regulation, design construction, maintenance, control, and user concerns are topics covered.

Scope: International. Updated monthly. 1968—.

Producer: Transportation Research Information Services.

Available: Dialog.

LIST OF PUBLISHERS

AAHPERD *see* American Alliance for Health, Physical Education, Recreation, and Dance.

AASHTO *see* American Association of State Highway and Transportation Officials.

ABA *see* American Bar Association.

ABBE Publishers Association of Washington, DC, 4111 Gallows Rd., Virginia Div., Annandale, VA 22003.

ABC-CLIO, Inc., P.O. Box 1911, Santa Barbara, CA 93116-1911.

ACA *see* American Correctional Association.

Academy of Criminal Justice Sciences, 402 Nunn Hall, Northern Kentucky University, Highland Heights, KY 41099-5998.

ACC Communications, Inc., P.O. Box 2440, Costa Mesa, CA 92628.

ACIR *see* U.S. Advisory Commission on Intergovernmental Relations.

Addison-Wesley Publishing Co., Inc., Rte. 128, Reading, MA 01867.

Administrative Office of United States Courts, 1 Columbus Circle, N.E., Washington, DC 20544.

AIDS Housing of Washington, 2001 Western Ave., Ste. 300, Seattle, WA, 98121.

Air and Waste Management Association, P.O. Box 2861, Pittsburgh, PA 15230.

Alexander Research & Communications, Inc., 215 Park Ave. S., Ste. 1301, New York, NY 10003-1601.

American Academy of Orthopaedic Surgeons, P.O. Box 75838, Chicago, IL 60675-5838.

American Alliance for Health, Physical Education, Recreation, and Dance, 1900 Association Drive, Reston, VA 22091.

American Arbitration Association, 140 W. 51st St., New York, NY 10020-1203.

American Association for the Advancement of Science, 1333 H St., N.W., 11th Fl., Washington, DC 20005.

American Association of Museums, 1225 Eye Street, N.W., Ste. 200, Washington, DC 20005.

American Association of Retired Persons, 601 E St., N.W., Washington, DC 20049, (202)434-6231.

American Association of State Highway and Transportation Officials, 444 N. Capitol St., N.W., Ste. 225, Washington, DC 20001.

American Banker/Bond Buyer, One State St. Plaza, New York, NY 10004, (212)943-6304.

American Bar Association, 750 N. Lake Shore Drive, Chicago, IL 60611.

American Chemical Society, 1155 16th St., N.W., Washington, DC 20036.

American Civil Defense Association, P.O. Box 910, Starke, FL 32091.

American Concrete Institute, P.O. Box 19150, Detroit, MI 48219-0150.

American Correctional Association, 8025 Laurel Lakes Court, Laurel, MD 20707-5075.

American Economic Development Council, 9801 W. Higgins Road, Ste. 540, Rosemont, IL 60018-4726.

American Finance Association, Stern School of Business, New York University, 100 Trinity Place, New York, NY 10006.

American Fire Sprinkler Association, 12459 Jupiter Rd., Ste. 142, Dallas, TX 75238-3200.

American Institute of Professional Geologists, 7828 Vance Dr., Arvada, CO 80003.

American Judicature Society, 25 E. Washington, Ste. 1600, Chicago, IL 60602-1805.

American Museum of Natural History, Central Park West at 79th St., New York, NY 10024-5192.

American Planning Association, 1313 E. 60th St., Chicago, IL 60637-2891.

American Public Power Association, 2301 M St., N.W., Washington, DC 20037.

American Public Transit Association, 1201 New York Ave., N.W., Ste. 400, Washington, DC 20005.

American Public Welfare Association, 810 First St., N.E., Ste. 500, Washington, DC 20002-4205.

American Public Works Association, 1313 E. 60th St., Chicago, IL 60637-2881.

American Real Estate and Urban Economics Association, School of Business, Rm. 428, Indiana University, Bloomington, IN 47405.

American Recycling Market, Inc., Box 577, Ogdenburg, NY 13669, (800)267-0707.

American Society for Public Administration, 1120 G St., N.W., Ste. 500, Washington, DC 20005.

American Society for Testing and Materials, 1916 Race St., Philadelphia, PA 19103.

American Society of Civil Engineers, 345 E. 47th St., New York, NY 10017-2398, (212)705-7520.

American Society of Criminology, 1314 Kennear Road, Columbus, OH 43212.

American Society of Transportation and Logistics, Inc., 3600 Chamberlain Ln., No. 232, Louisville, KY 40241-1989.

American Trucking Association, 2200 Mill Road, Alexandria, VA 22314-4654.

American Water Works Association, 6666 W. Quincy Ave., Denver, CO 80325.

Anderson Publishing Co., P.O. Box 1576, Cincinnati, OH 45201-1576.

APA *see* American Planning Association.

APPA *see* American Public Power Association.

APWA *see* American Public Works Association.

AREUEA *see* American Real Estate and Urban Economics Association.

Artech House, Inc., 685 Canton St., Norwood, MA 02062.

ASCE *see* American Society of Civil Engineers.

Ashgate Publishing Company, Old Post Road, Brookfield, VT 05036.

ASPA *see* American Society for Public Administration.

Aspen Publishers, Inc., 200 Orchard Ridge Dr., Ste. 200, Gaithersburg, MD 20878.

Association for Computing Machinery, 1515 Broadway, New York, NY 10036.

Association for Preservation Technology International, P.O. Box 8178, Fredericksburg, VA 22404.

Association of Academic Health Centers, 1400 16th St., N.W., Ste. 410, Washington, DC 20036.

Association of Bay Area Governments, P.O. Box 2050, Oakland, CA 94604-2050.

Association of Physical Plant Administrators of Universities and Colleges, 1446 Duke St., Alexandria, VA 22314-3492.

Association of Records Managers and Administrators, P.O. Box 8540, Prairie Village, KS 66208.

ASTM *see* American Society for Testing and Materials.

Auburn House, 88 Post Rd., W., Box 5007, Westport, CT 06881-5007.

Automated Office, Ltd., 1123 Broadway, New York, NY 10010.

Avery Architectural and Fine Arts Library *see* Columbia University.

AWWA *see* American Water Works Association.

Basil Blackwell Ltd., 108 Cowley Rd., Oxford OX41JF, England.

Baywood Publishing Co., Inc., 26 Austin Ave., Box 337, Amityville, NY 11701.

BCR Enterprises, Inc., 950 York Road, No. 203, Hinsdale, IL 60521-2939.

Bernan Press, 4611F Assembly Dr., Lanham, MD 20706-4391.

BNA *see* Bureau of National Affairs, Inc.

BNI Publications, Inc., 3055 Overland Ave., Los Angeles, CA 90034.

Bobit Publishing Co., 2512 Artesia Boulevard, Redondo Beach, CA 90278.

BOCA *see* Building Officials and Code Administrators International.

Boston University, School of Education, 605 Commonwealth Ave., Boston, MA 02215, (617)353-3295.

Bowker A&I Publishing, Reed Reference Publishing Group, 121 Chanlon Rd., New Providence, NJ 07974, (908)464-6800.

R. R. Bowker Co., 121 Chanlon Rd., New Providence, NJ 07974, (908)464-6800.

Bowling Green State University, Philosophy Documentation Center, Bowling Green, OH 43403-0189.

BPI Communications, 1515 Broadway, 39th Fl., New York, NY 10036.

Brady Communications, 113 Sylvan Ave, Rt. 9W, Englewood Cliffs, NJ 07632.

Paul H. Brookes Publishing Co., P.O. Box 10624, Baltimore, MD 21285-0624.

Brookings Institution, 1775 Massachusetts Ave., N.W., Washington, DC 20036-2188.

William C. Brown Publisher, 2460 Kerper Blvd., Dubuque, IA 52001.

BRS Information Technologies, 8000 Westpark Drive, McLean, VA 22102, (703)442-0900.

BTA Economic Research Institute, 901 Dove St., Ste. 158, Newport Beach, CA 92660.

Building Officials and Code Administrators International, 4051 Flossmoor Rd., Country Club Hills, IL 60478-5795.

Bureau of National Affairs, Inc., 1231 25th St., N.W., Washington, DC 20037, (202)452-4132.

Burwell Enterprises, 3724 F.M. 1960, Ste. 214, Houston, TX 77068.

Business Publishers, Inc., 951 Pershing Drive, Silver Spring, MD 20910-4464, (301)587-6300.

Butterworth-Heinemann, 80 Montvale Ave., Stoneham, MA 02180.

Buzzworm Inc., 2305 Canyon Blvd., Ste. 206, Boulder, CO 80302.

Bywood Publishing Co., 17 Galloway Ln., Peekskill, NY 10566-6101.

C.A.B. International, Wallingford, Oxon, OX10 8DE, England, 0491 32111.

Cahners Publishing Co., 8601 Georgia Ave., Ste. 300, Silver Spring, MD 20910.

Cahners Publishing Co., 275 Washington St., Newton, MA 02158-1630.

Callaghan & Co., 155 Pfingsten Road, Deerfield, IL 60015.

Cambridge Scientific Abstracts, 7200 Wisconsin Ave., Ste. 601, Bethesda, MD 20814, (301)961-6750.

Cambridge University Press, 40 W. 20th Street, New York, NY 10011.

Camelot Publishing Co., P.O. Box 1357, Ormond Beach, FL 32175-1357.

Canada Institute for Scientific and Technical Information, Montreal Road, Ottawa, Ontario K1A 052, Canada, (613)993-1210.

Canadian Parks-Recreation Association, 1600 James Naismith Drive, Gloucester, Ontario K1B 5N4, Canada.

CAN/OLE *see* Canada Institute for Scientific and Technical Information.

Capitol Publications, Inc., Telecom Publishing Group, Box 1455, Alexandria, VA 22313-2055, (703)739-6400.

Cardozo School of Law, 55 Fifth Ave., New York, NY 10003.

Carl Vinson Institute of Government *see* University of Georgia.

Cassell Publishing, 387 Park Ave., S., 5th Fl., New York, NY 10016.

Cato Institute, 1000 Massachusetts Ave., N.W., 6th Fl., Washington, DC 20001-5403.

CAUSE, 4840 Pearl E. Circle, Ste. 302E, Boulder, CO 80301.

Central United States Earthquake Consortium, 2630 E. Holmes Road, Memphis, TN 38118-8001.

Chapman and Hall *see* Routledge, Chapman and Hall.

Chatham House Publications, Inc., Box 1, Chatham, NJ 07928.

Child Welfare League of America, Inc., 440 First St., N.W., Washington, DC 20001.

CIO Publishers, Inc., 492 Old Connecticut Path, P.O. Box 9208, Framingham, MA 01701-9208.

City Hall Communications, P.O. Box 309, Seabrook, MD 20703-0309.

Claire B. Rubin and Associates, P.O. Box 2208, Arlington, VA 22202.

Clark Boardman Callaghan, 375 Hudson Street, New York, NY 10014.

CMP Publications, 600 Community Drive, Manhasset, NY 11030.

COGEL *see* Council on Governmental Ethics Laws.

Columbia University, Avery Architectural and Fine Arts Library, Broadway & 116th St., New York, NY 10027, (212)854-8404.

Columbia University Press, 562 W. 113th St., New York, NY 10025.

Communication Channels, Inc., 6255 Barfield Road, Atlanta, GA 30328-4369.

Community Association Institute Research Foundation, 1630 Duke St., Alexandria, VA 22314.

Community Nutrition Institute, 2001 S. St., N.W., Washington, DC 20009.

CompuServe Information Service, 5000 Arlington Centre Boulevard, Box 20102, Columbus, OH 43220, (614)457-8600.

Conference Board, Inc., 845 Third Ave., 5th Fl., New York, NY 10022.

Congressional Quarterly, Inc., 1414 22nd St., N.W., Washington, DC 20037.

Connect and Connect Software, 10101 Bubb Road, Cupertino, CA 95014, (408)973-0110.

Corporation for Enterprise Development, 777 N. Capital St., N.E., Ste. 801, Washington, DC 20002.

Council of Planning Librarians, 1313 E. 60th Street, Chicago, IL 60637-2897.

Council of State Governments, Iron Works Pike, P.O. Box 11910, Lexington, KY 40578-9989.

Council on Governmental Ethics Laws, Iron Works Pike, P.O. Box 11910, Lexington, KY 40578-1910.

CPL *see* Council of Planning Librarians.

CQ Press *see* Congressional Quarterly.

Crain Communications, Inc., 740 N. Rush St., Chicago, IL 60611-2590.

CRCS Publications, P.O. Box 1460, Sebastopol, CA 95472.

Creative Age Publications, 7628 Densmore Ave., Van Nuys, CA 91406-2088.

CRICOM PASE Inc., P.O. Box 309, Metuchen, NJ 08840.

Crisp Publications, Inc., 1200 Hamilton Ct., Menlo Park, CA 94025.

CUSEC *see* Central United States Earthquake Consortium.

Dance Magazine, Inc., 33 W. 60th St., New York, NY 10023.

Data Based Solutions, Inc., 4010 Morena Boulevard, Ste. 200, San Diego, CA 92117-4547.

Data-Star, Plaza Ste., 114 Jermyn St., London, SW1Y 6HJ, England, (71)930-5503.

Datapro Information Services Group, 600 Delran Pkwy., P.O. Box 1066, Delran, NJ 08075.

Marcel Dekker, 270 Madison Ave., New York, NY 10016.

DELPHI *see* General Videotex Corporation.

Department of City and Regional Planning *see* Ohio State University.

Paul M. Deutsch, Printing, 2211 Hillcrest St., Orlando, FL 32803.

Dialog Information Services, Inc., 3460 Hillview Ave., Palo Alto, CA 94304, (415)858-3785.

Diane Publishing Co., 600 Upland Ave., Upland, PA 19015.

DIMDI, Weisshausstrasse 27, Postfach 420580, D-5000 Cologne 41, Germany, (221)47 24-1.

DOE *see* U.S. Department of Energy.

Dow Jones News/Retrieval, P.O. Box 300, Princeton, NJ 08543-0300, (609)520-4000.

DOT *see* U. S. Department of Transportation.

DRI/McGraw-Hill, Data Products Division, 24 Hartwell Ave., Lexington, MA 02173, (617)863-5100.

Dryden Press, 301 Commerce St., Ft. Worth, TX 76102.

Earthquake Engineering Research Institute, 499 14th St., Ste. 320, Oakland, CA 94612-1902.

Economics and Technology, Inc., One Washington Mall, Boston, MA 02108.

EIS International, 1401 Rockville Pike, Ste. 500, Rockville, MD 20852.

E. Elgar *see* Ashgate Publishing Co.

Elsevier Advanced Technology Publications, Mayfield House, 256 Banbury Road, Oxford OX2 7DH, England, 0865 512242.

Elsevier Science Publishers B. V., P.O. Box 211, 1000 AE Amsterdam, The Netherlands.

Elsevier Science Publishers, Ltd., Crown House, Linton Road, Barking, Essex 1G11 8JU, England.

Elsevier Science Publishing Co., Inc., P.O. Box 882, Madison Square Station, New York, NY 10159.

Emergency Preparedness Canada, 2nd Fl., Jackson Bldg., 122 Bank St. W., Ottawa, Ontario K1A OW6, Canada.

Engineering Information, Inc., Castle Point on

the Hudson, Hoboken, NJ 07030, (201)216-8500.

Eno Foundation for Transportation, 270 Saugatuck Ave., Westport, CT 06880-0055.

Erlbaum, Lawrence, Associations, Inc., 365 Broadway, Hillsdale, NJ 07642.

ESA-IRS, Via Galileo Galilei, 1-00044 Frascati (Rome), Italy, 06941801.

ETSI/HRIN see Executive Telecom System.

Executive Enterprises Publications, Co., Inc., 22 W. 21st St., New York, NY 10010-6904.

Executive Telecom System International, The Human Resource Information Network, 9585 Valparaiso Court, Indianapolis, IN 46268, (317)872-2045.

FAA see Federal Aviation Administration.

Family Service America, 11700 W. Lake Park Drive, Milwaukee, WI 53224.

Federal Aviation Administration, International Research Program office, ARD-4, 800 Independence Ave., S.W., Washington, DC 20591.

Federal Emergency Management Agency, 500 C St., S.W., Rm. 429, Washington, DC 20472, (301)926-5376.

FEMA see Federal Emergency Management Agency.

FHWA see U.S. Federal Highway Administration.

Fire Buff House Publishers, P.O. Box 711, New Albany, IN 47151.

Fire Publications, Inc., c/o J. A. Ackerman, Pub., 9072 E. Artesia Boulevard, Bellflower, CA 90706.

Firefacts, NFPA, 1 Batterymarch Park, P.O. Box 9101, Quincy, MA 02269-9101, (617)770-3000.

Florida Conservation Foundation Books, 1251-B Miller Ave., Winter Park, FL 32789.

Florida League of Cities, Inc., P.O. Box 1757, Tallahassee, FL 32302.

Forecast Public Artworks, 2955 Bloomington, Minneapolis, MN 55407.

Friendship Publications, Inc., P.O. Box 1472, Spokane, WA 99210-1472.

Gale Research, Inc., 835 Penobscot Building, Detroit, MI 48226-4094.

GAO see U.S. General Accounting Office.

Garland Publishing, Inc., 717 Fifth Ave., Ste. 2500, New York, NY 10022.

Gas Industries, P.O. Box 558, Park Ridge, IL 60068.

General Videotex Corp./DELPHI, 3 Blackstone Street, Cambridge, MA 02139, (617)491-3393.

Georgia State University, College of Public and Urban Affairs, Box 4018, Atlanta, GA 30302-4018.

GFOA see Government Finance Officers Association.

Glenbridge Publishing, Ltd., 6010 W. Jewell Ave., Denver, CO 80232-7106.

Gordon & Breach Science Publishers, Inc., P.O. Box 786, Cooper Sta., New York, NY 10276.

Government Finance Officers Association, 180 N. Michigan Ave., Ste. 800, Chicago, IL 60601, (312)977-9700.

Government Information Services, 1611 N. Kent St., Ste. 508, Arlington, VA 22209.

Government Research Services, 701 Jackson, Topeka, KS 66603.

GPO see Superintendent of Documents, U.S. Government Printing Office.

Graham & Trotman, 835 Penobscot Bldg., Detroit, MI 48226-4094.

Great Britain Department of the Environment, Building Research Establishment Library, Bucknell's Lane, Garston, Watford Herts, WD2 7JR, England, 0923894040.

Greenwood Press, 88 Post Road West, Box 5007, Westport, CT 06881-5007.

Guilford Press, 72 Spring Street, New York, NY 10012.

Gulf Publishing Co., P.O. Box 2608, Houston, TX 77252.

H. C. I. Publications, 410 Archibald St., Kansas City, MO 64111-3046.

Halsted Press, 605 Third Ave., New York, NY 10158-0012.

Harcourt Brace & Co., 1250 Sixth Ave., San Diego, CA 92101.

Hare Publications, 6300 Yarrow Drive, Carlsbad, CA 92009-1597.

HarperCollins Publishers, Inc., 10 E. 53rd St., New York, NY 10022-5299.

Harvard University Press, 79 Garden Street, Cambridge, MA 02138.

Haworth Press, Inc., 10 Alice St., Binghamton, NY 13904-1580.

Hazardous Materials Control Resources Institute, 7237 Hanover Pky., Greenbelt, MD 20770-3602.

Hazardous Materials Publishing, P.O. Box 204, Barre, VT 05641.

Hill and Wang, 19 Union Sq., W., New York, NY 10003.

Horizon House Publications, 685 Canton St., Norwood, MA 02062.

Ellis Horword Ltd., Campus 400, Maylands Ave., Hemel Hempsted, Herts, HP2 7EZ, England.

Houghton Mifflin, 1 Beacon St., Boston, MA 02108.

HRIN see Executive Telecom System International.

HUD see U.S. Department of Housing and Urban Development.

Humanities Press International, Inc., 165 First Ave., Atlantic Highlands, NJ 07716-1289.

IAAO see International Association of Assessing Officers.

IACP see International Association of Chiefs of Police.

IAFC see International Association of Fire Chiefs.

ICHIEFS, 1329 18th Street, N.W., Washington, DC 20036-6516, (202)452-0684.

ICMA see International City/County Management Association.

IDD Information Services, Inc., 2 World Trade Center, 18th Fl., New York, NY 10048, (212)432-0045.

IDDIS see IDD Information Services, Inc.

IDG Communications, Inc., 375 Cochituate

Road, Box 9171, Framingham, MA 01701-9171.

IEEE see Institute of Electrical and Electronic Engineers.

IESNA see Illuminating Engineering Society of North America.

Illinois Commission on Intergovernmental Co-operation, State House, Springfield, IL 62706.

Illuminating Engineering Society of North America, 345 E. 47th St., New York, NY 10017.

ILR Press, Cornell University, Ithaca, NY 14851-0952.

Independent Computer Consultants Association, 933 Gardenview Office Parkway, St. Louis, MO 63141-5917, (314)997-4633.

Indiana University Press, 601 N. Morton St., Bloomington, IN 47404-3797.

Industrial Relations Research Institute, University of Wisconsin Press, Social Science Building, 1180 Observatory, Madison, WI 53706.

INFORM, 381 Park Ave., S., New York, NY 10016.

Information Access Company, 362 Lakeside Drive, Foster City, CA 94404, (415)358-4643.

Information Publications, 3790 El Camino Real, Ste. 162, Palo Alto, CA 94306.

Information Sources, Inc., 1173 Colusa Ave., P.O. Box 7848, Berkeley, CA 94707, (510)525-6220.

Infoworld Publishing, 155 Bovet Rd., Ste. 800, San Mateo, CA 94402.

Institute for Scientific Information, 3501 Market St., Philadelphia, PA 19104, (215)386-0100.

Institute of Electrical and Electronic Engineers, 345 E. 47th St., New York, NY 10017.

Institute of Transportation Engineers, 525 School St., S.W., Ste. 410, Washington, DC 20024-2729.

International Association of Arson Investigators, P.O. Box 91119, Louisville, KY 40291.

International Association of Assessing Officers, 1313 E. 60th St., Chicago, IL 60637-9990.

International Association of Chiefs of Police, 1110 N. Glebe Rd., Ste. 200, Arlington, VA 22201.

International Association of Fire Chiefs, 1329 18th St., N.W., Washington, DC 20036-0684, (202)833-3420.

International Association of Wildland Fire, P.O. Box 328, Fairfield, WA 99012-0328.

International City/County Management Association, 777 North Capitol St., N.E., Ste. 500, Washington, DC 20002-4201, (202)289-4262.

International Foundation of Employee Benefit Plans, 18700 W. Bluemound Road, P.O. Box 69, Brookfield, WI 53008-0069, (414)786-6700.

International Library Law Book Publishers, 101 Lakeforest Boulevard, Ste. 270, Gaithersburg, MD 20877.

International Personnel Management Association, 1617 Duke St., Alexandria, VA 22314.

International Research and Evaluation, 21098 IRE Control Center, Eagan, MN 55121, (612)888-9635.

International Research Center for Energy and

Economic Development, University of Colorado, Campus Box 263, Boulder, CO 80309-0263.

Interscience Enterprises Ltd., World Trade Centre Building, 110 Ave. Louis Casai, Case Postale 309, CH-1215 Geneva-Aeroport, Switzerland.

Intertec Publishing Corp., 707 Westchester Ave., Ste. 101, White Plains, NY 10604-3102.

Interweave Press, Inc., 201 E. Fourth St., Loveland, CO 80537.

IPMA see International Personnel Management Association.

ISI see Institute for Scientific Information.

Island Press, Star Rte 1, Box 38, Covelo, CA 95428.

Jane's Information Group, 1340 Braddock Pl., Ste. 300, Alexandria, VA 22314-1651.

JEMS Publishing Co., P.O. Box 2789, Carlsbad, CA 92018.

Johns Hopkins University Press, 701 W. 40th St., Ste. 275, Baltimore, MD 21211-2190.

Joint Assistance Centre, H-65 South Extension 1, New Delhi 110049, India.

Jossey-Bass Inc., 350 Sansome St., 5th Fl., San Francisco, CA 94104.

Journal of Commerce, 741 National Press Bldg., Washington, DC 20045.

Kendall/Hunt, 2460 Kerper Boulevard, Dubuque, IA 52001.

Key Communications Group, Inc., P.O. Box 42578, Washington, DC 20015-0578.

Kluwer Academic Publishers Group, P.O. Box 358, Accord Station, Hingham, MA 02018-0358.

Knowledge Index, 5000 Arlington Centre Blvd., Columbus, OH 43220, (614) 457-8600.

Knowledge Network for All Americans, 4350 Fairfax Dr., No. 740, Arlington, VA 22203-1619.

Krause Publications, Inc., 700 E. State St., Iola, WI 54990.

Labor Relations Press see LRP Publications.

Lakewood Publications, Inc., 50 S. Ninth St., Minneapolis, MN 55402.

Leadership, Incorporated, of Scottsdale, 7418 E. Helm Dr., Scottsdale, AZ 85260-2382.

Learned Information, 143 Old Marlton Pike, Medford, NJ 08055-8707, (609)654-6266.

Leicester University Press see St. Martin's Press.

Leisure Studies Association, E. & F. N. Spon, 2-6 Boundary Row, London SE 1 8HN, England.

Lewis Publishers, Inc., 121 S. Main St., P.O. Box 519, Chelsea, MI 48118.

Life Science Network (BIOSIS), 2100 Arch St., Philadelphia, PA 19103-1399, (215)587-4800.

Locke Science Publishing Co., P.O. Box 146413, Chicago, IL 60614.

Login Services Corp., 245 E. 6th St., Ste. 809, St. Paul, MN 55101-9006, (612)255-1133.

Longman Publishing Group, The Longman Bldg., 10 Bank St., White Plains, NY 10606-1951.

LRP Publications, P.O. Box 980, 747 Dresher Rd., Horsham, PA 19044-0980.

LSA see Leisure Studies Association.

MacLean-Hunter, Ltd., 777 Bay St., Toronto, Ontario M5W 1A7, Canada.

Macmillan London Ltd., 18-21 Cavaye Pl., London SW10 9PG, England.

Macmillan Publishing Co., 866 Third Ave., New York, NY 10022.

Madisen Publishing Division, P.O. Box 1936, Appleton, WI 54913.

Magazine ASAP, 362 Lakeside Dr., Foster City, CA 94404, (415)358-4643.

Maple Publishing, 134 W. Slade St., Palatine, IL 60067.

Maxwell Macmillan see Macmillan Publishing.

McFarland & Co., Inc., Box 611, Jefferson, NC 28640.

McGill-Queens University Press see University of Toronto Press.

McGraw-Hill, Inc., 1221 Ave. of the Americas, New York, NY 10020.

McGraw-Hill Information Services Co., Byte Publications, One Phoenix Mill Lane, Peterborough, NH 03458.

Mead Data Central, Inc., 9443 Springboro Pike, P.O. Box 933, Dayton, OH 45401, (513)865-6800.

Med-Index Publications, P.O. Box 526180, Salt Lake City, UT 84152-6180.

Mellen Research University Press, P.O. Box 450, Lewiston, NY 14092.

Michael Daniels, Publishers, P.O. Box 3233, Culver City, CA 90231-3233.

MIT Press, 55 Hayward St., Cambridge, MA 02142.

Monitor Leadership Directories, 1301 Pennsylvania Ave., N.W., Washington, DC 20004.

Monitor Publishing Co., 104 Fifth Ave., 2nd Fl., New York, NY 10011.

William Morrow & Co., 1350 Avenue of the Americas, New York, NY 10019.

Mortgage Bankers Association of America, 1125 15th St., N.W., Washington, DC 20005.

Mosby-Year Book, Inc., 11830 Westline Industrial Dr., St. Louis, MO 63146.

NAHB see National Association of Home Builders.

NAHRO see National Association of Housing and Redevelopment Officials.

NASW see National Association of Social Workers.

National Academy of Public Administration, 1120 G St., N.W., Ste. 850, Washington, DC 20005.

National Academy of Sciences, National Research Council, Transportation Information Service, 2101 Constitution Ave., N.W., Washington, DC 20418, (202)334-3250.

National Academy Press, 2101 Constitution Ave., N.W., Washington, DC 20418.

National Association of Counties, 440 First St., N.W., Washington, DC 20001-2023.

National Association of Home Builders, 1201 15th St., N.W., Washington, DC 20005, (202)737-0717.

National Association of Housing and Redevelopment Officials, 1320 18th St., N.W., Washington, DC 20036.

National Association of Search and Rescue Headquarters, P.O. Box 3709, Fairfax, VA 22038.

National Association of Social Workers, 750

First St., N.E., Washington, DC 20002, (202)336-8277.

National Association of Towns and Townships, 1522 K St., N.W., Ste. 730, Washington, DC 20005.

National Civic League, 1445 Market St., Ste. 300, Denver, CO 80202-1728, (303)571-4343.

National Conference of State Legislatures, 1560 Broadway, Ste. 700, Denver, CO 80202-5140.

National Coordinating Council on Emergency Management, 7297 Lee Highway, Ste. N, Falls Church, VA 22042.

National Council of Juvenile and Family Court Judges, P.O. Box 8978, University of Nevada, Reno, NV 89507.

National Directory of Children, Youth and Families Services, P.O. Box 1837, Longmont, CO 80502-1837.

National Economic Development and Law Center, 1950 Addison St., Berkeley, CA 94704.

National Emergency Training Center, 16825 S. Seton Ave., Emmitsburg, MD 21727, (800)638-1821, (301)447-1032.

National Fire Protection Association, 1 Batterymarch Park, Quincy, MA 02269-9101, (617)770-3000.

National Fire Sprinkler Association, Robin Hill Corporate Park, Route 22, P.O. Box 1000, Patterson, NY 12563.

National Institute for Urban Search and Rescue, P.O. Box 91648, Santa Barbara, CA 93190-1648, (805)-569-5066, (800)767-0093.

National Institute of Justice/National Criminal Justice Reference Service, P.O. Box 6000, Rockville, MD 20850, (301)251-5500.

National Journal, 1730 M St., N.W., Ste. 1100, Washington, DC 20036.

National League of Cities, 1301 Pennsylvania Ave., N.W., Washington, DC 20004-1763.

National Oceanic and Atmospheric Administration, 14th and Constitution Ave., N.W., Washington, DC 20230.

National Parks and Conservation Association, 1776 Massachusetts Ave., N.W., Washington, DC 20036.

National Recreation and Park Association, 3101 Park Center Drive, Alexandria, VA 22302.

National Register Publishing Co., 3004 Glenview Rd., Wilmette, IL 60091.

National Rehabilitation Association, 1910 Association Dr., Ste. 205, Reston, VA 22091-1502.

National Research Council, 2101 Constitution Ave., Washington, DC 20418.

National Search and Rescue Secretariat, 275 Slater St., 4th Fl., Ottawa, Ontario, Canada, K1A 0K2.

National Software Testing Laboratories, Inc., Plymouth Corporate Center, Box 1000, Plymouth Meeting, PA 19462.

National Solid Wastes Management Association, 1730 Rhode Island Ave., N.W., Ste. 1000, Washington, DC 20036.

National Tax Association, Tax Institute of America, 5310 E. Main St., Ste. 104, Columbus, OH 43213.

National Technical Information Service, 5285 Port Royal Road, Springfield, VA 22161.

National Telephone Cooperative Association, 2626 Pennsylvania Ave., N.W., Washington, DC 20037.

National Trust for Historic Preservation, 1785 Massachusetts Ave., N.W., Washington, DC 20036.

Natural Hazards Research and Applications Information Center, University of Colorado, Campus Box 482, Boulder, CO 80309-0482.

Natural Phenomena Hazards Project (DOE), Lawrence Livermore National Laboratory, P.O. Box 808, L-193, Livermore, CA 94551.

NCJRS see National Institute of Justice, National Criminal Justice Reference Service.

NCSL see National Conference of State Legislatures.

Nelson Publishing, 2504 N. Tamiami Trail, Nokomis, FL 34275.

Nelson-Hall, Inc., 111 N. Canal St., Chicago, IL 60606.

New York State Department of Environmental Conservation, Division of Solid Waste, 50 Wolf Road, Albany, NY 12233-4010.

NewsNet, Inc., 945 Haverford Road, Bryn Mawr, PA 19010, (215)527-8030.

NEXIS see Mead Data Central.

NFPA see National Fire Protection Association.

NHRAIC see Natural Hazards Research and Applications Information Center.

NIUSR see National Institute for Urban Search and Rescue.

NLC see National League of Cities.

North American Publishing Co., 401 N. Broad St., Philadelphia, PA 19108-9988.

North-Holland, P.O. Box 882, Madison Square Station, New York, NY 10159.

Northwestern University School of Law, 357 E. Chicago Ave., Chicago, IL 60611.

Noyes Data Corporation, 120 Mill Rd., Park Ridge, NJ 07656.

NRPA see National Recreation and Park Association.

NTIS see National Technical Information Service.

Numbers and Concepts Publishing, 2525 Arapahoe Ave., Ste. E4-221, Boulder, CO 80302.

O'Reilly and Associates, 103 Morris Street, Sebastopol, CA 95472.

OCLC Online Computer Library Center, Inc., 6565 Frantz Road, Dublin, OH 43017, (614)764-6000.

Odonian Press, Box 7776, Berkeley, CA 94707.

OECD/IEA Publications Office, 2 rue Andre Pascal, F-75775 Paris, CEDEX 16, France.

Office Publications, Inc., 1600 Summer St., Box 120031, Stamford, CT 06912-0031.

Ohio State University, Department of City and Regional Planning, 1070 Carmack Road, Columbus, OH 43210.

Old House Journal Corp., 2 Main St., Gloucester, MA 01930-5726.

Omnigraphics, Inc., Penobscot Building, Detroit, MI 48226.

Online, Inc., 11 Tannery Lane, Weston, CT 06883.

ORBIT Search Service, 8000 Westpark Drive, Ste. 400, McLean, VA 22102, (703)442-0900.

Oregon Historical Society Press, 1230 SW Park Ave., Portland, OR 92705-2483.

Oryx Press, 4041 N. Central Ave., Ste. 700, Phoenix, AZ 85012-3399, (602)265-2651.

Osiris Press, 445 Fifth Ave., Ste. 270, New York, NY 10016-0109.

Oxford University Press, 200 Madison Ave., New York, NY 10016.

Pacific Research Institute for Public Policy, 177 Post St., Ste. 500, San Francisco, CA 94108.

PAIS International see Public Affairs Information Service, Inc.

Paradigm Publishing, Inc., 280 Case Ave. E., St. Paul, MN 55101-4000.

Paramount Publishing, Ltd., 17-21 Shenley Road, Borehamwood, Herts WD6 1RT, England.

PCW Communications, Inc., 501 Second St., Ste. 600, San Francisco, CA 94107.

Peacock Press, Seldon Lane, Greenwich, CT 06831.

Pendragon Publishing, Ltd., 807 Manning Road, N.E., Ste. 200, Calgary, Alberta, T2E 7M8, Canada.

PennWell Publishing Co., One Technology Park Dr., Westford, MA 01886-0989.

PennWell Publishing Co., Park 80 W. Plaza 2, Saddle Brook, NJ 07662-5812.

Pergamon Press, Inc., 660 White Plains Rd., Tarrytown, NY 10591-5153.

Phillips Publishing, Inc., 7811 Montrose Rd., Potomac, MD 20854.

Philosophy Documentation Center see Bowling Green University.

Planning and Zoning Center Inc., 302 S. Waverly Road, Lansing, MI 48917.

Plenum Publishing Corp., 233 Spring St., New York, NY 10013-1578.

Police Foundation, 1001 22nd St., N.W., Ste. 200, Washington, DC 20037.

Political Woman, 276 Chatterton Parkway, White Plains, NY 10606.

Praeger Publishers, Inc., 88 Post Road W., Box 5007, Westport, CT 06881-5007.

Predicasts, 362 Lakeside Dr., Foster City, CA 94404, (415)358-4643.

Prentice-Hall, Inc., 15 Columbus Cir., New York, NY 10023.

Prime National Publishing Corp., 470 Boston Post Road, Weston, MA 02193.

Princeton Architectural Press, 37 E. Seventh St., New York, NY 10003.

Princeton University Press, 41 William St., Princeton, NJ 08540.

Privatization Center see Reason Foundation.

Professional Pride, 4308 S. 278th St., Auburn, WA 98001-9909.

Professional Publications, Inc., 1250 Fifth Ave., Belmont, CA 94002.

PTN Publishing Corp., 445 Broad Hollow Road, Ste. 21, Melville, NY 11747-4722.

PTS Newsletter Database see Predicasts.

Public Affairs Information Service, Inc., 521 W. 43rd St., New York, NY 10036-4396, (212)736-6629.

Public Safety Personnel Research Institute, Inc.,

5519 N. Cumberland Ave., Ste. 1008, Chicago, IL 60656-1498.

Public Technology, Inc., 1301 Pennsylvania Ave., N.W., Washington, DC 20004, (202)626-2400.

Public Utilities Reports, Inc., 2111 Wilson Blvd., Ste. 200, Arlington, VA 22201, (703)243-7000.

Public Works Journal Corp., 200 S. Broad St., Ridgewood, NJ 07451.

Quorum Books, 88 Post Road W., Box 5007, Westport, CT 06881-5007.

Rand Corporation, P.O. Box 2138, Santa Monica, CA 90406-2138.

Reason Foundation, 3415 S. Sepulveda Blvd., Ste. 400, Los Angeles, CA 90034, (310)391-2245.

Research Libraries Group, Inc., 1200 Villa St., Mountain View, CA 94041-1100, (415)962-9951.

RLIN see Research Libraries Group, Inc.

Routledge, Chapman and Hall, 29 W. 35th Street, New York, NY 10001-2291.

Russell Sage Foundation, 112 E. 64th St., New York, NY 10021.

Rutgers University Press, 109 Church Street, New Brunswick, NJ 08901.

SAE see Society of Automotive Engineers.

Sagamore Publishing, Inc., 302 W. Hill St., Box 673, Champaign, IL 61824-0673.

Sage Publications, Inc., 2455 Teller Road, Newbury Park, CA 91320.

W. B. Saunders, Curtis Center, Independence Square, W. Philadelphia, PA 19106-3399.

Scholarly Resources, Inc., 104 Greenhill Ave., Wilmington, DE 19805-1897.

Securities Data Co., 1180 Raymond Boulevard, 5th Fl., Newark, NJ 07102, (201)622-3100.

Seven Locks Press, P.O. Box 68, Arlington, VA 22210.

M. E. Sharpe, 80 Business Park Drive, Armonk, NY 10504.

Simmons-Boardman Publishing Corp., 345 Hudson St., New York, NY 10014.

Society for Advancement of Management, P.O. Box 889, Vinton, VA 24179.

Society of Automotive Engineers, Inc., 400 Commonwealth Dr., Warrendale, PA 15096-0001.

Society of Fire Protection Engineers, 1 Liberty Sq., Boston, MA 02109-9825.

Sociological Abstracts, Inc., P.O. Box 22206, San Diego, CA 92192, (619)695-8803.

South End Press, 116 Saint Botolph St., Boston, MA 02115.

Specialized Publication Services, Inc., P.O. Box 1915, Madison Square Station, New York, NY 10159.

Sport Information Resource Centre, 1600 James Naismith Dr., Gloucester, Ontario, Canada, K1B 5N4, (613)748-5658.

Springer Publishing Co., Inc., 536 Broadway, 11th Fl., New York, NY 10012.

Springer-Verlag New York, Inc., 175 Fifth Ave., New York, NY 10010.

St. Martin's Press, Inc., 175 Fifth Ave., New York, NY 10010.

Stanford Environmental Law Society, Stanford Law School, Stanford, CA 94305.

Stanton & Harper Books, 603 Elwell Ave., Greensboro, NC 27405.

State University of New York Press (SUNY), State University Plaza, Albany, NY 12246-0001.

STN International, FIZ Karlsruhe, P.O. Box 2465, W-7500 Karlsruhe 1, Germany, 07247 808555.

SUNY see State University of New York.

Superintendent of Documents, U.S. Government Printing Office, Washington, DC 20402-9371.

Sybex, Inc. 2021 Challenger Dr., Alameda, CA 94501.

TAB Books, Inc., P.O. Box 40, Blue Ridge Summit, PA 17294-0850.

Tax Analysts, 6830 N. Fairfax Drive, Arlington, VA 22213.

Taylor and Francis, 1900 Frost Road, Ste. 101, Bristol, PA 19007.

Technomic Publishing Co., 851 New Holland Ave., Box 3535, Lancaster, PA 17604.

Temple University Press, 1601 N. Broad St., University Services Building, Room 305, Philadelphia, PA 19122.

Third World Press, 7524 S. Cottage Grove, Box 730, Chicago, IL 60619.

Thomas Publishing Corp., 1325 G St., N.W., Ste. 900, Washington, DC 20005.

Thompson Publishing Group, 1725 N. Salisbury Blvd., Salisbury, MD 21801-3351.

Thomson Financial Networks, Inc., 11 Farnsworth St., Boston, MA 02210, (617)345-2000.

Time, Inc., Time-Life Bldg., New York, NY 10020, (212)522-1212.

Town and Country Planning Association, 17 Carlton House Terrace, London, SW1Y 5AS, England.

Trans-Atlantic Publications, Inc., 311 Bainbridge St., Philadelphia, PA 19147.

Transaction Publishers, Dept. 3092, Rutgers University, New Brunswick, NJ 08903.

Transporation Research Information Services, 2101 Constitution Ave., N.W., Washington, DC 20418, (202)334-3250.

Transportation Research Board, 2101 Constitution Ave., N.W., Washington, DC 20418, (202)334-3250.

TRB see Transportation Research Board.

TreeWorks, 526 W. Nittany Ave., State College, PA 16801-4058.

U.S. Advisory Commission on Intergovernmental Relations, 800 K St., N.W., Ste. 450-South, Washington, DC 20575.

U.S. Bureau of Justice Statistics, 633 Indiana Ave., N.W., Washington, DC 20531.

U.S. Bureau of Labor Statistics, 441 G St., N.W., Washington, DC 20212.

U.S. Bureau of the Census, Data Users Service Division, Washington, DC 20233, (301)763-2074.

U.S. Bureau of the Census, U.S. Department of Commerce, Washington, DC 20233.

U.S. Conference of Mayors, 1620 Eye St., N.W., Washington, DC 20006.

U.S. Department of Energy, Office of Scientific and Technical Information, P.O. Box 62, Oak Ridge, TN 37831, (615)576-1189.

U.S. Department of Housing and Urban Development, 451 Seventh St., S.W., Washington, DC 20410.

U.S. Department of Transportation, 400 Seventh St., S.W., Washington, DC 20590.

U.S. Federal Highway Administration, 400 Seventh Street, N.W., Washington, DC 20590.

U.S. General Accounting Office, P.O. Box 6015, Gaithersburg, MD 20877.

U.S. Geological Survey, NEIC, Box 25046 Federal Center Mail Stop 967, Denver, CO 80225 (303)236-1500.

U.S. Geological Survey, Water Resources Scientific Information Center, 425 National Center, Reston, VA 22092, (703)648-6820.

U.S. Government Printing Office see Superintendent of Documents.

U.S. National Institute of Justice, P.O. Box 6000, Rockville, MD 20850, (301)251-5500.

U.S. National Institute of Standards and Technology, Bldg. 224, Rm. A252, Gaithersburg, MD 20899, (301)975-6862.

ULI see Urban Land Institute.

UMI/Data Courier, 620 S. Third St., Louisville, KY 40202-2475, (502)583-4111.

University Microfilms International, 300 N. Zeeb Road, Ann Arbor, MI 48106, (313)761-4700.

University of Alabama, University Blvd., P.O. Box 870132, Tuscaloosa, AL 35401.

University of California, Institute of Governmental Studies, 102 Moses Hall, Berkeley, CA 94720.

University of California Press, 2120 Berkeley Way, Berkeley, CA 94720.

University of Chicago Press, 5801 S. Ellis Ave., 4th Fl., Chicago, IL 60637.

University of Georgia, Carl Vinson Institute of Government, Terrell Hall, Athens, GA 30602.

University of Illinois Press, 54 East Gregory Drive, Champaign, IL 61820.

University of Michigan Press, P.O. Box 1104, Ann Arbor, MI 48106.

University of New Mexico Press, 1720 Lomas Blvd., N.E., Albuquerque, NM 87131-1591.

University of Oklahoma Press, 1005 Asp Ave., Norman, OK 73019-0445.

University of Pennsylvania Press, 418 Service Drive, Blockley Hall, 13th Fl., Philadelphia, PA 19104-6097.

University of Pittsburgh Press, 127 N. Bellefield Ave., Pittsburgh, PA 15260.

University of Texas at Austin, Bureau of Business Research, P.O. Box 7459, Austin, TX 78713-7459.

University of Toledo, 2801 W. Bancroft St., Toledo, OH 43606.

University of Toronto Press, 340 Nagel Dr., Cheektowaga, NY 14225.

University of Wisconsin Press, 114 N. Murray St., Madison, WI 53715.

University Press of America, 4720 Boston Way, Lanham, MD 20706.

Urban Institute, 2100 M Street N.W., Washington, DC 20037.

Urban Land Institute, 625 Indiana Ave., N.W., Ste. 400, Washington, DC 20004-2930.

USCM see U.S. Conference of Mayors.

USGS see U.S. Geological Survey.

Van Nostrand Reinhold Co., 115 Fifth Ave., New York, NY 10003; order to: 7625 Empire Drive, Florence, KY 41022.

Venture Publishing, 1999 Cato Ave., State College, PA 16801.

Viking Penguin, 375 Hudson St., New York, NY 10014-3657.

Vintage Books, Mail Drop 28-2, 201 E. 50th St., New York, NY 10022.

VU/TEXT Information Services, 325 Chestnut St., Ste. 1300, Philadelphia, PA 19106, (215)574-4421.

Wadsworth Publishing Co., 10 Davis Dr., Belmont, CA 94002.

Wakeman/Walworth Inc., 300 N. Washington St., Alexandria, VA 22314.

Warren, Gorham, & Lamont, One Penn Plaza, New York, NY 10119.

Washington Post News Library, 1150 15th Street, N.W., 5th Fl., Washington, DC 20071, (202)334-7341.

Washington Researchers, Ltd., 2612 P St., N.W., Washington, DC 20007-3062, (202)333-3499.

Washington University, One Brookings Drive, Campus Box 1120, St. Louis, MO 63130.

Waste Management Information Bureau, United Kingdom Atomic Energy Authority, AEA Environment and Energy, Bldg. 7.12, Harwell Laboratory, Didcot, Oxon. OX11 ORA, England, 0235-433442.

Water Pollution Control Federation, 601 Wythe St., Alexandria, VA 22314-1994.

Waterfront Center, 1536 44th St., N.W., Washington, DC 20007.

WEFA Group, 401 City Line Ave., Ste. 300, Bala Cynwyd, PA 19004-1780, (215)660-6300.

West Publishing Co., 610 Opperman Dr., Eagan, MN 55123, (612)687-7000.

WESTLAW see West Publishing Co.

Westview Press, 5500 Central Ave., Boulder, CO 80301-2847.

John Wiley and Sons, One Wiley Dr., Somerset, NJ 08875-1272.

Willow Tree Press, Inc., 124 Willow Tree Rd., Monsey, NY 10952, (914)362-8376.

H. W. Wilson, 950 University Ave., Bronx, NY 10452, (212)588-8400.

Wilsonline see H. W. Wilson.

Windcrest see TAB Books.

World Resources Institute, 1709 New York Ave., N.W., Washington, DC 20006.

Yale University Press, 302 Temple Street, New Haven, CT 06511.

Ziff-Davis Publishing Co., 10 Presidents Landing, Medford, MA 02155-5146.

Ziff-Davis Publishing Co., 8601 Georgia Ave., 300, Silver Spring, MD 20910.

List of Authors and Contributors

Authors and Contributors

David R. Berman is a professor of political science at Arizona State University. He has written books and numerous articles on state and local government, politics, and public policy. Before coming to Arizona State, he was a research associate with the National League of Cities. Professor Berman holds a Ph.D and a master of arts degree from American University and a bachelor's degree from Rockford College.

Evan Berman is assistant professor of Political Science at the University of Miami, School of Business Administration, with teaching and research interests in public administration and public policy. He has worked for the National Science Foundation, and U.S. Congress (Office of Technology Assessment). He has a Ph.D. from the George Washington University, an a M.A. and B.Sc. from the University of Amsterdam (The Netherlands).

Eugene P. Boyd is a public policy analyst with the Congressional Research Service of the Library of Congress where he conducts research and policy analysis of federal housing, community and economic development and related urban policy issues, legislation, and programs in support of members of Congress and congressional committees. He also has worked as a housing and information specialist for the Planning and Development Division of the Prince George's County Maryland Housing Authority. Mr. Boyd holds a bachelor's degree in urban studies from Virginia Commonwealth University and has undertaken graduate studies in city and regional planning at Howard University.

Victor S. DeSantis, assistant professor of public administration at the University of North Texas, is conducting research on the effect of organizational structures and government institutions on local policy areas such as public finances and economic development. DeSantis served previously as the data coordinator and manager of statistical analysis at ICMA. He holds M.A. and Ph.D. degrees from the School of Public Affairs at American University.

Eleanor Ferrall is librarian emerita of Hayden Library at Arizona State University. She served as reference subject specialist for the university's School of Public Affairs and School of Justice Studies. As associate faculty, she taught graduate courses in library research for both schools. She is a published writer and regular book review contributor.

Gerard Hoetmer is assistant executive director, research and development and public policy for ICMA. His projects have dealt with local government fire service, emergency management, code administration, and police management. Hoetmer is a member of the NFPA Committee 1201 on Public Fire Services, the International Conference of Building Officials Executive Board Advisory Council, the IAFC Fire Department Accreditation Committee, and the National Science Foundation's Natural Hazards Advisory Committee. He has written and edited many publications on public safety issues, including *The Principles and Practices of Emergency Management* with Dr. Thomas Drabek. Hoetmer is the former assistant to the fire chief in Aurora, Colorado, and holds a master's degree in public administration and finance from the University of Colorado.

Kenneth L. Kraemer is professor of information technology (IT) and management in the Graduate School of Management at the University of California, Irvine. His research and teaching focuses on the implications of IT for organizations, the management of IT services, and the globalization of IT production. He is currently comparing the U.S. and Twelve Asia-Pacific countries in their development of national IT infrastructure such as national information highways. He consults to state and local governments and has done work for HUD, OTA, and the United Nations. He received his masters and PhD from the University of Southern California.

Mike Milakovich is Associate Professor of Political Science at the University of Miami, School of Business Administration with teaching and research interests in public policy, quality management, criminal justice, and health care administration. Prior to affiliating with the University of Miami, he was a visiting research fellow at the University of Chicago Law School and he taught at the University of North Carolina (Greensboro). He received a bachelor's degree from the University of California at Santa Barbara and master's and doctoral degrees from the Indiana University.

Donald F. Norris is director of the Maryland Institute for Policy Analysis and Research (MIPAR) and associate professor of policy sciences at the University of Maryland Baltimore County. Norris has authored and edited several books, has published several articles, and has served on several editorial boards. Norris is currently a member of the editorial board of *Social Science Computer Review*. Norris' research activities include demographic, social, and economic change in the Baltimore area, the structure and politics of metropolitan governmental cooperation, and public welfare reform. He has conducted a computer survey in Maryland. Norris holds a bachelor's degree from Memphis State University and an MA and Ph.D. from the University of Virginia.

Rosemary O'Leary is an attorney and a faculty member of the department of public administration at the Maxwell Graduate School of Citizenship and Public Affairs at Syracuse University. She also is an adjunct faculty member at the State University of New York College of Environmental Science and Forestry. O'Leary has served as an attorney and as the director of policy and planning for an environmental agency in the Midwest. She has published extensively in the areas of environmental policy, environmental law, and law and public policy and has won national research awards. Her book, *Environmental Change: Federal Courts and the EPA*, was published in 1993. She is a member of the board of editors of four national journals. O'Leary is Chair of the Environment and Natural Resources Administration section of the American Society for Public Administration.

Tari Renner is chair of the political science department at Illinois Wesleyan University. He was Formerly an associate professor in the political science department at Duquesne University. Prior to his position at Duquesne, he was the senior statistical analyst for ICMA, where he was responsible for the design, data collection, and analysis of local government survey research projects. Renner holds a bachelor's degree from the University of South Florida and a master's and Ph.D. in political science from The American University.

Jonathan West chairs the Department of Political Science and is director of the Master's of Public Administration program at the University of Miami with research and teaching interests in public administration and public policy. Prior to joining UM in 1981, he served on the faculties of the University of Arizona and the University of Houston. West also worked as a management analyst in the Office of the Surgeon General, Department of Defense in Washington, D.C. He holds a bachelor's degree from the University of Utah and master's and doctor's degrees from Northwestern University.

Charles R. Wise is professor of public affairs and associate dean for Bloomington in the School of Public and Environmental Affairs of Indiana University. Wise served in the U.S. Department of Justice as special assistant for policy analysis in the Office of Legislative Affairs and then as director of intergovernmental relations. Wise also served as research consultant with the U.S. Air Safety Commission.

Wise held numerous positions in the American Society of Public Administration and the National Association of Schools of Public Affairs and Administration. Wise was managing editor of *Public Administration Review* and has three times received the Mosher Award for best academic article to appear in that journal. Wise is the author of *The Dynamics of Legislation: Leadership and Policy Change in the Congressional Process* and has published extensively in professional journals.

Sherman M. Wyman is an associate professor at the School of Urban and Public Affairs and Coordinator of the MPA program at the University of Texas at Arlington. Previously Wyman was director of the City Management Graduate Program at the University of Kansas and head of the Bureau of Governmental Research and Service at Denver University. He holds a bachelor's degree from Stanford University, an MPA from Syracuse, and a Ph.D. in public administration from the University of Southern California. A Fulbright Scholar in comparative local governments in Norway from 1960–61, Wyman has held a variety of urban management and planning posts in addition to consulting assignments. His research interests and publications focus on regional and urban management, organizational change, and local economic development.

Cumulative Index, 1990–1994

Cumulative Index, 1990–1994

The cumulative index comprises the years 1990 through 1994 of *The Municipal Year Book*.

Urban administrators and others involved in local government, as well as students, scholars, researchers, and others who refer frequently to *The Municipal Year Book*, should find this index a valuable tool.

Entries for the years 1990 through 1992 appear exactly as indexed in the Cumulative Index to *The Municipal Year Book 1992*. The years 1993 and 1994 are included in this Cumulative Index. Entries for 1970, 1971, 1972, 1973, and 1974 can be found in the 1975, 1976, 1977, and 1978 editions, respectively, of *The Municipal Year Book*. Entries for 1975 and 1976 can be found in the 1980 edition, and entries for 1977, 1978, 1979, 1980, 1981, 1982, 1983, 1984, 1985, 1986, 1987, and 1988 can be found in the 1981, 1982, 1983, 1984, 1985, 1986, 1987, 1988, 1989, 1990, 1991, and 1992 editions, respectively.

How To Use This Index. Entries run in chronological order, starting with 1990. The **year** is in **boldface** numerals, followed by a colon (e.g., **93:**); the relevant page numbers follow. Years are separated by semicolons.

Page numbers followed by the words *table(s)* or *figure(s)* indicate that those particular pages contain table(s) and/or figure(s). The term *PICSs* refers to both *Profiles of Individual Cities and Profiles of Individual Counties*.

The Municipal Year Book 1994
  Volume 61

Composition by
  EPS Group
  Hanover, Maryland

Printing and binding by
  Kingsport Press
  Kingsport, Tennessee

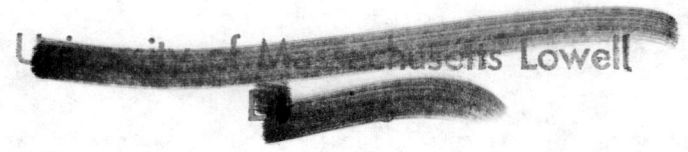